D0080959

SIXTH EDITION

OPTIONS, FUTURES, AND OTHER DERIVATIVES

SIXTH EDITION

OPTIONS, FUTURES, AND OTHER DERIVATIVES

John C. Hull

Maple Financial Group Professor of Derivatives and Risk Management
Director, Bonham Center for Finance
Joseph L. Rotman School of Management
University of Toronto

Prentice Hall
Upper Saddle River, New Jersey 07458

Library of Congress Cataloging-in-Publication Data

Hull, John, 1946–
Options, futures, and other derivatives / John Hull. — 6th ed.
p. cm.
Includes bibliographical references and index.
ISBN 0-13-149908-4 (alk. paper)
1. Futures. 2. Stock options 3. Derivative securities. I. Title.

HG6024.A3H85 2005
332.64'5—dc22

2005047692

Executive Editor: David Alexander
Editorial Director: Jeff Shelstad
Assistant Editor: Francesca Calogero
Editorial Assistant: Michael Dittamo
Media Project Manager: Nancy Welcher
Marketing Manager: Sharon Koch
Marketing Assistant: Tina Panagiotou
Managing Editor (Production): Cynthia Regan
Production Editor: Melissa Owens
Permissions Supervisor: Charles Morris
Manufacturing Buyer: Diane Peirano
Cover Design: Bruce Kenselaar
Cover Illustration/Photo: Getty Images
Director, Image Resource Center: Melinda Reo
Manager, Rights and Permissions: Zina Arabia
Manager, Visual Research: Beth Brenzel
Manager, Cover Visual Research & Permissions: Karen Sanatar
Manager, Print Production: Christy Mahon
Editing and Page Composition: The Geometric Press
Printer/Binder: Hamilton Printing Company

Credits and acknowledgments borrowed from other sources and reproduced, with permission, in this textbook appear on appropriate page within text.

Pearson Education LTD.
Pearson Education Singapore, Pte. Ltd
Pearson Education, Canada, Ltd
Pearson Education – Japan
Pearson Education Australia PTY, Limited
Pearson Education North Asia Ltd
Pearson Educación de Mexico, S.A. de C.V.
Pearson Education Malaysia, Pte. Ltd

10 9 8 7 6 5 4
ISBN 0-13-149908-4

To Michelle

CONTENTS IN BRIEF

Contents

BUSINESS SNAPSHOTS

TECHNICAL NOTES

Available on the Author's Website
www.rotman.utoronto.ca/~hull

1. Convexity Adjustments to Eurodollar Futures
2. Properties of the Lognormal Distribution
3. Warrant Valuation When Value of Equity plus Warrants Is Lognormal
4. Exact Procedure for Valuing American Calls on Stocks Paying a Single Dividend
5. Calculation of the Cumulative Probability in a Bivariate Normal Distribution
6. Differential Equation for Price of a Derivative on a Stock Paying a Known Dividend Yield
7. Differential Equation for Price of a Derivative on a Futures Price
8. Analytic Approximation for Valuing American Options
9. Generalized Tree-Building Procedure
10. The Cornish–Fisher Expansion to Estimate VaR
11. Manipulation of Credit Transition Matrices
12. Calculation of Cumulative Noncentral Chi-Square Distribution
13. Efficient Procedure for Valuing American-Style Lookback Options
14. The Hull–White Two-Factor Model
15. Valuing Options on Coupon-Bearing Bonds in a One-Factor Interest Rate Model
16. Construction of an Interest Rate Tree with Nonconstant Time Steps and Nonconstant Parameters
17. The Process for the Short Rate in an HJM Term Structure Model
18. Valuation of a Compounding Swap
19. Valuation of an Equity Swap
20. A Generalization of the Risk-Neutral Valuation Result

Preface

It is sometimes hard for me to believe that the first edition of this book was only 330 pages and 13 chapters long! Over the last 15 years I have had to expand and adapt the book to keep up with the fast pace of change in derivatives markets.

Like earlier editions, the book serves several markets. It is appropriate for graduate courses in business, economics, and financial engineering. It can be used on advanced undergraduate courses when students have good quantitative skills. Many practitioners involved in derivatives markets find the book useful. I am pleased that half the purchasers of the book have historically been analysts, traders, and other market practitioners.

One of the key decisions that must be made by an author who is writing in the area of derivatives concerns the use of mathematics. If the level of mathematical sophistication is too high, the material is likely to be inaccessible to many students and practitioners. If it is too low, some important issues will inevitably be treated in a rather superficial way. I have tried to be particularly careful about the way I use both mathematics and notation in the book. Nonessential mathematical material has been either eliminated or included in end-of-chapter appendices and in the technical notes on my website. Concepts that are likely to be new to many readers have been explained carefully, and many numerical examples have been included.

The book provides a comprehensive treatment of derivatives and risk management. It assumes that the reader has taken introductory courses in finance and in probability and statistics. No prior knowledge of options, futures contracts, swaps, or other derivative instruments is assumed. It is not therefore necessary for students to take an elective course in investments prior to taking a course based on this book.

There are many different ways *Options, Futures, and Other Derivatives* can be used in the classroom. Instructors teaching a first course in derivatives may wish to spend most time on the first half of the book; those teaching more advanced courses will find that many different combinations of chapters in the second half of the book can be used. I find the material in Chapter 32 works well at the end of either an introductory or an advanced course.

What's New?

Material has been updated and improved throughout the book. The changes in this edition include:

1. Complete rewrites of the chapters on credit risk and credit derivatives (Chapters 20 and 21) to reflect market developments in these important areas. The rewrites result in chapters that are up to date and easier to teach from than the corresponding chapters in the fifth edition.

2. The opening six chapters have been replaced by seven chapters that cover forward, futures, and swap contracts in a more student-friendly way. The chapter on hedging has been moved to Chapter 3. Chapter 4 is now devoted to understanding how interest rates are calculated and used. Chapter 5 covers the determination of futures and forward prices. Chapter 6 deals with interest rate futures, and Chapter 7 covers swaps.
3. Over 50 highlighted descriptions of real-world situations and interesting issues, referred to as *Business Snapshots*, illustrate points being made in the text.
4. There is more discussion of how models can be implemented with Excel (see, for example, Monte Carlo simulation in Chapter 17, GARCH models in Chapter 19, and the variance-gamma model in Chapter 24). Excel Spreadsheets illustrating model implementations are available from my website.
5. A series of Technical Notes are available from my website. This means that less purely technical material needs to be included in the book. As a result, the presentation is streamlined and more student friendly.
6. DerivaGem Version 1.51 is included. One change from the previous version of DerivaGem is that spreadsheets are now unlocked in the Calculator.
7. The binomial tree chapter (Chapter 11) and the swaps chapter (Chapter 7) have been extended so that there is a more complete coverage of these topics at one place in the book.
8. There is a new chapter on "Convexity, Timing, and Quanto Adjustments". Previously the material in this chapter was included in the chapters on "Martingales and Measures" and "Interest Rate Derivatives: The Standard Market Models".
9. Sequencing of chapters in the second half of the book has been changed to better meet the needs of students and instructors.
10. Many new topics are included. For example, I cover the size of derivatives markets in Chapter 1, Basel II in Chapter 20, and the variance-gamma model in Chapter 24. Other topics are discussed in more depth than in the fifth edition. For example, there is more on convexity adjustments to Eurodollar futures (Chapter 5), copula models (Chapters 20 and 21), and executive stock options (Chapters 8 and 13).
11. One change has been made to the mathematical notation. δt, δx, etc., have been replaced by Δt, Δx, etc. (This reverses a change in the previous edition where I was trying to avoid overworking Δ—but found that the change was not popular!)
12. New end-of-chapter problems have been added.

The whole book (including end-of-chapter references) has been fully updated and many changes have been made to improve the presentation of material.

Software

Version 1.51 of DerivaGem is included with this book. This consists of two Excel applications: the *Options Calculator* and the *Applications Builder*. The Options Calculator consists of easy-to-use software for valuing a wide range of options. The worksheets are now unlocked. The Applications Builder consists of a number of Excel functions from which users can build their own applications. It includes a number of sample applications and enables students to explore the properties of options and numerical procedures more easily. It also allows more interesting assignments to be designed.

The software is described more fully at the end of the book. Updates to the software can be downloaded from my website

www.rotman.utoronto.ca/~hull

Slides

Several hundred PowerPoint slides can be downloaded from my website. Instructors who adopt the text are welcome to adapt the slides to meet their own needs.

Solutions Manual

As in the fifth edition, end-of-chapter problems are divided into two groups: "Questions and Problems" and "Assignment Questions". Solutions to the Questions and Problems are in *Options, Futures, and Other Derivatives: Solutions Manual* (ISBN: 0-13-149906-8), which is published by Prentice Hall and can be purchased by students.

Technical Notes

A new feature of the sixth edition is the use of Technical Notes. These elaborate on points made in the text and can be downloaded from my website.

www.rotman.utoronto.ca/~hull

By not including the Technical Notes in the book, I was able to streamline the presentation of material so that it is more student friendly.

Online Training

In conjunction with Learning Dividends, Inc., I have developed e-Learning material entitled *Hull on Derivatives* to accompany the first half of the book. This consists of 14 modules with fully animated and narrated instruction. For more information visit

www.hullonderivatives.com

Acknowledgments

Many people have played a part in the production of this book. Academics, students, and practitioners who have made excellent and useful suggestions include Farhang Aslani, Jas Badyal, Emilio Barone, Giovanni Barone-Adesi, Alex Bergier, George Blazenko, Laurence Booth, Phelim Boyle, Peter Carr, Don Chance, J.-P. Chateau, Ren-Raw Chen, Dan Cline, George Constantinides, Michel Crouhy, Emanuel Derman, Brian Donaldson, Dieter Dorp, Scott Drabin, Jerome Duncan, Steinar Ekern, David Forfar, David Fowler, Louis Gagnon, Richard Goldfarb, Dajiang Guo, Jörgen Hallbeck, Ian Hawkins, Michael Hemler, Steve Heston, Bernie Hildebrandt, Michelle Hull, Andrew Karolyi, Kiyoshi Kato, Kevin Kneafsy, Iain MacDonald, Bill Margrabe, Eddie Mizzi, Izzy Nelkin, Neil Pearson, Paul Potvin, Shailendra Pandit, Eric Reiner, Richard Rendleman, Gordon Roberts, Chris Robinson, Cheryl Rosen, John Rumsey, Ani Sanyal, Klaus Schurger, Eduardo Schwartz, Michael Selby, Piet Sercu, Duane Stock, Edward Thorpe, Yisong Tian, Alan Tucker, P.V. Viswanath, George Wang, Jason Wei, Bob Whaley, Alan White, Hailiang Yang, Victor Zak, and Jozef Zemek.

I am particularly grateful to Eduardo Schwartz, who read the original manuscript for the first edition and made many comments that led to significant improvements, and to Richard Rendleman and George Constantinides, who made specific suggestions that led to improvements in more recent editions.

The first five editions of this book were very popular with practitioners and their comments and suggestions have led to many improvements in the book. I would particularly like to thank Dan Cline and David Forfar. The students in my elective courses on derivatives at the University of Toronto have also played a significant role the evolution of the book. Yves Noth from the University of St. Gallen provided excellent research assistance for this edition.

Alan White, a colleague at the University of Toronto, deserves a special acknowledgment. Alan and I have been carrying out joint research in the area of derivatives for the last 22 years. During that time we have spent countless hours discussing different issues concerning derivatives. Many of the new ideas in this book, and many of the new ways used to explain old ideas, are as much Alan's as mine. Alan read the original version of this book very carefully and made many excellent suggestions for improvement. He has also done most of the development work on the DerivaGem software.

Special thanks are due to many people at Prentice Hall for their enthusiasm, advice, and encouragement. I would particularly like to thank David Alexander, my editor, and Francesca Calogero, the finance assistant editor. I am also grateful to Scott Barr, Leah Jewell, Paul Donnelly, and Maureen Riopelle, who at different times have played key roles in the development of the book.

I welcome comments on the book from readers. My email address is:

hull@rotman.utoronto.ca

John Hull
Joseph L. Rotman School of Management
University of Toronto

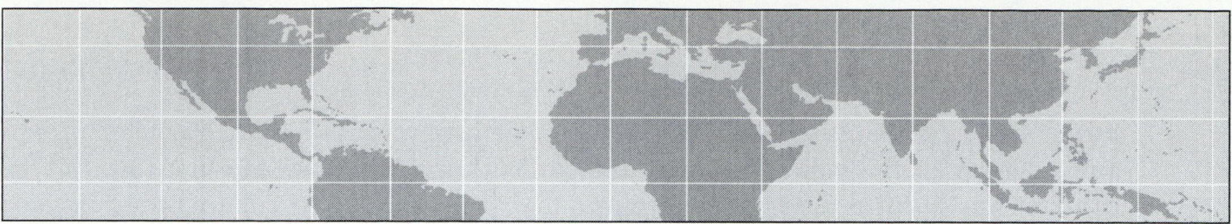

CHAPTER 1 Introduction

In the last 25 years derivatives have become increasingly important in the world of finance. Futures and options are now traded actively on many exchanges throughout the world. Many different types of forward contracts, swaps, options, and other derivatives are regularly traded by financial institutions, fund managers, and corporate treasurers in the over-the-counter market. Derivatives are added to bond issues, used in executive compensation plans, embedded in capital investment opportunities, and so on. We have now reached the stage where anyone who works in finance needs to understand how derivatives work, how they are used, and how they are priced.

A *derivative* can be defined as a financial instrument whose value depends on (or derives from) the values of other, more basic, underlying variables. Very often the variables underlying derivatives are the prices of traded assets. A stock option, for example, is a derivative whose value is dependent on the price of a stock. However, derivatives can be dependent on almost any variable, from the price of hogs to the amount of snow falling at a certain ski resort.

Since the first edition of this book was published in 1988 there have been many developments in derivatives markets. There is now active trading in credit derivatives, electricity derivatives, weather derivatives, and insurance derivatives. Many new types of interest rate, foreign exchange, and equity derivative products have been created. There have been many new ideas in risk management and risk measurement. Analysts have also become more aware of the need to analyze what are known as *real options*. (These are the options acquired by a company when it invests in real assets such as real estate, plant, and equipment.) This edition of the book reflects all these developments.

In this opening chapter we take a first look at forward, futures, and options markets and provide an overview of how they are used by hedgers, speculators, and arbitrageurs. Later chapters will give more details and elaborate on many of the points made here.

1.1 EXCHANGE-TRADED MARKETS

A derivatives exchange is a market where individuals trade standardized contracts that have been defined by the exchange. Derivatives exchanges have existed for a long time. The Chicago Board of Trade (CBOT, www.cbot.com) was established in 1848 to bring farmers and merchants together. Initially its main task was to standardize the quantities and qualities of the grains that were traded. Within a few years the first futures-type contract was developed. It was known as a *to-arrive contract*. Speculators soon became interested in the contract and found trading the contract to be an attractive alternative to trading the grain itself. A rival futures exchange, the Chicago Mercantile Exchange (CME, www.cme.com), was established in 1919. Now futures exchanges exist all over the world.

The Chicago Board Options Exchange (CBOE, www.cboe.com) started trading call option contracts on 16 stocks in 1973. Options had traded prior to 1973, but the CBOE succeeded in creating an orderly market with well-defined contracts. Put option contracts started trading on the exchange in 1977. The CBOE now trades options on well over 1,000 stocks and many different stock indices. Like futures, options have proved to be very popular contracts. Many other exchanges throughout the world now trade options. The underlying assets include foreign currencies and futures contracts as well as stocks and stock indices.

Electronic Markets

Traditionally derivatives traders have used what is known as the *open outcry system*. This involves traders physically meeting on the floor of the exchange, shouting, and using a complicated set of hand signals to indicate the trades they would like to carry out. Exchanges are increasingly replacing the open outcry system by *electronic trading*. This involves traders entering their desired trades at a keyboard and a computer being used to match buyers and sellers. The open outcry system has its advocates, but, as time passes, exchanges are increasingly turning to electronic trading.

1.2 OVER-THE-COUNTER MARKETS

Not all trading is done on exchanges. The *over-the-counter market* is an important alternative to exchanges and, measured in terms of the total volume of trading, has become much larger than the exchange-traded market. It is a telephone- and computer-linked network of dealers who do not physically meet. Trades are done over the phone and are usually between two financial institutions or between a financial institution and one of its clients (typically a corporate treasurer or fund manager). Financial institutions often act as market makers for the more commonly traded instruments. This means that they are always prepared to quote both a bid price (a price at which they are prepared to buy) and an offer price (a price at which they are prepared to sell).

Telephone conversations in the over-the-counter market are usually taped. If there is a dispute about what was agreed, the tapes are replayed to resolve the issue. Trades in the over-the-counter market are typically much larger than trades in the exchange-traded market. A key advantage of the over-the-counter market is that the terms of a contract do not have to be those specified by an exchange. Market participants are free to negotiate any mutually attractive deal. A disadvantage is that there is usually some credit risk in an over-the-counter trade (i.e., there is a small risk that the contract will not be honored). As we shall see in the next chapter, exchanges have organized themselves to eliminate virtually all credit risk.

Figure 1.1 Size of over-the-counter and exchange-traded derivatives markets.

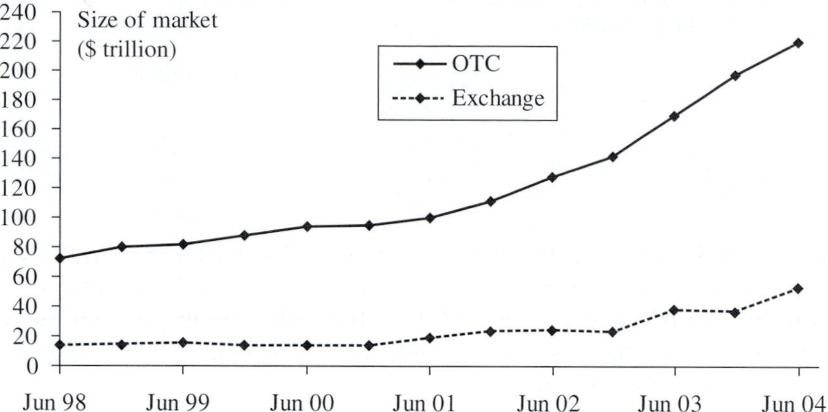

Market Size

Both the over-the-counter and the exchange-traded market for derivatives are huge. Although the statistics that are collected for the two markets are not exactly comparable, it is clear that the over-the-counter market is much larger than the exchange-traded market. The Bank for International Settlements (www.bis.org) started collecting statistics on the markets in 1998. Figure 1.1 compares (a) the estimated total principal amounts underlying transactions that were outstanding in the over-the counter markets between June 1998 and June 2004 and (b) the estimated total value of the assets underlying exchange-traded contracts during the same period. Using these measures, we see that, by June 2004, the over-the-counter market had grown to $220.1 trillion (approximately five times the world gross domestic product) and the exchange-traded market had grown to $49.0 trillion.

In interpreting these numbers, we should bear in mind that the principal underlying an over-the-counter transaction is not the same as its value. An example of an over-the-counter contract is an agreement to buy 100 million US dollars with British pounds at a predetermined exchange rate in 1 year. The total principal amount underlying this transaction is $100 million. However, the value of the contract might be only $1 million. The Bank for International Settlements estimates the gross market value of all over-the-counter contracts outstanding in June 2004 to be about $6.4 trillion.[1]

1.3 FORWARD CONTRACTS

A relatively simple derivative is a *forward contract*. It is an agreement to buy or sell an asset at a certain future time for a certain price. It can be contrasted with a *spot*

[1] A contract that is worth $1 million to one side and –$1 million to the other side would be counted as having a gross market value of $1 million.

Table 1.1 Spot and forward quotes for the USD/GBP exchange rate, June 3, 2003 (GBP = British pound; USD = US dollar; quote is number of USD per GBP).

	Bid	*Offer*
Spot	1.6281	1.6285
1-month forward	1.6248	1.6253
3-month forward	1.6187	1.6192
6-month forward	1.6094	1.6100

contract, which is an agreement to buy or sell an asset today. A forward contract is traded in the over-the-counter market—usually between two financial institutions or between a financial institution and one of its clients.

One of the parties to a forward contract assumes a *long position* and agrees to buy the underlying asset on a certain specified future date for a certain specified price. The other party assumes a *short position* and agrees to sell the asset on the same date for the same price.

Forward contracts on foreign exchange are very popular. Most large banks employ both spot traders and forward traders. Spot traders are trading a foreign currency for almost immediate delivery. Forward traders are trading for delivery at a future time. Table 1.1 provides the quotes on the exchange rate between the British pound (GBP) and the US dollar (USD) that might be made by a large international bank on June 3, 2003. The quote is for the number of USD per GBP. The first row indicates that the bank is prepared to buy GBP (also known as sterling) in the spot market (i.e., for virtually immediate delivery) at the rate of \$1.6281 per GBP and sell sterling in the spot market at \$1.6285 per GBP. The second, third, and fourth rows indicate that the bank is prepared to buy sterling in 1, 3, and 6 months at \$1.6248, \$1.6187, and \$1.6094 per GBP, respectively, and to sell sterling in 1, 3, and 6 months at \$1.6253, \$1.6192, and \$1.6100 per GBP, respectively.

Forward contracts can be used to hedge foreign currency risk. Suppose that, on June 3, 2003, the treasurer of a US corporation knows that the corporation will pay £1 million in 6 months (i.e., on December 3, 2003) and wants to hedge against exchange rate moves. Using the quotes in Table 1.1, the treasurer can agree to buy £1 million 6 months forward at an exchange rate of 1.6100. The corporation then has a long forward contract on GBP. It has agreed that on December 3, 2003, it will buy £1 million from the bank for \$1.61 million. The bank has a short forward contract on GBP. It has agreed that on December 3, 2003, it will sell £1 million for \$1.61 million. Both sides have made a binding commitment.

Payoffs from Forward Contracts

Consider the position of the corporation in the trade we have just described. What are the possible outcomes? The forward contract obligates the corporation to buy £1 million for \$1,610,000. If the spot exchange rate rose to, say, 1.7000, at the end of the 6 months, the forward contract would be worth \$90,000 ($= \$1,700,000 - \$1,610,000$) to the corporation. It would enable 1 million pounds to be purchased at 1.6100 rather than

Figure 1.2 Payoffs from forward contracts: (a) long position, (b) short position. Delivery price = K; price of asset at contract maturity = S_T.

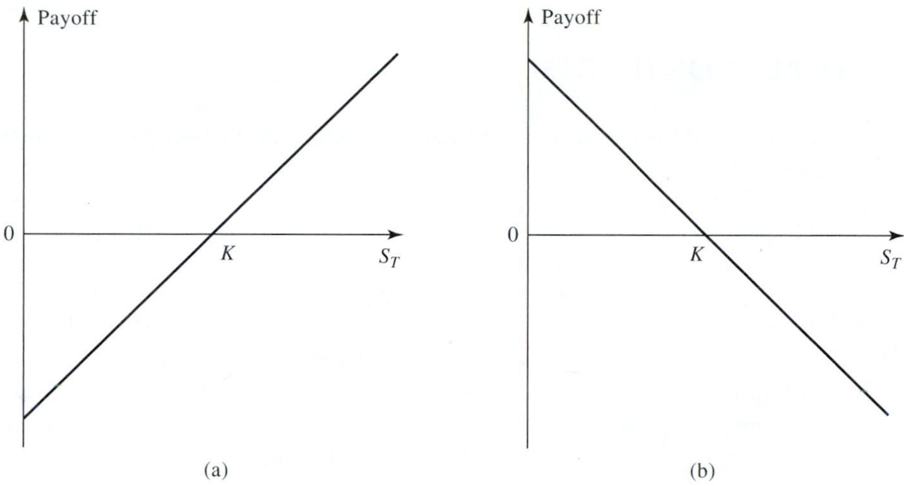

at $1.7000. Similarly, if the spot exchange rate fell to 1.5000 at the end of the 6 months, the forward contract would have a negative value to the corporation of $110,000 because it would lead to the corporation paying $110,000 more than the market price for the sterling.

In general, the payoff from a long position in a forward contract on one unit of an asset is

$$S_T - K$$

where K is the delivery price and S_T is the spot price of the asset at maturity of the contract. This is because the holder of the contract is obligated to buy an asset worth S_T for K. Similarly, the payoff from a short position in a forward contract on one unit of an asset is

$$K - S_T$$

These payoffs can be positive or negative. They are illustrated in Figure 1.2. Because it costs nothing to enter into a forward contract, the payoff from the contract is also the trader's total gain or loss from the contract.

Forward Prices and Spot Prices

We shall be discussing in some detail the relationship between spot and forward prices in Chapter 5. For a quick preview of why the two are related, consider a stock that pays no dividend and is worth $60. You can borrow or lend money for 1 year at 5%. What should the 1-year forward price of the stock be?

The answer is $60 grossed up at 5% for 1 year, or $63. If the forward price is more than this, say $67, you could borrow $60, buy one share of the stock, and sell it forward for $67. After paying off the loan, you would net a profit of $4 in 1 year. If the forward price is less than $63, say $58, an investor owning the stock as part of a portfolio would sell the stock for $60 and enter into a forward contract to buy it back for $58 in 1 year. The proceeds of investment would be invested at 5% to earn $3. The investor would end up $5 better off than if the stock were kept in the portfolio for the year.

1.4 FUTURES CONTRACTS

Like a forward contract, a futures contract is an agreement between two parties to buy or sell an asset at a certain time in the future for a certain price. Unlike forward contracts, futures contracts are normally traded on an exchange. To make trading possible, the exchange specifies certain standardized features of the contract. As the two parties to the contract do not necessarily know each other, the exchange also provides a mechanism that gives the two parties a guarantee that the contract will be honored.

The largest exchanges on which futures contracts are traded are the Chicago Board of Trade (CBOT) and the Chicago Mercantile Exchange (CME). On these and other exchanges throughout the world, a very wide range of commodities and financial assets form the underlying assets in the various contracts. The commodities include pork bellies, live cattle, sugar, wool, lumber, copper, aluminum, gold, and tin. The financial assets include stock indices, currencies, and Treasury bonds. Futures prices are regularly reported in the financial press. Suppose that, on September 1, the December futures price of gold is quoted as $300. This is the price, exclusive of commissions, at which traders can agree to buy or sell gold for December delivery. It is determined on the floor of the exchange in the same way as other prices (i.e., by the laws of supply and demand). If more traders want to go long than to go short, the price goes up; if the reverse is true, then the price goes down.

Further details on issues such as margin requirements, daily settlement procedures, delivery procedures, bid–offer spreads, and the role of the exchange clearinghouse are given in Chapter 2.

1.5 OPTIONS

Options are traded both on exchanges and in the over-the-counter market. There are two basic types of option. A *call option* gives the holder the right to buy the underlying asset by a certain date for a certain price. A *put option* gives the holder the right to sell the underlying asset by a certain date for a certain price. The price in the contract is known as the *exercise price* or *strike price*; the date in the contract is known as the *expiration date* or *maturity*. *American options* can be exercised at any time up to the expiration date. *European options* can be exercised only on the expiration date itself.[2] Most of the options that are traded on exchanges are American. In the exchange-traded equity option market, one contract is usually an agreement to buy or sell 100 shares. European options are generally easier to analyze than American options, and some of the properties of an American option are frequently deduced from those of its European counterpart.

It should be emphasized that an option gives the holder the right to do something.

[2] Note that the terms *American* and *European* do not refer to the location of the option or the exchange. Some options trading on North American exchanges are European.

Table 1.2 Prices of options on Intel, May 29, 2003; stock price = $20.83.

	Calls			*Puts*		
Strike price ($)	*June*	*July*	*Oct.*	*June*	*July*	*Oct.*
20.00	1.25	1.60	2.40	0.45	0.85	1.50
22.50	0.20	0.45	1.15	1.85	2.20	2.85

The holder does not have to exercise this right. This is what distinguishes options from forwards and futures, where the holder is obligated to buy or sell the underlying asset. However, whereas it costs nothing to enter into a forward or futures contract, there is a cost to acquiring an option.

The largest exchange in the world for trading stock options is the Chicago Board Options Exchange (CBOE; www.cboe.com). Table 1.2 gives the closing prices of some of the American options trading on Intel on May 29, 2003. The option strike prices are $20 and $22.50. The maturities are June 2003, July 2003, and October 2003. The June options have an expiration date on June 21, 2003, the July options have an expiration date on July 19, 2003, and the October options have an expiration date on October 18, 2003. Intel's stock price at the close of trading on May 29, 2003, was $20.83.

Suppose an investor instructs a broker to buy one October call option contract on Intel with a strike price of $22.50. The broker will relay these instructions to a trader at the CBOE. This trader will then find another trader who wants to sell 1 October call contract on Intel with a strike price of $22.50, and a price will be agreed. We assume that the price is $1.15, as indicated in Table 1.2. This is the price for an option to buy one share. In the United States, one stock option contract is a contract to buy or sell 100 shares. Therefore the investor must arrange for $115 to be remitted to the exchange through the broker. The exchange will then arrange for this amount to be passed on to the party on the other side of the transaction.

In our example the investor has obtained at a cost of $115 the right to buy 100 Intel shares for $22.50 each. The party on the other side of the transaction has received $115 and has agreed to sell 100 Intel shares for $22.50 per share if the investor chooses to exercise the option. If the price of Intel does not rise above $22.50 before October 18, 2003, the option is not exercised and the investor loses $115. But if the Intel share price does well and the option is exercised when it is $30, the investor is able to buy 100 shares at $22.50 per share when they are worth $30 per share. This leads to a gain of $750, or $635 when the initial cost of the options is taken into account.

An alternative trade for the investor would be the purchase of one July put option contract with a strike price of $20. From Table 1.2 we see that this would cost 100×0.85, or $85. The investor would obtain at a cost of $85 the right to sell 100 Intel shares for $20 per share prior to July 19, 2003. If the Intel share price stays above $20, the option is not exercised and the investor loses $85. But if the investor exercises when the stock price is $15, he or she makes a gain of $500 by buying 100 Intel shares at $15 and selling them for $20. The net profit after the cost of the option is taken into account is $415.

Figure 1.3 Net profit per share from (a) purchasing a contract consisting of 100 Intel October call options with a strike price of $22.50 and (b) purchasing a contract consisting of 100 Intel July put options with a strike price of $20.00.

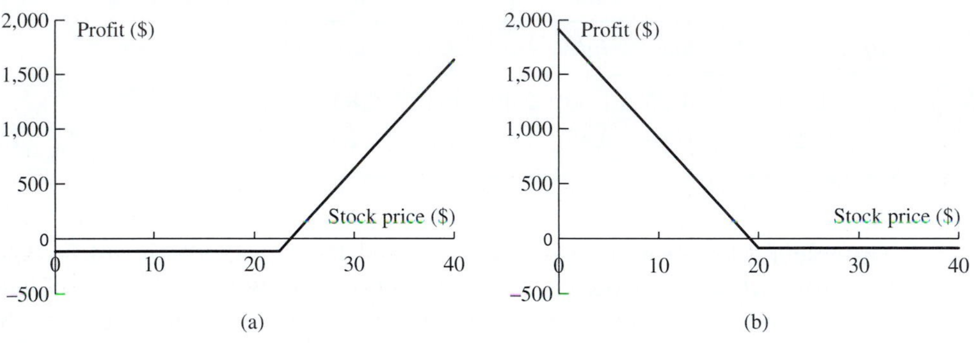

The options trading on the CBOE are American. If we assume for simplicity that they are European, so that they can be exercised only at maturity, the investor's profit as a function of the final stock price is shown in Figure 1.3.

Further details about the operation of options markets and how prices such as those in Table 1.2 are determined by traders are given in later chapters. At this stage we note that there are four types of participants in options markets:

1. Buyers of calls
2. Sellers of calls
3. Buyers of puts
4. Sellers of puts

Buyers are referred to as having *long positions*; sellers are referred to as having *short positions*. Selling an option is also known as *writing the option*.

1.6 TYPES OF TRADERS

Derivatives markets have been outstandingly successful. The main reason is that they have attracted many different types of traders and have a great deal of liquidity. When an investor wants to take one side of a contract, there is usually no problem in finding someone that is prepared to take the other side.

Three broad categories of traders can be identified: hedgers, speculators, and arbitrageurs. Hedgers use derivatives to reduce the risk that they face from potential future movements in a market variable. Speculators use them to bet on the future direction of a market variable. Arbitrageurs take offsetting positions in two or more instruments to lock in a profit. As described in Business Snapshot 1.1, hedge funds have become big users of derivatives for all three purposes.

In the next few sections, we will consider the activities of each type of trader in more detail.

Business Snapshot 1.1 Hedge Funds

Hedge funds have become major users of derivatives for hedging, speculation, and arbitrage. A hedge fund is similar to a mutual fund in that it invests funds on behalf of clients. However, unlike mutual funds, hedge funds are not required to register under US federal securities law. This is because they accept funds only from financially sophisticated individuals and do not publicly offer their securities. Mutual funds are subject to regulations requiring that shares in the funds be fairly priced, that the shares be redeemable at any time, that investment policies be disclosed, that the use of leverage be limited, that no short positions are taken, and so on. Hedge funds are relatively free of these regulations. This gives them a great deal of freedom to develop sophisticated, unconventional, and proprietary investment strategies. The fees charged by hedge fund managers are dependent on the fund's performance and are relatively high—typically 1% to 2% of the amount invested plus 20% of the profits. Hedge funds have grown in popularity with about $1 trillion being invested throughout the world for clients in 2004. "Funds of funds" have been set up to invest in a portfolio of other hedge funds.

The investment strategy followed by a hedge fund manager often involves using derivatives to set up a speculative or arbitrage position. Once the strategy has been defined, the hedge fund manager must:

1. Evaluate the risks to which the fund is exposed
2. Decide which risks are acceptable and which will be hedged
3. Devise strategies (usually involving derivatives) to hedge the unacceptable risks

Here are some examples of the labels used for hedge funds together with the trading strategies followed:

Convertible arbitrage: Take a long position in a convertible bond combined with an actively managed short position in the underlying equity.

Distressed securities: Buy securities issued by companies in bankruptcy or close to bankruptcy.

Emerging markets: Invest in debt and equity of companies in developing or emerging countries and in the debt of the countries themselves.

Growth fund: Invest in growth stocks, hedging with the short sales of options.

Macro or global: Use derivatives to speculate on interest rate and foreign exchange rate moves.

Market neutral: Purchase securities considered to be undervalued and sell securities considered to be overvalued in such a way that the exposure to the overall direction of the market is zero.

1.7 HEDGERS

In this section we illustrate how hedgers can reduce their risks with forward contracts and options.

An Example of Hedging Using Forward Contracts

Suppose that it is June 3, 2003, and ImportCo, a company based in the United States, knows that it will have to pay £10 million on September 3, 2003, for goods it has purchased from a British supplier. The USD–GBP exchange rate quotes made by a financial institution are shown in Table 1.1. ImportCo could hedge its foreign exchange risk by buying pounds (GBP) from the financial institution in the 3-month forward market at 1.6192. This would have the effect of fixing the price to be paid to the British exporter at $16,192,000.

Consider next another US company, which we will refer to as ExportCo, that is exporting goods to the United Kingdom and, on June 3, 2003, knows that it will receive £30 million 3 months later. ExportCo can hedge its foreign exchange risk by selling £30 million in the 3-month forward market at an exchange rate of 1.6187. This would have the effect of locking in the US dollars to be realized for the sterling at $48,561,000.

Note that a company might do better if it chooses not to hedge than if it chooses to hedge. Alternatively, it might do worse. Consider ImportCo. If the exchange rate is 1.5000 on September 3 and the company has not hedged, the £10 million that it has to pay will cost $15,000,000, which is less than $16,192,000. On the other hand, if the exchange rate is 1.7000, the £10 million will cost $17,000,000—and the company will wish that it had hedged! The position of ExportCo if it does not hedge is the reverse. If the exchange rate in September proves to be less than 1.6187, the company will wish that it had hedged; if the rate is greater than 1.6187, it will be pleased that it had not done so.

This example illustrates a key aspect of hedging. The cost of, or price received for, the underlying asset is assured. However, there is no guarantee that the outcome with hedging will be better than the outcome without hedging.

An Example of Hedging Using Options

Options can also be used for hedging. Consider an investor who in May 2003 owns 1,000 Microsoft shares. The current share price is $28 per share. The investor is concerned about a possible share price decline in the next 2 months and wants protection. The investor could buy ten July put option contracts on Microsoft on the Chicago Board Options Exchange with a strike price of $27.50. This would give the investor the right to sell a total of 1,000 shares for a price of $27.50. If the quoted option price is $1, then each option contract would cost $100 \times \$1 = \$100$ and the total cost of the hedging strategy would be $10 \times \$100 = \$1{,}000$.

The strategy costs $1,000 but guarantees that the shares can be sold for at least $27.50 per share during the life of the option. If the market price of Microsoft falls below $27.50, the options can be exercised, so that $27,500 is realized for the entire holding. When the cost of the options is taken into account, the amount realized is $26,500. If the market price stays above $27.50, the options are not exercised and expire worthless. However, in this case the value of the holding is always above $27,500 (or above $26,500 when the cost of the options is taken into account). Figure 1.4 shows the net value of the portfolio (after taking the cost of the options into account) as a function of Microsoft's stock price in 2 months. The dotted line shows the value of the portfolio assuming no hedging.

Figure 1.4 Value of Microsoft holding in 2 months with and without hedging.

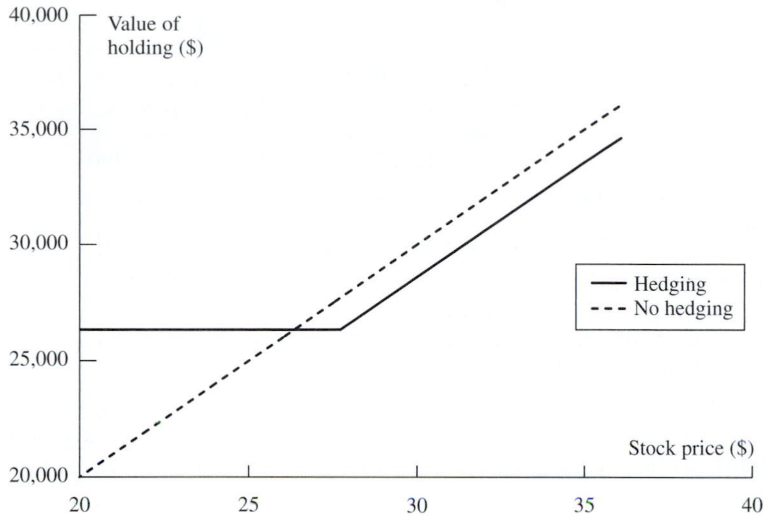

A Comparison

There is a fundamental difference between the use of forward contracts and options for hedging. Forward contracts are designed to neutralize risk by fixing the price that the hedger will pay or receive for the underlying asset. Option contracts, by contrast, provide insurance. They offer a way for investors to protect themselves against adverse price movements in the future while still allowing them to benefit from favorable price movements. Unlike forwards, options involve the payment of an up-front fee.

1.8 SPECULATORS

We now move on to consider how futures and options markets can be used by speculators. Whereas hedgers want to avoid exposure to adverse movements in the price of an asset, speculators wish to take a position in the market. Either they are betting that the price of the asset will go up or they are betting that it will go down.

An Example of Speculation Using Futures

Consider a US speculator who in February thinks that the British pound will strengthen relative to the US dollar over the next 2 months and is prepared to back that hunch to the tune of £250,000. One thing the speculator can do is purchase £250,000 in the spot market in the hope that the sterling can be sold later at a higher price. (The sterling once purchased would be kept in an interest-bearing account.) Another possibility is to take a long position in four CME April futures contracts on sterling. (Each futures contract is for the purchase of £62,500.) Table 1.3 summarizes the two alternatives on the assumption that the current exchange rate is 1.6470 dollars per pound and the April

Table 1.3 Speculation using spot and futures contracts. One futures contract is on £62,500.

	February trade	
	Buy £250,000 Spot price = 1.6470	*Buy 4 futures contracts Futures price = 1.6410*
Investment	$411,750	$20,000
Profit if April spot = 1.7000	$13,250	$14,750
Profit if April spot = 1.6000	−$11,750	−$10,250

futures price is 1.6410 dollars per pound. If the exchange rate turns out to be 1.7000 dollars per pound in April, the futures contract alternative enables the speculator to realize a profit of $(1.7000 - 1.6410) \times 250{,}000 = \$14{,}750$. The spot market alternative leads to 250,000 units of an asset being purchased for $1.6470 in February and sold for $1.7000 in April, so that a profit of $(1.7000 - 1.6470) \times 250{,}000 = \$13{,}250$ is made. If the exchange rate falls to 1.6000 dollars per pound, the futures contract gives rise to a $(1.6410 - 1.6000) \times 250{,}000 = \$10{,}250$ loss, whereas the spot market alternative gives rise to a loss of $(1.6470 - 1.6000) \times 250{,}000 = \$11{,}750$. The alternatives appear to give rise to slightly different profits and losses. But these calculations do not reflect the interest that is earned or paid. As shown in Chapter 5, when the interest earned in sterling and the interest foregone on the dollars used to buy the sterling are taken into account, the profit or loss from the two alternatives is the same.

What then is the difference between the two alternatives? The first alternative of buying sterling requires an up-front investment of $411,750. In contrast, the second alternative requires only a small amount of cash—perhaps $20,000—to be deposited by the speculator in what is termed a "margin account". (Margin accounts are discussed in Chapter 2.) The futures market allows the speculator to obtain leverage. With a relatively small initial outlay, the investor is able to take a large speculative position.

An Example of Speculation Using Options

Options can also be used for speculation. Suppose that it is October and a speculator considers that Amazon.com is likely to increase in value over the next 2 months. The

Table 1.4 Comparison of profits (losses) from two alternative strategies for using $2,000 to speculate on Amazon.com stock in October.

	December stock price	
Investor's strategy	*$15*	*$27*
Buy 100 shares	($500)	$700
Buy 2,000 call options	($2,000)	$7,000

stock price is currently \$20, and a 2-month call option with a \$22.50 strike price is currently selling for \$1. Table 1.4 illustrates two possible alternatives, assuming that the speculator is willing to invest \$2,000. One alternative is to purchase 100 shares; the other involves the purchase of 2,000 call options (i.e., 20 call option contracts). Suppose that the speculator's hunch is correct and the price of Amazon.com's shares rises to \$27 by December. The first alternative of buying the stock yields a profit of

$$100 \times (\$27 - \$20) = \$700$$

However, the second alternative is far more profitable. A call option on Amazon.com with a strike price of \$22.50 gives a payoff of \$4.50, because it enables something worth \$27 to be bought for \$22.50. The total payoff from the 2,000 options that are purchased under the second alternative is

$$2{,}000 \times \$4.50 = \$9{,}000$$

Subtracting the original cost of the options yields a net profit of

$$\$9{,}000 - \$2{,}000 = \$7{,}000$$

The options strategy is, therefore, 10 times more profitable than the strategy of buying the stock.

Options also give rise to a greater potential loss. Suppose the stock price falls to \$15 by December. The first alternative of buying stock yields a loss of

$$100 \times (\$20 - \$15) = \$500$$

Because the call options expire without being exercised, the options strategy would lead to a loss of \$2,000—the original amount paid for the options. Figure 1.5 shows the profit or loss from the two strategies as a function of the price of Amazon.com in 2 months.

Figure 1.5 Profit or loss from two alternative strategies for speculating on Amazon.com's stock price.

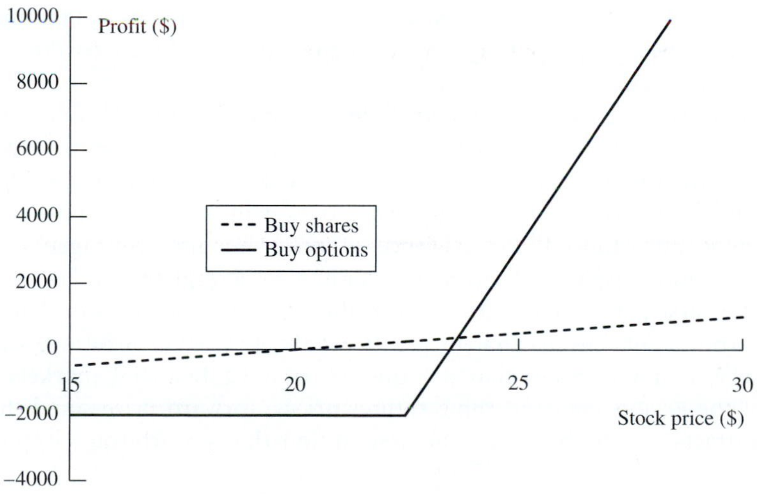

Options like futures provide a form of leverage. For a given investment, the use of options magnifies the financial consequences. Good outcomes become very good, while bad outcomes become very bad!

A Comparison

Futures and options are similar instruments for speculators in that they both provide a way in which a type of leverage can be obtained. However, there is an important difference between the two. When a speculator uses futures, the potential loss as well as the potential gain is very large. When options are used, no matter how bad things get, the speculator's loss is limited to the amount paid for the options.

1.9 ARBITRAGEURS

Arbitrageurs are a third important group of participants in futures, forward, and options markets. Arbitrage involves locking in a riskless profit by simultaneously entering into transactions in two or more markets. In later chapters we will see how arbitrage is sometimes possible when the futures price of an asset gets out of line with its spot price. We will also examine how arbitrage can be used in options markets. This section illustrates the concept of arbitrage with a very simple example.

Let us consider a stock that is traded on both the New York Stock Exchange (www.nyse.com) and the London Stock Exchange (www.stockex.co.uk). Suppose that the stock price is \$172 in New York and £100 in London at a time when the exchange rate is \$1.7500 per pound. An arbitrageur could simultaneously buy 100 shares of the stock in New York and sell them in London to obtain a risk-free profit of

$$100 \times [(\$1.75 \times 100) - \$172]$$

or \$300 in the absence of transactions costs. Transactions costs would probably eliminate the profit for a small investor. However, a large investment bank faces very low transactions costs in both the stock market and the foreign exchange market. It would find the arbitrage opportunity very attractive and would try to take as much advantage of it as possible.

Arbitrage opportunities such as the one just described cannot last for long. As arbitrageurs buy the stock in New York, the forces of supply and demand will cause the dollar price to rise. Similarly, as they sell the stock in London, the sterling price will be driven down. Very quickly the two prices will become equivalent at the current exchange rate. Indeed, the existence of profit-hungry arbitrageurs makes it unlikely that a major disparity between the sterling price and the dollar price could ever exist in the first place. Generalizing from this example, we can say that the very existence of arbitrageurs means that in practice only very small arbitrage opportunities are observed in the prices that are quoted in most financial markets. In this book most of the arguments concerning futures prices, forward prices, and the values of option contracts will be based on the assumption that no arbitrage opportunities exist.

Business Snapshot 1.2 The Barings Bank Disaster

Derivatives are very versatile instruments. They can be used for hedging, speculation, and arbitrage. One of the risks faced by a company that trades derivatives is that an employee who has a mandate to hedge or to look for arbitrage opportunities may become a speculator.

Nick Leeson, an employee of Barings Bank in the Singapore office in 1995, had a mandate to look for arbitrage opportunities between the Nikkei 225 futures prices on the Singapore exchange and those on the Osaka exchange. Over time Leeson moved from being an arbitrageur to being a speculator without anyone in the Barings London head office fully understanding that he had changed the way he was using derivatives. He began to make losses, which he was able to hide. He then began to take bigger speculative positions in an attempt to recover the losses, but only succeeded in making the losses worse.

By the time Leeson was found out, his total loss was close to 1 billion dollars. As a result, Barings—a bank that had been in existence for 200 years—was wiped out. One of the lessons from Barings is that it is important to define unambiguous risk limits for traders and then monitor carefully what they do to make sure that these limits are adhered to.

1.10 DANGERS

Derivatives are very versatile instruments. As we have seen, they can be used for hedging, for speculation, and for arbitrage. It is this very versatility that can cause problems. Sometimes traders who have a mandate to hedge risks or follow an arbitrage strategy become (consciously or unconsciously) speculators. The results can be disastrous. One example of this is provided by the activities of Nick Leeson at Barings Bank (see Business Snapshot 1.2).[3]

To avoid the sort of problems Barings encountered, it is very important for both financial and nonfinancial corporations to set up controls to ensure that derivatives are being used for their intended purpose. Risk limits should be set and the activities of traders should be monitored daily to ensure that these risk limits are adhered to.

SUMMARY

One of the exciting developments in finance over the last 25 years has been the growth of derivatives markets. In many situations, both hedgers and speculators find it more attractive to trade a derivative on an asset than to trade the asset itself. Some derivatives are traded on exchanges; others are traded by financial institutions, fund managers, and corporations in the over-the-counter market, or added to new issues of debt and equity securities. Much of this book is concerned with the valuation of derivatives. The aim is to present a unifying framework within which all derivatives—not just options or futures—can be valued.

[3] The movie *Rogue Trader* provides a good dramatization of the failure of Barings Bank.

In this chapter we have taken a first look at forward, futures, and options contracts. A forward or futures contract involves an obligation to buy or sell an asset at a certain time in the future for a certain price. There are two types of options: calls and puts. A call option gives the holder the right to buy an asset by a certain date for a certain price. A put option gives the holder the right to sell an asset by a certain date for a certain price. Forwards, futures, and options trade on a wide range of different underlying assets.

Derivatives have been very successful innovations in capital markets. Three main types of traders can be identified: hedgers, speculators, and arbitrageurs. Hedgers are in the position where they face risk associated with the price of an asset. They use derivatives to reduce or eliminate this risk. Speculators wish to bet on future movements in the price of an asset. They use derivatives to get extra leverage. Arbitrageurs are in business to take advantage of a discrepancy between prices in two different markets. If, for example, they see the futures price of an asset getting out of line with the cash price, they will take offsetting positions in the two markets to lock in a profit.

FURTHER READING

Chancellor, E. *Devil Take the Hindmost—A History of Financial Speculation*. New York: Farra Straus Giroux, 1999.

Merton, R. C. "Finance Theory and Future Trends: The Shift to Integration," *Risk*, 12, 7 (July 1999): 48–51.

Miller, M. H. "Financial Innovation: Achievements and Prospects," *Journal of Applied Corporate Finance*, 4 (Winter 1992): 4–11.

Rawnsley, J. H. *Total Risk: Nick Leeson and the Fall of Barings Bank*. New York: Harper Collins, 1995.

Zhang, P. G. *Barings Bankruptcy and Financial Derivatives*. Singapore: World Scientific, 1995.

Questions and Problems (Answers in Solutions Manual)

1.1. What is the difference between a long forward position and a short forward position?

1.2. Explain carefully the difference between hedging, speculation, and arbitrage.

1.3. What is the difference between entering into a long forward contract when the forward price is \$50 and taking a long position in a call option with a strike price of \$50?

1.4. Explain carefully the difference between selling a call option and buying a put option.

1.5. An investor enters into a short forward contract to sell 100,000 British pounds for US dollars at an exchange rate of 1.5000 US dollars per pound. How much does the investor gain or lose if the exchange rate at the end of the contract is (a) 1.4900 and (b) 1.5200?

1.6. A trader enters into a short cotton futures contract when the futures price is 50 cents per pound. The contract is for the delivery of 50,000 pounds. How much does the trader gain or lose if the cotton price at the end of the contract is (a) 48.20 cents per pound and (b) 51.30 cents per pound?

1.7. Suppose that you write a put contract with a strike price of \$40 and an expiration date in 3 months. The current stock price is \$41 and the contract is on 100 shares. What have you committed yourself to? How much could you gain or lose?

1.8. What is the difference between the over-the-counter market and the exchange-traded market? What are the bid and offer quotes of a market maker in the over-the-counter market?

1.9. You would like to speculate on a rise in the price of a certain stock. The current stock price is \$29, and a 3-month call with a strike price of \$30 costs \$2.90. You have \$5,800 to invest. Identify two alternative investment strategies, one in the stock and the other in an option on the stock. What are the potential gains and losses from each?

1.10. Suppose that you own 5,000 shares worth \$25 each. How can put options be used to provide you with insurance against a decline in the value of your holding over the next 4 months?

1.11. When first issued, a stock provides funds for a company. Is the same true of a stock option? Discuss.

1.12. Explain why a forward contract can be used for either speculation or hedging.

1.13. Suppose that a March call option to buy a share for \$50 costs \$2.50 and is held until March. Under what circumstances will the holder of the option make a profit? Under what circumstances will the option be exercised? Draw a diagram illustrating how the profit from a long position in the option depends on the stock price at maturity of the option.

1.14. Suppose that a June put option to sell a share for \$60 costs \$4 and is held until June. Under what circumstances will the seller of the option (i.e., the party with the short position) make a profit? Under what circumstances will the option be exercised? Draw a diagram illustrating how the profit from a short position in the option depends on the stock price at maturity of the option.

1.15. It is May and a trader writes a September call option with a strike price of \$20. The stock price is \$18 and the option price is \$2. Describe the trader's cash flows if the option is held until September and the stock price is \$25 at that time.

1.16. A trader writes a December put option with a strike price of \$30. The price of the option is \$4. Under what circumstances does the trader make a gain?

1.17. A company knows that it is due to receive a certain amount of a foreign currency in 4 months. What type of option contract is appropriate for hedging?

1.18. A United States company expects to have to pay 1 million Canadian dollars in 6 months. Explain how the exchange rate risk can be hedged using (a) a forward contract and (b) an option.

1.19. A trader enters into a short forward contract on 100 million yen. The forward exchange rate is \$0.0080 per yen. How much does the trader gain or lose if the exchange rate at the end of the contract is (a) \$0.0074 per yen and (b) \$0.0091 per yen?

1.20. The Chicago Board of Trade offers a futures contract on long-term Treasury bonds. Characterize the traders likely to use this contract.

1.21. "Options and futures are zero-sum games." What do you think is meant by this statement?

1.22. Describe the profit from the following portfolio: a long forward contract on an asset and a long European put option on the asset with the same maturity as the forward contract and a strike price that is equal to the forward price of the asset at the time the portfolio is set up.

1.23. In the 1980s, Bankers Trust developed *index currency option notes* (ICONs). These are bonds in which the amount received by the holder at maturity varies with a foreign exchange rate. One example was its trade with the Long Term Credit Bank of Japan. The ICON specified that if the yen–US dollar exchange rate, S_T, is greater than 169 yen per dollar at maturity (in 1995), the holder of the bond receives \$1,000. If it is less than 169 yen per dollar, the amount received by the holder of the bond is

$$1{,}000 - \max\left[0,\ 1{,}000\left(\frac{169}{S_T} - 1\right)\right]$$

When the exchange rate is below 84.5, nothing is received by the holder at maturity. Show that this ICON is a combination of a regular bond and two options.

1.24. On July 1, 2005, a company enters into a forward contract to buy 10 million Japanese yen on January 1, 2006. On September 1, 2005, it enters into a forward contract to sell 10 million Japanese yen on January 1, 2006. Describe the payoff from this strategy.

1.25. Suppose that sterling/USD spot and forward exchange rates are as follows:

Spot	1.6080
90-day forward	1.6056
180-day forward	1.6018

What opportunities are open to an arbitrageur in the following situations?
(a) A 180-day European call option to buy £1 for \$1.57 costs 2 cents.
(b) A 90-day European put option to sell £1 for \$1.64 costs 2 cents.

Assignment Questions

1.26. The price of gold is currently \$500 per ounce. The forward price for delivery in 1 year is \$700. An arbitrageur can borrow money at 10% per annum. What should the arbitrageur do? Assume that the cost of storing gold is zero and that gold provides no income.

1.27. The current price of a stock is \$94, and 3-month European call options with a strike price of \$95 currently sell for \$4.70. An investor who feels that the price of the stock will increase is trying to decide between buying 100 shares and buying 2,000 call options (= 20 contracts). Both strategies involve an investment of \$9,400. What advice would you give? How high does the stock price have to rise for the option strategy to be more profitable?

1.28. On May 29, 2003, an investor owns 100 Intel shares. As indicated in Table 1.2, the share price is \$20.83 and an October put option with a strike price of \$20 costs \$1.50. The investor is comparing two alternatives to limit downside risk. The first is to buy 1 October put option contract with a strike price of \$20. The second involves instructing a broker to sell the 100 shares as soon as Intel's price reaches \$20. Discuss the advantages and disadvantages of the two strategies.

1.29. A bond issued by Standard Oil worked as follows. The holder received no interest. At the bond's maturity the company promised to pay \$1,000 plus an additional amount based on the price of oil at that time. The additional amount was equal to the product of 170 and the excess (if any) of the price of a barrel of oil at maturity over \$25. The maximum additional amount paid was \$2,550 (which corresponds to a price of \$40 per barrel). Show that the bond is a combination of a regular bond, a long position in call options on oil with a strike price of \$25, and a short position in call options on oil with a strike price of \$40.

1.30. Suppose that in the situation of Table 1.1 a corporate treasurer said: "I will have £1 million to sell in 6 months. If the exchange rate is less than 1.59, I want you to give me 1.59. If it is greater than 1.63, I will accept 1.63. If the exchange rate is between 1.59 and 1.63, I will sell the sterling for the exchange rate." How could you use options to satisfy the treasurer?

1.31. Describe how foreign currency options can be used for hedging in the situation considered in Section 1.7 so that (a) ImportCo is guaranteed that its exchange rate will be less than 1.4600, and (b) ExportCo is guaranteed that its exchange rate will be at least 1.4200. Use DerivaGem to calculate the cost of setting up the hedge in each case assuming that the exchange rate volatility is 12%, interest rates in the United States are 3%, and interest rates in Britain are 4.4%. Assume that the current exchange rate is the average of the bid and offer in Table 1.1.

1.32. A trader buys a European call option and sells a European put option. The options have the same underlying asset, strike price, and maturity. Describe the trader's position. Under what circumstances does the price of the call equal the price of the put?

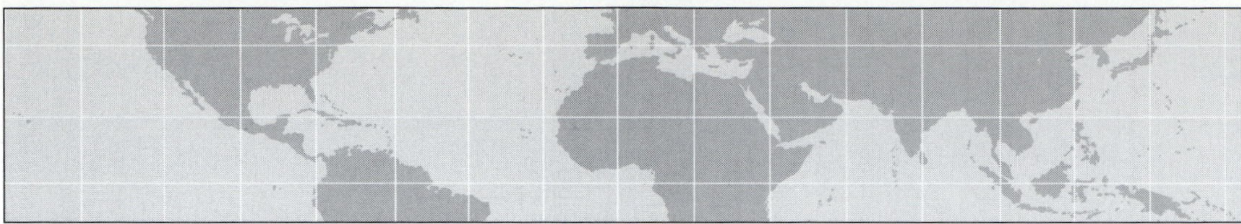

CHAPTER 2

Mechanics of Futures Markets

In Chapter 1 we explained that both futures and forward contracts are agreements to buy or sell an asset at a future time for a certain price. Futures contracts are traded on an organized exchange, and the contract terms are standardized by that exchange. By contrast, forward contracts are private agreements between two financial institutions or between a financial institution and one of its corporate clients.

This chapter covers the details of how futures markets work. We examine issues such as the specification of contracts, the operation of margin accounts, the organization of exchanges, the regulation of markets, the way in which quotes are made, and the treatment of futures transactions for accounting and tax purposes. We compare futures contracts with forward contracts and explain the difference between the payoffs realized from them.

2.1 BACKGROUND

As we saw in Chapter 1, futures contracts are now traded actively all over the world. The two largest futures exchanges in the United States are the Chicago Board of Trade (CBOT, www.cbot.com) and the Chicago Mercantile Exchange (CME, www.cme.com). The largest exchanges in Europe are the London International Financial Futures and Options Exchange (www.liffe.com), Eurex (www.eurexchange.com), and Euronext (www.euronext.com). Other large exchanges include Bolsa de Mercadorias y Futuros (www.bmf.com.br) in São Paulo, the Tokyo International Financial Futures Exchange (www.tiffe.or.jp), the Singapore International Monetary Exchange (www.simex.com.sg), and the Sydney Futures Exchange (www.sfe.com.au). For a more complete list, see the table at the end of this book.

We examine how a futures contract comes into existence by considering the corn futures contract traded on the Chicago Board of Trade (CBOT). On March 5 an investor in New York might call a broker with instructions to buy 5,000 bushels of corn for delivery in July of the same year. The broker would immediately pass these instructions on to a trader on the floor of the CBOT. The broker would request a long position in one contract because each corn contract on the CBOT is for the delivery of exactly 5,000 bushels. At about the same time, another investor in Kansas might

Business Snapshot 2.1 The Unanticipated Delivery of a Futures Contract

This story (which may well be apocryphal) was told to the author of this book by a senior executive of a financial institution. It concerns a new employee of the financial institution who had not previously worked in the financial sector. One of the clients of the financial institution regularly entered into a long futures contract on live cattle for hedging purposes and issued instructions to close out the position on the last day of trading. (Live cattle futures contracts trade on the Chicago Mercantile Exchange and each contract is on 40,000 pounds of cattle.) The new employee was given responsibility for handling the account.

When the time came to close out a contract the employee noted that the client was long one contract and instructed a trader at the exchange go long (not short) one contract. The result of this mistake was that the financial institution ended up with a long position in two live cattle futures contracts. By the time the mistake was spotted trading in the contract had ceased. The financial institution (not the client) was responsible for the mistake. As a result, it started to look into the details of the delivery arrangements for live cattle futures contracts—something it had never done before. Under the terms of the contract, cattle could be delivered by the party with the short position to a number of different locations in the United States during the delivery month. Because it was long, the financial institution could do nothing but wait for a party with a short position to issue a *notice of intention to deliver* to the exchange and for the exchange to assign that notice to the financial institution.

It eventually received a notice from the exchange and found that it would receive live cattle at a location 2,000 miles away the following Tuesday. The new employee was dispatched to the location to handle things. It turned out that the location had a cattle auction every Tuesday. The party with the short position that was making delivery bought cattle at the auction and then immediately delivered them. Unfortunately the cattle could not be resold until the next cattle auction the following Tuesday. The employee was therefore faced with the problem of making arrangements for the cattle to be housed and fed for a week. This was a great start to a first job in the financial sector!

instruct a broker to sell 5,000 bushels of corn for July delivery. This broker would then pass instructions to short one contract to a trader on the floor of the CBOT. The two floor traders would meet, agree on a price to be paid for the corn in July, and the deal would be done.

The investor in New York who agreed to buy has a *long futures position* in one contract; the investor in Kansas who agreed to sell has a *short futures position* in one contract. The price agreed to on the floor of the exchange is the current *futures price* for July corn. We will suppose the price is 170 cents per bushel. This price, like any other price, is determined by the laws of supply and demand. If, at a particular time, more traders wish to sell rather than buy July corn, the price will go down. New buyers then enter the market so that a balance between buyers and sellers is maintained. If more traders wish to buy rather than sell July corn, the price goes up. New sellers then enter the market and a balance between buyers and sellers is maintained.

Closing Out Positions

The vast majority of futures contracts do not lead to delivery. The reason is that most traders choose to close out their positions prior to the delivery period specified in the contract. Closing out a position means entering into the opposite type of trade from the original one. For example, the New York investor who bought a July corn futures contract on March 5 can close out the position by selling (i.e., shorting) one July corn futures contract on April 20. The Kansas investor who sold (i.e., shorted) a July contract on March 5 can close out the position by buying one July contract on April 20. In each case, the investor's total gain or loss is determined by the change in the futures price between March 5 and April 20.

Delivery is so unusual that traders sometimes forget how the delivery process works (see Business Snapshot 2.1). Nevertheless we will spend part of this chapter reviewing the delivery arrangements in futures contracts. This is because it is the possibility of final delivery that ties the futures price to the spot price.[1]

2.2 THE SPECIFICATION OF A FUTURES CONTRACT

The major exchanges that trade futures contracts are listed at the end of this book. When developing a new contract, the exchange must specify in some detail the exact nature of the agreement between the two parties. In particular, it must specify the asset, the contract size (exactly how much of the asset will be delivered under one contract), where delivery will be made, and when delivery will be made.

Sometimes alternatives are specified for the grade of the asset that will be delivered or for the delivery locations. As a general rule, it is the party with the short position (the party that has agreed to sell the asset) that chooses what will happen when alternatives are specified by the exchange. When the party with the short position is ready to deliver, it files a *notice of intention to deliver* with the exchange. This notice indicates selections it has made with respect to the grade of asset that will be delivered and the delivery location.

The Asset

When the asset is a commodity, there may be quite a variation in the quality of what is available in the marketplace. When the asset is specified, it is therefore important that the exchange stipulate the grade or grades of the commodity that are acceptable. The New York Cotton Exchange has specified the asset in its orange juice futures contract as

> US Grade A, with Brix value of not less than 57 degrees, having a Brix value to acid ratio of not less than 13 to 1 nor more than 19 to 1, with factors of color and flavor each scoring 37 points or higher and 19 for defects, with a minimum score 94.

The Chicago Mercantile Exchange in its random-length lumber futures contract has specified that

> Each delivery unit shall consist of nominal 2×4s of random lengths from 8 feet to 20 feet, grade-stamped Construction and Standard, Standard and Better, or #1 and #2;

---

[1] As mentioned in Chapter 1, the spot price is the price for almost immediate delivery.

> however, in no case may the quantity of Standard grade or #2 exceed 50%. Each delivery unit shall be manufactured in California, Idaho, Montana, Nevada, Oregon, Washington, Wyoming, or Alberta or British Columbia, Canada, and contain lumber produced from grade-stamped Alpine fir, Englemann spruce, hem-fir, lodgepole pine, and/or spruce pine fir.

For some commodities a range of grades can be delivered, but the price received depends on the grade chosen. For example, in the Chicago Board of Trade corn futures contract, the standard grade is "No. 2 Yellow", but substitutions are allowed with the price being adjusted in a way established by the exchange.

The financial assets in futures contracts are generally well defined and unambiguous. For example, there is no need to specify the grade of a Japanese yen. However, there are some interesting features of the Treasury bond and Treasury note futures contracts traded on the Chicago Board of Trade. The underlying asset in the Treasury bond contract is any long-term US Treasury bond that has a maturity of greater than 15 years and is not callable within 15 years. In the Treasury note futures contract, the underlying asset is any long-term Treasury note with a maturity of no less than 6.5 years and no more than 10 years from the date of delivery. In both cases, the exchange has a formula for adjusting the price received according to the coupon and maturity date of the bond delivered. This is discussed in Chapter 6.

The Contract Size

The contract size specifies the amount of the asset that has to be delivered under one contract. This is an important decision for the exchange. If the contract size is too large, many investors who wish to hedge relatively small exposures or who wish to take relatively small speculative positions will be unable to use the exchange. On the other hand, if the contract size is too small, trading may be expensive as there is a cost associated with each contract traded.

The correct size for a contract clearly depends on the likely user. Whereas the value of what is delivered under a futures contract on an agricultural product might be $10,000 to $20,000, it is much higher for some financial futures. For example, under the Treasury bond futures contract traded on the Chicago Board of Trade, instruments with a face value of $100,000 are delivered.

In some cases exchanges have introduced "mini" contracts to attract smaller investors. For example, the CME's Mini Nasdaq 100 contract is on 20 times the Nasdaq 100 index, whereas the regular contract is on 100 times the index.

Delivery Arrangements

The place where delivery will be made must be specified by the exchange. This is particularly important for commodities that involve significant transportation costs. In the case of the Chicago Mercantile Exchange's random-length lumber contract, the delivery location is specified as

> On track and shall either be unitized in double-door boxcars or, at no additional cost to the buyer, each unit shall be individually paper-wrapped and loaded on flatcars. Par delivery of hem-fir in California, Idaho, Montana, Nevada, Oregon, and Washington, and in the province of British Columbia.

When alternative delivery locations are specified, the price received by the party with the short position is sometimes adjusted according to the location chosen by that party. For example, in the case of the corn futures contract traded by the Chicago Board of Trade, delivery can be made at Chicago, Burns Harbor, Toledo, or St. Louis. However, deliveries at Toledo and St. Louis are made at a discount of 4 cents per bushel from the Chicago contract price.

Delivery Months

A futures contract is referred to by its delivery month. The exchange must specify the precise period during the month when delivery can be made. For many futures contracts, the delivery period is the whole month.

The delivery months vary from contract to contract and are chosen by the exchange to meet the needs of market participants. For example, corn futures traded on the Chicago Board of Trade have delivery months of March, May, July, September, and December. At any given time, contracts trade for the closest delivery month and a number of subsequent delivery months. The exchange specifies when trading in a particular month's contract will begin. The exchange also specifies the last day on which trading can take place for a given contract. Trading generally ceases a few days before the last day on which delivery can be made.

Price Quotes

The futures price is quoted in a way that is convenient and easy to understand. For example, crude oil futures prices on the New York Mercantile Exchange are quoted in dollars per barrel to two decimal places (i.e., to the nearest cent). Treasury bond and Treasury note futures prices on the Chicago Board of Trade are quoted in dollars and thirty-seconds of a dollar. The minimum price movement that can occur in trading is consistent with the way in which the price is quoted. Thus, it is $0.01 per barrel for the oil futures and one thirty-second of a dollar for the Treasury bond and Treasury note futures.

Price Limits and Position Limits

For most contracts, daily price movement limits are specified by the exchange. If the price moves down by an amount equal to the daily price limit, the contract is said to be *limit down*. If it moves up by the limit, it is said to be *limit up*. A *limit move* is a move in either direction equal to the daily price limit. Normally, trading ceases for the day once the contract is limit up or limit down. However, in some instances the exchange has the authority to step in and change the limits.

The purpose of daily price limits is to prevent large price movements from occurring because of speculative excesses. However, limits can become an artificial barrier to trading when the price of the underlying commodity is advancing or declining rapidly. Whether price limits are, on balance, good for futures markets is controversial.

Position limits are the maximum number of contracts that a speculator may hold. The purpose of the limits is to prevent speculators from exercising undue influence on the market.

2.3 CONVERGENCE OF FUTURES PRICE TO SPOT PRICE

As the delivery period for a futures contract is approached, the futures price converges to the spot price of the underlying asset. When the delivery period is reached, the futures price equals—or is very close to—the spot price.

To see why this is so, we first suppose that the futures price is above the spot price during the delivery period. Traders then have a clear arbitrage opportunity:

1. Short a futures contract
2. Buy the asset
3. Make delivery

These steps are certain to lead to a profit equal to the amount by which the futures price exceeds the spot price. As traders exploit this arbitrage opportunity, the futures price will fall. Suppose next that the futures price is below the spot price during the delivery period. Companies interested in acquiring the asset will find it attractive to enter into a long futures contract and then wait for delivery to be made. As they do so, the futures price will tend to rise.

The result is that the futures price is very close to the spot price during the delivery period. Figure 2.1 illustrates the convergence of the futures price to the spot price. In Figure 2.1(a) the futures price is above the spot price prior to the delivery period. In Figure 2.1(b) the futures price is below the spot price prior to the delivery period. The circumstances under which these two patterns are observed are discussed in Chapter 5.

2.4 DAILY SETTLEMENT AND MARGINS

If two investors get in touch with each other directly and agree to trade an asset in the future for a certain price, there are obvious risks. One of the investors may regret the

Figure 2.1 Relationship between futures price and spot price as the delivery period is approached: (a) Futures price above spot price; (b) futures price below spot price.

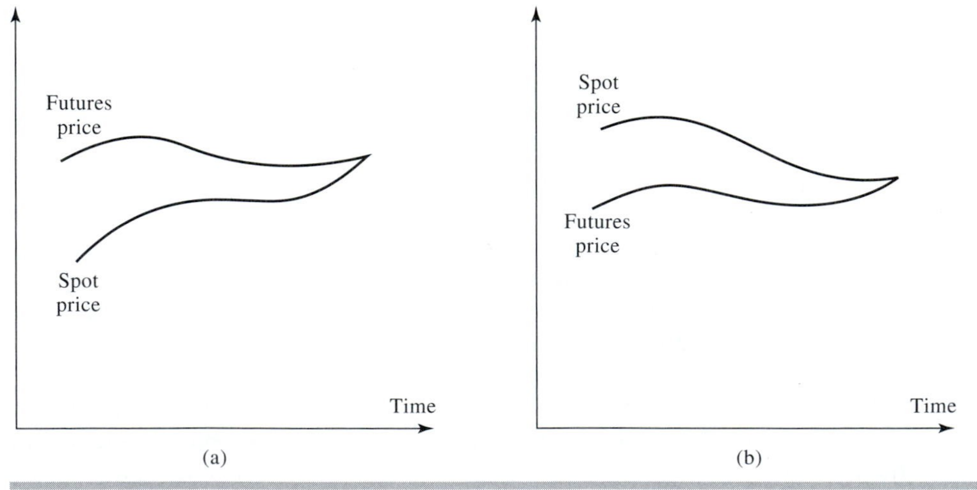

deal and try to back out. Alternatively, the investor simply may not have the financial resources to honor the agreement. One of the key roles of the exchange is to organize trading so that contract defaults are avoided. This is where margins come in.

The Operation of Margins

To illustrate how margins work, we consider an investor who contacts his or her broker on Thursday, June 5, to buy two December gold futures contracts on the New York Commodity Exchange (COMEX). We suppose that the current futures price is $400 per ounce. Because the contract size is 100 ounces, the investor has contracted to buy a total of 200 ounces at this price. The broker will require the investor to deposit funds in a *margin account*. The amount that must be deposited at the time the contract is entered into is known as the *initial margin*. We suppose this is $2,000 per contract, or $4,000 in total. At the end of each trading day, the margin account is adjusted to reflect the investor's gain or loss. This practice is referred to as *marking to market* the account.

Suppose, for example, that by the end of June 5 the futures price has dropped from $400 to $397. The investor has a loss of $600 (= 200 × $3), because the 200 ounces of December gold, which the investor contracted to buy at $400, can now be sold for only $397. The balance in the margin account would therefore be reduced by $600 to $3,400. Similarly, if the price of December gold rose to $403 by the end of the first day, the balance in the margin account would be increased by $600 to $4,600. A trade is first marked to market at the close of the day on which it takes place. It is then marked to market at the close of trading on each subsequent day.

Note that marking to market is not merely an arrangement between broker and client. When there is a decrease in the futures price so that the margin account of an investor with a long position is reduced by $600, the investor's broker has to pay the exchange $600 and the exchange passes the money on to the broker of an investor with a short position. Similarly, when there is an increase in the futures price, brokers for parties with short positions pay money to the exchange and brokers for parties with long positions receive money from the exchange. Later we will examine in more detail the mechanism by which this happens.

The investor is entitled to withdraw any balance in the margin account in excess of the initial margin. To ensure that the balance in the margin account never becomes negative a *maintenance margin*, which is somewhat lower than the initial margin, is set. If the balance in the margin account falls below the maintenance margin, the investor receives a margin call and is expected to top up the margin account to the initial margin level the next day. The extra funds deposited are known as a *variation margin*. If the investor does not provide the variation margin, the broker closes out the position by selling the contract. In the case of the investor considered earlier, closing out the position would involve neutralizing the existing contract by selling 200 ounces of gold for delivery in December.

Table 2.1 illustrates the operation of the margin account for one possible sequence of futures prices in the case of the investor considered earlier. The maintenance margin is assumed for the purpose of the illustration to be $1,500 per contract, or $3,000 in total. On June 13 the balance in the margin account falls $340 below the maintenance margin level. This drop triggers a margin call from the broker for an additional $1,340. Table 2.1 assumes that the investor does in fact provide this margin by the close of trading on June 16. On June 19 the balance in the margin account again falls below the maintenance

Table 2.1 Operation of margins for a long position in two gold futures contracts. The initial margin is \$2,000 per contract, or \$4,000 in total, and the maintenance margin is \$1,500 per contract, or \$3,000 in total. The contract is entered into on June 5 at \$400 and closed out on June 26 at \$392.30. The numbers in the second column, except the first and the last, represent the futures prices at the close of trading.

Day	*Futures price (\$)*	*Daily gain (loss) (\$)*	*Cumulative gain (loss) (\$)*	*Margin account balance (\$)*	*Margin call (\$)*
	400.00			4,000	
June 5	397.00	(600)	(600)	3,400	
June 6	396.10	(180)	(780)	3,220	
June 9	398.20	420	(360)	3,640	
June 10	397.10	(220)	(580)	3,420	
June 11	396.70	(80)	(660)	3,340	
June 12	395.40	(260)	(920)	3,080	
June 13	393.30	(420)	(1,340)	2,660	1,340
June 16	393.60	60	(1,280)	4,060	
June 17	391.80	(360)	(1,640)	3,700	
June 18	392.70	180	(1,460)	3,880	
June 19	387.00	(1,140)	(2,600)	2,740	1,260
June 20	387.00	0	(2,600)	4,000	
June 23	388.10	220	(2,380)	4,220	
June 24	388.70	120	(2,260)	4,340	
June 25	391.00	460	(1,800)	4,800	
June 26	392.30	260	(1,540)	5,060	

margin level, and a margin call for \$1,260 is sent out. The investor provides this margin by the close of trading on June 20. On June 26 the investor decides to close out the position by selling two contracts. The futures price on that day is \$392.30, and the investor has a cumulative loss of \$1,540. Note that the investor has excess margin on June 16, 23, 24, and 25. Table 2.1 assumes that the excess is not withdrawn.

Further Details

Many brokers allow an investor to earn interest on the balance in a margin account. The balance in the account does not, therefore, represent a true cost, provided that the interest rate is competitive with what could be earned elsewhere. To satisfy the initial margin requirements (but not subsequent margin calls), an investor can sometimes deposit securities with the broker. Treasury bills are usually accepted in lieu of cash at about 90% of their face value. Shares are also sometimes accepted in lieu of cash—but at about 50% of their market value.

The effect of the marking to market is that a futures contract is settled daily rather than all at the end of its life. At the end of each day, the investor's gain (loss) is added to (subtracted from) the margin account, bringing the value of the contract back to zero. A futures contract is in effect closed out and rewritten at a new price each day.

Minimum levels for initial and maintenance margins are set by the exchange. Individual brokers may require greater margins from their clients than those specified by the exchange. However, they cannot require lower margins than those specified by the exchange. Margin levels are determined by the variability of the price of the underlying asset. The higher this variability, the higher the margin levels. The maintenance margin is usually about 75% of the initial margin.

Margin requirements may depend on the objectives of the trader. A bona fide hedger, such as a company that produces the commodity on which the futures contract is written, is often subject to lower margin requirements than a speculator. The reason is that there is deemed to be less risk of default. Day trades and spread transactions often give rise to lower margin requirements than do hedge transactions. In a *day trade* the trader announces to the broker an intent to close out the position in the same day. In a *spread transaction* the trader simultaneously takes a long position in a contract on an asset for one maturity month and a short position in a contract on the same asset for another maturity month.

Note that margin requirements are the same on short futures positions as they are on long futures positions. It is just as easy to take a short futures position as it is to take a long one. The spot market does not have this symmetry. Taking a long position in the spot market involves buying the asset for immediate delivery and presents no problems. Taking a short position involves selling an asset that you do not own. This is a more complex transaction that may or may not be possible in a particular market. It is discussed further in Chapter 5.

The Clearinghouse and Clearing Margins

The *exchange clearinghouse* is an adjunct of the exchange and acts as an intermediary in futures transactions. It guarantees the performance of the parties to each transaction. The clearinghouse has a number of members, who must post funds with the exchange. Brokers who are not members themselves must channel their business through a member. The main task of the clearinghouse is to keep track of all the transactions that take place during a day, so that it can calculate the net position of each of its members.

Just as an investor is required to maintain a margin account with a broker, a clearinghouse member is required to maintain a margin account with the clearinghouse. This is known as a *clearing margin*. The margin accounts for clearinghouse members are adjusted for gains and losses at the end of each trading day in the same way as are the margin accounts of investors. However, in the case of the clearinghouse member, there is an original margin, but no maintenance margin. Every day the account balance for each contract must be maintained at an amount equal to the original margin times the number of contracts outstanding. Thus, depending on transactions during the day and price movements, the clearinghouse member may have to add funds to its margin account at the end of the day. Alternatively, it may find it can remove funds from the account at this time. Brokers who are not clearinghouse members must maintain a margin account with a clearinghouse member.

In determining clearing margins, the exchange clearinghouse calculates the number of contracts outstanding on either a gross or a net basis. The *gross basis* simply adds

Business Snapshot 2.2 Long-Term Capital Management's Big Loss

Long-Term Capital Management (LTCM), a hedge fund formed in the mid-1990s, always collateralized its transactions. The hedge fund's investment strategy was known as convergence arbitrage. A very simple example of what it might do is the following. It would find two bonds, X and Y, issued by the same company that promised the same payoffs, with X being less liquid (i.e., less actively traded) than Y. The market always places a value on liquidity. As a result the price of X would be less than the price of Y. LTCM would buy X, short Y, and wait, expecting the prices of the two bonds to converge at some future time.

When interest rates increased, the company expected both bonds to move down in price by about the same amount, so that the collateral it paid on bond X would be about the same as the collateral it received on bond Y. Similarly, when interest rates decreased, LTCM expected both bonds to move up in price by about the same amount, so that the collateral it received on bond X would be about the same as the collateral it paid on bond Y. It therefore expected that there would be no significant outflow of funds as a result of its collateralization agreements.

In August 1998, Russia defaulted on its debt and this led to what is termed a "flight to quality" in capital markets. One result was that investors valued liquid instruments more highly than usual and the spreads between the prices of the liquid and illiquid instruments in LTCM's portfolio increased dramatically. The prices of the bonds LTCM had bought went down and the prices of those it had shorted increased. It was required to post collateral on both. The company was highly leveraged and unable to make the payments required under the collateralization agreements. The result was that positions had to be closed out and there was a total loss of about $4 billion. If the company had been less highly leveraged it would probably have been able to survive the flight to quality and could have waited for the prices of the liquid and illiquid bonds to become closer to each other.

the total of all long positions entered into by clients to the total of all the short positions entered into by clients. The net basis allows these to be offset against each other. Suppose a clearinghouse member has two clients: one with a long position in 20 contracts, the other with a short position in 15 contracts. Gross margining would calculate the clearing margin on the basis of 35 contracts; net margining would calculate the clearing margin on the basis of 5 contracts. Most exchanges currently use net margining.

Credit Risk

The whole purpose of the margining system is to ensure that traders do not walk away from their commitments. Overall the system has been very successful. Investors entering into contracts at major exchanges have always had their contracts honored. Futures exchanges were tested on October 19, 1987, when the S&P 500 index declined by over 20% and investors with long positions in S&P futures found they had negative margin balances. Some of the investors walked away from their positions (even though they were legally obliged to make good on their contracts). As a result some brokers went bankrupt because, without their clients' money, they were unable to meet margin calls on contracts they entered into on behalf of their clients. However, everyone who had a short futures position on the S&P 500 got paid off.

Collateralization in OTC Markets

Credit risk has traditionally been a feature of the over-the-counter markets. There is always a chance that the party on the other side of an over-the-counter trade will default. It is interesting that, in an attempt to reduce credit risk, the over-the-counter market is now imitating the margining system adopted by exchanges with a procedure known as *collateralization*.

Consider two participants in the over-the-counter market, company A and company B, with an outstanding over-the-counter contract. They could enter into a collateralization agreement where they value the contract each day using a pre-agreed valuation methodology. If from one day to the next the value of the contract to company A increases, company B is required to pay collateral equal to this increase to company A. Similarly, if the value of the contract to company A decreases, company A is required to pay collateral equal to the decrease to company B.

Collateralization significantly reduces the credit risk in over-the-counter contracts and is discussed further in Chapter 20. Collateralization agreements were used by a hedge fund, Long-Term Capital Management (LTCM), in the 1990s. They allowed LTCM to be highly leveraged. The contracts did provide credit risk protection, but as described in Business Snapshot 2.2 the high leverage left the hedge fund vulnerable to other risks.

2.5 NEWSPAPER QUOTES

Many newspapers carry futures prices. Table 2.2 shows the prices for commodities as they appeared in the *Wall Street Journal* of Thursday, February 5, 2004. The prices refer to the trading that took place on the previous day (i.e., Wednesday, February 4, 2004). The prices for index futures, currency futures, and interest rate futures are given in Chapters 3, 5, and 6, respectively.

The asset underlying the futures contract, the exchange that the contract is traded on, the contract size, and how the price is quoted are all shown at the top of each section in Table 2.2. The first asset is corn, traded on the Chicago Board of Trade. The contract size is 5,000 bushels, and the price is quoted in cents per bushel. The months in which particular contracts are traded are shown in the first column. Corn contracts with maturities in March 2004, May 2004, July 2004, September 2004, December 2004, March 2005, and December 2005 were traded on February 4, 2004.

Prices

The first three numbers in each row show the opening price, the highest price achieved in trading during the day, and the lowest price achieved in trading during the day. The opening price is representative of the prices at which contracts were trading immediately after the opening bell. For March 2004 corn on February 4, 2004, the opening price was 273.25 cents per bushel and, during the day, the price traded between 269.25 and 274.75 cents.

Table 2.2 Commodity futures quotes from the *Wall Street Journal*, February 5, 2004. (Columns show month, open, high, low, settle, change, lifetime high, lifetime low, and open interest, respectively.)

Exchange Abbreviations

For commodity futures and futures options

CBT-Chicago Board of Trade;
CME-Chicago Mercantile Exchange;
CSCE-Coffee, Sugar & Cocoa Exchange, New York;
CMX-COMEX (Div. of New York Mercantile Exchange);
EUREX-European Exchange;
FINEX-Financial Exchange (Div. of New York Cotton Exchange);
IPE-International Petroleum Exchange;
KC-Kansas City Board of Trade;
LIFFE-London International Financial Futures Exchange;
MATIF-Marche a Terme International de France;
ME-Montreal Exchange;
MPLS-Minneapolis Grain Exchange;
NQLX-NQLX (unit of Euronext.liffe)
NYCE-New York Cotton Exchange;
NYFE-New York Futures Exchange (Sub. of New York Cotton Exchange);
NYM-New York Mercantile Exchange;
ONE-OneChicago
SFE-Sydney Futures Exchange;
SGX-Singapore Exchange Ltd.;

Futures prices reflect day and overnight trading
Open interest reflects previous day's trading

Wednesday, February 4, 2004

Grain and Oilseed Futures

Corn (CBT)-5,000 bu.; cents per bu.

	OPEN	HIGH	LOW	SETTLE	CHG	LIFETIME HIGH	LIFETIME LOW	OPEN INT
Mar	273.25	274.75	269.25	270.25	-2.75	281.50	219.00	292,145
May	278.00	279.75	274.00	275.25	-2.75	285.75	224.50	130,369
July	280.50	282.50	277.00	278.25	-2.25	288.50	227.75	79,647
Sept	274.50	276.00	272.50	272.50	-2.75	283.00	229.75	14,330
Dec	270.75	273.00	268.50	270.00	-.75	278.75	232.50	105,132
Mr05	274.25	276.00	272.25	273.50	-1.00	281.50	239.00	7,662
Dec	252.50	252.75	252.50	252.75	-.25	258.00	235.00	1,364

Est vol 54,315; vol Tue 81,306; open int 632,256, +1,555.

Oats (CBT)-5,000 bu.; cents per bu.

	OPEN	HIGH	LOW	SETTLE	CHG	LIFETIME HIGH	LIFETIME LOW	OPEN INT
Mar	156.25	156.25	153.00	153.00	-3.00	164.75	131.00	4,361
May	158.50	158.50	155.75	155.75	-3.25	163.75	135.00	1,403

Est vol 543; vol Tue 1,134; open int 6,487, +277.

Soybeans (CBT)-5,000 bu.; cents per bu.

	OPEN	HIGH	LOW	SETTLE	CHG	LIFETIME HIGH	LIFETIME LOW	OPEN INT
Mar	803.00	813.00	802.00	805.75	3.25	855.00	508.00	110,983
May	805.00	811.50	804.00	805.75	1.25	853.50	515.50	83,539
July	795.50	799.50	791.50	792.00	-3.00	842.00	520.00	37,181
Aug	765.50	770.00	760.00	760.50	-5.25	804.00	521.00	8,682
Sept	714.00	714.00	705.00	706.50	-5.50	748.00	528.00	4,033
Nov	643.50	646.50	635.00	636.50	-8.25	678.00	483.00	22,489
Ja05	643.00	643.00	638.00	638.00	-7.00	678.00	573.00	440

Est vol 51,149; vol Tue 69,055; open int 267,713, -1,819.

Soybean Meal (CBT)-100 tons; $ per ton.

	OPEN	HIGH	LOW	SETTLE	CHG	LIFETIME HIGH	LIFETIME LOW	OPEN INT
Mar	246.80	249.80	246.50	247.00	.20	268.80	152.50	46,742
May	247.00	249.80	246.40	246.50	-.40	268.20	153.00	59,488
July	243.40	245.50	242.30	242.40	-1.00	263.20	152.50	32,077
Aug	234.80	235.50	232.80	233.00	-1.10	251.20	154.00	11,892
Sept	221.00	222.00	218.80	219.30	-.90	234.50	154.00	9,574
Oct	192.50	192.50	189.00	190.00	-1.40	206.00	150.50	7,015
Dec	189.00	189.00	185.50	185.60	-2.60	202.50	150.00	15,868
Ja05	188.00	188.00	185.50	185.80	-2.40	203.00	161.50	882

Est vol 20,000; vol Tue 33,272; open int 184,147, -2,396.

Soybean Oil (CBT)-60,000 lbs.; cents per lb.

	OPEN	HIGH	LOW	SETTLE	CHG	LIFETIME HIGH	LIFETIME LOW	OPEN INT
Mar	29.86	30.13	29.75	29.86	...	30.37	19.00	70,068
May	29.75	30.02	29.66	29.76	.04	30.19	19.01	64,391
July	29.80	29.80	29.40	29.45	-.02	29.87	19.01	41,093
Aug	29.08	29.15	28.85	28.90	-.05	29.20	19.05	5,103
Sept	28.25	28.25	27.95	28.00	-.02	28.35	19.01	6,754
Oct	26.90	27.00	26.80	26.90	-.15	27.10	19.00	5,429
Dec	25.90	25.90	25.75	25.78	-.19	26:30	18.98	10,994

Est vol 17,571; vol Tue 33,871; open int 204,766, +2,177.

Rough Rice (CBT)-2,000 cwt.; cents per cwt.

	OPEN	HIGH	LOW	SETTLE	CHG	LIFETIME HIGH	LIFETIME LOW	OPEN INT
Mar	776.00	784.50	770.00	773.00	-1.00	925.00	680.00	5,418
July	816.00	816.00	809.00	809.00	-1.00	939.00	761.00	541

Est vol 409; vol Tue 973; open int 7,275, -63.

Wheat (CBT)-5,000 bu.; cents per bu.

	OPEN	HIGH	LOW	SETTLE	CHG	LIFETIME HIGH	LIFETIME LOW	OPEN INT
Mar	380.50	382.00	375.25	376.00	-4.50	421.50	301.50	75,392
May	386.75	387.00	381.00	382.50	-4.25	413.00	290.00	28,178
July	381.00	381.50	377.00	377.25	-4.25	404.00	298.00	25,753
Sept	382.00	383.50	381.00	381.50	-3.50	402.00	326.00	1,803
Dec	391.50	392.00	388.50	390.50	-3.50	410.00	330.00	3,219

Est vol 18,516; vol Tue 24,710; open int 134,517, +36.

Wheat (KC)-5,000 bu.; cents per bu.

	OPEN	HIGH	LOW	SETTLE	CHG	LIFETIME HIGH	LIFETIME LOW	OPEN INT
Mar	386.00	387.50	380.00	380.50	-7.00	416.00	314.00	35,068
May	385.75	387.00	379.00	380.50	-6.75	412.00	315.00	14,006
July	383.50	384.00	380.00	380.50	-4.75	408.00	313.00	11,690
Sept	384.50	386.00	383.50	386.00	-2.00	405.00	330.50	1,938
Dec	392.50	393.50	390.00	390.00	-5.50	408.50	341.00	1,273

Est vol 19,427; vol Tue 10,017; open int 63,983, -463.

Wheat (MPLS)-5,000 bu.; cents per bu.

	OPEN	HIGH	LOW	SETTLE	CHG	LIFETIME HIGH	LIFETIME LOW	OPEN INT
Mar	412.00	413.25	409.00	411.00	-2.50	423.75	343.75	13,938
May	407.00	407.25	401.50	402.25	-4.75	420.00	349.50	7,993
July	400.00	400.00	395.00	395.00	-5.50	411.00	352.00	4,185
Sept	396.50	396.50	391.50	391.50	-5.50	403.00	346.00	4,898
Dec	400.00	401.00	395.75	396.00	-5.00	408.00	355.00	1,037

Est vol 7,695; vol Tue 6,203; open int 32,066, -868.

Livestock Futures

Cattle-Feeder (CME)-50,000 lbs.; cents per lb.

	OPEN	HIGH	LOW	SETTLE	CHG	LIFETIME HIGH	LIFETIME LOW	OPEN INT
Mar	83.70	83.80	82.22	82.22	-1.50	97.45	77.50	5,192
Apr	85.30	85.40	83.92	83.92	-1.50	94.90	78.30	2,260
May	85.85	85.85	84.35	84.35	-1.50	93.90	79.10	3,739
Aug	88.10	88.20	86.77	86.77	-1.50	93.25	81.60	2,316
Sept	87.75	87.75	87.00	87.00	-1.50	92.00	81.70	297
Oct	88.25	88.25	87.00	87.00	-1.50	92.00	81.95	317

Est vol 1,472; vol Tue 1,739; open int 14,199, +22.

Cattle-Live (CME)-40,000 lbs.; cents per lb.

	OPEN	HIGH	LOW	SETTLE	CHG	LIFETIME HIGH	LIFETIME LOW	OPEN INT
Feb	76.30	76.45	74.82	74.82	-1.50	94.95	71.00	18,526
Apr	72.87	73.05	71.37	71.37	-1.50	85.55	68.60	42,771
June	69.95	70.15	68.42	68.42	-1.50	78.75	66.50	15,578
Aug	72.45	72.55	70.95	70.95	-1.50	77.20	68.00	8,444
Oct	75.50	75.55	74.02	74.20	-1.32	78.80	69.50	10,518
Dec	77.07	77.15	75.65	76.12	-1.02	78.90	72.00	3,520

Est vol 16,156; vol Tue 10,727; open int 100,345, +316.

Hogs-Lean (CME)-40,000 lbs.; cents per lb.

	OPEN	HIGH	LOW	SETTLE	CHG	LIFETIME HIGH	LIFETIME LOW	OPEN INT
Feb	59.80	59.97	58.97	59.42	.50	63.00	50.75	5,560
Apr	59.67	60.00	58.70	58.87	-.47	62.40	53.55	28,654
May	60.55	60.85	60.30	60.65	-.05	63.90	55.90	1,621
June	65.00	65.10	64.05	64.60	-.15	67.10	58.40	8,907
July	61.70	61.80	61.25	61.47	-.02	63.85	56.90	2,289
Aug	59.70	59.80	59.25	59.65	.10	61.37	55.00	1,521
Oct	52.50	52.85	52.25	52.25	-.35	54.65	49.00	919
Dec	52.40	53.15	52.25	52.37	-.12	53.97	49.00	522

Est vol 10,289; vol Tue 8,924; open int 50,055, -1,609.

Pork Bellies (CME)-40,000 lbs.; cents per lb.

	OPEN	HIGH	LOW	SETTLE	CHG	LIFETIME HIGH	LIFETIME LOW	OPEN INT
Feb	86.30	87.67	86.30	87.30	1.17	93.40	76.40	831
Mar	87.30	88.25	87.30	88.02	1.30	93.15	76.90	879
May	89.05	89.50	88.75	89.50	1.67	94.15	79.40	385

Est vol 669; vol Tue 883; open int 2,270, -26.

Food and Fiber Futures

Lumber (CME)-110,000 bd. ft., $ per 1,000 bd. ft.

	OPEN	HIGH	LOW	SETTLE	CHG	LIFETIME HIGH	LIFETIME LOW	OPEN INT
Mar	334.20	344.50	334.00	344.50	10.00	365.00	256.20	2,408
May	336.60	346.60	336.60	346.60	10.00	357.50	263.10	686
July	337.90	344.00	335.10	343.20	6.80	354.90	282.00	233

Est vol 889; vol Tue 286; open int 3,368, -22.

Milk (CME)-200,000 lbs., cents per lb.

	OPEN	HIGH	LOW	SETTLE	CHG	LIFETIME HIGH	LIFETIME LOW	OPEN INT
Feb	11.74	11.75	11.72	11.75	.05	11.90	10.95	2,554
Mar	12.20	12.26	12.20	12.20	.05	12.35	11.05	2,525
Apr	12.65	12.75	12.60	12.73	.13	12.75	11.00	1,988
May	12.88	13.00	12.87	12.95	.13	13.00	11.00	1,948
June	13.13	13.26	13.12	13.26	.16	13.32	11.41	1,761
July	13.74	13.95	13.72	13.86	.12	13.95	11.60	1,676
Aug	14.18	14.25	14.13	14.20	.02	14.28	11.65	1,723
Sept	14.55	14.75	14.55	14.65	.05	14.75	12.10	1,900
Oct	13.94	14.15	13.89	14.05	.11	14.15	11.89	1,513
Nov	12.95	13.20	12.95	13.20	.25	13.30	11.39	1,169
Dec	12.40	12.45	12.40	12.45	.05	12.50	11.30	809

Est vol 1,437; vol Tue 842; open int 19,736, +289.

	OPEN	HIGH	LOW	SETTLE	CHG	LIFETIME HIGH	LIFETIME LOW	OPEN INT
Cocoa (CSCE)-10 metric tons; $ per ton.								
Mar	1,606	1,615	1,578	1,581	−19	2,358	1,250	22,360
May	1,596	1,599	1,565	1,569	−21	2,265	1,345	13,766
July	1,595	1,596	1,572	1,564	−23	2,307	1,350	12,922
Sept	1,590	1,590	1,562	1,563	−24	2,402	1,370	8,710
Est vol 9,057; vol Tue 9,675; open int 87,295, −1,218.								
Coffee (CSCE)-37,500 lbs.; cents per lb.								
Mar	73.75	74.00	71.60	72.60	−2.05	83.00	59.65	59,048
May	75.60	75.80	73.70	74.65	−1.95	82.00	61.75	26,054
July	77.00	77.70	75.70	76.45	−1.95	82.50	63.90	8,737
Sept	78.40	79.20	77.40	78.15	−1.90	83.45	65.75	7,837
Dec	80.15	81.25	80.15	80.75	−1.90	85.95	68.50	4,577
Mr05	83.40	83.70	83.40	83.30	−1.85	87.90	71.00	2,948
Est vol 32,220; vol Tue 15,761; open int 109,783, +1,170.								
Sugar-World (CSCE)-112,000 lbs.; cents per lb.								
Mar	5.74	5.77	5.66	5.68	−.07	7.65	5.50	131,494
May	5.94	5.97	5.87	5.88	−.07	7.32	5.54	50,135
July	5.97	6.00	5.92	5.93	−.06	6.95	5.50	37,213
Oct	6.09	6.10	6.02	6.03	−.06	6.88	5.55	25,822
Mr05	6.33	6.33	6.27	6.28	−.04	6.82	6.24	11,411
May	6.32	6.33	6.30	6.30	−.03	6.57	6.20	4,813
July	6.28	6.29	6.28	6.25	−.03	6.42	6.15	2,901
Est vol 23,839; vol Tue 32,525; open int 265,575, −1,048.								
Sugar-Domestic (CSCE)-112,000 lbs.; cents per lb.								
Mar	20.35	20.40	20.35	20.40	.04	22.02	20.20	884
May	20.35	20.35	20.35	20.35	...	22.07	20.15	3,835
July	20.50	20.50	20.50	20.50	...	22.10	20.25	3,280
Sept	20.74	20.74	20.74	20.74	−.01	22.07	20.63	3,087
Nov	21.05	21.05	21.05	21.05	...	21.70	20.94	855
Ja05	20.80	20.80	20.80	20.80	...	21.40	20.80	285
Est vol 43; vol Tue 203; open int 12,510, −112.								
Cotton (NYCE)-50,000 lbs.; cents per lb.								
Mar	69.10	69.90	68.70	69.25	.35	86.00	45.60	43,633
May	71.20	71.95	70.75	71.27	.44	86.00	51.50	27,184
July	72.35	73.00	71.80	72.30	.35	85.50	56.75	8,924
Dec	68.00	68.25	67.50	67.75	.05	71.00	59.00	6,330
Est vol 12,611; vol Tue 21,022; open int 88,074, +239.								
Orange Juice (NYCE)-15,000 lbs.; cents per lb.								
Mar	61.20	62.00	60.80	61.65	.25	103.50	60.60	25,803
May	64.50	64.70	64.00	64.45	.25	105.00	63.50	7,488
July	67.20	67.30	66.50	67.05	.35	106.00	66.40	1,518
Sept	69.40	70.00	69.40	69.40	.20	86.80	69.25	774
Nov	71.30	71.30	71.30	71.90	−.10	91.50	71.30	491
Est vol 1,846; vol Tue 1,259; open int 36,251, −123.								
Metal Futures								
Copper-High (CMX)-25,000 lbs.; cents per lb.								
Feb	116.90	117.30	116.90	117.35	0.60	117.30	67.20	1,033
Mar	116.85	117.55	116.50	117.45	0.60	117.55	69.75	65,863
Apr	116.55	116.90	116.55	117.10	0.60	116.90	71.95	941
May	116.05	116.70	115.95	116.55	0.45	116.70	70.90	8,263
June	116.00	116.15	115.75	115.95	0.40	116.15	73.50	724
July	115.00	115.45	115.00	115.30	0.35	115.45	70.90	6,549
Aug	114.30	114.70	114.30	114.70	0.40	114.70	73.65	486
Sept	113.90	114.00	113.90	114.05	0.40	114.00	70.95	2,211
Oct	113.25	113.25	113.25	113.45	0.40	113.25	74.00	388
Nov	112.55	112.70	112.45	112.85	0.40	112.70	79.00	287
Dec	111.85	112.35	111.60	112.20	0.35	112.35	74.20	4,135
Mr05	110.55	110.55	110.50	110.40	0.25	110.55	74.40	322
Est vol 11,000; vol Tue 8,170; open int 91,868, −170.								
Gold (CMX)-100 troy oz.; $ per troy oz.								
Feb	399.80	401.30	398.50	401.00	1.80	431.50	322.00	5,090
Apr	400.70	401.80	399.40	401.70	1.80	432.30	320.00	143,464
June	401.40	403.00	400.50	402.70	1.80	432.00	287.00	29,868
Aug	403.10	403.10	402.00	403.70	1.80	431.30	324.70	8,621
Dec	404.10	405.50	403.00	405.50	1.70	434.50	290.00	22,312
Est vol 40,000; vol Tue 40,608; open int 236,512, −4,897.								
Platinum (NYM)-50 troy oz.; $ per troy oz.								
Apr	824.00	824.00	812.00	820.60	−5.70	868.00	677.00	6,816
July	...	...	...	810.60	−5.70	852.00	801.00	292
Est vol 602; vol Tue 808; open int 7,126, −95.								
Silver (CMX)-5,000 troy oz.; cnts per troy oz.								
Feb	611.5	611.5	611.5	614.5	2.4	611.5	611.5	240
Mar	613.0	618.5	607.0	614.8	2.5	679.5	437.0	78,208
May	614.5	620.0	608.5	616.2	2.6	681.0	445.0	7,153
July	616.5	621.0	611.0	617.4	2.6	673.0	436.0	5,063
Dec	618.5	623.0	613.0	619.9	2.6	677.0	440.0	12,458
Dc05	627.0	627.0	627.0	624.6	3.9	675.0	436.0	1,564
Est vol 16,000; vol Tue 15,059; open int 107,432, −482.								
Petroleum Futures								
Crude Oil, Light Sweet (NYM)-1,000 bbls.; $ per bbl.								
Mar	34.09	34.45	32.95	33.10	−1.00	35.25	20.35	196,160
Apr	32.82	33.25	31.85	31.99	−0.83	34.50	20.35	91,932
May	32.11	32.20	31.25	31.32	−0.72	33.85	20.35	42,864
June	31.55	31.65	30.80	30.84	−0.63	33.25	20.53	39,700
July	31.00	31.10	30.40	30.37	−0.60	32.60	20.86	29,920
Aug	30.57	30.60	30.10	29.93	−0.58	32.15	20.84	19,040
Sept	30.21	30.21	29.65	29.58	−0.56	31.61	20.82	26,690
Oct	29.93	29.93	29.93	29.33	−0.54	31.20	23.75	17,830
Nov	29.59	29.70	29.59	29.11	−0.53	30.85	24.75	14,370
Dec	29.60	29.60	29.00	28.92	−0.52	30.69	16.35	51,129
Ja05	29.00	29.00	29.00	28.67	−0.50	30.33	23.25	15,606
Feb	28.75	28.75	28.75	28.48	−0.49	30.07	23.85	5,061
June	28.24	28.24	28.24	27.79	−0.45	29.05	22.40	10,556
Dec	27.42	27.52	27.20	27.03	−0.39	28.31	17.00	25,454
Dc06	26.77	26.77	26.60	26.38	−0.39	27.65	19.10	16,726
Dc07	26.45	26.50	26.40	26.18	−0.34	27.35	19.50	9,971
Dc08	26.50	26.50	26.50	26.18	−0.34	27.15	19.75	7,354
Est vol 225,976; vol Tue 219,163; open int 663,890, +1,691.								
Heating Oil No. 2 (NYM)-42,000 gal.; $ per gal.								
Mar	.9142	.9280	.8830	.8897	−.0245	1.0129	.6370	64,063
Apr	.8770	.8840	.8505	.8586	−.0166	.9417	.6275	22,296
May	.8436	.8436	.8200	.8251	−.0151	.8881	.6140	10,010
June	.8174	.8185	.7950	.8016	−.0136	.8581	.6354	11,337
July	.7800	.7910	.7800	.7896	−.0131	.8380	.6415	7,713
Aug	.7925	.7925	.7750	.7876	−.0126	.8373	.6455	5,437
Oct	.8050	.8050	.8050	.7986	−.0121	.8425	.6655	1,466
Nov	.8100	.8100	.8100	.8046	−.0121	.8480	.6820	1,548
Dec	.8175	.8175	.8100	.8106	−.0121	.8540	.6937	10,047
Est vol 66,129; vol Tue 49,216; open int 141,064, +3,503.								
Gasoline-NY Unleaded (NYM)-42,000 gal.; $ per gal.								
Mar	1.0015	1.0150	.9740	.9857	−.0158	1.0410	.7325	67,894
Apr	1.0475	1.0530	1.0190	1.0305	−.0124	1.0800	.7975	27,871
May	1.0310	1.0310	1.0130	1.0150	−.0119	1.0655	.8080	13,375
June	1.0050	1.0100	.9920	.9895	−.0109	1.0410	.8070	6,390
July	.9550	.9650	.9550	.9615	−.0104	1.0100	.9300	3,617
Sept	.9090	.9090	.9050	.8940	−.0089	.9380	.8530	5,260
Est vol 46,056; vol Tue 48,469; open int 131,831, +2,200.								
Natural Gas (NYM)-10,000 MMBtu.; $ per MMBtu								
Mar	5.670	5.790	5.560	5.654	.003	7.500	3.150	51,734
Apr	5.350	5.420	5.280	5.340	.015	6.010	2.970	23,196
May	5.180	5.270	5.180	5.210	.020	5.668	3.030	25,805
June	5.220	5.260	5.190	5.210	.020	5.612	3.010	19,336
July	5.230	5.274	5.200	5.235	.020	5.622	3.040	17,676
Aug	5.260	5.294	5.220	5.250	.020	5.624	3.120	13,402
Sept	5.220	5.265	5.180	5.218	.020	5.640	3.100	13,093
Oct	5.230	5.240	5.200	5.225	.017	5.580	3.100	14,742
Nov	5.430	5.460	5.400	5.423	.017	5.735	3.270	10,289
Dec	5.610	5.660	5.580	5.613	.015	5.912	3.460	12,860
Ja05	5.745	5.800	5.710	5.750	.015	6.027	3.520	9,971
Feb	5.710	5.720	5.680	5.710	.015	5.991	3.400	9,752
Mar	5.570	5.570	5.505	5.540	.020	5.740	3.640	8,955
May	4.880	4.880	4.880	4.900	.020	5.000	3.500	4,187
June	4.920	4.920	4.920	4.925	.020	5.020	3.530	4,518
July	4.950	4.950	4.950	4.961	.020	5.050	3.560	10,788
Aug	4.950	4.950	4.950	4.971	.020	5.065	3.230	5,319
Dec	5.290	5.290	5.290	5.311	.015	5.400	3.960	4,389
Est vol 46,926; vol Tue 45,710; open int 307,861, −1,771.								
Brent Crude (IPE)-1,000 net bbls.; $ per bbl.								
Mar	29.52	29.80	28.85	28.88	−0.62	32.10	23.00	81,701
Apr	29.28	29.53	28.62	28.66	−0.63	31.54	22.95	82,264
May	29.10	29.34	28.45	28.48	−0.66	31.18	21.97	22,069
June	28.88	29.07	28.25	28.29	−0.65	30.83	23.45	27,498
July	28.69	28.83	28.29	28.08	−0.65	30.55	23.65	10,450
Aug	28.10	28.51	28.10	27.87	−0.64	30.20	24.00	9,032
Sept	28.25	28.29	27.88	27.65	−0.64	29.77	24.40	11,307
Oct	27.94	28.08	27.94	27.45	−0.63	39.45	20.90	5,806
Nov	27.73	27.88	27.73	27.27	−0.61	38.85	24.15	5,352
Dec	27.65	27.70	27.17	27.10	−0.59	38.83	25.32	24,112
Ja05	27.44	27.45	27.35	26.88	−0.57	28.70	22.43	3,611
Dec	26.00	26.00	25.90	25.65	−0.34	26.90	21.91	20,253
Dc06	25.30	25.30	25.30	25.05	−0.29	26.05	24.10	3,400
Est vol 113,000; vol Tue 113,278; open int 321,427, −3,267.								

Source: Reprinted by permission of Dow Jones, Inc., via Copyright Clearance Center, Inc.,

Settlement Price

The fourth number is the *settlement price*. This is the price used for calculating daily gains and losses and margin requirements. It is usually calculated as the price at which the contract traded immediately before the bell signaling the end of trading for the day. The fifth number is the change in the settlement price from the previous day. For the March 2004 corn futures contract, the settlement price was 270.25 cents on February 4, 2004, down 2.75 cents from February 3, 2004.

In the case of the March 2004 corn futures, an investor with a long position in one contract would find his or her margin account balance reduced by $137.50 (= 5,000 × 2.75 cents) between February 3, 2004, and February 4, 2004. Similarly, an investor with a short position in one contract would find that the margin balance increased by $137.50 between these two dates.

Lifetime Highs and Lows

The sixth and seventh numbers show the highest futures price and the lowest futures price achieved in the trading of the particular contract over its lifetime. The March 2004 corn contract had traded for well over a year on February 4, 2004. During this period the highest and lowest prices achieved were 281.50 cents and 219.00 cents.

Open Interest and Volume of Trading

The final column in Table 2.2 shows the *open interest* for each contract. This is the total number of contracts outstanding. The open interest is the number of long positions or, equivalently, the number of short positions. Because of the problems in compiling the data, the open-interest information is one trading day older than the price information. Thus, in the *Wall Street Journal* of February 5, 2004, the open interest is for the close of trading on February 3, 2004. For the March 2004 corn futures contract, the open interest was 292,145 contracts.

At the end of each section, Table 2.2 shows the estimated volume of trading in contracts of all maturities on February 4, 2004, and the actual volume of trading in these contracts on February 3, 2004. It also shows the total open interest for all contracts on February 3, 2004, and the change in this open interest from the previous trading day. For all corn futures contracts, the estimated trading volume was 54,315 contracts on February 4, 2004, and the actual trading volume was 81,306 contracts on February 3, 2004. The open interest for all corn futures contracts was 632,256 on February 3, 2004, up 1,555 from the previous trading day.

Sometimes the volume of trading in a day is greater than the open interest at the end of the day. This is indicative of a large number of day trades.

Patterns of Futures Prices

A number of different patterns of futures prices can be picked out from Table 2.2. Figure 2.2 shows the pattern of (settlement) futures prices for the gold contract trading on the New York Commodity Exchange and the Brent crude oil contract trading on the International Petroleum Exchange. The futures price of gold increases as the time to maturity increases. This is known as a normal market. By contrast, the futures price of crude oil is a decreasing function of maturity. This is known as an *inverted market*.

Figure 2.2 Settlement futures price as a function of time to maturity on February 4, 2004, for (a) gold and (b) Brent crude oil.

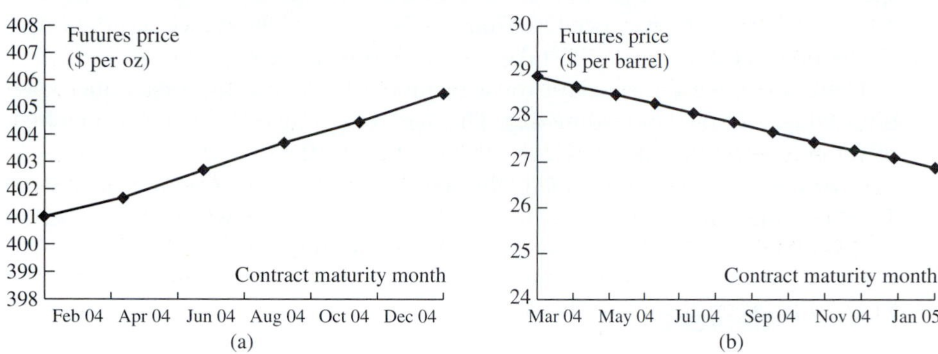

Other commodities show mixed patterns. For example, the futures price of heating oil first decreases, then increases with maturity.

2.6 DELIVERY

As mentioned earlier in this chapter, very few of the futures contracts that are entered into lead to delivery of the underlying asset. Most are closed out early. Nevertheless, it is the possibility of eventual delivery that determines the futures price. An understanding of delivery procedures is therefore important.

The period during which delivery can be made is defined by the exchange and varies from contract to contract. The decision on when to deliver is made by the party with the short position, whom we shall refer to as investor A. When investor A decides to deliver, investor A's broker issues a notice of intention to deliver to the exchange clearinghouse. This notice states how many contracts will be delivered and, in the case of commodities, also specifies where delivery will be made and what grade will be delivered. The exchange then chooses a party with a long position to accept delivery.

Suppose that the party on the other side of investor A's futures contract when it was entered into was investor B. It is important to realize that there is no reason to expect that it will be investor B who takes delivery. Investor B may well have closed out his or her position by trading with investor C, investor C may have closed out his or her position by trading with investor D, and so on. The usual rule chosen by the exchange is to pass the notice of intention to deliver on to the party with the oldest outstanding long position. Parties with long positions must accept delivery notices. However, if the notices are transferable, long investors have a short period of time, usually half an hour, to find another party with a long position that is prepared to accept the notice from them.

In the case of a commodity, taking delivery usually means accepting a warehouse receipt in return for immediate payment. The party taking delivery is then responsible for all warehousing costs. In the case of livestock futures, there may be costs associated with feeding and looking after the animals. In the case of financial futures, delivery is usually made by wire transfer. For all contracts the price paid is usually based on the settlement price immediately preceding the date of the notice of intention to deliver. If specified by the exchange, this price is adjusted for grade, location of delivery, and so on. The whole delivery procedure from the issuance of the notice of intention to deliver to the delivery itself generally takes about two to three days.

There are three critical days for a contract. These are the first notice day, the last notice day, and the last trading day. The *first notice day* is the first day on which a notice of intention to make delivery can be submitted to the exchange. The *last notice day* is the last such day. The *last trading day* is generally a few days before the last notice day. To avoid the risk of having to take delivery, an investor with a long position should close out his or her contracts prior to the first notice day.

Cash Settlement

Some financial futures, such as those on stock indices, are settled in cash because it is inconvenient or impossible to deliver the underlying asset. In the case of the futures contract on the S&P 500, for example, delivering the underlying asset would involve delivering a portfolio of 500 stocks. When a contract is settled in cash, all outstanding contracts are declared closed on a particular day. The final settlement price is set equal to the spot price of the underlying asset at either the opening or close of trading on that day. For example, in the S&P 500 futures contract trading on the Chicago Mercantile Exchange, all contracts are declared closed on the third Friday of the delivery month and the final settlement price is the opening price of the index on that day.

2.7 TYPES OF TRADERS AND TYPES OF ORDERS

There are two main types of traders executing trades: commission brokers and locals. *Commission brokers* are following the instructions of their clients and charge a commission for doing so; *locals* are trading on their own account.

Individuals taking positions, whether locals or the clients of commission brokers, can be categorized as hedgers, speculators, or arbitrageurs, as discussed in Chapter 1. Speculators can be classified as scalpers, day traders, or position traders. *Scalpers* are watching for very short-term trends and attempt to profit from small changes in the contract price. They usually hold their positions for only a few minutes. *Day traders* hold their positions for less than one trading day. They are unwilling to take the risk that adverse news will occur overnight. *Position traders* hold their positions for much longer periods of time. They hope to make significant profits from major movements in the markets.

Orders

The simplest type of order placed with a broker is a *market order*. It is a request that a trade be carried out immediately at the best price available in the market. However, there are many other types of orders. We will consider those that are more commonly used.

A *limit order* specifies a particular price. The order can be executed only at this price or at one more favorable to the investor. Thus, if the limit price is $30 for an investor wanting to take a long position, the order will be executed only at a price of $30 or less. There is, of course, no guarantee that the order will be executed at all, because the limit price may never be reached.

A *stop order* or *stop-loss order* also specifies a particular price. The order is executed at the best available price once a bid or offer is made at that particular price or a less-favorable price. Suppose a stop order to sell at $30 is issued when the market price is $35. It becomes an order to sell when and if the price falls to $30. In effect, a stop order becomes a market order as soon as the specified price has been hit. The purpose of a stop order is usually to close out a position if unfavorable price movements take place. It limits the loss that can be incurred.

A *stop–limit order* is a combination of a stop order and a limit order. The order becomes a limit order as soon as a bid or offer is made at a price equal to or less favorable than the stop price. Two prices must be specified in a stop–limit order: the stop price and the limit price. Suppose that at the time the market price is $35, a stop–limit order to buy is issued with a stop price of $40 and a limit price of $41. As soon as there is a bid or offer at $40, the stop–limit becomes a limit order at $41. If the stop price and the limit price are the same, the order is sometimes called a *stop-and-limit order*.

A *market-if-touched* (MIT) *order* is executed at the best available price after a trade occurs at a specified price or at a price more favorable than the specified price. In effect, an MIT becomes a market order once the specified price has been hit. An MIT is also known as a *board order*. Consider an investor who has a long position in a futures contract and is issuing instructions that would lead to closing out the contract. A stop order is designed to place a limit on the loss that can occur in the event of unfavorable price movements. By contrast, a market-if-touched order is designed to ensure that profits are taken if sufficiently favorable price movements occur.

A *discretionary order* or *market-not-held order* is traded as a market order except that execution may be delayed at the broker's discretion in an attempt to get a better price.

Some orders specify time conditions. Unless otherwise stated, an order is a day order and expires at the end of the trading day. A *time-of-day order* specifies a particular period of time during the day when the order can be executed. An *open order* or a *good-till-canceled order* is in effect until executed or until the end of trading in the particular contract. A *fill-or-kill order*, as its name implies, must be executed immediately on receipt or not at all.

2.8 REGULATION

Futures markets in the United States are currently regulated federally by the Commodity Futures Trading Commission (CFTC; www.cftc.gov), which was established in 1974. This body is responsible for licensing futures exchanges and approving contracts. All new contracts and changes to existing contracts must be approved by the CFTC. To be approved, the contract must have some useful economic purpose. Usually this means that it must serve the needs of hedgers as well as speculators.

The CFTC looks after the public interest. It is responsible for ensuring that prices are communicated to the public and that futures traders report their outstanding positions if they are above certain levels. The CFTC also licenses all individuals who offer their services to the public in futures trading. The backgrounds of these individuals are investigated, and there are minimum capital requirements. The CFTC deals with complaints brought by the public and ensures that disciplinary action is taken against individuals when appropriate. It has the authority to force exchanges to take disciplinary action against members who are in violation of exchange rules.

With the formation of the National Futures Association (NFA; www.nfa.futures.org) in 1982, some of responsibilities of the CFTC were shifted to the futures industry itself. The NFA is an organization of individuals who participate in the futures industry. Its objective is to prevent fraud and to ensure that the market operates in the best interests of the general public. The NFA requires its members to pass an exam. It is authorized to monitor trading and take disciplinary action when appropriate. The agency has set up an efficient system for arbitrating disputes between individuals and its members.

From time to time, other bodies, such as the Securities and Exchange Commission (SEC; www.sec.gov), the Federal Reserve Board (www.federalreserve.gov), and the US Treasury Department (www.treas.gov), have claimed jurisdictional rights over some aspects of futures trading. These bodies are concerned with the effects of futures trading on the spot markets for securities such as stocks, Treasury bills, and Treasury bonds. The SEC currently has an effective veto over the approval of new stock or bond index futures contracts. However, the basic responsibility for all futures and options on futures rests with the CFTC.

Trading Irregularities

Most of the time futures markets operate efficiently and in the public interest. However, from time to time, trading irregularities do come to light. One type of trading irregularity occurs when an investor group tries to "corner the market".[2] The investor group takes a huge long futures position and also tries to exercise some control over the supply of the underlying commodity. As the maturity of the futures contracts is approached, the investor group does not close out its position, so that the number of outstanding futures contracts may exceed the amount of the commodity available for delivery. The holders of short positions realize that they will find it difficult to deliver and become desperate to close out their positions. The result is a large rise in both futures and spot prices. Regulators usually deal with this type of abuse of the market by increasing margin requirements or imposing stricter position limits or prohibiting trades that increase a speculator's open position or requiring market participants to close out their positions.

Other types of trading irregularity can involve the traders on the floor of the exchange. These received some publicity early in 1989, when it was announced that the FBI had carried out a two-year investigation, using undercover agents, of trading on the Chicago Board of Trade and the Chicago Mercantile Exchange. The investigation was initiated because of complaints filed by a large agricultural concern. The alleged offenses included overcharging customers, not paying customers the full proceeds of sales, and traders using their knowledge of customer orders to trade first for themselves (an offence known as *front running*).

---

[2] Possibly the best known example of this was the attempt by the Hunt brothers to corner the silver market in 1979–80. Between the middle of 1979 and the beginning of 1980, their activities led to a price rise from $9 per ounce to $50 per ounce.

2.9 ACCOUNTING AND TAX

The full details of the accounting and tax treatment of futures contracts are beyond the scope of this book. A trader who wants detailed information on this should consult experts. In this section we provide some general background information.

Accounting

Accounting standards require changes in the market value of a futures contract to be recognized when they occur unless the contract qualifies as a hedge. If the contract does qualify as a hedge, gains or losses are generally recognized for accounting purposes in the same period in which the gains or losses from the item being hedged are recognized. The latter treatment is referred to as *hedge accounting*.

Consider a company with a December year end. In September 2004 it takes a long position in a March 2005 corn futures contract and closes out the position at the end of February 2005. Suppose that the futures prices are 250 cents per bushel when the contract is entered into, 270 cents per bushel at the end of 2004, and 280 cents per bushel when the contract is closed out. The contract is for the delivery of 5,000 bushels. If the contract does not qualify as a hedge, the gains for accounting purposes are

$$5{,}000 \times (2.70 - 2.50) = \$1{,}000$$

in 2004 and

$$5{,}000 \times (2.80 - 2.70) = \$500$$

in 2005. If the company is hedging the purchase of 5,000 bushels of corn in February 2005 so that the contract qualifies for hedge accounting, the entire gain of $1,500 is realized in 2005 for accounting purposes.

The treatment of hedging gains and losses is sensible. If the company is hedging the purchase of 5,000 bushels of corn in February 2005, the effect of the futures contract is to ensure that the price paid is close to 250 cents per bushel. The accounting treatment reflects that this price is paid in 2005. The 2004 accounts for the company are unaffected by the futures transaction.

In June 1998, the Financial Accounting Standards Board issued FASB Statement No. 133, Accounting for Derivative Instruments and Hedging Activities (FAS 133). FAS 133 applies to all types of derivatives (including futures, forwards, swaps, and options). It requires all derivatives to be included on the balance sheet at fair market value.[3] It increases disclosure requirements. It also gives companies far less latitude than previously in using hedge accounting. For hedge accounting to be used, the hedging instrument must be highly effective in offsetting exposures and an assessment of this effectiveness is required every three months. A similar standard IAS 39 has now been issued by the International Accounting Standards Board.

Tax

Under the US tax rules, two key issues are the nature of a taxable gain or loss and the timing of the recognition of the gain or loss. Gains or losses are either classified as capital gains or losses or alternatively as part of ordinary income.

[3] Previously the attraction of derivatives in some situations was that they were "off-balance-sheet" items.

For a corporate taxpayer, capital gains are taxed at the same rate as ordinary income, and the ability to deduct losses is restricted. Capital losses are deductible only to the extent of capital gains. A corporation may carry back a capital loss for three years and carry it forward for up to five years. For a noncorporate taxpayer, short-term capital gains are taxed at the same rate as ordinary income, but long-term capital gains are subject to a maximum capital gains tax rate of 15%. (Long-term capital gains are gains from the sale of a capital asset held for longer than one year; short-term capital gains are the gains from the sale of a capital asset held one year or less.) For a noncorporate taxpayer, capital losses are deductible to the extent of capital gains plus ordinary income up to $3,000 and can be carried forward indefinitely.

Generally, positions in futures contracts are treated as if they are closed out on the last day of the tax year. For the noncorporate taxpayer, this gives rise to capital gains and losses that are treated as if they were 60% long term and 40% short term without regard to the holding period. This is referred to as the "60/40" rule. A noncorporate taxpayer may elect to carry back for three years any net losses from the 60/40 rule to offset any gains recognized under the rule in the previous three years.

Hedging transactions are exempt from this rule. The definition of a hedge transaction for tax purposes is different from that for accounting purposes. The tax regulations define a hedging transaction as a transaction entered into in the normal course of business primarily for one of the following reasons:

1. To reduce the risk of price changes or currency fluctuations with respect to property that is held or to be held by the taxpayer for the purposes of producing ordinary income
2. To reduce the risk of price or interest rate changes or currency fluctuations with respect to borrowings made by the taxpayer

The hedging transaction must be identified before the end of the day on which the taxpayer enters into the transaction. The asset being hedged must be identified within 35 days. Gains or losses from hedging transactions are treated as ordinary income. The timing of the recognition of gains or losses from hedging transactions generally matches the timing of the recognition of income or deduction from the hedged items.

2.10 FORWARD vs. FUTURES CONTRACTS

The main differences between forward and futures contracts are summarized in Table 2.3. Both contracts are agreements to buy or sell an asset for a certain price at a certain future time. A forward contract is traded in the over-the-counter market and there is no standard contract size or standard delivery arrangements. A single delivery date is usually specified and the contract is usually held to the end of its life and then settled. A futures contract is a standardized contract traded on an exchange. A range of delivery dates is usually specified. It is settled daily and usually closed out prior to maturity.

Profits from Forward and Futures Contracts

Suppose that the sterling exchange rate for a 90-day forward contract is 1.6000 and that this rate is also the futures price for a contract that will be delivered in exactly 90 days. What is the difference between the gains and losses under the two contracts?

Table 2.3 Comparison of forward and futures contracts.

Forward	*Futures*
Private contract between two parties	Traded on an exchange
Not standardized	Standardized contract
Usually one specified delivery date	Range of delivery dates
Settled at end of contract	Settled daily
Delivery or final cash settlement usually takes place	Contract is usually closed out prior to maturity
Some credit risk	Virtually no credit risk

Under the forward contract, the whole gain or loss is realized at the end of the life of the contract. Under the futures contract, the gain or loss is realized day by day because of the daily settlement procedures. Suppose that investor A is long £1 million in a 90-day forward contract and investor B is long £1 million in 90-day futures contracts. (Because each futures contract is for the purchase or sale of £62,500, investor B must purchase a total of 16 contracts.) Assume that the spot exchange rate in 90 days proves to be 1.8000 dollars per pound. Investor A makes a gain of \$200,000 on the 90th day. Investor B makes the same gain—but spread out over the 90-day period. On some days investor B may realize a loss, whereas on other days he or she makes a gain. However, in total, when losses are netted against gains, there is a gain of \$200,000 over the 90-day period.

Foreign Exchange Quotes

Both forward and futures contracts trade actively on foreign currencies. However, there is a difference in the way exchange rates are quoted in the two markets. Futures prices are always quoted as the number of US dollars per unit of the foreign currency or as the number of US cents per unit of the foreign currency. Forward prices are always quoted in the same way as spot prices. This means that, for the British pound, the euro, the Australian dollar, and the New Zealand dollar, the forward quotes show the number of US dollars per unit of the foreign currency and are directly comparable with futures quotes. For other major currencies, forward quotes show the number of units of the foreign currency per US dollar (USD). Consider the Canadian dollar (CAD). A futures price quote of 0.7050 USD per CAD corresponds to a forward price quote of 1.4184 CAD per USD ($1.4184 = 1/0.7050$).

SUMMARY

A very high proportion of the futures contracts that are traded do not lead to the delivery of the underlying asset. They are closed out before the delivery period is reached. However, it is the possibility of final delivery that drives the determination of the futures price. For each futures contract, there is a range of days during which delivery can be made and a well-defined delivery procedure. Some contracts, such as those on stock indices, are settled in cash rather than by delivery of the underlying asset.

The specification of contracts is an important activity for a futures exchange. The two sides to any contract must know what can be delivered, where delivery can take place, and when delivery can take place. They also need to know details on the trading hours, how prices will be quoted, maximum daily price movements, and so on. New contracts must be approved by the Commodity Futures Trading Commission before trading starts.

Margins are an important aspect of futures markets. An investor keeps a margin account with his or her broker. The account is adjusted daily to reflect gains or losses, and from time to time the broker may require the account to be topped up if adverse price movements have taken place. The broker either must be a clearinghouse member or must maintain a margin account with a clearinghouse member. Each clearinghouse member maintains a margin account with the exchange clearinghouse. The balance in the account is adjusted daily to reflect gains and losses on the business for which the clearinghouse member is responsible.

Information on futures prices is collected in a systematic way at exchanges and relayed within a matter of seconds to investors throughout the world. Many daily newspapers such as the *Wall Street Journal* carry a summary of the previous day's trading.

Forward contracts differ from futures contracts in a number of ways. Forward contracts are private arrangements between two parties, whereas futures contracts are traded on exchanges. There is generally a single delivery date in a forward contract, whereas futures contracts frequently involve a range of such dates. Because they are not traded on exchanges, forward contracts need not be standardized. A forward contract is not usually settled until the end of its life, and most contracts do in fact lead to delivery of the underlying asset or a cash settlement at this time.

In the next few chapters we shall examine in more detail the ways in which forward and futures contracts can be used for hedging. We shall also look at how forward and futures prices are determined.

FURTHER READING

Duffie, D. *Futures Markets*. Upper Saddle River, NJ: Prentice Hall, 1989.

Gastineau, G. L., D. J. Smith, and R. Todd. *Risk Management, Derivatives, and Financial Analysis under SFAS No. 133*. The Research Foundation of AIMR and Blackwell Series in Finance, 2001.

Jorion, P. "Risk Management Lessons from Long-Term Capital Management," *European Financial Management*, 6, 3 (September 2000): 277–300.

Kawaller, I. G. and P. D. Koch. "Meeting the Highly Effective Expectation Criterion for Hedge Accounting," *Journal of Derivatives*, 7, 4 (Summer 2000): 79–87.

Lowenstein, R. *When Genius Failed: The Rise and Fall of Long-Term Capital Management*. New York: Random House, 2000.

Warwick, B., F. J. Jones, and R. J. Teweles. *The Futures Game*. 3rd edn. New York: McGraw-Hill, 1998.

Questions and Problems (Answers in Solutions Manual)

2.1. Distinguish between the terms *open interest* and *trading volume*.

2.2. What is the difference between a *local* and a *commission broker*?

2.3. Suppose that you enter into a short futures contract to sell July silver for $5.20 per ounce on the New York Commodity Exchange. The size of the contract is 5,000 ounces. The initial margin is $4,000, and the maintenance margin is $3,000. What change in the futures price will lead to a margin call? What happens if you do not meet the margin call?

2.4. Suppose that in September 2006 you take a long position in a contract on May 2007 crude oil futures. You close out your position in March 2007. The futures price (per barrel) is $18.30 when you enter into your contract, $20.50 when you close out your position, and $19.10 at the end of December 2006. One contract is for the delivery of 1,000 barrels. What is your total profit? When is it realized? How is it taxed if you are (a) a hedger and (b) a speculator? Assume that you have a December 31 year-end.

2.5. What does a stop order to sell at $2 mean? When might it be used? What does a limit order to sell at $2 mean? When might it be used?

2.6. What is the difference between the operation of the margin accounts administered by a clearinghouse and those administered by a broker?

2.7. What differences exist in the way prices are quoted in the foreign exchange futures market, the foreign exchange spot market, and the foreign exchange forward market?

2.8. The party with a short position in a futures contract sometimes has options as to the precise asset that will be delivered, where delivery will take place, when delivery will take place, and so on. Do these options increase or decrease the futures price? Explain your reasoning.

2.9. What are the most important aspects of the design of a new futures contract?

2.10. Explain how margins protect investors against the possibility of default.

2.11. An investor enters into two long July futures contracts on orange juice. Each contract is for the delivery of 15,000 pounds. The current futures price is 160 cents per pound, the initial margin is $6,000 per contract, and the maintenance margin is $4,500 per contract. What price change would lead to a margin call? Under what circumstances could $2,000 be withdrawn from the margin account?

2.12. Show that if the futures price of a commodity is greater than the spot price during the delivery period than there is an arbitrage opportunity. Does an arbitrage opportunity exist if the futures price is less than the spot price? Explain your answer.

2.13. Explain the difference between a market-if-touched order and a stop order.

2.14. Explain what a stop–limit order to sell at 20.30 with a limit of 20.10 means.

2.15. At the end of one day a clearinghouse member is long 100 contracts, and the settlement price is $50,000 per contract. The original margin is $2,000 per contract. On the following day the member becomes responsible for clearing an additional 20 long contracts, entered into at a price of $51,000 per contract. The settlement price at the end of this day is $50,200. How much does the member have to add to its margin account with the exchange clearinghouse?

2.16. On July 1, 2006, a US company enters into a forward contract to buy 10 million GBP on January 1, 2007. On September 1, 2006, it enters into a forward contract to sell 10 million

GBP on January 1, 2007. Describe the profit or loss the company will make in dollars as a function of the forward exchange rates on July 1, 2006, and September 1, 2006.

2.17. The forward price on the Swiss franc for delivery in 45 days is quoted as 1.8204. The futures price for a contract that will be delivered in 45 days is 0.5479. Explain these two quotes. Which is more favorable for an investor wanting to sell Swiss francs?

2.18. Suppose you call your broker and issue instructions to sell one July hogs contract. Describe what happens.

2.19. "Speculation in futures markets is pure gambling. It is not in the public interest to allow speculators to trade on a futures exchange." Discuss this viewpoint.

2.20. Identify the contracts with the highest open interest in Table 2.2. Consider each of the following sections separately: grains and oilseeds, livestock, food and fiber, metals, and petroleum.

2.21. What do you think would happen if an exchange started trading a contract in which the quality of the underlying asset was incompletely specified?

2.22. "When a futures contract is traded on the floor of the exchange, it may be the case that the open interest increases by one, stays the same, or decreases by one." Explain this statement.

2.23. Suppose that on October 24, 2006, you take a short position in an April 2007 live cattle futures contract. You close out your position on January 21, 2007. The futures price (per pound) is 61.20 cents when you enter into the contract, 58.30 cents when you close out your position, and 58.80 cents at the end of December 2006. One contract is for the delivery of 40,000 pounds of cattle. What is your total profit? How is it taxed if you are (a) a hedger and (b) a speculator?

2.24. A cattle farmer expects to have 120,000 pounds of live cattle to sell in 3 months. The live cattle futures contract on the Chicago Mercantile Exchange is for the delivery of 40,000 pounds of cattle. How can the farmer use the contract for hedging? From the farmer's viewpoint, what are the pros and cons of hedging?

2.25. It is now July 2005. A mining company has just discovered a small deposit of gold. It will take 6 months to construct the mine. The gold will then be extracted on a more or less continuous basis for 1 year. Futures contracts on gold are available on the New York Commodity Exchange. There are delivery months every 2 months from August 2005 to December 2006. Each contract is for the delivery of 100 ounces. Discuss how the mining company might use futures markets for hedging.

Assignment Questions

2.26. A company enters into a short futures contract to sell 5,000 bushels of wheat for 250 cents per bushel. The initial margin is $3,000 and the maintenance margin is $2,000. What price change would lead to a margin call? Under what circumstances could $1,500 be withdrawn from the margin account?

2.27. Suppose that there are no storage costs for corn and the interest rate for borrowing or lending is 5% per annum. How could you make money on February 4, 2004, by trading March 2004 and May 2004 contracts. Use Table 2.2.

2.28. What position is equivalent to a long forward contract to buy an asset at K on a certain date and a put option to sell it for K on that date.

2.29. The author's Web page (www.rotman.utoronto.ca/~hull/data) contains daily closing prices for the December 2001 crude oil futures contract and the December 2001 gold futures contract. (Both contracts are traded on NYMEX.) You are required to download the data and answer the following:

(a) How high do the maintenance margin levels for oil and gold have to be set so that there is a 1% chance that an investor with a balance slightly above the maintenence margin level on a particular day has a negative balance 2 days later (i.e. 1 day after a margin call)? How high do they have to be for a 0.1% chance? Assume daily price changes are normally distributed with mean zero.

(b) Imagine an investor who starts with a long position in the oil contract at the beginning of the period covered by the data and keeps the contract for the whole of the period of time covered by the data. Margin balances in excess of the initial margin are withdrawn. Use the maintenance margin you calculated in part (a) for a 1% risk level and assume that the maintenance margin is 75% of the initial margin. Calculate the number of margin calls and the number of times the investor has a negative margin balance and therefore an incentive to walk away. Assume that all margin calls are met in your calculations. Repeat the calculations for an investor who starts with a short position in the gold contract.

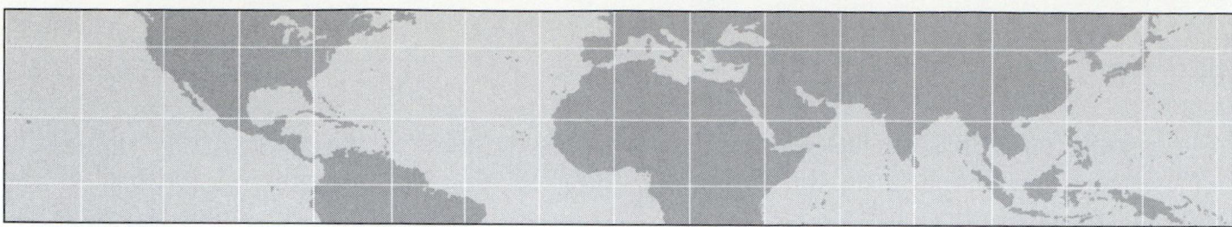

CHAPTER 3 Hedging Strategies Using Futures

Many of the participants in futures markets are hedgers. Their aim is to use futures markets to reduce a particular risk that they face. This risk might relate to the price of oil, a foreign exchange rate, the level of the stock market, or some other variable. A *perfect hedge* is one that completely eliminates the risk. Perfect hedges are rare. For the most part, therefore, a study of hedging using futures contracts is a study of the ways in which hedges can be constructed so that they perform as close to perfect as possible.

In this chapter we consider a number of general issues associated with the way hedges are set up. When is a short futures position appropriate? When is a long futures position appropriate? Which futures contract should be used? What is the optimal size of the futures position for reducing risk? At this stage, we restrict our attention to what might be termed *hedge-and-forget* strategies. We assume that no attempt is made to adjust the hedge once it has been put in place. The hedger simply takes a futures position at the beginning of the life of the hedge and closes out the position at the end of the life of the hedge. In Chapter 15 we will examine dynamic hedging strategies in which the hedge is monitored closely and frequent adjustments are made.

Throughout this chapter we will ignore the daily settlement of futures contracts. This means that we can ignore the time value of money in most situations because all cash flows occur at the time the hedge is closed out.

3.1 BASIC PRINCIPLES

When an individual or company chooses to use futures markets to hedge a risk, the objective is usually to take a position that neutralizes the risk as far as possible. Consider a company that knows it will gain \$10,000 for each 1 cent increase in the price of a commodity over the next 3 months and lose \$10,000 for each 1 cent decrease in the price during the same period. To hedge, the company's treasurer should take a short futures position that is designed to offset this risk. The futures position should lead to a loss of \$10,000 for each 1 cent increase in the price of the commodity over the 3 months and a gain of \$10,000 for each 1 cent decrease in the price during this period. If the price of the commodity goes down, the gain on the futures position offsets the loss on the rest of the company's business. If the price of the commodity goes up, the loss on the futures position is offset by the gain on the rest of the company's business.

Short Hedges

A *short hedge* is a hedge, such as the one just described, that involves a short position in futures contracts. A short hedge is appropriate when the hedger already owns an asset and expects to sell it at some time in the future. For example, a short hedge could be used by a farmer who owns some hogs and knows that they will be ready for sale at the local market in two months. A short hedge can also be used when an asset is not owned right now but will be owned at some time in the future. Consider, for example, a US exporter who knows that he or she will receive euros in 3 months. The exporter will realize a gain if the euro increases in value relative to the US dollar and will sustain a loss if the euro decreases in value relative to the US dollar. A short futures position leads to a loss if the euro increases in value and a gain if it decreases in value. It has the effect of offsetting the exporter's risk.

To provide a more detailed illustration of the operation of a short hedge in a specific situation, we assume that it is May 15 today and that an oil producer has just negotiated a contract to sell 1 million barrels of crude oil. It has been agreed that the price that will apply in the contract is the market price on August 15. The oil producer is therefore in the position where it will gain \$10,000 for each 1 cent increase in the price of oil over the next 3 months and lose \$10,000 for each 1 cent decrease in the price during this period. Suppose that on May 15 the spot price is \$19 per barrel and the crude oil futures price on the New York Mercantile Exchange (NYMEX) for August delivery is \$18.75 per barrel. Because each futures contract on NYMEX is for the delivery of 1,000 barrels, the company can hedge its exposure by shorting 1,000 futures contracts. If the oil producer closes out its position on August 15, the effect of the strategy should be to lock in a price close to \$18.75 per barrel.

To illustrate what might happen, suppose that the spot price on August 15 proves to be \$17.50 per barrel. The company realizes \$17.5 million for the oil under its sales contract. Because August is the delivery month for the futures contract, the futures price on August 15 should be very close to the spot price of \$17.50 on that date. The company therefore gains approximately

$$\$18.75 - \$17.50 = \$1.25$$

per barrel, or \$1.25 million in total from the short futures position. The total amount realized from both the futures position and the sales contract is therefore approximately \$18.75 per barrel, or \$18.75 million in total.

For an alternative outcome, suppose that the price of oil on August 15 proves to be \$19.50 per barrel. The company realizes \$19.50 for the oil and loses approximately

$$\$19.50 - \$18.75 = \$0.75$$

per barrel on the short futures position. Again, the total amount realized is approximately \$18.75 million. It is easy to see that in all cases the company ends up with approximately \$18.75 million.

Long Hedges

Hedges that involve taking a long position in a futures contract are known as *long hedges*. A long hedge is appropriate when a company knows it will have to purchase a certain asset in the future and wants to lock in a price now.

Suppose that it is now January 15. A copper fabricator knows it will require 100,000 pounds of copper on May 15 to meet a certain contract. The spot price of copper is 140 cents per pound, and the futures price for May delivery is 120 cents per pound. The fabricator can hedge its position by taking a long position in four May futures contracts on the COMEX division of NYMEX and closing its position on May 15. Each contract is for the delivery of 25,000 pounds of copper. The strategy has the effect of locking in the price of the required copper at close to 120 cents per pound.

Suppose that the price of copper on May 15 proves to be 125 cents per pound. Because May is the delivery month for the futures contract, this should be very close to the futures price. The fabricator therefore gains approximately

$$100{,}000 \times (\$1.25 - \$1.20) = \$5{,}000$$

on the futures contracts. It pays $100{,}000 \times \$1.25 = \$125{,}000$ for the copper, making the total cost approximately $\$125{,}000 - \$5{,}000 = \$120{,}000$. For an alternative outcome, suppose that the futures price is 105 cents per pound on May 15. The fabricator then loses approximately

$$100{,}000 \times (\$1.20 - \$1.05) = \$15{,}000$$

on the futures contract and pays $100{,}000 \times \$1.05 = \$105{,}000$ for the copper. Again, the total cost is approximately \$120,000, or 120 cents per pound.

Note that it is better for the company to use futures contracts than to buy the copper on January 15 in the spot market. If it does the latter, it will pay 140 cents per pound instead of 120 cents per pound and will incur both interest costs and storage costs. For a company using copper on a regular basis, this disadvantage would be offset by the convenience of having the copper on hand.[1] However, for a company that knows it will not require the copper until May 15, the futures contract alternative is likely to be preferred.

Long hedges can be used to manage an existing short position. Consider an investor who has shorted a certain stock. (See Section 5.2 for a discussion of shorting.) Part of the risk faced by the investor is related to the performance of the whole stock market. The investor can neutralize this risk with a long position in index futures contracts. This type of hedging strategy is discussed further later in the chapter.

The examples we have looked at assume that the futures position is closed out in the delivery month. The hedge has the same basic effect if delivery is allowed to happen. However, making or taking delivery can be costly and inconvenient. For this reason, delivery is not usually made even when the hedger keeps the futures contract until the delivery month. As will be discussed later, hedgers with long positions usually avoid any possibility of having to take delivery by closing out their positions before the delivery period.

We have also assumed in the two examples that there is no daily settlement. In practice, daily settlement does have a small effect on the performance of a hedge. As

[1] See Chapter 5 for a discussion of convenience yields.

explained in Chapter 2, it means that the payoff from the futures contract is realized day by day throughout the life of the hedge rather than all at the end.

3.2 ARGUMENTS FOR AND AGAINST HEDGING

The arguments in favor of hedging are so obvious that they hardly need to be stated. Most companies are in the business of manufacturing, or retailing or wholesaling, or providing a service. They have no particular skills or expertise in predicting variables such as interest rates, exchange rates, and commodity prices. It makes sense for them to hedge the risks associated with these variables as they arise. The companies can then focus on their main activities—for which presumably they do have particular skills and expertise. By hedging, they avoid unpleasant surprises such as sharp rises in the price of a commodity.

In practice, many risks are left unhedged. In the rest of this section we will explore some of the reasons.

Hedging and Shareholders

One argument sometimes put forward is that the shareholders can, if they wish, do the hedging themselves. They do not need the company to do it for them. This argument is, however, open to question. It assumes that shareholders have as much information about the risks faced by a company as does the company's management. In most instances, this is not the case. The argument also ignores commissions and other transactions costs. These are less expensive per dollar of hedging for large transactions than for small transactions. Hedging is therefore likely to be less expensive when carried out by the company than when it is carried out by individual shareholders. Indeed, the size of futures contracts makes hedging by individual shareholders impossible in many situations.

One thing that shareholders can do far more easily than a corporation is diversify risk. A shareholder with a well-diversified portfolio may be immune to many of the risks faced by a corporation. For example, in addition to holding shares in a company that uses copper, a well-diversified shareholder may hold shares in a copper producer, so that there is very little overall exposure to the price of copper. If companies are acting in the best interests of well-diversified shareholders, it can be argued that hedging is unnecessary in many situations. However, the extent to which managers are in practice influenced by this type of argument is open to question.

Hedging and Competitors

If hedging is not the norm in a certain industry, it may not make sense for one particular company to choose to be different from all others. Competitive pressures within the industry may be such that the prices of the goods and services produced by the industry fluctuate to reflect raw material costs, interest rates, exchange rates, and so on. A company that does not hedge can expect its profit margins to be roughly constant. However, a company that does hedge can expect its profit margins to fluctuate!

To illustrate this point, consider two manufacturers of gold jewelry, SafeandSure

Table 3.1 Danger in hedging when competitors do not hedge.

Change in gold price	*Effect on price of gold jewelry*	*Effect on profits of TakeaChance Co.*	*Effect on profits of SafeandSure Co.*
Increase	Increase	None	Increase
Decrease	Decrease	None	Decrease

Company and TakeaChance Company. We assume that most companies in the industry do not hedge against movements in the price of gold and that TakeaChance Company is no exception. However, SafeandSure Company has decided to be different from its competitors and to use futures contracts to hedge its purchase of gold over the next 18 months. If the price of gold goes up, economic pressures will tend to lead to a corresponding increase in the wholesale price of the jewelry, so that TakeaChance Company's profit margin is unaffected. By contrast, SafeandSure Company's profit margin will increase after the effects of the hedge have been taken into account. If the price of gold goes down, economic pressures will tend to lead to a corresponding decrease in the wholesale price of the jewelry. Again, TakeaChance Company's profit margin is unaffected. However, SafeandSure Company's profit margin goes down. In extreme conditions, SafeandSure Company's profit margin could become negative as a result of the "hedging" carried out! The situation is summarized in Table 3.1.

This example emphasizes the importance of looking at the big picture when hedging. All the implications of price changes on a company's profitability should be taken into account in the design of a hedging strategy to protect against the price changes.

Other Considerations

It is important to realize that a hedge using futures contracts can result in a decrease or an increase in a company's profits relative to the position it would be in with no hedging. In the example involving the oil producer considered earlier, if the price of oil goes down, the company loses money on its sale of 1 million barrels of oil, and the futures position leads to an offsetting gain. The treasurer can be congratulated for having had the foresight to put the hedge in place. Clearly, the company is better off than it would be with no hedging. Other executives in the organization, it is hoped, will appreciate the contribution made by the treasurer. If the price of oil goes up, the company gains from its sale of the oil, and the futures position leads to an offsetting loss. The company is in a worse position than it would be with no hedging. Although the hedging decision was perfectly logical, the treasurer may in practice have a difficult time justifying it. Suppose that the price of oil at the end of the hedge is \$21.75, so that the company loses \$3 per barrel on the futures contract. We can imagine a conversation such as the following between the treasurer and the president:

PRESIDENT: This is terrible. We've lost \$3 million in the futures market in the space of three months. How could it happen? I want a full explanation.

TREASURER: The purpose of the futures contracts was to hedge our exposure to the price of oil, not to make a profit. Don't forget we made \$3 million from the favorable effect of the oil price increases on our business.

Business Snapshot 3.1 Hedging by Gold Mining Companies

It is natural for a gold mining company to consider hedging against changes in the price of gold. Typically it takes several years to extract all the gold from a mine. Once a gold mining company decides to go ahead with production at a particular mine, it has a big exposure to the price of gold. Indeed a mine that looks profitable at the outset could become unprofitable if the price of gold plunges.

Gold mining companies are careful to explain their hedging strategies to potential shareholders. Some gold mining companies do not hedge. They tend to attract shareholders who buy gold stocks because they want to benefit when the price of gold increases and are prepared to accept the risk of a loss from a decrease in the price of gold. Other companies choose to hedge. They estimate the number of ounces they will produce each month for the next few years and enter into short futures or forward contracts to lock in the price that will be received.

Suppose you are Goldman Sachs and have just entered into a forward contract with a gold mining company whereby you agree to buy a large amount of gold at a fixed price. How do you hedge your risk? The answer is that you borrow gold from a central bank and sell it at the current market price. (The central banks of many countries hold large amounts of gold.) At the end of the life of the forward contract, you buy gold from the gold mining company under the terms of the forward contract and use it to repay the central bank. The central bank charges a fee (perhaps 1.5% per annum), known as the gold lease rate for lending its gold in this way.

PRESIDENT: What's that got to do with it? That's like saying that we do not need to worry when our sales are down in California because they are up in New York.

TREASURER: If the price of oil had gone down...

PRESIDENT: I don't care what would have happened if the price of oil had gone down. The fact is that it went up. I really do not know what you were doing playing the futures markets like this. Our shareholders will expect us to have done particularly well this quarter. I'm going to have to explain to them that your actions reduced profits by $3 million. I'm afraid this is going to mean no bonus for you this year.

TREASURER: That's unfair. I was only...

PRESIDENT: Unfair! You are lucky not to be fired. You lost $3 million.

TREASURER: It all depends on how you look at it...

It is easy to see why many treasurers are reluctant to hedge! Hedging reduces risk for the company. However, it may increase risk for the treasurer if others do not fully understand what is being done. The only real solution to this problem involves ensuring that all senior executives within the organization fully understand the nature of hedging before a hedging program is put in place. Ideally, hedging strategies are set by a company's board of directors and are clearly communicated to both the company's management and the shareholders. (See Business Snapshot 3.1 for a discussion of hedging by gold mining companies.)

3.3 BASIS RISK

The hedges in the examples considered so far have been almost too good to be true. The hedger was able to identify the precise date in the future when an asset would be bought or sold. The hedger was then able to use futures contracts to remove almost all the risk arising from the price of the asset on that date. In practice, hedging is often not quite as straightforward. Some of the reasons are as follows:

1. The asset whose price is to be hedged may not be exactly the same as the asset underlying the futures contract.
2. The hedger may be uncertain as to the exact date when the asset will be bought or sold.
3. The hedge may require the futures contract to be closed out before its delivery month.

These problems give rise to what is termed *basis risk*. This concept will now be explained.

The Basis

The *basis* in a hedging situation is as follows:[2]

$$\text{Basis} = \text{Spot price of asset to be hedged} - \text{Futures price of contract used}$$

If the asset to be hedged and the asset underlying the futures contract are the same, the basis should be zero at the expiration of the futures contract. Prior to expiration, the basis may be positive or negative. The spot price should equal the futures price for a very short maturity contract. From Table 2.2 and Figure 2.2, we see that the basis is negative for some assets (e.g., gold) and positive for others (e.g., Brent crude oil).

When the spot price increases by more than the futures price, the basis increases. This is referred to as a *strengthening of the basis*. When the futures price increases by more than the spot price, the basis declines. This is referred to as a *weakening of the basis*. Figure 3.1 illustrates how a basis might change over time in a situation where the basis is positive prior to expiration of the futures contract.

To examine the nature of basis risk, we will use the following notation:

S_1: Spot price at time t_1
S_2: Spot price at time t_2
F_1: Futures price at time t_1
F_2: Futures price at time t_2
b_1: Basis at time t_1
b_2: Basis at time t_2

We will assume that a hedge is put in place at time t_1 and closed out at time t_2. As an example, we will consider the case where the spot and futures prices at the time the hedge is initiated are \$2.50 and \$2.20, respectively, and that at the time the hedge is closed out they are \$2.00 and \$1.90, respectively. This means that $S_1 = 2.50$, $F_1 = 2.20$, $S_2 = 2.00$, and $F_2 = 1.90$.

---

[2] This is the usual definition. However, the alternative definition Basis = Futures price − Spot price is sometimes used, particularly when the futures contract is on a financial asset.

Figure 3.1 Variation of basis over time.

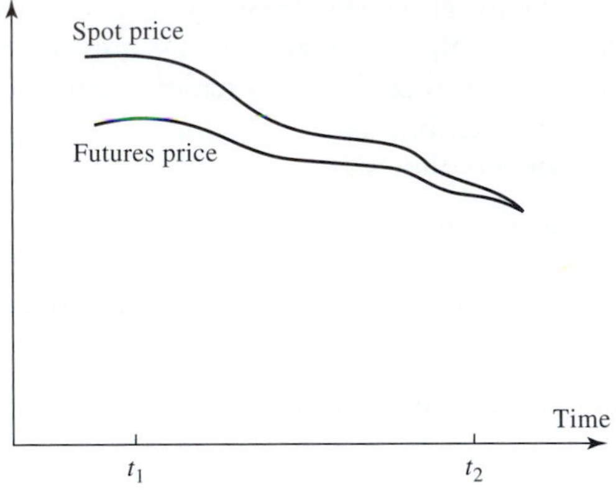

From the definition of the basis, we have

$$b_1 = S_1 - F_1 \quad \text{and} \quad b_2 = S_2 - F_2$$

and, in our example, $b_1 = 0.30$ and $b_2 = 0.10$.

Consider first the situation of a hedger who knows that the asset will be sold at time t_2 and takes a short futures position at time t_1. The price realized for the asset is S_2 and the profit on the futures position is $F_1 - F_2$. The effective price that is obtained for the asset with hedging is therefore

$$S_2 + F_1 - F_2 = F_1 + b_2$$

In our example, this is \$2.30. The value of F_1 is known at time t_1. If b_2 were also known at this time, a perfect hedge would result. The hedging risk is the uncertainty associated with b_2 and is known as *basis risk*. Consider next a situation where a company knows it will buy the asset at time t_2 and initiates a long hedge at time t_1. The price paid for the asset is S_2 and the loss on the hedge is $F_1 - F_2$. The effective price that is paid with hedging is therefore

$$S_2 + F_1 - F_2 = F_1 + b_2$$

This is the same expression as before and is \$2.30 in the example. The value of F_1 is known at time t_1, and the term b_2 represents basis risk.

Note that basis risk can lead to an improvement or a worsening of a hedger's position. Consider a short hedge. If the basis strengthens unexpectedly, the hedger's position improves; if the basis weakens unexpectedly, the hedger's position worsens. For a long hedge, the reverse holds. If the basis strengthens unexpectedly, the hedger's position worsens; if the basis weakens unexpectedly, the hedger's position improves.

The asset that gives rise to the hedger's exposure is sometimes different from the asset underlying the hedge. The basis risk is then usually greater. Define S_2^* as the price of the asset underlying the futures contract at time t_2. As before, S_2 is the price of the asset being hedged at time t_2. By hedging, a company ensures that the price that will be paid (or received) for the asset is

$$S_2 + F_1 - F_2$$

This can be written as

$$F_1 + (S_2^* - F_2) + (S_2 - S_2^*)$$

The terms $S_2^* - F_2$ and $S_2 - S_2^*$ represent the two components of the basis. The $S_2^* - F_2$ term is the basis that would exist if the asset being hedged were the same as the asset underlying the futures contract. The $S_2 - S_2^*$ term is the basis arising from the difference between the two assets.

Choice of Contract

One key factor affecting basis risk is the choice of the futures contract to be used for hedging. This choice has two components:

1. The choice of the asset underlying the futures contract
2. The choice of the delivery month

If the asset being hedged exactly matches an asset underlying a futures contract, the first choice is generally fairly easy. In other circumstances, it is necessary to carry out a careful analysis to determine which of the available futures contracts has futures prices that are most closely correlated with the price of the asset being hedged.

The choice of the delivery month is likely to be influenced by several factors. In the examples given earlier in this chapter, we assumed that, when the expiration of the hedge corresponds to a delivery month, the contract with that delivery month is chosen. In fact, a contract with a later delivery month is usually chosen in these circumstances. The reason is that futures prices are in some instances quite erratic during the delivery month. Moreover, a long hedger runs the risk of having to take delivery of the physical asset if the contract is held during the delivery month. Taking delivery can be expensive and inconvenient.

In general, basis risk increases as the time difference between the hedge expiration and the delivery month increases. A good rule of thumb is therefore to choose a delivery month that is as close as possible to, but later than, the expiration of the hedge. Suppose delivery months are March, June, September, and December for a particular contract. For hedge expirations in December, January, and February, the March contract will be chosen; for hedge expirations in March, April, and May, the June contract will be chosen; and so on. This rule of thumb assumes that there is sufficient liquidity in all contracts to meet the hedger's requirements. In practice, liquidity tends to be greatest in short-maturity futures contracts. Therefore, in some situations, the hedger may be inclined to use short-maturity contracts and roll them forward. This strategy is discussed later in the chapter.

Example 3.1

It is March 1. A US company expects to receive 50 million Japanese yen at the end of July. Yen futures contracts on the Chicago Mercantile Exchange have delivery months of March, June, September, and December. One contract is for the delivery of 12.5 million yen. The company therefore shorts four September yen futures contracts on March 1. When the yen are received at the end of July, the company closes out its position. We suppose that the futures price on March 1 in cents per yen is 0.7800 and that the spot and futures prices when the contract is closed out are 0.7200 and 0.7250, respectively.

The gain on the futures contract is 0.7800 − 0.7250 = 0.0550 cents per yen. The basis is 0.7200 − 0.7250 = −0.0050 cents per yen when the contract is closed out. The effective price obtained in cents per yen is the final spot price plus the gain on the futures:

$$0.7200 + 0.0550 = 0.7750$$

This can also be written as the initial futures price plus the final basis:

$$0.7800 + (-0.0050) = 0.7750$$

The total amount received by the company for the 50 million yen is 50 × 0.00775 million dollars, or $387,500.

Example 3.2

It is June 8 and a company knows that it will need to purchase 20,000 barrels of crude oil at some time in October or November. Oil futures contracts are currently traded for delivery every month on NYMEX and the contract size is 1,000 barrels. The company therefore decides to use the December contract for hedging and takes a long position in 20 December contracts. The futures price on June 8 is $18.00 per barrel. The company finds that it is ready to purchase the crude oil on November 10. It therefore closes out its futures contract on that date. The spot price and futures price on November 10 are $20.00 per barrel and $19.10 per barrel.

The gain on the futures contract is 19.10 − 18.00 = $1.10 per barrel. The basis when the contract is closed out is 20.00 − 19.10 = $0.90 per barrel. The effective price paid (in dollars per barrel) is the final spot price less the gain on the futures, or

$$20.00 - 1.10 = 18.90$$

This can also be calculated as the initial futures price plus the final basis,

$$18.00 + 0.90 = 18.90$$

The total price paid is 18.90 × 20,000 = $378,000.

3.4 CROSS HEDGING

In the examples considered up to now, the asset underlying the futures contract has been the same as the asset whose price is being hedged. *Cross hedging* occurs when the two assets are different. Consider, for example, an airline that is concerned about the future price of jet fuel. Because there is no futures contract on jet fuel, it might choose to use heating oil futures contracts to hedge its exposure.

The *hedge ratio* is the ratio of the size of the position taken in futures contracts to the size of the exposure. When the asset underlying the futures contract is the same as the asset being hedged, it is natural to use a hedge ratio of 1.0. This is the hedge ratio we have used in the examples considered so far. For instance, in Example 3.2, the hedger's exposure was on 20,000 barrels of oil, and futures contracts were entered into for the delivery of exactly this amount of oil.

When cross hedging is used, setting the hedge ratio equal to 1.0 is not always optimal. The hedger should choose a value for the hedge ratio that minimizes the variance of the value of the hedged position. We now consider how the hedger can do this.

Calculating the Minimum Variance Hedge Ratio

We will use the following notation:

ΔS: Change in spot price, S, during a period of time equal to the life of the hedge

ΔF: Change in futures price, F, during a period of time equal to the life of the hedge

σ_S: Standard deviation of ΔS

σ_F: Standard deviation of ΔF

ρ: Coefficient of correlation between ΔS and ΔF

h^*: Hedge ratio that minimizes the variance of the hedger's position

In the appendix at the end of this chapter, we show that

$$h^* = \rho \frac{\sigma_S}{\sigma_F} \tag{3.1}$$

The optimal hedge ratio is the product of the coefficient of correlation between ΔS and ΔF and the ratio of the standard deviation of ΔS to the standard deviation of ΔF. Figure 3.2 shows how the variance of the value of the hedger's position depends on the hedge ratio chosen.

If $\rho = 1$ and $\sigma_F = \sigma_S$, the hedge ratio, h^*, is 1.0. This result is to be expected, because in this case the futures price mirrors the spot price perfectly. If $\rho = 1$ and $\sigma_F = 2\sigma_S$, the hedge ratio h^* is 0.5. This result is also as expected, because in this case the futures price always changes by twice as much as the spot price.

The optimal hedge ratio, h^*, is the slope of the best-fit line when ΔS is regressed against ΔF, as indicated in Figure 3.3. This is intuitively reasonable, because we require h^* to correspond to the ratio of changes in ΔS to changes in ΔF. The *hedge effectiveness* can be

Figure 3.2 Dependence of variance of hedger's position on hedge ratio.

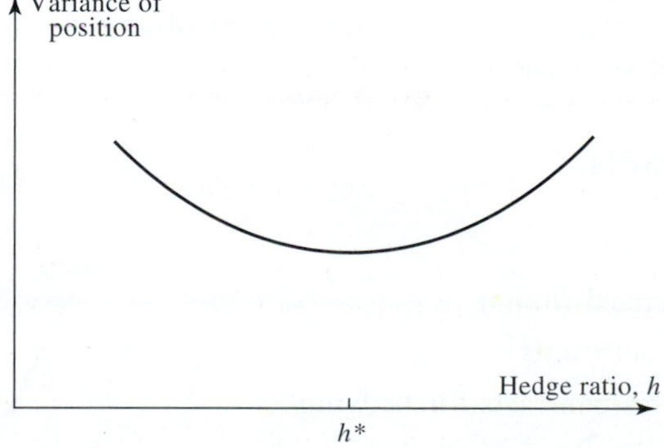

Figure 3.3 Regression of change in spot price against change in futures price.

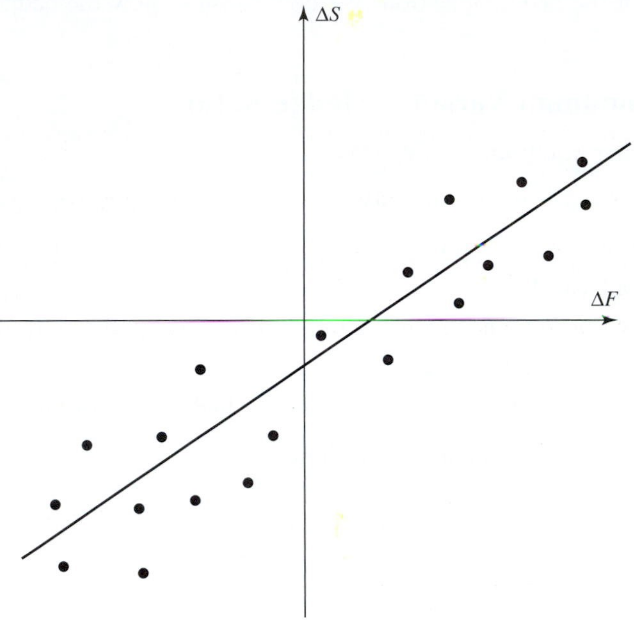

defined as the proportion of the variance that is eliminated by hedging. This is the R^2 from the regression of ΔS against ΔF and equals ρ^2, or

$$h^{*2}\frac{\sigma_F^2}{\sigma_S^2}$$

The parameters ρ, σ_F, and σ_S in equation (3.1) are usually estimated from historical data on ΔS and ΔF. (The implicit assumption is that the future will in some sense be like the past.) A number of equal nonoverlapping time intervals are chosen, and the values of ΔS and ΔF for each of the intervals are observed. Ideally, the length of each time interval is the same as the length of the time interval for which the hedge is in effect. In practice, this sometimes severely limits the number of observations that are available, and a shorter time interval is used.

Optimal Number of Contracts

Define variables as follows:

N_A: Size of position being hedged (units)
Q_F: Size of one futures contract (units)
N^*: Optimal number of futures contracts for hedging

The futures contracts used should have a face value of h^*N_A. The number of futures contracts required is therefore given by

$$N^* = \frac{h^* N_A}{Q_F} \tag{3.2}$$

Example 3.3

An airline expects to purchase 2 million gallons of jet fuel in 1 month and decides to use heating oil futures for hedging.[3] We suppose that Table 3.2 gives, for 15 successive months, data on the change, ΔS, in the jet fuel price per gallon and the corresponding change, ΔF, in the futures price for the contract on heating oil that would be used for hedging price changes during the month. The number of observations, which we will denote by n, is 15. We will denote the ith observations on ΔF and ΔS by x_i and y_i, respectively. From Table 3.2, we have

$$\sum x_i = -0.013 \qquad \sum x_i^2 = 0.0138$$
$$\sum y_i = 0.003 \qquad \sum y_i^2 = 0.0097$$
$$\sum x_i y_i = 0.0107$$

Table 3.2 Data to calculate minimum variance hedge ratio when heating oil futures contract is used to hedge purchase of jet fuel.

Month i	*Change in futures price per gallon* $(= x_i)$	*Change in fuel price per gallon* $(= y_i)$
1	0.021	0.029
2	0.035	0.020
3	−0.046	−0.044
4	0.001	0.008
5	0.044	0.026
6	−0.029	−0.019
7	−0.026	−0.010
8	−0.029	−0.007
9	0.048	0.043
10	−0.006	0.011
11	−0.036	−0.036
12	−0.011	−0.018
13	0.019	0.009
14	−0.027	−0.032
15	0.029	0.023

[3] For an account of how Delta Airlines used heating oil to hedge its future purchases of jet fuel, see A. Ness, "Delta Wins on Fuel," *Risk*, June 2001, p. 8.

Standard formulas from statistics give the estimate of σ_F as

$$\sqrt{\frac{\sum x_i^2}{n-1} - \frac{\left(\sum x_i\right)^2}{n(n-1)}} = 0.0313$$

The estimate of σ_S is

$$\sqrt{\frac{\sum y_i^2}{n-1} - \frac{\left(\sum y_i\right)^2}{n(n-1)}} = 0.0263$$

The estimate of ρ is

$$\frac{n\sum x_i y_i - \sum x_i \sum y_i}{\sqrt{\left[n\sum x_i^2 - \left(\sum x_i\right)^2\right]\left[n\sum y_i^2 - \left(\sum y_i\right)^2\right]}} = 0.928$$

From equation (3.1), the minimum variance hedge ratio, h^*, is therefore

$$0.928 \times \frac{0.0263}{0.0313} = 0.78$$

Each heating oil contract traded on NYMEX is on 42,000 gallons of heating oil. From equation (3.2), the optimal number of contracts is

$$\frac{0.78 \times 2{,}000{,}000}{42{,}000} = 37.14$$

or, rounding to the nearest whole number, 37.

3.5 STOCK INDEX FUTURES

We now move on to consider stock index futures and how they are used to hedge or manage exposures to equity prices.

A *stock index* tracks changes in the value of a hypothetical portfolio of stocks. The weight of a stock in the portfolio equals the proportion of the portfolio invested in the stock. The percentage increase in the stock index over a small interval of time is set equal to the percentage increase in the value of the hypothetical portfolio. Dividends are usually not included in the calculation so that the index tracks the capital gain/loss from investing in the portfolio.[4]

If the hypothetical portfolio of stocks remains fixed, the weights assigned to individual stocks in the portfolio do not remain fixed. When the price of one particular stock in the portfolio rises more sharply than others, more weight is automatically given to that stock. Some indices are constructed from a hypothetical portfolio consisting of one of each of a number of stocks. The weights assigned to the stocks are then proportional to their market prices, with adjustments being made when there are stock splits. Other indices are constructed so that weights are proportional to market capitalization (stock price × number of shares outstanding). The underlying portfolio is then automatically adjusted to reflect stock splits, stock dividends, and new equity issues.

[4] An exception to this is a *total return index*. This is calculated by assuming that dividends on the hypothetical portfolio are reinvested in the portfolio.

Stock Indices

Table 3.3 shows futures prices for contracts on a number of different stock indices as they were reported in the *Wall Street Journal* of February 5, 2004. The prices refer to the close of trading on February 4, 2004.

The *Dow Jones Industrial Average* is based on a portfolio consisting of 30 blue-chip stocks in the United States. The weights given to the stocks are proportional to their prices. The Chicago Board of Trade trades two contracts on the index. One is on $10 times the index. The other (the Mini DJ Industrial Average) is on $5 times the index.

Table 3.3 Index futures quotes from *Wall Street Journal*, February 5, 2004: Columns show month, open, high, low, settle, change, lifetime high, lifetime low, and open interest, respectively.

Index Futures

DJ Industrial Average (CBT)-$10 x index

Mar	10446	10507	10418	10440	-38	10687	8580	36,831
June	...	...	...	10419	-38	10475	9000	581

Est vol 11,816; vol Tue 182; open int 37,455, -65.
Idx prl: Hi 10524.22; Lo 10447.18; Close 10470.74, -34.44.

Mini DJ Industrial Average (CBT)-$5 x index

Mar	10446	10506	10417	10440	-38	10687	9069	46,175

Vol Wed 70,499; open int 48,145, -1,739.

DJ-AIG Commodity Index (CBT)-$100 x index

Feb	...	...	...	439.3	-3.5	456.2	452.1	2,351

Est vol 1,150; vol Tue 220; open int 2,571, unch.
Idx prl: Hi 139.159; Lo 137.163; Close 137.350, -1.171.

S&P 500 Index (CME)-$250 x index

Mar	113290	113360	112300	112390	-910	123950	77700	585,763
June	112620	113100	112250	112290	-910	115350	78000	21,212

Est vol 46,110; vol Tue 45,600; open int 610,710, +107.
Idx prl: Hi 1136.03; Lo 1124.74; Close 1126.52, -9.51.

Mini S&P 500 (CME)-$50 x index

Mar	113300	113350	112200	112400	-900	115500	98650	539,366

Vol Wed 595,531; open int 550,820, -18,936.

S&P Midcap 400 (CME)-$500 x index

Mar	584.50	586.00	580.30	580.80	-6.00	603.25	559.75	15,879

Est vol 582; vol Tue 672; open int 15,880, -98.
Idx prl: Hi 587.39; Lo 580.91; Close 581.63, -5.76.

Nasdaq 100 (CME)-$100 x index

Mar	148850	148850	146200	146300	-2400	150900	146200	72,861

Est vol 14,295; vol Tue 9,985; open int 72,918, -246.
Idx prl: Hi 1482.35; Lo 1461.01; Close 1462.61, -29.24.

Mini Nasdaq 100 (CME)-$20 x index

Mar	1488.0	1489.0	1461.5	1463.0	-24.0	1563.0	1307.0	249,320

Vol Wed 257,039; open int 250,794, +4,618.

GSCI (CME)-$250 x nearby index

Feb	264.50	266.10	258.50	258.50	-5.50	274.50	251.50	14,534

Est vol 243; vol Tue 104; open int 14,901, +31.
Idx prl: Hi 265.61; Lo 258.87; Close 259.53, -4.02.

TRAKRS Long-Short Tech (CME)-$1 x index

July	40.30	40.30	39.82	39.82	-1.40	45.25	19.76	410,834

Est vol 87; vol Tue 150; open int 410,834, +150.
Idx prl: Hi 40.03; Lo 38.16; Close 38.56, -1.47.

Russell 2000 (CME)-$500 x index

Mar	576.50	576.50	563.50	563.75	-14.40	585.75	557.50	22,953

Est vol 3,572; vol Tue 969; open int 22,953, -42.
Idx prl: Hi 579.15; Lo 564.03; Close 564.03, -15.12.

Russell 1000 (NYFE)-$500 x index

Mar	...	...	...	601.00	-5.05	618.00	603.00	77,631

Est vol 79; vol Tue 66; open int 77,631, -72.
Idx prl: Hi 607.34; Lo 601.23; close 602.10, -5.24.

NYSE Composite Index (NYFE)-$50 x index

Mar	...	...	...	6509.50	-57.00	6556.00	6115.00	1,260

Est vol 0; vol Tue 0; open int 1,260, unch.
Idx prl: Hi 6574.76; Lo 6520.91; Close 6526.10, -48.72.

U.S. Dollar Index (FINEX)-$1,000 x index

Mar	87.04	87.30	86.92	87.02	.04	103.18	85.10	16,414
June	...	...	...	87.43	.04	88.37	85.71	2,116

Est vol 2,500; vol Tue 2,272; open int 18,543, +610.
Idx prl: Hi 87.10; Lo 86.70; open int 86.84, +.05.

Nikkei 225 Stock Average (CME)-$5 x index

Mar	10400.	10510.	10360.	10380.	-265	11155.	7670.	30,555

Est vol 3,558; vol Tue 2,468; open int 30,730, +33.
Index: Hi 10627.26; Lo 10418.77; Close 10447.25, -194.67.

Share Price Index (SFE)-AUD 25 x index

Mar	3257.0	3267.0	3250.0	3254.0	-2.0	3346.0	2700.0	160,822
June	3264.0	3278.0	3264.0	3266.0	-2.0	3350.0	2700.0	3,931

Est vol 10,928; vol Tue 10,169; open int 167,890, +2,133.
Index: Hi 3273.5; Lo 3263.6; Close 3265.6, +1.3.

CAC-40 Stock Index (MATIF)-€10 x index

Feb	3626.0	3632.5	3603.0	3614.0	-29.5	3729.5	3531.5	346,178
Mar	3630.0	3634.5	3610.5	3620.0	-29.5	3734.5	2885.0	130,956
June	3563.5	3563.5	3562.5	3560.5	-29.0	3651.5	3282.0	8,810

Est vol 77,301; vol Tue 76,586; open int 489,860, +19,063.
Index: Hi 3625.38; Lo 3602.94; Close 3607.57, -30.64.

Xetra DAX (EUREX)-€25 x index

Mar	4050.0	4056.0	4018.0	4029.5	-31.0	4190.0	3237.5	286,286
June	4065.0	4074.5	4042.5	4050.5	-31.0	4210.0	3251.0	10,167
Sept	4086.5	4096.0	4064.0	4072.0	-31.5	4231.0	3961.0	2,874

Vol Wed 113,473; open int 299,327, -1,522.
Index: Hi 4050.08; Lo 4008.80; Close 4028.37, -29.14.

FTSE 100 Index (LIFFE)-£10 x index

Mar	4340.0	4386.5	4339.5	4376.0	10.0	4509.5	3895.5	426,561
June	4352.0	4385.5	4352.0	4384.5	9.5	4514.0	4019.5	17,929
Sept	4372.5	4374.5	4372.5	4394.5	10.0	4526.5	4288.5	10,192

Vol Wed 59,473; open int 462,529, +1,934.
Index: Hi 4409.30; Lo 4369.10; Close 4398.50, +7.90.

DJ Euro STOXX 50 Index (EUREX)-€10 x index

Mar	2834.0	2841.0	2820.0	2821.0	-27.0	2921.0	2376.0	1,226,828
June	2797.0	2800.0	2785.0	2783.0	-27.0	2883.0	2364.0	88,041
Sept	2796.0	2796.0	2787.0	2782.0	-27.0	2881.0	2709.0	14,454

Vol Wed 384,795; open int 1,329,323, -2,788.
Index: Hi 2839.55; Lo 2816.18; Close 2819.92, -21.34.

DJ STOXX 50 Index (EUREX)-€10 x index

Mar	2675.0	2689.0	2671.0	2674.0	-14.0	2757.0	2393.0	39,662
June	...	...	...	2653.0	-14.0	...	...	640

Vol Wed 1,895; open int 40,302, +513.
Index: Hi 2698.24; Lo 2681.59; Close 2689.82, -5.23.

Source: Reprinted by permission of Dow Jones, Inc., via Copyright Clearance Center, Inc.,

The *Standard & Poor's 500 (S&P 500) Index* is based on a portfolio of 500 different stocks: 400 industrials, 40 utilities, 20 transportation companies, and 40 financial institutions. The weights of the stocks in the portfolio at any given time are proportional to their market capitalizations. This index accounts for 80% of the market capitalization of all the stocks listed on the New York Stock Exchange. The Chicago Mercantile Exchange (CME) trades two contracts on the S&P 500. One is on $250 times the index; the other (the Mini S&P 500 contract) is on $50 times the index. The *Standard & Poor's MidCap 400 Index* is similar to the S&P 500, but based on a portfolio of 400 stocks that have somewhat lower market capitalizations.

The *Nasdaq 100* is based on 100 stocks using the National Association of Securities Dealers Automatic Quotations Service. The CME trades two contracts. One is on $100 times the index; the other (the Mini Nasdaq 100 contract) is on $20 times the index.

The *Russell 2000 Index* is an index of the prices of 2,000 small capitalization stocks in the United States. The *Russell 1000 Index* is an index of the prices of the 1,000 largest capitalization stocks in the United States. The *NYSE Composite Index* is an index of all stocks trading on the New York Stock Exchange. The *US Dollar Index* is a trade-weighted index of the values of six foreign currencies (the euro, yen, pound, Canadian dollar, Swedish krona, and Swiss franc). The *Nikkei 225 Stock Average* is based on a portfolio of 225 of the largest stocks trading on the Tokyo Stock Exchange. Stocks are weighted according to their prices. One futures contract (traded on the CME) is on $5 times the index.

The *Share Price Index* is the All Ordinaries Share Price Index, a broadly based index of Australian stocks. The *CAC-40 Index* is based on 40 large stocks trading in France. The *Xetra DAX Index* is based on 30 stocks trading in Germany. The *FTSE 100 Index* is based on a portfolio of 100 major UK stocks listed on the London Stock Exchange. The *DJ Euro Stoxx 50 Index* and the *DJ Stoxx 50 Index* are two different indices of blue-chip European stocks compiled by Dow Jones and its European partners. The futures contracts on these indices trade on Eurex and are on 10 times the values of the indices measured in euros.

The other indices shown in Table 3.3 are not stock indices. The DJ-AIG commodity index and the GSCI index futures contract are designed to track commodity prices. The TRAKRS long–short tech index is an unusual index designed to reflect the performance of a portfolio that is long individual technology stocks and short financial instruments representing technology sectors.

As we mentioned in Chapter 2, futures contracts on stock indices are settled in cash, not by delivery of the underlying asset. All contracts are marked to market to either the opening price or the closing price of the index on the last trading day, and the positions are then deemed to be closed. For example, contracts on the S&P 500 are closed out at the opening price of the S&P 500 index on the third Friday of the delivery month.

Hedging an Equity Portfolio

Stock index futures can be used to hedge a well-diversified equity portfolio. Define:

P: Current value of the portfolio

A: Current value of the stocks underlying one futures contract

If the portfolio mirrors the index, the optimal hedge ratio, h^*, equals 1.0 and equation (3.2) shows that the number of futures contracts that should be shorted is

$$N^* = \frac{P}{A} \tag{3.3}$$

Suppose, for example, that a portfolio worth \$1 million mirrors the S&P 500. The current value of the index is 1,000, and each futures contract is on \$250 times the index. In this case $P = 1{,}000{,}000$ and $A = 250{,}000$, so that four contracts should be shorted to hedge the portfolio.

When the portfolio does not exactly mirror the index, we can use the parameter beta (β) from the capital asset pricing model to determine the appropriate hedge ratio. Beta is the slope of the best-fit line obtained when excess return on the portfolio over the risk-free rate is regressed against the excess return of the market over the risk-free rate. When $\beta = 1.0$, the return on the portfolio tends to mirror the return on the market; when $\beta = 2.0$, the excess return on the portfolio tends to be twice as great as the excess return on the market; when $\beta = 0.5$, it tends to be half as great; and so on.

A portfolio with a β of 2.0 is twice as sensitive to market movements as a portfolio with a beta 1.0. It is therefore necessary to use twice as many contracts to hedge the portfolio. Similarly, a portfolio with a beta of 0.5 is half as sensitive to market movements as a portfolio with a beta of 1.0 and we should use half as many contracts to hedge it. In general, $h^* = \beta$, so that equation (3.2) gives

$$N^* = \beta \frac{P}{A} \tag{3.4}$$

This formula assumes that the maturity of the futures contract is close to the maturity of the hedge and ignores the daily settlement of the futures contract.[5]

We illustrate that this formula gives good results with an example. Suppose that

Value of S&P 500 index = 1,000

Value of portfolio = \$5,000,000

Risk-free interest rate = 4% per annum

Dividend yield on index = 1% per annum

Beta of portfolio = 1.5

We assume that a futures contract on the S&P 500 with 4 months to maturity is used to hedge the value of the portfolio over the next 3 months and that the current futures price of this contract is 1,010. One futures contract is for delivery of \$250 times the index. It follows that $A = 250 \times 1{,}000 = 250{,}000$ and from equation (3.4), the number of futures contracts that should be shorted to hedge the portfolio is

$$1.5 \times \frac{5{,}000{,}000}{250{,}000} = 30$$

[5] It can be shown that one way of taking account of daily settlement is to replace A by the value of the futures contract in equation (3.4) (see Problem 5.23). For a discussion of this, see R. J. Rendleman, "A Reconciliation of Potentially Conflicting Approaches to Hedging with Futures," *Advances in Futures and Options Research*, 6 (1993): 81–92. A strategy known as *tailing the hedge*, where the hedge position is adjusted every day, is then in theory necessary.

Suppose the index turns out to be 900 in 3 months and the futures price is 902. The gain from the short futures position is then

$$30 \times (1010 - 902) \times 250 = \$810{,}000$$

The loss on the index is 10%. The index pays a dividend of 1% per annum, or 0.25% per 3 months. When dividends are taken into account, an investor in the index would therefore earn –9.75% in the 3-month period. The risk-free interest rate is approximately 1% per 3 months. Because the portfolio has a β of 1.5, the capital asset pricing model gives

$$\text{Expected return on portfolio} - \text{Risk-free interest rate} = 1.5 \times (\text{Return on index} - \text{Risk-free interest rate})$$

It follows that the expected return (%) on the portfolio during the 3 months is

$$1.0 + [1.5 \times (-9.75 - 1.0)] = -15.125$$

The expected value of the portfolio (inclusive of dividends) at the end of the 3 months is therefore

$$\$5{,}000{,}000 \times (1 - 0.15125) = \$4{,}243{,}750$$

It follows that the expected value of the hedger's position, including the gain on the hedge, is

$$\$4{,}243{,}750 + \$810{,}000 = \$5{,}053{,}750$$

Table 3.4 summarizes these calculations together with similar calculations for other values of the index at maturity. It can be seen that the total expected value of the hedger's position in 3 months is almost independent of the value of the index.

The only thing we have not covered in this example is the relationship between futures prices and spot prices. We will see in Chapter 5 that the 1,010 assumed for the futures

Table 3.4 Performance of stock index hedge.

Value of index in three months:	900	950	1,000	1,050	1,100
Futures price of index today:	1,010	1,010	1,010	1,010	1,010
Futures price of index in three months:	902	952	1,003	1,053	1,103
Gain on futures position:	810,000	435,000	52,500	−322,500	−697,500
Return on market:	−9.750%	−4.750%	0.250%	5.250%	10.250%
Expected return on portfolio:	−15.125%	−7.625%	−0.125%	7.375%	14.875%
Expected portfolio value in three months (including dividends):	4,243,750	4,618,750	4,993,750	5,368,750	5,743,750
Total expected value of position in three months:	5,053,750	5,053,750	5,046,250	5,046,250	5,046,250

price today is roughly what we would expect given the interest rate and dividend we are assuming. The same is true of the futures prices in 3 months shown in Table 3.4.[6]

Reasons for Hedging an Equity Portfolio

Table 3.4 shows that the hedging scheme results in a value for the hedger's position at the end of the 3-month period being about 1% higher than at the beginning of the 3-month period. There is no surprise here. The risk-free rate is 4% per annum, or 1% per 3 months. The hedge results in the investor's position growing at the risk-free rate.

It is natural to ask why the hedger should go to the trouble of using futures contracts. To earn the risk-free interest rate, the hedger can simply sell the portfolio and invest the proceeds in risk-free instruments such as Treasury bills.

One answer to this question is that hedging can be justified if the hedger feels that the stocks in the portfolio have been chosen well. In these circumstances, the hedger might be very uncertain about the performance of the market as a whole, but confident that the stocks in the portfolio will outperform the market (after appropriate adjustments have been made for the beta of the portfolio). A hedge using index futures removes the risk arising from market moves and leaves the hedger exposed only to the performance of the portfolio relative to the market. Another reason for hedging may be that the hedger is planning to hold a portfolio for a long period of time and requires short-term protection in an uncertain market situation. The alternative strategy of selling the portfolio and buying it back later might involve unacceptably high transaction costs.

Changing the Beta of a Portfolio

In the example in Table 3.4, the beta of the hedger's portfolio is reduced to zero. Sometimes futures contracts are used to change the beta of a portfolio to some value other than zero. Continuing with our earlier example:

$$\text{Value of S\&P 500 index} = 1{,}000$$

$$\text{Value of portfolio} = \$5{,}000{,}000$$

$$\text{Beta of portfolio} = 1.5$$

Because each contract is on \$250 times the index, $A = 250{,}000$. To completely hedge the portfolio, equation (3.4) shows that the number of contracts shorted should be

$$1.5 \times \frac{5{,}000{,}000}{250{,}000} = 30$$

To reduce the beta of the portfolio from 1.5 to 0.75, the number of contracts shorted should be 15 rather than 30; to increase the beta of the portfolio to 2.0, a long position in 10 contracts should be taken; and so on. In general, to change the beta of the

[6] The calculations in Table 3.4 assume that the dividend yield on the index is predictable, the risk-free interest rate remains constant, and the return on the index over the 3-month period is perfectly correlated with the return on the portfolio. In practice, these assumptions do not hold perfectly, and the hedge works rather less well than is indicated by Table 3.4.

portfolio from β to β^*, where $\beta > \beta^*$, a short position in

$$(\beta - \beta^*)\frac{P}{A}$$

contracts is required. When $\beta < \beta^*$, a long position in

$$(\beta^* - \beta)\frac{P}{A}$$

contracts is required.

Exposure to the Price of an Individual Stock

Some exchanges do trade futures contracts on selected individual stocks, but in most cases a position in an individual stock can only be hedged using a stock index futures contract.

Hedging an exposure to the price of an individual stock using index futures contracts is similar to hedging a well-diversified stock portfolio. The number of index futures contracts that the hedger should short into is given by $\beta P/A$, where β is the beta of the stock, P is the total value of the shares owned, and A is the current value of the stocks underlying one index futures contract. Note that although the number of contracts entered into is calculated in the same way as it is when a portfolio of stocks is being hedged, the performance of the hedge is considerably worse. The hedge provides protection only against the risk arising from market movements, and this risk is a relatively small proportion of the total risk in the price movements of individual stocks. The hedge is appropriate when an investor feels that the stock will outperform the market but is unsure about the performance of the market. It can also be used by an investment bank that has underwritten a new issue of the stock and wants protection against moves in the market as a whole.

Consider an investor who in June holds 20,000 IBM shares, each worth \$100. The investor feels that the market will be very volatile over the next month but that IBM has a good chance of outperforming the market. The investor decides to use the August futures contract on the S&P 500 to hedge the position during the 1-month period. The β of IBM is estimated at 1.1. The current level of the index is 900, and the current futures price for the August contract on the S&P 500 is 908. Each contract is for delivery of \$250 times the index. In this case $P = 20{,}000 \times 100 = 2{,}000{,}000$ and $A = 900 \times 250 = 225{,}000$. The number of contracts that should be shorted is therefore

$$1.1 \times \frac{2{,}000{,}000}{225{,}000} = 9.78$$

Rounding to the nearest integer, the hedger shorts 10 contracts, closing out the position 1 month later. Suppose IBM rises to \$125 during the month, and the futures price of the S&P 500 rises to 1080. The investor gains $20{,}000 \times (\$125 - \$100) = \$500{,}000$ on IBM while losing $10 \times 250 \times (1080 - 908) = \$430{,}000$ on the futures contracts.

In this example, the hedge offsets a gain on the underlying asset with a loss on the futures contracts. The offset might seem to be counterproductive. However, it cannot be emphasized often enough that the purpose of a hedge is to reduce risk. A hedge tends to make unfavorable outcomes less unfavorable but also to make favorable outcomes less favorable.

3.6 ROLLING THE HEDGE FORWARD

Sometimes the expiration date of the hedge is later than the delivery dates of all the futures contracts that can be used. The hedger must then roll the hedge forward by closing out one futures contract and taking the same position in a futures contract with a later delivery date. Hedges can be rolled forward many times. Consider a company that wishes to use a short hedge to reduce the risk associated with the price to be received for an asset at time T. If there are futures contracts 1, 2, 3, ..., n (not all necessarily in existence at the present time) with progressively later delivery dates, the company can use the following strategy:

Time t_1: Short futures contract 1
Time t_2: Close out futures contract 1
Short futures contract 2
Time t_3: Close out futures contract 2
Short futures contract 3
⋮
Time t_n: Close out futures contract $n-1$
Short futures contract n
Time T: Close out futures contract n

Suppose that in April 2004 a company realizes that it will have 100,000 barrels of oil to sell in June 2005 and decides to hedge its risk with a hedge ratio of 1.0. The current spot price is \$19. Although futures contracts are traded with maturities stretching several years into the future, we suppose that only the first 6 delivery months have sufficient liquidity to meet the company's needs. The company therefore shorts 100 October 2004 contracts. In September 2004 it rolls the hedge forward into the March 2005 contract. In February 2005 it rolls the hedge forward again into the July 2005 contract.

One possible outcome is shown in Table 3.5. The October 2004 contract is shorted at \$18.20 per barrel and closed out at \$17.40 per barrel for a profit of \$0.80 per barrel; the March 2005 contract is shorted at \$17.00 per barrel and closed out at \$16.50 per barrel for a profit of \$0.50 per barrel. The July 2005 contract is shorted at \$16.30 per barrel and closed out at \$15.90 per barrel for a profit of \$0.40 per barrel. The final spot price is \$16.

The dollar gain per barrel of oil from the short futures contracts, ignoring the time value of money, is

$$(18.20 - 17.40) + (17.00 - 16.50) + (16.30 - 15.90) = 1.70$$

Table 3.5 Data for the example on rolling oil hedge forward.

Date	*Apr. 2004*	*Sept. 2004*	*Feb. 2005*	*June 2005*
Oct. 2004 futures price	18.20	17.40		
Mar. 2005 futures price		17.00	16.50	
July 2005 futures price			16.30	15.90
Spot price	19.00			16.00

Business Snapshot 3.2 Metallgesellschaft: Hedging Gone Awry

Sometimes rolling hedges forward can lead to cash flow pressures. The problem was illustrated dramatically by the activities of a German company, Metallgesellschaft (MG), in the early 1990s.

MG sold a huge volume of 5- to 10-year heating oil and gasoline fixed-price supply contracts to its customers at 6 to 8 cents above market prices. It hedged its exposure with long positions in short-dated futures contracts that were rolled forward. As it turned out, the price of oil fell and there were margin calls on the futures positions. Considerable short-term cash flow pressures were placed on MG. The members of MG who devised the hedging strategy argued that these short-term cash outflows were offset by positive cash flows that would ultimately be realized on the long-term fixed-price contracts. However, the company's senior management and its bankers became concerned about the huge cash drain. As a result, the company closed out all the hedge positions and agreed with its customers that the fixed-price contracts would be abandoned. The outcome was a loss to MG of $1.33 billion.

The oil price declined from $19 to $16. Receiving only $1.70 per barrel compensation for a price decline of $3.00 may appear unsatisfactory. However, we cannot expect total compensation for a price decline when futures prices are below spot prices. The best we can hope for is to lock in the futures price that would apply to a June 2005 contract if it were actively traded.

The daily settlement of futures contracts can cause a mismatch between the timing of the cash flows on hedge and the timing of the cash flows from the position being hedged. In situations where the hedge is rolled forward so that it lasts a long time this can lead to serious problems (see Business Snapshot 3.2).

SUMMARY

This chapter has discussed various ways in which a company can take a position in futures contracts to offset an exposure to the price of an asset. If the exposure is such that the company gains when the price of the asset increases and loses when the price of the asset decreases, a short hedge is appropriate. If the exposure is the other way round (i.e., the company gains when the price of the asset decreases and loses when the price of the asset increases), a long hedge is appropriate.

Hedging is a way of reducing risk. As such, it should be welcomed by most executives. In reality, there are a number of theoretical and practical reasons why companies do not hedge. On a theoretical level, we can argue that shareholders, by holding well-diversified portfolios, can eliminate many of the risks faced by a company. They do not require the company to hedge these risks. On a practical level, a company may find that it is increasing rather than decreasing risk by hedging if none of its competitors does so. Also, a treasurer may fear criticism from other executives if the company makes a gain from movements in the price of the underlying asset and a loss on the hedge.

An important concept in hedging is basis risk. The basis is the difference between the spot price of an asset and its futures price. Basis risk is created by a hedger's uncertainty as to what the basis will be at maturity of the hedge.

The hedge ratio is the ratio of the size of the position taken in futures contracts to the size of the exposure. It is not always optimal to use a hedge ratio of 1.0. If the hedger wishes to minimize the variance of a position, a hedge ratio different from 1.0 may be appropriate. The optimal hedge ratio is the slope of the best-fit line obtained when changes in the spot price are regressed against changes in the futures price.

Stock index futures can be used to hedge the systematic risk in an equity portfolio. The number of futures contracts required is the beta of the portfolio multiplied by the ratio of the value of the portfolio to the value of the assets underlying one futures contract. Stock index futures can also be used to change the beta of a portfolio without changing the stocks comprising the portfolio.

When there is no liquid futures contract that matures later than the expiration of the hedge, a strategy known as rolling the hedge forward may be appropriate. This involves entering into a sequence of futures contracts. When the first futures contract is near expiration, it is closed out and the hedger enters into a second contract with a later delivery month. When the second contract is close to expiration, it is closed out and the hedger enters into a third contract with a later delivery month; and so on. The result of all this is the creation of a long-dated futures contract by trading a series of short-dated contracts.

FURTHER READING

Allayannis, G. and J. Weston. "The Use of Foreign Currency Derivatives and Firm Market Value," *Review of Financial Studies*, 14, 1 (Spring 2001): 243–76.

Bodnar, G. M., G. S. Hayt, and R. C. Marston. "1998 Wharton Survey of Financial Risk Management by U.S. Non-Financial Firms" *Financial Management*, 2, 4 (1998): 70–91.

Brown, G. W. "Managing Foreign Exchange Risk with Derivatives." *Journal of Financial Economics*, 60 (2001): 401–48.

Culp, C. and M. H. Miller. "Metallgesellschaft and the Economics of Synthetic Storage," *Journal of Applied Corporate Finance*, 7, 4 (Winter 1995): 62–76.

Ederington, L. H. "The Hedging Performance of the New Futures Market," *Journal of Finance*, 34 (March 1979): 157–70.

Edwards, F. R. and M. S. Canter. "The Collapse of Metallgesellschaft: Unhedgeable Risks, Poor Hedging Strategy, or Just Bad Luck?" *Journal of Applied Corporate Finance*, 8, 1 (Spring 1995): 86–105.

Geczy, C., B. A. Minton, and C. Schrand. "Why Firms Use Currency Derivatives," *Journal of Finance*, 52, 4 (1997): 1323–54.

Graham, J. R. and C. W. Smith, Jr. "Tax Incentives to Hedge," *Journal of Finance*, 54, 6 (1999): 2241–62.

Haushalter, G. D. "Financing Policy, Basis Risk, and Corporate Hedging: Evidence from Oil and Gas Producers," *Journal of Finance*, 55, 1 (2000): 107–52.

Mello, A. S. and J. E. Parsons. "Hedging and Liquidity," *Review of Financial Studies*, 13 (Spring 2000): 127–53.

Neuberger, A. J. "Hedging Long-Term Exposures with Multiple Short-Term Futures Contracts," *Review of Financial Studies*, 12 (1999): 429–59.

Petersen, M. A. and S. R. Thiagarajan, "Risk Management and Hedging: With and Without Derivatives," *Financial Management*, 29, 4 (Winter 2000): 5–30.

Stulz, R. M. "Optimal Hedging Policies," *Journal of Financial and Quantitative Analysis*, 19 (June 1984): 127–40.

Tufano, P. "Who Manages Risk? An Empirical Examination of Risk Management Practices in the Gold Mining Industry," *Journal of Finance*, 51, 4 (1996): 1097–1138.

Tufano, P. "The Determinants of Stock Price Exposure: Financial Engineering and the Gold Mining Industry," *Journal of Finance*, 53, 3 (1998): 1015–52.

Questions and Problems (Answers in Solutions Manual)

3.1. Under what circumstances are (a) a short hedge and (b) a long hedge appropriate?

3.2. Explain what is meant by *basis risk* when futures contracts are used for hedging.

3.3. Explain what is meant by a *perfect hedge*. Does a perfect hedge always lead to a better outcome than an imperfect hedge? Explain your answer.

3.4. Under what circumstances does a minimum variance hedge portfolio lead to no hedging at all?

3.5. Give three reasons that the treasurer of a company might not hedge the company's exposure to a particular risk.

3.6. Suppose that the standard deviation of quarterly changes in the prices of a commodity is \$0.65, the standard deviation of quarterly changes in a futures price on the commodity is \$0.81, and the coefficient of correlation between the two changes is 0.8. What is the optimal hedge ratio for a 3-month contract? What does it mean?

3.7. A company has a \$20 million portfolio with a beta of 1.2. It would like to use futures contracts on the S&P 500 to hedge its risk. The index is currently standing at 1080, and each contract is for delivery of \$250 times the index. What is the hedge that minimizes risk? What should the company do if it wants to reduce the beta of the portfolio to 0.6?

3.8. In the Chicago Board of Trade's corn futures contract, the following delivery months are available: March, May, July, September, and December. State the contract that should be used for hedging when the expiration of the hedge is in (a) June, (b) July, and (c) January.

3.9. Does a perfect hedge always succeed in locking in the current spot price of an asset for a future transaction? Explain your answer.

3.10. Explain why a short hedger's position improves when the basis strengthens unexpectedly and worsens when the basis weakens unexpectedly.

3.11. Imagine you are the treasurer of a Japanese company exporting electronic equipment to the United States. Discuss how you would design a foreign exchange hedging strategy and the arguments you would use to sell the strategy to your fellow executives.

3.12. Suppose that in Example 3.2 of Section 3.3 the company decides to use a hedge ratio of 0.8. How does the decision affect the way in which the hedge is implemented and the result?

3.13. "If the minimum variance hedge ratio is calculated as 1.0, the hedge must be perfect." Is this statement true? Explain your answer.

3.14. "If there is no basis risk, the minimum variance hedge ratio is always 1.0." Is this statement true? Explain your answer.

3.15. "For an asset where futures prices are usually less than spot prices, long hedges are likely to be particularly attractive." Explain this statement.

3.16. The standard deviation of monthly changes in the spot price of live cattle is (in cents per pound) 1.2. The standard deviation of monthly changes in the futures price of live cattle for the closest contract is 1.4. The correlation between the futures price changes and the spot price changes is 0.7. It is now October 15. A beef producer is committed to purchasing 200,000 pounds of live cattle on November 15. The producer wants to use the December live cattle futures contracts to hedge its risk. Each contract is for the delivery of 40,000 pounds of cattle. What strategy should the beef producer follow?

3.17. A corn farmer argues "I do not use futures contracts for hedging. My real risk is not the price of corn. It is that my whole crop gets wiped out by the weather." Discuss this viewpoint. Should the farmer estimate his or her expected production of corn and hedge to try to lock in a price for expected production?

3.18. On July 1, an investor holds 50,000 shares of a certain stock. The market price is $30 per share. The investor is interested in hedging against movements in the market over the next month and decides to use the September Mini S&P 500 futures contract. The index is currently 1,500 and one contract is for delivery of $50 times the index. The beta of the stock is 1.3. What strategy should the investor follow?

3.19. Suppose that in Table 3.5 the company decides to use a hedge ratio of 1.5. How does the decision affect the way the hedge is implemented and the result?

3.20. A futures contract is used for hedging. Explain why the marking to market of the contract can give rise to cash flow problems.

3.21. An airline executive has argued: "There is no point in our using oil futures. There is just as much chance that the price of oil in the future will be less than the futures price as there is that it will be greater than this price." Discuss the executive's viewpoint.

3.22. Suppose that the 1-year gold lease rate is 1.5% and the 1-year risk-free rate is 5.0%. Both rates are compounded annually. Use the discussion in Business Snapshot 3.1 to calculate the maximum 1-year forward price Goldman Sachs should quote for gold when the spot price is $400.

Assignment Questions

3.23. The following table gives data on monthly changes in the spot price and the futures price for a certain commodity. Use the data to calculate a minimum variance hedge ratio.

Spot price change	+0.50	+0.61	−0.22	−0.35	+0.79
Futures price change	+0.56	+0.63	−0.12	−0.44	+0.60
Spot price change	+0.04	+0.15	+0.70	−0.51	−0.41
Futures price change	−0.06	+0.01	+0.80	−0.56	−0.46

3.24. It is July 16. A company has a portfolio of stocks worth $100 million. The beta of the portfolio is 1.2. The company would like to use the CME December futures contract on the S&P 500 to change the beta of the portfolio to 0.5 during the period July 16 to November 16. The index is currently 1,000, and each contract is on $250 times the index.

(a) What position should the company take?

(b) Suppose that the company changes its mind and decides to increase the beta of the portfolio from 1.2 to 1.5. What position in futures contracts should it take?

3.25. It is now October 2004. A company anticipates that it will purchase 1 million pounds of copper in each of February 2005, August 2005, February 2006, and August 2006. The company has decided to use the futures contracts traded in the COMEX division of the New York Mercantile Exchange to hedge its risk. One contract is for the delivery of 25,000 pounds of copper. The initial margin is $2,000 per contract and the maintenance margin is $1,500 per contract. The company's policy is to hedge 80% of its exposure. Contracts with maturities up to 13 months into the future are considered to have sufficient liquidity to meet the company's needs. Devise a hedging strategy for the company.

Assume the market prices (in cents per pound) today and at future dates are as follows:

Date	*Oct. 2004*	*Feb. 2005*	*Aug. 2005*	*Feb. 2006*	*Aug. 2006*
Spot price	72.00	69.00	65.00	77.00	88.00
Mar. 2005 futures price	72.30	69.10			
Sept. 2005 futures price	72.80	70.20	64.80		
Mar. 2006 futures price		70.70	64.30	76.70	
Sept. 2006 futures price			64.20	76.50	88.20

What is the impact of the strategy you propose on the price the company pays for copper? What is the initial margin requirement in October 2004? Is the company subject to any margin calls?

3.26. A fund manager has a portfolio worth $50 million with a beta of 0.87. The manager is concerned about the performance of the market over the next 2 months and plans to use 3-month futures contracts on the S&P 500 to hedge the risk. The current level of the index is 1250, one contract is on 250 times the index, the risk-free rate is 6% per annum, and the dividend yield on the index is 3% per annum. The current 3-month futures price is 1259.

(a) What position should the fund manager take to eliminate all exposure to the market over the next 2 months?

(b) Calculate the effect of your strategy on the fund manager's returns if the level of the market in 2 months is 1,000, 1,100, 1,200, 1,300, and 1,400. Assume that the 1-month futures price is 0.25% higher than the index level at this time.

APPENDIX

PROOF OF THE MINIMUM VARIANCE HEDGE RATIO FORMULA

Suppose we expect to sell N_A units of an asset at time t_2 and choose to hedge at time t_1 by shorting futures contracts on N_F units of a similar asset. The hedge ratio, which we will denote by h, is

$$h = \frac{N_F}{N_A} \tag{3A.1}$$

We will denote the total amount realized for the asset when the profit or loss on the hedge is taken into account by Y, so that

$$Y = S_2 N_A - (F_2 - F_1) N_F$$

or

$$Y = S_1 N_A + (S_2 - S_1) N_A - (F_2 - F_1) N_F \tag{3A.2}$$

where S_1 and S_2 are the asset prices at times t_1 and t_2, and F_1 and F_2 are the futures prices at times t_1 and t_2. From equation (3A.1), the expression for Y in equation (3A.2) can be written

$$Y = S_1 N_A + N_A(\Delta S - h\,\Delta F) \tag{3A.3}$$

where

$$\Delta S = S_2 - S_1 \quad \text{and} \quad \Delta F = F_2 - F_1$$

Because S_1 and N_A are known at time t_1, the variance of Y in equation (3A.3) is minimized when the variance of $\Delta S - h\,\Delta F$ is minimized. The variance of $\Delta S - h\,\Delta F$ is

$$v = \sigma_S^2 + h^2\sigma_F^2 - 2h\rho\sigma_S\sigma_F$$

where σ_S, σ_F, and ρ are as defined in Section 3.4, so that

$$\frac{dv}{dh} = 2h\sigma_F^2 - 2\rho\sigma_S\sigma_F$$

Setting this equal to zero, and noting that d^2v/dh^2 is positive, we see that the value of h that minimizes the variance is $h = \rho\sigma_S/\sigma_F$.

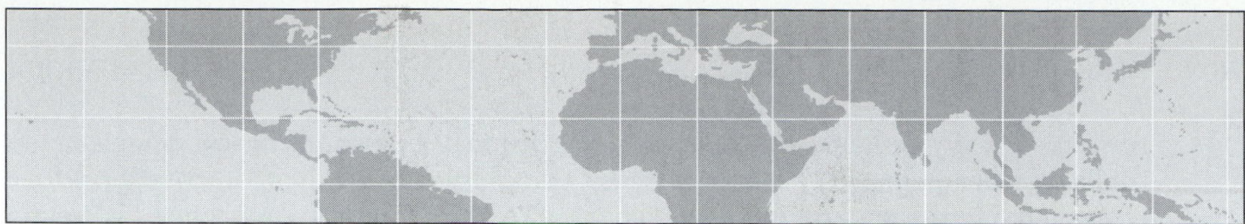

CHAPTER 4 Interest Rates

Interest rates are a factor in the valuation of virtually all derivatives and will feature prominently in much of the material that will be presented in the rest of this book. In this chapter we cover some fundamental issues concerned with the way interest rates are measured and analyzed. We explain the compounding frequency used to define an interest rate and the meaning of continuously compounded interest rates, which are used extensively in the analysis of derivatives. We cover zero rates, par yields, and yield curves, discuss bond pricing, and outline a procedure commonly used by a derivatives trading desk to calculate zero-coupon Treasury interest rates. We cover forward rates and forward rate agreements and review different theories of the term structure of interest rates. Finally we explain the use of duration and convexity measures to determine the sensitivity of bond prices to interest rate changes.

Chapter 6 will cover interest rate futures and show how the duration measure can be used when interest rate exposures are hedged. For ease of exposition we will ignore day count conventions throughout this chapter. The nature of these conventions and their impact on calculations will be discussed in Chapters 6 and 7.

4.1 TYPES OF RATES

An interest rate in a particular situation defines the amount of money a borrower promises to pay the lender. For any given currency, many different types of interest rates are regularly quoted. These include mortgage rates, deposit rates, prime borrowing rates, and so on. The interest rate applicable in a situation depends on the credit risk. This is the risk that there will be a default by the borrower of funds, so that the interest and principal are not paid to the lender as promised. The higher the credit risk, the higher the interest rate that is promised by the borrower.

Treasury Rates

Treasury rates are the rates an investor earns on Treasury bills and Treasury bonds. These are the instruments used by a government to borrow in its own currency. Japanese Treasury rates are the rates at which the Japanese government borrows in yen; US Treasury rates are the rates at which the US government borrows in US dollars; and so on. It is usually assumed that there is no chance that a government will default on an obligation denominated in its own currency.[1] Treasury rates are therefore totally risk-free rates in the sense that an investor who buys a Treasury bill or Treasury bond is certain that interest and principal payments will be made as promised.

Treasury rates are important because they are used to price Treasury bonds and are sometimes used to define the payoff from a derivative. However, derivatives traders (particularly those active in the over-the-counter market) do not usually use Treasury rates as risk-free rates. Instead they use LIBOR rates.

LIBOR

LIBOR is short for *London Interbank Offer Rate*. A LIBOR quote by a particular bank is the rate of interest at which the bank is prepared to make a large wholesale deposit with other banks. Large banks and other financial institutions quote 1-month, 3-month, 6-month, and 12-month LIBOR in all major currencies. Here 1-month LIBOR is the rate at which 1-month deposits are offered, 3-month LIBOR is the rate at which 3-month deposits are offered, and so on.

A deposit with a bank can be regarded as a loan to that bank. A bank must therefore satisfy certain creditworthiness criteria in order to be able to accept a LIBOR quote from another bank and receive deposits from that bank at LIBOR. Typically it must have to have a AA credit rating.[2]

AA-rated financial institutions regard LIBOR as their short-term opportunity cost of capital. They can borrow short-term funds at the LIBOR quotes of other financial institutions. Their own LIBOR quotes determine the rate at which surplus funds are lent to other financial institutions. LIBOR rates are not totally free of credit risk. There is a small chance that a AA-rated financial institution will default on a LIBOR loan. However, they are close to risk-free. Derivatives traders regard LIBOR rates as a better indication of the "true" risk-free rate than Treasury rates, because a number of tax and regulatory issues cause Treasury rates to be artifically low (see Business Snapshot 4.1). To be consistent with the normal practice in derivatives markets, the term "risk-free rate" in this book should be interpreted as the LIBOR rate.[3]

In addition to quoting LIBOR rates, large banks also quote LIBID rates. This is the *London Interbank Bid Rate* and is the rate at which they will accept deposits from other banks. At any specified time, there is usually a small spread between the quoted LIBID and LIBOR rates (with LIBOR higher than LIBID). The rates themselves are determined by active trading between banks and are continually changing so that the supply of funds in the interbank market equals the demand for funds in that market. For example, if more banks want to borrow US dollars for 3 months than lend US dollars for 3 months, the 3-month US LIBID and LIBOR rates quoted by banks will increase. Similarly, if more banks want to lend 3-month funds than borrow these funds, the 3-month LIBID and LIBOR rates will decrease. LIBOR and LIBID trade in what is known as the *Eurocurrency market*. This market is outside the control of any one government.

---

[1] The reason for this is that the government can always meet its obligation by printing more money.

[2] The best credit rating given to a company by the rating agency S&P is AAA. The second best is AA. The corresponding ratings from the rival rating agency Moody's are Aaa and Aa, respectively.

[3] As we shall see in Chapter 7, it is more accurate to say that the risk-free rate should be interpreted as the rate derived from LIBOR, swap, and Eurodollar futures quotes.

Business Snapshot 4.1 What Is the Risk-Free Rate?

It is natural to assume that the rates on Treasury bills and Treasury bonds are the correct benchmark risk-free rates for derivative traders working for financial institutions. In fact, these derivative traders usually use LIBOR rates as short-term risk-free rates. This is because they regard LIBOR as their opportunity cost of capital (see Section 4.1). Traders argue that Treasury rates are too low to be used as risk-free rates because:

1. Treasury bills and Treasury bonds must be purchased by financial institutions to fulfill a variety of regulatory requirements. This increases demand for these Treasury instruments driving the price up and the yield down.
2. The amount of capital a bank is required to hold to support an investment in Treasury bills and bonds is substantially smaller than the capital required to support a similar investment in other instruments with very low risk.
3. In the United States, Treasury instruments are given a favorable tax treatment compared with most other fixed-income investments because they are not taxed at the state level.

LIBOR is approximately equal to the short-term borrowing rate of a AA-rated company. It is therefore not a perfect proxy for the risk-free rate. There is a small chance that a AA borrower will default within the life of a LIBOR loan. Nevertheless, traders feel it is the best proxy for them to use. LIBOR rates are quoted out to 12 months. As we shall see in Chapter 7, the Eurodollar futures market and the swap market are used to extend the trader's proxy for the risk-free rate beyond 12 months.

Repo Rates

Sometimes trading activities are funded with a *repo* or *repurchase agreement*. This is a contract where an investment dealer who owns securities agrees to sell them to another company now and buy them back later at a slightly higher price. The other company is providing a loan to the investment dealer. The difference between the price at which the securities are sold and the price at which they are repurchased is the interest it earns. The interest rate is referred to as the *repo rate*. If structured carefully, the loan involves very little credit risk. If the borrower does not honor the agreement, the lending company simply keeps the securities. If the lending company does not keep to its side of the agreement, the original owner of the securities keeps the cash.

The most common type of repo is an *overnight repo*, in which the agreement is renegotiated each day. However, longer-term arrangements, known as *term repos*, are sometimes used.

4.2 MEASURING INTEREST RATES

A statement by a bank that the interest rate on 1-year deposits is 10% per annum sounds straightforward and unambiguous. In fact, its precise meaning depends on the way the interest rate is measured.

Table 4.1 Effect of the compounding frequency on the value of \$100 at the end of 1 year when the interest rate is 10% per annum.

Compounding frequency	*Value of \$100 at end of year (\$)*
Annually ($m = 1$)	110.00
Semiannually ($m = 2$)	110.25
Quarterly ($m = 4$)	110.38
Monthly ($m = 12$)	110.47
Weekly ($m = 52$)	110.51
Daily ($m = 365$)	110.52

If the interest rate is measured with annual compounding, the bank's statement that the interest rate is 10% means that \$100 grows to

$$\$100 \times 1.1 = \$110$$

at the end of 1 year. When the interest rate is measured with semiannual compounding, it means that we earn 5% every 6 months, with the interest being reinvested. In this case \$100 grows to

$$\$100 \times 1.05 \times 1.05 = \$110.25$$

at the end of 1 year. When the interest rate is measured with quarterly compounding, the bank's statement means that we earn 2.5% every 3 months, with the interest being reinvested. The \$100 then grows to

$$\$100 \times 1.025^4 = \$110.38$$

at the end of 1 year. Table 4.1 shows the effect of increasing the compounding frequency further.

The compounding frequency defines the units in which an interest rate is measured. A rate expressed with one compounding frequency can be converted into an equivalent rate with a different compounding frequency. For example, from Table 4.1 we see that 10.25% with annual compounding is equivalent to 10% with semiannual compounding. We can think of the difference between one compounding frequency and another to be analogous to the difference between kilometers and miles. They are two different units of measurement.

To generalize our results, suppose that an amount A is invested for n years at an interest rate of R per annum. If the rate is compounded once per annum, the terminal value of the investment is

$$A(1+R)^n$$

If the rate is compounded m times per annum, the terminal value of the investment is

$$A\left(1+\frac{R}{m}\right)^{mn} \tag{4.1}$$

When $m = 1$, the rate is sometimes referred to as the *equivalent annual interest rate*.

Continuous Compounding

The limit as the compounding frequency, m, tends to infinity is known as *continuous compounding*.[4] With continuous compounding, it can be shown that an amount A invested for n years at rate R grows to

$$Ae^{Rn} \tag{4.2}$$

where $e = 2.71828$. The exponential function, e^x, is built into most calculators, so the computation of the expression in equation (4.2) presents no problems. In the example in Table 4.1, $A = 100$, $n = 1$, and $R = 0.1$, so that the value to which A grows with continuous compounding is

$$100e^{0.1} = \$110.52$$

This is (to two decimal places) the same as the value with daily compounding. For most practical purposes, continuous compounding can be thought of as being equivalent to daily compounding. Compounding a sum of money at a continuously compounded rate R for n years involves multiplying it by e^{Rn}. Discounting it at a continuously compounded rate R for n years involves multiplying by e^{-Rn}.

In this book, interest rates will be measured with continuous compounding except where stated otherwise. Readers used to working with interest rates that are measured with annual, semiannual, or some other compounding frequency may find this a little strange at first. However, continuously compounded interest rates are used to such a great extent in pricing derivatives that it makes sense to get used to working with them now.

Suppose that R_c is a rate of interest with continuous compounding and R_m is the equivalent rate with compounding m times per annum. From the results in equations (4.1) and (4.2), we have

$$Ae^{R_c n} = A\left(1 + \frac{R_m}{m}\right)^{mn}$$

or

$$e^{R_c} = \left(1 + \frac{R_m}{m}\right)^{m}$$

This means that

$$R_c = m \ln\left(1 + \frac{R_m}{m}\right) \tag{4.3}$$

and

$$R_m = m(e^{R_c/m} - 1) \tag{4.4}$$

These equations can be used to convert a rate with a compounding frequency of m times per annum to a continuously compounded rate and vice versa. The natural logarithm function $\ln x$, which is built into most calculators, is the *inverse* of the exponential function, so that, if $y = \ln x$, then $x = e^y$.

Example 4.1

Consider an interest rate that is quoted as 10% per annum with semiannual compounding. From equation (4.3) with $m = 2$ and $R_m = 0.1$, the equivalent rate

[4] Actuaries sometimes refer to a continuously compounded rate as the *force of interest*.

with continuous compounding is

$$2\ln\left(1+\frac{0.1}{2}\right)=0.09758$$

or 9.758% per annum.

Example 4.2

Suppose that a lender quotes the interest rate on loans as 8% per annum with continuous compounding, and that interest is actually paid quarterly. From equation (4.4) with $m = 4$ and $R_c = 0.08$, the equivalent rate with quarterly compounding is

$$4(e^{0.08/4}-1)=0.0808$$

or 8.08% per annum. This means that on a \$1,000 loan, interest payments of \$20.20 would be required each quarter.

4.3 ZERO RATES

The n-year zero-coupon interest rate is the rate of interest earned on an investment that starts today and lasts for n years. All the interest and principal is realized at the end of n years. There are no intermediate payments. The n-year zero-coupon interest rate is sometimes also referred to as the n-year *spot rate*, the n-year *zero rate*, or just the n-year zero. Suppose a 5-year zero rate with continuous compounding is quoted as 5% per annum. This means that \$100, if invested for 5 years, grows to

$$100\times e^{0.05\times 5}=128.40$$

Many of the interest rates we observe directly in the market are not pure zero rates. Consider a 5-year government bond that provides a 6% coupon. The price of this bond does not by itself determine the 5-year Treasury zero rate because some of the return on the bond is realized in the form of coupons prior to the end of year 5. Later in this chapter we will discuss how we can determine Treasury zero rates from the market prices of coupon-bearing bonds.

4.4 BOND PRICING

Most bonds provide coupons periodically. The bond's principal (which is also known as its par value or face value) is received at the end of its life. The theoretical price of a bond can be calculated as the present value of all the cash flows that will be received by the owner of the bond. Sometimes bond traders use the same discount rate for all the cash flows underlying a bond, but a more accurate approach is to use a different zero rate for each cash flow.

To illustrate this, consider the situation where Treasury zero rates, measured with continuous compounding, are as in Table 4.2. (We explain later how these can be calculated.) Suppose that a 2-year Treasury bond with a principal of \$100 provides coupons at the rate of 6% per annum semiannually. To calculate the present value of the first coupon of \$3, we discount it at 5.0% for 6 months; to calculate the present

Table 4.2 Treasury zero rates.

Maturity (years)	*Zero rate (%)* *(continuously compounded)*
0.5	5.0
1.0	5.8
1.5	6.4
2.0	6.8

value of the second coupon of \$3, we discount it at 5.8% for 1 year; and so on. Therefore the theoretical price of the bond is

$$3e^{-0.05\times 0.5} + 3e^{-0.058\times 1.0} + 3e^{-0.064\times 1.5} + 103e^{-0.068\times 2.0} = 98.39$$

or \$98.39.

Bond Yield

A bond's yield is the discount rate that, when applied to all cash flows, gives a bond price equal to its market price. Suppose that the theoretical price of the bond we have been considering, \$98.39, is also its market value (i.e., the market's price of the bond is in exact agreement with the data in Table 4.2). If y is the yield on the bond, expressed with continuous compounding, we have

$$3e^{-y\times 0.5} + 3e^{-y\times 1.0} + 3e^{-y\times 1.5} + 103e^{-y\times 2.0} = 98.39$$

This equation can be solved using an iterative ("trial and error") procedure to give $y = 6.76\%$.[5]

Par Yield

The *par yield* for a certain bond maturity is the coupon rate that causes the bond price to equal its par value. (The par value is the same as the principal value.) Usually the bond is assumed to provide semiannual coupons. Suppose that the coupon on a 2-year bond in our example is c per annum (or $\frac{1}{2}c$ per 6 months). Using the zero rates in Table 4.2, the value of the bond is equal to its par value of 100 when

$$\frac{c}{2}e^{-0.05\times 0.5} + \frac{c}{2}e^{-0.058\times 1.0} + \frac{c}{2}e^{-0.064\times 1.5} + \left(100 + \frac{c}{2}\right)e^{-0.068\times 2.0} = 100$$

This equation can be solved in a straightforward way to give $c = 6.87$. The 2-year par yield is therefore 6.87% per annum with semiannual compounding (or 6.75% with continuous compounding).

More generally, if d is the present value of \$1 received at the maturity of the bond, A is the value of an annuity that pays one dollar on each coupon payment date, and m

[5] One way of solving nonlinear equations of the form $f(y) = 0$, such as this one, is to use the Newton–Raphson method. We start with an estimate y_0 of the solution and produce successively better estimates $y_1, y_2, y_3, \dots$ using the formula $y_{i+1} = y_i - f(y_i)/f'(y_i)$, where $f'(y)$ denotes the derivative of f with respect to y.

is the number of coupon payments per year, then the par yield c must satisfy

$$100 = A\frac{c}{m} + 100d$$

so that

$$c = \frac{(100 - 100d)m}{A}$$

In our example, $m = 2$, $d = e^{-0.068\times 2} = 0.87284$, and

$$A = e^{-0.05\times 0.5} + e^{-0.058\times 1.0} + e^{-0.064\times 1.5} + e^{-0.068\times 2.0} = 3.70027$$

The formula confirms that the par yield is 6.87% per annum. Note that this is a rate expressed with semiannual compounding; with continuous compounding, it would be 6.75% per annum.

4.5 DETERMINING TREASURY ZERO RATES

We now discuss how Treasury zero rates can be calculated from the prices of Treasury bonds. The most popular approach is known as the *bootstrap method.* To illustrate the nature of the method, consider the data in Table 4.3 on the prices of five bonds. Because the first three bonds pay no coupons, the zero rates corresponding to the maturities of these bonds can easily be calculated. The 3-month bond provides a return of 2.5 in 3 months on an initial investment of 97.5. With quarterly compounding, the 3-month zero rate is $(4 \times 2.5)/97.5 = 10.256\%$ per annum. Equation (4.3) shows that, when the rate is expressed with continuous compounding, it becomes

$$4\ln\left(1 + \frac{0.10256}{4}\right) = 0.10127$$

or 10.127% per annum. The 6-month bond provides a return of 5.1 in 6 months on an initial investment of 94.9. With semiannual compounding the 6-month rate is $(2 \times 5.1)/94.9 = 10.748\%$ per annum. Equation (4.3) shows that, when the rate is

Table 4.3 Data for bootstrap method.

Bond principal (\$)	*Time to maturity* (*years*)	*Annual coupon** (\$)	*Bond price* (\$)
100	0.25	0	97.5
100	0.50	0	94.9
100	1.00	0	90.0
100	1.50	8	96.0
100	2.00	12	101.6

* Half the stated coupon is assumed to be paid every 6 months.

expressed with continuous compounding, it becomes

$$2\ln\left(1+\frac{0.10748}{2}\right)=0.10469$$

or 10.469% per annum. Similarly, the 1-year rate with continuous compounding is

$$\ln\left(1+\frac{10}{90}\right)=0.10536$$

or 10.536% per annum.

The fourth bond lasts 1.5 years. The payments are as follows:

6 months: \$4
1 year: \$4
1.5 years: \$104

From our earlier calculations, we know that the discount rate for the payment at the end of 6 months is 10.469% and that the discount rate for the payment at the end of 1 year is 10.536%. We also know that the bond's price, \$96, must equal the present value of all the payments received by the bondholder. Suppose the 1.5-year zero rate is denoted by R. It follows that

$$4e^{-0.10469\times 0.5}+4e^{-0.10536\times 1.0}+104e^{-R\times 1.5}=96$$

This reduces to

$$e^{-1.5R}=0.85196$$

or

$$R=-\frac{\ln(0.85196)}{1.5}=0.10681$$

The 1.5-year zero rate is therefore 10.681%. This is the only zero rate that is consistent with the 6-month rate, 1-year rate, and the data in Table 4.3.

The 2-year zero rate can be calculated similarly from the 6-month, 1-year, and 1.5-year zero rates, and the information on the last bond in Table 4.3. If R is the 2-year zero rate, then

$$6e^{-0.10469\times 0.5}+6e^{-0.10536\times 1.0}+6e^{-0.10681\times 1.5}+106e^{-R\times 2.0}=101.6$$

This gives $R=0.10808$, or 10.808%.

The rates we have calculated are summarized in Table 4.4. A chart showing the zero

Table 4.4 Continuously compounded zero rates determined from data in Table 4.3.

Maturity (years)	*Zero rate (%) (continuously compounded)*
0.25	10.127
0.50	10.469
1.00	10.536
1.50	10.681
2.00	10.808

Figure 4.1 Zero rates given by the bootstrap method.

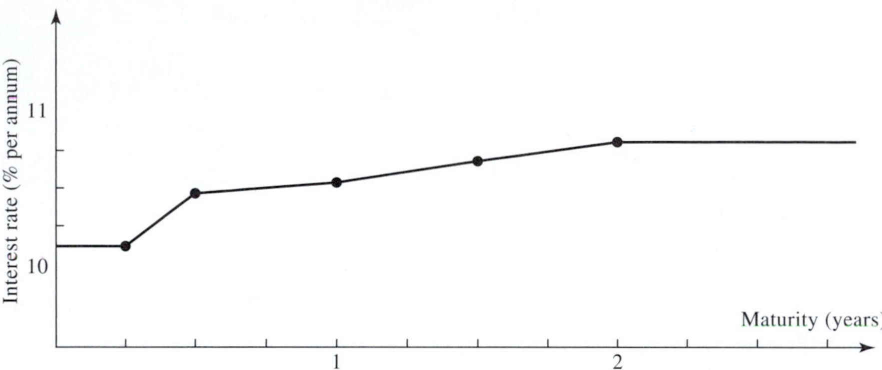

rate as a function of maturity is known as the *zero curve*. A common assumption is that the zero curve is linear between the points determined using the bootstrap method. (This means that the 1.25-year zero rate is $0.5 \times 10.536 + 0.5 \times 10.681 = 10.6085\%$ in our example.) It is also usually assumed that the zero curve is horizontal prior to the first point and horizontal beyond the last point. Figure 4.1 shows the zero curve for our data using these assumptions. By using longer maturity bonds, the zero curve would be more accurately determined beyond 2 years.

In practice, we do not usually have bonds with maturities equal to exactly 1.5 years, 2 years, 2.5 years, and so on. The approach often used by analysts is to interpolate between the bond price data before it is used to calculate the zero curve. For example, if they know that a 2.3-year bond with a coupon of 6% sells for 98 and a 2.7-year bond with a coupon of 6.5% sells for 99, it might be assumed that a 2.5-year bond with a coupon of 6.25% would sell for 98.5.

4.6 FORWARD RATES

Forward interest rates are the rates of interest implied by current zero rates for periods of time in the future. To illustrate how they are calculated, we suppose that a particular set of zero rates are as shown in the second column of Table 4.5. The rates are assumed to be continuously compounded. Thus, the 3% per annum rate for 1 year means that, in return for an investment of \$100 today, an investor receives $100e^{0.03\times 1} = \$103.05$ in 1 year; the 4% per annum rate for 2 years means that, in return for an investment of \$100 today, the investor receives $100e^{0.04\times 2} = \$108.33$ in 2 years; and so on.

The forward interest rate in Table 4.5 for year 2 is 5% per annum. This is the rate of interest that is implied by the zero rates for the period of time between the end of the first year and the end of the second year. It can be calculated from the 1-year zero interest rate of 3% per annum and the 2-year zero interest rate of 4% per annum. It is the rate of interest for year 2 that, when combined with 3% per annum for year 1, gives 4% overall for the 2 years. To show that the correct answer is 5% per annum, suppose that \$100 is invested. A rate of 3% for the first year and 5% for the second year gives

$$100e^{0.03\times 1}e^{0.05\times 1} = \$108.33$$

at the end of the second year. A rate of 4% per annum for 2 years gives

$$100e^{0.04\times 2}$$

which is also \$108.33. This example illustrates the general result that when interest rates are continuously compounded and rates in successive time periods are combined, the overall equivalent rate is simply the average rate during the whole period. In our example, 3% for the first year and 5% for the second year average to 4% over the 2 years. The result is only approximately true when the rates are not continuously compounded.

The forward rate for the year 3 is the rate of interest that is implied by a 4% per annum 2-year zero rate and a 4.6% per annum 3-year zero rate. It is 5.8% per annum. The reason is that an investment for 2 years at 4% per annum combined with an investment for one year at 5.8% per annum gives an overall average return for the three years of 4.6% per annum. The other forward rates can be calculated similarly and are shown in the third column of the table. In general, if R_1 and R_2 are the zero rates for maturities T_1 and T_2, respectively, and R_F is the forward interest rate for the period of time between T_1 and T_2, then

$$R_F = \frac{R_2T_2 - R_1T_1}{T_2 - T_1} \tag{4.5}$$

To illustrate this formula, consider the calculation of the year-4 forward rate from the data in Table 4.5: $T_1 = 3$, $T_2 = 4$, $R_1 = 0.046$, and $R_2 = 0.05$, and the formula gives $R_F = 0.062$.

Equation (4.5) can be written as

$$R_F = R_2 + (R_2 - R_1)\frac{T_1}{T_2 - T_1} \tag{4.6}$$

This shows that if the zero curve is upward sloping between T_1 and T_2, so that $R_2 > R_1$, then $R_F > R_2$ (i.e., the forward rate is greater than both zero rates). Similarly if the zero curve is downward sloping with $R_2 < R_1$, then $R_F < R_2$ (i.e., the forward rate is less

Table 4.5 Calculation of forward rates.

Year (n)	*Zero rate for an n-year investment (% per annum)*	*Forward rate for nth year (% per annum)*
1	3.0	
2	4.0	5.0
3	4.6	5.8
4	5.0	6.2
5	5.3	6.5

Business Snapshot 4.2 Orange County's Yield Curve Plays

Suppose an investor can borrow or lend at the rates given in Table 4.5 and thinks that 1-year interest rates will not change much over the next 5 years. The investor can borrow 1-year funds and invest for 5-years. The 1-year borrowings can be rolled over for further 1-year periods at the end of the first, second, third, and fourth years. If interest rates do stay about the same, this strategy will yield a profit of about 2.3% per year, because interest will be received at 5.3% and paid at 3%. This type of trading strategy is known as a *yield curve play*. The investor is speculating that rates in the future will be quite different from the forward rates observed in the market today. (In our example, forward rates observed in the market today for future 1-year periods are 5%, 5.8%, 6.2%, and 6.5%.)

Robert Citron, the Treasurer at Orange County, used yield curve plays similar to the one we have just described very successfully in 1992 and 1993. The profit from Mr. Citron's trades became an important contributor to Orange County's budget and he was re-elected. (No one listened to his opponent in the election who said his trading strategy was too risky.)

In 1994 Mr. Citron expanded his yield curve plays. He invested heavily in *inverse floaters*. These pay a rate of interest equal to a fixed rate of interest minus a floating rate. He also leveraged his position by borrowing in the repo market. If short-term interest rates had remained the same or declined he would have continued to do well. As it happened, interest rates rose sharply during 1994. On December 1, 1994, Orange County announced that its investment portfolio had lost \$1.5 billion and several days later it filed for bankruptcy protection.

than both zero rates). Taking limits as T_2 approaches T_1 in equation (4.6) and letting the common value of the two be T, we obtain

$$R_F = R + T\frac{\partial R}{\partial T}$$

where R is the zero rate for a maturity of T. The value of R_F obtained in this way is known as the *instantaneous forward rate* for a maturity of T. This is the forward rate that is applicable to a very short future time period that begins at time T.

Assuming that the zero rates for borrowing and investing are the same (which is close to the truth for a large financial institution), an investor can lock in the forward rate for a future time period. Suppose, for example, that the zero rates are as in Table 4.5. If an investor borrows \$100 at 3% for 1 year and then invests the money at 4% for 2 years, the result is a cash outflow of $100e^{0.03\times 1} = \$103.05$ at the end of year 1 and an inflow of $100e^{0.04\times 2} = \$108.33$ at the end of year 2. Because $108.33 = 103.05e^{0.05}$, a return equal to the forward rate (5%) is earned on \$103.05 during the second year. Suppose next that the investor borrows \$100 for four years at 5% and invests it for three years at 4.6%. The result is a cash inflow of $100e^{0.046\times 3} = \$114.80$ at the end of the third year and a cash outflow of $100e^{0.05\times 4} = \$122.14$ at the end of the fourth year. Because $122.14 = 114.80e^{0.062}$, money is being borrowed for the fourth year at the forward rate of 6.2%.

If an investor thinks that rates in the future will be different from today's forward rates there are many trading strategies that the investor will find attractive (see Business

Snapshot 4.2). One of these involves entering into a contract known as a *forward rate agreement*. We will now discuss how this contract works and how it is valued.

4.7 FORWARD RATE AGREEMENTS

A forward rate agreement (FRA) is an over-the-counter agreement that a certain interest rate will apply to either borrowing or lending a certain principal during a specified future period of time. The assumption underlying the contract is that the borrowing or lending would normally be done at LIBOR.

Consider a forward rate agreement where a company X is agreeing to lend money to company Y for the period of time between T_1 and T_2. Define:

R_K: The rate of interest agreed to in the FRA

R_F: The forward LIBOR interest rate for the period between times T_1 and T_2, calculated today[6]

R_M: The actual LIBOR interest rate observed in the market at time T_1 for the period between times T_1 and T_2

L: The principal underlying the contract

We will depart from our usual assumption of continuous compounding and assume that the rates R_K, R_F, and R_M are all measured with a compounding frequency reflecting their maturity. This means that if $T_2 - T_1 = 0.5$, they are expressed with semiannual compounding; if $T_2 - T_1 = 0.25$, they are expressed with quarterly compounding; and so on.

Normally company X would earn R_M from the LIBOR loan. The FRA means that it will earn R_K. The extra interest rate (which may be negative) that it earns as a result of entering into the FRA is $R_K - R_M$. The interest rate is set at time T_1 and paid at time T_2. The extra interest rate therefore leads to a cash flow to company X at time T_2 of

$$L(R_K - R_M)(T_2 - T_1) \tag{4.7}$$

Similarly there is a cash flow to company Y at time T_2 of

$$L(R_M - R_K)(T_2 - T_1) \tag{4.8}$$

From equations (4.7) and (4.8), we see that there is another interpretation of the FRA. It is an agreement where company X will receive interest on the principal between T_1 and T_2 at the fixed rate of R_K and pay interest at the realized market rate of R_M. Company Y will pay interest on the principal between T_1 and T_2 at the fixed rate of R_K and receive interest at R_M.

Usually FRAs are settled at time T_1 rather than T_2. The payoff must then be discounted from time T_2 to T_1. For company X, the time T_1 payoff is

$$\frac{L(R_K - R_M)(T_2 - T_1)}{1 + R_M(T_2 - T_1)}$$

---

[6] LIBOR forward rates are calculated as described in Section 4.6 from the LIBOR/swap zero curve, which is calculated as described in Section 7.6.

and, for company Y, the time T_1 payoff is

$$\frac{L(R_M - R_K)(T_2 - T_1)}{1 + R_M(T_2 - T_1)}$$

Example 4.3

Suppose that a company enters into an FRA that specifies it will receive a fixed rate of 4% on a principal of \$1 million for a 3-month period starting in 3 years. If 3-month LIBOR proves to be 4.5% for the 3-month period the cash flow to the lender will be

$$1{,}000{,}000 \times (0.04 - 0.045) \times 0.25 = -\$1{,}250$$

at the 3.25-year point. This is equivalent to a cash flow of

$$-\frac{1{,}250}{1 + 0.045 \times 0.25} = -\$1{,}236.09$$

at the 3-year point. The cash flow to the party on the opposite side of the transaction will be +\$1,250 at the 3.25-year point or +\$1,236.09 at the 3-year point. (All interest rates in this example are expressed with quarterly compounding.)

Valuation

To value an FRA we first note that it is always worth zero when $R_K = R_F$.[7] This is because, as noted in Section 4.6, a large financial institution can at no cost lock in the forward rate for a future time period. For example, it can ensure that it earns the forward rate for the time period between years 2 and 3 by borrowing for a certain amount of money for 2 years and investing it for 3 years. Similarly, it can ensure that it pays the forward rate for the time period between years 2 and 3 by borrowing for a certain amount of money for 3 years and investing it for 2 years.

Compare two FRAs. The first promises that the LIBOR forward rate R_F will be earned on a principal of L between times T_1 and T_2; the second promises that R_K will be earned on the same principal between the same two dates. The two contracts are the same except for the interest payments received at time T_2. The excess of the value of the second contract over the first is, therefore, the present value of the difference between these interest payments, or

$$L(R_K - R_F)(T_2 - T_1)e^{-R_2T_2}$$

where R_2 is the continously compounded riskless zero rate for a maturity T_2.[8] Because the value of the FRA where R_F is earned is zero, the value of the FRA where R_K is earned is

$$V_{\text{FRA}} = L(R_K - R_F)(T_2 - T_1)e^{-R_2T_2} \quad \textbf{(4.9)}$$

Similarly, the value of an FRA where R_K is paid is

$$V_{\text{FRA}} = L(R_F - R_K)(T_2 - T_1)e^{-R_2T_2} \quad \textbf{(4.10)}$$

---

[7] It is usually the case that R_K is set equal to R_F when the FRA is first initiated.

[8] Note that R_K, R_M, and R_F are expressed with a compounding frequency corresponding to $T_2 - T_1$, whereas R_2 is expressed with continuous compounding.

Example 4.4

Suppose that LIBOR zero and forward rates are as in Table 4.5. Consider an FRA where we will receive a rate of 6%, measured with annual compounding, on a principal of \$1 million between the end of year 1 and the end of year 2. In this case, the forward rate is 5% with continuous compounding or 5.127% with annual compounding. From equation (4.9), it follows that the value of the FRA is

$$1{,}000{,}000(0.06 - 0.05127)e^{-0.04\times 2} = \$8{,}058$$

By comparing equations (4.7) and (4.9), we see that an FRA can be valued if we

1. Calculate the payoff on the assumption that forward rates are realized, that is, on the assumption that $R_M = R_F$.
2. Discount this payoff at the risk-free rate.

4.8 DURATION

The *duration* of a bond, as its name implies, is a measure of how long on average the holder of the bond has to wait before receiving cash payments. A zero-coupon bond that lasts n years has a duration of n years. However, a coupon-bearing bond lasting n years has a duration of less than n years, because the holder receives some of the cash payments prior to year n.

Suppose that a bond provides the holder with cash flows c_i at time t_i $(1 \leqslant i \leqslant n)$. The price, B, and yield, y (continuously compounded), are related by

$$B = \sum_{i=1}^{n} c_i e^{-yt_i} \tag{4.11}$$

The duration, D, of the bond is defined as

$$D = \frac{\sum_{i=1}^{n} t_i c_i e^{-yt_i}}{B} \tag{4.12}$$

This can be written

$$D = \sum_{i=1}^{n} t_i \left[\frac{c_i e^{-yt_i}}{B}\right]$$

The term in square brackets is the ratio of the present value of the cash flow at time t_i to the bond price. The bond price is the present value of all payments. The duration is therefore a weighted average of the times when payments are made, with the weight applied to time t_i being equal to the proportion of the bond's total present value provided by the cash flow at time t_i. The sum of the weights is 1.0.

When a small change Δy in the yield is considered, it is approximately true that

$$\Delta B = \frac{dB}{dy}\Delta y \tag{4.13}$$

Table 4.6 Calculation of duration.

Time (years)	*Cash flow ($)*	*Present value*	*Weight*	*Time × weight*
0.5	5	4.709	0.050	0.025
1.0	5	4.435	0.047	0.047
1.5	5	4.176	0.044	0.066
2.0	5	3.933	0.042	0.083
2.5	5	3.704	0.039	0.098
3.0	105	73.256	0.778	2.333
Total:	130	94.213	1.000	2.653

From equation (4.11), this becomes

$$\Delta B = -\Delta y \sum_{i=1}^{n} c_i t_i e^{-yt_i} \quad \textbf{(4.14)}$$

(Note that there is a negative relationship between B and y. When bond yields increase, bond prices decrease. When bond yields decrease, bond prices increase.) From equations (4.12) and (4.14), we can derive the key duration relationship

$$\Delta B = -BD\,\Delta y \quad \textbf{(4.15)}$$

This can be written

$$\frac{\Delta B}{B} = -D\,\Delta y \quad \textbf{(4.16)}$$

Equation (4.16) is an approximate relationship between percentage changes in a bond price and changes in its yield. It is easy to use and is the reason why duration, which was first suggested by Macaulay in 1938, has become such a popular measure.

Consider a 3-year 10% coupon bond with a face value of $100. Suppose that the yield on the bond is 12% per annum with continuous compounding. This means that $y = 0.12$. Coupon payments of $5 are made every 6 months. Table 4.6 shows the calculations necessary to determine the bond's duration. The present values of the bond's cash flows, using the yield as the discount rate, are shown in column 3 (e.g., the present value of the first cash flow is $5e^{-0.12\times 0.5} = 4.709$). The sum of the numbers in column 3 gives the bond's price as 94.213. The weights are calculated by dividing the numbers in column 3 by 94.213. The sum of the numbers in column 5 gives the duration as 2.653 years.

Small changes in interest rates are often measured in *basis points*. As mentioned earlier, a basis point is 0.01% per annum. The following example investigates the accuracy of the duration relationship in equation (4.15).

Example 4.5

For the bond in Table 4.6, the bond price, B, is 94.213 and the duration, D, is 2.653, so that equation (4.15) gives

$$\Delta B = -94.213 \times 2.653\,\Delta y$$

or

$$\Delta B = -249.95\,\Delta y$$

When the yield on the bond increases by 10 basis points (= 0.1%), it follows that $\Delta y = +0.001$. The duration relationship predicts that $\Delta B = -249.95 \times 0.001 = -0.250$, so that the bond price goes down to $94.213 - 0.250 = 93.963$. How accurate is this? When the bond yield increases by 10 basis points to 12.1%, the bond price is

$$5e^{-0.121\times0.5} + 5e^{-0.121\times1.0} + 5e^{-0.121\times1.5} + 5e^{-0.121\times2.0} + 5e^{-0.121\times2.5} + 105e^{-0.121\times3.0} = 93.963$$

which is (to three decimal places) the same as that predicted by the duration relationship.

Modified Duration

The preceding analysis is based on the assumption that y is expressed with continuous compounding. If y is expressed with annual compounding, it can be shown that the approximate relationship in equation (4.15) becomes

$$\Delta B = -\frac{BD\,\Delta y}{1+y}$$

More generally, if y is expressed with a compounding frequency of m times per year, then

$$\Delta B = -\frac{BD\,\Delta y}{1+y/m}$$

A variable D^*, defined by

$$D^* = \frac{D}{1+y/m}$$

is sometimes referred to as the bond's *modified duration*. It allows the duration relationship to be simplified to

$$\Delta B = -BD^*\Delta y \tag{4.17}$$

when y is expressed with a compounding frequency of m times per year. The following example investigates the accuracy of the modified duration relationship.

Example 4.6

The bond in Table 4.6 has a price of 94.213 and a duration of 2.653. The yield, expressed with semiannual compounding is 12.3673%. The modified duration, D^*, is given by

$$D^* = \frac{2.653}{1+0.123673/2} = 2.499$$

From equation (4.17),

$$\Delta B = -94.213 \times 2.4985\,\Delta y$$

or

$$\Delta B = -235.39\,\Delta y$$

When the yield (semiannually compounded) increases by 10 basis points (= 0.1%), we have $\Delta y = +0.001$. The duration relationship predicts that we expect ΔB to be $-235.39 \times 0.001 = -0.235$, so that the bond price goes down to $94.213 - 0.235 = 93.978$. How accurate is this? When the bond yield (semiannually compounded) increases by 10 basis points to 12.4673% (or to 12.0941% with continuous compounding), an exact calculation similar to that in the previous example shows that the bond price becomes 93.978. This shows that the modified duration calculation gives good accuracy.

Bond Portfolios

The duration, D, of a bond portfolio can be defined as a weighted average of the durations of the individual bonds in the portfolio, with the weights being proportional to the bond prices. Equations (4.15) to (4.17) then apply, with B being defined as the value of the bond portfolio. They estimate the change in the value of the bond portfolio for a small change Δy in the yields of all the bonds.

It is important to realize that, when duration is used for bond portfolios, there is an implicit assumption that the yields of all bonds will change by the same amount. When the bonds have widely differing maturities, this happens only when there is a parallel shift in the zero-coupon yield curve. We should therefore interpret equations (4.15) to (4.17) as providing estimates of the impact on the price of a bond portfolio of a small parallel shift, Δy, in the zero curve.

4.9 CONVEXITY

The duration relationship applies only to small changes in yields. This is illustrated in Figure 4.2, which shows the relationship between the percentage change in value and change in yield for two bond portfolios having the same duration. The gradients of the two curves are the same at the origin. This means that both bond portfolios change in value by the same percentage for small yield changes and is consistent with equation (4.16). For large yield changes, the portfolios behave differently. Portfolio X has more curvature in its relationship with yields than portfolio Y. A factor known as *convexity* measures this curvature and can be used to improve the relationship in equation (4.16).

A measure of convexity is

$$C = \frac{1}{B}\frac{d^2B}{dy^2} = \frac{\sum_{i=1}^{n} c_i t_i^2 e^{-yt_i}}{B}$$

From Taylor series expansions, we obtain a more accurate expression than equation (4.13), given by

$$\Delta B = \frac{dB}{dy}\Delta y + \tfrac{1}{2}\frac{d^2B}{dy^2}\Delta y^2$$

This leads to

$$\frac{\Delta B}{B} = -D\,\Delta y + \tfrac{1}{2}C(\Delta y)^2$$

The convexity of a bond portfolio tends to be greatest when the portfolio provides payments evenly over a long period of time. It is least when the payments are

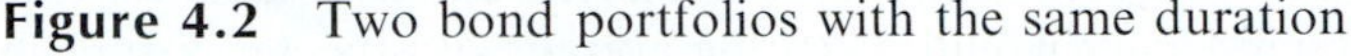

Figure 4.2 Two bond portfolios with the same duration.

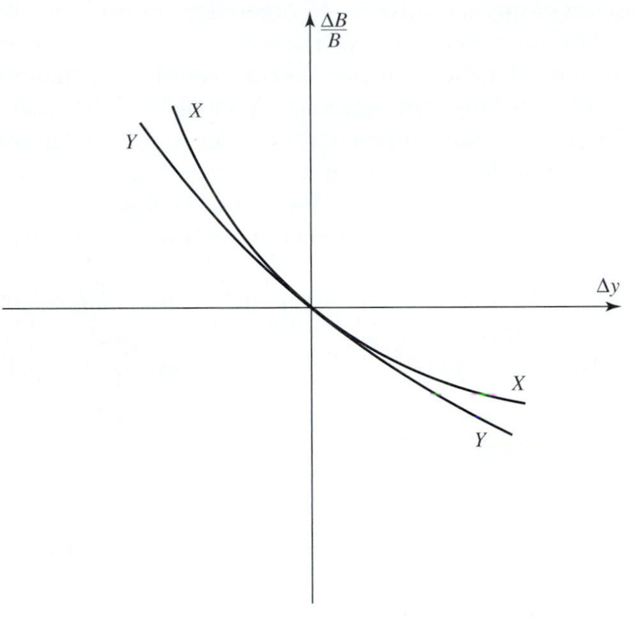

concentrated around one particular point in time. By matching convexity as well as duration, a company can make itself immune to relatively large parallel shifts in the zero curve. However, it is still exposed to nonparallel shifts.

4.10 THEORIES OF THE TERM STRUCTURE OF INTEREST RATES

It is natural to ask what determines the shape of the zero curve. Why is it sometimes downward-sloping, sometimes upward-sloping, and sometimes partly upward-sloping and partly downward-sloping? A number of different theories have been proposed. The simplest is *expectations theory*, which conjectures that long-term interest rates should reflect expected future short-term interest rates. More precisely, it argues that a forward interest rate corresponding to a certain future period is equal to the expected future zero interest rate for that period. Another idea, *market segmentation theory*, conjectures that there need be no relationship between short-, medium-, and long-term interest rates. Under the theory, a major investor such as a large pension fund invests in bonds of a certain maturity and does not readily switch from one maturity to another. The short-term interest rate is determined by supply and demand in the short-term bond market; the medium-term interest rate is determined by supply and demand in the medium-term bond market; and so on.

The theory that is in some ways most appealing is *liquidity preference theory*, which argues that forward rates should always be higher than expected future zero rates. The basic assumption underlying the theory is that investors prefer to preserve their liquidity and invest funds for short periods of time. Borrowers, on the other hand, usually prefer to borrow at fixed rates for long periods of time. If the interest rates offered by banks and other financial intermediaries corresponded to expectations theory, long-term interest rates would equal the average of expected future short-term interest rates. In the absence of any incentive to do otherwise, investors would tend to deposit their funds for short time periods, and borrowers would tend to choose to borrow for long time periods. Financial intermediaries would then find themselves financing substantial amounts of long-term fixed-rate loans with short-term deposits. Excessive interest rate risk would result. In practice, in order to match depositors with borrowers and avoid interest rate risk, financial intermediaries raise long-term interest rates relative to expected future short-term interest rates. This strategy reduces the demand for long-term fixed-rate borrowing and encourages investors to deposit their funds for long terms.

Liquidity preference theory leads to a situation in which forward rates are greater than expected future zero rates. It is also consistent with the empirical result that yield curves tend to be upward-sloping more often than they are downward-sloping.

SUMMARY

Two important interest rates for derivative traders are Treasury rates and LIBOR rates. Treasury rates are the rates paid by a government on borrowings in its own currency. LIBOR rates are short-term lending rates offered by banks in the interbank market.

The compounding frequency used for an interest rate defines the units in which it is measured. The difference between an annually compounded rate and a quarterly compounded rate is analogous to the difference between a distance measured in miles and a distance measured in kilometers. Traders frequently use continuous compounding when analyzing the value of derivatives.

Many different types of interest rates are quoted in financial markets and calculated by analysts. The n-year zero rate or n-year spot rate is the rate applicable to an investment lasting for n years when all of the return is realized at the end. The par yield on a bond of a certain maturity is the coupon rate that causes the bond to sell for its par value. Forward rates are the rates applicable to future periods of time implied by today's zero rates.

The method most commonly used to calculate zero rates is known as the bootstrap method. It involves starting with short-term instruments and moving progressively to longer-term instruments, making sure that the zero rates calculated at each stage are consistent with the prices of the instruments. It is used daily by trading desks to calculate a Treasury zero-rate curve.

A forward rate agreement (FRA) is an over-the-counter agreement that a certain interest rate will apply for either borrowing or lending a certain principal at LIBOR during a specified future period of time. An FRA can be valued by assuming that forward rates are realized and discounting the resulting payoff.

An important concept in interest rate markets is *duration*. Duration measures the sensitivity of the value of a bond portfolio to a small parallel shift in the zero-coupon yield curve. Specifically,

$$\Delta B = -BD\,\Delta y$$

where B is the value of the bond portfolio, D is the duration of the portfolio, Δy is the size of a small parallel shift in the zero curve, and ΔB is the resultant effect on the value of the bond portfolio.

FURTHER READING

Allen, S. L., and A. D. Kleinstein. *Valuing Fixed-Income Investments and Derivative Securities*. New York: New York Institute of Finance, 1991.

Fabozzi, F. J. *Fixed-Income Mathematics: Analytical and Statistical Techniques*, New York: McGraw-Hill, 1996.

Fabozzi, F. J. *Duration, Convexity, and Other Bond Risk Measures*, Frank J. Fabozzi Assoc., 1999.

Grinblatt, M., and F. A. Longstaff. "Financial Innovation and the Role of Derivatives Securities: An Empirical Analysis of the Treasury Strips Program," *Journal of Finance*, 55, 3 (2000): 1415–36.

Jorion, P. *Big Bets Gone Bad: Derivatives and Bankruptcy in Orange County*. New York: Academic Press, 1995.

Stigum, M., and F. L. Robinson. *Money Markets and Bond Calculations*. Chicago: Irwin, 1996.

Questions and Problems (Answers in Solutions Manual)

4.1. A bank quotes you an interest rate of 14% per annum with quarterly compounding. What is the equivalent rate with (a) continuous compounding and (b) annual compounding?

4.2. What is meant by LIBOR and LIBID. Which is higher?

4.3. The 6-month and 1-year zero rates are both 10% per annum. For a bond that has a life of 18 months and pays a coupon of 8% per annum (with semiannual payments and one having just been made), the yield is 10.4% per annum. What is the bond's price? What is the 18-month zero rate? All rates are quoted with semiannual compounding.

4.4. An investor receives \$1,100 in one year in return for an investment of \$1,000 now. Calculate the percentage return per annum with:
(a) Annual compounding
(b) Semiannual compounding
(c) Monthly compounding
(d) Continuous compounding

4.5. Suppose that zero interest rates with continuous compounding are as follows:

Maturity (months)	*Rate (% per annum)*
3	8.0
6	8.2
9	8.4
12	8.5
15	8.6
18	8.7

Calculate forward interest rates for the second, third, fourth, fifth, and sixth quarters.

4.6. Assuming that zero rates are as in Problem 4.5, what is the value of an FRA that enables the holder to earn 9.5% for a 3-month period starting in 1 year on a principal of $1,000,000? The interest rate is expressed with quarterly compounding.

4.7. The term structure of interest rates is upward-sloping. Put the following in order of magnitude:
(a) The 5-year zero rate
(b) The yield on a 5-year coupon-bearing bond
(c) The forward rate corresponding to the period between 5 and 5.25 years in the future
What is the answer to this question when the term structure of interest rates is downward-sloping?

4.8. What does duration tell you about the sensitivity of a bond portfolio to interest rates. What are the limitations of the duration measure?

4.9. What rate of interest with continuous compounding is equivalent to 15% per annum with monthly compounding?

4.10. A deposit account pays 12% per annum with continuous compounding, but interest is actually paid quarterly. How much interest will be paid each quarter on a $10,000 deposit?

4.11. Suppose that 6-month, 12-month, 18-month, 24-month, and 30-month zero rates are, respectively, 4%, 4.2%, 4.4%, 4.6%, and 4.8% per annum, with continuous compounding. Estimate the cash price of a bond with a face value of 100 that will mature in 30 months and pays a coupon of 4% per annum semiannually.

4.12. A 3-year bond provides a coupon of 8% semiannually and has a cash price of 104. What is the bond's yield?

4.13. Suppose that the 6-month, 12-month, 18-month, and 24-month zero rates are 5%, 6%, 6.5%, and 7%, respectively. What is the 2-year par yield?

4.14. Suppose that zero interest rates with continuous compounding are as follows:

Maturity (years)	*Rate (% per annum)*
1	2.0
2	3.0
3	3.7
4	4.2
5	4.5

Calculate forward interest rates for the second, third, fourth, and fifth years.

4.15. Use the rates in Problem 4.14 to value an FRA where you will pay 5% for the third year on $1 million.

4.16. A 10-year 8% coupon bond currently sells for $90. A 10-year 4% coupon bond currently sells for $80. What is the 10-year zero rate? (*Hint*: Consider taking a long position in two of the 4% coupon bonds and a short position in one of the 8% coupon bonds.)

4.17. Explain carefully why liquidity preference theory is consistent with the observation that the term structure of interest rates tends to be upward-sloping more often than it is downward-sloping.

4.18. "When the zero curve is upward-sloping, the zero rate for a particular maturity is greater than the par yield for that maturity. When the zero curve is downward-sloping the reverse is true." Explain why this is so.

4.19. Why are US Treasury rates significantly lower than other rates that are close to risk-free?

4.20. Why does a loan in the repo market involve very little credit risk?

4.21. Explain why an FRA is equivalent to the exchange of a floating rate of interest for a fixed rate of interest.

4.22. A 5-year bond with a yield of 11% (continuously compounded) pays an 8% coupon at the end of each year.
(a) What is the bond's price?
(b) What is the bond's duration?
(c) Use the duration to calculate the effect on the bond's price of a 0.2% decrease in its yield.
(d) Recalculate the bond's price on the basis of a 10.8% per annum yield and verify that the result is in agreement with your answer to (c).

4.23. The cash prices of 6-month and 1-year Treasury bills are 94.0 and 89.0. A 1.5-year bond that will pay coupons of $4 every 6 months currently sells for $94.84. A 2-year bond that will pay coupons of $5 every 6 months currently sells for $97.12. Calculate the 6-month, 1-year, 1.5-year, and 2-year zero rates.

Assignment Questions

4.24. An interest rate is quoted as 5% per annum with semiannual compounding. What is the equivalent rate with (a) annual compounding, (b) monthly compounding, and (c) continuous compounding.

4.25. The 6-month, 12-month, 18-month, and 24-month zero rates are 4%, 4.5%, 4.75%, and 5%, with semiannual compounding.
(a) What are the rates with continuous compounding?
(b) What is the forward rate for the 6-month period beginning in 18 months?
(c) What is the value of an FRA that promises to pay you 6% (compounded semiannually) on a principal of $1 million for the 6-month period starting in 18 months?

4.26. What is the 2-year par yield when the zero rates are as in Problem 4.25? What is the yield on a 2-year bond that pays a coupon equal to the par yield?

4.27. The following table gives the prices of bonds:

Bond principal ($)	*Time to maturity* (*years*)	*Annual coupon** ($)	*Bond price* ($)
100	0.50	0.0	98
100	1.00	0.0	95
100	1.50	6.2	101
100	2.00	8.0	104

* Half the stated coupon is assumed to be paid every six months.

(a) Calculate zero rates for maturities of 6 months, 12 months, 18 months, and 24 months.

(b) What are the forward rates for the following periods: 6 months to 12 months, 12 months to 18 months, and 18 months to 24 months?
(c) What are the 6-month, 12-month, 18-month, and 24-month par yields for bonds that provide semiannual coupon payments?
(d) Estimate the price and yield of a 2-year bond providing a semiannual coupon of 7% per annum.

4.28. Portfolio A consists of a 1-year zero-coupon bond with a face value of $2,000 and a 10-year zero-coupon bond with a face value of $6,000. Portfolio B consists of a 5.95-year zero-coupon bond with a face value of $5,000. The current yield on all bonds is 10% per annum.
(a) Show that both portfolios have the same duration.
(b) Show that the percentage changes in the values of the two portfolios for a 0.1% per annum increase in yields are the same.
(c) What are the percentage changes in the values of the two portfolios for a 5% per annum increase in yields?

CHAPTER 5

Determination of Forward and Futures Prices

In this chapter we examine how forward prices and futures prices are related to the spot price of the underlying asset. Forward contracts are easier to analyze than futures contracts because there is no daily settlement—only a single payment at maturity. Luckily it can be shown that the forward price and futures price of an asset are usually very close when the maturities of the two contracts are the same.

In the first part of the chapter we derive some important general results on the relationship between forward prices and spot prices. We then use the results to examine the relationship between futures prices and spot prices for contracts on stock indices, foreign exchange, and commodities. We will consider interest rate futures contracts in the next chapter.

5.1 INVESTMENT ASSETS vs. CONSUMPTION ASSETS

When considering forward and futures contracts, it is important to distinguish between investment assets and consumption assets. An *investment asset* is an asset that is held for investment purposes by significant numbers of investors. Stocks and bonds are clearly investment assets. Gold and silver are also examples of investment assets. Note that investment assets do not have to be held exclusively for investment. (Silver, for example, has a number of industrial uses.) However, they do have to satisfy the requirement that they are held by significant numbers of investors solely for investment. A *consumption asset* is an asset that is held primarily for consumption. It is not usually held for investment. Examples of consumption assets are commodities such as copper, oil, and pork bellies.

As we shall see later in this chapter, we can use arbitrage arguments to determine the forward and futures prices of an investment asset from its spot price and other observable market variables. We cannot do this for consumption assets.

5.2 SHORT SELLING

Some of the arbitrage strategies presented in this chapter involve *short selling*. This trade, usually simply referred to as "shorting", involves selling an asset that is not owned. It is something that is possible for some—but not all—investment assets. We will illustrate how it works by considering a short sale of shares of a stock.

Suppose an investor instructs a broker to short 500 IBM shares. The broker will carry out the instructions by borrowing the shares from another client and selling them in the market in the usual way. The investor can maintain the short position for as long as desired, provided there are always shares for the broker to borrow. At some stage, however, the investor will close out the position by purchasing 500 IBM shares. These are then replaced in the account of the client from which the shares were borrowed. The investor takes a profit if the stock price has declined and a loss if it has risen. If, at any time while the contract is open, the broker runs out of shares to borrow, the investor is *short-squeezed* and is forced to close out the position immediately, even if not ready to do so.

An investor with a short position must pay to the broker any income, such as dividends or interest, that would normally be received on the securities that have been shorted. The broker will transfer such income to the account of the client from whom the securities have been borrowed. Consider the position of an investor who shorts 500 shares in April when the price per share is \$120 and closes out the position by buying them back in July when the price per share is \$100. Suppose that a dividend of \$1 per share is paid in May. The investor receives $500 \times \$120 = \$60{,}000$ in April when the short position is initiated. The dividend leads to a payment by the investor of $500 \times \$1 = \$500$ in May. The investor also pays $500 \times \$100 = \$50{,}000$ for shares when the position is closed out in July. The net gain, therefore, is

$$\$60{,}000 - \$500 - \$50{,}000 = \$9{,}500$$

Table 5.1 illustrates this example and shows that the cash flows from the short sale are the mirror image of the cash flows from purchasing the shares in April and selling them in July.

The investor is required to maintain a *margin account* with the broker. The margin account consists of cash or marketable securities deposited by the investor with the broker to guarantee that the investor will not walk away from the short position if the share price increases. It is similar to the margin account discussed in Chapter 2 for

Table 5.1 Cash flows from short sale and purchase of shares.

	Purchase of shares	
April:	Purchase 500 shares for \$120	−\$60,000
May:	Receive dividend	+\$500
July:	Sell 500 shares for \$100 per share	+\$50,000
		Net profit = −\$9,500
	Short sale of shares	
April:	Borrow 500 shares and sell them for \$120	+\$60,000
May:	Pay dividend	−\$500
July:	Buy 500 shares for \$100 per share	−\$50,000
	Replace borrowed shares to close short position	
		Net profit = +\$9,500

futures contracts. An initial margin is required and if there are adverse movements (i.e., increases) in the price of the asset that is being shorted, additional margin may be required. The margin account does not represent a cost to the investor. This is because interest is usually paid on the balance in margin accounts and, if the interest rate offered is unacceptable, marketable securities such as Treasury bills can be used to meet margin requirements. The proceeds of the sale of the asset belong to the investor and normally form part of the initial margin.

Regulators in the United States currently allow a stock to be shorted only on an *uptick*—that is, when the most recent movement in the price of the stock was an increase. An exception is made when traders are shorting a basket of stocks replicating a stock index.

5.3 ASSUMPTIONS AND NOTATION

In this chapter we will assume that the following are all true for some market participants:

1. The market participants are subject to no transaction costs when they trade.
2. The market participants are subject to the same tax rate on all net trading profits.
3. The market participants can borrow money at the same risk-free rate of interest as they can lend money.
4. The market participants take advantage of arbitrage opportunities as they occur.

Note that we do not require these assumptions to be true for all market participants. All that we require is that they be true—or at least approximately true—for a few key market participants such as large investment banks. It is the trading activities of these key market participants and their eagerness to take advantage of arbitrage opportunities as they occur that determine the relationship between forward and spot prices.

The following notation will be used throughout this chapter:

T: Time until delivery date in a forward or futures contract (in years)

S_0: Price of the asset underlying the forward or futures contract today

F_0: Forward or futures price today

r: Zero-coupon risk-free rate of interest per annum, expressed with continuous compounding, for an investment maturing at the delivery date (i.e., in T years)

The risk-free rate, r, is in theory the rate at which money is borrowed or lent when there is no credit risk, so that the money is certain to be repaid. As mentioned in Chapter 4, financial institutions and other participants in derivatives markets assume that LIBOR rates rather than Treasury rates are risk-free rates.

5.4 FORWARD PRICE FOR AN INVESTMENT ASSET

The easiest forward contract to value is one written on an investment asset that provides the holder with no income. Non-dividend-paying stocks and zero-coupon bonds are examples of such investment assets.

Illustration

Consider a long forward contract to purchase a non-dividend-paying stock in 3 months.[1] Assume the current stock price is \$40 and the 3-month risk-free interest rate is 5% per annum.

Suppose first that the forward price is relatively high at \$43. An arbitrageur can borrow \$40 at the risk-free interest rate of 5% per annum, buy one share, and short a forward contract to sell one share in 3 months. At the end of the 3 months, the arbitrageur delivers the share and receives \$43. The sum of money required to pay off the loan is

$$40e^{0.05\times 3/12} = \$40.50$$

By following this strategy, the arbitrageur locks in a profit of \$43.00 − \$40.50 = \$2.50 at the end of the 3-month period.

Suppose next that the forward price is relatively low at \$39. An arbitrageur can short one share, invest the proceeds of the short sale at 5% per annum for 3 months, and take a long position in a 3-month forward contract. The proceeds of the short sale grow to $40e^{0.05\times 3/12}$, or \$40.50 in 3 months. At the end of the 3 months, the arbitrageur pays \$39, takes delivery of the share under the terms of the forward contract, and uses it to close out the short position. A net gain of

$$\$40.50 - \$39.00 = \$1.50$$

is therefore made at the end of the 3 months. The two trading strategies we have considered are summarized in Table 5.2.

Under what circumstances do arbitrage opportunities such as those in Table 5.2 not exist? The first arbitrage works when the forward price is greater than \$40.50. The

Table 5.2 Arbitrage opportunities when forward price is out of line with spot price for asset providing no income. (Asset price = \$40; interest rate = 5%; maturity of forward contract = 3 months.)

Forward Price = \$43	***Forward Price = \$39***
Action now:	*Action now*:
Borrow \$40 at 5% for 3 months	Short 1 unit of asset to realize \$40
Buy one unit of asset	Invest \$40 at 5% for 3 months
Enter into forward contract to sell asset in 3 months for \$43	Enter into a forward contract to buy asset in 3 months for \$39
Action in 3 months:	*Action in 3 months*:
Sell asset for \$43	Buy asset for \$39
Use \$40.50 to repay loan with interest	Close short position
	Receive \$40.50 from investment
Profit realized = \$2.50	Profit realized = \$1.50

[1] Forward contracts on individual stocks are relatively rare. However, they form useful examples for developing our ideas. Futures on individual stocks started trading in the United States in November 2002.

Business Snapshot 5.1 Kidder Peabody's Embarrassing Mistake

Investment banks have developed a way of creating a zero-coupon bond, called a *strip*, from a coupon-bearing Treasury bond by selling each of the cash flows underlying the coupon-bearing bond as a separate security. Joseph Jett, a trader working for Kidder Peabody, had a relatively simple trading strategy. He would buy strips and sell them in the forward market. As equation (5.1) shows, the forward price of a security providing no income is always higher than the spot price. Suppose, for example, that the 3-month interest rate is 4% per annum and the spot price of a strip is \$70. The 3-month forward price of the strip is $70e^{0.04\times 3/12} = \$70.70$.

Kidder Peabody's computer system reported a profit on each of Jett's trades equal to the excess of the forward price over the spot price (\$0.70 in our example). In fact this profit was nothing more than the cost of financing the purchase of the strip. But by rolling his contracts forward Jett was able to prevent this cost from accruing to him.

The result was that the system reported a profit of \$100 million on Jett's trading (and Jett received a big bonus) when in fact there was a loss in the region of \$350 million. This shows that even large financial institutions can get relatively simple things wrong!

second arbitrage works when the forward price is less than \$40.50. We deduce that for there to be no arbitrage the forward price must be exactly \$40.50.

A Generalization

To generalize this example, we consider a forward contract on an investment asset with price S_0 that provides no income. Using our notation, T is the time to maturity, r is the risk-free rate, and F_0 is the forward price. The relationship between F_0 and S_0 is

$$F_0 = S_0 e^{rT} \tag{5.1}$$

If $F_0 > S_0 e^{rT}$, arbitrageurs can buy the asset and short forward contracts on the asset. If $F_0 < S_0 e^{rT}$, they can short the asset and enter into long forward contracts on it.[2] In our example, $S_0 = 40$, $r = 0.05$, and $T = 0.25$, so that equation (5.1) gives

$$F_0 = 40e^{0.05\times 0.25} = \$40.50$$

which is in agreement with our earlier calculations.

A long forward contract and a spot purchase both lead to the asset being owned at time T. The forward price is higher than the spot price because of the cost of financing the spot purchase of the asset during the life of the forward contract. This point was overlooked by Kidder Peabody, much to its cost (see Business Snapshot 5.1).

[2] For another way of seeing that equation (5.1) is correct, consider the following strategy: buy one unit of the asset and enter into a short forward contract to sell it for F_0 at time T. This costs S_0 and is certain to lead to a cash inflow of F_0 at time T. Therefore S_0 must equal the present value of F_0; that is, $S_0 = F_0 e^{-rT}$, or equivalently $F_0 = S_0 e^{rT}$.

Example 5.1

Consider a 4-month forward contract to buy a zero-coupon bond that will mature 1 year from today. (This means that the bond will have 8 months to go when the forward contract matures.) The current price of the bond is \$930. We assume that the 4-month risk-free rate of interest (continuously compounded) is 6% per annum. Because zero-coupon bonds provide no income, we can use equation (5.1) with $T = 4/12$, $r = 0.06$, and $S_0 = 930$. The forward price, F_0, is given by

$$F_0 = 930e^{0.06\times 4/12} = \$948.79$$

This would be the delivery price in a contract negotiated today.

What If Short Sales Are Not Possible?

Short sales are not possible for all investment assets. As it happens, this does not matter. To derive equation (5.1), we do not need to be able to short the asset. All that we require is that there be a significant number of people who hold the asset purely for investment (and by definition this is always true of an investment asset). If the forward price is too low, they will find it attractive to sell the asset and take a long position in a forward contract.

Suppose the underlying asset is gold and assume no storage costs or income. If $F_0 > S_0e^{rT}$, an investor can adopt the following strategy:

1. Borrow S_0 dollars at an interest rate r for T years.
2. Buy 1 ounce of gold.
3. Short a forward contract on 1 ounce of gold.

At time T, 1 ounce of gold is sold for F_0. An amount S_0e^{rT} is required to repay the loan at this time and the investor makes a profit of $F_0 - S_0e^{rT}$.

Suppose next that $F_0 < S_0e^{rT}$. In this case an investor who owns 1 ounce of gold can

1. Sell the gold for S_0.
2. Invest the proceeds at interest rate r for time T.
3. Take a long position in a forward contract on 1 ounce of gold.

At time T, the cash invested has grown to S_0e^{rT}. The gold is repurchased for F_0 and the investor makes a profit of $S_0e^{rT} - F_0$ relative to the position the investor would have been in if the gold had been kept.

As in the non-dividend-paying stock example considered earlier, we can expect the forward price to adjust so that neither of the two arbitrage opportunities we have considered exists. This means that the relationship in equation (5.1) must hold.

5.5 KNOWN INCOME

In this section we consider a forward contract on an investment asset that will provide a perfectly predictable cash income to the holder. Examples are stocks paying known dividends and coupon-bearing bonds. We adopt the same approach as in the previous section. We first look at a numerical example and then review the formal arguments.

Illustration

Consider a long forward contract to purchase a coupon-bearing bond whose current price is \$900. We will suppose that the forward contract matures in 9 months. We will also suppose that a coupon payment of \$40 is expected after 4 months. We assume that the 4-month and 9-month risk-free interest rates (continuously compounded) are, respectively, 3% and 4% per annum.

Suppose first that the forward price is relatively high at \$910. An arbitrageur can borrow \$900 to buy the bond and short a forward contract. The coupon payment has a present value of $40e^{-0.03\times 4/12} = \$39.60$. Of the \$900, \$39.60 is therefore borrowed at 3% per annum for 4 months so that it can be repaid with the coupon payment. The remaining \$860.40 is borrowed at 4% per annum for 9 months. The amount owing at the end of the 9-month period is $860.40e^{0.04\times 0.75} = \$886.60$. A sum of \$910 is received for the bond under the terms of the forward contract. The arbitrageur therefore makes a net profit of

$$910.00 - 886.60 = \$23.40$$

Suppose next that the forward price is relatively low at \$870. An investor can short the bond and enter into a long forward contract. Of the \$900 realized from shorting the bond, \$39.60 is invested for 4 months at 3% per annum so that it grows into an amount sufficient to pay the coupon on the bond. The remaining \$860.40 is invested for 9 months at 4% per annum and grows to \$886.60. Under the terms of the forward contract, \$870 is paid to buy the bond and the short position is closed out. The investor therefore gains

$$886.60 - 870 = \$16.60$$

The two strategies we have considered are summarized in Table 5.3.[3] The first strategy in Table 5.3 produces a profit when the forward price is greater than \$886.60, whereas the second strategy produces a profit when the forward price is less than \$886.60. It follows that if there are no arbitrage opportunities then the forward price must be \$886.60.

A Generalization

We can generalize from this example to argue that, when an investment asset will provide income with a present value of I during the life of a forward contract, we have

$$F_0 = (S_0 - I)e^{rT} \tag{5.2}$$

In our example, $S_0 = 900.00$, $I = 40e^{-0.03\times 4/12} = 39.60$, $r = 0.04$, and $T = 0.75$, so that

$$F_0 = (900.00 - 39.60)e^{0.04\times 0.75} = \$886.60$$

This is in agreement with our earlier calculation. Equation (5.2) applies to any investment asset that provides a known cash income.

If $F_0 > (S_0 - I)e^{rT}$, an arbitrageur can lock in a profit by buying the asset and shorting a forward contract on the asset; if $F_0 < (S_0 - I)e^{rT}$, an arbitrageur can lock

[3] If shorting the bond is not possible, investors who already own the bond will sell it and buy a forward contract on the bond increasing the value of their position by \$16.60. This is similar to the strategy we described for gold in Section 5.4.

Table 5.3 Arbitrage opportunities when 9-month forward price is out of line with spot price for asset providing known cash income. (Asset price = \$900; income of \$40 occurs at 4 months; 4-month and 9-month rates are, respectively, 3% and 4% per annum.)

Forward price = \$910	***Forward price = \$870***
Action now:	*Action now*:
Borrow \$900: \$39.60 for 4 months and \$860.40 for 9 months	Short 1 unit of asset to realize \$900
Buy 1 unit of asset	Invest \$39.40 for 4 months and \$860.40 for 9 months
Enter into forward contract to sell asset in 9 months for \$910	Enter into a forward contract to buy asset in 9 months for \$870
Action in 4 months:	*Action in 4 months*:
Receive \$40 of income on asset	Receive \$40 from 4-month investment
Use \$40 to repay first loan with interest	Pay income of \$40 on asset
Action in 9 months:	*Action in 9 months*:
Sell asset for \$910	Receive \$886.60 from 9-month investment
Use \$886.60 to repay second loan with interest	Buy asset for \$870
	Close out short position
Profit realized = \$23.40	Profit realized = \$16.60

in a profit by shorting the asset and taking a long position in a forward contract. If short sales are not possible, investors who own the asset will find it profitable to sell the asset and enter into long forward contracts.[4]

Example 5.2

Consider a 10-month forward contract on a stock with a price of \$50. We assume that the risk-free rate of interest (continuously compounded) is 8% per annum for all maturities. We also assume that dividends of \$0.75 per share are expected after 3 months, 6 months, and 9 months. The present value of the dividends, I, is

$$I = 0.75e^{-0.08\times 3/12} + 0.75e^{-0.08\times 6/12} + 0.75e^{-0.08\times 9/12} = 2.162$$

The variable T is 10 months, so that the forward price, F_0, from equation (5.2), is given by

$$F_0 = (50 - 2.162)e^{0.08\times 10/12} = \$51.14$$

If the forward price were less than this, an arbitrageur would short the stock spot and buy forward contracts. If the forward price were greater than this, an arbitrageur would short forward contracts and buy the stock spot.

[4] For another way of seeing that equation (5.2) is correct, consider the following strategy: buy one unit of the asset and enter into a short forward contract to sell it for F_0 at time T. This costs S_0 and is certain to lead to a cash inflow of F_0 at time T and an income with a present value of I. The initial outflow is S_0. The present value of the inflows is $I + F_0e^{-rT}$. Hence, $S_0 = I + F_0e^{-rT}$, or equivalently $F_0 = (S_0 - I)e^{rT}$.

5.6 KNOWN YIELD

We now consider the situation where the asset underlying a forward contract provides a known yield rather than a known cash income. This means that the income is known when expressed as a percentage of the asset's price at the time the income is paid. Suppose that an asset is expected to provide a yield of 5% per annum. This could mean that income is paid once a year and is equal to 5% of the asset price at the time it is paid, in which case the yield would then be 5% with annual compounding. Alternatively, it could mean that income is paid twice a year and is equal to 2.5% of the asset price at the time it is paid, in which case the yield would then be 5% per annum with semiannual compounding. In Section 4.2 we explained that we will normally measure interest rates with continuous compounding. Similarly, we will normally measure yields with continuous compounding. Formulas for translating a yield measured with one compounding frequency to a yield measured with another compounding frequency are the same as those given for interest rates in Section 4.2.

Define q as the average yield per annum on an asset during the life of a forward contract with continuous compounding. It can be shown (see Problem 5.20) that

$$F_0 = S_0 e^{(r-q)T} \tag{5.3}$$

Example 5.3

Consider a 6-month forward contract on an asset that is expected to provide income equal to 2% of the asset price once during a 6-month period. The risk-free rate of interest (with continuous compounding) is 10% per annum. The asset price is \$25. In this case, $S_0 = 25$, $r = 0.10$, and $T = 0.5$. The yield is 4% per annum with semiannual compounding. From equation (4.3), this is 3.96% per annum with continuous compounding. It follows that $q = 0.0396$, so that from equation (5.3) the forward price, F_0, is given by

$$F_0 = 25e^{(0.10-0.0396)\times 0.5} = \$25.77$$

5.7 VALUING FORWARD CONTRACTS

The value of a forward contract at the time it is first entered into is zero. At a later stage, it may prove to have a positive or negative value. It is important for banks and other financial institutions to value the contract each day. (This is referred to as marking to market the contract.) Using the notation introduced earlier, we suppose K is the delivery price for a contract that was negotiated some time ago, the delivery date is T years from today, and r is the T-year risk-free interest rate. The variable F_0 is the forward price that would be applicable if we negotiated the contract today. We also define

f: Value of forward contract today

It is important to be clear about the meaning of the variables F_0, K, and f. If today happens to be the day when the contract is first negotiated, the delivery price (K) is set equal to the forward price (F_0) and the value of the contract (f) is 0. As time passes, K

stays the same (because it is part of the definition of the contract), but F_0 changes and f becomes either positive or negative.

A general result, applicable to all long forward contracts (both those on investment assets and those on consumption assets), is

$$f = (F_0 - K)e^{-rT} \tag{5.4}$$

To see why equation (5.4) is correct, we use an argument analogous to the one we used for forward rate agreements in Section 4.7. We compare a long forward contract that has a delivery price of F_0 with an otherwise identical long forward contract that has a delivery price of K. The difference between the two is only in the amount that will be paid for the underlying asset at time T. Under the first contract, this amount is F_0; under the second contract, it is K. A cash outflow difference of $F_0 - K$ at time T translates to a difference of $(F_0 - K)e^{-rT}$ today. The contract with a delivery price F_0 is therefore less valuable than the contract with delivery price K by an amount $(F_0 - K)e^{-rT}$. The value of the contract that has a delivery price of F_0 is by definition zero. It follows that the value of the contract with a delivery price of K is $(F_0 - K)e^{-rT}$. This proves equation (5.4). Similarly, the value of a short forward contract with delivery price K is

$$(K - F_0)e^{-rT}$$

Example 5.4

A long forward contract on a non-dividend-paying stock was entered into some time ago. It currently has 6 months to maturity. The risk-free rate of interest (with continuous compounding) is 10% per annum, the stock price is \$25, and the delivery price is \$24. In this case, $S_0 = 25$, $r = 0.10$, $T = 0.5$, and $K = 24$. From equation (5.1), the 6-month forward price, F_0, is given by

$$F_0 = 25e^{0.1\times 0.5} = \$26.28$$

From equation (5.4), the value of the forward contract is

$$f = (26.28 - 24)e^{-0.1\times 0.5} = \$2.17$$

Equation (5.4) shows that we can value a long forward contract on an asset by making the assumption that the price of the asset at the maturity of the forward contract equals the forward price F_0. To see this, note that when we make the assumption, a long forward contract provides a payoff at time T of $F_0 - K$. This has a present value of $(F_0 - K)e^{-rT}$, which is the value of f in equation (5.4). Similarly, we can value a short forward contract on the asset by assuming that the current forward price of the asset is realized. These results are analogous to the result in Section 4.7 that we can value a forward rate agreement on the assumption that forward rates are realized.

Using equation (5.4) in conjunction with equation (5.1) gives the following expression for the value of a forward contract on an investment asset that provides no income

$$f = S_0 - Ke^{-rT} \tag{5.5}$$

Similarly, using equation (5.4) in conjunction with equation (5.2) gives the following

Business Snapshot 5.2 A Systems Error?

A foreign exchange trader working for a bank enters into a long forward contract to buy 1 million pounds sterling at an exchange rate of 1.6000 in 3 months. At the same time, another trader on the next desk takes a long position in 16 contracts for 3-month futures on sterling. The futures price is 1.6000 and each contract is on 62,500 pounds. The positions taken by the forward and futures traders are therefore the same. Within minutes of the positions being taken the forward and the futures prices both increase to 1.6040. The bank's systems show that the futures trader has made a profit of \$4,000, while the forward trader has made a profit of only \$3,900. The forward trader immediately calls the bank's systems department to complain. Does the forward trader have a valid complaint?

The answer is no! The daily settlement of futures contracts ensures that the futures trader realizes an almost immediate profit corresponding to the increase in the futures price. If the forward trader closed out the position by entering into a short contract at 1.6040, the forward trader would have contracted to buy 1 million pounds at 1.6000 in 3 months and sell 1 million pounds at 1.6040 in 3 months. This would lead to a \$4,000 profit—but in 3 months, not today. The forward trader's profit is the present value of \$4,000. This is consistent with equation (5.4).

The forward trader can gain some consolation from the fact that gains and losses are treated symmetrically. If the forward/futures prices dropped to 1.5960 instead of rising to 1.6040, then the futures trader would take a loss of \$4,000 while the forward trader would take a loss of only \$3,900.

expression for the value of a long forward contract on an investment asset that provides a known income with present value I:

$$f = S_0 - I - Ke^{-rT} \tag{5.6}$$

Finally, using equation (5.4) in conjunction with equation (5.3) gives the following expression for the value of a long forward contract on an investment asset that provides a known yield at rate q:

$$f = S_0 e^{-qT} - Ke^{-rT} \tag{5.7}$$

When a futures price changes, the gain or loss on a futures contract is calculated as the change in the futures price multiplied by the size of the position. This gain is realized almost immediately because of the way futures contracts are settled daily. Equation (5.4) shows that, when a forward price changes, the gain or loss is the present value of the change in the forward price multiplied by the size of the position. The difference between the gain/loss on forward and futures contracts can cause confusion on a foreign exchange trading desk (see Business Snapshot 5.2).

5.8 ARE FORWARD PRICES AND FUTURES PRICES EQUAL?

The appendix at the end of this chapter provides an arbitrage argument to show that when the risk-free interest rate is constant and the same for all maturities, the forward price for a contract with a certain delivery date is the same as the futures price for a contract with that delivery date. The argument in the appendix can be extended to cover situations where the interest rate is a known function of time.

When interest rates vary unpredictably (as they do in the real world), forward and futures prices are in theory no longer the same. The proof of the relationship between the two is beyond the scope of this book. However, we can get a sense of the nature of the relationship by considering the situation where the price of the underlying asset, S, is strongly positively correlated with interest rates. When S increases, an investor who holds a long futures position makes an immediate gain because of the daily settlement procedure. The positive correlation indicates that it is likely that interest rates have also increased. The gain will therefore tend to be invested at a higher than average rate of interest. Similarly, when S decreases, the investor will incur an immediate loss. This loss will tend to be financed at a lower than average rate of interest. An investor holding a forward contract rather than a futures contract is not affected in this way by interest rate movements. It follows that a long futures contract will be more attractive than a similar long forward contract. Hence, when S is strongly positively correlated with interest rates, futures prices will tend to be higher than forward prices. When S is strongly negatively correlated with interest rates, a similar argument shows that forward prices will tend to be higher than futures prices.

The theoretical differences between forward and futures prices for contracts that last only a few months are in most circumstances sufficiently small to be ignored. In practice, there are a number of factors not reflected in theoretical models that may cause forward and futures prices to be different. These include taxes, transactions costs, and the treatment of margins. The risk that the counterparty will default is generally less in the case of a futures contract because of the role of the exchange clearinghouse. Also, in some instances, futures contracts are more liquid and easier to trade than forward contracts. Despite all these points, for most purposes it is reasonable to assume that forward and futures prices are the same. This is the assumption we will usually make in this book. We will use the symbol F_0 to represent both the futures price and the forward price of an asset today.

As the life of a futures contract increases, the differences between forward and futures contracts are liable to become significant. It is then dangerous to assume that forward and futures prices are perfect substitutes for each other. This point is particularly relevant to Eurodollar futures contracts because they have maturities as long as 10 years. Eurodollar futures contracts are covered in Chapter 6.

5.9 FUTURES PRICES OF STOCK INDICES

We introduced futures on stock indices in Section 3.5 and showed how a stock index futures contract is a useful tool in managing equity portfolios. Table 3.3 shows futures prices for a number of different indices. We are now in a position to consider how index futures prices are determined.

A stock index can usually be regarded as the price of an investment asset that pays dividends.[5] The investment asset is the portfolio of stocks underlying the index, and the dividends paid by the investment asset are the dividends that would be received by the

[5] Occasionally this is not the case: see Business Snapshot 5.3.

Business Snapshot 5.3 The CME Nikkei 225 Futures Contract

The arguments in this chapter on how index futures prices are determined require that the index be the value of an investment asset. This means that it must be the value of a portfolio of assets that can be traded. The asset underlying the Chicago Mercantile Exchange's futures contract on the Nikkei 225 Index does not qualify, and the reason why is quite subtle. Suppose that S is the value of the Nikkei 225 Index. This is the value of a portfolio of 225 Japanese stocks measured in yen. The variable underlying the CME futures contract on the Nikkei 225 has a *dollar value* of $5S$. In other words, the futures contract takes a variable that is measured in yen and treats it as though it is dollars.

We cannot invest in a portfolio whose value will always be $5S$ dollars. The best we can do is to invest in one that is always worth $5S$ yen or in one that is always worth $5QS$ dollars, where Q is the dollar value of 1 yen. The variable $5S$ dollars is not, therefore, the price of an investment asset and equation (5.8) does not apply.

CME's Nikkei 225 futures contract is an example of a *quanto*. A quanto is a derivative where the underlying asset is measured in one currency and the payoff is in another currency. Quantos will be discussed further in Chapter 27.

holder of this portfolio. It is usually assumed that the dividends provide a known yield rather than a known cash income. If q is the dividend yield rate, equation (5.3) gives the futures price, F_0, as

$$F_0 = S_0 e^{(r-q)T} \tag{5.8}$$

Note that in Table 3.3 the futures price of the Dow Jones Industrial Average for the June contract is less than that for the March contract. This indicates that on February 4, 2004, the dividend yield, q, was greater than the risk-free rate, r.

Example 5.5

Consider a 3-month futures contract on the S&P 500. Suppose that the stocks underlying the index provide a dividend yield of 1% per annum, that the current value of the index is 800, and that the continuously compounded risk-free interest rate is 6% per annum. In this case, $r = 0.06$, $S_0 = 800$, $T = 0.25$, and $q = 0.01$. Hence, the futures price, F_0, is given by

$$F_0 = 800e^{(0.06-0.01)\times 0.25} = \$810.06$$

In practice, the dividend yield on the portfolio underlying an index varies week by week throughout the year. For example, a large proportion of the dividends on the NYSE stocks are paid in the first week of February, May, August, and November each year. The chosen value of q should represent the average annualized dividend yield during the life of the contract. The dividends used for estimating q should be those for which the ex-dividend date is during the life of the futures contract. Looking at Table 3.3 of Chapter 3, we see that the settlement prices for futures contracts on the S&P 500 Index appear to be decreasing with the maturity of the futures contract at about 0.4% per annum. This corresponds to the situation where the dividend yield exceeds the risk-free rate by about 0.4% per annum.

Business Snapshot 5.4 Index Arbitrage in October 1987

To do index arbitrage, a trader must be able to trade both the index futures contract and the portfolio of stocks underlying the index very quickly at the prices quoted in the market. In normal market conditions this is possible using program trading, and the relationship in equation (5.8) holds well. Examples of days when the market was anything but normal are October 19 and 20 of 1987. On what is termed "Black Monday", October 19, 1987, the market fell by more than 20%, and the 604 million shares traded on the New York Stock Exchange easily exceeded all previous records. The exchange's systems were overloaded, and orders placed to buy or sell shares on that day could be delayed by up to two hours before being executed.

For most of October 19, 1987, futures prices were at a significant discount to the underlying index. For example, at the close of trading the S&P 500 Index was at 225.06 (down 57.88 on the day), whereas the futures price for December delivery on the S&P 500 was 201.50 (down 80.75 on the day). This was largely because the delays in processing orders made index arbitrage impossible. On the next day, Tuesday, October 20, 1987, the New York Stock Exchange placed temporary restrictions on the way in which program trading could be done. This also made index arbitrage very difficult and the breakdown of the traditional linkage between stock indices and stock index futures continued. At one point the futures price for the December contract was 18% less than the S&P 500 Index. However, after a few days the market returned to normal, and the activities of arbitrageurs ensured that equation (5.8) governed the relationship between futures and spot prices of indices.

Index Arbitrage

If $F_0 > S_0e^{(r-q)T}$, profits can be made by buying the stocks underlying the index at the spot price (i.e., for immediate delivery) and shorting futures contracts. If $F_0 < S_0e^{(r-q)T}$, profits can be made by doing the reverse—that is, shorting or selling the stocks underlying the index and taking a long position in futures contracts. These strategies are known as *index arbitrage*. When $F_0 < S_0e^{(r-q)T}$, index arbitrage is often done by a pension fund that owns an indexed portfolio of stocks. When $F_0 > S_0e^{(r-q)T}$, it is often done by a corporation holding short-term money market investments. For indices involving many stocks, index arbitrage is sometimes accomplished by trading a relatively small representative sample of stocks whose movements closely mirror those of the index. Often index arbitrage is implemented through *program trading*. This involves using a computer system to generate the trades.

Most of the time the activities of arbitrageurs ensure that equation (5.8) holds, but occasionally arbitrage is impossible and the futures price does get out of line with the spot price (see Business Snapshot 5.4).

5.10 FORWARD AND FUTURES CONTRACTS ON CURRENCIES

We now move on to consider forward and futures foreign currency contracts from the perspective of a US investor. The underlying asset in such contracts is a certain number of units of the foreign currency. We will therefore define the variable S_0 as the current spot price in dollars of one unit of the foreign currency and F_0 as the forward or futures

Figure 5.1 Two ways of converting 1,000 units of a foreign currency to dollars at time T. Here, S_0 is spot exchange rate, F_0 is forward exchange rate, and r and r_f are the dollar and foreign risk-free rates.

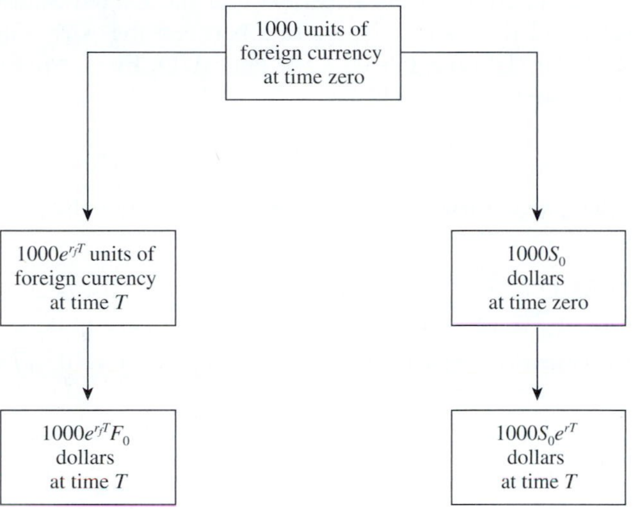

price in dollars of one unit of the foreign currency. This is consistent with the way we have defined S_0 and F_0 for other assets underlying forward and futures contracts. However, as mentioned in Section 2.10, it does not necessarily correspond to the way spot and forward exchange rates are quoted. For major exchange rates other than the British pound, euro, Australian dollar, and New Zealand dollar, a spot or forward exchange rate is normally quoted as the number of units of the currency that are equivalent to one US dollar.

A foreign currency has the property that the holder of the currency can earn interest at the risk-free interest rate prevailing in the foreign country. For example, the holder can invest the currency in a foreign-denominated bond. We define r_f as the value of the foreign risk-free interest rate when money is invested for time T. The variable r is the US dollar risk-free rate when money is invested for this period of time.

The relationship between F_0 and S_0 is

$$F_0 = S_0e^{(r-r_f)T} \tag{5.9}$$

This is the well-known interest rate parity relationship from international finance. The reason it is true is illustrated in Figure 5.1. Suppose that an individual starts with 1,000 units of the foreign currency. There are two ways it can be converted to dollars at time T. One is by investing it for T years at r_f and entering into a forward contract to sell the proceeds for dollars at time T. This generates $1{,}000e^{r_fT}F_0$ dollars. The other is by exchanging the foreign currency for dollars in the spot market and investing the proceeds for T years at rate r. This generates $1{,}000S_0e^{rT}$ dollars. In the absence of arbitrage opportunities, the two strategies must give the same result. Hence,

$$1{,}000e^{r_fT}F_0 = 1{,}000S_0e^{rT}$$

so that

$$F_0 = S_0 e^{(r-r_f)T}$$

Example 5.6

Suppose that the 2-year interest rates in Australia and the United States are 5% and 7%, respectively, and the spot exchange rate between the Australian dollar (AUD) and the US dollar (USD) is 0.6200 USD per AUD. From equation (5.9), the 2-year forward exchange rate should be

$$0.62e^{(0.07-0.05)\times 2} = 0.6453$$

Suppose first that the 2-year forward exchange rate is less than this, say 0.6300. An arbitrageur can:

1. Borrow 1,000 AUD at 5% per annum for 2 years, convert to 620 USD and invest the USD at 7% (both rates are continuously compounded).
2. Enter into a forward contract to buy 1,105.17 AUD for $1{,}105.17 \times 0.63 =$ 696.26 USD.

The 620 USD that are invested at 7% grow to $620e^{0.07\times 2} = 713.17$ USD in 2 years. Of this, 696.26 USD are used to purchase 1,105.17 AUD under the terms of the forward contract. This is exactly enough to repay principal and interest on the 1,000 AUD that are borrowed ($1{,}000e^{0.05\times 2} = 1{,}105.17$). The strategy therefore gives rise to a riskless profit of $713.17 - 696.26 = 16.91$ USD. (If this does not sound very exciting, consider following a similar strategy where you borrow 100 million AUD!)

Suppose next that the 2-year forward rate is 0.6600 (greater than the 0.6453 value given by equation (5.9)). An arbitrageur can:

1. Borrow 1,000 USD at 7% per annum for 2 years, convert to $1{,}000/0.6200 =$ 1,612.90 AUD, and invest the AUD at 5%.
2. Enter into a forward contract to sell 1,782.53 AUD for $1{,}782.53 \times 0.66 =$ 1,176.47 USD.

The 1,612.90 AUD that are invested at 5% grow to $1{,}612.90e^{0.05\times 2} = 1{,}782.53$ AUD in 2 years. The forward contract has the effect of converting this to 1,176.47 USD. The amount needed to payoff the USD borrowings is $1{,}000e^{0.07\times 2} = 1{,}150.27$ USD. The strategy therefore gives rise to a riskless profit of $1{,}176.47 - 1{,}150.27 = 26.20$ USD.

Table 5.4 shows currency futures quotes on February 4, 2004. In the case of the first eight contracts the quotes are US dollars (or cents) per unit of the foreign currency. This is the usual quotation convention for futures contracts. Equation (5.9) applies with r equal to the US risk-free rate and r_f equal to the foreign risk-free rate.

On February 4, 2004, interest rates on the Japanese yen and Swiss franc were lower than the interest rate on the US dollar. This corresponds to the $r > r_f$ situation and explains why futures prices for these currencies increase with maturity in Table 5.4. On the Canadian dollar, the British pound, the Australian dollar, the Mexican peso, and the euro, interest rates were higher than in the United States. This corresponds to the $r_f > r$ situation and explains why the futures prices of these currencies decrease with maturity.

Table 5.4 Foreign exchange futures quotes from the *Wall Street Journal* on February 5, 2004. (Columns show month, open, high, low, settle, change, lifetime high, lifetime low, and open interest, respectively.)

Currency Futures								
Japanese Yen (CME)-¥12,500,000; $ per ¥								
Mar	.9490	.9507	.9476	.9497	.0011	.9515	.8240	161,371
June	.9524	.9529	.9510	.9526	.0011	.9532	.8496	8,070
Est vol 6,229; vol Tue 14,298; open int 169,516, +4,280.								
Canadian Dollar (CME)-CAD 100,000; $ per CAD								
Mar	.7466	.7500	.7431	.7485	.0015	.7863	.6150	57,248
June	.7450	.7480	.7421	.7465	.0015	.7850	.6201	3,453
Sept	.7448	.7460	.7414	.7449	.0015	.7815	.6505	1,635
Dec	.7440	.7445	.7405	.7433	.0015	.7800	.6940	787
Est vol 6,009; vol Tue 12,621; open int 63,329, −2,093.								
British Pound (CME)-£62,500; $ per £								
Mar	1.8335	1.8338	1.8225	1.8277	−.0049	1.8488	1.5654	66,330
June	1.8200	1.8200	1.8060	1.8135	−.0051	1.8373	1.6080	127
Est vol 6,429; vol Tue 14,952; open int 66,822, +2,521.								
Swiss Franc (CME)-CHF 125,000; $ per CHF								
Mar	.8018	.8020	.7970	.8002	−.0008	.8249	.7060	40,580
June	...	...	...	.8019	−.0008	.8248	.7117	216
Est vol 4,223; vol Tue 9,933; open int 40,899, +458.								
Australian Dollar (CME)-AUD 100,000; $ per AUD								
Mar	.7605	.7614	.7545	.7578	−.0034	.7769	.5193	50,309
June	.7490	.7500	.7490	.7494	−.0034	.7686	.5645	843
Est vol 3,108; vol Tue 10,590; open int 51,677, −1,877.								
Mexican Peso (CME)-MXN 500,000; $ per MXN								
Mar	.08990	.09050	.08857	.08920	−00057	.09330	.08600	36,882
June	.08900	.08915	.08780	.08812	−00060	.09125	.08495	594
Est vol 12,680; vol Tue 6,785; open int 38,120, −303.								
Euro/US Dollar (CME)-€125,000; $ per €								
Mar	1.2532	1.2565	1.2478	1.2520	−.0013	1.2875	1.0425	122,318
June	1.2492	1.2520	1.2460	1.2491	−.0013	1.2837	1.0570	1,293
Est vol 20,357; vol Tue 69,168; open int 124,312, +3,721.								
Euro/US Dollar (FINEX)-€200,000; $ per €								
Mar	...	...	...	1.2520	−.0012	1.2841	1.4720	510
Est vol 191; vol Tue 93; open int 512, −12.								
Euro/Japanese Yen (FINEX)-€100,000; ¥ per €								
Mar	131.85	131.85	131.61	131.85	−.28	136.44	130.45	7,752
Est vol 67; vol Tue 287; open int 7,752, +76.								
Euro/British Pound (FINEX)-€100,000; £ per €								
Mar	.6840	.6843	.6832	.6852	.0013	.7094	.6832	9,964
Est vol 198; vol Tue 454; open int 9,964, +360.								

Source: Reprinted by permission of Dow Jones, Inc., via Copyright Clearance Center, Inc.

The last two contracts in Table 5.4 involve exchange rates relative to the euro. The quotes are yen per euro and pounds per euro. To use equation (5.9), for the euro/yen contract, we can measure S_0 and F_0 as yen per euro, define r as the yen interest rate and r_f as the euro interest rate. Similarly, to use equation (5.9), for the euro/pound contract we can measure S_0 and F_0 as pounds per euro, define r as the sterling interest rate and r_f as the euro interest rate.

Example 5.7

The futures price of the Canadian dollar in Table 5.4 appears to be decreasing at a rate of about 1.0% per annum with the maturity of the contract. (The September 2004 settlement price of 0.7449 is about 0.5% below the March 2004 settlement price of 0.7485.) The decrease suggests that short-term interest rates were about 1% per annum higher in the Canada than in the United States on February 4, 2004.

A Foreign Currency as an Asset Providing a Known Yield

Equation (5.9) is identical to equation (5.3) with q replaced by r_f. This is not a coincidence. A foreign currency can be regarded as an investment asset paying a known yield. The yield is the risk-free rate of interest in the foreign currency.

To understand this, we note that the value of interest paid in a foreign currency depends on the value of the foreign currency. Suppose that the interest rate on British pounds is 5% per annum. To a US investor the British pound provides an income equal to 5% of the value of the British pound per annum. In other words it is an asset that provides a yield of 5% per annum.

5.11 FUTURES ON COMMODITIES

We now move on to consider futures contracts on commodities. First we consider the futures prices of commodities that are investment assets such as gold and silver.[6] We then move on to consider the futures prices of consumption assets.

Income and Storage Costs

As explained in Business Snapshot 3.1, the hedging strategies of gold producers leads to a requirement on the part of investment banks to borrow gold. Gold owners such as central banks charge interest in the form of what is known as the *gold lease rate* when they lend gold. The same is true of silver. Gold and silver can therefore provide income to the holder. Like other commodities they also have storage costs.

Equation (5.1) shows that, in the absence of storage costs and income, the forward price of a commodity that is an investment asset is given by

$$F_0 = S_0 e^{rT} \tag{5.10}$$

Storage costs can be treated as negative income. If U is the present value of all the storage costs, net of income, during the life of a forward contract, it follows from equation (5.2) that

$$F_0 = (S_0 + U)e^{rT} \tag{5.11}$$

Example 5.8

Consider a 1-year futures contract on an investment asset that provides no income. It costs \$2 per unit to store the asset, with the payment being made at the end of the year. Assume that the spot price is \$450 per unit and the risk-free rate is 7% per annum for all maturities. This corresponds to $r = 0.07$, $S_0 = 450$, $T = 1$, and

$$U = 2e^{-0.07\times 1} = 1.865$$

From equation (5.11), the theoretical futures price, F_0, is given by

$$F_0 = (450 + 1.865)e^{0.07\times 1} = \$484.63$$

If the actual futures price is greater than 484.63, an arbitrageur can buy the asset and short 1-year futures contracts to lock in a profit. If the actual futures price is less than 484.63, an investor who already owns the asset can improve the return by selling the asset and buying futures contracts.

If the storage costs incurred at any time are proportional to the price of the commodity, they can be treated as negative yield. In this case, from equation (5.3),

$$F_0 = S_0 e^{(r+u)T} \tag{5.12}$$

[6] Recall that, for an asset to be an investment asset, it need not be held solely for investment purposes. What is required is that some individuals hold it for investment purposes and that these individuals be prepared to sell their holdings and go long forward contracts, if the latter look more attractive. This explains why silver, although it has significant industrial uses, is an investment asset.

where u denotes the storage costs per annum as a proportion of the spot price net of any yield earned on the asset.

Consumption Commodities

Commodities that are consumption assets rather than investment assets usually provide no income, but can be subject to significant storage costs. We now review the arbitrage strategies used to determine futures prices from spot prices carefully.[7] Suppose that, instead of equation (5.11), we have

$$F_0 > (S_0 + U)e^{rT} \tag{5.13}$$

To take advantage of this opportunity, an arbitrageur can implement the following strategy:

1. Borrow an amount $S_0 + U$ at the risk-free rate and use it to purchase one unit of the commodity and to pay storage costs.
2. Short a forward contract on one unit of the commodity.

If we regard the futures contract as a forward contract, this strategy leads to a profit of $F_0 - (S_0 + U)e^{rT}$ at time T. There is no problem in implementing the strategy for any commodity. However, as arbitrageurs do so, there will be a tendency for S_0 to increase and F_0 to decrease until equation (5.13) is no longer true. We conclude that equation (5.13) cannot hold for any significant length of time.

Suppose next that

$$F_0 < (S_0 + U)e^{rT} \tag{5.14}$$

When the commodity is an investment asset, we can argue that many investors hold the commodity solely for investment. When they observe the inequality in equation (5.14), they will find it profitable to do the following:

1. Sell the commodity, save the storage costs, and invest the proceeds at the risk-free interest rate.
2. Take a long position in a forward contract.

The result is a riskless profit at maturity of $(S_0 + U)e^{rT} - F_0$ relative to the position the investors would have been in if they had held the commodity. It follows that equation (5.14) cannot hold for long. Because neither equation (5.13) nor (5.14) can hold for long, we must have $F_0 = (S_0 + U)e^{rT}$.

This argument cannot be used for commodities that are not to any significant extent held for investment. Individuals and companies who keep such a commodity in their inventory do so because of its consumption value—not because of its value as an investment. They are reluctant to sell the commodity and buy forward contracts, because forward contracts cannot be consumed. There is therefore nothing to stop equation (5.14) from holding, and all we can assert for a consumption commodity is

$$F_0 \leqslant (S_0 + U)e^{rT} \tag{5.15}$$

---

[7] For some commodities the spot price depends on the delivery location. We assume that the delivery location for spot and futures are the same.

If storage costs are expressed as a proportion u of the spot price, the equivalent result is

$$F_0 \leqslant S_0 e^{(r+u)T} \tag{5.16}$$

Convenience Yields

We do not necessarily have equality in equations (5.15) and (5.16) because users of a consumption commodity may feel that ownership of the physical commodity provides benefits that are not obtained by holders of futures contracts. For example, an oil refiner is unlikely to regard a futures contract on crude oil in the same way as crude oil held in inventory. The crude oil in inventory can be an input to the refining process, whereas a futures contract cannot be used for this purpose. In general, ownership of the physical asset enables a manufacturer to keep a production process running and perhaps profit from temporary local shortages. A futures contract does not do the same. The benefits from holding the physical asset are sometimes referred to as the *convenience yield* provided by the commodity. If the dollar amount of storage costs is known and has a present value U, then the convenience yield y is defined such that

$$F_0 e^{yT} = (S_0 + U)e^{rT}$$

If the storage costs per unit are a constant proportion, u, of the spot price, then y is defined so that

$$F_0 e^{yT} = S_0 e^{(r+u)T}$$

or

$$F_0 = S_0 e^{(r+u-y)T} \tag{5.17}$$

The convenience yield simply measures the extent to which the left-hand side is less than the right-hand side in equation (5.15) or (5.16). For investment assets the convenience yield must be zero; otherwise, there are arbitrage opportunities. Figure 2.2 of Chapter 2 shows that the futures prices of crude oil tended to decrease as the time to maturity of the contract increased on February 4, 2004. This pattern suggests that the convenience yield, y, is greater than $r + u$ for oil on this date.

The convenience yield reflects the market's expectations concerning the future availability of the commodity. The greater the possibility that shortages will occur, the higher the convenience yield. If users of the commodity have high inventories, there is very little chance of shortages in the near future and the convenience yield tends to be low. On the other hand, low inventories tend to lead to high convenience yields.

5.12 THE COST OF CARRY

The relationship between futures prices and spot prices can be summarized in terms of the *cost of carry*. This measures the storage cost plus the interest that is paid to finance the asset less the income earned on the asset. For a non-dividend-paying stock, the cost of carry is r, because there are no storage costs and no income is earned; for a stock index, it is $r - q$, because income is earned at rate q on the asset. For a currency, it is $r - r_f$; for a commodity that provides income at rate q and requires storage costs at rate u, it is $r - q + u$; and so on.

Define the cost of carry as c. For an investment asset, the futures price is

$$F_0 = S_0 e^{cT} \tag{5.18}$$

For a consumption asset, it is

$$F_0 = S_0 e^{(c-y)T} \tag{5.19}$$

where y is the convenience yield.

5.13 DELIVERY OPTIONS

Whereas a forward contract normally specifies that delivery is to take place on a particular day, a futures contract often allows the party with the short position to choose to deliver at any time during a certain period. (Typically the party has to give a few days' notice of its intention to deliver.) The choice introduces a complication into the determination of futures prices. Should the maturity of the futures contract be assumed to be the beginning, middle, or end of the delivery period? Even though most futures contracts are closed out prior to maturity, it is important to know when delivery would have taken place in order to calculate the theoretical futures price.

If the futures price is an increasing function of the time to maturity, it can be seen from equation (5.19) that $c > y$, so that the benefits from holding the asset (including convenience yield and net of storage costs) are less than the risk-free rate. It is usually optimal in such a case for the party with the short position to deliver as early as possible, because the interest earned on the cash received outweighs the benefits of holding the asset. As a rule, futures prices in these circumstances should be calculated on the basis that delivery will take place at the beginning of the delivery period. If futures prices are decreasing as time to maturity increases ($c < y$), the reverse is true. It is then usually optimal for the party with the short position to deliver as late as possible, and futures prices should, as a rule, be calculated on this assumption.

5.14 FUTURES PRICES AND EXPECTED FUTURE SPOT PRICES

We refer to the market's average opinion about what the spot price of an asset will be at a certain future time as the *expected spot price* of the asset at that time. Suppose that it is now June and the September futures price of corn is 200 cents. It is interesting to ask what the expected spot price of corn in September is. Is it less than 200 cents, greater than 200 cents, or exactly equal to 200 cents? As illustrated in Figure 2.1, the futures price converges to the spot price at maturity. If the expected spot price is less than 200 cents, the market must be expecting the September futures price to decline, so that traders with short positions gain and traders with long positions lose. If the expected spot price is greater than 200 cents, the reverse must be true. The market must be expecting the September futures price to increase, so that traders with long positions gain while those with short positions lose.

Keynes and Hicks

Economists John Maynard Keynes and John Hicks argued that, if hedgers tend to hold short positions and speculators tend to hold long positions, the futures price of an asset will be below the expected spot price.[8] This is because speculators require compensation for the risks they are bearing. They will trade only if they can expect to make money on average. Hedgers will lose money on average, but they are likely to be prepared to accept this because the futures contract reduces their risks. If hedgers tend to hold long positions while speculators hold short positions, Keynes and Hicks argued that the futures price will be above the expected spot price for a similar reason.

Risk and Return

The modern approach to explaining the relationship between futures prices and expected spot prices is based on the relationship between risk and expected return in the economy. In general, the higher the risk of an investment, the higher the expected return demanded by an investor. Readers familiar with the capital asset pricing model will know that there are two types of risk in the economy: systematic and nonsystematic. Nonsystematic risk should not be important to an investor. It can be almost completely eliminated by holding a well-diversified portfolio. An investor should not therefore require a higher expected return for bearing nonsystematic risk. Systematic risk, in contrast, cannot be diversified away. It arises from a correlation between returns from the investment and returns from the whole stock market. An investor generally requires a higher expected return than the risk-free interest rate for bearing positive amounts of systematic risk. Also, an investor is prepared to accept a lower expected return than the risk-free interest rate when the systematic risk in an investment is negative.

The Risk in a Futures Position

Let us consider a speculator who takes a long position in a futures contract that lasts for T years in the hope that the spot price of the asset will be above the futures price at the end of the life of the futures contract. We ignore daily settlement and assume that the futures contract can be treated as a forward contract. We suppose that the speculator puts the present value of the futures price into a risk-free investment while simultaneously taking a long futures position. The proceeds of the risk-free investment are used to buy the asset on the delivery date. The asset is then immediately sold for its market price. The cash flows to the speculator are as follows:

Today: $-F_0e^{-rT}$

End of futures contract: $+S_T$

where F_0 is the futures price today, S_T is the price of the asset at time T at the end of the futures contract, and r is the risk-free return on funds invested for time T.

How do we value this investment? The discount rate we should use for the expected cash flow at time T equals an investor's required return on the investment. Suppose that k is an investor's required return for this investment. The present value of this investment is

$$-F_0e^{-rT} + E(S_T)e^{-kT}$$

[8] See: J. M. Keynes, *A Treatise on Money*. London: Macmillan, 1930; and J. R. Hicks, *Value and Capital*. Oxford: Clarendon Press, 1939.

where E denotes expected value. We can assume that all investments in securities markets are priced so that they have zero net present value. This means that

$$-F_0 e^{-rT} + E(S_T)e^{-kT} = 0$$

or

$$F_0 = E(S_T)e^{(r-k)T} \tag{5.20}$$

As we have just discussed, the returns investors require on an investment depend on its systematic risk. The investment we have been considering is in essence an investment in the asset underlying the futures contract. If the returns from this asset are uncorrelated with the stock market, the correct discount rate to use is the risk-free rate r, so we should set $k = r$. Equation (5.20) then gives

$$F_0 = E(S_T)$$

This shows that the futures price is an unbiased estimate of the expected future spot price when the return from the underlying asset is uncorrelated with the stock market.

If the return from the asset is positively correlated with the stock market, $k > r$ and equation (5.20) leads to $F_0 < E(S_T)$. This shows that, when the asset underlying the futures contract has positive systematic risk, we should expect the futures price to understate the expected future spot price. An example of an asset that has positive systematic risk is a stock index. The expected return of investors on the stocks underlying an index is generally more than the risk-free rate, r. The dividends provide a return of q. The expected increase in the index must therefore be more than $r - q$. Equation (5.8) is therefore consistent with the prediction that the futures price understates the expected future stock price for a stock index.

If the return from the asset is negatively correlated with the stock market, $k < r$ and equation (5.20) gives $F_0 > E(S_T)$. This shows that, when the asset underlying the futures contract has negative systematic risk, we should expect the futures price to overstate the expected future spot price.

Normal Backwardation and Contango

When the futures price is below the expected future spot price, the situation is known as *normal backwardation*; and when the futures price is above the expected future spot price, the situation is known as *contango*.

SUMMARY

For most purposes, the futures price of a contract with a certain delivery date can be considered to be the same as the forward price for a contract with the same delivery date. It can be shown that in theory the two should be exactly the same when interest rates are perfectly predictable.

For the purposes of understanding futures (or forward) prices, it is convenient to divide futures contracts into two categories: those in which the underlying asset is held for investment by a significant number of investors and those in which the underlying asset is held primarily for consumption purposes.

Table 5.5 Summary of results for a contract with time to maturity T on an investment asset with price S_0 when the risk-free interest rate for a T-year period is r.

Asset	*Forward/futures price*	*Value of long forward contract with delivery price K*
Provides no income:	S_0e^{rT}	$S_0 - Ke^{-rT}$
Provides known income with present value I:	$(S_0 - I)e^{rT}$	$S_0 - I - Ke^{-rT}$
Provides known yield q:	$S_0e^{(r-q)T}$	$S_0e^{-qT} - Ke^{-rT}$

In the case of investment assets, we have considered three different situations:

1. The asset provides no income.
2. The asset provides a known dollar income.
3. The asset provides a known yield.

The results are summarized in Table 5.5. They enable futures prices to be obtained for contracts on stock indices, currencies, gold, and silver. Storage costs can be treated as negative income.

In the case of consumption assets, it is not possible to obtain the futures price as a function of the spot price and other observable variables. Here the parameter known as the asset's convenience yield becomes important. It measures the extent to which users of the commodity feel that ownership of the physical asset provides benefits that are not obtained by the holders of the futures contract. These benefits may include the ability to profit from temporary local shortages or the ability to keep a production process running. We can obtain an upper bound for the futures price of consumption assets using arbitrage arguments, but we cannot nail down an equality relationship between futures and spot prices.

The concept of cost of carry is sometimes useful. The cost of carry is the storage cost of the underlying asset plus the cost of financing it minus the income received from it. In the case of investment assets, the futures price is greater than the spot price by an amount reflecting the cost of carry. In the case of consumption assets, the futures price is greater than the spot price by an amount reflecting the cost of carry net of the convenience yield.

If we assume the capital asset pricing model is true, the relationship between the futures price and the expected future spot price depends on whether the return on the asset is positively or negatively correlated with the return on the stock market. Positive correlation will tend to lead to a futures price lower than the expected future spot price, whereas negative correlation will tend to lead to a futures price higher than the expected future spot price. Only when the correlation is zero will the theoretical futures price be equal to the expected future spot price.

FURTHER READING

Cox, J. C., J. E. Ingersoll, and S. A. Ross. "The Relation between Forward Prices and Futures Prices," *Journal of Financial Economics*, 9 (December 1981): 321–46.

Ghon, R. S. and R. P. Chang. "Intra-day Arbitrage in Foreign Exchange and Eurocurrency Markets," *Journal of Finance*, 47, 1 (1992): 363–380.

Jarrow, R. A., and G. S. Oldfield. "Forward Contracts and Futures Contracts," *Journal of Financial Economics*, 9 (December 1981): 373–82.

Kane, E. J. "Market Incompleteness and Divergences between Forward and Futures Interest Rates," *Journal of Finance*, 35 (May 1980): 221–34.

Pindyck, R. S. "Inventories and the Short-Run Dynamics of Commodity Prices," *Rand Journal of Economics*, 25, 1 (1994): 141–159.

Richard, S., and M. Sundaresan. "A Continuous-Time Model of Forward and Futures Prices in a Multigood Economy," *Journal of Financial Economics*, 9 (December 1981): 347–72.

Routledge, B. R., D. J. Seppi, and C. S. Spatt. "Equilibrium Forward Curves for Commodities," Journal of Finance, 55, 3 (2000) 1297–1338.

Questions and Problems (Answers in Solutions Manual)

5.1. Explain what happens when an investor shorts a certain share.

5.2. What is the difference between the forward price and the value of a forward contract?

5.3. Suppose that you enter into a 6-month forward contract on a non-dividend-paying stock when the stock price is $30 and the risk-free interest rate (with continuous compounding) is 12% per annum. What is the forward price?

5.4. A stock index currently stands at 350. The risk-free interest rate is 8% per annum (with continuous compounding) and the dividend yield on the index is 4% per annum. What should the futures price for a 4-month contract be?

5.5. Explain carefully why the futures price of gold can be calculated from its spot price and other observable variables whereas the futures price of copper cannot.

5.6. Explain carefully the meaning of the terms *convenience yield* and *cost of carry*. What is the relationship between futures price, spot price, convenience yield, and cost of carry?

5.7. Explain why a foreign currency can be treated as an asset providing a known yield.

5.8. Is the futures price of a stock index greater than or less than the expected future value of the index? Explain your answer.

5.9. A 1-year long forward contract on a non-dividend-paying stock is entered into when the stock price is $40 and the risk-free rate of interest is 10% per annum with continuous compounding.

(a) What are the forward price and the initial value of the forward contract?

(b) Six months later, the price of the stock is $45 and the risk-free interest rate is still 10%. What are the forward price and the value of the forward contract?

5.10. The risk-free rate of interest is 7% per annum with continuous compounding, and the dividend yield on a stock index is 3.2% per annum. The current value of the index is 150. What is the 6-month futures price?

5.11. Assume that the risk-free interest rate is 9% per annum with continuous compounding and that the dividend yield on a stock index varies throughout the year. In February, May, August, and November, dividends are paid at a rate of 5% per annum. In other months, dividends are paid at a rate of 2% per annum. Suppose that the value of the index on July 31, 2006, is 300. What is the futures price for a contract deliverable on December 31, 2006?

5.12. Suppose that the risk-free interest rate is 10% per annum with continuous compounding and that the dividend yield on a stock index is 4% per annum. The index is standing at 400, and the futures price for a contract deliverable in four months is 405. What arbitrage opportunities does this create?

5.13. Estimate the difference between short-term interest rates in Mexico and the United States on February 4, 2004, from the information in Table 5.4.

5.14. The 2-month interest rates in Switzerland and the United States are, respectively, 3% and 8% per annum with continuous compounding. The spot price of the Swiss franc is \$0.6500. The futures price for a contract deliverable in 2 months is \$0.6600. What arbitrage opportunities does this create?

5.15. The spot price of silver is \$9 per ounce. The storage costs are \$0.24 per ounce per year payable quarterly in advance. Assuming that interest rates are 10% per annum for all maturities, calculate the futures price of silver for delivery in 9 months.

5.16. Suppose that F_1 and F_2 are two futures contracts on the same commodity with times to maturity, t_1 and t_2, where $t_2 > t_1$. Prove that

$$F_2 \leqslant F_1 e^{r(t_2 - t_1)}$$

where r is the interest rate (assumed constant) and there are no storage costs. For the purposes of this problem, assume that a futures contract is the same as a forward contract.

5.17. When a known future cash outflow in a foreign currency is hedged by a company using a forward contract, there is no foreign exchange risk. When it is hedged using futures contracts, the marking-to-market process does leave the company exposed to some risk. Explain the nature of this risk. In particular, consider whether the company is better off using a futures contract or a forward contract when:
(a) The value of the foreign currency falls rapidly during the life of the contract.
(b) The value of the foreign currency rises rapidly during the life of the contract.
(c) The value of the foreign currency first rises and then falls back to its initial value.
(d) The value of the foreign currency first falls and then rises back to its initial value.
Assume that the forward price equals the futures price.

5.18. It is sometimes argued that a forward exchange rate is an unbiased predictor of future exchange rates. Under what circumstances is this so?

5.19. Show that the growth rate in an index futures price equals the excess return of the index over the risk-free rate. Assume that the risk-free interest rate and the dividend yield are constant.

5.20. Show that equation (5.3) is true by considering an investment in the asset combined with a short position in a futures contract. Assume that all income from the asset is reinvested in the asset. Use an argument similar to that in footnotes 2 and 4 and explain in detail what an arbitrageur would do if equation (5.3) did not hold.

5.21. Explain carefully what is meant by the expected price of a commodity on a particular future date. Suppose that on February 4, 2004, speculators tended to be short crude oil futures and hedgers tended to be long crude oil futures. What does the Keynes and Hicks argument imply about the expected future price of oil? Use Table 2.2.

5.22. The Value Line Index is designed to reflect changes in the value of a portfolio of over 1,600 equally weighted stocks. Prior to March 9, 1988, the change in the index from one day to the next was calculated as the *geometric* average of the changes in the prices of the stocks underlying the index. In these circumstances, does equation (5.8) correctly relate the futures price of the index to its cash price? If not, does the equation overstate or understate the futures price?

5.23. A US company is interested in using the futures contracts traded on the CME to hedge its Australian dollar exposure. Define r as the interest rate (all maturities) on the US dollar and r_f as the interest rate (all maturities) on the Australian dollar. Assume that r and r_f are constant and that the company uses a contract expiring at time T to hedge an exposure at time t ($T > t$).
(a) Show that the optimal hedge ratio is $e^{(r_f - r)(T-t)}$.
(b) Show that, when t is 1 day, the optimal hedge ratio is almost exactly S_0/F_0, where S_0 is the current spot price of the currency and F_0 is the current futures price of the currency for the contract maturing at time T.
(c) Show that the company can take account of the daily settlement of futures contracts for a hedge that lasts longer than 1 day by adjusting the hedge ratio so that it always equals the spot price of the currency divided by the futures price of the currency.

Assignment Questions

5.24. A stock is expected to pay a dividend of $1 per share in 2 months and in 5 months. The stock price is $50, and the risk-free rate of interest is 8% per annum with continuous compounding for all maturities. An investor has just taken a short position in a 6-month forward contract on the stock.
(a) What are the forward price and the initial value of the forward contract?
(b) Three months later, the price of the stock is $48 and the risk-free rate of interest is still 8% per annum. What are the forward price and the value of the short position in the forward contract?

5.25. A bank offers a corporate client a choice between borrowing cash at 11% per annum and borrowing gold at 2% per annum. (If gold is borrowed, interest must be repaid in gold. Thus, 100 ounces borrowed today would require 102 ounces to be repaid in 1 year.) The risk-free interest rate is 9.25% per annum, and storage costs are 0.5% per annum. Discuss whether the rate of interest on the gold loan is too high or too low in relation to the rate of interest on the cash loan. The interest rates on the two loans are expressed with annual compounding. The risk-free interest rate and storage costs are expressed with continuous compounding.

5.26. A company that is uncertain about the exact date when it will pay or receive a foreign currency may try to negotiate with its bank a forward contract that specifies a period during which delivery can be made. The company wants to reserve the right to choose the exact delivery date to fit in with its own cash flows. Put yourself in the position of the bank. How would you price the product that the company wants?

5.27. A trader owns gold as part of a long-term investment portfolio. The trader can buy gold for $450 per ounce and sell it for $449 per ounce. The trader can borrow funds at 6% per year and invest funds at 5.5% per year (both interest rates are expressed with annual compounding). For what range of 1-year forward prices of gold does the trader have no arbitrage opportunities? Assume there is no bid–offer spread for forward prices.

5.28. A company enters into a forward contract with a bank to sell a foreign currency for K_1 at time T_1. The exchange rate at time T_1 proves to be S_1 ($> K_1$). The company asks the bank if it can roll the contract forward until time T_2 ($> T_1$) rather than settle at time T_1. The bank agrees to a new delivery price, K_2. Explain how K_2 should be calculated.

APPENDIX

PROOF THAT FORWARD AND FUTURES PRICES ARE EQUAL WHEN INTEREST RATES ARE CONSTANT

This appendix demonstrates that forward and futures prices are equal when interest rates are constant. Suppose that a futures contract lasts for n days and that F_i is the futures price at the end of day i ($0 < i < n$). Define δ as the risk-free rate per day (assumed constant). Consider the following strategy:[9]

1. Take a long futures position of e^{δ} at the end of day 0 (i.e., at the beginning of the contract).
2. Increase long position to $e^{2\delta}$ at the end of day 1.
3. Increase long position to $e^{3\delta}$ at the end of day 2.

   And so on.

This strategy is summarized in Table 5.6. By the beginning of day i, the investor has a long position of $e^{\delta i}$. The profit (possibly negative) from the position on day i is

$$(F_i - F_{i-1})e^{\delta i}$$

Assume that the profit is compounded at the risk-free rate until the end of day n. Its value at the end of day n is

$$(F_i - F_{i-1})e^{\delta i}e^{(n-i)\delta} = (F_i - F_{i-1})e^{n\delta}$$

The value at the end of day n of the entire investment strategy is therefore

$$\sum_{i=1}^{n}(F_i - F_{i-1})e^{n\delta}$$

This is

$$[(F_n - F_{n-1}) + (F_{n-1} - F_{n-2}) + \cdots + (F_1 - F_0)]e^{n\delta} = (F_n - F_0)e^{n\delta}$$

Because F_n is the same as the terminal asset spot price, S_T, the terminal value of the investment strategy can be written

$$(S_T - F_0)e^{n\delta}$$

Table 5.6 The investment strategy to show that futures and forward prices are equal.

Day	0	1	2	...	$n-1$	n
Futures price	F_0	F_1	F_2	...	F_{n-1}	F_n
Futures position	e^{δ}	$e^{2\delta}$	$e^{3\delta}$	...	$e^{n\delta}$	0
Gain/loss	0	$(F_1 - F_0)e^{\delta}$	$(F_2 - F_1)e^{2\delta}$	...	...	$(F_n - F_{n-1})e^{n\delta}$
Gain/loss compounded to day n	0	$(F_1 - F_0)e^{n\delta}$	$(F_2 - F_1)e^{n\delta}$	...	...	$(F_n - F_{n-1})e^{n\delta}$

[9] This strategy was proposed by J. C. Cox, J. E. Ingersoll, and S. A. Ross, "The Relation between Forward Prices and Futures Prices," *Journal of Financial Economics* 9 (December 1981): 321–46.

An investment of F_0 in a risk-free bond combined with the strategy involving futures just given yields

$$F_0e^{n\delta} + (S_T - F_0)e^{n\delta} = S_Te^{n\delta}$$

at time T. No investment is required for all the long futures positions described. It follows that an amount F_0 can be invested to give an amount $S_Te^{n\delta}$ at time T.

Suppose next that the forward price at the end of day 0 is G_0. Investing G_0 in a riskless bond and taking a long forward position of $e^{n\delta}$ forward contracts also guarantees an amount $S_Te^{n\delta}$ at time T. Thus, there are two investment strategies—one requiring an initial outlay of F_0 and the other requiring an initial outlay of G_0—both of which yield $S_Te^{n\delta}$ at time T. It follows that, in the absence of arbitrage opportunities,

$$F_0 = G_0$$

In other words, the futures price and the forward price are identical. Note that in this proof there is nothing special about the time period of 1 day. The futures price based on a contract with weekly settlements is also the same as the forward price when corresponding assumptions are made.

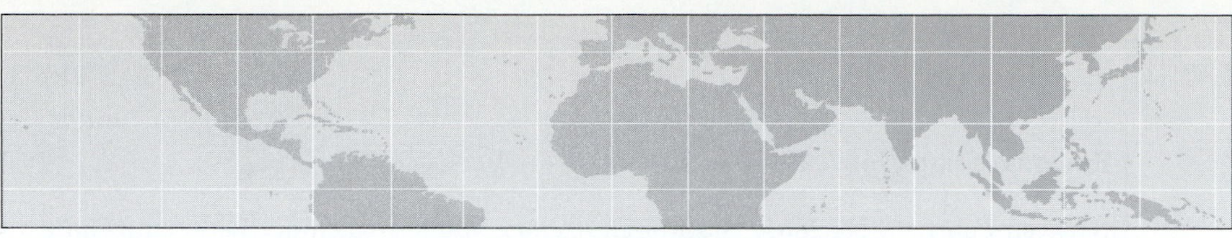

CHAPTER 6

Interest Rate Futures

So far we have covered futures contracts on commodities, stock indices, and foreign currencies. We have seen how they work, how they are used for hedging, and how futures prices are set. We now move on to consider interest rate futures.

In this chapter we explain the popular Treasury bond and Eurodollar futures contracts that trade in the United States. Many of the other interest rate futures contracts throughout the world have been modeled on these contracts. We also show how interest rate futures contracts, when used in conjunction with the duration measure introduced in Chapter 4, can be used to hedge a company's exposure to interest rate movements.

6.1 DAY COUNT CONVENTIONS

As a preliminary to the material in this chapter, we consider day count conventions. The day count defines the way in which interest accrues over time. Generally, we know the interest earned over some reference period (e.g., the time between coupon payments), and we are interested in calculating the interest earned over some other period.

The day count convention is usually expressed as X/Y. When we are calculating the interest earned between two dates, X defines the way in which the number of days between the two dates is calculated, and Y defines the way in which the total number of days in the reference period is measured. The interest earned between the two dates is

$$\frac{\text{Number of days between dates}}{\text{Number of days in reference period}} \times \text{Interest earned in reference period}$$

Three day count conventions that are commonly used in the United States are:

1. Actual/actual (in period)
2. 30/360
3. Actual/360

Business Snapshot 6.1 Day Counts Can Be Deceptive

Between February 28, 2005, and March 1, 2005, you have a choice between owning a US government bond and a US corporate bond. They pay the same coupon and have the same quoted price. Which would you prefer?

It sounds as though you should be indifferent, but in fact you should have a marked preference for the corporate bond. Under the 30/360 day count convention used for corporate bonds, there are 3 days between February 28, 2002, and March 1, 2002. Under the actual/actual (in period) day count convention used for government bonds, there is only 1 day. You would earn approximately three times as much interest by holding the corporate bond!

US Treasury Bonds

The actual/actual (in period) day count is used for Treasury bonds in the United States. This means that the interest earned between two dates is based on the ratio of the actual days elapsed to the actual number of days in the period between coupon payments. Suppose that the bond principal is \$100, coupon payment dates are March 1 and September 1, the coupon rate is 8%, and we wish to calculate the interest earned between March 1 and July 3. The reference period is from March 1 to September 1. There are 184 (actual) days in this period, and interest of \$4 is earned during the period. There are 124 (actual) days between March 1 and July 3. The interest earned between March 1 and July 3 is therefore

$$\frac{124}{184} \times 4 = 2.6957$$

US Corporate and Municipal Bonds

The 30/360 day count is used for corporate and municipal bonds in the United States. This means that we assume 30 days per month and 360 days per year when carrying out calculations. With the 30/360 day count, the total number of days between March 1 and September 1 is 180. The total number of days between March 1 and July 3 is $(4 \times 30) + 2 = 122$. In a corporate bond with the same terms as the Treasury bond just considered, the interest earned between March 1 and July 3, therefore, would be

$$\frac{122}{180} \times 4 = 2.7111$$

As shown in Business Snapshot 6.1, sometimes the 30/360 day count convention has surprising consequences.

US Money Market Instruments

The actual/360 day count is used for money market instruments in the United States. This indicates that the reference period is 360 days. The interest earned during part of a year is calculated by dividing the actual number of elapsed days by 360 and multiplying by the rate. The interest earned in 90 days is therefore exactly one-fourth of the quoted rate, and the interest earned in a whole year of 365 days is 365/360 times the quoted rate.

The prices of money market instruments are sometimes quoted using a *discount rate*. This is the interest earned as a percentage of the final face value rather than as a percentage of the initial price paid for the instrument. An example is Treasury bills in the United States. If the price of a 91-day Treasury bill is quoted as 8, this means that the annualized rate of interest earned is 8% of the face value. Suppose that the face value is \$100. Interest of \$2.0222 (= \$100 × 0.08 × 91/360) is earned over the 91-day life. This corresponds to a true rate of interest of 2.0222/(100 − 2.0222) = 2.064% for the 91-day period. In general, the relationship between the cash price and quoted price of a Treasury bill in the United States is

$$P = \frac{360}{n}(100 - Y)$$

where P is the quoted price, Y is the cash price, and n is the remaining life of the Treasury bill measured in calendar days.

6.2 QUOTATIONS FOR TREASURY BONDS

Treasury bond prices in the United States are quoted in dollars and thirty-seconds of a dollar. The quoted price is for a bond with a face value of \$100. Thus, a quote of 90-05 indicates that the quoted price for a bond with a face value of \$100,000 is \$90,156.25.

The quoted price, which traders refer to as the *clean price*, is not the same as the cash price, which traders refer to as the *dirty price*. In general,

$$\text{Cash price} = \text{Quoted price} + \text{Accrued interest since last coupon date}$$

To illustrate this formula, suppose that it is March 5, 2007, and the bond under consideration is an 11% coupon bond maturing on July 10, 2012, with a quoted price of 95-16 or \$95.50. Because coupons are paid semiannually on government bonds (and the final coupon is at maturity), the most recent coupon date is January 10, 2007, and the next coupon date is July 10, 2007. The number of days between January 10, 2007, and March 5, 2007, is 54, whereas the number of days between January 10, 2007, and July 10, 2007, is 181. On a bond with \$100 face value, the coupon payment is \$5.50 on January 10 and July 10. The accrued interest on March 5, 2007, is the share of the July 10 coupon accruing to the bondholder on March 5, 2007. Because actual/actual in period is used for Treasury bonds (see Section 6.1), this is

$$\frac{54}{181} \times \$5.5 = \$1.64$$

The cash price per \$100 face value for the bond is therefore

$$\$95.5 + \$1.64 = \$97.14$$

Thus, the cash price of a \$100,000 bond is \$97,140.

Table 6.1 Interest rate futures quotes from the *Wall Street Journal* on February 5, 2004. (Columns show month, open, high, low, settle, change, lifetime high, lifetime low, and open interest, respectively.)

Interest Rate Futures

Treasury Bonds (CBT)-$100,000; pts 32nds of 100%

Mar	111-25	111-31	109-18	111-17	–3	116-23	101-00	467,134
June	110-09	110-12	109-16	110-03	–3	116-15	104-00	31,215

Est vol 183,502; vol Tue 208,442; open int 499,090, +8,789.

Treasury Notes (CBT)-$100,000; pts 32nds of 100%

Mar	113-29	14-005	113-15	113-22	–4.5	116-10	106-29	1,130,409
June	112-17	112-17	111-29	112-03	–4.5	113-18	107-13	147,892

Est vol 489,439; vol Tue 623,701; open int 1,278,301, –9,178.

5 Yr. Treasury Notes (CBT)-$100,000; pts 32nds of 100%

Mar	12-215	112-24	12-125	112-17	–3.5	19-215	09-145	882,174

Est vol 219,841; vol Tue 268,683; open int 948,759, +6,645.

2 Yr. Treasury Notes (CBT)-$200,000; pts 32nds of 100%

Mar	07-132	07-142	07-102	07-127	–.2	07-205	106-02	164,711

Est vol 15,846; vol Tue 11,507; open int 166,044, +168.

30 Day Federal Funds (CBT)-$5,000,000; 100 - daily avg.

Feb	99.000	99.000	98.995	99.000	...	99.890	98.700	64,359
Mar	99.00	99.00	98.99	98.99	...	99.16	98.74	48,219
Apr	99.00	99.00	98.99	98.99	...	99.17	89.96	71,817
May	98.96	98.96	98.95	98.96	...	99.79	98.40	37,989
June	98.94	98.95	98.94	98.95	...	98.97	98.38	27,460
July	98.87	98.87	98.86	98.87	...	98.93	98.20	26,248
Aug	98.77	98.78	98.77	98.78	.01	98.85	98.24	4,137
Sept	98.70	98.71	98.68	98.71	–.01	98.79	98.22	5,260

Est vol 15,789; vol Tue 16,390; open int 286,642, –49,041.

10 Yr. Interest Rate Swaps (CBT)-$100,000; pts 32nds of 100%

Mar	111-15	111-19	111-03	111-10	–6	113-05	107-20	39,568

Est vol 1,060; vol Tue 968; open int 39,569, +269.

10 Yr. Muni Note Index (CBT)-$1,000 x index

Mar	103-13	103-21	103-08	103-15	1	105-04	99-21	2,249

Est vol 269; vol Tue 194; open int 2,249, +6.
Index: Close 104-15; Yield 4.44.

1 Month Libor (CME)-$3,000,000; pts of 100%

	OPEN	HIGH	LOW	SETTLE	CHG	YIELD	CHG	OPEN INT
Feb	98.90	98.90	98.89	98.89	...	1.11	...	29,195
Mar	98.89	98.89	98.89	98.89	...	1.11	...	11,060
Apr	98.86	98.86	98.86	98.86	...	1.14	...	8,279
May	98.83	98.83	98.82	98.82	...	1.18	...	2,550
Oct	98.44	98.44	98.43	98.44	...	1.56	...	51,960

Est vol 1,215; vol Tue 2,781; open int 171,119, +1,172.

Eurodollar (CME)-$1,000,000; pts of 100%

	OPEN	HIGH	LOW	SETTLE	CHG	YIELD	CHG	OPEN INT
Feb	98.86	98.86	98.86	98.86	...	1.14	...	32,246
Mar	98.84	98.84	98.83	98.84	...	1.16	...	827,925
Apr	98.80	98.80	98.79	98.80	...	1.20	...	35,531
May	98.75	98.75	98.74	98.74	...	1.26	...	14,543
June	98.69	98.69	98.66	98.68	...	1.32	...	838,794
July	98.58	98.58	98.57	98.58	...	1.42	...	2,150
Sept	98.41	98.43	98.38	98.41	...	1.59	...	794,586
Dec	98.04	98.06	98.00	98.03	...	1.97	...	600,750
Mr05	97.65	97.67	97.58	97.63	...	2.37	...	419,479
June	97.24	97.26	97.19	97.23	...	2.77	...	330,839
Sept	96.88	96.90	96.82	96.86	...	3.14	...	260,971
Dec	96.56	96.59	96.51	96.55	...	3.45	...	191,396
Mr06	96.32	96.33	96.25	96.30	–.01	3.70	.01	172,526
June	96.10	96.11	96.04	96.07	–.01	3.93	.01	128,625
Sept	95.91	95.91	95.83	95.86	–.01	4.14	.01	119,346
Dec	95.69	95.71	95.63	95.66	–.02	4.34	.02	105,045
Mr07	95.47	95.53	95.46	95.49	–.02	4.51	.02	75,659
June	95.34	95.38	95.30	95.33	–.03	4.67	.03	66,675
Sept	95.19	95.23	95.16	95.18	–.03	4.82	.03	73,288
Dec	95.05	95.09	95.02	95.04	–.03	4.96	.03	59,439
Mr08	94.92	94.97	94.90	94.92	–.03	5.08	.03	46,996
June	94.80	94.86	94.79	94.81	–.03	5.19	.03	50,074
Sept	94.71	94.75	94.68	94.71	–.03	5.29	.03	34,029
Dec	94.65	94.65	94.57	94.60	–.03	5.40	.03	26,470
Ju09	94.42	94.47	94.41	94.43	–.03	5.57	.03	9,247
Sept	94.34	94.40	94.34	94.35	–.03	5.65	.03	8,400
Dec	94.26	94.31	94.25	94.27	–.03	5.73	.03	4,633
Mr10	94.19	94.19	94.18	94.19	–.04	5.81	.04	8,192
June	94.12	94.12	94.11	94.12	–.04	5.88	.04	6,761
Sept	94.05	94.05	94.04	94.05	–.04	5.95	.04	4,683

Est vol 780,408; vol Tue 779,833; open int 5,375,781, +11,885.

Euroyen (CME)-¥100,000,000; pts of 100%

	OPEN	HIGH	LOW	SETTLE	CHG	LIFETIME HIGH	LIFETIME LOW	OPEN INT
Mar	99.91	99.91	99.91	99.91	...	99.92	99.14	11,530
June	99.91	99.91	99.91	99.91	...	99.92	99.41	9,096
Sept	99.89	99.89	99.89	99.89	...	99.90	99.35	12,320
Mr05	99.82	99.82	99.82	99.82	...	99.84	99.27	4,726

Est vol 431; vol Tue 25; open int 49,808, +775.

Short Sterling (LIFFE)-£500,000; pts of 100%

	OPEN	HIGH	LOW	SETTLE	CHG	LIFETIME HIGH	LIFETIME LOW	OPEN INT
Feb	95.82	95.82	95.82	95.82	...	95.89	95.80	1,913
Mar	95.76	95.77	95.75	95.76	...	96.80	93.01	188,159
June	95.57	95.58	95.54	95.56	...	96.71	93.04	201,882
Sept	95.37	95.40	95.34	95.36	...	96.59	93.35	153,843
Dec	95.21	95.24	95.19	95.20	...	96.48	93.25	139,045
Mr05	95.10	95.13	95.06	95.08	...	96.38	93.29	83,684
June	95.01	95.04	94.98	94.99	...	96.30	93.29	72,583
Sept	94.95	94.97	94.91	94.92	...	96.23	94.06	70,992
Dec	94.88	94.91	94.85	94.86	...	96.15	94.06	35,228
Mr06	94.82	94.84	94.80	94.82	.02	96.10	94.05	27,988
June	94.77	94.81	94.75	94.77	.02	95.97	94.04	28,423
Sept	94.74	94.78	94.72	94.74	.02	95.75	94.32	15,264
Dec	94.74	94.75	94.71	94.72	.02	95.83	94.25	6,356
Mr07	94.69	94.69	94.69	94.71	.02	95.82	94.33	527
June	94.71	94.71	94.71	94.70	.02	95.73	94.66	639

Est vol 142,996; vol Tue 184,402; open int 1,028,552, –284.

Long Gilt (LIFFE)-£100,000; pts of 100%

	OPEN	HIGH	LOW	SETTLE	CHG	LIFETIME HIGH	LIFETIME LOW	OPEN INT
Mar	107.95	108.41	107.95	108.12	.26	109.73	105.39	159,338

Est vol 50,453; vol Tue 36,817; open int 159,339, –153.

3 Month Euribor (LIFFE)-€1,000,000; pts of 100%

	OPEN	HIGH	LOW	SETTLE	CHG	LIFETIME HIGH	LIFETIME LOW	OPEN INT
Feb	97.92	97.93	97.92	97.93	.01	97.96	97.77	13,595
Mar	97.94	97.95	97.93	97.94	.01	98.29	93.83	562,698
June	97.91	97.92	97.89	97.90	.02	98.21	93.79	511,614
Sept	97.77	97.78	97.75	97.76	.03	98.08	93.73	428,741
Dec	97.55	97.57	97.53	97.55	.04	97.91	93.64	436,055
Mr05	97.32	97.34	97.30	97.31	.03	97.77	94.07	301,516
June	97.09	97.10	97.06	97.07	.03	97.60	94.29	197,768
Sept	96.88	96.89	96.84	96.86	.02	97.44	94.29	119,907
Dec	96.68	96.69	96.65	96.66	.02	97.28	94.41	95,512
Mr06	96.51	96.53	96.48	96.50	.02	97.14	94.40	41,992
June	96.35	96.36	96.32	96.33	.02	96.96	94.66	37,197
Sept	96.20	96.21	96.17	96.18	.02	96.81	94.58	22,947
Dec	96.03	96.04	96.01	96.02	.02	96.60	94.62	11,645
Mr07	95.93	95.93	95.93	95.90	.02	96.48	94.57	4,473
June	95.79	95.79	95.79	95.80	.02	96.29	94.57	2,490
Sept	95.69	95.69	95.69	95.70	.02	96.21	95.26	2,204

Est vol 547,848; vol Tue 533,760; open int 2,791,222, +50,205.

3 Month Euroswiss (LIFFE)-CHF 1,000,000; pts of 100%

	OPEN	HIGH	LOW	SETTLE	CHG	LIFETIME HIGH	LIFETIME LOW	OPEN INT
Mar	99.73	99.74	99.72	99.73	...	99.75	96.32	95,989
June	99.61	99.61	99.56	99.57	–.02	99.63	96.98	81,441
Sept	99.37	99.39	99.35	99.36	–.01	99.41	97.60	41,632
Dec	99.14	99.14	99.11	99.12	–.01	99.17	98.00	32,364
Mr05	98.87	98.87	98.86	98.87	–.01	98.93	97.90	7,335
June	98.65	98.65	98.61	98.62	–.01	98.68	97.74	9,694
Sept	98.43	98.44	98.36	98.41	–.02	98.47	97.75	4,732
Dec	98.21	98.22	98.14	98.19	–.01	98.24	97.92	2,745

Est vol 14,180; vol Tue 21,649; open int 275,932, –1,537.

Canadian Bankers Acceptance (ME)-CAD 1,000,000

	OPEN	HIGH	LOW	SETTLE	CHG	LIFETIME HIGH	LIFETIME LOW	OPEN INT
Mar	97.71	97.71	97.67	97.68	–0.02	97.78	93.77	70,087
June	97.78	97.78	97.72	97.75	–0.03	97.88	95.34	97,819
Sept	97.71	97.71	97.65	97.68	–0.03	97.81	94.22	35,605
Dec	97.51	97.51	97.45	97.47	–0.04	97.62	94.10	17,196
Mr05	97.21	97.21	97.16	97.18	–0.04	97.33	94.45	9,163
Sept	96.53	96.53	96.53	96.51	–0.04	96.64	95.21	1,200

Est vol 24,925; vol Tue 21,162; open int 238,828, +585.

10 Yr. Canadian Govt. Bonds (ME)-CAD 100,000

	OPEN	HIGH	LOW	SETTLE	CHG	LIFETIME HIGH	LIFETIME LOW	OPEN INT
Mar	110.58	110.64	110.07	110.39	–0.22	111.61	106.90	90,003

Est vol 6,222; vol Tue 12,898; open int 90,003, +6,036.

3 Yr. Commonwealth T-Bonds (SFE)-AUD 100,000								
Mar	94.38	94.48	94.37	94.47	0.09	94.56	93.96	609,295
Est vol 130,882; vol Tue 72,788; open int 609,295, +83,322.								

Euroyen (SGX)-¥100,000,000; pts of 100%								
Mar	99.91	99.91	99.91	99.91	...	99.92	98.19	60,509
June	99.91	99.91	99.91	99.92	0.01	99.92	99.45	71,194
Sept	99.89	99.90	99.89	99.90	0.01	99.90	99.34	43,155
Dec	99.87	99.87	99.87	99.87	...	99.87	99.22	45,234
Mr05	99.81	99.82	99.81	99.82	0.01	99.85	99.18	23,103
June	99.78	99.78	99.78	99.78	0.01	99.85	99.10	20,948
Sept	99.70	99.71	99.70	99.71	0.02	99.74	98.95	14,023
Dec	99.61	99.62	99.61	99.61	0.01	99.77	98.80	3,635
Mr06	99.50	99.50	99.50	99.50	0.01	99.76	98.84	3,405
June	99.42	99.42	99.42	99.43	0.02	99.75	98.55	1,380
Dec	99.23	99.23	99.23	99.23	0.02	99.71	98.35	1,851
Est vol 3,160; vol Tue 5,292; open int 295,306, −1,880.								

5 Yr. Euro-BOBL (EUREX)-€100,000; pts of 100%								
Mar	111.59	111.66	111.47	111.56	...	112.06	108.71	743,330
June	110.79	110.80	110.71	110.75	...	111.16	109.50	7,545
vol Wed 582,579; open int 750,875, +21,654.								

10 Yr. Euro-BUND (EUREX)-€100,000; pts of 100%								
Mar	114.30	114.45	114.15	114.26	−0.02	117.76	110.73	945,187
June	113.31	113.43	113.26	113.28	−0.01	114.11	110.62	27,345
vol Wed 841,211; open int 972,534, −23,916.								

2 Yr. Euro-SCHATZ (EUREX)-€100,000; pts of 100%								
Mar	106.18	106.20	106.13	106.17	...	106.35	104.95	683,537
June	105.80	105.84	105.79	105.80	...	105.88	105.21	28,066
vol Wed 437,442; open int 711,603, +22,620.								

Source: Reprinted by permission of Dow Jones, Inc., via Copyright Clearance Center, Inc.

6.3 TREASURY BOND FUTURES

Table 6.1 shows interest rate futures quotes as they appeared in the *Wall Street Journal* on February 5, 2004. One of the most popular long-term interest rate futures contracts is the Treasury bond futures contract traded on the Chicago Board of Trade (CBOT). In this contract, any government bond that has more than 15 years to maturity on the first day of the delivery month and is not callable within 15 years from that day can be delivered. As will be explained later in this section, the CBOT has developed a procedure for adjusting the price received by the party with the short position according to the particular bond delivered.

The Treasury note and 5-year Treasury note futures contract in the United States are also very popular. With Treasury note futures, any government bond (or note) with a maturity between $6\frac{1}{2}$ and 10 years can be delivered. In the 5-year Treasury note futures contract, the bond delivered has a life that is about 4 or 5 years.

The remaining discussion in this section focuses on CBOT Treasury bond futures. The Treasury note futures traded in the United States and many other futures contracts in the rest of the world are designed in a similar way to CBOT Treasury bond futures, so that many of the points we will make are applicable to these contracts as well.

Quotes

Treasury bond futures prices are quoted in the same way as the Treasury bond prices themselves (see Section 6.2). Table 6.1 shows that the settlement price on February 4, 2004, for the June 2004 contract was 110-03, or $110\frac{3}{32}$. One contract involves the delivery of \$100,000 face value of the bond. Thus, a \$1 change in the quoted futures price would lead to a \$1,000 change in the value of the futures contract. Delivery can take place at any time during the delivery month.

Conversion Factors

As mentioned, the Treasury bond futures contract allows the party with the short position to choose to deliver any bond that has a maturity of more than 15 years and that is not callable within 15 years. When a particular bond is delivered, a parameter known as its *conversion factor* defines the price received by the party with the short position. The quoted price applicable to the delivery is the product of the conversion factor and the most recent settlement price. Taking accrued interest into account, as described in Section 6.2, the cash received for each \$100 face value of bond delivered is

$$(\text{Settlement price} \times \text{Conversion factor}) + \text{Accrued interest}$$

Each contract is for the delivery of \$100,000 face value of bonds. Suppose the settlement price is 90-00, the conversion factor for the bond delivered is 1.3800, and the accrued interest on this bond at the time of delivery is \$3 per \$100 face value. The cash received by the party with the short position (and paid by the party with the long position) is then

$$(1.3800 \times 90.00) + 3.00 = \$127.20$$

per \$100 face value. A party with the short position in one contract would deliver bonds with a face value of \$100,000 and receive \$127,200.

The conversion factor for a bond is equal to the quoted price the bond would have per dollar of principal on the first day of the delivery month on the assumption that the interest rate for all maturities equals 6% per annum (with semiannual compounding). The bond maturity and the times to the coupon payment dates are rounded down to the nearest 3 months for the purposes of the calculation. The practice enables the CBOT to produce comprehensive tables. If, after rounding, the bond lasts for an exact number of 6-month periods, the first coupon is assumed to be paid in 6 months. If, after rounding, the bond does not last for an exact number of 6-month periods (i.e., there are an extra 3 months), the first coupon is assumed to be paid after 3 months and accrued interest is subtracted.

As a first example of these rules, consider a 10% coupon bond with 20 years and 2 months to maturity. For the purposes of calculating the conversion factor, the bond is assumed to have exactly 20 years to maturity. The first coupon payment is assumed to be made after 6 months. Coupon payments are then assumed to be made at 6-month intervals until the end of the 20 years when the principal payment is made. Assume that the face value is \$100. When the discount rate is 6% per annum with semiannual compounding (or 3% per 6 months), the value of the bond is

$$\sum_{i=1}^{40} \frac{5}{1.03^i} + \frac{100}{1.03^{40}} = \$146.23$$

Dividing by the face value gives a conversion factor of 1.4623.

As a second example of the rules, consider an 8% coupon bond with 18 years and 4 months to maturity. For the purposes of calculating the conversion factor, the bond is assumed to have exactly 18 years and 3 months to maturity. Discounting all the payments back to a point in time 3 months from today at 6% per annum (compounded semiannually) gives a value of

$$4 + \sum_{i=1}^{36} \frac{4}{1.03^i} + \frac{100}{1.03^{36}} = \$125.83$$

The interest rate for a 3-month period is $\sqrt{1.03} - 1$, or 1.4889%. Hence, discounting back to the present gives the bond's value as $125.83/1.014889 = \$123.99$. Subtracting the accrued interest of 2.0, this becomes \$121.99. The conversion factor is therefore 1.2199.

Cheapest-to-Deliver Bond

At any given time during the delivery month, there are many bonds that can be delivered in the CBOT Treasury bond futures contract. These vary widely as far as coupon and maturity are concerned. The party with the short position can choose which of the available bonds is "cheapest" to deliver. Because the party with the short position receives

$$(\text{Settlement price} \times \text{Conversion factor}) + \text{Accrued interest}$$

and the cost of purchasing a bond is

$$\text{Quoted bond price} + \text{Accrued interest}$$

the cheapest-to-deliver bond is the one for which

$$\text{Quoted bond price} - (\text{Settlement price} \times \text{Conversion factor})$$

is least. Once the party with the short position has decided to deliver, it can determine the cheapest-to-deliver bond by examining each of the bonds in turn.

Example 6.1

The party with the short position has decided to deliver and is trying to choose between the three bonds in Table 6.2. Assume the most recent settlement price is 93-08, or 93.25.

Table 6.2 Deliverable bonds in the Example 6.1.

Bond	*Quoted bond price ($)*	*Conversion factor*
1	99.50	1.0382
2	143.50	1.5188
3	119.75	1.2615

The cost of delivering each of the bonds is as follows:

Bond 1: $99.50 - (93.25 \times 1.0382) = \$2.69$

Bond 2: $143.50 - (93.25 \times 1.5188) = \$1.87$

Bond 3: $119.75 - (93.25 \times 1.2615) = \$2.12$

The cheapest-to-deliver bond is Bond 2.

A number of factors determine the cheapest-to-deliver bond. When bond yields are in excess of 6%, the conversion factor system tends to favor the delivery of low-coupon long-maturity bonds. When yields are less than 6%, the system tends to favor the delivery of high-coupon short-maturity bonds. Also, when the yield curve is upward-sloping, there is a tendency for bonds with a long time to maturity to be favored, whereas when it is downward-sloping, there is a tendency for bonds with a short time to maturity to be delivered.

In addition to the cheapest-to-deliver bond option, the party with a short position has an option known as the wild card play. This is described in Business Snapshot 6.2.

Business Snapshot 6.2 The Wild Card Play

Trading in the CBOT Treasury bond futures contract ceases at 2:00 p.m. Chicago time. However, Treasury bonds themselves continue trading in the spot market until 4:00 p.m. Furthermore, a trader with a short futures position has until 8:00 p.m. to issue to the clearinghouse a notice of intention to deliver. If the notice is issued, the invoice price is calculated on the basis of the settlement price that day. This is the price at which trading was conducted just before the closing bell at 2:00 p.m.

This practice gives rise to an option known as the *wild card play*. If bond prices decline after 2:00 p.m. on the first day of the delivery month, the party with the short position can issue a notice of intention to deliver at, say, 3:45 p.m. and proceed to buy cheapest-to-deliver bonds for delivery at the 2:00 p.m. futures price. If the bond price does not decline, the party with the short position keeps the position open and waits until the next day when the same strategy can be used.

As with the other options open to the party with the short position, the wild card play is not free. Its value is reflected in the futures price, which is lower than it would be without the option.

Determining the Futures Price

An exact theoretical futures price for the Treasury bond contract is difficult to determine because the short party's options concerned with the timing of delivery and choice of the bond that is delivered cannot easily be valued. However, if we assume that both the cheapest-to-deliver bond and the delivery date are known, the Treasury bond futures contract is a futures contract on a security providing the holder with known income.[1] Equation (5.2) then shows that the futures price, F_0, is related to the spot price, S_0, by

$$F_0 = (S_0 - I)e^{rT} \qquad \textbf{(6.1)}$$

where I is the present value of the coupons during the life of the futures contract, T is the time until the futures contract matures, and r is the risk-free interest rate applicable to a time period of length T.

Example 6.2

Suppose that, in a Treasury bond futures contract, it is known that the cheapest-to-deliver bond will be a 12% coupon bond with a conversion factor of 1.4000. Suppose also that it is known that delivery will take place in 270 days. Coupons are payable semiannually on the bond. As illustrated in Figure 6.1, the last coupon date was 60 days ago, the next coupon date is in 122 days, and the coupon date thereafter is in 305 days. The term structure is flat, and the rate of interest (with continuous compounding) is 10% per annum. Assume that the current quoted bond price is \$120. The cash price of the bond is obtained by adding to this quoted price the proportion of the next coupon payment that accrues to the

[1] In practice, for the purposes of determining the cheapest-to-deliver in this calculation, analysts usually assume that zero rates at the maturity of the futures contract will equal today's forward rates.

Figure 6.1 Time chart for Example 6.2.

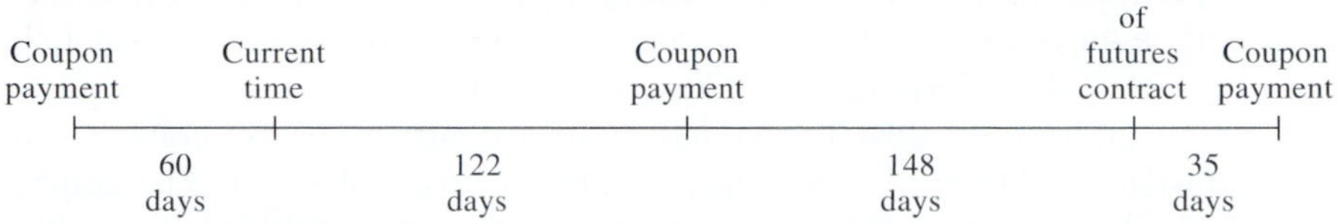

Coupon payment		Current time		Coupon payment		Maturity of futures contract		Coupon payment
	60 days		122 days		148 days		35 days	

holder. The cash price is therefore

$$120 + \frac{60}{60 + 122} \times 6 = 121.978$$

A coupon of \$6 will be received after 122 days (= 0.3342 years). The present value of this is

$$6e^{-0.1 \times 0.3342} = 5.803$$

The futures contract lasts for 270 days (= 0.7397 years). The cash futures price, if the contract were written on the 12% bond, would therefore be

$$(121.978 - 5.803)e^{0.1 \times 0.7397} = 125.094$$

At delivery, there are 148 days of accrued interest. The quoted futures price, if the contract were written on the 12% bond, is calculated by subtracting the accrued interest

$$125.094 - 6 \times \frac{148}{148 + 35} = 120.242$$

From the definition of the conversion factor, 1.4000 standard bonds are considered equivalent to each 12% bond. The quoted futures price should therefore be

$$\frac{120.242}{1.4000} = 85.887$$

6.4 EURODOLLAR FUTURES

The most popular interest rate futures contract in the United States is the 3-month Eurodollar futures contract traded on the Chicago Mercantile Exchange (CME). A Eurodollar is a dollar deposited in a US or foreign bank outside the United States. The Eurodollar interest rate is the rate of interest earned on Eurodollars deposited by one bank with another bank. It is essentially the same as the London Interbank Offer Rate (LIBOR) introduced in Chapter 4.

Three-month Eurodollar futures contracts are futures contracts on the 3-month (90-day) Eurodollar interest rate. They allow an investor to lock in an interest rate on \$1 million for a future 3-month period. The 3-month period to which the interest rate applies starts on the third Wednesday of the delivery month. The contracts have delivery months of March, June, September, and December for up to 10 years into the future. This means that in 2004 an investor can use Eurodollar futures to lock in an interest rate for 3-month periods that are as far into the future as 2014. (Table 6.1 shows quotes out to 2010.) Short-maturity contracts trade for months other than March, June, September, and December. For example, from Table 6.1 we see that Eurodollar futures with maturities in February, April, May, and July 2004 trade on February 4, 2004. However, these have relatively low open interest.

To understand how Eurodollar futures contracts work, consider the March 2005 contract in Table 6.1. This has a settlement price of 97.63. The contract ends on the third Wednesday of the delivery month. In the case of this contract, the third Wednesday of the delivery month is March 16, 2005. The contract is marked to market in the usual way until that date. However, on March 16, 2005, the settlement price is set equal to $100 - R$, where R is the actual 3-month Eurodollar interest rate on that day, expressed with quarterly compounding and an actual/360 day count convention. (Thus, if the 3-month Eurodollar interest rate on March 16, 2005, turned out to be 2%, the final settlement price would be 98.) There is a final marking to market reflecting this settlement price and all contracts are declared closed.

The contract is designed so that a 1 basis point (= 0.01) move in the futures quote corresponds to a gain or loss of $25 per contract. When a Eurodollar futures quote increases by 1 basis point, a trader who is long one contract gains $25 and a trader who is short one contract loses $25. Similarly, when the quote decreases by 1 basis point a trader who is long one contract loses $25 and a trader who is short one contract gains $25. This is consistent with the point made earlier: that the contract locks in an interest rate on $1 million dollars for 3 months. When an interest rate per year changes by 1 basis point, the interest earned on 1 million dollars for 3 months changes by

$$1{,}000{,}000 \times 0.0001 \times 0.25 = 25$$

or $25. Because the futures quote is 100 minus the futures interest rate, an investor who is long gains when interest rates fall and an investor who is short gains when interest rates rise.

Example 6.3

On February 4, 2004, an investor wants to lock in the interest rate that will be earned on $5 million for 3 months starting on March 16, 2005. The investor goes long five March05 Eurodollar futures contracts at 97.63. On March 16, 2005, the 3-month LIBOR interest rate is 2%, so that the final settlement price proves to be 98.00. The investor gains $5 \times 25 \times (9{,}800 - 9{,}763) = \$4{,}625$ on the long futures position. The interest earned on the $5 million for 3 months at 2% is

$$5{,}000{,}000 \times 0.25 \times 0.02 = 25{,}000$$

or $25,000. The gain on the futures contract brings this up to $29,625. This is the interest that would have been earned if the interest rate had been 2.37% ($5{,}000{,}000 \times 0.25 \times 0.0237 = 29{,}625$). This illustration shows that the futures trade has the effect of locking in an interest rate equal to 2.37%, or (100 − 97.63)%.

The exchange defines the contract price as

$$10{,}000[100 - 0.25(100 - Q)] \tag{6.2}$$

where Q is the quote. Thus, the settlement price of 97.63 for the March 2005 contract in

Table 6.1 corresponds to a contract price of

$$10{,}000[100 - 0.25(100 - 97.63)] = \$994{,}075$$

In Example 6.3, the final contract price is

$$10{,}000[100 - 0.25(100 - 98)] = \$995{,}000$$

and the difference between the initial and final contract price is \$925, so that an investor with a long position in five contracts gains 5×925 dollars, or \$4,625, as in Example 6.3. This is consistent with the "\$25 per 1 basis point move" rule.

We can see that the interest rate term structure in the United States was upward-sloping on February 4, 2004. The futures rate for a 3-month period beginning in March 17, 2004, was 1.16%; for a 3-month period beginning March 16, 2005, it was 2.37%; for a 3-month period beginning March 21, 2007, it was 4.51%; and for a 3-month period beginning March 17, 2010, it was 5.81%.

Other contracts similar to the CME Eurodollar futures contract trade on interest rates in other countries. As shown in Table 6.1, the CME trades Euroyen contracts. The London International Financial Futures and Options Exchange trades 3-month Euribor contracts (i.e., contracts on the 3-month LIBOR rate for the euro) and 3-month Euroswiss futures.

Forward vs. Futures Interest Rates

The Eurodollar futures contract is similar to a forward rate agreement (FRA: see Section 4.7) in that it locks in an interest rate for a future period. For short maturities (up to a year or so), the two contracts can be assumed to be the same and the Eurodollar futures interest rate can be assumed to be the same as the corresponding forward interest rate. For longer-dated contracts, differences between the contracts become important. Compare a Eurodollar futures contract on an interest rate for the period between times T_1 and T_2 with an FRA for the same period. The Eurodollar futures contract is settled daily. The final settlement is at time T_1 and reflects the realized interest rate for the period between times T_1 and T_2. By contrast the FRA is not settled daily and the final settlement reflecting the realized interest rate between times T_1 and T_2 is made at time T_2.[2]

There are therefore two components to the difference between a Eurodollar futures contract and an FRA. These are:

1. The difference between a Eurodollar futures contract and a similar contract where there is no daily settlement. The latter is a forward contract where a payoff equal to the difference between the forward interest rate and the realized interest rate is paid at time T_1.
2. The difference between a forward contract where there is settlement at time T_1 and a forward contract where there is settlement at time T_2.

These two components to the difference between the contracts cause some confusion in practice. Both decrease the forward rate relative to the futures rate, but for long-dated contracts the reduction caused by the second difference is much smaller than that

[2] As mentioned in Section 4.7, settlement may occur at time T_1, but it is then equal to the present value of the normal forward contract payoff at time T_2.

caused by the first. The reason why the first difference (daily settlement) decreases the forward rate follows from the arguments in Section 5.8. Suppose you have a contract where the payoff is $R_M - R_F$ at time T_1, where R_F is a predetermined rate for the period between T_1 and T_2, and R_M is the realized rate for this period, and you have the option to switch to daily settlement. In this case daily settlement leads to cash inflows when rates are high and cash outflows when rates are low. You would therefore find switching to daily settlement to be attractive because you tend to have more money in your margin account when rates are high. As a result the market would therefore set R_F higher for the daily settlement alternative (reducing your cumulative expected payoff). To put this the other way round, switching from daily settlement to settlement at time T_1 reduces R_F.

To understand the reason why the second difference reduces the forward rate, suppose that the payoff of $R_M - R_F$ is at time T_2 instead of T_1 (as it is for a regular FRA). If R_M is high, the payoff is positive. Because rates are high, the cost to you of having the payoff that you receive at time T_2 rather than time T_1 is relatively high. If R_M is low, the payoff is negative. Because rates are low, the benefit to you of having the payoff you make at time T_2 rather than time T_1 is relatively low. Overall you would rather have the payoff at time T_1. If it is at time T_2 rather than T_1, you must be compensated by a reduction in R_F.[3]

Analysts make what is known as a *convexity adjustment* to account for the total differences between the two rates. One popular adjustment is[4]

$$\text{Forward rate} = \text{Futures rate} - \tfrac{1}{2}\sigma^2 T_1 T_2 \tag{6.3}$$

where, as above, T_1 is the time to maturity of the futures contract and T_2 is the time to the maturity of the rate underlying the futures contract. The variable σ is the standard deviation of the change in the short-term interest rate in 1 year. Both rates are expressed with continuous compounding.[5] A typical value for σ is 1.2% or 0.012.

Example 6.4

Consider the situation where $\sigma = 0.012$ and we wish to calculate the forward rate when the 8-year Eurodollar futures price quote is 94. In this case $t_1 = 8$, $t_2 = 8.25$, and the convexity adjustment is

$$\tfrac{1}{2} \times 0.012^2 \times 8 \times 8.25 = 0.00475$$

or 0.475% (47.5 basis points). The futures rate is 6% per annum on an actual/360 basis with quarterly compounding. This corresponds to 1.5% per 90 days or an annual rate of $(365/90)\ln 1.015 = 6.038\%$ with continuous compounding and an actual/365 day count. The estimate of the forward rate given by equation (6.3), therefore, is $6.038 - 0.475 = 5.563\%$ per annum with continuous compounding. Table 6.3 shows how the size of the adjustment increases with the time to maturity.

---

[3] Quantifying the effect of this type of timing difference on the value of a derivative is discussed further in Chapter 27.

[4] See Technical Note 1 on the author's website for a proof of this.

[5] This formula is based on the Ho–Lee interest rate model, which will be discussed in Chapter 28. See T. S. Y. Ho and S.-B. Lee, "Term structure movements and pricing interest rate contingent claims," *Journal of Finance*, 41 (December 1986), 1011–29.

Table 6.3 Convexity adjustment for the futures rate in Example 6.4.

Maturity of futures (years)	*Convexity adjustments (basis points)*
2	3.2
4	12.2
6	27.0
8	47.5
10	73.8

We can see from Table 6.3 that the size of the adjustment is roughly proportional to the square of the time to maturity of the futures contract. Thus the convexity adjustment for the 8-year contract is approximately 16 times that for a 2-year contract.

Using Eurodollar Futures to Extend the LIBOR Zero Curve

The LIBOR zero curve out to 1 year is determined by the 1-month, 3-month, 6-month, and 12-month LIBOR rates. Once the convexity adjustment just described has been made, Eurodollar futures are often used to extend the zero curve. Suppose that the ith Eurodollar futures contract matures at time T_i ($i = 1, 2, \dots$). It is usually assumed that the forward interest rate calculated from the ith futures contract applies exactly to the period T_i to T_{i+1}. (In practice this is close to true.) This enables a bootstrap procedure to be used to determine zero rates. Suppose that F_i is the forward rate calculated from the ith Eurodollar futures contract and R_i is the zero rate for a maturity T_i. From equation (4.5), we have

$$F_i = \frac{R_{i+1}T_{i+1} - R_iT_i}{T_{i+1} - T_i}$$

so that

$$R_{i+1} = \frac{F_i(T_{i+1} - T_i) + R_iT_i}{T_{i+1}} \tag{6.4}$$

Other Euro rates such as Euroswiss, Euroyen, and Euribor are used in a similar way.

Example 6.5

The 400-day LIBOR zero rate has been calculated as 4.80% with continuous compounding and, from Eurodollar futures quotes, it has been calculated that (a) the forward rate for a 90-day period beginning in 400 days is 5.30% with continuous compounding, (b) the forward rate for a 90-day period beginning in 491 days is 5.50% with continuous compounding, and (c) the forward rate for a 90-day period beginning in 589 days is 5.60% with continuous compounding. We can use equation (6.4) to obtain the 491-day rate as

$$\frac{0.053 \times 91 + 0.048 \times 400}{491} = 0.04893$$

or 4.893%. Similarly we can use the second forward rate to obtain the 589-day rate as

$$\frac{0.055 \times 98 + 0.04893 \times 491}{589} = 0.04994$$

or 4.994%. The next forward rate of 5.60% would be used to determine the zero curve out to the maturity of the next Eurodollar futures contract. (Note that, even though the rate underlying the Eurodollar futures contract is a 90-day rate, it is assumed to apply to the 91 or 98 days elapsing between Eurodollar contract maturities.)

6.5 DURATION-BASED HEDGING STRATEGIES

We discussed duration in Section 4.8. Consider the situation where a position in an asset that is interest rate dependent, such as a bond portfolio or a money market security, is being hedged using an interest rate futures contract. Define:

F_C: Contract price for the interest rate futures contract

D_F: Duration of the asset underlying the futures contract at the maturity of the futures contract

P: Forward value of the portfolio being hedged at the maturity of the hedge (in practice, this is usually assumed to be the same as the value of the portfolio today)

D_P: Duration of the portfolio at the maturity of the hedge

If we assume that the change in the yield, Δy, is the same for all maturities, which means that only parallel shifts in the yield curve can occur, it is approximately true that

$$\Delta P = -PD_P \, \Delta y$$

To a reasonable approximation, it is also true that

$$\Delta F_C = -F_C D_F \, \Delta y$$

The number of contracts required to hedge against an uncertain Δy, therefore, is

$$N^* = \frac{PD_P}{F_C D_F} \qquad \textbf{(6.5)}$$

This is the *duration-based hedge ratio*. It is sometimes also called the *price sensitivity hedge ratio*.[6] Using it has the effect of making the duration of the entire position zero.

When the hedging instrument is a Treasury bond futures contract, the hedger must base D_F on an assumption that one particular bond will be delivered. This means that the hedger must estimate which of the available bonds is likely to be cheapest to deliver at the time the hedge is put in place. If, subsequently, the interest rate environment changes so that it looks as though a different bond will be cheapest to deliver, then the hedge has to be adjusted and its performance may be worse than anticipated.

When hedges are constructed using interest rate futures, it is important to bear in

[6] For a more detailed discussion of equation (6.5), see R. J. Rendleman, "Duration-Based Hedging with Treasury Bond Futures," *Journal of Fixed Income* 9, 1 (June 1999): 84–91.

mind that interest rates and futures prices move in opposite directions. When interest rates go up, an interest rate futures price goes down. When interest rates go down, the reverse happens, and the interest rate futures price goes up. Thus, a company in a position to lose money if interest rates drop should hedge by taking a long futures position. Similarly, a company in a position to lose money if interest rates rise should hedge by taking a short futures position.

The hedger tries to choose the futures contract so that the duration of the underlying asset is as close as possible to the duration of the asset being hedged. Eurodollar futures tend to be used for exposures to short-term interest rates, whereas Treasury bond and Treasury note futures contracts are used for exposures to longer-term rates.

Example 6.6

It is August 2 and a fund manager with $10 million invested in government bonds is concerned that interest rates are expected to be highly volatile over the next 3 months. The fund manager decides to use the December T-bond futures contract to hedge the value of the portfolio. The current futures price is 93-02, or 93.0625. Because each contract is for the delivery of $100,000 face value of bonds, the futures contract price is $93,062.50.

We suppose that the duration of the bond portfolio in 3 months will be 6.80 years. The cheapest-to-deliver bond in the T-bond contract is expected to be a 20-year 12% per annum coupon bond. The yield on this bond is currently 8.80% per annum, and the duration will be 9.20 years at maturity of the futures contract.

The fund manager requires a short position in T-bond futures to hedge the bond portfolio. If interest rates go up, a gain will be made on the short futures position, but a loss will be made on the bond portfolio. If interest rates decrease, a loss will be made on the short position, but there will be a gain on the bond portfolio. The number of bond futures contracts that should be shorted can be calculated from equation (6.5) as

$$\frac{10{,}000{,}000}{93{,}062.50} \times \frac{6.80}{9.20} = 79.42$$

Rounding to the nearest whole number, the portfolio manager should short 79 contracts.

6.6 HEDGING PORTFOLIOS OF ASSETS AND LIABILITIES

Financial institutions frequently attempt to hedge themselves against interest rate risk by ensuring that the average duration of their assets equals the average duration of their liabilities. (The liabilities can be regarded as short positions in bonds.) This strategy is known as *duration matching* or *portfolio immunization*. When implemented, it ensures that a small parallel shift in interest rates will have little effect on the value of the portfolio of assets and liabilities. The gain (loss) on the assets should offset the loss (gain) on the liabilities.

Duration matching does not immunize a portfolio against nonparallel shifts in the zero curve. This is a weakness of the approach. In practice, short-term rates are usually more volatile than, and are not perfectly correlated with, long-term rates. Sometimes it

Business Snapshot 6.3 Asset–Liability Management by Banks

In the 1960s interest rates were low and not very volatile. Many banks got into the habit of accepting short-term deposits and making long-term loans. In the 1970s interest rates rose and some of these banks found that they were funding the low-interest long-term loans made in the 1960s with relatively expensive short-term deposits. As a result there were some spectacular bank failures.

The asset–liability management (ALM) committees of banks now monitor their exposure to interest rates very carefully. Matching the durations of assets and liabilities is a first step, but this does not protect a bank against nonparallel shifts in the yield curve. A popular approach is known as *GAP management*. This involves dividing the zero-coupon yield curve into segments, known as *buckets*. The first bucket might be 0 to 1 month, the second 1 to 3 months, and so on. The ALM committee then investigates the effect on the values of both assets and liabilities of the zero rates corresponding to one bucket changing while those corresponding to all other buckets staying the same.

If there is a mismatch, corrective action is usually taken. Luckily banks today have many more tools to manage their exposures to interest rates than they had in the 1960s. These tools include swaps, FRAs, bond futures, Eurodollar futures, and other interest rate derivatives.

even happens that short- and long-term rates move in opposite directions to each other. Duration matching is therefore only a first step and financial institutions have developed other tools to help them manage their interest rate exposure. See Business Snapshot 6.3.

SUMMARY

Two very popular interest rate contracts are the Treasury bond and Eurodollar futures contracts that trade in the United States. In the Treasury bond futures contracts, the party with the short position has a number of interesting delivery options:

1. Delivery can be made on any day during the delivery month.
2. There are a number of alternative bonds that can be delivered.
3. On any day during the delivery month, the notice of intention to deliver at the 2:00 p.m. settlement price can be made any time up to 8:00 p.m.

These options all tend to reduce the futures price.

The Eurodollar futures contract is a contract on the 3-month rate on the third Wednesday of the delivery month. Eurodollar futures are frequently used to estimate LIBOR forward rates for the purpose of constructing a LIBOR zero curve. When long-dated contracts are used in this way, it is important to make what is termed a convexity adjustment to allow for the marking to market in the futures contract.

The concept of duration is important in hedging interest rate risk. It enables a hedger to assess the sensitivity of a bond portfolio to small parallel shifts in the yield curve. It also enables the hedger to assess the sensitivity of an interest rate futures price to small changes in the yield curve. The number of futures contracts necessary to protect the bond portfolio against small parallel shifts in the yield curve can therefore be calculated.

The key assumption underlying the duration-based hedging scheme is that all interest rates change by the same amount. This means that only parallel shifts in the term structure are allowed for. In practice, short-term interest rates are generally more volatile than are long-term interest rates, and hedge performance is liable to be poor if the duration of the bond underlying the futures contract differs markedly from the duration of the asset being hedged.

FURTHER READING

Burghardt, G., and W. Hoskins. "The Convexity Bias in Eurodollar Futures," *Risk*, 8, 3 (1995): 63–70.

Duffie, D. "Debt Management and Interest Rate Risk," in W. Beaver and G. Parker (eds.), *Risk Management: Challenges and Solutions*. New York: McGraw-Hill, 1994.

Grinblatt, M., and N. Jegadeesh. "The Relative Price of Eurodollar Futures and Forward Contracts," *Journal of Finance*, 51, 4 (September 1996): 1499–1522.

Questions and Problems (Answers in Solutions Manual)

6.1. A US Treasury bond pays a 7% coupon on January 7 and July 7. How much interest accrues per $100 of principal to the bondholder between July 7, 2004, and August 9, 2004? How would your answer be different if it were a corporate bond?

6.2. It is January 9, 2005. The price of a Treasury bond with a 12% coupon that matures on October 12, 2009, is quoted as 102-07. What is the cash price?

6.3. How is the conversion factor of a bond calculated by the Chicago Board of Trade? How is it used?

6.4. A Eurodollar futures price changes from 96.76 to 96.82. What is the gain or loss to an investor who is long two contracts?

6.5. What is the purpose of the convexity adjustment made to Eurodollar futures rates? Why is the convexity adjustment necessary?

6.6. The 350-day LIBOR rate is 3% with continuous compounding and the forward rate calculated from a Eurodollar futures contract that matures in 350 days is 3.2% with continuous compounding. Estimate the 440-day zero rate.

6.7. It is January 30. You are managing a bond portfolio worth $6 million. The duration of the portfolio in 6 months will be 8.2 years. The September Treasury bond futures price is currently 108-15, and the cheapest-to-deliver bond will have a duration of 7.6 years in September. How should you hedge against changes in interest rates over the next 6 months?

6.8. The price of a 90-day Treasury bill is quoted as 10.00. What continuously compounded return (on an actual/365 basis) does an investor earn on the Treasury bill for the 90-day period?

6.9. It is May 5, 2005. The quoted price of a government bond with a 12% coupon that matures on July 27, 2011, is 110-17. What is the cash price?

6.10. Suppose that the Treasury bond futures price is 101-12. Which of the following four bonds is cheapest to deliver?

Bond	*Price*	*Conversion factor*
1	125-05	1.2131
2	142-15	1.3792
3	115-31	1.1149
4	144-02	1.4026

6.11. It is July 30, 2005. The cheapest-to-deliver bond in a September 2005 Treasury bond futures contract is a 13% coupon bond, and delivery is expected to be made on September 30, 2005. Coupon payments on the bond are made on February 4 and August 4 each year. The term structure is flat, and the rate of interest with semiannual compounding is 12% per annum. The conversion factor for the bond is 1.5. The current quoted bond price is \$110. Calculate the quoted futures price for the contract.

6.12. An investor is looking for arbitrage opportunities in the Treasury bond futures market. What complications are created by the fact that the party with a short position can choose to deliver any bond with a maturity of over 15 years?

6.13. Suppose that the 9-month LIBOR interest rate is 8% per annum and the 6-month LIBOR interest rate is 7.5% per annum (both with actual/365 and continuous compounding). Estimate the 3-month Eurodollar futures price quote for a contract maturing in 6 months.

6.14. Suppose that the 300-day LIBOR zero rate is 4% and Eurodollar quotes for contracts maturing in 300, 398, and 489 days are 95.83, 95.62, and 95.48. Calculate 398-day and 489-day LIBOR zero rates. Assume no difference between forward and futures rates for the purposes of your calculations.

6.15. Suppose that a bond portfolio with a duration of 12 years is hedged using a futures contract in which the underlying asset has a duration of 4 years. What is likely to be the impact on the hedge of the fact that the 12-year rate is less volatile than the 4-year rate?

6.16. Suppose that it is February 20 and a treasurer realizes that on July 17 the company will have to issue \$5 million of commercial paper with a maturity of 180 days. If the paper were issued today, the company would realize \$4,820,000. (In other words, the company would receive \$4,820,000 for its paper and have to redeem it at \$5,000,000 in 180 days' time.) The September Eurodollar futures price is quoted as 92.00. How should the treasurer hedge the company's exposure?

6.17. On August 1, a portfolio manager has a bond portfolio worth \$10 million. The duration of the portfolio in October will be 7.1 years. The December Treasury bond futures price is currently 91-12 and the cheapest-to-deliver bond will have a duration of 8.8 years at maturity. How should the portfolio manager immunize the portfolio against changes in interest rates over the next 2 months?

6.18. How can the portfolio manager change the duration of the portfolio to 3.0 years in Problem 6.17?

6.19. Between October 30, 2006, and November 1, 2006, you have a choice between owning a US government bond paying a 12% coupon and a US corporate bond paying a 12% coupon. Consider carefully the day count conventions discussed in this chapter and decide which of the two bonds you would prefer to own. Ignore the risk of default.

6.20. Suppose that a Eurodollar futures quote is 88 for a contract maturing in 60 days. What is the LIBOR forward rate for the 60- to 150-day period? Ignore the difference between futures and forwards for the purposes of this question.

6.21. The 3-month Eurodollar futures price for a contract maturing in 6 years is quoted as 95.20. The standard deviation of the change in the short-term interest rate in 1 year is 1.1%. Estimate the forward LIBOR interest rate for the period between 6.00 and 6.25 years in the future.

6.22. Explain why the forward interest rate is less than the corresponding futures interest rate calculated from a Eurodollar futures contract.

Assignment Questions

6.23. Assume that a bank can borrow or lend money at the same interest rate in the LIBOR market. The 90-day rate is 10% per annum, and the 180-day rate is 10.2% per annum, both expressed with continuous compounding and actual/actual day count. The Eurodollar futures price for a contract maturing in 91 days is quoted as 89.5. What arbitrage opportunities are open to the bank?

6.24. A Canadian company wishes to create a Canadian LIBOR futures contract from a US Eurodollar futures contract and forward contracts on foreign exchange. Using an example, explain how the company should proceed. For the purposes of this problem, assume that a futures contract is the same as a forward contract.

6.25. The futures price for the June 2005 CBOT bond futures contract is 118-23.
- (a) Calculate the conversion factor for a bond maturing on January 1, 2021, paying a coupon of 10%.
- (b) Calculate the conversion factor for a bond maturing on October 1, 2026, paying a coupon of 7%.
- (c) Suppose that the quoted prices of the bonds in (a) and (b) are 169.00 and 136.00, respectively. Which bond is cheaper to deliver?
- (d) Assuming that the cheapest-to-deliver bond is actually delivered, what is the cash price received for the bond?

6.26. A portfolio manager plans to use a Treasury bond futures contract to hedge a bond portfolio over the next 3 months. The portfolio is worth $100 million and will have a duration of 4.0 years in 3 months. The futures price is 122, and each futures contract is on $100,000 of bonds. The bond that is expected to be cheapest to deliver will have a duration of 9.0 years at the maturity of the futures contract. What position in futures contracts is required?
- (a) What adjustments to the hedge are necessary if after 1 month the bond that is expected to be cheapest to deliver changes to one with a duration of 7 years?
- (b) Suppose that all rates increase over the next 3 months, but long-term rates increase less than short-term and medium-term rates. What is the effect of this on the performance of the hedge?

CHAPTER 7 Swaps

The first swap contracts were negotiated in the early 1980s. Since then the market has seen phenomenal growth. Swaps now occupy a position of central importance in the over-the-counter derivatives market.

A swap is an agreement between two companies to exchange cash flows in the future. The agreement defines the dates when the cash flows are to be paid and the way in which they are to be calculated. Usually the calculation of the cash flows involves the future value of an interest rate, an exchange rate, or other market variable.

A forward contract can be viewed as a simple example of a swap. Suppose it is March 1, 2006, and a company enters into a forward contract to buy 100 ounces of gold for $400 per ounce in 1 year. The company can sell the gold in 1 year as soon as it is received. The forward contract is therefore equivalent to a swap where the company agrees that on March 1, 2007, it will pay $40,000 and receive $100S$, where S is the market price of 1 ounce of gold on that date.

Whereas a forward contract is equivalent to the exchange of cash flows on just one future date, swaps typically lead to cash flow exchanges taking place on several future dates. In this chapter we examine how swaps are used and how they are valued. Our discussion centers on two popular swaps: plain vanilla interest rate swaps and fixed-for-fixed currency swaps. Other types of swaps are discussed in Chapter 30.

7.1 MECHANICS OF INTEREST RATE SWAPS

The most common type of swap is a "plain vanilla" interest rate swap. With this swap a company agrees to pay cash flows equal to interest at a predetermined fixed rate on a notional principal for a number of years. In return, it receives interest at a floating rate on the same notional principal for the same period of time.

LIBOR

The floating rate in most interest rate swap agreements is the London Interbank Offer Rate (LIBOR). We introduced this in Chapter 4. It is the rate of interest at which a bank is prepared to deposit money with other banks in the Eurocurrency market. Typically, 1-month, 3-month, 6-month, and 12-month LIBOR are quoted in all major currencies.

Just as prime is often the reference rate of interest for floating-rate loans in the domestic financial market, LIBOR is a reference rate of interest for loans in international financial markets. To understand how it is used, consider a 5-year bond with a rate of interest specified as 6-month LIBOR plus 0.5% per annum. The life of the bond is divided into 10 periods, each 6 months in length. For each period, the rate of interest is set at 0.5% per annum above the 6-month LIBOR rate at the beginning of the period. Interest is paid at the end of the period.

Illustration

Consider a hypothetical 3-year swap initiated on March 5, 2004, between Microsoft and Intel. We suppose Microsoft agrees to pay to Intel an interest rate of 5% per annum on a notional principal of $100 million, and in return Intel agrees to pay Microsoft the 6-month LIBOR rate on the same notional principal. Microsoft is the *fixed-rate payer*; Intel is the *floating-rate payer*. We assume the agreement specifies that payments are to be exchanged every 6 months and that the 5% interest rate is quoted with semiannual compounding. This swap is represented diagrammatically in Figure 7.1.

The first exchange of payments would take place on September 5, 2004, 6 months after the initiation of the agreement. Microsoft would pay Intel $2.5 million. This is the interest on the $100 million principal for 6 months at 5%. Intel would pay Microsoft interest on the $100 million principal at the 6-month LIBOR rate prevailing 6 months prior to September 5, 2004—that is, on March 5, 2004. Suppose that the 6-month LIBOR rate on March 5, 2004, is 4.2%. Intel pays Microsoft $0.5 \times 0.042 \times \$100 =$ $2.1 million.[1] Note that there is no uncertainty about this first exchange of payments because it is determined by the LIBOR rate at the time the contract is entered into.

The second exchange of payments would take place on March 5, 2005, a year after the initiation of the agreement. Microsoft would pay $2.5 million to Intel. Intel would pay interest on the $100 million principal to Microsoft at the 6-month LIBOR rate prevailing 6 months prior to March 5, 2005—that is, on September 5, 2004. Suppose that the 6-month LIBOR rate on September 5, 2004, is 4.8%. Intel pays $0.5 \times 0.048 \times \$100 =$ $2.4 million to Microsoft.

In total, there are six exchanges of payment on the swap. The fixed payments are always $2.5 million. The floating-rate payments on a payment date are calculated using the 6-month LIBOR rate prevailing 6 months before the payment date. An interest rate swap is generally structured so that one side remits the difference between the two payments to the other side. In our example, Microsoft would pay Intel $0.4 million (= $2.5 million – $2.1 million) on September 5, 2004, and $0.1 million (= $2.5 million – $2.4 million) on March 5, 2005.

Figure 7.1 Interest rate swap between Microsoft and Intel.

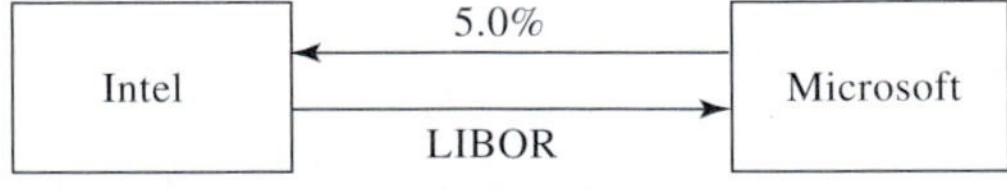

[1] The calculations here are simplified in that they ignore day count conventions. This point is discussed in more detail later in the chapter.

Table 7.1 Cash flows (millions of dollars) to Microsoft in a $100 million 3-year interest rate swap when a fixed rate of 5% is paid and LIBOR is received.

Date	*Six-month LIBOR rate (%)*	*Floating cash flow received*	*Fixed cash flow paid*	*Net cash flow*
Mar. 5, 2004	4.20			
Sept. 5, 2004	4.80	+2.10	−2.50	−0.40
Mar. 5, 2005	5.30	+2.40	−2.50	−0.10
Sept. 5, 2005	5.50	+2.65	−2.50	+0.15
Mar. 5, 2006	5.60	+2.75	−2.50	+0.25
Sept. 5, 2006	5.90	+2.80	−2.50	+0.30
Mar. 5, 2007		+2.95	−2.50	+0.45

Table 7.1 provides a complete example of the payments made under the swap for one particular set of 6-month LIBOR rates. The table shows the swap cash flows from the perspective of Microsoft. Note that the $100 million principal is used only for the calculation of interest payments. The principal itself is not exchanged. This is why it is termed the *notional principal.*

If the principal were exchanged at the end of the life of the swap, the nature of the deal would not be changed in any way. The principal is the same for both the fixed and floating payments. Exchanging $100 million for $100 million at the end of the life of the swap is a transaction that would have no financial value to either Microsoft or Intel. Table 7.2 shows the cash flows in Table 7.1 with a final exchange of principal added in. This provides an interesting way of viewing the swap. The cash flows in the third column of this table are the cash flows from a long position in a floating-rate bond. The cash flows in the fourth column of the table are the cash flows from a short position in a fixed-rate bond. The table shows that the swap can be regarded as the exchange of a fixed-rate bond for a floating-rate bond. Microsoft, whose position is described by Table 7.2, is long a floating-rate bond and short a fixed-rate bond. Intel is long a fixed-rate bond and short a floating-rate bond.

Table 7.2 Cash flows (millions of dollars) from Table 7.1 when there is a final exchange of principal.

Date	*Six-month LIBOR rate (%)*	*Floating cash flow received*	*Fixed cash flow paid*	*Net cash flow*
Mar. 5, 2004	4.20			
Sept. 5, 2004	4.80	+2.10	−2.50	−0.40
Mar. 5, 2005	5.30	+2.40	−2.50	−0.10
Sept. 5, 2005	5.50	+2.65	−2.50	+0.15
Mar. 5, 2006	5.60	+2.75	−2.50	+0.25
Sept. 5, 2006	5.90	+2.80	−2.50	+0.30
Mar. 5, 2007		+102.95	−102.50	+0.45

This characterization of the cash flows in the swap helps to explain why the floating rate in the swap is set 6 months before it is paid. On a floating-rate bond, interest is generally set at the beginning of the period to which it will apply and is paid at the end of the period. The calculation of the floating-rate payments in a "plain vanilla" interest rate swap such as the one in Table 7.2 reflects this.

Using the Swap to Transform a Liability

For Microsoft, the swap could be used to transform a floating-rate loan into a fixed-rate loan. Suppose that Microsoft has arranged to borrow $100 million at LIBOR plus 10 basis points. (One basis point is one-hundredth of 1%, so the rate is LIBOR plus 0.1%.) After Microsoft has entered into the swap, it has the following three sets of cash flows:

1. It pays LIBOR plus 0.1% to its outside lenders.
2. It receives LIBOR under the terms of the swap.
3. It pays 5% under the terms of the swap.

These three sets of cash flows net out to an interest rate payment of 5.1%. Thus, for Microsoft, the swap could have the effect of transforming borrowings at a floating rate of LIBOR plus 10 basis points into borrowings at a fixed rate of 5.1%.

For Intel, the swap could have the effect of transforming a fixed-rate loan into a floating-rate loan. Suppose that Intel has a 3-year $100 million loan outstanding on which it pays 5.2%. After it has entered into the swap, it has the following three sets of cash flows:

1. It pays 5.2% to its outside lenders.
2. It pays LIBOR under the terms of the swap.
3. It receives 5% under the terms of the swap.

These three sets of cash flows net out to an interest rate payment of LIBOR plus 0.2% (or LIBOR plus 20 basis points). Thus, for Intel, the swap could have the effect of transforming borrowings at a fixed rate of 5.2% into borrowings at a floating rate of LIBOR plus 20 basis points. These potential uses of the swap by Intel and Microsoft are illustrated in Figure 7.2.

Using the Swap to Transform an Asset

Swaps can also be used to transform the nature of an asset. Consider Microsoft in our example. The swap could have the effect of transforming an asset earning a fixed rate of interest into an asset earning a floating rate of interest. Suppose that Microsoft owns $100 million in bonds that will provide interest at 4.7% per annum over the next 3 years.

Figure 7.2 Microsoft and Intel use the swap to transform a liability.

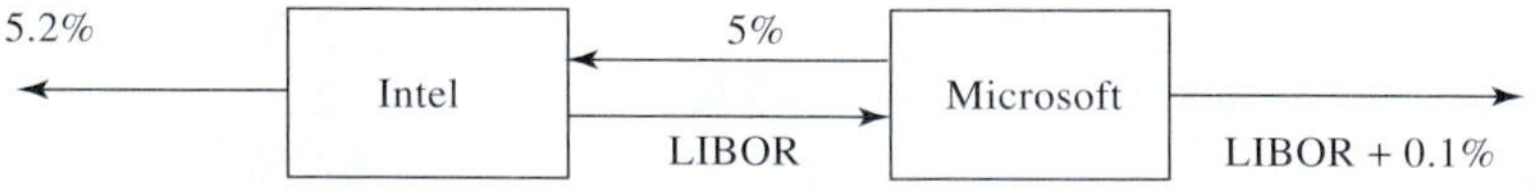

Figure 7.3 Microsoft and Intel use the swap to transform an asset.

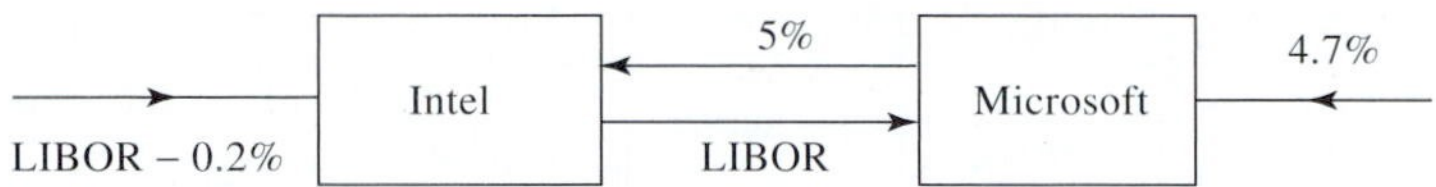

After Microsoft has entered into the swap, it has the following three sets of cash flows:

1. It receives 4.7% on the bonds.
2. It receives LIBOR under the terms of the swap.
3. It pays 5% under the terms of the swap.

These three sets of cash flows net out to an interest rate inflow of LIBOR minus 30 basis points. Thus, one possible use of the swap for Microsoft is to transform an asset earning 4.7% into an asset earning LIBOR minus 30 basis points.

Next, consider Intel. The swap could have the effect of transforming an asset earning a floating rate of interest into an asset earning a fixed rate of interest. Suppose that Intel has an investment of $100 million that yields LIBOR minus 20 basis points. After it has entered into the swap, it has the following three sets of cash flows:

1. It receives LIBOR minus 20 basis points on its investment.
2. It pays LIBOR under the terms of the swap.
3. It receives 5% under the terms of the swap.

These three sets of cash flows net out to an interest rate inflow of 4.8%. Thus, one possible use of the swap for Intel is to transform an asset earning LIBOR minus 20 basis points into an asset earning 4.8%. These potential uses of the swap by Intel and Microsoft are illustrated in Figure 7.3.

Role of Financial Intermediary

Usually two nonfinancial companies such as Intel and Microsoft do not get in touch directly to arrange a swap in the way indicated in Figures 7.2 and 7.3. They each deal with a financial intermediary such as a bank or other financial institution. "Plain vanilla" fixed-for-floating swaps on US interest rates are usually structured so that the financial institution earns about 3 or 4 basis points (0.03% or 0.04%) on a pair of offsetting transactions.

Figure 7.4 shows what the role of the financial institution might be in the situation in Figure 7.2. The financial institution enters into two offsetting swap transactions with

Figure 7.4 Interest rate swap from Figure 7.2 when financial institution is involved.

Figure 7.5 Interest rate swap from Figure 7.3 when financial institution is involved.

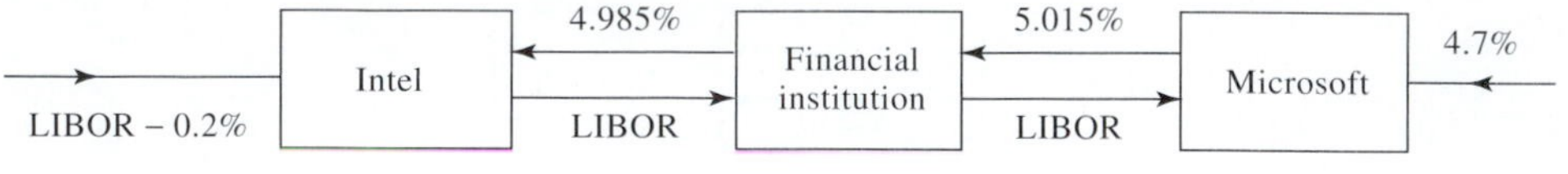

Intel and Microsoft. Assuming that both companies honor their obligations, the financial institution is certain to make a profit of 0.03% (3 basis points) per year multiplied by the notional principal of $100 million. This amounts to $30,000 per year for the 3-year period. Microsoft ends up borrowing at 5.115% (instead of 5.1%, as in Figure 7.2), and Intel ends up borrowing at LIBOR plus 21.5 basis points (instead of at LIBOR plus 20 basis points, as in Figure 7.2).

Figure 7.5 illustrates the role of the financial institution in the situation in Figure 7.3. The swap is the same as before and the financial institution is certain to make a profit of 3 basis points if neither company defaults. Microsoft ends up earning LIBOR minus 31.5 basis points (instead of LIBOR minus 30 basis points, as in Figure 7.3), and Intel ends up earning 4.785% (instead of 4.8%, as in Figure 7.3).

Note that in each case the financial institution has two separate contracts: one with Intel and the other with Microsoft. In most instances, Intel will not even know that the financial institution has entered into an offsetting swap with Microsoft, and vice versa. If one of the companies defaults, the financial institution still has to honor its agreement with the other company. The 3-basis-point spread earned by the financial institution is partly to compensate it for the risk that one of the two companies will default on the swap payments.

Market Makers

In practice, it is unlikely that two companies will contact a financial institution at the same time and want to take opposite positions in exactly the same swap. For this reason, many large financial institutions act as market makers for swaps. This means that they are prepared to enter into a swap without having an offsetting swap with another counterparty.[2] Market makers must carefully quantify and hedge the risks they are taking. Bonds, forward rate agreements, and interest rate futures are examples of the instruments that can be used for hedging by swap market makers. Table 7.3 shows quotes for plain vanilla US dollar swaps that might be posted by a market maker.[3] As mentioned earlier, the bid–offer spread is 3 to 4 basis points. The average of the bid and offer fixed rates is known as the *swap rate*. This is shown in the final column of Table 7.3.

Consider a new swap where the fixed rate equals the current swap rate. We can reasonably assume that the value of this swap is zero. (Why else would a market maker choose bid–offer quotes centered on the swap rate?) In Table 7.2 we saw that a swap can

[2] This is sometimes referred to as *warehousing* swaps.

[3] The standard swap in the United States is one where fixed payments made every 6 months are exchanged for floating LIBOR payments made every 3 months. In Table 7.1 we assumed that fixed and floating payments are exchanged every 6 months. As we shall see later, the fixed rate should in theory be the same, regardless of whether floating payments are made every 3 or every 6 months.

Table 7.3 Bid and offer fixed rates in the swap market and swap rates (percent per annum).

Maturity (years)	*Bid*	*Offer*	*Swap rate*
2	6.03	6.06	6.045
3	6.21	6.24	6.225
4	6.35	6.39	6.370
5	6.47	6.51	6.490
7	6.65	6.68	6.665
10	6.83	6.87	6.850

be characterized as the difference between a fixed-rate bond and a floating-rate bond. Define:

B_{fix}: Value of fixed-rate bond underlying the swap we are considering

B_{fl}: Value of floating-rate bond underlying the swap we are considering

Since the swap is worth zero, it follows that

$$B_{\text{fix}} = B_{\text{fl}} \tag{7.1}$$

We will use this result later in the chapter when discussing how the LIBOR/swap zero curve is determined.

7.2 DAY COUNT ISSUES

We discussed day count conventions in Section 6.1. The day count conventions affect payments on a swap, and some of the numbers calculated in the examples we have given do not exactly reflect these day count conventions. Consider, for example, the 6-month LIBOR payments in Table 7.1. Because it is a money market rate, 6-month LIBOR is quoted on an actual/360 basis. The first floating payment in Table 7.1, based on the LIBOR rate of 4.2%, is shown as \$2.10 million. Because there are 184 days between March 5, 2004, and September 5, 2004, it should be

$$100 \times 0.042 \times \frac{184}{360} = \$2.1467 \text{ million}$$

In general, a LIBOR-based floating-rate cash flow on a swap payment date is calculated as $LRn/360$, where L is the principal, R is the relevant LIBOR rate, and n is the number of days since the last payment date.

The fixed rate that is paid in a swap transaction is similarly quoted with a particular day count basis being specified. As a result, the fixed payments may not be exactly equal on each payment date. The fixed rate is usually quoted as actual/365 or 30/360. It is not therefore directly comparable with LIBOR because it applies to a full year. To make the rates comparable, either the 6-month LIBOR rate must be multiplied by 365/360 or the fixed rate must be multiplied by 360/365.

For ease of exposition, we will ignore day count issues in the calculations in the rest of this chapter.

Business Snapshot 7.1 Extract from Hypothetical Swap Confirmation

Trade date:	27-February-2004
Effective date:	5-March-2004
Business day convention (all dates):	Following business day
Holiday calendar:	US
Termination date:	5-March-2007
Fixed amounts	
Fixed-rate payer:	Microsoft
Fixed-rate notional principal:	USD 100 million
Fixed rate:	5.015% per annum
Fixed-rate day count convention:	Actual/365
Fixed-rate payment dates:	Each 5-March and 5-September, commencing 5-September-2004, up to and including 5-March-2007
Floating amounts	
Floating-rate payer:	Goldman Sachs
Floating-rate notional principal:	USD 100 million
Floating rate:	USD 6-month LIBOR
Floating-rate day count convention:	Actual/360
Floating-rate payment dates:	Each 5-March and 5-September, commencing 5-September-2004, up to and including 5-March-2007

7.3 CONFIRMATIONS

A *confirmation* is the legal agreement underlying a swap and is signed by representatives of the two parties. The drafting of confirmations has been facilitated by the work of the International Swaps and Derivatives Association (ISDA) in New York. This organization has produced a number of Master Agreements that consist of clauses defining in some detail the terminology used in swap agreements, what happens in the event of default by either side, and so on. In Business Snapshot 7.1, we show a possible extract from the confirmation for the swap shown in Figure 7.4 between Microsoft and a financial institution (assumed here to be Goldman Sachs). Almost certainly, the full confirmation would state that the provisions of an ISDA Master Agreement apply to the contract.

The confirmation specifies that the following business day convention is to be used and that the US calendar determines which days are business days and which days are holidays. This means that, if a payment date falls on a weekend or a US holiday, the payment is made on the next business day.[4] September 5, 2004, is a Sunday. The first

[4] Another business day convention that is sometimes specified is the *modified following* business day convention, which is the same as the following business day convention except that, when the next business day falls in a different month from the specified day, the payment is made on the immediately preceding business day. *Preceding* and *modified preceding* business day conventions are defined analogously.

exchange of payments in the swap between Microsoft and Goldman Sachs is therefore on Monday September 6, 2004.

7.4 THE COMPARATIVE-ADVANTAGE ARGUMENT

An explanation commonly put forward to explain the popularity of swaps concerns comparative advantages. Consider the use of an interest rate swap to transform a liability. Some companies, it is argued, have a comparative advantage when borrowing in fixed-rate markets, whereas other companies have a comparative advantage in floating-rate markets. To obtain a new loan, it makes sense for a company to go to the market where it has a comparative advantage. As a result, the company may borrow fixed when it wants floating, or borrow floating when it wants fixed. The swap is used to transform a fixed-rate loan into a floating-rate loan, and vice versa.

Illustration

Suppose that two companies, AAACorp and BBBCorp, both wish to borrow $10 million for 5 years and have been offered the rates shown in Table 7.4. AAACorp has a AAA credit rating; BBBCorp has a BBB credit rating.[5] We assume that BBBCorp wants to borrow at a fixed rate of interest, whereas AAACorp wants to borrow at a floating rate of interest linked to 6-month LIBOR. Because it has a worse credit rating than AAACorp, BBBCorp pays a higher rate of interest than AAACorp in both fixed and floating markets.

A key feature of the rates offered to AAACorp and BBBCorp is that the difference between the two fixed rates is greater than the difference between the two floating rates. BBBCorp pays 1.2% more than AAACorp in fixed-rate markets and only 0.7% more than AAACorp in floating-rate markets. BBBCorp appears to have a comparative advantage in floating-rate markets, whereas AAACorp appears to have a comparative advantage in fixed-rate markets.[6] It is this apparent anomaly that can lead to a swap being negotiated. AAACorp borrows fixed-rate funds at 4% per annum. BBBCorp borrows floating-rate funds at LIBOR plus 1% per annum. They then enter into a swap

Table 7.4 Borrowing rates that provide a basis for the comparative-advantage argument.

	Fixed	*Floating*
AAACorp	4.0%	6-month LIBOR + 0.3%
BBBCorp	5.2%	6-month LIBOR + 1.0%

[5] The credit ratings assigned to companies by S&P (in order of decreasing creditworthiness) are AAA, AA, A, BBB, BB, B, and CCC. The corresponding ratings assigned by Moody's are Aaa, Aa, A, Baa, Ba, B, and Caa, respectively.

[6] Note that BBBCorp's comparative advantage in floating-rate markets does not imply that BBBCorp pays less than AAACorp in this market. It means that the extra amount that BBBCorp pays over the amount paid by AAACorp is less in this market. One of my students summarized the situation as follows: "AAACorp pays more less in fixed-rate markets; BBBCorp pays less more in floating-rate markets."

Figure 7.6 Swap agreement between AAACorp and BBBCorp when rates in Table 7.4 apply.

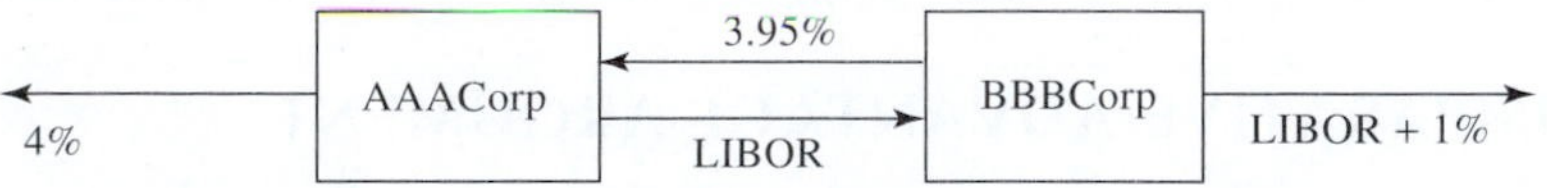

agreement to ensure that AAACorp ends up with floating-rate funds and BBBCorp ends up with fixed-rate funds.

To understand how this swap might work, we first assume that AAACorp and BBBCorp get in touch with each other directly. The sort of swap they might negotiate is shown in Figure 7.6. This is similar to our example in Figure 7.2. AAACorp agrees to pay BBBCorp interest at 6-month LIBOR on \$10 million. In return, BBBCorp agrees to pay AAACorp interest at a fixed rate of 3.95% per annum on \$10 million.

AAACorp has three sets of interest rate cash flows:

1. It pays 4% per annum to outside lenders.
2. It receives 3.95% per annum from BBBCorp.
3. It pays LIBOR to BBBCorp.

The net effect of the three cash flows is that AAACorp pays LIBOR plus 0.05% per annum. This is 0.25% per annum less than it would pay if it went directly to floating-rate markets. BBBCorp also has three sets of interest rate cash flows:

1. It pays LIBOR + 1% per annum to outside lenders.
2. It receives LIBOR from AAACorp.
3. It pays 3.95% per annum to AAACorp.

The net effect of the three cash flows is that BBBCorp pays 4.95% per annum. This is 0.25% per annum less than it would pay if it went directly to fixed-rate markets.

In this example, the swap has been structured so that the net gain to both sides is the same, 0.25%. This need not be the case. However, the total apparent gain from this type of interest rate swap arrangement is always $a - b$, where a is the difference between the interest rates facing the two companies in fixed-rate markets, and b is the difference between the interest rates facing the two companies in floating-rate markets. In this case, $a = 1.2\%$ and $b = 0.7\%$, so that the total gain is 0.5%.

If AAACorp and BBBCorp did not deal directly with each other and used a financial institution, an arrangement such as that shown in Figure 7.7 might result. (This is similar

Figure 7.7 Swap agreement between AAACorp and BBBCorp when rates in Table 7.4 apply and a financial intermediary is involved.

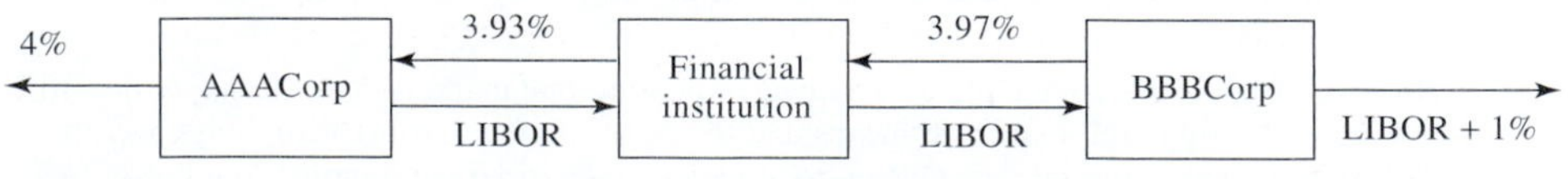

to the example in Figure 7.4.) In this case, AAACorp ends up borrowing at LIBOR + 0.07%, BBBCorp ends up borrowing at 4.97%, and the financial institution earns a spread of 4 basis points per year. The gain to AAACorp is 0.23%; the gain to BBBCorp is 0.23%; and the gain to the financial institution is 0.04%. The total gain to all three parties is 0.50% as before.

Criticism of the Comparative-Advantage Argument

The comparative-advantage argument we have just outlined for explaining the attractiveness of interest rate swaps is open to question. Why in Table 7.4 should the spreads between the rates offered to AAACorp and BBBCorp be different in fixed and floating markets? Now that the swap market has been in existence for some time, we might reasonably expect these types of differences to have been arbitraged away.

The reason that spread differentials appear to exist is due to the nature of the contracts available to companies in fixed and floating markets. The 4.0% and 5.2% rates available to AAACorp and BBBCorp in fixed-rate markets are 5-year rates (e.g., the rates at which the companies can issue 5-year fixed-rate bonds). The LIBOR + 0.3% and LIBOR + 1.0% rates available to AAACorp and BBBCorp in floating-rate markets are 6-month rates. In the floating-rate market, the lender usually has the opportunity to review the floating rates every 6 months. If the creditworthiness of AAACorp or BBBCorp has declined, the lender has the option of increasing the spread over LIBOR that is charged. In extreme circumstances, the lender can refuse to roll over the loan at all. The providers of fixed-rate financing do not have the option to change the terms of the loan in this way.[7]

The spreads between the rates offered to AAACorp and BBBCorp are a reflection of the extent to which BBBCorp is more likely than AAACorp to default. During the next 6 months, there is very little chance that either AAACorp or BBBCorp will default. As we look further ahead, default statistics show that on average the probability of a default by a company with a relatively low credit rating (such as BBBCorp) increases faster than the probability of a default by a company with a relatively high credit rating (such as AAACorp). This is why the spread between the 5-year rates is greater than the spread between the 6-month rates.

After negotiating a floating-rate loan at LIBOR + 1.0% and entering into the swap shown in Figure 7.7, BBBCorp appears to obtain a fixed-rate loan at 4.97%. The arguments just presented show that this is not really the case. In practice, the rate paid is 4.97% only if BBBCorp can continue to borrow floating-rate funds at a spread of 1.0% over LIBOR. If, for example, the credit rating of BBBCorp declines so that the floating-rate loan is rolled over at LIBOR + 2.0%, the rate paid by BBBCorp increases to 5.97%. The market expects that BBBCorp's spread over 6-month LIBOR will on average rise during the swap's life. BBBCorp's expected average borrowing rate when it enters into the swap is therefore greater than 4.97%.

The swap in Figure 7.7 locks in LIBOR + 0.07% for AAACorp for the whole of the next 5 years, not just for the next 6 months. This appears to be a good deal for AAACorp. The downside is that it is bearing the risk of a default by the financial institution. If it borrowed floating-rate funds in the usual way, it would not be bearing this risk.

[7] If the floating-rate loans are structured so that the spread over LIBOR is guaranteed in advance regardless of changes in credit rating, there is in practice little or no comparative advantage.

7.5 THE NATURE OF SWAP RATES

At this stage it is appropriate to examine the nature of swap rates and the relationship between swap and LIBOR markets. We explained in Section 4.1 that LIBOR is the rate of interest at which AA-rated banks borrow for periods between 1 and 12 months from other banks. As shown in Table 7.3, a swap rate is the average of (a) the fixed rate that a swap market maker is prepared to pay in exchange for receiving LIBOR (its bid rate) and (b) the fixed rate that it is prepared to receive in return for paying LIBOR (its offer rate).

Like LIBOR rates, swap rates are not risk-free lending rates. However, they are close to risk-free. A financial institution can earn the 5-year swap rate on a certain principal by doing the following:

1. Lend the principal for the first 6 months to a AA borrower and then relend it for successive 6 month periods to other AA borrowers; and
2. Enter into a swap to exchange the LIBOR income for the 5-year swap rate.

This shows that the 5-year swap rate is an interest rate with a credit risk corresponding to the situation where 10 consecutive 6-month LIBOR loans to AA companies are made. Similarly the 7-year swap rate is an interest rate with a credit risk corresponding to the situation where 14 consecutive 6-month LIBOR loans to AA companies are made. Swap rates of other maturities can be interpreted analogously.

Note that swap rates are less than AA borrowing rates. It is much more attractive to lend money for successive 6-month periods to borrowers who are always AA at the beginning of the periods than to lend it to one borrower for the whole 5 years when all we can be sure of is that the borrower is AA at the beginning of the 5 years.

7.6 DETERMINING LIBOR/SWAP ZERO RATES

We explained in Section 4.1 that derivative traders tend to use LIBOR rates as a proxies for risk-free rates when valuing derivatives. One problem with LIBOR rates is that direct observations are possible only for maturities out to 12 months. As described in Section 6.4, one way of extending the LIBOR zero curve beyond 12 months is to use Eurodollar futures. Typically Eurodollar futures are used to produce a LIBOR zero curve out to 2 years—and sometimes out to as far as 5 years. Traders then use swap rates to extend the LIBOR zero curve further. The resulting zero curve is sometimes referred to as the LIBOR zero curve and sometimes as the swap zero curve. To avoid any confusion, we will refer to it as the LIBOR/swap zero curve. We will now describe how swap rates are used in the determination of the LIBOR/swap zero curve.

The first point to note is that the value of a newly issued floating-rate bond that pays 6-month LIBOR is always equal to its principal value (or par value) when the LIBOR/swap zero curve is used for discounting.[8] The reason is that the bond provides a rate of interest of LIBOR, and LIBOR is the discount rate. The interest on the bond exactly matches the discount rate, and as a result the bond is fairly priced at par.

In equation (7.1), we showed that for a newly issued swap where the fixed rate equals the swap rate, $B_{\text{fix}} = B_{\text{fl}}$. We have just shown that B_{fl} equals the notional principal. It follows that B_{fix} also equals the swap's notional principal. Swap rates therefore define a

[8] The same is true of a newly issued bond that pays 1-month, 3-month, or 12-month LIBOR.

set of par yield bonds. For example, from the swap rates in Table 7.3, we can deduce that the 2-year LIBOR/swap par yield is 6.045%, the 3-year LIBOR/swap par yield is 6.225%, and so on.[9]

The usual method for determining the LIBOR/swap zero curve is the bootstrap method which we used to determine the Treasury zero curve in Section 4.5. LIBOR rates define the zero curve out to 1 year. Swap rates define par yield bonds that are used to determine longer-term rates.

Example 7.1

Suppose that the 6-month, 12-month, and 18-month LIBOR/swap zero rates have been determined as 4%, 4.5%, and 4.8% with continuous compounding and that the 2-year swap rate (for a swap where payments are made semiannually) is 5%. This 5% swap rate means that a bond with a principal of \$100 and a semiannual coupon of 5% per annum sells for par. It follows that, if R is the 2-year zero rate, then

$$2.5e^{-0.04\times 0.5} + 2.5e^{-0.045\times 1.0} + 2.5e^{-0.048\times 1.5} + 102.5e^{2R} = 100$$

Solving this, we obtain $R = 4.953\%$. (Note that this calculation is simplified in that it does not take the swap's day count conventions and holiday calendars into account. See Section 7.2.)

7.7 VALUATION OF INTEREST RATE SWAPS

We now move on to discuss the valuation of interest rate swaps. An interest rate swap is worth zero, or close to zero, when it is first initiated. After it has been in existence for some time, its value may become positive or negative. There are two valuation approaches. The first regards the swap as the difference between two bonds; the second regards it as a portfolio of FRAs.

Valuation in Terms of Bond Prices

Principal payments are not exchanged in an interest rate swap. However, as illustrated in Table 7.2, we can assume that principal payments are both received and paid at the end of the swap without changing its value. By doing this, we find that, from the point of view of the floating-rate payer, a swap can be regarded as a long position in a fixed-rate bond and a short position in a floating-rate bond, so that

$$V_{\text{swap}} = B_{\text{fix}} - B_{\text{fl}}$$

where V_{swap} is the value of the swap, B_{fl} is the value of the floating-rate bond (corresponding to payments that are made), and B_{fix} is the value of the fixed-rate bond (corresponding to payments that are received). Similarly, from the point of view of the fixed-rate payer, a swap is a long position in a floating-rate bond and a short

[9] Analysts frequently interpolate between swap rates before calculating the zero curve, so that they have swap rates for maturities at 6-month intervals. For example, for the data in Table 7.3 the 2.5-year swap rate would be assumed to be 6.135%; the 7.5-year swap rate would be assumed to be 6.696%; and so on.

position in a fixed-rate bond, so that the value of the swap is

$$V_{\text{swap}} = B_{\text{fl}} - B_{\text{fix}}$$

The value of the fixed rate bond, B_{fix}, can be determined as described in Section 4.4. To value the floating-rate bond, we note that the bond is worth the notional principal immediately after an interest payment. This is because at this time the bond is a "fair deal" where the borrower pays LIBOR for each subsequent accrual period.

Suppose that the notional principal is L, the next exchange of payments is at time t^*, and the floating payment that will be made at time t^* (which was determined at the last payment date) is k^*. Immediately after the payment $B_{\text{fl}} = L$ as just explained. It follows that immediately before the payment $B_{\text{fl}} = L + k^*$. The floating-rate bond can therefore be regarded as an instrument providing a single cash flow of $L + k^*$ at time t^*. Discounting this, the value of the floating-rate bond today is

$$(L + k^*)e^{-r^*t^*}$$

where r^* is the LIBOR/swap zero rate for a maturity of t^*.

Example 7.2

Suppose that a financial institution has agreed to pay 6-month LIBOR and receive 8% per annum (with semiannual compounding) on a notional principal of \$100 million. The swap has a remaining life of 1.25 years. The LIBOR rates with continuous compounding for 3-month, 9-month, and 15-month maturities are 10%, 10.5%, and 11%, respectively. The 6-month LIBOR rate at the last payment date was 10.2% (with semiannual compounding).

The calculations for valuing the swap in terms of bonds are summarized in Table 7.5. The fixed-rate bond has cash flows of 4, 4, and 104 on the three payment dates. The discount factors for these cash flows are, respectively,

$$e^{-0.1\times 0.25}, \quad e^{-0.105\times 0.75}, \quad e^{-0.11\times 1.25}$$

and are shown in the fourth column of Table 7.5. The table shows that the value of the fixed-rate bond (in millions of dollars) is 98.238.

In this example, $k^* = 0.5 \times 0.102 \times 100 = \$5.1$ million and $t^* = 0.25$, so that the floating-rate bond can be valued as though it produces a cash flow of \$105.1 million in 3 months. The table shows that the value of the floating bond (in millions of dollars) is 102.505.

Table 7.5 Valuing a swap in terms of bonds (\$ millions). Here, B_{fix} is fixed-rate bond underlying the swap, and B_{fl} is floating-rate bond underlying the swap.

Time	B_{fix} *cash flow*	B_{fl} *cash flow*	*Discount factor*	*Present value* B_{fix} *cash flow*	*Present value* B_{fl} *cash flow*
0.25	4.0	105.100	0.9753	3.901	102.505
0.75	4.0		0.9243	3.697	
1.25	104.0		0.8715	90.640	
Total:				98.238	102.505

The value of the swap is the difference between the two bond prices:

$$V_{\text{swap}} = 98.238 - 102.505 = -4.267$$

or -4.267 million dollars.

If the financial institution had been in the opposite position of paying fixed and receiving floating, the value of the swap would be +\$4.267 million. Note that our calculations do not take account of day count conventions and holiday calendars.

Valuation in Terms of FRAs

A swap can be characterized as a portfolio of forward rate agreements. Consider the swap between Microsoft and Intel in Figure 7.1. The swap is a 3-year deal entered into on March 5, 2004, with semiannual payments. The first exchange of payments is known at the time the swap is negotiated. The other five exchanges can be regarded as FRAs. The exchange on March 5, 2005, is an FRA where interest at 5% is exchanged for interest at the 6-month rate observed in the market on September 5, 2004; the exchange on September 5, 2005, is an FRA where interest at 5% is exchanged for interest at the 6-month rate observed in the market on March 5, 2005; and so on.

As shown at the end of Section 4.7, an FRA can be valued by assuming that forward interest rates are realized. Because it is nothing more than a portfolio of forward rate agreements, a plain vanilla interest rate swap can also be valued by making the assumption that forward interest rates are realized. The procedure is as follows:

1. Use the LIBOR/swap zero curve to calculate forward rates for each of the LIBOR rates that will determine swap cash flows.
2. Calculate swap cash flows on the assumption that the LIBOR rates will equal the forward rates.
3. Discount these swap cash flows (using the LIBOR/swap zero curve) to obtain the swap value.

Example 7.3

Consider again the situation in Example 7.2. Under the terms of the swap, a financial institution has agreed to pay 6-month LIBOR and receive 8% per annum (with semiannual compounding) on a notional principal of \$100 million. The swap has a remaining life of 1.25 years. The LIBOR rates with continuous compounding for 3-month, 9-month, and 15-month maturities are 10%, 10.5%, and 11%, respectively. The 6-month LIBOR rate at the last payment date was 10.2% (with semiannual compounding).

The calculations are summarized in Table 7.6. The first row of the table shows the cash flows that will be exchanged in 3 months. These have already been determined. The fixed rate of 8% will lead to a cash inflow of $100 \times 0.08 \times 0.5 = 4$ million. The floating rate of 10.2% (which was set 3 months ago) will lead to a cash outflow of $100 \times 0.102 \times 0.5 = 5.1$ million. The second row of the table shows the cash flows that will be exchanged in 9 months assuming that forward rates are realized. The cash inflow is 4.0 million as before. To calculate the cash outflow, we must first calculate the forward rate corresponding to the period between 3 and 9 months.

Table 7.6 Valuing swap in terms of FRAs ($ millions). Floating cash flows are calculated by assuming that forward rates will be realized.

Time	*Fixed cash flow*	*Floating cash flow*	*Net cash flow*	*Discount factor*	*Present value of net cash flow*
0.25	4.0	−5.100	−1.100	0.9753	−1.073
0.75	4.0	−5.522	−1.522	0.9243	−1.407
1.25	4.0	−6.051	−2.051	0.8715	−1.787
Total:					−4.267

From equation (4.5), this is

$$\frac{0.105 \times 0.75 - 0.10 \times 0.25}{0.5} = 0.1075$$

or 10.75% with continuous compounding. From equation (4.4), the forward rate becomes 11.044% with semiannual compounding. The cash outflow is therefore $100 \times 0.11044 \times 0.5 = 5.522$ million. The third row similarly shows the cash flows that will be exchanged in 15 months assuming that forward rates are realized. The discount factors for the three payment dates are, respectively,

$$e^{-0.1\times 0.25}, \quad e^{-0.105\times 0.75}, \quad e^{-0.11\times 1.25}$$

The present value of the exchange in three months is −1.073 million. The values of the FRAs corresponding to the exchanges in 9 months and 15 months are −1.407 and −1.787, respectively. The total value of the swap is −$4.267 million. This is in agreement with the value we calculated in Example 7.2 by decomposing the swap into bonds.

The fixed rate in an interest rate swap is chosen so that the swap is worth zero initially. This means that at the outset of a swap the sum of the values of the FRAs underlying the swap is zero. It does not mean that the value of each individual FRA is zero. In general, some FRAs will have positive values whereas others have negative values.

Consider the FRAs underlying the swap between Microsoft and Intel in Figure 7.1:

Value of FRA to Microsoft $>$ 0 when forward interest rate $>$ 5.0%

Value of FRA to Microsoft $=$ 0 when forward interest rate $=$ 5.0%

Value of FRA to Microsoft $<$ 0 when forward interest rate $<$ 5.0%

Suppose that the term structure of interest rates is upward-sloping at the time the swap is negotiated. This means that the forward interest rates increase as the maturity of the FRA increases. Since the sum of the values of the FRAs is zero, the forward interest rate must be less than 5.0% for the early payment dates and greater than 5.0% for the later payment dates. The value to Microsoft of the FRAs corresponding to early payment dates is therefore negative, whereas the value of the FRAs corresponding to later payment dates is positive. If the term structure of interest rates is downward-sloping at the time the swap is negotiated, the reverse is true. The impact of the shape of the term structure of interest rates on the values of the forward contracts underlying a swap is summarized in Figure 7.8.

Figure 7.8 Valuing of forward rate agreements underlying a swap as a function of maturity. In (a) the term structure of interest rates is upward-sloping and we receive fixed, or it is downward-sloping and we receive floating; in (b) the term structure of interest rates is upward-sloping and we receive floating, or it is downward-sloping and we receive fixed.

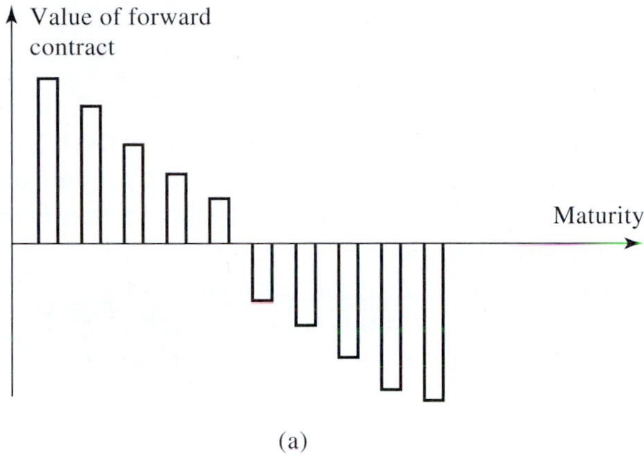

(a)

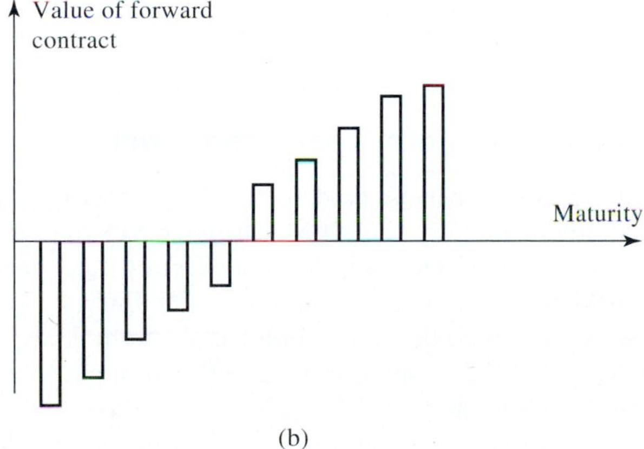

(b)

7.8 CURRENCY SWAPS

Another popular type of swap is known as a *currency swap*. In its simplest form, this involves exchanging principal and interest payments in one currency for principal and interest payments in another.

A currency swap agreement requires the principal to be specified in each of the two currencies. The principal amounts in each currency are usually exchanged at the beginning and at the end of the life of the swap. Usually the principal amounts are chosen to be approximately equivalent using the exchange rate at the swap's initiation. When they are exchanged at the end of the life of the swap, their values may be quite different.

Figure 7.9 A currency swap.

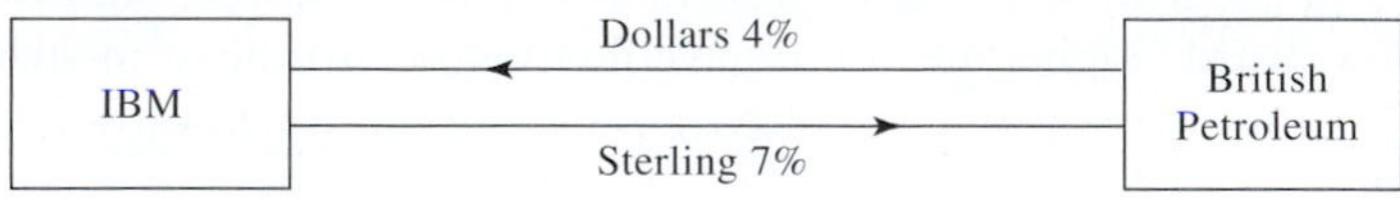

Illustration

Consider a hypothetical 5-year currency swap agreement between IBM and British Petroleum entered into on February 1, 2004. We suppose that IBM pays a fixed rate of interest of 7% in sterling and receives a fixed rate of interest of 4% in dollars from British Petroleum. Interest rate payments are made once a year and the principal amounts are \$15 million and £10 million. This is termed a *fixed-for-fixed* currency swap because the interest rate in both currencies is fixed. The swap is shown in Figure 7.9. Initially, the principal amounts flow in the opposite direction to the arrows in Figure 7.9. The interest payments during the life of the swap and the final principal payment flow in the same direction as the arrows. Thus, at the outset of the swap, IBM pays \$15 million and receives £10 million. Each year during the life of the swap contract, IBM receives \$0.60 million (= 4% of \$15 million) and pays £0.70 million (= 7% of £10 million). At the end of the life of the swap, it pays a principal of £10 million and receives a principal of \$15 million. These cash flows are shown in Table 7.7.

Use of a Currency Swap to Transform Loans and Assets

A swap such as the one just considered can be used to transform borrowings in one currency to borrowings in another. Suppose that IBM can issue \$15 million of US-dollar-denominated bonds at 4% interest. The swap has the effect of transforming this transaction into one where IBM has borrowed £10 million at 7% interest. The initial exchange of principal converts the proceeds of the bond issue from US dollars to sterling. The subsequent exchanges in the swap have the effect of swapping the interest and principal payments from dollars to sterling.

The swap can also be used to transform the nature of assets. Suppose that IBM can invest £10 million in the UK to yield 7% per annum for the next 5 years, but feels that

Table 7.7 Cash flows to IBM in currency swap.

Date	*Dollar cash flow (millions)*	*Sterling cash flow (millions)*
February 1, 2004	−15.00	+10.00
February 1, 2005	+0.60	−0.70
February 1, 2006	+0.60	−0.70
February 1, 2007	+0.60	−0.70
February 1, 2008	+0.60	−0.70
February 1, 2009	+15.60	−10.70

the US dollar will strengthen against sterling and prefers a US-dollar-denominated investment. The swap has the effect of transforming the UK investment into a \$15 million investment in the US yielding 4%.

Comparative Advantage

Currency swaps can be motivated by comparative advantage. To illustrate this, we consider another hypothetical example. Suppose the 5-year fixed-rate borrowing costs to General Motors and Qantas Airways in US dollars (USD) and Australian dollars (AUD) are as shown in Table 7.8. The data in the table suggest that Australian rates are higher than USD interest rates, and also that General Motors is more creditworthy than Qantas Airways, because it is offered a more favorable rate of interest in both currencies. From the viewpoint of a swap trader, the interesting aspect of Table 7.8 is that the spreads between the rates paid by General Motors and Qantas Airways in the two markets are not the same. Qantas Airways pays 2% more than General Motors in the US dollar market and only 0.4% more than General Motors in the AUD market.

This situation is analogous to that in Table 7.4. General Motors has a comparative advantage in the USD market, whereas Qantas Airways has a comparative advantage in the AUD market. In Table 7.4, where a plain vanilla interest rate swap was considered, we argued that comparative advantages are largely illusory. Here we are comparing the rates offered in two different currencies, and it is more likely that the comparative advantages are genuine. One possible source of comparative advantage is tax. General Motors' position might be such that USD borrowings lead to lower taxes on its worldwide income than AUD borrowings. Qantas Airways' position might be the reverse. (Note that we assume that the interest rates in Table 7.8 have been adjusted to reflect these types of tax advantages.)

We suppose that General Motors wants to borrow 20 million AUD and Qantas Airways wants to borrow 12 million USD and that the current exchange rate (USD per AUD) is 0.6000. This creates a perfect situation for a currency swap. General Motors and Qantas Airways each borrow in the market where they have a comparative advantage; that is, General Motors borrows USD whereas Qantas Airways borrows AUD. They then use a currency swap to transform General Motors' loan into an AUD loan and Qantas Airways' loan into a USD loan.

As already mentioned, the difference between the USD interest rates is 2%, whereas the difference between the AUD interest rates is 0.4%. By analogy with the interest rate swap case, we expect the total gain to all parties to be $2.0 - 0.4 = 1.6\%$ per annum.

There are many ways in which the swap can be arranged. Figure 7.10 shows one way swaps might be entered into with a financial institution. General Motors borrows USD and Qantas Airways borrows AUD. The effect of the swap is to transform the USD

Table 7.8 Borrowing rates providing basis for currency swap.

	*USD**	*AUD**
General Motors	5.0%	12.6%
Qantas Airways	7.0%	13.0%

* Quoted rates have been adjusted to reflect the differential impact of taxes.

Figure 7.10 A currency swap motivated by comparative advantage.

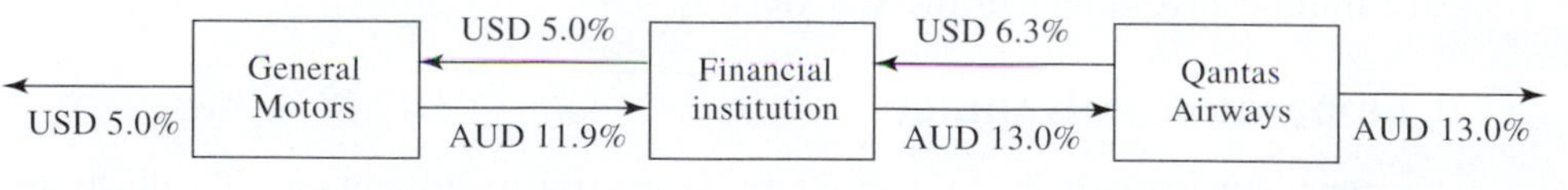

interest rate of 5% per annum to an AUD interest rate of 11.9% per annum for General Motors. As a result, General Motors is 0.7% per annum better off than it would be if it went directly to AUD markets. Similarly, Qantas exchanges an AUD loan at 13% per annum for a USD loan at 6.3% per annum and ends up 0.7% per annum better off than it would be if it went directly to USD markets. The financial institution gains 1.3% per annum on its USD cash flows and loses 1.1% per annum on its AUD flows. If we ignore the difference between the two currencies, the financial institution makes a net gain of 0.2% per annum. As predicted, the total gain to all parties is 1.6% per annum.

Each year the financial institution makes a gain of USD 156,000 (= 1.3% of 12 million) and incurs a loss of AUD 220,000 (= 1.1% of 20 million). The financial institution can avoid any foreign exchange risk by buying AUD 220,000 per annum in the forward market for each year of the life of the swap, thus locking in a net gain in USD.

It is possible to redesign the swap so that the financial institution makes a 0.2% spread in USD. Figures 7.11 and 7.12 present two alternatives. These alternatives are unlikely to be used in practice because they do not lead to General Motors and Qantas being free of foreign exchange risk.[10] In Figure 7.11, Qantas bears some foreign exchange risk because it pays 1.1% per annum in AUD and pays 5.2% per annum in USD. In Figure 7.12, General Motors bears some foreign exchange risk because it receives 1.1% per annum in USD and pays 13% per annum in AUD.

7.9 VALUATION OF CURRENCY SWAPS

Like interest rate swaps, fixed-for-fixed currency swaps can be decomposed into either the difference between two bonds or a portfolio of forward foreign exchange contracts.

Figure 7.11 Alternative arrangement for currency swap: Qantas Airways bears some foreign exchange risk.

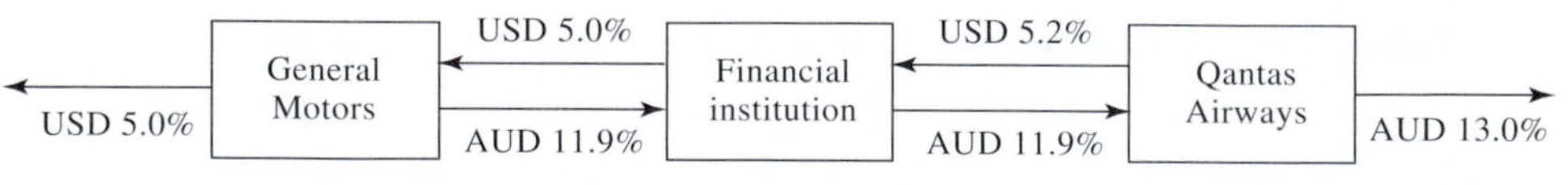

[10] Usually it makes sense for the financial institution to bear the foreign exchange risk, because it is in the best position to hedge the risk.

Figure 7.12 Alternative arrangement for currency swap: General Motors bears some foreign exchange risk.

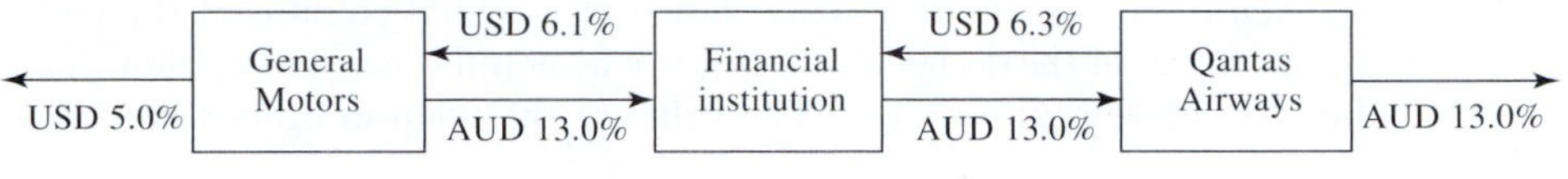

Valuation in Terms of Bond Prices

If we define V_{swap} as the value in US dollars of an outstanding swap where dollars are received and a foreign currency is paid, then

$$V_{\text{swap}} = B_D - S_0 B_F$$

where B_F is the value, measured in the foreign currency, of the bond defined by the foreign cash flows on the swap and B_D is the value of the bond defined by the domestic cash flows on the swap, and S_0 is the spot exchange rate (expressed as number of dollars per unit of foreign currency). The value of a swap can therefore be determined from LIBOR rates in the two currencies, the term structure of interest rates in the domestic currency, and the spot exchange rate.

Similarly, the value of a swap where the foreign currency is received and dollars are paid is

$$V_{\text{swap}} = S_0 B_F - B_D$$

Example 7.4

Suppose that the term structure of LIBOR/swap interest rates is flat in both Japan and the United States. The Japanese rate is 4% per annum and the US rate is 9% per annum (both with continuous compounding). A financial institution has entered into a currency swap in which it receives 5% per annum in yen and pays 8% per annum in dollars once a year. The principals in the two currencies are $10 million and 1,200 million yen. The swap will last for another 3 years, and the current exchange rate is 110 yen = $1.

The calculations are summarized in Table 7.9. In this case the cash flows from the dollar bond underlying the swap are as shown in the second column. The

Table 7.9 Valuation of currency swap in terms of bonds. (All amounts in millions.)

Time	*Cash flows on dollar bond ($)*	*Present value ($)*	*Cash flows forward on yen bond (yen)*	*Present value (yen)*
1	0.8	0.7311	60	57.65
2	0.8	0.6682	60	55.39
3	0.8	0.6107	60	53.22
3	10.0	7.6338	1,200	1,064.30
Total:		9.6439		1,230.55

present value of the cash flows using the dollar discount rate of 9% are shown in the third column. The cash flows from the yen bond underlying the swap are shown in the fourth column of the table. The present value of the cash flows using the yen discount rate of 4% are shown in the final column of the table.

The value of the dollar bond, B_D, is 9.6439 million dollars. The value of the yen bond is 1230.55 million yen. The value of the swap in dollars is therefore

$$\frac{1{,}230.55}{110} - 9.6439 = 1.5430 \text{ million}$$

Valuation as Portfolio of Forward Contracts

Each exchange of payments in a fixed-for-fixed currency swap is a forward contract. As shown in Section 5.7, forward foreign exchange contracts can be valued by assuming that forward exchange rates are realized. The forward exchange rates themselves can be calculated from equation (5.9).

Example 7.5

Consider again the situation in Example 7.4. The LIBOR/swap term structure of interest rates is flat in both Japan and the United States. The Japanese rate is 4% per annum and the US rate is 9% per annum (both with continuous compounding). A financial institution has entered into a currency swap in which it receives 5% per annum in yen and pays 8% per annum in dollars once a year. The principals in the two currencies are \$10 million and 1,200 million yen. The swap will last for another 3 years, and the current exchange rate is 110 yen = \$1.

The calculations are summarized in Table 7.10. The financial institution pays $0.08 \times 10 = \$0.8$ million dollars and receives $1{,}200 \times 0.05 = 60$ million yen each year. In addition, the dollar principal of \$10 million is paid and the yen principal of 1,200 is received at the end of year 3. The current spot rate is 0.009091 dollar per yen. In this case $r = 4\%$ and $r_f = 9\%$, so that, from equation (5.9), the 1-year forward rate is

$$0.009091\, e^{(0.09-0.04)\times 1} = 0.009557$$

The 2- and 3-year forward rates in Table 7.10 are calculated similarly. The forward contracts underlying the swap can be valued by assuming that the forward rates are realized. If the 1-year forward rate is realized, the yen cash flow in year 1

Table 7.10 Valuation of currency swap as a portfolio of forward contracts. (All amounts in millions.)

Time	*Dollar cash flow*	*Yen cash flow*	*Forward rate*	*Dollar value of yen cash flow*	*Net cash flow (\$)*	*Present value*
1	−0.8	60	0.009557	0.5734	−0.2266	−0.2071
2	−0.8	60	0.010047	0.6028	−0.1972	−0.1647
3	−0.8	60	0.010562	0.6337	−0.1663	−0.1269
3	−10.0	1200	0.010562	12.6746	+2.6746	2.0417
Total:						1.5430

is worth $60 \times 0.009557 = 0.5734$ million dollars and the net cash flow at the end of year 1 is $0.8 - 0.5734 = -0.2266$ million dollars. This has a present value of

$$-0.2266\, e^{-0.09 \times 1} = -0.2071$$

million dollars. This is the value of forward contract corresponding to the exchange of cash flows at the end of year 1. The value of the other forward contracts are calculated similarly. As shown in Table 7.10, the total value of the forward contracts is \$1.5430 million. This agrees with the value calculated for the swap in Example 7.4 by decomposing it into bonds.

The value of a currency swap is normally zero when it is first negotiated. If the two principals are worth exactly the same using the exchange rate at the start of the swap, the value of the swap is also zero immediately after the initial exchange of principal. However, as in the case of interest rate swaps, this does not mean that each of the individual forward contracts underlying the swap has zero value. It can be shown that, when interest rates in two currencies are significantly different, the payer of the currency with the high interest rate is in the position where the forward contracts corresponding to the early exchanges of cash flows have negative values, and the forward contract corresponding to final exchange of principals has a positive value. (This is the situation in our example in Table 7.10.) The payer of the currency with the low interest rate is likely to be in the opposite position; that is, the early exchanges of cash flows have positive values and the final exchange has a negative value.

For the payer of the low-interest currency, the swap will tend to have a negative value during most of its life. The forward contracts corresponding to the early exchanges of payments have positive values, and once these exchanges have taken place, there is a tendency for the remaining forward contracts to have, in total, a negative value. For the payer of the high-interest currency, the reverse is true. The value of the swap will tend to be positive during most of its life. These results are important when the credit risk in the swap is being evaluated.

7.10 CREDIT RISK

Contracts such as swaps that are private arrangements between two companies entail credit risks. Consider a financial institution that has entered into offsetting contracts with two companies (see Figure 7.4, 7.5, or 7.7). If neither party defaults, the financial institution remains fully hedged. A decline in the value of one contract will always be offset by an increase in the value of the other contract. However, there is a chance that one party will get into financial difficulties and default. The financial institution then still has to honor the contract it has with the other party.

Suppose that, some time after the initiation of the contracts in Figure 7.4, the contract with Microsoft has a positive value to the financial institution, whereas the contract with Intel has a negative value. If Microsoft defaults, the financial institution is liable to lose the whole of the positive value it has in this contract. To maintain a hedged position, it would have to find a third party willing to take Microsoft's position. To induce the third party to take the position, the financial institution would have to pay the third party an amount roughly equal to the value of its contract with Microsoft prior to the default.

A financial institution has credit-risk exposure from a swap only when the value of the swap to the financial institution is positive. What happens when this value is negative and the counterparty gets into financial difficulties? In theory, the financial institution could realize a windfall gain, because a default would lead to it getting rid of a liability. In practice, it is likely that the counterparty would choose to sell the contract to a third party or rearrange its affairs in some way so that its positive value in the contract is not lost. The most realistic assumption for the financial institution is therefore as follows. If the counterparty goes bankrupt, there will be a loss if the value of the swap to the financial institution is positive, and there will be no effect on the financial institution's position if the value of the swap to the financial institution is negative. This situation is summarized in Figure 7.13.

Potential losses from defaults on a swap are much less than the potential losses from defaults on a loan with the same principal. This is because the value of the swap is usually only a small fraction of the value of the loan. Potential losses from defaults on a currency swap are greater than on an interest rate swap. The reason is that, because principal amounts in two different currencies are exchanged at the end of the life of a currency swap, a currency swap is liable to have a greater value at the time of a default than an interest rate swap.

It is important to distinguish between the credit risk and market risk to a financial institution in any contract. As discussed earlier, the credit risk arises from the possibility of a default by the counterparty when the value of the contract to the financial institution is positive. The market risk arises from the possibility that market variables such as interest rates and exchange rates will move in such a way that the value of a contract to the financial institution becomes negative. Market risks can be hedged by entering into offsetting contracts; credit risks are less easy to hedge.

One of the more bizarre stories in swap markets is outlined in Business Snapshot 7.2. It concerns the British Local Authority, Hammersmith and Fulham and shows that, in

Figure 7.13 The credit exposure in a swap.

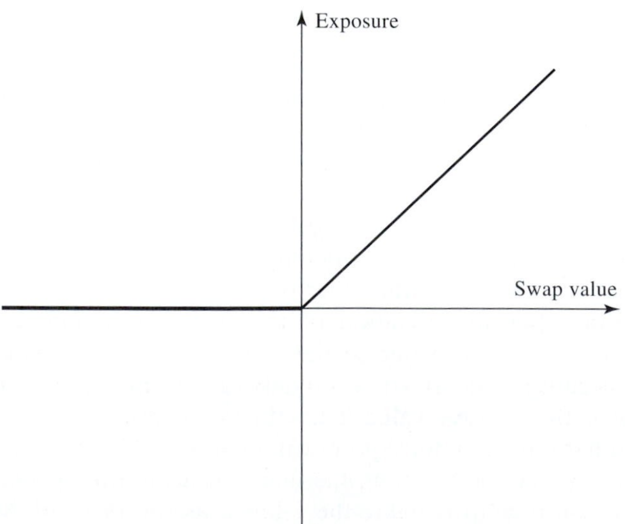

Business Snapshot 7.2 The Hammersmith and Fulham Story

Between 1987 to 1989 the London Borough of Hammersmith and Fulham in Great Britain entered into about 600 interest rate swaps and related instruments with a total notional principal of about 6 billion pounds. The transactions appear to have been entered into for speculative rather than hedging purposes. The two employees of Hammersmith and Fulham that were responsible for the trades had only a sketchy understanding of the risks they were taking and how the products they were trading worked.

By 1989, because of movements in sterling interest rates, Hammersmith and Fulham had lost several hundred million pounds on the swaps. To the banks on the other side of the transactions, the swaps were worth several hundred million pounds. The banks were concerned about credit risk. They had entered into offsetting swaps to hedge their interest rate risks. If Hammersmith and Fulham defaulted, the banks would still have to honor their obligations on the offsetting swaps and would take a huge loss.

What happened was something a little different from a default. Hammersmith and Fulham's auditor asked to have the transactions declared void because Hammersmith and Fulham did not have the authority to enter into the transactions. The British courts agreed. The case was appealed and went all the way to the House of Lords, Britain's highest court. The final decision was that Hammersmith and Fulham did not have the authority to enter into the swaps, but that they ought to have the authority to do so in the future for risk-management purposes. Needless to say, banks were furious that their contracts were overturned in this way by the courts.

addition to bearing market risk and credit risk, banks trading swaps also sometimes bear legal risk.

7.11 OTHER TYPES OF SWAPS

In this chapter we have covered interest rate swaps where LIBOR is exchanged for a fixed rate of interest and currency swaps where a fixed rate of interest in one currency is exchanged for a fixed rate of interest in another currency. Many other types of swaps are traded. We will discuss many of them in detail in later chapters, such as in Chapters 21, 26, and 30. At this stage, we will provide an overview.

Variations on the Standard Interest Rate Swap

In fixed-for-floating interest rate swaps, LIBOR is the most common reference floating interest rate. In the examples in this chapter, the tenor (i.e., payment frequency) of LIBOR has been 6 months, but swaps where the tenor of LIBOR is 1 month, 3 months, and 12 months trade regularly. The tenor on the floating side does not have to match the tenor on the fixed side. (Indeed, as pointed out in footnote 3, the standard interest rate swap in the United States is one where there are quarterly LIBOR payments and semiannual fixed payments.) LIBOR is the most common floating rate, but others such as the commercial paper (CP) rate are occasionally used. Sometimes floating-for-floating interest rates swaps are negotiated. For example, the 3-month CP rate plus 10 basis points might be exchanged for 3-month LIBOR with both being applied to the same principal. (This deal would allow a company to hedge its exposure when assets and liabilities are subject to different floating rates.)

The principal in a swap agreement can be varied throughout the term of the swap to meet the needs of a counterparty. In an *amortizing swap*, the principal reduces in a predetermined way. (This might be designed to correspond to the amortization schedule on a loan.) In a *step-up swap*, the principal increases in a predetermined way. (This might be designed to correspond to drawdowns on a loan agreement.) Deferred swaps or *forward swaps*, where the parties do not begin to exchange interest payments until some future date, are also sometimes arranged. Sometimes swaps are negotiated where the principal to which the fixed payments are applied is different from the principal to which the floating payments are applied.

A *constant maturity swap* (CMS swap) is an agreement to exchange a LIBOR rate for a swap rate. An example would be an agreement to exchange 6-month LIBOR applied to a certain principal for the 10-year swap rate applied to the same principal every 6 months for the next 5 years. A *constant maturity Treasury swap* (CMT swap) is a similar agreement to exchange a LIBOR rate for a particular Treasury rate (e.g., the 10-year Treasury rate).

In a *compounding swap*, interest on one or both sides is compounded forward to the end of the life of the swap according to preagreed rules and there is only one payment date at the end of the life of the swap. In a *LIBOR-in arrears* swap, the LIBOR rate observed on a payment date is used to calculate the payment on that date. (As explained in Section 7.1, in a standard deal the LIBOR rate observed on one payment date is used to determine the payment on the next payment date.) In an *accrual swap*, the interest on one side of the swap accrues only when the floating reference rate is in a certain range.

Other Currency Swaps

In this chapter we have considered fixed-for-fixed currency swaps. Another type of swap is a fixed-for-floating currency swap, whereby a floating rate (usually LIBOR) in one currency is exchanged for a fixed rate in another currency. This is a combination of a fixed-for-floating interest rate swap and a fixed-for-fixed currency swap and is known as a *cross-currency interest rate swap*. A further type of currency swap is a *floating-for-floating currency swap*, where a floating rate in one currency is exchanged for a floating rate in another currency.

Sometimes a rate observed in one currency is applied to a principal amount in another currency. One such deal might be where 3-month LIBOR observed in the United States is exchanged for 3-month LIBOR in Britain, with both principals being applied to a principal of 10 million British pounds. This type of swap is referred to as a *diff swap or a quanto*.

Equity Swaps

An *equity swap* is an agreement to exchange the total return (dividends and capital gains) realized on an equity index for either a fixed or a floating rate of interest. For example, the total return on the S&P 500 in successive 6-month periods might be exchanged for LIBOR, with both being applied to the same principal. Equity swaps can be used by portfolio managers to convert returns from a fixed or floating investment to the returns from investing in an equity index, and vice versa.

Options

Sometimes there are options embedded in a swap agreement. For example, in an *extendable swap*, one party has the option to extend the life of the swap beyond the specified period. In a *puttable swap*, one party has the option to terminate the swap early. Options on swaps, or *swaptions*, are also available. These provide one party with the right at a future time to enter into a swap where a predetermined fixed rate is exchanged for floating.

Commodity Swaps, Volatility Swaps, and Other Exotic Instuments

Commodity swaps are in essence a series of forward contracts on a commodity with different maturity dates and the same delivery prices. In a *volatility swap* there are a series of time periods. At the end of each period, one side pays a preagreed volatility, while the other side pays the historical volatility realized during the period. Both volatilities are multiplied by the same notional principal in calculating payments.

Swaps are limited only by the imagination of financial engineers and the desire of corporate treasurers and fund mangers for exotic structures. In Chapter 30, we will describe the famous 5/30 swap entered into between Procter and Gamble and Bankers Trust, where payments depended in a complex way on the 30-day commercial paper rate, a 30-year Treasury bond price, and the yield on a 5-year Treasury bond.

SUMMARY

The two most common types of swaps are interest rate swaps and currency swaps. In an interest rate swap, one party agrees to pay the other party interest at a fixed rate on a notional principal for a number of years. In return, it receives interest at a floating rate on the same notional principal for the same period of time. In a currency swap, one party agrees to pay interest on a principal amount in one currency. In return, it receives interest on a principal amount in another currency.

Principal amounts are not usually exchanged in an interest rate swap. In a currency swap, principal amounts are usually exchanged at both the beginning and the end of the life of the swap. For a party paying interest in the foreign currency, the foreign principal is received, and the domestic principal is paid at the beginning of the life of the swap. At the end of the life of the swap, the foreign principal is paid and the domestic principal is received.

An interest rate swap can be used to transform a floating-rate loan into a fixed-rate loan, or vice versa. It can also be used to transform a floating-rate investment to a fixed-rate investment, or vice versa. A currency swap can be used to transform a loan in one currency into a loan in another currency. It can also be used to transform an investment denominated in one currency into an investment denominated in another currency.

There are two ways of valuing interest rate and currency swaps. In the first, the swap is decomposed into a long position in one bond and a short position in another bond. In the second it is regarded as a portfolio of forward contracts.

When a financial institution enters into a pair of offsetting swaps with different counterparties, it is exposed to credit risk. If one of the counterparties defaults when the financial institution has positive value in its swap with that counterparty, the financial institution loses money because it still has to honor its swap agreement with the other counterparty.

FURTHER READING

Baz, J., and M. Pascutti. "Alternative Swap Contracts Analysis and Pricing," *Journal of Derivatives*, (Winter 1996): 7–21.

Brown, K. C., and D. J. Smith. *Interest Rate and Currency Swaps: A Tutorial*. Association for Investment Management and Research, 1996.

Cooper, I., and A. Mello. "The Default Risk in Interest Rate Swaps," *Journal of Finance*, 46, 2 (1991): 597–620.

Dattatreya, R. E., and K. Hotta. *Advanced Interest Rate and Currency Swaps: State-of-the-Art Products, Strategies, and Risk Management Applications*. Irwin, 1993.

Flavell, R. *Swaps and Other Instruments*. Chichester: Wiley, 2002.

Gupta, A., and M. G. Subrahmanyam. "An Empirical Examination of the Convexity Bias in the Pricing of Interest Rate Swaps," *Journal of Financial Economics*, 55, 2 (2000): 239–79.

Litzenberger, R. H. "Swaps: Plain and Fanciful," *Journal of Finance*, 47, 3 (1992): 831–50.

Minton, B. A. "An Empirical Examination of the Basic Valuation Models for Interest Rate Swaps," *Journal of Financial Economics*, 44, 2 (1997): 251–77.

Sun, T., S. Sundaresan, and C. Wang. "Interest Rate Swaps: An Empirical Investigation," *Journal of Financial Economics*, 34, 1 (1993): 77–99.

Titman, S. "Interest Rate Swaps and Corporate Financing Choices," *Journal of Finance*, 47, 4 (1992): 1503–16.

Questions and Problems (Answers in Solutions Manual)

7.1. Companies A and B have been offered the following rates per annum on a $20 million 5-year loan:

	Fixed rate	*Floating rate*
Company A:	12.0%	LIBOR + 0.1%
Company B:	13.4%	LIBOR + 0.6%

Company A requires a floating-rate loan; company B requires a fixed-rate loan. Design a swap that will net a bank, acting as intermediary, 0.1% per annum and that will appear equally attractive to both companies.

7.2. Company X wishes to borrow US dollars at a fixed rate of interest. Company Y wishes to borrow Japanese yen at a fixed rate of interest. The amounts required by the two companies are roughly the same at the current exchange rate. The companies have been quoted the following interest rates, which have been adjusted for the impact of taxes:

	Yen	*Dollars*
Company X:	5.0%	9.6%
Company Y:	6.5%	10.0%

Design a swap that will net a bank, acting as intermediary, 50 basis points per annum. Make the swap equally attractive to the two companies and ensure that all foreign exchange risk is assumed by the bank.

7.3. A $100 million interest rate swap has a remaining life of 10 months. Under the terms of the swap, 6-month LIBOR is exchanged for 12% per annum (compounded semiannually). The average of the bid–offer rate being exchanged for 6-month LIBOR in swaps of all maturities is currently 10% per annum with continuous compounding. The 6-month LIBOR rate was 9.6% per annum 2 months ago. What is the current value of the swap to the party paying floating? What is its value to the party paying fixed?

7.4. Explain what a swap rate is. What is the relationship between swap rates and par yields?

7.5. A currency swap has a remaining life of 15 months. It involves exchanging interest at 14% on £20 million for interest at 10% on $30 million once a year. The term structure of interest rates in both the United Kingdom and the United States is currently flat, and if the swap were negotiated today the interest rates exchanged would be 8% in dollars and 11% in sterling. All interest rates are quoted with annual compounding. The current exchange rate (dollars per pound sterling) is 1.6500. What is the value of the swap to the party paying sterling? What is the value of the swap to the party paying dollars?

7.6. Explain the difference between the credit risk and the market risk in a financial contract.

7.7. A corporate treasurer tells you that he has just negotiated a 5-year loan at a competitive fixed rate of interest of 5.2%. The treasurer explains that he achieved the 5.2% rate by borrowing at 6-month LIBOR plus 150 basis points and swapping LIBOR for 3.7%. He goes on to say that this was possible because his company has a comparative advantage in the floating-rate market. What has the treasurer overlooked?

7.8. Explain why a bank is subject to credit risk when it enters into two offsetting swap contracts.

7.9. Companies X and Y have been offered the following rates per annum on a $5 million 10-year investment:

	Fixed rate	*Floating rate*
Company X:	8.0%	LIBOR
Company Y:	8.8%	LIBOR

Company X requires a fixed-rate investment; company Y requires a floating-rate investment. Design a swap that will net a bank, acting as intermediary, 0.2% per annum and will appear equally attractive to X and Y.

7.10. A financial institution has entered into an interest rate swap with company X. Under the terms of the swap, it receives 10% per annum and pays 6-month LIBOR on a principal of $10 million for 5 years. Payments are made every 6 months. Suppose that company X defaults on the sixth payment date (at the end of year 3) when the interest rate (with semiannual compounding) is 8% per annum for all maturities. What is the loss to the financial institution? Assume that 6-month LIBOR was 9% per annum halfway through year 3.

7.11. A financial institution has entered into a 10-year currency swap with company Y. Under the terms of the swap, the financial institution receives interest at 3% per annum in Swiss francs and pays interest at 8% per annum in US dollars. Interest payments are exchanged once a year. The principal amounts are 7 million dollars and 10 million francs. Suppose that company Y declares bankruptcy at the end of year 6, when the exchange rate is $0.80 per franc. What is the cost to the financial institution? Assume that, at the end of year 6, the interest rate is 3% per annum in Swiss francs and 8% per annum in US dollars for all maturities. All interest rates are quoted with annual compounding.

7.12. Companies A and B face the following interest rates (adjusted for the differential impact of taxes):

	Company A	*Company B*
US dollars (floating rate):	LIBOR + 0.5%	LIBOR + 1.0%
Canadian dollars (fixed rate):	5.0%	6.5%

Assume that A wants to borrow US dollars at a floating rate of interest and B wants to borrow Canadian dollars at a fixed rate of interest. A financial institution is planning to arrange a swap and requires a 50-basis-point spread. If the swap is equally attractive to A and B, what rates of interest will A and B end up paying?

7.13. After it hedges its foreign exchange risk using forward contracts, is the financial institution's average spread in Figure 7.10 likely to be greater than or less than 20 basis points? Explain your answer.

7.14. "Companies with high credit risks are the ones that cannot access fixed-rate markets directly. They are the companies that are most likely to be paying fixed and receiving floating in an interest rate swap." Assume that this statement is true. Do you think it increases or decreases the risk of a financial institution's swap portfolio? Assume that companies are most likely to default when interest rates are high.

7.15. Why is the expected loss from a default on a swap less than the expected loss from the default on a loan with the same principal?

7.16. A bank finds that its assets are not matched with its liabilities. It is taking floating-rate deposits and making fixed-rate loans. How can swaps be used to offset the risk?

7.17. Explain how you would value a swap that is the exchange of a floating rate in one currency for a fixed rate in another currency.

7.18. The LIBOR zero curve is flat at 5% (continuously compounded) out to 1.5 years. Swap rates for 2- and 3-year semiannual pay swaps are 5.4% and 5.6%, respectively. Estimate the LIBOR zero rates for maturities of 2.0, 2.5, and 3.0 years. (Assume that the 2.5-year swap rate is the average of the 2- and 3-year swap rates.)

Assignment Questions

7.19. The 1-year LIBOR rate is 10%. A bank trades swaps where a fixed rate of interest is exchanged for 12-month LIBOR with payments being exchanged annually. The 2- and 3-year swap rates (expressed with annual compounding) are 11% and 12% per annum. Estimate the 2- and 3-year LIBOR zero rates.

7.20. Company A, a British manufacturer, wishes to borrow US dollars at a fixed rate of interest. Company B, a US multinational, wishes to borrow sterling at a fixed rate of interest. They have been quoted the following rates per annum (adjusted for differential tax effects):

	Sterling	*US dollars*
Company A	11.0%	7.0%
Company B	10.6%	6.2%

Design a swap that will net a bank, acting as intermediary, 10 basis points per annum and that will produce a gain of 15 basis points per annum for each of the two companies.

7.21. Under the terms of an interest rate swap, a financial institution has agreed to pay 10% per annum and to receive 3-month LIBOR in return on a notional principal of $100 million with payments being exchanged every 3 months. The swap has a remaining life of 14 months. The average of the bid and offer fixed rates currently being swapped for 3-month LIBOR is 12% per annum for all maturities. The 3-month LIBOR rate 1 month ago was 11.8% per annum. All rates are compounded quarterly. What is the value of the swap?

7.22. Suppose that the term structure of interest rates is flat in the United States and Australia. The USD interest rate is 7% per annum and the AUD rate is 9% per annum. The current value of the AUD is 0.62 USD. Under the terms of a swap agreement, a financial institution pays 8% per annum in AUD and receives 4% per annum in USD. The principals in the two currencies are $12 million USD and 20 million AUD. Payments are exchanged every year, with one exchange having just taken place. The swap will last 2 more years. What is the value of the swap to the financial institution? Assume all interest rates are continuously compounded.

7.23. Company X is based in the United Kingdom and would like to borrow $50 million at a fixed rate of interest for 5 years in US funds. Because the company is not well known in the United States, this has proved to be impossible. However, the company has been quoted 12% per annum on fixed-rate 5-year sterling funds. Company Y is based in the United States and would like to borrow the equivalent of $50 million in sterling funds for 5 years at a fixed rate of interest. It has been unable to get a quote but has been offered US dollar funds at 10.5% per annum. Five-year government bonds currently yield 9.5% per annum in the United States and 10.5% in the United Kingdom. Suggest an appropriate currency swap that will net the financial intermediary 0.5% per annum.

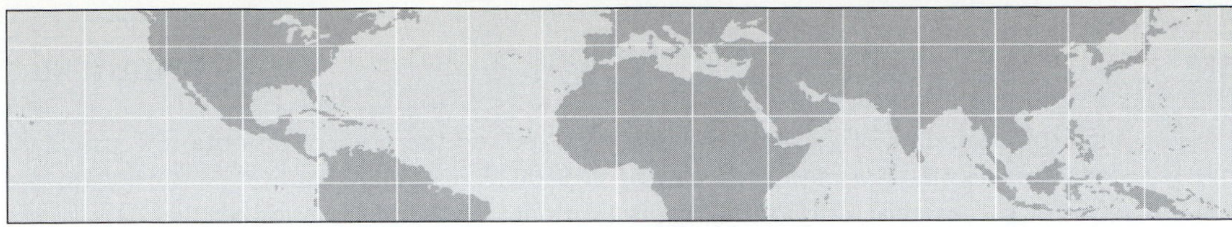

CHAPTER 8

Mechanics of Options Markets

We introduced options in Chapter 1. This chapter explains how options markets are organized, what terminology is used, how the contracts are traded, how margin requirements are set, and so on. Later chapters will examine such topics as trading strategies involving options, the determination of option prices, and the ways in which portfolios of options can be hedged. This chapter is concerned primarily with stock options. It presents some introductory material on currency options, index options, and futures options. More details concerning these instruments can be found in Chapter 14.

Options are fundamentally different from forward and futures contracts. An option gives the holder of the option the right to do something, but the holder does not have to exercise this right. By contrast, in a forward or futures contract, the two parties have committed themselves to some action. It costs a trader nothing (except for the margin requirements) to enter into a forward or futures contract, whereas the purchase of an option requires an up-front payment.

8.1 TYPES OF OPTIONS

As mentioned in Chapter 1, there are two basic types of options. A *call option* gives the holder of the option the right to buy an asset by a certain date for a certain price. A *put option* gives the holder the right to sell an asset by a certain date for a certain price. The date specified in the contract is known as the *expiration date* or the *maturity date*. The price specified in the contract is known as the *exercise price* or the *strike price*.

Options can be either American or European, a distinction that has nothing to do with geographical location. *American options* can be exercised at any time up to the expiration date, whereas *European options* can be exercised only on the expiration date itself. Most of the options that are traded on exchanges are American. However, European options are generally easier to analyze than American options, and some of the properties of an American option are frequently deduced from those of its European counterpart.

Call Options

Consider the situation of an investor who buys a European call option with a strike price of \$100 to purchase 100 eBay shares. Suppose that the current stock price is \$98, the expiration date of the option is in 4 months, and the price of an option to purchase one share is \$5. The initial investment is \$500. Because the option is European, the investor can exercise only on the expiration date. If the stock price on this date is less than \$100, the investor will clearly choose not to exercise. (There is no point in buying for \$100 a share that has a market value of less than \$100.) In these circumstances, the investor loses the whole of the initial investment of \$500. If the stock price is above \$100 on the expiration date, the option will be exercised. Suppose, for example, that the stock price is \$115. By exercising the option, the investor is able to buy 100 shares for \$100 per share. If the shares are sold immediately, the investor makes a gain of \$15 per share, or \$1,500, ignoring transactions costs. When the initial cost of the option is taken into account, the net profit to the investor is \$1,000.

Figure 8.1 shows how the investor's net profit or loss on an option to purchase one share varies with the final stock price in the example. It is important to realize that an investor sometimes exercises an option and makes a loss overall. Suppose that, in the example, eBay's stock price is \$102 at the expiration of the option. The investor would exercise the option for a gain of $100 \times (\$102 - \$100) = \$200$ and realize a loss overall of \$300 when the initial cost of the option is taken into account. It is tempting to argue that the investor should not exercise the option in these circumstances. However, not exercising would lead to an overall loss of \$500, which is worse than the \$300 loss when the investor exercises. In general, call options should always be exercised at the expiration date if the stock price is above the strike price.

Put Options

Whereas the purchaser of a call option is hoping that the stock price will increase, the purchaser of a put option is hoping that it will decrease. Consider an investor who buys a European put option to sell 100 shares in IBM with a strike price of \$70. Suppose that the current stock price is \$65, the expiration date of the option is in 3 months, and the

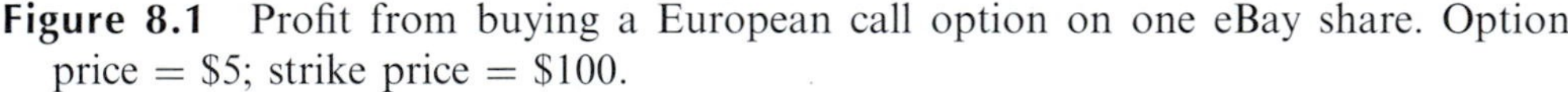

Figure 8.1 Profit from buying a European call option on one eBay share. Option price = \$5; strike price = \$100.

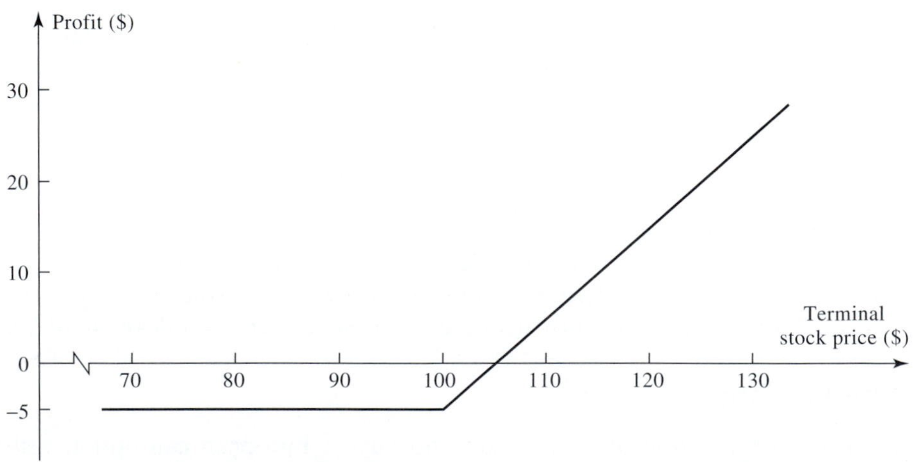

Figure 8.2 Profit from buying a European put option on one IBM share. Option price = \$7; strike price = \$70.

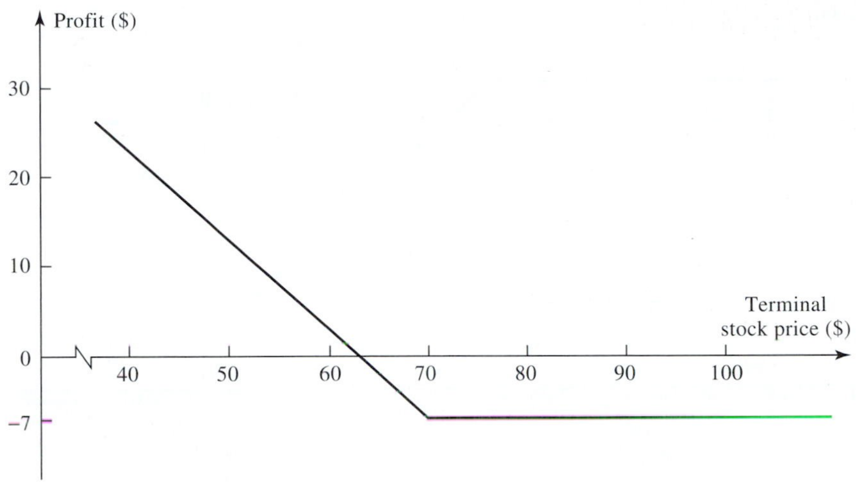

price of an option to sell one share is \$7. The initial investment is \$700. Because the option is European, it will be exercised only if the stock price is below \$70 on the expiration date. Suppose that the stock price is \$55 on this date. The investor can buy 100 shares for \$55 per share and, under the terms of the put option, sell the same shares for \$70 to realize a gain of \$15 per share, or \$1,500. (Again, transactions costs are ignored.) When the \$700 initial cost of the option is taken into account, the investor's net profit is \$800. There is no guarantee that the investor will make a gain. If the final stock price is above \$70, the put option expires worthless, and the investor loses \$700. Figure 8.2 shows the way in which the investor's profit or loss on an option to sell one share varies with the terminal stock price in this example.

Early Exercise

As already mentioned, exchange-traded stock options are generally American rather than European. That is, the investor in the foregoing examples would not have to wait until the expiration date before exercising the option. We will see later that there are some circumstances under which it is optimal to exercise American options prior to maturity.

8.2 OPTION POSITIONS

There are two sides to every option contract. On one side is the investor who has taken the long position (i.e., has bought the option). On the other side is the investor who has taken a short position (i.e., has sold or *written* the option). The writer of an option receives cash up front, but has potential liabilities later. The writer's profit or loss is the reverse of that for the purchaser of the option. Figures 8.3 and 8.4 show the variation of the profit or loss with the final stock price for writers of the options considered in Figures 8.1 and 8.2.

Figure 8.3 Profit from writing a European call option on one eBay share. Option price = \$5; strike price = \$100.

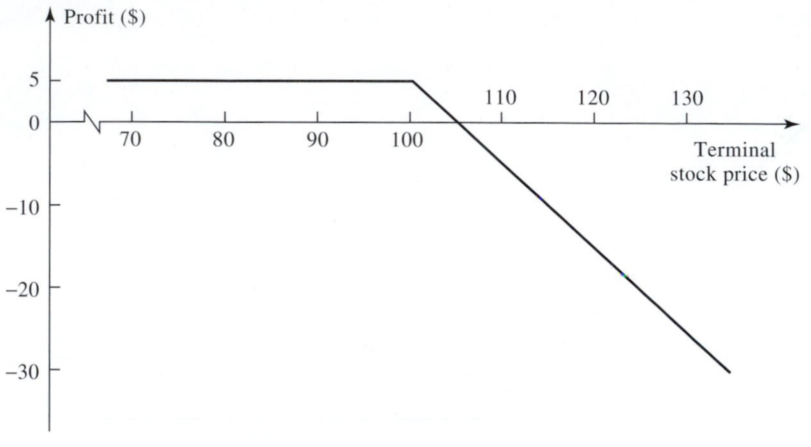

There are four types of option positions:

1. A long position in a call option
2. A long position in a put option
3. A short position in a call option
4. A short position in a put option

It is often useful to characterize European option positions in terms of the terminal value or payoff to the investor at maturity. The initial cost of the option is then not included in the calculation. If K is the strike price and S_T is the final price of the

Figure 8.4 Profit from writing a European put option on one IBM share. Option price = \$7; strike price = \$70.

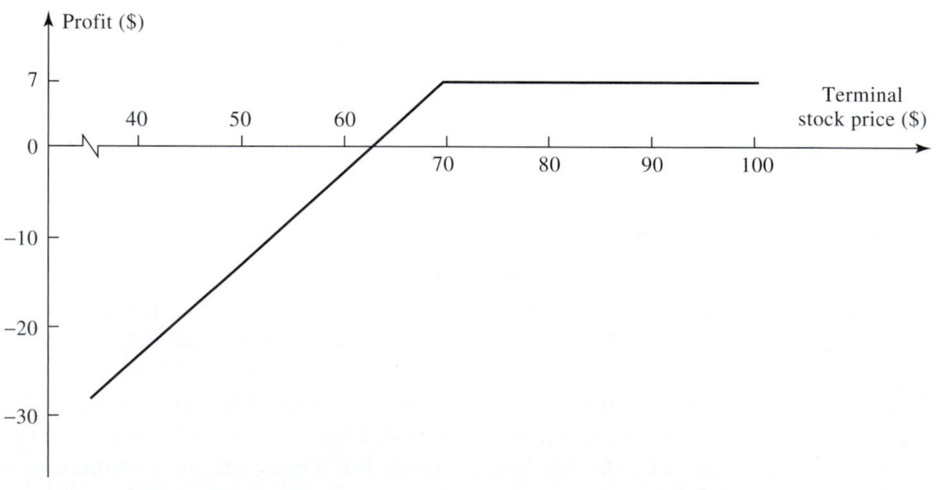

Figure 8.5 Payoffs from positions in European options: (a) long call; (b) short call; (c) long put; (d) short put. Strike price = K; price of asset at maturity = S_T.

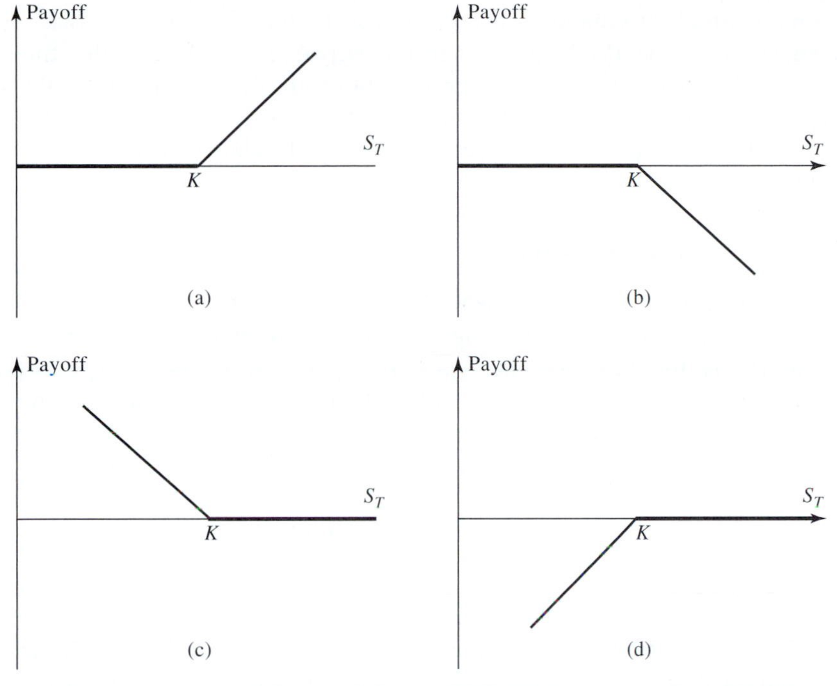

underlying asset, the payoff from a long position in a European call option is

$$\max(S_T - K, 0)$$

This reflects the fact that the option will be exercised if $S_T > K$ and will not be exercised if $S_T \leqslant K$. The payoff to the holder of a short position in the European call option is

$$-\max(S_T - K, 0) = \min(K - S_T, 0)$$

The payoff to the holder of a long position in a European put option is

$$\max(K - S_T, 0)$$

and the payoff from a short position in a European put option is

$$-\max(K - S_T, 0) = \min(S_T - K, 0)$$

Figure 8.5 illustrates these payoffs.

8.3 UNDERLYING ASSETS

This section provides a first look at options on stocks, currencies, stock indices, and futures.

Stock Options

Most trading in stock options is on exchanges. In the United States the exchanges trading stock options are the Chicago Board Options Exchange (www.cboe.com), the Philadelphia Stock Exchange (www.phlx.com), the American Stock Exchange (www.amex.com), the Pacific Exchange (www.pacifex.com), and the International Securities Exchange (www.iseoptions.com). Options trade on more than 1,000 different stocks. One contract gives the holder the right to buy or sell 100 shares at the specified strike price. This contract size is convenient because the shares themselves are normally traded in lots of 100.

Foreign Currency Options

Most currency options trading is now in the over-the-counter market, but there is some exchange trading. The major exchange for trading foreign currency options in the United States is the Philadelphia Stock Exchange. It offers both European and American contracts on a variety of different currencies. The size of one contract depends on the currency. For example, in the case of the British pound, one contract gives the holder the right to buy or sell £31,250; in the case of the Japanese yen, one contract gives the holder the right to buy or sell 6.25 million yen. Foreign currency options contracts are discussed further in Chapter 14.

Index Options

Many different index options currently trade throughout the world in both the over-the-counter market and the exchange-traded market. The most popular exchange-traded contracts in the United States are those on the S&P 500 Index (SPX), the S&P 100 Index (OEX), the Nasdaq 100 Index (NDX), and the Dow Jones Industrial Index (DJX). All of these trade on the Chicago Board Options Exchange. Most of the contracts are European. An exception is the contract on the S&P 100, which is American. One contract is usually to buy or sell 100 times the index at the specified strike price. Settlement is always in cash, rather than by delivering the portfolio underlying the index. Consider, for example, one call contract on the S&P 100 with a strike price of 980. If it is exercised when the value of the index is 992, the writer of the contract pays the holder $(992 - 980) \times 100 = \$1{,}200$. This cash payment is based on the index value at the end of the day on which exercise instructions are issued. Not surprisingly, investors usually wait until the end of a day before issuing these instructions. Index options are discussed further in Chapter 14.

Futures Options

When an exchange trades a particular futures contract it often also trades options on that contract. A futures option normally matures just before the delivery period in the futures contract. When a call option is exercised, the holder acquires from the writer a long position in the underlying futures contract plus a cash amount equal to the excess of the futures price over the strike price. When a put option is exercised, the holder acquires a short position in the underlying futures contract plus a cash amount equal to the excess of the strike price over the futures price. Futures options contracts are discussed further in Chapter 14.

8.4 SPECIFICATION OF STOCK OPTIONS

In the rest of this chapter, we will focus on stock options. As already mentioned, an exchange-traded stock option in the United States is an American-style option contract to buy or sell 100 shares of the stock. Details of the contract—the expiration date, the strike price, what happens when dividends are declared, how large a position investors can hold, and so on—are specified by the exchange.

Expiration Dates

One of the items used to describe a stock option is the month in which the expiration date occurs. Thus, a January call trading on IBM is a call option on IBM with an expiration date in January. The precise expiration date is the Saturday immediately following the third Friday of the expiration month. The last day on which options trade is the third Friday of the expiration month. An investor with a long position in an option normally has until 4:30 p.m. Central Time on that Friday to instruct a broker to exercise the option. The broker then has until 10:59 p.m. the next day to complete the paperwork notifying the exchange that exercise is to take place.

Stock options are on a January, February, or March cycle. The January cycle consists of the months of January, April, July, and October. The February cycle consists of the months of February, May, August, and November. The March cycle consists of the months of March, June, September, and December. If the expiration date for the current month has not yet been reached, options trade with expiration dates in the current month, the following month, and the next two months in the cycle. If the expiration date of the current month has passed, options trade with expiration dates in the next month, the next-but-one month, and the next two months of the expiration cycle. For example, IBM is on a January cycle. At the beginning of January, options are traded with expiration dates in January, February, April, and July; at the end of January, they are traded with expiration dates in February, March, April, and July; at the beginning of May, they are traded with expiration dates in May, June, July, and October; and so on. When one option reaches expiration, trading in another is started. Longer-term options, known as LEAPS (long-term equity anticipation securities), also trade on about 500 stocks in the United States. These have expiration dates up to 3 years into the future. The expiration dates for LEAPS on stocks are always in January.

Strike Prices

The exchange normally chooses the strike prices at which options can be written so that they are spaced \$2.50, \$5, or \$10 apart. Typically the spacing is \$2.50 when the stock price is between \$5 and \$25, \$5 when the stock price is between \$25 and \$200, and \$10 for stock prices above \$200. As will be explained shortly, stock splits and stock dividends can lead to nonstandard strike prices.

When a new expiration date is introduced, the two or three strike prices closest to the current stock price are usually selected by the exchange. If the stock price moves outside the range defined by the highest and lowest strike price, trading is usually introduced in an option with a new strike price. To illustrate these rules, suppose that the stock price is \$84 when trading begins in the October options. Call and put options would probably first be offered with strike prices of \$80, \$85, and \$90. If the stock price rose above \$90, it is likely that a strike price of \$95 would be offered; if it fell below \$80, it is likely that a strike price of \$75 would be offered; and so on.

Terminology

For any given asset at any given time, many different option contracts may be trading. Consider a stock that has four expiration dates and five strike prices. If call and put options trade with every expiration date and every strike price, there are a total of 40 different contracts. All options of the same type (calls or puts) are referred to as an *option class*. For example, IBM calls are one class, whereas IBM puts are another class. An *option series* consists of all the options of a given class with the same expiration date and strike price. In other words, an option series refers to a particular contract that is traded. The IBM 50 October calls are an option series.

Options are referred to as *in the money*, *at the money*, or *out of the money*. If S is the stock price and K is the strike price, a call option is in the money when $S > K$, at the money when $S = K$, and out of the money when $S < K$. A put option is in the money when $S < K$, at the money when $S = K$, and out of the money when $S > K$. Clearly, an option will be exercised only when it is in the money. In the absence of transactions costs, an in-the-money option will always be exercised on the expiration date if it has not been exercised previously.

The *intrinsic value* of an option is defined as the maximum of zero and the value the option would have if it were exercised immediately. For a call option, the intrinsic value is therefore $\max(S - K, 0)$. For a put option, it is $\max(K - S, 0)$. An in-the-money American option must be worth at least as much as its intrinsic value because the holder can realize a positive intrinsic value by exercising immediately. Often it is optimal for the holder of an in-the-money American option to wait rather than exercise immediately. The option is then said to have *time value*. The total value of an option can be thought of as the sum of its intrinsic value and its time value.

FLEX Options

The Chicago Board Options Exchange offers FLEX (short for flexible) options on equities and equity indices. These are options where the traders on the floor of the exchange agree to nonstandard terms. These nonstandard terms can involve a strike price or an expiration date that is different from what is usually offered by the exchange. It can also involve the option being European rather than American. FLEX options are an attempt by option exchanges to regain business from the over-the-counter markets. The exchange specifies a minimum size (e.g., 100 contracts) for FLEX option trades.

Dividends and Stock Splits

The early over-the-counter options were dividend protected. If a company declared a cash dividend, the strike price for options on the company's stock was reduced on the ex-dividend day by the amount of the dividend. Exchange-traded options are not usually adjusted for cash dividends. In other words, when a cash dividend occurs, there are no adjustments to the terms of the option contract. An exception is sometimes made for large cash dividends (see the Gucci Group example in Business Snapshot 8.1).

Exchange-traded options are adjusted for stock splits. A stock split occurs when the existing shares are "split" into more shares. For example, in a 3-for-1 stock split, three

Business Snapshot 8.1 Gucci Group's Large Dividend

When there is a large cash dividend (typically one more than 10% of the stock price), a committee of the Options Clearing Corporation (OCC) at the Chicago Board Options Exchange can decide to make adjustments to the terms of options traded on the exchange.

On May 28, 2003, Gucci Group NV (GUC) declared a cash dividend of 13.50 euros (approximately \$15.88) per common share and this was approved at the GUC annual shareholders meeting on July 16, 2003. The dividend was about 16% of the share price at the time it was declared. In this case, the OCC committee decided to adjust the terms of options. As a result, exercise of an option contract required the delivery of 100 shares plus $100 \times 15.88 = \$1,588$ of cash. The holder of a call contract paid 100 times the strike price on exercise and received \$1,588 of cash in addition to 100 shares. The holder of a put contract received 100 times the strike price on exercise and delivered \$1,588 of cash in addition to 100 shares. These adjustments had the effect of reducing the strike price by \$15.88.

Adjustments for large dividends are not always made. For example, Deutsche Terminbörse chose not to adjust the terms of options traded on that exchange when Daimler-Benz surprised the market on March 10, 1998, with a dividend equal to about 12% of its stock price.

new shares are issued to replace each existing share. Because a stock split does not change the assets or the earning ability of a company, we should not expect it to have any effect on the wealth of the company's shareholders. All else being equal, the 3-for-1 stock split should cause the stock price to go down to one-third of its previous value. In general, an n-for-m stock split should cause the stock price to go down to m/n of its previous value. The terms of option contracts are adjusted to reflect expected changes in a stock price arising from a stock split. After an n-for-m stock split, the strike price is reduced to m/n of its previous value, and the number of shares covered by one contract is increased to n/m of its previous value. If the stock price declines in the way expected, the positions of both the writer and the purchaser of a contract remain unchanged.

Example 8.1

Consider a call option to buy 100 shares of a company for \$30 per share. Suppose that the company makes a 2-for-1 stock split. The terms of the option contract are then changed so that it gives the holder the right to purchase 200 shares for \$15 per share.

Stock options are adjusted for stock dividends. A stock dividend involves a company issuing more shares to its existing shareholders. For example, a 20% stock dividend means that investors receive one new share for each five already owned. A stock dividend, like a stock split, has no effect on either the assets or the earning power of a company. The stock price can be expected to go down as a result of a stock dividend. The 20% stock dividend referred to is essentially the same as a 6-for-5 stock split. All else being equal, it should cause the stock price to decline to 5/6 of its previous value. The terms of an option are adjusted to reflect the expected price decline arising from a stock dividend in the same way as they are for that arising from a stock split.

Example 8.2

Consider a put option to sell 100 shares of a company for $15 per share. Suppose that the company declares a 25% stock dividend. This is equivalent to a 5-for-4 stock split. The terms of the option contract are changed so that it gives the holder the right to sell 125 shares for $12.

Adjustments are also made for rights issues. The basic procedure is to calculate the theoretical price of the rights and then to reduce the strike price by this amount.

Position Limits and Exercise Limits

The Chicago Board Options Exchange often specifies a *position limit* for option contracts. This defines the maximum number of option contracts that an investor can hold on one side of the market. For this purpose, long calls and short puts are considered to be on the same side of the market. Also considered to be on the same side are short calls and long puts. The *exercise limit* usually equals the position limit. It defines the maximum number of contracts that can be exercised by any individual (or group of individuals acting together) in any period of five consecutive business days. Options on the largest and most frequently traded stocks have positions limits of 75,000 contracts. Smaller capitalization stocks have position limits of 60,000, 31,500, 22,500, or 13,500 contracts.

Position limits and exercise limits are designed to prevent the market from being unduly influenced by the activities of an individual investor or group of investors. However, whether the limits are really necessary is a controversial issue.

8.5 NEWSPAPER QUOTES

Many newspapers carry options prices. Table 8.1 shows the prices as they appeared in the *Wall Street Journal* of Thursday February 5, 2004. They refer to the last trade on the previous day (Wednesday February 4, 2004).

The first part of the table shows the 40 most actively traded option contracts listed according to their volume of trading. The most active contract was the February 2004 contract on the Nasdaq 100 index. From the table we see that a call option contract on Cisco expiring in February 2004 with a strike price of $25 traded for $0.40 down $1.60 from the previous day. The closing price of Cisco's stock was $24.08. Similarly, a put option on Peoplesoft expiring in April 2004 with a strike price 20 traded for $0.50 down $0.35 from the previous day. Peoplesoft's stock price closed at $22.70. The second part of the table shows quotes for long-term options (LEAPS). For example, a Cisco call with a strike price of $30 expiring in January 2006 traded for $2.75, while the corresponding put traded for $7.20.

As mentioned earlier, one contract is for the purchase or sale of 100 shares. One contract therefore costs 100 times the price shown. Because most options are priced at less than $10 and some are priced at less than $1, investors do not have to be extremely wealthy to trade options.

The *Wall Street Journal* also shows at the end of the first part of the table the total call volume, put volume, call open interest, and put open interest for each exchange. As in the case of futures contracts, the volume is the total number of contracts traded on a day and the open interest is the number of contracts outstanding.

Table 8.1 Stock option quotes from the *Wall Street Journal* on February 5, 2004.

MOST ACTIVE LISTED OPTIONS

Wednesday, February 4, 2004

Composite volume and close for actively traded equity and LEAPS, or long-term options, with results for the corresponding put or call contract. Volume figures are unofficial. Open interest is total outstanding for all exchanges and reflects previous trading day. Close when possible is shown for the underlying stock or primary market. **XC**-Composite. **p**-Put. **o**-Strike price adjusted for split.

OPTION/STRIKE				VOL	EXCH	LAST	NET CHG	CLOSE	OPEN INT
Nasd100Tr	Feb	37		79,072	XC	0.45	-0.30	36.33	179,411
Nasd100Tr	Feb	37	p	77,716	XC	1.10	0.30	36.33	366,260
Cisco	Feb	25	p	65,470	XC	1.30	0.85	24.08	125,149
Nasd100Tr	Mar	37	p	50,099	XC	1.60	0.30	36.33	136,136
Cisco	Feb	25		45,922	XC	0.40	-1.60	24.08	53,363
Nasd100Tr	Feb	38	p	45,379	XC	1.80	0.40	36.33	256,982
Nasd100Tr	Mar	37		40,652	XC	1	-0.30	36.33	85,536
Cisco	Apr	27.50		37,154	XC	0.50	-0.70	24.08	50,310
Nasd100Tr	Feb	36	p	32,848	XC	0.60	0.20	36.33	272,591
Nasd100Tr	Feb	38		32,650	XC	0.20	-0.20	36.33	210,587
Cisco	Feb	27.50		28,459	XC	0.10	-0.55	24.08	159,880
Nasd100Tr	Mar	36	p	23,642	XC	1.15	0.25	36.33	132,833
SemiHTr	Feb	42.50	p	22,758	XC	2.30	0.70	40.58	55,469
JDS Uni	Mar	5		21,315	XC	0.30	-0.15	4.76	47,388
ATT Wrls	Jan 05	10	p	20,942	XC	0.50	-0.05	11.13	9,652
Cisco	Mar	27.50		20,475	XC	0.30	-0.70	24.08	26,565
Nasd100Tr	Jan 06	35		20,087	XC	6.40	-0.30	36.33	105,059
Nasd100Tr	Mar	38		18,915	XC	0.60	-0.25	36.33	65,878
Intel	Feb	30		18,538	XC	0.95	-0.80	30.02	28,975
JohnJn	Feb	55		17,424	XC	0.55	0.25	54.48	18,120
Cisco	Apr	25		16,786	XC	1.15	-1.40	24.08	35,860
ATT Wrls	Feb	11		16,696	XC	0.35	...	11.13	19,457
FordM	Jan 05	20		16,006	XC	0.35	0.05	13.89	17,243
Nasd100Tr	Feb	35	p	15,424	XC	0.25	...	36.33	80,784
ATT Wrls	Apr	11		14,865	XC	0.70	...	11.13	4,849
Pfizer	Feb	70		14,847	XC	1	0.35	38.27	19,623
Nasd100Tr	Feb	36		14,301	XC	0.95	-0.50	36.33	46,174
Nasd100Tr	Jun	35	p	13,821	XC	1.70	0.25	36.33	70,112
Peoplesoft	Apr	20	p	12,605	XC	0.50	-0.35	22.70	7,767
Peoplesoft	Mar	22.50	p	12,542	XC	1.05	-0.50	22.70	289
SemiHTr	Feb	40	p	12,235	XC	0.95	0.45	40.58	34,513
Pfizer	Mar	40		12,164	XC	0.40	0.15	38.27	9,707
Cisco	Mar	25		11,453	XC	0.85	-1.45	24.08	7,877
ATT Wrls	Jul	12.50		11,056	XC	0.30	-0.05	11.13	65,795
Conseco	Jun	15	p	11,006	XC	0.45	0.30	21.86	547
Nasd100Tr	Feb	39	p	10,906	XC	2.70	0.55	36.33	52,208
Pfizer	Mar	70		10,676	XC	1.45	0.40	38.27	42,155
WalMart	Feb	55		10,613	XC	1.10	0.15	55.39	47,678
Dellinc	Feb	32.50	p	10,542	XC	0.95	0.50	32.39	27,928
Cisco	Feb	27.50	p	10,526	XC	3.40	1.75	24.08	40,102

Volume & Open Interest Summaries

AMERICAN			
Call Vol:	507,923	Open Int:	45,122,029
Put Vol:	435,069	Open Int:	34,155,216
CHICAGO BOARD			
Call Vol:	803,225	Open Int:	59,856,094
Put Vol:	647,213	Open Int:	49,257,435
INTL SECURITIES			
Call Vol:	1,006,254	Open Int:	51,961,968
Put Vol:	704,231	Open Int:	41,896,347
PHILADELPHIA			
Call Vol:	424,568	Open Int:	43,397,779
Put Vol:	263,640	Open Int:	33,690,351
PACIFIC			
Call Vol:	234,706	Open Int:	54,541,910
Put Vol:	159,733	Open Int:	43,234,469
TOTAL			
Call Vol:	2,976,676		
Put Vol:	2,209,886		

LEAPS-LONG TERM OPTIONS

OPTION/STRIKE		EXP	-CALL- VOL	-CALL- LAST	-PUT- VOL	-PUT- LAST
AT&T	15	Jan 05	...	...	4450	0.80
19.14	17.50	Jan 05	315	2.80	3615	1.70
19.14	20	Jan 05	898	1.65	1414	3.20
ATT Wrls	10	Jan 05	430	1.70	20942	0.50
AMD	7.50	Jan 06	...	...	7520	0.95
14.13	17.50	Jan 05	3109	2.05	...	...
Amgen	70	Jan 05	1431	4.90	...	...
ApldMat	15	Jan 05	35	7.40	3040	0.85
21.38	17.50	Jan 05	10	5.40	6290	1.45
Broadcom	40	Jan 05	2255	6.30	120	7.30
Cisco	22.50	Jan 05	804	4.30	2899	2.40
24.08	25	Jan 05	4397	3.10	633	3.60
24.08	25	Jan 06	3272	4.60	228	4.60
24.08	30	Jan 05	5208	1.45	214	6.90
24.08	30	Jan 06	3147	2.75	40	7.20
24.08	40	Jan 06	1988	0.95	...	...
CompAsc	25	Jan 05	1800	4.70	300	3.10
ContlAir	10	Jan 06	...	...	1500	2.20
Corning	12.50	Jan 05	2622	1.90	160	2.20
11.99	12.50	Jan 06	3942	3.30	34	3.10
DJIA Diam	116	Jan 05	1500	1.85	...	...
Dell Inc	35	Jan 06	87	4.50	1623	5.90
DukeEgy	22.50	Jan 06	3457	2.05	...	...
ElPasoCp	5	Jan 05	...	...	3500	0.50
8.16	7.50	Jan 05	5302	1.85	1207	1.25
FordM	12.50	Jan 05	2079	2.60	2	1.30
13.89	12.50	Jan 06	2009	3.10	4011	1.90
13.89	15	Jan 06	3527	2.10	20	3.20
13.89	20	Jan 05	16006	0.35	...	...
FredMac	60	Jan 05	192	7.50	2550	5.30
GenMotrs	10	Jan 06	...	...	9100	0.20
47.97	15	Jan 06	...	...	3500	0.45
47.97	20	Jan 06	...	...	3690	0.75
47.97	40	Jan 06	2040	9.70	105	4.40
47.97	55	Jan 06	2245	3.40	...	...
Gillette	45	Jan 05	1450	0.40	...	...
HomeDp	30	Jan 05	...	...	1500	1.45
Intel	30	Jan 05	1127	4.10	2389	3.60
JohnJns	55	Jan 05	107	3.60	1457	4.20
LillyEli	65	Jan 05	52	10.50	1575	5.80
70.50	70	Jan 05	1862	8	1515	8
70.50	75	Jan 05	2445	5.80	...	...
Lucent	2.50	Jan 05	1885	1.90	20	0.20
4.20	5	Jan 05	3845	0.70	703	1.45
LucentT	5	Jan 06	2023	1.10	260	1.75
Lyondell	12.50	Jan 05	...	...	5016	1.10
Maxim	45	Jan 05	10	9.90	5000	5
48.69	55	Jan 05	5075	5	60	10.30
MicronT	22.50	Jan 06	...	...	5000	7.90
Microsft	22.50	Jan 05	22	5.80	1480	0.90
Microsoft	30	Jan 06	1912	2.85	...	...
Nasd100Tr	34	Jan 06	21	6.90	2510	3.40
36.33	35	Jan 05	1713	4.50	233	2.85
36.33	35	Jan 06	20087	6.40	37	4
36.33	38	Jan 06	1731	4.70	1956	5.30
36.33	47	Jan 05	1510	0.55	...	...
36.33	49	Jan 06	2500	1.35	...	...
NortelNw	7.50	Jan 05	1995	1.70	504	1.55
7.50	10	Jan 05	1822	0.95	66	3.40
Pfizer	40	Jan 05	1766	2.15	24	4.10
RylCarb	15	Jan 06	...	...	2250	0.45
SBC Com	20	Jan 06	47	6.20	1531	1.50
SwstAirl	15	Jan 06	5561	2.90	5151	2.90
SprntFON	20	Jan 06	...	...	2620	4.40
SunMicro	5	Jan 06	1784	1.45	241	1.20
TenetHlt	7.50	Jan 06	...	...	2010	1.15
TimeWarn	15	Jan 05	185	3.30	3205	0.90
17.19	15	Jan 06	24	4.10	5000	1.35
17.19	17.50	Jan 06	8	2.75	3649	2.40
17.19	20	Jan 06	2581	1.70	...	...
UltraPet	25	Jan 05	...	...	2000	4.10
Verizon	30	Jan 06	...	...	2714	2.55
WalMart	55	Jan 06	2033	6.80	2478	5.30
WinnDix	2.50	Jan 05	...	...	3080	0.40
XM Sat	5	Jan 06	...	...	2930	0.40

Volume & Open Interest Summaries

CHICAGO BOARD			
Call Vol:	31,142	Open Int:	5,520,851
Put Vol:	27,750	Open Int:	6,222,730
INTL SECURITIES			
Call Vol:	108,287	Open Int:	21,850,815
Put Vol:	75,548	Open Int:	20,174,219
PACIFIC			
Call Vol:	41,886	Open Int:	21,859,348
Put Vol:	43,151	Open Int:	20,109,861
TOTAL			
Call Vol:	181,315		
Put Vol:	146,449		

Source: Reprinted by permission of Dow Jones, Inc., via Copyright Clearance Center, Inc.

8.6 TRADING

Traditionally, exchanges have had to provide a large open area for individuals to meet and trade options. This is changing. Eurex, the large European derivatives exchange, is fully electronic, so traders do not have to physically meet.[1] The International Securities Exchange (www.iseoptions.com) launched the first all-electronic options market for equities in the United States in May 2000. The Chicago Board Options Exchange has CBOEdirect, and the CME has GLOBEX. Both are electronic systems that run side by side with their floor-based open-outcry markets.

Market Makers

Most options exchanges use market makers to facilitate trading. A market maker for a certain option is an individual who, when asked to do so, will quote both a bid and an offer price on the option. The bid is the price at which the market maker is prepared to buy, and the offer is the price at which the market maker is prepared to sell. At the time the bid and offer prices are quoted, the market maker does not know whether the trader who asked for the quotes wants to buy or sell the option. The offer is always higher than the bid, and the amount by which the offer exceeds the bid is referred to as the *bid–offer* spread. The exchange sets upper limits for the bid–offer spread. For example, it might specify that the spread be no more than \$0.25 for options priced at less than \$0.50, \$0.50 for options priced between \$0.50 and \$10, \$0.75 for options priced between \$10 and \$20, and \$1 for options priced over \$20.

The existence of the market maker ensures that buy and sell orders can always be executed at some price without any delays. Market makers therefore add liquidity to the market. The market makers themselves make their profits from the bid–offer spread. They use some of the schemes discussed later in this book to hedge their risks.

Offsetting Orders

An investor who has purchased an option can close out the position by issuing an offsetting order to sell the same option. Similarly, an investor who has written an option can close out the position by issuing an offsetting order to buy the same option. (In this respect options markets are similar to futures markets.) If, when an options contract is traded, neither investor is closing an existing position, the open interest increases by one contract. If one investor is closing an existing position and the other is not, the open interest stays the same. If both investors are closing existing positions, the open interest goes down by one contract.

8.7 COMMISSIONS

The types of orders that can be placed with a broker for options trading are similar to those for futures trading (see Section 2.7). A market order is to be executed immediately; a limit order specifies the least favorable price at which the order can be executed; and so on.

[1] Eurex has set up an all-electronic exchange in Chicago.

For a retail investor, commissions vary significantly from broker to broker. Discount brokers generally charge lower commissions than full-service brokers. The actual amount charged is often calculated as a fixed cost plus a proportion of the dollar amount of the trade. Table 8.2 shows the sort of schedule that might be offered by a discount broker. Thus, the purchase of eight contracts when the option price is \$3 would cost $\$20 + (0.02 \times \$2{,}400) = \$68$ in commissions.

If an option position is closed out by entering into an offsetting trade, the commission must be paid again. If the option is exercised, the commission is the same as it would be if the investor placed an order to buy or sell the underlying stock. Typically, this is 1% to 2% of the stock's value.

Consider an investor who buys one call contract with a strike price of \$50 when the stock price is \$49. We suppose the option price is \$4.50, so that the cost of the contract is \$450. Under the schedule in Table 8.2, the purchase or sale of one contract always costs \$30 (both the maximum and minimum commission is \$30 for the first contract). Suppose that the stock price rises and the option is exercised when the stock reaches \$60. Assuming that the investor pays 1.5% commission on stock trades, the commission payable when the option is exercised is

$$0.015 \times \$60 \times 100 = \$90$$

The total commission paid is therefore \$120, and the net profit to the investor is

$$\$1{,}000 - \$450 - \$120 = \$430$$

Note that selling the option for \$10 instead of exercising it would save the investor \$60 in commissions. (The commission payable when an option is sold is only \$30 in our example.) In general, the commission system tends to push retail investors in the direction of selling options rather than exercising them.

A hidden cost in option trading (and in stock trading) is the market maker's bid–offer spread. Suppose that, in the example just considered, the bid price was \$4.00 and the offer price was \$4.50 at the time the option was purchased. We can reasonably assume that a "fair" price for the option is halfway between the bid and the offer price, or \$4.25. The cost to the buyer and to the seller of the market maker system is the difference between the fair price and the price paid. This is \$0.25 per option, or \$25 per contract.

Table 8.2 A typical commission schedule for a discount broker.

Dollar amount of trade	*Commission**
< \$2,500	\$20 + 2% of dollar amount
\$2,500 to \$10,000	\$45 + 1% of dollar amount
> \$10,000	\$120 + 0.25% of dollar amount

* Maximum commission is \$30 per contract for the first five contracts plus \$20 per contract for each additional contract. Minimum commission is \$30 per contract for the first contract plus \$2 per contract for each additional contract.

8.8 MARGINS

When shares are purchased in the United States, an investor can either pay cash or borrow using a margin account. (This is known as *buying on margin*.) The initial margin is usually 50% of the value of the shares, and the maintenance margin is usually 25% of the value of the shares. The margin account operates like that for a futures contract (see Chapter 2).

When call and put options with maturities less than 9 months are purchased, the option price must be paid in full. Investors are not allowed to buy these options on margin because options already contain substantial leverage and buying on margin would raise this leverage to an unacceptable level. For options with maturities greater than 9 months investors can buy on margin, borrowing up to 25% of the option value.

An investor who writes options is required to maintain funds in a margin account. Both the investor's broker and the exchange want to be satisfied that the investor will not default if the option is exercised. The size of the margin required depends on the circumstances.

Writing Naked Options

A *naked option* is an option that is not combined with an offsetting position in the underlying stock. The initial margin required by the CBOE for a written naked call option is the greater of the following two calculations:

1. A total of 100% of the proceeds of the sale plus 20% of the underlying share price less the amount, if any, by which the option is out of the money
2. A total of 100% of the option proceeds plus 10% of the underlying share price

For a written naked put option, it is the greater of

1. A total of 100% of the proceeds of the sale plus 20% of the underlying share price less the amount, if any, by which the option is out of the money
2. A total of 100% of the option proceeds plus 10% of the exercise price

The 20% in the preceding calculations is replaced by 15% for options on a broadly based stock index because a stock index is usually less volatile than the price of an individual stock.

Example 8.3

An investor writes four naked call option contracts on a stock. The option price is \$5, the strike price is \$40, and the stock price is \$38. Because the option is \$2 out of the money, the first calculation gives

$$400 \times (5 + 0.2 \times 38 - 2) = \$4{,}240$$

The second calculation gives

$$400 \times (5 + 0.1 \times 38) = \$3{,}520$$

The initial margin requirement is therefore \$4,240. Note that, if the option had been a put, it would be \$2 in the money and the margin requirement would be

$$400 \times (5 + 0.2 \times 38) = \$5{,}040$$

In both cases the proceeds of the sale, \$2,000, can be used to form part of the margin account.

A calculation similar to the initial margin calculation (but with the current market price replacing the proceeds of sale) is repeated every day. Funds can be withdrawn from the margin account when the calculation indicates that the margin required is less than the current balance in the margin account. When the calculation indicates that a significantly greater margin is required, a margin call will be made.

Other Rules

In Chapter 10, we will examine option trading strategies such as covered calls, protective puts, spreads, combinations, straddles, and strangles. The CBOE has special rules for determining the margin requirements when these trading strategies are used. These are described in the *CBOE Margin Manual*, which is available on the CBOE website (www.cboe.com).

As an example of the rules, consider an investor who writes a covered call. This is a written call option when the shares that might have to be delivered are already owned. Covered calls are far less risky than naked calls, because the worst that can happen is that the investor is required to sell shares already owned at below their market value. No margin is required on the written option. However, the investor can borrow an amount equal to $0.5\min(S, K)$, rather than the usual $0.5S$, on the stock position.

8.9 THE OPTIONS CLEARING CORPORATION

The Options Clearing Corporation (OCC) performs much the same function for options markets as the clearinghouse does for futures markets (see Chapter 2). It guarantees that options writers will fulfill their obligations under the terms of options contracts and keeps a record of all long and short positions. The OCC has a number of members, and all options trades must be cleared through a member. If a brokerage house is not itself a member of an exchange's OCC, it must arrange to clear its trades with a member. Members are required to have a certain minimum amount of capital and to contribute to a special fund that can be used if any member defaults on an option obligation.

The writer of the option maintains a margin account with a broker, as described earlier.[2] The broker maintains a margin account with the OCC member that clears its trades. The OCC member in turn maintains a margin account with the OCC.

Exercising an Option

When an investor notifies a broker to exercise an option, the broker in turn notifies the OCC member that clears its trades. This member then places an exercise order with

[2] The margin requirements described in the previous section are the minimum requirements specified by the OCC. A brokerage house may require higher margins from its clients. However, it cannot require lower margins. Some brokerage houses do not allow their retail clients to write uncovered options at all.

the OCC. The OCC randomly selects a member with an outstanding short position in the same option. The member, using a procedure established in advance, selects a particular investor who has written the option. If the option is a call, this investor is required to sell stock at the strike price. If it is a put, the investor is required to buy stock at the strike price. The investor is said to be *assigned*. When an option is exercised, the open interest goes down by one.

At the expiration of the option, all in-the-money options should be exercised unless the transactions costs are so high as to wipe out the payoff from the option. Some brokerage firms will automatically exercise options for a client at expiration when it is in their client's interest to do so. Many exchanges also have rules for exercising options that are in the money at expiration.

8.10 REGULATION

Options markets are regulated in a number of different ways. Both the exchange and its Options Clearing Corporation have rules governing the behavior of traders. In addition, there are both federal and state regulatory authorities. In general, options markets have demonstrated a willingness to regulate themselves. There have been no major scandals or defaults by OCC members. Investors can have a high level of confidence in the way the market is run.

The Securities and Exchange Commission is responsible for regulating options markets in stocks, stock indices, currencies, and bonds at the federal level. The Commodity Futures Trading Commission is responsible for regulating markets for options on futures. The major options markets are in the states of Illinois and New York. These states actively enforce their own laws on unacceptable trading practices.

8.11 TAXATION

Determining the tax implications of options strategies can be tricky, and an investor who is in doubt about this should consult a tax specialist. In the United States, the general rule is that (unless the taxpayer is a professional trader) gains and losses from the trading of stock options are taxed as capital gains or losses. The way that capital gains and losses are taxed in the United States was discussed in Section 2.9. For both the holder and the writer of a stock option, a gain or loss is recognized when (a) the option expires unexercised or (b) the option position is closed out. If the option is exercised, the gain or loss from the option is rolled into the position taken in the stock and recognized when the stock position is closed out. For example, when a call option is exercised, the party with a long position is deemed to have purchased the stock at the strike price plus the call price. This is then used as a basis for calculating this party's gain or loss when the stock is eventually sold. Similarly, the party with the short call position is deemed to have sold the stock at the strike price plus the call price. When a put option is exercised, the seller of the option is deemed to have bought the stock for the strike price less the original put price and the purchaser of the option is deemed to have sold the stock for the strike price less the original put price.

Wash Sale Rule

One tax consideration in option trading in the United States is the wash sale rule. To understand this rule, imagine an investor who buys a stock when the price is \$60 and plans to keep it for the long term. If the stock price drops to \$40, the investor might be tempted to sell the stock and then immediately repurchase it, so that the \$20 loss is realized for tax purposes. To prevent this sort of thing, the tax authorities have ruled that when the repurchase is within 30 days of the sale (i.e., between 30 days before the sale and 30 days after the sale), any loss on the sale is not deductible. The disallowance also applies where, within the 61-day period, the taxpayer enters into an option or similar contract to acquire the stock. Thus, selling a stock at a loss and buying a call option within a 30-day period will lead to the loss being disallowed. The wash sale rule does not apply if the taxpayer is a dealer in stocks or securities and the loss is sustained in the ordinary course of business.

Constructive Sales

Prior to 1997, if a United States taxpayer shorted a security while holding a long position in a substantially identical security, no gain or loss was recognized until the short position was closed out. This means that short positions could be used to defer recognition of a gain for tax purposes. The situation was changed by the Tax Relief Act of 1997. An appreciated property is now treated as "constructively sold" when the owner does one of the following:

1. Enters into a short sale of the same or substantially identical property
2. Enters into a futures or forward contract to deliver the same or substantially identical property
3. Enters into one or more positions that eliminate substantially all of the loss and opportunity for gain

It should be noted that transactions reducing only the risk of loss or only the opportunity for gain should not result in constructive sales. Therefore an investor holding a long position in a stock can buy in-the-money put options on the stock without triggering a constructive sale.

Tax practitioners sometimes use options to minimize tax costs or maximize tax benefits (see Business Snapshot 8.2). Tax authorities in many jurisdictions have proposed legislation designed to combat the use of derivatives for tax purposes. Before entering into any tax-motivated transaction, a corporate treasurer or private individual should explore in detail how the structure could be unwound in the event of legislative change and how costly this process could be.

8.12 WARRANTS, EXECUTIVE STOCK OPTIONS, AND CONVERTIBLES

Usually, when a call option on a stock is exercised, the party with the short position acquires shares that have already been issued and sells them to the party with the long position for the strike price. The company whose stock underlies the option is not involved in any way. Warrants and executive stock options are call options that work slightly differently. They are written by a company on its own stock. When they are

Business Snapshot 8.2 Tax Planning Using Options

As a simple example of a possible tax planning strategy using options, suppose that Country A has a tax regime where the tax is low on interest and dividends and high on capital gains, while Country B has a tax regime where tax is high on interest and dividends and low on capital gains. It is advantageous for a company to receive the income from a security in Country A and the capital gain, if there is one, in Country B. The company would like to keep capital losses in Country A, where they can be used to offset capital gains on other items. All of this can be accomplished by arranging for a subsidiary company in Country A to have legal ownership of the security and for a subsidiary company in Country B to buy a call option on the security from the company in Country A, with the strike price of the option equal to the current value of the security. During the life of the option, income from the security is earned in Country A. If the security price rises sharply, the option will be exercised and the capital gain will be realized in Country B. If it falls sharply, the option will not be exercised and the capital loss will be realized in Country A.

exercised, the company satisfies the option holder by issuing more of its own stock and selling it to the option holder for the strike price. The exercise of a warrant or executive stock option therefore leads to an increase in the number of shares of the company's stock that are outstanding.

Warrants are call options that often come into existence as a result of a bond issue. They are added to the bond issue to make it more attractive to investors. Typically, a warrant lasts for a number of years. Once they have been created, they sometimes trade separately from the bonds to which they were originally attached.

Executive stock options are call options issued to executives to motivate them to act in the best interests of the company's shareholders (see Business Snapshot 8.3). Recently there has been a great deal of controversy about whether executive stock options should be expensed by companies on their income statements. Some companies and their accountants argue that there is no reliable way of doing this. Options experts contend that executive stock options can be valued at least as precisely as other items in financial statements. The valuation of warrants and executive stock options is discussed in Chapter 13.

A *convertible bond* is a bond issued by a company that can be converted into equity at certain times using a predetermined exchange ratio. It is therefore a bond with an embedded call option on the company's stock. Convertibles are like warrants and executive stock options in that their exercise leads to more shares being issued by the company. Convertible bonds are discussed in more detail in Chapter 21.

8.13 OVER-THE-COUNTER MARKETS

Most of this chapter has focused on exchange-traded options markets. The over-the-counter market for options has become increasingly important since the early 1980s and is now larger than the exchange-traded market. As explained in Chapter 1, in the over-the-counter market, financial institutions, corporate treasurers, and fund managers trade over the phone. There is a wide range of assets underlying the options. Over-the-counter

Business Snapshot 8.3 Executive Stock Options

Stock options became an increasingly popular type of compensation for executives and other employees in the 1990s and early 2000s. In a typical arrangement, an executive is granted a certain number of call options on the stock of the company for which he or she works. The options are at the money on the grant date. They often last for 10 years or even longer and there is a vesting period of up to 5 years. The options cannot be exercised during the vesting period, but can be exercised any time after the vesting period ends. If the executive leaves the company during the vesting period, the options are forfeited. If the executive leaves the company after the end of the vesting period, in-the-money options are exercised immediately while out-of-the-money options are forfeited. Options cannot be sold to another party by the executive.

One reason why executive stock options have been so attractive has been their accounting treatment. The compensation cost charged to the income statement for an employee stock option in the United States and other countries used to be its intrinsic value. Because most executive stock options are at the money when they are issued, this compensation cost was usually zero. In 1995, accounting standard FAS 123 was issued. This encouraged, but did not require, companies to expense the "fair value" of the options on their income statement. (If the fair value was not expensed on the income statement, it had to be reported in a footnote to the company's accounts.) At first very few companies chose to expense stock options voluntarily, but as the cost to the company of these options began to receive more publicity in the early 2000s more did so.

Accounting standards have now changed to require the expensing of stock options at their fair value on the income statement. In February 2004, the International Accounting Standards Board issued IAS 2, which required companies to start expensing stock options in 2005. In December 2004, FAS 123 was revised to require the expensing of executive stock options in the United States starting in 2005.

Executive stock options tend to be exercised earlier than similar exchange-traded or over-the-counter options because the executive is not allowed to sell the options. If an executive wants to realize cash from the options, he or she has to exercise the options and sell the stock. For this reason, valuing executive stock options is not as easy as valuing regular options. It requires a model of the executives' early exercise behavior.

options on foreign exchange and interest rates are particularly popular. The chief potential disadvantage of the over-the-counter market is that option writer may default. This means that the purchaser is subject to some credit risk. In an attempt to overcome this disadvantage, market participants are adopting a number of measures such as requiring counterparties to post collateral. This was discussed in Section 2.4.

The instruments traded in the over-the-counter market are often structured by financial institutions to meet the precise needs of their clients. Sometimes this involves choosing exercise dates, strike prices, and contract sizes that are different from those traded by the exchange. In other cases the structure of the option is different from standard calls and puts. The option is then referred to as an *exotic option*. Chapter 22 describes a number of different types of exotic options.

SUMMARY

There are two types of options: calls and puts. A call option gives the holder the right to buy the underlying asset for a certain price by a certain date. A put option gives the holder the right to sell the underlying asset by a certain date for a certain price. There are four possible positions in options markets: a long position in a call, a short position in a call, a long position in a put, and a short position in a put. Taking a short position in an option is known as writing it. Options are currently traded on stocks, stock indices, foreign currencies, futures contracts, and other assets.

An exchange must specify the terms of the option contracts it trades. In particular, it must specify the size of the contract, the precise expiration time, and the strike price. In the United States one stock option contract gives the holder the right to buy or sell 100 shares. The expiration of a stock option contract is 10:59 p.m. Central Time on the Saturday immediately following the third Friday of the expiration month. Options with several different expiration months trade at any given time. Strike prices are at $\$2\frac{1}{2}$, \$5, or \$10 intervals, depending on the stock price. The strike price is generally fairly close to the stock price when trading in an option begins.

The terms of a stock option are not normally adjusted for cash dividends. However, they are adjusted for stock dividends, stock splits, and rights issues. The aim of the adjustment is to keep the positions of both the writer and the buyer of a contract unchanged.

Most options exchanges use market makers. A market maker is an individual who is prepared to quote both a bid price (at which he or she is prepared to buy) and an offer price (at which he or she is prepared to sell). Market makers improve the liquidity of the market and ensure that there is never any delay in executing market orders. They themselves make a profit from the difference between their bid and offer prices (known as their bid–offer spread). The exchange has rules specifying upper limits for the bid–offer spread.

Writers of options have potential liabilities and are required to maintain margins with their brokers. If it is not a member of the Options Clearing Corporation, the broker will maintain a margin account with a firm that is a member. This firm will in turn maintain a margin account with the Options Clearing Corporation. The Options Clearing Corporation is responsible for keeping a record of all outstanding contracts, handling exercise orders, and so on.

Not all options are traded on exchanges. Many options are traded by phone in the over-the-counter market. An advantage of over-the-counter options is that they can be tailored by a financial institution to meet the particular needs of a corporate treasurer or fund manager.

FURTHER READING

Arzac, E. R. "PERCs, DECs, and Other Mandatory Convertibles," *Journal of Applied Corporate Finance*, 10, 1 (1997): 54–63.

Core, J. E., and W. R. Guay. "Stock Option Plans for Non-executive Employees," *Journal of Financial Economics*, 61, 2 (2001): 253–87.

Cox, J. C., and M. Rubinstein. *Options Markets*. Upper Saddle River, NJ: Prentice-Hall, 1985.

Hull, J. C., and A. White, "How to Value Employee Stock Options," *Financial Analysts Journal*, 60, 1 (January/February 2004): 114–19.

Rubinstein, M. "On the Accounting Valuation of Employee Stock Options," *Journal of Derivatives*, 3, 1 (Fall 1995): 8–24.

Questions and Problems (Answers in Solutions Manual)

8.1. An investor buys a European put on a share for \$3. The stock price is \$42 and the strike price is \$40. Under what circumstances does the investor make a profit? Under what circumstances will the option be exercised? Draw a diagram showing the variation of the investor's profit with the stock price at the maturity of the option.

8.2. An investor sells a European call on a share for \$4. The stock price is \$47 and the strike price is \$50. Under what circumstances does the investor make a profit? Under what circumstances will the option be exercised? Draw a diagram showing the variation of the investor's profit with the stock price at the maturity of the option.

8.3. An investor sells a European call option with strike price of K and maturity T and buys a put with the same strike price and maturity. Describe the investor's position.

8.4. Explain why brokers require margins when clients write options but not when they buy options.

8.5. A stock option is on a February, May, August, and November cycle. What options trade on (a) April 1 and (b) May 30?

8.6. A company declares a 2-for-1 stock split. Explain how the terms change for a call option with a strike price of \$60.

8.7. How is an executive stock option different from a regular exchange-traded or over-the-counter American-style stock option?

8.8. A corporate treasurer is designing a hedging program involving foreign currency options. What are the pros and cons of using (a) the Philadelphia Stock Exchange and (b) the over-the-counter market for trading?

8.9. Suppose that a European call option to buy a share for \$100.00 costs \$5.00 and is held until maturity. Under what circumstances will the holder of the option make a profit? Under what circumstances will the option be exercised? Draw a diagram illustrating how the profit from a long position in the option depends on the stock price at maturity of the option.

8.10. Suppose that a European put option to sell a share for \$60 costs \$8 and is held until maturity. Under what circumstances will the seller of the option (the party with the short position) make a profit? Under what circumstances will the option be exercised? Draw a diagram illustrating how the profit from a short position in the option depends on the stock price at maturity of the option.

8.11. Describe the terminal value of the following portfolio: a newly entered-into long forward contract on an asset and a long position in a European put option on the asset with the same maturity as the forward contract and a strike price that is equal to the forward price of the asset at the time the portfolio is set up. Show that the European put option has the same value as a European call option with the same strike price and maturity.

8.12. A trader buys a call option with a strike price of \$45 and a put option with a strike price of \$40. Both options have the same maturity. The call costs \$3 and the put costs \$4. Draw a diagram showing the variation of the trader's profit with the asset price.

8.13. Explain why an American option is always worth at least as much as a European option on the same asset with the same strike price and exercise date.

8.14. Explain why an American option is always worth at least as much as its intrinsic value.

8.15. Explain carefully the difference between writing a put option and buying a call option.

8.16. The treasurer of a corporation is trying to choose between options and forward contracts to hedge the corporation's foreign exchange risk. Discuss the advantages and disadvantages of each.

8.17. Consider an exchange-traded call option contract to buy 500 shares with a strike price of \$40 and maturity in 4 months. Explain how the terms of the option contract change when there is: (a) a 10% stock dividend; (b) a 10% cash dividend; and (c) a 4-for-1 stock split.

8.18. "If most of the call options on a stock are in the money, it is likely that the stock price has risen rapidly in the last few months." Discuss this statement.

8.19. What is the effect of an unexpected cash dividend on (a) a call option price and (b) a put option price?

8.20. Options on General Motors stock are on a March, June, September, and December cycle. What options trade on (a) March 1, (b) June 30, and (c) August 5?

8.21. Explain why the market maker's bid–offer spread represents a real cost to options investors.

8.22. A United States investor writes five naked call option contracts. The option price is \$3.50, the strike price is \$60.00, and the stock price is \$57.00. What is the initial margin requirement?

Assignment Questions

8.23. The price of a stock is \$40. The price of a 1-year European put option on the stock with a strike price of \$30 is quoted as \$7 and the price of a 1-year European call option on the stock with a strike price of \$50 is quoted as \$5. Suppose that an investor buys 100 shares, shorts 100 call options, and buys 100 put options. Draw a diagram illustrating how the investor's profit or loss varies with the stock price over the next year. How does your answer change if the investor buys 100 shares, shorts 200 call options, and buys 200 put options?

8.24. "If a company does not do better than its competitors but the stock market goes up, executives do very well from their stock options. This makes no sense." Discuss this viewpoint. Can you think of alternatives to the usual executive stock option plan that take the viewpoint into account.

8.25. Use DerivaGem to calculate the value of an American put option on a non-dividend-paying stock when the stock price is \$30, the strike price is \$32, the risk-free rate is 5%, the volatility is 30%, and the time to maturity is 1.5 years. (Choose binomial American for the "option type" and 50 time steps.)
(a) What is the option's intrinsic value?
(b) What is the option's time value?
(c) What would a time value of zero indicate? What is the value of an option with zero time value?
(d) Using a trial and error approach, calculate how low the stock price would have to be for the time value of the option to be zero.

8.26. On July 20, 2004, Microsoft surprised the market by announcing a \$3 dividend. The ex-dividend date was November 17, 2004, and the payment date was December 2, 2004. Its stock price at the time was about \$28. It also changed the terms of its employee stock options so that each exercise price was adjusted downward to

$$\text{Predividend exercise price} \times \frac{\text{Closing price} - \$3.00}{\text{Closing price}}$$

The number of shares covered by each stock option outstanding was adjusted upward to

$$\text{Number of shares predividend} \times \frac{\text{Closing price}}{\text{Closing price} - \$3.00}$$

"Closing Price" means the official NASDAQ closing price of a share of Microsoft common stock on the last trading day before the ex-dividend date. Evaluate this adjustment. Compare it with the system used by exchanges to adjust for extraordinary dividends (see Business Snapshot 8.1).

CHAPTER

Properties of Stock Options

In this chapter we look at the factors affecting stock option prices. We use a number of different arbitrage arguments to explore the relationships between European option prices, American option prices, and the underlying stock price. The most important of these relationships is put–call parity, which is a relationship between European call option prices and European put option prices.

The chapter examines whether American options should be exercised early. It shows that it is never optimal to exercise an American call option on a non-dividend-paying stock prior to the option's expiration, but that under some circumstances the early exercise of an American put option on such a stock is optimal.

9.1 FACTORS AFFECTING OPTION PRICES

There are six factors affecting the price of a stock option:

1. The current stock price, S_0
2. The strike price, K
3. The time to expiration, T
4. The volatility of the stock price, σ
5. The risk-free interest rate, r
6. The dividends expected during the life of the option

In this section we consider what happens to option prices when one of these factors changes, with all the others remaining fixed. The results are summarized in Table 9.1.

Figures 9.1 and 9.2 show how European call and put prices depend on the first five factors in the situation where $S_0 = 50$, $K = 50$, $r = 5\%$ per annum, $\sigma = 30\%$ per annum, $T = 1$ year, and there are no dividends. In this case the call price is 7.116 and the put price is 4.677.

Stock Price and Strike Price

If a call option is exercised at some future time, the payoff will be the amount by which the stock price exceeds the strike price. Call options therefore become more valuable as

Table 9.1 Summary of the effect on the price of a stock option of increasing one variable while keeping all others fixed.*

Variable	*European call*	*European put*	*American call*	*American put*
Current stock price	+	−	+	−
Strike price	−	+	−	+
Time to expiration	?	?	+	+
Volatility	+	+	+	+
Risk-free rate	+	−	+	−
Amount of future dividends	−	+	−	+

* + indicates that an increase in the variable causes the option price to increase; − indicates that an increase in the variable causes the option price to decrease; ? indicates that the relationship is uncertain.

the stock price increases and less valuable as the strike price increases. For a put option, the payoff on exercise is the amount by which the strike price exceeds the stock price. Put options therefore behave in the opposite way from call options: they become less valuable as the stock price increases and more valuable as the strike price increases. Figures 9.1(a–d) illustrate the way in which put and call prices depend on the stock price and strike price.

Time to Expiration

Now consider the effect of the expiration date. Both put and call American options become more valuable as the time to expiration increases. Suppose that we have two American options that differ only as far as the expiration date is concerned. The owner of the long-life option has all the exercise opportunities open to the owner of the short-life option—and more. The long-life option must therefore always be worth at least as much as the short-life option.

Although European put and call options usually become more valuable as the time to expiration increases (see, e.g., Figures 9.1(e, f)), this is not always the case. Consider two European call options on a stock: one with an expiration date in 1 month, the other with an expiration date in 2 months. Suppose that a very large dividend is expected in 6 weeks. The dividend will cause the stock price to decline, so that the short-life option could be worth more than the long-life option.

Volatility

The precise way in which volatility is defined is discussed in Chapter 13. Roughly speaking, the *volatility* of a stock price is a measure of how uncertain we are about future stock price movements. As volatility increases, the chance that the stock will do very well or very poorly increases. For the owner of a stock, these two outcomes tend to offset each other. However, this is not so for the owner of a call or put. The owner of a call benefits from price increases but has limited downside risk in the event of price decreases because the most the owner can lose is the price of the option. Similarly, the owner of a put benefits from price decreases, but has limited downside risk in the event of price increases. The values of both calls and puts therefore increase as volatility increases (see Figures 9.2(a, b)).

Risk-Free Interest Rate

The risk-free interest rate affects the price of an option in a less clear-cut way. As interest rates in the economy increase, the expected return required by investors from the stock

Figure 9.1 Effect of changes in stock price, strike price, and expiration date on option prices when $S_0 = 50$, $K = 50$, $r = 5\%$, $\sigma = 30\%$, and $T = 1$.

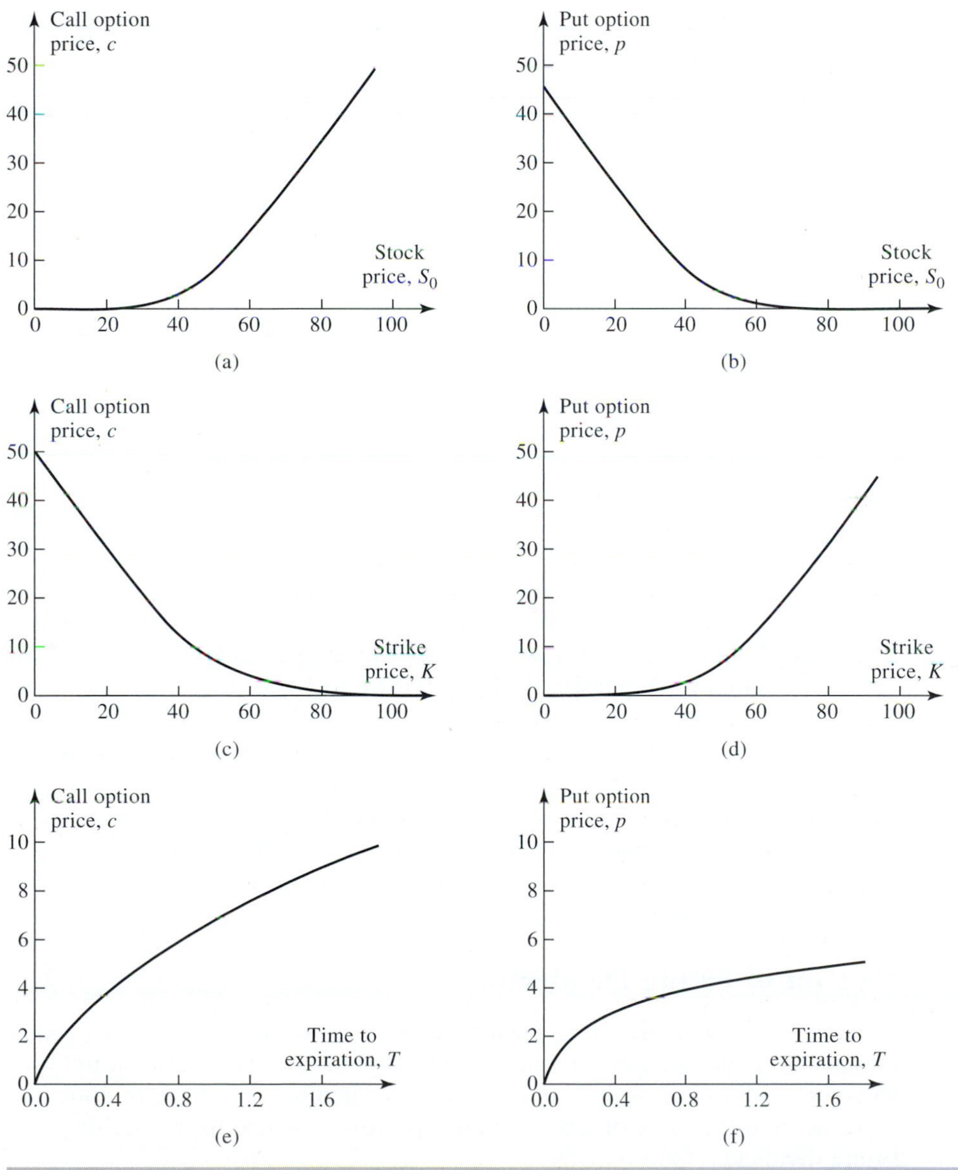

Figure 9.2 Effect of changes in volatility and risk-free interest rate on option prices when $S_0 = 50$, $K = 50$, $r = 5\%$, $\sigma = 30\%$, and $T = 1$.

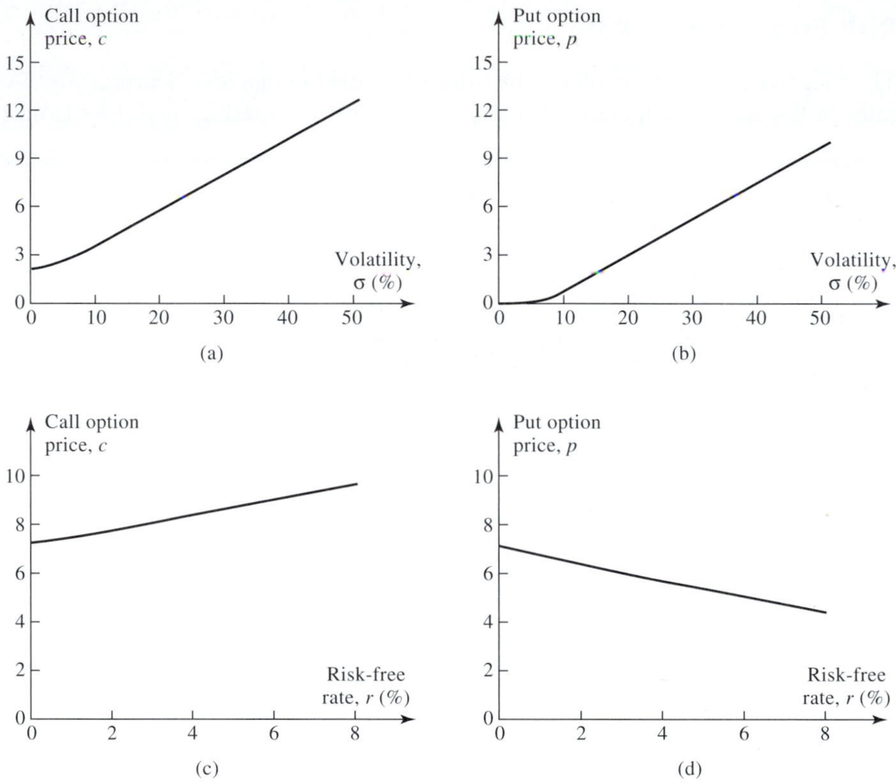

tends to increase. In addition, the present value of any future cash flow received by the holder of the option decreases. The combined impact of these two effects is to increase the value of call options and decrease the value of put options (see Figures 9.2(c, d)).

It is important to emphasize that we are assuming that interest rates change while all other variables stay the same. In particular we are assuming that interest rates change while the stock price remains the same. In practice, when interest rates rise (fall), stock prices tend to fall (rise). The net effect of an interest rate increase and the accompanying stock price decrease can be to decrease the value of a call option and increase the value of a put option. Similarly, the net effect of an interest rate decrease and the accompanying stock price increase can be to increase the value of a call option and decrease the value of a put option.

Amount of Future Dividends

Dividends have the effect of reducing the stock price on the ex-dividend date. This is bad news for the value of call options and good news for the value of put options. The value of a call option is therefore negatively related to the size of an anticipated future dividend, and the value of a put option is positively related to the size of an anticipated future dividend.

9.2 ASSUMPTIONS AND NOTATION

In this chapter we will make assumptions similar to those made for deriving forward and futures prices in Chapter 5. We assume that there are some market participants, such as large investment banks, for which the following statements are true:

1. There are no transactions costs.
2. All trading profits (net of trading losses) are subject to the same tax rate.
3. Borrowing and lending are possible at the risk-free interest rate.

We assume that these market participants are prepared to take advantage of arbitrage opportunities as they arise. As discussed in Chapters 1 and 5, this means that any available arbitrage opportunities disappear very quickly. For the purposes of our analysis, it is therefore reasonable to assume that there are no arbitrage opportunities.

We will use the following notation:

S_0: Current stock price
K: Strike price of option
T: Time to expiration of option
S_T: Stock price at maturity
r: Continuously compounded risk-free rate of interest for an investment maturing in time T
C: Value of American call option to buy one share
P: Value of American put option to sell one share
c: Value of European call option to buy one share
p: Value of European put option to sell one share

It should be noted that r is the nominal rate of interest, not the real rate of interest. We can assume that $r > 0$. Otherwise, a risk-free investment would provide no advantages over cash. (Indeed, if $r < 0$, cash would be preferable to a risk-free investment.)

9.3 UPPER AND LOWER BOUNDS FOR OPTION PRICES

In this section we derive upper and lower bounds for option prices. These bounds do not depend on any particular assumptions about the factors mentioned in Section 9.1 (except $r > 0$). If an option price is above the upper bound or below the lower bound, then there are profitable opportunities for arbitrageurs.

Upper Bounds

An American or European call option gives the holder the right to buy one share of a stock for a certain price. No matter what happens, the option can never be worth more than the stock. Hence, the stock price is an upper bound to the option price:

$$c \leqslant S_0 \quad \text{and} \quad C \leqslant S_0$$

If these relationships were not true, an arbitrageur could easily make a riskless profit by buying the stock and selling the call option.

An American or European put option gives the holder the right to sell one share of a stock for K. No matter how low the stock price becomes, the option can never be worth more than K. Hence,

$$p \leqslant K \quad \text{and} \quad P \leqslant K$$

For European options, we know that at maturity the option cannot be worth more than K. It follows that it cannot be worth more than the present value of K today:

$$p \leqslant Ke^{-rT}$$

If this were not true, an arbitrageur could make a riskless profit by writing the option and investing the proceeds of the sale at the risk-free interest rate.

Lower Bound for Calls on Non-Dividend-Paying Stocks

A lower bound for the price of a European call option on a non-dividend-paying stock is

$$S_0 - Ke^{-rT}$$

We first look at a numerical example and then consider a more formal argument.

Suppose that $S_0 = \$20$, $K = \$18$, $r = 10\%$ per annum, and $T = 1$ year. In this case,

$$S_0 - Ke^{-rT} = 20 - 18e^{-0.1} = 3.71$$

or \$3.71. Consider the situation where the European call price is \$3.00, which is less than the theoretical minimum of \$3.71. An arbitrageur can short the stock and buy the call to provide a cash inflow of \$20.00 − \$3.00 = \$17.00. If invested for 1 year at 10% per annum, the \$17.00 grows to $17e^{0.1} = \$18.79$. At the end of the year, the option expires. If the stock price is greater than \$18.00, the arbitrageur exercises the option for \$18.00, closes out the short position, and makes a profit of

$$\$18.79 - \$18.00 = \$0.79$$

If the stock price is less than \$18.00, the stock is bought in the market and the short position is closed out. The arbitrageur then makes an even greater profit. For example, if the stock price is \$17.00, the arbitrageur's profit is

$$\$18.79 - \$17.00 = \$1.79$$

For a more formal argument, we consider the following two portfolios:

Portfolio A: one European call option plus an amount of cash equal to Ke^{-rT}

Portfolio B: one share

In portfolio A, the cash, if it is invested at the risk-free interest rate, will grow to K in time T. If $S_T > K$, the call option is exercised at maturity and portfolio A is worth S_T. If $S_T < K$, the call option expires worthless and the portfolio is worth K. Hence, at time T, portfolio A is worth

$$\max(S_T, K)$$

Portfolio B is worth S_T at time T. Hence, portfolio A is always worth as much as, and can be worth more than, portfolio B at the option's maturity. It follows that in the absence of arbitrage opportunities this must also be true today. Hence,

$$c + Ke^{-rT} \geqslant S_0$$

or

$$c \geqslant S_0 - Ke^{-rT}$$

Because the worst that can happen to a call option is that it expires worthless, its value cannot be negative. This means that $c \geqslant 0$ and therefore

$$c \geqslant \max(S_0 - Ke^{-rT}, 0) \tag{9.1}$$

Example 9.1

Consider a European call option on a non-dividend-paying stock when the stock price is \$51, the strike price is \$50, the time to maturity is 6 months, and the risk-free rate of interest is 12% per annum. In this case, $S_0 = 51$, $K = 50$, $T = 0.5$, and $r = 0.12$. From equation (9.1), a lower bound for the option price is $S_0 - Ke^{-rT}$, or

$$51 - 50e^{-0.12\times0.5} = \$3.91$$

Lower Bound for European Puts on Non-Dividend-Paying Stocks

For a European put option on a non-dividend-paying stock, a lower bound for the price is

$$Ke^{-rT} - S_0$$

Again, we first consider a numerical example and then look at a more formal argument.

Suppose that $S_0 = \$37$, $K = \$40$, $r = 5\%$ per annum, and $T = 0.5$ years. In this case,

$$Ke^{-rT} - S_0 = 40e^{-0.05\times0.5} - 37 = \$2.01$$

Consider the situation where the European put price is \$1.00, which is less than the theoretical minimum of \$2.01. An arbitrageur can borrow \$38.00 for 6 months to buy both the put and the stock. At the end of the 6 months, the arbitrageur will be required to repay $38e^{0.05\times0.5} = \$38.96$. If the stock price is below \$40.00, the arbitrageur exercises the option to sell the stock for \$40.00, repays the loan, and makes a profit of

$$\$40.00 - \$38.96 = \$1.04$$

If the stock price is greater than \$40.00, the arbitrageur discards the option, sells the stock, and repays the loan for an even greater profit. For example, if the stock price is \$42.00, the arbitrageur's profit is

$$\$42.00 - \$38.96 = \$3.04$$

For a more formal argument, we consider the following two portfolios:

Portfolio C: one European put option plus one share

Portfolio D: an amount of cash equal to Ke^{-rT}

If $S_T < K$, then the option in portfolio C is exercised at option maturity, and the portfolio becomes worth K. If $S_T > K$, then the put option expires worthless, and the portfolio is worth S_T at this time. Hence, portfolio C is worth

$$\max(S_T,\ K)$$

in time T. Assuming the cash is invested at the risk-free interest rate, portfolio D is worth K in time T. Hence, portfolio C is always worth as much as, and can sometimes be worth more than, portfolio D in time T. It follows that in the absence of arbitrage opportunities portfolio C must be worth at least as much as portfolio D today. Hence,

$$p + S_0 \geqslant Ke^{-rT}$$

or

$$p \geqslant Ke^{-rT} - S_0$$

Because the worst that can happen to a put option is that it expires worthless, its value cannot be negative. This means that

$$p \geqslant \max(Ke^{-rT} - S_0,\ 0) \tag{9.2}$$

Example 9.2

Consider a European put option on a non-dividend-paying stock when the stock price is \$38, the strike price is \$40, the time to maturity is 3 months, and the risk-free rate of interest is 10% per annum. In this case $S_0 = 38$, $K = 40$, $T = 0.25$, and $r = 0.10$. From equation (9.2), a lower bound for the option price is $Ke^{-rT} - S_0$, or

$$40e^{-0.1\times 0.25} - 38 = \$1.01$$

9.4 PUT–CALL PARITY

We now derive an important relationship between p and c. Consider the following two portfolios that were used in the previous section:

Portfolio A: one European call option plus an amount of cash equal to Ke^{-rT}

Portfolio C: one European put option plus one share

Both are worth

$$\max(S_T,\ K)$$

at expiration of the options. Because the options are European, they cannot be exercised prior to the expiration date. The portfolios must therefore have identical values today. This means that

$$c + Ke^{-rT} = p + S_0 \tag{9.3}$$

This relationship is known as *put–call parity*. It shows that the value of a European call with a certain strike price and exercise date can be deduced from the value of a European put with the same strike price and exercise date, and vice versa.

If equation (9.3) does not hold, there are arbitrage opportunities. Suppose that the stock price is \$31, the strike price is \$30, the risk-free interest rate is 10% per annum, the price of a 3-month European call option is \$3, and the price of a three-month European put option is \$2.25. In this case,

$$c + Ke^{-rT} = 3 + 30e^{-0.1\times 3/12} = \$32.26$$

and

$$p + S_0 = 2.25 + 31 = \$33.25$$

Portfolio C is overpriced relative to portfolio A. The correct arbitrage strategy is to buy the securities in portfolio A and short the securities in portfolio C. The strategy involves buying the call and shorting both the put and the stock, generating a positive cash flow of

$$-3 + 2.25 + 31 = \$30.25$$

up front. When invested at the risk-free interest rate, this amount grows to

$$30.25e^{0.1\times 0.25} = \$31.02$$

in 3 months.

If the stock price at expiration of the option is greater than \$30, the call will be exercised; and if it is less than \$30, the put will be exercised. In either case, the investor ends up buying one share for \$30. This share can be used to close out the short position. The net profit is therefore

$$\$31.02 - \$30.00 = \$1.02$$

For an alternative situation, suppose that the call price is \$3 and the put price is \$1. In this case,

$$c + Ke^{-rT} = 3 + 30e^{-0.1\times 3/12} = \$32.26$$

and

$$p + S_0 = 1 + 31 = \$32.00$$

Portfolio A is overpriced relative to portfolio C. An arbitrageur can short the securities in portfolio A and buy the securities in portfolio C to lock in a profit. The strategy involves

Table 9.2 Arbitrage opportunities when put–call parity does not hold. Stock price = \$31; interest rate = 10%; call price = \$3. Both put and call have a strike price of \$30 and 3 months to maturity.

Three-month put price = \$2.25	***Three-month put price = \$1***
Action now:	*Action now*:
Buy call for \$3	Borrow \$29 for 3 months
Short put to realize \$2.25	Short call to realize \$3
Short the stock to realize \$31	Buy put for \$1
Invest \$30.25 for 3 months	Buy the stock for \$31
Action in 3 months if $S_T > 30$:	*Action in 3 months if* $S_T > 30$:
Receive \$31.02 from investment	Call exercised: sell stock for \$30
Exercise call to buy stock for \$30	Use \$29.73 to repay loan
Net profit = \$1.02	Net profit = \$0.27
Action in 3 months if $S_T < 30$:	*Action in 3 months if* $S_T < 30$:
Receive \$31.02 from investment	Exercise put to sell stock for \$3
Put exercised: buy stock for \$30	Use \$29.73 to repay loan
Net profit = \$1.02	Net profit = \$0.27

Business Snapshot 9.1 Put–Call Parity and Capital Structure

The pioneers of option pricing were Fischer Black, Myron Scholes, and Robert Merton. In the early 1970s, they showed that options can be used to characterize the capital structure of a company. Today this model is widely used by financial institutions to assess a company's credit risk.

To illustrate the model, consider a company that has assets that are financed with zero-coupon bonds and equity. Suppose that the bonds mature in 5 years at which time a principal payment of K is required. The company pays no dividends. If the assets are worth more than K in 5 years, the equity holders choose to repay the bondholders. If the assets are worth less than K, the equity holders choose to declare bankruptcy and the bondholders end up owning the company.

The value of the equity in 5 years is therefore $\max(A_T - K, 0)$, where A_T is the value of the company's assets at that time. This shows that the equity holders have a 5-year European call option on the assets of the company with a strike price of K. What about the bondholders? They get $\min(A_T, K)$ in 5 years. This is the same as $K - \max(K - A_T, 0)$. The bondholders have given the equity holders the right to sell the company's assets to them for K in 5 years. The bonds are therefore worth the present value of K minus the value of a 5-year European put option on the assets with a strike price of K.

To summarize, if c and p are the value of the call and put options, respectively, then

$$\text{Value of equity} = c$$

$$\text{Value of debt} = PV(K) - p$$

Denote the value of the assets of the company today by A_0. The value of the assets must equal the total value of the instruments used to finance the assets. This means that it must equal the sum of the value of the equity and the value of the debt, so that

$$A_0 = c + [PV(K) - p]$$

Rearranging this equation, we have

$$c + PV(K) = p + A_0$$

This is the put–call parity result in equation (9.3) for call and put options on the assets of the company.

shorting the call and buying both the put and the stock with an initial investment of

$$\$31 + \$1 - \$3 = \$29$$

When the investment is financed at the risk-free interest rate, a repayment of $29e^{0.1\times0.25} =$ \$29.73 is required at the end of the 3 months. As in the previous case, either the call or the put will be exercised. The short call and long put option position therefore leads to the stock being sold for \$30.00. The net profit is therefore

$$\$30.00 - \$29.73 = \$0.27$$

These examples are illustrated in Table 9.2. Business Snapshot 9.1 shows how options and put–call parity can help us understand the positions of the debt and equity holders in a company.

American Options

Put–call parity holds only for European options. However, it is possible to derive some results for American option prices. It can be shown (see Problem 9.18) that, when there are no dividends,

$$S_0 - K \leqslant C - P \leqslant S_0 - Ke^{-rT} \tag{9.4}$$

Example 9.3

An American call option on a non-dividend-paying stock with strike price \$20.00 and maturity in 5 months is worth \$1.50. Suppose that the current stock price is \$19.00 and the risk-free interest rate is 10% per annum. From equation (9.4), we have

$$19 - 20 \leqslant C - P \leqslant 19 - 20e^{-0.1\times 5/12}$$

or

$$1 \geqslant P - C \geqslant 0.18$$

showing that $P - C$ lies between \$1.00 and \$0.18. With C at \$1.50, P must lie between \$1.68 and \$2.50. In other words, upper and lower bounds for the price of an American put with the same strike price and expiration date as the American call are \$2.50 and \$1.68.

9.5 EARLY EXERCISE: CALLS ON A NON-DIVIDEND-PAYING STOCK

This section demonstrates that it is never optimal to exercise an American call option on a non-dividend-paying stock before the expiration date.

To illustrate the general nature of the argument, consider an American call option on a non-dividend-paying stock with 1 month to expiration when the stock price is \$50 and the strike price is \$40. The option is deep in the money, and the investor who owns the option might well be tempted to exercise it immediately. However, if the investor plans to hold the stock obtained by exercising the option for more than 1 month, this is not the best strategy. A better course of action is to keep the option and exercise it at the end of the month. The \$40 strike price is then paid out 1 month later than it would be if the option were exercised immediately, so that interest is earned on the \$40 for 1 month. Because the stock pays no dividends, no income from the stock is sacrificed. A further advantage of waiting rather than exercising immediately is that there is some chance (however remote) that the stock price will fall below \$40 in 1 month. In this case, the investor will not exercise in 1 month and will be glad that the decision to exercise early was not taken!

This argument shows that there are no advantages to exercising early if the investor plans to keep the stock for the remaining life of the option (1 month, in this case). What if the investor thinks the stock is currently overpriced and is wondering whether to exercise the option and sell the stock? In this case, the investor is better off selling the option than exercising it.[1] The option will be bought by another investor who does want to hold the stock. Such investors must exist: otherwise the current stock price would not be \$50. The price obtained for the option will be greater than its intrinsic value of \$10, for the reasons mentioned earlier.

[1] As an alternative strategy, the investor can keep the option and short the stock to lock in a better profit than \$10.

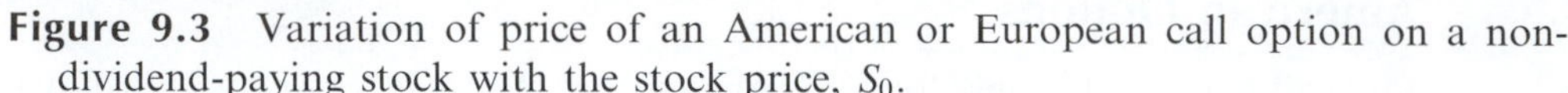

Figure 9.3 Variation of price of an American or European call option on a non-dividend-paying stock with the stock price, S_0.

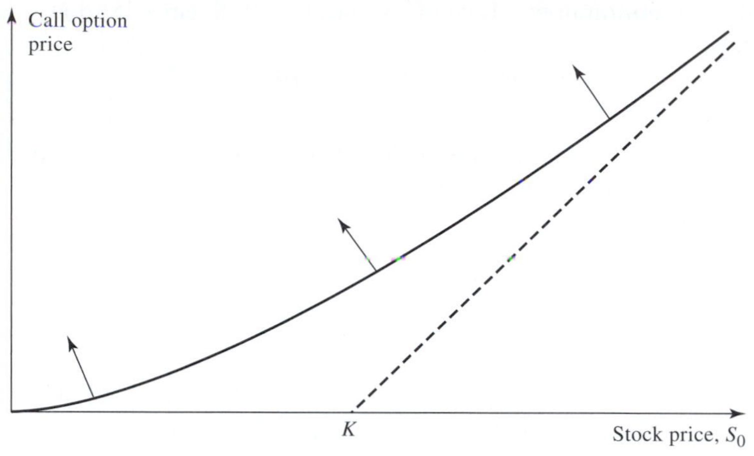

For a more formal argument, we can use equation (9.1):

$$c \geqslant S_0 - Ke^{-rT}$$

Because the owner of an American call has all the exercise opportunities open to the owner of the corresponding European call, we must have

$$C \geqslant c$$

Hence,

$$C \geqslant S_0 - Ke^{-rT}$$

Given $r > 0$, it follows that $C > S_0 - K$. If it were optimal to exercise early, C would equal $S_0 - K$. We deduce that it can never be optimal to exercise early.

Figure 9.3 shows the general way in which the call price varies with S_0. It indicates that the call price is always above its intrinsic value of $\max(S_0 - K, 0)$. As r or T or the volatility increases, the line relating the call price to the stock price moves in the direction indicated by the arrows (i.e., farther away from the intrinsic value).

To summarize, there are two reasons an American call on a non-dividend-paying stock should not be exercised early. One relates to the insurance that it provides. A call option, when held instead of the stock itself, in effect insures the holder against the stock price falling below the strike price. Once the option has been exercised and the strike price has been exchanged for the stock price, this insurance vanishes. The other reason concerns the time value of money. From the perspective of the option holder, the later the strike price is paid out, the better.

9.6 EARLY EXERCISE: PUTS ON A NON-DIVIDEND-PAYING STOCK

It can be optimal to exercise an American put option on a non-dividend-paying stock early. Indeed, at any given time during its life, a put option should always be exercised early if it is sufficiently deep in the money.

To illustrate this, consider an extreme situation. Suppose that the strike price is \$10 and the stock price is virtually zero. By exercising immediately, an investor makes an immediate gain of \$10. If the investor waits, the gain from exercise might be less than \$10, but it cannot be more than \$10 because negative stock prices are impossible. Furthermore, receiving \$10 now is preferable to receiving \$10 in the future. It follows that the option should be exercised immediately.

Like a call option, a put option can be viewed as providing insurance. A put option, when held in conjunction with the stock, insures the holder against the stock price falling below a certain level. However, a put option is different from a call option in that it may be optimal for an investor to forgo this insurance and exercise early in order to realize the strike price immediately. In general, the early exercise of a put option becomes more attractive as S_0 decreases, as r increases, and as the volatility decreases.

It will be recalled from equation (9.2) that

$$p \geqslant Ke^{-rT} - S_0$$

For an American put with price P, the stronger condition

$$P \geqslant K - S_0$$

must always hold because immediate exercise is always possible.

Figure 9.4 shows the general way in which the price of an American put varies with S_0. Provided that $r > 0$, it is always optimal to exercise an American put immediately when the stock price is sufficiently low. When early exercise is optimal, the value of the option is $K - S_0$. The curve representing the value of the put therefore merges into the put's intrinsic value, $K - S_0$, for a sufficiently small value of S_0. In Figure 9.4, this value of S_0 is shown as point A. The line relating the put price to the stock price moves in the direction indicated by the arrows when r decreases, when the volatility increases, and when T increases.

Because there are some circumstances when it is desirable to exercise an American put option early, it follows that an American put option is always worth more than the

Figure 9.4 Variation of price of an American put option with stock price, S_0.

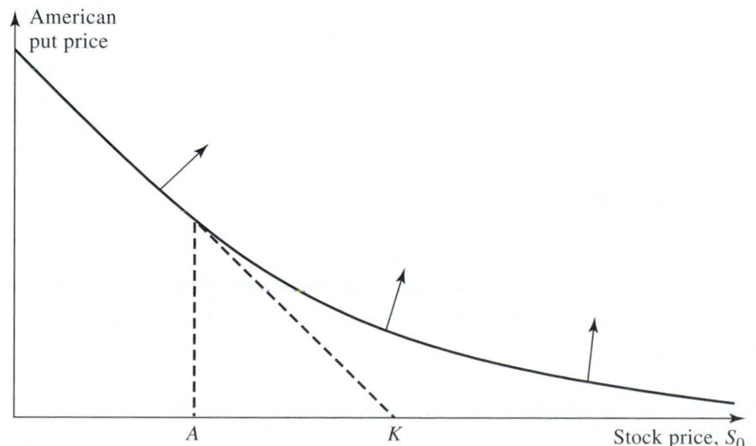

Figure 9.5 Variation of price of a European put option with the stock price, S_0.

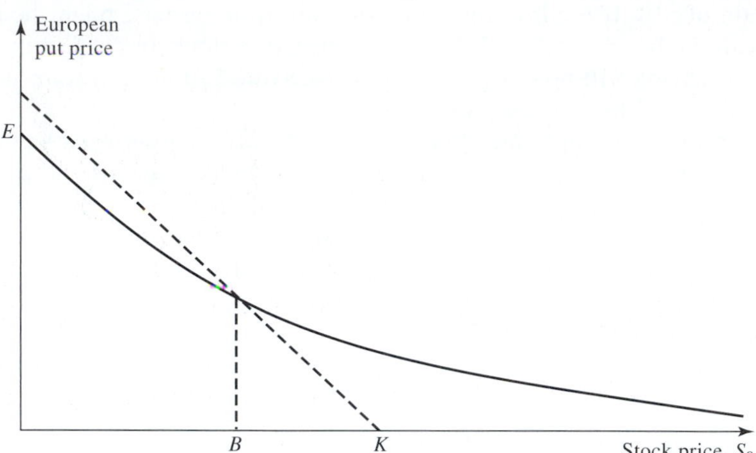

corresponding European put option. Furthermore, because an American put is sometimes worth its intrinsic value (see Figure 9.4), it follows that a European put option must sometimes be worth less than its intrinsic value. Figure 9.5 shows the variation of the European put price with the stock price. Note that point B in Figure 9.5, at which the price of the option is equal to its intrinsic value, must represent a higher value of the stock price than point A in Figure 9.4. Point E in Figure 9.5 is where $S_0 = 0$ and the European put price is Ke^{-rT}.

9.7 EFFECT OF DIVIDENDS

The results produced so far in this chapter have assumed that we are dealing with options on a non-dividend-paying stock. In this section we examine the impact of dividends. In the United States most exchange-traded stock options have a life of less than 1 year and dividends payable during the life of the option can usually be predicted with reasonable accuracy. We will use D to denote the present value of the dividends during the life of the option. In the calculation of D, a dividend is assumed to occur at the time of its ex-dividend date.

Lower Bound for Calls and Puts

We can redefine portfolios A and B as follows:

Portfolio A: one European call option plus an amount of cash equal to $D + Ke^{-rT}$
Portfolio B: one share

A similar argument to the one used to derive equation (9.1) shows that

$$c \geqslant S_0 - D - Ke^{-rT} \quad \textbf{(9.5)}$$

We can also redefine portfolios C and D as follows:

Portfolio C: one European put option plus one share

Portfolio D: an amount of cash equal to $D + Ke^{-rT}$

A similar argument to the one used to derive equation (9.2) shows that

$$p \geqslant D + Ke^{-rT} - S_0 \tag{9.6}$$

Early Exercise

When dividends are expected, we can no longer assert than an American call option will not be exercised early. Sometimes it is optimal to exercise an American call immediately prior to an ex-dividend date. It is never optimal to exercise a call at other times. This point is discussed further in the appendix to Chapter 13.

Put–Call Parity

Comparing the value at option maturity of the redefined portfolios A and C shows that, with dividends, the put–call parity result in equation (9.3) becomes

$$c + D + Ke^{-rT} = p + S_0 \tag{9.7}$$

Dividends cause equation (9.4) to be modified (see Problem 9.19) to

$$S_0 - D - K \leqslant C - P \leqslant S_0 - Ke^{-rT} \tag{9.8}$$

SUMMARY

There are six factors affecting the value of a stock option: the current stock price, the strike price, the expiration date, the stock price volatility, the risk-free interest rate, and the dividends expected during the life of the option. The value of a call generally increases as the current stock price, the time to expiration, the volatility, and the risk-free interest rate increase. The value of a call decreases as the strike price and expected dividends increase. The value of a put generally increases as the strike price, the time to expiration, the volatility, and the expected dividends increase. The value of a put decreases as the current stock price and the risk-free interest rate increase.

It is possible to reach some conclusions about the value of stock options without making any assumptions about the volatility of stock prices. For example, the price of a call option on a stock must always be worth less than the price of the stock itself. Similarly, the price of a put option on a stock must always be worth less than the option's strike price.

A European call option on a non-dividend-paying stock must be worth more than

$$\max(S_0 - Ke^{-rT}, 0)$$

where S_0 is the stock price, K is the strike price, r is the risk-free interest rate, and T is the time to expiration. A European put option on a non-dividend-paying stock must be worth more than

$$\max(Ke^{-rT} - S_0,\ 0)$$

When dividends with present value D will be paid, the lower bound for a European call option becomes

$$\max(S_0 - D - Ke^{-rT},\ 0)$$

and the lower bound for a European put option becomes

$$\max(Ke^{-rT} + D - S_0,\ 0)$$

Put–call parity is a relationship between the price, c, of a European call option on a stock and the price, p, of a European put option on a stock. For a non-dividend-paying stock, it is

$$c + Ke^{-rT} = p + S_0$$

For a dividend-paying stock, the put–call parity relationship is

$$c + D + Ke^{-rT} = p + S_0$$

Put–call parity does not hold for American options. However, it is possible to use arbitrage arguments to obtain upper and lower bounds for the difference between the price of an American call and the price of an American put.

In Chapter 13, we will carry the analyses in this chapter further by making specific assumptions about the probabilistic behavior of stock prices. The analysis will enable us to derive exact pricing formulas for European stock options. In Chapters 11 and 17, we will see how numerical procedures can be used to price American options.

FURTHER READING

Black, F., and M. Scholes. "The Pricing of Options and Corporate Liabilities," *Journal of Political Economy*, 81 (May/June 1973): 637–59.

Broadie, M., and J. Detemple. "American Option Valuation: New Bounds, Approximations, and a Comparison of Existing Methods," *Review of Financial Studies*, 9, 4 (1996): 1211–50.

Merton, R.C.. "On the Pricing of Corporate Debt: The Risk Structure of Interest Rates," *Journal of Finance*, 29, 2 (1974): 449–70.

Merton, R.C. "Theory of Rational Option Pricing," *Bell Journal of Economics and Management Science*, 4 (Spring 1973): 141–83.

Merton, R.C. "The Relationship between Put and Call Prices: Comment," *Journal of Finance*, 28 (March 1973): 183–84.

Stoll, H.R. "The Relationship between Put and Call Option Prices," *Journal of Finance*, 24 (December 1969): 801–24.

Questions and Problems (Answers in Solutions Manual)

9.1. List the six factors that affect stock option prices.

9.2. What is a lower bound for the price of a 4-month call option on a non-dividend-paying stock when the stock price is \$28, the strike price is \$25, and the risk-free interest rate is 8% per annum?

9.3. What is a lower bound for the price of a 1-month European put option on a non-dividend-paying stock when the stock price is \$12, the strike price is \$15, and the risk-free interest rate is 6% per annum?

9.4. Give two reasons why the early exercise of an American call option on a non-dividend-paying stock is not optimal. The first reason should involve the time value of money. The second should apply even if interest rates are zero.

9.5. "The early exercise of an American put is a trade-off between the time value of money and the insurance value of a put." Explain this statement.

9.6. Explain why an American call option on a dividend-paying stock is always worth at least as much as its intrinsic value. Is the same true of a European call option? Explain your answer.

9.7. The price of a non-dividend-paying stock is \$19 and the price of a 3-month European call option on the stock with a strike price of \$20 is \$1. The risk-free rate is 4% per annum. What is the price of a 3-month European put option with a strike price of \$20?

9.8. Explain why the arguments leading to put–call parity for European options cannot be used to give a similar result for American options.

9.9. What is a lower bound for the price of a 6-month call option on a non-dividend-paying stock when the stock price is \$80, the strike price is \$75, and the risk-free interest rate is 10% per annum?

9.10. What is a lower bound for the price of a 2-month European put option on a non-dividend-paying stock when the stock price is \$58, the strike price is \$65, and the risk-free interest rate is 5% per annum?

9.11. A 4-month European call option on a dividend-paying stock is currently selling for \$5. The stock price is \$64, the strike price is \$60, and a dividend of \$0.80 is expected in 1 month. The risk-free interest rate is 12% per annum for all maturities. What opportunities are there for an arbitrageur?

9.12. A 1-month European put option on a non-dividend-paying stock is currently selling for \$2.50. The stock price is \$47, the strike price is \$50, and the risk-free interest rate is 6% per annum. What opportunities are there for an arbitrageur?

9.13. Give an intuitive explanation of why the early exercise of an American put becomes more attractive as the risk-free rate increases and volatility decreases.

9.14. The price of a European call that expires in 6 months and has a strike price of \$30 is \$2. The underlying stock price is \$29, and a dividend of \$0.50 is expected in 2 months and again in 5 months. The term structure is flat, with all risk-free interest rates being 10%. What is the price of a European put option that expires in 6 months and has a strike price of \$30?

9.15. Explain carefully the arbitrage opportunities in Problem 9.14 if the European put price is \$3.

9.16. The price of an American call on a non-dividend-paying stock is \$4. The stock price is \$31, the strike price is \$30, and the expiration date is in 3 months. The risk-free interest rate is 8%. Derive upper and lower bounds for the price of an American put on the same stock with the same strike price and expiration date.

9.17. Explain carefully the arbitrage opportunities in Problem 9.16 if the American put price is greater than the calculated upper bound.

9.18. Prove the result in equation (9.4). (*Hint*: For the first part of the relationship, consider (a) a portfolio consisting of a European call plus an amount of cash equal to K, and (b) a portfolio consisting of an American put option plus one share.)

9.19. Prove the result in equation (9.8). (*Hint*: For the first part of the relationship, consider (a) a portfolio consisting of a European call plus an amount of cash equal to $D+K$, and (b) a portfolio consisting of an American put option plus one share.)

9.20. Regular call options on non-dividend-paying stocks should not be exercised early. However, there is a tendency for executive stock options to be exercised early even when the company pays no dividends (see Business Snapshot 8.3 for a discussion of executive stock options). Give a possible reason for this.

9.21. Use the software DerivaGem to verify that Figures 9.1 and 9.2 are correct.

Assignment Questions

9.22. A European call option and put option on a stock both have a strike price of \$20 and an expiration date in 3 months. Both sell for \$3. The risk-free interest rate is 10% per annum, the current stock price is \$19, and a \$1 dividend is expected in 1 month. Identify the arbitrage opportunity open to a trader.

9.23. Suppose that c_1, c_2, and c_3 are the prices of European call options with strike prices K_1, K_2, and K_3, respectively, where $K_3 > K_2 > K_1$ and $K_3 - K_2 = K_2 - K_1$. All options have the same maturity. Show that

$$c_2 \leqslant 0.5(c_1 + c_3)$$

(*Hint*: Consider a portfolio that is long one option with strike price K_1, long one option with strike price K_3, and short two options with strike price K_2.)

9.24. What is the result corresponding to that in Problem 9.23 for European put options?

9.25. Suppose that you are the manager and sole owner of a highly leveraged company. All the debt will mature in 1 year. If at that time the value of the company is greater than the face value of the debt, you will pay off the debt. If the value of the company is less than the face value of the debt, you will declare bankruptcy and the debt holders will own the company.

(a) Express your position as an option on the value of the company.
(b) Express the position of the debt holders in terms of options on the value of the company.
(c) What can you do to increase the value of your position?

9.26. Consider an option on a stock when the stock price is \$41, the strike price is \$40, the risk-free rate is 6%, the volatility is 35%, and the time to maturity is 1 year. Assume that a dividend of \$0.50 is expected after 6 months.

(a) Use DerivaGem to value the option assuming it is a European call.
(b) Use DerivaGem to value the option assuming it is a European put.
(c) Verify that put–call parity holds.
(d) Explore using DerivaGem what happens to the price of the options as the time to maturity becomes very large. For this purpose, assume there are no dividends. Explain the results you get.

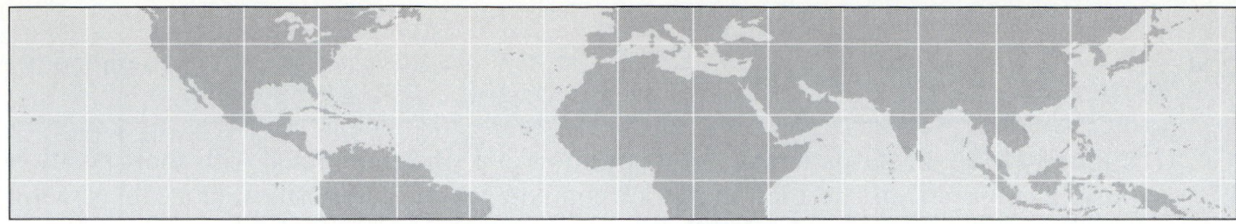

CHAPTER 10 Trading Strategies Involving Options

We discussed the profit pattern from an investment in a single stock option in Chapter 8. In this chapter we cover more fully the range of profit patterns obtainable using options. We assume that the underlying asset is a stock. Similar results can be obtained for other underlying assets, such as foreign currencies, stock indices, and futures contracts. The options used in the strategies we discuss are European. American options may lead to slightly different outcomes because of the possibility of early exercise.

In the first section we consider what happens when a position in a stock option is combined with a position in the stock itself. We then move on to examine the profit patterns obtained when an investment is made in two or more different options on the same stock. One of the attractions of options is that they can be used to create a wide range of different payoff functions. (A payoff function is the payoff as a function of the stock price.) If European options were available with every single possible strike price, any payoff function could in theory be created.

For ease of exposition the figures and tables showing the profit from a trading strategy will ignore the time value of money. The profit will be shown as the final payoff minus the initial cost. (In theory, it should be calculated as the present value of the final payoff minus the initial cost.)

10.1 STRATEGIES INVOLVING A SINGLE OPTION AND A STOCK

There are a number of different trading strategies involving a single option on a stock and the stock itself. The profits from these are illustrated in Figure 10.1. In this figure and in other figures throughout this chapter, the dashed line shows the relationship between profit and the stock price for the individual securities constituting the portfolio, whereas the solid line shows the relationship between profit and the stock price for the whole portfolio.

In Figure 10.1(a), the portfolio consists of a long position in a stock plus a short position in a call option. This is known as *writing a covered call*. The long stock position "covers" or protects the investor from the payoff on the short call that becomes necessary if there is a sharp rise in the stock price. In Figure 10.1(b), a short position in a stock is combined with a long position in a call option. This is the reverse of writing

Figure 10.1 Profit patterns (a) long position in a stock combined with short position in a call; (b) short position in a stock combined with long position in a call; (c) long position in a put combined with long position in a stock; (d) short position in a put combined with short position in a stock.

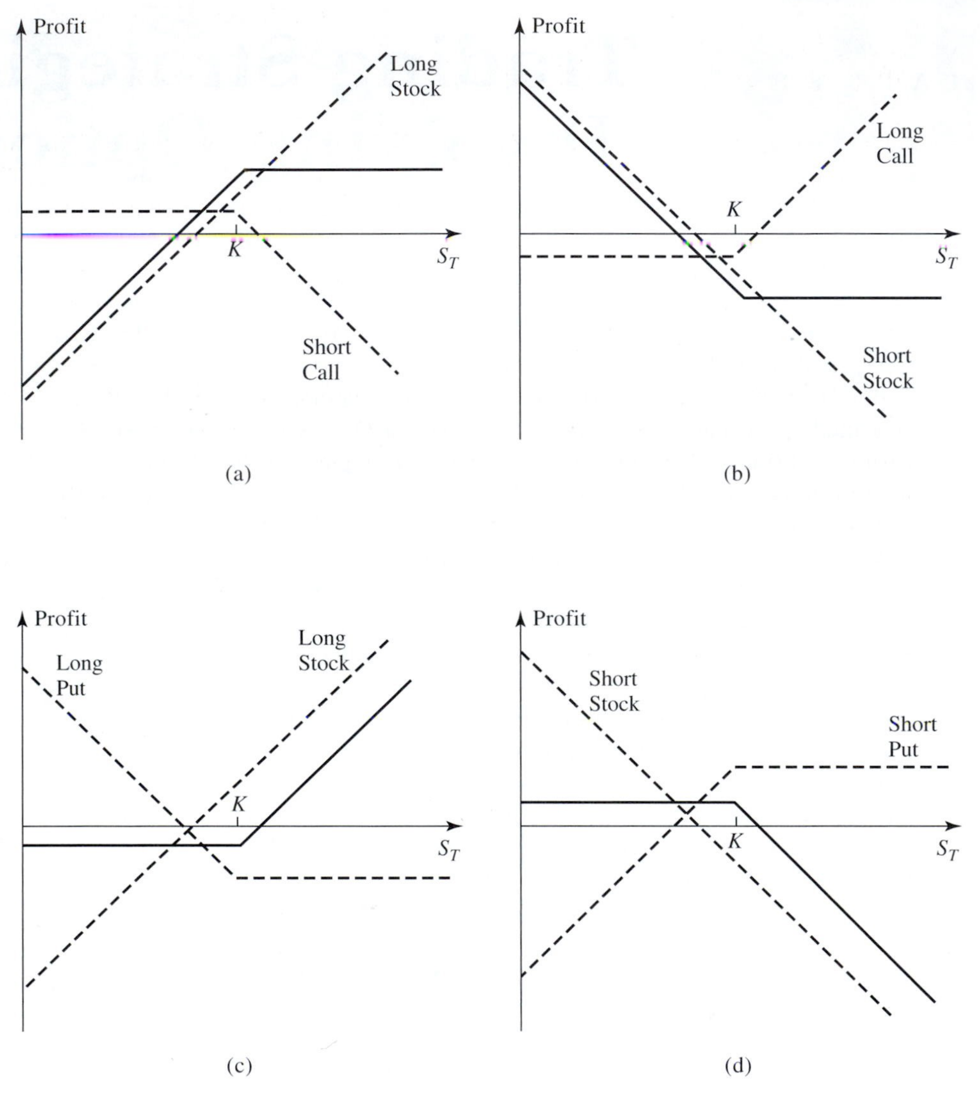

a covered call. In Figure 10.1(c), the investment strategy involves buying a put option on a stock and the stock itself. The approach is sometimes referred to as a *protective put* strategy. In Figure 10.1(d), a short position in a put option is combined with a short position in the stock. This is the reverse of a protective put.

The profit patterns in Figures 10.1 have the same general shape as the profit patterns discussed in Chapter 8 for short put, long put, long call, and short call, respectively. Put–call parity provides a way of understanding why this is so. From Chapter 9, the put–call parity relationship is

$$p + S_0 = c + Ke^{-rT} + D \tag{10.1}$$

where p is the price of a European put, S_0 is the stock price, c is the price of a European call, K is the strike price of both call and put, r is the risk-free interest rate, T is the time to maturity of both call and put, and D is the present value of the dividends anticipated during the life of the options.

Equation (10.1) shows that a long position in a put combined with a long position in the stock is equivalent to a long call position plus a certain amount ($= Ke^{-rT} + D$) of cash. This explains why the profit pattern in Figure 10.1(c) is similar to the profit pattern from a long call position. The position in Figure 10.1(d) is the reverse of that in Figure 10.1(c) and therefore leads to a profit pattern similar to that from a short call position.

Equation (10.1) can be rearranged to become

$$S_0 - c = Ke^{-rT} + D - p$$

In other words, a long position in a stock combined with a short position in a call is equivalent to a short put position plus a certain amount ($= Ke^{-rT} + D$) of cash. This equality explains why the profit pattern in Figure 10.1(a) is similar to the profit pattern from a short put position. The position in Figure 10.1(b) is the reverse of that in Figure 10.1(a) and therefore leads to a profit pattern similar to that from a long put position.

10.2 SPREADS

A spread trading strategy involves taking a position in two or more options of the same type (i.e., two or more calls or two or more puts).

Bull Spreads

One of the most popular types of spreads is a *bull spread*. This can be created by buying a call option on a stock with a certain strike price and selling a call option on the same

Figure 10.2 Profit from bull spread created using call options.

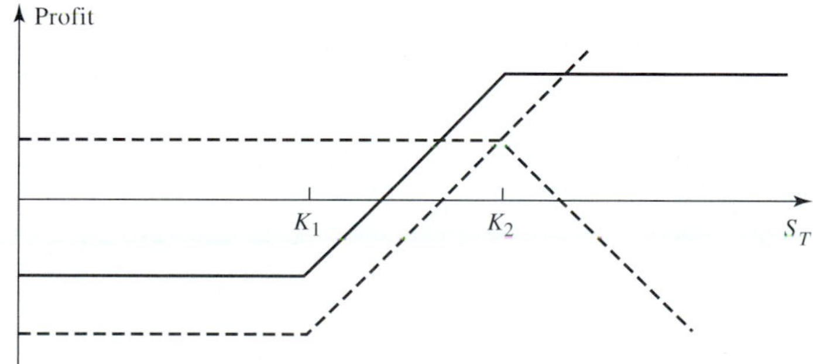

Table 10.1 Payoff from a bull spread created using calls.

Stock price range	*Payoff from long call option*	*Payoff from short call option*	*Total payoff*
$S_T \geqslant K_2$	$S_T - K_1$	$-(S_T - K_2)$	$K_2 - K_1$
$K_1 < S_T < K_2$	$S_T - K_1$	0	$S_T - K_1$
$S_T \leqslant K_1$	0	0	0

stock with a higher strike price. Both options have the same expiration date. The strategy is illustrated in Figure 10.2. The profits from the two option positions taken separately are shown by the dashed lines. The profit from the whole strategy is the sum of the profits given by the dashed lines and is indicated by the solid line. Because a call price always decreases as the strike price increases, the value of the option sold is always less than the value of the option bought. A bull spread, when created from calls, therefore requires an initial investment.

Suppose that K_1 is the strike price of the call option bought, K_2 is the strike price of the call option sold, and S_T is the stock price on the expiration date of the options. Table 10.1 shows the total payoff that will be realized from a bull spread in different circumstances. If the stock price does well and is greater than the higher strike price, the payoff is the difference between the two strike prices, or $K_2 - K_1$. If the stock price on the expiration date lies between the two strike prices, the payoff is $S_T - K_1$. If the stock price on the expiration date is below the lower strike price, the payoff is zero. The profit in Figure 10.2 is calculated by subtracting the initial investment from the payoff.

A bull spread strategy limits the investor's upside as well as downside risk. The strategy can be described by saying that the investor has a call option with a strike price equal to K_1 and has chosen to give up some upside potential by selling a call option with strike price K_2 ($K_2 > K_1$). In return for giving up the upside potential, the investor gets the

Figure 10.3 Profit from bull spread created using put options.

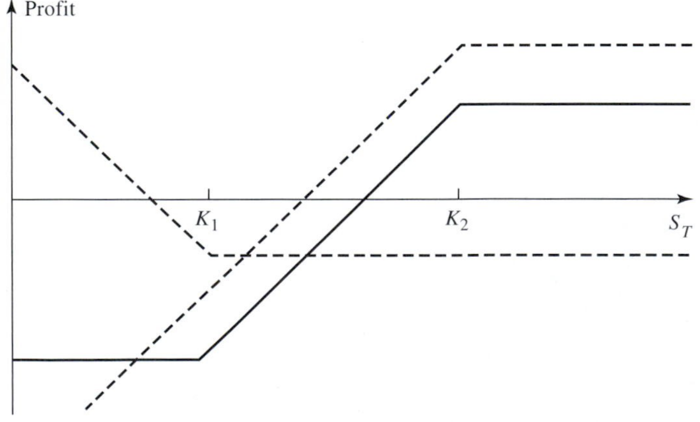

price of the option with strike price K_2. Three types of bull spreads can be distinguished:

1. Both calls are initially out of the money.
2. One call is initially in the money; the other call is initially out of the money.
3. Both calls are initially in the money.

The most aggressive bull spreads are those of type 1. They cost very little to set up and have a small probability of giving a relatively high payoff ($= K_2 - K_1$). As we move from type 1 to type 2 and from type 2 to type 3, the spreads become more conservative.

Example 10.1

An investor buys for \$3 a call with a strike price of \$30 and sells for \$1 a call with a strike price of \$35. The payoff from this bull spread strategy is \$5 if the stock price is above \$35, and zero if it is below \$30. If the stock price is between \$30 and \$35, the payoff is the amount by which the stock price exceeds \$30. The cost of the strategy is \$3 − \$1 = \$2. The profit is therefore as follows:

Stock price range	*Profit*
$S_T \leqslant 30$	-2
$30 < S_T < 35$	$S_T - 32$
$S_T \geqslant 35$	3

Bull spreads can also be created by buying a put with a low strike price and selling a put with a high strike price, as illustrated in Figure 10.3. Unlike the bull spread created from calls, bull spreads created from puts involve a positive up-front cash flow to the investor (ignoring margin requirements) and a payoff that is either negative or zero.

Bear Spreads

An investor who enters into a bull spread is hoping that the stock price will increase. By contrast, an investor who enters into a *bear spread* is hoping that the stock price will decline. Bear spreads can be created by buying a put with one strike price and selling a put with another strike price. The strike price of the option purchased is greater than the strike price of the option sold. (This is in contrast to a bull spread, where the strike

Figure 10.4 Profit from bear spread created using put options.

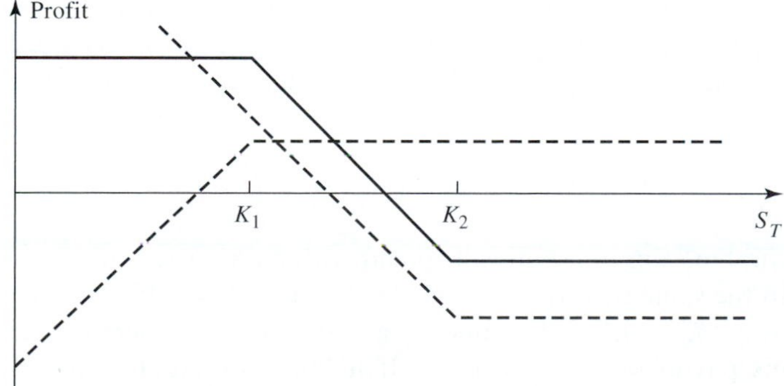

Table 10.2 Payoff from a bear spread created with put options.

Stock price range	*Payoff from long put option*	*Payoff from short put option*	*Total payoff*
$S_T \geqslant K_2$	0	0	0
$K_1 < S_T < K_2$	$K_2 - S_T$	0	$K_2 - S_T$
$S_T \leqslant K_1$	$K_2 - S_T$	$-(K_1 - S_T)$	$K_2 - K_1$

price of the option purchased is always less than the strike price of the option sold.) In Figure 10.4, the profit from the spread is shown by the solid line. A bear spread created from puts involves an initial cash outflow because the price of the put sold is less than the price of the put purchased. In essence, the investor has bought a put with a certain strike price and chosen to give up some of the profit potential by selling a put with a lower strike price. In return for the profit given up, the investor gets the price of the option sold.

Assume that the strike prices are K_1 and K_2, with $K_1 < K_2$. Table 10.2 shows the payoff that will be realized from a bear spread in different circumstances. If the stock price is greater than K_2, the payoff is zero. If the stock price is less than K_1, the payoff is $K_2 - K_1$. If the stock price is between K_1 and K_2, the payoff is $K_2 - S_T$. The profit is calculated by subtracting the initial cost from the payoff.

Example 10.2

An investor buys for \$3 a put with a strike price of \$35 and sells for \$1 a put with a strike price of \$30. The payoff from this bear spread strategy is zero if the stock price is above \$35, and \$5 if it is below \$30. If the stock price is between \$30 and \$35, the payoff is $35 - S_T$. The options cost \$3 – \$1 = \$2 up front. The profit is therefore as follows:

Stock price range	*Profit*
$S_T \leqslant 30$	+3
$30 < S_T < 35$	$33 - S_T$
$S_T \geqslant 35$	−2

Like bull spreads, bear spreads limit both the upside profit potential and the downside risk. Bear spreads can be created using calls instead of puts. The investor buys a call with a high strike price and sells a call with a low strike price, as illustrated in Figure 10.5. Bear spreads created with calls involve an initial cash inflow (ignoring margin requirements).

Box Spreads

A box spread is a combination of a bull call spread with strike prices K_1 and K_2 and a bear put spread with the same two strike prices. As shown in Table 10.3 the payoff from a box spread is always $K_2 - K_1$. The value of a box spread is therefore always the present value of this payoff or $(K_2 - K_1)e^{-rT}$. If it has a different value there is an arbitrage opportunity. If the market price of the box spread is too low, it is profitable to

Figure 10.5 Profit from bear spread created using call options.

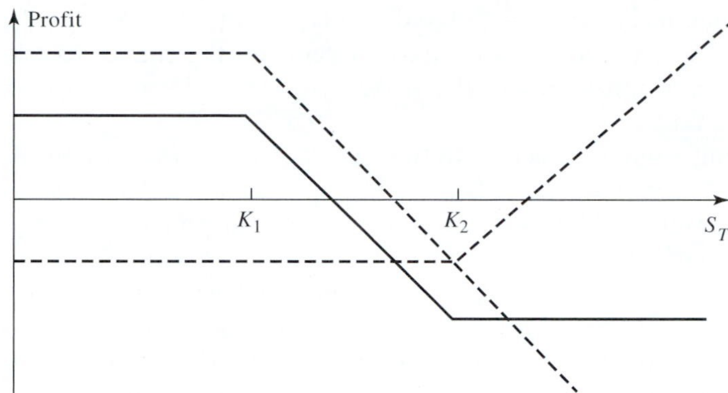

buy the box. This involves buying a call with strike price K_1, buying a put with strike price K_2, selling a call with strike price K_2, and selling a put with strike price K_1. If the market price of the box spread is too high, it is profitable to sell the box. This involves buying a call with strike price K_2, buying a put with strike price K_1, selling a call with strike price K_1, and selling a put with strike price K_2.

It is important to realize that a box-spread arbitrage only works with European options. Most of the options that trade on exchanges are American. As shown in Business Snapshot 10.1, inexperienced traders who treat American options as European are liable to lose money.

Butterfly Spreads

A *butterfly spread* involves positions in options with three different strike prices. It can be created by buying a call option with a relatively low strike price, K_1, buying a call option with a relatively high strike price, K_3, and selling two call options with a strike price, K_2, halfway between K_1 and K_3. Generally K_2 is close to the current stock price. The pattern of profits from the strategy is shown in Figure 10.6. A butterfly spread leads to a profit if the stock price stays close to K_2, but gives rise to a small loss if there is a significant stock price move in either direction. It is therefore an appropriate strategy for an investor who feels that large stock price moves are unlikely. The strategy requires a small investment initially. The payoff from a butterfly spread is shown in Table 10.5.

Table 10.3 Payoff from a box spread.

Stock price range	*Payoff from bull call spread*	*Payoff from bear put spread*	*Total payoff*
$S_T \geqslant K_2$	$K_2 - K_1$	0	$K_2 - K_1$
$K_1 < S_T < K_2$	$S_T - K_1$	$K_2 - S_T$	$K_2 - K_1$
$S_T \leqslant K_1$	0	$K_2 - K_1$	$K_2 - K_1$

Business Snapshot 10.1 Losing Money with Box Spreads

Suppose that a stock has a price of \$50 and a volatility of 30%. No dividends are expected and the risk-free rate is 8%. A trader offers you the chance to sell on the CBOE a 2-month box spread where the strike prices are \$55 and \$60 for \$5.10. Should you do the trade?

The trade certainly sounds attractive. In this case $K_1 = 55$, $K_2 = 60$, and the payoff is certain to be \$5 in 2 months. By selling the box spread for \$5.10 and investing the funds for 2 months you would have more than enough funds to meet the \$5 payoff in 2 months. The theoretical value of the box spread today is $5 \times e^{-0.08\times 2/12} = \$4.93$.

Unfortunately there is a snag. CBOE stock options are American and the \$5 payoff from the box spread is calculated on the assumption that the options comprising the box are European. Option prices for this example (calculated using DerivaGem) are shown in Table 10.4. A bull call spread where the strike prices are \$55 and \$60 costs 0.96 − 0.26 = \$0.70. (This is the same for both European and American options because, as we saw in Chapter 9, the price of a European call is the same as the price of an American call when there are no dividends.) A bear put spread with the same strike prices costs 9.46 − 5.23 = \$4.23 if the options are European and 10.00 − 5.44 = \$4.56 if they are American. The combined value of both spreads if they are created with European options is 0.70 + 4.23 = \$4.93. This is the theoretical box spread price calculated above. The combined value of buying both spreads if they are American is 0.70 + 4.56 = \$5.26. Selling a box spread created with American options for \$5.10 would not be a good trade. You would realize this almost immediately as the trade involves selling a \$60 strike put and this would be exercised against you almost as soon as you sold it!

Suppose that a certain stock is currently worth \$61. Consider an investor who feels that a significant price move in the next 6 months is unlikely. Suppose that the market prices of 6-month calls are as follows:

Strike price (\$)	Call price (\$)
55	10
60	7
65	5

Table 10.4 Values of 2-month European and American options on a non-dividend-paying stock. Stock price = \$50; interest rate = 8% per annum; and volatility = 30% per annum.

Option type	*Strike price*	*European option price*	*American option price*
Call	60	0.26	0.26
Call	55	0.96	0.96
Put	60	9.46	10.00
Put	55	5.23	5.44

Figure 10.6 Profit from butterfly spread using call options.

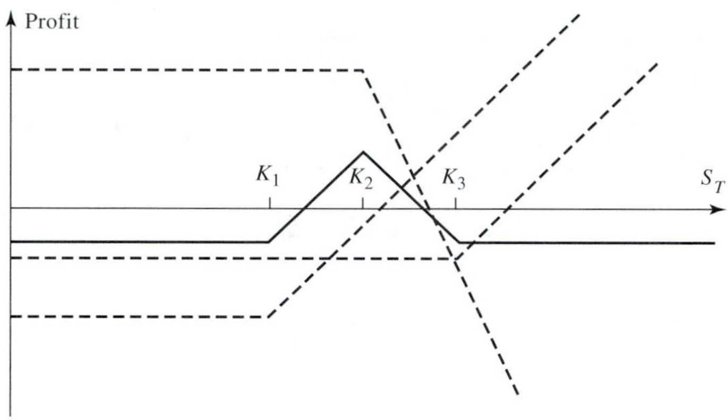

The investor could create a butterfly spread by buying one call with a \$55 strike price, buying one call with a \$65 strike price, and selling two calls with a \$60 strike price. It costs $\$10 + \$5 - (2 \times \$7) = \$1$ to create the spread. If the stock price in 6 months is greater than \$65 or less than \$55, the total payoff is zero, and the investor incurs a net loss of \$1. If the stock price is between \$56 and \$64, a profit is made. The maximum profit, \$4, occurs when the stock price in 6 months is \$60.

Butterfly spreads can be created using put options. The investor buys a put with a low strike price, buys a put with a high strike price, and sells two puts with an intermediate strike price, as illustrated in Figure 10.7. The butterfly spread in the example just considered would be created by buying a put with a strike price of \$55, buying a put with a strike price of \$65, and selling two puts with a strike price of \$60. If all options are European, the use of put options results in exactly the same spread as the use of call options. Put–call parity can be used to show that the initial investment is the same in both cases.

A butterfly spread can be sold or shorted by following the reverse strategy. Options are sold with strike prices of K_1 and K_3, and two options with the middle strike price K_2 are purchased. This strategy produces a modest profit if there is a significant movement in the stock price.

Table 10.5 Payoff from a butterfly spread.

Stock price range	*Payoff from first long call*	*Payoff from second long call*	*Payoff from short calls*	*Total payoff**
$S_T < K_1$	0	0	0	0
$K_1 < S_T < K_2$	$S_T - K_1$	0	0	$S_T - K_1$
$K_2 < S_T < K_3$	$S_T - K_1$	0	$-2(S_T - K_2)$	$K_3 - S_T$
$S_T > K_3$	$S_T - K_1$	$S_T - K_3$	$-2(S_T - K_2)$	0

* These payoffs are calculated using the relationship $K_2 = 0.5(K_1 + K_3)$.

Figure 10.7 Profit from butterfly spread using put options.

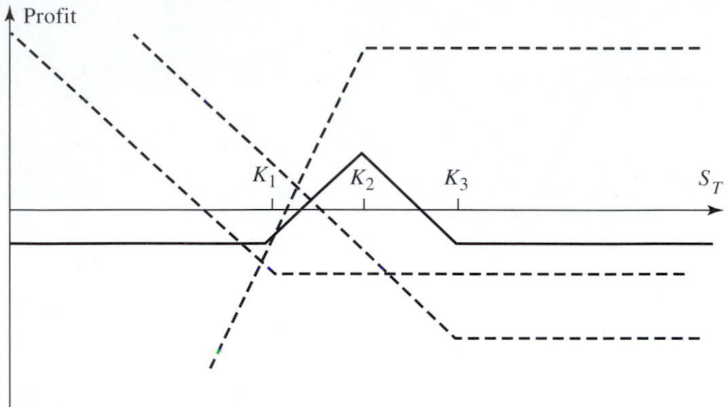

Calendar Spreads

Up to now we have assumed that the options used to create a spread all expire at the same time. We now move on to *calendar spreads* in which the options have the same strike price and different expiration dates.

A calendar spread can be created by selling a call option with a certain strike price and buying a longer-maturity call option with the same strike price. The longer the maturity of an option, the more expensive it usually is. A calendar spread therefore usually requires an initial investment. Profit diagrams for calendar spreads are usually produced so that they show the profit when the short-maturity option expires on the assumption that the long-maturity option is sold at that time. The profit pattern for a calendar spread produced from call options is shown in Figure 10.8. The pattern is

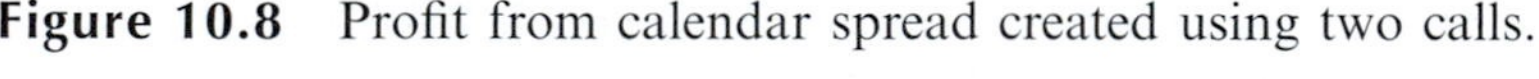

Figure 10.8 Profit from calendar spread created using two calls.

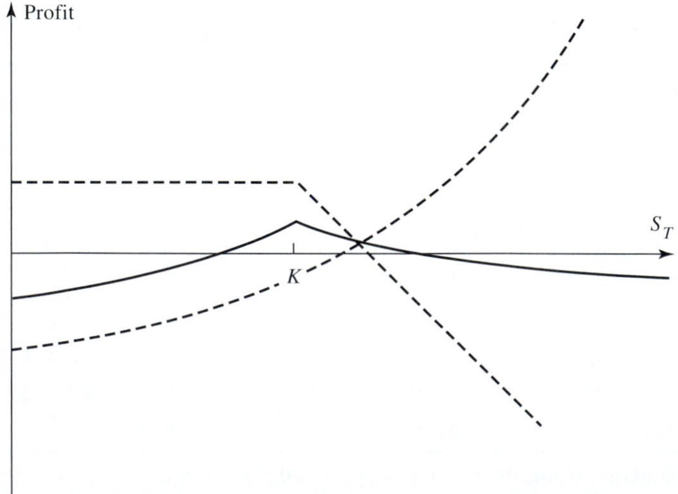

Figure 10.9 Profit from a calendar spread created using two puts.

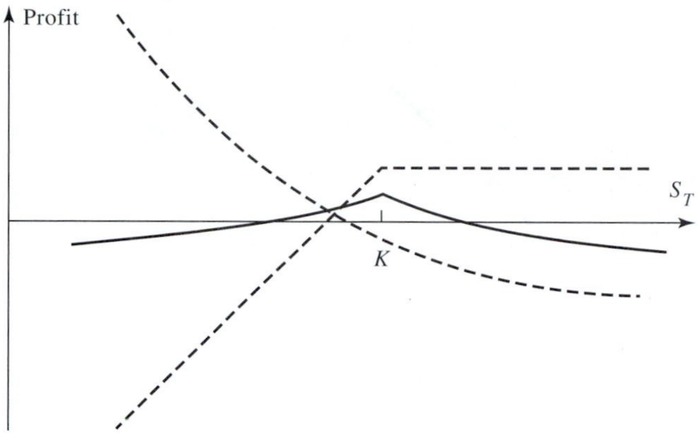

similar to the profit from the butterfly spread in Figure 10.6. The investor makes a profit if the stock price at the expiration of the short-maturity option is close to the strike price of the short-maturity option. However, a loss is incurred when the stock price is significantly above or significantly below this strike price.

To understand the profit pattern from a calendar spread, first consider what happens if the stock price is very low when the short-maturity option expires. The short-maturity option is worthless and the value of the long-maturity option is close to zero. The investor therefore incurs a loss that is close to the cost of setting up the spread initially. Consider next what happens if the stock price, S_T, is very high when the short-maturity option expires. The short-maturity option costs the investor $S_T - K$, and the long-maturity option is worth close to $S_T - K$, where K is the strike price of the options. Again, the investor makes a net loss that is close to the cost of setting up the spread initially. If S_T is close to K, the short-maturity option costs the investor either a small amount or nothing at all. However, the long-maturity option is still quite valuable. In this case a significant net profit is made.

In a *neutral calendar spread*, a strike price close to the current stock price is chosen. A *bullish calendar spread* involves a higher strike price, whereas a *bearish calendar spread* involves a lower strike price.

Calendar spreads can be created with put options as well as call options. The investor buys a long-maturity put option and sells a short-maturity put option. As shown in Figure 10.9, the profit pattern is similar to that obtained from using calls.

A *reverse calendar spread* is the opposite to that in Figures 10.8 and 10.9. The investor buys a short-maturity option and sells a long-maturity option. A small profit arises if the stock price at the expiration of the short-maturity option is well above or well below the strike price of the short-maturity option. However, a significant loss results if it is close to the strike price.

Diagonal Spreads

Bull, bear, and calendar spreads can all be created from a long position in one call and a short position in another call. In the case of bull and bear spreads, the calls have

Figure 10.10 Profit from a straddle.

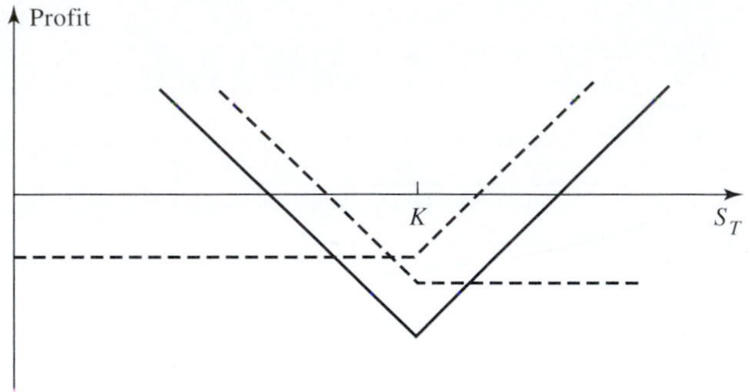

different strike prices and the same expiration date. In the case of calendar spreads, the calls have the same strike price and different expiration dates.

In a *diagonal spread* both the expiration date and the strike price of the calls are different. This increases the range of profit patterns that are possible.

10.3 COMBINATIONS

A *combination* is an option trading strategy that involves taking a position in both calls and puts on the same stock. We will consider straddles, strips, straps, and strangles.

Straddle

One popular combination is a *straddle*, which involves buying a call and put with the same strike price and expiration date. The profit pattern is shown in Figure 10.10. The strike price is denoted by K. If the stock price is close to this strike price at expiration of the options, the straddle leads to a loss. However, if there is a sufficiently large move in either direction, a significant profit will result. The payoff from a straddle is calculated in Table 10.6.

A straddle is appropriate when an investor is expecting a large move in a stock price but does not know in which direction the move will be. Consider an investor who feels that the price of a certain stock, currently valued at \$69 by the market, will move significantly in the next 3 months. The investor could create a straddle by buying both a put and a call with a strike price of \$70 and an expiration date in 3 months. Suppose that the call costs \$4 and the put costs \$3. If the stock price stays at \$69, it is easy to see

Table 10.6 Payoff from a straddle.

Range of stock price	*Payoff from call*	*Payoff from put*	*Total payoff*
$S_T \leqslant K$	0	$K - S_T$	$K - S_T$
$S_T > K$	$S_T - K$	0	$S_T - K$

Business Snapshot 10.2 How to Make Money from Trading Straddles

Suppose that a big move is expected in a company's stock price because there is a takeover bid for the company or the outcome of a major lawsuit involving the company is about to be announced. Should you trade a straddle?

A straddle seems a natural trading strategy in this case. However, if your view of the company's situation is much the same as that of other market participants, this view will be reflected in the prices of options. Options on the stock will be significantly more expensive than options on a similar stock for which no jump is expected. The V-shaped profit pattern from the straddle in Figure 10.10 will have moved downward, so that a bigger move in the stock price is necessary for you to make a profit.

For a straddle to be an effective strategy, you must believe that there are likely to be big movements in the stock price and these beliefs must be different from those of most other investors. Market prices incorporate the beliefs of market participants. To make money from any investment strategy, you must take a view that is different from most of the rest of the market—and you must be right!

that the strategy costs the investor \$6. (An up-front investment of \$7 is required, the call expires worthless, and the put expires worth \$1.) If the stock price moves to \$70, a loss of \$7 is experienced. (This is the worst that can happen.) However, if the stock price jumps up to \$90, a profit of \$13 is made; if the stock moves down to \$55, a profit of \$8 is made; and so on. As discussed in Business Snapshot 10.2 an investor should carefully consider whether the jump that he or she anticipates is already reflected in option prices before putting on a straddle trade.

The straddle in Figure 10.10 is sometimes referred to as a *bottom straddle* or *straddle purchase*. A *top straddle* or *straddle write* is the reverse position. It is created by selling a call and a put with the same exercise price and expiration date. It is a highly risky strategy. If the stock price on the expiration date is close to the strike price, a significant profit results. However, the loss arising from a large move is unlimited.

Figure 10.11 Profit from a strip and a strap.

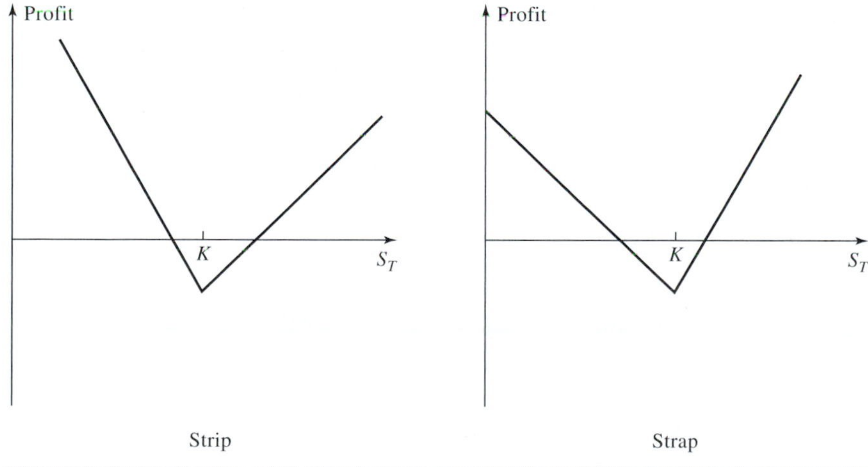

Figure 10.12 Profit from a strangle.

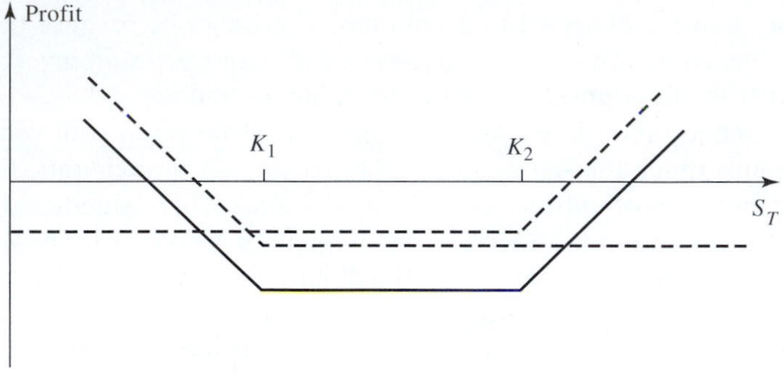

Strips and Straps

A *strip* consists of a long position in one call and two puts with the same strike price and expiration date. A *strap* consists of a long position in two calls and one put with the same strike price and expiration date. The profit patterns from strips and straps are shown in Figure 10.11. In a strip the investor is betting that there will be a big stock price move and considers a decrease in the stock price to be more likely than an increase. In a strap the investor is also betting that there will be a big stock price move. However, in this case, an increase in the stock price is considered to be more likely than a decrease.

Strangles

In a *strangle*, sometimes called a *bottom vertical combination*, an investor buys a put and a call with the same expiration date and different strike prices. The profit pattern that is obtained is shown in Figure 10.12. The call strike price, K_2, is higher than the put strike price, K_1. The payoff function for a strangle is calculated in Table 10.7.

A strangle is a similar strategy to a straddle. The investor is betting that there will be a large price move, but is uncertain whether it will be an increase or a decrease. Comparing Figures 10.12 and 10.10, we see that the stock price has to move farther in a strangle than in a straddle for the investor to make a profit. However, the downside risk if the stock price ends up at a central value is less with a strangle.

The profit pattern obtained with a strangle depends on how close together the strike prices are. The farther they are apart, the less the downside risk and the farther the stock price has to move for a profit to be realized.

Table 10.7 Payoff from a strangle.

Range of stock price	*Payoff from call*	*Payoff from put*	*Total payoff*
$S_T \leqslant K_1$	0	$K_1 - S_T$	$K_1 - S_T$
$K_1 < S_T < K_2$	0	0	0
$S_T \geqslant K_2$	$S_T - K_2$	0	$S_T - K_2$

Figure 10.13 Payoff from a butterfly spread.

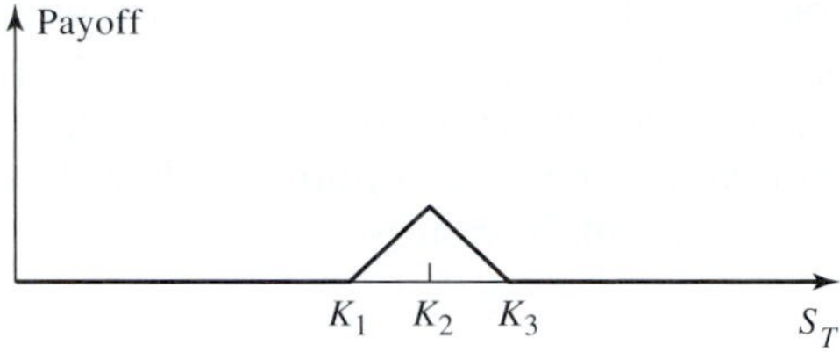

The sale of a strangle is sometimes referred to as a *top vertical combination*. It can be appropriate for an investor who feels that large stock price moves are unlikely. However, as with sale of a straddle, it is a risky strategy involving unlimited potential loss to the investor.

10.4 OTHER PAYOFFS

This chapter has demonstrated just a few of the ways in which options can be used to produce an interesting relationship between profit and stock price. If European options expiring at time T were available with every single possible strike price, any payoff function at time T could in theory be obtained. The easiest illustration of this involves a series of butterfly spreads. Recall that a butterfly spread is created by buying options with strike prices K_1 and K_3 and selling two options with strike price K_2, where $K_1 < K_2 < K_3$ and $K_3 - K_2 = K_2 - K_1$. Figure 10.13 shows the payoff from a butterfly spread. The pattern could be described as a spike. As K_1 and K_3 move closer together, the spike becomes smaller. Through the judicious combination of a large number of very small spikes, any payoff function can be approximated.

SUMMARY

A number of common trading strategies involve a single option and the underlying stock. For example, writing a covered call involves buying the stock and selling a call option on the stock; a protective put involves buying a put option and buying the stock. The former is similar to selling a put option; the latter is similar to buying a call option.

Spreads involve either taking a position in two or more calls or taking a position in two or more puts. A bull spread can be created by buying a call (put) with a low strike price and selling a call (put) with a high strike price. A bear spread can be created by buying a put (call) with a high strike price and selling a put (call) with a low strike price. A butterfly spread involves buying calls (puts) with a low and high strike price and selling two calls (puts) with some intermediate strike price. A calendar spread involves selling a call (put) with a short time to expiration and buying a call (put) with a longer time to expiration. A diagonal spread involves a long position in one option and a short position in another option such that both the strike price and the expiration date are different.

Combinations involve taking a position in both calls and puts on the same stock. A straddle combination involves taking a long position in a call and a long position in a put with the same strike price and expiration date. A strip consists of a long position in one call and two puts with the same strike price and expiration date. A strap consists of a long position in two calls and one put with the same strike price and expiration date. A strangle consists of a long position in a call and a put with different strike prices and the same expiration date. There are many other ways in which options can be used to produce interesting payoffs. It is not surprising that option trading has steadily increased in popularity and continues to fascinate investors.

FURTHER READING

Bharadwaj, A. and J. B. Wiggins. "Box Spread and Put–Call Parity Tests for the S&P Index LEAPS Markets," *Journal of Derivatives*, 8, 4 (Summer 2001): 62–71.

Chaput, J. S., and L. H. Ederington, "Option Spread and Combination Trading," *Journal of Derivatives*, 10, 4 (Summer 2003): 70–88.

McMillan, L. G. *Options as a Strategic Investment*. 4th edn., Upper Saddle River: Prentice-Hall, 2001.

Rendleman, R. J. "Covered Call Writing from an Expected Utility Perspective," *Journal of Derivatives*, 8, 3 (Spring 2001): 63–75.

Ronn, A. G. and E. I. Ronn. "The Box–Spread Arbitrage Conditions," *Review of Financial Studies*, 2, 1 (1989): 91–108.

Questions And Problems (Answers in Solutions Manual)

10.1. What is meant by a protective put? What position in call options is equivalent to a protective put?

10.2. Explain two ways in which a bear spread can be created.

10.3. When is it appropriate for an investor to purchase a butterfly spread?

10.4. Call options on a stock are available with strike prices of \$15, \$17$\frac{1}{2}$, and \$20, and expiration dates in 3 months. Their prices are \$4, \$2, and \$$\frac{1}{2}$, respectively. Explain how the options can be used to create a butterfly spread. Construct a table showing how profit varies with stock price for the butterfly spread.

10.5. What trading strategy creates a reverse calendar spread?

10.6. What is the difference between a strangle and a straddle?

10.7. A call option with a strike price of \$50 costs \$2. A put option with a strike price of \$45 costs \$3. Explain how a strangle can be created from these two options. What is the pattern of profits from the strangle?

10.8. Use put–call parity to relate the initial investment for a bull spread created using calls to the initial investment for a bull spread created using puts.

10.9. Explain how an aggressive bear spread can be created using put options.

10.10. Suppose that put options on a stock with strike prices \$30 and \$35 cost \$4 and \$7, respectively. How can the options be used to create (a) a bull spread and (b) a bear spread? Construct a table that shows the profit and payoff for both spreads.

10.11. Use put–call parity to show that the cost of a butterfly spread created from European puts is identical to the cost of a butterfly spread created from European calls.

10.12. A call with a strike price of \$60 costs \$6. A put with the same strike price and expiration date costs \$4. Construct a table that shows the profit from a straddle. For what range of stock prices would the straddle lead to a loss?

10.13. Construct a table showing the payoff from a bull spread when puts with strike prices K_1 and K_2, with $K_2 > K_1$, are used.

10.14. An investor believes that there will be a big jump in a stock price, but is uncertain as to the direction. Identify six different strategies the investor can follow and explain the differences among them.

10.15. How can a forward contract on a stock with a particular delivery price and delivery date be created from options?

10.16. "A box spread comprises four options. Two can be combined to create a long forward position and two can be combined to create a short forward position." Explain this statement.

10.17. What is the result if the strike price of the put is higher than the strike price of the call in a strangle?

10.18. One Australian dollar is currently worth \$0.64. A 1-year butterfly spread is set up using European call options with strike prices of \$0.60, \$0.65, and \$0.70. The risk-free interest rates in the United States and Australia are 5% and 4% respectively, and the volatility of the exchange rate is 15%. Use the DerivaGem software to calculate the cost of setting up the butterfly spread position. Show that the cost is the same if European put options are used instead of European call options.

Assignment Questions

10.19. Three put options on a stock have the same expiration date and strike prices of \$55, \$60, and \$65. The market prices are \$3, \$5, and \$8, respectively. Explain how a butterfly spread can be created. Construct a table showing the profit from the strategy. For what range of stock prices would the butterfly spread lead to a loss?

10.20. A diagonal spread is created by buying a call with strike price K_2 and exercise date T_2 and selling a call with strike price K_1 and exercise date T_1, where $T_2 > T_1$. Draw a diagram showing the profit when (a) $K_2 > K_1$ and (b) $K_2 < K_1$.

10.21. Draw a diagram showing the variation of an investor's profit and loss with the terminal stock price for a portfolio consisting of:

(a) One share and a short position in one call option
(b) Two shares and a short position in one call option
(c) One share and a short position in two call options
(d) One share and a short position in four call options

In each case, assume that the call option has an exercise price equal to the current stock price.

10.22. Suppose that the price of a non-dividend-paying stock is \$32, its volatility is 30%, and the risk-free rate for all maturities is 5% per annum. Use DerivaGem to calculate the cost of setting up the following positions:

(a) A bull spread using European call options with strike prices of \$25 and \$30 and a maturity of 6 months

(b) A bear spread using European put options with strike prices of \$25 and \$30 and a maturity of 6 months
(c) A butterfly spread using European call options with strike prices of \$25, \$30, and \$35 and a maturity of 1 year
(d) A butterfly spread using European put options with strike prices of \$25, \$30, and \$35 and a maturity of 1 year
(e) A straddle using options with a strike price of \$30 and a 6-month maturity
(f) A strangle using options with strike prices of \$25 and \$35 and a 6-month maturity

In each case provide a table showing the relationship between profit and final stock price. Ignore the impact of discounting.

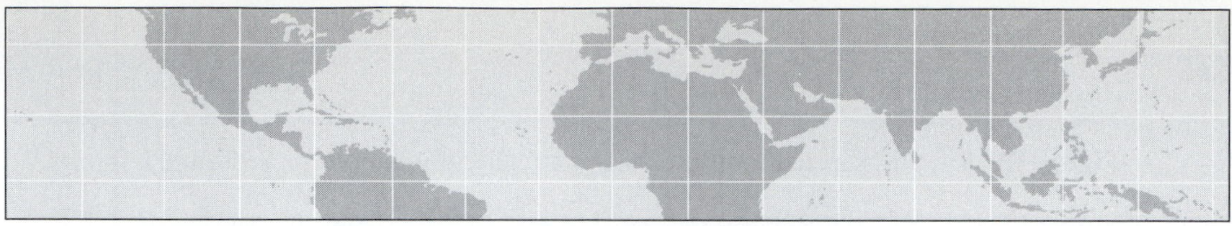

CHAPTER 11 Binomial Trees

A useful and very popular technique for pricing an option involves constructing a *binomial tree*. This is a diagram representing different possible paths that might be followed by the stock price over the life of an option. The underlying assumption is that the stock price follows a *random walk*. In each time step, it has a certain probability of moving up by a certain percentage amount and a certain probability of moving down by a certain percentage amount. In the limit, as the time step becomes smaller, this model leads to the lognormal assumption for stock prices that underlies the Black–Scholes model we will be discussing in Chapter 13.

In this chapter we will take a first look at binomial trees and their relationship to an important principle known as risk-neutral valuation. The general approach adopted here is similar to that in an important paper published by Cox, Ross, and Rubinstein in 1979. More details on numerical procedures involving binomial and trinomial trees are given in Chapter 17.

11.1 A ONE-STEP BINOMIAL MODEL

We start by considering a very simple situation. A stock price is currently \$20, and it is known that at the end of 3 months it will be either \$22 or \$18. We are interested in valuing a European call option to buy the stock for \$21 in 3 months. This option will have one of two values at the end of the 3 months. If the stock price turns out to be \$22, the value of the option will be \$1; if the stock price turns out to be \$18, the value of the option will be zero. The situation is illustrated in Figure 11.1.

It turns out that a relatively simple argument can be used to price the option in this example. The only assumption needed is that arbitrage opportunities do not exist. We set up a portfolio of the stock and the option in such a way that there is no uncertainty about the value of the portfolio at the end of the 3 months. We then argue that, because the portfolio has no risk, the return it earns must equal the risk-free interest rate. This enables us to work out the cost of setting up the portfolio and therefore the option's price. Because there are two securities (the stock and the stock option) and only two possible outcomes, it is always possible to set up the riskless portfolio.

Consider a portfolio consisting of a long position in Δ shares of the stock and a short position in one call option. We calculate the value of Δ that makes the portfolio riskless.

Figure 11.1 Stock price movements for numerical example in Section 11.1.

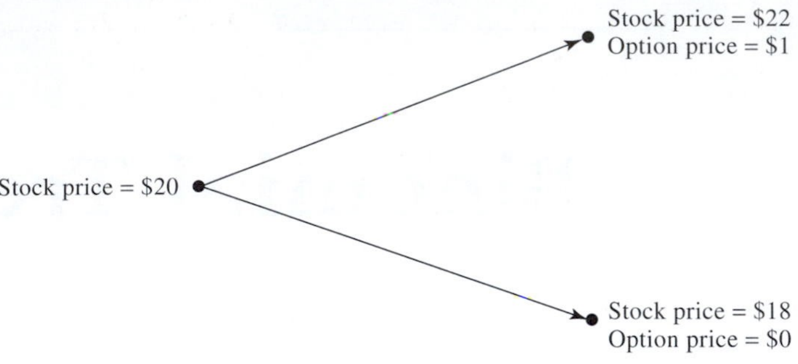

If the stock price moves up from \$20 to \$22, the value of the shares is 22Δ and the value of the option is 1, so that the total value of the portfolio is $22\Delta - 1$. If the stock price moves down from \$20 to \$18, the value of the shares is 18Δ and the value of the option is zero, so that the total value of the portfolio is 18Δ. The portfolio is riskless if the value of Δ is chosen so that the final value of the portfolio is the same for both alternatives. This means that

$$22\Delta - 1 = 18\Delta$$

or

$$\Delta = 0.25$$

A riskless portfolio is therefore

Long: 0.25 shares
Short: 1 option

If the stock price moves up to \$22, the value of the portfolio is

$$22 \times 0.25 - 1 = 4.5$$

If the stock price moves down to \$18, the value of the portfolio is

$$18 \times 0.25 = 4.5$$

Regardless of whether the stock price moves up or down, the value of the portfolio is always 4.5 at the end of the life of the option.

Riskless portfolios must, in the absence of arbitrage opportunities, earn the risk-free rate of interest. Suppose that in this case the risk-free rate is 12% per annum. It follows that the value of the portfolio today must be the present value of 4.5, or

$$4.5e^{-0.12\times 3/12} = 4.367$$

The value of the stock price today is known to be \$20. Suppose the option price is denoted by f. The value of the portfolio today is

$$20 \times 0.25 - f = 5 - f$$

It follows that

$$5 - f = 4.367$$

or

$$f = 0.633$$

This shows that, in the absence of arbitrage opportunities, the current value of the option must be 0.633. If the value of the option were more than 0.633, the portfolio would cost less than 4.367 to set up and would earn more than the risk-free rate. If the value of the option were less than 0.633, shorting the portfolio would provide a way of borrowing money at less than the risk-free rate.

A Generalization

We can generalize the argument just presented by considering a stock whose price is S_0 and an option on the stock whose current price is f. We suppose that the option lasts for time T and that during the life of the option the stock price can either move up from S_0 to a new level, S_0u, where $u > 1$, or down from S_0 to a new level, S_0d, where $d < 1$. The percentage increase in the stock price when there is an up movement is $u - 1$; the percentage decrease when there is a down movement is $1 - d$. If the stock price moves up to S_0u, we suppose that the payoff from the option is f_u; if the stock price moves down to S_0d, we suppose the payoff from the option is f_d. The situation is illustrated in Figure 11.2.

As before, we imagine a portfolio consisting of a long position in Δ shares and a short position in one option. We calculate the value of Δ that makes the portfolio riskless. If there is an up movement in the stock price, the value of the portfolio at the end of the life of the option is

$$S_0u\Delta - f_u$$

If there is a down movement in the stock price, the value becomes

$$S_0d\Delta - f_d$$

The two are equal when

$$S_0u\Delta - f_u = S_0d\Delta - f_d$$

or

$$\Delta = \frac{f_u - f_d}{S_0u - S_0d} \tag{11.1}$$

In this case, the portfolio is riskless and must earn the risk-free interest rate. Equation (11.1) shows that Δ is the ratio of the change in the option price to the change in the stock price as we move between the nodes.

Figure 11.2 Stock and option prices in a general one-step tree.

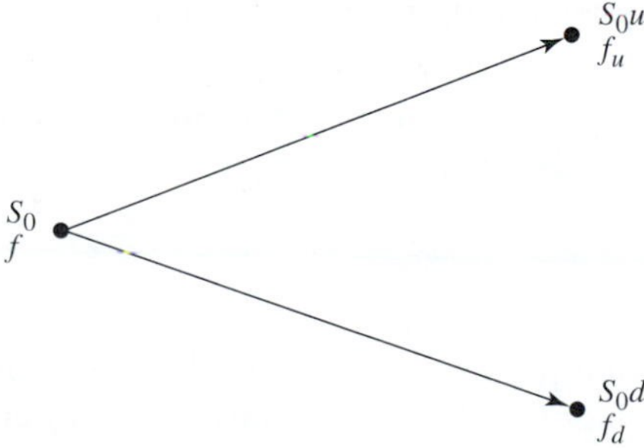

If we denote the risk-free interest rate by r, the present value of the portfolio is

$$(S_0 u\Delta - f_u)e^{-rT}$$

The cost of setting up the portfolio is

$$S_0\Delta - f$$

It follows that

$$S_0\Delta - f = (S_0 u\Delta - f_u)e^{-rT}$$

or

$$f = S_0\Delta(1 - ue^{-rT}) + f_u e^{-rT}$$

Substituting from equation (11.1) for Δ and simplifying, we can reduce this equation to

$$f = e^{-rT}[pf_u + (1-p)f_d] \tag{11.2}$$

where

$$p = \frac{e^{rT} - d}{u - d} \tag{11.3}$$

Equations (11.2) and (11.3) enable an option to be priced when stock price movements are given by a one-step binomial tree.

In the numerical example considered previously (see Figure 11.1), $u = 1.1$, $d = 0.9$, $r = 0.12$, $T = 0.25$, $f_u = 1$, and $f_d = 0$. From equation (11.3), we have

$$p = \frac{e^{0.12\times 3/12} - 0.9}{1.1 - 0.9} = 0.6523$$

and, from equation (11.2), we have

$$f = e^{-0.12\times 0.25}(0.6523 \times 1 + 0.3477 \times 0) = 0.633$$

The result agrees with the answer obtained earlier in this section.

Irrelevance of the Stock's Expected Return

The option pricing formula in equation (11.2) does not involve the probabilities of the stock price moving up or down. For example, we get the same option price when the probability of an upward movement is 0.5 as we do when it is 0.9. This is surprising and seems counterintuitive. It is natural to assume that, as the probability of an upward movement in the stock price increases, the value of a call option on the stock increases and the value of a put option on the stock decreases. This is not the case.

The key reason is that we are not valuing the option in absolute terms. We are calculating its value in terms of the price of the underlying stock. The probabilities of future up or down movements are already incorporated into the stock price: we do not need to take them into account again when valuing the option in terms of the stock price.

11.2 RISK-NEUTRAL VALUATION

Although we do not need to make any assumptions about the probabilities of up and down movements in order to derive equation (11.2), it is natural to interpret the variable p in equation (11.2) as the probability of an up movement in the stock price.

The variable $1 - p$ is then the probability of a down movement, and the expression

$$pf_u + (1 - p)f_d$$

is the expected payoff from the option. With this interpretation of p, equation (11.2) then states that the value of the option today is its expected future payoff discounted at the risk-free rate.

We now investigate the expected return from the stock when the probability of an up movement is p. The expected stock price at time T, $E(S_T)$, is given by

$$E(S_T) = pS_0u + (1 - p)S_0d$$

or

$$E(S_T) = pS_0(u - d) + S_0d$$

Substituting from equation (11.3) for p, we obtain

$$E(S_T) = S_0e^{rT} \tag{11.4}$$

showing that the stock price grows on average at the risk-free rate. Setting the probability of the up movement equal to p is therefore equivalent to assuming that the return on the stock equals the risk-free rate.

In a *risk-neutral world* all individuals are indifferent to risk. In such a world, investors require no compensation for risk, and the expected return on all securities is the risk-free interest rate. Equation (11.4) shows that we are assuming a risk-neutral world when we set the probability of an up movement to p. Equation (11.2) shows that the value of the option is its expected payoff in a risk-neutral world discounted at the risk-free rate.

This result is an example of an important general principle in option pricing known as *risk-neutral valuation*. The principle states that we can with complete impunity assume the world is risk neutral when pricing options. The resulting prices are correct not just in a risk-neutral world, but in other worlds as well.

The One-Step Binomial Example Revisited

We now return to the example in Figure 11.1 and illustrate that risk-neutral valuation gives the same answer as no-arbitrage arguments. In Figure 11.1, the stock price is currently \$20 and will move either up to \$22 or down to \$18 at the end of 3 months. The option considered is a European call option with a strike price of \$21 and an expiration date in 3 months. The risk-free interest rate is 12% per annum.

We define p as the probability of an upward movement in the stock price in a risk-neutral world. We can calculate p from equation (11.3). Alternatively, we can argue that the expected return on the stock in a risk-neutral world must be the risk-free rate of 12%. This means that p must satisfy

$$22p + 18(1 - p) = 20e^{0.12\times 3/12}$$

or

$$4p = 20e^{0.12\times 3/12} - 18$$

That is, p must be 0.6523.

At the end of the 3 months, the call option has a 0.6523 probability of being worth 1 and a 0.3477 probability of being worth zero. Its expected value is therefore

$$0.6523 \times 1 + 0.3477 \times 0 = 0.6523$$

In a risk-neutral world this should be discounted at the risk-free rate. The value of the option today is therefore

$$0.6523e^{-0.12\times3/12}$$

or \$0.633. This is the same as the value obtained earlier, demonstrating that no-arbitrage arguments and risk-neutral valuation give the same answer.

Real World vs. Risk-Neutral World

It should be emphasized that p is the probability of an up movement in a risk-neutral world. In general this is not the same as the probability of an up movement in the real world. In our example $p = 0.6523$. When the probability of an up movement is 0.6523, the expected return on both the stock and the option is the risk-free rate of 12%. Suppose that, in the real world, the expected return on the stock is 16% and p^* is the probability of an up movement. It follows that

$$22p^* + 18(1 - p^*) = 20e^{0.16\times3/12}$$

so that $p^* = 0.7041$.

The expected payoff from the option in the real world is then given by

$$p^* \times 1 + (1 - p^*) \times 0$$

This is 0.7041. Unfortunately it is not easy to know the correct discount rate to apply to the expected payoff in the real world. A position in a call option is riskier than a position in the stock. As a result the discount rate to be applied to the payoff from a call option is greater than 16%. Without knowing the option's value, we do not know how much greater than 16% it should be.[1] Using risk-neutral valuation is convenient

Figure 11.3 Stock prices in a two-step tree.

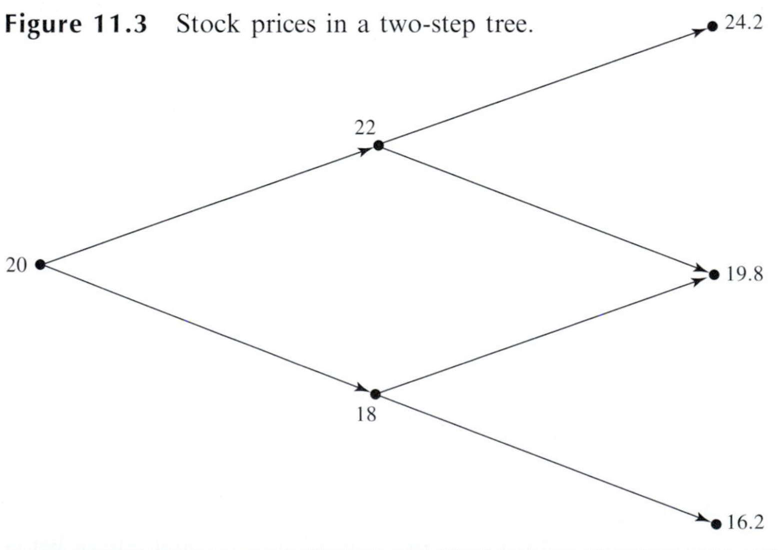

[1] Because the correct value of the option is 0.633, we can deduce that the correct discount rate is 42.58%. This is because $0.633 = 0.7041e^{-0.4258\times3/12}$.

because we know that in a risk-neutral world the expected return on all assets (and therefore the discount rate to use for all expected payoffs) is the risk-free rate.

11.3 TWO-STEP BINOMIAL TREES

We can extend the analysis to a two-step binomial tree such as that shown in Figure 11.3. Here the stock price starts at \$20 and in each of two time steps may go up by 10% or down by 10%. We suppose that each time step is 3 months long and the risk-free interest rate is 12% per annum. As before, we consider an option with a strike price of \$21.

The objective of the analysis is to calculate the option price at the initial node of the tree. This can be done by repeatedly applying the principles established earlier in the chapter. Figure 11.4 shows the same tree as Figure 11.3, but with both the stock price and the option price at each node. (The stock price is the upper number and the option price is the lower number.) The option prices at the final nodes of the tree are easily calculated. They are the payoffs from the option. At node D the stock price is 24.2 and the option price is $24.2 - 21 = 3.2$; at nodes E and F the option is out of the money and its value is zero.

At node C the option price is zero, because node C leads to either node E or node F and at both nodes the option price is zero. We calculate the option price at node B by focusing our attention on the part of the tree shown in Figure 11.5. Using the notation introduced earlier in the chapter, $u = 1.1$, $d = 0.9$, $r = 0.12$, and $T = 0.25$, so that $p = 0.6523$, and equation (11.2) gives the value of the option at node B as

$$e^{-0.12\times 3/12}(0.6523 \times 3.2 + 0.3477 \times 0) = 2.0257$$

Figure 11.4 Stock and option prices in a two-step tree. The upper number at each node is the stock price and the lower number is the option price.

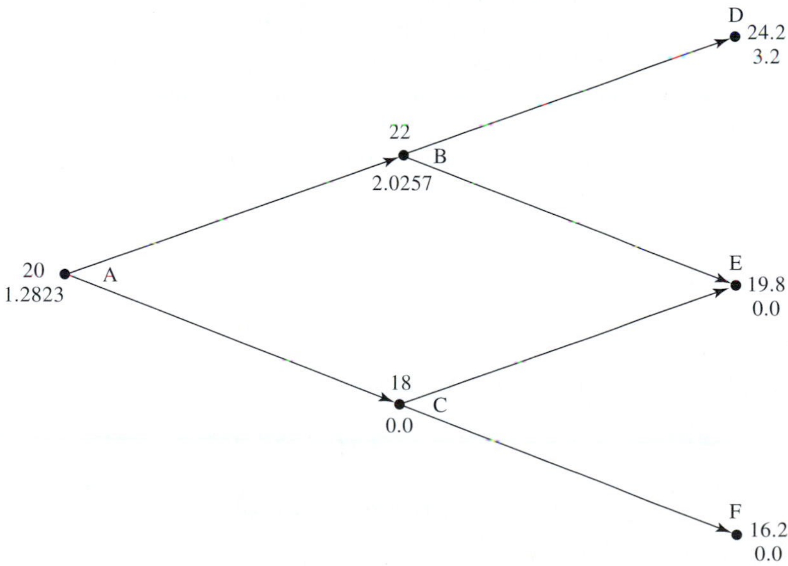

Figure 11.5 Evaluation of option price at node B.

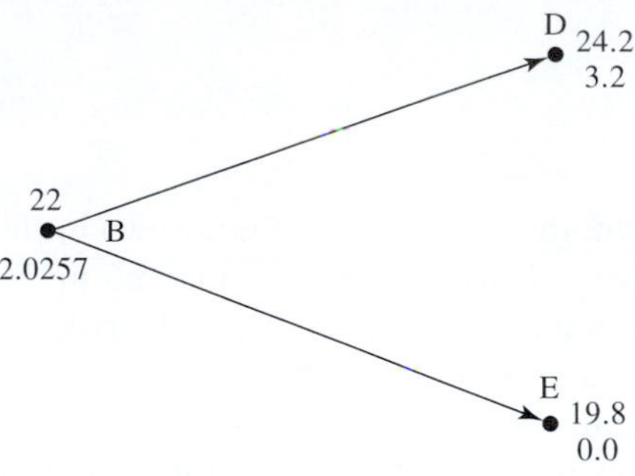

It remains for us to calculate to option price at the initial node A. We do so by focusing on the first step of the tree. We know that the value of the option at node B is 2.0257 and that at node C it is zero. Equation (11.2) therefore gives the value at node A as

$$e^{-0.12\times 3/12}(0.6523 \times 2.0257 + 0.3477 \times 0) = 1.2823$$

The value of the option is \$1.2823.

Note that this example was constructed so that u and d (the proportional up and down movements) were the same at each node of the tree and so that the time steps were of the same length. As a result, the risk-neutral probability, p, as calculated by equation (11.3) is the same at each node.

A Generalization

We can generalize the case of two time steps by considering the situation in Figure 11.6. The stock price is initially S_0. During each time step, it either moves up to u times its initial value or moves down to d times its initial value. The notation for the value of the option is shown on the tree. (For example, after two up movements the value of the option is f_{uu}.) We suppose that the risk-free interest rate is r and the length of the time step is Δt years.

Because the length of a time step is now Δt rather than T, equations (11.2) and (11.3) become

$$f = e^{-r\Delta t}[pf_u + (1-p)f_d] \tag{11.5}$$

$$p = \frac{e^{r\Delta t} - d}{u - d} \tag{11.6}$$

Repeated application of equation (11.5) gives

$$f_u = e^{-r\Delta t}[pf_{uu} + (1-p)f_{ud}] \tag{11.7}$$

$$f_d = e^{-r\Delta t}[pf_{ud} + (1-p)f_{dd}] \tag{11.8}$$

$$f = e^{-r\Delta t}[pf_u + (1-p)f_d] \tag{11.9}$$

Figure 11.6 Stock and option prices in general two-step tree.

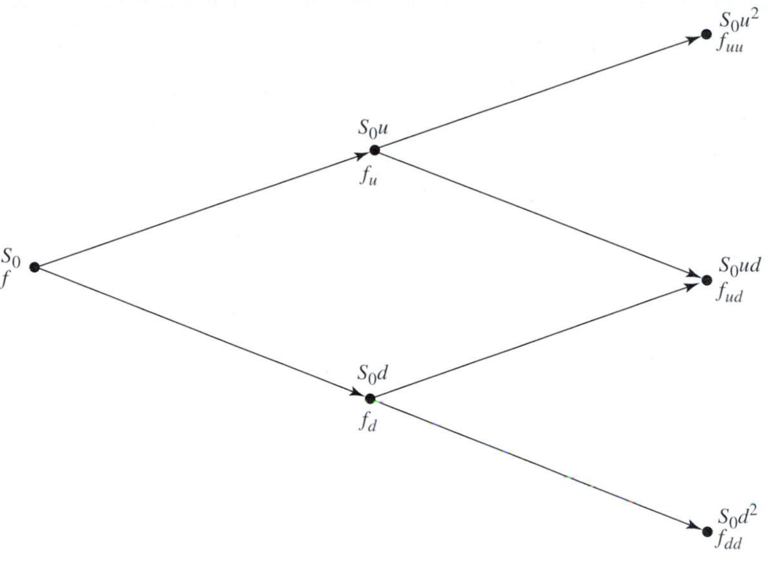

Substituting from equations (11.7) and (11.8) into (11.9), we get

$$f = e^{-2r\Delta t}[p^2 f_{uu} + 2p(1-p)f_{ud} + (1-p)^2 f_{dd}] \quad \textbf{(11.10)}$$

This is consistent with the principle of risk-neutral valuation mentioned earlier. The variables p^2, $2p(1-p)$, and $(1-p)^2$ are the probabilities that the upper, middle, and lower final nodes will be reached. The option price is equal to its expected payoff in a risk-neutral world discounted at the risk-free interest rate.

As we add more steps to the binomial tree, the risk-neutral valuation principle continues to hold. The option price is always equal to its expected payoff in a risk-neutral world discounted at the risk-free interest rate.

11.4 A PUT EXAMPLE

The procedures described in this chapter can be used to price puts as well as calls. Consider a 2-year European put with a strike price of \$52 on a stock whose current price is \$50. We suppose that there are two time steps of 1 year, and in each time step the stock price either moves up by 20% or moves down by 20%. We also suppose that the risk-free interest rate is 5%.

The tree is shown in Figure 11.7. In this case $u = 1.2$, $d = 0.8$, $\Delta t = 1$, and $r = 0.05$. From equation (11.6) the value of the risk-neutral probability, p, is given by

$$p = \frac{e^{0.05\times 1} - 0.8}{1.2 - 0.8} = 0.6282$$

The possible final stock prices are: \$72, \$48, and \$32. In this case, $f_{uu} = 0$, $f_{ud} = 4$,

Figure 11.7 Using a two-step tree to value a European put option. At each node, the upper number is the stock price and the lower number is the option price.

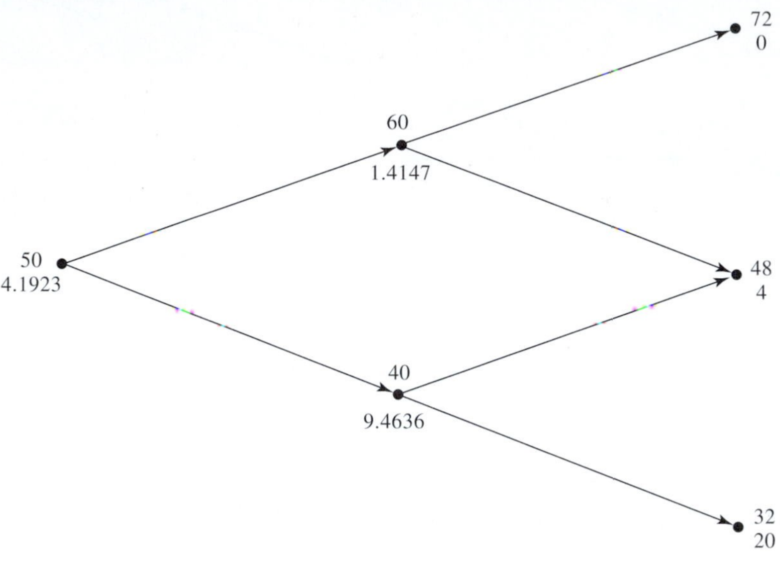

and $f_{dd} = 20$. From equation (11.10), we have

$$f = e^{-2\times 0.05\times 1}(0.6282^2 \times 0 + 2 \times 0.6282 \times 0.3718 \times 4 + 0.3718^2 \times 20) = 4.1923$$

The value of the put is \$4.1923. This result can also be obtained using equation (11.5) and working back through the tree one step at a time. Figure 11.7 shows the intermediate option prices that are calculated.

11.5 AMERICAN OPTIONS

Up to now all the options we have considered have been European. We now move on to consider how American options can be valued using a binomial tree such as that in Figure 11.4 or 11.7. The procedure is to work back through the tree from the end to the beginning, testing at each node to see whether early exercise is optimal. The value of the option at the final nodes is the same as for the European option. At earlier nodes the value of the option is the greater of

1. The value given by equation (11.5)
2. The payoff from early exercise

Figure 11.8 shows how Figure 11.7 is affected if the option under consideration is American rather than European. The stock prices and their probabilities are unchanged. The values for the option at the final nodes are also unchanged. At node B, equation (11.5) gives the value of the option as 1.4147, whereas the payoff from early exercise is negative ($= -8$). Clearly early exercise is not optimal at node B, and the value of the option at this node is 1.4147. At node C, equation (11.5) gives the value of the

Figure 11.8 Using a two-step tree to value an American put option. At each node, the upper number is the stock price and the lower number is the option price.

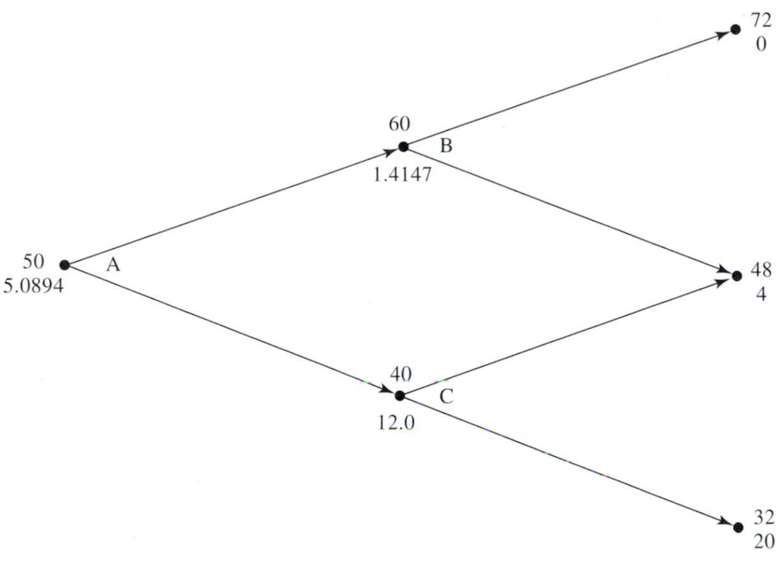

option as 9.4636, whereas the payoff from early exercise is 12. In this case, early exercise is optimal and the value of the option at the node is 12. At the initial node A, the value given by equation (11.5) is

$$e^{-0.05\times 1}(0.6282 \times 1.4147 + 0.3718 \times 12.0) = 5.0894$$

and the payoff from early exercise is 2. In this case early exercise is not optimal. The value of the option is therefore \$5.0894.

11.6 DELTA

At this stage it is appropriate to introduce *delta*, an important parameter in the pricing and hedging of options.

The delta of a stock option is the ratio of the change in the price of the stock option to the change in the price of the underlying stock. It is the number of units of the stock we should hold for each option shorted in order to create a riskless hedge. It is the same as the Δ introduced earlier in this chapter. The construction of a riskless hedge is sometimes referred to as *delta hedging*. The delta of a call option is positive, whereas the delta of a put option is negative.

From Figure 11.1, we can calculate the value of the delta of the call option being considered as

$$\frac{1-0}{22-18} = 0.25$$

This is because when the stock price changes from \$18 to \$22, the option price changes from \$0 to \$1.

In Figure 11.4 the delta corresponding to stock price movements over the first time step is

$$\frac{2.0257 - 0}{22 - 18} = 0.5064$$

The delta for stock price movements over the second time step is

$$\frac{3.2 - 0}{24.2 - 19.8} = 0.7273$$

if there is an upward movement over the first time step, and

$$\frac{0 - 0}{19.8 - 16.2} = 0$$

if there is a downward movement over the first time step.

From Figure 11.7, delta is

$$\frac{1.4147 - 9.4636}{60 - 40} = -0.4024$$

at the end of the first time step, and either

$$\frac{0 - 4}{72 - 48} = -0.1667 \quad \text{or} \quad \frac{4 - 20}{48 - 32} = -1.0000$$

at the end of the second time step.

The two-step examples show that delta changes over time. (In Figure 11.4, delta changes from 0.5064 to either 0.7273 or 0; and, in Figure 11.7, it changes from −0.4024 to either −0.1667 or −1.0000.) Thus, in order to maintain a riskless hedge using an option and the underlying stock, we need to adjust our holdings in the stock periodically. This is a feature of options that we will return to in Chapter 15.

11.7 MATCHING VOLATILITY WITH u AND d

In practice, when constructing a binomial tree to represent the movements in a stock price, we choose the parameters u and d to match the volatility of the stock price. To see how this is done, we suppose that the expected return on a stock (in the real world) is μ and its volatility is σ. Figure 11.9(a) shows stock price movements over the first step of a binomial tree. The step is of length Δt. The stock price starts at S_0 and moves either up to S_0u or down to S_0d. The probability of an up movement (in the real world) is assumed to be p^*.

The expected stock price at the end of the first time step is $S_0e^{\mu\Delta t}$. On the tree the expected stock price at this time is

$$p^*S_0u + (1 - p^*)S_0d$$

In order to match the expected return on the stock with the tree's parameters, we must therefore have

$$p^*S_0u + (1 - p^*)S_0d = S_0e^{\mu\Delta t}$$

Figure 11.9 Change in stock price in time Δt in (a) the real world and (b) the risk-neutral world.

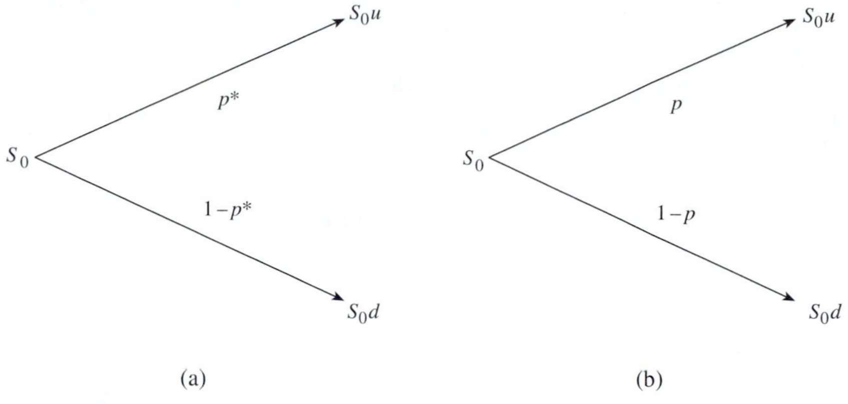

or

$$p^* = \frac{e^{\mu \Delta t} - d}{u - d} \tag{11.11}$$

As we will explain in Chapter 13, the volatility σ of a stock price is defined so that $\sigma\sqrt{\Delta t}$ is the standard deviation of the return on the stock price in a short period of time of length Δt. Equivalently, the variance of the return is $\sigma^2 \Delta t$. On the tree in Figure 11.9(a), the variance of the stock price return is[2]

$$p^* u^2 + (1 - p^*)d^2 - [p^* u + (1 - p^*)d]^2$$

In order to match the stock price volatility with the tree's parameters, we must therefore have

$$p^* u^2 + (1 - p^*)d^2 - [p^* u + (1 - p^*)d]^2 = \sigma^2 \Delta t \tag{11.12}$$

Substituting from equation (11.11) into equation (11.12), we get

$$e^{\mu \Delta t}(u + d) - ud - e^{2\mu \Delta t} = \sigma^2 \Delta t$$

When terms in Δt^2 and higher powers of Δt are ignored, one solution to this equation is[3]

$$u = e^{\sigma\sqrt{\Delta t}} \tag{11.13}$$

$$d = e^{-\sigma\sqrt{\Delta t}} \tag{11.14}$$

These are the values of u and d proposed by Cox, Ross, and Rubinstein (1979) for matching u and d.

[2] This uses the result that the variance of a variable X equals $E(X^2) - [E(X)]^2$, where E denotes expected value.

[3] We are here using the series expansion

$$e^x = 1 + x + \frac{x^2}{2!} + \frac{x^3}{3!} + \cdots$$

The analysis in Section 11.2 shows that we can replace the tree in Figure 11.9(a) by the tree in Figure 11.9(b), where the probability of an up movement is p, and then behave as though the world is risk neutral. The variable p is given by equation (11.6) as

$$p = \frac{a - d}{u - d} \tag{11.15}$$

where

$$a = e^{r\Delta t} \tag{11.16}$$

It is the risk-neutral probability of an up movement. In Figure 11.9(b), the expected stock price at the end of the time step is $S_0 e^{r\Delta t}$, as shown in equation (11.4). The variance of the stock price return is

$$pu^2 + (1-p)d^2 - [pu + (1-p)d]^2 = [e^{r\Delta t}(u+d) - ud - e^{2r\Delta t}]$$

Substituting for u and d from equations (11.13) and (11.14), we find this equals $\sigma^2 \Delta t$ when terms in Δt^2 and higher powers of Δt are ignored.

This analysis shows that when we move from the real world to the risk-neutral world the expected return on the stock changes, but its volatility remains the same (at least in the limit as Δt tends to zero). This is an illustration of an important general result known as *Girsanov's theorem*. When we move from a world with one set of risk preferences to a world with another set of risk preferences, the expected growth rates in variables change, but their volatilities remain the same. We will examine the impact of risk preferences on the behavior of market variables in more detail in Chapter 25. Moving from one set of risk preferences to another is sometimes referred to as *changing*

Figure 11.10 Two-step tree to value an American 2-year put option when the stock price is 50, strike price is 52, risk-free rate is 5%, and volatility is 30%.

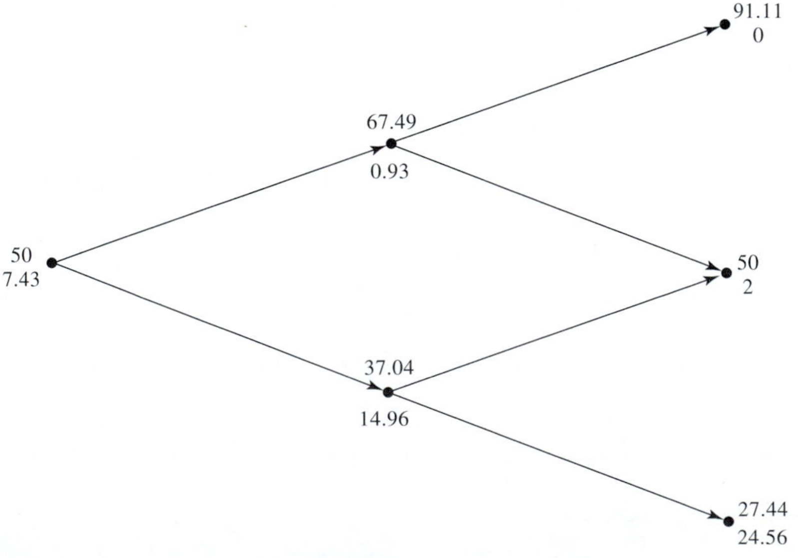

the measure. The real-world measure is sometimes referred to as the *P-measure*, while the risk-neutral world measure is referred to as the *Q-measure*.[4]

Consider again the American put option in Figures 11.8, where the stock price is \$50, the strike price is \$52, the risk-free rate is 5%, the life of the option is 2 years, and there are two time steps. In this case, $\Delta t = 1$. Suppose that the volatility σ is 30%. Then, from equations (11.13) to (11.16), we have

$$u = e^{0.3\times 1} = 1.3499, \qquad d = \frac{1}{1.3499} = 0.7408, \qquad a = e^{0.05\times 1} = 1.0513$$

and

$$p = \frac{1.053 - 0.7408}{1.3499 - 0.7408} = 0.5097$$

The tree is shown in Figure 11.10. The value of the put option is 7.43. This is different from the value obtained in Figure 11.8 by assuming $u = 1.2$ and $d = 0.8$.

11.8 INCREASING THE NUMBER OF STEPS

The binomial model presented above is unrealistically simple. Clearly, an analyst can expect to obtain only a very rough approximation to an option price by assuming that stock price movements during the life of the option consist of one or two binomial steps.

When binomial trees are used in practice, the life of the option is typically divided into 30 or more time steps. In each time step there is a binomial stock price movement. With 30 time steps there are 31 terminal stock prices and 2^{30}, or about 1 billion, possible stock price paths are considered.

The equations defining the tree are equations (11.13) to (11.16), regardless of the number of time steps. Suppose, for example, that there are five steps instead of two in the example we considered in Figure 11.10. The parameters would be $\Delta t = 2/5 = 0.4$, $r = 0.05$, and $\sigma = 0.3$. These values give $u = e^{0.3\times\sqrt{0.4}} = 1.2089$, $d = 1/1.2089 = 0.8272$, $a = e^{0.05\times 0.4} = 1.0202$, and $p = (1.0202 - 0.8272)/(1.2089 - 0.8272) = 0.5056$.

Using DerivaGem

The software accompanying this book, DerivaGem, is a useful tool for becoming comfortable with binomial trees. After loading the software in the way described at the end of this book, go to the Equity_FX_Index_Futures_Options worksheet. Choose Equity as the Underlying Type and select Binomial American as the Option Type. Enter the stock price, volatility, risk-free rate, time to expiration, exercise price, and tree steps, as 50, 30%, 5%, 2, 52, and 2, respectively. Click on the *Put* button and then on *Calculate*. The price of the option is shown as 7.428 in the box labeled Price. Now click on *Display Tree* and you will see the equivalent of Figure 11.10. (The red numbers in the software indicate the nodes where the option is exercised.)

Return to the Equity_FX_Index_Futures_Options worksheet and change the number of time steps to 5. Hit *Enter* and click on *Calculate*. You will find that the value of the option changes to 7.671. By clicking on *Display Tree* the five-step tree is displayed, together with the values of u, d, a, and p calculated above.

[4] With the notation we have been using, p is the probability under the Q-measure, while p^* is the probability under the P-measure.

DerivaGem can display trees that have up to 10 steps, but the calculations can be done for up to 500 steps. In our example, 500 steps gives the option price (to two decimal places) as 7.47. This is an accurate answer. By changing the Option Type to Binomial European we can use the tree to value a European option. Using 500 time steps the value of a European option with the same parameters as the American option is 6.76. (By changing the option type to Analytic European we can display the value the option using the Black–Scholes formula that will be presented in Chapter 13. This is also 6.76.)

By changing the Underlying Type, we can consider options on assets other than stocks. These will now be discussed.

11.9 OPTIONS ON OTHER ASSETS

We introduced options on indices, currencies, and futures contracts in Chapter 8 and will cover them in more detail in Chapter 14. It turns out that we can construct and use binomial trees for these options in exactly the same way as for options on stocks except that the equations for p change. As in the case of options on stocks, equation (11.2) applies so that the value at a node (before the possibility of early exercise is considered) is p times the value if there is an up movement plus $1 - p$ times the value if there is a down movement, discounted at the risk-free rate.

Options on Stocks Paying a Continuous Dividend Yield

Consider a stock paying a known dividend yield at rate q. The total return from dividends and capital gains in a risk-neutral world is r. The dividends provide a return of q. Capital gains must therefore provide a return of $r - q$. If the stock starts at S_0, its expected value after one time step of length Δt must be $S_0 e^{(r-q)\Delta t}$. This means that

$$pS_0u + (1 - p)S_0d = S_0e^{(r-q)\Delta t}$$

so that

$$p = \frac{e^{(r-q)\Delta t} - d}{u - d}$$

As in the case of options on non-dividend-paying stocks, we match volatility by setting $u = e^{\sigma\sqrt{\Delta t}}$ and $d = 1/u$. This means that we can use equations (11.13) to (11.16) except that we set $a = e^{(r-q)\Delta t}$.

Options on Stock Indices

When calculating a futures price for a stock index in Chapter 5 we assumed that the stocks underlying the index provided a dividend yield at rate q. We make a similar assumption here. The valuation of an option on a stock index is therefore very similar to the valuation of an option on a stock paying a known dividend yield.

Example 11.1

A stock index is currently 810 and has a volatility of 20% and a dividend yield of 2%. The risk-free rate is 5%. Figure 11.11 shows the output from DerivaGem for valuing a European 6-month call option with a strike price of 800 using a two-step tree.

Figure 11.11 Two-step tree to value an European 6-month call option on an index when the index level is 810, strike price is 800, risk-free rate is 5%, volatility is 20%, and dividend yield is 2%.

At each node:
Upper value = Underlying Asset Price
Lower value = Option Price
Shading indicates where option is exercised

Strike price = 800
Discount factor per step = 0.9876
Time step, dt = 0.2500 years, 91.25 days
Growth factor per step, a = 1.0075
Probability of up move, p = 0.5126
Up step size, u = 1.1052
Down step size, d = 0.9048

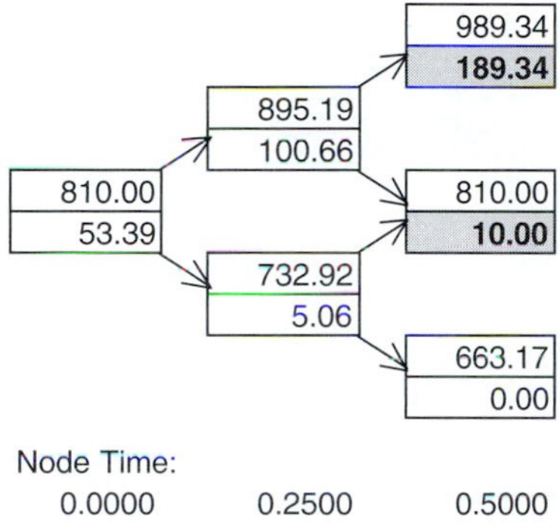

In this case,

$$\Delta t = 0.25, \qquad u = e^{0.20\times\sqrt{0.25}} = 1.1052,$$

$$d = 1/u = 0.9048, \qquad a = e^{(0.05-0.02)\times 0.25} = 1.0075$$

$$p = (1.0075 - 0.9048)/(1.1052 - 0.9048) = 0.5126$$

The value of the option is 53.39.

Options on Currencies

As pointed out in Section 5.10, a foreign currency can be regarded as an asset providing a yield at the foreign risk-free rate of interest, r_f. By analogy with the stock index case we can construct a tree for options on a currency by using equations (11.13) to (11.16) and setting $a = e^{(r-r_f)\Delta t}$.

Example 11.2

The Australian dollar is currently worth 0.6100 U.S. dollars and this exchange rate has a volatility of 12%. The Australian risk-free rate is 7% and the U.S. risk-free rate is 5%. Figure 11.12 shows the output from DerivaGem for valuing a 3-month American call option with a strike price of 0.6000 using a three-step tree.

Figure 11.12 Three-step tree to value an American 3-month call option on a currency when the value of the currency is 0.6100, strike price is 0.6000, risk-free rate is 5%, volatility is 12%, and foreign risk-free rate is 7%.

At each node:
Upper value = Underlying Asset Price
Lower value = Option Price
Shading indicates where option is exercised

Strike price = 0.6
Discount factor per step = 0.9958
Time step, dt = 0.0833 years, 30.42 days
Growth factor per step, a = 0.9983
Probability of up move, p = 0.4673
Up step size, u = 1.0352
Down step size, d = 0.9660

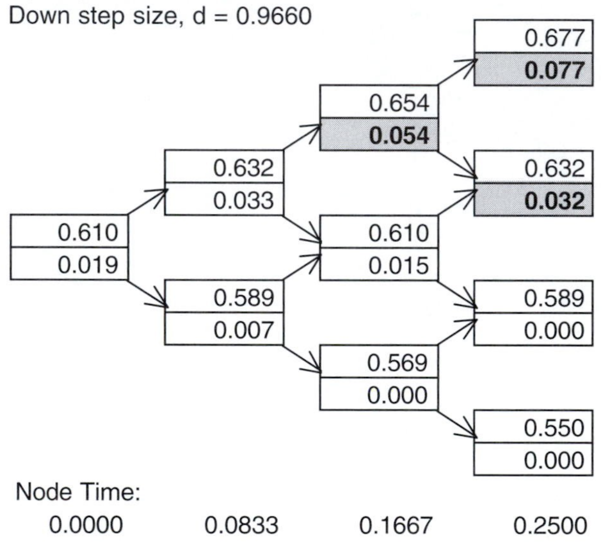

In this case,

$$\Delta t = 0.08333, \quad u = e^{0.12 \times \sqrt{0.08333}} = 1.0352$$
$$d = 1/u = 0.9660, \quad a = e^{(0.05-0.07)\times 0.08333} = 0.9983$$
$$p = (0.9983 - 0.9660)/(1.0352 - 0.9660) = 0.4673$$

The value of the option is 0.019.

Options on Futures

It costs nothing to take a long or a short position in a futures contract. It follows that in a risk-neutral world a futures price should have an expected growth rate of zero. (We discuss this point in more detail in Section 14.7.) Similarly to above, we define p as the probability of an up movement in the futures price, u as the percentage up movement, and d as the percentage down movement. If F_0 is the initial futures price, the expected futures price at the end of one time step of length Δt should also be F_0. This means that

$$pF_0u + (1 - p)F_0d = F_0$$

so that

$$p = \frac{1 - d}{u - d}$$

and we can use equations (11.13) to (11.16) with $a = 1$.

Example 11.3

A futures price is currently 31 and has a volatility of 30%. The risk-free rate is 5%. Figure 11.13 shows the output from DerivaGem for valuing a 9-month American put option with a strike price of 30 using a three-step tree.

Figure 11.13 Three-step tree to value an American 9-month put option on a futures contract when the futures price is 31, strike price is 30, risk-free rate is 5%, and volatility is 30%.

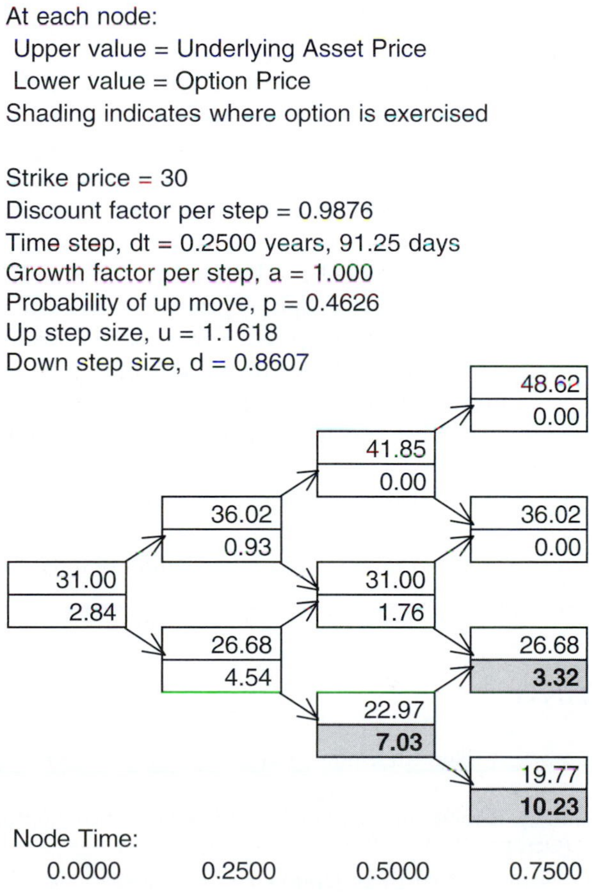

At each node:
Upper value = Underlying Asset Price
Lower value = Option Price
Shading indicates where option is exercised

Strike price = 30
Discount factor per step = 0.9876
Time step, dt = 0.2500 years, 91.25 days
Growth factor per step, a = 1.000
Probability of up move, p = 0.4626
Up step size, u = 1.1618
Down step size, d = 0.8607

Node Time: 0.0000	0.2500	0.5000	0.7500
			48.62 / 0.00
		41.85 / 0.00	
	36.02 / 0.93		36.02 / 0.00
31.00 / 2.84		31.00 / 1.76	
	26.68 / 4.54		26.68 / **3.32**
		22.97 / **7.03**	
			19.77 / **10.23**

In this case,

$$\Delta t = 0.25, \quad u = e^{0.3\sqrt{0.25}} = 1.1618$$
$$d = 1/u = 1/1.1618 = 0.8607, \quad a = 1,$$
$$p = (1 - 0.8607)/(1.1618 - 0.8607) = 0.4626$$

The value of the option is 2.84.

SUMMARY

This chapter has provided a first look at the valuation of options on stocks and other assets. In the simple situation where movements in the price of a stock during the life of an option are governed by a one-step binomial tree, it is possible to set up a portfolio consisting of a stock option and the stock that is riskless. In a world with no arbitrage opportunities, riskless portfolios must earn the risk-free interest. This enables the stock option to be priced in terms of the stock. It is interesting to note that no assumptions are required about the probabilities of up and down movements in the stock price at each node of the tree.

When stock price movements are governed by a multistep binomial tree, we can treat each binomial step separately and work back from the end of the life of the option to the beginning to obtain the current value of the option. Again only no-arbitrage arguments are used, and no assumptions are required about the probabilities of up and down movements in the stock price at each node.

A very important principle states that we can assume the world is risk-neutral when valuing an option. This chapter has shown, through both numerical examples and algebra, that no-arbitrage arguments and risk-neutral valuation are equivalent and lead to the same option prices.

The delta of a stock option, Δ, considers the effect of a small change in the underlying stock price on the change in the option price. It is the ratio of the change in the option price to the change in the stock price. For a riskless position, an investor should buy Δ shares for each option sold. An inspection of a typical binomial tree shows that delta changes during the life of an option. This means that to hedge a particular option position, we must change our holding in the underlying stock periodically.

Constructing binomial trees for valuing options on stock indices, currencies, and futures contracts is very similar to doing so for valuing options on stocks. In Chapter 17, we will return to binomial trees and give a more details on how they can be used in practice.

FURTHER READING

Coval, J. E. and T. Shumway. "Expected Option Returns," *Journal of Finance*, 56, 3 (2001): 983–1009.

Cox, J. C., S. A. Ross, and M. Rubinstein. "Option Pricing: A Simplified Approach." *Journal of Financial Economics* 7 (October 1979): 229–64.

Rendleman, R., and B. Bartter. "Two State Option Pricing." *Journal of Finance* 34 (1979): 1092–1110.

Questions and Problems (Answers in Solutions Manual)

11.1. A stock price is currently \$40. It is known that at the end of 1 month it will be either \$42 or \$38. The risk-free interest rate is 8% per annum with continuous compounding. What is the value of a 1-month European call option with a strike price of \$39?

11.2. Explain the no-arbitrage and risk-neutral valuation approaches to valuing a European option using a one-step binomial tree.

11.3. What is meant by the "delta" of a stock option?

11.4. A stock price is currently \$50. It is known that at the end of 6 months it will be either \$45 or \$55. The risk-free interest rate is 10% per annum with continuous compounding. What is the value of a 6-month European put option with a strike price of \$50?

11.5. A stock price is currently \$100. Over each of the next two 6-month periods it is expected to go up by 10% or down by 10%. The risk-free interest rate is 8% per annum with continuous compounding. What is the value of a 1-year European call option with a strike price of \$100?

11.6. For the situation considered in Problem 11.5, what is the value of a 1-year European put option with a strike price of \$100? Verify that the European call and European put prices satisfy put–call parity.

11.7. What are the formulas for u and d in terms of volatility?

11.8. Consider the situation in which stock price movements during the life of a European option are governed by a two-step binomial tree. Explain why it is not possible to set up a position in the stock and the option that remains riskless for the whole of the life of the option.

11.9. A stock price is currently \$50. It is known that at the end of 2 months it will be either \$53 or \$48. The risk-free interest rate is 10% per annum with continuous compounding. What is the value of a 2-month European call option with a strike price of \$49? Use no-arbitrage arguments.

11.10. A stock price is currently \$80. It is known that at the end of 4 months it will be either \$75 or \$85. The risk-free interest rate is 5% per annum with continuous compounding. What is the value of a 4-month European put option with a strike price of \$80? Use no-arbitrage arguments.

11.11. A stock price is currently \$40. It is known that at the end of 3 months it will be either \$45 or \$35. The risk-free rate of interest with quarterly compounding is 8% per annum. Calculate the value of a 3-month European put option on the stock with an exercise price of \$40. Verify that no-arbitrage arguments and risk-neutral valuation arguments give the same answers.

11.12. A stock price is currently \$50. Over each of the next two 3-month periods it is expected to go up by 6% or down by 5%. The risk-free interest rate is 5% per annum with continuous compounding. What is the value of a 6-month European call option with a strike price of \$51?

11.13. For the situation considered in Problem 11.12, what is the value of a 6-month European put option with a strike price of \$51? Verify that the European call and European put prices satisfy put–call parity. If the put option were American, would it ever be optimal to exercise it early at any of the nodes on the tree?

11.14. A stock price is currently \$25. It is known that at the end of 2 months it will be either \$23 or \$27. The risk-free interest rate is 10% per annum with continuous compounding. Suppose S_T is the stock price at the end of 2 months. What is the value of a derivative that pays off S_T^2 at this time?

11.15. Calculate u, d, and p when a binomial tree is constructed to value an option on a foreign currency. The tree step size is 1 month, the domestic interest rate is 5% per annum, the foreign interest rate is 8% per annum, and the volatility is 12% per annum.

Assignment Questions

11.16. A stock price is currently \$50. It is known that at the end of 6 months it will be either \$60 or \$42. The risk-free rate of interest with continuous compounding is 12% per annum. Calculate the value of a 6-month European call option on the stock with an exercise price of \$48. Verify that no-arbitrage arguments and risk-neutral valuation arguments give the same answers.

11.17. A stock price is currently \$40. Over each of the next two 3-month periods it is expected to go up by 10% or down by 10%. The risk-free interest rate is 12% per annum with continuous compounding.

(a) What is the value of a 6-month European put option with a strike price of \$42?

(b) What is the value of a 6-month American put option with a strike price of \$42?

11.18. Using a "trial-and-error" approach, estimate how high the strike price has to be in Problem 11.17 for it to be optimal to exercise the option immediately.

11.19. A stock price is currently \$30. During each 2-month period for the next 4 months it will increase by 8% or reduce by 10%. The risk-free interest rate is 5%. Use a two-step tree to calculate the value of a derivative that pays off $\max[(30 - S_T), 0]^2$, where S_T is the stock price in 4 months. If the derivative is American-style, should it be exercised early?

11.20. Consider a European call option on a non-dividend-paying stock where the stock price is \$40, the strike price is \$40, the risk-free rate is 4% per annum, the volatility is 30% per annum, and the time to maturity is 6 months.

(a) Calculate u, d, and p for a two-step tree.

(b) Value the option using a two-step tree.

(c) Verify that DerivaGem gives the same answer.

(d) Use DerivaGem to value the option with 5, 50, 100, and 500 time steps.

11.21. Repeat Problem 11.20 for an American put option on a futures contract. The strike price and the futures price are \$50, the risk-free rate is 10%, the time to maturity is 6 months, and the volatility is 40% per annum.

11.22. Footnote 1 shows that the correct discount rate to use for the real-world expected payoff in the case of the call option considered in Figure 11.1 is 42.6%. Show that if the option is a put rather than a call the discount rate is −52.5%. Explain why the two real-world discount rates are so different.

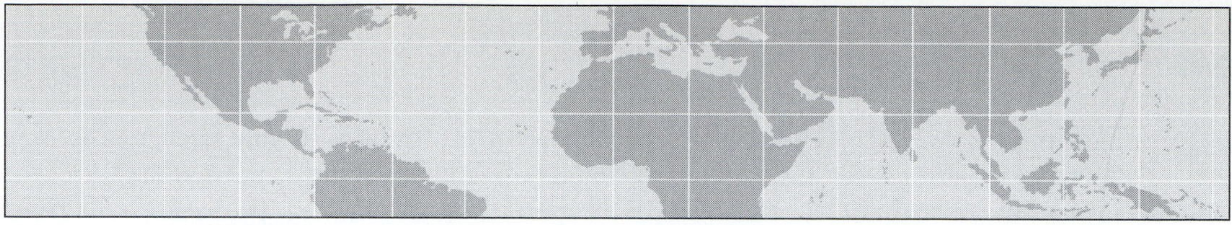

CHAPTER 12 Wiener Processes and Itô's Lemma

Any variable whose value changes over time in an uncertain way is said to follow a *stochastic process*. Stochastic processes can be classified as *discrete time* or *continuous time*. A discrete-time stochastic process is one where the value of the variable can change only at certain fixed points in time, whereas a continuous-time stochastic process is one where changes can take place at any time. Stochastic processes can also be classified as *continuous variable* or *discrete variable*. In a continuous-variable process, the underlying variable can take any value within a certain range, whereas in a discrete-variable process, only certain discrete values are possible.

This chapter develops a continuous-variable, continuous-time stochastic process for stock prices. Learning about this process is the first step to understanding the pricing of options and other more complicated derivatives. It should be noted that, in practice, we do not observe stock prices following continuous-variable, continuous-time processes. Stock prices are restricted to discrete values (e.g., multiples of a cent) and changes can be observed only when the exchange is open. Nevertheless, the continuous-variable, continuous-time process proves to be a useful model for many purposes.

Many people feel that continuous-time stochastic processes are so complicated that they should be left entirely to "rocket scientists". This is not so. The biggest hurdle to understanding these processes is the notation. Here we present a step-by-step approach aimed at getting the reader over this hurdle. We also explain an important result known as *Itô's lemma* that is central to the pricing of derivatives.

12.1 THE MARKOV PROPERTY

A *Markov process* is a particular type of stochastic process where only the present value of a variable is relevant for predicting the future. The past history of the variable and the way that the present has emerged from the past are irrelevant.

Stock prices are usually assumed to follow a Markov process. Suppose that the price of IBM stock is $100 now. If the stock price follows a Markov process, our predictions for the future should be unaffected by the price one week ago, one month ago, or one year ago. The only relevant piece of information is that the price is now \$100.[1] Predictions for the future are uncertain and must be expressed in terms of probability distributions. The Markov property implies that the probability distribution of the price at any particular future time is not dependent on the particular path followed by the price in the past.

The Markov property of stock prices is consistent with the weak form of market efficiency. This states that the present price of a stock impounds all the information contained in a record of past prices. If the weak form of market efficiency were not true, technical analysts could make above-average returns by interpreting charts of the past history of stock prices. There is very little evidence that they are in fact able to do this.

It is competition in the marketplace that tends to ensure that weak-form market efficiency holds. There are many, many investors watching the stock market closely. Trying to make a profit from it leads to a situation where a stock price, at any given time, reflects the information in past prices. Suppose that it was discovered that a particular pattern in stock prices always gave a 65% chance of subsequent steep price rises. Investors would attempt to buy a stock as soon as the pattern was observed, and demand for the stock would immediately rise. This would lead to an immediate rise in its price and the observed effect would be eliminated, as would any profitable trading opportunities.

12.2 CONTINUOUS-TIME STOCHASTIC PROCESSES

Consider a variable that follows a Markov stochastic process. Suppose that its current value is 10 and that the change in its value during 1 year is $\phi(0, 1)$, where $\phi(\mu, \sigma)$ denotes a probability distribution that is normally distributed with mean μ and standard deviation σ. What is the probability distribution of the change in the value of the variable during 2 years?

The change in 2 years is the sum of two normal distributions, each of which has a mean of zero and standard deviation of 1.0. Because the variable is Markov, the two probability distributions are independent. When we add two independent normal distributions, the result is a normal distribution where the mean is the sum of the means and the variance is the sum of the variances.[2] The mean of the change during 2 years in the variable we are considering is, therefore, zero and the variance of this change is 2.0. Hence, the change in the variable over 2 years is $\phi(0, \sqrt{2})$.

Consider next the change in the variable during 6 months. The variance of the change in the value of the variable during 1 year equals the variance of the change during the first 6 months plus the variance of the change during the second 6 months. We assume these are the same. It follows that the variance of the change during a 6-month period must be 0.5. Equivalently, the standard deviation of the change is $\sqrt{0.5}$, so that the probability distribution for the change in the value of the variable during 6 months is $\phi(0, \sqrt{0.5})$.

---

[1] Statistical properties of the stock price history of IBM may be useful in determining the characteristics of the stochastic process followed by the stock price (e.g., its volatility). The point being made here is that the particular path followed by the stock in the past is irrelevant.

[2] Variance is the square of standard deviation. The variance of a 1-year change in the value of the variable we are considering is therefore 1.0.

A similar argument shows that the change in the value of the variable during 3 months is $\phi(0, \sqrt{0.25})$. More generally, the change during any time period of length T is $\phi(0, \sqrt{T})$. In particular, the change during a very short time period of length Δt is $\phi(0, \sqrt{\Delta t})$.

The square root signs in these results may seem strange. They arise because, when Markov processes are considered, the variance of the changes in successive time periods are additive. The standard deviations of the changes in successive time periods are not additive. The variance of the change in the variable in our example is 1.0 per year, so that the variance of the change in 2 years is 2.0 and the variance of the change in 3 years is 3.0. The standard deviation of the change in 2 and 3 years is $\sqrt{2}$ and $\sqrt{3}$, respectively. Strictly speaking, we should not refer to the standard deviation of the variable as 1.0 per year. It should be "1.0 per square root of years". The results explain why uncertainty is sometimes referred to as being proportional to the square root of time.

Wiener Processes

The process followed by the variable we have been considering is known as a *Wiener process*. It is a particular type of Markov stochastic process with a mean change of zero and a variance rate of 1.0 per year. It has been used in physics to describe the motion of a particle that is subject to a large number of small molecular shocks and is sometimes referred to as *Brownian motion*.

Expressed formally, a variable z follows a Wiener process if it has the following two properties:

PROPERTY 1. *The change Δz during a small period of time Δt is*

$$\Delta z = \epsilon\sqrt{\Delta t} \tag{12.1}$$

where ϵ has a standardized normal distribution $\phi(0, 1)$.

PROPERTY 2. *The values of Δz for any two different short intervals of time, Δt, are independent.*

It follows from the first property that Δz itself has a normal distribution with

$$\text{mean of } \Delta z = 0$$
$$\text{standard deviation of } \Delta z = \sqrt{\Delta t}$$
$$\text{variance of } \Delta z = \Delta t$$

The second property implies that z follows a Markov process.

Consider the change in the value of z during a relatively long period of time, T. This can be denoted by $z(T) - z(0)$. It can be regarded as the sum of the changes in z in N small time intervals of length Δt, where

$$N = \frac{T}{\Delta t}$$

Thus,

$$z(T) - z(0) = \sum_{i=1}^{N} \epsilon_i \sqrt{\Delta t} \tag{12.2}$$

where the ϵ_i $(i = 1, 2, \ldots, N)$ are distributed $\phi(0, 1)$. We know from the second

Figure 12.1 How a Wiener process is obtained when $\Delta t \to 0$ in equation (12.1).

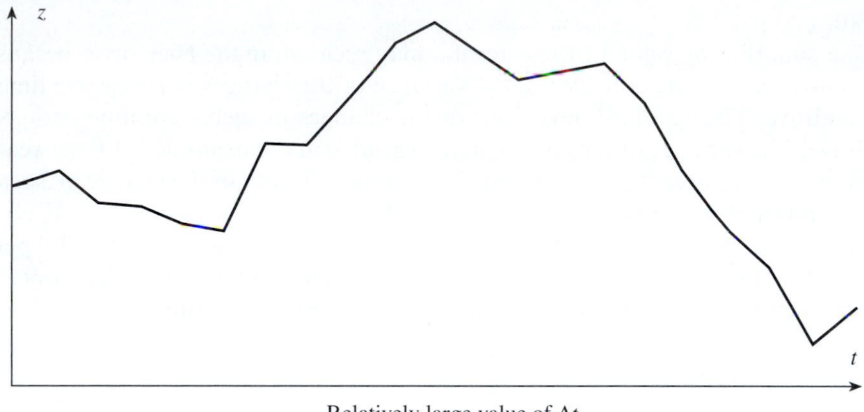

Relatively large value of Δt

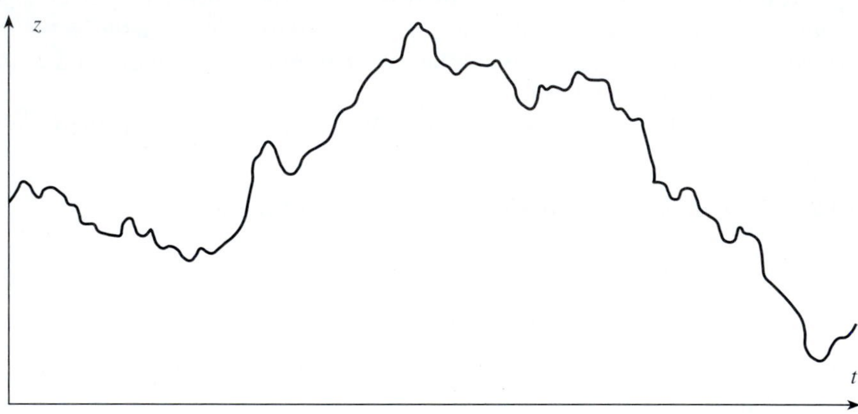

Smaller value of Δt

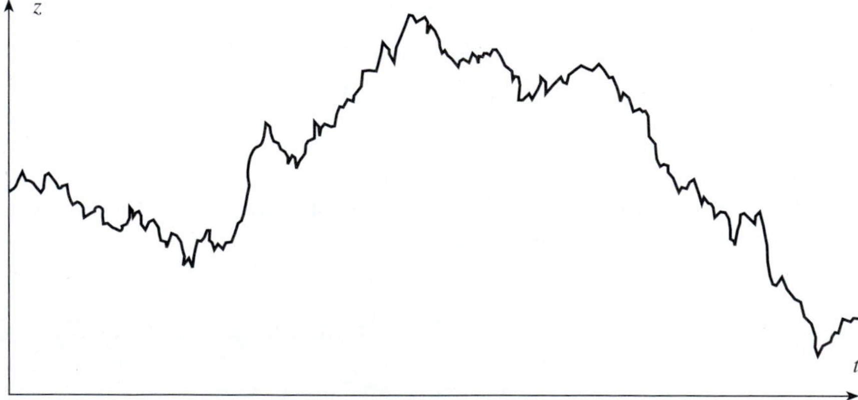

The true process obtained as $\Delta t \to 0$

property of Wiener processes that the ϵ_i are independent of each other. It follows from equation (12.2) that $z(T) - z(0)$ is normally distributed, with

$$\text{mean of } [z(T) - z(0)] = 0$$
$$\text{variance of}[z(T) - z(0)] = N\,\Delta t = T$$
$$\text{standard deviation of } [z(T) - z(0)] = \sqrt{T}$$

This is consistent with the discussion earlier in this section.

Example 12.1

Suppose that the value, z, of a variable that follows a Wiener process is initially 25 and that time is measured in years. At the end of 1 year, the value of the variable is normally distributed with a mean of 25 and a standard deviation of 1.0. At the end of 5 years, it is normally distributed with a mean of 25 and a standard deviation of $\sqrt{5}$, or 2.236. Our uncertainty about the value of the variable at a certain time in the future, as measured by its standard deviation, increases as the square root of how far we are looking ahead.

In ordinary calculus, it is usual to proceed from small changes to the limit as the small changes become closer to zero. Thus, $dx = a\,dt$ is the notation used to indicate that $\Delta x = a\,\Delta t$ in the limit as $\Delta t \to 0$. We use similar notational conventions in stochastic calculus. So, when we refer to dz as a Wiener process, we mean that it has the properties for Δz given above in the limit as $\Delta t \to 0$.

Figure 12.1 illustrates what happens to the path followed by z as the limit $\Delta t \to 0$ is approached. Note that the path is quite "jagged". This is because the size of a movement in z in time Δt is proportional to $\sqrt{\Delta t}$ and, when Δt is small, $\sqrt{\Delta t}$ is much bigger than Δt. Two intriguing properties of Wiener processes, related to this $\sqrt{\Delta t}$ property, are as follows:

1. The expected length of the path followed by z in any time interval is infinite.

2. The expected number of times z equals any particular value in any time interval is infinite.

Generalized Wiener Process

The mean change per unit time for a stochastic process is known as the *drift rate* and the variance per unit time is known as the *variance rate*. The basic Wiener process, dz, that has been developed so far has a drift rate of zero and a variance rate of 1.0. The drift rate of zero means that the expected value of z at any future time is equal to its current value. The variance rate of 1.0 means that the variance of the change in z in a time interval of length T equals T. A *generalized Wiener process* for a variable x can be defined in terms of dz as

$$dx = a\,dt + b\,dz \tag{12.3}$$

where a and b are constants.

To understand equation (12.3), it is useful to consider the two components on the right-hand side separately. The $a\,dt$ term implies that x has an expected drift rate of a per unit of time. Without the $b\,dz$ term, the equation is $dx = a\,dt$, which implies that $dx/dt = a$. Integrating with respect to time, we get

$$x = x_0 + at$$

where x_0 is the value of x at time 0. In a period of time of length T, the variable x increases by an amount aT. The $b\,dz$ term on the right-hand side of equation (12.3) can be regarded as adding noise or variability to the path followed by x. The amount of this noise or variability is b times a Wiener process. A Wiener process has a standard deviation of 1.0. It follows that b times a Wiener process has a standard deviation of b. In a small time interval Δt, the change Δx in the value of x is given by equations (12.1) and (12.3) as

$$\Delta x = a\,\Delta t + b\epsilon\sqrt{\Delta t}$$

where, as before, ϵ has a standard normal distribution. Thus Δx has a normal distribution with

$$\text{mean of } \Delta x = a\,\Delta t$$
$$\text{standard deviation of } \Delta x = b\sqrt{\Delta t}$$
$$\text{variance of } \Delta x = b^2\Delta t$$

Similar arguments to those given for a Wiener process show that the change in the value of x in any time interval T is normally distributed with

$$\text{mean of change in } x = aT$$
$$\text{standard deviation of change in } x = b\sqrt{T}$$
$$\text{variance of change in } x = b^2T$$

Thus, the generalized Wiener process given in equation (12.3) has an expected drift rate (i.e., average drift per unit of time) of a and a variance rate (i.e., variance per unit of time) of b^2. It is illustrated in Figure 12.2.

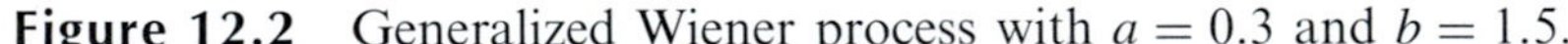

Figure 12.2 Generalized Wiener process with $a = 0.3$ and $b = 1.5$.

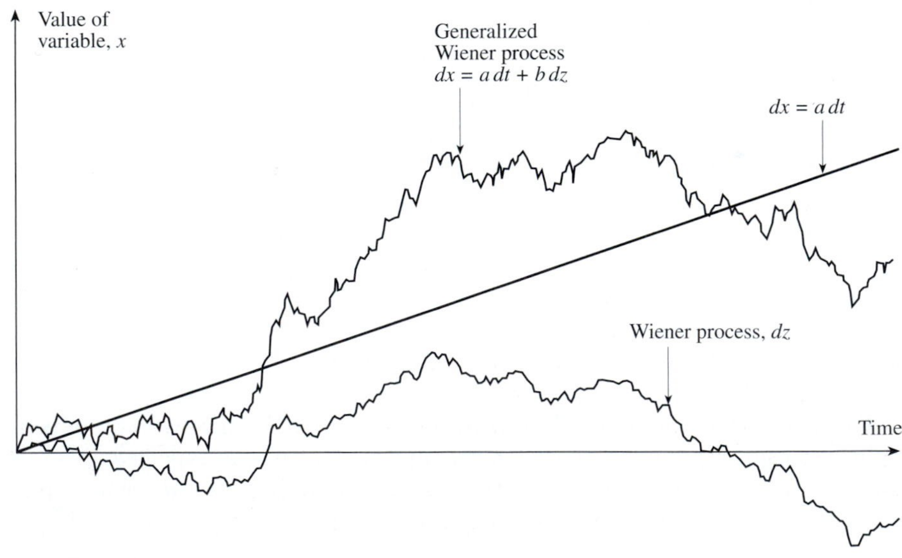

Example 12.2

Consider the situation where the cash position of a company, measured in thousands of dollars, follows a generalized Wiener process with a drift of 20 per year and a variance rate of 900 per year. Initially, the cash position is 50. At the end of 1 year the cash position will have a normal distribution with a mean of 70 and a standard deviation of $\sqrt{900}$, or 30. At the end of 6 months it will have a normal distribution with a mean of 60 and a standard deviation of $30\sqrt{0.5} = 21.21$. Our uncertainty about the cash position at some time in the future, as measured by its standard deviation, increases as the square root of how far ahead we are looking. Note that the cash position can become negative. (We can interpret this as a situation where the company is borrowing funds.)

Itô Process

A further type of stochastic process, known as an *Itô process*, can be defined. This is a generalized Wiener process in which the parameters a and b are functions of the value of the underlying variable x and time t. An Itô process can be written algebraically as

$$dx = a(x, t)\,dt + b(x, t)\,dz \tag{12.4}$$

Both the expected drift rate and variance rate of an Itô process are liable to change over time. In a small time interval between t and $t + \Delta t$, the variable changes from x to $x + \Delta x$, where

$$\Delta x = a(x, t)\Delta t + b(x, t)\epsilon\sqrt{\Delta t}$$

This relationship involves a small approximation. It assumes that the drift and variance rate of x remain constant, equal to $a(x, t)$ and $b(x, t)^2$, respectively, during the time interval between t and $t + \Delta t$.

12.3 THE PROCESS FOR A STOCK PRICE

In this section we discuss the stochastic process usually assumed for the price of a non-dividend-paying stock.

It is tempting to suggest that a stock price follows a generalized Wiener process; that is, that it has a constant expected drift rate and a constant variance rate. However, this model fails to capture a key aspect of stock prices. This is that the expected percentage return required by investors from a stock is independent of the stock's price. If investors require a 14% per annum expected return when the stock price is \$10, then, *ceteris paribus*, they will also require a 14% per annum expected return when it is \$50.

Clearly, the assumption of constant expected drift rate is inappropriate and needs to be replaced by the assumption that the expected return (i.e., expected drift divided by the stock price) is constant. If S is the stock price at time t, then the expected drift rate in S should be assumed to be μS for some constant parameter μ. This means that in a short interval of time, Δt, the expected increase in S is $\mu S\,\Delta t$. The parameter μ is the expected rate of return on the stock, expressed in decimal form.

If the volatility of the stock price is always zero, then this model implies that

$$\Delta S = \mu S\,\Delta t$$

In the limit, as $\Delta t \to 0$,

$$dS = \mu S\,dt$$

or

$$\frac{dS}{S} = \mu\,dt$$

Integrating between time 0 and time T, we get

$$S_T = S_0 e^{\mu T} \tag{12.5}$$

where S_0 and S_T are the stock price at time 0 and time T. Equation (12.5) shows that, when the variance rate is zero, the stock price grows at a continuously compounded rate of μ per unit of time.

In practice, of course, a stock price does exhibit volatility. A reasonable assumption is that the variability of the percentage return in a short period of time, Δt, is the same regardless of the stock price. In other words, an investor is just as uncertain of the percentage return when the stock price is \$50 as when it is \$10. This suggests that the standard deviation of the change in a short period of time Δt should be proportional to the stock price and leads to the model

$$dS = \mu S\,dt + \sigma S\,dz$$

or

$$\frac{dS}{S} = \mu\,dt + \sigma\,dz \tag{12.6}$$

Equation (12.6) is the most widely used model of stock price behavior. The variable σ is the volatility of the stock price. The variable μ is its expected rate of return. The model in equation (12.6) can be regarded as the limiting case of the random walk represented by the binomial trees in Chapter 11 as the time step becomes smaller.

Example 12.3

Consider a stock that pays no dividends, has a volatility of 30% per annum, and provides an expected return of 15% per annum with continuous compounding. In this case, $\mu = 0.15$ and $\sigma = 0.30$. The process for the stock price is

$$\frac{dS}{S} = 0.15\,dt + 0.30\,dz$$

If S is the stock price at a particular time and ΔS is the increase in the stock price in the next small interval of time,

$$\frac{\Delta S}{S} = 0.15\Delta t + 0.30\epsilon\sqrt{\Delta t}$$

where ϵ has a standard normal distribution. Consider a time interval of 1 week or 0.0192 year and suppose that the initial stock price is \$100. Then $\Delta t = 0.0192$, $S = 100$, and

$$\Delta S = 100(0.00288 + 0.0416\epsilon)$$

or

$$\Delta S = 0.288 + 4.16\epsilon$$

showing that the price increase has a normal distribution with mean \$0.288 and standard deviation \$4.16.

Discrete-Time Model

The model of stock price behavior we have developed is known as *geometric Brownian motion*. The discrete-time version of the model is

$$\frac{\Delta S}{S} = \mu\,\Delta t + \sigma\epsilon\sqrt{\Delta t} \tag{12.7}$$

or

$$\Delta S = \mu S\,\Delta t + \sigma S\epsilon\sqrt{\Delta t} \tag{12.8}$$

The variable ΔS is the change in the stock price, S, in a small time interval Δt, and ϵ has a standard normal distribution (i.e., a normal distribution with a mean of zero and standard deviation of 1.0). The parameter μ is the expected rate of return per unit of time from the stock and the parameter σ is the volatility of the stock price. In this chapter we will assume these parameters are constant.

The left-hand side of equation (12.7) is the return provided by the stock in a short period of time, Δt. The term $\mu\,\Delta t$ is the expected value of this return, and the term $\sigma\epsilon\sqrt{\Delta t}$ is the stochastic component of the return. The variance of the stochastic component (and, therefore, of the whole return) is $\sigma^2\Delta t$. This is consistent with the definition of the volatility σ given in Section 11.7; that is, σ is such that $\sigma\sqrt{\Delta t}$ is the standard deviation of the return in a short time period Δt.

Equation (12.7) shows that $\Delta S/S$ is normally distributed with mean $\mu\,\Delta t$ and standard deviation $\sigma\sqrt{\Delta t}$. In other words,

$$\frac{\Delta S}{S} \sim \phi(\mu\,\Delta t,\ \sigma\sqrt{\Delta t}) \tag{12.9}$$

Monte Carlo Simulation

A Monte Carlo simulation of a stochastic process is a procedure for sampling random outcomes for the process. We will use it as a way of developing some understanding of the nature of the stock price process in equation (12.6).

Suppose that the expected return from a stock is 14% per annum and that the standard deviation of the return (i.e., the volatility) is 20% per annum. Without notation, this means that $\mu = 0.14$ and $\sigma = 0.20$. Suppose that $\Delta t = 0.01$, so that we are considering changes in the stock price in time intervals of length 0.01 year. From equation (12.8), we have

$$\Delta S = 0.14 \times 0.01S + 0.2\sqrt{0.01}\,S\epsilon$$

or

$$\Delta S = 0.0014S + 0.02S\epsilon \tag{12.10}$$

A path for the stock price can be simulated by sampling repeatedly for ϵ from $\phi(0, 1)$ and substituting into equation (12.10). The expression =RAND( ) in Excel produces a random sample between 0 and 1. The inverse cumulative normal distribution is NORMSINV. The instruction to produce a random sample from a standard normal distribution in Excel is therefore =NORMSINV(RAND( )). Table 12.1 shows one path for a stock price that was sampled in this way. The initial stock price is assumed to be \$20. For the first period, ϵ is sampled as 0.52. From equation (12.10), the change during the first time period is

$$\Delta S = 0.0014 \times 20 + 0.02 \times 20 \times 0.52 = 0.236$$

Table 12.1 Simulation of stock price when $\mu = 0.14$ and $\sigma = 0.20$ during periods of length 0.01 year.

Stock price at start of period	*Random sample for ϵ*	*Change in stock price during period*
20.000	0.52	0.236
20.236	1.44	0.611
20.847	−0.86	−0.329
20.518	1.46	0.628
21.146	−0.69	−0.262
20.883	−0.74	−0.280
20.603	0.21	0.115
20.719	−1.10	−0.427
20.292	0.73	0.325
20.617	1.16	0.507
21.124	2.56	1.111

Therefore, at the beginning of the second time period, the stock price is \$20.236. The value of ϵ sampled for the next period is 1.44. From equation (12.10), the change during the second time period is

$$\Delta S = 0.0014 \times 20.236 + 0.02 \times 20.236 \times 1.44 = 0.611$$

So, at the beginning of the next period, the stock price is \$20.847; and so on. Note that, because the process we are simulating is Markov, the samples for ϵ should be independent of each other.[3]

Table 12.1 assumes that stock prices are measured to the nearest 0.001. It is important to realize that the table shows only one possible pattern of stock price movements. Different random samples would lead to different price movements. Any small time interval Δt can be used in the simulation. In the limit as $\Delta t \to 0$, a perfect description of the stochastic process obtained. The final stock price of 21.124 in Table 12.1 can be regarded as a random sample from the distribution of stock prices at the end of 10 time intervals (i.e., at the end of 1/10 of a year). By repeatedly simulating movements in the stock price, a complete probability distribution of the stock price at the end of this time is obtained. Monte Carlo simulation is discussed in more detail in Chapter 17.

12.4 THE PARAMETERS

The process for stock prices developed in this chapter involves two parameters, μ and σ. The parameter μ is the expected continuously compounded return earned by an investor per year. Most investors require higher expected returns to induce them to take higher risks. It follows that the value of μ should depend on the risk of the return from the stock.[4] It should also depend on the level of interest rates in the economy. The higher the level of interest rates, the higher the expected return required on any given stock.

[3] In practice, it is more efficient to sample $\ln S$ rather than S, as will be discussed in Section 17.6.

[4] More precisely, μ depends on that part of the risk that cannot be diversified away by the investor.

Fortunately, we do not have to concern ourselves with the determinants of μ in any detail because the value of a derivative dependent on a stock is, in general, independent of μ. The parameter σ, the stock price volatility, is, by contrast, critically important to the determination of the value of many derivatives. We will discuss procedures for estimating σ in Chapter 13. Typical values of σ for a stock are in the range 0.15 to 0.60 (i.e., 15% to 60%).

The standard deviation of the proportional change in the stock price in a small interval of time Δt is $\sigma\sqrt{\Delta t}$. As a rough approximation, the standard deviation of the proportional change in the stock price over a relatively long period of time T is $\sigma\sqrt{T}$. This means that, as an approximation, volatility can be interpreted as the standard deviation of the change in the stock price in 1 year. In Chapter 13, we will show that the volatility of a stock price is exactly equal to the standard deviation of the continuously compounded return provided by the stock in 1 year.

12.5 ITÔ'S LEMMA

The price of a stock option is a function of the underlying stock's price and time. More generally, we can say that the price of any derivative is a function of the stochastic variables underlying the derivative and time. A serious student of derivatives must, therefore, acquire some understanding of the behavior of functions of stochastic variables. An important result in this area was discovered by the mathematician K. Itô in 1951,[5] and is known as *Itô's lemma*.

Suppose that the value of a variable x follows the Itô process

$$dx = a(x,t)\,dt + b(x,t)\,dz \tag{12.11}$$

where dz is a Wiener process and a and b are functions of x and t. The variable x has a drift rate of a and a variance rate of b^2. Itô's lemma shows that a function G of x and t follows the process

$$dG = \left(\frac{\partial G}{\partial x}a + \frac{\partial G}{\partial t} + \tfrac{1}{2}\frac{\partial^2 G}{\partial x^2}b^2\right)dt + \frac{\partial G}{\partial x}b\,dz \tag{12.12}$$

where the dz is the same Wiener process as in equation (12.11). Thus, G also follows an Itô process, with a drift rate of

$$\frac{\partial G}{\partial x}a + \frac{\partial G}{\partial t} + \tfrac{1}{2}\frac{\partial^2 G}{\partial x^2}b^2$$

and a variance rate of

$$\left(\frac{\partial G}{\partial x}\right)^2 b^2$$

A completely rigorous proof of Itô's lemma is beyond the scope of this book. In the appendix to this chapter, we show that the lemma can be viewed as an extension of well-known results in differential calculus.

Earlier, we argued that

$$dS = \mu S\,dt + \sigma S\,dz \tag{12.13}$$

[5] See K. Itô, "On Stochastic Differential Equations," *Memoirs of the American Mathematical Society*, 4 (1951): 1–51.

with μ and σ constant, is a reasonable model of stock price movements. From Itô's lemma, it follows that the process followed by a function G of S and t is

$$dG = \left(\frac{\partial G}{\partial S}\mu S + \frac{\partial G}{\partial t} + \frac{1}{2}\frac{\partial^2 G}{\partial S^2}\sigma^2 S^2\right) dt + \frac{\partial G}{\partial S}\sigma S\, dz \tag{12.14}$$

Note that both S and G are affected by the same underlying source of uncertainty, dz. This proves to be very important in the derivation of the Black–Scholes results.

Application to Forward Contracts

To illustrate Itô's lemma, consider a forward contract on a non-dividend-paying stock. Assume that the risk-free rate of interest is constant and equal to r for all maturities. From equation (5.1), we have

$$F_0 = S_0 e^{rT}$$

where F_0 is the forward price at time zero, S_0 is the spot price at time zero, and T is the time to maturity of the forward contract.

We are interested in what happens to the forward price as time passes. We define F as the forward price at a general time t, and S as the stock price at time t, with $t < T$. The relationship between F and S is given by

$$F = Se^{r(T-t)} \tag{12.15}$$

Assuming that the process for S is given by equation (12.13), we can use Itô's lemma to determine the process for F. From equation (12.15), we have

$$\frac{\partial F}{\partial S} = e^{r(T-t)}, \qquad \frac{\partial^2 F}{\partial S^2} = 0, \qquad \frac{\partial F}{\partial t} = -rSe^{r(T-t)}$$

From equation (12.14), the process for F is given by

$$dF = \left[e^{r(T-t)}\mu S - rSe^{r(T-t)}\right] dt + e^{r(T-t)}\sigma S\, dz$$

Substituting F for $Se^{r(T-t)}$ gives

$$dF = (\mu - r)F\, dt + \sigma F\, dz \tag{12.16}$$

Like S, the forward price F follows geometric Brownian motion. It has an expected growth rate of $\mu - r$ rather than μ. The growth rate in F is the excess return of S over the risk-free rate.

12.6 THE LOGNORMAL PROPERTY

We now use Itô's lemma to derive the process followed by $\ln S$ when S follows the process in equation (12.13). We define

$$G = \ln S$$

Since

$$\frac{\partial G}{\partial S} = \frac{1}{S}, \qquad \frac{\partial^2 G}{\partial S^2} = -\frac{1}{S^2}, \qquad \frac{\partial G}{\partial t} = 0$$

it follows from equation (12.14) that the process followed by G is

$$dG = \left(\mu - \frac{\sigma^2}{2}\right) dt + \sigma\, dz \tag{12.17}$$

Since μ and σ are constant, this equation indicates that $G = \ln S$ follows a generalized Wiener process. It has constant drift rate $\mu - \sigma^2/2$ and constant variance rate σ^2. The change in $\ln S$ between time 0 and some future time T is therefore normally distributed, with mean $(\mu - \sigma^2/2)T$ and variance $\sigma^2 T$. This means that

$$\ln S_T - \ln S_0 \sim \phi\left[\left(\mu - \frac{\sigma^2}{2}\right)T,\ \sigma\sqrt{T}\right] \tag{12.18}$$

or

$$\ln S_T \sim \phi\left[\ln S_0 + \left(\mu - \frac{\sigma^2}{2}\right)T,\ \sigma\sqrt{T}\right] \tag{12.19}$$

where S_T is the stock price at a future time T, S_0 is the stock price at time 0, and $\phi(m, s)$ denotes a normal distribution with mean m and standard deviation s.

Equation (12.19) shows that $\ln S_T$ is normally distributed. A variable has a lognormal distribution if the natural logarithm of the variable is normally distributed. The model of stock price behavior we have developed in this chapter therefore implies that a stock's price at time T, given its price today, is lognormally distributed. The standard deviation of the logarithm of the stock price is $\sigma\sqrt{T}$. It is proportional to the square root of how far ahead we are looking.

SUMMARY

Stochastic processes describe the probabilistic evolution of the value of a variable through time. A Markov process is one where only the present value of the variable is relevant for predicting the future. The past history of the variable and the way in which the present has emerged from the past is irrelevant.

A Wiener process dz is a process describing the evolution of a normally distributed variable. The drift of the process is zero and the variance rate is 1.0 per unit time. This means that, if the value of the variable is x_0 at time 0, then at time T it is normally distributed with mean x_0 and standard deviation $\sqrt{T}$.

A generalized Wiener process describes the evolution of a normally distributed variable with a drift of a per unit time and a variance rate of b^2 per unit time, where a and b are constants. This means that if, as before, the value of the variable is x_0 at time 0, it is normally distributed with a mean of $x_0 + aT$ and a standard deviation of $b\sqrt{T}$ at time T.

An Itô process is a process where the drift and variance rate of x can be a function of both x itself and time. The change in x in a very short period of time is, to a good approximation, normally distributed, but its change over longer periods of time is liable to be nonnormal.

One way of gaining an intuitive understanding of a stochastic process for a variable is to simulate the behavior of the variable. This involves dividing a time interval into many small time steps and randomly sampling possible paths for the variable. The future probability distribution for the variable can then be calculated. Monte Carlo simulation is discussed further in Chapter 17.

Itô's lemma is a way of calculating the stochastic process followed by a function of a variable from the stochastic process followed by the variable itself. As we shall see in Chapter 13, Itô's lemma plays a very important part in the pricing of derivatives. A key point is that the Wiener process dz underlying the stochastic process for the variable is exactly the same as the Wiener process underlying the stochastic process for the function of the variable. Both are subject to the same underlying source of uncertainty.

The stochastic process usually assumed for a stock price is geometric Brownian motion. Under this process the return to the holder of the stock in a small period of time is normally distributed and the returns in two nonoverlapping periods are independent. The value of the stock price at a future time has a lognormal distribution. The Black–Scholes model, which we cover in the next chapter, is based on the geometric Brownian motion assumption.

FURTHER READING

On Efficient Markets and the Markov Property of Stock Prices

Brealey, R. A. *An Introduction to Risk and Return from Common Stock*, 2nd edn. Cambridge, MA: MIT Press, 1983.

Cootner, P. H. (ed.) *The Random Character of Stock Market Prices*. Cambridge, MA: MIT Press, 1964.

On Stochastic Processes

Cox, D. R., and H. D. Miller. *The Theory of Stochastic Processes*. London: Chapman and Hall, 1965.

Feller, W. *Probability Theory and Its Applications*, Vols. 1 and 2. New York: Wiley, 1950.

Karlin, S., and H. M. Taylor. *A First Course in Stochastic Processes*, 2nd edn. New York: Academic Press, 1975.

Neftci, S. *Introduction to Mathematics of Financial Derivatives*, New York: Academic Press, 1996.

Questions and Problems (Answers in Solutions Manual)

12.1. What would it mean to assert that the temperature at a certain place follows a Markov process? Do you think that temperatures do, in fact, follow a Markov process?

12.2. Can a trading rule based on the past history of a stock's price ever produce returns that are consistently above average? Discuss.

12.3. A company's cash position, measured in millions of dollars, follows a generalized Wiener process with a drift rate of 0.5 per quarter and a variance rate of 4.0 per quarter. How high does the company's initial cash position have to be for the company to have a less than 5% chance of a negative cash position by the end of 1 year?

12.4. Variables X_1 and X_2 follow generalized Wiener processes, with drift rates μ_1 and μ_2 and variances σ_1^2 and σ_2^2. What process does $X_1 + X_2$ follow if:
(a) The changes in X_1 and X_2 in any short interval of time are uncorrelated?
(b) There is a correlation ρ between the changes in X_1 and X_2 in any short time interval?

12.5. Consider a variable S that follows the process

$$dS = \mu\, dt + \sigma\, dz$$

For the first three years, $\mu = 2$ and $\sigma = 3$; for the next three years, $\mu = 3$ and $\sigma = 4$. If the initial value of the variable is 5, what is the probability distribution of the value of the variable at the end of year 6?

12.6. Suppose that G is a function of a stock price S and time. Suppose that σ_S and σ_G are the volatilities of S and G. Show that, when the expected return of S increases by $\lambda\sigma_S$, the growth rate of G increases by $\lambda\sigma_G$, where λ is a constant.

12.7. Stock A and stock B both follow geometric Brownian motion. Changes in any short interval of time are uncorrelated with each other. Does the value of a portfolio consisting of one of stock A and one of stock B follow geometric Brownian motion? Explain your answer.

12.8. The process for the stock price in equation (12.8) is

$$\Delta S = \mu S\,\Delta t + \sigma S\epsilon\sqrt{\Delta t}$$

where μ and σ are constant. Explain carefully the difference between this model and each of the following:

$$\Delta S = \mu\,\Delta t + \sigma\epsilon\sqrt{\Delta t}$$
$$\Delta S = \mu S\,\Delta t + \sigma\epsilon\sqrt{\Delta t}$$
$$\Delta S = \mu\,\Delta t + \sigma S\epsilon\sqrt{\Delta t}$$

Why is the model in equation (12.8) a more appropriate model of stock price behavior than any of these three alternatives?

12.9. It has been suggested that the short-term interest rate r follows the stochastic process

$$dr = a(b - r)\,dt + rc\,dz$$

where a, b, c are positive constants and dz is a Wiener process. Describe the nature of this process.

12.10. Suppose that a stock price S follows geometric Brownian motion with expected return μ and volatility σ:

$$dS = \mu S\,dt + \sigma S\,dz$$

What is the process followed by the variable S^n? Show that S^n also follows geometric Brownian motion.

12.11. Suppose that x is the yield to maturity with continuous compounding on a zero-coupon bond that pays off \$1 at time T. Assume that x follows the process

$$dx = a(x_0 - x)\,dt + sx\,dz$$

where a, x_0, and s are positive constants and dz is a Wiener process. What is the process followed by the bond price?

Assignment Questions

12.12. Suppose that a stock price has an expected return of 16% per annum and a volatility of 30% per annum. When the stock price at the end of a certain day is \$50, calculate the following:

(a) The expected stock price at the end of the next day.
(b) The standard deviation of the stock price at the end of the next day.
(c) The 95% confidence limits for the stock price at the end of the next day.

12.13. A company's cash position, measured in millions of dollars, follows a generalized Wiener process with a drift rate of 0.1 per month and a variance rate of 0.16 per month. The initial cash position is 2.0.

(a) What are the probability distributions of the cash position after 1 month, 6 months, and 1 year?

(b) What are the probabilities of a negative cash position at the end of 6 months and 1 year?

(c) At what time in the future is the probability of a negative cash position greatest?

12.14. Suppose that x is the yield on a perpetual government bond that pays interest at the rate of \$1 per annum. Assume that x is expressed with continuous compounding, that interest is paid continuously on the bond, and that x follows the process

$$dx = a(x_0 - x)\,dt + sx\,dz$$

where a, x_0, and s are positive constants, and dz is a Wiener process. What is the process followed by the bond price? What is the expected instantaneous return (including interest and capital gains) to the holder of the bond?

12.15. If S follows the geometric Brownian motion process in equation (12.6), what is the process followed by

(a) $y = 2S$

(b) $y = S^2$

(c) $y = e^S$

(d) $y = e^{r(T-t)}/S$

In each case express the coefficients of dt and dz in terms of y rather than S.

12.16. A stock price is currently 50. Its expected return and volatility are 12% and 30%, respectively. What is the probability that the stock price will be greater than 80 in 2 years? (*Hint*: $S_T > 80$ when $\ln S_T > \ln 80$.)

APPENDIX

DERIVATION OF ITÔ'S LEMMA

In this appendix, we show how Itô's lemma can be regarded as a natural extension of other, simpler results. Consider a continuous and differentiable function G of a variable x. If Δx is a small change in x and ΔG is the resulting small change in G, a well-known result from ordinary calculus is

$$\Delta G \approx \frac{dG}{dx}\Delta x \tag{12A.1}$$

In other words, ΔG is approximately equal to the rate of change of G with respect to x multiplied by Δx. The error involves terms of order Δx^2. If more precision is required, a Taylor series expansion of ΔG can be used:

$$\Delta G = \frac{dG}{dx}\Delta x + \tfrac{1}{2}\frac{d^2G}{dx^2}\Delta x^2 + \tfrac{1}{6}\frac{d^3G}{dx^3}\Delta x^3 + \cdots$$

For a continuous and differentiable function G of two variables x and y, the result analogous to equation (12A.1) is

$$\Delta G \approx \frac{\partial G}{\partial x}\Delta x + \frac{\partial G}{\partial y}\Delta y \tag{12A.2}$$

and the Taylor series expansion of ΔG is

$$\Delta G = \frac{\partial G}{\partial x}\Delta x + \frac{\partial G}{\partial y}\Delta y + \tfrac{1}{2}\frac{\partial^2 G}{\partial x^2}\Delta x^2 + \frac{\partial^2 G}{\partial x\,\partial y}\Delta x\,\Delta y + \tfrac{1}{2}\frac{\partial^2 G}{\partial y^2}\Delta y^2 + \cdots \tag{12A.3}$$

In the limit, as Δx and Δy tend to zero, equation (12A.3) becomes

$$dG = \frac{\partial G}{\partial x}dx + \frac{\partial G}{\partial y}dy \tag{12A.4}$$

We now extend equation (12A.4) to cover functions of variables following Itô processes. Suppose that a variable x follows the Itô process

$$dx = a(x, t)\,dt + b(x, t)\,dz \tag{12A.5}$$

and that G is some function of x and of time t. By analogy with equation (12A.3), we can write

$$\Delta G = \frac{\partial G}{\partial x}\Delta x + \frac{\partial G}{\partial t}\Delta t + \tfrac{1}{2}\frac{\partial^2 G}{\partial x^2}\Delta x^2 + \frac{\partial^2 G}{\partial x\,\partial t}\Delta x\,\Delta t + \tfrac{1}{2}\frac{\partial^2 G}{\partial t^2}\Delta t^2 + \cdots \tag{12A.6}$$

Equation (12A.5) can be discretized to

$$\Delta x = a(x, t)\,\Delta t + b(x, t)\epsilon\sqrt{\Delta t}$$

or, if arguments are dropped,

$$\Delta x = a\,\Delta t + b\epsilon\sqrt{\Delta t} \tag{12A.7}$$

This equation reveals an important difference between the situation in equation (12A.6) and the situation in equation (12A.3). When limiting arguments were used to move from equation (12A.3) to equation (12A.4), terms in Δx^2 were ignored because they were second-order terms. From equation (12A.7), we have

$$\Delta x^2 = b^2 \epsilon^2 \Delta t + \text{terms of higher order in } \Delta t \qquad \textbf{(12A.8)}$$

This shows that the term involving Δx^2 in equation (12A.6) has a component that is of order Δt and cannot be ignored.

The variance of a standardized normal distribution is 1.0. This means that

$$E(\epsilon^2) - [E(\epsilon)]^2 = 1$$

where E denotes expected value. Since $E(\epsilon) = 0$, it follows that $E(\epsilon^2) = 1$. The expected value of $\epsilon^2 \Delta t$, therefore, is Δt. It can be shown that the variance of $\epsilon^2 \Delta t$ is of order Δt^2 and that, as a result, we can treat $\epsilon^2 \Delta t$ as nonstochastic and equal to its expected value, Δt, as Δt tends to zero. It follows from equation (12A.8) that Δx^2 becomes non-stochastic and equal to $b^2 dt$ as Δt tends to zero. Taking limits as Δx and Δt tend to zero in equation (12A.6), and using this last result, we obtain

$$dG = \frac{\partial G}{\partial x} dx + \frac{\partial G}{\partial t} dt + \tfrac{1}{2} \frac{\partial^2 G}{\partial x^2} b^2 dt \qquad \textbf{(12A.9)}$$

This is Itô's lemma. If we substitute for dx from equation (12A.5), equation (12A.9) becomes

$$dG = \left(\frac{\partial G}{\partial x} a + \frac{\partial G}{\partial t} + \tfrac{1}{2} \frac{\partial^2 G}{\partial x^2} b^2 \right) dt + \frac{\partial G}{\partial x} b \, dz$$

CHAPTER 13

The Black–Scholes–Merton Model

In the early 1970s, Fischer Black, Myron Scholes, and Robert Merton made a major breakthrough in the pricing of stock options.[1] This involved the development of what has become known as the Black–Scholes (or Black–Scholes–Merton) model. The model has had a huge influence on the way that traders price and hedge options. It has also been pivotal to the growth and success of financial engineering in the last 20 years. In 1997, the importance of the model was recognized when Robert Merton and Myron Scholes were awarded the Nobel prize for economics. Sadly, Fischer Black died in 1995, otherwise he too would undoubtedly have been one of the recipients of this prize.

This chapter shows how the Black–Scholes model for valuing European call and put options on a non-dividend-paying stock is derived. It explains how volatility can be either estimated from historical data or implied from option prices using the model. It shows how the risk-neutral valuation argument introduced in Chapter 11 can be used. It also shows how the Black–Scholes model can be extended to deal with European call and put options on dividend-paying stocks and presents some results on the pricing of American call options on dividend-paying stocks.

13.1 LOGNORMAL PROPERTY OF STOCK PRICES

The model of stock price behavior used by Black, Scholes, and Merton is the model we developed in Chapter 12. It assumes that percentage changes in the stock price in a short period of time are normally distributed. We define

μ: Expected return on stock per year

σ: Volatility of the stock price per year

The mean of the percentage change in the stock price in time Δt is $\mu\,\Delta t$ and the

[1] See F. Black and M. Scholes, "The Pricing of Options and Corporate Liabilities," *Journal of Political Economy*, 81 (May/June 1973): 637–59; R.C. Merton, "Theory of Rational Option Pricing," *Bell Journal of Economics and Management Science*, 4 (Spring 1973): 141–83.

standard deviation of this percentage change is $\sigma\sqrt{\Delta t}$, so that

$$\frac{\Delta S}{S} \sim \phi(\mu\, \Delta t,\ \sigma\sqrt{\Delta t}) \tag{13.1}$$

where ΔS is the change in the stock price S in time Δt, and $\phi(m, s)$ denotes a normal distribution with mean m and standard deviation s.

As shown in Section 12.6, the model implies that

$$\ln S_T - \ln S_0 \sim \phi\left[\left(\mu - \frac{\sigma^2}{2}\right)T,\ \sigma\sqrt{T}\right]$$

From this, it follows that

$$\ln\frac{S_T}{S_0} \sim \phi\left[\left(\mu - \frac{\sigma^2}{2}\right)T,\ \sigma\sqrt{T}\right] \tag{13.2}$$

and

$$\ln S_T \sim \phi\left[\ln S_0 + \left(\mu - \frac{\sigma^2}{2}\right)T,\ \sigma\sqrt{T}\right] \tag{13.3}$$

where S_T is the stock price at a future time T and S_0 is the stock price at time 0. Equation (13.3) shows that $\ln S_T$ is normally distributed, so that S_T has a lognormal distribution. The mean of $\ln S_T$ is $\ln S_0 + (\mu - \sigma^2/2)T$ and the standard deviation is $\sigma\sqrt{T}$.

Example 13.1

Consider a stock with an initial price of \$40, an expected return of 16% per annum, and a volatility of 20% per annum. From equation (13.3), the probability distribution of the stock price S_T in 6 months' time is given by

$$\ln S_T \sim \phi[\ln 40 + (0.16 - 0.2^2/2) \times 0.5,\ 0.2\sqrt{0.5}\,]$$

$$\ln S_T \sim \phi(3.759,\ 0.141)$$

There is a 95% probability that a normally distributed variable has a value within 1.96 standard deviations of its mean. Hence, with 95% confidence,

$$3.759 - 1.96 \times 0.141 < \ln S_T < 3.759 + 1.96 \times 0.141$$

This can be written

$$e^{3.759-1.96\times0.141} < S_T < e^{3.759+1.96\times0.141}$$

or

$$32.55 < S_T < 56.56$$

Thus, there is a 95% probability that the stock price in 6 months will lie between 32.55 and 56.56.

A variable that has a lognormal distribution can take any value between zero and infinity. Figure 13.1 illustrates the shape of a lognormal distribution. Unlike the normal distribution, it is skewed so that the mean, median, and mode are all different. From equation (13.3) and the properties of the lognormal distribution, it can be shown that the expected value $E(S_T)$ of S_T is given by

$$E(S_T) = S_0 e^{\mu T} \tag{13.4}$$

Figure 13.1 Lognormal distribution.

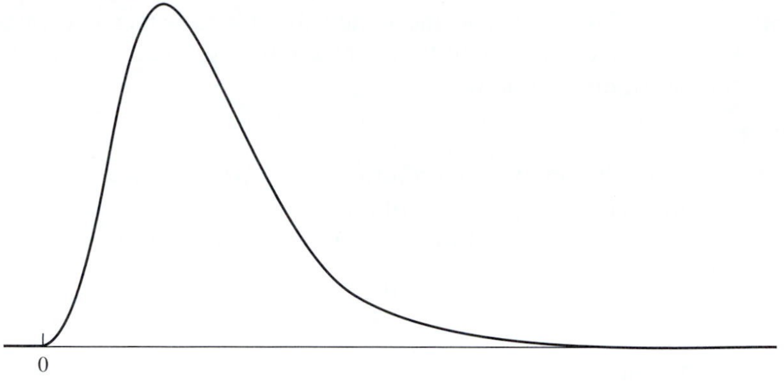

This fits in with the definition of μ as the expected rate of return. The variance $\text{var}(S_T)$ of S_T, can be shown to be given by[2]

$$\text{var}(S_T) = S_0^2 e^{2\mu T}(e^{\sigma^2 T} - 1) \tag{13.5}$$

Example 13.2

Consider a stock where the current price is \$20, the expected return is 20% per annum, and the volatility is 40% per annum. The expected stock price, $E(S_T)$, and the variance of the stock price, $\text{var}(S_T)$, in 1 year, are given by

$$E(S_T) = 20e^{0.2\times 1} = 24.43 \quad \text{and} \quad \text{var}(S_T) = 400e^{2\times 0.2\times 1}(e^{0.4^2\times 1} - 1) = 103.54$$

The standard deviation of the stock price in 1 year is $\sqrt{103.54}$, or 10.18.

13.2 THE DISTRIBUTION OF THE RATE OF RETURN

The lognormal property of stock prices can be used to provide information on the probability distribution of the continuously compounded rate of return earned on a stock between times 0 and T. If we define the continuously compounded rate of return per annum realized between times 0 and T as x, it follows that

$$S_T = S_0 e^{xT}$$

so that

$$x = \frac{1}{T}\ln\frac{S_T}{S_0} \tag{13.6}$$

From equation (13.2), it follows that

$$x \sim \phi\left(\mu - \frac{\sigma^2}{2}, \frac{\sigma}{\sqrt{T}}\right) \tag{13.7}$$

[2] See Technical Note 2 on the author's website for a proof of the results in equations (13.4) and (13.5). For a more extensive discussion of the properties of the lognormal distribution, see J. Aitchison and J. A. C. Brown, *The Lognormal Distribution*. Cambridge University Press, 1966.

Thus, the continuously compounded rate of return per annum is normally distributed with mean $\mu - \sigma^2/2$ and standard deviation $\sigma/\sqrt{T}$. As T increases, the standard deviation of x declines. To understand the reason for this, consider two cases: $T = 1$ and $T = 20$. We are more certain about the average return per year over 20 years than we are about the return in any one year.

Example 13.3

Consider a stock with an expected return of 17% per annum and a volatility of 20% per annum. The probability distribution for the average rate of return (continuously compounded) realized over 3 years is normal, with mean

$$0.17 - \frac{0.2^2}{2} = 0.15$$

or 15% per annum, and standard deviation

$$\frac{0.2}{\sqrt{3}} = 0.1155$$

or 11.55% per annum. Because there is a 95% chance that a normally distributed variable will lie within 1.96 standard deviations of its mean, we can be 95% confident that the average return realized over 3 years will be between −7.6% and +37.6% per annum.

13.3 THE EXPECTED RETURN

The expected return, μ, required by investors from a stock depends on the riskiness of the stock. The higher the risk, the higher the expected return. It also depends on the level of interest rates in the economy. The higher the level of interest rates, the higher the expected return required on any given stock. Fortunately, we do not have to concern ourselves with the determinants of μ in any detail. It turns out that the value of a stock option, when expressed in terms of the value of the underlying stock, does not depend on μ at all. Nevertheless, there is one aspect of the expected return from a stock that frequently causes confusion.

Equation (13.1) shows that $\mu\,\Delta t$ is the expected percentage change in the stock price in a very short period of time, Δt. It is natural to assume from this that μ is the expected continuously compounded return on the stock. However, this is not the case. The continuously compounded return, x, actually realized over a period of time of length T is given by equation (13.6) as

$$x = \frac{1}{T}\ln\frac{S_T}{S_0}$$

and, as indicated in equation (13.7), the expected value $E(x)$ of x is $\mu - \sigma^2/2$.

The reason why the expected continuously compounded return is different from μ is subtle, but important. Suppose we consider a very large number of very short periods of time of length Δt. Define S_i as the stock price at the end of the ith interval and ΔS_i as $S_{i+1} - S_i$. Under the assumptions we are making for stock price behavior, the average of the returns on the stock in each interval is close to μ. In other words, $\mu\,\Delta t$ is close to the arithmetic mean of the $\Delta S_i/S_i$. However, the expected return over the whole period

Business Snapshot 13.1 Mutual Fund Returns Can Be Misleading

The difference between μ and $\mu - \sigma^2/2$ is closely related to an issue in the reporting of mutual fund returns. Suppose that the following is a sequence of returns per annum reported by a mutual fund manager over the last five years (measured using annual compounding):

$$15\%, \quad 20\%, \quad 30\%, \quad -20\%, \quad 25\%$$

The arithmetic mean of the returns, calculated by taking the sum of the returns and dividing by 5, is 14%. However, an investor would actually earn less than 14% per annum by leaving the money invested in the fund for 5 years. The dollar value of \$100 at the end of the 5 years would be

$$100 \times 1.15 \times 1.20 \times 1.30 \times 0.80 \times 1.25 = \$179.40$$

By contrast, a 14% return with annual compounding would give

$$100 \times 1.14^5 = \$192.54$$

The return that gives \$179.40 at the end of five years is 12.4%. This is because

$$100 \times (1.124)^5 = 179.40$$

What average return should the fund manager report? It is tempting for the manager to make a statement such as: "The average of the returns per year that we have realized in the last 5 years is 14%." Although true, this is misleading. It is much less misleading to say: "The average return realized by someone who invested with us for the last 5 years is 12.4% per year." In some jurisdictions, regulations require fund managers to report returns the second way.

This phenomenon is an example of a result that is well known by mathematicians. The geometric mean of a set of numbers (not all the same) is always less than the arithmetic mean. In our example, the return multipliers each year are 1.15, 1.20, 1.30, 0.80, and 1.25. The arithmetic mean of these numbers is 1.140, but the geometric mean is only 1.124.

covered by the data, expressed with a compounding interval of Δt, is close to $\mu - \sigma^2/2$, not μ.[3] Business Snapshot 13.1 provides a numerical example concerning the mutual fund industry to illustrate the point being made here. For a mathematical explanation of what is going on, we start with equation (13.4):

$$E(S_T) = S_0 e^{\mu T}$$

Taking logarithms, we get

$$\ln[E(S_T)] = \ln(S_0) + \mu T$$

It is now tempting to set $\ln[E(S_T)] = E[\ln(S_T)]$, so that $E[\ln(S_T)] - \ln(S_0) = \mu T$, or $E[\ln(S_T/S_0)] = \mu T$, which leads to $E(R) = \mu$. However, we cannot do this because ln

[3] The arguments in this section show that the term "expected return" is ambiguous. It can refer either to μ or to $\mu - \sigma^2/2$. Unless otherwise stated, it will be used to refer to μ throughout this book.

is a nonlinear function. In fact, $\ln[E(S_T)] > E[\ln(S_T)]$, so that $E[\ln(S_T/S_0)] < \mu T$, which leads to $E(x) < \mu$. (As pointed out above, $E(x) = \mu - \sigma^2/2$.)

13.4 VOLATILITY

The volatility σ of a stock is a measure of our uncertainty about the returns provided by the stock. Stocks typically have a volatility between 15% and 60%.

From equation (13.7), the volatility of a stock price can be defined as the standard deviation of the return provided by the stock in 1 year when the return is expressed using continuous compounding.

When T is small, equation (13.1) shows that $\sigma\sqrt{T}$ is approximately equal to the standard deviation of the percentage change in the stock price in time T. Suppose that $\sigma = 0.3$, or 30%, per annum and the current stock price is \$50. The standard deviation of the percentage change in the stock price in 1 week is approximately

$$30 \times \sqrt{\frac{1}{52}} = 4.16\%$$

A one-standard-deviation move in the stock price in 1 week is therefore 50×0.0416, or \$2.08.

Equation (13.1) shows that our uncertainty about a future stock price, as measured by its standard deviation, increases—at least approximately—with the square root of how far ahead we are looking. For example, the standard deviation of the stock price in 4 weeks is approximately twice the standard deviation in 1 week.

Estimating Volatility from Historical Data

To estimate the volatility of a stock price empirically, the stock price is usually observed at fixed intervals of time (e.g., every day, week, or month).

Define:

$n + 1$: Number of observations

S_i: Stock price at end of ith interval, with $i = 0, 1, \dots, n$

τ: Length of time interval in years

and let

$$u_i = \ln\left(\frac{S_i}{S_{i-1}}\right)$$

for $i = 1, 2, \dots, n$.

The usual estimate, s, of the standard deviation of the u_i is given by

$$s = \sqrt{\frac{1}{n-1}\sum_{i=1}^{n}(u_i - \bar{u})^2}$$

or

$$s = \sqrt{\frac{1}{n-1}\sum_{i=1}^{n}u_i^2 - \frac{1}{n(n-1)}\left(\sum_{i=1}^{n}u_i\right)^2}$$

where $\bar{u}$ is the mean of the u_i.

From equation (13.2), the standard deviation of the u_i is $\sigma\sqrt{\tau}$. The variable s is therefore an estimate of $\sigma\sqrt{\tau}$. It follows that σ itself can be estimated as $\hat{\sigma}$, where

$$\hat{\sigma} = \frac{s}{\sqrt{\tau}}$$

The standard error of this estimate can be shown to be approximately $\hat{\sigma}/\sqrt{2n}$.

Choosing an appropriate value for n is not easy. More data generally lead to more accuracy, but σ does change over time and data that are too old may not be relevant for predicting the future volatility. A compromise that seems to work reasonably well is to use closing prices from daily data over the most recent 90 to 180 days. An often-used rule of thumb is to set n equal to the number of days to which the volatility is to be applied. Thus, if the volatility estimate is to be used to value a 2-year option, daily data for the last 2 years are used. More sophisticated approaches to estimating volatility involving GARCH models are discussed in Chapter 19.

Example 13.4

Table 13.1 shows a possible sequence of stock prices during 21 consecutive trading days. In this case,

$$\sum u_i = 0.09531 \text{ and } \sum u_i^2 = 0.00326$$

Table 13.1 Computation of volatility.

Day	*Closing stock price (dollars)*	*Price relative* S_i/S_{i-1}	*Daily return* $u_i = \ln(S_i/S_{i-1})$
0	20.00		
1	20.10	1.00500	0.00499
2	19.90	0.99005	0.01000
3	20.00	1.00503	0.00501
4	20.50	1.02500	0.02469
5	20.25	0.98780	−0.01227
6	20.90	1.03210	0.03159
7	20.90	1.00000	0.00000
8	20.90	1.00000	0.00000
9	20.75	0.99282	−0.00720
10	20.75	1.00000	0.00000
11	21.00	1.01205	0.01198
12	21.10	1.00476	0.00475
13	20.90	0.99052	−0.00952
14	20.90	1.00000	0.00000
15	21.25	1.01675	0.01661
16	21.40	1.00706	0.00703
17	21.40	1.00000	0.00000
18	21.25	0.99299	−0.00703
19	21.75	1.02353	0.02326
20	22.00	1.01149	0.01143

and the estimate of the standard deviation of the daily return is

$$\sqrt{\frac{0.00326}{19} - \frac{0.09531^2}{380}} = 0.01216$$

or 1.216%. Assuming that there are 252 trading days per year, $\tau = 1/252$ and the data give an estimate for the volatility per annum of $0.01216\sqrt{252} = 0.193$, or 19.3%. The standard error of this estimate is

$$\frac{0.193}{\sqrt{2 \times 20}} = 0.031$$

or 3.1% per annum.

The foregoing analysis assumes that the stock pays no dividends, but it can be adapted to accommodate dividend-paying stocks. The return, u_i, during a time interval that includes an ex-dividend day is given by

$$u_i = \ln \frac{S_i + D}{S_{i-1}}$$

where D is the amount of the dividend. The return in other time intervals is still

$$u_i = \ln \frac{S_i}{S_{i-1}}$$

However, as tax factors play a part in determining returns around an ex-dividend date, it is probably best to discard altogether data for intervals that include an ex-dividend date.

Trading Days vs. Calendar Days

An important issue is whether time should be measured in calendar days or trading days when volatility parameters are being estimated and used. As shown in Business Snapshot 13.2, research shows that volatility is much higher when the exchange is open for trading than when it is closed. As a result, practitioners tend to ignore days when the exchange is closed when estimating volatility from historical data and when calculating the life of an option. The volatility per annum is calculated from the volatility per trading day using the formula

$$\begin{matrix}\text{Volatility}\\ \text{per annum}\end{matrix} = \begin{matrix}\text{Volatility}\\ \text{per trading day}\end{matrix} \times \sqrt{\begin{matrix}\text{Number of trading days}\\ \text{per annum}\end{matrix}}$$

This is what we did in Example 13.4 when calculating volatility from the data in Table 13.1. The number of trading days in a year is usually assumed to be 252 for stocks.

The life of an option is also usually measured using trading days rather than calendar days. It is calculated as T years, where

$$T = \frac{\text{Number of trading days until option maturity}}{252}$$

Business Snapshot 13.2 What Causes Volatility?

It is natural to assume that the volatility of a stock is caused by new information reaching the market. This new information causes people to revise their opinions about the value of the stock. The price of the stock changes and volatility results. This view of what causes volatility is not supported by research. With several years of daily stock price data, researchers can calculate:

1. The variance of stock price returns between the close of trading on one day and the close of trading on the next day when there are no intervening nontrading days
2. The variance of the stock price returns between the close of trading on Friday and the close of trading on Monday

The second variance is the variance of returns over a 3-day period. The first is a variance over a 1-day period. We might reasonably expect the second variance to be three times as great as the first variance. Fama (1965), French (1980), and French and Roll (1986) show that this is not the case. These three research studies estimate the second variance to be, respectively, 22%, 19%, and 10.7% higher than the first variance.

At this stage you might be tempted to argue that these results are explained by more news reaching the market when the market is open for trading. But research by Roll (1984) does not support this explanation. Roll looked at the prices of orange juice futures. By far the most important news for orange juice futures prices is news about the weather and news about the weather is equally likely to arrive at any time. When Roll did a similar analysis to that just described for stocks, he found that the second (Friday-to-Monday) variance is only 1.54 times the first variance.

The only reasonable conclusion from all this is that volatility is to a large extent caused by trading itself. (Traders usually have no difficulty accepting this conclusion!)

13.5 CONCEPTS UNDERLYING THE BLACK–SCHOLES–MERTON DIFFERENTIAL EQUATION

The Black–Scholes–Merton differential equation is an equation that must be satisfied by the price of any derivative dependent on a non-dividend-paying stock. The equation is derived in the next section. Here we consider the nature of the arguments we will use.

The arguments are similar to the no-arbitrage arguments we used to value stock options in Chapter 11 for the situation where stock price movements are binomial. They involve setting up a riskless portfolio consisting of a position in the derivative and a position in the stock. In the absence of arbitrage opportunities, the return from the portfolio must be the risk-free interest rate, r. This leads to the Black-Scholes-Merton differential equation.

The reason a riskless portfolio can be set up is that the stock price and the derivative price are both affected by the same underlying source of uncertainty: stock price movements. In any short period of time, the price of the derivative is perfectly correlated with the price of the underlying stock. When an appropriate portfolio of the stock and the derivative is established, the gain or loss from the stock position

Figure 13.2 Relationship between call price and stock price. Current stock price is S_0.

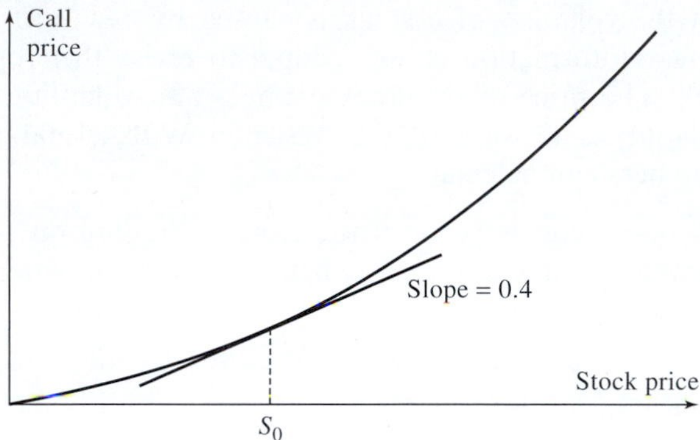

always offsets the gain or loss from the derivative position so that the overall value of the portfolio at the end of the short period of time is known with certainty.

Suppose, for example, that at a particular point in time the relationship between a small change ΔS in the stock price and the resultant small change Δc in the price of a European call option is given by

$$\Delta c = 0.4\,\Delta S$$

This means that the slope of the line representing the relationship between c and S is 0.4, as indicated in Figure 13.2. The riskless portfolio would consist of:

1. A long position in 0.4 shares
2. A short position in one call option

There is one important difference between the Black–Scholes–Merton analysis and our analysis using a binomial model in Chapter 11. In Black–Scholes–Merton, the position in the stock and the derivative is riskless for only a very short period of time. (Theoretically, it remains riskless only for an instantaneously short period of time.) To remain riskless, it must be adjusted, or *rebalanced*, frequently.[4] For example, the relationship between Δc and ΔS in our example might change from $\Delta c = 0.4\,\Delta S$ today to $\Delta c = 0.5\,\Delta S$ in 2 weeks. This would mean that, in order to maintain the riskless position, an extra 0.1 share would have to be purchased for each call option sold. It is nevertheless true that the return from the riskless portfolio in any very short period of time must be the risk-free interest rate. This is the key element in the Black–Scholes analysis and leads to their pricing formulas.

Assumptions

The assumptions we use to derive the Black–Scholes–Merton differential equation are as follows:

1. The stock price follows the process developed in Chapter 12 with μ and σ constant.
2. The short selling of securities with full use of proceeds is permitted.

[4] We discuss the rebalancing of portfolios in more detail in Chapter 15.

3. There are no transactions costs or taxes. All securities are perfectly divisible.
4. There are no dividends during the life of the derivative.
5. There are no riskless arbitrage opportunities.
6. Security trading is continuous.
7. The risk-free rate of interest, r, is constant and the same for all maturities.

As we discuss in later chapters, some of these assumptions can be relaxed. For example, σ and r can be known functions of t. We can even allow interest rates to be stochastic provided that the stock price distribution at maturity of the option is still lognormal.

13.6 DERIVATION OF THE BLACK–SCHOLES–MERTON DIFFERENTIAL EQUATION

The stock price process we are assuming is the one we developed in Section 12.3:

$$dS = \mu S\,dt + \sigma S\,dz \tag{13.8}$$

Suppose that f is the price of a call option or other derivative contingent on S. The variable f must be some function of S and t. Hence, from equation (12.14),

$$df = \left(\frac{\partial f}{\partial S}\mu S + \frac{\partial f}{\partial t} + \tfrac{1}{2}\frac{\partial^2 f}{\partial S^2}\sigma^2 S^2\right) dt + \frac{\partial f}{\partial S}\sigma S\,dz \tag{13.9}$$

The discrete versions of equations (13.8) and (13.9) are

$$\Delta S = \mu S\,\Delta t + \sigma S\,\Delta z \tag{13.10}$$

and

$$\Delta f = \left(\frac{\partial f}{\partial S}\mu S + \frac{\partial f}{\partial t} + \tfrac{1}{2}\frac{\partial^2 f}{\partial S^2}\sigma^2 S^2\right) \Delta t + \frac{\partial f}{\partial S}\sigma S\,\Delta z \tag{13.11}$$

where ΔS and Δf are the changes in f and S in a small time interval Δt. Recall from the discussion of Itô's lemma in Section 12.5 that the Wiener processes underlying f and S are the same. In other words, the Δz $(= \epsilon\sqrt{\Delta t})$ in equations (13.10) and (13.11) are the same. It follows that, by choosing a portfolio of the stock and the derivative, the Wiener process can be eliminated.

The appropriate portfolio is

-1: derivative

$+\partial f/\partial S$: shares

The holder of this portfolio is short one derivative and long an amount $\partial f/\partial S$ of shares. Define Π as the value of the portfolio. By definition

$$\Pi = -f + \frac{\partial f}{\partial S}S \tag{13.12}$$

The change $\Delta\Pi$ in the value of the portfolio in the time interval Δt is given by

$$\Delta\Pi = -\Delta f + \frac{\partial f}{\partial S}\Delta S \tag{13.13}$$

Substituting equations (13.10) and (13.11) into equation (13.13) yields

$$\Delta\Pi = \left(-\frac{\partial f}{\partial t} - \tfrac{1}{2}\frac{\partial^2 f}{\partial S^2}\sigma^2 S^2\right)\Delta t \tag{13.14}$$

Because this equation does not involve Δz, the portfolio must be riskless during time Δt. The assumptions listed in the preceding section imply that the portfolio must instantaneously earn the same rate of return as other short-term risk-free securities. If it earned more than this return, arbitrageurs could make a riskless profit by borrowing money to buy the portfolio; if it earned less, they could make a riskless profit by shorting the portfolio and buying risk-free securities. It follows that

$$\Delta\Pi = r\Pi\,\Delta t \tag{13.15}$$

where r is the risk-free interest rate. Substituting from equations (13.12) and (13.14) into (13.15), we obtain

$$\left(\frac{\partial f}{\partial t} + \tfrac{1}{2}\frac{\partial^2 f}{\partial S^2}\sigma^2 S^2\right)\Delta t = r\left(f - \frac{\partial f}{\partial S}S\right)\Delta t$$

so that

$$\frac{\partial f}{\partial t} + rS\frac{\partial f}{\partial S} + \tfrac{1}{2}\sigma^2 S^2\frac{\partial^2 f}{\partial S^2} = rf \tag{13.16}$$

Equation (13.16) is the Black–Scholes–Merton differential equation. It has many solutions, corresponding to all the different derivatives that can be defined with S as the underlying variable. The particular derivative that is obtained when the equation is solved depends on the *boundary conditions* that are used. These specify the values of the derivative at the boundaries of possible values of S and t. In the case of a European call option, the key boundary condition is

$$f = \max(S - K,\ 0) \quad \text{when } t = T$$

In the case of a European put option, it is

$$f = \max(K - S,\ 0) \quad \text{when } t = T$$

One point that should be emphasized about the portfolio used in the derivation of equation (13.16) is that it is not permanently riskless. It is riskless only for an infinitesimally short period of time. As S and t change, $\partial f/\partial S$ also changes. To keep the portfolio riskless, it is therefore necessary to frequently change the relative proportions of the derivative and the stock in the portfolio.

Example 13.5

A forward contract on a non-dividend-paying stock is a derivative dependent on the stock. As such, it should satisfy equation (13.16). From equation (5.5), we know that the value of the forward contract, f, at a general time t is given in terms of the stock price S at this time by

$$f = S - Ke^{-r(T-t)}$$

where K is the delivery price. This means that

$$\frac{\partial f}{\partial t} = -rKe^{-r(T-t)}, \qquad \frac{\partial f}{\partial S} = 1, \qquad \frac{\partial^2 f}{\partial S^2} = 0$$

When these are substituted into the left-hand side of equation (13.16), we obtain

$$-rKe^{-r(T-t)} + rS$$

This equals rf, showing that equation (13.16) is indeed satisfied.

The Prices of Tradeable Derivatives

Any function $f(S, t)$ that is a solution of the differential equation (13.16) is the theoretical price of a derivative that could be traded. If a derivative with that price existed, it would not create any arbitrage opportunities. Conversely, if a function $f(S, t)$ does not satisfy the differential equation (13.16), it cannot be the price of a derivative without creating arbitrage opportunities for traders.

To illustrate this point, consider first the function e^S. This does not satisfy the differential equation (13.16). It is therefore not a candidate for being the price of a derivative dependent on the stock price. If an instrument whose price was always e^S existed, there would be an arbitrage opportunity. As a second example, consider the function

$$\frac{e^{(\sigma^2 - 2r)(T-t)}}{S}$$

This does satisfy the differential equation, and so is, in theory, the price of a tradeable security. (It is the price of a derivative that pays off $1/S_T$ at time T.) For other examples of tradeable derivatives, see Problems 13.11, 13.12, 13.23, and 13.28.

13.7 RISK-NEUTRAL VALUATION

We introduced risk-neutral valuation in connection with the binomial model in Chapter 11. It is without doubt the single most important tool for the analysis of derivatives. It arises from one key property of the Black–Scholes–Merton differential equation (13.16). This property is that the equation does not involve any variables that are affected by the risk preferences of investors. The variables that do appear in the equation are the current stock price, time, stock price volatility, and the risk-free rate of interest. All are independent of risk preferences.

The Black–Scholes–Merton differential equation would not be independent of risk preferences if it involved the expected return, μ, on the stock. This is because the value of μ does depend on risk preferences. The higher the level of risk aversion by investors, the higher μ will be for any given stock. It is fortunate that μ happens to drop out in the derivation of the differential equation.

Because the Black–Scholes–Merton differential equation is independent of risk preferences, an ingenious argument can be used. If risk preferences do not enter the equation, they cannot affect its solution. Any set of risk preferences can, therefore, be used when evaluating f. In particular, the very simple assumption that all investors are risk neutral can be made.

In a world where investors are risk neutral, the expected return on all investment assets is the risk-free rate of interest, r. The reason is that risk-neutral investors do not require a premium to induce them to take risks. It is also true that the present value of any cash flow in a risk-neutral world can be obtained by discounting its expected value at the risk-free rate. The assumption that the world is risk neutral does, therefore, considerably simplify the analysis of derivatives.

Consider a derivative that provides a payoff at one particular time. It can be valued using risk-neutral valuation by using the following procedure:

1. Assume that the expected return from the underlying asset is the risk-free interest rate, r (i.e., assume $\mu = r$).
2. Calculate the expected payoff from the derivative.
3. Discount the expected payoff at the risk-free interest rate.

It is important to appreciate that risk-neutral valuation (or the assumption that all investors are risk neutral) is merely an artificial device for obtaining solutions to the Black–Scholes differential equation. The solutions that are obtained are valid in all worlds, not just those where investors are risk neutral. When we move from a risk-neutral world to a risk-averse world, two things happen. The expected growth rate in the stock price changes and the discount rate that must be used for any payoffs from the derivative changes. It happens that these two changes always offset each other exactly.

Application to Forward Contracts on a Stock

We valued forward contracts on a non-dividend-paying stock in Section 5.7. In Example 13.5, we verified that the pricing formula satisfies the Black–Scholes differential equation. In this section we derive the pricing formula from risk-neutral valuation. We make the assumption that interest rates are constant and equal to r. This is somewhat more restrictive than the assumption in Chapter 5.

Consider a long forward contract that matures at time T with delivery price, K. As indicated in Figure 1.2, the value of the contract at maturity is

$$S_T - K$$

where S_T is the stock price at time T. From the risk-neutral valuation argument, the value of the forward contract at time 0 is its expected value at time T in a risk-neutral world discounted at the risk-free rate of interest. Denoting the value of the forward contract at time zero by f, this means that

$$f = e^{-rT}\hat{E}(S_T - K)$$

where $\hat{E}$ denotes the expected value in a risk-neutral world. Since K is a constant, this equation becomes

$$f = e^{-rT}\hat{E}(S_T) - Ke^{-rT} \tag{13.17}$$

The expected return μ on the stock becomes r in a risk-neutral world. Hence, from equation (13.4), we have

$$\hat{E}(S_T) = S_0 e^{rT} \tag{13.18}$$

Substituting equation (13.18) into equation (13.17) gives

$$f = S_0 - Ke^{-rT} \tag{13.19}$$

This is in agreement with equation (5.5).

13.8 BLACK–SCHOLES PRICING FORMULAS

The Black–Scholes formulas for the prices at time 0 of a European call option on a non-dividend-paying stock and a European put option on a non-dividend-paying stock are

$$c = S_0 N(d_1) - Ke^{-rT} N(d_2) \tag{13.20}$$

and

$$p = Ke^{-rT} N(-d_2) - S_0 N(-d_1) \tag{13.21}$$

where

$$d_1 = \frac{\ln(S_0/K) + (r + \sigma^2/2)T}{\sigma\sqrt{T}}$$

$$d_2 = \frac{\ln(S_0/K) + (r - \sigma^2/2)T}{\sigma\sqrt{T}} = d_1 - \sigma\sqrt{T}$$

The function $N(x)$ is the cumulative probability distribution function for a standardized normal distribution. In other words, it is the probability that a variable with a standard normal distribution, $\phi(0, 1)$, will be less than x. It is illustrated in Figure 13.3. The remaining variables should be familiar. The variables c and p are the European call and European put price, S_0 is the stock price at time zero, K is the strike price, r is the

Figure 13.3 Shaded area represents $N(x)$.

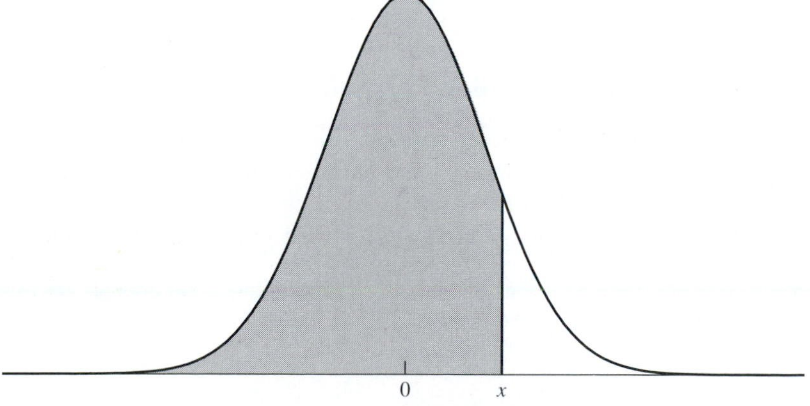

continuously compounded risk-free rate, σ is the stock price volatility, and T is the time to maturity of the option.

One way of deriving the Black–Scholes formulas is by solving the differential equation (13.16) subject to the boundary condition mentioned in Section 13.6.[5] Another approach is to use risk-neutral valuation. Consider a European call option. The expected value of the option at maturity in a risk-neutral world is

$$\hat{E}[\max(S_T - K, 0)]$$

where, as before, $\hat{E}$ denotes the expected value in a risk-neutral world. From the risk-neutral valuation argument, the European call option price c is this expected value discounted at the risk-free rate of interest, that is,

$$c = e^{-rT}\hat{E}[\max(S_T - K, 0)] \tag{13.22}$$

The appendix at the end of this chapter shows that this equation leads to the result in equation (13.20).

To provide an interpretation of the terms in equation (13.20), we note that it can be written

$$c = e^{-rT}[S_0 N(d_1)e^{rT} - KN(d_2)] \tag{13.23}$$

The expression $N(d_2)$ is the probability that the option will be exercised in a risk-neutral world, so that $KN(d_2)$ is the strike price times the probability that the strike price will be paid. The expression $S_0 N(d_1)e^{rT}$ is the expected value of a variable that is equal to S_T if $S_T > K$ and to zero otherwise in a risk-neutral world.

Since the European price equals the American price when there are no dividends (see Section 9.5), equation (13.20) also gives the value of an American call option on a non-dividend-paying stock. Unfortunately, no exact analytic formula for the value of an American put option on a non-dividend-paying stock has been produced. Numerical procedures for calculating American put values are discussed in Chapter 17.

When the Black–Scholes formula is used in practice the interest rate r is set equal to the zero-coupon risk-free interest rate for a maturity T. As we show in later chapters, this is theoretically correct when r is a known function of time. It is also theoretically correct when the interest rate is stochastic provided that the stock price at time T is lognormal and the volatility parameter is chosen appropriately. As mentioned earlier, time is normally measured as the number of trading days left in the life of the option divided by the number of trading days in 1 year.

Properties of the Black–Scholes Formulas

We now show that the Black–Scholes formulas have the right general properties by considering what happens when some of the parameters take extreme values.

When the stock price, S_0, becomes very large, a call option is almost certain to be exercised. It then becomes very similar to a forward contract with delivery price K.

[5] The differential equation gives the call and put prices at a general time t. For example, the call price that satisfies the differential equation is $c = SN(d_1) - Ke^{-r(T-t)}N(d_2)$, where

$$d_1 = \frac{\ln(S/K) + (r + \sigma^2/2)(T - t)}{\sigma\sqrt{T - t}}$$

and $d_2 = d_1 - \sigma\sqrt{T - t}$. See Problem 13.17 to prove that the differential equation is satisfied.

From equation (5.5), we expect the call price to be

$$S_0 - Ke^{-rT}$$

This is, in fact, the call price given by equation (13.20) because, when S_0 becomes very large, both d_1 and d_2 become very large, and $N(d_1)$ and $N(d_2)$ are both close to 1.0. When the stock price becomes very large, the price of a European put option, p, approaches zero. This is consistent with equation (13.21) because $N(-d_1)$ and $N(-d_2)$ are both close to zero.

Consider next what happens when the volatility σ approaches zero. Because the stock is virtually riskless, its price will grow at rate r to S_0e^{rT} at time T and the payoff from a call option is

$$\max(S_0e^{rT} - K, 0)$$

Discounting at rate r, the value of the call today is

$$e^{-rT}\max(S_0e^{rT} - K, 0) = \max(S_0 - Ke^{-rT}, 0)$$

To show that this is consistent with equation (13.20), consider first the case where $S_0 > Ke^{-rT}$. This implies that $\ln(S_0/K) + rT > 0$. As σ tends to zero, d_1 and d_2 tend to $+\infty$, so that $N(d_1)$ and $N(d_2)$ tend to 1.0 and equation (13.20) becomes

$$c = S_0 - Ke^{-rT}$$

When $S_0 < Ke^{-rT}$, it follows that $\ln(S_0/K) + rT < 0$. As σ tends to zero, d_1 and d_2 tend to $-\infty$, so that $N(d_1)$ and $N(d_2)$ tend to zero and equation (13.20) gives a call price of zero. The call price is therefore always $\max(S_0 - Ke^{-rT}, 0)$ as σ tends to zero. Similarly, it can be shown that the put price is always $\max(Ke^{-rT} - S_0, 0)$ as σ tends to zero.

13.9 CUMULATIVE NORMAL DISTRIBUTION FUNCTION

The only problem in implementing equations (13.20) and (13.21) is in calculating the cumulative normal distribution function, $N(x)$. Tables for $N(x)$ are provided at the end of this book. The NORMSDIST function calculates $N(x)$ in Excel. A polynomial approximation that gives six-decimal-place accuracy is[6]

$$N(x) = \begin{cases} 1 - N'(x)(a_1k + a_2k^2 + a_3k^3 + a_4k^4 + a_5k^5) & \text{when } x \geqslant 0 \\ 1 - N(-x) & \text{when } x < 0 \end{cases}$$

where

$$k = \frac{1}{1 + \gamma x}, \quad \gamma = 0.2316419$$

$$a_1 = 0.319381530, \quad a_2 = -0.356563782$$

$$a_3 = 1.781477937, \quad a_4 = -1.821255978, \quad a_5 = 1.330274429$$

---

[6] See M. Abramowitz and I. Stegun, *Handbook of Mathematical Functions*. New York: Dover Publications, 1972.

and

$$N'(x) = \frac{1}{\sqrt{2\pi}} e^{-x^2/2}$$

Example 13.6

The stock price 6 months from the expiration of an option is \$42, the exercise price of the option is \$40, the risk-free interest rate is 10% per annum, and the volatility is 20% per annum. This means that $S_0 = 42$, $K = 40$, $r = 0.1$, $\sigma = 0.2$, $T = 0.5$,

$$d_1 = \frac{\ln(42/40) + (0.1 + 0.2^2/2) \times 0.5}{0.2\sqrt{0.5}} = 0.7693$$

$$d_2 = \frac{\ln(42/40) + (0.1 - 0.2^2/2) \times 0.5}{0.2\sqrt{0.5}} = 0.6278$$

and

$$Ke^{-rT} = 40e^{-0.05} = 38.049$$

Hence, if the option is a European call, its value c is given by

$$c = 42N(0.7693) - 38.049N(0.6278)$$

If the option is a European put, its value p is given by

$$p = 38.049N(-0.6278) - 42N(-0.7693)$$

Using the polynomial approximation,

$$N(0.7693) = 0.7791, \qquad N(-0.7693) = 0.2209$$

$$N(0.6278) = 0.7349, \qquad N(-0.6278) = 0.2651$$

so that

$$c = 4.76, \qquad p = 0.81$$

Ignoring the time value of money, the stock price has to rise by \$2.76 for the purchaser of the call to break even. Similarly, the stock price has to fall by \$2.81 for the purchaser of the put to break even.

13.10 WARRANTS AND EXECUTIVE STOCK OPTIONS

The exercise of a regular call option on a company has no effect on the number of the company's shares outstanding. If the writer of the option does not own the company's shares, he or she must buy them in the market in the usual way and then sell them to the option holder for the strike price. As explained in Chapter 8, warrants and executive stock options are different from regular call options in that exercise leads to the company issuing more shares and then selling them to the option holder for the strike price. As the strike price is less than the market price, this dilutes the interest of the existing shareholders.

How should potential dilution affect the way we value outstanding warrants and executive stock options? The answer is that it should not! Assuming markets are

Business Snapshot 13.3 Warrants, Executive Stock Options, and Dilution

Consider a company with 100,000 shares each worth \$50. It surprises the market with an announcement that it is granting 100,000 stock options to its employees with a strike price of \$50 and a vesting period of 3 years. If the market sees little benefit to the shareholders from the employee stock options in the form of reduced salaries and more highly motivated managers, the stock price will decline immediately after the announcement of the employee stock options. If the stock price declines to \$45. The dilution cost to the current shareholders is \$5 per share or \$500,000 in total.

Suppose that the company does well during the vesting period so that by the end of the vesting period the share price is \$100. Suppose further that all the options are exercised at this point. The payoff to the employees is \$50 per option. It is tempting to argue that there will be further dilution in that 100,000 shares worth \$100 per share are now merged with 100,000 shares for which only \$50 is paid, so that (a) the share price reduces to \$75 and (b) the payoff to the option holders is only \$25 per option. However, this argument is flawed. The exercise of the options is anticipated by the market and already reflected in the share price. The payoff from each option exercised is \$50.

This example illustrates the general point that when markets are efficient the impact of dilution from executive stock options or warrants is reflected in the stock price as soon as they are announced and does not need to be taken into account again when the options are valued.

efficient the stock price will reflect potential dilution from all outstanding warrants and executive stock options. This is explained in Business Snapshot 13.3.[7]

Consider next the situation a company is in when it is contemplating a new issue of warrants (or executive stock options). We suppose that the company is interested in calculating the cost of the issue assuming that there are no compensating benefits. We assume that the company has N shares worth S_0 each and the number of new options contemplated is M, with each option giving the holder the right to buy one share for K. The value of the company today is NS_0. This value does not change as a result of the warrant issue. Suppose that without the warrant issue the share price will be S_T at the warrant's maturity. This means that (with or without the warrant issue) the total value of the equity and the warrants at time T will NS_T. If the warrants are exercised, there is a cash inflow from the strike price increasing this to $NS_T + MK$. This value is distributed among $N + M$ shares, so that the share price immediately after exercise becomes

$$\frac{NS_T + MK}{N + M}$$

Therefore the payoff to an option holder if the option is exercised is

$$\frac{NS_T + MK}{N + M} - K$$

[7] Analysts sometimes assume that the sum of the values of the warrants and the equity (rather than just the value of the equity) is lognormal. The result is a Black–Scholes type of equation for the value of the warrant in terms of the value of the warrant. See Technical Note 3 on the author's website for an explanation of this model.

or

$$\frac{N}{N+M}(S_T - K)$$

This shows that the value of each option is the value of

$$\frac{N}{N+M}$$

regular call options on the company's stock. Therefore the total cost of the options is M times this.

Example 13.7

A company with 1 million shares worth \$40 each is considering issuing 200,000 warrants each giving holder the right to buy one share with a strike price of \$60 in 5 years. It wants to know the cost of this. The interest rate is 3% per annum, and the volatility is 30% per annum. The company pays no dividends. From equation (13.20), the value of a 5-year European call option on the stock is \$7.04. In this case, $N = 1{,}000{,}000$ and $M = 200{,}000$, so that the value of each warrant is

$$\frac{1{,}000{,}000}{1{,}000{,}000 + 200{,}000} \times 7.04 = 5.87$$

or \$5.87. The total cost of the warrant issue is $200{,}000 \times 5.87 = \$1.17$ million. Assuming the market perceives no benefits from the warrant issue, we expect the stock price to decline by \$1.17 to \$38.83.

13.11 IMPLIED VOLATILITIES

The one parameter in the Black–Scholes pricing formulas that cannot be directly observed is the volatility of the stock price. In Section 13.4, we discussed how this can be estimated from a history of the stock price. In practice, traders usually work with what are known as *implied volatilities*. These are the volatilities implied by option prices observed in the market.

To illustrate how implied volatilities are calculated, suppose that the value of a European call option on a non-dividend-paying stock is 1.875 when $S_0 = 21$, $K = 20$, $r = 0.1$, and $T = 0.25$. The implied volatility is the value of σ that, when substituted into equation (13.20), gives $c = 1.875$. Unfortunately, it is not possible to invert equation (13.20) so that σ is expressed as a function of S_0, K, r, T, and c. However, an iterative search procedure can be used to find the implied σ. For example, we can start by trying $\sigma = 0.20$. This gives a value of c equal to 1.76, which is too low. Because c is an increasing function of σ, a higher value of σ is required. We can next try a value of 0.30 for σ. This gives a value of c equal to 2.10, which is too high and means that σ must lie between 0.20 and 0.30. Next, a value of 0.25 can be tried for σ. This also proves to be too high, showing that σ lies between 0.20 and 0.25. Proceeding in this way, we can halve the range for σ at each iteration and the correct value of σ can be calculated to any required accuracy.[8] In this example, the implied volatility is 0.235, or 23.5%, per

[8] This method is presented for illustration. Other more powerful methods, such as the Newton–Raphson method, are often used in practice (see footnote 5 of Chapter 4). DerivaGem can be used to calculate implied volatilities.

annum. A similar procedure can be used in conjunction with binomial trees to find implied volatilities for American options.

Implied volatilities are used to monitor the market's opinion about the volatility of a particular stock. Traders like to calculate implied volatilities from actively traded options on a certain asset and interpolate between them to calculate the appropriate volatility for pricing a less actively traded option on the same stock. We explain this procedure in Chapter 16. It is important to note that the prices of deep-in-the-money and deep-out-of-the-money options are relatively insensitive to volatility. Implied volatilities calculated from these options, therefore, tend to be unreliable.

13.12 DIVIDENDS

Up to now, we have assumed that the stock upon which the option is written pays no dividends. In this section, we modify the Black–Scholes model to take account of dividends. We assume that the amount and timing of the dividends during the life of an option can be predicted with certainty. For short-life options this is not an unreasonable assumption. For long-life options it is usual to assume that the dividend yield rather the cash dividend payments are known. Options can then be valued as will be described in the next chapter. The date on which the dividend is paid should be assumed to be the ex-dividend date. On this date the stock price declines by the amount of the dividend.[9]

European Options

European options can be analyzed by assuming that the stock price is the sum of two components: a riskless component that corresponds to the known dividends during the life of the option and a risky component. The riskless component, at any given time, is the present value of all the dividends during the life of the option discounted from the ex-dividend dates to the present at the risk-free rate. By the time the option matures, the dividends will have been paid and the riskless component will no longer exist. The Black–Scholes formula is therefore correct if S_0 is equal to the risky component of the stock price and σ is the volatility of the process followed by the risky component.[10] Operationally, this means that the Black–Scholes formula can be used provided that the stock price is reduced by the present value of all the dividends during the life of the option, the discounting being done from the ex-dividend dates at the risk-free rate. A dividend is counted as being during the life of the option only if its ex-dividend date occurs during the life of the option.

[9] For tax reasons the stock price may go down by somewhat less than the cash amount of the dividend. To take account of this phenomenon, we need to interpret the word 'dividend' in the context of option pricing as the reduction in the stock price on the ex-dividend date caused by the dividend. Thus, if a dividend of \$1 per share is anticipated and the share price normally goes down by 80% of the dividend on the ex-dividend date, the dividend should be assumed to be \$0.80 for the purposes of the analysis.

[10] In theory, this is not quite the same as the volatility of the stochastic process followed by the whole stock price. The volatility of the risky component is approximately equal to the volatility of the whole stock price multiplied by $S_0/(S_0 - D)$, where D is the present value of the dividends. However, an adjustment is only necessary when volatilities are estimated using historical data. An implied volatility is calculated after the present value of dividends have been subtracted from the stock price and is the volatility of the risky component.

Example 13.8

Consider a European call option on a stock when there are ex-dividend dates in two months and five months. The dividend on each ex-dividend date is expected to be \$0.50. The current share price is \$40, the exercise price is \$40, the stock price volatility is 30% per annum, the risk-free rate of interest is 9% per annum, and the time to maturity is six months. The present value of the dividends is

$$0.5e^{-0.1667\times 0.09} + 0.5e^{-0.4167\times 0.09} = 0.9741$$

The option price can therefore be calculated from the Black–Scholes formula, with $S_0 = 40 - 0.9741 = 39.0259$, $K = 40$, $r = 0.09$, $\sigma = 0.3$, and $T = 0.5$:

$$d_1 = \frac{\ln(39.0259/40) + (0.09 + 0.3^2/2)\times 0.5}{0.3\sqrt{0.5}} = 0.2017$$

$$d_2 = \frac{\ln(39.0259/40) + (0.09 - 0.3^2/2)\times 0.5}{0.3\sqrt{0.5}} = -0.0104$$

Using the polynomial approximation in Section 13.9 gives us

$$N(d_1) = 0.5800, \qquad N(d_2) = 0.4959$$

and, from equation (13.20), the call price is

$$39.0259 \times 0.5800 - 40e^{-0.09\times 0.5} \times 0.4959 = 3.67$$

or \$3.67.

American Options

Consider next American call options. In Section 9.5, we showed that in the absence of dividends American options should never be exercised early. An extension to the argument shows that when there are dividends, it is optimal to exercise only at a time immediately before the stock goes ex-dividend. We assume that n ex-dividend dates are anticipated and that they are at times $t_1, t_2, \dots, t_n$, with $t_1 < t_2 < \cdots < t_n$. The dividends corresponding to these times will be denoted by $D_1, D_2, \dots, D_n$, respectively.

We start by considering the possibility of early exercise just prior to the final ex-dividend date (i.e., at time t_n). If the option is exercised at time t_n, the investor receives

$$S(t_n) - K$$

where $S(t)$ denotes the stock price at time t. If the option is not exercised, the stock price drops to $S(t_n) - D_n$. As shown by equation (9.5), the value of the option is then greater than

$$S(t_n) - D_n - Ke^{-r(T-t_n)}$$

It follows that, if

$$S(t_n) - D_n - Ke^{-r(T-t_n)} \geqslant S(t_n) - K$$

that is,

$$D_n \leqslant K\left[1 - e^{-r(T-t_n)}\right] \qquad \textbf{(13.24)}$$

it cannot be optimal to exercise at time t_n. On the other hand, if

$$D_n > K\left[1 - e^{-r(T-t_n)}\right] \tag{13.25}$$

for any reasonable assumption about the stochastic process followed by the stock price, it can be shown that it is always optimal to exercise at time t_n for a sufficiently high value of $S(t_n)$. The inequality in (13.25) will tend to be satisfied when the final ex-dividend date is fairly close to the maturity of the option (i.e., $T - t_n$ is small) and the dividend is large.

Consider next time t_{n-1}, the penultimate ex-dividend date. If the option is exercised immediately prior to time t_{n-1}, the investor receives $S(t_{n-1}) - K$. If the option is not exercised at time t_{n-1}, the stock price drops to $S(t_{n-1}) - D_{n-1}$ and the earliest subsequent time at which exercise could take place is t_n. Hence, from equation (9.5), a lower bound to the option price if it is not exercised at time t_{n-1} is

$$S(t_{n-1}) - D_{n-1} - Ke^{-r(t_n - t_{n-1})}$$

It follows that if

$$S(t_{n-1}) - D_{n-1} - Ke^{-r(t_n - t_{n-1})} \geqslant S(t_{n-1}) - K$$

or

$$D_{n-1} \leqslant K\left[1 - e^{-r(t_n - t_{n-1})}\right]$$

it is not optimal to exercise immediately prior to time t_{n-1}. Similarly, for any $i < n$, if

$$D_i \leqslant K\left[1 - e^{-r(t_{i+1} - t_i)}\right] \tag{13.26}$$

it is not optimal to exercise immediately prior to time t_i.

The inequality in (13.26) is approximately equivalent to

$$D_i \leqslant Kr(t_{i+1} - t_i)$$

Assuming that K is fairly close to the current stock price, the dividend yield on the stock has to be either close to or above the risk-free rate of interest for this inequality not to be satisfied. This is often not the case.

We can conclude from this analysis that, in many circumstances, the most likely time for the early exercise of an American call is immediately before the final ex-dividend date, t_n. Furthermore, if inequality (13.26) holds for $i = 1, 2, \dots, n-1$ and inequality (13.24) holds, we can be certain that early exercise is never optimal.

Black's Approximation

Black suggests an approximate procedure for taking account of early exercise in call options.[11] This involves calculating, as described earlier in this section, the prices of European options that mature at times T and t_n, and then setting the American price equal to the greater of the two. This approximation seems to work well in most cases.[12]

---

[11] See F. Black, "Fact and Fantasy in the Use of Options," *Financial Analysts Journal*, 31 (July/August 1975): 36–41, 61–72.

[12] For an exact formula, suggested by Roll, Geske, and Whaley, for valuing calls when there is only one ex-dividend date, see Technical Note 4 on the author's website. This involves the cumulative bivariate normal distribution function. A procedure for calculating this function is given in Technical Note 5 also on the author's website.

Example 13.9

Consider the situation in Example 13.8, but suppose that the option is American rather than European. In this case $D_1 = D_2 = 0.5$, $S_0 = 40$, $K = 40$, $r = 0.09$, $t_1 = 2/12$, and $t_2 = 5/12$. Since

$$K\big[1 - e^{-r(t_2-t_1)}\big] = 40(1 - e^{-0.09\times 0.25}) = 0.89$$

is greater than 0.5, it follows (see inequality (13.26)) that the option should never be exercised immediately before the first ex-dividend date. In addition, since

$$K\big[1 - e^{-r(T-t_2)}\big] = 40(1 - e^{-0.09\times 0.0833}) = 0.30$$

is less than 0.5, it follows (see inequality (13.25)) that, when it is sufficiently deep in the money, the option should be exercised immediately before the second ex-dividend date.

We now use Black's approximation to value the option. The present value of the first dividend is

$$0.5e^{-0.1667\times 0.09} = 0.4926$$

so that the value of the option, on the assumption that it expires just before the final ex-dividend date, can be calculated using the Black–Scholes formula with $S_0 = 40 - 0.4926 = 39.5074$, $K = 40$, $r = 0.09$, $\sigma = 0.30$, and $T = 0.4167$. It is \$3.52. Black's approximation involves taking the greater of this and the value of the option when it can only be exercised at the end of 6 months. From Example 13.8, we know that the latter is \$3.67. Black's approximation, therefore, gives the value of the American call as \$3.67.

The value of the option given by DerivaGem using "Binomial American" with 500 time steps is \$3.72. There are two reasons for differences between the Binomial Model (BM) and Black's approximation (BA). The first concerns the timing of the early exercise decision; the second concerns the way volatility is applied. The timing of the early exercise decision tends to make BM greater than BA. In BA, the assumption is that the holder has to decide today whether the option will be exercised after 5 months or after 6 months; BM allows the decision on early exercise at the 5-month point to depend on the stock price. The way in which volatility is applied tends to make BA greater than BM. In BA, when we assume exercise takes place after 5 months, the volatility is applied to the stock price less the present value of the first dividend; when we assume exercise takes place after 6 months, the volatility is applied to the stock price less the present value of both dividends.

SUMMARY

We started this chapter by examining the properties of the process for stock prices introduced in Chapter 12. The process implies that the price of a stock at some future time, given its price today, is lognormal. It also implies that the continuously compounded return from the stock in a period of time is normally distributed. Our uncertainty about future stock prices increases as we look further ahead. The standard deviation of the logarithm of the stock price is proportional to the square root of how far ahead we are looking.

To estimate the volatility σ of a stock price empirically, the stock price is observed at fixed intervals of time (e.g., every day, every week, or every month). For each time period, the natural logarithm of the ratio of the stock price at the end of the time period to the stock price at the beginning of the time period is calculated. The volatility is estimated as the standard deviation of these numbers divided by the square root of the length of the time period in years. Usually, days when the exchanges are closed are ignored in measuring time for the purposes of volatility calculations.

The differential equation for the price of any derivative dependent on a stock can be obtained by creating a riskless position in the option and the stock. Because the derivative and the stock price both depend on the same underlying source of uncertainty, this can always be done. The position that is created remains riskless for only a very short period of time. However, the return on a riskless position must always be the risk-free interest rate if there are to be no arbitrage opportunities.

The expected return on the stock does not enter into the Black–Scholes differential equation. This leads to a useful result known as risk-neutral valuation. This result states that when valuing a derivative dependent on a stock price, we can assume that the world is risk neutral. This means that we can assume that the expected return from the stock is the risk-free interest rate, and then discount expected payoffs at the risk-free interest rate. The Black–Scholes equations for European call and put options can be derived by either solving their differential equation or by using risk-neutral valuation.

An implied volatility is the volatility that, when used in conjunction with the Black–Scholes option pricing formula, gives the market price of the option. Traders monitor implied volatilities and commonly use the implied volatilities from actively traded options to estimate the appropriate volatility to use to price a less actively traded option on the same asset. Empirical results show that the volatility of a stock is much higher when the exchange is open than when it is closed. This suggests that, to some extent, trading itself causes stock price volatility.

The Black–Scholes results can be extended to cover European call and put options on dividend-paying stocks. The procedure is to use the Black–Scholes formula with the stock price reduced by the present value of the dividends anticipated during the life of the option, and the volatility equal to the volatility of the stock price net of the present value of these dividends.

In theory, American call options are liable to be exercised early, immediately before any ex-dividend date. In practice, only the final ex-dividend date usually needs to be considered. Fischer Black has suggested an approximation. This involves setting the American call option price equal to the greater of two European call option prices. The first European call option expires at the same time as the American call option; the second expires immediately prior to the final ex-dividend date.

FURTHER READING

On the Distribution of Stock Price Changes

Blattberg, R., and N. Gonedes, "A Comparison of the Stable and Student Distributions as Statistical Models for Stock Prices," *Journal of Business*, 47 (April 1974): 244–80.

Fama, E. F., "The Behavior of Stock Market Prices," *Journal of Business*, 38 (January 1965): 34–105.

Kon, S. J., "Models of Stock Returns—A Comparison," *Journal of Finance*, 39 (March 1984): 147–65.

Richardson, M., and T. Smith, "A Test for Multivariate Normality in Stock Returns," *Journal of Business*, 66 (1993): 295–321.

On the Black–Scholes Analysis

Black, F. "Fact and Fantasy in the Use of Options and Corporate Liabilities," *Financial Analysts Journal*, 31 (July/August 1975): 36–41, 61–72.

Black, F. "How We Came Up with the Option Pricing Formula," *Journal of Portfolio Management*, 15, 2 (1989): 4–8.

Black, F., and M. Scholes, "The Pricing of Options and Corporate Liabilities," *Journal of Political Economy*, 81 (May/June 1973): 637–59.

Merton, R. C., "Theory of Rational Option Pricing," *Bell Journal of Economics and Management Science*, 4 (Spring 1973): 141–83.

On Risk-Neutral Valuation

Cox, J. C., and S. A. Ross, "The Valuation of Options for Alternative Stochastic Processes," *Journal of Financial Economics*, 3 (1976): 145–66.

Smith, C. W., "Option Pricing: A Review," *Journal of Financial Economics*, 3 (1976): 3–54.

On the Causes of Volatility

Fama, E. F. "The Behavior of Stock Market Prices." *Journal of Business*, 38 (January 1965): 34–105.

French, K. R. "Stock Returns and the Weekend Effect." *Journal of Financial Economics, 8 (March 1980): 55–69.*

French, K. R., and R. Roll "Stock Return Variances: The Arrival of Information and the Reaction of Traders." *Journal of Financial Economics*, 17 (September 1986): 5–26.

Roll R. "Orange Juice and Weather," *American Economic Review*, 74, 5 (December 1984): 861–80.

Questions and Problems (Answers in Solutions Manual)

13.1. What does the Black–Scholes stock option pricing model assume about the probability distribution of the stock price in one year? What does it assume about the continuously compounded rate of return on the stock during the year?

13.2. The volatility of a stock price is 30% per annum. What is the standard deviation of the percentage price change in one trading day?

13.3. Explain the principle of risk-neutral valuation.

13.4. Calculate the price of a 3-month European put option on a non-dividend-paying stock with a strike price of \$50 when the current stock price is \$50, the risk-free interest rate is 10% per annum, and the volatility is 30% per annum.

13.5. What difference does it make to your calculations in Problem 13.4 if a dividend of \$1.50 is expected in 2 months?

13.6. What is *implied volatility*? How can it be calculated?

13.7. A stock price is currently \$40. Assume that the expected return from the stock is 15% and that its volatility is 25%. What is the probability distribution for the rate of return (with continuous compounding) earned over a 2-year period?

13.8. A stock price follows geometric Brownian motion with an expected return of 16% and a volatility of 35%. The current price is \$38.

(a) What is the probability that a European call option on the stock with an exercise price of \$40 and a maturity date in 6 months will be exercised?

(b) What is the probability that a European put option on the stock with the same exercise price and maturity will be exercised?

13.9. Using the notation in this chapter, prove that a 95% confidence interval for S_T is between

$$S_0 e^{(\mu-\sigma^2/2)T-1.96\sigma\sqrt{T}} \quad \text{and} \quad S_0 e^{(\mu-\sigma^2/2)T+1.96\sigma\sqrt{T}}$$

13.10. A portfolio manager announces that the average of the returns realized in each year of the last 10 years is 20% per annum. In what respect is this statement misleading?

13.11. Assume that a non-dividend-paying stock has an expected return of μ and a volatility of σ. An innovative financial institution has just announced that it will trade a security that pays off a dollar amount equal to $\ln S_T$ at time T, where S_T denotes the value of the stock price at time T.

(a) Use risk-neutral valuation to calculate the price of the security at time t in terms of the stock price, S, at time t.

(b) Confirm that your price satisfies the differential equation (13.16).

13.12. Consider a derivative that pays off S_T^n at time T, where S_T is the stock price at that time. When the stock price follows geometric Brownian motion, it can be shown that its price at time t ($t \leqslant T$) has the form

$$h(t, T)S^n$$

where S is the stock price at time t and h is a function only of t and T.

(a) By substituting into the Black–Scholes–Merton partial differential equation, derive an ordinary differential equation satisfied by $h(t, T)$.

(b) What is the boundary condition for the differential equation for $h(t, T)$?

(c) Show that

$$h(t, T) = e^{[0.5\sigma^2 n(n-1)+r(n-1)](T-t)}$$

where r is the risk-free interest rate and σ is the stock price volatility.

13.13. What is the price of a European call option on a non-dividend-paying stock when the stock price is \$52, the strike price is \$50, the risk-free interest rate is 12% per annum, the volatility is 30% per annum, and the time to maturity is 3 months?

13.14. What is the price of a European put option on a non-dividend-paying stock when the stock price is \$69, the strike price is \$70, the risk-free interest rate is 5% per annum, the volatility is 35% per annum, and the time to maturity is 6 months?

13.15. Consider an American call option on a stock. The stock price is \$70, the time to maturity is 8 months, the risk-free rate of interest is 10% per annum, the exercise price is \$65, and the volatility is 32%. A dividend of \$1 is expected after 3 months and again after 6 months. Show that it can never be optimal to exercise the option on either of the two dividend dates. Use DerivaGem to calculate the price of the option.

13.16. A call option on a non-dividend-paying stock has a market price of \$$2\frac{1}{2}$. The stock price is \$15, the exercise price is \$13, the time to maturity is 3 months, and the risk-free interest rate is 5% per annum. What is the implied volatility?

13.17. With the notation used in this chapter:

(a) What is $N'(x)$?

(b) Show that $SN'(d_1) = Ke^{-r(T-t)}N'(d_2)$, where S is the stock price at time t and

$$d_1 = \frac{\ln(S/K) + (r + \sigma^2/2)(T-t)}{\sigma\sqrt{T-t}}$$

$$d_2 = \frac{\ln(S/K) + (r - \sigma^2/2)(T-t)}{\sigma\sqrt{T-t}}$$

(c) Calculate $\partial d_1/\partial S$ and $\partial d_2/\partial S$.

(d) Show that when

$$c = SN(d_1) - Ke^{-r(T-t)}N(d_2)$$

it follows that

$$\frac{\partial c}{\partial t} = -rKe^{-r(T-t)}N(d_2) - SN'(d_1)\frac{\sigma}{2\sqrt{T-t}}$$

where c is the price of a call option on a non-dividend-paying stock.

(e) Show that $\partial c/\partial S = N(d_1)$.

(f) Show that c satisfies the Black–Scholes differential equation.

(g) Show that c satisfies the boundary condition for a European call option, i.e., that $c = \max(S - K, 0)$ as $t \longrightarrow T$.

13.18. Show that the Black–Scholes formulas for call and put options satisfy put–call parity.

13.19. A stock price is currently \$50 and the risk-free interest rate is 5%. Use the DerivaGem software to translate the following table of European call options on the stock into a table of implied volatilities, assuming no dividends. Are the option prices consistent with the assumptions underlying Black–Scholes?

	Maturity (months)		
Strike price (\$)	*3*	*6*	*12*
45	7.0	8.3	10.5
50	3.7	5.2	7.5
55	1.6	2.9	5.1

13.20. Explain carefully why Black's approach to evaluating an American call option on a dividend-paying stock may give an approximate answer even when only one dividend is anticipated. Does the answer given by Black's approach understate or overstate the true option value? Explain your answer.

13.21. Consider an American call option on a stock. The stock price is \$50, the time to maturity is 15 months, the risk-free rate of interest is 8% per annum, the exercise price is \$55, and the volatility is 25%. Dividends of \$1.50 are expected in 4 months and 10 months. Show that it can never be optimal to exercise the option on either of the two dividend dates. Calculate the price of the option.

13.22. Show that the probability that a European call option will be exercised in a risk-neutral world is, with the notation introduced in this chapter, $N(d_2)$. What is an expression for the value of a derivative that pays off \$100 if the price of a stock at time T is greater than K?

13.23. Show that S^{-2r/σ^2} could be the price of a traded security.

13.24. A company has an issue of executive stock options outstanding. Should dilution be taken into account when the options are valued? Explain your answer.

13.25. A company's stock price is \$50 and 10 million shares are outstanding. The company is considering giving its employees 3 million at-the-money 5-year call options. Option exercises will be handled by issuing more shares. The stock price volatility is 25%, the 5-year risk-free rate is 5% and the company does not pay dividends. Estimate the cost to the company of the employee stock option issue.

Assignment Questions

13.26. A stock price is currently \$50. Assume that the expected return from the stock is 18% and its volatility is 30%. What is the probability distribution for the stock price in 2 years? Calculate the mean and standard deviation of the distribution. Determine the 95% confidence interval.

13.27. Suppose that observations on a stock price (in dollars) at the end of each of 15 consecutive weeks are as follows:

30.2, 32.0, 31.1, 30.1, 30.2, 30.3, 30.6, 33.0, 32.9, 33.0, 33.5, 33.5, 33.7, 33.5, 33.2

Estimate the stock price volatility. What is the standard error of your estimate?

13.28. A financial institution plans to offer a security that pays off a dollar amount equal to S_T^2 at time T.

(a) Use risk-neutral valuation to calculate the price of the security at time t in terms of the stock price S at time t. (*Hint*: The expected value of S_T^2 can be calculated from the mean and variance of S_T given in Section 13.1.)

(b) Confirm that your price satisfies the differential equation (13.16).

13.29. Consider an option on a non-dividend-paying stock when the stock price is \$30, the exercise price is \$29, the risk-free interest rate is 5%, the volatility is 25% per annum, and the time to maturity is 4 months.

(a) What is the price of the option if it is a European call?

(b) What is the price of the option if it is an American call?

(c) What is the price of the option if it is a European put?

(d) Verify that put–call parity holds.

13.30. Assume that the stock in Problem 13.29 is due to go ex-dividend in $1\frac{1}{2}$ months. The expected dividend is 50 cents.

(a) What is the price of the option if it is a European call?

(b) What is the price of the option if it is a European put?

(c) If the option is an American call, are there any circumstances under which it will be exercised early?

13.31. Consider an American call option when the stock price is \$18, the exercise price is \$20, the time to maturity is 6 months, the volatility is 30% per annum, and the risk-free interest rate is 10% per annum. Two equal dividends are expected during the life of the option with ex-dividend dates at the end of 2 months and 5 months. Assume the dividends are 40 cents. Use Black's approximation and the DerivaGem software to value the option. How high can the dividends be without the American option being worth more than the corresponding European option?

APPENDIX

PROOF OF THE BLACK–SCHOLES–MERTON FORMULA

We will prove the Black–Scholes result by first proving another key result that will also be useful in future chapters.

Key Result

If V is lognormally distributed and the standard deviation of $\ln V$ is w, then

$$E[\max(V - K, 0)] = E(V)N(d_1) - KN(d_2) \tag{13A.1}$$

where

$$d_1 = \frac{\ln[E(V)/K] + w^2/2}{w}$$

$$d_2 = \frac{\ln[E(V)/K] - w^2/2}{w}$$

and E denotes the expected value.

Proof of Key Result

Define $g(V)$ as the probability density function of V. It follows that

$$E[\max(V - K, 0)] = \int_K^{\infty} (V - K)g(V)\,dV \tag{13A.2}$$

The variable $\ln V$ is normally distributed with standard deviation w. From the properties of the lognormal distribution, the mean of $\ln V$ is m, where[13]

$$m = \ln[E(V)] - w^2/2 \tag{13A.3}$$

Define a new variable

$$Q = \frac{\ln V - m}{w} \tag{13A.4}$$

This variable is normally distributed with a mean of zero and a standard deviation of 1.0. Denote the density function for Q by $h(Q)$ so that

$$h(Q) = \frac{1}{\sqrt{2\pi}} e^{-Q^2/2}$$

Using equation (13A.4) to convert the expression on the right-hand side of equation (13A.2) from an integral over V to an integral over Q, we get

$$E[\max(V - K, 0)] = \int_{(\ln K - m)/w}^{\infty} (e^{Qw+m} - K)\,h(Q)\,dQ$$

or

$$E[\max(V - K, 0)] = \int_{(\ln K - m)/w}^{\infty} e^{Qw+m} h(Q)dQ - K \int_{(\ln K - m)/w}^{\infty} h(Q)dQ \tag{13A.5}$$

[13] For a proof of this, see Technical Note 2 on the author's website.

Now

$$\begin{aligned} e^{Qw+m}h(Q) &= \frac{1}{\sqrt{2\pi}} e^{(-Q^2+2Qw+2m)/2} \\ &= \frac{1}{\sqrt{2\pi}} e^{[-(Q-w)^2+2m+w^2]/2} \\ &= \frac{e^{m+w^2/2}}{\sqrt{2\pi}} e^{[-(Q-w)^2]/2} \\ &= e^{m+w^2/2} h(Q-w) \end{aligned}$$

This means that equation (13A.5) becomes

$$E[\max(V-K,\ 0)] = e^{m+w^2/2} \int_{(\ln K-m)/w}^{\infty} h(Q-w)\,dQ - K \int_{(\ln K-m)/w}^{\infty} h(Q)\,dQ \qquad \textbf{(13A.6)}$$

If we define $N(x)$ as the probability that a variable with a mean of zero and a standard deviation of 1.0 is less than x, the first integral in equation (13A.6) is

$$1 - N[(\ln K - m)/w - w]$$

or

$$N[(-\ln K + m)/w + w]$$

Substituting for m from equation (13A.3) leads to

$$N\left(\frac{\ln[E(V)/K] + w^2/2}{w}\right) = N(d_1)$$

Similarly the second integral in equation (13A.6) is $N(d_2)$. Equation (13A.6), therefore, becomes

$$E[\max(V-K,\ 0)] = e^{m+w^2/2} N(d_1) - KN(d_2)$$

Substituting for m from equation (13A.3) gives the key result.

The Black–Scholes–Merton Result

We now consider a call option on a non-dividend-paying stock maturing at time T. The strike price is K, the risk-free rate is r, the current stock price is S_0, and the volatility is σ. As shown in equation (13.22), the call price c is given by

$$c = e^{-rT} \hat{E}[\max(S_T - K,\ 0)] \qquad \textbf{(13A.7)}$$

where S_T is the stock price at time T and $\hat{E}$ denotes the expectation in a risk-neutral world. Under the stochastic process assumed by Black–Scholes, S_T is lognormal. Also, from equations (13.3) and (13.4), $\hat{E}(S_T) = S_0 e^{rT}$ and the standard deviation of $\ln S_T$ is $\sigma\sqrt{T}$.

From the key result just proved, equation (13A.7) implies

$$c = e^{-rT}[S_0 e^{rT} N(d_1) - KN(d_2)]$$

or

$$c = S_0 N(d_1) - Ke^{-rT} N(d_2)$$

where

$$d_1 = \frac{\ln[\hat{E}(S_T)/K] + \sigma^2 T/2}{\sigma\sqrt{T}} = \frac{\ln(S_0/K) + (r + \sigma^2/2)T}{\sigma\sqrt{T}}$$

and

$$d_2 = \frac{\ln[\hat{E}(S_T)/K] - \sigma^2 T/2}{\sigma\sqrt{T}} = \frac{\ln(S_0/K) + (r - \sigma^2/2)T}{\sigma\sqrt{T}}$$

CHAPTER 14 Options on Stock Indices, Currencies, and Futures

In this chapter we tackle the problem of valuing options on stock indices, currencies, and futures contracts. As a first step, we produce results for options on a stock paying a known dividend yield. We then argue that stock indices, currencies, and futures prices are analogous to stocks paying known dividend yield. This enables the results for options on a stock paying a dividend yield to be applied to value options on these other assets.

14.1 RESULTS FOR A STOCK PAYING A KNOWN DIVIDEND YIELD

This section provides a simple rule that enables results produced for European options on a non-dividend-paying stock to be extended so that they apply to European options on a stock paying a known dividend yield.

Dividends cause stock prices to reduce on the ex-dividend date by the amount of the dividend payment. The payment of a dividend yield at rate q therefore causes the growth rate in the stock price to be less than it would otherwise be by an amount q. If, with a dividend yield of q, the stock price grows from S_0 today to S_T at time T, then in the absence of dividends it would grow from S_0 today to $S_T e^{qT}$ at time T. Alternatively, in the absence of dividends, it would grow from $S_0 e^{-qT}$ today to S_T at time T.

This argument shows that we get the same probability distribution for the stock price at time T in each of the following two cases:

1. The stock starts at price S_0 and provides a dividend yield at rate q.
2. The stock starts at price $S_0 e^{-qT}$ and pays no dividends.

This leads to a simple rule. When valuing a European option lasting for time T on a stock paying a known dividend yield at rate q, we reduce the current stock price from S_0 to $S_0 e^{-qT}$ and then value the option as though the stock pays no dividends.

Lower Bounds for Option Prices

As a first application of this rule, consider the problem of determining bounds for the price of a European option on a stock providing a dividend yield equal to q. Substituting S_0e^{-qT} for S_0 in equation (9.1), we see that the lower bound for the European call option price c is

$$c \geqslant \max(S_0e^{-qT} - Ke^{-rT},\ 0) \tag{14.1}$$

To obtain a lower bound for a European put option, we can similarly replace S_0 by S_0e^{-qT} in equation (9.2), to get

$$p \geqslant \max(Ke^{-rT} - S_0e^{-qT},\ 0) \tag{14.2}$$

These results can also be proved using no-arbitrage arguments (see Problem 14.36).

Put–Call Parity

Replacing S_0 by S_0e^{-qT} in equation (9.3), we obtain put–call parity for a stock providing a dividend yield equal to q:

$$c + Ke^{-rT} = p + S_0e^{-qT} \tag{14.3}$$

This result can also be proved using no-arbitrage arguments (see Problem 14.36).

14.2 OPTION PRICING FORMULAS

By replacing S_0 by S_0e^{-qT} in the Black–Scholes formulas, equations (13.20) and (13.21), we obtain the price c of a European call and the price p of a European put on a stock providing a dividend yield at rate q as

$$c = S_0e^{-qT}N(d_1) - Ke^{-rT}N(d_2) \tag{14.4}$$

$$p = Ke^{-rT}N(-d_2) - S_0e^{-qT}N(-d_1) \tag{14.5}$$

Since

$$\ln\left(\frac{S_0e^{-qT}}{K}\right) = \ln\frac{S_0}{K} - qT$$

the parameters d_1 and d_2 are given by

$$d_1 = \frac{\ln(S_0/K) + (r - q + \sigma^2/2)T}{\sigma\sqrt{T}}$$

$$d_2 = \frac{\ln(S_0/K) + (r - q - \sigma^2/2)T}{\sigma\sqrt{T}} = d_1 - \sigma\sqrt{T}$$

These results were first derived by Merton.[1] As discussed in Section 13.12, the word "dividend" should be defined as the reduction of the stock price on the ex-dividend date arising from any dividends declared. If the dividend yield is not constant during the life of the option, equations (14.4) and (14.5) are still true, with q equal to the average

[1] See R. Merton, "Theory of Rational Option Pricing," *Bell Journal of Economics and Management Science*, 4 (Spring 1973): 141–83.

annualized dividend yield during the life of the option. The dividend yield should be expressed with continuous compounding (see Section 5.6).

Differential Equation and Risk-Neutral Valuation

To prove the results in equations (14.4) and (14.5) more formally, we can either solve the differential equation that the option price must satisfy or use risk-neutral valuation.

When we include a dividend yield of q in the analysis in Section 13.6, the differential equation (13.16) becomes[2]

$$\frac{\partial f}{\partial t} + (r-q)S\frac{\partial f}{\partial S} + \tfrac{1}{2}\sigma^2 S^2 \frac{\partial^2 f}{\partial S^2} = rf \qquad \textbf{(14.6)}$$

Like equation (13.16), this does not involve any variable affected by risk preferences. Therefore, the risk-neutral valuation procedure, described in Section 13.7, can be used.

In a risk-neutral world, the total return from the stock must be r. The dividends provide a return of q. The expected growth rate in the stock price must therefore be $r-q$. So the risk-neutral process for the stock price is given by

$$dS = (r-q)S\,dt + \sigma S\,dz \qquad \textbf{(14.7)}$$

To value a derivative dependent on a stock that provides a dividend yield equal to q, we set the expected growth rate of the stock equal to $r-q$ and discount the expected payoff at rate r. When the expected growth rate in the stock price is $r-q$, the expected stock price at time T is $S_0e^{(r-q)T}$. A similar analysis to that in the appendix of Chapter 13 gives the expected payoff in a risk-neutral world as

$$e^{(r-q)T}S_0N(d_1) - KN(d_2)$$

where d_1 and d_2 are defined as above. Discounting at rate r for time T leads to equation (14.4).

Binomial Trees

Binomial trees can be used to value an option on a stock paying a known dividend yield in the way described in Chapter 11. To match the stock price volatility, we set

$$u = e^{\sigma\sqrt{\Delta t}} \quad \text{and} \quad d = e^{-\sigma\sqrt{\Delta t}}$$

where Δt is the length of the time step. The risk-neutral probability p of an up movement is chosen so that the expected return is $r-q$. This means that

$$pSu + (1-p)Sd = Se^{(r-q)\Delta t}$$

or

$$p = \frac{a-d}{u-d}$$

where

$$a = e^{(r-q)\Delta t}$$

This was the result we used in Section 11.9.

---

[2] See Technical Note 6 on the author's website for a proof of this.

14.3 OPTIONS ON STOCK INDICES

As discussed in Chapter 8, several exchanges trade options on stock indices. Some of the indices track the movement of the market as a whole. Others are based on the performance of a particular sector (e.g., computer technology, oil and gas, transportation, or telecommunications).

Quotes

Table 14.1 shows quotes for options on the Dow Jones Industrial Average (DJX) and S&P 500 (SPX) as they appeared in the Money and Investing section of the *Wall Street*

Table 14.1 Quotes for stock index options from the *Wall Street Journal*, February 5, 2004.

Wednesday, Feb. 4, 2004
Volume, last, net change and open interest for all contracts. Volume figures are unofficial. Open interest reflects previous trading day. p-Put c-Call. The totals for call and put volume are midday figures

CHICAGO

	STRIKE	VOL	LAST	NET CHG	OPEN INT
DJ INDUS AVG(DJX)					
Mar	90 p	5	0.15	−0.05	5,844
Mar	92 p	105	0.20	0.05	14,161
Apr	92 p	1	0.55	0.05	40
Mar	96 p	310	0.40	...	11,814
Feb	98 p	40	0.10	−0.05	7,602
Mar	98 p	775	0.60	0.05	4,211
Feb	99 c	10	5.90	0.10	328
Feb	99 p	200	0.15	...	2,190
Apr	99 p	3	1.35	0.05	606
Feb	100 p	179	0.20	...	6,935
Mar	100 p	3	0.90	0.05	21,574
Apr	100 p	3	1.35	−0.05	2,248
Mar	101 c	10	4.80	−0.70	3,075
Mar	101 p	3	1	−0.10	4,772
Feb	102 p	151	0.40	−0.10	2,925
Apr	102 p	2,133	2	0.15	2,206
Feb	104 c	40	1.75	−0.05	5,265
Feb	104 p	422	1.05	0.15	7,282
Mar	104 c	378	2.50	−0.30	11,255
Mar	104 p	458	2.10	0.20	12,458
Apr	104 p	5	2.85	0.10	1,799
Feb	105 c	2,068	1.05	−0.15	13,467
Feb	105 p	2,335	1.50	0.20	15,555
Mar	105 c	646	1.90	−0.15	39,444
Mar	105 p	122	2.35	0.05	21,489
Apr	105 c	200	2.75	0.05	1,914
Apr	105 p	102	3	...	895
Feb	106 c	1,071	0.65	−0.10	4,647
Feb	106 p	65	2.10	0.15	3,485
Mar	106 p	30	3	0.25	5,426
Apr	106 p	5	3.80	0.20	1,547
Feb	107 c	118	0.35	−0.10	4,414
Mar	107 p	2	3.50	...	125
Apr	107 c	10	1.50	−0.75	617
Apr	107 p	5	4.30	0.20	742
Feb	108 c	6	0.20	−0.10	3,305
Feb	108 p	2	3.90	0.40	2,585
Mar	108 c	182	0.85	...	11,472
Mar	108 p	41	4	...	614
Apr	108 p	40	5	0.20	88
Feb	112 p	23	7.30	0.10	435
Call Vol.........8,251				Open Int..313,904	
Put Vol....... 14,484				Open Int..370,073	
S & P 500(SPX)					
Feb	850 p	10	0.05	...	1,434
Mar	850 p	430	0.40	0.10	29,388
Apr	850 p	10	1.05	...	311
Feb	875 p	5	0.05	...	613
Apr	875 p	5	1.65	0.20	16
Mar	900 p	5	0.80	...	37,089
Apr	900 p	85	1.90	−0.15	2
Feb	925 c	140	199.50	2.50	690
Feb	925 p	4	0.10	−0.05	3,579
Mar	925 p	96	1.05	0.05	14,592
Feb	950 p	200	0.40	0.30	17,129
Feb	975 p	2,090	0.25	0.10	18,301
Mar	975 c	10	155	6.50	9,718
Mar	975 p	360	2.05	0.05	40,001
Apr	975 p	26	5.20	1.20	2,027
Feb	995 p	23	0.30	...	13,445
Mar	995 p	2,004	2.70	0.10	27,317
Apr	995 p	4	5.70	...	2,658
Feb	1005 p	256	0.35	0.05	36,093
Mar	1005 c	11	125	−12.50	2,370
Mar	1005 p	1,173	2.90	−0.10	25,947
Feb	1025 c	10	100.50	−9.50	5,757
Feb	1025 p	6,227	0.60	0.05	45,995
Mar	1025 p	515	4.60	0.50	55,930
Apr	1025 p	225	9	1.00	5,171
Feb	1035 p	306	0.70	...	2,864
Feb	1040 p	10	1	0.25	4,270
Feb	1050 c	1,789	76.30	−15.20	9,986
Feb	1050 p	1,929	1.10	...	42,107
Mar	1050 c	10	84	−5.80	19,676
Mar	1050 p	36	6.90	0.90	48,190
Feb	1055 p	130	1.40	0.10	3,134
Mar	1060 c	1	73	−6.50	3,391
Mar	1060 p	2,305	8.10	1.30	7,272
Mar	1070 p	600	9	0.90	7,919
Feb	1075 c	27	57.80	−3.70	11,711
Feb	1075 p	11,023	2.70	0.60	28,638
Mar	1075 c	16	64.50	−3.50	33,222
Mar	1075 p	519	10.40	1.80	38,840
Apr	1075 p	185	16.40	1.30	1,138
Feb	1085 c	4	48.80	−0.20	204
Feb	1085 p	583	3.70	1.00	6,492
Mar	1085 p	305	12	2.50	5,608
Feb	1090 c	30	43.60	−5.40	319
Feb	1090 p	85	4	0.70	5,371
Feb	1100 c	447	31.30	−8.10	21,191
Feb	1100 p	2,617	6.40	2.10	32,392
Mar	1100 c	33	40.50	−6.50	40,878
Mar	1100 p	4,203	15.80	1.80	44,776
Apr	1100 c	32	50	−4.50	462
Apr	1100 p	8,895	24	4.00	9,380
Feb	1105 p	124	7.20	1.70	1,734
Feb	1110 c	6	26.50	−5.50	13
Feb	1110 p	3,828	8.50	2.20	6,048
Mar	1110 c	11	34.40	−9.80	20,786
Mar	1110 p	688	18.10	2.10	18,829
Feb	1115 c	4	20.60	−5.20	973
Feb	1115 p	115	10.30	3.10	9,530
Feb	1120 c	93	18	−6.00	152
Feb	1120 p	255	12.10	3.50	6,774
Feb	1125 c	1,803	14	−7.00	19,486
Feb	1125 p	1,570	14.50	4.50	32,185
Mar	1125 c	4,980	24.70	−4.90	80,288
Mar	1125 p	4,764	25	4.00	78,162
Apr	1125 c	36	32.90	−4.80	2,641
Apr	1125 p	327	32	3.20	2,931
Feb	1130 c	1,156	11.30	−5.20	4,741
Feb	1130 p	2,693	16.60	4.20	11,001
Mar	1130 c	2,829	21.50	−5.00	12,667
Mar	1130 p	2,864	27	3.80	13,475
Feb	1135 c	322	9	−4.50	1,262
Feb	1135 p	396	19.90	5.60	2,600
Mar	1135 c	413	19.90	−4.10	9,978
Mar	1135 p	851	30	5.00	9,651
Feb	1140 c	1,779	7	−5.00	6,401
Feb	1140 p	948	22	5.50	8,040
Mar	1140 c	1,401	18	−3.00	3,698
Mar	1140 p	1	30	2.00	2,151
Feb	1145 c	52	6.60	−2.90	944
Feb	1145 p	47	26	5.00	1,584
Feb	1150 c	3,479	4.20	−3.30	26,943
Feb	1150 p	943	28.70	6.20	6,483
Mar	1150 c	520	13	−3.70	35,491
Mar	1150 p	52	38	5.00	23,226
Apr	1150 c	23	20.60	−3.40	2,122
Feb	1155 c	179	3.80	−2.00	1,557
Feb	1160 c	1,351	2.55	−1.85	6,062
Feb	1160 p	126	37	7.80	1,159
Mar	1160 c	402	10	−2.90	2,098
Maf	1160 p	1	45	1.00	14
Feb	1170 c	3,054	1.50	−0.90	6,733
Feb	1170 p	13	42.80	3.80	261
Feb	1175 c	1,617	1.15	−0.85	28,065
Feb	1175 p	55	49	6.00	2,196
Mar	1175 c	614	6	−2.00	26,761
Mar	1175 p	3	57.10	8.10	2,304
Apr	1175 c	558	12.20	−1.50	2,095
Feb	1180 c	420	0.80	−0.55	1,543
Feb	1185 c	7	0.85	−0.25	731
Feb	1190 c	86	0.50	−0.35	2,597
Mar	1190 c	104	4.70	...	...
Feb	1200 c	1,259	0.35	−0.20	22,677
Feb	1200 p	16	70.70	5.70	315
Mar	1200 c	1,965	3	−0.50	23,307
Mar	1200 p	1	73.40	4.90	463
Apr	1200 c	25	7	−0.60	3,481
Feb	1210 c	10	0.25	−0.10	1,424
Feb	1215 c	13	0.25	−0.15	963
Feb	1225 c	72	0.10	−0.10	5,124
Mar	1225 c	1	1.20	−0.30	3,018
Mar	1225 p	2	96.90	−4.60	11
Apr	1225 c	20	3.20	−0.50	2,845
Feb	1250 c	55	0.05	−0.10	8,403
Mar	1250 c	14	0.55	−0.05	11,441
Mar	1250 p	30	120	0.50	515
Apr	1250 c	3	1.50	−0.40	410
Call Vol......... 37,739				Open Int.1,200,003	
Put Vol......... 85,508				Open Int.1,976,864	
LEAPS-LONG TERM					
DJ INDUS AVG - CB					
Dec 05	76 p	10	2	...	...
Dec 05	104 c	1	9.20	0.40	11,701
Dec 05	108 c	500	6.90	0.40	82
Dec 05	108 p	500	10	1.00	20
Call Vol............ 501				Open Int... 13,617	
Put Vol............ 510				Open Int... 12,357	
S & P 500 - CB					
Dec 04	80 c	60	33.10	...	7,895
Dec 05	80 p	10	1.75	0.05	12,238
Dec 04	90 p	132	1.60	0.20	38,870
Dec 05	90 c	61	26	...	24,696
Dec 05	90 p	3	3.50	0.50	18,418
Dec 04	95 p	10	2.20	0.05	5,595
Dec 04	100 p	87	3.10	0.15	25,728
Dec 05	100 p	10	5	0.30	28,972
Dec 04	105 p	8	4.30	0.10	2,324
Dec 04	110 p	12	5.60	0.60	25,390
Dec 06	110 c	11	14.70	−1.00	4,328
Dec 06	110 p	10	9.10	0.70	33,811
Dec 04	120 c	4	3.40	−0.20	9,911
Call Vol............ 136				Open Int. 480,710	
Put Vol............ 282				Open.Int. 435,054	

Source: Reprinted by permission of Dow Jones, Inc., via Copyright Clearance Center, Inc.

Journal on Thursday February 5, 2004. The *Wall Street Journal* also shows quotes for options on a number of other indices including the Nasdaq 100 (NDX), Russell 2000 (RUT), and S&P 100 (OEX). All the options trade on the Chicago Board Options Exchange and all are European, except the contract on the S&P 100, which is American. The quotes refer to the price at which the last trade was made on Wednesday, February 4, 2004. The closing prices of the DJX and SPX on February 4, 2004, were 104.71 and 1,126.52, respectively.

One index option contract is on 100 times the index. (Note that the Dow Jones index used for index options is 0.01 times the usually quoted Dow Jones index.) Index options are settled in cash. This means that, on exercise of the option, the holder of a call option contract receives $(S - K) \times 100$ in cash and the writer of the contract pays this amount in cash, where S is the value of the index at the close of trading on the day of the exercise and K is the strike price. Similarly, the holder of a put option contract receives $(K - S) \times 100$ in cash and the writer of the contract pays this amount in cash.

Table 14.1 shows that, in addition to relatively short-dated options, the exchanges trade longer-maturity contracts known as LEAPS. The acronym LEAPS stands for "long-term equity anticipation securities" and was originated by the CBOE. LEAPS are exchange-traded options that last up to 3 years. (Note when interpreting Table 14.1 that the S&P 500 index is divided by 10 for the purpose of defining LEAPS contracts.) The usual expiration month for LEAPS on indices is December. As mentioned in Chapter 8, the CBOE and several other exchanges also trade LEAPS on many individual stocks. These have expirations in January.

The CBOE also trades *flex options* on indices. As mentioned in Chapter 8, these are options where the trader can choose the expiration date, the strike price, and whether the option is American or European.

Valuation

In valuing index futures in Chapter 5, we assumed that the index could be treated as a security paying a known dividend yield. In valuing index options, we make similar assumptions. This means that equations (14.1) and (14.2) provide a lower bound for European index options; equation (14.3) is the put–call parity result for European index options; and equations (14.4) and (14.5) can be used to value European options on an index. In all cases, S_0 is equal to the value of the index, σ is equal to the volatility of the index, and q is equal to the average annualized dividend yield (continuously compounded) on the index during the life of the option. The calculation of q should include only dividends whose ex-dividend date occurs during the life of the option.

In the United States ex-dividend dates tend to occur during the first week of February, May, August, and November. At any given time, the correct value of q is therefore likely to depend on the life of the option. This is even more true for some foreign indices. In Japan, for example, all companies tend to use the same ex-dividend dates.

Example 14.1

Consider a European call option on the S&P 500 that is 2 months from maturity. The current value of the index is 930, the exercise price is 900, the risk-free interest rate is 8% per annum, and the volatility of the index is 20% per annum. Dividend yields of 0.2% and 0.3% are expected in the first month and the second month, respectively. In this case, $S_0 = 930$, $K = 900$, $r = 0.08$, $\sigma = 0.2$, and $T = 2/12$. The total dividend yield during the option's life is $0.2 + 0.3 = 0.5\%$. This is 3% per annum. Hence, $q = 0.03$, and

$$d_1 = \frac{\ln(930/900) + (0.08 - 0.03 + 0.2^2/2) \times 2/12}{0.2\sqrt{2/12}} = 0.5444$$

$$d_2 = \frac{\ln(930/900) + (0.08 - 0.03 - 0.2^2/2) \times 2/12}{0.2\sqrt{2/12}} = 0.4628$$

$$N(d_1) = 0.7069, \qquad N(d_2) = 0.6782$$

so that the call price c is given by equation (14.4) as

$$c = 930 \times 0.7069e^{-0.03\times 2/12} - 900 \times 0.6782e^{-0.08\times 2/12} = 51.83$$

One contract would cost \$5,183.

If the absolute amount of the dividend that will be paid on the stocks underlying the index (rather than the dividend yield) is assumed to be known, the basic Black–Scholes formula can be used with the initial stock price being reduced by the present value of the dividends. This is the approach recommended in Chapter 13 for a stock paying known dividends. However, it may be difficult to implement for a broadly based stock index because it requires a knowledge of the dividends expected on every stock underlying the index.

Binomial Trees

In some circumstances it is optimal to exercise American put and call options on an index prior to the expiration date. Binomial trees can be used to value American-style index options as discussed in Section 11.9. An example of the use of binomial trees for index options is in Example 11.1 and Figure 11.11.

Portfolio Insurance

Portfolio managers can use index options to limit their downside risk. Suppose that the value of an index today is S_0. Consider a manager in charge of a well-diversified portfolio whose beta is 1.0. A beta of 1.0 implies that the returns from the portfolio mirror those from the index. Assuming the dividend yield from the portfolio is the same as the dividend yield from the index, the percentage changes in the value of the portfolio can be expected to be approximately the same as the percentage changes in the value of the index. Each contract on the S&P 500 is on 100 times the index. It follows that the value of the portfolio is protected against the possibility of the index falling below K if, for each $100S_0$ dollars in the portfolio, the manager buys one put option contract with strike price K. Suppose that the manager's portfolio is worth \$500,000 and the value of the index is 1,000. The portfolio is worth 500 times the index. The manager can obtain insurance against the value of the portfolio dropping below \$450,000 in the next 3 months by buying five put option contracts with a strike price

Business Snapshot 14.1 Can We Guarantee that Stocks Will Beat Bonds in the Long Run?

It is often said that if you are a long-term investor you should buy stocks rather than bonds. Consider a US fund manager who is trying to persuade investors to buy as a long-term investment an equity fund that is expected to mirror the S&P 500. The manager might be tempted to offer purchasers of the fund a guarantee that their return will be at least as good as the return on risk-free bonds over the next 10 years. Historically stocks have outperformed bonds in the United States over almost any 10-year period. It appears that the fund manager would not be giving much away.

In fact, this type of guarantee is surprisingly expensive. Suppose that an equity index is 1,000 today, the dividend yield on the index is 1% per annum, the volatility of the index is 15% per annum, and the 10-year risk-free rate is 5% per annum. To outperform bonds, the stocks underlying the index must earn more than 5% per annum. The dividend yield will provide 1% per annum. The capital gains on the stocks must therefore provide 4% per annum. This means that we require the index level to be at least $1{,}000e^{0.04\times 10} = 1{,}492$ in 10 years.

A guarantee that the return on \$1,000 invested in the index will be greater than the return on \$1,000 invested in bonds over the next 10 years is therefore equivalent to the right to sell the index for 1,492 in 10 years. This is a European put option on the index and can be valued from equation (14.5) with $S_0 = 1{,}000$, $K = 1{,}492$, $r = 5\%$, $\sigma = 15\%$, $T = 10$, and $q = 1\%$. The value of the put option is 169.7. This shows that the guarantee contemplated by the fund manager is worth about 17% of the fund—hardly something that should be given away!

of 900. Suppose that the risk-free rate is 12%, the dividend yield on the index is 4%, and the volatility of the index is 22%. The parameters of the option are:

$$S_0 = 1000, \quad K = 900, \quad r = 0.12, \quad \sigma = 0.22, \quad T = 0.25, \quad q = 0.04$$

From equation (14.5), the value of the option is \$6.48. The cost of the insurance is therefore $5 \times 100 \times 6.48 = \$3{,}240$.

To illustrate how the insurance works, consider the situation where the index drops to 880 in 3 months. The portfolio will be worth about \$440,000. The payoff from the options will be $5 \times (900 - 880) \times 100 = \$10,000$, bringing the total value of the portfolio up to the insured value of \$450,000 (or \$446,760 when the cost of the options are taken into account).

It is sometimes argued that the return from stocks is certain to beat the return from bonds in the long run. If this were true, long-dated portfolio insurance where the strike price equaled the future value of a bond portfolio would not cost very much. In fact, as indicated in Business Snapshot 14.1, it is quite expensive.

When the Portfolio's Beta Is Not 1.0

If the portfolio's returns are not expected to equal those of an index, the capital asset pricing model can be used. This model asserts that the expected excess return of a portfolio over the risk-free interest rate equals beta times the excess return of a market index over the risk-free interest rate. Suppose that the \$500,000 portfolio just considered

Table 14.2 Relationship between value of index and value of portfolio for beta = 2.0.

Value of index in 3 months	*Value of portfolio in 3 months ($)*
1,080	570,000
1,040	530,000
1,000	490,000
960	450,000
920	410,000
880	370,000

has a beta of 2.0 instead of 1.0. As before, we assume that the S&P 500 index is currently 1,000, the risk-free rate is 12% and the dividend yield on the index is 4%. Table 14.2 shows the expected relationship between the level of the index and the value of the portfolio in 3 months. To illustrate the sequence of calculations necessary to derive Table 14.2, Table 14.3 shows the calculations for the case when the value of the index in 3 months proves to be 1,040.

Suppose that S_0 is the value of the index. It can be shown that, for each $100S_0$ dollars in the portfolio, a total of beta put contracts should be purchased. The strike price should be the value that the index is expected to have when the value of the portfolio reaches the insured value. Assume that the required insured value is $450,000, as in the beta = 1.0 case. Table 14.2 shows that the appropriate strike price for the put options purchased is 960. The option parameters are:

$$S = 1000, \quad K = 960, \quad r = 0.12, \quad \sigma = 0.22, \quad T = 0.25, \quad q = 0.04$$

and equation (14.5) gives the value of the option as $19.21. In this case, $100S_0 = \$100{,}000$ and beta = 2.0, so that two put contracts are required for each $100,000 in the portfolio.

Table 14.3 Calculations for Table 14.2 when the value of the index is 1,040 in 3 months.

Value of index in 3 months:	1,040
Return from change in index:	40/1,000, or 4% per 3 months
Dividends from index:	$0.25 \times 4 = 1\%$ per 3 months
Total return from index:	$4 + 1 = 5\%$ per 3 months
Risk-free interest rate:	$0.25 \times 12 = 3\%$ per 3 months
Excess return from index over risk-free interest rate:	$5 - 3 = 2\%$ per 3 months
Excess return from portfolio over risk-free interest rate:	$2 \times 2 = 4\%$ per 3 months
Return from portfolio:	$3 + 4 = 7\%$ per 3 months
Dividends from portfolio:	$0.25 \times 4 = 1\%$ per 3 months
Increase in value of portfolio:	$7 - 1 = 6\%$ per 3 months
Value of portfolio:	$\$500,000 \times 1.06 = \$530,000$

Since the portfolio is worth \$500,000, a total of 10 contracts should be purchased. The total cost of the insurance is therefore $10 \times 100 \times 19.21 = \$19{,}210$.

To illustrate that the required result is obtained, consider what happens if the value of the index falls to 880. As shown in Table 14.2, the value of the portfolio is then about \$370,000. The put options pay off $(960 - 880) \times 10 \times 100 = \$80{,}000$, and this is exactly what is necessary to move the total value of the portfolio manager's position up from \$370,000 to the required level of \$450,000. (After the cost of the options are taken into account the value of the portfolio is \$430,790.)

There are two reasons why the cost of hedging increases as the beta of a portfolio increases: more put options are required, and they have a higher strike price.

14.4 CURRENCY OPTIONS

Currency options are primarily traded in the over-the-counter market. The advantage of this market is that large trades are possible with strike prices, expiration dates, and other features tailored to meet the needs of corporate treasurers. European and American options do trade on the Philadelphia Stock Exchange in the United States, but the exchange-traded market is much smaller than the over-the-counter market.

For a corporation wishing to hedge a foreign exchange exposure, foreign currency options are an interesting alternative to forward contracts. A company due to receive sterling at a known time in the future can hedge its risk by buying put options on sterling that mature at that time. The strategy guarantees that the value of the sterling will not be less than the strike price, while allowing the company to benefit from any favorable exchange-rate movements. Similarly, a company due to pay sterling at a known time in the future can hedge by buying calls on sterling that mature at that time. The approach guarantees that the cost of the sterling will not be greater than a certain amount while allowing the company to benefit from favorable exchange-rate movements. Whereas a forward contract locks in the exchange rate for a future transaction, an option provides a type of insurance. This insurance is not free. It costs nothing to enter into a forward transaction, whereas options require a premium to be paid up front.

Valuation

To value currency options, we define S_0 as the spot exchange rate. To be precise, S_0 is the value of one unit of the foreign currency in US dollars. As explained in Section 5.10, a foreign currency is analogous to a stock paying a known dividend yield. The owner of foreign currency receives a yield equal to the risk-free interest rate, r_f, in the foreign currency. Equations (14.1) and (14.2), with q replaced by r_f, provide bounds for the European call price, c, and the European put price, p:

$$c \geqslant S_0 e^{-r_f T} - K e^{-rT}$$

$$p \geqslant K e^{-rT} - S_0 e^{-r_f T}$$

Equation (14.3), with q replaced by r_f, provides the put–call parity result for currency options:

$$c + K e^{-rT} = p + S_0 e^{-r_f T}$$

Finally, equations (14.4) and (14.5) provide the pricing formulas for currency options when q is replaced by r_f:

$$c = S_0 e^{-r_f T} N(d_1) - K e^{-rT} N(d_2) \tag{14.7}$$

$$p = K e^{-rT} N(-d_2) - S_0 e^{-r_f T} N(-d_1) \tag{14.8}$$

where

$$d_1 = \frac{\ln(S_0/K) + (r - r_f + \sigma^2/2)T}{\sigma\sqrt{T}}$$

$$d_2 = \frac{\ln(S_0/K) + (r - r_f - \sigma^2/2)T}{\sigma\sqrt{T}} = d_1 - \sigma\sqrt{T}$$

Both the domestic interest rate, r, and the foreign interest rate, r_f, are the rates for a maturity T. Put and call options on a currency are symmetrical in that a put option to sell currency A for currency B at an exercise price K is the same as a call option to buy B with A at $1/K$.

Example 14.2

Consider a 4-month European call option on the British pound. Suppose that the current exchange rate is 1.6000, the exercise price is 1.6000, the risk-free interest rate in the United States is 8% per annum, the risk-free interest rate in Britain is 11% per annum, and the option price is 4.3 cents. In this case, $S_0 = 1.6$, $K = 1.6$, $r = 0.08$, $r_f = 0.11$, $T = 0.3333$, and $c = 0.043$. The implied volatility can be calculated by trial and error. A volatility of 20% gives an option price of 0.0639, a volatility of 10% gives an option price of 0.0285, and so on. The implied volatility is 14.1%.

From equation (5.9), the forward rate F_0 for a maturity T is given by

$$F_0 = S_0 e^{(r - r_f)T}$$

Thus, equations (14.7) and (14.8) can be simplified to

$$c = e^{-rT}[F_0 N(d_1) - K N(d_2)] \tag{14.9}$$

$$p = e^{-rT}[K N(-d_2) - F_0 N(-d_1)] \tag{14.10}$$

where

$$d_1 = \frac{\ln(F_0/K) + \sigma^2 T/2}{\sigma\sqrt{T}}$$

$$d_2 = \frac{\ln(F_0/K) - \sigma^2 T/2}{\sigma\sqrt{T}} = d_1 - \sigma\sqrt{T}$$

Note that, for equations (14.9) and (14.10), to be the correct equations for valuing a European option on the spot foreign exchange rate, the maturities of the forward contract and the option must be the same.

Binomial Trees

In some circumstances it is optimal to exercise American currency options prior to maturity. Thus, American currency options are worth more than their European counterparts. In general, call options on high-interest currencies and put options on low-interest currencies are the most likely to be exercised prior to maturity. The reason is that a high-interest currency is expected to depreciate and a low-interest currency is expected to appreciate. Binomial trees can be used to value American-style currency options as described in Section 11.9. An example of the valuation of a currency option is given in Example 11.2 and Figure 11.12.

14.5 FUTURES OPTIONS

Options on futures contracts, or futures options, are now traded on many different exchanges. They are American-style options and require the delivery of an underlying futures contract when exercised. If a call futures option is exercised, the holder acquires a long position in the underlying futures contract plus a cash amount equal to the most recent settlement futures price minus the strike price. If a put futures option is exercised, the holder acquires a short position in the underlying futures contract plus a cash amount equal to the strike price minus the most recent settlement futures price. As the following examples show, the effective payoff from a call futures option is the futures price at the time of exercise less the strike price; the effective payoff from a put futures option is the strike price less the futures price at the time of exercise.

Example 14.3

Suppose it is August 15 and an investor has one September futures call option contract on copper with a strike price of 70 cents per pound. One futures contract is on 25,000 pounds of copper. Suppose that the futures price of copper for delivery in September is currently 81 cents, and at the close of trading on August 14 (the last settlement) it was 80 cents. If the option is exercised, the investor receives a cash amount of

$$25{,}000 \times (80 - 70)\,\text{cents} = \$2{,}500$$

plus a long position in a futures contract to buy 25,000 pounds of copper in September. If desired, the position in the futures contract can be closed out immediately. This would leave the investor with the $2,500 cash payoff plus an amount

$$25{,}000 \times (81 - 80)\,\text{cents} = \$250$$

reflecting the change in the futures price since the last settlement. The total payoff from exercising the option on August 15 is $2,750, which equals $25{,}000(F - K)$, where F is the futures price at the time of exercise and K is the strike price.

Example 14.4

An investor has one December futures put option on corn with a strike price of 200 cents per bushel. One futures contract is on 5,000 bushels of corn. Suppose that the current futures price of corn for delivery in December is 180, and the most recent settlement price is 179 cents. If the option is exercised, the investor receives a cash amount of

$$5{,}000 \times (200 - 179)\,\text{cents} = \$1{,}050$$

plus a short position in a futures contract to sell 5,000 bushels of corn in December.

If desired, the position in the futures contract can be closed out. This would leave the investor with the \$1,050 cash payoff minus an amount

$$5{,}000 \times (180 - 179)\,\text{cents} = \$50$$

reflecting the change in the futures price since the last settlement. The net payoff from exercise is \$1,000, which equals $5{,}000(K - F)$, where F is the futures price at the time of exercise and K is the strike price.

Quotes

Futures options are referred to by the month in which the underlying futures contract matures—not by the expiration month of the option. As mentioned earlier, futures options are American. The expiration date of a futures option contract is usually on, or a few days before, the earliest delivery date of the underlying futures contract. (For example, the CBOT Treasury bond futures option expires on the Friday preceding by at least two business days the end of the month before the futures contract expiration month.) An exception is the CME mid-curve Eurodollar contract, where the futures contract expires either one or two years after the options contract.

Table 14.4 shows quotes for futures options as they appeared in the *Wall Street Journal* on February 5, 2004. The most popular contracts (as measured by open interest) are those on corn, soybeans, cotton, sugar-world, crude oil, natural gas, gold, Treasury bonds, Treasury notes, 5-year Treasury notes, 30-day federal funds, Eurodollars, 1-year and 2-year mid-curve Eurodollars, Euribor, Eurobunds, and the S&P 500.

Options on Interest Rate Futures

The most actively traded interest rate options offered by exchanges in the United States are those on Treasury bond futures, Treasury note futures, and Eurodollar futures. Table 14.4 shows the closing prices for these instruments on February 4, 2004.

A Treasury bond futures option is an option to enter a Treasury bond futures contract. As mentioned in Chapter 6, one Treasury bond futures contract is for the delivery of \$100,000 of Treasury bonds. The price of a Treasury bond futures option is quoted as a percentage of the face value of the underlying Treasury bonds to the nearest sixty-fourth of 1%. Table 14.4 gives the price of the March call futures option on a Treasury bond on February 4, 2004, as 2-06, or $2\frac{6}{64}\%$ of the bond principal, when the strike price is 110. This means that one contract costs \$2,093.75. The quotes for options on Treasury notes are similar.

An option on Eurodollar futures is an option to enter into a Eurodollar futures contract. As explained in Chapter 6, when the Eurodollar futures quote changes by 1 basis point, or 0.01%, there is a gain or loss on a Eurodollar futures contract of \$25. Similarly, in the pricing of options on Eurodollar futures, 1 basis point represents \$25. The *Wall Street Journal* quote for the CME Eurodollar futures contract in Table 14.4 should be multiplied by 10 to get the CME quote in basis points. For example, the 5.90 quote for the CME March call futures option when the strike price is 98.25 in Table 14.4 indicates that the CME quote is 59.0 basis points and one contract costs $59.0 \times \$25 = \$1{,}475.00$.

Table 14.4 Closing prices of futures options on February 4, 2004.

Wednesday, February 4, 2004

Final or settlement prices of selected contracts. Volume and open interest are totals in all contract months.

Grain and Oilseed

Corn (CBT)

5,000 bu.; cents per bu.

STRIKE	CALLS-SETTLE			PUTS-SETTLE		
Price	Mar	May	Jly	Mar	May	Jly
260	11.875	20.250	26.750	1.625	5.250	8.500
270	5.500	14.750	21.250	5.250	9.500	13.500
280	2.250	10.500	17.250	12.000	15.500	19.000
290	.750	7.375	14.000	20.500	22.000	25.625
300	.250	5.125	11.375	30.000	29.625	32.625
310	.125	3.500	9.250	...	...	...

Est vol 14,610 Tu 8,885 calls 6,364 puts
Op int Tues 323,990 calls 227,010 puts

Soybeans (CBT)

5,000 bu.; cents per bu.

Price	Mar	May	Jly	Mar	May	Jly
760	47.500	58.500	60.000	1.875	13.000	28.500
780	31.250	46.500	50.250	5.500	20.750	38.500
800	18.875	36.250	42.000	13.125	30.750	50.000
820	10.250	28.500	35.000	24.500	42.250	62.750
840	5.125	22.000	29.500	39.375	56.000	77.000
860	2.500	17.000	24.750	56.625	70.750	92.000

Est vol 17,482 Tu 16,204 calls 6,863 puts
Op int Tues 153,237 calls 125,007 puts

Soybean Meal (CBT)

100 tons; $ per ton

Price	Mar	May	Jly	Mar	May	Jly
235	...	...	...	...	...	...
240	9.00	13.50	14.50	2.00	7.25	11.75
245	...	...	...	...	...	...
250	3.75	9.30	10.90	6.75	12.60	18.25
255	...	...	...	...	...	...
260	1.35	6.50	8.50	14.40	19.75	25.70

Est vol 2,445 Tu 2,767 calls 2,418 puts
Op int Tues 39,831 calls 36,748 puts

Soybean Oil (CBT)

60,000 lbs.; cents per lb.

Price	Mar	May	Jly	Mar	May	Jly
290	1.080	1.770	2.070	.250	1.000	1.620
295	.750	1.545	1.870	.400	1.280	...
300	.550	1.325	1.700	.700	1.570	2.240
305	...	...	...	...	...	...
310	.250	1.000	1.410	...	...	...
315	...	...	...	...	...	...

Est vol 6,036 Tu 2,484 calls 2,045 puts
Op int Tues 55,851 calls 44,819 puts

Wheat (CBT)

5,000 bu.; cents per bu.

Price	Mar	May	Jly	Mar	May	Jly
360	19.250	32.375	34.500	3.250	10.000	17.250
370	12.750	26.500	29.750	6.750	14.000	22.500
380	8.000	21.500	25.250	12.000	19.000	28.000
390	4.500	17.500	21.500	18.500	25.000	34.250
400	2.500	14.125	18.250	26.375	31.500	41.000
410	1.375	11.250	15.500	35.250	38.625	48.000

Est vol 4,768 Tu 2,369 calls 1,615 puts
Op int Tues 76,609 calls 56,869 puts

Wheat (KC)

5,000 bu.; cents per bu.

Price	Mar	May	Jly	Mar	May	Jly
360	22.500	30.625	36.375	2.000	10.250	16.000
370	15.000	24.875	31.250	4.500	14.500	20.750
380	9.125	20.000	26.625	8.625	19.500	26.125
390	5.250	16.125	22.750	14.750	25.625	32.125
400	2.875	14.000	19.375	22.375	32.500	38.750
410	2.000	10.500	16.500	31.000	...	...

Est vol 2,045 Tu 437 calls 315 puts
Op int Tues 21,347 calls 19,365 puts

Food and Fiber

Cotton (NYCE)

50,000 lbs.; cents per lb.

STRIKE	CALLS-SETTLE			PUTS-SETTLE		
Price	Mar	May	Jly	Mar	May	Jly
67	2.44	5.85	7.13	.19	1.60	1.87
68	1.64	5.21	6.47	.39	1.95	2.20
69	.90	4.60	5.86	.65	2.34	2.58
70	.46	4.04	5.28	1.21	2.78	3.00
71	.28	3.54	4.75	2.03	3.27	3.46
72	.15	3.07	4.25	2.90	3.80	3.95

Est vol 9,021 Tu 8,443 calls 5,904 puts
Op int Tues 217,446 calls 113,615 puts

Orange Juice (NYCE)

15,000 lbs.; cents per lb.

Price	Mar	May	Jly	Mar	May	Jly
50	11.65	14.45	17.10	.05	.15	.25
55	6.75	9.75	12.60	.10	.40	.75
60	2.40	5.75	8.25	.75	1.35	1.40
65	.45	3.05	5.05	3.50	3.50	3.00
70	.15	1.55	2.95	8.35	7.05	5.90
75	.10	.80	1.70	13.35	11.40	9.55

Est vol 412 Tu 1,547 calls 843 puts
Op int Tues 42,351 calls 14,369 puts

Coffee (CSCE)

37,500 lbs.; cents per lb.

Price	Mar	Apr	May	Mar	Apr	May
67.5	5.40	8.17	9.06	0.30	0.98	1.94
70	3.35	6.38	7.53	0.75	1.85	2.90
72.5	1.85	4.94	6.24	1.75	2.79	4.10
75	1.00	3.82	5.18	3.30	4.17	5.52
77.5	0.49	2.98	4.30	5.39	5.82	7.14
80	0.23	2.34	3.58	7.63	7.68	8.91

Est vol 9,420 Tu 2,864 calls 2,718 puts
Op int Tues 78,119 calls 38,500 puts

Sugar-World (CSCE)

112,000 lbs.; cents per lb.

Price	Mar	Apr	May	Mar	Apr	May
450	1.19	1.39	1.40	0.01	0.01	0.02
500	0.69	0.89	0.93	0.01	0.02	0.06
550	0.25	0.47	0.55	0.07	0.09	0.17
600	0.02	0.18	0.27	0.34	0.30	0.39
650	0.01	0.05	0.12	0.83	0.67	0.74
700	0.01	0.01	0.06	1.33	1.13	1.17

Est vol 2,533 Tu 1,814 calls 1,889 puts
Op int Tues 154,632 calls 112,414 puts

Cocoa (CSCE)

10 metric tons; $ per ton

Price	Mar	Apr	May	Mar	Apr	May
1500	84	108	133	3	39	64
1550	42	78	105	11	59	86
1600	14	54	81	33	85	112
1650	4	36	61	73	117	142
1700	1	24	45	120	155	176
1750	1	15	34	170	196	214

Est vol 1,663 Tu 439 calls 341 puts
Op int Tues 18,472 calls 15,125 puts

Petroleum

Crude Oil (NYM)

1,000 bbls.; $ per bbl.

Price	Mar	Apr	May	Mar	Apr	May
3200	1.53	1.36	1.39	0.43	1.37	2.07
3250	1.20	1.12	1.18	0.60	1.63	2.36
3300	0.91	0.93	1.00	0.81	1.94	2.67
3350	0.66	0.75	0.84	1.06	2.26	3.01
3400	0.49	0.61	0.70	1.39	2.62	3.37
3450	0.33	0.50	0.00	1.73	3.00	...

Est vol 43,517 Tu 13,264 calls 17,244 puts
Op int Tues 341,383 calls 486,295 puts

Heating Oil No.2 (NYM)

42,000 gal.; $ per gal.

STRIKE	CALLS-SETTLE			PUTS-SETTLE		
Price	Mar	Apr	May	Mar	Apr	May
87	.0437	.0426	.0335	.0240	.0540	...
88	.0381	.0386	.0303	.0284	.0600	.0850
89	.0330	.0348	.0275	.0333	.0661	...
90	.0290	.0314	.0248	.0393	.0727	...
91	.0245	.0282	.0224	.0448	.0795	...
92	.0210	.0254	...	.0513	.0866	...

Est vol 815 Tu 800 calls 300 puts
Op int Tues 27,374 calls 19,492 puts

Gasoline-Unlead (NYM)

42,000 gal.; $ per gal.

Price	Mar	Apr	May	Mar	Apr	May
97	.0462	...	.0932	.0305	.0301	.0484
98	.0409	.0842	.0877	.0352	.0338	.0528
99	.0361	...	.0823	.0404	.0378	.0574
100	.0318	.0725	.0773	.0461	.0421	.0623
101	.0279	.0671	.0724	.0522	.0466	.0674
102	.0243	.0619	.0680	.0586	.0514	...

Est vol 2,854 Tu 1,831 calls 1,008 puts
Op int Tues 21,736 calls 17,368 puts

Natural Gas (NYM)

10,000 MMBtu.; $ per MMBtu.

Price	Mar	Apr	May	Mar	Apr	May
555	.382	.276	...	.278	.486	...
560	.358	.260	.238	.304	.519	...
565	.334	.244	...	.330	.553	...
570	.313	.230	.210	.359	.589	...
575	.293	.216	.197	.389	.625	...
580	.275	.203	.185	.421	.662	...

Est vol 37,627 Tu 17,111 calls 19,795 puts
Op int Tues 316,788 calls 386,608 puts

Brent Crude (IPE)

1,000 net bbls.; $ per bbl.

Price	Mar	Apr	May	Mar	Apr	May
	Data not available from source.				...	...
...	...	...				...
	...	...	...	...	...	...
	...	...	...	...	...	...
	...	...	...	...	...	...
	...	...	...	...	...	...
	...	...	...	...	...	...

Est vol Tu calls puts
Op int Tues calls puts

Livestock

Cattle-Feeder (CME)

50,000 lbs.; cents per lb.

Price	Mar	Apr	May	Mar	Apr	May
8000	4.00	5.50	6.28	3.00	2.80	3.10
8100	...	...	...	...	...	...
8200	2.50	4.00	...	3.50	3.30	3.90
8300	2.10	...	...	4.10	...	...
8400	1.60	3.10	4.00	4.60	4.40	4.80
8500	1.20	...	...	5.20	...	...

Est vol 534 Tu 183 calls 261 puts
Op int Tues 3,298 calls 5,427 puts

Cattle-Live (CME)

40,000 lbs.; cents per lb.

Price	Feb	Mar	Apr	Feb	Mar	Apr
73	1.50	...	2.00	0.50	...	4.05
74	0.80	...	1.70	0.80	...	4.75
75	0.35	...	1.50	1.35	...	5.55
76	0.18	...	1.25	2.18	...	6.28
77	0.08	...	1.05	3.08	...	7.08
78	0.03	...	0.85	4.03	...	7.88

Est vol 1,903 Tu 690 calls 855 puts
Op int Tues 40,381 calls 42,076 puts

Hogs-Lean (CME)

40,000 lbs.; cents per lb.

Price	Feb	Apr	May	Feb	Apr	May
57	2.63	3.80	...	0.20	1.93	...
58	1.78	3.18	4.80	0.35	2.30	2.18
59	1.08	2.65	...	0.65	2.78	...
60	0.53	2.15	3.63	1.10	3.28	2.98
61	0.28	1.73	...	...	...	...
62	0.15	1.35	2.68	2.73	...	...

Est vol 243 Tu 207 calls 358 puts
Op int Tues 5,619 calls 6,176 puts

Continued on next page

Table 14.4—Continued

STRIKE CALLS-SETTLE PUTS-SETTLE

Metals

Copper (CMX)

25,000 lbs.; cents per lb.

Price	Mar	Apr	May	Mar	Apr	May
114	5.00	6.00	7.15	1.55	2.90	4.65
116	3.70	4.90	6.15	2.25	3.80	5.60
118	2.55	3.95	5.20	3.10	4.85	6.65
120	1.75	3.10	4.40	4.30	6.00	7.85
122	1.15	1.80	3.70	5.70	9.65	9.10
124	0.70	1.00	3.05	7.25	13.90	10.50

Est vol 1,650 Tu 247 calls 23 puts
Op int Tues 12,848 calls 3,638 puts

Gold (CMX)

100 troy ounces; $ per troy ounce

Price	Mar	Apr	Jun	Mar	Apr	Jun
390	13.50	16.80	21.80	1.90	5.10	9.20
395	10.00	13.70	19.00	3.30	7.00	11.40
400	7.00	11.00	17.50	5.30	9.30	14.90
405	4.80	8.80	14.30	8.10	12.10	16.60
410	3.20	6.60	12.50	11.50	14.90	19.70
415	2.10	5.50	10.80	15.40	18.80	23.00

Est vol 18,000 Tu 4,487 calls 5,463 puts
Op int Tues 306,159 calls 227,854 puts

Silver (CMX)

5,000 troy ounces; cts per troy ounce

Price	Mar	Apr	May	Mar	Apr	May
610	20.30	30.50	38.40	15.50	24.40	32.20
620	15.90	26.30	34.30	21.10	30.10	38.10
625	14.00	24.40	32.40	24.20	33.20	41.20
630	12.40	22.70	30.70	27.60	36.40	44.40
640	9.70	19.50	27.50	34.90	43.20	51.20
650	7.60	16.80	24.70	42.70	50.50	58.40

Est vol 1,800 Tu 1,474 calls 1,954 puts
Op int Tues 66,669 calls 26,556 puts

Interest Rate

T-Bonds (CBT)

$100,000; points and 64ths of 100%

Price	Mar	Apr	May	Mar	Apr	May
110	2-06	2-03	2-35	0-36	1-61	2-29
111	1-28	1-36	...	0-58	2-30	...
112	0-58	1-11	1-42	1-24	3-04	...
113	0-34	0-54	...	2-00	3-48	...
114	0-19	0-39	...	2-49	4-32	...
115	0-10	0-27	0-49	3-40	5-20	...

Est vol 23,701;
Tu vol 14,191 calls 17,000 puts
Op int Tues 412,644 calls 444,891 puts

T-Notes (CBT)

$100,000; points and 64ths of 100%

Price	Mar	Apr	May	Mar	Apr	May
112	2-00	1-30	1-52	0-20	1-25	1-46
113	1-17	1-00	...	0-37	1-58	...
114	0-44	0-41	0-59	1-00	...	...
115	0-20	0-24	0-40	1-40	...	...
116	0-08	0-14	0-26	2-28	...	...
117	0-03	0-08	0-16	...	...	...

Est vol 150,806 Tu 61,052 calls 65,301 puts
Op int Tues 1,045,055 calls 1,083,950 puts

5 Yr Treas Notes (CBT)

$100,000; points and 64ths of 100%

Price	Mar	Apr	May	Mar	Apr	May
11150	1-16	0-49	0-62	0-15	1-08	1-21
11200	0-56	0-36	...	0-22	1-27	...
11250	0-36	0-25	...	0-34	...	...
11300	0-22	0-17	...	0-52	...	...
11350	0-12	0-11	...	1-10	...	...
11400	0-06	...	...	1-36	...	...

Est vol 17,994 Tu 4,736 calls 25,086 puts
Op int Tues 125,023 calls 426,615 puts

30 Day Federal Funds (CBT)

$5,000,000; 100 minus daily average

Price	Feb	Mar	Apr	Feb	Mar	Apr
988750	.127	.117	.120	.002	.002	.005
989375	.065	.062	.060	.002	.007	.007
990000	.007	.007	.007	.007	.017	.017
990625	...	.002	.002	...	...	...
991250	.002	.002	...	...	...	...
991875	...	...	...	...	...	...

Est vol 330 Tu 1,199 calls 1,303 puts
Op int Tues 128,420 calls 162,873 puts

Eurodollar (CME)

$ million; pts. of 100%

Price	Feb	Mar	Apr	Feb	Mar	Apr
9825	...	5.90	...	0.00	0.00	0.12
9850	...	3.42	2.22	0.00	0.02	0.37
9875	0.95	1.02	0.45	0.05	0.12	1.10
9900	...	0.05	0.02	...	1.65	...
9925	...	0.00	...	...	4.10	...
9950	...	0.00	...	...	6.60	...

Est vol 288,753;
Tu vol 83,303 calls 142,595 puts
Op int Tues 4,268,863 calls 4,408,535 puts

1 Yr. Mid-Curve Eurodlr (CME)

$1,000,000 contract units; pts. of 100%

Price	Feb	Mar	Apr	Feb	Mar	Apr
9725	4.02	4.65	2.75	0.17	0.80	2.95
9750	2.05	2.87	1.60	0.70	1.52	...
9775	0.70	1.55	0.82	1.85	2.70	...
9800	0.15	0.65	0.35	3.80	4.30	...
9825	0.02	0.20	0.15	...	6.35	...
9850	0.00	0.05	...	...	...	...

Est vol 210,600 Tu 61,545 calls 129,840 puts
Op int Tues 934,544 calls 932,093 puts

2 Yr. Mid-Curve Eurodlr (CME)

$1,000,000 contract units; pts. of 100%

Price	Mar	Jun	Sep	Mar	Jun	Sep
9575	6.00	5.70	...	0.50	2.45	...
9600	4.00	4.10	4.05	1.00	3.35	5.40
9625	2.45	2.82	2.90	1.95	4.57	...
9650	1.27	1.85	...	3.27	6.07	...
9675	0.60	1.12	...	5.10	...	...
9700	0.17	0.50	...	7.17	...	...

Est vol 800 Tu 8,400 calls 0 puts
Op int Tues 158,035 calls 33,178 puts

Euribor (LIFFE)

Euro 1,000,000

Price	Feb	Mar	Apr	Feb	Mar	Apr
97750	0.18	0.19	0.17	...	0.00	0.02
97875	0.06	0.07	0.08	0.00	0.01	0.06
98000	0.01	0.03	0.03	0.07	0.09	0.13
98125	...	0.01	0.01	0.19	0.20	0.24
98250	...	0.00	0.00	0.31	0.32	0.35
98375	...	...	0.00	0.44	0.44	0.48

Vol Wd 327,805 calls 29,183 puts
Op int Tues 5,655,304 calls 1,807,541 puts

Euro-BUND (EUREX)

100,000; pts. In 100%

Price	Mar	Apr	May	Mar	Apr	May
11350	1.01	0.78	1.02	0.25	1.00	1.24
11400	0.68	0.56	0.78	0.42	1.28	1.50
11450	0.42	0.39	0.61	0.66	1.61	1.83
11500	0.22	0.26	0.46	0.96	1.98	2.18
11550	0.11	0.17	0.34	1.35	2.39	2.56
11600	0.06	0.10	...	1.80	2.82	...

Vol Wd 35,857 calls 42,186 puts
Op int Tues 366,384 calls 479,188 puts

Currency

Japanese Yen (CME)

12,500,000 yen; cents per 100 yen

Price	Feb	Mar	Apr	Feb	Mar	Apr
9400	1.03	1.72	2.30	0.06	0.75	1.04
9450	0.60	1.44	2.03	0.13	0.97	1.27
9500	0.30	1.19	1.78	0.33	1.22	1.52
9550	0.13	0.98	1.56	0.66	...	...
9600	0.06	0.81	1.36	1.09	1.84	...
9650	0.04	0.67	...	...	...	...

Est vol 1,352 Tu 1,271 calls 531 puts
Op int Tues 23,459 calls 20,676 puts

Canadian Dollar (CME)

100,000 Can.$, cents per Can.$

Price	Feb	Mar	Apr	Feb	Mar	Apr
7400	...	1.35	...	0.07	0.50	...
7450	0.51	1.04	...	0.16	0.69	...
7500	0.23	0.77	1.03	0.38	0.92	1.38
7550	0.10	0.57	...	0.75	1.22	...
7600	0.05	0.42	...	1.19	1.57	...
7650	0.02	0.31	...	1.67	1.96	...

Est vol 419 Tu 219 calls 163 puts
Op int Tues 12,761 calls 9,409 puts

British Pound (CME)

62,500 pounds; cents per pound

Price	Feb	Mar	Apr	Feb	Mar	Apr
1810	2.01	3.13	...	0.24	1.36	...
1820	1.13	2.53	...	0.36	1.76	...
1830	0.68	2.04	...	0.91	2.27	...
1840	0.34	1.60	...	1.57	2.83	...
1850	0.16	1.24	1.66	...	...	...
1860	0.08	0.96	1.42	3.31	...	...

Est vol 755 Tu 242 calls 625 puts
Op int Tues 6,257 calls 5,097 puts

Swiss Franc (CME)

125,000 francs; cents per franc

Price	Feb	Mar	Apr	Feb	Mar	Apr
7900	1.10	1.70	...	0.08	0.68	...
7950	0.69	1.39	...	0.17	0.87	...
8000	0.37	1.11	...	0.35	1.09	...
8050	0.18	0.89	...	0.66	1.37	...
8100	0.10	0.71	...	1.08	1.69	...
8150	0.05	0.55	...	1.53	2.03	...

Est vol 189 Tu 44 calls 384 puts
Op int Tues 1,690 calls 2,356 puts

Euro Fx (CME)

125,000 euros; cents per euro

Price	Feb	Mar	Apr	Feb	Mar	Apr
12400	1.35	2.36	2.82	0.15	1.16	1.91
12450	0.98	2.07	2.55	0.28	1.37	2.14
12500	0.66	1.81	2.31	0.46	1.61	2.40
12550	0.42	1.56	2.08	0.72	1.86	2.67
12600	0.26	1.34	1.87	1.06	2.14	2.96
12650	0.15	1.14	1.68	1.45	2.44	3.27

Est vol 3,767 Tu 3,252 calls 2,088 puts
Op int Tues 39,137 calls 43,286 puts

Index

DJ Industrial Avg (CBOT)

$100 times premium

Price	Feb	Mar	Apr	Feb	Mar	Apr
102	28.50	37.00	42.40	4.50	13.25	20.50
103	21.00	30.00	35.50	7.00	16.25	...
104	14.50	24.00	29.75	10.50	20.00	...
105	9.00	18.50	24.25	15.00	24.50	...
106	5.50	14.00	19.50	21.50	30.00	...
107	3.00	10.00	...	29.00	...	...

Est vol 124 Tu 111 calls 72 puts
Op int Tues 5,861 calls 5,480 puts

S&P 500 Stock Index (CME)

$250 times premium

Price	Feb	Mar	Apr	Feb	Mar	Apr
1115	19.70	29.90	37.80	10.80	21.00	29.90
1120	16.60	26.90	34.90	12.70	23.00	32.00
1125	13.80	24.00	32.00	14.90	25.10	34.10
1130	11.30	21.40	29.30	17.40	27.50	36.40
1135	9.10	19.00	26.80	20.20	30.10	...
1140	7.20	16.70	24.30	23.30	32.80	41.30

Est vol 14,455 Tu 4,759 calls 10,464 puts
Op int Tues 88,723 calls 228,763 puts

Other Options

Nasdaq 100 (CME)

$100 times NASDAQ 100 Index

Price	Feb	Mar	Apr	Feb	Mar	Apr
1460	...	...	...	...	...	...

Est vol 41 Tu 3 calls 2 puts
Op int Tues 2,185 calls 958 puts

NYSE Composite (NYFE)

$50 times premium

Price	Feb	Mar	Apr	Feb	Mar	Apr
6500	7450	12100	16400	6500	11150	16450

Est vol 0 Tu 3 calls 20 puts
Op int Tues 1 calls 9,514 puts

Source: Reprinted by permission of Dow Jones, Inc., via Copyright Clearance Center, Inc.

Interest rate futures option contracts work in the same way as the other futures options contracts discussed in this chapter. For example, the payoff from a call is $\max(F - K, 0)$, where F is the futures price at the time of exercise and K is the strike price. In addition to the cash payoff, the option holder obtains a long position in the futures contract when the option is exercised and the option writer obtains a corresponding short position.

Interest rate futures prices increase when bond prices increase (i.e., when interest rates fall). They decrease when bond prices decrease (i.e., when interest rates rise). An investor who thinks that short-term interest rates will rise can speculate by buying put options on Eurodollar futures, whereas an investor who thinks the rates will fall can speculate by buying call options on Eurodollar futures. An investor who thinks that long-term interest rates will rise can speculate by buying put options on Treasury note futures or Treasury bond futures, whereas an investor who thinks the rates will fall can speculate by buying call options on these instruments.

Example 14.5

It is February and the futures price for the June Eurodollar contract is 93.82 (corresponding to a 3-month Eurodollar interest rate of 6.18% per annum). The price of a call option on the contract with a strike price of 94.00 is quoted at the CME as 0.1, or 10 basis points (corresponding to a *Wall Street Journal* quote of 1.00). This option could be attractive to an investor who feels that interest rates are likely to come down. Suppose that short-term interest rates do drop by about 100 basis points and the investor exercises the call when the Eurodollar futures price is 94.78 (corresponding to a 3-month Eurodollar interest rate of 5.22% per annum). The payoff is $25 \times (94.78 - 94.00) = \$1{,}950$. The cost of the contract is $10 \times 25 = \$250$. The investor's profit is therefore \$1,700.

Example 14.6

It is August and the futures price for the December Treasury bond contract traded on the CBOT is 96-09 (or $96\frac{9}{32} = 96.28125$). The yield on long-term government bonds is about 6.4% per annum. An investor who feels that this yield will fall by December might choose to buy December calls with a strike price of 98. Assume that the price of these calls is 1-04 (or $1\frac{4}{64} = 1.0625\%$ of the principal). If long-term rates fall to 6% per annum and the Treasury bond futures price rises to 100-00, the investor will make a net profit per \$100 of bond futures of

$$100.00 - 98.00 - 1.0625 = 0.9375$$

Since one option contract is for the purchase or sale of instruments with a face value of \$100,000, the investor would make a profit of \$937.50 per option contract bought.

Reasons for the Popularity of Futures Options

It is natural to ask why people choose to trade options on futures rather than options on the underlying asset. The main reason appears to be that a futures contract is, in many circumstances, more liquid and easier to trade than the underlying asset. Furthermore, a futures price is known immediately from trading on the futures exchange, whereas the spot price of the underlying asset may not be so readily available.

Consider Treasury bonds. The market for Treasury bond futures is much more active than the market for any particular Treasury bond. Moreover, a Treasury bond futures price is known immediately from trading on the CBOT. By contrast, the current market price of a bond can be obtained only by contacting one or more dealers. It is not surprising that investors would rather take delivery of a Treasury bond futures contract than Treasury bonds.

Futures on commodities are also often easier to trade than the commodities themselves. For example, it is much easier and more convenient to make or take delivery of a live-hogs futures contract than it is to make or take delivery of the hogs themselves.

An important point about a futures option is that exercising it does not usually lead to delivery of the underlying asset. This is because, in most circumstances, the underlying futures contract is closed out prior to delivery. Futures options are therefore normally eventually settled in cash. This is appealing to many investors, particularly those with limited capital who may find it difficult to come up with the funds to buy the underlying asset when an option is exercised.

Another advantage sometimes cited for futures options is that futures and futures options are traded in pits side by side in the same exchange. This facilitates hedging, arbitrage, and speculation. It also tends to make the markets more efficient.

A final point is that futures options tend to entail lower transactions costs than spot options in many situations.

Put–Call Parity

In Chapter 9, we derived a put–call parity relationship for European stock options. We now present a similar argument to derive a put–call parity relationship for European futures options on the assumption that there is no difference between the payoffs from futures and forward contracts.

Consider European call and put futures options, both with strike price K and time to expiration T. We can form two portfolios:

Portfolio A: a European call futures option plus an amount of cash equal to Ke^{-rT}

Portfolio B: a European put futures option plus a long futures contract plus an amount of cash equal to F_0e^{-rT}

In portfolio A, the cash can be invested at the risk-free rate r and will grow to K at time T. Let F_T be the futures price at maturity of the option. If $F_T > K$, the call option in portfolio A is exercised and portfolio A is worth F_T. If $F_T \leqslant K$, the call is not exercised and portfolio A is worth K. The value of portfolio A at time T is therefore given by

$$\max(F_T, K)$$

In portfolio B, the cash can be invested at the risk-free rate to grow to F_0 at time T. The put option provides a payoff of $\max(K - F_T, 0)$. The futures contract provides a payoff of $F_T - F_0$. The value of portfolio B at time T is therefore given by

$$F_0 + (F_T - F_0) + \max(K - F_T, 0) = \max(F_T, K)$$

Since the two portfolios have the same value at time T and there are no early exercise opportunities, it follows that they are worth the same today. The value of portfolio A today is

$$c + Ke^{-rT}$$

where c is the price of the call futures option. The marking-to-market process ensures that the futures contract in portfolio B is worth zero today. Therefore, portfolio B is worth

$$p + F_0 e^{-rT}$$

where p is the price of the put futures option. Hence,

$$c + Ke^{-rT} = p + F_0 e^{-rT} \tag{14.11}$$

This is the same as put–call parity for options on a non-dividend-paying stock in equation (9.3) except that the stock price is replaced by the futures price times e^{-rT}

For American options, the put–call parity relationship is (see Problem 14.38)

$$F_0 e^{-rT} - K \leqslant C - P \leqslant F_0 - Ke^{-rT}$$

Example 14.7

Suppose that the price of a European call option on silver futures for delivery in 6 months is \$0.56 per ounce when the exercise price is \$8.50. Assume that the silver futures price for delivery in 6 months is currently \$8.00 and the risk-free interest rate for an investment that matures in 6 months is 10% per annum. From a rearrangement of equation (14.11), the price of a European put option on silver futures with the same maturity and exercise price as the call option is

$$0.56 + 8.50e^{-0.1\times 0.5} - 8.00e^{-0.1\times 0.5} = 1.04$$

14.6 VALUATION OF FUTURES OPTIONS USING BINOMIAL TREES

This section examines, more formally than in Chapter 11, how binomial trees can be used to price futures options. The key difference between futures options and stock options is that there are no up-front costs when a futures contract is entered into.

Suppose that the current futures price is 30 and it is expected to move either up to 33 or down to 28 over the next month. We consider a 1-month call option on the futures with a strike price of 29 and ignore daily settlement. The situation is shown in Figure 14.1. If the futures price proves to be 33, then the payoff from the option is 4 and the value of the futures contract is 3. If the futures price proves to be 28, then the payoff from the option is zero and the value of the futures contract is -2.[3]

To set up a riskless hedge, we consider a portfolio consisting of a short position in one option contract and a long position in Δ futures contracts. If the futures price moves up to 33, the value of the portfolio is $3\Delta - 4$; if it moves down to 28, the value of the portfolio is -2Δ. The portfolio is riskless when these are the same—that is,

---

[3] There is an approximation here in that the gain or loss on the futures contract is not realized at time T. It is realized day by day between time 0 and time T. However, as the length of the time step in a binomial tree becomes shorter, the approximation becomes better, and in the limit, as the time step tends to zero, an accurate answer is obtained.

Figure 14.1 Futures price movements in numerical example.

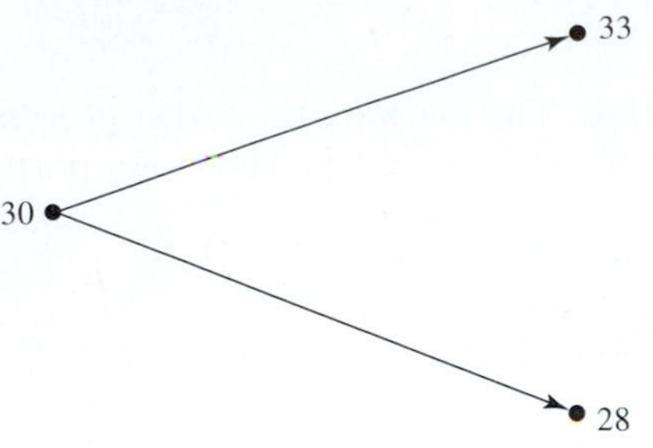

when

$$3\Delta - 4 = -2\Delta$$

or $\Delta = 0.8$.

For this value of Δ, we know the portfolio will be worth $3 \times 0.8 - 4 = -1.6$ in 1 month. Assume a risk-free interest rate of 6%. The value of the portfolio today must be

$$-1.6e^{-0.06\times 0.08333} = -1.592$$

The portfolio consists of one short option and Δ futures contracts. Since the value of the futures contract today is zero, the value of the option today must be 1.592.

A Generalization

We can generalize this analysis by considering a futures price that starts at F_0 and is anticipated to rise to F_0u or move down to F_0d over the time period T. We consider a derivative maturing at the end of the time period, and we suppose that its payoff is f_u if the futures price moves up and f_d if it moves down. The situation is summarized in Figure 14.2.

The riskless portfolio in this case consists of a short position in one option combined with a long position in Δ futures contracts, where

$$\Delta = \frac{f_u - f_d}{F_0u - F_0d}$$

Figure 14.2 Futures price and option price in general situation.

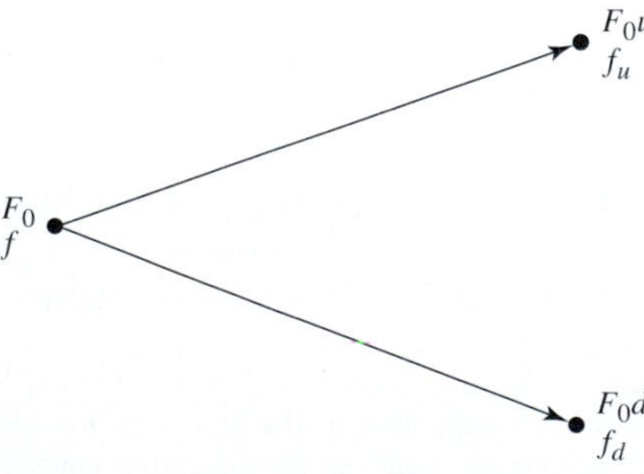

The value of the portfolio at the end of the time period, then, is always

$$(F_0u - F_0)\Delta - f_u$$

Denoting the risk-free interest rate by r, we obtain the value of the portfolio today as

$$[(F_0u - F_0)\Delta - f_u]e^{-rT}$$

Another expression for the present value of the portfolio is $-f$, where f is the value of the option today. It follows that

$$-f = [(F_0u - F_0)\Delta - f_u]e^{-rT}$$

Substituting for Δ and simplifying reduces this equation to

$$f = e^{-rT}[pf_u + (1-p)f_d] \qquad \textbf{(14.12)}$$

where

$$p = \frac{1-d}{u-d} \qquad \textbf{(14.13)}$$

In the numerical example in Figure 14.1, $u = 1.1$, $d = 0.9333$, $r = 0.06$, $T = 0.08333$, $f_u = 4$, and $f_d = 0$. From equation (14.13), we have

$$p = \frac{1 - 0.9333}{1.1 - 0.9333} = 0.4$$

and, from equation (14.12),

$$f = e^{-0.06\times 0.08333}(0.4 \times 4 + 0.6 \times 0) = 1.592$$

This result agrees with the answer obtained for this example earlier.

Multistep Trees

In practice, trees are used to value American-style futures options in the same way as they are used to value options on stocks. This is explained in Section 11.9. An example is in Example 11.3 and Figure 11.13.

14.7 THE DRIFT OF FUTURES PRICES IN A RISK-NEUTRAL WORLD

There is a general result that allows us to use the analysis in Section 14.1 for futures options. This result is that in a risk-neutral world a futures price behaves in the same way as a stock paying a dividend yield at the domestic risk-free interest rate r.

One clue that this might be so is given by noting that the equation for p in a binomial tree for a futures price is the same as that for a stock paying a dividend yield equal to q when $q = r$. Another clue is that the put–call parity relationship for futures options prices is the same as that for options on a stock paying a dividend yield at rate q when the stock price is replaced by the futures price and $q = r$.

To prove the result formally, we calculate the drift of a futures price in a risk-neutral world. We define F_t as the futures price at time t. If we enter into a long futures contract today, its value is zero. At time Δt (the first time it is marked to market) it provides a payoff of $F_{\Delta t} - F_0$. If r is the very-short-term (Δt-period) interest rate at time 0, risk-neutral valuation gives the value of the contract at time 0 as

$$e^{-r\Delta t}\hat{E}[F_{\Delta t} - F_0]$$

where $\hat{E}$ denotes expectations in a risk-neutral world. We must therefore have

$$e^{-r\Delta t}\hat{E}(F_{\Delta t} - F_0) = 0$$

showing that

$$\hat{E}(F_{\Delta t}) = F_0$$

Similarly, $\hat{E}(F_{2\Delta t}) = F_{\Delta t}$, $\hat{E}(F_{3\Delta t}) = F_{2\Delta t}$, and so on. Putting many results like this together, we see that

$$\hat{E}(F_T) = F_0$$

for any time T

The drift of the futures price in a risk-neutral world is therefore zero. From equation (14.7), then, the futures price behaves like a stock providing a dividend yield q equal to r. This result is a very general one. It is true for all futures prices and does not depend on any assumptions about interest rates, volatilities, etc.[4]

The usual assumption made for the process followed by a futures price F in the risk-neutral world is

$$dF = \sigma F\,dz \tag{14.14}$$

where σ is a constant.

Differential Equation

For another way of seeing that a futures price behaves like a stock paying a dividend yield at rate q, we can derive the differential equation satisfied by a derivative dependent on a futures price in the same way as we derived the differential equation for a derivative dependent on a non-dividend-paying stock in Section 13.6. This is[5]

$$\frac{\partial f}{\partial t} + \tfrac{1}{2}\frac{\partial^2 f}{\partial F^2}\sigma^2 F^2 = rf \tag{14.15}$$

It has the same form as equation (14.6) with q set equal to r. This confirms that, for the purpose of valuing derivatives, a futures price can be treated in the same way as a stock providing a dividend yield at rate r.

14.8 BLACK'S MODEL FOR VALUING FUTURES OPTIONS

European futures options can be valued by extending the results we have produced. Fischer Black was the first to show this in a paper published in 1976.[6] The underlying

[4] As we will discover in Chapter 25, a more precise statement of the result is: "A futures price has zero drift in the traditional risk-neutral world where the numeraire is the money market account." A zero-drift stochastic process is known as a martingale. A forward price is a martingale in a different risk-neutral world. This is one where the numeraire is a zero-coupon bond maturing at time T.

[5] See Technical Note 7 on the author's website for a proof of this.

[6] See F. Black, "The Pricing of Commodity Contracts," *Journal of Financial Economics*, 3 (March 1976): 167–79.

assumption is that futures prices have the same lognormal property that we assumed for stock prices in Chapter 13. The European call price c and the European put price p for a futures option are given by equations (14.4) and (14.5) with S_0 replaced by F_0 and $q = r$:

$$c = e^{-rT}[F_0 N(d_1) - KN(d_2)] \tag{14.16}$$

$$p = e^{-rT}[KN(-d_2) - F_0 N(-d_1)] \tag{14.17}$$

where

$$d_1 = \frac{\ln(F_0/K) + \sigma^2 T/2}{\sigma\sqrt{T}}$$

$$d_2 = \frac{\ln(F_0/K) - \sigma^2 T/2}{\sigma\sqrt{T}} = d_1 - \sigma\sqrt{T}$$

and σ is the volatility of the futures price. When the cost of carry and the convenience yield are functions only of time, it can be shown that the volatility of the futures price is the same as the volatility of the underlying asset. Note that Black's model does not require the option contract and the futures contract to mature at the same time.

Example 14.8

Consider a European put futures option on crude oil. The time to the option's maturity is 4 months, the current futures price is \$20, the exercise price is \$20, the risk-free interest rate is 9% per annum, and the volatility of the futures price is 25% per annum. In this case, $F_0 = 20$, $K = 20$, $r = 0.09$, $T = 4/12$, $\sigma = 0.25$, and $\ln(F_0/K) = 0$, so that

$$d_1 = \frac{\sigma\sqrt{T}}{2} = 0.07216$$

$$d_2 = -\frac{\sigma\sqrt{T}}{2} = -0.07216$$

$$N(-d_1) = 0.4712, \qquad N(-d_2) = 0.5288$$

and the put price p is given by

$$p = e^{-0.09\times 4/12}(20 \times 0.5288 - 20 \times 0.4712) = 1.12$$

or \$1.12.

14.9 FUTURES OPTIONS vs. SPOT OPTIONS

In this section we compare options on futures and options on spot when they have the same strike price and time to maturity. An *option on spot* or *spot option* is a regular option to buy or sell the underlying asset in the spot market.

The payoff from a European spot call option with strike price K is

$$\max(S_T - K, 0)$$

where S_T is the spot price at the option's maturity. The payoff from a European futures call option with the same strike price is

$$\max(F_T - K, 0)$$

where F_T is the futures price at the option's maturity. If the European futures option matures at the same time as the futures contract, $F_T = S_T$ and the two options are in theory equivalent. If the European call futures option matures before the futures contract, it is worth more than the corresponding spot option in a normal market (where futures prices are higher than spot prices) and less than the corresponding spot option in an inverted market (where futures prices are lower than spot prices).

Similarly, a European futures put option is worth the same as its spot option counterpart when the futures option matures at the same time as the futures contract. If the European put futures option matures before the futures contract, it is worth less than the corresponding spot option in a normal market and more than the corresponding spot option in an inverted market.

Results for American Options

Traded futures options are, in practice, usually American. Assuming that the risk-free rate of interest, r, is positive, there is always some chance that it will be optimal to exercise an American futures option early. American futures options are, therefore, worth more than their European counterparts.

It is not generally true that an American futures option is worth the same as the corresponding American spot option when the futures and options contracts have the same maturity. Suppose, for example, that there is a normal market with futures prices consistently higher than spot prices prior to maturity. This is the case with most stock indices, gold, silver, low-interest currencies, and some commodities. An American call futures option must be worth more than the corresponding American spot call option. The reason is that in some situations the futures option will be exercised early, in which case it will provide a greater profit to the holder. Similarly, an American put futures option must be worth less than the corresponding American spot put option. If there is an inverted market with futures prices consistently lower than spot prices, as is the case with high-interest currencies and some commodities, the reverse must be true. American call futures options are worth less than the corresponding American spot call option, whereas American put futures options are worth more than the corresponding American spot put option.

The differences just described between American futures options and American spot options hold true when the futures contract expires later than the options contract as well as when the two expire at the same time. In fact, the differences tend to be greater the later the futures contract expires.

SUMMARY

The Black–Scholes formula for valuing European options on a non-dividend-paying stock can be extended to cover European options on a stock providing a known dividend yield. This is a useful result because a number of other assets on which options are written can be considered to be analogous to a stock providing a dividend yield. In particular:

1. An index is analogous to a stock providing a dividend yield. The dividend yield is the average dividend yield on the stocks composing the index.

2. A foreign currency is analogous to a stock providing a dividend yield where the dividend yield is the foreign risk-free interest rate.
3. A futures price is analogous to a stock providing a dividend yield where the dividend yield is equal to the domestic risk-free interest rate.

The extension to Black–Scholes can, therefore, be used to value European options on indices, foreign currencies, and futures contracts.

Index options are settled in cash. Upon exercise of an index call option, the holder receives the amount by which the index exceeds the strike price at close of trading. Similarly, upon exercise of an index put option, the holder receives the amount by which the strike price exceeds the index at close of trading. Index options can be used for portfolio insurance. If the portfolio has a β of 1.0, it is appropriate to buy one put option for each $100S_0$ dollars in the portfolio, where S_0 is the value of the index; otherwise, β put options should be purchased for each $100S_0$ dollars in the portfolio, where β is the beta of the portfolio calculated using the capital asset pricing model. The strike price of the put options purchased should reflect the level of insurance required.

Currency options are traded both on organized exchanges and over the counter. They can be used by corporate treasurers to hedge foreign exchange exposure. For example, a US corporate treasurer who knows that sterling will be received at a certain time in the future can hedge by buying put options that mature at that time. Similarly, a US corporate treasurer who knows that the company will be paying sterling at a certain time in the future can hedge by buying call options that mature at that time.

Futures options require the delivery of the underlying futures contract upon exercise. When a call is exercised, the holder acquires a long futures position plus a cash amount equal to the excess of the futures price over the strike price. Similarly, when a put is exercised, the holder acquires a short position plus a cash amount equal to the excess of the strike price over the futures price. The futures contract that is delivered typically expires slightly later than the option. If we assume that the two expiration dates are the same, a European futures option is worth exactly the same as the corresponding European spot option. However, this is not true of American options. If the futures market is normal, an American call futures option is worth more than the corresponding American spot call option, while an American put futures is worth less than the corresponding American spot put option. If the futures market is inverted, the reverse is true.

FURTHER READING

General

Merton, R. C. "Theory of Rational Option Pricing," *Bell Journal of Economics and Management Science*, 4 (Spring 1973): 141–83.

Bodie, Z. "On the Risk of Stocks in the Long Run," *Financial Analysts Journal*, 51, 3 (1995): 18–22.

On Options on Currencies

Amin, K., and R. A. Jarrow. "Pricing Foreign Currency Options under Stochastic Interest Rates," *Journal of International Money and Finance*, 10 (1991): 310–29.

Biger, N., and J. C. Hull. "The Valuation of Currency Options," *Financial Management*, 12 (Spring 1983): 24–28.

Garman, M. B., and S. W. Kohlhagen. "Foreign Currency Option Values," *Journal of International Money and Finance*, 2 (December 1983): 231–37.

Giddy, I. H. and G. Dufey. "Uses and Abuses of Currency Options," *Journal of Applied Corporate Finance*, 8, 3 (1995): 49–57.

Grabbe, J. O. "The Pricing of Call and Put Options on Foreign Exchange," *Journal of International Money and Finance*, 2 (December 1983): 239–53.

Jorion, P. "Predicting Volatility in the Foreign Exchange Market," *Journal of Finance* 50, 2 (1995): 507–28.

On Options on Futures

Black, F. "The Pricing of Commodity Contracts," *Journal of Financial Economics*, 3 (March 1976): 167–79.

Hilliard, J. E., and J. Reis. "Valuation of Commodity Futures and Options under Stochastic Convenience Yields, Interest Rates, and Jump Diffusions in the Spot," *Journal of Financial and Quantitative Analysis*, 33, 1 (March 1998): 61–86.

Miltersen, K. R., and E. S. Schwartz. "Pricing of Options on Commodity Futures with Stochastic Term Structures of Convenience Yields and Interest Rates," *Journal of Financial and Quantitative Analysis*, 33, 1 (March 1998), 33–59.

Questions and Problems (Answers in Solutions Manual)

14.1. A portfolio is currently worth $10 million and has a beta of 1.0. The S&P 100 is currently standing at 500. Explain how a put option on the S&P 100 with a strike of 480 can be used to provide portfolio insurance.

14.2. "Once we know how to value options on a stock paying a dividend yield, we know how to value options on stock indices, currencies, and futures." Explain this statement.

14.3. A stock index is currently 300, the dividend yield on the index is 3% per annum, and the risk-free interest rate is 8% per annum. What is a lower bound for the price of a 6-month European call option on the index when the strike price is 290?

14.4. A currency is currently worth $0.80. Over each of the next 2 months it is expected to increase or decrease in value by 2%. The domestic and foreign risk-free interest rates are 6% and 8%, respectively. What is the value of a 2-month European call option with a strike price of $0.80?

14.5. Explain the difference between a call option on yen and a call option on yen futures.

14.6. Explain how currency options can be used for hedging.

14.7. Calculate the value of a 3-month at-the-money European call option on a stock index when the index is at 250, the risk-free interest rate is 10% per annum, the volatility of the index is 18% per annum, and the dividend yield on the index is 3% per annum.

14.8. Consider an American call futures option where the futures contract and the option contract expire at the same time. Under what circumstances is the futures option worth more than the corresponding American option on the underlying asset?

14.9. Calculate the value of an 8-month European put option on a currency with a strike price of 0.50. The current exchange rate is 0.52, the volatility of the exchange rate is 12%, the domestic risk-free interest rate is 4% per annum, and the foreign risk-free interest rate is 8% per annum.

14.10. Why are options on bond futures more actively traded than options on bonds?

14.11. "A futures price is like a stock paying a dividend yield." What is the dividend yield?

14.12. A futures price is currently 50. At the end of 6 months it will be either 56 or 46. The risk-free interest rate is 6% per annum. What is the value of a 6-month European call option with a strike price of 50?

14.13. Calculate the value of a 5-month European put futures option when the futures price is $19, the strike price is $20, the risk-free interest rate is 12% per annum, and the volatility of the futures price is 20% per annum.

14.14. A total return index tracks the return, including dividends, on a certain portfolio. Explain how you would value (a) forward contracts and (b) European options on the index.

14.15. The S&P 100 index currently stands at 696 and has a volatility of 30% per annum. The risk-free rate of interest is 7% per annum and the index provides a dividend yield of 4% per annum. Calculate the value of a 3-month European put with strike price 700.

14.16. What is the put–call parity relationship for European currency options?

14.17. A foreign currency is currently worth $1.50. The domestic and foreign risk-free interest rates are 5% and 9%, respectively. Calculate a lower bound for the value of a 6-month call option on the currency with a strike price of $1.40 if it is (a) European and (b) American.

14.18. Consider a stock index currently standing at 250. The dividend yield on the index is 4% per annum and the risk-free rate is 6% per annum. A 3-month European call option on the index with a strike price of 245 is currently worth $10. What is the value of a 3-month European put option on the index with a strike price of 245?

14.19. Would you expect the volatility of a stock index to be greater or less than the volatility of a typical stock? Explain your answer.

14.20. Does the cost of portfolio insurance increase or decrease as the beta of the portfolio increases? Explain your answer.

14.21. Suppose that a portfolio is worth $60 million and the S&P 500 is at 1200. If the value of the portfolio mirrors the value of the index, what options should be purchased to provide protection against the value of the portfolio falling below $54 million in 1 year's time?

14.22. Consider again the situation in Problem 14.21. Suppose that the portfolio has a beta of 2.0, that the risk-free interest rate is 5% per annum, and that the dividend yield on both the portfolio and the index is 3% per annum. What options should be purchased to provide protection against the value of the portfolio falling below $54 million in 1 year's time?

14.23. Suppose you buy a put option contract on October gold futures with a strike price of $400 per ounce. Each contract is for the delivery of 100 ounces. What happens if you exercise when the October futures price is $377 and the most recent settlement price is $380?

14.24. Suppose you sell a call option contract on April live-cattle futures with a strike price of 70 cents per pound. Each contract is for the delivery of 40,000 pounds. What happens if the contract is exercised when the futures price is 76 cents and the most recent settlement price is 75 cents?

14.25. Consider a 2-month call futures option with a strike price of 40 when the risk-free interest rate is 10% per annum. The current futures price is 47. What is a lower bound for the value of the futures option if it is (a) European and (b) American?

14.26. Consider a 4-month put futures option with a strike price of 50 when the risk-free interest rate is 10% per annum. The current futures price is 47. What is a lower bound for the value of the futures option if it is (a) European and (b) American?

14.27. A futures price is currently 60. It is known that over each of the next two 3-month periods it will either rise by 10% or fall by 10%. The risk-free interest rate is 8% per annum. What is the value of a 6-month European call option on the futures with a strike price of 60? If the call were American, would it ever be worth exercising it early?

14.28. In Problem 14.27, what is the value of a 6-month European put option on futures with a strike price of 60? If the put were American, would it ever be worth exercising it early? Verify that the call prices calculated in Problem 14.27 and the put prices calculated here satisfy put–call parity relationships.

14.29. A futures price is currently 25, its volatility is 30% per annum, and the risk-free interest rate is 10% per annum. What is the value of a 9-month European call on the futures with a strike price of 26?

14.30. A futures price is currently 70, its volatility is 20% per annum, and the risk-free interest rate is 6% per annum. What is the value of a 5-month European put on the futures with a strike price of 65?

14.31. Suppose that a futures price is currently 35. A European call option and a European put option on the futures with a strike price of 34 are both priced at 2 in the market. The risk-free interest rate is 10% per annum. Identify an arbitrage opportunity. Both options have 1 year to maturity.

14.32. "The price of an at-the-money European call futures option always equals the price of a similar at-the-money European put futures option." Explain why this statement is true.

14.33. Suppose that a futures price is currently 30. The risk-free interest rate is 5% per annum. A 3-month American call futures option with a strike price of 28 is worth 4. Calculate bounds for the price of a 3-month American put futures option with a strike price of 28.

14.34. Can an option on the yen/euro exchange rate be created from two options, one on the dollar/euro exchange rate, and the other on the dollar–yen exchange rate? Explain your answer.

14.35. A corporation knows that in 3 months it will have $5 million to invest for 90 days at LIBOR minus 50 basis points and wishes to ensure that the rate obtained will be at least 6.5%. What position in exchange-traded interest rate options should it take?

14.36. Prove the results in equations (14.1), (14.2), and (14.3) using the following portfolios:

Portfolio A: one European call option plus an amount of cash equal to Ke^{-rT}
Portfolio B: e^{-qT} shares, with dividends being reinvested in additional shares
Portfolio C: one European put option plus e^{-qT} shares, with dividends on the shares being reinvested in additional shares
Portfolio D: an amount of cash equal to Ke^{-rT}

14.37. Show that, if C is the price of an American call with strike price K and maturity T on a stock providing a dividend yield of q, and P is the price of an American put on the same stock with the same strike price and exercise date, then

$$S_0e^{-qT} - K \leqslant C - P \leqslant S_0 - Ke^{-rT}$$

where S_0 is the stock price, r is the risk-free interest rate, and $r > 0$. (*Hint*: To obtain the first half of the inequality, consider possible values of:

Portfolio A: a European call option plus an amount K invested at the risk-free rate

Portfolio B: an American put option plus e^{-qT} of stock with dividends being reinvested in the stock

To obtain the second half of the inequality, consider possible values of:

Portfolio C: an American call option plus an amount Ke^{-rT} invested at the risk-free rate

Portfolio D: a European put option plus one stock, with dividends being reinvested in the stock.)

14.38. Show that, if C is the price of an American call option on a futures contract when the strike price is K and the maturity is T, and P is the price of an American put on the same futures contract with the same strike price and exercise date, then

$$F_0e^{-rT} - K \leqslant C - P \leqslant F_0 - Ke^{-rT}$$

where F_0 is the futures price and r is the risk-free rate. Assume that $r > 0$ and that there is no difference between forward and futures contracts. (*Hint*: Use an analogous approach to that indicated for Problem 14.37.)

14.39. If the price of currency A expressed in terms of the price of currency B follows the process

$$dS = (r_B - r_A)S\,dt + \sigma S\,dz$$

where r_A is the risk-free interest rate in currency A and r_B is the risk-free interest rate in currency B. What is the process followed by the price of currency B expressed in terms of currency A?

Assignment Questions

14.40. Use the DerivaGem software to calculate implied volatilities for the March 104 call and the March 104 put on the Dow Jones Industrial Average (DJX) in Table 14.1. The value of the DJX on February 4, 2004, was 104.71. Assume that the risk-free rate was 1.2% and that the dividend yield was 3.5%. The options expire on March 20, 2004. Are the quotes for the two options consistent with put–call parity?

14.41. A stock index currently stands at 300. It is expected to increase or decrease by 10% over each of the next two time periods of 3 months. The risk-free interest rate is 8% and the dividend yield on the index is 3%. What is the value of a 6-month put option on the index with a strike price of 300 if it is (a) European and (b) American?

14.42. Suppose that the spot price of the Canadian dollar is US \$0.75 and that the Canadian dollar/US dollar exchange rate has a volatility of 4% per annum. The risk-free rates of interest in Canada and the United States are 9% and 7% per annum, respectively. Calculate the value of a European call option to buy one Canadian dollar for US \$0.75 in 9 months. Use put–call parity to calculate the price of a European put option to sell one Canadian dollar for US \$0.75 in 9 months. What is the price of a call option to buy US \$0.75 with one Canadian dollar in 9 months?

14.43. A mutual fund announces that the salaries of its fund managers will depend on the performance of the fund. If the fund loses money, the salaries will be zero. If the fund makes a profit, the salaries will be proportional to the profit. Describe the salary of a fund manager as an option. How is a fund manager motivated to behave with this type of remuneration package?

14.44. A futures price is currently 40. It is known that at the end of 3 months the price will be either 35 or 45. What is the value of a 3-month European call option on the futures with a strike price of 42 if the risk-free interest rate is 7% per annum?

14.45. Calculate the implied volatility of soybean futures prices from the following information concerning a European put on soybean futures:

Current futures price	525
Exercise price	525
Risk-free rate	6% per annum
Time to maturity	5 months
Put price	20

14.46. Use the DerivaGem software to calculate implied volatilities for the July options on corn futures in Table 14.4. Assume the futures prices in Table 2.2 apply and that the risk-free rate is 1.1% per annum. Treat the options as American and use 100 time steps. The options mature on June 19, 2004. Can you draw any conclusions from the pattern of implied volatilities you obtain?

CHAPTER 15 The Greek Letters

A financial institution that sells an option to a client in the over-the-counter markets is faced with the problem of managing its risk. If the option happens to be the same as one that is traded on an exchange, the financial institution can neutralize its exposure by buying on the exchange the same option as it has sold. But when the option has been tailored to the needs of a client and does not correspond to the standardized products traded by exchanges, hedging the exposure is far more difficult.

In this chapter we discuss some of the alternative approaches to this problem. We cover what are commonly referred to as the "Greek letters", or simply the "Greeks". Each Greek letter measures a different dimension to the risk in an option position and the aim of a trader is to manage the Greeks so that all risks are acceptable. The analysis presented in this chapter is applicable to market makers in options on an exchange as well as to traders working in the over-the-counter market for financial institutions.

Toward the end of the chapter, we will consider the creation of options synthetically. This turns out to be very closely related to the hedging of options. Creating an option position synthetically is essentially the same task as hedging the opposite option position. For example, creating a long call option synthetically is the same as hedging a short position in the call option.

15.1 ILLUSTRATION

In the next few sections we use as an example the position of a financial institution that has sold for \$300,000 a European call option on 100,000 shares of a non-dividend-paying stock. We assume that the stock price is \$49, the strike price is \$50, the risk-free interest rate is 5% per annum, the stock price volatility is 20% per annum, the time to maturity is 20 weeks (0.3846 years), and the expected return from the stock is 13% per annum.[1] With our usual notation, this means that

$$S_0 = 49, \quad K = 50, \quad r = 0.05, \quad \sigma = 0.20, \quad T = 0.3846, \quad \mu = 0.13$$

The Black–Scholes price of the option is about \$240,000. The financial institution has

[1] As shown in Chapters 11 and 13, the expected return is irrelevant to the pricing of an option. It is given here because it can have some bearing on the effectiveness of a hedging scheme.

therefore sold the option for \$60,000 more than its theoretical value, but it is faced with the problem of hedging the risks.[2]

15.2 NAKED AND COVERED POSITIONS

One strategy open to the financial institution is to do nothing. This is sometimes referred to as adopting a *naked position*. It is a strategy that works well if the stock price is below \$50 at the end of the 20 weeks. The option then costs the financial institution nothing and it makes a profit of \$300,000. A naked position works less well if the call is exercised because the financial institution then has to buy 100,000 shares at the market price prevailing in 20 weeks to cover the call. The cost to the financial institution is 100,000 times the amount by which the stock price exceeds the strike price. For example, if after 20 weeks the stock price is \$60, the option costs the financial institution \$1,000,000. This is considerably greater than the \$300,000 charged for the option.

As an alternative to a naked position, the financial institution can adopt a *covered position*. This involves buying 100,000 shares as soon as the option has been sold. If the option is exercised, this strategy works well, but in other circumstances it could lead to a significant loss. For example, if the stock price drops to \$40, the financial institution loses \$900,000 on its stock position. This is considerably greater than the \$300,000 charged for the option.[3]

Neither a naked position nor a covered position provides a good hedge. If the assumptions underlying the Black–Scholes formula hold, the cost to the financial institution should always be \$240,000 on average for both approaches.[4] But on any one occasion the cost is liable to range from zero to over \$1,000,000. A good hedge would ensure that the cost is always close to \$240,000.

15.3 A STOP-LOSS STRATEGY

One interesting hedging scheme that is sometimes proposed involves a *stop-loss strategy*. To illustrate the basic idea, consider an institution that has written a call option with strike price K to buy one unit of a stock. The hedging scheme involves buying one unit of the stock as soon as its price rises above K and selling it as soon as its price falls below K. The objective is to hold a naked position whenever the stock price is less than K and a covered position whenever the stock price is greater than K. The scheme is designed to ensure that at time T the institution owns the stock if the option closes in the money and does not own it if the option closes out of the money. The strategy appears to produce payoffs that are the same as the payoffs on the option. In the situation illustrated in Figure 15.1, it involves buying the stock at time t_1, selling it at time t_2, buying it at time t_3, selling it at time t_4, buying it at time t_5, and delivering it at time T.

[2] A call option on a non-dividend-paying stock is a convenient example with which to develop our ideas. The points that will be made apply to other types of options and to other derivatives.

[3] Put–call parity shows that the exposure from writing a covered call is the same as the exposure from writing a naked put.

[4] More precisely, the present value of the expected cost is \$240,000 for both approaches assuming that appropriate risk-adjusted discount rates are used.

Figure 15.1 A stop-loss strategy.

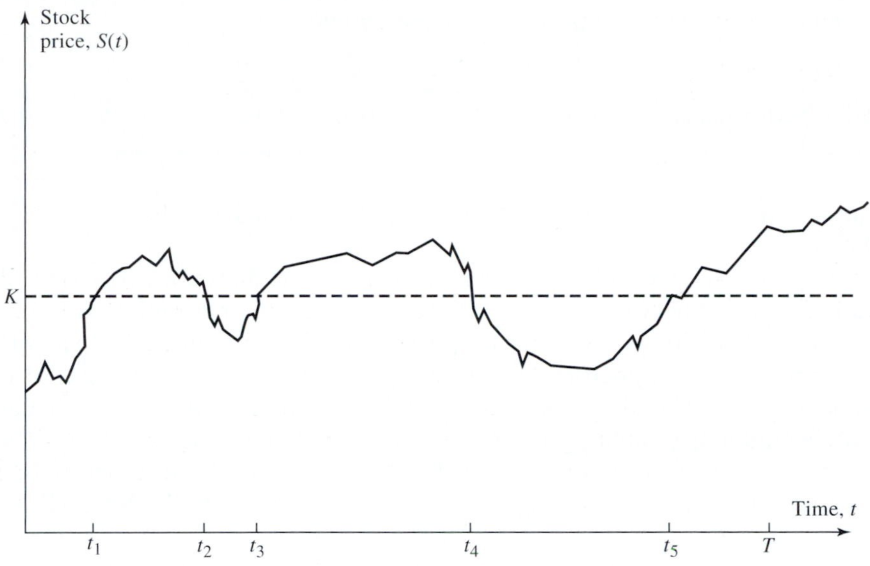

As usual, we denote the initial stock price by S_0. The cost of setting up the hedge initially is S_0 if $S_0 > K$ and zero otherwise. It seems as though the total cost, Q, of writing and hedging the option is the option's intrinsic value:

$$Q = \max(S_0 - K, 0) \tag{15.1}$$

This is because all purchases and sales subsequent to time 0 are made at price K. If this were in fact correct, the hedging scheme would work perfectly in the absence of transactions costs. Furthermore, the cost of hedging the option would always be less than its Black–Scholes price. Thus, an investor could earn riskless profits by writing options and hedging them.

There are two basic reasons why equation (15.1) is incorrect. The first is that the cash flows to the hedger occur at different times and must be discounted. The second is that purchases and sales cannot be made at exactly the same price K. This second point is critical. If we assume a risk-neutral world with zero interest rates, we can justify ignoring the time value of money. But we cannot legitimately assume that both purchases and sales are made at the same price. If markets are efficient, the hedger cannot know whether, when the stock price equals K, it will continue above or below K.

As a practical matter, purchases must be made at a price $K + \epsilon$ and sales must be made at a price $K - \epsilon$, for some small positive number ϵ. Thus, every purchase and subsequent sale involves a cost (apart from transaction costs) of 2ϵ. A natural response on the part of the hedger is to monitor price movements more closely, so that ϵ is reduced. Assuming that stock prices change continuously, ϵ can be made arbitrarily small by monitoring the stock prices closely. But as ϵ is made smaller, trades tend to occur more frequently. Thus, the lower cost per trade is offset by the

Table 15.1 Performance of stop-loss strategy. The performance measure is the ratio of the standard deviation of the cost of writing the option and hedging it to the theoretical price of the option.

Δt (weeks)	5	4	2	1	0.5	0.25
Hedge performance	1.02	0.93	0.82	0.77	0.76	0.76

increased frequency of trading. As $\epsilon \to 0$, the expected number of trades tends to infinity.[5]

A stop-loss strategy, although superficially attractive, does not work particularly well as a hedging scheme. Consider its use for an out-of-the-money option. If the stock price never reaches the strike price K, the hedging scheme costs nothing. If the path of the stock price crosses the strike price level many times, the scheme is quite expensive. Monte Carlo simulation can be used to assess the overall performance of stop-loss hedging. This involves randomly sampling paths for the stock price and observing the results of using the scheme. Table 15.1 shows the results for the option considered earlier. It assumes that the stock price is observed at the end of time intervals of length Δt.[6] The hedge performance measure is the ratio of the standard deviation of the cost of hedging the option to the Black–Scholes option price. Each result is based on 1,000 sample paths for the stock price and has a standard error of about 2%. A perfect hedge would have a hedge performance measure of zero. In this case it appears to be impossible to produce a value for the hedge performance measure below 0.70 regardless of how small Δt is made.

15.4 DELTA HEDGING

Most traders use more sophisticated hedging schemes than those mentioned so far. These involve calculating measures such as delta, gamma, and vega. In this section we consider the role played by delta.

The *delta* (Δ) of an option was introduced in Chapter 11. It is defined as the rate of change of the option price with respect to the price of the underlying asset. It is the slope of the curve that relates the option price to the underlying asset price. Suppose that the delta of a call option on a stock is 0.6. This means that when the stock price changes by a small amount, the option price changes by about 60% of that amount. Figure 15.2 shows the relationship between a call price and the underlying stock price. When the stock price corresponds to point A, the option price corresponds to point B, and Δ is the slope of the line indicated. In general,

$$\Delta = \frac{\partial c}{\partial S}$$

where c is the price of the call option and S is the stock price.

[5] As mentioned in Section 12.2, the expected number of times a Wiener process equals any particular value in a given time interval is infinite.

[6] The precise hedging rule used was as follows. If the stock price moves from below K to above K in a time interval of length Δt, it is bought at the end of the interval. If it moves from above K to below K in the time interval, it is sold at the end of the interval; otherwise, no action is taken.

Figure 15.2 Calculation of delta.

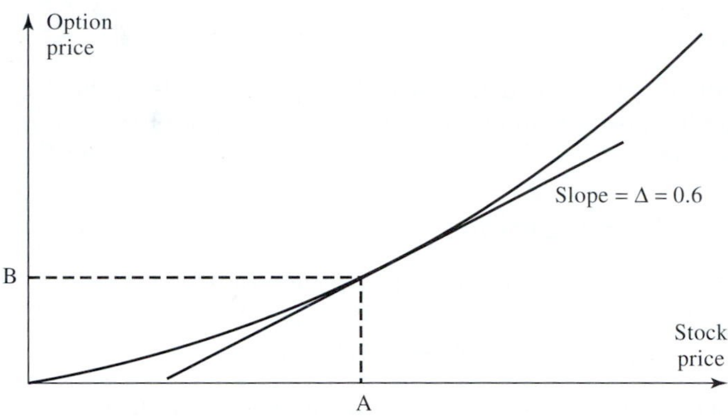

Suppose that, in Figure 15.2, the stock price is \$100 and the option price is \$10. Imagine an investor who has sold 20 call option contracts—that is, options to buy 2,000 shares. The investor's position could be hedged by buying $0.6 \times 2{,}000 = 1{,}200$ shares. The gain (loss) on the option position would then tend to be offset by the loss (gain) on the stock position. For example, if the stock price goes up by \$1 (producing a gain of \$1,200 on the shares purchased), the option price will tend to go up by $0.6 \times \$1 = \$0.60$ (producing a loss of \$1,200 on the options written); if the stock price goes down by \$1 (producing a loss of \$1,200 on the shares purchased), the option price will tend to go down by \$0.60 (producing a gain of \$1,200 on the options written).

In this example, the delta of the investor's option position is

$$0.6 \times (-2{,}000) = -1{,}200$$

In other words, the investor loses $1{,}200\Delta S$ on the short option position when the stock price increases by ΔS. The delta of the stock is 1.0, so that the long position in 1,200 shares has a delta of +1,200. The delta of the investor's overall position is, therefore, zero. The delta of the stock position offsets the delta of the option position. A position with a delta of zero is referred to as being *delta neutral.*

It is important to realize that, because delta changes, the investor's position remains delta hedged (or delta neutral) for only a relatively short period of time. The hedge has to be adjusted periodically. This is known as *rebalancing*. In our example, at the end of 3 days the stock price might increase to \$110. As indicated by Figure 15.2, an increase in the stock price leads to an increase in delta. Suppose that delta rises from 0.60 to 0.65. An extra $0.05 \times 2{,}000 = 100$ shares would then have to be purchased to maintain the hedge.

The delta-hedging scheme just described is an example of a *dynamic-hedging scheme*. It can be contrasted with *static-hedging schemes*, where the hedge is set up initially and never adjusted. Static hedging schemes are sometimes also referred to as *hedge-and-forget schemes.* Delta is closely related to the Black–Scholes–Merton analysis. As explained in Chapter 13, Black, Scholes, and Merton showed that it is possible to set up a riskless portfolio consisting of a position in an option on a stock and a position in the stock. Expressed in terms of Δ, the Black–Scholes portfolio is

-1: option

$+\Delta$: shares of the stock

Using our new terminology, we can say that Black and Scholes valued options by setting up a delta-neutral position and arguing that the return on the position should be the risk-free interest rate.

Delta of European Stock Options

For a European call option on a non-dividend-paying stock, it can be shown (see Problem 13.17) that

$$\Delta(\text{call}) = N(d_1)$$

where d_1 is defined as in equation (13.20). Using delta hedging for a short position in a European call option therefore involves keeping a long position of $N(d_1)$ shares at any given time. Similarly, using delta hedging for a long position in a European call option involves maintaining a short position of $N(d_1)$ shares at any given time.

For a European put option on a non-dividend-paying stock, delta is given by

$$\Delta(\text{put}) = N(d_1) - 1$$

Delta is negative, which means that a long position in a put option should be hedged with a long position in the underlying stock, and a short position in a put option should be hedged with a short position in the underlying stock. Figure 15.3 shows the variation of the delta of a call option and a put option with the stock price. Figure 15.4 shows the variation of delta with the time to maturity for in-the-money, at-the-money, and out-of-the-money call options.

Figure 15.3 Variation of delta with stock price for (a) a call option and (b) a put option on a non-dividend-paying stock.

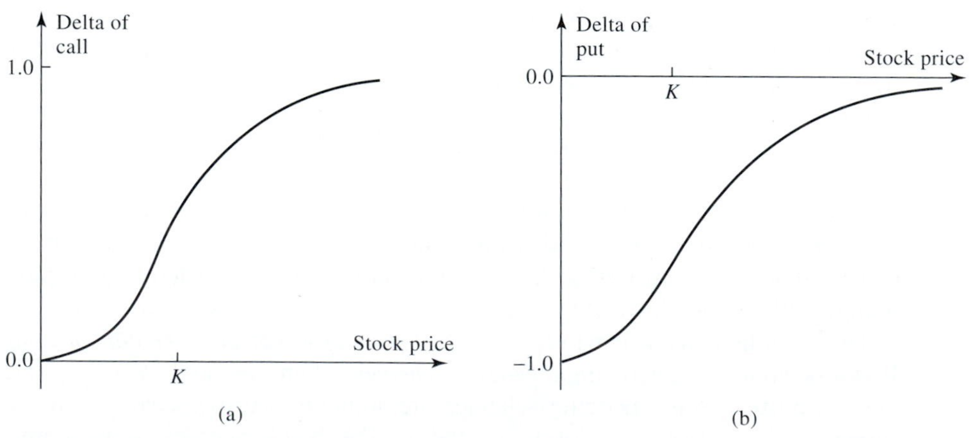

Figure 15.4 Typical patterns for variation of delta with time to maturity for a call option.

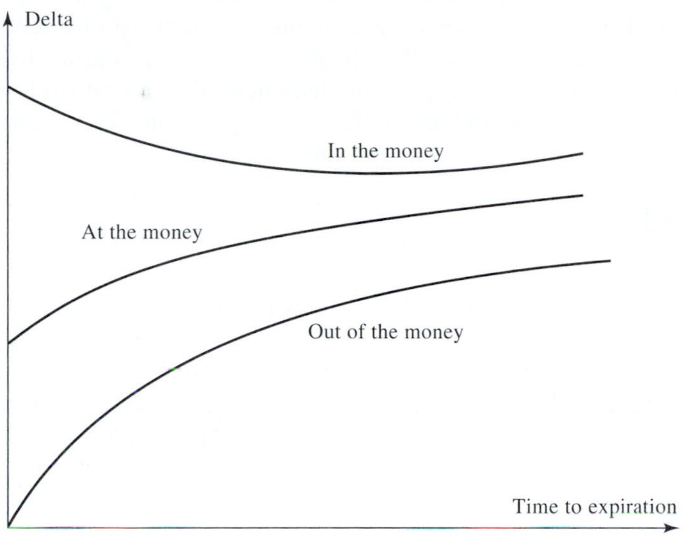

Delta of Other European Options

For European call options on an asset paying a yield q,

$$\Delta(\text{call}) = e^{-qT}N(d_1)$$

where d_1 is defined by equation (14.4). For European put options on the asset,

$$\Delta(\text{put}) = e^{-qT}[N(d_1) - 1]$$

When the asset is a stock index, these formulas are correct with q equal to the dividend yield on the index. When the asset is a currency, they are correct with q equal to the foreign risk-free rate, r_f. When the asset is a futures contract, they are correct with q equal to the domestic risk-free rate, r, and $S_0 = F_0$ in the definition of d_1. (In the latter case, delta gives the rate of change of the option price with respect to the futures price.)

Example 15.1

A US bank has sold 6-month put options on £1 million with a strike price of 1.6000 and wishes to make its portfolio delta neutral. Suppose that the current exchange rate is 1.6200, the risk-free interest rate in the United Kingdom is 13% per annum, the risk-free interest rate in the United States is 10% per annum, and the volatility of sterling is 15%. In this case, $S_0 = 1.6200$, $K = 1.6000$, $r = 0.10$, $r_f = 0.13$, $\sigma = 0.15$, and $T = 0.5$. The delta of a put option on a currency is

$$[N(d_1) - 1]e^{-r_f T}$$

where d_1 is given by equation (14.7). It can be shown that

$$d_1 = 0.0287 \quad \text{and} \quad N(d_1) = 0.5115$$

so that the delta of the put option is -0.458. This is the delta of a long position in one put option. (It means that, when the exchange rate increases by ΔS, the price of the put goes down by 45.8% of ΔS.) The delta of the bank's total short option position is +458,000. To make the position delta neutral, we must therefore add a short sterling position of £458,000 to the option position. This short sterling position has a delta of $-458{,}000$ and neutralizes the delta of the option position.

Delta of Forward Contracts

The concept of delta can be applied to financial instruments other than options. Consider a forward contract on a non-dividend-paying stock. Equation (5.5) shows that the value of a forward contract is $S_0 - Ke^{-rT}$, where K is the delivery price and T is the forward contract's time to maturity. When the price of the stock changes by ΔS, with all else remaining the same, the value of a forward contract on the stock also changes by ΔS. The delta of a forward contract on one share of the stock is therefore always 1.0. This means that a short forward contract on one share can be hedged by purchasing one share; a long forward contract on one share can be hedged by shorting one share.[7]

For an asset providing a dividend yield at rate q, equation (5.7) shows that the forward contract's delta is e^{-qT}. In the case of a stock index, q is set equal to the dividend yield on the index. For a currency, it is set equal to the foreign risk-free rate, r_f.

Delta of a Futures Contract

From equation (5.1), the futures price for a contract on a non-dividend-paying stock is S_0e^{rT}, where T is the time to maturity of the futures contract. This shows that when the price of the stock changes by ΔS, with all else remaining the same, the futures price changes by $\Delta S\, e^{rT}$. Since futures contracts are marked to market daily, the holder of a long futures contract makes an almost immediate gain of this amount. The delta of a futures contract is therefore e^{rT}. For a futures contract on an asset providing a dividend yield at rate q, equation (5.3) shows similarly that delta is $e^{(r-q)T}$. It is interesting that the impact of marking to market is to make the deltas of futures and forward contracts slightly different. This is true even when interest rates are constant and the forward price equals the futures price.

Sometimes a futures contract is used to achieve a delta-neutral position. Define:

T: Maturity of futures contract

H_A: Required position in asset for delta hedging

H_F: Alternative required position in futures contracts for delta hedging

If the underlying asset is a non-dividend-paying stock, the analysis we have just given shows that

$$H_F = e^{-rT} H_A \qquad \textbf{(15.2)}$$

[7] These are hedge-and-forget schemes. Since delta is always 1.0, no changes need to be made to the position in the stock during the life of the contract.

When the underlying asset pays a dividend yield q,

$$H_F = e^{-(r-q)T} H_A \tag{15.3}$$

For a stock index, we set q equal to the dividend yield on the index; for a currency we set it equal to the foreign risk-free rate, r_f, so that

$$H_F = e^{-(r-r_f)T} H_A \tag{15.4}$$

Example 15.2

Consider the option in the previous example where hedging using the currency requires a short position of 458,000 pounds sterling. From equation (15.4), hedging using 9-month currency futures requires a short futures position of

$$e^{-(0.10-0.13)\times 9/12} 458{,}000$$

or £468,442. Because each futures contract is for the purchase or sale of £62,500, seven contracts should be shorted (seven being the nearest whole number to 468,442/62,500).

Dynamic Aspects of Delta Hedging

Tables 15.2 and 15.3 provide two examples of the operation of delta hedging for the example in Section 15.1. The hedge is assumed to be adjusted or rebalanced weekly. The initial value of delta can be calculated from the data in Section 15.1 as 0.522. This means that, as soon as the option is written, \$2,557,800 must be borrowed to buy 52,200 shares at a price of \$49. The rate of interest is 5%. An interest cost of approximately \$2,500 is therefore incurred in the first week.

In Table 15.2 the stock price falls by the end of the first week to \$48.12. The delta declines to 0.458, and 6,400 of shares are sold to maintain the hedge. The strategy realizes \$308,000 in cash, and the cumulative borrowings at the end of Week 1 are reduced to \$2,252,300. During the second week, the stock price reduces to \$47.37, delta declines again, and so on. Toward the end of the life of the option, it becomes apparent that the option will be exercised and delta approaches 1.0. By Week 20, therefore, the hedger has a fully covered position. The hedger receives \$5 million for the stock held, so that the total cost of writing the option and hedging it is \$263,300.

Table 15.3 illustrates an alternative sequence of events such that the option closes out of the money. As it becomes clear that the option will not be exercised, delta approaches zero. By Week 20 the hedger has a naked position and has incurred costs totaling \$256,600.

In Tables 15.2 and 15.3, the costs of hedging the option, when discounted to the beginning of the period, are close to but not exactly the same as the Black–Scholes price of \$240,000. If the hedging scheme worked perfectly, the cost of hedging would, after discounting, be exactly equal to the Black–Scholes price for every simulated stock price path. The reason for the variation in the cost of delta hedging is that the hedge is rebalanced only once a week. As rebalancing takes place more frequently, the variation in the cost of hedging is reduced. Of course, the examples in Tables 15.2 and 15.3 are idealized in that they assume that the volatility is constant and there are no transaction costs.

Table 15.2 Simulation of delta hedging. Option closes in the money and cost of hedging is $263,300.

Week	*Stock price*	*Delta*	*Shares purchased*	*Cost of shares purchased ($000)*	*Cumulative cost including interest ($000)*	*Interest cost ($000)*
0	49.00	0.522	52,200	2,557.8	2,557.8	2.5
1	48.12	0.458	(6,400)	(308.0)	2,252.3	2.2
2	47.37	0.400	(5,800)	(274.7)	1,979.8	1.9
3	50.25	0.596	19,600	984.9	2,966.6	2.9
4	51.75	0.693	9,700	502.0	3,471.5	3.3
5	53.12	0.774	8,100	430.3	3,905.1	3.8
6	53.00	0.771	(300)	(15.9)	3,893.0	3.7
7	51.87	0.706	(6,500)	(337.2)	3,559.5	3.4
8	51.38	0.674	(3,200)	(164.4)	3,398.5	3.3
9	53.00	0.787	11,300	598.9	4,000.7	3.8
10	49.88	0.550	(23,700)	(1,182.2)	2,822.3	2.7
11	48.50	0.413	(13,700)	(664.4)	2,160.6	2.1
12	49.88	0.542	12,900	643.5	2,806.2	2.7
13	50.37	0.591	4,900	246.8	3,055.7	2.9
14	52.13	0.768	17,700	922.7	3,981.3	3.8
15	51.88	0.759	(900)	(46.7)	3,938.4	3.8
16	52.87	0.865	10,600	560.4	4,502.6	4.3
17	54.87	0.978	11,300	620.0	5,126.9	4.9
18	54.62	0.990	1,200	65.5	5,197.3	5.0
19	55.87	1.000	1,000	55.9	5,258.2	5.1
20	57.25	1.000	0	0.0	5,263.3	

Table 15.4 shows statistics on the performance of delta hedging obtained from 1,000 random stock price paths in our example. As in Table 15.1, the performance measure is the ratio of the standard deviation of the cost of hedging the option to the Black–Scholes price of the option. It is clear that delta hedging is a great improvement over a stop-loss strategy. Unlike a stop-loss strategy, the performance of a delta-hedging strategy gets steadily better as the hedge is monitored more frequently.

Delta hedging aims to keep the value of the financial institution's position as close to unchanged as possible. Initially, the value of the written option is $240,000. In the situation depicted in Table 15.2, the value of the option can be calculated as $414,500 in Week 9. Thus, the financial institution has lost $174,500 on its short option position. Its cash position, as measured by the cumulative cost, is $1,442,900 worse in Week 9 than in Week 0. The value of the shares held has increased from $2,557,800 to $4,171,100. The net effect of all this is that the value of the financial institution's position has changed by only $4,100 during the 9-week period.

Table 15.3 Simulation of delta hedging. Option closes out of the money and cost of hedging is $256,600.

Week	*Stock price*	*Delta*	*Shares purchased*	*Cost of shares purchased ($000)*	*Cumulative cost including interest ($000)*	*Interest cost ($000)*
0	49.00	0.522	52,200	2,557.8	2,557.8	2.5
1	49.75	0.568	4,600	228.9	2,789.2	2.7
2	52.00	0.705	13,700	712.4	3,504.3	3.4
3	50.00	0.579	(12,600)	(630.0)	2,877.7	2.8
4	48.38	0.459	(12,000)	(580.6)	2,299.9	2.2
5	48.25	0.443	(1,600)	(77.2)	2,224.9	2.1
6	48.75	0.475	3,200	156.0	2,383.0	2.3
7	49.63	0.540	6,500	322.6	2,707.9	2.6
8	48.25	0.420	(12,000)	(579.0)	2,131.5	2.1
9	48.25	0.410	(1,000)	(48.2)	2,085.4	2.0
10	51.12	0.658	24,800	1,267.8	3,355.2	3.2
11	51.50	0.692	3,400	175.1	3,533.5	3.4
12	49.88	0.542	(15,000)	(748.2)	2,788.7	2.7
13	49.88	0.538	(400)	(20.0)	2,771.4	2.7
14	48.75	0.400	(13,800)	(672.7)	2,101.4	2.0
15	47.50	0.236	(16,400)	(779.0)	1,324.4	1.3
16	48.00	0.261	2,500	120.0	1,445.7	1.4
17	46.25	0.062	(19,900)	(920.4)	526.7	0.5
18	48.13	0.183	12,100	582.4	1,109.6	1.1
19	46.63	0.007	(17,600)	(820.7)	290.0	0.3
20	48.12	0.000	(700)	(33.7)	256.6	

Where the Cost Comes From

The delta-hedging scheme in Tables 15.2 and 15.3 in effect creates a long position in the option synthetically. This neutralizes the short position arising from the option that has been written. The scheme generally involves selling stock just after the price has gone down and buying stock just after the price has gone up. It might be termed a buy-high, sell-low scheme! The cost of $240,000 comes from the average difference between the price paid for the stock and the price realized for it.

Table 15.4 Performance of delta hedging. The performance measure is the ratio of the standard deviation of the cost of writing the option and hedging it to the theoretical price of the option.

Time between hedge rebalancing (weeks):	5	4	2	1	0.5	0.25
Performance measure:	0.43	0.39	0.26	0.19	0.14	0.09

Delta of a Portfolio

The delta of a portfolio of options or other derivatives dependent on a single asset whose price is S is

$$\frac{\partial \Pi}{\partial S}$$

where Π is the value of the portfolio.

The delta of the portfolio can be calculated from the deltas of the individual options in the portfolio. If a portfolio consists of a quantity w_i of option i ($1 \leqslant i \leqslant n$), the delta of the portfolio is given by

$$\Delta = \sum_{i=1}^{n} w_i \, \Delta_i$$

where Δ_i is the delta of ith option. The formula can be used to calculate the position in the underlying asset or in a futures contract on the underlying asset necessary to make the delta of the portfolio zero. When this position has been taken, the portfolio is referred to as being *delta neutral.*

Suppose a financial institution in the United States has the following three positions in options on the Australian dollar:

1. A long position in 100,000 call options with strike price 0.55 and an expiration date in 3 months. The delta of each option is 0.533.
2. A short position in 200,000 call options with strike price 0.56 and an expiration date in 5 months. The delta of each option is 0.468.
3. A short position in 50,000 put options with strike price 0.56 and an expiration date in 2 months. The delta of each option is −0.508.

The delta of the whole portfolio is

$$100{,}000 \times 0.533 - 200{,}000 \times 0.468 - 50{,}000 \times (-0.508) = -14{,}900$$

This means that the portfolio can be made delta neutral with a long position of 14,900 Australian dollars.

A 6-month forward contract could also be used to achieve delta neutrality here. Suppose that the risk-free rate of interest is 8% per annum in Australia and 5% in the United States ($r = 0.05$ and $r_f = 0.08$). The delta of a forward contract maturing at time T on one Australian dollar is $e^{-r_f T}$ or $e^{-0.08\times 0.5} = 0.9608$. The long position in Australian dollar forward contracts for delta neutrality is therefore $14{,}900/0.9608 = 15{,}508$.

Another alternative is to use a 6-month futures contract. From equation (15.4), the long position in Australian dollar futures for delta neutrality is

$$14{,}900e^{-(0.05-0.08)\times 0.5} = 15{,}125$$

Transaction Costs

Maintaining a delta-neutral position in a single option and the underlying asset, in the way that has just been described, is liable to be prohibitively expensive because of the transactions costs incurred on trades. For a large portfolio of options, delta neutrality is more feasible. Only one trade in the underlying asset is necessary to zero out delta for the whole portfolio. The hedging transactions costs are absorbed by the profits on many different trades.

15.5 THETA

The *theta* (Θ) of a portfolio of options is the rate of change of the value of the portfolio with respect to the passage of time with all else remaining the same. Theta is sometimes referred to as the *time decay* of the portfolio. For a European call option on a non-dividend-paying stock, it can be shown from the Black–Scholes formula that

$$\Theta(\text{call}) = -\frac{S_0 N'(d_1)\sigma}{2\sqrt{T}} - rKe^{-rT}N(d_2)$$

where d_1 and d_2 are defined as in equation (13.20) and

$$N'(x) = \frac{1}{\sqrt{2\pi}}e^{-x^2/2} \qquad \textbf{(15.5)}$$

For a European put option on the stock (see Problem 13.17),

$$\Theta(\text{put}) = -\frac{S_0 N'(d_1)\sigma}{2\sqrt{T}} + rKe^{-rT}N(-d_2)$$

For a European call option on an asset paying a dividend at rate q,

$$\Theta(\text{call}) = -\frac{S_0 N'(d_1)\sigma e^{-qT}}{2\sqrt{T}} + qS_0N(d_1)e^{-qT} - rKe^{-rT}N(d_2)$$

where d_1 and d_2 are defined as in equation (14.4), and, for a European put option on the asset,

$$\Theta(\text{put}) = -\frac{S_0 N'(d_1)\sigma e^{-qT}}{2\sqrt{T}} - qS_0N(-d_1)e^{-qT} + rKe^{-rT}N(-d_2)$$

When the asset is a stock index, these last two equations are true with q equal to the dividend yield on the index. When it is a currency, they are true with q equal to the foreign risk-free rate, r_f. When it is a futures contract, they are true with $S_0 = F_0$ and $q = r$.

In these formulas, time is measured in years. Usually, when theta is quoted, time is measured in days, so that theta is the change in the portfolio value when 1 day passes with all else remaining the same. We can measure theta either "per calendar day" or "per trading day". To obtain the theta per calendar day, the formula for theta must be divided by 365; to obtain theta per trading day, it must be divided by 252. (DerivaGem measures theta per calendar day.)

Example 15.3

Consider a 4-month put option on a stock index. The current value of the index is 305, the strike price is 300, the dividend yield is 3% per annum, the risk-free interest rate is 8% per annum, and the volatility of the index is 25% per annum. In this case, $S_0 = 305$, $K = 300$, $q = 0.03$, $r = 0.08$, $\sigma = 0.25$, and $T = 0.3333$. The option's theta is

$$-\frac{S_0 N'(d_1)\sigma e^{-qT}}{2\sqrt{T}} - qS_0N(-d_1)e^{-qT} + rKe^{-rT}N(-d_2) = -18.15$$

The theta is $-18.15/365 = -0.0497$ per calendar day or $-18.15/252 = -0.0720$ per trading day.

Figure 15.5 Variation of theta of a European call option with stock price.

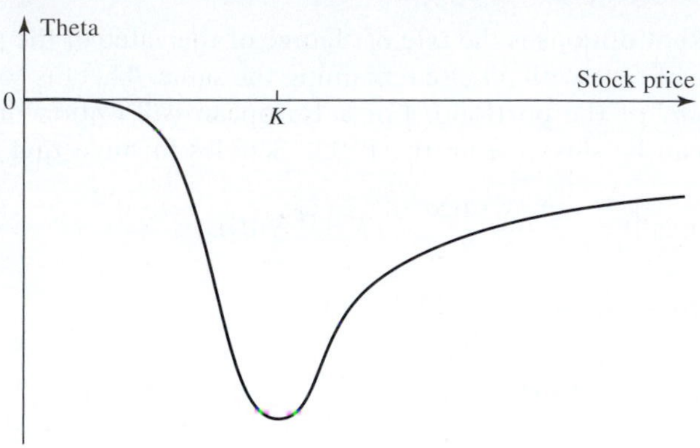

Theta is usually negative for an option.[8] This is because, as the time to maturity decreases with all else remaining the same, the option tends to become less valuable. The variation of Θ with stock price for a call option on a stock is shown in Figure 15.5. When the stock price is very low, theta is close to zero. For an at-the-money call option, theta is large and negative. As the stock price becomes larger, theta tends to $-rKe^{-rT}$. Figure 15.6 shows typical patterns for the variation of Θ with the time to maturity for in-the-money, at-the-money, and out-of-the-money call options.

Figure 15.6 Typical patterns for variation of theta of a European call option with time to maturity.

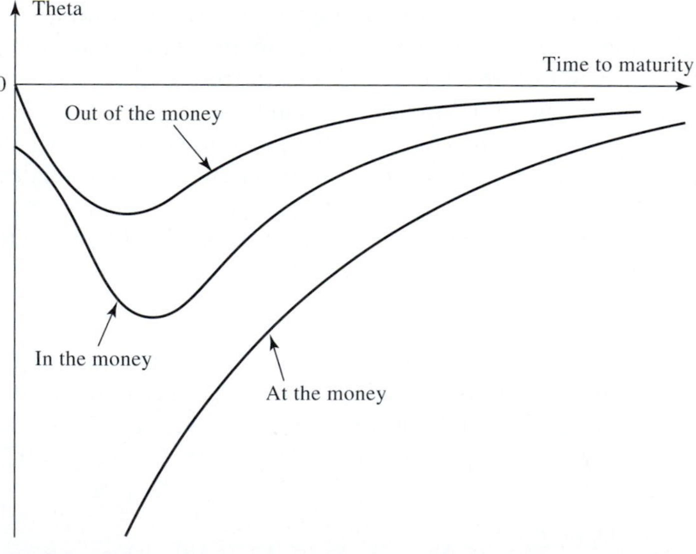

[8] An exception to this could be an in-the-money European put option on a non-dividend-paying stock or an in-the-money European call option on a currency with a very high interest rate.

Theta is not the same type of hedge parameter as delta. There is uncertainty about the future stock price, but there is no uncertainty about the passage of time. It makes sense to hedge against changes in the price of the underlying asset, but it does not make any sense to hedge against the effect of the passage of time on an option portfolio. In spite of this, many traders regard theta as a useful descriptive statistic for a portfolio. This is because, as we shall see later, in a delta-neutral portfolio theta is a proxy for gamma.

15.6 GAMMA

The *gamma* (Γ) of a portfolio of options on an underlying asset is the rate of change of the portfolio's delta with respect to the price of the underlying asset. It is the second partial derivative of the portfolio with respect to asset price:

$$\Gamma = \frac{\partial^2 \Pi}{\partial S^2}$$

If gamma is small, delta changes slowly, and adjustments to keep a portfolio delta neutral need to be made only relatively infrequently. However, if gamma is large in absolute terms, delta is highly sensitive to the price of the underlying asset. It is then quite risky to leave a delta-neutral portfolio unchanged for any length of time. Figure 15.7 illustrates this point. When the stock price moves from S to S', delta hedging assumes that the option price moves from C to C', when in fact it moves from C to C''. The difference between C' and C'' leads to a hedging error. This error depends on the curvature of the relationship between the option price and the stock price. Gamma measures this curvature.[9]

Suppose that ΔS is the price change of an underlying asset during a small interval of time, Δt, and $\Delta \Pi$ is the corresponding price change in the portfolio. The appendix at

Figure 15.7 Hedging error introduced by nonlinearity.

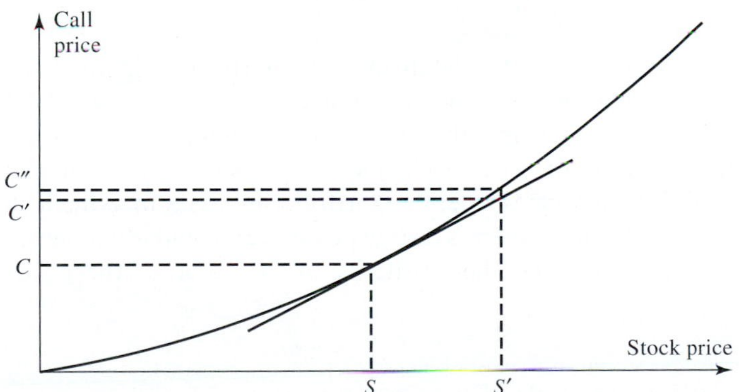

[9] Indeed, the gamma of an option is sometimes referred to as its *curvature* by practitioners.

Figure 15.8 Alternative relationships between $\Delta\Pi$ and ΔS for a delta-neutral portfolio with (a) slightly positive gamma, (b) large positive gamma, (c) slightly negative gamma, and (d) large negative gamma.

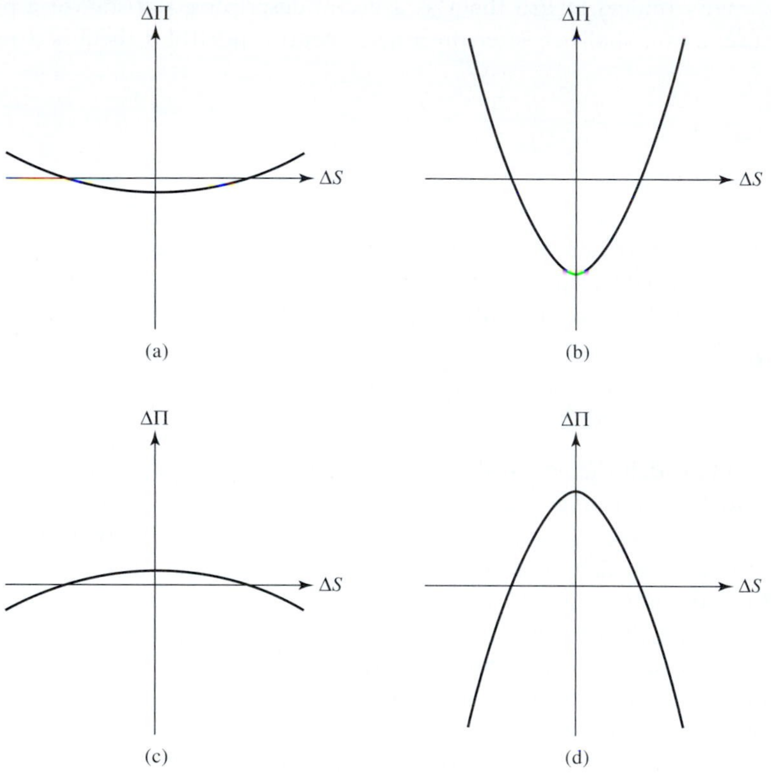

the end of this chapter shows that, if terms of order higher than Δt are ignored, we have

$$\Delta\Pi = \Theta\,\Delta t + \tfrac{1}{2}\Gamma\,\Delta S^2 \qquad \textbf{(15.6)}$$

for a delta-neutral portfolio, where Θ is the theta of the portfolio. Figure 15.8 shows the nature of this relationship between $\Delta\Pi$ and ΔS. When gamma is positive, theta tends to be negative. The portfolio declines in value if there is no change in S, but increases in value if there is a large positive or negative change in S. When gamma is negative, theta tends to be positive and the reverse is true; the portfolio increases in value if there is no change in S but decreases in value if there is a large positive or negative change in S. As the absolute value of gamma increases, the sensitivity of the value of the portfolio to S increases.

Example 15.4

Suppose that the gamma of a delta-neutral portfolio of options on an asset is $-10{,}000$. Equation (15.6) shows that, if a change of $+2$ or -2 in the price of the asset occurs over a short period of time, there is an unexpected decrease in the value of the portfolio of approximately $0.5 \times 10{,}000 \times 2^2 = \$20{,}000$.

Making a Portfolio Gamma Neutral

A position in the underlying asset itself or a forward contract on the underlying asset both have zero gamma and cannot be used to change the gamma of a portfolio. What is required is a position in an instrument such as an option that is not linearly dependent on the underlying asset.

Suppose that a delta-neutral portfolio has a gamma equal to Γ, and a traded option has a gamma equal to Γ_T. If the number of traded options added to the portfolio is w_T, the gamma of the portfolio is

$$w_T \Gamma_T + \Gamma$$

Hence, the position in the traded option necessary to make the portfolio gamma neutral is $-\Gamma/\Gamma_T$. Including the traded option is likely to change the delta of the portfolio, so the position in the underlying asset then has to be changed to maintain delta neutrality. Note that the portfolio is gamma neutral only for a short period of time. As time passes, gamma neutrality can be maintained only if the position in the traded option is adjusted so that it is always equal to $-\Gamma/\Gamma_T$.

Making a delta-neutral portfolio gamma neutral can be regarded as a first correction for the fact that the position in the underlying asset cannot be changed continuously when delta hedging is used. Delta neutrality provides protection against relatively small stock price moves between rebalancing. Gamma neutrality provides protection against larger movements in this stock price between hedge rebalancing. Suppose that a portfolio is delta neutral and has a gamma of $-3{,}000$. The delta and gamma of a particular traded call option are 0.62 and 1.50, respectively. The portfolio can be made gamma neutral by including in the portfolio a long position of

$$\frac{3{,}000}{1.5} = 2{,}000$$

in the call option. However, the delta of the portfolio will then change from zero to $2{,}000 \times 0.62 = 1{,}240$. A quantity, 1,240, of the underlying asset must therefore be sold from the portfolio to keep it delta neutral.

Calculation of Gamma

For a European call or put option on a non-dividend-paying stock, the gamma is given by

$$\Gamma = \frac{N'(d_1)}{S_0 \sigma \sqrt{T}}$$

where d_1 is defined as in equation (13.20) and $N'(x)$ is as given by equation (15.5). The gamma of a long position is always positive and varies with S_0 in the way indicated in Figure 15.9. The variation of gamma with time to maturity for out-of-the-money, at-the-money, and in-the-money options is shown in Figure 15.10. For an at-the-money option, gamma increases as the time to maturity decreases. Short-life at-the-money options have very high gammas, which means that the value of the option holder's position is highly sensitive to jumps in the stock price.

Figure 15.9 Variation of gamma with stock price for an option.

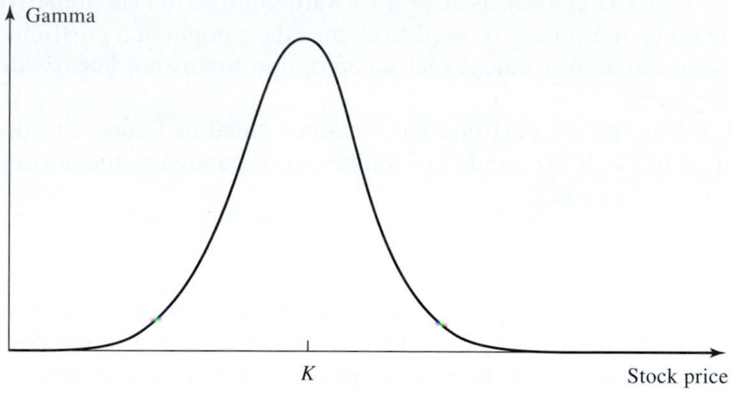

For a European call or put option on an asset paying a continuous dividend at rate q,

$$\Gamma = \frac{N'(d_1)\, e^{-qT}}{S_0 \sigma \sqrt{T}}$$

where d_1 is as in equation (14.4). When the asset is a stock index, q is set equal to the dividend yield on the index. When it is a currency, q is set equal to the foreign risk-free rate, r_f. When it is a futures contract, $S_0 = F_0$ and $q = r$.

Figure 15.10 Variation of gamma with time to maturity for a stock option.

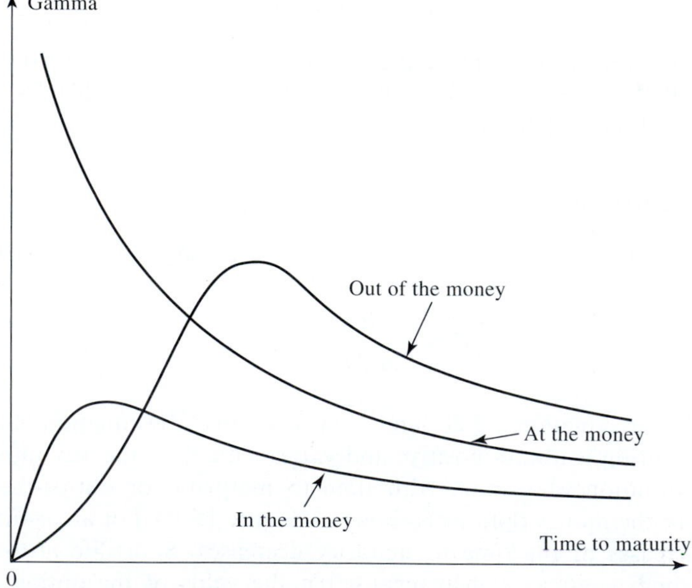

Example 15.5

Consider a 4-month put option on a stock index. The current value of the index is 305, the strike price is 300, the dividend yield is 3% per annum, the risk-free interest rate is 8% per annum, and volatility of the index is 25% per annum. In this case, $S_0 = 305$, $K = 300$, $q = 0.03$, $r = 0.08$, $\sigma = 0.25$, and $T = 4/12$. The gamma of the index option is given by

$$\frac{N'(d_1)e^{-qT}}{S_0\sigma\sqrt{T}} = 0.00857$$

Thus, an increase of 1 in the index (from 305 to 306) increases the delta of the option by approximately 0.00857.

15.7 RELATIONSHIP BETWEEN DELTA, THETA, AND GAMMA

The price of a single derivative dependent on a non-dividend-paying stock must satisfy the differential equation (13.16). It follows that the value Π of a portfolio of such derivatives also satisfies the differential equation

$$\frac{\partial \Pi}{\partial t} + rS\frac{\partial \Pi}{\partial S} + \tfrac{1}{2}\sigma^2 S^2 \frac{\partial^2 \Pi}{\partial S^2} = r\Pi$$

Since

$$\Theta = \frac{\partial \Pi}{\partial t}, \qquad \Delta = \frac{\partial \Pi}{\partial S}, \qquad \Gamma = \frac{\partial^2 \Pi}{\partial S^2}$$

it follows that

$$\Theta + rS\Delta + \tfrac{1}{2}\sigma^2 S^2 \Gamma = r\Pi \tag{15.7}$$

Similar results can be produced for other underlying assets (see Problem 15.19).

For a delta-neutral portfolio, $\Delta = 0$ and

$$\Theta + \tfrac{1}{2}\sigma^2 S^2 \Gamma = r\Pi$$

This shows that, when Θ is large and positive, gamma of a portfolio tends to be large and negative, and vice versa. This is consistent with the way in which Figure 15.8 has been drawn and explains why theta can be regarded as a proxy for gamma in a delta-neutral portfolio.

15.8 VEGA

Up to now we have implicitly assumed that the volatility of the asset underlying a derivative is constant. In practice, volatilities change over time. This means that the value of a derivative is liable to change because of movements in volatility as well as because of changes in the asset price and the passage of time.

The *vega* of a portfolio of derivatives, $\mathcal{V}$, is the rate of change of the value of the portfolio with respect to the volatility of the underlying asset.[10]

$$\mathcal{V} = \frac{\partial \Pi}{\partial \sigma}$$

If vega is high in absolute terms, the portfolio's value is very sensitive to small changes in volatility. If vega is low in absolute terms, volatility changes have relatively little impact on the value of the portfolio.

A position in the underlying asset has zero vega. However, the vega of a portfolio can be changed by adding a position in a traded option. If $\mathcal{V}$ is the vega of the portfolio and $\mathcal{V}_T$ is the vega of a traded option, a position of $-\mathcal{V}/\mathcal{V}_T$ in the traded option makes the portfolio instantaneously vega neutral. Unfortunately, a portfolio that is gamma neutral will not in general be vega neutral, and vice versa. If a hedger requires a portfolio to be both gamma and vega neutral, at least two traded derivatives dependent on the underlying asset must usually be used.

Example 15.6

Consider a portfolio that is delta neutral, with a gamma of $-5{,}000$ and a vega of $-8{,}000$. A traded option has a gamma of 0.5, a vega of 2.0, and a delta of 0.6. The portfolio can be made vega neutral by including a long position in 4,000 traded options. This would increase delta to 2,400 and require that 2,400 units of the asset be sold to maintain delta neutrality. The gamma of the portfolio would change from $-5{,}000$ to $-3{,}000$.

To make the portfolio gamma and vega neutral, we suppose that there is a second traded option with a gamma of 0.8, a vega of 1.2, and a delta of 0.5. If w_1 and w_2 are the quantities of the two traded options included in the portfolio, we require that

$$-5{,}000 + 0.5w_1 + 0.8w_2 = 0$$

and

$$-8{,}000 + 2.0w_1 + 1.2w_2 = 0$$

The solution to these equations is $w_1 = 400$, $w_2 = 6{,}000$. The portfolio can therefore be made gamma and vega neutral by including 400 of the first traded option and 6,000 of the second traded option. The delta of the portfolio after the addition of the positions in the two traded options is $400 \times 0.6 + 6{,}000 \times 0.5 = 3{,}240$. Hence, 3,240 units of the asset would have to be sold to maintain delta neutrality.

For a European call or put option on a non-dividend-paying stock, vega is given by

$$\mathcal{V} = S_0\sqrt{T}\,N'(d_1)$$

where d_1 is defined as in equation (13.20). The formula for $N'(x)$ is given in equation (15.5). For a European call or put option on an asset providing a dividend yield at rate q,

$$\mathcal{V} = S_0\sqrt{T}\,N'(d_1)\,e^{-qT}$$

[10] Vega is the name given to one of the "Greek letters" in option pricing, but it is not one of the letters in the Greek alphabet.

Figure 15.11 Variation of vega with stock price for an option.

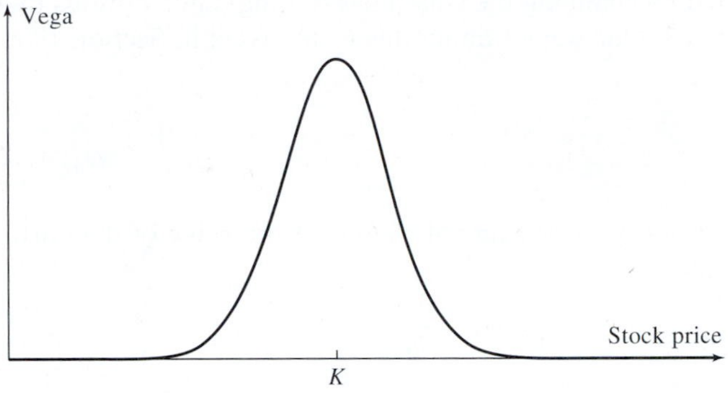

where d_1 is defined as in equation (14.4). When the asset is a stock index, q is set equal to the dividend yield on the index. When it is a currency, q is set equal to the foreign risk-free rate, r_f. When it is a futures contract, $S_0 = F_0$ and $q = r$.

The vega of a long position in a regular European or American option is always positive. The general way in which vega varies with S_0 is shown in Figure 15.11.

Example 15.7

Consider a 4-month put option on a stock index. The current value of the index is 305, the strike price is 300, the dividend yield is 3% per annum, the risk-free interest rate is 8% per annum, and the volatility of the index is 25% per annum. In this case $S_0 = 305$, $K = 300$, $q = 0.03$, $r = 0.08$, $\sigma = 0.25$, and $T = 4/12$. The option's vega is given by

$$S_0\sqrt{T}\,N'(d_1)\,e^{-qT} = 66.44$$

Thus a 1% (0.01) increase in volatility (from 25% to 26%) increases the value of the option by approximately 0.6644 ($= 0.01 \times 66.44$).

Calculating vega from the Black–Scholes model and its extensions may seem strange because one of the assumptions underlying Black–Scholes is that volatility is constant. It would be theoretically more correct to calculate vega from a model in which volatility is assumed to be stochastic. However, it turns out that the vega calculated from a stochastic volatility model is very similar to the Black–Scholes vega, so the practice of calculating vega from a model in which volatility is constant works reasonably well.[11]

Gamma neutrality protects against large changes in the price of the underlying asset between hedge rebalancing. Vega neutrality protects for a variable σ. As might be expected, whether it is best to use an available traded option for vega or gamma hedging depends on the time between hedge rebalancing and the volatility of the volatility.[12]

[11] See J. C. Hull and A. White, "The Pricing of Options on Assets with Stochastic Volatilities," *Journal of Finance* 42 (June 1987): 281–300; J. C. Hull and A. White, "An Analysis of the Bias in Option Pricing Caused by a Stochastic Volatility," *Advances in Futures and Options Research* 3 (1988): 27–61.

[12] For a discussion of this issue, see J. C. Hull and A. White, "Hedging the Risks from Writing Foreign Currency Options," *Journal of International Money and Finance* 6 (June 1987): 131–52.

When volatilities change, the implied volatilities of short-dated options tend to change by more than the implied volatilities of long-dated options. The vega of a portfolio is therefore often calculated by changing the volatilities of long-dated options by less than that of short-dated options. One way of doing this is discussed in Section 19.6.

15.9 RHO

The *rho* of a portfolio of options is the rate of change of the value of the portfolio with respect to the interest rate:

$$\text{rho} = \frac{\partial \Pi}{\partial r}$$

It measures the sensitivity of the value of a portfolio to interest rates. For a European call option on a non-dividend-paying stock,

$$\text{rho (call)} = KTe^{-rT}N(d_2)$$

where d_2 is defined as in equation (13.20). For a European put option,

$$\text{rho (put)} = -KTe^{-rT}N(-d_2)$$

These same formulas apply to European call and put options on stocks and stock indices paying known dividend yields when d_2 is as in equation (14.4).

Example 15.8

Consider a 4-month put option on a stock index. The current value of the index is 305, the strike price is 300, the dividend yield is 3% per annum, the risk-free interest rate is 8% per annum, and the volatility of the index is 25% per annum. In this case, $S_0 = 305$, $K = 300$, $q = 0.03$, $r = 0.08$, $\sigma = 0.25$, and $T = 4/12$. The option's rho is

$$-KTe^{-rT}N(-d_2) = -42.6$$

This means that for a 1% (0.01) change in the risk-free interest rate (from 8% to 9%) the value of the option decreases by 0.426 ($= 0.01 \times 42.6$).

In the case of currency options, there are two rhos corresponding to the two interest rates. The rho corresponding to the domestic interest rate is given by the formulas already presented with d_2 as in equation (14.7). The rho corresponding to the foreign interest rate for a European call on a currency is

$$-Te^{-r_f T}S_0N(d_1)$$

and for a European put it is

$$Te^{-r_f T}S_0N(-d_1)$$

where d_1 is given by equation (14.7).

For a European call futures option, rho is $-cT$ and for a European put futures option rho is $-pT$, where c and p are the European call and put option prices, respectively.

Business Snapshot 15.1 Dynamic Hedging in Practice

In a typical arrangement at a financial institution, the responsibility for a portfolio of derivatives dependent on a particular underlying asset is assigned to one trader or to a group of traders working together. For example, one trader at Goldman Sachs might be assigned responsibility for all derivatives dependent on the value of the Australian dollar. A computer system calculates the value of the portfolio and Greek letters for the portfolio. Limits are defined for each Greek letter and special permission is required if a trader wants to exceed a limit at the end of a trading day.

The delta limit is often expressed as the equivalent maximum position in the underlying asset. For example, the delta limit of Goldman Sachs on Microsoft might be \$10 million. If the Microsoft stock price is \$50 this means that the absolute value of delta as we have calculated it can be no more that 200,000. The vega limit is usually expressed as a maximum dollar exposure per 1% change in the volatility.

As a matter of course, options traders make themselves delta neutral—or close to delta neutral—at the end of each day. Gamma and vega are monitored, but are not usually managed on a daily basis. Financial institutions often find that their business with clients involves writing options and that as a result they accumulate negative gamma and vega. They are then always looking out for opportunities to manage their gamma and vega risks by buying options at competitive prices.

There is one aspect of an options portfolio that mitigates problems of managing gamma and vega somewhat. Options are often close to the money when they are first sold, so that they have relatively high gammas and vegas. But after some time has elapsed, the underlying asset price has often changed enough for them to become deep out of the money or deep in the money. Their gammas and vegas are then very small and of little consequence. The nightmare scenario for an options trader is where written options remain very close to the money as the maturity date is approached.

15.10 THE REALITIES OF HEDGING

In an ideal world, traders working for financial institutions would be able to rebalance their portfolios very frequently in order to maintain a zero delta, a zero gamma, and a zero vega. In practice, this is not possible. When managing a large portfolio dependent on a single underlying asset, traders usually make delta zero, or close to zero, at least once a day by trading the underlying asset. Unfortunately, a zero gamma and a zero vega are less easy to achieve because it is difficult to find options or other nonlinear derivatives that can be traded in the volume required at competitive prices (see discussion of dynamic hedging in Business Snapshot 15.1)

There are big economies of scale in being an options trader. As noted earlier, maintaining delta neutrality for an individual option on, say, the S&P 500 by trading daily would be prohibitively expensive. But it is realistic to do this for a portfolio of several hundred options on the S&P 500. This is because the cost of daily rebalancing (either by trading the stocks underlying the index or by trading index futures) is covered by the profit on many different trades.

15.11 SCENARIO ANALYSIS

In addition to monitoring risks such as delta, gamma, and vega, option traders often also carry out a scenario analysis. The analysis involves calculating the gain or loss on their portfolio over a specified period under a variety of different scenarios. The time period chosen is likely to depend on the liquidity of the instruments. The scenarios can be either chosen by management or generated by a model.

Consider a bank with a portfolio of options on a foreign currency. There are two main variables on which the value of the portfolio depends. These are the exchange rate and the exchange-rate volatility. Suppose that the exchange rate is currently 1.0000 and its volatility is 10% per annum. The bank could calculate a table such as Table 15.5 showing the profit or loss experienced during a 2-week period under different scenarios. This table considers seven different exchange rates and three different volatilities. Because a one-standard-deviation move in the exchange rate during a 2-week period is about 0.02, the exchange rate moves considered are approximately one, two, and three standard deviations.

In Table 15.5, the greatest loss is in the lower right corner of the table. The loss corresponds to the volatility increasing to 12% and the exchange rate moving up to 1.06. Usually the greatest loss in a table such as 15.5 occurs at one of the corners, but this is not always so. Consider, for example, the situation where a bank's portfolio consists of a short position in a butterfly spread (see Section 10.2). The greatest loss will be experienced if the exchange rate stays where it is.

15.12 PORTFOLIO INSURANCE

A portfolio manager is often interested in acquiring a put option on his or her portfolio. This provides protection against market declines while preserving the potential for a gain if the market does well. One approach (discussed in Section 14.3) is to buy put options on a market index such as the S&P 500. An alternative is to create the options synthetically.

Creating an option synthetically involves maintaining a position in the underlying asset (or futures on the underlying asset) so that the delta of the position is equal to the delta of the required option. The position necessary to create an option synthetically is the reverse of that necessary to hedge it. This is because the procedure for hedging an option involves the creation of an equal and opposite option synthetically.

Table 15.5 Profit or loss realized in 2 weeks under different scenarios ($ million).

Volatility	*Exchange rate*						
	0.94	*0.96*	*0.98*	*1.00*	*1.02*	*1.04*	*1.06*
8%	+102	+55	+25	+6	−10	−34	−80
10%	+80	+40	+17	+2	−14	−38	−85
12%	+60	+25	+9	−2	−18	−42	−90

There are two reasons why it may be more attractive for the portfolio manager to create the required put option synthetically than to buy it in the market. The first is that options markets do not always have the liquidity to absorb the trades that managers of large funds would like to carry out. The second is that fund managers often require strike prices and exercise dates that are different from those available in exchange-traded options markets.

The synthetic option can be created from trading the portfolio or from trading in index futures contracts. We first examine the creation of a put option by trading the portfolio. Recall that the delta of a European put on the portfolio is

$$\Delta = e^{-qT}[N(d_1) - 1] \qquad \textbf{(15.8)}$$

where, with our usual notation,

$$d_1 = \frac{\ln(S_0/K) + (r - q + \sigma^2/2)T}{\sigma\sqrt{T}}$$

S_0 is the value of the portfolio, K is the strike price, r is the risk-free rate, q is the dividend yield on the portfolio, σ is the volatility of the portfolio, and T is the life of the option. The volatility of the portfolio can usually be assumed to be its beta times the volatility of a well-diversified market index.

To create the put option synthetically, the fund manager should ensure that at any given time a proportion

$$e^{-qT}[1 - N(d_1)]$$

of the stocks in the original portfolio has been sold and the proceeds invested in riskless assets. As the value of the original portfolio declines, the delta of the put given by equation (15.8) becomes more negative and the proportion of the original portfolio sold must be increased. As the value of the original portfolio increases, the delta of the put becomes less negative and the proportion of the original portfolio sold must be decreased (i.e., some of the original portfolio must be repurchased).

Using this strategy to create portfolio insurance means that at any given time funds are divided between the stock portfolio on which insurance is required and riskless assets. As the value of the stock portfolio increases, riskless assets are sold and the position in the stock portfolio is increased. As the value of the stock portfolio declines, the position in the stock portfolio is decreased and riskless assets are purchased. The cost of the insurance arises from the fact that the portfolio manager is always selling after a decline in the market and buying after a rise in the market.

Example 15.9

A portfolio is worth \$90 million. To protect against market downturns the managers of the portfolio require a 6-month European put option on the portfolio with a strike price of \$87 million. The risk-free rate is 9% per annum, the dividend yield is 3% per annum, and the volatility of the portfolio is 25% per annum. The S&P 500 index stands at 900. As the portfolio is considered to mimic the S&P 500 fairly closely, one alternative is to buy 1,000 put option contracts on the S&P 500 with a strike price of 870. Another alternative is to create the required option synthetically. In this case, $S_0 = 90$ million, $K = 87$ million,

$r = 0.09$, $q = 0.03$, $\sigma = 0.25$, and $T = 0.5$, so that

$$d_1 = \frac{\ln(90/87) + (0.09 - 0.03 + 0.25^2/2)0.5}{0.25\sqrt{0.5}} = 0.4499$$

and the delta of the required option is initially

$$e^{-qT}[N(d_1) - 1] = -0.3215$$

This shows that 32.15% of the portfolio should be sold initially to match the delta of the required option. The amount of the portfolio sold must be monitored frequently. For example, if the value of the portfolio reduces to \$88 million after 1 day, the delta of the required option changes to 0.3679 and a further 4.64% of the original portfolio should be sold. If the value of the portfolio increases to \$92 million, the delta of the required option changes to -0.2787 and 4.28% of the original portfolio should be repurchased.

Use of Index Futures

Using index futures to create options synthetically can be preferable to using the underlying stocks because the transaction costs associated with trades in index futures are generally lower than those associated with the corresponding trades in the underlying stocks. The dollar amount of the futures contracts shorted as a proportion of the value of the portfolio should from equations (15.3) and (15.8) be

$$e^{-qT}e^{-(r-q)T^*}[1 - N(d_1)] = e^{q(T^*-T)}e^{-rT^*}[1 - N(d_1)]$$

where T^* is the maturity of the futures contract. If the portfolio is worth A_1 times the index and each index futures contract is on A_2 times the index, the number of futures contracts shorted at any given time should be

$$e^{q(T^*-T)}e^{-rT^*}[1 - N(d_1)]\frac{A_1}{A_2}$$

Example 15.10

Suppose that in the previous example futures contracts on the S&P 500 maturing in 9 months are used to create the option synthetically. In this case initially $T = 0.5$, $T^* = 0.75$, $A_1 = 100{,}000$, $A_2 = 250$, and $d_1 = 0.4499$, so that the number of futures contracts shorted should be

$$e^{q(T^*-T)}e^{-rT^*}[1 - N(d_1)]\frac{A_1}{A_2} = 122.96$$

or 123, rounding to the nearest whole number. As time passes and the index changes, the position in futures contracts must be adjusted.

This analysis assumes that the portfolio mirrors the index. When this is not the case, it is necessary to (a) calculate the portfolio's beta, (b) find the position in options on the index that gives the required protection, and (c) choose a position in index futures to create the options synthetically. As discussed in Section 14.3, the strike price for the options should be the expected level of the market index when the portfolio reaches its insured value. The number of options required is beta times the number that would be required if the portfolio had a beta of 1.0.

Business Snapshot 15.2 Was Portfolio Insurance to Blame for the Crash of 1987?

On Monday, October 19, 1987, the Dow Jones Industrial Average dropped by more than 20%. Many people feel that portfolio insurance played a major role in this crash. In October 1987 between \$60 billion and \$90 billion of equity assets were subject to portfolio insurance schemes where put options were created synthetically in the way discussed in Section 15.12. During the period Wednesday, October 14, 1987, to Friday, October 16, 1987, the market declined by about 10%, with much of this decline taking place on Friday afternoon. The portfolio insurance schemes should have generated at least \$12 billion of equity or index futures sales as a result of this decline. In fact, portfolio insurers had time to sell only \$4 billion and they approached the following week with huge amounts of selling already dictated by their models. It is estimated that on Monday, October 19, sell programs by three portfolio insurers accounted for almost 10% of the sales on the New York Stock Exchange, and that portfolio insurance sales amounted to 21.3% of all sales in index futures markets. It is likely that the decline in equity prices was exacerbated by investors other than portfolio insurers selling heavily because they anticipated the actions of portfolio insurers.

Because the market declined so fast and the stock exchange systems were overloaded, many portfolio insurers were unable to execute the trades generated by their models and failed to obtain the protection they required. Needless to say, the popularity of portfolio insurance schemes has declined significantly since 1987. One of the morals of this story is that it is dangerous to follow a particular trading strategy—even a hedging strategy—when many other market participants are doing the same thing.

15.13 STOCK MARKET VOLATILITY

We discussed in Chapter 13 the issue of whether volatility is caused solely by the arrival of new information or whether trading itself generates volatility. Portfolio insurance schemes such as those just described have the potential to increase volatility. When the market declines, they cause portfolio managers either to sell stock or to sell index futures contracts. Either action may accentuate the decline (see Business Snapshot 15.2). The sale of stock is liable to drive down the market index further in a direct way. The sale of index futures contracts is liable to drive down futures prices. This creates selling pressure on stocks via the mechanism of index arbitrage (see Chapter 5), so that the market index is liable to be driven down in this case as well. Similarly, when the market rises, the portfolio insurance schemes cause portfolio managers either to buy stock or to buy futures contracts. This may accentuate the rise.

In addition to formal portfolio insurance schemes, we can speculate that many investors consciously or subconsciously follow portfolio insurance schemes of their own. For example, an investor may be inclined to enter the market when it is rising but will sell when it is falling to limit the downside risk.

Whether portfolio insurance schemes (formal or informal) affect volatility depends on how easily the market can absorb the trades that are generated by portfolio insurance. If portfolio insurance trades are a very small fraction of all trades, there is likely to be no effect. As portfolio insurance becomes more popular, it is liable to have a destabilizing effect on the market.

SUMMARY

Financial institutions offer a variety of option products to their clients. Often the options do not correspond to the standardized products traded by exchanges. The financial institutions are then faced with the problem of hedging their exposure. Naked and covered positions leave them subject to an unacceptable level of risk. One course of action that is sometimes proposed is a stop-loss strategy. This involves holding a naked position when an option is out of the money and converting it to a covered position as soon as the option moves into the money. Although superficially attractive, the strategy does not provide a good hedge.

The delta (Δ) of an option is the rate of change of its price with respect to the price of the underlying asset. Delta hedging involves creating a position with zero delta (sometimes referred to as a delta-neutral position). Because the delta of the underlying asset is 1.0, one way of hedging is to take a position of $-\Delta$ in the underlying asset for each long option being hedged. The delta of an option changes over time. This means that the position in the underlying asset has to be frequently adjusted.

Once an option position has been made delta neutral, the next stage is often to look at its gamma (Γ). The gamma of an option is the rate of change of its delta with respect to the price of the underlying asset. It is a measure of the curvature of the relationship between the option price and the asset price. The impact of this curvature on the performance of delta hedging can be reduced by making an option position gamma neutral. If Γ is the gamma of the position being hedged, this reduction is usually achieved by taking a position in a traded option that has a gamma of $-\Gamma$.

Delta and gamma hedging are both based on the assumption that the volatility of the underlying asset is constant. In practice, volatilities do change over time. The vega of an option or an option portfolio measures the rate of change of its value with respect to volatility. A trader who wishes to hedge an option position against volatility changes can make the position vega neutral. As with the procedure for creating gamma neutrality, this usually involves taking an offsetting position in a traded option. If the trader wishes to achieve both gamma and vega neutrality, two traded options are usually required.

Two other measures of the risk of an option position are theta and rho. Theta measures the rate of change of the value of the position with respect to the passage of time, with all else remaining constant. Rho measures the rate of change of the value of the position with respect to the interest rate, with all else remaining constant.

In practice, option traders usually rebalance their portfolios at least once a day to maintain delta neutrality. It is usually not feasible to maintain gamma and vega neutrality on a regular basis. Typically a trader monitors these measures. If they get too large, either corrective action is taken or trading is curtailed.

Portfolio managers are sometimes interested in creating put options synthetically for the purposes of insuring an equity portfolio. They can do so either by trading the portfolio or by trading index futures on the portfolio. Trading the portfolio involves splitting the portfolio between equities and risk-free securities. As the market declines, more is invested in risk-free securities. As the market increases, more is invested in equities. Trading index futures involves keeping the equity portfolio intact and selling index futures. As the market declines, more index futures are sold; as it rises, fewer are sold. This type of portfolio insurance works well in normal market conditions. On Monday, October 19, 1987, when the Dow Jones Industrial Average dropped very sharply, it worked badly. Portfolio insurers were unable to sell either stocks or index futures fast enough to protect their positions.

FURTHER READING

Taleb, N. N., *Dynamic Hedging: Managing Vanilla and Exotic Options*. New York: Wiley, 1996.

Questions and Problems (Answers in Solutions Manual)

15.1. Explain how a stop-loss hedging scheme can be implemented for the writer of an out-of-the-money call option. Why does it provide a relatively poor hedge?

15.2. What does it mean to assert that the delta of a call option is 0.7? How can a short position in 1,000 options be made delta neutral when the delta of each option is 0.7?

15.3. Calculate the delta of an at-the-money 6-month European call option on a non-dividend-paying stock when the risk-free interest rate is 10% per annum and the stock price volatility is 25% per annum.

15.4. What does it mean to assert that the theta of an option position is −0.1 when time is measured in years? If a trader feels that neither a stock price nor its implied volatility will change, what type of option position is appropriate?

15.5. What is meant by the gamma of an option position? What are the risks in the situation where the gamma of a position is large and negative and the delta is zero?

15.6. "The procedure for creating an option position synthetically is the reverse of the procedure for hedging the option position." Explain this statement.

15.7. Why did portfolio insurance not work well on October 19, 1987?

15.8. The Black–Scholes price of an out-of-the-money call option with an exercise price of \$40 is \$4. A trader who has written the option plans to use a stop-loss strategy. The trader's plan is to buy at \$40.10 and to sell at \$39.90. Estimate the expected number of times the stock will be bought or sold.

15.9. Suppose that a stock price is currently \$20 and that a call option with an exercise price of \$25 is created synthetically using a continually changing position in the stock. Consider the following two scenarios:
(a) Stock price increases steadily from \$20 to \$35 during the life of the option.
(b) Stock price oscillates wildly, ending up at \$35.
Which scenario would make the synthetically created option more expensive? Explain your answer.

15.10. What is the delta of a short position in 1,000 European call options on silver futures? The options mature in 8 months, and the futures contract underlying the option matures in 9 months. The current 9-month futures price is \$8 per ounce, the exercise price of the options is \$8, the risk-free interest rate is 12% per annum, and the volatility of silver is 18% per annum.

15.11. In Problem 15.10, what initial position in 9-month silver futures is necessary for delta hedging? If silver itself is used, what is the initial position? If 1-year silver futures are used, what is the initial position? Assume no storage costs for silver.

15.12. A company uses delta hedging to hedge a portfolio of long positions in put and call options on a currency. Which of the following would give the most favorable result?
(a) A virtually constant spot rate
(b) Wild movements in the spot rate
Explain your answer.

15.13. Repeat Problem 15.12 for a financial institution with a portfolio of short positions in put and call options on a currency.

15.14. A financial institution has just sold 1,000 7-month European call options on the Japanese yen. Suppose that the spot exchange rate is 0.80 cent per yen, the exercise price is 0.81 cent per yen, the risk-free interest rate in the United States is 8% per annum, the risk-free interest rate in Japan is 5% per annum, and the volatility of the yen is 15% per annum. Calculate the delta, gamma, vega, theta, and rho of the financial institution's position. Interpret each number.

15.15. Under what circumstances is it possible to make a European option on a stock index both gamma neutral and vega neutral by adding a position in one other European option?

15.16. A fund manager has a well-diversified portfolio that mirrors the performance of the S&P 500 and is worth $360 million. The value of the S&P 500 is 1,200, and the portfolio manager would like to buy insurance against a reduction of more than 5% in the value of the portfolio over the next 6 months. The risk-free interest rate is 6% per annum. The dividend yield on both the portfolio and the S&P 500 is 3%, and the volatility of the index is 30% per annum.
(a) If the fund manager buys traded European put options, how much would the insurance cost?
(b) Explain carefully alternative strategies open to the fund manager involving traded European call options, and show that they lead to the same result.
(c) If the fund manager decides to provide insurance by keeping part of the portfolio in risk-free securities, what should the initial position be?
(d) If the fund manager decides to provide insurance by using 9-month index futures, what should the initial position be?

15.17. Repeat Problem 15.16 on the assumption that the portfolio has a beta of 1.5. Assume that the dividend yield on the portfolio is 4% per annum.

15.18. Show by substituting for the various terms in equation (15.7) that the equation is true for:
(a) A single European call option on a non-dividend-paying stock
(b) A single European put option on a non-dividend-paying stock
(c) Any portfolio of European put and call options on a non-dividend-paying stock

15.19. What is the equation corresponding to equation (15.7) for (a) a portfolio of derivatives on a currency and (b) a portfolio of derivatives on a futures contract?

15.20. Suppose that $70 billion of equity assets are the subject of portfolio insurance schemes. Assume that the schemes are designed to provide insurance against the value of the assets declining by more than 5% within 1 year. Making whatever estimates you find necessary, use the DerivaGem software to calculate the value of the stock or futures contracts that the administrators of the portfolio insurance schemes will attempt to sell if the market falls by 23% in a single day.

15.21. Does a forward contract on a stock index have the same delta as the corresponding futures contract? Explain your answer.

15.22. A bank's position in options on the dollar/euro exchange rate has a delta of 30,000 and a gamma of −80,000. Explain how these numbers can be interpreted. The exchange rate (dollars per euro) is 0.90. What position would you take to make the position delta neutral? After a short period of time, the exchange rate moves to 0.93. Estimate the new delta. What additional trade is necessary to keep the position delta neutral? Assuming the bank did set up a delta-neutral position originally, has it gained or lost money from the exchange-rate movement?

15.23. Use the put–call parity relationship to derive, for a non-dividend-paying stock, the relationship between:
(a) The delta of a European call and the delta of a European put
(b) The gamma of a European call and the gamma of a European put
(c) The vega of a European call and the vega of a European put
(d) The theta of a European call and the theta of a European put

Assignment Questions

15.24. Consider a 1-year European call option on a stock when the stock price is \$30, the strike price is \$30, the risk-free rate is 5%, and the volatility is 25% per annum. Use the DerivaGem software to calculate the price, delta, gamma, vega, theta, and rho of the option. Verify that delta is correct by changing the stock price to \$30.1 and recomputing the option price. Verify that gamma is correct by recomputing the delta for the situation where the stock price is \$30.1. Carry out similar calculations to verify that vega, theta, and rho are correct. Use the DerivaGem Applications Builder functions to plot the option price, delta, gamma, vega, theta, and rho against the stock price for the stock option.

15.25. A financial institution has the following portfolio of over-the-counter options on sterling:

Type	*Position*	*Delta of option*	*Gamma of option*	*Vega of option*
Call	−1,000	0.50	2.2	1.8
Call	−500	0.80	0.6	0.2
Put	−2,000	−0.40	1.3	0.7
Call	−500	0.70	1.8	1.4

A traded option is available with a delta of 0.6, a gamma of 1.5, and a vega of 0.8.
(a) What position in the traded option and in sterling would make the portfolio both gamma neutral and delta neutral?
(b) What position in the traded option and in sterling would make the portfolio both vega neutral and delta neutral?

15.26. Consider again the situation in Problem 15.25. Suppose that a second traded option with a delta of 0.1, a gamma of 0.5, and a vega of 0.6 is available. How could the portfolio be made delta, gamma, and vega neutral?

15.27. A deposit instrument offered by a bank guarantees that investors will receive a return during a 6-month period that is the greater of (a) zero and (b) 40% of the return provided by a market index. An investor is planning to put $100,000 in the instrument. Describe the payoff as an option on the index. Assuming that the risk-free rate of interest is 8% per annum, the dividend yield on the index is 3% per annum, and the volatility of the index is 25% per annum, is the product a good deal for the investor?

15.28. The formula for the price c of a European call futures option in terms of the futures price F_0 is given in Chapter 14 as

$$c = e^{-rT}[F_0N(d_1) - KN(d_2)]$$

where

$$d_1 = \frac{\ln(F_0/K) + \sigma^2T/2}{\sigma\sqrt{T}} \quad \text{and} \quad d_2 = d_1 - \sigma\sqrt{T}$$

and K, r, T, and σ are the strike price, interest rate, time to maturity, and volatility, respectively.

(a) Prove that $F_0N'(d_1) = KN'(d_2)$.

(b) Prove that the delta of the call price with respect to the futures price is $e^{-rT}N(d_1)$.

(c) Prove that the vega of the call price is $F_0\sqrt{T}N'(d_1)e^{-rT}$.

(d) Prove the formula for the rho of a call futures option given at the end of Section 15.9.

The delta, gamma, theta, and vega of a call futures option are the same as those for a call option on a stock paying dividends at rate q, with q replaced by r and S_0 replaced by F_0. Explain why the same is not true of the rho of a call futures option.

15.29. Use DerivaGem to check that equation (15.7) is satisfied for the option considered in Section 15.1. (*Note*: DerivaGem produces a value of theta "per calendar day". The theta in equation (15.7) is "per year".)

15.30. Use the DerivaGem Application Builder functions to reproduce Table 15.2. (In Table 15.2 the stock position is rounded to the nearest 100 shares.) Calculate the gamma and theta of the position each week. Calculate the change in the value of the portfolio each week and check whether equation (15.6) is approximately satisfied. (*Note*: DerivaGem produces a value of theta "per calendar day". The theta in equation (15.6) is "per year".)

APPENDIX

TAYLOR SERIES EXPANSIONS AND HEDGE PARAMETERS

A Taylor series expansion of the change in the portfolio value in a short period of time shows the role played by different Greek letters. If the volatility of the underlying asset is assumed to be constant, the value Π of the portfolio is a function of the asset price S, and time t. The Taylor series expansion gives

$$\Delta\Pi = \frac{\partial\Pi}{\partial S}\Delta S + \frac{\partial\Pi}{\partial t}\Delta t + \frac{1}{2}\frac{\partial^2\Pi}{\partial S^2}\Delta S^2 + \frac{1}{2}\frac{\partial^2\Pi}{\partial t^2}\Delta t^2 + \frac{\partial^2\Pi}{\partial S\,\partial t}\Delta S\,\Delta t + \cdots \tag{15A.1}$$

where $\Delta\Pi$ and ΔS are the change in Π and S in a small time interval Δt. Delta hedging eliminates the first term on the right-hand side. The second term is nonstochastic. The third term (which is of order Δt) can be made zero by ensuring that the portfolio is gamma neutral as well as delta neutral. Other terms are of order higher than Δt.

For a delta-neutral portfolio, the first term on the right-hand side of equation (15A.1) is zero, so that

$$\Delta\Pi = \Theta\,\Delta t + \tfrac{1}{2}\Gamma\,\Delta S^2$$

when terms of order higher than Δt are ignored. This is equation (15.6).

When the volatility of the underlying asset is uncertain, Π is a function of σ, S, and t. Equation (15A.1) then becomes

$$\Delta\Pi = \frac{\partial\Pi}{\partial S}\Delta S + \frac{\partial\Pi}{\partial\sigma}\Delta\sigma + \frac{\partial\Pi}{\partial t}\Delta t + \frac{1}{2}\frac{\partial^2\Pi}{\partial S^2}\Delta S^2 + \frac{1}{2}\frac{\partial^2\Pi}{\partial\sigma^2}\Delta\sigma^2 + \cdots$$

where $\Delta\sigma$ is the change in σ in time Δt. In this case, delta hedging eliminates the first term on the right-hand side. The second term is eliminated by making the portfolio vega neutral. The third term is nonstochastic. The fourth term is eliminated by making the portfolio gamma neutral. Traders sometimes define other Greek letters to correspond to higher-order terms in the expansion.

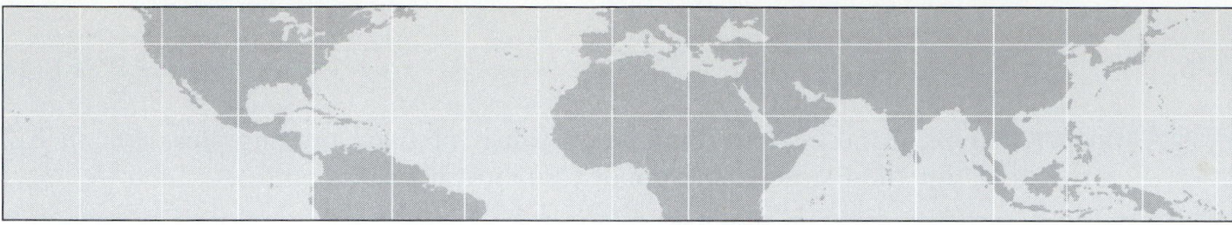

CHAPTER 16 Volatility Smiles

How close are the market prices of options to those predicted by Black–Scholes? Do traders really use Black–Scholes when determining a price for an option? Are the probability distributions of asset prices really lognormal? In this chapter we answer these questions. We explain that traders do use the Black–Scholes model—but not in exactly the way that Black and Scholes originally intended. This is because they allow the volatility used to price an option to depend on its strike price and time to maturity.

A plot of the implied volatility of an option as a function of its strike price is known as a *volatility smile*. In this chapter we describe the volatility smiles that traders use in equity and foreign currency markets. We explain the relationship between a volatility smile and the risk-neutral probability distribution being assumed for the future asset price. We also discuss how option traders allow volatility to be a function of option maturity and how they use volatility surfaces as pricing tools.

16.1 PUT–CALL PARITY REVISITED

Put–call parity, which we explained in Chapter 9, provides a good starting point for understanding volatility smiles. It is an important relationship between the price c of a European call and the price p of a European put:

$$p + S_0e^{-qT} = c + Ke^{-rT} \tag{16.1}$$

The call and the put have the same strike price, K, and time to maturity, T. The variable S_0 is the price of the underlying asset today, r is the risk-free interest rate for maturity T, and q is the yield on the asset.

A key feature of the put–call parity relationship is that it is based on a relatively simple no-arbitrage argument. It does not require any assumption about the probability distribution of the asset price in the future. It is true both when the asset price distribution is lognormal and when it is not lognormal.

Suppose that, for a particular value of the volatility, p_{BS} and c_{BS} are the values of European put and call options calculated using the Black–Scholes model. Suppose further that p_{mkt} and c_{mkt} are the market values of these options. Because put–call parity holds for the Black–Scholes model, we must have

$$p_{\text{BS}} + S_0 e^{-qT} = c_{\text{BS}} + Ke^{-rT}$$

In the absence of arbitrage opportunities, it also holds for the market prices, so that

$$p_{\text{mkt}} + S_0 e^{-qT} = c_{\text{mkt}} + Ke^{-rT}$$

Subtracting these two equations, we get

$$p_{\text{BS}} - p_{\text{mkt}} = c_{\text{BS}} - c_{\text{mkt}} \tag{16.2}$$

This shows that the dollar pricing error when the Black–Scholes model is used to price a European put option should be exactly the same as the dollar pricing error when it is used to price a European call option with the same strike price and time to maturity.

Suppose that the implied volatility of the put option is 22%. This means that $p_{\text{BS}} = p_{\text{mkt}}$ when a volatility of 22% is used in the Black–Scholes model. From equation (16.2), it follows that $c_{\text{BS}} = c_{\text{mkt}}$ when this volatility is used. The implied volatility of the call is, therefore, also 22%. This argument shows that the implied volatility of a European call option is always the same as the implied volatility of a European put option when the two have the same strike price and maturity date. To put this another way, for a given strike price and maturity, the correct volatility to use in conjunction with the Black–Scholes model to price a European call should always be the same as that used to price a European put. This is also approximately true for American options. It follows that when traders refer to the relationship between implied volatility and strike price, or to the relationship between implied volatility and maturity, they do not need to state whether they are talking about calls or puts. The relationship is the same for both.

Example 16.1

The value of the Australian dollar is \$0.60. The risk-free interest rate is 5% per annum in the United States and 10% per annum in Australia. The market price of a European call option on the Australian dollar with a maturity of 1 year and a strike price of \$0.59 is 0.0236. DerivaGem shows that the implied volatility of the call is 14.5%. For there to be no arbitrage, the put–call parity relationship in equation (16.1) must apply with q equal to the foreign risk-free rate. The price p of a European put option with a strike price of \$0.59 and maturity of 1 year therefore satisfies

$$p + 0.60e^{-0.10\times 1} = 0.0236 + 0.59e^{-0.05\times 1}$$

so that $p = 0.0419$. DerivaGem shows that, when the put has this price, its implied volatility is also 14.5%. This is what we expect from the analysis just given.

16.2 FOREIGN CURRENCY OPTIONS

The volatility smile used by traders to price foreign currency options has the general form shown in Figure 16.1. The volatility is relatively low for at-the-money options. It becomes progressively higher as an option moves either into the money or out of the money.

Figure 16.1 Volatility smile for foreign currency options.

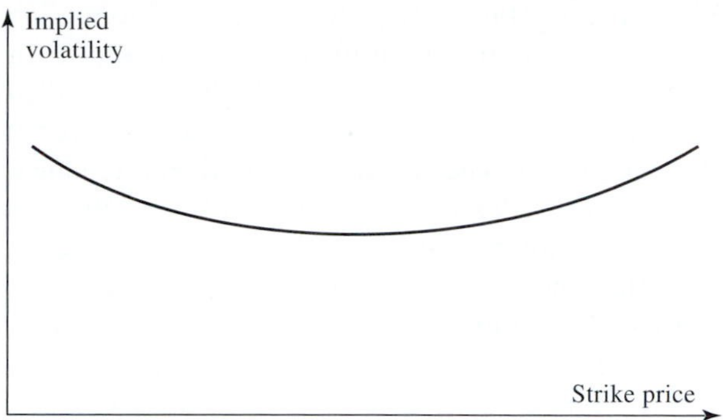

In the appendix at the end of this chapter we show how to determine the risk-neutral probability distribution for an asset price at a future time from the volatility smile given by options maturing at that time. We refer to this as the *implied distribution*. The volatility smile in Figure 16.1 corresponds to the probability distribution shown by the solid line in Figure 16.2. A lognormal distribution with the same mean and standard deviation as the implied distribution is shown by the dashed line in Figure 16.2. It can be seen that the implied distribution has heavier tails than the lognormal distribution.[1]

Figure 16.2 Implied and lognormal distribution for foreign currency options.

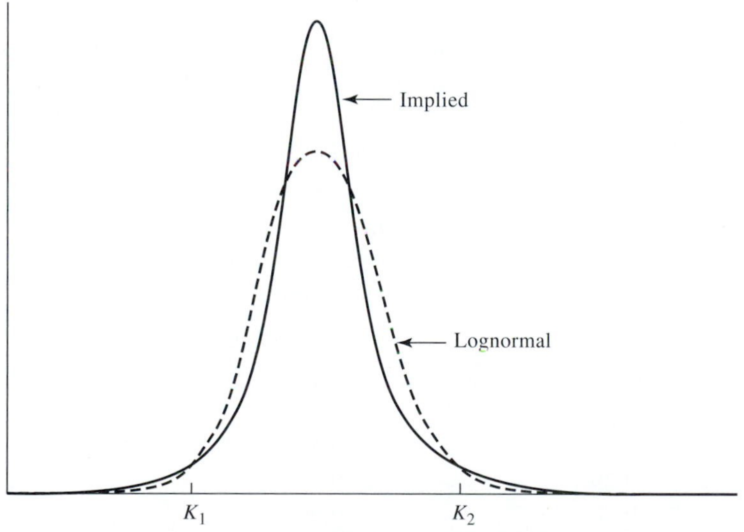

[1] This is known as *kurtosis*. Note that, in addition to having a heavier tail, the implied distribution is more "peaked". Both small and large movements in the exchange rate are more likely than with the lognormal distribution. Intermediate movements are less likely.

To see that Figures 16.1 and 16.2 are consistent with each other, consider first a deep-out-of-the-money call option with a high strike price of K_2. This option pays off only if the exchange rate proves to be above K_2. Figure 16.2 shows that the probability of this is higher for the implied probability distribution than for the lognormal distribution. We therefore expect the implied distribution to give a relatively high price for the option. A relatively high price leads to a relatively high implied volatility—and this is exactly what we observe in Figure 16.1 for the option. The two figures are therefore consistent with each other for high strike prices. Consider next a deep-out-of-the-money put option with a low strike price of K_1. This option pays off only if the exchange rate proves to be below K_1. Figure 16.2 shows that the probability of this is also higher for implied probability distribution than for the lognormal distribution. We therefore expect the implied distribution to give a relatively high price, and a relatively high implied volatility, for this option as well. Again, this is exactly what we observe in Figure 16.1.

Empirical Results

We have just shown that the smile used by traders for foreign currency options implies that they consider that the lognormal distribution understates the probability of extreme movements in exchange rates. To test whether they are right, Table 16.1 examines the daily movements in 12 different exchange rates over a 10-year period.[2] The first step in the production of the table is to calculate the standard deviation of daily percentage change in each exchange rate. The next stage is to note how often the actual percentage change exceeded one standard deviation, two standard deviations, and so on. The final stage is to calculate how often this would have happened if the percentage changes had been normally distributed. (The lognormal model implies that percentage changes are almost exactly normally distributed over a one-day time period.)

Daily changes exceed three standard deviations on 1.34% of days. The lognormal model predicts that this should happen on only 0.27% of days. Daily changes exceed four, five, and six standard deviations on 0.29%, 0.08%, and 0.03% of days, respectively. The lognormal model predicts that we should hardly ever observe this happening. The table therefore provides evidence to support the existence of heavy tails and the volatility smile used by traders. Business Snapshot 16.1 shows how you

Table 16.1 Percentage of days when daily exchange rate moves are greater than one, two,..., six standard deviations (SD = standard deviation of daily change).

	Real world	*Lognormal model*
>1 SD	25.04	31.73
>2 SD	5.27	4.55
>3 SD	1.34	0.27
>4 SD	0.29	0.01
>5 SD	0.08	0.00
>6 SD	0.03	0.00

[2] This table is taken from J. C. Hull and A. White, "Value at Risk When Daily Changes in Market Variables Are Not Normally Distributed." *Journal of Derivatives*, 5, No. 3 (Spring 1998): 9–19.

> **Business Snapshot 16.1** Making Money from Foreign Currency Options
>
> Suppose that most market participants think that exchange rates are lognormally distributed. They will be comfortable using the same volatility to value all options on a particular exchange rate. You have just done the analysis in Table 16.1 and know that the lognormal assumption is not a good one for exchange rates. What should you do?
>
> The answer is that you should buy deep-out-the-money call and put options on a variety of different currencies and wait. These options will be relatively inexpensive and more of them will close in the money than the lognormal model predicts. The present value of your payoffs will on average be much greater than the cost of the options.
>
> In the mid-1980s a few traders knew about the heavy tails of foreign exchange probability distributions. Everyone else thought that the lognormal assumption of Black–Scholes was reasonable. The few traders who were well informed followed the strategy we have described—and made lots of money. By the late 1980s everyone realized that foreign currency options should be priced with a volatility smile and the trading opportunity disappeared.

could have made money if you had done the analysis in Table 16.1 ahead of the rest of the market.

Reasons for the Smile in Foreign Currency Options

Why are exchange rates not lognormally distributed? Two of the conditions for an asset price to have a lognormal distribution are:

1. The volatility of the asset is constant.
2. The price of the asset changes smoothly with no jumps.

In practice, neither of these conditions is satisfied for an exchange rate. The volatility of an exchange rate is far from constant, and exchange rates frequently exhibit jumps.[3] It turns out that the effect of both a nonconstant volatility and jumps is that extreme outcomes become more likely. The impact of jumps and nonconstant volatility depends on the option maturity. The percentage impact of a nonconstant volatility on prices becomes more pronounced as the maturity of the option is increased, but the volatility smile created by the nonconstant volatility usually becomes less pronounced. The percentage impact of jumps on both prices and the volatility smile becomes less pronounced as the maturity of the option is increased. When we look at sufficiently long-dated options, jumps tend to get "averaged out" so that the stock price distribution when there are jumps is almost indistinguishable from the one obtained when the stock price changes smoothly.

16.3 EQUITY OPTIONS

The volatility smile for equity options has been studied by Rubinstein (1985, 1994) and Jackwerth and Rubinstein (1996). Prior to 1987 there was no marked volatility smile.

[3] Often the jumps are in response to the actions of central banks.

Figure 16.3 Volatility smile for equities.

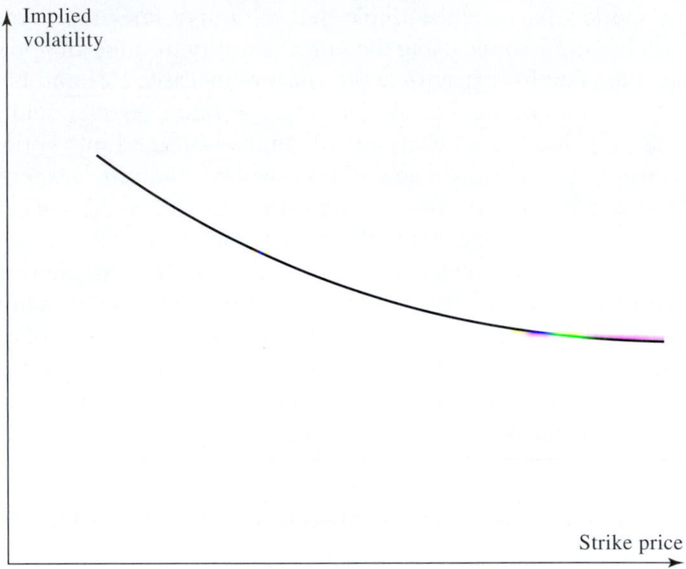

Since 1987 the volatility smile used by traders to price equity options (both on individual stocks and on stock indices) has the general form shown in Figure 16.3. This is sometimes referred to as a *volatility skew*. The volatility decreases as the strike price increases. The volatility used to price a low-strike-price option (i.e., a deep-out-of-the-money put or a deep-in-the-money call) is significantly higher than that used to price a high-strike-price option (i.e., a deep-in-the-money put or a deep-out-of-the-money call).

The volatility smile for equity options corresponds to the implied probability distribution given by the solid line in Figure 16.4. A lognormal distribution with the same

Figure 16.4 Implied distribution and lognormal distribution for equity options.

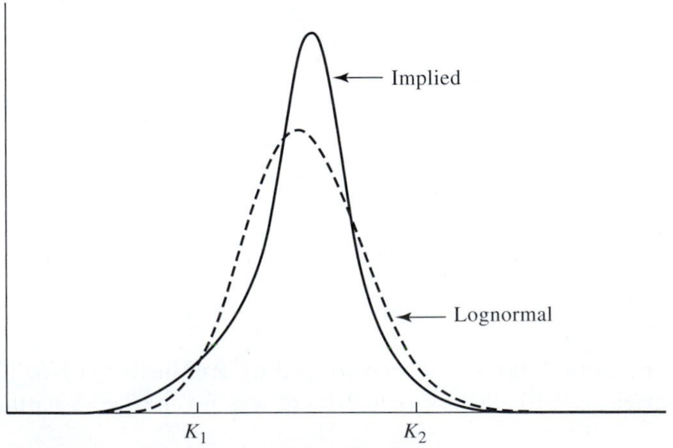

Business Snapshot 16.2 Crashophobia

It is interesting that the pattern in Figure 16.3 for equities has existed only since the stock market crash of October 1987. Prior to October 1987, implied volatilities were much less dependent on strike price. This has led Mark Rubinstein to suggest that one reason for the equity volatility smile may be "crashophobia". Traders are concerned about the possibility of another crash similar to October 1987, and they price options accordingly.

There is some empirical support for this explanation. Declines in the S&P 500 tend to be accompanied by a steepening of the volatility skew. When the S&P increases, the skew tends to become less steep.

mean and standard deviation as the implied distribution is shown by the dotted line. It can be seen that the implied distribution has a heavier left tail and a less heavy right tail than the lognormal distribution.

To see that Figures 16.3 and 16.4 are consistent with each other, we proceed as for Figures 16.1 and 16.2 and consider options that are deep out of the money. From Figure 16.4 a deep-out-of-the-money call with a strike price of K_2 has a lower price when the implied distribution is used than when the lognormal distribution is used. This is because the option pays off only if the stock price proves to be above K_2, and the probability of this is lower for the implied probability distribution than for the lognormal distribution. Therefore, we expect the implied distribution to give a relatively low price for the option. A relatively low price leads to a relatively low implied volatility—and this is exactly what we observe in Figure 16.4 for the option. Consider next a deep-out-of-the-money put option with a strike price of K_1. This option pays off only if the stock price proves to be below K_1. Figure 16.3 shows that the probability of this is higher for implied probability distribution than for the lognormal distribution. We therefore expect the implied distribution to give a relatively high price, and a relatively high implied volatility, for this option. Again, this is exactly what we observe in Figure 16.3.

The Reason for the Smile in Equity Options

One possible explanation for the smile in equity options concerns leverage. As a company's equity declines in value, the company's leverage increases. This means that the equity becomes more risky and its volatility increases. As a company's equity increases in value, leverage decreases. The equity then becomes less risky and its volatility decreases. This argument shows that we can expect the volatility of equity to be a decreasing function of price and is consistent with Figures 16.3 and 16.4. Another explanation is crashophobia (see Business Snapshot 16.2).

16.4 THE VOLATILITY TERM STRUCTURE AND VOLATILITY SURFACES

In addition to a volatility smile, traders use a volatility term structure when pricing options. This means that the volatility used to price an at-the-money option depends on the maturity of the option. Volatility tends to be an increasing function of maturity when short-dated volatilities are historically low. This is because there is then an expectation that volatilities will increase. Similarly, volatility tends to be an decreasing

Table 16.2 Volatility surface.

	Strike price				
	0.90	*0.95*	*1.00*	*1.05*	*1.10*
1 month	14.2	13.0	12.0	13.1	14.5
3 month	14.0	13.0	12.0	13.1	14.2
6 month	14.1	13.3	12.5	13.4	14.3
1 year	14.7	14.0	13.5	14.0	14.8
2 year	15.0	14.4	14.0	14.5	15.1
5 year	14.8	14.6	14.4	14.7	15.0

function of maturity when short-dated volatilities are historically high. This is because there is then an expectation that volatilities will decrease.

Volatility surfaces combine volatility smiles with the volatility term structure to tabulate the volatilities appropriate for pricing an option with any strike price and any maturity. An example of a volatility surface that might be used for foreign currency options is given in Table 16.2.

One dimension of Table 16.2 is strike price; the other is time to maturity. The main body of the table shows implied volatilities calculated from the Black–Scholes model. At any given time, some of the entries in the table are likely to correspond to options for which reliable market data are available. The implied volatilities for these options are calculated directly from their market prices and entered into the table. The rest of the table is determined using linear interpolation.

When a new option has to be valued, financial engineers look up the appropriate volatility in the table. For example, when valuing a 9-month option with a strike price of 1.05, a financial engineer would interpolate between 13.4 and 14.0 in Table 16.2 to obtain a volatility of 13.7%. This is the volatility that would be used in the Black–Scholes formula or a binomial tree.

The shape of the volatility smile depends on the option maturity. As illustrated in Table 16.2, the smile tends to become less pronounced as the option maturity increases. Define T as the time to maturity and F_0 as the forward price of the asset. Some financial engineers choose to define the volatility smile as the relationship between implied volatility and

$$\frac{1}{\sqrt{T}}\ln\left(\frac{K}{F_0}\right)$$

rather than as the relationship between the implied volatility and K. The smile is then usually much less dependent on the time to maturity.[4]

The Role of the Model

How important is the pricing model if traders are prepared to use a different volatility for every option? It can be argued that the Black–Scholes model is no more than a sophisticated interpolation tool used by traders for ensuring that an option is priced

[4] For a discussion of this approach, see S. Natenberg *Option Pricing and Volatility: Advanced Trading Strategies and Techniques*, 2nd edn. McGraw-Hill, 1994; R. Tompkins *Options Analysis: A State of the Art Guide to Options Pricing*, Burr Ridge, IL: Irwin, 1994.

consistently with the market prices of other actively traded options. If traders stopped using Black–Scholes and switched to another plausible model, then the volatility surface and the shape of the smile would change, but arguably the dollar prices quoted in the market would not change appreciably.

16.5 GREEK LETTERS

The volatility smile complicates the calculation of Greek letters. Derman describes a number of volatility regimes or rules of thumb that are sometimes assumed by traders.[5] The simplest of these is known as the *sticky strike rule*. This assumes that the implied volatility of an option remains constant from one day to the next. It means that Greek letters calculated using the Black–Scholes assumptions are correct provided that the volatility used for an option is its current implied volatility.

A more complicated rule is known as the *sticky delta* rule. This assumes that the relationship we observe between an option price and S/K today will apply tomorrow. As the price of the underlying asset changes, the implied volatility of the option is assumed to change to reflect the option's "moneyness" (i.e., the extent to which it is in or out of the money). If we use the sticky delta rule, the formulas for Greek letters given in the Chapter 15 are no longer correct. For example, delta of a call option is given by

$$\frac{\partial c_{\text{BS}}}{\partial S} + \frac{\partial c_{\text{BS}}}{\partial \sigma_{\text{imp}}} \frac{\partial \sigma_{\text{imp}}}{\partial S}$$

where c_{BS} is the Black-Scholes price of the option expressed as a function of the asset price S and the implied volatility σ_{imp}. Consider the impact of this formula on the delta of an equity call option. From Figure 16.3, volatility is a decreasing function of the strike price K. Alternatively it can be regarded as an increasing function of S/K. Under the sticky delta model, therefore, the volatility increases as the asset price increases, so that

$$\frac{\partial \sigma_{\text{imp}}}{\partial S} > 0$$

As a result, delta is higher than that given by the Black–Scholes assumptions.

It turns out that the sticky strike and sticky delta rules do not correspond to internally consistent models (except when the volatility smile is flat for all maturities). A model that can be made exactly consistent with the smiles is known as the *implied volatility function* model or the *implied tree model*. We will explain this model in Chapter 24.

In practice, banks try to ensure that their exposure to the most commonly observed changes in the volatility surface is reasonably small. One technique for identifying these changes is principal components analysis, which we discuss in Chapter 18.

16.6 WHEN A SINGLE LARGE JUMP IS ANTICIPATED

Let us now consider an example of how an unusual volatility smile might arise in equity markets. Suppose that a stock price is currently \$50 and an important news

[5] See E. Derman, "Regimes of Volatility," *Risk*, April 1999, 54–59

Figure 16.5 Effect of a single large jump. The solid line is the true distribution; the dashed line is the lognormal distribution.

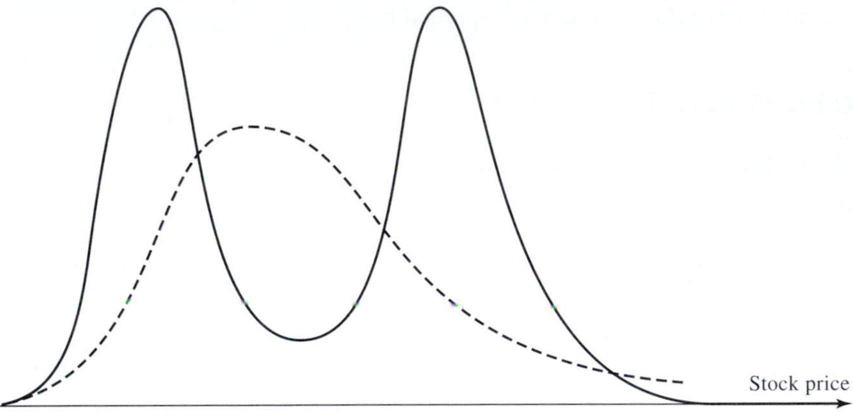

announcement due in a few days is expected either to increase the stock price by \$8 or to reduce it by \$8. (This announcement could concern the outcome of a takeover attempt or the verdict in an important lawsuit.) The probability distribution of the stock price in, say, 1 month might then consist of a mixture of two lognormal distributions, the first corresponding to favorable news, the second to unfavorable news. The situation is illustrated in Figure 16.5. The solid line shows the mixtures-of-lognormals distribution for the stock price in 1 month; the dashed line shows a lognormal distribution with the same mean and standard deviation as this distribution.

The true probability distribution is bimodal (certainly not lognormal). One easy way to investigate the general effect of a bimodal stock price distribution is to consider the extreme case where the distribution is binomial. This is what we will now do.

Suppose that the stock price is currently \$50 and that it is known that in 1 month it will be either \$42 or \$58. Suppose further that the risk-free rate is 12% per annum. The situation is illustrated in Figure 16.6 . Options can be valued using the binomial model from Chapter 11. In this case $u = 1.16$, $d = 0.84$, $a = 1.0101$, and $p = 0.5314$. The results from valuing a range of different options are shown in Table 16.3. The first column shows alternative strike prices; the second column shows prices of 1-month European call options; the third column shows the prices of one-month European put option prices;

Figure 16.6 Change in stock price in 1 month.

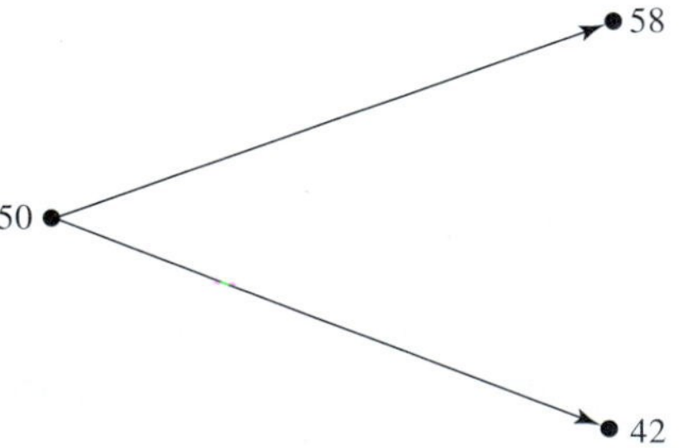

Table 16.3 Implied volatilities in situation where true distribution is binomial.

Strike price ($)	*Call price* ($)	*Put price* ($)	*Implied volatility* (%)
42	8.42	0.00	0.0
44	7.37	0.93	58.8
46	6.31	1.86	66.6
48	5.26	2.78	69.5
50	4.21	3.71	69.2
52	3.16	4.64	66.1
54	2.10	5.57	60.0
56	1.05	6.50	49.0
58	0.00	7.42	0.0

the fourth column shows implied volatilities. (As shown in Section 16.1, the implied volatility of a European put option is the same as that of a European call option when they have the same strike price and maturity.) Figure 16.7 shows the volatility smile. It is actually a "frown" (the opposite of that observed for currencies) with volatilities declining as we move out of or into the money. The volatility implied from an option with a strike price of 50 will overprice an option with a strike price of 44 or 56.

SUMMARY

The Black–Scholes model and its extensions assume that the probability distribution of the underlying asset at any given future time is lognormal. This assumption is not the

Figure 16.7 Volatility smile for situation in Table 16.3.

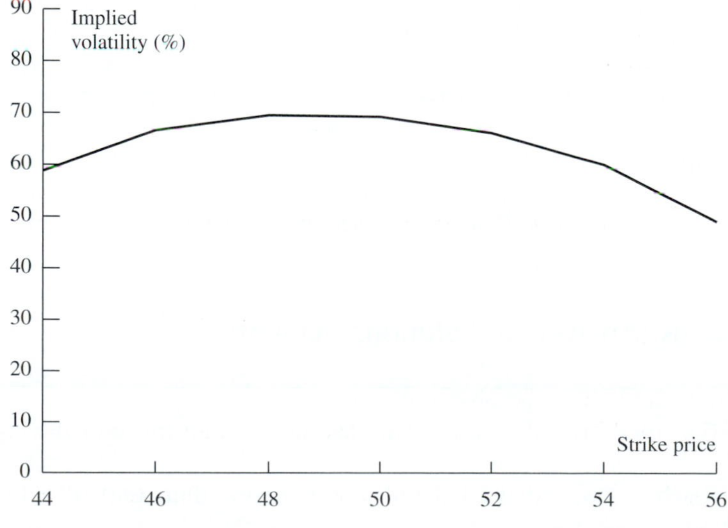

one made by traders. They assume the probability distribution of an equity price has a heavier left tail and a less heavy right tail than the lognormal distribution. They also assume that the probability distribution of an exchange rate has a heavier right tail and a heavier left tail than the lognormal distribution.

Traders use volatility smiles to allow for nonlognormality. The volatility smile defines the relationship between the implied volatility of an option and its strike price. For equity options, the volatility smile tends to be downward sloping. This means that out-of-the-money puts and in-the-money calls tend to have high implied volatilities whereas out-of-the-money calls and in-the-money puts tend to have low implied volatilities. For foreign currency options, the volatility smile is U-shaped. Both out-of-the-money and in-the-money options have higher implied volatilities than at-the-money options.

Often traders also use a volatility term structure. The implied volatility of an option then depends on its life. When volatility smiles and volatility term structures are combined, they produce a volatility surface. This defines implied volatility as a function of both the strike price and the time to maturity.

FURTHER READING

Bakshi, G., C. Cao, and Z. Chen. "Empirical Performance of Alternative Option Pricing Models," *Journal of Finance*, 52, No. 5 (December 1997): 2004–49.

Bates, D. S. "Post-'87 Crash Fears in the S&P Futures Market," *Journal of Econometrics*, 94 (January/February 2000): 181–238.

Derman, E. "Regimes of Volatility," *Risk*, April 1999: 55–59.

Ederington, L. H., and W. Guan. "Why Are Those Options Smiling," *Journal of Derivatives*, 10, 2 (2002): 9–34.

Jackwerth, J. C., and M. Rubinstein. "Recovering Probability Distributions from Option Prices," *Journal of Finance*, 51 (December 1996): 1611–31.

Lauterbach, B., and P. Schultz. "Pricing Warrants: An Empirical Study of the Black–Scholes Model and Its Alternatives," *Journal of Finance*, 4, No. 4 (September 1990): 1181–1210.

Melick, W. R., and C. P. Thomas. "Recovering an Asset's Implied Probability Density Function from Option Prices: An Application to Crude Oil during the Gulf Crisis," *Journal of Financial and Quantitative Analysis*, 32, 1 (March 1997): 91–115.

Rubinstein, M. "Nonparametric Tests of Alternative Option Pricing Models Using All Reported Trades and Quotes on the 30 Most Active CBOE Option Classes from August 23, 1976, through August 31, 1978," *Journal of Finance*, 40 (June 1985): 455–80.

Rubinstein, M. "Implied Binomial Trees," *Journal of Finance*, 49, 3 (July 1994): 771–818.

Xu, X., and S. J. Taylor. "The Term Structure of Volatility Implied by Foreign Exchange Options," *Journal of Financial and Quantitative Analysis*, 29 (1994): 57–74.

Questions and Problems (Answers in Solutions Manual)

16.1. What volatility smile is likely to be observed when:

(a) Both tails of the stock price distribution are less heavy than those of the lognormal distribution?

(b) The right tail is heavier, and the left tail is less heavy, than that of a lognormal distribution?

16.2. What volatility smile is observed for equities?

16.3. What volatility smile is likely to be caused by jumps in the underlying asset price? Is the pattern likely to be more pronounced for a 2-year option than for a 3-month option?

16.4. A European call and put option have the same strike price and time to maturity. The call has an implied volatility of 30% and the put has an implied volatility of 25%. What trades would you do?

16.5. Explain carefully why a distribution with a heavier left tail and less heavy right tail than the lognormal distribution gives rise to a downward sloping volatility smile.

16.6. The market price of a European call is \$3.00 and its price given by Black–Scholes model with a volatility of 30% is \$3.50. The price given by this Black–Scholes model for a European put option with the same strike price and time to maturity is \$1.00. What should the market price of the put option be? Explain the reasons for your answer.

16.7. Explain what is meant by "crashophobia".

16.8. A stock price is currently \$20. Tomorrow, news is expected to be announced that will either increase the price by \$5 or decrease the price by \$5. What are the problems in using Black–Scholes to value 1-month options on the stock?

16.9. What volatility smile is likely to be observed for 6-month options when the volatility is uncertain and positively correlated to the stock price?

16.10. What problems do you think would be encountered in testing a stock option pricing model empirically?

16.11. Suppose that a central bank's policy is to allow an exchange rate to fluctuate between 0.97 and 1.03. What pattern of implied volatilities for options on the exchange rate would you expect to see?

16.12. Option traders sometimes refer to deep-out-of-the-money options as being options on volatility. Why do you think they do this?

16.13. A European call option on a certain stock has a strike price of \$30, a time to maturity of 1 year, and an implied volatility of 30%. A European put option on the same stock has a strike price of \$30, a time to maturity of 1 year, and an implied volatility of 33%. What is the arbitrage opportunity open to a trader? Does the arbitrage work only when the lognormal assumption underlying Black–Scholes holds? Explain carefully the reasons for your answer.

16.14. Suppose that the result of a major lawsuit affecting Microsoft is due to be announced tomorrow. Microsoft's stock price is currently \$60. If the ruling is favorable to Microsoft, the stock price is expected to jump to \$75. If it is unfavorable, the stock is expected to jump to \$50. What is the risk-neutral probability of a favorable ruling? Assume that the volatility of Microsoft's stock will be 25% for 6 months after the ruling if the ruling is favorable and 40% if it is unfavorable. Use DerivaGem to calculate the relationship between implied volatility and strike price for 6-month European options on Microsoft today. Microsoft does not pay dividends. Assume that the 6-month risk-free rate is 6%. Consider call options with strike prices of 30, 40, 50, 60, 70, and 80.

16.15. An exchange rate is currently 0.8000. The volatility of the exchange rate is quoted as 12% and interest rates in the two countries are the same. Using the lognormal assumption, estimate the probability that the exchange rate in 3 months will be (a) less than 0.7000, (b) between 0.7000 and 0.7500, (c) between 0.7500 and 0.8000, (d) between

0.8000 and 0.8500, (e) between 0.8500 and 0.9000, and (f) greater than 0.9000. Based on the volatility smile usually observed in the market for exchange rates, which of these estimates would you expect to be too low and which would you expect to be too high?

16.16. A stock price is \$40. A 6-month European call option on the stock with a strike price of \$30 has an implied volatility of 35%. A 6-month European call option on the stock with a strike price of \$50 has an implied volatility of 28%. The 6-month risk-free rate is 5% and no dividends are expected. Explain why the two implied volatilities are different. Use DerivaGem to calculate the prices of the two options. Use put–call parity to calculate the prices of 6-month European put options with strike prices of \$30 and \$50. Use DerivaGem to calculate the implied volatilities of these two put options.

16.17. "The Black–Scholes model is used by traders as an interpolation tool." Discuss this view.

Assignment Questions

16.18. A company's stock is selling for \$4. The company has no outstanding debt. Analysts consider the liquidation value of the company to be at least \$300,000 and there are 100,000 shares outstanding. What volatility smile would you expect to see?

16.19. A company is currently awaiting the outcome of a major lawsuit. This is expected to be known within 1 month. The stock price is currently \$20. If the outcome is positive, the stock price is expected to be \$24 at the end of 1 month. If the outcome is negative, it is expected to be \$18 at this time. The 1-month risk-free interest rate is 8% per annum.
(a) What is the risk-neutral probability of a positive outcome?
(b) What are the values of 1-month call options with strike prices of \$19, \$20, \$21, \$22, and \$23?
(c) Use DerivaGem to calculate a volatility smile for 1-month call options.
(d) Verify that the same volatility smile is obtained for 1-month put options.

16.20. A futures price is currently \$40. The risk-free interest rate is 5%. Some news is expected tomorrow that will cause the volatility over the next 3 months to be either 10% or 30%. There is a 60% chance of the first outcome and a 40% chance of the second outcome. Use DerivaGem to calculate a volatility smile for 3-month options.

16.21. Data for a number of foreign currencies are provided on the author's website:

`http://www.rotman.utoronto.ca/~hull`

Choose a currency and use the data to produce a table similar to Table 16.1.

16.22. Data for a number of stock indices are provided on the author's website:

`http://www.rotman.utoronto.ca/~hull`

Choose an index and test whether a three-standard-deviation down movement happens more often than a three-standard-deviation up movement.

16.23. Consider a European call and a European put with the same strike price and time to maturity. Show that they change in value by the same amount when the volatility increases from a level σ_1 to a new level σ_2 within a short period of time. (*Hint*: Use put–call parity.)

APPENDIX

DETERMINING IMPLIED RISK-NEUTRAL DISTRIBUTIONS FROM VOLATILITY SMILES

The price of a European call option on an asset with strike price K and maturity T is given by

$$c = e^{-rT} \int_{S_T=K}^{\infty} (S_T - K)\, g(S_T)\, dS_T$$

where r is the interest rate (assumed constant), S_T is the asset price at time T, and g is the risk-neutral probability density function of S_T. Differentiating once with respect to K, we obtain

$$\frac{\partial c}{\partial K} = -e^{-rT} \int_{S_T=K}^{\infty} g(S_T)\, dS_T$$

Differentiating again with respect to K, we have

$$\frac{\partial^2 c}{\partial K^2} = e^{-rT}\, g(K)$$

This shows that the probability density function g is given by

$$g(K) = e^{rT} \frac{\partial^2 c}{\partial K^2}$$

This result, which is from Breeden and Litzenberger (1978), allows risk-neutral probability distributions to be estimated from volatility smiles.[6] Suppose that c_1, c_2, and c_3 are the prices of T-year European call options with strike prices of $K - \delta$, K, and $K + \delta$, respectively. Assuming δ is small, an estimate of $g(K)$ is

$$e^{rT} \frac{c_1 + c_3 - 2c_2}{\delta^2}$$

[6] See D. T. Breeden and R. H. Litzenberger, "Prices of State-Contingent Claims Implicit in Option Prices," *Jounal of Business*, 51 (1978), 621–51.

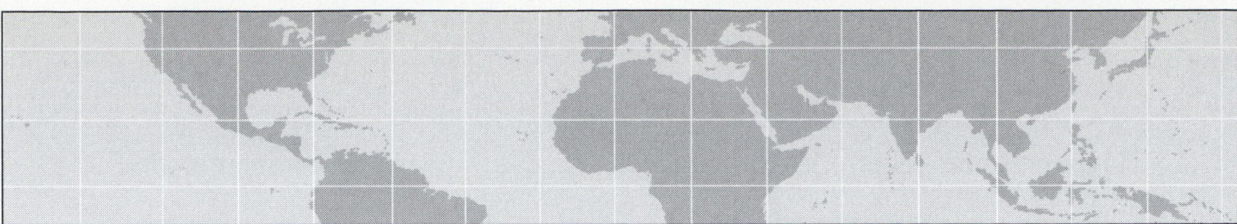

CHAPTER 17 Basic Numerical Procedures

This chapter discusses three numerical procedures for valuing derivatives when exact formulas are not available. The first involves representing the asset price movements in the form of a tree and was introduced in Chapter 11. The second involves Monte Carlo simulation, which we encountered briefly in Chapter 12 when explaining stochastic processes. The third involves finite difference methods.

Monte Carlo simulation is usually used for derivatives where the payoff is dependent on the history of the underlying variable or where there are several underlying variables. Trees and finite difference methods are usually used for American options and other derivatives where the holder has early exercise decisions to make prior to maturity. In addition to valuing a derivative, all the procedures can be used to calculate Greek letters such as delta, gamma, and vega.

The basic procedures we discuss in this chapter can be used to handle most of the derivatives valuations problems that are encountered in practice. However, sometimes they have to be adapted to cope with particular situations. We discuss this in Chapter 24.

17.1 BINOMIAL TREES

We introduced binomial trees in Chapter 11. They can be used to value either European or American options. The Black–Scholes formulas and their extensions that we presented in Chapters 13 and 14 provide analytic valuations for European options.[1] There are no analytic valuations for American options. Binomial trees are therefore most useful for valuing these types of options.[2]

As explained in Chapter 11, the binomial tree valuation approach involves dividing the life of the option into a large number of small time intervals of length Δt. It assumes that in each time interval the price of the underlying asset moves from its initial value of

[1] The Black–Scholes formulas are based on the same set of assumptions as binomial trees. As one might expect, in the limit as the number of time steps is increased, the price given for a European option by the binomial method converges to the Black–Scholes price.

[2] Some analytic approximations for valuing American options have been suggested. The most well-known one is the quadratic approximation approach. See Technical Note 8 on the author's website for a description of this approach.

Figure 17.1 Asset price movements in time Δt under the binomial model.

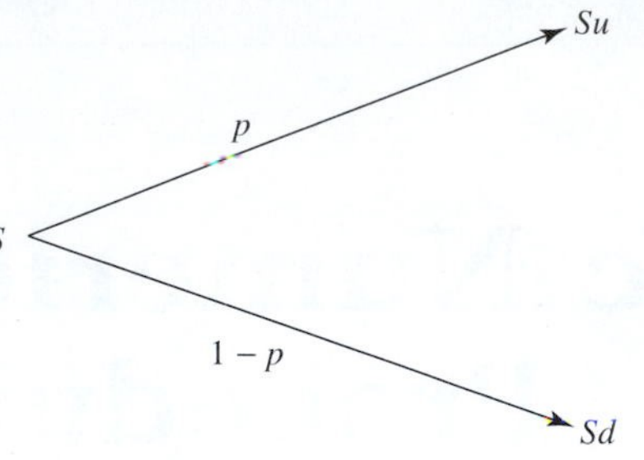

S to one of two new values, Su and Sd. The approach is illustrated in Figure 17.1. In general, $u > 1$ and $d < 1$. The movement from S to Su, therefore, is an "up" movement and the movement from S to Sd is a "down" movement. The probability of an up movement will be denoted by p. The probability of a down movement is $1 - p$.

Risk-Neutral Valuation

The risk-neutral valuation principle, explained in Chapters 11 and 13, states that an option (or other derivative) can be valued on the assumption that the world is risk neutral. This means that for valuation purposes we can use the following procedure:

1. Assume that the expected return from all traded assets is the risk-free interest rate.
2. Value payoffs from the derivative by calculating their expected values and discounting at the risk-free interest rate.

This principle is a key element of the ways in which trees are used.

Determination of p, u, and d

The parameters p, u, and d must give correct values for the mean and variance of asset price changes during a time interval of length Δt. Because we are working in a risk-neutral world, the expected return from the asset is the risk-free interest rate, r. Suppose that the asset provides a yield of q. The expected return in the form of capital gains must be $r - q$. This means that the expected value of the asset price at the end of a time interval of length Δt must be $Se^{(r-q)\Delta t}$, where S is the stock price at the beginning of the time interval. It follows that

$$Se^{(r-q)\Delta t} = pSu + (1 - p)Sd \tag{17.1}$$

or

$$e^{(r-q)\Delta t} = pu + (1 - p)d \tag{17.2}$$

As explained in Section 13.4, the variance of the percentage change in the stock price in a small time interval of length Δt is $\sigma^2\Delta t$. The variance of a variable Q is defined as $E(Q^2) - [E(Q)]^2$. There is a probability p that the percentage change is u and $1 - p$ that it is d. The expected percentage change is $e^{(r-q)\Delta t}$. It follows that

$$pu^2 + (1 - p)d^2 - e^{2(r-q)\Delta t} = \sigma^2\Delta t$$

Substituting for p from equation (17.2) gives

$$e^{(r-q)\Delta t}(u+d) - ud - e^{2(r-q)\Delta t} = \sigma^2 \Delta t \tag{17.3}$$

Equations (17.2) and (17.3) impose two conditions on p, u, and d. A third condition used by Cox, Ross, and Rubinstein (1979) is[3]

$$u = \frac{1}{d}$$

A solution to equations (17.2) and (17.3) when terms of higher order than Δt are ignored is[4]

$$p = \frac{a-d}{u-d} \tag{17.4}$$

$$u = e^{\sigma\sqrt{\Delta t}} \tag{17.5}$$

$$d = e^{-\sigma\sqrt{\Delta t}} \tag{17.6}$$

where

$$a = e^{(r-q)\Delta t} \tag{17.7}$$

The variable a is sometimes referred to as the *growth factor*. Equations (17.4) to (17.7) are the same as those in Section 11.9.

Tree of Asset Prices

Figure 17.2 illustrates the complete tree of asset prices that is considered when the binomial model is used. At time zero, the asset price, S_0, is known. At time Δt, there are two possible asset prices, $S_0 u$ and $S_0 d$; at time $2\Delta t$, there are three possible asset prices, $S_0 u^2$, S_0, and $S_0 d^2$; and so on. In general, at time $i\,\Delta t$, we consider $i+1$ asset prices. These are

$$S_0 u^j d^{i-j}, \quad j = 0, 1, \dots, i$$

Note that the relationship $u = 1/d$ is used in computing the asset price at each node of the tree in Figure 17.2. For example, $S_0 u^2 d = S_0 u$. Note also that the tree recombines in the sense that an up movement followed by a down movement leads to the same asset price as a down movement followed by an up movement.

Working Backward through the Tree

Options are evaluated by starting at the end of the tree (time T) and working backward. The value of the option is known at time T. For example, a put option is worth $\max(K - S_T, 0)$ and a call option is worth $\max(S_T - K, 0)$, where S_T is the asset price at time T and K is the strike price. Because a risk-neutral world is being assumed, the

---

[3] See J.C. Cox, S.A. Ross, and M. Rubinstein, "Option Pricing: A Simplified Approach," *Journal of Financial Economics*, 7 (October 1979), 229–63.

[4] To see this, we note that equations (17.4) and (17.7) satisfy the condition in equation (17.2) exactly. The exponential function e^x can be expanded as $1 + x + x^2/2 + \cdots$. When terms of higher order than Δt are ignored, equation (17.5) implies that $u = 1 + \sigma\sqrt{\Delta t} + \frac{1}{2}\sigma^2\,\Delta t$ and equation (17.6) implies that $d = 1 - \sigma\sqrt{\Delta t} + \frac{1}{2}\sigma^2\,\Delta t$. Also, $e^{(r-q)\Delta t} = 1 + (r-q)\Delta t$ and $e^{2(r-q)\Delta t} = 1 + 2(r-q)\Delta t$. By substitution we see that equation (17.3) is satisfied when terms of higher order than Δt are ignored.

Figure 17.2 Tree used to value an option.

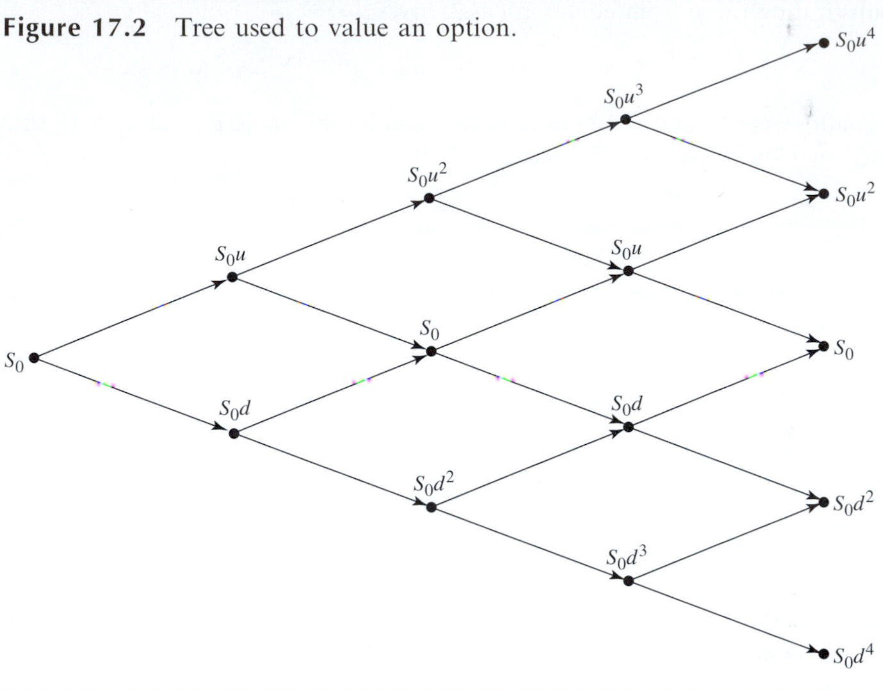

value at each node at time $T - \Delta t$ can be calculated as the expected value at time T discounted at rate r for a time period Δt. Similarly, the value at each node at time $T - 2\Delta t$ can be calculated as the expected value at time $T - \Delta t$ discounted for a time period Δt at rate r, and so on. If the option is American, it is necessary to check at each node to see whether early exercise is preferable to holding the option for a further time period Δt. Eventually, by working back through all the nodes, we are able to obtain the value of the option at time zero.

Example 17.1

Consider a 5-month American put option on a non-dividend-paying stock when the stock price is \$50, the strike price is \$50, the risk-free interest rate is 10% per annum, and the volatility is 40% per annum. With our usual notation, this means that $S_0 = 50$, $K = 50$, $r = 0.10$, $\sigma = 0.40$, $T = 0.4167$, and $q = 0$. Suppose that we divide the life of the option into five intervals of length 1 month ($= 0.0833$ year) for the purposes of constructing a binomial tree. Then $\Delta t = 0.0833$ and, using equations (17.4) to (17.7), we have

$$u = e^{\sigma\sqrt{\Delta t}} = 1.1224, \qquad d = e^{-\sigma\sqrt{\Delta t}} = 0.8909, \qquad a = e^{r\Delta t} = 1.0084$$

$$p = \frac{a-d}{u-d} = 0.5073, \qquad 1 - p = 0.4927$$

Figure 17.3 shows the binomial tree produced by DerivaGem. At each node there are two numbers. The top one shows the stock price at the node; the lower one shows the value of the option at the node. The probability of an up movement is always 0.5073; the probability of a down movement is always 0.4927.

Figure 17.3 Binomial tree from DerivaGem for American put on non-dividend-paying stock (Example 17.1).

At each node:
Upper value = Underlying Asset Price
Lower value = Option Price
Shading indicates where option is exercised

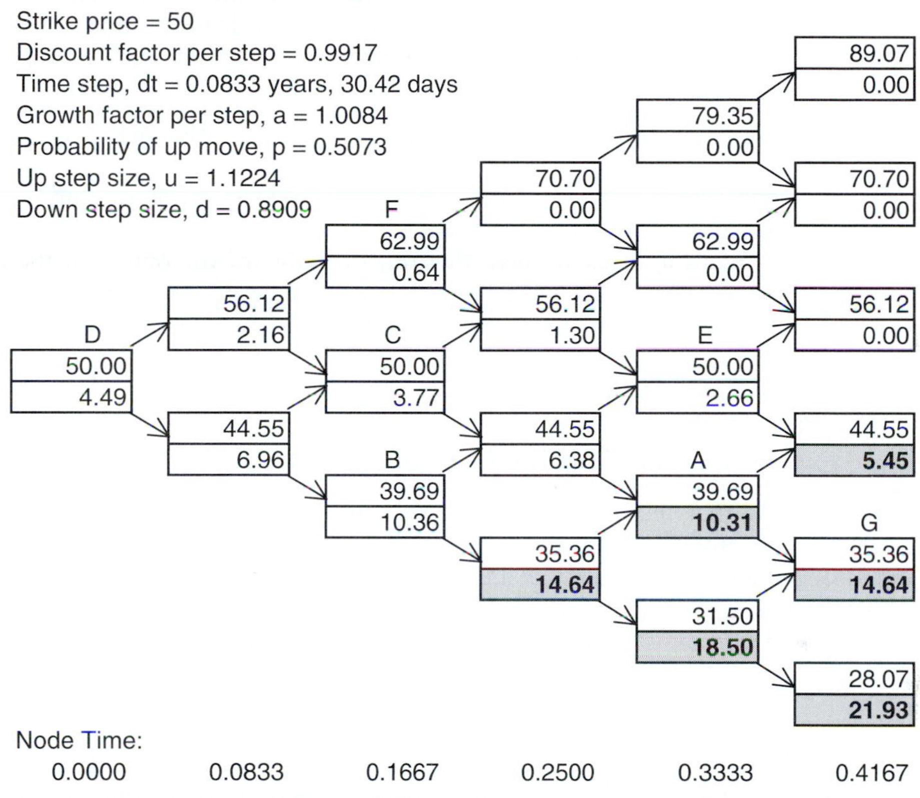

The stock price at the jth node ($j = 0, 1, \ldots, i$) at time $i\,\Delta t$ ($i = 0, 1, \ldots, 5$) is calculated as $S_0 u^j d^{i-j}$. For example, the stock price at node A ($i = 4$, $j = 1$) (i.e., the second node up at the end of the fourth time step) is $50 \times 1.1224 \times 0.8909^3 =$ \$39.69. The option prices at the final nodes are calculated as $\max(K - S_T, 0)$. For example, the option price at node G is $50.00 - 35.36 = 14.64$. The option prices at the penultimate nodes are calculated from the option prices at the final nodes. First, we assume no exercise of the option at the nodes. This means that the option price is calculated as the present value of the expected option price one time step later. For example, at node E, the option price is calculated as

$$(0.5073 \times 0 + 0.4927 \times 5.45)e^{-0.10\times0.0833} = 2.66$$

whereas at node A it is calculated as

$$(0.5073 \times 5.45 + 0.4927 \times 14.64)e^{-0.10\times0.0833} = 9.90$$

We then check to see if early exercise is preferable to waiting. At node E, early exercise would give a value for the option of zero because both the stock price and strike price are \$50. Clearly it is best to wait. The correct value for the option at node E, therefore, is \$2.66. At node A, it is a different story. If the option is exercised, it is worth \$50.00 – \$39.69, or \$10.31. This is more than \$9.90. If node A is reached, then the option should be exercised and the correct value for the option at node A is \$10.31.

Option prices at earlier nodes are calculated in a similar way. Note that it is not always best to exercise an option early when it is in the money. Consider node B. If the option is exercised, it is worth \$50.00 – \$39.69, or \$10.31. However, if it is held, it is worth

$$(0.5073 \times 6.38 + 0.4927 \times 14.64)e^{-0.10\times 0.0833} = 10.36$$

The option should, therefore, not be exercised at this node, and the correct option value at the node is \$10.36.

Working back through the tree, the value of the option at the initial node is \$4.49. This is our numerical estimate for the option's current value. In practice, a smaller value of Δt, and many more nodes, would be used. DerivaGem shows that with 30, 50, 100, and 500 time steps we get values for the option of 4.263, 4.272, 4.278, and 4.283.

Expressing the Approach Algebraically

Suppose that the life of an American put option on a non-dividend-paying stock is divided into N subintervals of length Δt. We will refer to the jth node at time $i\,\Delta t$ as the (i, j) node, where $0 \leqslant i \leqslant N$ and $0 \leqslant j \leqslant i$). Define $f_{i,j}$ as the value of the option at the (i, j) node. The stock price at the (i, j) node is $S_0 u^j d^{i-j}$. Since the value of an American put at its expiration date is $\max(K - S_T, 0)$, we know that

$$f_{N,j} = \max(K - S_0 u^j d^{N-j}, 0), \quad j = 0, 1, \dots, N$$

There is a probability p of moving from the (i, j) node at time $i\,\Delta t$ to the $(i+1, j+1)$ node at time $(i+1)\,\Delta t$, and a probability $1 - p$ of moving from the (i, j) node at time $i\,\Delta t$ to the $(i+1, j)$ node at time $(i+1)\,\Delta t$. Assuming no early exercise, risk-neutral valuation gives

$$f_{i,j} = e^{-r\Delta t}[p f_{i+1,j+1} + (1-p) f_{i+1,j}]$$

for $0 \leqslant i \leqslant N-1$ and $0 \leqslant j \leqslant i$. When early exercise is taken into account, this value for $f_{i,j}$ must be compared with the option's intrinsic value, and we obtain

$$f_{i,j} = \max\{K - S_0 u^j d^{i-j},\ e^{-r\Delta t}[p f_{i+1,j+1} + (1-p) f_{i+1,j}]\}$$

Note that, because the calculations start at time T and work backward, the value at time $i\,\Delta t$ captures not only the effect of early exercise possibilities at time $i\,\Delta t$, but also the effect of early exercise at subsequent times.

In the limit as Δt tends to zero, an exact value for the American put is obtained. In practice, $N = 30$ usually gives reasonable results. Figure 17.4 shows the convergence of the option price in the example we have been considering. This figure was calculated

Figure 17.4 Convergence of the price of the option in Example 17.1 calculated from the DerivaGem Application Builder functions.

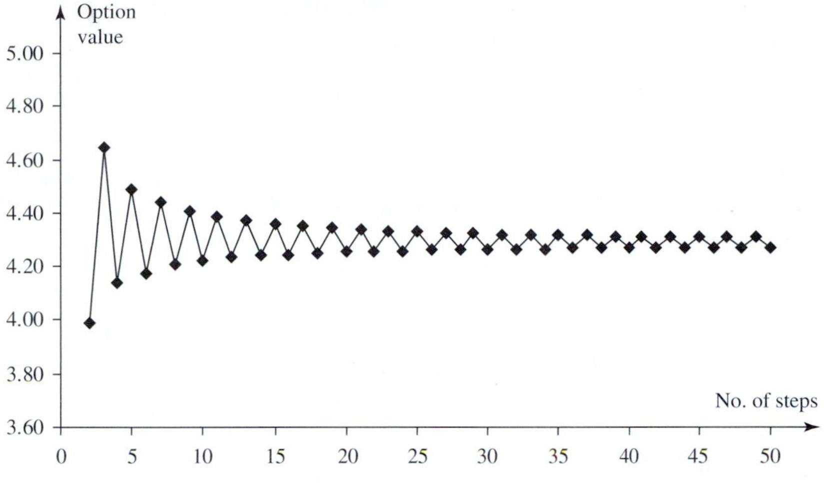

using the Application Builder functions provided with the DerivaGem software (see Sample Application A).

Estimating Delta and Other Greek Letters

It will be recalled that the delta (Δ) of an option is the rate of change of its price with respect to the underlying stock price. It can be calculated as

$$\frac{\Delta f}{\Delta S}$$

where ΔS is a small change in the stock price and Δf is the corresponding small change in the option price. At time Δt, we have an estimate f_{11} for the option price when the stock price is $S_0 u$ and an estimate f_{10} for the option price when the stock price is $S_0 d$. In other words, when $\Delta S = S_0 u - S_0 d$, $\Delta f = f_{11} - f_{10}$. Therefore an estimate of delta at time Δt is

$$\Delta = \frac{f_{11} - f_{10}}{S_0 u - S_0 d} \tag{17.8}$$

To determine gamma (Γ), note that we have two estimates of Δ at time $2\Delta t$. When $S = (S_0 u^2 + S_0)/2$ (halfway between the second and third node), delta is $(f_{22} - f_{21})/(S_0 u^2 - S_0)$; when $S = (S_0 + S_0 d^2)/2$ (halfway between the first and second node), delta is $(f_{21} - f_{20})/(S_0 - S_0 d^2)$. The difference between the two values of S is h, where

$$h = 0.5(S_0 u^2 - S_0 d^2)$$

Gamma is the change in delta divided by h:

$$\Gamma = \frac{[(f_{22} - f_{21})/(S_0 u^2 - S_0)] - [(f_{21} - f_{20})/(S_0 - S_0 d^2)]}{h} \tag{17.9}$$

These procedures provide estimates of delta at time Δt and of gamma at time $2\Delta t$. In practice, they are usually used as estimates of delta and gamma at time zero as well.[5]

A further hedge parameter that can be obtained directly from the tree is theta (Θ). This is the rate of change of the option price with time when all else is kept constant. If the tree starts at time zero, an estimate of theta is

$$\Theta = \frac{f_{21} - f_{00}}{2\Delta t} \tag{17.10}$$

Vega can be calculated by making a small change, $\Delta\sigma$, in the volatility and constructing a new tree to obtain a new value of the option. (The time step Δt should be kept the same.) The estimate of vega is

$$\mathcal{V} = \frac{f^* - f}{\Delta\sigma}$$

where f and f^* are the estimates of the option price from the original and the new tree, respectively. Rho can be calculated similarly.

Example 17.2

Consider again Example 17.1. From Figure 17.3, we have $f_{1,0} = 6.96$ and $f_{1,1} = 2.16$. Equation (17.8) gives an estimate for delta of

$$\frac{2.16 - 6.96}{56.12 - 44.55} = -0.41$$

From equation (17.9), an estimate of the gamma of the option can be obtained from the values at nodes B, C, and F as

$$\frac{[(0.64 - 3.77)/(62.99 - 50.00)] - [(3.77 - 10.36)/(50.00 - 39.69)]}{11.65} = 0.03$$

From equation (17.10), an estimate of the theta of the option can be obtained from the values at nodes D and C as

$$\frac{3.77 - 4.49}{0.1667} = -4.3 \quad \text{per year}$$

or -0.012 per calendar day. These are only rough estimates. They become progressively better as the number of time steps on the tree is increased. Using 50 time steps, DerivaGem provides estimates of -0.415, 0.034, and -0.0117 for delta, gamma, and theta, respectively. By making small changes to parameters and recomputing values, vega and rho are estimated as 0.123 and -0.072, respectively.

17.2 USING THE BINOMIAL TREE FOR OPTIONS ON INDICES, CURRENCIES, AND FUTURES CONTRACTS

As explained in Chapters 11 and 14, stock indices, currencies, and futures contracts can, for the purposes of option valuation, be considered as assets providing known yields. In

[5] If slightly more accuracy is required for delta and gamma, we can start the binomial tree at time $-2\Delta t$ and assume that the stock price is S_0 at this time. This leads to the option price being calculated for three different stock prices at time zero.

the case of a stock index, the relevant yield is the dividend yield on the stock portfolio underlying the index; in the case of a currency, it is the foreign risk-free interest rate; in the case of a futures contract, it is the domestic risk-free interest rate. The binomial tree approach can therefore be used to value options on stock indices, currencies, and futures contracts provided that q in equation (17.7) is interpreted appropriately.

Example 17.3

Consider a 4-month American call option on index futures where the current futures price is 300, the exercise price is 300, the risk-free interest rate is 8% per annum, and the volatility of the index is 30% per annum. We divide the life of the option into four 1-month periods for the purposes of constructing the tree. In this case, $F_0 = 300$, $K = 300$, $r = 0.08$, $\sigma = 0.3$, $T = 0.3333$, and $\Delta t = 0.0833$. Because a futures contract is analogous to a stock paying dividends at a rate r, q should be set equal to r in equation (17.7). This gives $a = 1$. The other parameters

Figure 17.5 Binomial tree produced by DerivaGem for American call option on an index futures contract (Example 17.3).

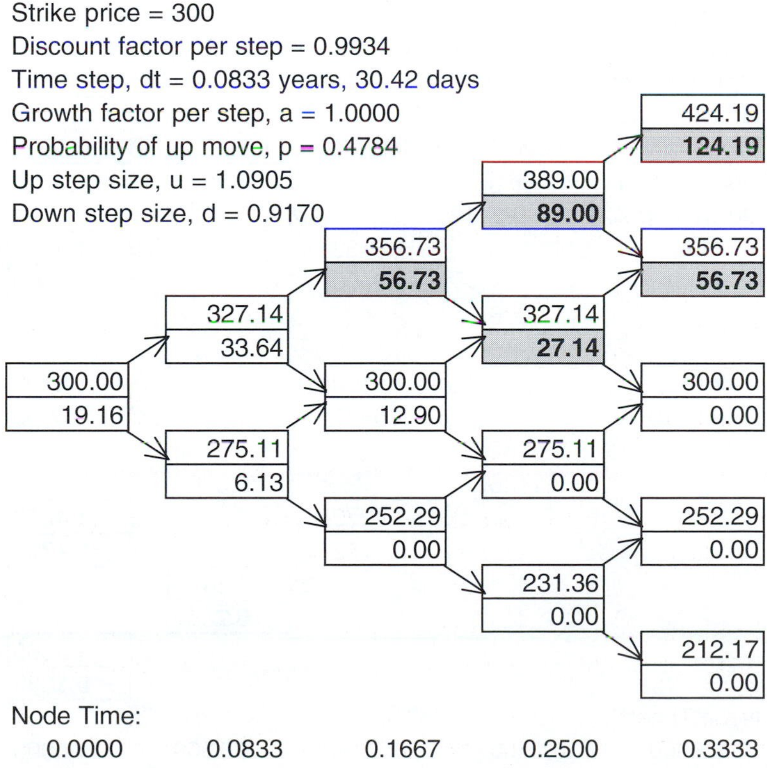

necessary to construct the tree are

$$u = e^{\sigma\sqrt{\Delta t}} = 1.0905, \qquad d = \frac{1}{u} = 0.9170$$
$$p = \frac{a-d}{u-d} = 0.4784, \qquad 1 - p = 0.5216$$

The tree, as produced by DerivaGem, is shown in Figure 17.5. (The upper number is the futures price; the lower number is the option price.) The estimated value of the option is 19.16. More accuracy is obtained using more steps. With 50 time steps, DerivaGem gives a value of 20.18; with 100 time steps it gives 20.22.

Example 17.4

Consider a 1-year American put option on the British pound. The current exchange rate is 1.6100, the strike price is 1.6000, the US risk-free interest rate is 8%

Figure 17.6 Binomial tree produced by DerivaGem for American put option on a currency (Example 17.4).

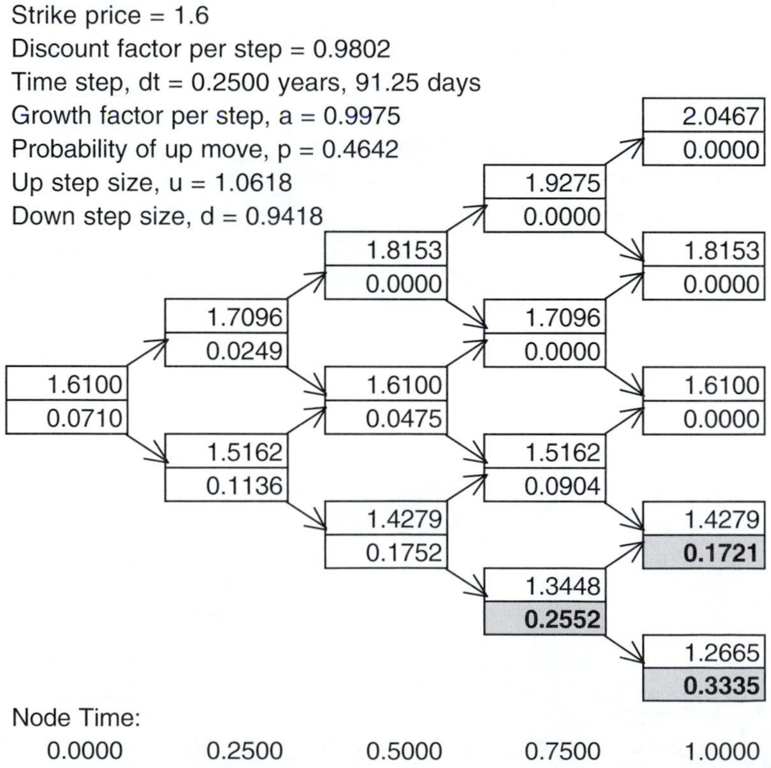

per annum, the sterling risk-free interest rate is 9% per annum, and the volatility of the sterling exchange rate is 12% per annum. In this case, $S_0 = 1.61$, $K = 1.60$, $r = 0.08$, $r_f = 0.09$, $\sigma = 0.12$, and $T = 1.0$. We divide the life of the option into four 3-month periods for the purposes of constructing the tree, so that $\Delta t = 0.25$. In this case, $q = r_f$ and equation (17.7) gives

$$a = e^{(0.08-0.09)\times 0.25} = 0.9975$$

The other parameters necessary to construct the tree are

$$u = e^{\sigma\sqrt{\Delta t}} = 1.0618, \qquad d = \frac{1}{u} = 0.9418$$

$$p = \frac{a-d}{u-d} = 0.4642, \qquad 1 - p = 0.5358$$

The tree, as produced by DerivaGem, is shown in Figure 17.6. (The upper number is the exchange rate; the lower number is the option price.) The estimated value of the option is \$0.0710. (Using 50 time steps, DerivaGem gives the value of the option as 0.0738; with 100 time steps it also gives 0.0738.)

17.3 BINOMIAL MODEL FOR A DIVIDEND-PAYING STOCK

We now move on to the more tricky issue of how the binomial model can be used for a dividend-paying stock. As in Chapter 13, the word *dividend* will, for the purposes of our discussion, be used to refer to the reduction in the stock price on the ex-dividend date as a result of the dividend.

Known Dividend Yield

If it is assumed that there is a single dividend, and the dividend yield (i.e., the dividend as a percentage of the stock price) is known, the tree takes the form shown in Figure 17.7 and can be analyzed in similar manner to that just described. If the time $i\,\Delta t$ is prior to the stock going ex-dividend, the nodes on the tree correspond to stock prices

$$S_0 u^j d^{i-j}, \quad j = 0, 1, \dots, i$$

where u and d are defined as in equations (17.5) and (17.6). If the time $i\,\Delta t$ is after the stock goes ex-dividend, the nodes correspond to stock prices

$$S_0(1-\delta)u^j d^{i-j}, \quad j = 0, 1, \dots, i$$

where δ is the dividend yield. Several known dividend yields during the life of an option can be dealt with similarly. If δ_i is the total dividend yield associated with all ex-dividend dates between time zero and time $i\,\Delta t$, the nodes at time $i\,\Delta t$ correspond to stock prices

$$S_0(1-\delta_i)u^j d^{i-j}$$

Known Dollar Dividend

In some situations, the most realistic assumption is that the dollar amount of the dividend rather than the dividend yield is known in advance. If the volatility of the stock, σ, is assumed constant, the tree then takes the form shown in Figure 17.8. It does not recombine, which means that the number of nodes that have to be evaluated, particularly if there are several dividends, is liable to become very large. Suppose that there is only one dividend, that the ex-dividend date, τ, is between $k\,\Delta t$ and $(k+1)\,\Delta t$, and that the dollar amount of the dividend is D. When $i \leqslant k$, the nodes on the tree at time $i\,\Delta t$ correspond to stock prices

$$S_0 u^j d^{i-j}, \quad j = 0, 1, 2, \dots, i$$

as before. When $i = k+1$, the nodes on the tree correspond to stock prices

$$S_0 u^j d^{i-j} - D, \quad j = 0, 1, 2, \dots, i$$

When $i = k+2$, the nodes on the tree correspond to stock prices

$$(S_0 u^j d^{i-1-j} - D)u \quad \text{and} \quad (S_0 u^j d^{i-1-j} - D)d$$

for $j = 0, 1, 2, \dots, i-1$, so that there are $2i$ rather than $i+1$ nodes. When $i = k+m$, there are $m(k+2)$ rather than $k+m+1$ nodes.

The problem can be simplified by assuming, as in the analysis of European options in Section 13.12, that the stock price has two components: a part that is uncertain and a part that is the present value of all future dividends during the life of the option. Suppose, as before, that there is only one ex-dividend date, τ, during the life of the

Figure 17.7 Tree when stock pays a known dividend yield at one particular time.

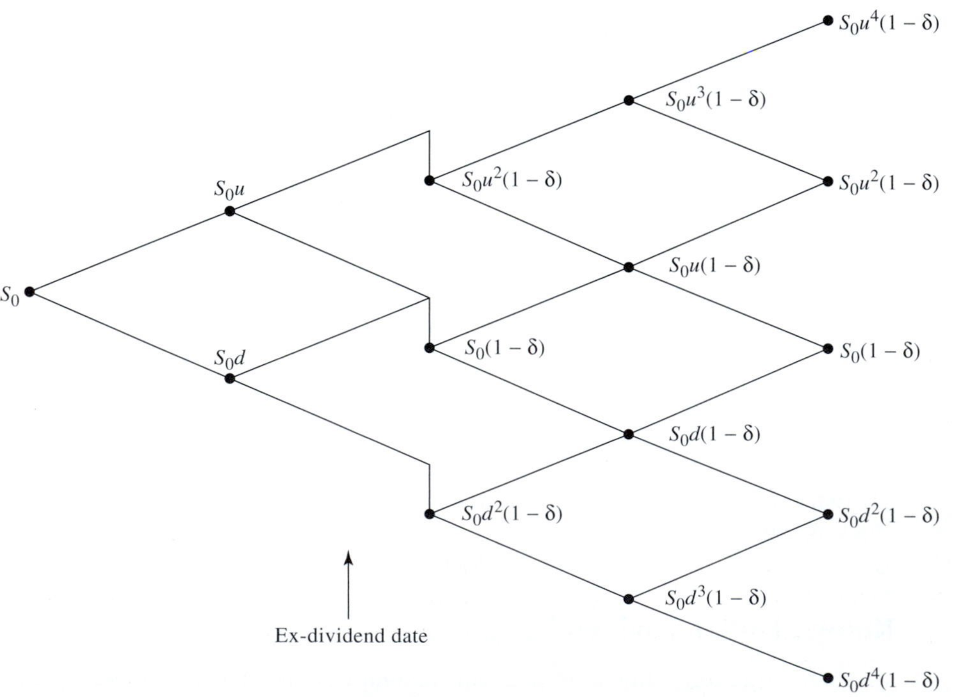

Figure 17.8 Tree when dollar amount of dividend is assumed known and volatility is assumed constant.

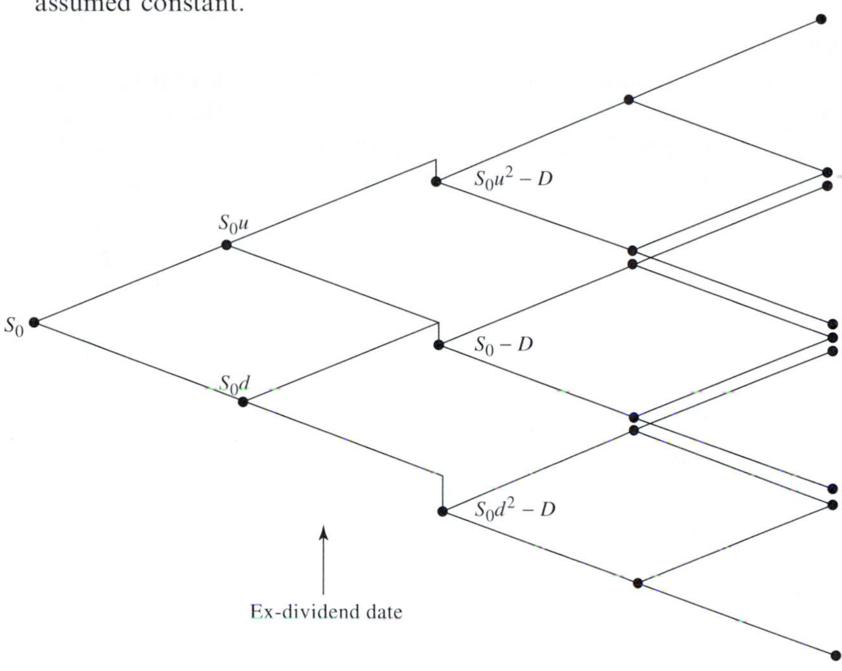

option and that $k\,\Delta t \leqslant \tau \leqslant (k+1)\,\Delta t$. The value of the uncertain component, S^*, at time $i\,\Delta t$ is given by

$$S^* = S \quad \text{when } i\,\Delta t > \tau$$

and

$$S^* = S - De^{-r(\tau - i\Delta t)} \quad \text{when } i\,\Delta t \leqslant \tau$$

where D is the dividend. Define σ^* as the volatility of S^* and assume that σ^* is constant.[6] The parameters p, u, and d can be calculated from equations (17.4), (17.5), (17.6), and (17.7) with σ replaced by σ^* and a tree can be constructed in the usual way to model S^*. By adding to the stock price at each node, the present value of future dividends (if any), the tree can be converted into another tree that models S. Suppose that S_0^* is the value of S^* at time zero. At time $i\,\Delta t$, the nodes on this tree correspond to the stock prices

$$S_0^* u^j d^{i-j} + De^{-r(\tau - i\,\Delta t)}, \quad j = 0, 1, \dots, i$$

when $i\,\Delta t < \tau$ and

$$S_0^* u^j d^{i-j}, \quad j = 0, 1, \dots, i$$

when $i\,\Delta t > \tau$. This approach, which has the advantage of being consistent with the approach for European options in Section 13.12, succeeds in achieving a situation where

[6] As mentioned in Section 13.12, σ^* is in theory slightly greater than σ, the volatility of S. In practice, the use of implied volatilities avoids the need for analysts to distinguish between σ and σ^*.

the tree recombines so that there are $i+1$ nodes at time $i\,\Delta t$. It can be generalized in a straightforward way to deal with the situation where there are several dividends.

Example 17.5

Consider a 5-month American put option on a stock that is expected to pay a single dividend of \$2.06 during the life of the option. The initial stock price is \$52, the strike price is \$50, the risk-free interest rate is 10% per annum, the volatility is 40% per annum, and the ex-dividend date is in $3\frac{1}{2}$ months.

We first construct a tree to model S^*, the stock price less the present value of future dividends during the life of the option. At time zero, the present value of the dividend is

$$2.06e^{-0.2917\times 0.1} = 2.00$$

Figure 17.9 Tree produced by DerivaGem for Example 17.5.

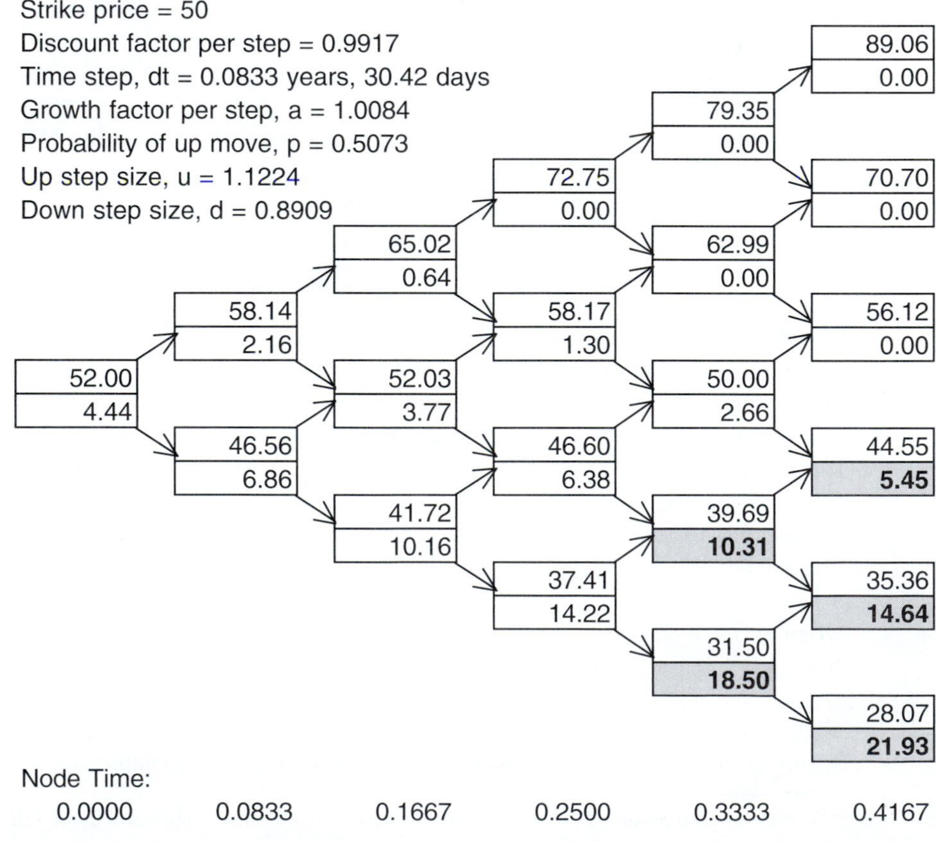

The initial value of S^* is therefore 50.00. Assuming that the 40% per annum volatility refers to S^*, we find that Figure 17.3 provides a binomial tree for S^*. (This is because S^* has the same initial value and volatility as the stock price that Figure 17.3 was based upon.) Adding the present value of the dividend at each node leads to Figure 17.9, which is a binomial model for S. The probabilities at each node are, as in Figure 17.3, 0.5073 for an up movement and 0.4927 for a down movement. Working back through the tree in the usual way gives the option price as $4.44. (Using 50 time steps, DerivaGem gives a value for the option of 4.202; using 100 steps it gives 4.212.)

When the option lasts a long time (say, 3 or more years) it is usually more appropriate to assume a known dividend yield rather than a known cash dividend because the latter cannot reasonably be assumed to be the same for all the stock prices that might be encountered in the future.[7] Often for convenience the dividend yield is assumed to be paid continuously. Valuing an option on a dividend paying stock is then similar to valuing an option on a stock index.

Control Variate Technique

A technique known as the *control variate technique* can improve the accuracy of the pricing of an American option.[8] This involves using the same tree to calculate both the value of the American option, f_A, and the value of the corresponding European option, f_E. We also calculate the Black–Scholes price of the European option, f_{BS}. The error given by the tree in the pricing of the European option is assumed equal to that given by the tree in the pricing of the American option. This gives the estimate of the price of the American option as

$$f_A + f_{\text{BS}} - f_E$$

To illustrate this approach, Figure 17.10 values the option in Figure 17.3 on the assumption that it is European. The price obtained is $4.32. From the Black–Scholes formula, the true European price of the option is $4.08. The estimate of the American price in Figure 17.3 is $4.49. The control variate estimate of the American price, therefore, is

$$4.49 + 4.08 - 4.32 = 4.25$$

A good estimate of the American price, calculated using 100 steps, is 4.278. The control variate approach does, therefore, produce a considerable improvement over the basic tree estimate of 4.49 in this case.

The control variate technique in effect involves using the tree to calculate the difference between the European and the American price rather than the American price itself. We give a further application of the control variate technique when we discuss Monte Carlo simulation later in the chapter.

---

[7] Another problem is that, for long-dated options, S^* is significantly less than S_0 and volatility estimates can be very high.

[8] See J. Hull and A. White, "The Use of the Control Variate Technique in Option Pricing," *Journal of Financial and Quantitative Analysis*, 23 (September 1988): 237–51.

Figure 17.10 Tree, as produced by DerivaGem, for European version of option in Figure 17.3. At each node, the upper number is the stock price, and the lower number is the option price.

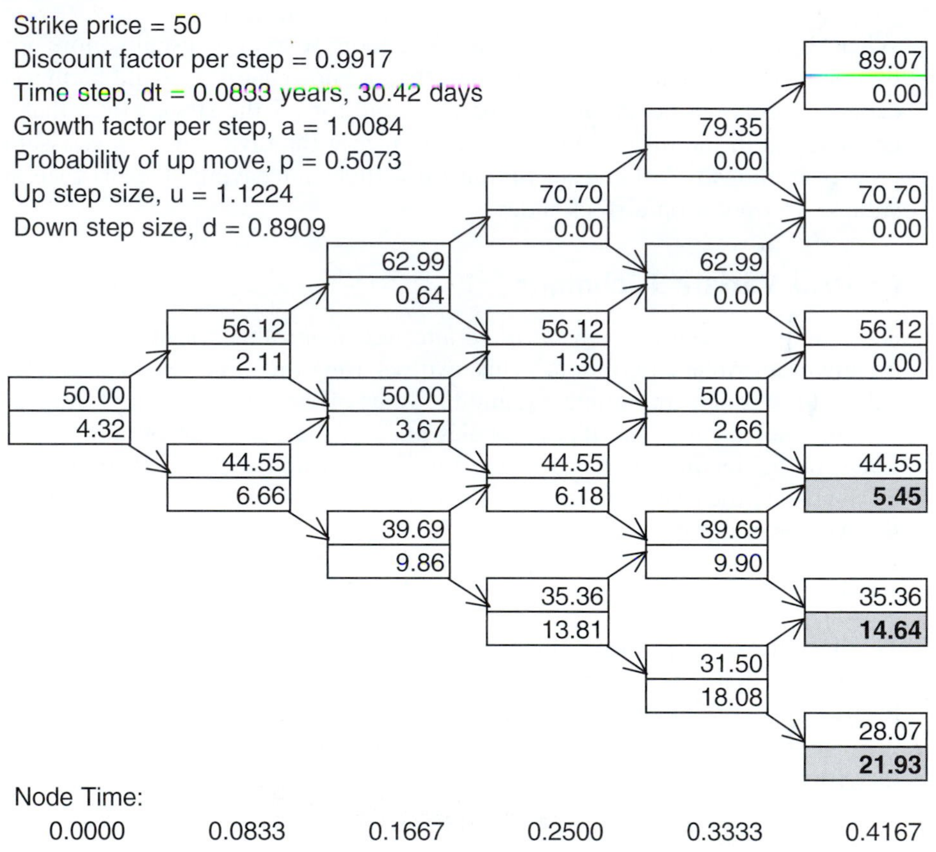

17.4 ALTERNATIVE PROCEDURES FOR CONSTRUCTING TREES

The Cox, Ross, and Rubinstein approach is not the only way of building a binomial tree. Instead of imposing the assumption $u = 1/d$ on equations (17.2) and (17.3), we can set $p = 0.5$. A solution to the equations when terms of higher order than Δt are ignored is then

$$u = e^{(r-q-\sigma^2/2)\Delta t+\sigma\sqrt{\Delta t}}$$

$$d = e^{(r-q-\sigma^2/2)\Delta t-\sigma\sqrt{\Delta t}}$$

This allows trees with $p = 0.5$ to be built for options on indices, foreign exchange, and futures.

This alternative tree-building procedure has the advantage over the Cox, Ross, and Rubinstein approach that the probabilities are always 0.5 regardless of the value of σ or the number of time steps.[9] Its disadvantage is that it is not as straightforward to calculate delta, gamma, and rho from the tree because the tree is no longer centered at the initial stock price.

Example 17.6

Consider a 9-month American call option on the Canadian dollar. The current exchange rate is 0.7900, the strike price is 0.7950, the US risk-free interest rate is 6% per annum, the Canadian risk-free interest rate is 10% per annum, and the

Figure 17.11 Binomial tree for American call option on the Canadian dollar. At each node, upper number is spot exchange rate and lower number is option price. All probabilities are 0.5.

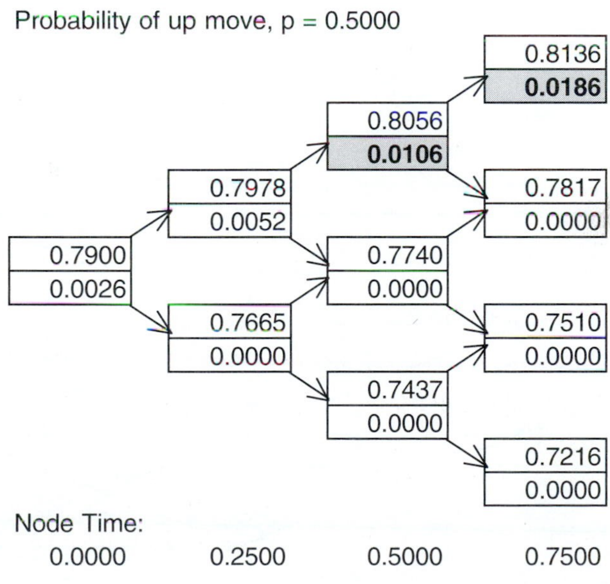

[9] When time steps are so large that $\sigma < |(r-q)\sqrt{\Delta t}|$, the Cox, Ross, and Rubinstein tree gives negative probabilities. The alternative procedure described here does not have that drawback.

volatility of the exchange rate is 4% per annum. In this case, $S_0 = 0.79$, $K = 0.795$, $r = 0.06$, $r_f = 0.10$, $\sigma = 0.04$, and $T = 0.75$. We divide the life of the option into 3-month periods for the purposes of constructing the tree, so that $\Delta t = 0.25$. We set the probabilities on each branch to 0.5 and

$$u = e^{(0.06-0.10-0.0016/2)0.25+0.04\sqrt{0.25}} = 1.0098$$
$$d = e^{(0.06-0.10-0.0016/2)0.25-0.04\sqrt{0.25}} = 0.9703$$

The tree for the exchange rate is shown in Figure 17.11. The tree gives the value of the option as \$0.0026.

Trinomial Trees

Trinomial trees can be used as an alternative to binomial trees. The general form of the tree is as shown in Figure 17.12. Suppose that p_u, p_m, and p_d are the probabilities of up, middle, and down movements at each node and Δt is the length of the time step. For a non-dividend-paying stock, parameter values that match the mean and standard deviation of price changes when terms of higher order than Δt are ignored are

$$u = e^{\sigma\sqrt{3\Delta t}}, \qquad d = \frac{1}{u}$$

$$p_d = -\sqrt{\frac{\Delta t}{12\sigma^2}}\left(r - q - \frac{\sigma^2}{2}\right) + \frac{1}{6}, \qquad p_m = \frac{2}{3}, \qquad p_u = \sqrt{\frac{\Delta t}{12\sigma^2}}\left(r - q - \frac{\sigma^2}{2}\right) + \frac{1}{6}$$

Figure 17.12 Trinomial stock price tree.

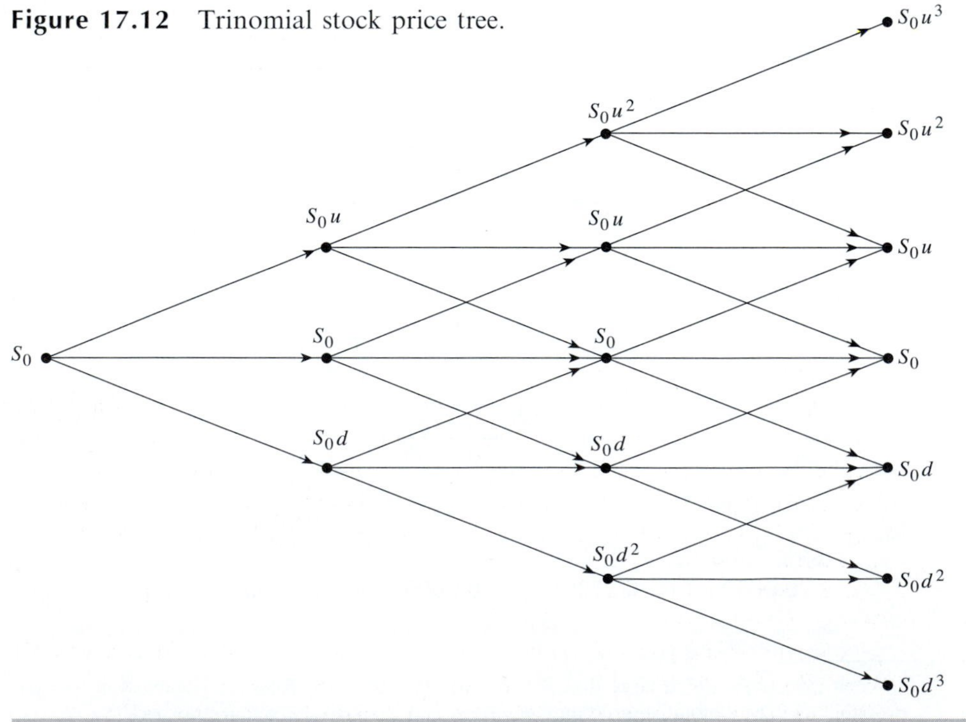

Calculations for a trinomial tree are analogous to those for a binomial tree. We work from the end of the tree to the beginning. At each node we calculate the value of exercising and the value of continuing. The value of continuing is

$$e^{-r\Delta t}(p_u f_u + p_m f_m + p_d f_d)$$

where f_u, f_m, and f_d are the values of the option at the subsequent up, middle, and down nodes, respectively. The trinomial tree approach proves to be equivalent to the explicit finite difference method, which will be described in Section 17.8.

Figlewski and Gao have proposed an enhancement of the trinomial tree method, which they call the *adaptive mesh model*. In this, a high-resolution (small-Δt) tree is grafted onto a low-resolution (large-Δt) tree.[10] When valuing a regular American option, high resolution is most useful for the parts of the tree close to the strike price at the end of the life of the option.

17.5 TIME-DEPENDENT PARAMETERS

Up to now we have assumed that r, q, r_f, and σ are constants. In practice, they are usually assumed to be time dependent. The values of these variables between times t and $t + \Delta t$ are assumed to be equal to their forward values.[11]

We can make r and q (or r_f) a function of time in a Cox–Ross–Rubinstein binomial tree. We set

$$a = e^{[f(t)-g(t)]\Delta t} \tag{17.11}$$

for nodes at time t, where $f(t)$ is the forward interest rate between times t and $t + \Delta t$ and $g(t)$ is the forward value of q between these times. This does not change the geometry of the tree because u and d do not depend on a. The probabilities on the branches emanating from nodes at time t are:[12]

$$p = \frac{e^{[f(t)-g(t)]\Delta t} - d}{u - d} \tag{17.12}$$

$$1 - p = \frac{u - e^{[f(t)-g(t)]\Delta t}}{u - d}$$

The rest of the way that we use the tree is the same as before, except that when discounting between times t and $t + \Delta t$ we use $f(t)$.

Making σ a function of time in a binomial tree is more challenging. One approach is to make the lengths of time steps inversely proportional to the variance rate. The values of u and d are then always the same and the tree recombines. Suppose that $\sigma(t)$ is the volatility for a maturity t so that $\sigma(t)^2 t$ is the cumulative variance by time t. Define $V = \sigma(T)^2 T$, where T is the life of the tree, and let t_i be the end of the ith time step. If there is a total

[10] See S. Figlewski and B. Gao, "The Adaptive Mesh Model: A New Approach to Efficient Option Pricing," *Journal of Financial Economics*, 53 (1999): 313–51.

[11] The forward dividend yield and forward variance rate are calculated in the same way as the forward interest rate. (The variance rate is the square of the volatility.)

[12] For a sufficiently large number of time steps, these probabilities are always positive.

Business Snapshot 17.1 Calculating Pi with Monte Carlo Simulation

Suppose the sides of the square in Figure 17.13 are one unit in length. Imagine that you fire darts randomly at the square and calculate the percentage that lie in the circle. What should you find? The square has an area of 1.0 and the circle has a radius of 0.5 The area of the circle is π times the radius squared or $\pi/4$. It follows that the percentage of darts that lie in the circle should be $\pi/4$. We can estimate π by multiplying the percentage that lie in the circle by 4.

We can use an Excel spreadsheet to simulate the dart throwing as illustrated in Table 17.1. We define both cell A1 and cell B1 as =RAND(). A1 and B1 are random numbers between 0 and 1 and define how far to the right and how high up the dart lands in the square in Figure 17.13. We then define cell C1 as

```
=IF((A1-0.5)^2+(B1-0.5)^2<0.5^2,4,0)
```

This has the effect of setting C1 equal to 4 if the dart lies in the circle and 0 otherwise.

Define the next 99 rows of the spreadsheet similarly to the first one. (This is a "select and drag" operation in Excel.) Define C102 as =AVERAGE(C1:C100) and C103 as =STDEV(C1:C100). C102 (which is 3.04 in Table 17.1) is an estimate of π calculated from 100 random trials. C103 is the standard deviation of our results and as we will see in Example 17.7 can be used to assess the accuracy of the estimate. Increasing the number of trials improves accuracy—but convergence to the correct value of 3.14162 is slow.

of N time steps, we choose t_i to satisfy $\sigma(t_i)^2 t_i = iV/N$. The variance between times t_{i-1} and t_i is then V/N for all i.

With a trinomial tree, a generalized tree-building procedure can be used to match time-dependent interest rates and volatilities (see Technical Note 9 on the author's website).

17.6 MONTE CARLO SIMULATION

We now explain Monte Carlo simulation, a quite different approach for valuing derivatives from binomial trees. Business Snapshot 17.1 illustrates the random sampling idea underlying Monte Carlo simulation by showing how a simple Excel program can be constructed to estimate π.

Figure 17.13 Calculation of π by throwing darts.

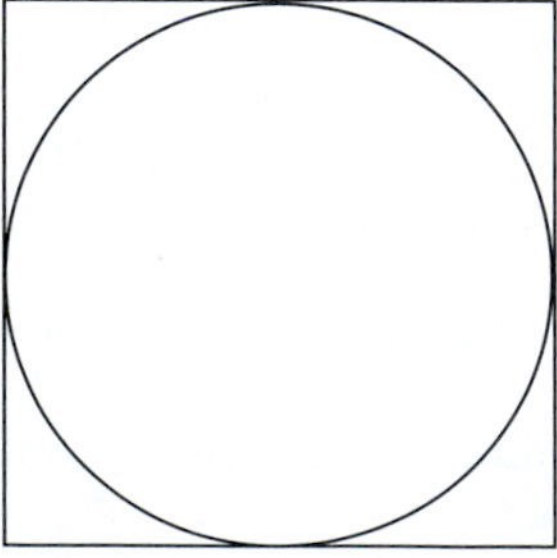

Table 17.1 Sample spreadsheet calculations in Business Snapshot 17.1.

	A	*B*	*C*
1	0.207	0.690	4
2	0.271	0.520	4
3	0.007	0.221	0
⋮	⋮	⋮	⋮
100	0.198	0.403	4
101			
102		Mean:	3.04
103		SD:	1.69

When used to value an option, Monte Carlo simulation uses the risk-neutral valuation result. We sample paths to obtain the expected payoff in a risk-neutral world and then discount this payoff at the risk-free rate. Consider a derivative dependent on a single market variable S that provides a payoff at time T. Assuming that interest rates are constant, we can value the derivative as follows:[13]

1. Sample a random path for S in a risk-neutral world.
2. Calculate the payoff from the derivative.
3. Repeat steps 1 and 2 to get many sample values of the payoff from the derivative in a risk-neutral world.
4. Calculate the mean of the sample payoffs to get an estimate of the expected payoff in a risk-neutral world.
5. Discount the expected payoff at the risk-free rate to get an estimate of the value of the derivative.

Suppose that the process followed by the underlying market variable in a risk-neutral world is

$$dS = \hat{\mu} S\, dt + \sigma S\, dz \tag{17.13}$$

where dz is a Wiener process, $\hat{\mu}$ is the expected return in a risk-neutral world, and σ is the volatility.[14] To simulate the path followed by S, we can divide the life of the derivative into N short intervals of length Δt and approximate equation (17.13) as

$$S(t + \Delta t) - S(t) = \hat{\mu} S(t)\, \Delta t + \sigma S(t) \epsilon \sqrt{\Delta t} \tag{17.14}$$

where $S(t)$ denotes the value of S at time t, ϵ is a random sample from a normal distribution with mean zero and standard deviation of 1.0. This enables the value of S at time Δt to be calculated from the initial value of S, the value at time $2\,\Delta t$ to be calculated from the value at time Δt, and so on. An illustration of the procedure is in Section 12.3. One simulation trial involves constructing a complete path for S using N random samples from a normal distribution.

[13] We discuss how Monte Carlo simulation can be used with stochastic interest rates in Section 25.4.

[14] If S is the price of a non-dividend-paying stock then $\hat{\mu} = r$, if it is an exchange rate then $\hat{\mu} = r - r_f$, and so on. Note that the volatility is the same in a risk-neutral world as in the real world, as shown in Section 11.7.

In practice, it is usually more accurate to simulate $\ln S$ rather than S. From Itô's lemma the process followed by $\ln S$ is

$$d\ln S = \left(\hat{\mu} - \frac{\sigma^2}{2}\right)dt + \sigma\,dz \tag{17.15}$$

so that

$$\ln S(t+\Delta t) - \ln S(t) = \left(\hat{\mu} - \frac{\sigma^2}{2}\right)\Delta t + \sigma\epsilon\sqrt{\Delta t}$$

or equivalently

$$S(t+\Delta t) = S(t)\exp\left[\left(\hat{\mu} - \frac{\sigma^2}{2}\right)\Delta t + \sigma\epsilon\sqrt{\Delta t}\right] \tag{17.16}$$

This equation is used to construct a path for S.

The advantage of working with $\ln S$ is that it follows a generalized Wiener process. This means that the equation

$$\ln S(T) - \ln S(0) = \left(\hat{\mu} - \frac{\sigma^2}{2}\right)T + \sigma\epsilon\sqrt{T}$$

is true for all T.[15] It follows that

$$S(T) = S(0)\exp\left[\left(\hat{\mu} - \frac{\sigma^2}{2}\right)T + \sigma\epsilon\sqrt{T}\right] \tag{17.17}$$

This equation can be used to value derivatives that provide a nonstandard payoff at time T. As indicated in Business Snapshot 17.2, it can also be used to check the Black–Scholes formulas.

The key advantage of Monte Carlo simulation is that it can be used when the payoff depends on the path followed by the underlying variable S as well as when it depends only on the final value of S. (For example, is can be used when payoffs depend on the average value of S.) Payoffs can occur at several times during the life of the derivative rather than all at the end. Any stochastic process for S can be accommodated. As will be shown shortly, the procedure can also be extended to accommodate situations where the payoff from the derivative depends on several underlying market variables. The drawbacks of Monte Carlo simulation are that it is computationally very time consuming and cannot easily handle situations where there are early exercise opportunities.[16]

Derivatives Dependent on More than One Market Variable

Consider the situation where the payoff from a derivative depends on n variables θ_i ($1 \leqslant i \leqslant n$). Define s_i as the volatility of θ_i, $\hat{m}_i$ as the expected growth rate of θ_i in a risk-neutral world, and ρ_{ik} as the instantaneous correlation between θ_i and θ_k.[17] As in the

[15] By contrast, equation (17.14) is true only in the limit as Δt tends to zero.

[16] As we will discuss in Chapter 24, a number of researchers have suggested ways Monte Carlo simulation can be extended to value American options.

[17] Note that s_i, $\hat{m}_i$, and ρ_{ik} are not necessarily constant; they may depend on the θ_i.

Business Snapshot 17.2 Checking Black–Scholes

The Black–Scholes formula for a European call option can be checked by using a binomial tree with a very large number of time steps. An alternative way of checking it is to use Monte Carlo simulation. Table 17.2 shows a spreadsheet that can be constructed. The cells C2, D2, E2, F2, and G2 contain S_0, K, r, σ, and T, respectively. Cells D4, E4, and F4 calculate d_1, d_2, and the Black–Scholes price, respectively. (The Black–Scholes price is 4.817 in the sample spreadsheet.)

NORMSINV is the inverse cumulative function for the standard normal distribution. It follows that NORMSINV(RAND())gives a random sample from a standard normal distribution. We set cell A1 as

=$C$2*EXP(($E$2−$F$2*$F$2/2)*$G$2+$F$2*NORMSINV(RAND())*SQRT($G$2))

This is random sample from the set of all stock prices at time T. We set cell B1 as

=EXP(−$E$2*$G$2)*MAX(A1−$D$2,0)

This is the present value of the payoff from a call option. We define the next 999 rows of the spreadsheet similarly to the first one. (This is a "select and drag" operation in Excel.) Define B1002 as AVERAGE(B1:B1000) and B1003 as STDEV(B1:B1000). B1002 (which is 4.98 in the sample spreadsheet) is an estimate of the value of the option. This should be not too far from the Black–Scholes price. As we shall see in Example 17.8, B1003 can be used to assess the accuracy of the estimate.

single-variable case, the life of the derivative must be divided into N subintervals of length Δt. The discrete version of the process for θ_i is then

$$\theta_i(t+\Delta t)-\theta_i(t)=\hat{m}_i\theta_i(t)\,\Delta t+s_i\theta_i(t)\epsilon_i\sqrt{\Delta t} \tag{17.18}$$

where ϵ_i is a random sample from a standard normal distribution. The coefficient of correlation between ϵ_i and ϵ_k is ρ_{ik} $(1 \leqslant i; k \leqslant n)$. One simulation trial involves obtaining N samples of the ϵ_i $(1 \leqslant i \leqslant n)$ from a multivariate standardized normal distribution. These are substituted into equation (17.18) to produce simulated paths for each θ_i, thereby enabling a sample value for the derivative to be calculated.

Table 17.2 Monte Carlo simulation to check Black–Scholes

	A	*B*	*C*	*D*	*E*	*F*	*G*
1	45.95	0	S_0	K	r	σ	T
2	54.49	4.38	50	50	0.05	0.3	0.5
3	50.09	0.09		d_1	d_2	BS price	
4	47.46	0		0.2239	0.0118	4.817	
5	44.93	0					
⋮	⋮	⋮					
1000	68.27	17.82					
1001							
1002	Mean:	4.98					
1003	SD:	7.68					

Generating the Random Samples from Normal Distributions

An approximate sample from a univariate standardized normal distribution can be obtained from the formula

$$\epsilon = \sum_{i=1}^{12} R_i - 6 \tag{17.19}$$

where the R_i ($1 \leqslant i \leqslant 12$) are independent random numbers between 0 and 1, and ϵ is the required sample from $\phi(0, 1)$. This approximation is satisfactory for most purposes. An alternative approach in Excel is to use =NORMSINV(RAND()) as in Business Snapshot 17.2.

When two correlated samples ϵ_1 and ϵ_2 from standard normal distributions are required, an appropriate procedure is as follows. Independent samples x_1 and x_2 from a univariate standardized normal distribution are obtained as just described. The required samples ϵ_1 and ϵ_2 are then calculated as follows:

$$\epsilon_1 = x_1$$
$$\epsilon_2 = \rho x_1 + x_2\sqrt{1-\rho^2}$$

where ρ is the coefficient of correlation.

More generally, consider the situation where we require n correlated samples from normal distributions with the correlation between sample i and sample j being ρ_{ij}. We first sample n independent variables x_i ($1 \leqslant i \leqslant n$), from univariate standardized normal distributions. The required samples, ϵ_i ($1 \leqslant i \leqslant n$), are then defined as follows:

$$\epsilon_1 = \alpha_{11}x_1$$
$$\epsilon_2 = \alpha_{21}x_1 + \alpha_{22}x_2$$
$$\epsilon_3 = \alpha_{31}x_1 + \alpha_{32}x_2 + \alpha_{33}x_3$$

and so on. We choose the coefficients α_{ij} so that the correlations and variances are correct. This can be done step by step as follows. Set $\alpha_{11} = 1$; choose α_{21} so that $\alpha_{21}\alpha_{11} = \rho_{21}$; choose α_{22} so that $\alpha_{21}^2 + \alpha_{22}^2 = 1$; choose α_{31} so that $\alpha_{31}\alpha_{11} = \rho_{31}$; choose α_{32} so that $\alpha_{31}\alpha_{21} + \alpha_{32}\alpha_{22} = \rho_{32}$; choose α_{33} so that $\alpha_{31}^2 + \alpha_{32}^2 + \alpha_{33}^2 = 1$; and so on.[18] This procedure is known as the *Cholesky decomposition*.

Number of Trials

The accuracy of the result given by Monte Carlo simulation depends on the number of trials. It is usual to calculate the standard deviation as well as the mean of the discounted payoffs given by the simulation trials. Denote the mean by μ and the standard deviation by ω. The variable μ is the simulation's estimate of the value of the derivative. The standard error of the estimate is

$$\frac{\omega}{\sqrt{M}}$$

where M is the number of trials. A 95% confidence interval for the price f of the

---

[18] If the equations for the α's do not have real solutions, the assumed correlation structure is internally inconsistent This will be discussed further in Chapter 19.

derivative is therefore given by

$$\mu - \frac{1.96\omega}{\sqrt{M}} < f < \mu + \frac{1.96\omega}{\sqrt{M}}$$

This shows that our uncertainty about the value of the derivative is inversely proportional to the square root of the number of trials. To double the accuracy of a simulation, we must quadruple the number of trials; to increase the accuracy by a factor of 10, the number of trials must increase by a factor of 100; and so on.

Example 17.7

In Table 17.1, π is calculated as the average of 100 numbers. The standard deviation of the numbers is 1.69. In this case, $\omega = 1.69$ and $M = 100$, so that the standard error of the estimate is $1.69/\sqrt{100} = 0.169$. The spreadsheet therefore gives a 95% confidence interval for π as $(3.04 - 1.96 \times 0.169)$ to $(3.04 + 1.96 \times 0.169)$ or 2.71 to 3.37.

Example 17.8

In Table 17.2, the value of the option is calculated as the average of 1000 numbers. The standard deviation of the numbers is 7.68. In this case, $\omega = 7.68$ and $M = 1000$. The standard error of the estimate is $7.68/\sqrt{1000} = 0.24$. The spreadsheet therefore gives a 95% confidence interval for the option value as $(4.98 - 1.96 \times 0.24)$ to $(4.98 + 1.96 \times 0.24)$, or 4.51 to 5.45.

Applications

Monte Carlo simulation tends to be numerically more efficient than other procedures when there are three or more stochastic variables. This is because the time taken to carry out a Monte Carlo simulation increases approximately linearly with the number of variables, whereas the time taken for most other procedures increases exponentially with the number of variables. One advantage of Monte Carlo simulation is that it can provide a standard error for the estimates that it makes. Another is that it is an approach that can accommodate complex payoffs and complex stochastic processes. Also, it can be used when the payoff depends on some function of the whole path followed by a variable, not just its terminal value.

Calculating the Greek Letters

The Greek letters discussed in Chapter 15 can be calculated using Monte Carlo simulation. Suppose that we are interested in the partial derivative of f with respect to x, where f is the value of the derivative and x is the value of an underlying variable or a parameter. First, Monte Carlo simulation is used in the usual way to calculate an estimate $\hat{f}$ for the value of the derivative. A small increase Δx is then made in the value of x, and a new value for the derivative, $\hat{f}^*$, is calculated in the same way as $\hat{f}$. An estimate for the hedge parameter is given by

$$\frac{\hat{f}^* - \hat{f}}{\Delta x}$$

In order to minimize the standard error of the estimate, the number of time intervals, N, the random number streams, and the number of trials, M, should be the same for calculating both $\hat{f}$ and $\hat{f}^*$.

Sampling through a Tree

Instead of implementing Monte Carlo simulation by randomly sampling from the stochastic process for an underlying variable, we can use an N-step binomial tree and sample from the 2^N paths that are possible. Suppose we have a binomial tree where the probability of an "up" movement is 0.6. The procedure for sampling a random path through the tree is as follows. At each node, we sample a random number between 0 and 1. If the number is less than 0.4, we take the down path. If it is greater than 0.4, we take the up path. Once we have a complete path from the initial node to the end of the tree, we can calculate a payoff. This completes the first trial. A similar procedure is used to complete more trials. The mean of the payoffs is discounted at the risk-free rate to get an estimate of the value of the derivative.[19]

Example 17.9

Suppose that the tree in Figure 17.3 is used to value an option that pays off $\max(S_{\text{ave}} - 50, 0)$, where S_{ave} is the average stock price during the 5 months (with the first and last stock price being included in the average). This is known as an Asian option. When ten simulation trials are used one possible result is shown in Table 17.3.

Table 17.3 Monte Carlo simulation to value Asian option from the tree in Figure 17.3. Payoff is amount by which average stock price exceeds \$50. U = up movement; D = down movement.

Trial	*Path*	*Average stock price*	*Option payoff*
1	UUUUD	64.98	14.98
2	UUUDD	59.82	9.82
3	DDDUU	42.31	0.00
4	UUUUU	68.04	18.04
5	UUDDU	55.22	5.22
6	UDUUD	55.22	5.22
7	DDUDD	42.31	0.00
8	UUDDU	55.22	5.22
9	UUUDU	62.25	12.25
10	DDUUD	45.56	0.00
Average			7.08

The value of the option is calculated as the average payoff discounted at the risk-free rate. In this case, the average payoff is \$7.08 and the risk-free rate is 10% and so the calculated value is $7.08e^{-0.1\times 5/12} = 6.79$. (This illustrates the methodology. In practice, we would have to use more time steps on the tree and many more simulation trials to get an accurate answer.)

[19] See D. Mintz, "Less is More," *Risk*, July 1997: 42–45, for a discussion of how sampling through a tree can be made efficient.

17.7 VARIANCE REDUCTION PROCEDURES

If the simulation is carried out as described so far, a very large number of trials is usually necessary to estimate f with reasonable accuracy. This is very expensive in terms of computation time. In this section, we examine a number of variance reduction procedures that can lead to dramatic savings in computation time.

Antithetic Variable Technique

In the antithetic variable technique, a simulation trial involves calculating two values of the derivative. The first value f_1 is calculated in the usual way; the second value f_2 is calculated by changing the sign of all the random samples from standard normal distributions. (If ϵ is a sample used to calculate f_1, then $-\epsilon$ is the corresponding sample used to calculate f_2.) The sample value of the derivative calculated from a simulation trial is the average of f_1 and f_2. This works well because when one value is above the true value, the other tends to be below, and vice versa.

Denote $\bar{f}$ as the average of f_1 and f_2:

$$\bar{f} = \frac{f_1 + f_2}{2}$$

The final estimate of the value of the derivative is the average of the $\bar{f}$'s. If $\bar{\omega}$ is the standard deviation of the $\bar{f}$'s, and M is the number of simulation trials (i.e., the number of pairs of values calculated), then the standard error of the estimate is

$$\bar{\omega}/\sqrt{M}$$

This is usually much less than the standard error calculated using $2M$ random trials.

Control Variate Technique

We have already given one example of the control variate technique in connection with the use of trees to value American options (see Section 17.3). The control variate technique is applicable when there are two similar derivatives, A and B. Derivative A is the security being valued; derivative B is similar to derivative A and has an analytic solution available. Two simulations using the same random number streams and the same Δt are carried out in parallel. The first is used to obtain an estimate f_A^* of the value of A; the second is used to obtain an estimate f_B^*, of the value of B. A better estimate f_A of the value of A is then obtained using the formula

$$f_A = f_A^* - f_B^* + f_B \tag{17.20}$$

where f_B is the known true value of B calculated analytically. Hull and White provide an example of the use of the control variate technique when evaluating the effect of stochastic volatility on the price of a European call option.[20] In this case, f_A is the estimated value of the option assuming stochastic volatility and f_B is its Black–Scholes value assuming constant volatility.

[20] See J. Hull and A. White, "The Pricing of Options on Assets with Stochastic Volatilities," *Journal of Finance*, 42 (June 1987): 281–300.

Importance Sampling

Importance sampling is best explained with an example. Suppose that we wish to calculate the price of a deep-out-of-the-money European call option with strike price K and maturity T. If we sample values for the underlying asset price at time T in the usual way, most of the paths will lead to zero payoff. This is a waste of computation time because the zero-payoff paths contribute very little to the determination of the value of the option. We therefore try to choose only important paths, that is, paths where the stock price is above K at maturity.

Suppose F is the unconditional probability distribution function for the stock price at time T and q, the probability of the stock price being greater than K at maturity, is known analytically. Then $G = F/q$ is the probability distribution of the stock price conditional on the stock price being greater than K. To implement importance sampling, we sample from G rather than F. The estimate of the value of the option is the average discounted payoff multiplied by q.

Stratified Sampling

Sampling representative values rather than random values from a probability distribution usually gives more accuracy. Stratified sampling is a way of doing this. Suppose we wish to take 1000 samples from a probability distribution we would divide the distribution into 1000 equally likely intervals and choose a representative value (typically the mean or median) for each interval.

In the case of a standard normal distribution when there are n intervals, we can calculate the representative value for the ith interval as

$$N^{-1}\left(\frac{i - 0.5}{n}\right)$$

where N^{-1} is the inverse cumulative normal distribution. For example, when $n = 4$ the representative values corresponding to the four intervals are $N^{-1}(0.125)$, $N^{-1}(0.375)$, $N^{-1}(0.625)$, $N^{-1}(0.875)$. The function N^{-1} can be calculated using the NORMSINV function in Excel.

Moment Matching

Moment matching involves adjusting the samples taken from a standardized normal distribution so that the first, second, and possibly higher moments are matched. Suppose that we sample from a normal distribution with mean 0 and standard deviation 1 to calculate the change in the value of a particular variable over a particular time period. Suppose that the samples are ϵ_i $(1 \leqslant i \leqslant n)$. To match the first two moments, we calculate the mean of the samples, m, and the standard deviation of the samples, s. We then define adjusted samples ϵ_i^* $(1 \leqslant i \leqslant n)$ as

$$\epsilon_i^* = \frac{\epsilon_i - m}{s}$$

These adjusted samples have the correct mean of 0 and the correct standard deviation of 1.0. We use the adjusted samples for all calculations.

Moment matching saves computation time, but can lead to memory problems because every number sampled must be stored until the end of the simulation. Moment matching is sometimes termed *quadratic resampling*. It is often used in conjunction with the antithetic variable technique. Because the latter automatically matches all odd moments, the goal of moment matching then becomes that of matching the second moment and, possibly, the fourth moment.

Using Quasi-Random Sequences

A quasi-random sequence (also called a *low-discrepancy* sequence) is a sequence of representative samples from a probability distribution.[21] Descriptions of the use of quasi-random sequences appear in Brotherton-Ratcliffe, and Press *et al.*[22] Quasi-random sequences can have the desirable property that they lead to the standard error of an estimate being proportional to $1/M$ rather than $1/\sqrt{M}$, where M is the sample size.

Quasi-random sampling is similar to stratified sampling. The objective is to sample representative values for the underlying variables. In stratified sampling, it is assumed that we know in advance how many samples will be taken. A quasi-random sampling scheme is more flexible. The samples are taken in such a way that we are always "filling in" gaps between existing samples. At each stage of the simulation, the sampled points are roughly evenly spaced throughout the probability space.

Figure 17.14 shows points generated in two dimensions using a procedure suggested by Sobol'.[23] It can be seen that successive points do tend to fill in the gaps left by previous points.

17.8 FINITE DIFFERENCE METHODS

Finite difference methods value a derivative by solving the differential equation that the derivative satisfies. The differential equation is converted into a set of difference equations, and the difference equations are solved iteratively.

To illustrate the approach, we consider how it might be used to value an American put option on a stock paying a dividend yield of q. The differential equation that the option must satisfy is, from equation (14.6),

$$\frac{\partial f}{\partial t} + (r-q)S\frac{\partial f}{\partial S} + \tfrac{1}{2}\sigma^2 S^2 \frac{\partial^2 f}{\partial S^2} = rf \tag{17.21}$$

Suppose that the life of the option is T. We divide this into N equally spaced intervals of length $\Delta t = T/N$. A total of $N+1$ times are therefore considered

$$0,\ \Delta t,\ 2\,\Delta t,\ \ldots,\ T$$

---

[21] The term *quasi-random* is a misnomer. A quasi-random sequence is totally deterministic.

[22] See R. Brotherton-Ratcliffe, "Monte Carlo Motoring," *Risk*, December 1994: 53–58; W. H. Press, S. A. Teukolsky, W. T. Vetterling, and B. P. Flannery, *Numerical Recipes in C: The Art of Scientific Computing*, 2nd edn. Cambridge University Press, 1992.

[23] See I. M. Sobol', *USSR Computational Mathematics and Mathematical Physics*, 7, 4 (1967): 86–112. A description of Sobol's procedure is in W. H. Press, S. A. Teukolsky, W. T. Vetterling, and B. P. Flannery, *Numerical Recipes in C: The Art of Scientific Computing*, 2nd edn. Cambridge University Press, 1992.

Figure 17.14 First 1024 points of a Sobol' sequence.

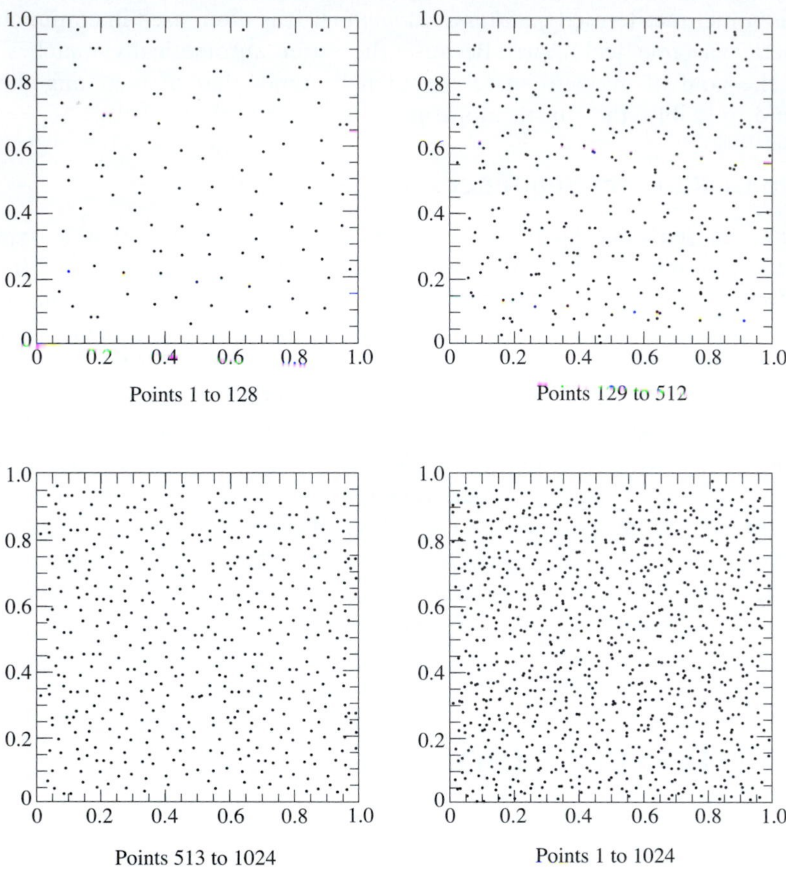

Suppose that S_{max} is a stock price sufficiently high that, when it is reached, the put has virtually no value. We define $\Delta S = S_{max}/M$ and consider a total of $M+1$ equally spaced stock prices:

$$0, \ \Delta S, \ 2\,\Delta S, \ \ldots, \ S_{max}$$

The level S_{max} is chosen so that one of these is the current stock price.

The time points and stock price points define a grid consisting of a total of $(M+1)(N+1)$ points, as shown in Figure 17.15. The (i, j) point on the grid is the point that corresponds to time $i\,\Delta t$ and stock price $j\,\Delta S$. We will use the variable $f_{i,j}$ to denote the value of the option at the (i, j) point.

Implicit Finite Difference Method

For an interior point (i, j) on the grid, $\partial f/\partial S$ can be approximated as

$$\frac{\partial f}{\partial S} = \frac{f_{i,j+1} - f_{i,j}}{\Delta S} \tag{17.22}$$

or as

$$\frac{\partial f}{\partial S} = \frac{f_{i,j} - f_{i,j-1}}{\Delta S} \tag{17.23}$$

Equation (17.22) is known as the *forward difference approximation*; equation (17.23) is known as the *backward difference approximation*. We use a more symmetrical approximation by averaging the two:

$$\frac{\partial f}{\partial S} = \frac{f_{i,j+1} - f_{i,j-1}}{2\,\Delta S} \tag{17.24}$$

For $\partial f/\partial t$, we will use a forward difference approximation so that the value at time $i\,\Delta t$ is related to the value at time $(i+1)\,\Delta t$:

$$\frac{\partial f}{\partial t} = \frac{f_{i+1,j} - f_{i,j}}{\Delta t} \tag{17.25}$$

The backward difference approximation for $\partial f/\partial S$ at the (i, j) point is given by equation (17.23). The backward difference at the $(i, j+1)$ point is

$$\frac{f_{i,j+1} - f_{i,j}}{\Delta S}$$

Figure 17.15 Grid for finite difference approach.

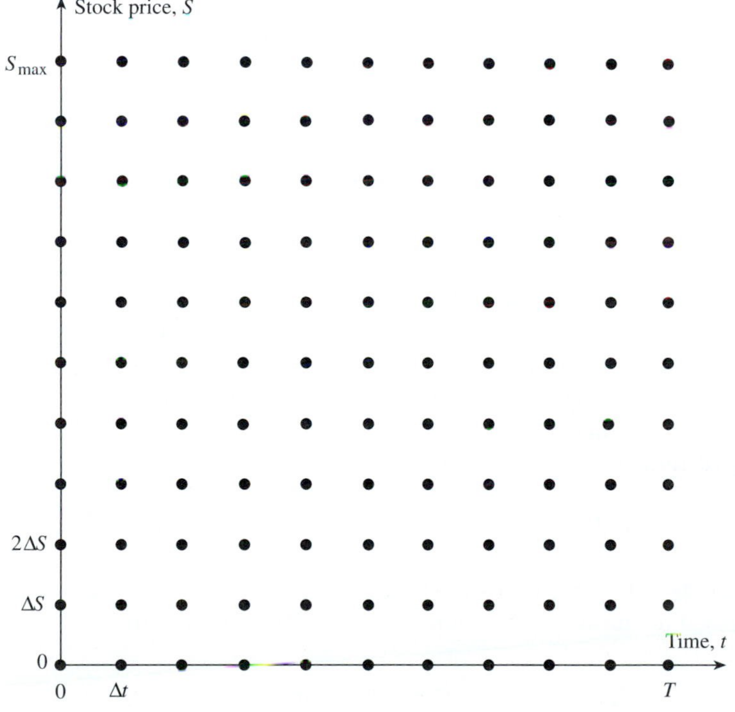

Hence a finite difference approximation for $\partial^2 f/\partial S^2$ at the (i, j) point is

$$\frac{\partial^2 f}{\partial S^2} = \left(\frac{f_{i,j+1} - f_{i,j}}{\Delta S} - \frac{f_{i,j} - f_{i,j-1}}{\Delta S}\right) \Big/ \Delta S$$

or

$$\frac{\partial^2 f}{\partial S^2} = \frac{f_{i,j+1} + f_{i,j-1} - 2f_{i,j}}{\Delta S^2} \tag{17.26}$$

Substituting equations (17.24), (17.25), and (17.26) into the differential equation (17.21) and noting that $S = j\,\Delta S$ gives

$$\frac{f_{i+1,j} - f_{i,j}}{\Delta t} + (r-q)j\,\Delta S\frac{f_{i,j+1} - f_{i,j-1}}{2\,\Delta S} + \tfrac{1}{2}\sigma^2 j^2 \Delta S^2 \frac{f_{i,j+1} + f_{i,j-1} - 2f_{i,j}}{\Delta S^2} = rf_{i,j}$$

for $j = 1, 2, \dots, M-1$ and $i = 0, 1 \dots, N-1$. Rearranging terms, we obtain

$$a_j f_{i,j-1} + b_j f_{i,j} + c_j f_{i,j+1} = f_{i+1,j} \tag{17.27}$$

where

$$a_j = \tfrac{1}{2}(r-q)j\,\Delta t - \tfrac{1}{2}\sigma^2 j^2 \Delta t$$

$$b_j = 1 + \sigma^2 j^2 \Delta t + r\,\Delta t$$

$$c_j = -\tfrac{1}{2}(r-q)j\,\Delta t - \tfrac{1}{2}\sigma^2 j^2 \Delta t$$

The value of the put at time T is $\max(K - S_T,\ 0)$, where S_T is the stock price at time T. Hence,

$$f_{N,j} = \max(K - j\,\Delta S,\ 0), \quad j = 0, 1, \dots, M \tag{17.28}$$

The value of the put option when the stock price is zero is K. Hence,

$$f_{i,0} = K, \quad i = 0, 1, \dots, N \tag{17.29}$$

We assume that the put option is worth zero when $S = S_{\max}$, so that

$$f_{i,M} = 0, \quad i = 0, 1, \dots, N \tag{17.30}$$

Equations (17.28), (17.29), and (17.30) define the value of the put option along the three edges of the grid in Figure 17.15, where $S = 0$, $S = S_{\max}$, and $t = T$. It remains to use equation (17.27) to arrive at the value of f at all other points. First the points corresponding to time $T - \Delta t$ are tackled. Equation (17.27) with $i = N-1$ gives

$$a_j\, f_{N-1,j-1} + b_j\, f_{N-1,j} + c_j\, f_{N-1,j+1} = f_{N,j} \tag{17.31}$$

for $j = 1, 2, \dots, M-1$. The right-hand sides of these equations are known from equation (17.28). Furthermore, from equations (17.29) and (17.30),

$$f_{N-1,0} = K \tag{17.32}$$

$$f_{N-1,M} = 0 \tag{17.33}$$

Equations (17.31) are therefore $M-1$ simultaneous equations that can be solved for the $M-1$ unknowns: $f_{N-1,1}, f_{N-1,2}, \dots, f_{N-1,M-1}$.[24] After this has been done, each value of $f_{N-1,j}$ is compared with $K - j\,\Delta S$. If $f_{N-1,j} < K - j\,\Delta S$, early exercise at time $T-\Delta t$ is optimal and $f_{N-1,j}$ is set equal to $K - j\,\Delta S$. The nodes corresponding to time $T - 2\,\Delta t$ are handled in a similar way, and so on. Eventually, $f_{0,1}, f_{0,2}, f_{0,3}, \dots, f_{0,M-1}$ are obtained. One of these is the option price of interest.

The control variate technique can be used in conjunction with finite difference methods. The same grid is used to value an option similar to the one under consideration but for which an analytic valuation is available. Equation (17.20) is then used.

Example 17.10

Table 17.4 shows the result of using the implicit finite difference method as just described for pricing the American put option in Example 17.1. Values of 20, 10, and 5 were chosen for M, N, and ΔS, respectively. Thus, the option price is evaluated at \$5 stock price intervals between \$0 and \$100 and at half-month time intervals throughout the life of the option. The option price given by the grid is \$4.07. The same grid gives the price of the corresponding European option as \$3.91. The true European price given by the Black–Scholes formula is \$4.08. The control variate estimate of the American price is therefore

$$4.07 + 4.08 - 3.91 = \$4.24$$

Explicit Finite Difference Method

The implicit finite difference method has the advantage of being very robust. It always converges to the solution of the differential equation as ΔS and Δt approach zero.[25] One of the disadvantages of the implicit finite difference method is that $M-1$ simultaneous equations have to be solved in order to calculate the $f_{i,j}$ from the $f_{i+1,j}$. The method can be simplified if the values of $\partial f/\partial S$ and $\partial^2 f/\partial S^2$ at point (i, j) on the grid are assumed to be the same as at point $(i+1, j)$. Equations (17.24) and (17.26) then become

$$\frac{\partial f}{\partial S} = \frac{f_{i+1,j+1} - f_{i+1,j-1}}{2\,\Delta S}$$

$$\frac{\partial^2 f}{\partial S^2} = \frac{f_{i+1,j+1} + f_{i+1,j-1} - 2f_{i+1,j}}{\Delta S^2}$$

The difference equation is

$$\frac{f_{i+1,j} - f_{i,j}}{\Delta t} + (r-q)j\,\Delta S\,\frac{f_{i+1,j+1} - f_{i+1,j-1}}{2\Delta S} + \tfrac{1}{2}\sigma^2 j^2 \Delta S^2\,\frac{f_{i+1,j+1} + f_{i+1,j-1} - 2f_{i+1,j}}{\Delta S^2} = r f_{i,j}$$

[24] This does not involve inverting a matrix. The $j=1$ equation in (17.31) can be used to express $f_{N-1,2}$ in terms of $f_{N-1,1}$; the $j=2$ equation, when combined with the $j=1$ equation, can be used to express $f_{N-1,3}$ in terms of $f_{N-1,1}$; and so on. The $j = M-2$ equation, together with earlier equations, enables $f_{N-1,M-1}$ to be expressed in terms of $f_{N-1,1}$. The final $j = M-1$ equation can then be solved for $f_{N-1,1}$, which can then be used to determine the other $f_{N-1,j}$.

[25] A general rule in finite difference methods is that ΔS should be kept proportional to $\sqrt{\Delta t}$ as they approach zero.

Table 17.4 Grid to value American option in Example 17.1 using implicit finite difference methods.

Stock price (dollars)	*Time to maturity (months)*										
	5	*4.5*	*4*	*3.5*	*3*	*2.5*	*2*	*1.5*	*1*	*0.5*	*0*
100	0.00	0.00	0.00	0.00	0.00	0.00	0.00	0.00	0.00	0.00	0.00
95	0.02	0.02	0.01	0.01	0.00	0.00	0.00	0.00	0.00	0.00	0.00
90	0.05	0.04	0.03	0.02	0.01	0.01	0.00	0.00	0.00	0.00	0.00
85	0.09	0.07	0.05	0.03	0.02	0.01	0.01	0.00	0.00	0.00	0.00
80	0.16	0.12	0.09	0.07	0.04	0.03	0.02	0.01	0.00	0.00	0.00
75	0.27	0.22	0.17	0.13	0.09	0.06	0.03	0.02	0.01	0.00	0.00
70	0.47	0.39	0.32	0.25	0.18	0.13	0.08	0.04	0.02	0.00	0.00
65	0.82	0.71	0.60	0.49	0.38	0.28	0.19	0.11	0.05	0.02	0.00
60	1.42	1.27	1.11	0.95	0.78	0.62	0.45	0.30	0.16	0.05	0.00
55	2.43	2.24	2.05	1.83	1.61	1.36	1.09	0.81	0.51	0.22	0.00
50	4.07	3.88	3.67	3.45	3.19	2.91	2.57	2.17	1.66	0.99	0.00
45	6.58	6.44	6.29	6.13	5.96	5.77	5.57	5.36	5.17	5.02	5.00
40	10.15	10.10	10.05	10.01	10.00	10.00	10.00	10.00	10.00	10.00	10.00
35	15.00	15.00	15.00	15.00	15.00	15.00	15.00	15.00	15.00	15.00	15.00
30	20.00	20.00	20.00	20.00	20.00	20.00	20.00	20.00	20.00	20.00	20.00
25	25.00	25.00	25.00	25.00	25.00	25.00	25.00	25.00	25.00	25.00	25.00
20	30.00	30.00	30.00	30.00	30.00	30.00	30.00	30.00	30.00	30.00	30.00
15	35.00	35.00	35.00	35.00	35.00	35.00	35.00	35.00	35.00	35.00	35.00
10	40.00	40.00	40.00	40.00	40.00	40.00	40.00	40.00	40.00	40.00	40.00
5	45.00	45.00	45.00	45.00	45.00	45.00	45.00	45.00	45.00	45.00	45.00
0	50.00	50.00	50.00	50.00	50.00	50.00	50.00	50.00	50.00	50.00	50.00

or

$$f_{i,j} = a_j^* f_{i+1,j-1} + b_j^* f_{i+1,j} + c_j^* f_{i+1,j+1} \tag{17.34}$$

where

$$a_j^* = \frac{1}{1+r\,\Delta t}\left(-\tfrac{1}{2}(r-q)j\,\Delta t + \tfrac{1}{2}\sigma^2 j^2 \Delta t\right)$$

$$b_j^* = \frac{1}{1+r\,\Delta t}(1 - \sigma^2 j^2 \Delta t)$$

$$c_j^* = \frac{1}{1+r\,\Delta t}\left(\tfrac{1}{2}(r-q)j\,\Delta t + \tfrac{1}{2}\sigma^2 j^2 \Delta t\right)$$

This creates what is known as the *explicit finite difference method.*[26] Figure 17.16 shows the difference between the implicit and explicit methods. The implicit method leads to equation (17.27), which gives a relationship between three different values of the option at time $i\,\Delta t$ (i.e., $f_{i,j-1}$, $f_{i,j}$, and $f_{i,j+1}$) and one value of the option at time $(i+1)\,\Delta t$

[26] We also obtain the explicit finite difference method if we use the backward difference approximation instead of the forward difference approximation for $\partial f/\partial t$.

Figure 17.16 Difference between implicit and explicit finite difference methods.

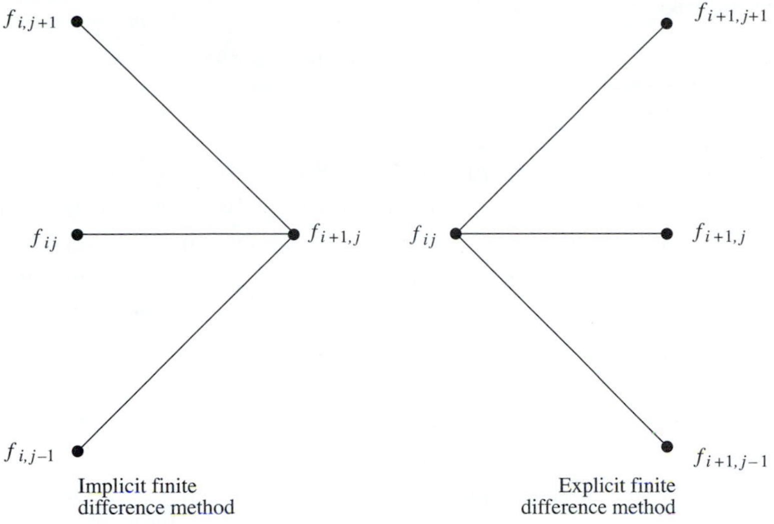

(i.e., $f_{i+1,j}$). The explicit method leads to equation (17.34), which gives a relationship between one value of the option at time $i\,\Delta t$ (i.e., $f_{i,j}$) and three different values of the option at time $(i+1)\,\Delta t$ (i.e., $f_{i+1,j-1}$, $f_{i+1,j}$, $f_{i+1,j+1}$).

Example 17.11

Table 17.5 shows the result of using the explicit version of the finite difference method for pricing the American put option in Example 17.1. As in Example 17.10, values of 20, 10, and 5 were chosen for M, N, and ΔS, respectively. The option price given by the grid is \$4.26.[27]

Change of Variable

It is computationally more efficient to use finite difference methods with ln S rather than S as the underlying variable. Define $Z = \ln S$. Equation (17.21) becomes

$$\frac{\partial f}{\partial t} + \left(r - q - \frac{\sigma^2}{2}\right)\frac{\partial f}{\partial Z} + \tfrac{1}{2}\sigma^2 \frac{\partial^2 f}{\partial Z^2} = rf$$

The grid then evaluates the derivative for equally spaced values of Z rather than for equally spaced values of S. The difference equation for the implicit method becomes

$$\frac{f_{i+1,j} - f_{i,j}}{\Delta t} + (r - q - \sigma^2/2)\frac{f_{i,j+1} - f_{i,j-1}}{2\Delta Z} + \tfrac{1}{2}\sigma^2 \frac{f_{i,j+1} + f_{i,j-1} - 2f_{i,j}}{\Delta Z^2} = rf_{i,j}$$

or

$$\alpha_j f_{i,j-1} + \beta_j f_{i,j} + \gamma_j f_{i,j+1} = f_{i+1,j} \qquad \textbf{(17.35)}$$

[27] The negative numbers and other inconsistencies in the top left-hand part of the grid will be explained later.

Table 17.5 Grid to value American option in Example 17.1 using explicit finite difference method.

Stock price (dollars)	*Time to maturity (months)*										
	5	*4.5*	*4*	*3.5*	*3*	*2.5*	*2*	*1.5*	*1*	*0.5*	*0*
100	0.00	0.00	0.00	0.00	0.00	0.00	0.00	0.00	0.00	0.00	0.00
95	0.06	0.00	0.00	0.00	0.00	0.00	0.00	0.00	0.00	0.00	0.00
90	−0.11	0.05	0.00	0.00	0.00	0.00	0.00	0.00	0.00	0.00	0.00
85	0.28	−0.05	0.05	0.00	0.00	0.00	0.00	0.00	0.00	0.00	0.00
80	−0.13	0.20	0.00	0.05	0.00	0.00	0.00	0.00	0.00	0.00	0.00
75	0.46	0.06	0.20	0.04	0.06	0.00	0.00	0.00	0.00	0.00	0.00
70	0.32	0.46	0.23	0.25	0.10	0.09	0.00	0.00	0.00	0.00	0.00
65	0.91	0.68	0.63	0.44	0.37	0.21	0.14	0.00	0.00	0.00	0.00
60	1.48	1.37	1.17	1.02	0.81	0.65	0.42	0.27	0.00	0.00	0.00
55	2.59	2.39	2.21	1.99	1.77	1.50	1.24	0.90	0.59	0.00	0.00
50	4.26	4.08	3.89	3.68	3.44	3.18	2.87	2.53	2.07	1.56	0.00
45	6.76	6.61	6.47	6.31	6.15	5.96	5.75	5.50	5.24	5.00	5.00
40	10.28	10.20	10.13	10.06	10.01	10.00	10.00	10.00	10.00	10.00	10.00
35	15.00	15.00	15.00	15.00	15.00	15.00	15.00	15.00	15.00	15.00	15.00
30	20.00	20.00	20.00	20.00	20.00	20.00	20.00	20.00	20.00	20.00	20.00
25	25.00	25.00	25.00	25.00	25.00	25.00	25.00	25.00	25.00	25.00	25.00
20	30.00	30.00	30.00	30.00	30.00	30.00	30.00	30.00	30.00	30.00	30.00
15	35.00	35.00	35.00	35.00	35.00	35.00	35.00	35.00	35.00	35.00	35.00
10	40.00	40.00	40.00	40.00	40.00	40.00	40.00	40.00	40.00	40.00	40.00
5	45.00	45.00	45.00	45.00	45.00	45.00	45.00	45.00	45.00	45.00	45.00
0	50.00	50.00	50.00	50.00	50.00	50.00	50.00	50.00	50.00	50.00	50.00

where

$$\alpha_j = \frac{\Delta t}{2\Delta Z}(r - q - \sigma^2/2) - \frac{\Delta t}{2\Delta Z^2}\sigma^2$$

$$\beta_j = 1 + \frac{\Delta t}{\Delta Z^2}\sigma^2 + r\,\Delta t$$

$$\gamma_j = -\frac{\Delta t}{2\Delta Z}(r - q - \sigma^2/2) - \frac{\Delta t}{2\Delta Z^2}\sigma^2$$

The difference equation for the explicit method becomes

$$\frac{f_{i+1,j} - f_{i,j}}{\Delta t} + (r - q - \sigma^2/2)\,\frac{f_{i+1,j+1} - f_{i+1,j-1}}{2\Delta Z} + \tfrac{1}{2}\sigma^2\,\frac{f_{i+1,j+1} + f_{i+1,j-1} - 2f_{i+1,j}}{\Delta Z^2} = rf_{i,j}$$

or

$$\alpha_j^*\,f_{i+1,j-1} + \beta_j^*\,f_{i+1,j} + \gamma_j^*\,f_{i+1,j+1} = f_{i,j} \tag{17.36}$$

where

$$\alpha_j^* = \frac{1}{1 + r\,\Delta t}\left[-\frac{\Delta t}{2\Delta Z}(r - q - \sigma^2/2) + \frac{\Delta t}{2\Delta Z^2}\sigma^2\right] \tag{17.37}$$

$$\beta_j^* = \frac{1}{1 + r\,\Delta t}\left(1 - \frac{\Delta t}{\Delta Z^2}\sigma^2\right) \tag{17.38}$$

$$\gamma_j^* = \frac{1}{1 + r\,\Delta t}\left[\frac{\Delta t}{2\Delta Z}(r - q - \sigma^2/2) + \frac{\Delta t}{2\Delta Z^2}\sigma^2\right] \tag{17.39}$$

The change of variable approach has the property that α_j, β_j, and γ_j as well as α_j^*, β_j^*, and γ_j^* are independent of j. It can be shown that it is numerically most efficient to set $\Delta Z = \sigma\sqrt{3\Delta t}$.

Relation to Trinomial Tree Approaches

The explicit finite difference method is equivalent to the trinomial tree approach.[28] In the expressions for a_j^*, b_j^*, and c_j^* in equation (17.34), we can interpret terms as follows:

$-\frac{1}{2}(r - q)j\,\Delta t + \frac{1}{2}\sigma^2 j^2\,\Delta t$: Probability of stock price decreasing from $j\,\Delta S$ to $(j - 1)\Delta S$ in time Δt.

$1 - \sigma^2 j^2\,\Delta t$: Probability of stock price remaining unchanged at $j\,\Delta S$ in time Δt.

$\frac{1}{2}(r - q)j\,\Delta t + \frac{1}{2}\sigma^2 j^2\,\Delta t$: Probability of stock price increasing from $j\,\Delta S$ to $(j + 1)\Delta S$ in time Δt.

This interpretation is illustrated in Figure 17.17. The three probabilities sum to unity. They give the expected increase in the stock price in time Δt as $(r - q)j\,\Delta S\,\Delta t = (r - q)S\,\Delta t$. This is the expected increase in a risk-neutral world. For small values

Figure 17.17 Interpretation of explicit finite difference method as a trinomial tree.

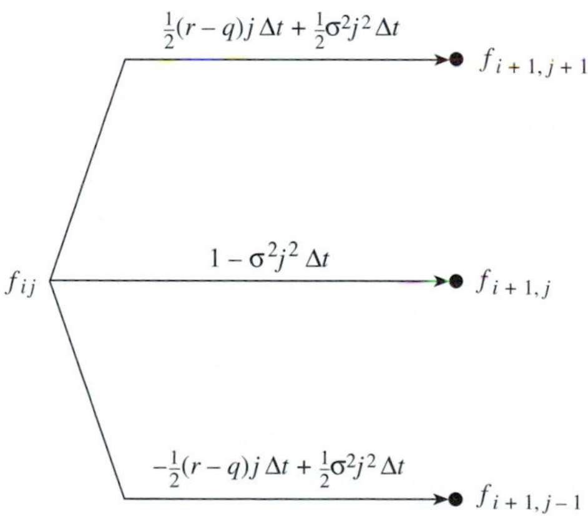

[28] It can also be shown that the implicit finite difference method is equivalent to a multinomial tree approach where there are $M + 1$ branches emanating from each node.

of Δt, they also give the variance of the change in the stock price in time Δt as $\sigma^2 j^2 \Delta S^2 \Delta t = \sigma^2 S^2 \Delta t$. This corresponds to the stochastic process followed by S. The value of f at time $i\,\Delta t$ is calculated as the expected value of f at time $(i+1)\,\Delta t$ in a risk-neutral world discounted at the risk-free rate.

For the explicit version of the finite difference method to work well, the three "probabilities"

$$-\tfrac{1}{2}(r-q)j\,\Delta t + \tfrac{1}{2}\sigma^2 j^2 \Delta t,$$

$$1 - \sigma^2 j^2 \Delta t$$

$$\tfrac{1}{2}(r-q)j\,\Delta t + \tfrac{1}{2}\sigma^2 j^2 \Delta t$$

should all be positive. In Example 17.11, $1 - \sigma^2 j^2 \Delta t$ is negative when $j \geqslant 13$ (i.e., when $S \geqslant 65$). This explains the negative option prices and other inconsistencies in the top left-hand part of Table 17.5. This example illustrates the main problem associated with the explicit finite difference method. Because the probabilities in the associated tree may be negative, it does not necessarily produce results that converge to the solution of the differential equation.[29]

When the change-of-variable approach is used (see equations (17.36) to (17.39)), the probability that $Z = \ln S$ will decrease by ΔZ, stay the same, and increase by ΔZ are

$$-\frac{\Delta t}{2\Delta Z}(r - q - \sigma^2/2) + \frac{\Delta t}{2\Delta Z^2}\sigma^2$$

$$1 - \frac{\Delta t}{\Delta z^2}\sigma^2$$

$$\frac{\Delta t}{2\Delta Z}(r - q - \sigma^2/2) + \frac{\Delta t}{2\Delta Z^2}\sigma^2$$

respectively. These movements in Z correspond to the stock price changing from S to $Se^{-\Delta Z}$, S, and $Se^{\Delta Z}$, respectively. If we set $\Delta Z = \sigma\sqrt{3\Delta t}$, then the tree and the probabilities are identical to those for the trinomial tree approach discussed in Section 17.4.

Other Finite Difference Methods

Many of the other finite difference methods that have been proposed have some of the features of the explicit finite difference method and some features of the implicit finite difference method.

In what is known as the *hopscotch method*, we alternate between the explicit and implicit calculations as we move from node to node. This is illustrated in Figure 17.18. At each time, we first do all the calculations at the "explicit nodes" in the usual way. We can then deal with the "implicit nodes" without solving a set of simultaneous equations because the values at the adjacent nodes have already been calculated.

[29] J. Hull and A. White, "Valuing Derivative Securities Using the Explicit Finite Difference Method," *Journal of Financial and Quantitative Analysis*, 25 (March 1990): 87–100, show how this problem can be overcome. In the situation considered here it is sufficient to construct the grid in $\ln S$ rather than S to ensure convergence.

Figure 17.18 The hopscotch method. I indicates node at which implicit calculations are done; E indicates node at which explicit calculations are done.

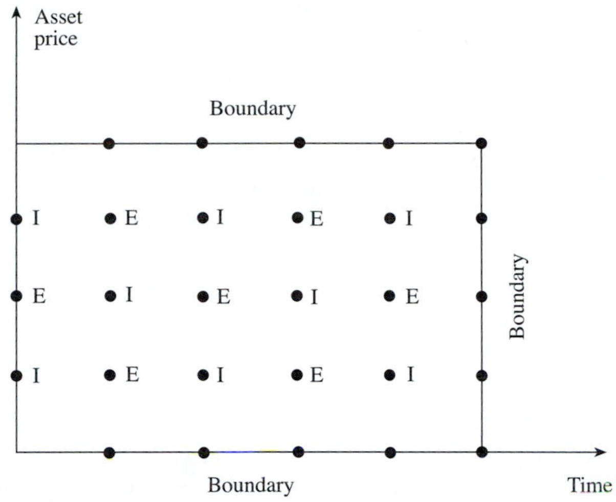

The *Crank–Nicolson* scheme is an average of the explicit and implicit methods. For the implicit method, equation (17.27) gives

$$f_{i,j} = a_j f_{i-1,j-1} + b_j f_{i-1,j} + c_j f_{i-1,j+1}$$

For the explicit method, equation (17.34) gives

$$f_{i-1,j} = a_j^* f_{i,j-1} + b_j^* f_{i,j} + c_j^* f_{i,j+1}$$

The Crank–Nicolson method averages these two equations to obtain

$$f_{i,j} + f_{i-1,j} = a_j f_{i-1,j-1} + b_j f_{i-1,j} + c_j f_{i-1,j+1} + a_j^* f_{i,j-1} + b_j^* f_{i,j} + c_j^* f_{i,j+1}$$

Putting

$$g_{i,j} = f_{i,j} - a_j^* f_{i,j-1} - b_j^* f_{i,j} - c_j^* f_{i,j+1}$$

we obtain

$$g_{i,j} = a_j f_{i-1,j-1} + b_j f_{i-1,j} + c_j f_{i-1,j+1} - f_{i-1,j}$$

This shows that implementing the Crank–Nicolson method is similar to implementing the implicit finite difference method. The advantage of the Crank–Nicolson method is that it has faster convergence than either the explicit or implicit method.

Applications of Finite Difference Methods

Finite difference methods can be used for the same types of derivative pricing problems as tree approaches. They can handle American-style as well as European-style derivatives but cannot easily be used in situations where the payoff from a derivative depends on the past history of the underlying variable. Finite difference methods can, at the expense of a considerable increase in computer time, be used when there are several state variables. The grid in Figure 17.15 then becomes multidimensional.

The method for calculating Greek letters is similar to that used for trees. Delta, gamma, and theta can be calculated directly from the $f_{i,j}$ values on the grid. For vega, it is necessary to make a small change to volatility and recalculate the value of the derivative using the same grid.

SUMMARY

We have presented three different numerical procedures for valuing derivatives when no analytic solution is available. These involve the use of trees, Monte Carlo simulation, and finite difference methods.

Binomial trees assume that, in each short interval of time Δt, a stock price either moves up by a multiplicative amount u or down by a multiplicative amount d. The sizes of u and d and their associated probabilities are chosen so that the change in the stock price has the correct mean and standard deviation in a risk-neutral world. Derivative prices are calculated by starting at the end of the tree and working backwards. For an American option, the value at a node is the greater of (a) the value if it is exercised immediately and (b) the discounted expected value if it is held for a further period of time Δt.

Monte Carlo simulation involves using random numbers to sample many different paths that the variables underlying the derivative could follow in a risk-neutral world. For each path, the payoff is calculated and discounted at the risk-free interest rate. The arithmetic average of the discounted payoffs is the estimated value of the derivative.

Finite difference methods solve the underlying differential equation by converting it to a difference equation. They are similar to tree approaches in that the computations work back from the end of the life of the derivative to the beginning. The explicit method is functionally the same as using a trinomial tree. The implicit finite difference method is more complicated but has the advantage that the user does not have to take any special precautions to ensure convergence.

In practice, the method that is chosen is likely to depend on the characteristics of the derivative being evaluated and the accuracy required. Monte Carlo simulation works forward from the beginning to the end of the life of a derivative. It can be used for European-style derivatives and can cope with a great deal of complexity as far as the payoffs are concerned. It becomes relatively more efficient as the number of underlying variables increases. Tree approaches and finite difference methods work from the end of the life of a security to the beginning and can accommodate American-style as well as European-style derivatives. However, they are difficult to apply when the payoffs depend on the past history of the state variables as well as on their current values. Also, they are liable to become computationally very time consuming when three or more variables are involved.

FURTHER READING

General

Clewlow, L., and C. Strickland, *Implementing Derivatives Models*. Chichester: Wiley, 1998.

Press, W. H., S. A. Teukolsky, W. T. Vetterling, and B. P. Flannery, *Numerical Recipes in C: The Art of Scientific Computing*, 2nd edn. Cambridge University Press, 1992.

On Tree Approaches

Cox, J. C, S. A. Ross, and M. Rubinstein. "Option Pricing: A Simplified Approach," *Journal of Financial Economics*, 7 (October 1979): 229–64.

Figlewski, S., and B. Gao. "The Adaptive Mesh Model: A New Approach to Efficient Option Pricing," *Journal of Financial Economics*, 53 (1999): 313–51.

Hull, J. C., and A. White, "The Use of the Control Variate Technique in Option Pricing," *Journal of Financial and Quantitative Analysis*, 23 (September 1988): 237–51.

Rendleman, R., and B. Bartter, "Two State Option Pricing," *Journal of Finance*, 34 (1979): 1092–1110.

On Monte Carlo Simulation

Boyle, P. P., "Options: A Monte Carlo Approach," *Journal of Financial Economics*, 4 (1977): 323–38.

Boyle, P. P., M. Broadie, and P. Glasserman. "Monte Carlo Methods for Security Pricing," *Journal of Economic Dynamics and Control*, 21 (1997): 1267–1322.

Broadie, M., P. Glasserman, and G. Jain. "Enhanced Monte Carlo Estimates for American Option Prices," *Journal of Derivatives*, 5 (Fall 1997): 25–44.

On Finite Difference Methods

Hull, J. C., and A. White, "Valuing Derivative Securities Using the Explicit Finite Difference Method," *Journal of Financial and Quantitative Analysis*, 25 (March 1990): 87–100.

Wilmott, P., *Derivatives: The Theory and Practice of Financial Engineering*. Chichester: Wiley, 1998.

Questions and Problems (Answers in Solutions Manual)

17.1. Which of the following can be estimated for an American option by constructing a single binomial tree: delta, gamma, vega, theta, rho?

17.2. Calculate the price of a 3-month American put option on a non-dividend-paying stock when the stock price is \$60, the strike price is \$60, the risk-free interest rate is 10% per annum, and the volatility is 45% per annum. Use a binomial tree with a time interval of 1 month.

17.3. Explain how the control variate technique is implemented when a tree is used to value American options.

17.4. Calculate the price of a 9-month American call option on corn futures when the current futures price is 198 cents, the strike price is 200 cents, the risk-free interest rate is 8% per annum, and the volatility is 30% per annum. Use a binomial tree with a time interval of 3 months.

17.5. Consider an option that pays off the amount by which the final stock price exceeds the average stock price achieved during the life of the option. Can this be valued using the binomial tree approach? Explain your answer.

17.6. "For a dividend-paying stock, the tree for the stock price does not recombine; but the tree for the stock price less the present value of future dividends does recombine." Explain this statement.

17.7. Show that the probabilities in a Cox, Ross, and Rubinstein binomial tree are negative when the condition in footnote 9 holds.

17.8. Use stratified sampling with 100 trials to improve the estimate of π in Business Snapshot 17.1 and Table 17.1.

17.9. Explain why the Monte Carlo simulation approach cannot easily be used for American-style derivatives.

17.10. A 9-month American put option on a non-dividend-paying stock has a strike price of \$49. The stock price is \$50, the risk-free rate is 5% per annum, and the volatility is 30% per annum. Use a three-step binomial tree to calculate the option price.

17.11. Use a three-time-step tree to value a 9-month American call option on wheat futures. The current futures price is 400 cents, the strike price is 420 cents, the risk-free rate is 6%, and the volatility is 35% per annum. Estimate the delta of the option from your tree.

17.12. A 3-month American call option on a stock has a strike price of \$20. The stock price is \$20, the risk-free rate is 3% per annum, and the volatility is 25% per annum. A dividend of \$2 is expected in 1.5 months. Use a three-step binomial tree to calculate the option price.

17.13. A 1-year American put option on a non-dividend-paying stock has an exercise price of \$18. The current stock price is \$20, the risk-free interest rate is 15% per annum, and the volatility of the stock price is 40% per annum. Use the DerivaGem software with four 3-month time steps to estimate the value of the option. Display the tree and verify that the option prices at the final and penultimate nodes are correct. Use DerivaGem to value the European version of the option. Use the control variate technique to improve your estimate of the price of the American option.

17.14. A 2-month American put option on a stock index has an exercise price of 480. The current level of the index is 484, the risk-free interest rate is 10% per annum, the dividend yield on the index is 3% per annum, and the volatility of the index is 25% per annum. Divide the life of the option into four half-month periods and use the tree approach to estimate the value of the option.

17.15. How can the control variate approach improve the estimate of the delta of an American option when the tree approach is used?

17.16. Suppose that Monte Carlo simulation is being used to evaluate a European call option on a non-dividend-paying stock when the volatility is stochastic. How could the control variate and antithetic variable technique be used to improve numerical efficiency? Explain why it is necessary to calculate six values of the option in each simulation trial when both the control variate and the antithetic variable technique are used.

17.17. Explain how equations (17.27) to (17.30) change when the implicit finite difference method is being used to evaluate an American call option on a currency.

17.18. An American put option on a non-dividend-paying stock has 4 months to maturity. The exercise price is \$21, the stock price is \$20, the risk-free rate of interest is 10% per annum, and the volatility is 30% per annum. Use the explicit version of the finite difference approach to value the option. Use stock price intervals of \$4 and time intervals of 1 month.

17.19. The spot price of copper is \$0.60 per pound. Suppose that the futures prices (dollars per pound) are as follows:

3 months	0.59
6 months	0.57
9 months	0.54
12 months	0.50

The volatility of the price of copper is 40% per annum and the risk-free rate is 6% per annum. Use a binomial tree to value an American call option on copper with an exercise price of \$0.60 and a time to maturity of 1 year. Divide the life of the option into four 3-month periods for the purposes of constructing the tree. (*Hint*: As explained in Section 14.7, the futures price of a variable is its expected future price in a risk-neutral world.)

17.20. Use the binomial tree in Problem 17.19 to value a security that pays off x^2 in 1 year where x is the price of copper.

17.21. When do the boundary conditions for $S = 0$ and $S \to \infty$ affect the estimates of derivative prices in the explicit finite difference method?

17.22. How would you use the antithetic variable method to improve the estimate of the European option in Business Snapshot 17.2 and Table 17.2?

17.23. A company has issued a 3-year convertible bond that has a face value of \$25 and can be exchanged for two of the company's shares at any time. The company can call the issue when the share price is greater than or equal to \$18. Assuming that the company will force conversion at the earliest opportunity, what are the boundary conditions for the price of the convertible? Describe how you would use finite difference methods to value the convertible assuming constant interest rates. Assume there is no risk of the company defaulting.

17.24. Provide formulas that can be used for obtaining three random samples from standard normal distributions when the correlation between sample i and sample j is $\rho_{i,j}$.

Assignment Questions

17.25. An American put option to sell a Swiss franc for dollars has a strike price of \$0.80 and a time to maturity of 1 year. The volatility of the Swiss franc is 10%, the dollar interest rate is 6%, the Swiss franc interest rate is 3%, and the current exchange rate is 0.81. Use a three-time-step tree to value the option. Estimate the delta of the option from your tree.

17.26. A 1-year American call option on silver futures has an exercise price of \$9.00. The current futures price is \$8.50, the risk-free rate of interest is 12% per annum, and the volatility of the futures price is 25% per annum. Use the DerivaGem software with four 3-month time steps to estimate the value of the option. Display the tree and verify that the option prices at the final and penultimate nodes are correct. Use DerivaGem to value the European version of the option. Use the control variate technique to improve your estimate of the price of the American option.

17.27. A 6-month American call option on a stock is expected to pay dividends of \$1 per share at the end of the second month and the fifth month. The current stock price is \$30, the exercise price is \$34, the risk-free interest rate is 10% per annum, and the volatility of the part of the stock price that will not be used to pay the dividends is 30% per annum. Use the DerivaGem software with the life of the option divided into six time steps to estimate the value of the option. Compare your answer with that given by Black's approximation (see Section 13.12).

17.28. The current value of the British pound is \$1.60 and the volatility of the pound/dollar exchange rate is 15% per annum. An American call option has an exercise price of \$1.62 and a time to maturity of 1 year. The risk-free rates of interest in the United States and the United Kingdom are 6% per annum and 9% per annum, respectively. Use the explicit finite difference method to value the option. Consider exchange rates at intervals of 0.20 between 0.80 and 2.40 and time intervals of 3 months.

17.29. Answer the following questions concerned with the alternative procedures for constructing trees in Section 17.4:

(a) Show that the binomial model in Section 17.4 is exactly consistent with the mean and variance of the change in the logarithm of the stock price in time Δt.

(b) Show that the trinomial model in Section 17.4 is consistent with the mean and variance of the change in the logarithm of the stock price in time Δt when terms of order $(\Delta t)^2$ and higher are ignored.

(c) Construct an alternative to the trinomial model in Section 17.4 so that the probabilities are 1/6, 2/3, and 1/6 on the upper, middle, and lower branches emanating from each node. Assume that the branching is from S to Su, Sm, or Sd with $m^2 = ud$. Match the mean and variance of the change in the logarithm of the stock price exactly.

17.30. The DerivaGem Application Buider functions enable you to investigate how the prices of options calculated from a binomial tree converge to the correct value as the number of time steps increases. (See Figure 17.4 and Sample Application A in DerivaGem.) Consider a put option on a stock index where the index level is 900, the strike price is 900, the risk-free rate is 5%, the dividend yield is 2%, and the time to maturity is 2 years.

(a) Produce results similar to Sample Application A on convergence for the situation where the option is European and the volatility of the index is 20%.

(b) Produce results similar to Sample Application A on convergence for the situation where the option is American and the volatility of the index is 20%.

(c) Produce a chart showing the pricing of the American option when the volatility is 20% as a function of the number of time steps when the control variate technique is used.

(d) Suppose that the price of the American option in the market is 85.0. Produce a chart showing the implied volatility estimate as a function of the number of time steps.

CHAPTER 18 Value at Risk

In Chapter 15 we examined measures such as delta, gamma, and vega for describing different aspects of the risk in a portfolio of derivatives. A financial institution usually calculates each of these measures each day for every market variable to which it is exposed. Often there are hundreds, or even thousands, of these market variables. A delta–gamma–vega analysis, therefore, leads to a huge number of different risk measures being produced each day. These risk measures provide valuable information for a trader who is responsible for managing the part of the financial institution's portfolio that is dependent on the particular market variable. However, they do not provide a way of measuring the total risk to which the financial institution is exposed.

Value at Risk (VaR) is an attempt to provide a single number summarizing the total risk in a portfolio of financial assets. It has become widely used by corporate treasurers and fund managers as well as by financial institutions. Central bank regulators also use VaR in determining the capital a bank is required to keep to reflect the market risks it is bearing.

In this chapter we explain the VaR measure and describe the two main approaches for calculating it. These are known as the *historical simulation* approach and the *model-building* approach.

18.1 THE VaR MEASURE

When using the value-at-risk measure, we are interested in making a statement of the following form:

> We are X percent certain that we will not lose more than V dollars in the next N days.

The variable V is the VaR of the portfolio. It is a function of two parameters: the time horizon (N days) and the confidence level ($X\%$). It is the loss level over N days that we are $X\%$ certain will not be exceeded. Bank regulators require banks to calculate VaR with $N = 10$ and $X = 99$ (see the discussion in Business Snapshot 18.1).

In general, when N days is the time horizon and $X\%$ is the confidence level, VaR is the loss corresponding to the $(100 - X)$th percentile of the distribution of the change in the value of the portfolio over the next N days. For example, when $N = 5$ and $X = 97$, VaR is the third percentile of the distribution of changes in the value of the portfolio

Business Snapshot 18.1 How Bank Regulators Use VaR

The Basel Committee on Bank Supervision is a committee of the world's bank regulators that meets regularly in Basel, Switzerland. In 1988 it published what has become known as *The 1988 BIS Accord*, or simply *The Accord*. This is an agreement between the regulators on how the capital a bank is required to hold for credit risk should be calculated. Several years later the Basel Committee published *The 1996 Amendment*, which was implemented in 1998 and required banks to hold capital for market risk as well as credit risk. *The Amendment* distinguishes between a bank's trading book and its banking book. The banking book consists primarily of loans and is not usually revalued on a regular basis for managerial and accounting purposes. The trading book consists of the myriad of different instrument that are traded by the bank (stocks, bonds, swaps, forward contracts, options, etc.) and is normally revalued daily.

The 1996 BIS Amendment calculates capital for the trading book using the VaR measure with $N = 10$ and $X = 99$. This means that it focuses on the revaluation loss over a 10-day period that is expected to be exceeded only 1% of the time. The capital it requires the bank to hold is k times this VaR measure (with an adjustment for what are termed specific risks). The multiplier k is chosen on a bank-by-bank basis by the regulators and must be at least 3.0. For a bank with excellent well-tested VaR estimation procedures, it is likely that k will be set equal to the minimum value of 3.0. For other banks it may be higher.

over the next 5 days. VaR is illustrated for the situation where the change in the value of the portfolio is approximately normally distributed in Figure 18.1.

VaR is an attractive measure because it is easy to understand. In essence, it asks the simple question "How bad can things get?" This is the question all senior managers want answered. They are very comfortable with the idea of compressing all the Greek letters for all the market variables underlying a portfolio into a single number.

If we accept that it is useful to have a single number to describe the risk of a portfolio, an interesting question is whether VaR is the best alternative. Some researchers have

Figure 18.1 Calculation of VaR from the probability distribution of the change in the portfolio value; confidence level is $X\%$.

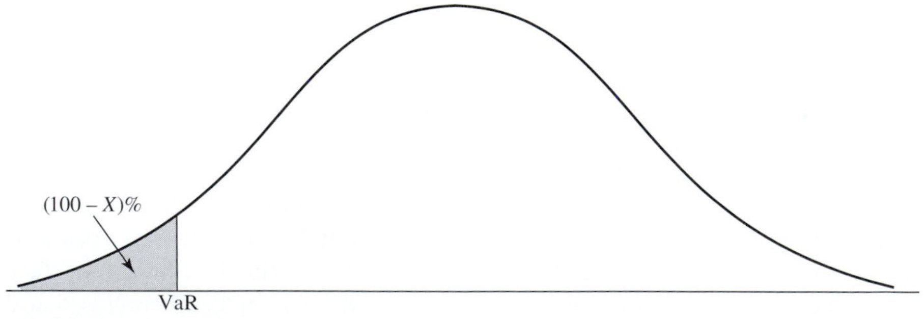

Figure 18.2 Alternative situation to Figure 18.1. VaR is the same, but the potential loss is larger.

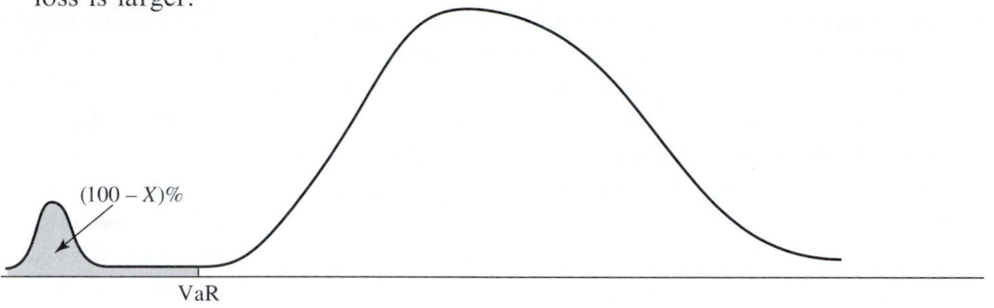

argued that VaR may tempt traders to choose a portfolio with a return distribution similar to that in Figure 18.2. The portfolios in Figures 18.1 and 18.2 have the same VaR, but the portfolio in Figure 18.2 is much riskier because potential losses are much larger.

A measure that deals with the problem we have just mentioned is *Conditional VaR* (C-VaR).[1] Whereas VaR asks the question "How bad can things get?", C-VaR asks "If things do get bad, how much can we expect to lose?" C-VaR is the expected loss during an N-day period conditional that we are in the $(100 - X)\%$ left tail of the distribution. For example, with $X = 99$ and $N = 10$, C-VaR is the average amount we lose over a 10-day period assuming that a 1% worst-case event occurs.

In spite of its weaknesses, VaR (not C-VaR) is the most popular measure of risk among both regulators and risk managers. We will therefore devote most of the rest of this chapter to how it can be measured.

The Time Horizon

In theory, VaR has two parameters. These are N, the time horizon measured in days, and X, the confidence interval. In practice analysts almost invariably set $N = 1$ in the first instance. This is because there is not enough data to estimate directly the behavior of market variables over periods of time longer than 1 day. The usual assumption is

$$N\text{-day VaR} = 1\text{-day VaR} \times \sqrt{N}$$

This formula is exactly true when the changes in the value of the portfolio on successive days have independent identical normal distributions with mean zero. In other cases it is an approximation.

As explained in Business Snapshot 18.1, regulators require a bank's capital to be at least three times the 10-day 99% VaR. Given the way a 10-day VaR is calculated, this minimum capital level is, to all intents and purposes $3 \times \sqrt{10} = 9.49$ times the 1-day 99% VaR.

---

[1] This measure, which is also known as *expected shortfall* or *tail loss*, was suggested by P. Artzner, F. Delbaen, J.-M. Eber, and D. Heath, "Coherent Measures of Risk," *Mathematical Finance*, 9 (1999): 203–28. These authors define certain properties that a good risk measure should have and show that the standard VaR measure does not have all of them.

18.2 HISTORICAL SIMULATION

Historical simulation is one popular way of estimating VaR. It involves using past data in a very direct way as a guide to what might happen in the future. Suppose that we wish to calculate VaR for a portfolio using a 1-day time horizon, a 99% confidence level, and 500 days of data. The first step is to identify the market variables affecting the portfolio. These will typically be exchange rates, equity prices, interest rates, and so on. We then collect data on the movements in these market variables over the most recent 500 days. This provides us with 500 alternative scenarios for what can happen between today and tomorrow. Scenario 1 is where the percentage changes in the values of all variables are the same as they were on the first day for which we have collected data; scenario 2 is where they are the same as on the second day for which we have data; and so on. For each scenario we calculate the dollar change in the value of the portfolio between today and tomorrow. This defines a probability distribution for daily changes in the value of our portfolio. The fifth-worst daily change is the first percentile of the distribution. The estimate of VaR is the loss when we are at this first percentile point. Assuming that the last 500 days are a good guide to what could happen during the next day, we are 99% certain that we will not take a loss greater than our VaR estimate.

The historical simulation methodology is illustrated in Tables 18.1 and 18.2. Table 18.1 shows observations on market variables over the last 500 days. The observations are taken at some particular point in time during the day (usually the close of trading). We denote the first day for which we have data as Day 0; the second as Day 1; and so on. Today is Day 500; tomorrow is Day 501.

Table 18.2 shows the values of the market variables tomorrow if their percentage changes between today and tomorrow are the same as they were between Day $i-1$ and Day i for $1 \leqslant i \leqslant 500$. The first row in Table 18.2 shows the values of market variables tomorrow assuming their percentage changes between today and tomorrow are the same as they were between Day 0 and Day 1; the second row shows the values of market variables tomorrow assuming their percentage changes between Day 1 and Day 2 occur; and so on. The 500 rows in Table 18.2 are the 500 scenarios considered.

Table 18.1 Data for VaR historical simulation calculation.

Day	*Market variable 1*	*Market variable 2*	...	*Market variable n*
0	20.33	0.1132	...	65.37
1	20.78	0.1159	...	64.91
2	21.44	0.1162	...	65.02
3	20.97	0.1184	...	64.90
⋮	⋮	⋮	⋮	⋮
498	25.72	0.1312	...	62.22
499	25.75	0.1323	...	61.99
500	25.85	0.1343	...	62.10

Table 18.2 Scenarios generated for tomorrow (Day 501) using data in Table 18.1.

Scenario number	*Market variable 1*	*Market variable 2*	...	*Market variable n*	*Portfolio value (\$ millions)*	*Change in value (\$ millions)*
1	26.42	0.1375	...	61.66	23.71	0.21
2	26.67	0.1346	...	62.21	23.12	−0.38
3	25.28	0.1368	...	61.99	22.94	−0.56
⋮	⋮	⋮	⋮	⋮	⋮	⋮
499	25.88	0.1354	...	61.87	23.63	0.13
500	25.95	0.1363	...	62.21	22.87	−0.63

Define v_i as the value of a market variable on Day i and suppose that today is Day m. The ith scenario assumes that the value of the market variable tomorrow will be

$$v_m \frac{v_i}{v_{i-1}}$$

In our example, $m = 500$. For the first variable, the value today, v_{500}, is 25.85. Also $v_0 = 20.33$ and $v_1 = 20.78$. It follows that the value of the first market variable in the first scenario is

$$25.85 \times \frac{20.78}{20.33} = 26.42$$

The penultimate column of Table 18.2 shows the value of the portfolio tomorrow for each of the 500 scenarios. We suppose the value of the portfolio today is \$23.50 million. This leads to the numbers in the final column for the change in the value between today and tomorrow for all the different scenarios. For Scenario 1 the change in value is +\$210,000, for Scenario 2 it is −\$380,000, and so on.

We are interested in the 1-percentile point of the distribution of changes in the portfolio value. Because there are a total of 500 scenarios in Table 18.2 we can estimate this as the fifth worst number in the final column of the table. Alternatively, we can use the techniques of what is known as *extreme value theory* to smooth the numbers in the left tail of the distribution in an attempt to obtain a more accurate estimate of the 1% point of the distribution.[2] As mentioned in the previous section, the N-day VaR for a 99% confidence level is calculated as $\sqrt{N}$ times the 1-day VaR.

Each day the VaR estimate in our example would be updated using the most recent 500 days of data. Consider, for example, what happens on Day 501. We find out new values for all the market variables and are able to calculate a new value for our portfolio.[3] We then go through the procedure we have outlined to calculate a new VaR. We use data on the market variables from Day 1 to Day 501. (This gives us the required 500 observations on the percentage changes in market variables; the Day-0

[2] See P. Embrechts, C. Kluppelberg, and T. Mikosch. *Modeling Extremal Events for Insurance and Finance*. New York: Springer, 1997; A. J. McNeil, "Extreme Value Theory for Risk Managers," in *Internal Modeling and CAD II*. London, Risk Books, 1999, and available from www.math.ethz.ch/~mcneil.

[3] Note that the portfolio's composition may have changed between Day 500 and Day 501.

values of the market variables are no longer used.) Similarly, on Day 502, we use data from Day 2 to Day 502 to determine VaR, and so on.

18.3 MODEL-BUILDING APPROACH

The main alternative to historical simulation is the model-building approach. Before getting into the details of the approach, it is appropriate to mention one issue concerned with the units for measuring volatility.

Daily Volatilities

In option pricing we usually measure time in years, and the volatility of an asset is usually quoted as a "volatility per year". When using the model-building approach to calculate VaR, we usually measure time in days and the volatility of an asset is usually quoted as a "volatility per day".

What is the relationship between the volatility per year used in option pricing and the volatility per day used in VaR calculations? Let us define σ_{year} as the volatility per year of a certain asset and σ_{day} as the equivalent volatility per day of the asset. Assuming 252 trading days in a year, we can use equation (13.2) to write the standard deviation of the continuously compounded return on the asset in 1 year as either σ_{year} or $\sigma_{\text{day}}\sqrt{252}$. It follows that

$$\sigma_{\text{year}} = \sigma_{\text{day}}\sqrt{252}$$

or

$$\sigma_{\text{day}} = \frac{\sigma_{\text{year}}}{\sqrt{252}}$$

so that daily volatility is about 6% of annual volatility.

As pointed out in Section 13.4, σ_{day} is approximately equal to the standard deviation of the percentage change in the asset price in one day. For the purposes of calculating VaR we assume exact equality. We define the daily volatility of an asset price (or any other variable) as equal to the standard deviation of the percentage change in one day.

Our discussion in the next few sections assumes that we have estimates of daily volatilities and correlations. In Chapter 19, we discuss how the estimates can be produced.

Single-Asset Case

We now consider how VaR is calculated using the model-building approach in a very simple situation where the portfolio consists of a position in a single stock. The portfolio we consider is one consisting of $10 million in shares of Microsoft. We suppose that $N = 10$ and $X = 99$, so that we are interested in the loss level over 10 days that we are 99% confident will not be exceeded. Initially, we consider a 1-day time horizon.

We assume that the volatility of Microsoft is 2% per day (corresponding to about 32% per year). Because the size of the position is $10 million, the standard deviation of daily changes in the value of the position is 2% of $10 million, or $200,000.

It is customary in the model-building approach to assume that the expected change in a market variable over the time period considered is zero. This is not strictly true, but it is a reasonable assumption. The expected change in the price of a market variable over a short time period is generally small when compared with the standard deviation of the change. Suppose, for example, that Microsoft has an expected return of 20% per annum. Over a 1-day period, the expected return is 0.20/252, or about 0.08%, whereas the standard deviation of the return is 2%. Over a 10-day period, the expected return is 0.08×10, or about 0.8%, whereas the standard deviation of the return is $2\sqrt{10}$, or about 6.3%.

So far, we have established that the change in the value of the portfolio of Microsoft shares over a 1-day period has a standard deviation of \$200,000 and (at least approximately) a mean of zero. We assume that the change is normally distributed.[4] From the tables at the end of this book, $N(-2.33) = 0.01$. This means that there is a 1% probability that a normally distributed variable will decrease in value by more than 2.33 standard deviations. Equivalently, it means that we are 99% certain that a normally distributed variable will not decrease in value by more than 2.33 standard deviations. The 1-day 99% VaR for our portfolio consisting of a \$10 million position in Microsoft is therefore

$$2.33 \times 200{,}000 = \$466{,}000$$

As discussed earlier, the N-day VaR is calculated as $\sqrt{N}$ times the 1-day VaR. The 10-day 99% VaR for Microsoft is therefore

$$466{,}000 \times \sqrt{10} = \$1{,}473{,}621$$

Consider next a portfolio consisting of a \$5 million position in AT&T, and suppose the daily volatility of AT&T is 1% (approximately 16% per year). A similar calculation to that for Microsoft shows that the standard deviation of the change in the value of the portfolio in 1 day is

$$5{,}000{,}000 \times 0.01 = 50{,}000$$

Assuming the change is normally distributed, the 1-day 99% VaR is

$$50{,}000 \times 2.33 = \$116{,}500$$

and the 10-day 99% VaR is

$$116{,}500 \times \sqrt{10} = \$368{,}405$$

Two-Asset Case

Now consider a portfolio consisting of both \$10 million of Microsoft shares and \$5 million of AT&T shares. We suppose that the returns on the two shares have a bivariate normal distribution with a correlation of 0.3. A standard result in statistics tells us that, if two variables X and Y have standard deviations equal to σ_X and σ_Y with the coefficient of correlation between them equal to ρ, the standard deviation of $X + Y$ is given by

$$\sigma_{X+Y} = \sqrt{\sigma_X^2 + \sigma_Y^2 + 2\rho\sigma_X\sigma_Y}$$

[4] To be consistent with the option pricing assumption in Chapter 13, we could assume that the price of Microsoft is lognormal tomorrow. Because 1 day is such a short period of time, this is almost indistinguishable from the assumption we do make—that the change in the stock price between today and tomorrow is normal.

To apply this result, we set X equal to the change in the value of the position in Microsoft over a 1-day period and Y equal to the change in the value of the position in AT&T over a 1-day period, so that

$$\sigma_X = 200{,}000 \quad \text{and} \quad \sigma_Y = 50{,}000$$

The standard deviation of the change in the value of the portfolio consisting of both stocks over a 1-day period is therefore

$$\sqrt{200{,}000^2 + 50{,}000^2 + 2 \times 0.3 \times 200{,}000 \times 50{,}000} = 220{,}227$$

The mean change is assumed to be zero. The change is normally distributed. So the 1-day 99% VaR is therefore

$$220{,}227 \times 2.33 = \$513{,}129$$

The 10-day 99% VaR is $\sqrt{10}$ times this, or $1,622,657.

The Benefits of Diversification

In the example we have just considered:

1. The 10-day 99% VaR for the portfolio of Microsoft shares is $1,473,621.
2. The 10-day 99% VaR for the portfolio of AT&T shares is $368,405.
3. The 10-day 99% VaR for the portfolio of both Microsoft and AT&T shares is $1,622,657.

The amount

$$(1{,}473{,}621 + 368{,}405) - 1{,}622{,}657 = \$219{,}369$$

represents the benefits of diversification. If Microsoft and AT&T were perfectly correlated, the VaR for the portfolio of both Microsoft and AT&T would equal the VaR for the Microsoft portfolio plus the VaR for the AT&T portfolio. Less than perfect correlation leads to some of the risk being "diversified away".[5]

18.4 LINEAR MODEL

The examples we have just considered are simple illustrations of the use of the linear model for calculating VaR. Suppose that we have a portfolio worth P consisting of n assets with an amount α_i being invested in asset i ($1 \leqslant i \leqslant n$). We define Δx_i as the return on asset i in 1 day. It follows that the dollar change in the value of our investment in asset i in 1 day is $\alpha_i \, \Delta x_i$ and

$$\Delta P = \sum_{i=1}^{n} \alpha_i \, \Delta x_i \tag{18.1}$$

where ΔP is the dollar change in the value of the whole portfolio in 1 day.

[5] Harry Markowitz was one of the first researchers to study the benefits of diversification to a portfolio manager. He was awarded a Nobel prize for this research in 1990. See H. Markowitz, "Portfolio Selection," *Journal of Finance*, 7, 1 (March 1952): 77–91.

In the example considered in the previous section, \$10 million was invested in the first asset (Microsoft) and \$5 million was invested in the second asset (AT&T), so that (in millions of dollars) $\alpha_1 = 10$, $\alpha_2 = 5$, and

$$\Delta P = 10\Delta x_1 + 5\Delta x_2$$

If we assume that the Δx_i in equation (18.1) are multivariate normal, ΔP is normally distributed. To calculate VaR, we therefore need to calculate only the mean and standard deviation of ΔP. We assume, as discussed in the previous section, that the expected value of each Δx_i is zero. This implies that the mean of ΔP is zero.

To calculate the standard deviation of ΔP, we define σ_i as the daily volatility of the ith asset and ρ_{ij} as the coefficient of correlation between returns on asset i and asset j. This means that σ_i is the standard deviation of Δx_i, and ρ_{ij} is the coefficient of correlation between Δx_i and Δx_j. The variance of ΔP, which we will denote by σ_P^2, is given by

$$\sigma_P^2 = \sum_{i=1}^{n}\sum_{j=1}^{n} \rho_{ij}\alpha_i\alpha_j\sigma_i\sigma_j$$

This equation can also be written

$$\sigma_P^2 = \sum_{i=1}^{n} \alpha_i^2\sigma_i^2 + 2\sum_{i=1}^{n}\sum_{j<i} \rho_{ij}\alpha_i\alpha_j\sigma_i\sigma_j \tag{18.2}$$

The standard deviation of the change over N days is $\sigma_P\sqrt{N}$, and the 99% VaR for an N-day time horizon is $2.33\sigma_P\sqrt{N}$.

In the example considered in the previous section, $\sigma_1 = 0.02$, $\sigma_2 = 0.01$, and $\rho_{12} = 0.3$. As already noted, $\alpha_1 = 10$ and $\alpha_2 = 5$, so that

$$\sigma_P^2 = 10^2 \times 0.02^2 + 5^2 \times 0.01^2 + 2 \times 10 \times 5 \times 0.3 \times 0.02 \times 0.01 = 0.0485$$

and $\sigma_P = 0.220$. This is the standard deviation of the change in the portfolio value per day (in millions of dollars). The 10-day 99% VaR is $2.33 \times 0.220 \times \sqrt{10} =$ \$1.623 million. This agrees with the calculation in the previous section.

Handling Interest Rates

It is out of the question to define a separate market variable for every single bond price or interest rate to which a company is exposed. Some simplifications are necessary when the model-building approach is used. One possibility is to assume that only parallel shifts in the yield curve occur. It is then necessary to define only one market variable: the size of the parallel shift. The changes in the value of bond portfolio can then be calculated using the duration relationship

$$\Delta P = -DP\Delta y$$

where P is the value of the portfolio, ΔP is the its change in P in one day, D is the modified duration of the portfolio, and Δy is the parallel shift in 1 day.

This approach does not usually give enough accuracy. The procedure usually followed is to choose as market variables the prices of zero-coupon bonds with standard maturities: 1 month, 3 months, 6 months, 1 year, 2 years, 5 years, 7 years, 10 years, and 30 years. For the purposes of calculating VaR, the cash flows from instruments in the portfolio are mapped into cash flows occurring on the standard maturity dates. Consider a \$1 million position in a Treasury bond lasting 1.2 years that pays a coupon of 6% semiannually. Coupons are paid in 0.2, 0.7, and 1.2 years, and the principal is paid in 1.2 years. This bond is, therefore, in the first instance regarded as a \$30,000 position in 0.2-year zero-coupon bond plus a \$30,000 position in a 0.7-year zero-coupon bond plus a \$1.03 million position in a 1.2-year zero-coupon bond. The position in the 0.2-year bond is then replaced by an equivalent position in 1-month and 3-month zero-coupon bonds; the position in the 0.7-year bond is replaced by an equivalent position in 6-month and 1-year zero-coupon bonds; and the position in the 1.2-year bond is replaced by an equivalent position in 1-year and 2-year zero-coupon bonds. The result is that the position in the 1.2-year coupon-bearing bond is for VaR purposes regarded as a position in zero-coupon bonds having maturities of 1 month, 3 months, 6 months, 1 year, and 2 years.

This procedure is known as *cash-flow mapping*. One way of doing it is explained in the appendix at the end of this chapter.

Applications of the Linear Model

The simplest application of the linear model is to a portfolio with no derivatives consisting of positions in stocks, bonds, foreign exchange, and commodities. In this case, the change in the value of the portfolio is linearly dependent on the percentage changes in the prices of the assets comprising the portfolio. Note that, for the purposes of VaR calculations, all asset prices are measured in the domestic currency. The market variables considered by a large bank in the United States are therefore likely to include the value of the Nikkei 225 index measured in dollars, the price of a 10-year sterling zero-coupon bond measured in dollars, and so on.

An example of a derivative that can be handled by the linear model is a forward contract to buy a foreign currency. Suppose the contract matures at time T. It can be regarded as the exchange of a foreign zero-coupon bond maturing at time T for a domestic zero-coupon bond maturing at time T. For the purposes of calculating VaR, the forward contract is therefore treated as a long position in the foreign bond combined with a short position in the domestic bond. Each bond can be handled using a cash-flow mapping procedure.

Consider next an interest rate swap. As explained in Chapter 7, this can be regarded as the exchange of a floating-rate bond for a fixed-rate bond. The fixed-rate bond is a regular coupon-bearing bond. The floating-rate bond is worth par just after the next payment date. It can be regarded as a zero-coupon bond with a maturity date equal to the next payment date. The interest rate swap therefore reduces to a portfolio of long and short positions in bonds and can be handled using a cash-flow mapping procedure.

The Linear Model and Options

We now consider how the linear model can be used when there are options. Consider first a portfolio consisting of options on a single stock whose current price is S. Suppose that the delta of the position (calculated in the way described in Chapter 15) is δ.[6] Since δ

[6] Normally we denote the delta and gamma of a portfolio by Δ and Γ. In this section and the next, we use the lower case Greek letters δ and γ to avoid overworking Δ.

is the rate of change of the value of the portfolio with S, it is approximately true that

$$\delta = \frac{\Delta P}{\Delta S}$$

or

$$\Delta P = \delta\,\Delta S \tag{18.3}$$

where ΔS is the dollar change in the stock price in 1 day and ΔP is, as usual, the dollar change in the portfolio in 1 day. We define Δx as the percentage change in the stock price in 1 day, so that

$$\Delta x = \frac{\Delta S}{S}$$

It follows that an approximate relationship between ΔP and Δx is

$$\Delta P = S\delta\,\Delta x$$

When we have a position in several underlying market variables that includes options, we can derive an approximate linear relationship between ΔP and the Δx_i similarly. This relationship is

$$\Delta P = \sum_{i=1}^{n} S_i\delta_i\,\Delta x_i \tag{18.4}$$

where S_i is the value of the ith market variable and δ_i is the delta of the portfolio with respect to the ith market variable. This corresponds to equation (18.1):

$$\Delta P = \sum_{i=1}^{n} \alpha_i\,\Delta x_i \tag{18.5}$$

with $\alpha_i = S_i\delta_i$. Equation (18.2) can therefore be used to calculate the standard deviation of ΔP.

Example 18.1

A portfolio consists of options on Microsoft and AT&T. The options on Microsoft have a delta of 1,000, and the options on AT&T have a delta of 20,000. The Microsoft share price is \$120, and the AT&T share price is \$30. From equation (18.4), it is approximately true that

$$\Delta P = 120 \times 1{,}000 \times \Delta x_1 + 30 \times 20{,}000 \times \Delta x_2$$

or

$$\Delta P = 120{,}000\Delta x_1 + 600{,}000\Delta x_2$$

where Δx_1 and Δx_2 are the returns from Microsoft and AT&T in 1 day and ΔP is the resultant change in the value of the portfolio. (The portfolio is assumed to be equivalent to an investment of \$120,000 in Microsoft and \$600,000 in AT&T.) Assuming that the daily volatility of Microsoft is 2% and the daily volatility of AT&T is 1% and the correlation between the daily changes is 0.3, the standard deviation of ΔP (in thousands of dollars) is

$$\sqrt{(120 \times 0.02)^2 + (600 \times 0.01)^2 + 2 \times 120 \times 0.02 \times 600 \times 0.01 \times 0.3} = 7.099$$

Since $N(-1.65) = 0.05$, the 5-day 95% VaR is $1.65 \times \sqrt{5} \times 7{,}099 = \$26{,}193$.

18.5 QUADRATIC MODEL

When a portfolio includes options, the linear model is an approximation. It does not take account of the gamma of the portfolio. As discussed in Chapter 15, delta is defined as the rate of change of the portfolio value with respect to an underlying market variable and gamma is defined as the rate of change of the delta with respect to the market variable. Gamma measures the curvature of the relationship between the portfolio value and an underlying market variable.

Figure 18.3 shows the impact of a nonzero gamma on the probability distribution of the value of the portfolio. When gamma is positive, the probability distribution tends to be positively skewed; when gamma is negative, it tends to be negatively skewed. Figures 18.4 and 18.5 illustrate the reason for this result. Figure 18.4 shows the relationship between the value of a long call option and the price of the underlying asset. A long call is an example of an option position with positive gamma. The figure shows that, when the probability distribution for the price of the underlying asset at the end of 1 day is normal, the probability distribution for the option price is positively skewed.[7] Figure 18.5 shows the relationship between the value of a short call position and the price of the underlying asset. A short call position has a negative gamma. In this case, we see that a normal distribution for the price of the underlying asset at the end of 1 day gets mapped into a negatively skewed distribution for the value of the option position.

The VaR for a portfolio is critically dependent on the left tail of the probability distribution of the portfolio value. For example, when the confidence level used is 99%, the VaR is the value in the left tail below which there is only 1% of the distribution. As indicated in Figures 18.3(a) and 18.4, a positive gamma portfolio tends to have a less heavy left tail than the normal distribution. If we assume the distribution is normal, we will tend to calculate a VaR that is too high. Similarly, as indicated in Figures 18.3(b) and 18.5, a negative gamma portfolio tends to have a heavier left tail than the normal distribution. If we assume the distribution is normal, we will tend to calculate a VaR that is too low.

For a more accurate estimate of VaR than that given by the linear model, we can use both delta and gamma measures to relate ΔP to the Δx_i. Consider a portfolio

Figure 18.3 Probability distribution for value of portfolio: (a) positive gamma; (b) negative gamma.

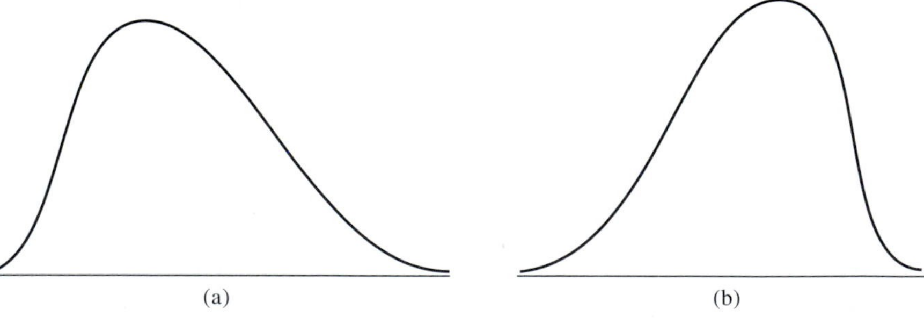

[7] As mentioned in footnote 4, we can use the normal distribution as an approximation to the lognormal distribution in VaR calculations.

Figure 18.4 Translation of normal probability distribution for asset into probability distribution for value of a long call on asset.

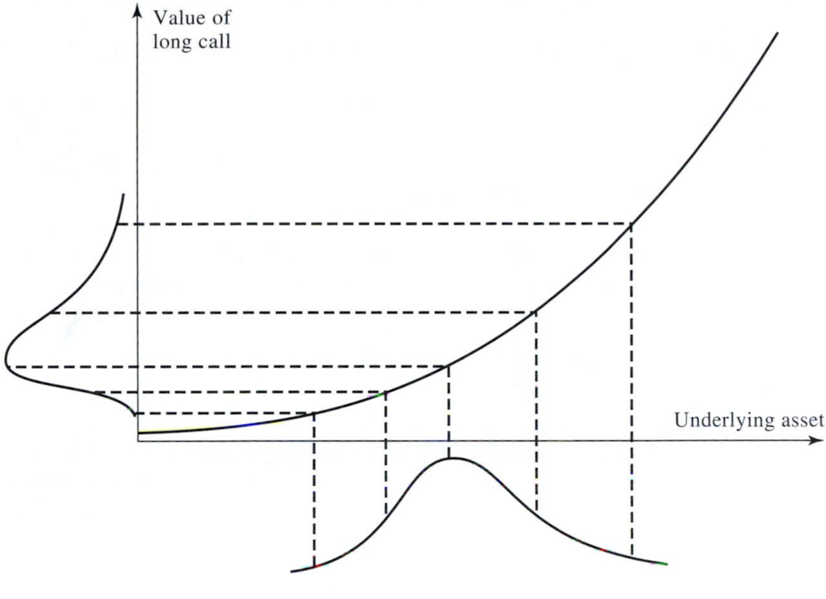

Figure 18.5 Translation of normal probability distribution for asset into probability distribution for value of a short call on asset.

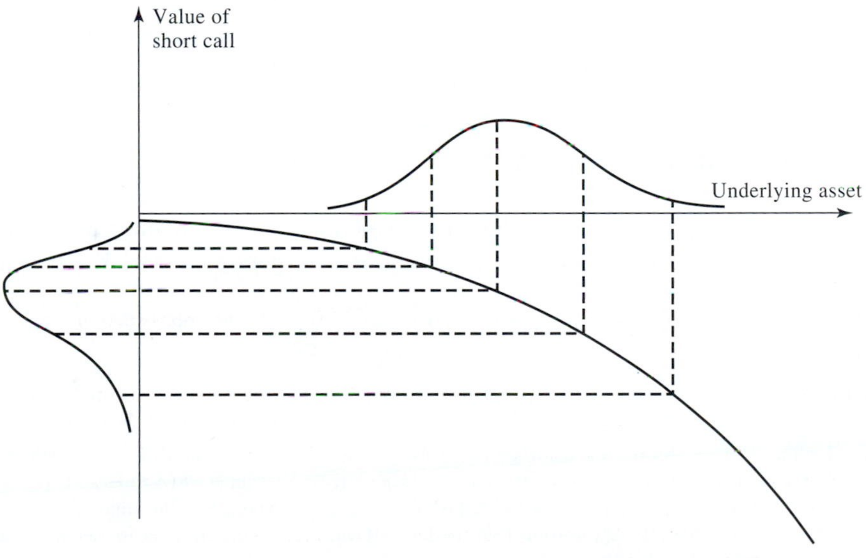

dependent on a single asset whose price is S. Suppose δ and γ are the delta and gamma of the portfolio. From the appendix to Chapter 15, the equation

$$\Delta P = \delta\,\Delta S + \tfrac{1}{2}\gamma(\Delta S)^2$$

is an improvement over the approximation in equation (18.3).[8] Setting

$$\Delta x = \frac{\Delta S}{S}$$

reduces this to

$$\Delta P = S\delta\,\Delta x + \tfrac{1}{2}S^2\gamma(\Delta x)^2 \qquad \textbf{(18.6)}$$

More generally for a portfolio with n underlying market variables, with each instrument in the portfolio being dependent on only one of the market variables, equation (18.6) becomes

$$\Delta P = \sum_{i=1}^{n} S_i\delta_i\,\Delta x_i + \sum_{i=1}^{n} \tfrac{1}{2}S_i^2\gamma_i\,(\Delta x_i)^2$$

where S_i is the value of the ith market variable, and δ_i and γ_i are the delta and gamma of the portfolio with respect to the ith market variable. When individual instruments in the portfolio may be dependent on more than one market variable, this equation takes the more general form

$$\Delta P = \sum_{i=1}^{n} S_i\delta_i\,\Delta x_i + \sum_{i=1}^{n}\sum_{j=1}^{n} \frac{1}{2}S_iS_j\gamma_{ij}\,\Delta x_i\,\Delta x_j \qquad \textbf{(18.7)}$$

where γ_{ij} is a "cross gamma" defined as

$$\gamma_{ij} = \frac{\partial^2 P}{\partial S_i\,\partial S_j}$$

Equation (18.7) is not as easy to work with as equation (18.5), but it can be used to calculate moments for ΔP. A result in statistics known as the Cornish–Fisher expansion can be used to estimate percentiles of the probability distribution from the moments.[9]

18.6 MONTE CARLO SIMULATION

As an alternative to the approaches described so far, we can implement the model-building approach using Monte Carlo simulation to generate the probability distribution

[8] The Taylor series expansion in the appendix to Chapter 15 suggests the approximation

$$\Delta P = \Theta\,\Delta t + \delta\,\Delta S + \tfrac{1}{2}\gamma(\Delta S)^2$$

when terms of higher order than Δt are ignored. In practice, the $\Theta\,\Delta t$ term is so small that it is usually ignored.

[9] See Technical Note 10 on the author's website for details of the calculation of moments and the use of Cornish–Fisher expansions. When there is a single underlying variable, $E(\Delta P) = 0.5S^2\Gamma\sigma^2$, $E(\Delta P^2) = S^2\Delta^2\sigma^2 + 0.75S^4\Gamma^2\sigma^4$, and $E(\Delta P^3) = 4.5S^4\Delta^2\Gamma\sigma^4 + 1.875S^6\Gamma^3\sigma^6$, where S is the value of the variable and σ is its daily volatility. Sample Application E in the DerivaGem Application Builder implements the Cornish–Fisher expansion method for this case.

for ΔP. Suppose we wish to calculate a 1-day VaR for a portfolio. The procedure is as follows:

1. Value the portfolio today in the usual way using the current values of market variables.
2. Sample once from the multivariate normal probability distribution of the Δx_i.[10]
3. Use the values of the Δx_i that are sampled to determine the value of each market variable at the end of one day.
4. Revalue the portfolio at the end of the day in the usual way.
5. Subtract the value calculated in Step 1 from the value in Step 4 to determine a sample ΔP.
6. Repeat Steps 2 to 5 many times to build up a probability distribution for ΔP.

The VaR is calculated as the appropriate percentile of the probability distribution of ΔP. Suppose, for example, that we calculate 5,000 different sample values of ΔP in the way just described. The 1-day 99% VaR is the value of ΔP for the 50th worst outcome; the 1-day VaR 95% is the value of ΔP for the 250th worst outcome; and so on.[11] The N-day VaR is usually assumed to be the 1-day VaR multiplied by $\sqrt{N}$.[12]

The drawback of Monte Carlo simulation is that it tends to be slow because a company's complete portfolio (which might consist of hundreds of thousands of different instruments) has to be revalued many times.[13] One way of speeding things up is to assume that equation (18.7) describes the relationship between ΔP and the Δx_i. We can then jump straight from Step 2 to Step 5 in the Monte Carlo simulation and avoid the need for a complete revaluation of the portfolio. This is sometimes referred to as the *partial simulation approach*.

18.7 COMPARISON OF APPROACHES

We have discussed two methods for estimating VaR: the historical simulation approach and the model-building approach. The advantages of the model-building approach are that results can be produced very quickly and it can be used in conjunction with volatility updating schemes such as those we will describe in the next chapter. The main disadvantage of the model-building approach is that it assumes that the market variables have a multivariate normal distribution. In practice, daily changes in market variables often have distributions that are quite different from normal (see, e.g., Table 16.1).

The historical simulation approach has the advantage that historical data determine the joint probability distribution of the market variables. It also avoids the need for cash-flow mapping (see Problem 18.2). The main disadvantages of historical simulation

[10] One way of doing so is given in Chapter 17.

[11] As in the case of historical simulation, extreme value theory can be used to "smooth the tails" so that better estimates of extreme percentiles are obtained.

[12] This is only approximately true when the portfolio includes options, but it is the assumption that is made in practice for most VaR calculation methods.

[13] An approach for limiting the number of portfolio revaluations is proposed in F. Jamshidian and Y. Zhu "Scenario simulation model: theory and methodology," *Finance and Stochastics*, 1 (1997), 43–67.

are that it is computationally slow and does not easily allow volatility updating schemes to be used.[14]

One disadvantage of the model-building approach is that it tends to give poor results for low-delta portfolios (see Problem 18.21).

18.8 STRESS TESTING AND BACK TESTING

In addition to calculating VaR, many companies carry out what is known as a *stress test* of their portfolio. Stress testing involves estimating how the portfolio would have performed under some of the most extreme market moves seen in the last 10 to 20 years.

For example, to test the impact of an extreme movement in US equity prices, a company might set the percentage changes in all market variables equal to those on October 19, 1987 (when the S&P 500 moved by 22.3 standard deviations). If this is considered to be too extreme, the company might choose January 8, 1988 (when the S&P 500 moved by 6.8 standard deviations). To test the effect of extreme movements in UK interest rates, the company might set the percentage changes in all market variables equal to those on April 10, 1992 (when 10-year bond yields moved by 7.7 standard deviations).

The scenarios used in stress testing are also sometimes generated by senior management. One technique sometimes used is to ask senior management to meet periodically and "brainstorm" to develop extreme scenarios that might occur given the current economic environment and global uncertainties.

Stress testing can be considered as a way of taking into account extreme events that do occur from time to time but that are virtually impossible according to the probability distributions assumed for market variables. A 5-standard-deviation daily move in a market variable is one such extreme event. Under the assumption of a normal distribution, it happens about once every 7,000 years, but, in practice, it is not uncommon to see a 5-standard-deviation daily move once or twice every 10 years.

Whatever the method used for calculating VaR, an important reality check is *back testing*. It involves testing how well the VaR estimates would have performed in the past. Suppose that we are calculating a 1-day 99% VaR. Back testing would involve looking at how often the loss in a day exceeded the 1-day 99% VaR that would have been calculated for that day. If this happened on about 1% of the days, we can feel reasonably comfortable with the methodology for calculating VaR. If it happened on, say, 7% of days, the methodology is suspect.

18.9 PRINCIPAL COMPONENTS ANALYSIS

One approach to handling the risk arising from groups of highly correlated market variables is principal components analysis. This takes historical data on movements in the market variables and attempts to define a set of components or factors that explain the movements.

---

[14] For a way of adapting the historical simulation approach to incorporate volatility updating, see J. Hull and A. White. "Incorporating volatility updating into the historical simulation method for value-at-risk," *Journal of Risk* 1, No. 1 (1998): 5–19.

Table 18.3 Factor loadings for US Treasury data.

	PC1	*PC2*	*PC3*	*PC4*	*PC5*	*PC6*	*PC7*	*PC8*	*PC9*	*PC10*
3m	0.21	−0.57	0.50	0.47	−0.39	−0.02	0.01	0.00	0.01	0.00
6m	0.26	−0.49	0.23	−0.37	0.70	0.01	−0.04	−0.02	−0.01	0.00
12m	0.32	−0.32	−0.37	−0.58	−0.52	−0.23	−0.04	−0.05	0.00	0.01
2y	0.35	−0.10	−0.38	0.17	0.04	0.59	0.56	0.12	−0.12	−0.05
3y	0.36	0.02	−0.30	0.27	0.07	0.24	−0.79	0.00	−0.09	−0.00
4y	0.36	0.14	−0.12	0.25	0.16	−0.63	0.15	0.55	−0.14	−0.08
5y	0.36	0.17	−0.04	0.14	0.08	−0.10	0.09	−0.26	0.71	0.48
7y	0.34	0.27	0.15	0.01	0.00	−0.12	0.13	−0.54	0.00	−0.68
10y	0.31	0.30	0.28	−0.10	−0.06	0.01	0.03	−0.23	−0.63	0.52
30y	0.25	0.33	0.46	−0.34	−0.18	0.33	−0.09	0.52	0.26	−0.13

The approach is best illustrated with an example. The market variables we will consider are 10 US Treasury rates with maturities between 3 months and 30 years. Tables 18.3 and 18.4 shows results produced by Frye for these market variables using 1,543 daily observations between 1989 and 1995.[15] The first column in Table 18.3 shows the maturities of the rates that were considered. The remaining 10 columns in the table show the 10 factors (or principal components) describing the rate moves. The first factor, shown in the column labeled PC1, corresponds to a roughly parallel shift in the yield curve. When we have one unit of that factor, the 3-month rate increases by 0.21 basis points, the 6-month rate increases by 0.26 basis points, and so on. The second factor is shown in the column labeled PC2. It corresponds to a "twist" or "steepening" of the yield curve. Rates between 3 months and 2 years move in one direction; rates between 3 years and 30 years move in the other direction. The third factor corresponds to a "bowing" of the yield curve. Rates at the short end and long end of the yield curve move in one direction; rates in the middle move in the other direction. The interest rate move for a particular factor is known as *factor loading*. In our example, the first factor's loading for the three-month rate is 0.21.[16]

Because there are 10 rates and 10 factors, the interest rate changes observed on any given day can always be expressed as a linear sum of the factors by solving a set of 10 simultaneous equations. The quantity of a particular factor in the interest rate changes on a particular day is known as the *factor score* for that day.

The importance of a factor is measured by the standard deviation of its factor score. The standard deviations of the factor scores in our example are shown in Table 18.4 and

Table 18.4 Standard deviation of factor scores (basis points).

PC1	*PC2*	*PC3*	*PC4*	*PC5*	*PC6*	*PC7*	*PC8*	*PC9*	*PC10*
17.49	6.05	3.10	2.17	1.97	1.69	1.27	1.24	0.80	0.79

[15] See J. Frye, "Principals of Risk: Finding VAR through Factor-Based Interest Rate Scenarios," in *VAR: Understanding and Applying Value at Risk*, pp. 275–88. London: Risk Publications, 1997.

[16] The factor loadings have the property that the sum of their squares for each factor is 1.0.

the factors are listed in order of their importance. The numbers in Table 18.4 are measured in basis points. A quantity of the first factor equal to one standard deviation, therefore, corresponds to the 3-month rate moving by $0.21 \times 17.49 = 3.67$ basis points, the 6-month rate moving by $0.26 \times 17.49 = 4.55$ basis points, and so on.

The technical details of how the factors are determined are not covered here. It is sufficient for us to note that the factors are chosen so that the factor scores are uncorrelated. For instance, in our example, the first factor score (amount of parallel shift) is uncorrelated with the second factor score (amount of twist) across the 1,543 days. The variances of the factor scores (i.e., the squares of the standard deviations) have the property that they add up to the total variance of the data. From Table 18.4, the total variance of the original data (i.e., sum of the variance of the observations on the 3-month rate, the variance of the observations on the 6-month rate, and so on) is

$$17.49^2 + 6.05^2 + 3.10^2 + \cdots + 0.79^2 = 367.9$$

From this it can be seen that the first factor accounts for $17.49^2/367.9 = 83.1\%$ of the variance in the original data; the first two factors account for $(17.49^2 + 6.05^2)/367.9 = 93.1\%$ of the variance in the data; the third factor accounts for a further 2.8% of the variance. This shows most of the risk in interest rate moves is accounted for by the first two or three factors. It suggests that we can relate the risks in a portfolio of interest rate dependent instruments to movements in these factors instead of considering all 10 interest rates. The three most important factors from Table 18.3 are plotted in Figure 18.6.[17]

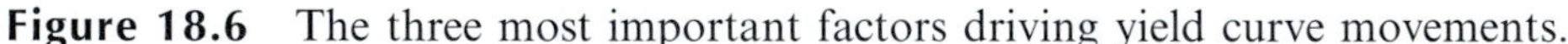

Figure 18.6 The three most important factors driving yield curve movements.

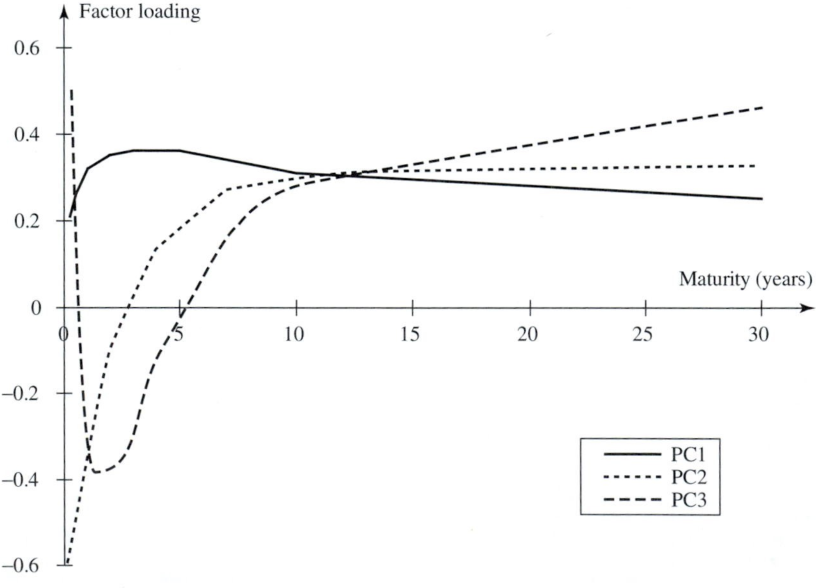

[17] Similar results to those described here, in respect of the nature of the factors and the amount of the total risk they account for, are obtained when a principal components analysis is used to explain the movements in almost any yield curve in any country.

Using Principal Components Analysis to Calculate VaR

To illustrate how a principal components analysis can be used to calculate VaR, suppose we have a portfolio with the exposures to interest rate moves shown in Table 18.5. A 1-basis-point change in the 1-year rate causes the portfolio value to increase by \$10 million, a 1-basis-point change in the 2-year rate causes it to increase by \$4 million, and so on. We use the first two factors to model rate moves. (As mentioned above, this captures over 90% of the uncertainty in rate moves.) Using the data in Table 18.3, our exposure to the first factor (measured in millions of dollars per factor score basis point) is

$$10 \times 0.32 + 4 \times 0.35 - 8 \times 0.36 - 7 \times 0.36 + 2 \times 0.36 = -0.08$$

and our exposure to the second factor is

$$10 \times (-0.32) + 4 \times (-0.10) - 8 \times 0.02 - 7 \times 0.14 + 2 \times 0.17 = -4.40$$

Suppose that f_1 and f_2 are the factor scores (measured in basis points). The change in the portfolio value is, to a good approximation, given by

$$\Delta P = -0.08 f_1 - 4.40 f_2$$

The factor scores are uncorrelated and have the standard deviations given in Table 18.4. The standard deviation of ΔP is therefore

$$\sqrt{0.08^2 \times 17.49^2 + 4.40^2 \times 6.05^2} = 26.66$$

Hence, the 1-day 99% VaR is $26.66 \times 2.33 = 62.12$. Note that the data in Table 18.5 are such that we have very little exposure to the first factor and significant exposure to the second factor. Using only one factor would significantly understate VaR (see Problem 18.13). The duration-based method for handling interest rates, mentioned in Section 18.4, would also significantly understate VaR as it considers only parallel shifts in the yield curve.

A principal components analysis can in theory be used for market variables other than interest rates. Suppose that a financial institution has exposures to a number of different stock indices. A principal components analysis can be used to identify factors describing movements in the indices and the most important of these can be used to replace the market indices in a VaR analysis. How effective a principal components analysis is for a group of market variables depends on how closely correlated they are.

As explained earlier in the chapter, VaR is usually calculated by relating the actual changes in a portfolio to percentage changes in market variables (the Δx_i). For a VaR calculation, it may therefore be most appropriate to carry out a principal components analysis on percentage changes in market variables rather than actual changes.

Table 18.5 Change in portfolio value for a 1-basis-point rate move (\$ millions).

1-year rate	*2-year rate*	*3-year rate*	*4-year rate*	*5-year rate*
+10	+4	−8	−7	+2

SUMMARY

A value at risk (VaR) calculation is aimed at making a statement of the form: "We are X percent certain that we will not lose more than V dollars in the next N days." The variable V is the VaR, $X\%$ is the confidence level, and N days is the time horizon.

One approach to calculating VaR is historical simulation. This involves creating a database consisting of the daily movements in all market variables over a period of time. The first simulation trial assumes that the percentage changes in each market variable are the same as those on the first day covered by the database; the second simulation trial assumes that the percentage changes are the same as those on the second day; and so on. The change in the portfolio value, ΔP, is calculated for each simulation trial, and the VaR is calculated as the appropriate percentile of the probability distribution of ΔP.

An alternative is the model-building approach. This is relatively straightforward if two assumptions can be made:

1. The change in the value of the portfolio (ΔP) is linearly dependent on percentage changes in market variables.
2. The percentage changes in market variables are multivariate normally distributed.

The probability distribution of ΔP is then normal, and there are analytic formulas for relating the standard deviation of ΔP to the volatilities and correlations of the underlying market variables. The VaR can be calculated from well-known properties of the normal distribution.

When a portfolio includes options, ΔP is not linearly related to the percentage changes in market variables. From knowledge of the gamma of the portfolio, we can derive an approximate quadratic relationship between ΔP and percentage changes in market variables. Monte Carlo simulation can then be used to estimate VaR.

In the next chapter we discuss how volatilities and correlations can be estimated and monitored.

FURTHER READING

Artzner P., F. Delbaen, J.-M. Eber, and D. Heath. "Coherent Measures of Risk," *Mathematical Finance*, 9 (1999): 203–28.

Basak, S., and A. Shapiro. "Value-at-Risk-Based Risk Management: Optimal Policies and Asset Prices," *Review of Financial Studies*, 14, 2 (2001): 371–405.

Beder, T. "VaR: Seductive but Dangerous," *Financial Analysts Journal*, 51, 5 (1995): 12–24.

Boudoukh, J., M. Richardson, and R. Whitelaw. "The Best of Both Worlds," *Risk*, May 1998: 64–67.

Dowd, K. *Beyond Value at Risk: The New Science of Risk Management*. New York: Wiley, 1998.

Duffie, D., and J. Pan. "An Overview of Value at Risk," *Journal of Derivatives*, 4, 3 (Spring 1997): 7–49.

Embrechts, P., C. Kluppelberg, and T. Mikosch. *Modeling Extremal Events for Insurance and Finance*. New York: Springer, 1997.

Frye, J. "Principals of Risk: Finding VAR through Factor-Based Interest Rate Scenarios" in *VAR: Understanding and Applying Value at Risk*, pp. 275–88. London: Risk Publications, 1997.

Hendricks, D. "Evaluation of Value-at-Risk Models Using Historical Data,"*Economic Policy Review*, Federal Reserve Bank of New York, 2 (April 1996): 39–69.

Hopper, G. "Value at Risk: A New Methodology for Measuring Portfolio Risk," *Business Review*, Federal Reserve Bank of Philadelphia, July/August 1996: 19–29.

Hua P., and P. Wilmott, "Crash Courses," *Risk*, June 1997: 64–67.

Hull, J. C., and A. White. "Value at Risk When Daily Changes in Market Variables Are Not Normally Distributed," *Journal of Derivatives*, 5 (Spring 1998): 9–19.

Hull, J. C., and A. White. "Incorporating Volatility Updating into the Historical Simulation Method for Value at Risk," *Journal of Risk*, 1, 1 (1998): 5–19.

Jackson, P., D. J. Maude, and W. Perraudin. "Bank Capital and Value at Risk." *Journal of Derivatives*, 4, 3 (Spring 1997): 73–90.

Jamshidian, F., and Y. Zhu. "Scenario Simulation Model: Theory and Methodology," *Finance and Stochastics*, 1 (1997): 43–67.

Jorion, P. *Value at Risk*, 2nd edn. McGraw-Hill, 2001.

Longin, F. M. "Beyond the VaR," *Journal of Derivatives*, 8, 4 (Summer 2001): 36–48.

Marshall, C., and M. Siegel. "Value at Risk: Implementing a Risk Measurement Standard," *Journal of Derivatives* 4, 3 (Spring 1997): 91–111.

McNeil, A. J. "Extreme Value Theory for Risk Managers," in *Internal Modeling and CAD II*, London: Risk Books, 1999. See also: www.math.ethz.ch/~mcneil.

Neftci, S. N. "Value at Risk Calculations, Extreme Events and Tail Estimation," *Journal of Derivatives*, 7, 3 (Spring 2000): 23–38.

Rich, D. "Second Generation VaR and Risk-Adjusted Return on Capital," *Journal of Derivatives*, 10, 4 (Summer 2003): 51–61.

Questions and Problems (Answers in Solutions Manual)

18.1. Consider a position consisting of a \$100,000 investment in asset A and a \$100,000 investment in asset B. Assume that the daily volatilities of both assets are 1% and that the coefficient of correlation between their returns is 0.3. What is the 5-day 99% VaR for the portfolio?

18.2. Describe three ways of handling instruments that are dependent on interest rates when the model-building approach is used to calculate VaR. How would you handle these instruments when historical simulation is used to calculate VaR?

18.3. A financial institution owns a portfolio of options on the US dollar–sterling exchange rate. The delta of the portfolio is 56.0. The current exchange rate is 1.5000. Derive an approximate linear relationship between the change in the portfolio value and the percentage change in the exchange rate. If the daily volatility of the exchange rate is 0.7%, estimate the 10-day 99% VaR.

18.4. Suppose you know that the gamma of the portfolio in the previous question is 16.2. How does this change your estimate of the relationship between the change in the portfolio value and the percentage change in the exchange rate?

18.5. Suppose that the daily change in the value of a portfolio is, to a good approximation, linearly dependent on two factors, calculated from a principal components analysis. The delta of a portfolio with respect to the first factor is 6 and the delta with respect to the second factor is −4. The standard deviations of the factor are 20 and 8, respectively. What is the 5-day 90% VaR?

18.6. Suppose that a company has a portfolio consisting of positions in stocks, bonds, foreign exchange, and commodities. Assume that there are no derivatives. Explain the assumptions underlying (a) the linear model and (b) the historical simulation model for calculating VaR.

18.7. Explain how an interest rate swap is mapped into a portfolio of zero-coupon bonds with standard maturities for the purposes of a VaR calculation.

18.8. Explain the difference between value at risk and conditional value at risk.

18.9. Explain why the linear model can provide only approximate estimates of VaR for a portfolio containing options.

18.10. Verify that the 0.3-year zero-coupon bond in the cash-flow mapping example in the appendix to this chapter is mapped into a \$37,397 position in a 3-month bond and a \$11,793 position in a 6-month bond.

18.11. Suppose that the 5-year rate is 6%, the 7-year rate is 7% (both expressed with annual compounding), the daily volatility of a 5-year zero-coupon bond is 0.5%, and the daily volatility of a 7-year zero-coupon bond is 0.58%. The correlation between daily returns on the two bonds is 0.6. Map a cash flow of \$1,000 received at time 6.5 years into a position in a 5-year bond and a position in a 7-year bond using the approach in the appendix. What cash flows in 5 and 7 years are equivalent to the 6.5-year cash flow?

18.12. Some time ago a company entered into a forward contract to buy £1 million for \$1.5 million. The contract now has 6 months to maturity. The daily volatility of a 6-month zero-coupon sterling bond (when its price is translated to dollars) is 0.06% and the daily volatility of a 6-month zero-coupon dollar bond is 0.05%. The correlation between returns from the two bonds is 0.8. The current exchange rate is 1.53. Calculate the standard deviation of the change in the dollar value of the forward contract in 1 day. What is the 10-day 99% VaR? Assume that the 6-month interest rate in both sterling and dollars is 5% per annum with continuous compounding.

18.13. The text calculates a VaR estimate for the example in Table 18.5 assuming two factors. How does the estimate change if you assume (a) one factor and (b) three factors.

18.14. A bank has a portfolio of options on an asset. The delta of the options is −30 and the gamma is −5. Explain how these numbers can be interpreted. The asset price is 20 and its volatility is 1% per day. Adapt Sample Application E in the DerivaGem Application Builder software to calculate VaR.

18.15. Suppose that in Problem 18.14 the vega of the portfolio is −2 per 1% change in the annual volatility. Derive a model relating the change in the portfolio value in 1 day to delta, gamma, and vega. Explain without doing detailed calculations how you would use the model to calculate a VaR estimate.

Assignment Questions

18.16. A company has a position in bonds worth \$6 million. The modified duration of the portfolio is 5.2 years. Assume that only parallel shifts in the yield curve can take place and that the standard deviation of the daily yield change (when yield is measured in percent) is 0.09. Use the duration model to estimate the 20-day 90% VaR for the portfolio. Explain carefully the weaknesses of this approach to calculating VaR. Explain two alternatives that give more accuracy.

18.17. Consider a position consisting of a \$300,000 investment in gold and a \$500,000 investment in silver. Suppose that the daily volatilities of these two assets are 1.8% and 1.2%, respectively, and that the coefficient of correlation between their returns is 0.6. What is the 10-day 97.5% VaR for the portfolio? By how much does diversification reduce the VaR?

18.18. Consider a portfolio of options on a single asset. Suppose that the delta of the portfolio is 12, the value of the asset is \$10, and the daily volatility of the asset is 2%. Estimate the 1-day 95% VaR for the portfolio from the delta. Suppose next that the gamma of the portfolio is -2.6. Derive a quadratic relationship between the change in the portfolio value and the percentage change in the underlying asset price in one day. How would you use this in a Monte Carlo simulation?

18.19. A company has a long position in a 2-year bond and a 3-year bond, as well as a short position in a 5-year bond. Each bond has a principal of \$100 and pays a 5% coupon annually. Calculate the company's exposure to the 1-year, 2-year, 3-year, 4-year, and 5-year rates. Use the data in Tables 18.3 and 18.4 to calculate a 20-day 95% VaR on the assumption that rate changes are explained by (a) one factor, (b) two factors, and (c) three factors. Assume that the zero-coupon yield curve is flat at 5%.

18.20. A bank has written a call option on one stock and a put option on another stock. For the first option the stock price is 50, the strike price is 51, the volatility is 28% per annum, and the time to maturity is 9 months. For the second option the stock price is 20, the strike price is 19, the volatility is 25% per annum, and the time to maturity is 1 year. Neither stock pays a dividend, the risk-free rate is 6% per annum, and the correlation between stock price returns is 0.4. Calculate a 10-day 99% VaR:
(a) Using only deltas
(b) Using the partial simulation approach
(c) Using the full simulation approach

18.21. A common complaint of risk managers is that the model-building approach (either linear or quadratic) does not work well when delta is close to zero. Test what happens when delta is close to zero by using Sample Application E in the DerivaGem Application Builder software. (You can do this by experimenting with different option positions and adjusting the position in the underlying to give a delta of zero.) Explain the results you get.

APPENDIX
CASH-FLOW MAPPING

In this appendix we explain one procedure for mapping cash flows to standard maturity dates. We will illustrate the procedure by considering a simple example of a portfolio consisting of a long position in a single Treasury bond with a principal of $1 million maturing in 0.8 years. We suppose that the bond provides a coupon of 10% per annum payable semiannually. This means that the bond provides coupon payments of $50,000 in 0.3 years and 0.8 years. It also provides a principal payment of $1 million in 0.8 years. The Treasury bond can therefore be regarded as a position in a 0.3-year zero-coupon bond with a principal of $50,000 and a position in a 0.8-year zero-coupon bond with a principal of $1,050,000.

The position in the 0.3-year zero-coupon bond is mapped into an equivalent position in 3-month and 6-month zero-coupon bonds. The position in the 0.8-year zero-coupon bond is mapped into an equivalent position in 6-month and 1-year zero-coupon bonds. The result is that the position in the 0.8-year coupon-bearing bond is, for VaR purposes, regarded as a position in zero-coupon bonds having maturities of 3 months, 6 months, and 1 year.

The Mapping Procedure

Consider the $1,050,000 that will be received in 0.8 years. We suppose that zero rates, daily bond price volatilities, and correlations between bond returns are as shown in Table 18.6.

The first stage is to interpolate between the 6-month rate of 6.0% and the 1-year rate of 7.0% to obtain a 0.8-year rate of 6.6%. (Annual compounding is assumed for all rates.) The present value of the $1,050,000 cash flow to be received in 0.8 years is

$$\frac{1{,}050{,}000}{1.066^{0.8}} = 997{,}662$$

We also interpolate between the 0.1% volatility for the 6-month bond and the 0.2% volatility for the 1-year bond to get a 0.16% volatility for the 0.8-year bond.

Table 18.6 Data to illustrate mapping procedure.

Maturity:	*3-month*	*6-month*	*1-year*
Zero rate (% with annual compounding):	5.50	6.00	7.00
Bond price volatility (% per day):	0.06	0.10	0.20

Correlation between daily returns	*3-month bond*	*6-month bond*	*1-year bond*
3-month bond	1.0	0.9	0.6
6-month bond	0.9	1.0	0.7
1-year bond	0.6	0.7	1.0

Table 18.7 The cash-flow mapping result.

	$50,000 received in 0.3 years	*$1,050,000 received in 0.8 years*	*Total*
Position in 3-month bond ($):	37,397		37,397
Position in 6-month bond ($):	11,793	319,589	331,382
Position in 1-year bond ($):		678,074	678,074

Suppose we allocate α of the present value to the 6-month bond and $1-\alpha$ of the present value to the 1-year bond. Using equation (18.2) and matching variances, we obtain

$$0.0016^2 = 0.001^2\alpha^2 + 0.002^2(1-\alpha)^2 + 2 \times 0.7 \times 0.001 \times 0.002\alpha(1-\alpha)$$

This is a quadratic equation that can be solved in the usual way to give $\alpha = 0.320337$. This means that 32.0337% of the value should be allocated to a 6-month zero-coupon bond and 67.9663% of the value should be allocated to a 1-year zero coupon bond. The 0.8-year bond worth $997,662 is therefore replaced by a 6-month bond worth

$$997{,}662 \times 0.320337 = \$319{,}589$$

and a 1-year bond worth

$$997{,}662 \times 0.679663 = \$678{,}074$$

This cash-flow mapping scheme has the advantage that it preserves both the value and the variance of the cash flow. Also, it can be shown that the weights assigned to the two adjacent zero-coupon bonds are always positive.

For the $50,000 cash flow received at time 0.3 years, we can carry out similar calculations (see Problem 18.10). It turns out that the present value of the cash flow is $49,189. It can be mapped into a position worth $37,397 in a 3-month bond and a position worth $11,793 in a 6-month bond.

The results of the calculations are summarized in Table 18.7. The 0.8-year coupon-bearing bond is mapped into a position worth $37,397 in a 3-month bond, a position worth $331,382 in a 6-month bond, and a position worth $678,074 in a 1-year bond. Using the volatilities and correlations in Table 18.6, equation (18.2) gives the variance of the change in the price of the 0.8-year bond with $n = 3$, $\alpha_1 = 37{,}397$, $\alpha_2 = 331{,}382$, $\alpha_3 = 678{,}074$, $\sigma_1 = 0.0006$, $\sigma_2 = 0.001$, $\sigma_3 = 0.002$, and $\rho_{12} = 0.9$, $\rho_{13} = 0.6$, $\rho_{23} = 0.7$. This variance is 2,628,518. The standard deviation of the change in the price of the bond is therefore $\sqrt{2{,}628{,}518} = 1{,}621.3$. Because we are assuming that the bond is the only instrument in the portfolio, the 10-day 99% VaR is

$$1621.3 \times \sqrt{10} \times 2.33 = 11{,}946$$

or about $11,950.

CHAPTER 19 Estimating Volatilities and Correlations

In this chapter we explain how historical data can be used to produce estimates of the current and future levels of volatilities and correlations. The chapter is relevant both to the calculation of value at risk using the model-building approach and to the valuation of derivatives. When calculating value at risk, we are most interested in the current levels of volatilities and correlations because we are assessing possible changes in the value of a portfolio over a very short period of time. When valuing derivatives, forecasts of volatilities and correlations over the whole life of the derivative are usually required.

The chapter considers models with imposing names such as exponentially weighted moving average (EWMA), autoregressive conditional heteroscedasticity (ARCH), and generalized autoregressive conditional heteroscedasticity (GARCH). The distinctive feature of the models is that they recognize that volatilities and correlations are not constant. During some periods, a particular volatility or correlation may be relatively low, whereas during other periods it may be relatively high. The models attempt to keep track of the variations in the volatility or correlation through time.

19.1 ESTIMATING VOLATILITY

Define σ_n as the volatility of a market variable on day n, as estimated at the end of day $n-1$. The square of the volatility, σ_n^2, on day n is the *variance rate*. We described the standard approach to estimating σ_n from historical data in Section 13.4. Suppose that the value of the market variable at the end of day i is S_i. The variable u_i is defined as the continuously compounded return during day i (between the end of day $i-1$ and the end of day i):

$$u_i = \ln \frac{S_i}{S_{i-1}}$$

An unbiased estimate of the variance rate per day, σ_n^2, using the most recent m observations on the u_i is

$$\sigma_n^2 = \frac{1}{m-1} \sum_{i=1}^{m} (u_{n-i} - \bar{u})^2 \tag{19.1}$$

where $\bar{u}$ is the mean of the u_is:

$$\bar{u} = \frac{1}{m}\sum_{i=1}^{m} u_{n-i}$$

For the purposes of monitoring daily volatility, the formula in equation (19.1) is usually changed in a number of ways:

1. u_i is defined as the percentage change in the market variable between the end of day $i-1$ and the end of day i, so that:[1]

$$u_i = \frac{S_i - S_{i-1}}{S_{i-1}} \tag{19.2}$$

2. $\bar{u}$ is assumed to be zero.[2]
3. $m-1$ is replaced by m.[3]

These three changes make very little difference to the estimates that are calculated, but they allow us to simplify the formula for the variance rate to

$$\sigma_n^2 = \frac{1}{m}\sum_{i=1}^{m} u_{n-i}^2 \tag{19.3}$$

where u_i is given by equation (19.2).[4]

Weighting Schemes

Equation (19.3) gives equal weight to $u_{n-1}^2, u_{n-2}^2, \ldots, u_{n-m}^2$. Our objective is to estimate the current level of volatility, σ_n. It therefore makes sense to give more weight to recent data. A model that does this is

$$\sigma_n^2 = \sum_{i=1}^{m} \alpha_i u_{n-i}^2 \tag{19.4}$$

The variable α_i is the amount of weight given to the observation i days ago. The α's are positive. If we choose them so that $\alpha_i < \alpha_j$ when $i > j$, less weight is given to older observations. The weights must sum to unity, so we have

$$\sum_{i=1}^{m} \alpha_i = 1$$

---

[1] This is consistent with the point made in Section 18.3 about the way that volatility is defined for the purposes of VaR calculations.

[2] As explained in Section 18.3, this assumption usually has very little effect on estimates of the variance because the expected change in a variable in one day is very small when compared with the standard deviation of changes.

[3] Replacing $m-1$ by m moves us from an unbiased estimate of the variance to a maximum likelihood estimate. Maximum likelihood estimates are discussed later in the chapter.

[4] Note that the u's in this chapter play the same role as the Δx's in Chapter 18. Both are daily percentage changes in market variables. In the case of the u's, the subscripts count observations made on different days on the same market variable. In the case of the Δx's, they count observations made on the same day on different market variables. The use of subscripts for σ is similarly different between the two chapters. In this chapter, the subscripts refer to days; in Chapter 18 they referred to market variables.

An extension of the idea in equation (19.4) is to assume that there is a long-run average variance rate and that this should be given some weight. This leads to the model that takes the form

$$\sigma_n^2 = \gamma V_L + \sum_{i=1}^{m} \alpha_i u_{n-i}^2 \tag{19.5}$$

where V_L is the long-run variance rate and γ is the weight assigned to V_L. Because the weights must sum to unity, we have

$$\gamma + \sum_{i=1}^{m} \alpha_i = 1$$

This is known as an ARCH(m) model. It was first suggested by Engle.[5] The estimate of the variance is based on a long-run average variance and m observations. The older an observation, the less weight it is given. Defining $\omega = \gamma V_L$, the model in equation (19.5) can be written

$$\sigma_n^2 = \omega + \sum_{i=1}^{m} \alpha_i u_{n-i}^2 \tag{19.6}$$

In the next two sections we discuss two important approaches to monitoring volatility using the ideas in equations (19.4) and (19.5).

19.2 THE EXPONENTIALLY WEIGHTED MOVING AVERAGE MODEL

The exponentially weighted moving average (EWMA) model is a particular case of the model in equation (19.4) where the weights α_i decrease exponentially as we move back through time. Specifically, $\alpha_{i+1} = \lambda \alpha_i$, where λ is a constant between 0 and 1.

It turns out that this weighting scheme leads to a particularly simple formula for updating volatility estimates. The formula is

$$\sigma_n^2 = \lambda \sigma_{n-1}^2 + (1-\lambda) u_{n-1}^2 \tag{19.7}$$

The estimate, σ_n, of the volatility for day n (made at the end of day $n-1$) is calculated from σ_{n-1} (the estimate that was made at the end of day $n-2$ of the volatility for day $n-1$) and u_{n-1} (the most recent daily percentage change).

To understand why equation (19.7) corresponds to weights that decrease exponentially, we substitute for σ_{n-1}^2 to get

$$\sigma_n^2 = \lambda[\lambda \sigma_{n-2}^2 + (1-\lambda) u_{n-2}^2] + (1-\lambda) u_{n-1}^2$$

or

$$\sigma_n^2 = (1-\lambda)(u_{n-1}^2 + \lambda u_{n-2}^2) + \lambda^2 \sigma_{n-2}^2$$

Substituting in a similar way for σ_{n-2}^2 gives

$$\sigma_n^2 = (1-\lambda)(u_{n-1}^2 + \lambda u_{n-2}^2 + \lambda^2 u_{n-3}^2) + \lambda^3 \sigma_{n-3}^2$$

---

[5] See R. Engle "Autoregressive Conditional Heteroscedasticity with Estimates of the Variance of UK Inflation," *Econometrica*, 50 (1982): 987–1008.

Continuing in this way, we see that

$$\sigma_n^2 = (1-\lambda)\sum_{i=1}^{m}\lambda^{i-1}u_{n-i}^2 + \lambda^m\sigma_{n-m}^2$$

For large m, the term $\lambda^m\sigma_{n-m}^2$ is sufficiently small to be ignored, so that equation (19.7) is the same as equation (19.4) with $\alpha_i = (1-\lambda)\lambda^{i-1}$. The weights for the u_i decline at rate λ as we move back through time. Each weight is λ times the previous weight.

Example 19.1

Suppose that λ is 0.90, the volatility estimated for a market variable for day $n-1$ is 1% per day, and during day $n-1$ the market variable increased by 2%. This means that $\sigma_{n-1}^2 = 0.01^2 = 0.0001$ and $u_{n-1}^2 = 0.02^2 = 0.0004$. Equation (19.7) gives

$$\sigma_n^2 = 0.9 \times 0.0001 + 0.1 \times 0.0004 = 0.00013$$

The estimate of the volatility, σ_n, for day n is therefore $\sqrt{0.00013}$, or 1.14%, per day. Note that the expected value of u_{n-1}^2 is σ_{n-1}^2, or 0.0001. In this example, the realized value of u_{n-1}^2 is greater than the expected value, and as a result our volatility estimate increases. If the realized value of u_{n-1}^2 had been less than its expected value, our estimate of the volatility would have decreased.

The EWMA approach has the attractive feature that relatively little data need to be stored. At any given time, we need to remember only the current estimate of the variance rate and the most recent observation on the value of the market variable. When we get a new observation on the value of the market variable, we calculate a new daily percentage change and use equation (19.7) to update our estimate of the variance rate. The old estimate of the variance rate and the old value of the market variable can then be discarded.

The EWMA approach is designed to track changes in the volatility. Suppose there is a big move in the market variable on day $n-1$, so that u_{n-1}^2 is large. From equation (19.7) this causes our estimate of the current volatility to move upward. The value of λ governs how responsive the estimate of the daily volatility is to the most recent daily percentage change. A low value of λ leads to a great deal of weight being given to the u_{n-1}^2 when σ_n is calculated. In this case, the estimates produced for the volatility on successive days are themselves highly volatile. A high value of λ (i.e., a value close to 1.0) produces estimates of the daily volatility that respond relatively slowly to new information provided by the daily percentage change.

The RiskMetrics database, which was originally created by J. P. Morgan and made publicly available in 1994, uses the EWMA model with $\lambda = 0.94$ for updating daily volatility estimates in its RiskMetrics database. The company found that, across a range of different market variables, this value of λ gives forecasts of the variance rate that come closest to the realized variance rate.[6] The realized variance rate on a particular day was calculated as an equally weighted average of the u_i^2 on the subsequent 25 days (see Problem 19.17).

[6] See J. P. Morgan, *RiskMetrics Monitor*, Fourth Quarter, 1995. We will explain an alternative (maximum likelihood) approach to estimating parameters later in the chapter.

19.3 THE GARCH(1,1) MODEL

We now move on to discuss what is known as the GARCH(1,1) model, proposed by Bollerslev in 1986.[7] The difference between the GARCH(1,1) model and the EWMA model is analogous to the difference between equation (19.4) and equation (19.5). In GARCH(1,1), σ_n^2 is calculated from a long-run average variance rate, V_L, as well as from σ_{n-1} and u_{n-1}. The equation for GARCH(1,1) is

$$\sigma_n^2 = \gamma V_L + \alpha u_{n-1}^2 + \beta \sigma_{n-1}^2 \qquad \textbf{(19.8)}$$

where γ is the weight assigned to V_L, α is the weight assigned to u_{n-1}^2, and β is the weight assigned to σ_{n-1}^2. Because the weights must sum to one, we have

$$\gamma + \alpha + \beta = 1$$

The EWMA model is a particular case of GARCH(1,1) where $\gamma = 0$, $\alpha = 1 - \lambda$, and $\beta = \lambda$.

The "(1,1)" in GARCH(1,1) indicates that σ_n^2 is based on the most recent observation of u^2 and the most recent estimate of the variance rate. The more general GARCH(p,q) model calculates σ_n^2 from the most recent p observations on u^2 and the most recent q estimates of the variance rate.[8] GARCH(1,1) is by far the most popular of the GARCH models.

Setting $\omega = \gamma V_L$, the GARCH(1,1) model can also be written

$$\sigma_n^2 = \omega + \alpha u_{n-1}^2 + \beta \sigma_{n-1}^2 \qquad \textbf{(19.9)}$$

This is the form of the model that is usually used for the purposes of estimating the parameters. Once ω, α, and β have been estimated, we can calculate γ as $1 - \alpha - \beta$. The long-term variance V_L can then be calculated as ω/γ. For a stable GARCH(1,1) process we require $\alpha + \beta < 1$. Otherwise the weight applied to the long-term variance is negative.

Example 19.2

Suppose that a GARCH(1,1) model is estimated from daily data as

$$\sigma_n^2 = 0.000002 + 0.13 u_{n-1}^2 + 0.86 \sigma_{n-1}^2$$

This corresponds to $\alpha = 0.13$, $\beta = 0.86$, and $\omega = 0.000002$. Because $\gamma = 1 - \alpha - \beta$, it follows that $\gamma = 0.01$. Because $\omega = \gamma V_L$, it follows that $V_L = 0.0002$. In other words, the long-run average variance per day implied by the model is 0.0002. This corresponds to a volatility of $\sqrt{0.0002} = 0.014$, or 1.4%, per day.

---

[7] See T. Bollerslev, "Generalized Autoregressive Conditional Heteroscedasticity," *Journal of Econometrics*, 31 (1986): 307–27.

[8] Other GARCH models have been proposed that incorporate asymmetric news. These models are designed so that σ_n depends on the sign of u_{n-1}. Arguably, the models are more appropriate for equities than GARCH(1,1). As mentioned in Chapter 16, the volatility of an equity's price tends to be inversely related to the price so that a negative u_{n-1} should have a bigger effect on σ_n than the same positive u_{n-1}. For a discussion of models for handling asymmetric news, see D. Nelson, "Conditional Heteroscedasticity and Asset Returns: A New Approach," *Econometrica*, 59 (1990): 347–70; R. F. Engle and V. Ng, "Measuring and Testing the Impact of News on Volatility," *Journal of Finance*, 48 (1993): 1749–78.

Suppose that the estimate of the volatility on day $n-1$ is 1.6% per day, so that $\sigma_{n-1}^2 = 0.016^2 = 0.000256$, and that on day $n-1$ the market variable decreased by 1%, so that $u_{n-1}^2 = 0.01^2 = 0.0001$. Then

$$\sigma_n^2 = 0.000002 + 0.13 \times 0.0001 + 0.86 \times 0.000256 = 0.00023516$$

The new estimate of the volatility is therefore $\sqrt{0.00023516} = 0.0153$, or 1.53%, per day.

The Weights

Substituting for σ_{n-1}^2 in equation (19.9), we obtain

$$\sigma_n^2 = \omega + \alpha u_{n-1}^2 + \beta(\omega + \alpha u_{n-2}^2 + \beta\sigma_{n-2}^2)$$

or

$$\sigma_n^2 = \omega + \beta\omega + \alpha u_{n-1}^2 + \alpha\beta u_{n-2}^2 + \beta^2\sigma_{n-2}^2$$

Substituting for σ_{n-2}^2, we get

$$\sigma_n^2 = \omega + \beta\omega + \beta^2\omega + \alpha u_{n-1}^2 + \alpha\beta u_{n-2}^2 + \alpha\beta^2 u_{n-3}^2 + \beta^3\sigma_{n-3}^2$$

Continuing in this way, we see that the weight applied to u_{n-i}^2 is $\alpha\beta^{i-1}$. The weights decline exponentially at rate β. The parameter β can be interpreted as a "decay rate". It is similar to λ in the EWMA model. It defines the relative importance of the observations on the u's in determining the current variance rate. For example, if $\beta = 0.9$, then u_{n-2}^2 is only 90% as important as u_{n-1}^2; u_{n-3}^2 is 81% as important as u_{n-1}; and so on. The GARCH(1,1) model is similar to the EWMA model except that, in addition to assigning weights that decline exponentially to past u^2, it also assigns some weight to the long-run average volatility.

Mean Reversion

The GARCH (1,1) model recognizes that over time the variance tends to get pulled back to a long-run average level of V_L. The amount of weight assigned to V_L is $\gamma = 1 - \alpha - \beta$. The GARCH(1,1) is equivalent to a model where the variance V follows the stochastic process

$$dV = a(V_L - V)\,dt + \xi V\,dz$$

where time is measured in days, $a = 1 - \alpha - \beta$, and $\xi = \alpha\sqrt{2}$ (see Problem 19.14). This is a mean-reverting model. The variance has a drift that pulls it back to V_L at rate a. When $V > V_L$, the variance has a negative drift; when $V_L < V$, it has a positive drift. Superimposed on the drift is a volatility ξ. We will discuss this type of model further in Chapter 24.

19.4 CHOOSING BETWEEN THE MODELS

In practice, variance rates do tend to be mean reverting. The GARCH(1,1) model incorporates mean reversion, whereas the EWMA model does not. GARCH (1,1) is therefore theoretically more appealing than the EWMA model.

In the next section, we will discuss how best-fit parameters ω, α, and β in GARCH(1,1) can be estimated. When the parameter ω is zero, the GARCH(1, 1) reduces to EWMA. In circumstances where the best-fit value of ω turns out to be negative, the GARCH(1, 1) model is not stable and it makes sense to switch to the EWMA model.

19.5 MAXIMUM LIKELIHOOD METHODS

It is now appropriate to discuss how the parameters in the models we have been considering are estimated from historical data. The approach used is known as the *maximum likelihood method*. It involves choosing values for the parameters that maximize the chance (or likelihood) of the data occurring.

To illustrate the method, we start with a very simple example. Suppose that we sample 10 stocks at random on a certain day and find that the price of one of them declined on that day and the prices of the other nine either remained the same or increased. What is our best estimate of the probability of a price decline? The natural answer is 0.1. Let us see if this is what the maximum likelihood method gives.

Suppose that the probability of a price decline is p. The probability that one particular stock declines in price and the other nine do not is $p(1-p)^9$. (There is a probability p that the stock will decline and $1-p$ that the other nine will not.) Using the maximum likelihood approach, the best estimate of p is the one that maximizes $p(1-p)^9$. Differentiating this expression with respect to p and setting the result equal to zero, we find that $p = 0.1$ maximizes the expression. This shows that the maximum likelihood estimate of p is 0.1, as expected.

Estimating a Constant Variance

Our next example of maximum likelihood methods considers the problem of estimating a variance of a variable X from m observations on X when the underlying distribution is normal with zero mean. We assume that the observations are $u_1, u_2, \dots, u_m$ and that the mean of the underlying distribution is zero. Denote the variance by v. The likelihood of u_i being observed is the probability density function for X when $X = u_i$. This is

$$\frac{1}{\sqrt{2\pi v}} \exp\left(\frac{-u_i^2}{2v}\right)$$

The likelihood of m observations occurring in the order in which they are observed is

$$\prod_{i=1}^{m} \left[\frac{1}{\sqrt{2\pi v}} \exp\left(\frac{-u_i^2}{2v}\right)\right] \tag{19.10}$$

Using the maximum likelihood method, the best estimate of v is the value that maximizes this expression.

Maximizing an expression is equivalent to maximizing the logarithm of the expression. Taking logarithms of the expression in equation (19.10) and ignoring constant multiplicative factors, it can be seen that we wish to maximize

$$\sum_{i=1}^{m} \left[-\ln(v) - \frac{u_i^2}{v}\right] \tag{19.11}$$

or

$$-m \ln(v) - \sum_{i=1}^{m} \frac{u_i^2}{v}$$

Differentiating this expression with respect to v and setting the result equation to zero, we see that the maximum likelihood estimator of v is[9]

$$\frac{1}{m}\sum_{i=1}^{m} u_i^2$$

Estimating GARCH (1,1) Parameters

We now consider how the maximum likelihood method can be used to estimate the parameters when GARCH (1,1) or some other volatility updating scheme is used. Define $v_i = \sigma_i^2$ as the variance estimated for day i. We assume that the probability distribution of u_i conditional on the variance is normal. A similar analysis to the one just given shows the best parameters are the ones that maximize

$$\prod_{i=1}^{m}\left[\frac{1}{\sqrt{2\pi v_i}} \exp\left(\frac{-u_i^2}{2v_i}\right)\right]$$

Taking logarithms, we see that this is equivalent to maximizing

$$\sum_{i=1}^{m}\left[-\ln(v_i) - \frac{u_i^2}{v_i}\right] \tag{19.12}$$

This is the same as the expression in equation (19.11), except that v is replaced by v_i. We search iteratively to find the parameters in the model that maximize the expression in equation (19.12).

The spreadsheet in Table 19.1 indicates how the calculations could be organized for the GARCH(1,1) model. The table analyzes data on the Japanese yen exchange rate between January 6, 1988, and August 15, 1997. The numbers in the table are based on trial estimates of the three GARCH(1,1) parameters: ω, α, and β. The first column in the table records the date. The second column counts the days. The third column shows the exchange rate, S_i, at the end of day i. The fourth column shows the proportional change in the exchange rate between the end of day $i-1$ and the end of day i. This is $u_i = (S_i - S_{i-1})/S_{i-1}$. The fifth column shows the estimate of the variance rate, $v_i = \sigma_i^2$, for day i made at the end of day $i-1$. On day 3, we start things off by setting the variance equal to u_2^2. On subsequent days, equation (19.9) is used. The sixth column tabulates the likelihood measure, $-\ln(v_i) - u_i^2/v_i$. The values in the fifth and sixth columns are based on the current trial estimates of ω, α, and β. We are interested in choosing ω, α, and β to maximize the sum of the numbers in the sixth column. This involves an iterative search procedure.[10]

---

[9] This confirms the point made in footnote 3.

[10] As discussed later, a general purpose algorithm such as Solver in Microsoft's Excel can be used. Alternatively, a special purpose algorithm, such as Levenberg–Marquardt, can be used. See, e.g., W. H. Press, B. P. Flannery, S. A. Teukolsky, and W. T. Vetterling. *Numerical Recipes in C: The Art of Scientific Computing*, Cambridge University Press, 1988.

Table 19.1 Estimation of parameters in GARCH(1,1) model.

Date	*Day i*	S_i	u_i	$v_i = \sigma_i^2$	$-\ln(v_i) - u_i^2/v_i$
06-Jan-88	1	0.007728			
07-Jan-88	2	0.007779	0.006599		
08-Jan-88	3	0.007746	−0.004242	0.00004355	9.6283
11-Jan-88	4	0.007816	0.009037	0.00004198	8.1329
12-Jan-88	5	0.007837	0.002687	0.00004455	9.8568
13-Jan-88	6	0.007924	0.011101	0.00004220	7.1529
⋮	⋮	⋮	⋮	⋮	⋮
13-Aug-97	2421	0.008643	0.003374	0.00007626	9.3321
14-Aug-97	2422	0.008493	−0.017309	0.00007092	5.3294
15-Aug-97	2423	0.008495	0.000144	0.00008417	9.3824
					22,063.5763

Trial estimates of GARCH parameters
$\omega = 0.00000176 \quad \alpha = 0.0626 \quad \beta = 0.8976$

In our example, the optimal values of the parameters turn out to be

$$\omega = 0.00000176, \quad \alpha = 0.0626, \quad \beta = 0.8976$$

and the maximum value of the function in equation (19.12) is 22,063.5763. The numbers shown in Table 19.1 were calculated on the final iteration of the search for the optimal ω, α, and β.

The long-term variance rate, V_L, in our example is

$$\frac{\omega}{1-\alpha-\beta} = \frac{0.00000176}{0.0398} = 0.00004422$$

The long-term volatility is $\sqrt{0.00004422}$, or 0.665%, per day.

Figure 19.1 shows the way the GARCH (1,1) volatility for the Japanese yen changed over the 10-year period covered by the data. Most of the time, the volatility was between 0.4% and 0.8% per day, but volatilities over 1% were experienced during some periods.

An alternative and more robust approach to estimating parameters in GARCH(1,1) is known as *variance targeting*.[11] This involves setting the long-run average variance rate, V_L, equal to the sample variance calculated from the data (or to some other value that is believed to be reasonable). The value of ω then equals $V_L(1-\alpha-\beta)$ and only two parameters have to be estimated. For the data in Table 19.1, the sample variance is 0.00004341, which gives a daily volatility of 0.659%. Setting V_L equal to the sample variance, the values of α and β that maximize the objective function in equation (19.12) are 0.0607 and 0.8990, respectively. The value of the objective function is 22,063.5274, only marginally below the value of 22,063.5763 obtained using the earlier procedure.

When the EWMA model is used, the estimation procedure is relatively simple. We set $\omega = 0$, $\alpha = 1-\lambda$, and $\beta = \lambda$, and only one parameter has to be estimated. In the data in Table 19.1, the value of λ that maximizes the objective function in equation (19.12) is 0.9686 and the value of the objective function is 21,995.8377.

[11] See R. Engle and J. Mezrich, "GARCH for Groups," *Risk*, August 1996: 36–40.

Figure 19.1 Daily volatility of the yen/USD exchange rate, 1988–1997.

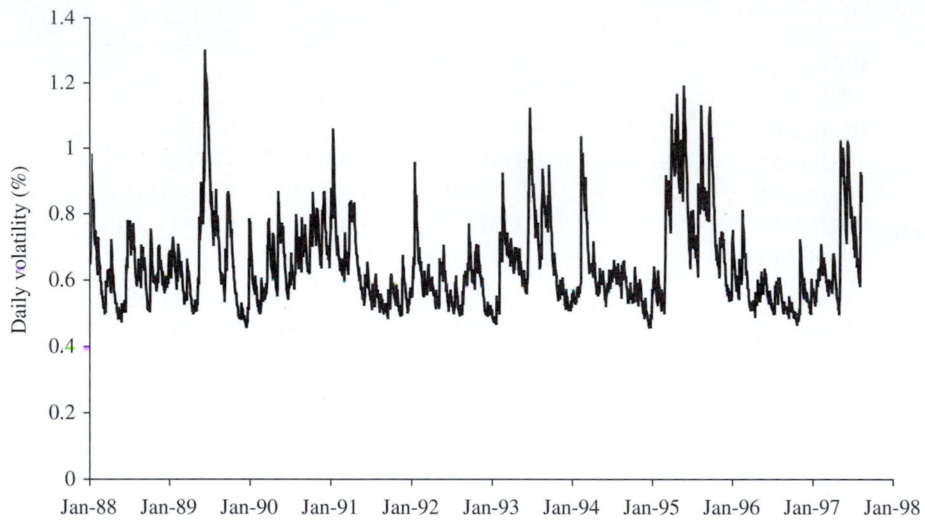

Both GARCH (1,1) and the EWMA method can be implemented by using the Solver routine in Excel to search for the values of the parameters that maximize the likelihood function. The routine works well provided that we structure our spreadsheet so that the parameters we are searching for have roughly equal values. For example, in GARCH (1,1) we could let cells A1, A2, and A3 contain $\omega \times 10^5$, α, and 0.1β. We could then set B1 = A1/100000, B2 = A2, and B3 = 10 ∗ A3. We would use B1, B2, and B3 to calculate the likelihood function. We would ask Solver to calculate the values of A1, A2, and A3 that maximize the likelihood function.

How Good Is the Model?

The assumption underlying a GARCH model is that volatility changes with the passage of time. During some periods volatility is relatively high; during other periods it is relatively low. To put this another way, when u_i^2 is high, there is a tendency for u_{i+1}^2, $u_{i+2}^2, \ldots$ to be high; when u_i^2 is low, there is a tendency for $u_{i+1}^2, u_{i+2}^2, \ldots$ to be low. We can test how true this is by examining the autocorrelation structure of the u_i^2.

Let us assume the u_i^2 do exhibit autocorrelation. If a GARCH model is working well, it should remove the autocorrelation. We can test whether it has done so by considering the autocorrelation structure for the variables u_i^2/σ_i^2. If these show very little autocorrelation, our model for σ_i has succeeded in explaining autocorrelations in the u_i^2.

Table 19.2 shows results for the yen/dollar exchange rate data referred to above. The first column shows the lags considered when the autocorrelation is calculated. The second shows autocorrelations for u_i^2; the third shows autocorrelations for u_i^2/σ_i^2.[12] The table shows that the autocorrelations are positive for u_i^2 for all lags between 1 and 15. In the case of u_i^2/σ_i^2, some of the autocorrelations are positive and some are negative. They are all much smaller in magnitude than the autocorrelations for u_i^2.

[12] For a series x_i, the autocorrelation with a lag of k is the coefficient of correlation between x_i and x_{i+k}.

Table 19.2 Autocorrelations before and after the use of a GARCH model.

Time lag	*Autocorrelation for* u_i^2	*Autocorrelation for* u_i^2/σ_i^2
1	0.072	0.004
2	0.041	−0.005
3	0.057	0.008
4	0.107	0.003
5	0.075	0.016
6	0.066	0.008
7	0.019	−0.033
8	0.085	0.012
9	0.054	0.010
10	0.030	−0.023
11	0.038	−0.004
12	0.038	−0.021
13	0.057	−0.001
14	0.040	0.002
15	0.007	−0.028

The GARCH model appears to have done a good job in explaining the data. For a more scientific test, we can use what is known as the Ljung–Box statistic.[13] If a certain series has m observations the Ljung–Box statistic is

$$m\sum_{k=1}^{K} w_k \eta_k^2$$

where η_k is the autocorrelation for a lag of k, K is the number of lags considered, and

$$w_k = \frac{m+2}{m-k}$$

For $K = 15$, zero autocorrelation can be rejected with 95% confidence when the Ljung–Box statistic is greater than 25.

From Table 19.2, the Ljung–Box Statistic for the u_i^2 series is about 123. This is strong evidence of autocorrelation. For the u_i^2/σ_i^2 series, the Ljung–Box statistic is 8.2, suggesting that the autocorrelation has been largely removed by the GARCH model.

19.6 USING GARCH(1,1) TO FORECAST FUTURE VOLATILITY

The variance rate estimated at the end of day $n-1$ for day n, when GARCH(1,1) is used, is

$$\sigma_n^2 = (1-\alpha-\beta)V_L + \alpha u_{n-1}^2 + \beta\sigma_{n-1}^2$$

[13] See G. M. Ljung and G. E. P. Box, "On a Measure of Lack of Fit in Time Series Models," *Biometrica*, 65 (1978): 297–303.

so that

$$\sigma_n^2 - V_L = \alpha(u_{n-1}^2 - V_L) + \beta(\sigma_{n-1}^2 - V_L)$$

On day $n + t$ in the future, we have

$$\sigma_{n+t}^2 - V_L = \alpha(u_{n+t-1}^2 - V_L) + \beta(\sigma_{n+t-1}^2 - V_L)$$

The expected value of u_{n+t-1}^2 is σ_{n+t-1}^2. Hence,

$$E[\sigma_{n+t}^2 - V_L] = (\alpha + \beta)E[\sigma_{n+t-1}^2 - V_L]$$

where E denotes expected value. Using this equation repeatedly yields

$$E[\sigma_{n+t}^2 - V_L] = (\alpha + \beta)^t(\sigma_n^2 - V_L)$$

or

$$E[\sigma_{n+t}^2] = V_L + (\alpha + \beta)^t(\sigma_n^2 - V_L) \tag{19.13}$$

This equation forecasts the volatility on day $n + t$ using the information available at the end of day $n - 1$. In the EWMA model, $\alpha + \beta = 1$ and equation (19.13) shows that the expected future variance rate equals the current variance rate. When $\alpha + \beta < 1$, the final term in the equation becomes progressively smaller as t increases. Figure 19.2 shows the expected path followed by the variance rate for situations where the current variance rate is different from V_L. As mentioned earlier, the variance rate exhibits mean reversion with a reversion level of V_L and a reversion rate of $1 - \alpha - \beta$. Our forecast of the future variance rate tends towards V_L as we look further and further ahead. This analysis emphasizes the point that we must have $\alpha + \beta < 1$ for a stable GARCH(1,1) process. When $\alpha + \beta > 1$, the weight given to the long-term average variance is negative and the process is "mean fleeing" rather than "mean reverting".

In the yen-dollar exchange rate example considered earlier $\alpha + \beta = 0.9602$ and $V_L = 0.00004422$. Suppose that our estimate of the current variance rate per day is 0.00006. (This corresponds to a volatility of 0.77% per day.) In 10 days the expected variance rate is

$$0.00004422 + 0.9602^{10}(0.00006 - 0.00004422) = 0.00005473$$

The expected volatility per day is 0.74%, still well above the long-term volatility of 0.665% per day. However, the expected variance rate in 100 days is

$$0.00004422 + 0.9602^{100}(0.00006 - 0.00004422) = 0.00004449$$

and the expected volatility per day is 0.667%, very close to the long-term volatility.

Volatility Term Structures

Suppose it is day n. Define:

$$V(t) = E(\sigma_{n+t}^2)$$

and

$$a = \ln\frac{1}{\alpha + \beta}$$

Figure 19.2 Expected path for the variance rate when (a) current variance rate is above long-term variance rate and (b) current variance rate is below long-term variance rate.

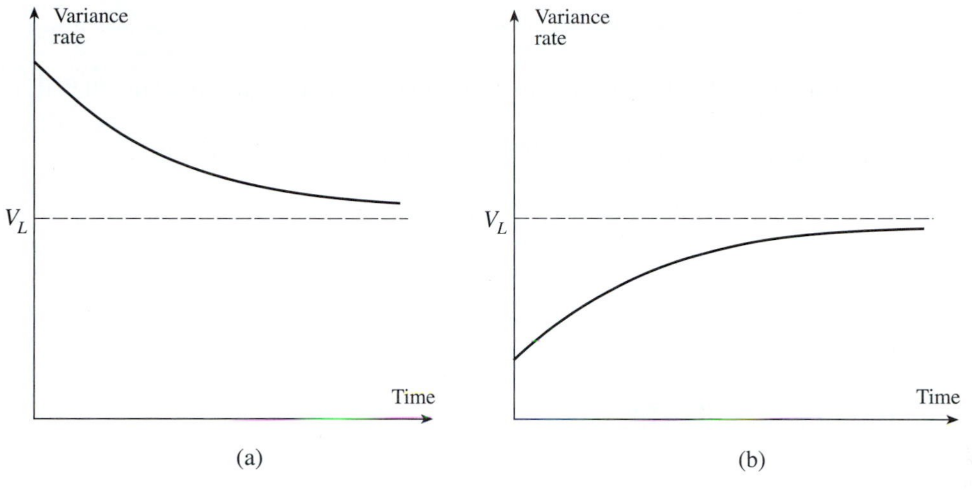

so that equation (19.13) becomes

$$V(t) = V_L + e^{-at}[V(0) - V_L]$$

Here, $V(t)$ is an estimate of the instantaneous variance rate in t days. The average variance rate per day between today and time T is given by

$$\frac{1}{T}\int_0^T V(t)\,dt = V_L + \frac{1 - e^{-aT}}{aT}[V(0) - V_L]$$

The longer the life of the option, the closer this is to V_L. Define $\sigma(T)$ as the volatility per annum that should be used to price a T-day option under GARCH(1,1). Assuming 252 days per year, $\sigma(T)^2$ is 252 times the average variance rate per day, so that

$$\sigma(T)^2 = 252\left(V_L + \frac{1 - e^{-aT}}{aT}[V(0) - V_L]\right) \tag{19.14}$$

As we discussed in Chapter 16, the market prices of different options on the same asset are often used to calculate a *volatility term structure*. This is the relationship between the implied volatilities of the options and their maturities. Equation (19.14) can be used to estimate a volatility term structure based on the GARCH(1,1) model. The estimated volatility term structure is not usually the same as the actual volatility term structure. However, as we will show, it is often used to predict the way that the actual volatility term structure will respond to volatility changes.

When the current volatility is above the long-term volatility, the GARCH(1,1) model estimates a downward-sloping volatility term structure. When the current volatility is below the long-term volatility, it estimates an upward-sloping volatility

Table 19.3 Yen/dollar volatility term structure predicted from GARCH(1, 1).

Option life (days)	10	30	50	100	500
Option volatility (% per annum)	12.00	11.59	11.33	11.00	10.65

term structure. In the case of the yen/dollar exchange rate, $a = \ln(1/0.9602) = 0.0406$ and $V_L = 0.00004422$. Suppose that the current variance rate per day, $V(0)$, is estimated as 0.00006 per day. It follows from equation (19.14) that

$$\sigma(T)^2 = 252\left(0.00004422 + \frac{1 - e^{-0.0406T}}{0.0406T}(0.00006 - 0.000044220)\right)$$

where T is measured in days. Table 19.3 shows the volatility per year for different values of T.

Impact of Volatility Changes

Equation (19.14) can be written

$$\sigma(T)^2 = 252\left[V_L + \frac{1 - e^{-aT}}{aT}\left(\frac{\sigma(0)^2}{252} - V_L\right)\right]$$

When $\sigma(0)$ changes by $\Delta\sigma(0)$, $\sigma(T)$ changes by

$$\frac{1 - e^{-aT}}{aT}\frac{\sigma(0)}{\sigma(T)}\Delta\sigma(0) \tag{19.15}$$

Table 19.4 shows the effect of a volatility change on options of varying maturities for our yen/dollar exchange rate example. We assume as before that $V(0) = 0.00006$, so that $\sigma(0) = 12.30\%$. The table considers a 100-basis-point change in the instantaneous volatility from 12.30% per year to 13.30% per year. This means that $\Delta\sigma(0) = 0.01$, or 1%.

Many financial institutions use analyses such as this when determining the exposure of their books to volatility changes. Rather than consider an across-the-board increase of 1% in implied volatilities when calculating vega, they relate the size of the volatility increase that is considered to the maturity of the option. Based on Table 19.4, a 0.84% volatility increase would be considered for a 10-day option, a 0.61% increase for a 30-day option, a 0.46% increase for a 50-day option, and so on.

Table 19.4 Impact of 1% change in the instantaneous volatility predicted from GARCH(1, 1).

Option life (days)	10	30	50	100	500
Increase in volatility (%)	0.84	0.61	0.46	0.27	0.06

19.7 CORRELATIONS

The discussion so far has centered on the estimation and forecasting of volatility. As explained in Chapter 18, correlations also play a key role in the calculation of VaR. In this section, we show how correlation estimates can be updated in a similar way to volatility estimates.

The correlation between two variables X and Y can be defined as

$$\frac{\text{cov}(X, Y)}{\sigma_X \sigma_Y}$$

where σ_X and σ_Y are the standard deviations of X and Y and cov(X, Y) is the covariance between X and Y. The covariance between X and Y is defined as

$$E[(X - \mu_X)(Y - \mu_Y)]$$

where μ_X and μ_Y are the means of X and Y, and E denotes the expected value. Although it is easier to develop intuition about the meaning of a correlation than it is for a covariance, it is covariances that are the fundamental variables of our analysis.[14]

Define x_i and y_i as the percentage changes in X and Y between the end of day $i-1$ and the end of day i:

$$x_i = \frac{X_i - X_{i-1}}{X_{i-1}}, \qquad y_i = \frac{Y_i - Y_{i-1}}{Y_{i-1}}$$

where X_i and Y_i are the values of X and Y at the end of day i. We also define the following:

$\sigma_{x,n}$: Daily volatility of variable X, estimated for day n

$\sigma_{y,n}$: Daily volatility of variable Y, estimated for day n

cov$_n$: Estimate of covariance between daily changes in X and Y, calculated on day n.

Our estimate of the correlation between X and Y on day n is

$$\frac{\text{cov}_n}{\sigma_{x,n}\,\sigma_{y,n}}$$

Using an equal-weighting scheme and assuming that the means of x_i and y_i are zero, equation (19.3) shows that we can estimate the variance rates of X and Y from the most recent m observations as

$$\sigma_{x,n}^2 = \frac{1}{m}\sum_{i=1}^{m} x_{n-i}^2, \qquad \sigma_{y,n}^2 = \frac{1}{m}\sum_{i=1}^{m} y_{n-i}^2$$

A similar estimate for the covariance between X and Y is

$$\text{cov}_n = \frac{1}{m}\sum_{i=1}^{m} x_{n-i}\, y_{n-i} \qquad \textbf{(19.16)}$$

[14] An analogy here is that variance rates were the fundamental variables for the EWMA and GARCH schemes in first part of this chapter, even though volatilities are easier to understand.

One alternative for updating covariances is an EWMA model similar to equation (19.7). The formula for updating the covariance estimate is then

$$\text{cov}_n = \lambda\,\text{cov}_{n-1} + (1-\lambda)x_{n-1}\,y_{n-1}$$

A similar analysis to that presented for the EWMA volatility model shows that the weights given to observations on the $x_i\,y_i$ decline as we move back through time. The lower the value of λ, the greater the weight that is given to recent observations.

Example 19.3

Suppose that $\lambda = 0.95$ and that the estimate of the correlation between two variables X and Y on day $n-1$ is 0.6. Suppose further that the estimate of the volatilities for the X and Y on day $n-1$ are 1% and 2%, respectively. From the relationship between correlation and covariance, the estimate of the covariance between the X and Y on day $n-1$ is

$$0.6 \times 0.01 \times 0.02 = 0.00012$$

Suppose that the percentage changes in X and Y on day $n-1$ are 0.5% and 2.5%, respectively. The variance and covariance for day n would be updated as follows:

$$\sigma_{x,n}^2 = 0.95 \times 0.01^2 + 0.05 \times 0.005^2 = 0.00009625$$

$$\sigma_{y,n}^2 = 0.95 \times 0.02^2 + 0.05 \times 0.025^2 = 0.00041125$$

$$\text{cov}_n = 0.95 \times 0.00012 + 0.05 \times 0.005 \times 0.025 = 0.00012025$$

The new volatility of X is $\sqrt{0.00009625} = 0.981\%$ and the new volatility of Y is $\sqrt{0.00041125} = 2.028\%$. The new coefficient of correlation between X and Y is

$$\frac{0.00012025}{0.00981 \times 0.02028} = 0.6044$$

GARCH models can also be used for updating covariance estimates and forecasting the future level of covariances. For example, the GARCH(1,1) model for updating a covariance is

$$\text{cov}_n = \omega + \alpha x_{n-1}\,y_{n-1} + \beta\,\text{cov}_{n-1}$$

and the long-term average covariance is $\omega/(1-\alpha-\beta)$. Formulas similar to those in equations (19.13) and (19.14) can be developed for forecasting future covariances and calculating the average covariance during the life of an option.[15]

Consistency Condition for Covariances

Once all the variances and covariances have been calculated, a variance–covariance matrix can be constructed. When $i \neq j$, the (i, j) element of this matrix shows the covariance between variable i and variable j. When $i = j$, it shows the variance of variable i.

[15] The ideas in this chapter can be extended to multivariate GARCH models, where an entire variance–covariance matrix is updated in a consistent way. For a discussion of alternative approaches, see R. Engle and J. Mezrich, "GARCH for Groups," *Risk*, August 1996: 36–40.

Not all variance–covariance matrices are internally consistent. The condition for an $N \times N$ variance–covariance matrix Ω to be internally consistent is

$$w^{\mathsf{T}} \Omega w \geqslant 0 \tag{19.17}$$

for all $N \times 1$ vectors w, where w^{T} is the transpose of w. A matrix that satisfies this property is known as *positive-semidefinite*.

To understand why the condition in equation (19.17) must hold, suppose that w^{T} is $[w_1, w_2, \dots, w_n]$. The expression $w^{\mathsf{T}} \Omega w$ is the variance of $w_1 x_1 + w_2 x_2 + \cdots + w_n x_n$, where x_i is the value of variable i. As such, it cannot be negative.

To ensure that a positive-semidefinite matrix is produced, variances and covariances should be calculated consistently. For example, if variances are calculated by giving equal weight to the last m data items, the same should be done for covariances. If variances are updated using an EWMA model with $\lambda = 0.94$, the same should be done for covariances.

An example of a variance–covariance matrix that is not internally consistent is

$$\begin{bmatrix} 1 & 0 & 0.9 \\ 0 & 1 & 0.9 \\ 0.9 & 0.9 & 1 \end{bmatrix}$$

The variance of each variable is 1.0, and so the covariances are also coefficients of correlation. The first variable is highly correlated with the third variable and the second variable is highly correlated with the third variable. However, there is no correlation at all between the first and second variables. This seems strange. When we set w equal to $(1, 1, -1)$, we find that the condition in equation (19.17) is not satisfied, proving that the matrix is not positive-semidefinite.[16]

SUMMARY

Most popular option pricing models, such as Black–Scholes, assume that the volatility of the underlying asset is constant. This assumption is far from perfect. In practice, the volatility of an asset, like the asset's price, is a stochastic variable. Unlike the asset price, it is not directly observable. This chapter has discussed schemes for attempting to keep track of the current level of volatility.

We define u_i as the percentage change in a market variable between the end of day $i - 1$ and the end of day i. The variance rate of the market variable (that is, the square of its volatility) is calculated as a weighted average of the u_i^2. The key feature of the schemes that have been discussed here is that they do not give equal weight to the observations on the u_i^2. The more recent an observation, the greater the weight assigned to it. In the EWMA and the GARCH(1,1) models, the weights assigned to observations decrease exponentially as the observations become older. The GARCH(1,1) model differs from the EWMA model in that some weight is also assigned to the long-run average variance rate. Both the EWMA and GARCH(1,1) models have structures that enable forecasts of the future level of variance rate to be produced relatively easily.

[16] It can be shown that the condition for a 3×3 matrix of correlations to be internally consistent is

$$\rho_{12}^2 + \rho_{13}^2 + \rho_{23}^2 - 2\rho_{12}\rho_{13}\rho_{23} \leqslant 1$$

where ρ_{ij} is the coefficient of correlation between variables i and j.

Maximum likelihood methods are usually used to estimate parameters from historical data in GARCH(1,1) and similar models. These methods involve using an iterative procedure to determine the parameter values that maximize the chance or likelihood that the historical data will occur. Once its parameters have been determined, a model can be judged by how well it removes autocorrelation from the u_i^2.

For every model that is developed to track variances, there is a corresponding model that can be developed to track covariances. The procedures described here can therefore be used to update the complete variance–covariance matrix used in value at risk calculations.

FURTHER READING

Bollerslev, T. "Generalized Autoregressive Conditional Heteroscedasticity," *Journal of Econometrics*, 31 (1986): 307–27.

Cumby, R., S. Figlewski, and J. Hasbrook. "Forecasting Volatilities and Correlations with EGARCH Models," *Journal of Derivatives*, 1, 2 (Winter 1993): 51–63.

Engle, R. F. "Autoregressive Conditional Heteroscedasticity with Estimates of the Variance of UK Inflation," *Econometrica* 50 (1982): 987–1008.

Engle R. F., and J. Mezrich. "Grappling with GARCH," *Risk*, September 1995: 112–117.

Engle, R. F., and J. Mezrich, "GARCH for Groups," *Risk*, August 1996: 36–40.

Engle, R. F., and V. Ng, "Measuring and Testing the Impact of News on Volatility," *Journal of Finance*, 48 (1993): 1749–78.

Nelson, D. "Conditional Heteroscedasticity and Asset Returns: A New Approach," *Econometrica*, 59 (1990): 347–70.

Noh, J., R. F. Engle, and A. Kane. "Forecasting Volatility and Option Prices of the S&P 500 Index," *Journal of Derivatives*, 2 (1994): 17–30.

Questions and Problems (Answers in Solutions Manual)

19.1. Explain the exponentially weighted moving average (EWMA) model for estimating volatility from historical data.

19.2. What is the difference between the exponentially weighted moving average model and the GARCH(1,1) model for updating volatilities?

19.3. The most recent estimate of the daily volatility of an asset is 1.5% and the price of the asset at the close of trading yesterday was \$30.00. The parameter λ in the EWMA model is 0.94. Suppose that the price of the asset at the close of trading today is \$30.50. How will this cause the volatility to be updated by the EWMA model?

19.4. A company uses an EWMA model for forecasting volatility. It decides to change the parameter λ from 0.95 to 0.85. Explain the likely impact on the forecasts.

19.5. The volatility of a certain market variable is 30% per annum. Calculate a 99% confidence interval for the size of the percentage daily change in the variable.

19.6. A company uses the GARCH(1,1) model for updating volatility. The three parameters are ω, α, and β. Describe the impact of making a small increase in each of the parameters while keeping the others fixed.

19.7. The most recent estimate of the daily volatility of the US dollar/sterling exchange rate is 0.6% and the exchange rate at 4 p.m. yesterday was 1.5000. The parameter λ in the EWMA model is 0.9. Suppose that the exchange rate at 4 p.m. today proves to be 1.4950. How would the estimate of the daily volatility be updated?

19.8. Assume that S&P 500 at close of trading yesterday was 1,040 and the daily volatility of the index was estimated as 1% per day at that time. The parameters in a GARCH(1,1) model are $\omega = 0.000002$, $\alpha = 0.06$, and $\beta = 0.92$. If the level of the index at close of trading today is 1,060, what is the new volatility estimate?

19.9. Suppose that the daily volatilities of asset A and asset B, calculated at the close of trading yesterday, are 1.6% and 2.5%, respectively. The prices of the assets at close of trading yesterday were \$20 and \$40 and the estimate of the coefficient of correlation between the returns on the two assets was 0.25. The parameter λ used in the EWMA model is 0.95.
(a) Calculate the current estimate of the covariance between the assets.
(b) On the assumption that the prices of the assets at close of trading today are \$20.5 and \$40.5, update the correlation estimate.

19.10. The parameters of a GARCH(1,1) model are estimated as $\omega = 0.000004$, $\alpha = 0.05$, and $\beta = 0.92$. What is the long-run average volatility and what is the equation describing the way that the variance rate reverts to its long-run average? If the current volatility is 20% per year, what is the expected volatility in 20 days?

19.11. Suppose that the current daily volatilities of asset X and asset Y are 1.0% and 1.2%, respectively. The prices of the assets at close of trading yesterday were \$30 and \$50 and the estimate of the coefficient of correlation between the returns on the two assets made at this time was 0.50. Correlations and volatilities are updated using a GARCH(1,1) model. The estimates of the model's parameters are $\alpha = 0.04$ and $\beta = 0.94$. For the correlation $\omega = 0.000001$, and for the volatilities $\omega = 0.000003$. If the prices of the two assets at close of trading today are \$31 and \$51, how is the correlation estimate updated?

19.12. Suppose that the daily volatility of the FTSE 100 stock index (measured in pounds sterling) is 1.8% and the daily volatility of the dollar/sterling exchange rate is 0.9%. Suppose further that the correlation between the FTSE 100 and the dollar/sterling exchange rate is 0.4. What is the volatility of the FTSE 100 when it is translated to US dollars? Assume that the dollar/sterling exchange rate is expressed as the number of US dollars per pound sterling. (*Hint*: When $Z = XY$, the percentage daily change in Z is approximately equal to the percentage daily change in X plus the percentage daily change in Y.)

19.13. Suppose that in Problem 19.12 the correlation between the S&P 500 Index (measured in dollars) and the FTSE 100 Index (measured in sterling) is 0.7, the correlation between the S&P 500 Index (measured in dollars) and the dollar/sterling exchange rate is 0.3, and the daily volatility of the S&P 500 index is 1.6%. What is the correlation between the S&P 500 index (measured in dollars) and the FTSE 100 index when it is translated to dollars? (*Hint*: For three variables X, Y, and Z, the covariance between $X + Y$ and Z equals the covariance between X and Z plus the covariance between Y and Z.)

19.14. Show that the GARCH (1,1) model $\sigma_n^2 = \omega + \alpha u_{n-1}^2 + \beta\sigma_{n-1}^2$ in equation (19.9) is equivalent to the stochastic volatility model $dV = a(V_L - V)\,dt + \xi V\,dz$, where time is measured in days, V is the square of the volatility of the asset price, and

$$a = 1 - \alpha - \beta, \qquad V_L = \frac{\omega}{1 - \alpha - \beta}, \qquad \xi = \alpha\sqrt{2}$$

What is the stochastic volatility model when time is measured in years? (*Hint*: The variable u_{n-1} is the return on the asset price in time Δt. It can be assumed to be normally distributed with mean zero and standard deviation σ_{n-1}. It follows that the mean of u_{n-1}^2 and u_{n-1}^4 are σ_{n-1}^2 and $3\sigma_{n-1}^4$, respectively.)

Assignment Questions

19.15. Suppose that the price of gold at close of trading yesterday was \$300 and its volatility was estimated as 1.3% per day. The price at the close of trading today is \$298. Update the volatility estimate using
(a) The EWMA model with $\lambda = 0.94$
(b) The GARCH(1, 1) model with $\omega = 0.000002$, $\alpha = 0.04$, and $\beta = 0.94$

19.16. Suppose that in Problem 19.15 the price of silver at the close of trading yesterday was \$8, its volatility was estimated as 1.5% per day, and its correlation with gold was estimated as 0.8. The price of silver at the close of trading today is unchanged at \$8. Update the volatility of silver and the correlation between silver and gold using the two models in Problem 19.15. In practice, is the ω parameter likely to be the same for gold and silver?

19.17. An Excel spreadsheet containing over 900 days of daily data on a number of different exchange rates and stock indices can be downloaded from the author's website:

http://www.rotman.utoronto.ca/~hull

Choose one exchange rate and one stock index. Estimate the value of λ in the EWMA model that minimizes the value of $\sum_i (v_i - \beta_i)^2$, where v_i is the variance forecast made at the end of day $i-1$ and β_i is the variance calculated from data between day i and day $i+25$. Use the Solver tool in Excel. Set the variance forecast at the end of the first day equal to the square of the return on that day to start the EWMA calculations.

19.18. Suppose that the parameters in a GARCH (1,1) model are $\alpha = 0.03$, $\beta = 0.95$, and $\omega = 0.000002$.
(a) What is the long-run average volatility?
(b) If the current volatility is 1.5% per day, what is your estimate of the volatility in 20, 40, and 60 days?
(c) What volatility should be used to price 20-, 40-, and 60-day options?
(d) Suppose that there is an event that increases the current volatility by 0.5% to 2% per day. Estimate the effect on the volatility in 20, 40, and 60 days.
(e) Estimate by how much the event increases the volatilities used to price 20-, 40-, and 60-day options? Make estimates using both equation (19.14) and equation (19.15).

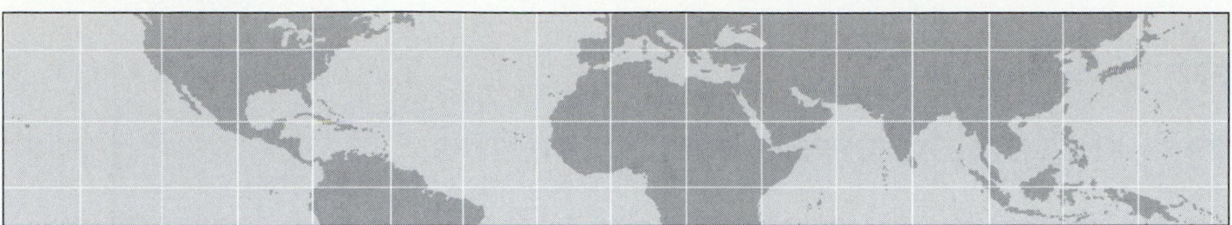

CHAPTER 20 Credit Risk

The value-at-risk measure we covered in Chapter 18 and the Greek letters we studied in Chapter 15 are aimed at quantifying market risk. In this chapter we consider another important risk for financial institutions: credit risk. Most financial institutions devote considerable resources to the measurement and management of credit risk. Regulators have for many years required banks to keep capital to reflect the credit risks they are bearing. (This capital is in addition to the capital, described in Business Snapshot 18.1, that they are required to keep for market risk.)

Credit risk arises from the possibility that borrowers and counterparties in derivatives transactions may default. In this chapter we focus on the quantification of credit risk. We discuss a number of different approaches to estimating the probability that a company will default and explain the key difference between risk-neutral and real-world probabilities of default. We examine the nature of the credit risk in over-the-counter derivatives transactions and discuss the clauses derivatives dealers write into their contracts to reduce credit risk. Finally we cover default correlation, Gaussian copula models, and the estimation of credit value at risk.

Chapter 21 will discuss credit derivatives and show how ideas introduced in this chapter can be used to value these instruments.

20.1 CREDIT RATINGS

Rating agencies such as Moody's and S&P are in the business of providing ratings describing the creditworthiness of corporate bonds. Using the Moody's system, the best rating is Aaa. Bonds with this rating are considered to have almost no chance of defaulting. The next best rating is Aa. Following that comes A, Baa, Ba, B, and Caa. Only bonds with ratings of Baa or above are considered to be *investment grade*. The S&P ratings corresponding to Moody's Aaa, Aa, A, Baa, Ba, B, and Caa are AAA, AA, A, BBB, BB, B, and CCC, respectively. To create finer rating measures, Moody's divides the Aa rating category into Aa1, Aa2, and Aa3; it divides A into A1, A2 and A3; and so on. Similarly S&P divides its AA rating category into AA+, AA, and AA−; it divides its A rating category into A+, A, and A−; and so on. (Only the Aaa category for Moody's and the AAA category for S&P are not subdivided.)

20.2 HISTORICAL DEFAULT PROBABILITIES

Table 20.1 is typical of the data that is produced by rating agencies. It shows the default experience through time of companies that started with a certain credit rating. For example, Table 20.1 shows that a bond issue with an initial credit rating of Baa has a 0.20% chance of defaulting by the end of the first year, a 0.57% chance of defaulting by the end of the second year, and so on. The probability of a bond defaulting during a particular year can be calculated from the table. For example, the probability that a bond initially rated Baa will default during the second year of its life is $0.57 - 0.20 = 0.37\%$.

Table 20.1 shows that, for investment grade bonds, the probability of default in a year tends to be an increasing function of time (e.g., the probabilities of an A-rated bond defaulting during years 1, 2, 3, 4, and 5 are 0.02%, 0.07%, 0.14%, 0.15%, and 0.16%, respectively). This is because the bond issuer is initially considered to be creditworthy, and the more time that elapses, the greater the possibility that its financial health will decline. For bonds with a poor credit rating, the probability of default is often a decreasing function of time (e.g., the probabilities that a Caa-rated bond will default during years 1, 2, 3, 4, and 5 are 23.65%, 13.55%, 10.82%, 7.54%, and 5.27%, respectively). The reason here is that, for a bond with a poor credit rating, the next year or two may be critical. If the issuer survives this period, its financial health is likely to have improved.

Default Intensities

From Table 20.1 we can calculate the probability of a Caa bond defaulting during the third year as $48.02 - 37.20 = 10.82\%$. We will refer to this as the *unconditional default probability*. It is the probability of default during the third year as seen at time 0. The probability that the Caa-rated bond will survive until the end of year 2 is $100 - 37.20 = 62.80\%$. The probability that it will default during the third year conditional on no earlier default is therefore 0.1082/0.6280, or 17.23%. Conditional default probabilities are referred to as *default intensities* or *hazard rates*.

The 17.23% we have just calculated is for a 1-year time period. Suppose instead that we consider a short time period of length Δt. The default intensity $\lambda(t)$ at time t is then defined so that $\lambda(t)\,\Delta t$ is the probability of default between time t and $t + \Delta t$ conditional on no earlier default. If $V(t)$ is the cumulative probability of the company surviving to

Table 20.1 Average cumulative default rates (%), 1970–2003. (Source: Moody's)

Term (years)	*1*	*2*	*3*	*4*	*5*	*7*	*10*	*15*	*20*
Aaa	0.00	0.00	0.00	0.04	0.12	0.29	0.62	1.21	1.55
Aa	0.02	0.03	0.06	0.15	0.24	0.43	0.68	1.51	2.70
A	0.02	0.09	0.23	0.38	0.54	0.91	1.59	2.94	5.24
Baa	0.20	0.57	1.03	1.62	2.16	3.24	5.10	9.12	12.59
Ba	1.26	3.48	6.00	8.59	11.17	15.44	21.01	30.88	38.56
B	6.21	13.76	20.65	26.66	31.99	40.79	50.02	59.21	60.73
Caa	23.65	37.20	48.02	55.56	60.83	69.36	77.91	80.23	80.23

time t (i.e., no default by time t), then

$$V(t + \Delta t) - V(t) = -\lambda(t)V(t)\,\Delta t$$

Taking limits

$$\frac{dV(t)}{dt} = -\lambda(t)V(t)$$

from which we get

$$V(t) = e^{-\int_0^t \lambda(\tau)d\tau}$$

Define $Q(t)$ as the probability of default by time t. It follows that

$$Q(t) = 1 - e^{-\int_0^t \lambda(\tau)d\tau}$$

or

$$Q(t) = 1 - e^{\bar{\lambda}(t)t} \tag{20.1}$$

where $\bar{\lambda}(t)$ is the average default intensity between time 0 and time t.

20.3 RECOVERY RATES

When a company goes bankrupt, those that are owed money by the company file claims against the assets of the company.[1] Sometimes there is a reorganization in which these creditors agree to a partial payment of their claims. In other cases the assets are sold by the liquidator and the proceeds are used to meet the claims as far as possible. Some claims typically have priorities over other claims and are met more fully.

The recovery rate for a bond is normally defined as the bond's market value immediately after a default, as a percent of its face value. Table 20.2 provides historical data on average recovery rates for different categories of bonds in the United States. It shows that senior secured debt holders had an average recovery rate of 51.6 cents per dollar of face value while junior subordinated debt holders had an average recovery rate of only 24.5 cents per dollar of face value.

Recovery rates are significantly negatively correlated with default rates. Moody's looked at average recovery rates and average default rates each year between 1982

Table 20.2 Recovery rates on corporate bonds as a percentage of face value, 1982–2003. (Source: Moody's)

Class	*Average recovery rate (%)*
Senior secured	51.6
Senior unsecured	36.1
Senior subordinated	32.5
Subordinated	31.1
Junior subordinated	24.5

[1] In the United States, the claim made by a bondholder is the bond's face value plus accrued interest.

and 2003. It found that the following relationship provides a good fit to the data:[2]

$$\text{Average recovery rate} = 50.3 - 6.3 \times \text{Average default rate}$$

where both the average recovery rate and the average default rate are measured as percentages.

20.4 ESTIMATING DEFAULT PROBABILITIES FROM BOND PRICES

The probability of default for a company can be estimated from the prices of bonds it has issued. The usual assumption is that the only reason a corporate bond sells for less than a similar risk-free bond is the possibility of default.[3]

Consider first an approximate calculation. Suppose that a bond yields 200 basis points more than a similar risk-free bond and that the expected recovery rate in the event of a default is 40%. The holder of a corporate bond must be expecting to lose 200 basis points (or 2% per year) from defaults. Given the recovery rate of 40%, this leads to an estimate of the probability of a default per year conditional on no earlier default of $0.02/(1 - 0.4)$, or 3.33%. In general,

$$h = \frac{s}{1 - R} \tag{20.2}$$

where h is the default intensity per year, s is the spread of the corporate bond yield over the risk-free rate, and R is the expected recovery rate.

A More Exact Calculation

For a more exact calculation, suppose that the corporate bond we have been considering lasts for 5 years, provides a coupon 6% per annum (paid semiannually) and that the yield on the corporate bond is 7% per annum (with continuous compounding). The yield on a similar risk-free bond is 5% (with continuous compounding). The yields imply that the price of the corporate bond is 95.34 and the price of the risk-free bond is 104.09. The expected loss from default over the 5-year life of the bond is therefore $104.09 - 95.34$, or \$8.75. Suppose that the probability of default per year (assumed in this simple example to be the same each year) is Q. Table 20.3 calculates the expected loss from default in terms of Q on the assumption that defaults can happen at times 0.5, 1.5, 2.5, 3.5, and 4.5 years (immediately before coupon payment dates). Risk-free rates for all maturities are assumed to be 5% (with continuous compounding).

To illustrate the calculations, consider the 3.5 year row in Table 20.2. The expected value of the risk-free bond at time 3.5 years (calculated using forward interest rates) is

$$3 + 3e^{-0.05\times0.5} + 3e^{-0.05\times1.0} + 103e^{-0.05\times1.5} = 104.34$$

[2] See D. T. Hamilton, P. Varma, S. Ou, and R. Cantor, "Default and Recovery Rates of Corporate Bond Issuers," Moody's Investor's Services, January 2004. The R^2 of the regression is 0.6. The correlation is also identified and discussed in E. I. Altman, B. Brady, A. Resti, and A. Sironi, "The Link between Default and Recovery Rates: Implications for Credit Risk Models and Procyclicality," Working Paper, New York University, 2003.

[3] This assumption is not perfect. In practice the price of a corporate bond is affected by its liquidity. The lower the liquidity, the lower the price.

Table 20.3 Calculation of loss from default on a bond in terms of the default probabilities per year, Q. Notional principal = $100.

Time (years)	*Default probability*	*Recovery amount ($)*	*Risk-free value ($)*	*Loss given default ($)*	*Discount factor*	*PV of expected loss ($)*
0.5	Q	40	106.73	66.73	0.9753	$65.08Q$
1.5	Q	40	105.97	65.97	0.9277	$61.20Q$
2.5	Q	40	105.17	65.17	0.8825	$57.52Q$
3.5	Q	40	104.34	64.34	0.8395	$54.01Q$
4.5	Q	40	103.46	63.46	0.7985	$50.67Q$
Total						$288.48Q$

Given the definition of recovery rates in the previous section, the amount recovered if there is a default is 40, so that the loss given default is 104.34 – 40, or $64.34. The present value of this loss is 54.01. The expected loss is therefore $54.01Q$.

The total expected loss is $288.48Q$. Setting this equal to 8.75, we obtain a value for Q equal to 3.03%. The calculations we have given assume that the default probability is the same in each year and that defaults take place at just one time during the year. We can extend the calculations to assume that defaults can take place more frequently. Also, instead of assuming a constant unconditional probability of default we can assume a constant default intensity or assume a particular pattern for the variation of default probabilities with time. With several bonds we can estimate several parameters describing the term structure of default probabilities. Suppose, for example, we have bonds maturing in 3, 5, 7, and 10 years. We could use the first bond to estimate a default probability per year for the first 3 years, the second bond to estimate default probability per year for years 4 and 5, the third bond to estimate a default probability for years 6 and 7, and the fourth bond to estimate a default probability for years 8, 9, and 10 (see Problems 20.15 and 20.27). The approach is analogous to the bootstrap procedure in Section 4.5 for calculating a zero-coupon yield curve.

The Risk-Free Rate

A key issue when bond prices are used to estimate default probabilities is the meaning of the terms "risk-free rate" and "risk-free bond". In equation (20.2), the spread s is the excess of the corporate bond yield over the yield on a similar risk-free bond. In Table 20.3, the risk-free value of the bond must be calculated using the risk-free rate. The benchmark risk-free rate that is usually used in quoting corporate bond yields is the yield on similar Treasury bonds. (For example, a bond trader might quote the yield on a particular corporate bond as being a spread of 250 basis points over Treasuries.)

As discussed in Section 4.1, traders usually use LIBOR/swap rates as proxies for risk-free rates when valuing derivatives. Traders also often use LIBOR/swap rates as risk-free rates when calculating default probabilities. For example, when they determine default probabilities from bond prices, the spread s in equation (20.2) is the spread of the bond yield over the LIBOR/swap rate. Also, the risk-free discount rates used in the calculations in Table 20.3 are LIBOR/swap zero rates.

Credit default swaps (which will be discussed in the next chapter) can be used to imply the risk-free rate assumed by traders. The rate used appears to be approximately equal to the LIBOR/swap rate minus 10 basis points on average.[4] This estimate is plausible. As explained in Section 7.5, the credit risk in a swap rate is the credit risk from making a series of 6-month loans to AA-rated counterparties and 10 basis points is a reasonable default risk premium for a AA-rated 6-month instrument.

Asset Swaps

In practice, traders often use asset swap spreads as a way of extracting default probabilities from bond prices. This is because asset swap spreads provide a direct estimate of the spread of bond yields over the LIBOR/swap curve.

To explain how asset swaps work, consider the situation where an asset swap spread for a particular bond is quoted as 150 basis points. There are three possible situations:

1. The bond sells for its par value of 100. The swap then involves one side (company A) paying the coupon on the bond and the other side (company B) paying LIBOR plus 150 basis points.[5]
2. The bond sells below its par value, say, for 95. The swap is then structured so that in addition to the coupons company A pays \$5 per \$100 of notional principal at the outset.
3. The underlying bond sells above par, say, for 108. Company B would then make a payment of \$8 per \$100 of principal at the outset.

The effect of all this is that the present value of the asset swap spread is the amount by which the price of the corporate bond is exceeded by the price of a similar risk-free bond where the risk-free rate is assumed to be given by the LIBOR/swap curve (see Problem 20.24). Consider again the example in Table 20.3 where the LIBOR/swap zero curve is flat at 5%. Suppose that instead of knowing the bond's price we know that the asset swap spread is 150 basis points. This means that the amount by which the value of the risk-free bond exceeds the value of the corporate bond is the present value of 150 basis points per year for 5 years. Assuming semiannual payments, this is \$6.55 per \$100 of principal.

The total loss in Table 20.3 would in this case be set equal to \$6.55. This means that the default probability per year, Q, would be 6.55/288.48, or 2.27%.

20.5 COMPARISON OF DEFAULT PROBABILITY ESTIMATES

The default probabilities estimated from historical data are much less than those derived from bond prices. Table 20.4 illustrates this.[6] It shows, for companies that start

[4] See J. Hull, M. Predescu, and A. White, "The Relationship between Credit Default Swap Spreads, Bond Yields, and Credit Rating Announcements," *Journal of Banking and Finance*, 28 (November 2004): 2789-2811.

[5] Note that it is the promised coupons that are exchanged. The exchanges take place regardless of whether the bond defaults.

[6] Tables 20.4 and 20.5 are taken from J. Hull, M. Predescu, and A. White, "Bond Prices, Default Probabilities, and Risk Premiums" *Journal of Credit Risk*, forthcoming.

with a particular rating, the average annual default intensity over 7 years calculated from (a) historical data and (b) bond prices.

The calculation of default intensities using historical data are based on equation (20.1) and Table 20.1. From equation (20.1), we have

$$\bar{\lambda}(7) = -\tfrac{1}{7}\ln[1 - Q(7)]$$

where $\bar{\lambda}(t)$ is the average default intensity (or hazard rate) by time t and $Q(t)$ is the cumulative probability of default by time t. The values of $Q(7)$ are taken directly from Table 20.1. Consider, for example, an A-rated company. The value of $Q(7)$ is 0.0091. The average 7-year default intensity is therefore

$$\bar{\lambda}(7) = -\tfrac{1}{7}\ln(0.9909) = 0.0013$$

or 0.13%.

The calculations using bond prices are based on equation (20.2) and bond yields published by Merrill Lynch. The results shown are averages between December 1996 and July 2004. The recovery rate is assumed to be 40% and, for the reasons discussed in the previous section, the risk-free interest rate is assumed to be the 7-year swap rate minus 10 basis points. For example, for A-rated bonds the average Merrill Lynch yield was 6.274%. The average swap rate was 5.605%, so that the average risk-free rate was 5.505%. This gives the average 7-year default probability as

$$\frac{0.06274 - 0.05505}{1 - 0.4} = 0.0128$$

or 1.28%.

Table 20.4 shows that the ratio of the default probability backed out of bond prices to the default probability calculated from historical data tends to decline as the credit quality declines with the ratio very high for investment grade companies. The difference between the two default probabilities tends to increase as credit quality declines.

Table 20.5 provides another way of looking at these results. It shows the excess return over the risk-free rate (still assumed to be the 7-year swap rate minus 10 basis points) earned by investors in bonds with different credit rating. Consider again an A-rated bond. The average spread over Treasuries is 120 basis points. Of this, 43 basis points are

Table 20.4 Seven-year average default intensities (% per annum).

Rating	*Historical default intensity*	*Default intensity from bonds*	*Ratio*	*Difference*
Aaa	0.04	0.67	16.8	0.63
Aa	0.06	0.78	13.0	0.72
A	0.13	1.28	9.8	1.15
Baa	0.47	2.38	5.1	1.91
Ba	2.47	5.07	2.1	2.67
B	7.69	9.02	1.2	1.53
Caa	16.90	21.30	1.3	4.40

Table 20.5 Expected excess return on bonds (basis points).

Rating	*Bond yield spread over Treasuries*	*Spread of risk-free rate over Treasuries*	*Spread for historical defaults*	*Expected excess return*
Aaa	83	43	2	38
Aa	90	43	4	43
A	120	43	8	69
Baa	186	43	28	115
Ba	347	43	144	160
B	585	43	449	93
Caa	1321	43	1014	264

accounted for by the average spread between 7-year Treasuries and our proxy for the risk-free rate. A spread of 8 basis points is necessary to cover expected defaults. (This equals the real-world probability of default from Table 20.4 times 1 minus the assumed recovery rate of 0.4.) This leaves an expected excess return (after expected defaults have been taken into account) of 69 basis points.

Tables 20.4 and 20.5 show that a large percentage difference between default probability estimates translates into a small (but significant) expected excess return on the bond. For Aaa-rated bonds the ratio of the two default probabilities is 16.8, but the expected excess return is only 38 basis points. The expected return tends to increase as credit quality declines.[7]

Real-World vs. Risk-Neutral Probabilities

The default probabilities implied from bond yields are risk-neutral probabilities of default. To explain why this is so, consider the calculations of default probabilities in Table 20.3. The calculations assume that expected default losses can be discounted at the risk-free rate. The risk-neutral valuation principle shows that this is a valid procedure providing the expected losses are calculated in a risk-neutral world. This means that the default probability Q in Table 20.3 must be a risk-neutral probability.

By contrast, the default probabilities implied from historical data are real-world default probabilities (sometimes also called *physical probabilities*). The expected excess return in Table 20.5 arises directly from the difference between real-world and risk-neutral default probabilities. If there were no expected excess return, then the real-world and risk-neutral default probabilities would be the same, and vice versa.

Why do we see such big differences between real-world and risk-neutral default probabilities? As we have just argued, this is the same as asking why corporate bond traders earn more than the risk-free rate on average. There are a number of potential reasons:

1. Corporate bonds are relatively illiquid and bond traders demand an extra return to compensate for this.

[7] The results for B-rated bonds in Tables 20.4 and 20.5 run counter to the overall pattern.

2. The subjective default probabilities of bond traders may be much higher than the those given in Tables 20.1. Bond traders may be allowing for depression scenarios much worse than anything seen during the period from 1970 to 2003.[8]
3. Bonds do not default independently of each other. This is the most important reason for the results in Tables 20.4 and 20.5. There are periods of time when default rates are very low and periods of time when they are very high.[9] This gives rise to systematic risk (i.e., risk that cannot be diversified away) and bond traders should require an expected excess return for bearing the risk. The variation in default rates from year to year may be due to overall economic conditions or it may be because a default by one company has a ripple effect resulting in defaults by other companies. (The latter is referred to by researchers as *credit contagion.*)
4. Bond returns are highly skewed with limited upside. As a result it is much more difficult to diversify risks in a bond portfolio than in an equity portfolio.[10] A very large number of different bonds must be held. In practice, many bond portfolios are far from fully diversified. As a result bond traders may require an extra return for bearing unsystematic risk in addition to the systematic risk mentioned above.

At this stage it is natural to ask whether we should use real-world or risk-neutral default probabilities in the analysis of credit risk. The answer depends on the purpose of the analysis. When valuing credit derivatives or estimating the impact of default risk on the pricing of instruments we should use risk-neutral default probabilities. This is because the analysis calculates the present value of expected future cash flows and almost invariably (implicitly or explicitly) involves using risk-neutral valuation. When carrying out scenario analyses to calculate potential future losses from defaults, we should use real-world default probabilities.

20.6 USING EQUITY PRICES TO ESTIMATE DEFAULT PROBABILITIES

When we use a table such as Table 20.1 to estimate a company's real-world probability of default, we are relying on the company's credit rating. Unfortunately, credit ratings are revised relatively infrequently. This has led some analysts to argue that equity prices can provide more up-to-date information for estimating default probabilities.

In 1974, Merton proposed a model where a company's equity is an option on the assets of the company.[11] Suppose, for simplicity, that a firm has one zero-coupon bond

[8] In addition to producing Table 20.1, which is based on the 1970 to 2003 period, Moody's produces a similar table based on the 1920 to 2003 period. When this table is used, historical default intensities for investment grade bonds in Table 20.4 rise somewhat. The Aaa default intensity increases from 4 to 6 basis points; the Aa increases from 6 to 22 basis points; the A increases from from 13 to 29 basis points; the Baa increases from 46 to 73 basis points.

[9] Evidence for this can be obtained by looking at the defaults rates in different years. Moody's statistics show that between 1970 and 2003 the default rate per year ranged from a low 0.09% in 1979 to a high of 3.81% in 2001.

[10] See J. D. Amato and E. M. Remolona, "The Credit Spread Puzzle," *BIS Quarterly Review*, 5, December 2003: 51–63.

[11] See R. Merton "On the Pricing of Corporate Debt: The Risk Structure of Interest Rates," *Journal of Finance*, 29 (1974): 449–70.

outstanding and that the bond matures at time T. Define:

V_0: Value of company's assets today
V_T: Value of company's assets at time T
E_0: Value of company's equity today
E_T: Value of company's equity at time T
D: Amount of debt interest and principal due to be repaid at time T
σ_V: Volatility of assets (assumed constant)
σ_E: Instantaneous volatility of equity.

If $V_T < D$, it is (at least in theory) rational for the company to default on the debt at time T. The value of the equity is then zero. If $V_T > D$, the company should make the debt repayment at time T and the value of the equity at this time is $V_T - D$. Merton's model, therefore, gives the value of the firm's equity at time T as

$$E_T = \max(V_T - D, 0)$$

This shows that the equity is a call option on the value of the assets with a strike price equal to the repayment required on the debt. The Black–Scholes formula gives the value of the equity today as

$$E_0 = V_0 N(d_1) - De^{-rT} N(d_2) \quad \textbf{(20.3)}$$

where

$$d_1 = \frac{\ln V_0/D + (r + \sigma_V^2/2)T}{\sigma_V\sqrt{T}} \quad \text{and} \quad d_2 = d_1 - \sigma_V\sqrt{T}$$

The value of the debt today is $V_0 - E_0$.

The risk-neutral probability that the company will default on the debt is $N(-d_2)$. To calculate this, we require V_0 and σ_V. Neither of these are directly observable. However, if the company is publicly traded, we can observe E_0. This means that equation (20.3) provides one condition that must be satisfied by V_0 and σ_V. We can also estimate σ_E. From Itô's lemma,

$$\sigma_E E_0 = \frac{\partial E}{\partial V}\sigma_V V_0$$

or

$$\sigma_E E_0 = N(d_1)\sigma_V V_0 \quad \textbf{(20.4)}$$

This provides another equation that must be satisfied by V_0 and σ_V. Equations (20.3) and (20.4) provide a pair of simultaneous equations that can be solved for V_0 and σ_V.[12]

Example 20.1

The value of a company's equity is \$3 million and the volatility of the equity is 80%. The debt that will have to be paid in 1 year is \$10 million. The risk-free rate is 5% per annum. In this case $E_0 = 3$, $\sigma_E = 0.80$, $r = 0.05$, $T = 1$, and $D = 10$. Solving equations (20.3) and (20.4) yields $V_0 = 12.40$ and $\sigma_V = 0.2123$. The parameter, d_2 is 1.1408, so that the probability of default is $N(-d_2) = 0.127$, or 12.7%. The market value of the debt is $V_0 - E_0$, or 9.40. The present value of the promised payment on the debt is $10e^{-0.05\times 1} = 9.51$. The expected loss on the

[12] To solve two nonlinear equations of the form $F(x, y) = 0$ and $G(x, y) = 0$, we can use the Solver routine in Excel to find the values of x and y that minimize $[F(x, y)]^2 + [G(x, y)]^2$.

debt is therefore (9.51 − 9.40)/9.51, or about 1.2% of its no-default value. Comparing this with the probability of default gives the expected recovery in the event of a default as (12.7 − 1.2)/12.7, or about 91%.

The basic Merton model we have just presented has been extended in a number of ways. For example, one version of the model assumes that a default occurs whenever the value of the assets falls below a barrier level.

How well do the default probabilities produced by Merton's model and its extensions correspond to actual default experience? The answer is that Merton's model and its extensions produce a good ranking of default probabilities (risk-neutral or real-world). This means that monotonic transformation can be used to convert the probability of default output from Merton's model into a good estimate of either the real-world or risk-neutral default probability.[13]

20.7 CREDIT RISK IN DERIVATIVES TRANSACTIONS

The credit exposure on a derivatives transaction is more complicated than that on a loan. This is because the claim that will be made in the event of a default is more uncertain. Consider a financial institution that has one derivatives contract outstanding with a counterparty. We can distinguish three possible situations:

1. Contract is always a liability to the financial institution
2. Contract is always an asset to the financial institution
3. Contract can become either an asset or a liability to the financial institution

An example of a derivatives contract in the first category is a short option position; an example in the second category is a long option position; an example in the third category is a forward contract.

Derivatives in the first category have no credit risk to the financial institution. If the counterparty goes bankrupt, there will be no loss. The derivative is one of the counterparty's assets. It is likely to be retained, closed out, or sold to a third party. The result is no loss (or gain) to the financial institution.

Derivatives in the second category always have credit risk to the financial institution. If the counterparty goes bankrupt, a loss is likely to be experienced. The derivative is one of the counterparty's liabilities. The financial institution has to make a claim against the assets of the counterparty and may receive some percentage of the value of the derivative.

Derivatives in the third category may or may not have credit risk. If the counterparty defaults when the value of the derivative is positive to the financial institution, a claim will be made against the assets of the counterparty and a loss is likely to be experienced. If the counterparty defaults when the value is negative to the financial institution, no loss is made because the derivative will be retained, closed out, or sold to a third party.[14]

[13] Moody's KMV provides a service that transforms a default probability produced by Merton's model into a real-world default probability (which it refers to as an EDF, short for expected default frequency). CreditGrades use Merton's model to estimate credit spreads, which are closely linked to risk-neutral default probabilities.

[14] Note that a company usually defaults because of the total value of its assets and liabilities, not because of the value of any one transaction.

Adjusting Derivatives' Valuations for Counterparty Default Risk

How should a financial institution (or end-user of derivatives) adjust the value of a derivative to allow for counterparty credit risk? Consider a derivative that has a value of f_0 today assuming no defaults. Let us suppose that defaults can take place at times $t_1, t_2, \dots, t_n$ and that the value of the derivative to the financial institution (assuming no defaults) at time t_i is f_i. Define the risk-neutral probability of default at time t_i as q_i and the expected recovery rate as R.[15]

The exposure at time t_i is the financial institution's potential loss. This is $\max(f_i, 0)$. Assume that the expected recovery in the event of a default is R times the exposure. Assume also that the recovery rate and the probability of default is independent of the value of the derivative. The risk-neutral expected loss from default at time t_i is

$$q_i(1-R)\hat{E}[\max(f_i, 0)]$$

where $\hat{E}$ denotes expected value in a risk-neutral world. Taking present values leads to the cost of defaults being

$$\sum_{i=1}^{n} u_i v_i \tag{20.5}$$

where u_i equals $q_i(1-R)$ and v_i is the value today of an instrument that pays off the exposure on the derivative under consideration at time t_i.

Consider again the three categories of derivatives mentioned earlier. The first category (where the derivative is always a liability to the financial institution) is easy to deal with. The value of f_i is always negative and so the total expected loss from defaults given by equation (20.5) is always zero. The financial institution needs to make no adjustments for the cost of defaults. (Of course, the counterparty may want to take account of the possibility of the financial institution defaulting in its own pricing.)

For the second category (where the derivative is always an asset to the financial institution) f_i is always positive. The expression $\max(f_i, 0)$ is always equal to f_i. Since v_i is the present value of f_i, it always equals f_0.[16] The expected loss from default is therefore f_0 times the total probability of default during the life of the derivative times $1 - R$.

Example 20.2

> Consider a 2-year over-the-counter option with a value (assuming no defaults) of \$3. Suppose that the company selling the option has a risk-neutral probability of defaulting during the 2-year period of 4% and the recovery in the event of a default is 25%. The expected cost of defaults is $3 \times 0.04 \times (1 - 0.25)$, or \$0.09. The buyer of the option should therefore be prepared to pay only \$2.91.

For the third category of derivatives, the sign of f_i is uncertain. The variable v_i is a call option on f_i with a strike price of zero. One way of calculating v_i is to simulate the underlying market variables over the life of the derivative. Sometimes approximate analytic calculations are possible (see, e.g., Problems 20.17 and 20.18).

---

[15] The probability of default could be calculated from bond prices in the way described in Section 20.4.

[16] This assumes no payoffs from the derivative prior to time t_i.

The analyses we have presented assume that the probability of default is independent of the value of the derivative. This is likely to be a reasonable approximation in circumstances when the derivative is a small part of the portfolio of the counterparty or when the counterparty is using the derivative for hedging purposes. When a counterparty wants to enter into a large derivatives transaction for speculative purposes a financial institution should be wary. When the transaction has a large negative value for the counterparty (and a large positive value for the financial institution), the chance of counterparty declaring bankruptcy may be much higher than when the situation is the other way round.

20.8 CREDIT RISK MITIGATION

In many instances the analysis we just have presented overstates the credit risk in a derivatives transaction. This is because there are a number of clauses that derivatives dealers include in their contracts to mitigate credit risk.

Netting

A clause that has become standard in over-the-counter derivatives contracts is known as *netting*. This states that if a company defaults on one contract it has with a counterparty then it must default on all outstanding contracts with the counterparty.

Netting has been successfully tested in the courts in most jurisdictions. It can substantially reduce credit risk for a financial institution. Consider, for example, a financial institution that has three contracts outstanding with a particular counterparty. The contracts are worth +\$10 million, +\$30 million, and −\$25 million to the financial institution. Suppose the counterparty runs into financial difficulties and defaults on its outstanding obligations. To the counterparty the three contracts have values of −\$10 million, −\$30 million, and +\$25 million, respectively. Without netting, the counterparty would default on the first two contracts and retain the third for a loss to the financial institution of \$40 million. With netting, it is compelled to default on all three contracts for a loss to the financial institution of \$15 million.[17]

Suppose a financial institution has a portfolio of N derivatives contracts with a particular counterparty. Suppose that the no-default value of the ith contract is V_i and the amount recovered in the event of default is the recovery rate times this no default value. Without netting, the financial institution loses

$$(1 - R)\sum_{i=1}^{N} \max(V_i, 0)$$

where R is the recovery rate. With netting, it loses

$$(1 - R)\max\left(\sum_{i=1}^{N} V_i, 0\right)$$

Without netting, its loss is the payoff from a portfolio of call options on the contract values where each option has a strike price of zero. With netting, it is the payoff from a

[17] Note that if the third contract were worth −\$45 million to the financial institution instead of −\$25 million, the counterparty would choose not to default and there would be no loss to the financial institution.

single option on the value of the portfolio of contracts. The value of an option on a portfolio is never greater than, and is often considerably less than, the value of the corresponding portfolio of options.

We can extend the analysis presented in the previous section so that equation (20.5) gives the present value of the expected loss from all contracts with a counterparty when netting agreements are in place. This is achieved by redefining v_i in the equation as the present value of a derivative that pays off the exposure at time t_i on the portfolio of all contracts with a counterparty.

A challenging task for a financial institution when considering whether it should enter into a new derivatives contract with a counterparty is to calculate the incremental effect on expected credit losses. This can be done by using equation (20.5) in the way just described to calculate expected default costs with and without the contract. It is interesting to note that, because of netting, the incremental effect of a new contract on expected default losses can be negative. This happens when the value of the new contract is negatively correlated with the value of existing contracts.

Collateralization

Another clause frequently used to mitigate credit risks is known as *collateralization*. Suppose that a company and a financial institution have entered into a number of derivatives contracts. A typical collateralization agreement specifies that the contracts be marked to market periodically using a pre-agreed formula. If the total value of the contracts to the financial institution is above a certain threshold level on a certain day, it can ask the company to post collateral. The amount of collateral posted when added to collateral already posted by the company is equal to the difference between the value of the contract to the financial institution and the threshold level. When the contract moves in favor of the company so that the difference between value of the contract to the financial institution and the threshold level is less than the total margin already posted, the company can reclaim margin. In the event of a default by the company, the financial institution can seize the collateral. If the company does not post collateral as required, the financial institution can close out the contracts.

Suppose, for example, that the threshold level for the company is \$10 million and contract is marked to market daily for the purposes of collateralization. If on a particular day the value of the contract to financial institution is \$10.5 million, it can ask for \$0.5 million of collateral. If the next day the value of the contract rises further to \$11.4 million it can ask for a further \$0.9 million of collateral. If the value of the contract falls to \$10.9 million on the following day, the company can ask for \$0.5 million of the collateral to be returned. Note that the threshold (\$10 million in this case) can be regarded as a line of credit that the financial institution is prepared to grant to the company.

The margin must be deposited by the company with the financial institution in cash or in the form of acceptable securities such as bonds. The securities are subject to a discount known as a *haircut* applied to their market value for the purposes of margin calculations. Interest is normally paid on cash.

If the collateralization agreement is a two-way agreement a threshold will also be specified for the financial institution. The company can then ask the financial institution to post collateral when the mark-to-market value of the outstanding contracts to the company exceeds the threshold.

Collateralization agreements provide a great deal of protection against the possibility of default (just as the margin accounts discussed in Chapter 2 provide protection for people who trade on an exchange). However, the threshold amount is not subject to protection. Furthermore, even when the threshold is zero, the protection is not total. When a company gets into financial difficulties, it is likely to stop responding to requests to post collateral. By the time the counterparty exercises its right to close out contracts, their value may have moved further in its favor.

Downgrade Triggers

Another credit mitigation technique used by a financial institution is known as a *downgrade trigger*. This is a clause stating that if the credit rating of the counterparty falls below a certain level, say Baa, the financial institution has the option to close out a derivatives contract at its market value. (As in the case of collateralization agreements, a formula for determining the market value must be agreed in advance.)

Downgrade triggers do not provide protection from a big jump in a company's credit rating (for example, from A to default). Also, downgrade triggers work well only if relatively little use is made of them. If a company has entered into many downgrade triggers with its counterparties, they are liable to provide relatively little protection to the counterparties (see Business Snapshot 20.1).

20.9 DEFAULT CORRELATION

The term *default correlation* is used to describe the tendency for two companies to default at about the same time. There are a number of reasons why default correlations exist. Companies in the same industry or the same geographic region tend to be affected similarly by external events and as a result may experience financial difficulties at the same time. Economic conditions generally cause average default rates to be higher in some years than in other years. A default by one company may cause a default by another—the credit contagion effect mentioned in Section 20.5. Default correlation means that credit risk cannot be completely diversified away and is the major reason why risk-neutral default probabilities are greater than real-world default probabilities (see Section 20.5).

Default correlation is important to the determination of probability distributions for default losses from a portfolio of exposures to different counterparties. Two types of default correlation models that have been suggested by researchers are referred to as *reduced form models* and *structural models*.

Reduced form models assume that the default intensities for different companies follow stochastic processes and are correlated with macroeconomic variables. When the default intensity for company A is high there is a tendency for the default intensity for company B to be high. This induces a default correlation between the two companies.

Reduced form models are mathematically attractive and reflect the tendency for economic cycles to generate default correlations. Their main disadvantage is that the range of default correlations that can be achieved is limited. Even when there is a perfect correlation between two default intensities, the corresponding correlation between defaults in any chosen period of time is usually quite low. This is liable to be a problem in some circumstances. For example, when two companies operate in the

> **Business Snapshot 20.1** Downgrade Triggers and Enron's Bankruptcy
>
> In December 2001, Enron, one of the largest companies in the United States, went bankrupt. Right up to the last few days, it had an investment grade credit rating. The Moody's rating immediately prior to default was Baa3 and the S&P rating was BBB−. The default was, however, anticipated to some extent by the stock market because Enron's stock price fell sharply in the period leading up to the bankruptcy. The probability of default estimated by models such as the one described in Section 20.6 increased sharply during this period.
>
> Enron had entered into a huge number of derivatives contracts with downgrade triggers. The downgrade triggers stated that, if its credit rating fell below investment grade (i.e., below Baa3/BBB−), its counterparties would have the option of closing out contracts. Suppose that Enron had been downgraded to below investment grade in, say, October 2001. The contracts that counterparties would choose to close out would be those with negative values to Enron (and positive values to the counterparties). So, Enron would have been required to make huge cash payments to its counterparties. It would not have been able to do this and immediate bankruptcy would result.
>
> This example illustrates that downgrade triggers provide protection only when relatively little use is made of them. When a company enters into a huge number of contracts with downgrade triggers, they may actually cause a company to go bankrupt prematurely. In Enron's case, we could argue that it was going to go bankrupt anyway and accelerating the event by two months would not have done any harm. In fact, Enron did have a chance of survival in October 2001. Attempts were being made to work out a deal with another energy company, Dynergy, and so forcing bankruptcy in October 2001 was not in the interests of either creditors or shareholders.
>
> The credit rating companies found themselves in a difficult position. If they downgraded Enron to recognize its deteriorating financial position, they were signing its death warrant. If they did not do so, there was a chance of Enron surviving.

same industry and the same country or when the financial health of one company is for some reason heavily dependent on the financial health of another company, a relatively high default correlation may be warranted. One approach to solving this problem is by extending the model so that the default intensity exhibits large jumps.

Structural models are based on a model similar to Merton's model (see Section 20.6). A company defaults if the value of its assets is below a certain level. Default correlation between companies A and B is introduced into the model by assuming that the stochastic process followed by the assets of company A is correlated with the stochastic process followed by the assets of company B. Structural models have the advantage over reduced form models that the correlation can be made as high as desired. Their main disadvantage is that they are liable to be computationally quite slow.

The Gaussian Copula Model for Time to Default

A reduced form default correlation model that has become a popular practical tool is the Gaussian copula model for the time to default. This quantifies the correlation between the times to default for two different companies. The model implicitly assumes that all companies will default eventually. But in any application of the model we are typically only interested in the possibility of defaults over the next 1 year, 5 years, or 10 years. We are therefore only interested in the left tail of the distribution of the time to default.

The model can be used in conjunction with either real-world or risk-neutral default probabilities. The left tail of the real-world probability distribution for the time to default of a company can be estimated from data produced by rating agencies such as that in Table 20.1. The left tail of the risk-neutral probability distribution of the time to default can be estimated from bond prices using the approach in Section 20.4.

Define t_1 as the time to default of company 1 and t_2 as the time to default of company 2. If the probability distributions of t_1 and t_2 were normal, we could assume that the joint probability distribution of t_1 and t_2 is bivariate normal. As it happens, the probability distribution of a company's time to default is not even approximately normal. This is where a Gaussian copula model comes in. We transform t_1 and t_2 into new variables x_1 and x_2 using

$$x_1 = N^{-1}[Q_1(t_1)], \qquad x_2 = N^{-1}[Q_2(t_2)]$$

where Q_1 and Q_2 are the cumulative probability distributions for t_1 and t_2, respectively, and N^{-1} is the inverse of the cumulative normal distribution ($u = N^{-1}(v)$ when $v = N(u)$). These are "percentile-to-percentile" transformations. The 5-percentile point in the probability distribution for t_1 is transformed to $x_1 = -1.645$, which is the 5-percentile point in the standard normal distribution; the 10-percentile point in the probability distribution for t_1 is transformed to $x_1 = -1.282$, which is the 10-percentile point in the standard normal distribution, and so on. The t_2-to-x_2 transformation is similar.

By construction, x_1 and x_2 have normal distributions with mean zero and unit standard deviation. We assume that the joint distribution of x_1 and x_2 is bivariate normal with correlation ρ_{12}. This assumption is referred to as using a *Gaussian copula*. The assumption is convenient because it means that the joint probability distribution of t_1 and t_2 is fully defined by the cumulative default probability distributions Q_1 and Q_2 for t_1 and t_2, together with a single correlation parameter ρ_{12}.

The attraction of the Gaussian copula model is that it can be extended to many companies. Suppose that we are considering n companies and that t_i is the time to default of the ith company. We transform each t_i into a new variable, x_i, that has a standard normal distribution. The transformation is the percentile-to-percentile transformation

$$x_i = N^{-1}[Q_i(t_i)]$$

where Q_i is the cumulative probability distribution for t_i. We then assume that the x_i are multivariate normal. The default correlation between t_i and t_j is measured as the correlation between x_i and x_j. This is referred to as the copula correlation.[18]

The Gaussian copula approach is a useful way representing the correlation structure between variables that are not normally distributed. It allows the correlation structure of the variables to be estimated separately from their marginal (unconditional) distributions. Although the variables themselves are not multivariate normal, the approach assumes that after a transformation is applied to each variable they are multivariate normal.

---

[18] As an approximation, the copula correlation between t_i and t_j is often assumed to be the correlation between the equity returns for companies i and j.

Example 20.3

Suppose that we wish to simulate defaults during the next 5 years in 10 companies. The copula default correlations between each pair of companies is 0.2. For each company the cumulative probability of a default during the next 1, 2, 3, 4, 5 years is 1%, 3%, 6%, 10%, 15%, respectively. When a Gaussian copula is used we sample from a multivariate normal distribution to obtain the x_i $(1 \leqslant i \leqslant 10)$ with the pairwise correlation between the x_i being 0.2. We then convert the x_i to t_i, a time to default. When the sample from the normal distribution is less than $N^{-1}(0.01) = -2.33$, a default takes place within the first year; when the sample is between -2.33 and $N^{-1}(0.03) = -1.88$, a default takes place during the second year; when the sample is between -1.88 and $N^{-1}(0.06) = -1.55$, a default takes place during the third year; when the sample is between -1.55 and $N^{-1}(0.10) = -1.28$, a default takes place during the fourth year; when the sample is between -1.28 and $N^{-1}(0.15) = -1.04$, a default takes place during the fifth year. When the sample is greater than -1.04, there is no default during the 5 years.

Using Factors to Define the Correlation Structure

To avoid defining a different correlation between x_i and x_j for each pair of companies i and j in the Gaussian copula model, a one-factor model is often used. The assumption is that

$$x_i = a_i M + \sqrt{1 - a_i^2}\, Z_i \tag{20.6}$$

Here M is a common factor affecting defaults for all companies and Z_i is a factor affecting only company i. The variables M and the Z_i have independent standard normal distributions. The a_i are constant parameters between -1 and $+1$. The correlation between x_i and x_j is $a_i a_j$.[19]

Suppose that the probability that company i will default by a particular time T is $Q_i(T)$. Under the Gaussian copula model, a default happens when $N(x_i) < Q_i(T)$ or $x_i < N^{-1}[Q_i(T)]$. From equation (20.6), this condition is

$$a_i M + \sqrt{1 - a_i^2}\, Z_i < N^{-1}[Q_i(T)]$$

or

$$Z_i < \frac{N^{-1}[Q_i(T)] - a_i M}{\sqrt{1 - a_i^2}}$$

Conditional on the value of the factor M, the probability of default is therefore

$$Q_i(T \mid M) = N\left(\frac{N^{-1}[Q_i(T)] - a_i M}{\sqrt{1 - a_i^2}}\right) \tag{20.7}$$

A particular case of the one-factor Gaussian model is where the probability distributions of default are the same for all i and the correlations between x_i and x_j is the same for all i and j. Suppose that $Q_i(T) = Q(T)$ for all i and that the common correlation

[19] The parameter a_i is sometimes approximated as the correlation of company i's equity returns with a well-diversified market index.

is ρ, so that $a_i = \sqrt{\rho}$ for all i. Equation (20.7) becomes

$$Q(T|M) = N\left(\frac{N^{-1}[Q(T)] - \sqrt{\rho}\,M}{\sqrt{1-\rho}}\right) \tag{20.8}$$

Binomial Correlation Measure

An alternative correlation measure used by rating agencies is the *binomial correlation measure*. For two companies A and B, this is the coefficient of correlation between:

1. A variable that equals 1 if company A defaults between times 0 and T, and 0 otherwise; and
2. A variable that equals 1 if company B defaults between times 0 and T, and 0 otherwise.

The measure is

$$\beta_{AB}(T) = \frac{P_{AB}(T) - Q_A(T)Q_B(T)}{\sqrt{[Q_A(T) - Q_A(T)^2][Q_B(T) - Q_B(T)^2]}} \tag{20.9}$$

where $P_{AB}(T)$ is the joint probability of A and B defaulting between time 0 and time T, $Q_A(T)$ is the cumulative probability that company A will default by time T, and $Q_B(T)$ is the cumulative probability that company B will default by time T. Typically $\beta_{AB}(T)$ depends on T, the length of the time period considered. Usually it increases as T increases.

From the definition of a Gaussian copula model, $P_{AB}(T) = M[x_A(T), x_B(T); \rho_{AB}]$, where $x_A(T) = N^{-1}(Q_A(T))$ and $x_B(T) = N^{-1}(Q_B(T))$ are the transformed times to default for companies A and B, and ρ_{AB} is the Gaussian copula correlation for the times to default for A and B. Here, $M(a, b; \rho)$ is the probability that, in a bivariate normal distribution where the correlation between the variables is ρ, the first variable is less than a and the second variable is less than b.[20] It follows that

$$\beta_{AB}(T) = \frac{M[x_A(T), x_B(T); \rho_{AB}] - Q_A(T)Q_B(T)}{\sqrt{[Q_A(T) - Q_A(T)^2][Q_B(T) - Q_B(T)^2]}} \tag{20.10}$$

This shows that, if $Q_A(T)$ and $Q_B(T)$ are known, $\beta_{AB}(T)$ can be calculated from ρ_{AB} and vice versa. Usually ρ_{AB} is markedly greater than $\beta_{AB}(T)$. This illustrates the important point that the magnitude of a correlation measure depends on the way it is defined.

Example 20.4

Suppose that the probability of company A defaulting in a 1-year period is 1% and the probability of company B defaulting in a 1-year period is also 1%. In this case, $x_A(1) = x_B(1) = N^{-1}(0.01) = -2.326$. If ρ_{AB} is 0.20, $M(x_A(1), x_B(1), \rho_{AB}) = 0.000337$ and equation (20.10) shows that $\beta_{AB}(T) = 0.024$ when $T = 1$.

20.10 CREDIT VaR

Credit value at risk can be defined analogously to the way we defined value at risk for market risks in Chapter 18. For example, a credit VaR with a confidence level of 99.9%

[20] See Technical Note 5 on the author's website for the calculation of $M(a, b; \rho)$.

and a 1-year time horizon is the credit loss that we are 99.9% confident will not be exceeded over 1 year.

Consider a bank with a very large portfolio of similar loans. As an approximation we assume that the probability of default is the same for each loan and the correlation between each pair of loans is the same. When the Gaussian copula model for time to default is used, the right-hand side of equation (20.8) is approximately equal to the percentage of defaults by time T as a function of M. The factor M has a standard normal distribution. We are $X\%$ certain that its value will be greater than $N^{-1}(1-X) = -N^{-1}(X)$. We are therefore $X\%$ certain that the percentage of losses over T years on a large portfolio will be less than $V(X, T)$, where

$$V(X, T) = N\left(\frac{N^{-1}[Q(T)] + \sqrt{\rho}\,N^{-1}(X)}{\sqrt{1-\rho}}\right) \tag{20.11}$$

This result was first produced by Vasicek.[21] As in equation (20.8), $Q(T)$ is the probability of default by time T and ρ is the copula correlation between any pair of loans.

A rough estimate of the credit VaR when an $X\%$ confidence level is used and the time horizon is T is therefore $L(1-R)V(X, T)$, where L is the size of the loan portfolio and R is the recovery rate. The contribution of a particular loan of size L_i to the credit VaR is $L_i(1-R)V(X, T)$. This model underlies the formulas that regulators are planning to use for credit risk capital (see Business Snapshot 20.2).

Example 20.4

Suppose that a bank has a total of \$100 million of retail exposures. The 1-year probability of default averages 2% and the recovery rate averages 60%. The copula correlation parameter is estimated as 0.1. In this case,

$$V(0.999, 1) = N\left(\frac{N^{-1}(0.02) + \sqrt{0.1}\,N^{-1}(0.999)}{\sqrt{1-0.1}}\right) = 0.128$$

showing that the 99.9% worst case default rate is 12.8%. The 1-year 99.9% credit VaR is therefore $100 \times 0.128 \times (1-0.6)$ or \$5.13 million.

CreditMetrics

Many bank's have developed other procedures for calculating credit VaR for internal use. One popular approach is known as CreditMetrics. This involves estimating a probability distribution of credit losses by carrying out a Monte Carlo simulation of the credit rating changes of all counterparties. Suppose we are interested in determining the probability distribution of losses over a 1-year period. On each simulation trial, we sample to determine the credit rating changes and defaults of all counterparties during the year. We then revalue our outstanding contracts to determine the total of credit losses for the year. After a large number of simulation trials, we obtain a probability distribution for credit losses. This can be used to calculate credit VaR.

This approach is liable to be computationally quite time intensive. However, it has the advantage that credit losses are defined as those arising from credit downgrades as well as defaults. Also the impact of credit mitigation clauses such as those described Section 20.8 can be approximately incorporated into the analysis.

---

[21] See O. Vasicek, "Probability of Loss on a Loan Portfolio," Working Paper, KMV, 1987.

Business Snapshot 20.2 Basel II

The Basel Committee on Bank Supervision is planning an overhaul of its procedures for calculating the capital banks are required to keep for the risks they are bearing. This is known as Basel II. No changes are planned to the way market risk capital is calculated (see Business Snapshot 18.1). A new capital requirement for operational risk is planned and significant changes have been proposed for the way in which capital is calculated for credit risk.

For banks eligible to use the Internal Ratings Based (IRB) approach, credit risk capital for a transaction is calculated as

$$UDR \times LGD \times EAD \times MatAd$$

Here UDR, the unexpected default rate, is the excess of the 99.9% worst case 1-year default rate over the expected 1-year default rate. It is calculated, using equation (20.11), as $V(X, T) - Q(T)$ with $X = 99.9\%$ and $T = 1$. The variable LGD is the percentage loss given default (similar to the variable we have been denoting by $1 - R$); EAD is the exposure at default; $MatAd$ is a maturity adjustment.

The rules for determining these numbers are complicated. For UDR, the 1-year probability of default, $Q(1)$, and a correlation parameter ρ are required. The 1-year probability of default is estimated by the bank and the rules for determining the correlation parameter depend on the type of exposure (retail, corporate, sovereign, etc.). For retail exposures, banks also determine LGD and EAD internally. For corporate exposures, banks using the "Advanced IRB" determine LGD and EAD internally, but for banks using the "Foundation IRB" approach there are rules prescribed for determining LGD and EAD. The maturity adjustment is an increasing function of the maturity of the instrument and equals 1.0 when the maturity of the instrument is in 1 year.

Table 20.6 is typical of the historical data provided by rating agencies on credit rating changes and could be used as a basis for a CreditMetrics Monte Carlo simulation. It shows the percentage probability of a bond moving from one rating category to another during a 1-year period. For example, a bond that starts with an A credit rating has a 91.84% chance of still having an A rating at the end of 1 year. It has a 0.02% chance of defaulting during the year, a 0.13% chance of dropping to B, and so on.[22]

In sampling to determine credit losses, the credit rating changes for different counterparties should not be assumed to be independent. A Gaussian copula model can be used to construct a joint probability distribution of rating changes similarly to the way it is used in the previous section to describe the joint probability distribution of times to default. The copula correlation between the rating transitions for two companies is usually set equal correlation between their equity returns using a factor model similar to that in Section 20.9.

As an illustration of the CreditMetrics approach suppose that we are simulating the rating change of a Aaa and a Baa company over a 1-year period using the transition matrix in Table 20.6. Suppose that the correlation between the equities of the two

[22] Technical Note 11 on the author's website explains how a table such as Table 20.6 can be used to calculate transition matrices for periods other than 1 year.

Table 20.6 One-year ratings transition matrix (probabilities expressed as percentages). From results reported by Moody's in 2004 with adjustments for the WR category.

Initial rating	*Rating at year-end*							
	Aaa	*Aa*	*A*	*Baa*	*Ba*	*B*	*Caa*	*Default*
Aaa	92.18	7.06	0.73	0.00	0.02	0.00	0.00	0.00
Aa	1.17	90.85	7.63	0.26	0.07	0.01	0.00	0.02
A	0.05	2.39	91.84	5.07	0.50	0.13	0.01	0.02
Baa	0.05	0.24	5.20	88.48	4.88	0.80	0.16	0.18
Ba	0.01	0.05	0.50	5.45	85.13	7.05	0.55	1.27
B	0.01	0.03	0.13	0.43	6.52	83.21	3.04	6.64
Caa	0.00	0.00	0.00	0.58	1.74	4.18	67.99	25.50
Default	0.00	0.00	0.00	0.00	0.00	0.00	0.00	100.00

companies is 0.2. On each simulation trial, we would sample two variables x_A and x_B from normal distributions so that their correlation is 0.2. The variable x_A determines the new rating of the Aaa company and variable x_B determines the new rating of the Baa company. Since $N^{-1}(0.9218) = 1.4173$, $N^{-1}(0.9218 + 0.0706) = 2.4276$, and $N^{-1}(0.9218 + 0.0706 + 0.0073) = 3.4319$, the Aaa company stays Aaa-rated if $x_A < 1.4173$, it becomes Aa-rated if $1.4173 \leqslant x_A < 2.4276$, and it becomes A-rated if $2.4276 \leqslant x_A < 3.4319$. Similarly, since $N^{-1}(0.0005) = -3.2905$, $N^{-1}(0.0005 + 0.0024) = -2.7589$, and $N^{-1}(0.0005 + 0.0024 + 0.0520) = -1.5991$, the Baa company becomes Aaa-rated if $x_B < -3.2905$, it becomes Aa-rated if $-3.2905 \leqslant x_B < -2.7589$, and it becomes A-rated if $-2.7589 \leqslant x_B < -1.5991$. The Aaa-rated company never defaults. The BBB-rated company defaults when $x_B > N^{-1}(0.9982)$, that is, when $x_B > 2.9113$.

SUMMARY

The probability that a company will default during a particular period of time in the future can be estimated from historical data, bond prices, or equity prices. The default probabilities calculated from bond prices are risk-neutral probabilities, whereas those calculated from historical data are real-world probabilities. Real-world probabilities should be used for scenario analysis and the calculation of credit VaR. Risk-neutral probabilities should be used for valuing credit-sensitive instruments. Risk-neutral default probabilities are significantly higher than real-world probabilities.

The expected loss experienced from a counterparty default is reduced by what is known as netting. This is a clause in most contracts written by a financial institution stating that, if a counterparty defaults on one contract it has with the financial institution, it must default on all contracts it has with the financial institution. Losses are also reduced by collateralization and downgrade triggers. Collateralization requires a counterparty to post collateral and a downgrade trigger gives a company the option to close out a contract if the credit rating of a counterparty falls below a specified level.

Credit VaR can be defined similarly to the way VaR is defined for market risk. One approach to calculating it is the Gaussian copula model of time to default. This has been used by regulators in their proposals for changes to the calculation of capital for credit risk. Another popular approach for calculating credit VaR is CreditMetrics. This uses a Gaussian copula model for credit rating changes.

FURTHER READING

Altman, E. I., "Measuring Corporate Bond Mortality and Performance," *Journal of Finance*, 44 (1989): 902–22.

Duffie, D., and K. Singleton, "Modeling Term Structures of Defaultable Bonds," *Review of Financial Studies*, 12 (1999): 687–720.

Finger, C. C, "A Comparison of Stochastic Default Rate Models," *RiskMetrics Journal*, 1 (November 2000): 49–73.

Hull, J., M. Predescu, and A. White, "Relationship between Credit Default Swap Spreads, Bond Yields, and Credit Rating Announcements," *Journal of Banking and Finance*, 28 (November 2004): 2789–2811.

Kealhofer, S., "Quantifying Default Risk I: Default Prediction," *Financial Analysts Journal*, 59, 1 (2003a): 30–44.

Kealhofer, S., "Quantifying Default Risk II: Debt Valuation," *Financial Analysts Journal*, 59, 3 (2003b): 78–92.

Li, D. X. "On Default Correlation: A Copula Approach," *Journal of Fixed Income*, March 2000: 43–54.

Litterman, R., and T. Iben, "Corporate Bond Valuation and the Term Structure of Credit Spreads," *Journal of Portfolio Management*, Spring 1991: 52–64.

Merton, R. C., "On the Pricing of Corporate Debt: The Risk Structure of Interest Rates," *Journal of Finance*, 29 (1974): 449–70.

Rodriguez, R. J., "Default Risk, Yield Spreads, and Time to Maturity," *Journal of Financial and Quantitative Analysis*, 23 (1988): 111–17.

Questions and Problems (Answers in the Solutions Manual)

20.1. The spread between the yield on a 3-year corporate bond and the yield on a similar risk-free bond is 50 basis points. The recovery rate is 30%. Estimate the average default intensity per year over the 3-year period.

20.2. Suppose that in Problem 20.1 the spread between the yield on a 5-year bond issued by the same company and the yield on a similar risk-free bond is 60 basis points. Assume the same recovery rate of 30%. Estimate the average default intensity per year over the 5-year period. What do your results indicate about the average default intensity in years 4 and 5?

20.3. Should researchers use real-world or risk-neutral default probabilities for (a) calculating credit value at risk and (b) adjusting the price of a derivative for defaults?

20.4. How are recovery rates usually defined?

20.5. Explain the difference between an unconditional default probability density and a default intensity.

20.6. Verify (a) that the numbers in the second column of Table 20.4 are consistent with the numbers in Table 20.1 and (b) that the numbers in the fourth column of Table 20.5 are consistent with the numbers in Table 20.4 and a recovery rate of 40%.

20.7. Describe how netting works. A bank already has one transaction with a counterparty on its books. Explain why a new transaction by a bank with a counterparty can have the effect of increasing or reducing the bank's credit exposure to the counterparty.

20.8. Suppose that the measure $\beta_{AB}(T)$ in equation (20.9) is the same in the real world and the risk-neutral world. Is the same true of the Gaussian copula measure, ρ_{AB}?

20.9. What is meant by a "haircut" in a collateralization agreement. A company offers to post its own equity as collateral. How would you respond?

20.10. Explain the difference between the Gaussian copula model for the time to default and CreditMetrics as far as the following are concerned: (a) the definition of a credit loss and (b) the way in which default correlation is modeled.

20.11. Suppose that the probability of company A defaulting during a 2-year period is 0.2 and the probability of company B defaulting during this period is 0.15. If the Gaussian copula measure of default correlation is 0.3, what is the binomial correlation measure?

20.12. Suppose that the LIBOR/swap curve is flat at 6% with continuous compounding and a 5-year bond with a coupon of 5% (paid semiannually) sells for 90.00. How would an asset swap on the bond be structured? What is the asset swap spread that would be calculated in this situation?

20.13. Show that the value of a coupon-bearing corporate bond is the sum of the values of its constituent zero-coupon bonds when the amount claimed in the event of default is the no-default value of the bond, but that this is not so when the claim amount is the face value of the bond plus accrued interest.

20.14. A 4-year corporate bond provides a coupon of 4% per year payable semiannually and has a yield of 5% expressed with continuous compounding. The risk-free yield curve is flat at 3% with continuous compounding. Assume that defaults can take place at the end of each year (immediately before a coupon or principal payment) and that the recovery rate is 30%. Estimate the risk-neutral default probability on the assumption that it is the same each year.

20.15. A company has issued 3- and 5-year bonds with a coupon of 4% per annum payable annually. The yields on the bonds (expressed with continuous compounding) are 4.5% and 4.75%, respectively. Risk-free rates are 3.5% with continuous compounding for all maturities. The recovery rate is 40%. Defaults can take place halfway through each year. The risk-neutral default rates per year are Q_1 for years 1 to 3 and Q_2 for years 4 and 5. Estimate Q_1 and Q_2.

20.16. Suppose that a financial institution has entered into a swap dependent on the sterling interest rate with counterparty X and an exactly offsetting swap with counterparty Y. Which of the following statements are true and which are false:

(a) The total present value of the cost of defaults is the sum of the present value of the cost of defaults on the contract with X plus the present value of the cost of defaults on the contract with Y.

(b) The expected exposure in 1 year on both contracts is the sum of the expected exposure on the contract with X and the expected exposure on the contract with Y.

(c) The 95% upper confidence limit for the exposure in 1 year on both contracts is the sum of the 95% upper confidence limit for the exposure in 1 year on the contract with X and the 95% upper confidence limit for the exposure in 1 year on the contract with Y.

Explain your answers.

20.17. A company enters into a 1-year forward contract to sell \$100 for AUD150. The contract is initially at the money. In other words, the forward exchange rate is 1.50. The 1-year dollar risk-free rate of interest is 5% per annum. The 1-year dollar rate of interest at which the counterparty can borrow is 6% per annum. The exchange rate volatility is 12% per annum. Estimate the present value of the cost of defaults on the contract? Assume that defaults are recognized only at the end of the life of the contract.

20.18. Suppose that in Problem 20.17, the 6-month forward rate is also 1.50 and the 6-month dollar risk-free interest rate is 5% per annum. Suppose further that the 6-month dollar rate of interest at which the counterparty can borrow is 5.5% per annum. Estimate the present value of the cost of defaults assuming that defaults can occur either at the 6-month point or at the 1-year point? (If a default occurs at the 6-month point, the company's potential loss is the market value of the contract.)

20.19. "A long forward contract subject to credit risk is a combination of a short position in a no-default put and a long position in a call subject to credit risk." Explain this statement.

20.20. Explain why the credit exposure on a matched pair of forward contracts resembles a straddle.

20.21. Explain why the impact of credit risk on a matched pair of interest rate swaps tends to be less than that on a matched pair of currency swaps.

20.22. "When a bank is negotiating currency swaps, it should try to ensure that it is receiving the lower interest rate currency from a company with a low credit risk." Explain why.

20.23. Does put–call parity hold when there is default risk? Explain your answer.

20.24. Suppose that in an asset swap B is the market price of the bond per dollar of principal, B^* is the default-free value of the bond per dollar of principal, and V is the present value of the asset swap spread per dollar of principal. Show that $V = B - B^*$.

20.25. Show that under Merton's model in Section 20.6 the credit spread on a T-year zero-coupon bond is $\ln[N(d_2) + N(-d_1)/L]/T$, where $L = De^{-rT}/V_0$.

Assignment Questions

20.26. Suppose a 3-year corporate bond provides a coupon of 7% per year payable semiannually and has a yield of 5% (expressed with semiannual compounding). The yields for all maturities on risk-free bonds is 4% per annum (expressed with semiannual compounding). Assume that defaults can take place every 6 months (immediately before a coupon payment) and the recovery rate is 45%. Estimate the default probabilities assuming (a) that the unconditional default probabilities are the same on each possible default date and (b) that the default probabilities conditional on no earlier default are the same on each possible default date.

20.27. A company has 1- and 2-year bonds outstanding, each providing a coupon of 8% per year payable annually. The yields on the bonds (expressed with continuous compounding) are 6.0% and 6.6%, respectively. Risk-free rates are 4.5% for all maturities. The recovery rate is 35%. Defaults can take place halfway through each year. Estimate the risk-neutral default rate each year.

20.28. Explain carefully the distinction between real-world and risk-neutral default probabilities. Which is higher? A bank enters into a credit derivative where it agrees to pay $100 at the end of 1 year if a certain company's credit rating falls from A to Baa or lower during the year. The 1-year risk-free rate is 5%. Using Table 20.6, estimate a value for the derivative. What assumptions are you making? Do they tend to overstate or understate the value of the derivative.

20.29. The value of a company's equity is $4 million and the volatility of its equity is 60%. The debt that will have to be repaid in 2 years is $15 million. The risk-free interest rate is 6% per annum. Use Merton's model to estimate the expected loss from default, the probability of default, and the recovery rate in the event of default. Explain why Merton's model gives a high recovery rate. (*Hint*: The Solver function in Excel can be used for this question.)

20.30. Suppose that a bank has a total of $10 million of exposures of a certain type. The 1-year probability of default averages 1% and the recovery rate averages 40%. The copula correlation parameter is 0.2. Estimate the 99.5% 1-year credit VaR.

CHAPTER 21 Credit Derivatives

The most exciting developments in derivatives markets since the late 1990s have been in the credit derivatives area. In 2000 the total notional principal for outstanding credit derivatives contracts was about $800 billion. By 2003 this had grown to over $3 trillion. Credit derivatives are contracts where the payoff depends on the creditworthiness of one or more companies or countries. In this chapter we explain how credit derivatives work and discuss some valuation issues.

Credit derivatives allow companies to trade credit risks in much the same way that they trade market risks. Banks and other financial institutions used to be in the position where they could do little once they had assumed a credit risk except wait (and hope for the best). Now they can actively manage their portfolios of credit risks, keeping some and entering into credit derivatives contracts to protect themselves from others. As indicated in Business Snapshot 21.1, banks have been the biggest buyers of credit protection and insurance companies have been the biggest sellers.

21.1 CREDIT DEFAULT SWAPS

The most popular credit derivative is a *credit default swap* (CDS). This is a contract that provides insurance against the risk of a default by particular company. The company is known as the *reference entity* and a default by the company is known as a *credit event*. The buyer of the insurance obtains the right to sell bonds issued by the company for their face value when a credit event occurs and the seller of the insurance agrees to buy the bonds for their face value when a credit event occurs.[1] The total face value of the bonds that can be sold is known as the credit default swap's *notional principal*.

The buyer of the CDS makes periodic payments to the seller until the end of the life of the CDS or until a credit event occurs. These payments are typically made in arrears every quarter, every half year, or every year. The settlement in the event of a default involves either physical delivery of the bonds or a cash payment.

An example will help to illustrate how a typical deal is structured. Suppose that two

[1] The face value (or par value) of a bond is the principal amount that the issuer will repay at maturity if it does not default.

Business Snapshot 21.1 Who Bears the Credit Risk?

Traditionally banks have been in the business of making loans and then bearing the credit risk that the borrower will default. But this is changing. Banks have for some time been reluctant to keep loans on their balance sheets. This is because, after the capital required by regulators has been accounted for, the average return earned on loans is often less attractive than that on other assets. During the 1990s, banks created asset-backed securities (similar to the mortgage-backed securities discussed in Chapter 29) to pass loans (and their credit risk) on to investors. In the late 1990s and early 2000s, banks have made extensive use of credit derivatives to shift the credit risk in their loans to other parts of the financial system.

If banks have been net buyers of credit protection, who have been net sellers? The answer is insurance companies. Insurance companies are not regulated in the same way as banks and as a result are sometimes more willing to bear credit risks than banks.

The result of all this is that the financial institution bearing the credit risk of a loan is often different from the financial institution that did the original credit checks. Whether this proves to be good for the overall health of the financial system remains to be seen.

parties enter into a 5-year credit default swap on March 1, 2004. Assume that the notional principal is \$100 million and the buyer agrees to pay 90 basis points annually for protection against default by the reference entity.

The CDS is shown in Figure 21.1. If the reference entity does not default (i.e., there is no credit event), the buyer receives no payoff and pays \$900,000 on March 1 of each of the years 2005, 2006, 2007, 2008, and 2009. If there is a credit event, a substantial payoff is likely. Suppose that the buyer notifies the seller of a credit event on June 1, 2007 (a quarter of the way into the fourth year). If the contract specifies physical settlement, the buyer has the right to sell bonds issued by the reference entity with a face value of \$100 million for \$100 million. If the contract requires cash settlement, an independent calculation agent will poll dealers to determine the mid-market value of the cheapest deliverable bond a predesignated number of days after the credit event. Suppose this bond is worth \$35 per \$100 of face value. The cash payoff would be \$65 million.

The regular quarterly, semiannual, or annual payments from the buyer of protection to the seller of protection cease when there is a credit event. However, because these payments are made in arrears, a final accrual payment by the buyer is usually required. In our example, the buyer would be required to pay to the seller the amount of the annual payment accrued between March 1, 2007, and June 1, 2007 (approximately \$225,000), but no further payments would be required.

Figure 21.1 Credit default swap.

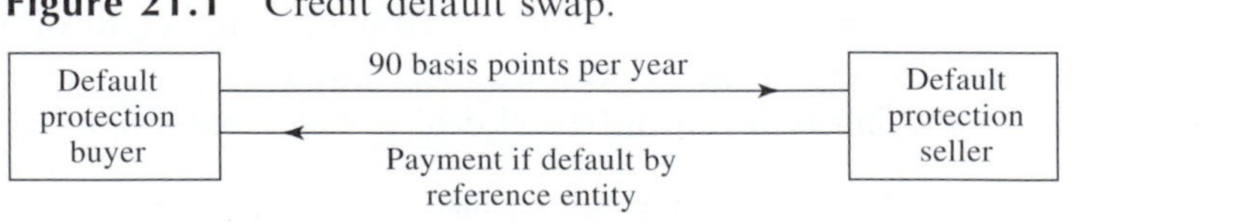

The total amount paid per year, as a percent of the notional principal, to buy protection is known as the *CDS spread.* Several large banks are market makers in the credit default swap market. When quoting on a new 5-year credit default swap on Ford Motor Credit, a market maker might bid 250 basis points and offer 260 basis points. This means that the market maker is prepared to buy protection on Ford by paying 250 basis points per year (i.e., 2.5% of the principal per year) and to sell protection on Ford for 260 basis points per year (i.e., 2.6% of the principal per year).

Credit Default Swaps and Bond Yields

A CDS can be used to hedge a position in a corporate bond. Suppose that an investor buys a 5-year corporate bond yielding 7% per year for its face value and at the same time enters into a 5-year CDS to buy protection against the issuer of the bond defaulting. Suppose that the CDS spread is 2% per annum. The effect of the CDS is to convert the corporate bond to a risk-free bond (at least approximately). If the bond issuer does not default the investor earns 5% per year (when the CDS spread is netted against the corporate bond yield). If the bond does default the investor earns 5% up to the time of the default. Under the terms of the CDS, the investor is then able to exchange the bond for its face value. This face value can be invested at the risk-free rate for the remainder of the 5 years.

The n-year CDS spread should be approximately equal to the excess of the par yield on an n-year corporate bond over the par yield on an n-year risk-free bond. If it is markedly less than this, an investor can earn more than the risk-free rate by buying the corporate bond and buying protection. If it is markedly greater than this, an investor can borrow at less than the risk-free rate by shorting the corporate bond and selling CDS protection. These are not perfect arbitrages, but they do give a good guide to the relationship between CDS spreads and bond yields. CDS spreads can be used to imply the risk-free rates used by market participants. As discussed in Section 20.4, the average implied risk-free rate appears to be approximately equal to the LIBOR/swap rate minus 10 basis points.

The Cheapest-to-Deliver Bond

As explained in Section 20.3 the recovery rate on a bond is defined as the value of the bond immediately after default as a percent of face value. This means that the payoff from a CDS is $L(1 - R)$, where L is the notional principal and R is the recovery rate.

Usually a CDS specifies that a number of different bonds can be delivered in the event of a default. The bonds typically have the same seniority, but they may not sell for the same percentage of face value immediately after a default.[2] This gives the holder of a CDS a cheapest-to-deliver bond option. When a default happens the buyer of protection (or the calculation agent in the event of cash settlement) will review alternative deliverable bonds and choose for delivery the one that can be purchased most cheaply.

[2] There are a number of reasons for this. The claim that is made in the event of a default is typically equal to the bond's face value plus accrued interest. Bonds with high accrued interest at the time of default therefore tend to have higher prices immediately after default. Also the market may judge that in the event of a reorganization of the company some bond holders will fare better than others.

21.2 CREDIT INDICES

Participants in credit derivatives markets have developed indices to track credit default swap spreads. In 2004, there were agreements between different producers of indices which led to some consolidation. Among the indices now used are:

1. The 5- and 10-year CDX NA IG indices tracking the credit spread for 125 investment grade North American companies; and
2. The 5- and 10-year iTraxx Europe indices tracking the credit spread for 125 investment grade European companies

In addition to monitoring credit spreads, indices provide a way market participants can easily buy or sell a portfolio of credit default swaps. For example, an investment bank, acting as market maker might quote the CDX NA IG 5-year index as bid 65 basis points and offer 66 basis points. An investor could then buy $800,000 of 5-year CDS protection on each the 125 underlying companies for $660,000 per year. The investor can sell $800,000 million of 5-year CDS protection on each of the 125 underlying names for $650,000 per year. When a company defaults, the annual payment is reduced by $660,000/125 = $5,280.[3]

21.3 VALUATION OF CREDIT DEFAULT SWAPS

Mid-market CDS spreads on individual reference entities (i.e., the average of the bid and offer CDS spreads quoted by brokers) can be calculated from default probability estimates. We will illustrate how this is done with a simple example.

Suppose that the probability of a reference entity defaulting during a year conditional on no earlier default is 2%.[4] Table 21.1 shows survival probabilities and unconditional default probabilities (i.e., default probabilities as seen at time zero) for each of the 5 years. The probability of a default during the first year is 0.02 and the probability the

Table 21.1 Unconditional default probabilities and survival probabilities.

Time (years)	*Default probability*	*Survival probability*
1	0.0200	0.9800
2	0.0196	0.9604
3	0.0192	0.9412
4	0.0188	0.9224
5	0.0184	0.9039

[3] The index is slightly lower than the average of the credit default swap spreads for the companies in the portfolio. To understand the reason for this, consider two companies, one with a spread of 1000 basis points and the other with a spread of 10 basis points. To buy protection on both companies would cost slightly less than 505 basis points per company. This is because the 1000 basis points is not expected to be paid for as long as the 10 basis points and should therefore carry less weight.

[4] As mentioned in Section 20.2, conditional default probabilities are known as default intensities.

Table 21.2 Calculation of the present value of expected payments. Payment = s per annum.

Time (years)	*Probability of survival*	*Expected payment*	*Discount factor*	*PV of expected payment*
1	0.9800	0.9800s	0.9512	0.9322s
2	0.9604	0.9604s	0.9048	0.8690s
3	0.9412	0.9412s	0.8607	0.8101s
4	0.9224	0.9224s	0.8187	0.7552s
5	0.9039	0.9039s	0.7788	0.7040s
Total				4.0704s

reference entity will survive until the end of the first year is 0.98. The probability of a default during the second year is $0.02 \times 0.98 = 0.0196$ and the probability of survival until the end of the second year is $0.98 \times 0.98 = 0.9604$. The probability of default during the third year is $0.02 \times 0.9604 = 0.0192$, and so on.

We will assume that defaults always happen halfway through a year and that payments on the credit default swap are made once a year, at the end of each year. We also assume that the risk-free (LIBOR) interest rate is 5% per annum with continuous compounding and the recovery rate is 40%. There are three parts to the calculation. These are shown in Tables 21.2, 21.3, and 21.4.

Table 21.2 shows the calculation of the expected present value of the payments made on the CDS assuming that payments are made at the rate of s per year and the notional principal is \$1. For example, there is a 0.9412 probability that the third payment of s is made. The expected payment is therefore 0.9412s and its present value is $0.9412se^{-0.05\times 3} = 0.8101s$. The total present value of the expected payments is 4.0704s.

Table 21.3 shows the calculation of the expected present value of the payoff assuming a notional principal of \$1. As mentioned earlier, we are assuming that defaults always happen halfway through a year. For example, there is a 0.0192 probability of a payoff halfway through the third year. Given that the recovery rate is 40% the expected payoff at this time is $0.0192 \times 0.6 \times 1 = 0.0115$. The present value of the expected payoff is $0.0115e^{-0.05\times 2.5} = 0.0102$. The total present value of the expected payoffs is \$0.0511.

Table 21.3 Calculation of the present value of expected payoff. Notional principal = \$1.

Time (years)	*Probability of default*	*Recovery rate*	*Expected payoff (\$)*	*Discount factor*	*PV of expected payoff (\$)*
0.5	0.0200	0.4	0.0120	0.9753	0.0117
1.5	0.0196	0.4	0.0118	0.9277	0.0109
2.5	0.0192	0.4	0.0115	0.8825	0.0102
3.5	0.0188	0.4	0.0113	0.8395	0.0095
4.5	0.0184	0.4	0.0111	0.7985	0.0088
Total					0.0511

Table 21.4 Calculation of the present value of accrual payment.

Time (years)	*Probability of default*	*Expected accrual payment*	*Discount factor*	*PV of expected accrual payment*
0.5	0.0200	$0.0100s$	0.9753	$0.0097s$
1.5	0.0196	$0.0098s$	0.9277	$0.0091s$
2.5	0.0192	$0.0096s$	0.8825	$0.0085s$
3.5	0.0188	$0.0094s$	0.8395	$0.0079s$
4.5	0.0184	$0.0092s$	0.7985	$0.0074s$
Total				$0.0426s$

As a final step we evaluate in Table 21.4 the accrual payment made in the event of a default. For example, there is a 0.0192 probability that there will be a final accrual payment halfway through the third year. The accrual payment is $0.5s$. The expected accrual payment at this time is therefore $0.0192 \times 0.5s = 0.0096s$. Its present value is $0.0096se^{-0.05\times 2.5} = 0.0085s$. The total present value of the expected accrual payments is $0.0426s$.

From Tables 21.2 and 21.4, the present value of the expected payments is

$$4.0704s + 0.0426s = 4.1130s$$

From Table 21.3, the present value of the expected payoff is 0.0511. Equating the two, we obtain the CDS spread for a new CDS as

$$4.1130s = 0.0511$$

or $s = 0.0124$. The mid-market spread should be 0.0124 times the principal or 124 basis points per year. This example is designed to illustrate the calculation methodology. In practice, we are likely to find that calculations are more extensive than those in Tables 21.2 to 21.4 because (a) payments are often made more frequently than once a year and (b) we might want to assume that defaults can happen more frequently than once a year.

Marking to Market a CDS

At the time it is negotiated, a CDS, like most other swaps, is worth close to zero. Later it may have a positive or negative value. Suppose, for example the credit default swap in our example had been negotiated some time ago for a spread of 150 basis points, the present value of the payments by the buyer would be $4.1130 \times 0.0150 = 0.0617$ and the present value of the payoff would be 0.0511 as above. The value of swap to the seller would therefore be $0.0617 - 0.0511$, or 0.0106 times the principal. Similarly the mark-to-market value of the swap to the buyer of protection would be -0.0106 times the principal.

Estimating Default Probabilities

The default probabilities used to value a CDS should be risk-neutral default probabilities, not real-world default probabilities (see Section 20.5 for a discussion of the difference between the two). Risk-neutral default probabilities can be estimated from bond prices or asset swaps as explained in Chapter 20. An alternative is to imply them

Table 21.5 Calculation of the present value of expected payoff from a binary credit default swap. Principal = $1.

Time (years)	*Probability of default*	*Expected payoff ($)*	*Discount factor*	*PV of expected payoff ($)*
0.5	0.0200	0.0200	0.9753	0.0195
1.5	0.0196	0.0196	0.9277	0.0182
2.5	0.0192	0.0192	0.8825	0.0170
3.5	0.0188	0.0188	0.8395	0.0158
4.5	0.0184	0.0184	0.7985	0.0147
Total				0.0852

from CDS quotes. The latter approach is similar to the practice in options markets of implying volatilities from the prices of actively traded options.

Suppose we change the example in Tables 21.2, 21.3 and 21.4 so that we do not know the default probabilities. Instead we know that the mid-market CDS spread for a newly issued 5-year CDS is 100 basis points per year. We can reverse engineer our calculations to conclude that the implied default probability per year (conditional on no earlier default) is 1.61% per year.[5]

Binary Credit Default Swaps

A binary credit default swap is structured similarly to a regular credit default swap except that the payoff is a fixed dollar amount. Suppose that in the example we have considered in Tables 21.1 to 21.4 the payoff is $1, instead of $(1 - R)$ dollars, and the swap spread is s. Tables 21.1, 21.2 and 21.4 are the same, but Table 21.3 is replaced by Table 21.5. The CDS spread for a new binary CDS is given by

$$4.1130s = 0.0852$$

so that the CDS spread, s, is 0.0207 or 207 basis points.

How Important is the Recovery Rate?

Whether we use CDS spreads or bond prices to estimate default probabilities we need an estimate of the recovery rate. However, provided that we use the same recovery rate for (a) estimating risk-neutral default probabilities and (b) valuing a CDS, the value of the CDS (or the estimate of the CDS spread) is not very sensitive to the recovery rate. This is because the implied probabilities of default are approximately proportional to $1/(1 - R)$ and the payoffs from a CDS are proportional to $1 - R$.

This argument does not apply to the valuation of binary CDS. Implied probabilities of default are still proportional to $1/(1 - R)$. However, for a binary CDS, the payoffs from the CDS are independent of R. If we have CDS spread for both a plain vanilla CDS and a binary CDS, we can estimate both the recovery rate and the default probability (see Problem 21.25).

[5] Ideally we would like to estimate a different default probability for each year instead of a single default intensity. We could do this if we had spreads for 1-, 2-, 3-, 4-, and 5-year CDS swaps or bond prices.

Business Snapshot 21.2 Is the CDS Market a Fair Game?

There is one important difference between credit default swaps and the other over-the-counter derivatives that we have considered in this book. The other over-the-counter derivatives depend on interest rates, exchange rates, equity indices, commodity prices, and so on. There is no reason to assume that any one market participant has better information than any other market participant about these variables.

Credit default swaps spreads depend on the probability that a particular company will default during a particular period of time. Arguably some market participants have more information to estimate this probability than others. A financial institution that works closely with a particular company by providing advice, making loans, and handling new issues of securities is likely to have more information about the creditworthiness of the company than another financial institution that has no dealings with the company. Economists refer to this as an *asymmetric information* problem.

Whether asymmetric information will curtail the expansion of the credit default swap market remains to be seen. Financial institutions emphasize that the decision to buy protection against the risk of default by a company is normally made by a risk manager and is not based on any special information that many exist elsewhere in the financial institution about the company.

The Future of the CDS Market

The market for credit default swaps has grown rapidly in the late 1990s and early 2000s. Credit default swaps account for about 70% of all credit derivatives. They have become important tools for managing credit risk. A financial institution can reduce its credit exposure to particular companies by buying protection. It can also use CDSs to diversify credit risk. For example, if a financial institution has too much credit exposure to a particular business sector, it can buy protection against defaults by companies in the sector and at the same time sell protection against default by companies in other unrelated sectors.

Some market participants think the growth of the CDS market will continue and that it will be as big as the interest rate swap market by 2010. Others are less optimistic. There is a potential asymmetric information problem in the CDS market that is not present in other over-the-counter derivatives markets (see Business Snapshot 21.2).

21.4 CDS FORWARDS AND OPTIONS

Once the CDS market was well established, it was natural for derivatives dealers to trade forwards and options on credit default swap spreads.[6]

A forward credit default swap is the obligation to buy or sell a particular credit default swap on a particular reference entity at a particular future time T. If the reference entity defaults before time T, the forward contract ceases to exist. Thus a bank could enter into a forward contract to sell 5-year protection on Ford Motor

[6] The valuation of these instruments is discussed in J. C. Hull and A. White, "The Valuation of Credit Default Swap Options," *Journal of Derivatives*, 10, 5 (Spring 2003): 40–50.

Credit for 280 basis points starting in 1 year. If Ford defaults during the next year, the bank's obligation under the forward contract ceases to exist.

A credit default swap option is an option to buy or sell a particular credit default swap on a particular reference entity at a particular future time T. For example, an investor could negotiate the right to buy 5-year protection on Ford Motor Credit starting in 1 year for 280 basis points. This is a call option. If the 5-year CDS spread for Ford in 1 year turns out to be more than 280 basis points, the option will be exercised; otherwise it will not be exercised. The cost of the option would be paid up front. Similarly an investor might negotiate the right to sell 5-year protection on Ford Motor Credit for 280 basis points starting in 1 year. This is a put option. If the 5-year CDS spread for Ford in 1 year turns out to be less than 280 basis points the option will be exercised; otherwise it will not be exercised. Again the cost of the option would be paid up front. Like CDS forwards, CDS options are usually structured so that they will cease to exist if the reference entity defaults before option maturity.

An option contract that has become popular in the credit derivatives market is a call option on a basket of reference entities. If there are m reference entities in the basket that have not defaulted by the option maturity, the option gives the holder the right to buy a portfolio of CDSs on the names for mK basis points, where K is the strike price. In addition, the holder gets the usual CDS payoff on any reference entities that do default during the life of the contract.

21.5 TOTAL RETURN SWAPS

A *total return swap* is a type of credit derivative. It is an agreement to exchange the total return on a bond (or any portfolio of assets) for LIBOR plus a spread. The total return includes coupons, interest, and the gain or loss on the asset over the life of the swap.

An example of a total return swap is a 5-year agreement with a notional principal of \$100 million to exchange the total return on a corporate bond for LIBOR plus 25 basis points. This is illustrated in Figure 21.2. On coupon payment dates the payer pays the coupons earned on an investment of \$100 million in the bond. The receiver pays interest at a rate of LIBOR plus 25 basis points on a principal of \$100 million. (LIBOR is set on one coupon date and paid on the next as in a plain vanilla interest rate swap.) At the end of the life of the swap there is a payment reflecting the change in value of the bond. For example, if the bond increases in value by 10% over the life of the swap, the payer is required to pay \$10 million (= 10% of \$100 million) at the end of the 5 years. Similarly, if the bond decreases in value by 15%, the receiver is required to pay \$15 million at the end of the 5 years. If there is a default on the bond, the swap is usually terminated and the receiver makes a final payment equal to the excess of \$100 million over the market value of the bond.

Figure 21.2 Total return swap.

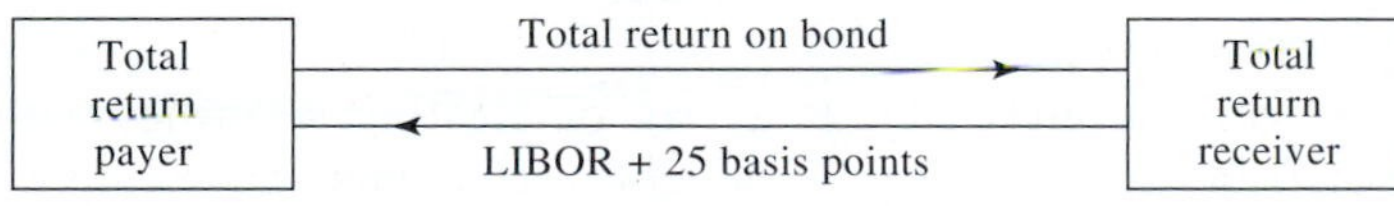

If we add the notional principal to both sides at the end of the life of the swap, we can characterize the total return swap as follows. The payer pays the cash flows on an investment of $100 million in the corporate bond. The receiver pays the cash flows on a $100 million bond paying LIBOR plus 25 basis points. If the payer owns the corporate bond, the total return swap allows it to pass the credit risk on the bond to the receiver. If it does not own the bond, the total return swap allows it to take a short position in the bond.

Total return swaps are often used as a financing tool. One scenario that could lead to the swap in Figure 21.2 is as follows. The receiver wants financing to invest $100 million in the reference bond. It approaches the payer (which is likely to be a financial institution) and agrees to the swap. The payer then invests $100 million in the bond. This leaves the receiver in the same position as it would have been if it had borrowed money at LIBOR plus 25 basis points to buy the bond. The payer retains ownership of the bond for the life of the swap and faces less credit risk than it would have done if it had lent money to the receiver to finance the purchase of the bond, with the bond being used as collateral for the loan. If the receiver defaults the payer does not have the legal problem of trying to realize on the collateral. Total return swaps are similar to repos (see Section 4.1) in that they are structured to minimize credit risk when securities are being financed.

The spread over LIBOR received by the payer is compensation for bearing the risk that the receiver will default. The payer will lose money if the receiver defaults at a time when the reference bond's price has declined. The spread therefore depends on the credit quality of the receiver, the credit quality of the bond issuer, and the default correlation between the two.

There are a number of variations on the standard deal we have described. Sometimes, instead of there being a cash payment for the change in value of the bond, there is physical settlement where the payer exchanges the underlying asset for the notional principal at the end of the life of the swap. Sometimes the change-in-value payments are made periodically rather than all at the end.

21.6 BASKET CREDIT DEFAULT SWAPS

In what is referred to as a *basket credit default swap* there are a number of reference entities. An *add-up basket* CDS provides a payoff when any of the reference entities default. A *first-to-default* CDS provides a payoff only when the first default occurs. A *second-to-default* CDS provides a payoff only when the second default occurs. More generally an *nth-to-default* CDS provides a payoff only when the nth default occurs. Payoffs are calculated in the same way as for a regular CDS. After the relevant default has occurred, there is a settlement. The swap then terminates and there are no further payments by either party.

21.7 COLLATERALIZED DEBT OBLIGATIONS

A collateralized debt obligation (CDO) is a way of creating securities with widely different risk characteristics from a portfolio of debt instruments. An example is shown in Figure 21.3. In this four types of securities (or tranches) are created from a portfolio

Figure 21.3 Collateralized debt obligation.

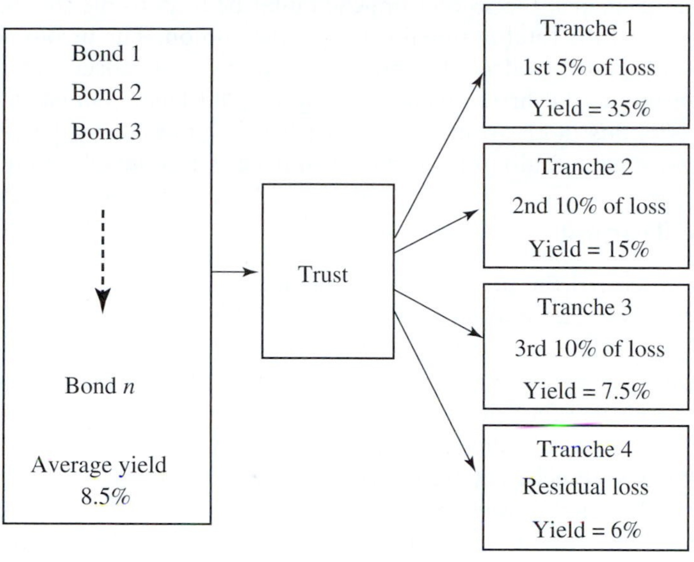

of bonds. The first tranche has 5% of the total bond principal and absorbs all credit losses from the portfolio during the life of the CDO until they have reached 5% of the total bond principal. The second tranche has 10% of the principal and absorbs all losses during the life of the CDO in excess of 5% of the principal up to a maximum of 15% of the principal. The third tranche has 10% of the principal and absorbs all losses in excess of 15% of the principal up to a maximum of 25% of the principal. The fourth tranche has 75% of the principal absorbs all losses in excess of 25% of the principal. The yields in Figure 21.3 are the rates of interest paid to tranche holders. These rates are paid on the balance of the principal remaining in the tranche after losses have been paid. Consider the first tranche. Initially the return of 35% is paid on the whole amount invested by the tranche 1 holders. But after losses equal to 1% of the total bond principal have been experienced, tranche 1 holders have lost 20% of their investment and the return is paid on only 80% of the original amount invested. Tranche 1 is referred to the *equity tranche*. A default loss of 2.5% on the bond portfolio translates into a loss of 50% of the tranche's principal. Tranche 4 by contrast is usually given an Aaa rating. Defaults on the bond portfolio must exceed 25% before the holders of this tranche are responsible for any credit losses.

The creator of the CDO normally retains the equity tranche and sells the remaining tranches in the market. A CDO provides a way of creating high quality debt from average quality (or even low quality) debt.

Synthetic CDOs

The CDO in Figure 21.3 is referred to as a *cash CDO*. An alternative structure which has become popular is a *synthetic CDO* where the creator of the CDO sells a portfolio of credit default swaps to third parties. It then passes on the default risk to the synthetic CDO's tranche holders. Analogously to Figure 21.3, the first tranche might be responsible for the payoffs on the credit default swaps until they have reached 5% of the total notional principal; the second tranche might be responsible for the payoffs between 5% and 15% of the total notional principal; and so on. The income from the credit default swaps is distributed to the tranches in a way that reflects the risk they are bearing. For example, the first tranche might get 3,000 basis points; the second tranche 1,000 basis points, and so on. As in a cash CDO this would be paid on a principal that declined as defaults for which the tranche is responsible occur.

Single Tranche Trading

In Section 21.2 we discussed the portfolios of 125 companies that are used to generate CDX and iTraxx indices. The market uses these portfolios to define standard CDO tranches. The trading of these standard tranches is known as *single tranche trading*. A single tranche trade is an agreement where one side agrees to sell protection against losses on a tranche and the other side agrees to buy the protection. The tranche is not part of a synthetic CDO but cash flows are calculated in the same way as if it were part of a synthetic CDO. The tranche is referred to as "unfunded" because it has not been created by selling credit default swaps or buying bonds.

In the case of the CDX NA IG index, the equity tranche covers losses between 0% and 3% of the principal. The second tranche, which is referred to as the *mezzanine tranche*, covers losses between 3% and 7%. The remaining tranches cover losses from 7% and 10%, 10% to 15%, and 15% to 30%. In the case of the iTraxx Europe index, the equity tranche covers losses between 0% and 3%. The mezzanine tranche covers losses between 3% and 6%. The remaining tranches cover losses from 6% to 9%, 9% to 12%, and 12% to 22%.

Table 21.6 shows the mid-market quotes for 5-year CDX and iTraxx tranches on August 4, 2004. On that date the CDX index level was 63.25 basis points and the iTraxx index was 42 basis points. For example, the mid-market price of mezzanine protection for the CDX IG NA was 347 basis points per year while that for iTraxx Europe was 168 basis points per year. Note that the equity tranche is quoted differently from the other tranches. The market quote of 41.75% for CDX means that the protection seller receives an initial payment of 41.75% of the principal plus a spread of 500 basis points per year. Similarly the market quote of 27.6% for iTraxx means that the protection seller receives an initial payment of 27.6% of the principal plus a spread of 500 basis points per year.

Table 21.6 Five-year CDX IG NA and iTraxx Europe tranches on August 4, 2004. Quotes are in basis points except for 0%–3% tranche. (*Source*: GFI)

CDX IG NA					
Tranche	0%–3%	3%–7%	7%–10%	10%–15%	15%–30%
Quote	41.8%	347	135.5	47.5	14.5
iTraxx Europe					
Tranche	0%–3%	3%–6%	6%–9%	9%–12%	12%–22%
Quote	27.6%	168	70	43	20

21.8 VALUATION OF A BASKET CDS AND CDO

The spread for an nth-to-default CDS or the tranche of a CDO is critically dependent on default correlation. Suppose that a basket of 100 reference entities is used to define a 5-year nth-to-default CDS and that each reference entity has a risk-neutral probability of 2% of defaulting during the 5 years. When the default correlation between the reference entities is zero the binomial distribution shows that the probability of one or more defaults during the 5 years is 86.74% and the probability of 10 or more defaults is 0.0034%. A first-to-default CDS is therefore quite valuable whereas a tenth-to-default CDS is worth almost nothing.

As the default correlation increases the probability of one or more defaults declines and the probability of 10 or more defaults increases. In the limit where the default correlation between the reference entities is perfect the probability of one or more defaults equals the probability of ten or more defaults and is 2%. This is because in this extreme situation the reference entities are essentially the same. Either they all default (with probability 2%) or none of them default (with probability 98%).

The valuation of a tranche of a CDO is similarly dependent on default correlation. If the correlation is low the junior equity tranche is very risky and the senior tranches are very safe. As the default correlation increases the junior tranches become less risky and the senior tranches become more risky. In the limit where the default correlation is perfect the tranches are equally risky.

Using the Gaussian Copula Model of Time to Default

The one-factor Gaussian copula model of time to default presented above has become the standard market model for valuing an nth-to-default CDS or a tranche of a CDO.

Consider a portfolio of N reference entities. From equation (20.7)

$$Q_i(T \mid M) = N\left(\frac{N^{-1}[Q_i(T)] - a_i M}{\sqrt{1 - a_i^2}}\right) \tag{21.1}$$

where $Q_i(T \mid M)$ is the probability of the ith entity defaulting by time T conditional on the value of the factor, M. Denote the probability of more than k defaults by time T as $P(k, T)$ and the corresponding probability conditional on the value of M as $P(k, T \mid M)$. When we fix the value of M, the default probabilities are independent. This facilitates the calculation of $P(k, T \mid M)$.

In the standard market model it is assumed that the time-to-default distribution is the same for all reference entities in the portfolio and that the copula correlation is the same for all pairs of reference entities.[7] This means that $Q_i(T \mid M) = Q(T \mid M)$ is the same for all i and equation (20.8) can be used instead of equation (20.7), so that

$$Q(T \mid M) = N\left(\frac{N^{-1}[Q(T)] - \sqrt{\rho} M}{\sqrt{1 - \rho}}\right) \tag{21.2}$$

[7] For a discussion of the more general model where these assumptions are not made, see J. C. Hull and A. White, "Vauation of a CDO and nth-to-Default Swap without Monte Carlo Simulation," *Journal of Derivatives*, 12, 2 (Winter 2004), 823.

Business Snapshot 21.3 Correlation Smiles

Credit derivatives dealers imply default correlations from the spreads on tranches. If the implied correlations were the same for all tranches, we could deduce that market prices are consistent with the one-factor Gaussian copula model for time to default. In practice, we find that the implied correlations for the most junior (equity) and most senior tranches are higher than those for the intermediate tranches. For example, in Table 21.6, the implied correlations for the five CDX IG NA tranches (starting with the equity tranche) are 21.0%, 4.2%, 17.7%, 19.0%, and 27.4%. Similarly the implied correlations for the corresponding iTraxx Europe tranches are 20.4%, 5.5%, 16.1%, 23.3%, and 31.1%.

The existence of a volatility smile in options markets indicates that the Black–Scholes model (although widely used) does not reflect the beliefs of market participants (see Chapter 16). In the same way, the existence of a correlation smile in CDO markets indicates that the one-factor Gaussian copula model (although widely used) does not reflect the beliefs of market participants.

From the properties of the binomial distribution,

$$P(k, T \mid M) = \frac{N!}{(N-k)!\,k!} Q(T \mid M)^k [1 - Q(T \mid M)]^{N-k}$$

The probability that the nth default will happen between times T_1 and T_2 conditional on M is $P(n, T_2 \mid M) - P(n, T_1 \mid M)$. This gives the probability distribution for the time of the nth default conditional on M. The factor M has a standard normal probability distribution. By integrating over the distribution for M we obtain the unconditional probability distribution for the time of the nth default.[8] With this distribution in hand, we can value an nth-to-default CDS in exactly the way as a regular CDS. To value the tranche of a CDO, we calculate expected payoffs and payments on the tranche conditional on M and then integrate over M.

Derivatives dealers calculate the implied copula correlation, ρ, in equation (21.2) from the spreads quoted in the market for nth-to-default CDSs and tranches of CDOs and tend to quote these rather than the spreads themselves. This is similar to the practice in options markets of quoting Black–Scholes implied volatilities rather than dollar prices. As discussed in Business Snapshot 21.3, there is a correlation smile phenomenon in CDO markets similar to the volatility smile phenomenon in options markets.

21.9 CONVERTIBLE BONDS

Convertible bonds are bonds issued by a company where the holder has the option to exchange the bonds for the company's stock at certain times in the future. The *conversion ratio* is the number of shares of stock obtained for one bond (this can be a function of time). The bonds are almost always callable (i.e., the issuer has the right to buy them back at certain times at a predetermined prices). The holder always has the right to convert the

[8] Integration over M can be accomplished in a fast and efficient way using a procedure known as Gaussian quadrature.

bond once it has been called. The call feature is therefore usually a way of forcing conversion earlier than the holder would otherwise choose. Sometimes the holder's call option is conditional on the price of the company's stock being above a certain level.

Credit risk plays an important role in the valuation of convertibles. If we ignore credit risk, we will get poor prices because the coupons and principal payments on the bond will be overvalued.

Ingersoll provides a way of valuing convertibles using a model similar to Merton's (1974) model discussed in Section 20.6.[9] He assumes geometric Brownian motion for the issuer's total assets and models the company's equity, its convertible debt, and its other debt as claims contingent on the value of the assets. Credit risk is taken into account because the debt holders get repaid in full only if the value of the assets exceeds the amount owing to them.

A simpler model that is widely used in practice involves modeling the issuer's stock price. It is assumed that the stock follows geometric Brownian motion except that there is a probability $\lambda\,\Delta t$ that there will be a default in each short period of time Δt. In the event of a default the stock price falls to zero and there is a recovery on the bond. The variable λ is the risk-neutral default intensity introduced in Section 20.2.

We can represent the stock price process by varying the usual binomial tree so that at each node there is:

1. A probability p_u of a percentage up movement of size u over the next time period of length Δt
2. A probability p_d of a percentage down movement of size d over the next time period of length Δt
3. A probability $\lambda\,\Delta t$, or more accurately $1 - e^{-\lambda \Delta t}$, that there will be a default with the stock price moving to zero over the next time period of length Δt

Parameter values, chosen to match the first two moments of the stock price distribution, are:

$$p_u = \frac{a - de^{-\lambda\Delta t}}{u - d}, \qquad p_d = \frac{ue^{-\lambda\Delta t} - a}{u - d}, \qquad u = e^{\sqrt{(\sigma^2 - \lambda)\Delta t}}, \qquad d = \frac{1}{u}$$

where $a = e^{(r-q)\Delta t}$, r is the risk-free rate, and q is the dividend yield on the stock.

The life of the tree is set equal to the life of the convertible bond. The value of the convertible at the final nodes of the tree is calculated based on any conversion options that the holder has at that time. We then roll back through the tree. At nodes where the terms of the instrument allow conversion we test whether conversion is optimal. We also test whether the position of the issuer can be improved by calling the bonds. If so, we assume that the bonds are called and retest whether conversion is optimal. This is equivalent to setting the value at a node equal to

$$\max[\min(Q_1, Q_2), Q_3]$$

where Q_1 is the value given by the rollback (assuming that the bond is neither converted nor called at the node), Q_2 is the call price, and Q_3 is the value if conversion takes place.

[9] See J.E. Ingersoll, "A Contingent Claims Valuation of Convertible Securities," *Journal of Financial Economics*, 4, (May 1977), 289–322.

Example 21.1

Consider a 9-month zero-coupon bond issued by company XYZ with a face value of \$100. Suppose that it can be exchanged for two shares of company XYZ's stock at any time during the 9 months. Assume also that it is callable for \$113 at any time. The initial stock price is \$50, its volatility is 30% per annum, and there are no dividends. The default intensity λ is 1% per year, and all risk-free rates for all maturities are 5%. We assume that in the event of a default the bond is worth \$40 (i.e., the recovery rate as it is usually defined is 40%).

Figure 21.4 shows the stock price tree that can be used to value the convertible when there are three time steps ($\Delta t = 0.25$). The upper number at each node is the stock price; the lower number is the price of the convertible bond. The tree parameters are:

$$u = e^{\sqrt{(0.09-0.01)\times 0.25}} = 1.1519, \quad d = 1/u = 0.8681$$
$$a = e^{0.05\times 0.25} = 1.0126, \quad p_u = 0.5167, \quad p_d = 0.4808$$

The probability of a default (i.e., of moving to the lowest nodes on the tree is $1 - e^{-0.01\times 0.25} = 0.002497$. At the three default nodes the stock price is zero and the bond price is 40.

We first consider the final nodes. At nodes G and H the bond should be converted and is worth twice the stock price. At nodes I and J the bond should not be converted and is worth 100.

We then move back through the tree calculating the value at earlier nodes. Consider for example node E. The value if the bond is converted is $2 \times 50 = \$100$. If it is not converted, then there is (a) a probability 0.5167 that it will move to node H, where the bond is worth 115.19, (b) a 0.4808 probability that it will move down to node I, where the bond is worth 100, and (c) a 0.002497

Figure 21.4 Tree for valuing convertible. Upper number at each node is stock price; lower number is convertible bond price.

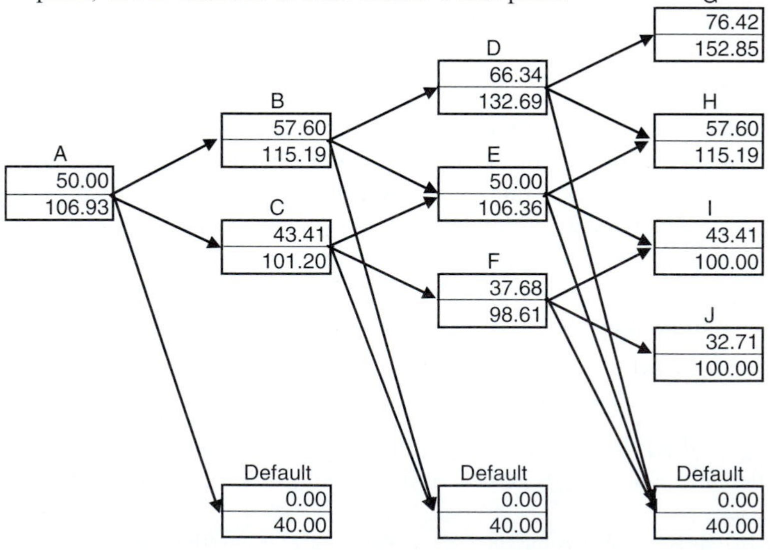

probability that it will default and be worth 40. The value of the bond if it is not converted is therefore

$$(0.5167 \times 115.19 + 0.4808 \times 100 + 0.002497 \times 40) \times e^{-0.05\times 0.25} = 106.36$$

This is more than the value of 100 that it would have if converted. We deduce that it is not worth converting the bond at node E. Finally, we note that the bond issuer would not call the bond at node E because this would be offering 113 for a bond worth 106.36.

As another example consider node B. The value of the bond if it is converted is $2 \times 57.596 = 115.19$. If it is not converted a similar calculation to that just given for node E gives its value as 118.31. The convertible bond holder will therefore choose not to convert. However, at this stage the bond issuer will call the bond for 113 and the bond holder will then decide that converting is better than being called. The value of the bond at node B is therefore 115.19. A similar argument is used to arrive at the value at node D. With no conversion the value is 132.79. However, the bond is called, forcing conversion and reducing the value at the node to 132.69.

The value of the convertible is its value at the initial node A, or 106.93.

When interest is paid on the debt, it must be taken into account. At each node when valuing the bond on the assumption that it is not converted, we include the present value of any interest payable on the bond in the next time step. The risk-neutral default intensity λ can be estimated from either bond prices or credit default swap spreads. In a more general implementation, λ, σ, and r are functions of time. This can be handled using a trinomial rather than a binomial tree (see Section 17.4).

One disadvantage of the model we have presented is that the probability of default is independent of the stock price. This has led some researchers to suggest an implicit finite difference method implementation of the model where the default intensity λ is a function of the stock price as well as time.[10]

SUMMARY

Credit derivatives enable banks and other financial institutions to actively manage their credit risks. They can be used to transfer credit risk from one company to another and to diversify credit risk by swapping one type of exposure for another.

The most common credit derivative is a credit default swap. This is a contract where one company buys insurance against another company defaulting on its obligations. The payoff is usually the difference between the face value of a bond issued by the second company and its value immediately after a default. Credit default swaps can be analyzed by calculating the present value of the expected payments and the present value of the expected payoff.

A forward credit default swap is an obligation to enter into a particular credit default swap on a particular date. A credit default swap option is the right to enter into a

[10] See, e.g., L. Andersen and D. Buffum, "Calibration and Implementation of Convertible Bond Models," *Journal of Computational Finance*, 7, 1 (Winter 2003/04), 1–34. These authors suggest assuming that the default intensity is inversely proportional to S^{α}, where S is the stock price and α is a positive constant.

particular credit default swap on a particular date. Both instruments cease to exist if the reference entity defaults before the date.

A total return swap is an instrument where the total return on a portfolio of credit-sensitive assets is exchanged for LIBOR plus a spread. Total return swaps are often used as financing vehicles. A company wanting to purchase a portfolio of bonds will approach a financial institution, who will buy the bonds on its behalf. The financial institution will then enter into a total return swap where it pays the return on the bonds to the company and receives LIBOR. The advantage of this type of arrangement is that the financial institution reduces its exposure to defaults by the company.

An nth-to-default CDS is defined as a CDS that pays off when the nth default occurs in a portfolio of companies. In a collateralized debt obligation a number of different securities are created from a portfolio of corporate bonds or commercial loans. There are rules for determining how credit losses are allocated to the securities. The result of the rules is that securities with both very high and very low credit ratings are created from the portfolio. A synthetic collateralized debt obligation creates a similar set of securities from credit default swaps. The standard market model for pricing both an nth-to-default CDS and tranches of a CDO is the one-factor Gaussian copula model for time to default.

Convertible bonds are bonds that can be converted to the issuer's equity according to prespecified terms. Credit risk has to be considered in the valuation of a convertible bond. This is because, if the bond is not converted, the promised payments on the bond are subject to credit risk. One popular procedure for valuing convertible bonds is to model equity prices on the assumption that there is a certain default intensity. In the event of a default the equity price drops to zero and the debt drops to a price reflecting its recovery rate.

FURTHER READING

Andersen, L., J. Sidenius, and S. Basu, "All Your Hedges in One Basket," *Risk*, November 2003.

Das S. *Credit Derivatives: Trading & Management of Credit & Default Risk*. Singapore: Wiley, 1998.

Hull, J. C., and A. White, "Valuation of a CDO and nth-to-Default Swap without Monte Carlo Simulation," *Journal of Derivatives*, 12, 2 (Winter 2004), 8–23.

Tavakoli, J. M., *Credit Derivatives: A Guide to Instruments and Applications*. New York: Wiley, 1998.

Schonbucher, P. J., *Credit Derivatives Pricing Models*. New York: Wiley, 2003.

Questions and Problems (Answers in Solutions Manual)

21.1. Explain the difference between a regular credit default swap and a binary credit default swap.

21.2. A credit default swap requires a semiannual payment at the rate of 60 basis points per year. The principal is $300 million and the credit default swap is settled in cash. A default occurs after 4 years and 2 months, and the calculation agent estimates that the price of the cheapest deliverable bond is 40% of its face value shortly after the default. List the cash flows and their timing for the seller of the credit default swap.

21.3. Explain the two ways a credit default swap can be settled.

21.4. Explain how a CDO and a synthetic CDO are created.

21.5. Explain what a first-to-default credit default swap is. Does its value increase or decrease as the default correlation between the companies in the basket increases? Explain.

21.6. Explain the difference between risk-neutral and real-world probabilities.

21.7. Explain why a total return swap can be useful as a financing tool.

21.8. Suppose that the risk-free zero curve is flat at 7% per annum with continuous compounding and that defaults can occur halfway through each year in a new 5-year credit default swap. Suppose that the recovery rate is 30% and the default probabilities each year conditional on no earlier default is 3%. Estimate the credit default swap spread. Assume payments are made annually.

21.9. What is the value of the swap in Problem 21.8 per dollar of notional principal to the protection buyer if the credit default swap spread is 150 basis points?

21.10. What is the credit default swap spread in Problem 21.8 if it is a binary CDS?

21.11. How does a 5-year nth-to-default credit default swap work? Consider a basket of 100 reference entities where each reference entity has a probability of defaulting in each year of 1%. As the default correlation between the reference entities increases what would you expect to happen to the value of the swap when (a) $n = 1$ and (b) $n = 25$. Explain your answer.

21.12. How is the recovery rate of a bond usually defined?

21.13. Show that the spread for a new plain vanilla CDS should be $(1 - R)$ times the spread for a similar new binary CDS, where R is the recovery rate.

21.14. Verify that if the CDS spread for the example in Tables 21.1 to 21.4 is 100 basis points and the probability of default in a year (conditional on no earlier default) must be 1.61%. How does the probability of default change when the recovery rate is 20% instead of 40%? Verify that your answer is consistent with the implied probability of default being approximately proportional to $1/(1 - R)$, where R is the recovery rate.

21.15. A company enters into a total return swap where it receives the return on a corporate bond paying a coupon of 5% and pays LIBOR. Explain the difference between this and a regular swap where 5% is exchanged for LIBOR.

21.16. Explain how forward contracts and options on credit default swaps are structured.

21.17. "The position of a buyer of a credit default swap is similar to the position of someone who is long a risk-free bond and short a corporate bond." Explain this statement.

21.18. Why is there a potential asymmetric information problem in credit default swaps?

21.19. Does valuing a CDS using real-world default probabilities rather than risk-neutral default probabilities overstate or understate its value? Explain your answer.

21.20. What is the difference between a total return swap and an asset swap?

21.21. Consider an 18-month zero-coupon bond with a face value of $100 that can be converted into five shares of the company's stock at any time during its life. Suppose that the current share price is $20, no dividends are paid on the stock, the risk-free rate for all maturities is 6% per annum with continuous compounding, and the share price volatility is 25% per annum. Assume that the default intensity is 3% per year and the recovery rate is 35%. The bond is callable at $110. Use a three-time-step tree to calculate the value of the bond. What is the value of the conversion option (net of the issuer's call option)?

21.22. Suppose that in a one-factor Gaussian copula model the 5-year probability of default for each of 125 names is 3% and the pairwise copula correlation is 0.2. Calculate, for factor values of −2, −1, 0, 1, and 2:
(a) The default probability conditional on the factor value
(b) The probability of more than 10 defaults conditional on the factor value when the factor value

21.23. What is a CDO squared? How about a CDO cubed?

Assignment Questions

21.24. Suppose that the risk-free zero curve is flat at 6% per annum with continuous compounding and that defaults can occur at times 0.25 years, 0.75 years, 1.25 years, and 1.75 years in a 2-year plain vanilla credit default swap with semiannual payments. Suppose that the recovery rate is 20% and the unconditional probabilities of default (as seen at time zero) are 1% at times 0.25 years and 0.75 years, and 1.5% at times 1.25 years and 1.75 years. What is the credit default swap spread? What would the credit default spread be if the instrument were a binary credit default swap?

21.25. Assume that the default probability for a company in a year, conditional on no earlier defaults is λ and the recovery rate is R. The risk-free interest rate is 5% per annum. Default always occurs halfway through a year. The spread for a 5-year plain vanilla CDS where payments are made annually is 120 basis points and the spread for a 5-year binary CDS where payments are made annually is 160 basis points. Estimate R and λ.

21.26. Explain how you would expect the yields offered on the various tranches in a CDO to change when the correlation between the bonds in the portfolio increases.

21.27. Suppose that:
(a) The yield on a 5-year risk-free bond is 7%.
(b) The yield on a 5-year corporate bond issued by company X is 9.5%.
(c) A 5-year credit default swap providing insurance against company X defaulting costs 150 basis points per year.

What arbitrage opportunity is there in this situation? What arbitrage opportunity would there be if the credit default spread were 300 basis points instead of 150 basis points? Give two reasons why arbitrage opportunities such as those you identify are less than perfect.

21.28. A 3-year convertible bond with a face value of $100 has been issued by company ABC. It pays a coupon of $5 at the end of each year. It can be converted into ABC's equity at the end of the first year or at the end of the second year. At the end of the first year, it can be exchanged for 3.6 shares immediately after the coupon date. At the end of the second year, it can be exchanged for 3.5 shares immediately after the coupon date. The current stock price is $25 and the stock price volatility is 25%. No dividends are paid on the stock. The risk-free interest rate is 5% with continuous compounding. The yield on bonds issued by ABC is 7% with continuous compounding and the recovery rate is 30%.
(a) Use a three-step tree to calculate the value of the bond.
(b) How much is the conversion option worth?

(c) What difference does it make to the value of the bond and the value of the conversion option if the bond is callable any time within the first 2 years for $115?

(d) Explain how your analysis would change if there were a dividend payment of $1 on the equity at the 6-month, 18-month, and 30-month points. Detailed calculations are not required.

(*Hint*: Use equation (20.2) to estimate the default intensity.)

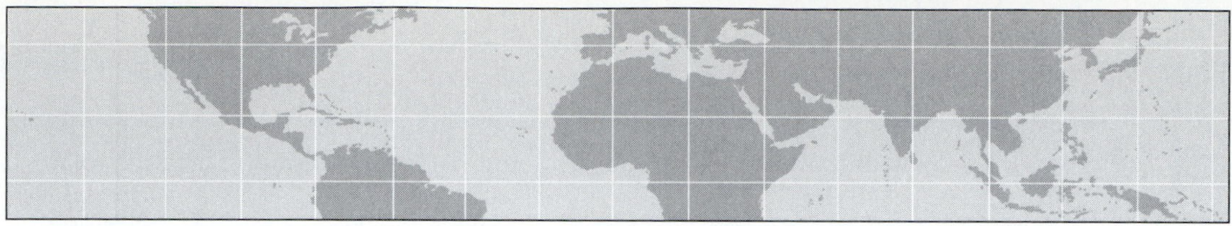

CHAPTER 22 Exotic Options

Derivatives such as European and American call and put options are what are termed *plain vanilla products*. They have standard well-defined properties and trade actively. Their prices or implied volatilities are quoted by exchanges or by brokers on a regular basis. One of the exciting aspects of the over-the-counter derivatives market is the number of nonstandard products that have been created by financial engineers. These products are termed *exotic options*, or simply *exotics*. Although they are usually a relatively small part of its portfolio, these exotics are important to an investment bank because they are generally much more profitable than plain vanilla products.

Exotic products are developed for a number of reasons. Sometimes they meet a genuine hedging need in the market; sometimes there are tax, accounting, legal, or regulatory reasons why corporate treasurers, fund managers, and financial institutions find exotic products attractive; sometimes the products are designed to reflect a view on potential future movements in particular market variables; occasionally an exotic product is designed by an investment bank to appear more attractive than it is to an unwary corporate treasurer or fund manager.

In this chapter we describe different types of exotic options and discuss their valuation. We use a categorization of exotic options similar to that in an excellent series of articles written by Eric Reiner and Mark Rubinstein for *Risk* magazine in 1991 and 1992. We assume that the asset provides a yield at rate q. As discussed in Chapter 14, for an option on a stock index we set q equal to the dividend yield on the index; for an option on a currency we set q equal to the foreign risk-free rate; and for an option on a futures contract we set q equal to the domestic risk-free rate. Most of the options discussed in this chapter can be valued using the DerivaGem software.

22.1 PACKAGES

A *package* is a portfolio consisting of standard European calls, standard European puts, forward contracts, cash, and the underlying asset itself. We discussed a number of different types of packages in Chapter 10: bull spreads, bear spreads, butterfly spreads, calendar spreads, straddles, strangles, and so on.

Figure 22.1 Payoffs from (a) short position and (b) long position in a range forward contract.

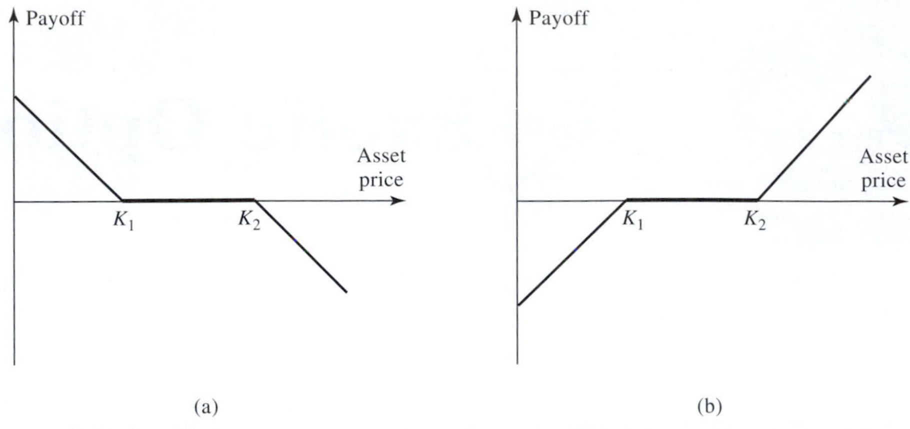

Often a package is structured by traders so that it has zero cost initially. An example is a *range forward contract*.[1] Figure 22.1 shows the payoff from short and long range forward contracts. A short range forward contract consists of a long position in a put with a low strike price, K_1, and a short position in a call with a high strike price, K_2. It guarantees that the underlying asset can be sold for a price between K_1 and K_2 at the maturity of the options. A long range forward contract consists of a short position in a put with the low strike price, K_1, and a long position in a call with the high strike price, K_2. It guarantees that the underlying asset can be purchased for a price between K_1 and K_2 at the maturity of the options. The value of the call usually equals the value of the put when the contract is initiated. As K_1 and K_2 are moved closer to each other, the price that will be received or paid for the asset at maturity becomes more certain. In the limit when $K_1 = K_2$, the range forward contract becomes a regular forward contract.

It is worth noting that any derivative can be converted into a zero-cost product by deferring payment until maturity. Consider a European call option. If c is the cost of the option when payment is made at time zero, then $A = ce^{rT}$ is the cost when payment is made at time T, the maturity of the option. The payoff is then $\max(S_T - K,\ 0) - A$ or $\max(S_T - K - A,\ -A)$. When the strike price, K, equals the forward price, other names for a deferred payment option are break forward, Boston option, forward with optional exit, and cancelable forward.

22.2 NONSTANDARD AMERICAN OPTIONS

In a standard American option, exercise can take place at any time during the life of the option and the exercise price is always the same. In practice, the American options that are traded in the over-the-counter market sometimes have nonstandard features.

[1] Other names used for a range forward contract are zero-cost collar, flexible forward, cylinder option, option fence, min–max, and forward band.

For example:

1. Early exercise may be restricted to certain dates. The instrument is then known as a *Bermudan option*.
2. Early exercise may be allowed during only part of the life of the option. For example, there may be an initial "lock out" period with no early exercise.
3. The strike price may change during the life of the option.

The warrants issued by corporations on their own stock often have some or all of these features. For example, in a 7-year warrant, exercise might be possible on particular dates during years 3 to 7, with the strike price being \$30 during years 3 and 4, \$32 during the next 2 years, and \$33 during the final year.

Nonstandard American options can usually be valued using a binomial tree. At each node, the test (if any) for early exercise is adjusted to reflect the terms of the option.

22.3 FORWARD START OPTIONS

Forward start options are options that will start at some time in the future. Executive options, which were discussed in Business Snapshot 8.3, can be viewed as a type of forward start option. This is because a company commits (implicitly or explicitly) to granting at-the-money options to employees in the future.

Consider a forward start at-the-money European call option that will start at time T_1 and mature at time T_2. Suppose that the asset price is S_0 at time zero and the S_1 at time T_1. To value the option, we note from the European option pricing formulas in Chapters 13 and 14 that the value of an at-the-money call option is proportional to the asset price. The value of the forward start option at time T_1 is therefore cS_1/S_0, where c is the value at time zero of an at-the-money option that lasts for $T_2 - T_1$. Using risk-neutral valuation, the value of the forward start option at time zero is

$$e^{-rT_1}\hat{E}\left[c\frac{S_1}{S_0}\right]$$

where $\hat{E}$ denotes the expected value in a risk-neutral world. Because c and S_0 are known and $\hat{E}[S_1] = S_0 e^{(r-q)T_1}$, it follows that the value of the forward start option is ce^{-qT_1}. For a non-dividend-paying stock, $q = 0$ and the value of the forward start option is exactly the same as the value of a regular at-the-money option with the same life as the forward start option.

22.4 COMPOUND OPTIONS

Compound options are options on options. There are four main types of compound options: a call on a call, a put on a call, a call on a put, and a put on a put. Compound options have two strike prices and two exercise dates. Consider, for example, a call on a call. On the first exercise date, T_1, the holder of the compound option is entitled to pay the first strike price, K_1, and receive a call option. The call option gives the holder the right to buy the underlying asset for the second strike price, K_2, on the second exercise date, T_2. The compound option will be exercised on the first exercise date only if the value of the option on that date is greater than the first strike price.

When the usual geometric Brownian motion assumption is made, European-style compound options can be valued analytically in terms of integrals of the bivariate normal distribution.[2] With our usual notation, the value at time zero of a European call option on a call option is

$$S_0e^{-qT_2}M(a_1, b_1; \sqrt{T_1/T_2}) - K_2e^{-rT_2}M(a_2, b_2; \sqrt{T_1/T_2}) - e^{-rT_1}K_1N(a_2)$$

where

$$a_1 = \frac{\ln(S_0/S^*) + (r - q + \sigma^2/2)T_1}{\sigma\sqrt{T_1}}, \qquad a_2 = a_1 - \sigma\sqrt{T_1}$$

$$b_1 = \frac{\ln(S_0/K_2) + (r - q + \sigma^2/2)T_2}{\sigma\sqrt{T_2}}, \qquad b_2 = b_1 - \sigma\sqrt{T_2}$$

The function $M(a, b : \rho)$ is the cumulative bivariate normal distribution function that the first variable will be less than a and the second will be less than b when the coefficient of correlation between the two is ρ.[3] The variable S^* is the asset price at time T_1 for which the option price at time T_1 equals K_1. If the actual asset price is above S^* at time T_1, the first option will be exercised; if it is not above S^*, the option expires worthless.

With similar notation, the value of a European put on a call is

$$K_2e^{-rT_2}M(-a_2, b_2; -\sqrt{T_1/T_2}) - S_0e^{-qT_2}M(-a_1, b_1; -\sqrt{T_1/T_2}) + e^{-rT_1}K_1N(-a_2)$$

The value of a European call on a put is

$$K_2e^{-rT_2}M(-a_2, -b_2; \sqrt{T_1/T_2}) - S_0e^{-qT_2}M(-a_1, -b_1; \sqrt{T_1/T_2}) - e^{-rT_1}K_1N(-a_2)$$

The value of a European put on a put is

$$S_0e^{-qT_2}M(a_1, -b_1; -\sqrt{T_1/T_2}) - K_2e^{-rT_2}M(a_2, -b_2; -\sqrt{T_1/T_2}) + e^{-rT_1}K_1N(a_2)$$

22.5 CHOOSER OPTIONS

A *chooser* option (sometimes referred to as an *as you like it* option) has the feature that, after a specified period of time, the holder can choose whether the option is a call or a put. Suppose that the time when the choice is made is T_1. The value of the chooser option at this time is

$$\max(c, p)$$

where c is the value of the call underlying the option and p is the value of the put underlying the option.

If the options underlying the chooser option are both European and have the same strike price, put–call parity can be used to provide a valuation formula. Suppose that S_1

---

[2] See R. Geske, "The Valuation of Compound Options," *Journal of Financial Economics*, 7 (1979): 63–81; M. Rubinstein, "Double Trouble," *Risk*, December 1991/January 1992: 53–56.

[3] See Technical Note 5 on the author's website for a numerical procedure for calculating M.

is the asset price at time T_1, K is the strike price, T_2 is the maturity of the options, and r is the risk-free interest rate. Put–call parity implies that

$$\begin{aligned}\max(c, p) &= \max(c,\ c + Ke^{-r(T_2-T_1)} - S_1e^{-q(T_2-T_1)}) \\ &= c + e^{-q(T_2-T_1)}\max(0,\ Ke^{-(r-q)(T_2-T_1)} - S_1)\end{aligned}$$

This shows that the chooser option is a package consisting of:

1. A call option with strike price K and maturity T_2
2. $e^{-q(T_2-T_1)}$ put options with strike price $Ke^{-(r-q)(T_2-T_1)}$ and maturity T_1

As such, it can readily be valued.

More complex chooser options can be defined where the call and the put do not have the same strike price and time to maturity. They are then not packages and have features that are somewhat similar to compound options.

22.6 BARRIER OPTIONS

Barrier options are options where the payoff depends on whether the underlying asset's price reaches a certain level during a certain period of time.

A number of different types of barrier options regularly trade in the over-the-counter market. They are attractive to some market participants because they are less expensive than the corresponding regular options. These barrier options can be classified as either *knock-out options* or *knock-in options*. A knock-out option ceases to exist when the underlying asset price reaches a certain barrier; a knock-in option comes into existence only when the underlying asset price reaches a barrier.

Equations (14.4) and (14.5) show that the values at time zero of a regular call and put option are

$$c = S_0e^{-qT}N(d_1) - Ke^{-rT}N(d_2)$$

$$p = Ke^{-rT}N(-d_2) - S_0e^{-qT}N(-d_1)$$

where

$$d_1 = \frac{\ln(S_0/K) + (r - q + \sigma^2/2)T}{\sigma\sqrt{T}}$$

$$d_2 = \frac{\ln(S_0/K) + (r - q - \sigma^2/2)T}{\sigma\sqrt{T}} = d_1 - \sigma\sqrt{T}$$

A *down-and-out call* is one type of knock-out option. It is a regular call option that ceases to exist if the asset price reaches a certain barrier level H. The barrier level is below the initial asset price. The corresponding knock-in option is a *down-and-in call*. This is a regular call that comes into existence only if the asset price reaches the barrier level.

If H is less than or equal to the strike price, K, the value of a down-and-in call at time zero is given by

$$c_{\text{di}} = S_0e^{-qT}(H/S_0)^{2\lambda}N(y) - Ke^{-rT}(H/S_0)^{2\lambda-2}N(y - \sigma\sqrt{T})$$

where

$$\lambda = \frac{r - q + \sigma^2/2}{\sigma^2}$$

$$y = \frac{\ln[H^2/(S_0K)]}{\sigma\sqrt{T}} + \lambda\sigma\sqrt{T}$$

Because the value of a regular call equals the value of a down-and-in call plus the value of a down-and-out call, the value of a down-and-out call is given by

$$c_{\text{do}} = c - c_{\text{di}}$$

If $H \geqslant K$, then

$$c_{\text{do}} = S_0N(x_1)e^{-qT} - Ke^{-rT}N(x_1 - \sigma\sqrt{T}) - S_0e^{-qT}(H/S_0)^{2\lambda}N(y_1) + Ke^{-rT}(H/S_0)^{2\lambda-2}N(y_1 - \sigma\sqrt{T})$$

and

$$c_{\text{di}} = c - c_{\text{do}}$$

where

$$x_1 = \frac{\ln(S_0/H)}{\sigma\sqrt{T}} + \lambda\sigma\sqrt{T}$$

$$y_1 = \frac{\ln(H/S_0)}{\sigma\sqrt{T}} + \lambda\sigma\sqrt{T}$$

An *up-and-out call* is a regular call option that ceases to exist if the asset price reaches a barrier level, H, that is higher than the current asset price. An *up-and-in call* is a regular call option that comes into existence only if the barrier is reached. When H is less than or equal to K, the value of the up-and-out call, c_{uo}, is zero and the value of the up-and-in call, c_{ui}, is c. When H is greater than K,

$$c_{\text{ui}} = S_0N(x_1)e^{-qT} - Ke^{-rT}N(x_1 - \sigma\sqrt{T}) - S_0e^{-qT}(H/S_0)^{2\lambda}[N(-y) - N(-y_1)] + Ke^{-rT}(H/S_0)^{2\lambda-2}[N(-y + \sigma\sqrt{T}) - N(-y_1 + \sigma\sqrt{T})]$$

and

$$c_{\text{uo}} = c - c_{\text{ui}}$$

Put barrier options are defined similarly to call barrier options. An *up-and-out put* is a put option that ceases to exist when a barrier, H, that is greater than the current asset price is reached. An *up-and-in put* is a put that comes into existence only if the barrier is reached. When the barrier, H, is greater than or equal to the strike price, K, their prices are

$$p_{\text{ui}} = -S_0e^{-qT}(H/S_0)^{2\lambda}N(-y) + Ke^{-rT}(H/S_0)^{2\lambda-2}N(-y + \sigma\sqrt{T})$$

and

$$p_{\text{uo}} = p - p_{\text{ui}}$$

When H is less than or equal to K,

$$p_{\text{uo}} = -S_0N(-x_1)e^{-qT} + Ke^{-rT}N(-x_1 + \sigma\sqrt{T}) + S_0e^{-qT}(H/S_0)^{2\lambda}N(-y_1) - Ke^{-rT}(H/S_0)^{2\lambda-2}N(-y_1 + \sigma\sqrt{T})$$

and

$$p_{ui} = p - p_{uo}$$

A *down-and-out put* is a put option that ceases to exist when a barrier less than the current asset price is reached. A *down-and-in put* is a put option that comes into existence only when the barrier is reached. When the barrier is greater than the strike price, $p_{do} = 0$ and $p_{di} = p$. When the barrier is less than the strike price,

$$p_{di} = -S_0N(-x_1)e^{-qT} + Ke^{-rT}N(-x_1 + \sigma\sqrt{T}) + S_0e^{-qT}(H/S_0)^{2\lambda}[N(y) - N(y_1)] \\ - Ke^{-rT}(H/S_0)^{2\lambda-2}[N(y - \sigma\sqrt{T}) - N(y_1 - \sigma\sqrt{T})]$$

and

$$p_{do} = p - p_{di}$$

All of these valuations make the usual assumption that the probability distribution for the asset price at a future time is lognormal. An important issue for barrier options is the frequency that the asset price, S, is observed for purposes of determining whether the barrier has been reached. The analytic formulas given in this section assume that S is observed continuously and sometimes this is the case.[4] Often, the terms of a contract state that S is observed periodically; for example, once a day at 12 noon. Broadie, Glasserman, and Kou provide a way of adjusting the formulas we have just given for the situation where the price of the underlying is observed discretely.[5] The barrier level H is replaced by $He^{0.5826\sigma\sqrt{T/m}}$ for an up-and-in or up-and-out option and by $He^{-0.5826\sigma\sqrt{T/m}}$ for a down-and-in or down-and-out option, where m is the number of times the asset price is observed (so that T/m is the time interval between observations).

Barrier options often have quite different properties from regular options. For example, sometimes vega is negative. Consider an up-and-out call option when the asset price is close to the barrier level. As volatility increases the probability that the barrier will be hit increases. As a result, a volatility increase can cause the price of the barrier option to decrease in these circumstances.

22.7 BINARY OPTIONS

Binary options are options with discontinuous payoffs. A simple example of a binary option is a *cash-or-nothing call*. This pays off nothing if the asset price ends up below the strike price at time T and pays a fixed amount, Q, if it ends up above the strike price. In a risk-neutral world, the probability of the asset price being above the strike price at the maturity of an option is, with our usual notation, $N(d_2)$. The value of a cash-or-nothing call is therefore $Qe^{-rT}N(d_2)$. A *cash-or-nothing put* is defined analogously to a cash-or-nothing call. It pays off Q if the asset price is below the strike price and nothing if it is above the strike price. The value of a cash-or-nothing put is $Qe^{-rT}N(-d_2)$.

Another type of binary option is an *asset-or-nothing call*. This pays off nothing if the

[4] One way to track whether a barrier has been reached from below (above) is to send a limit order to the exchange to sell (buy) the asset at the barrier price and see whether the order is filled.

[5] M. Broadie, P. Glasserman, and S. G. Kou, "A Continuity Correction for Discrete Barrier Options," *Mathematical Finance* 7, 4 (October 1997): 325–49.

underlying asset price ends up below the strike price and pays an amount equal to the asset price itself if it ends up above the strike price. With our usual notation, the value of an asset-or-nothing call is $S_0e^{-qT}N(d_1)$. An *asset-or-nothing put* pays off nothing if the underlying asset price ends up above the strike price and an amount equal to the asset price if it ends up below the strike price. The value of an asset-or-nothing put is $S_0e^{-qT}N(-d_1)$.

A regular European call option is equivalent to a long position in an asset-or-nothing call and a short position in a cash-or-nothing call where the cash payoff on the cash-or-nothing call equals the strike price. Similarly, a regular European put option is equivalent to a long position in a cash-or-nothing put and a short position in an asset-or-nothing put where the cash payoff on the cash-or-nothing put equals the strike price.

22.8 LOOKBACK OPTIONS

The payoffs from lookback options depend on the maximum or minimum asset price reached during the life of the option. The payoff from a European-style lookback call is the amount that the final asset price exceeds the minimum asset price achieved during the life of the option. The payoff from a European-style lookback put is the amount by which the maximum asset price achieved during the life of the option exceeds the final asset price.

Valuation formulas have been produced for European lookbacks.[6] The value of a European lookback call at time zero is

$$S_0e^{-qT}N(a_1) - S_0e^{-qT}\frac{\sigma^2}{2(r-q)}N(-a_1) - S_{\min}e^{-rT}\left[N(a_2) - \frac{\sigma^2}{2(r-q)}e^{Y_1}N(-a_3)\right]$$

where

$$a_1 = \frac{\ln(S_0/S_{\min}) + (r-q+\sigma^2/2)T}{\sigma\sqrt{T}}$$

$$a_2 = a_1 - \sigma\sqrt{T},$$

$$a_3 = \frac{\ln(S_0/S_{\min}) + (-r+q+\sigma^2/2)T}{\sigma\sqrt{T}}$$

$$Y_1 = -\frac{2(r-q-\sigma^2/2)\ln(S_0/S_{\min})}{\sigma^2}$$

and $S_{\min}$ is the minimum asset price achieved to date. (If the lookback has just been originated, $S_{\min} = S_0$.) See Problem 22.23 for the $r = q$ case.

The value of a European lookback put is

$$S_{\max}e^{-rT}\left[N(b_1) - \frac{\sigma^2}{2(r-q)}e^{Y_2}N(-b_3)\right] + S_0e^{-qT}\frac{\sigma^2}{2(r-q)}N(-b_2) - S_0e^{-qT}N(b_2)$$

[6] See B. Goldman, H. Sosin, and M. A. Gatto, "Path-Dependent Options: Buy at the Low, Sell at the High," *Journal of Finance*, 34 (December 1979): 1111–27.; M. Garman, "Recollection in Tranquility," *Risk*, March (1989): 16–19.

where

$$b_1 = \frac{\ln(S_{max}/S_0) + (-r + q + \sigma^2/2)T}{\sigma\sqrt{T}}$$

$$b_2 = b_1 - \sigma\sqrt{T}$$

$$b_3 = \frac{\ln(S_{max}/S_0) + (r - q - \sigma^2/2)T}{\sigma\sqrt{T}}$$

$$Y_2 = \frac{2(r - q - \sigma^2/2)\ln(S_{max}/S_0)}{\sigma^2}$$

and S_{max} is the maximum asset price achieved to date. (If the lookback has just been originated, then $S_{max} = S_0$.)

Example 22.1

Consider a newly issued lookback put on a non-dividend-paying stock where the stock price is 50, the stock price volatility is 40% per annum, the risk-free rate is 10% per annum, and the time to maturity is 3 months. In this case, $S_{max} = 50$, $S_0 = 50$, $r = 0.1$, $q = 0$, $\sigma = 0.4$, and $T = 0.25$. From the formulas just given, $b_1 = -0.025$, $b_2 = -0.225$, $b_3 = 0.025$, and $Y_2 = 0$, so that the value of the lookback put is 7.79. A newly issued lookback call on the same stock is worth 8.04.

A lookback call is a way that the holder can buy the underlying asset at the lowest price achieved during the life of the option. Similarly, a lookback put is a way that the holder can sell the underlying asset at the highest price achieved during the life of the option. The underlying asset in a lookback option is often a commodity. As with barrier options, the value of a lookback option is liable to be sensitive to the frequency that the asset price is observed for the purposes of computing the maximum or minimum. The formulas above assume that the asset price is observed continuously. Broadie, Glasserman, and Kou provide a way of adjusting the formulas we have just given for the situation where the asset price is observed discretely.[7]

22.9 SHOUT OPTIONS

A *shout option* is a European option where the holder can "shout" to the writer at one time during its life. At the end of the life of the option, the option holder receives either the usual payoff from a European option or the intrinsic value at the time of the shout, whichever is greater. Suppose the strike price is \$50 and the holder of a call shouts when the price of the underlying asset is \$60. If the final asset price is less than \$60, the holder receives a payoff of \$10. If it is greater than \$60, the holder receives the excess of the asset price over \$50.

A shout option has some of the same features as a lookback option, but is considerably less expensive. It can be valued by noting that if the holder shouts at a time τ when the asset price is S_τ the payoff from the option is

$$\max(0,\ S_T - S_\tau) + (S_\tau - K)$$

---

[7] M. Broadie, P. Glasserman, and S.G. Kou, "Connecting Discrete and Continuous Path-Dependent Options," *Finance and Stochastics*, 2 (1998): 1–28.

where, as usual, K is the strike price and S_T is the asset price at time T. The value at time τ if the holder shouts is therefore the present value of $S_\tau - K$ plus the value of a European option with strike price S_τ. The latter can be calculated using Black–Scholes formulas.

We value a shout option by constructing a binomial or trinomial tree for the underlying asset in the usual way. As we roll back through the tree, we calculate at each node the value of the option if we shout and the value if we do not shout. The option's price at the node is the greater of the two. The procedure for valuing a shout option is therefore similar to the procedure for valuing a regular American option.

22.10 ASIAN OPTIONS

Asian options are options where the payoff depends on the average price of the underlying asset during at least some part of the life of the option. The payoff from an *average price call* is $\max(0, S_{\text{ave}} - K)$ and that from an *average price put* is $\max(0, K - S_{\text{ave}})$, where S_{ave} is the average value of the underlying asset calculated over a predetermined averaging period. Average price options are less expensive than regular options and are arguably more appropriate than regular options for meeting some of the needs of corporate treasurers. Suppose that a US corporate treasurer expects to receive a cash flow of 100 million Australian dollars spread evenly over the next year from the company's Australian subsidiary. The treasurer is likely to be interested in an option that guarantees that the average exchange rate realized during the year is above some level. An average price put option can achieve this more effectively than regular put options.

Another type of Asian option is an average strike option. An *average strike call* pays off $\max(0, S_T - S_{\text{ave}})$ and an *average strike put* pays off $\max(0, S_{\text{ave}} - S_T)$. Average strike options can guarantee that the average price paid for an asset in frequent trading over a period of time is not greater than the final price. Alternatively, it can guarantee that the average price received for an asset in frequent trading over a period of time is not less than the final price.

If the underlying asset price, S, is assumed to be lognormally distributed and S_{ave} is a geometric average of the S's, analytic formulas are available for valuing European average price options.[8] This is because the geometric average of a set of lognormally distributed variables is also lognormal. Consider a newly issued option that will provide a payoff at time T based on the geometric average calculated between time zero and time T. In a risk-neutral world, it can be shown that the probability distribution of the geometric average of a asset price over a certain period is the same as that of the asset price at the end of the period if the asset's expected growth rate is set equal to $(r - q - \sigma^2/6)/2$ (rather than $r - q$) and its volatility is set equal to $\sigma/\sqrt{3}$ (rather than σ). The geometric average price option can, therefore, be treated like a regular option with the volatility set equal to $\sigma/\sqrt{3}$ and the dividend yield equal to

$$r - \tfrac{1}{2}\left(r - q - \frac{\sigma^2}{6}\right) = \tfrac{1}{2}\left(r + q + \frac{\sigma^2}{6}\right)$$

[8] See A. Kemna and A. Vorst, "A Pricing Method for Options Based on Average Asset Values," *Journal of Banking and Finance*, 14 (March 1990): 113–29.

When, as is nearly always the case, Asian options are defined in terms of arithmetic averages, exact analytic pricing formulas are not available. This is because the distribution of the arithmetic average of a set of lognormal distributions does not have analytically tractable properties. However, the distribution is approximately lognormal and this leads to a good analytic approximation for valuing average price options. We calculate the first two moments of the probability distribution of the arithmetic average in a risk-neutral world exactly and then fit a lognormal distribution to the moments.[9]

Consider a newly issued Asian option that provides a payoff at time T based on the arithmetic average between time zero and time T. The first moment, M_1, and the second moment, M_2, of the average in a risk-neutral world can be shown to be

$$M_1 = \frac{e^{(r-q)T} - 1}{(r-q)T} S_0$$

and

$$M_2 = \frac{2e^{[2(r-q)+\sigma^2]T} S_0^2}{(r-q+\sigma^2)(2r-2q+\sigma^2)T^2} + \frac{2S_0^2}{(r-q)T^2}\left[\frac{1}{2(r-q)+\sigma^2} - \frac{e^{(r-q)T}}{r-q+\sigma^2}\right]$$

when $q \neq r$ (see Problem 22.23 for the $q = r$ case).

If we assume that the average asset price is lognormal, we can regard an option on the average as like an option on a futures contract and use equations (14.16) and (14.17) with

$$F_0 = M_1 \tag{22.1}$$

and

$$\sigma^2 = \frac{1}{T}\ln\left(\frac{M_2}{M_1^2}\right) \tag{22.2}$$

Example 22.2

Consider a newly issued average price call option on a non-dividend-paying stock where the stock price is 50, the strike price is 50, the stock price volatility is 40% per annum, the risk-free rate is 10% per annum, and the time to maturity is 1 year. In this case, $S_0 = 50$, $K = 50$, $r = 0.1$, $q = 0$, $\sigma = 0.4$, and $T = 1$. If the average is a geometric average, we can value the option as a regular option with the volatility equal to $0.4/\sqrt{3}$, or 23.09%, and dividend yield equal to $(0.1 + 0.4^2/6)/2$, or 6.33%. The value of the option is 5.13. If the average is an arithmetic average, we first calculate $M_1 = 52.59$ and $M_2 = 2{,}922.76$. When we assume the average is lognormal, the option has the same value as an option on a futures contract. From equations (22.1) and (22.2), $F_0 = 52.59$ and $\sigma = 23.54\%$. DerivaGem gives the value of the option as 5.62.

The formulas just given for M_1 and M_2 assume that the average is calculated from continuous observations on the asset price. The appendix to this chapter shows how M_1 and M_2 can be obtained when the average is calculated from observations on the asset price at discrete points in time.

We can modify the analysis to accommodate the situation where the option is not newly issued and some prices used to determine the average have already been observed. Suppose that the averaging period is composed of a period of length t_1 over which

[9] See S. M. Turnbull and L. M. Wakeman, "A Quick Algorithm for Pricing European Average Options," *Journal of Financial and Quantitative Analysis*, 26 (September 1991): 377–89.

prices have already been observed and a future period of length t_2 (the remaining life of the option). Suppose that the average asset price during the first time period is $\bar{S}$. The payoff from an average price call is

$$\max\left(\frac{\bar{S}t_1 + S_{\text{ave}}t_2}{t_1 + t_2} - K,\ 0\right)$$

where S_{ave} is the average asset price during the remaining part of the averaging period. This is the same as

$$\frac{t_2}{t_1 + t_2}\max(S_{\text{ave}} - K^*,\ 0)$$

where

$$K^* = \frac{t_1 + t_2}{t_2}K - \frac{t_1}{t_2}\bar{S}$$

When $K^* > 0$, the option can be valued in the same way as a newly issued Asian option provided that we change the strike price from K to K^* and multiply the result by $t_2/(t_1 + t_2)$. When $K^* < 0$ the option is certain to be exercised and can be valued as a forward contract. The value is

$$\frac{t_2}{t_1 + t_2}[M_1e^{-rt_2} - K^*e^{-rt_2}]$$

22.11 OPTIONS TO EXCHANGE ONE ASSET FOR ANOTHER

Options to exchange one asset for another (sometimes referred to as *exchange options*) arise in various contexts. An option to buy yen with Australian dollars is, from the point of view of a US investor, an option to exchange one foreign currency asset for another foreign currency asset. A stock tender offer is an option to exchange shares in one stock for shares in another stock.

Consider a European option to give up an asset worth U_T at time T and receive in return an asset worth V_T. The payoff from the option is

$$\max(V_T - U_T,\ 0)$$

A formula for valuing this option was first produced by Margrabe.[10] Suppose that the asset prices, U and V, both follow geometric Brownian motion with volatilities σ_U and σ_V. Suppose further that the instantaneous correlation between U and V is ρ, and the yields provided by U and V are q_U and q_V, respectively. The value of the option at time zero is

$$V_0e^{-q_VT}N(d_1) - U_0e^{-q_UT}N(d_2) \tag{22.3}$$

where

$$d_1 = \frac{\ln(V_0/U_0) + (q_U - q_V + \hat{\sigma}^2/2)T}{\hat{\sigma}\sqrt{T}}, \qquad d_2 = d_1 - \hat{\sigma}\sqrt{T}$$

and

$$\hat{\sigma} = \sqrt{\sigma_U^2 + \sigma_V^2 - 2\rho\sigma_U\sigma_V}$$

and U_0 and V_0 are the values of U and V at times zero.

---

[10] See W. Margrabe, "The Value of an Option to Exchange One Asset for Another," *Journal of Finance*, 33 (March 1978): 177–86.

This result will be proved in Chapter 25. It is interesting to note that equation (22.3) is independent of the risk-free rate r. This is because, as r increases, the growth rate of both asset prices in a risk-neutral world increases, but this is exactly offset by an increase in the discount rate. The variable $\hat{\sigma}$ is the volatility of V/U. Comparisons with equation (14.4) show that the option price is the same as the price of U_0 European call options on an asset worth V/U when the strike price is 1.0, the risk-free interest rate is q_U, and the dividend yield on the asset is q_V. Mark Rubinstein shows that the American version of this option can be characterized similarly for valuation purposes.[11] It can be regarded as U_0 American options to buy an asset worth V/U for 1.0 when the risk-free interest rate is q_U and the dividend yield on the asset is q_V. The option can therefore be valued as described in Chapter 17 using a binomial tree.

An option to obtain the better or worse of two assets can be regarded as a position in one of the assets combined with an option to exchange it for the other asset:

$$\min(U_T, V_T) = V_T - \max(V_T - U_T, 0)$$
$$\max(U_T, V_T) = U_T + \max(V_T - U_T, 0)$$

22.12 OPTIONS INVOLVING SEVERAL ASSETS

Options involving two or more risky assets are sometimes referred to as *rainbow options*. One example is the bond futures contract traded on the CBOT described in Chapter 5. The party with the short position is allowed to choose between a large number of different bonds when making delivery.

Probably the most popular option involving several assets is a *basket option*. This is an option where the payoff is dependent on the value of a portfolio (or basket) of assets. The assets are usually either individual stocks or stock indices or currencies. A European basket option can be valued with Monte Carlo simulation, by assuming that the assets follow correlated geometric Brownian motion processes. A much faster approach is to calculate the first two moments of the basket at the maturity of the option in a risk-neutral world, and then assume that value of the basket is lognormally distributed at that time. The option can then be regarded as an option on a futures contract with the parameters shown in equations (22.1) and (22.2). The appendix to this chapter shows how the moments of the value of the basket at a future time can be calculated from the volatilities of, and correlations between, the assets. Correlations are typically estimated from historical data.

22.13 STATIC OPTIONS REPLICATION

If we try using the techniques described in Chapter 15 for hedging exotic options, we find that some are easy to handle while others are very difficult because of discontinuities (see Business Snapshot 22.1). For the difficult cases, a technique known as static options replication is sometimes useful.[12] This involves searching for a portfolio of

[11] See M. Rubinstein, "One for Another," *Risk*, July/August 1991: 30–32

[12] See E. Derman, D. Ergener, and I. Kani, "Static Options Replication," *Journal of Derivatives* 2, 4 (Summer 1995): 78–95.

Business Snapshot 22.1 Is Delta Hedging Easier or More Difficult for Exotics?

As described in Chapter 15 we can approach the hedging of exotic options by creating a delta neutral position and rebalancing frequently to maintain delta neutrality. When we do this we find some exotic options are easier to hedge than plain vanilla options and some are more difficult.

An example of an exotic option that is relatively easy to hedge is an average price option where the averaging period is the whole life of the option. As time passes, we observe more of the asset prices that will be used in calculating the final average. This means that our uncertainty about the payoff decreases with the passage of time. As a result, the option becomes progressively easier to hedge. In the final few days, the delta of the option always approaches zero because price movements during this time have very little impact on the payoff.

By contrast barrier options are relatively difficult to hedge. Consider a down-and-out call option on a currency when the exchange rate is 0.0005 above the barrier. If the barrier is hit, the option is worth nothing. If the barrier is not hit, the option may prove to be quite valuable. The delta of the option is discontinuous at the barrier making conventional hedging very difficult.

actively traded options that approximately replicates the exotic option. Shorting this position provides the hedge. The basic principle underlying static options replication is as follows. If two portfolios are worth the same on a certain boundary, they are also worth the same at all interior points of the boundary.

Consider as an example a 9-month up-and-out call option on a non-dividend-paying stock where the stock price is 50, the strike price is 50, the barrier is 60, the risk-free interest rate is 10% per annum, and the volatility is 30% per annum. Suppose that $f(S, t)$ is the value of the option at time t for a stock price of S. We can use any boundary in (S, t) space for the purposes of producing the replicating portfolio. A convenient one to choose is shown in Figure 22.2. It is defined by $S = 60$ and $t = 0.75$. The values of the up-and-out option on the boundary are given by

$$f(S, 0.75) = \max(S - 50, 0) \quad \text{when } S < 60$$

$$f(60, t) = 0 \quad \text{when } 0 \leqslant t \leqslant 0.75$$

There are many ways that we can approximately match these boundary values using regular options. The natural instrument to match the first boundary is a regular 9-month European call option with a strike price of 50. The first instrument introduced into the replicating portfolio is therefore likely to be one unit of this option. (We refer to this option as option A.) One way of then proceeding is as follows. We divide the life of the option into a number of time steps and choose options that satisfy the second boundary condition at the beginning of each time step.

Suppose that we choose time steps of 3 months. The next instrument we choose should lead to the second boundary being matched at $t = 0.5$. In other words, it should lead to the value of the complete replicating portfolio being zero when $t = 0.5$ and $S = 60$. The option should have the property that it has zero value on the first boundary since this has already been matched. One possibility is a regular 9-month European call

Figure 22.2 Boundary points used for static options replication example.

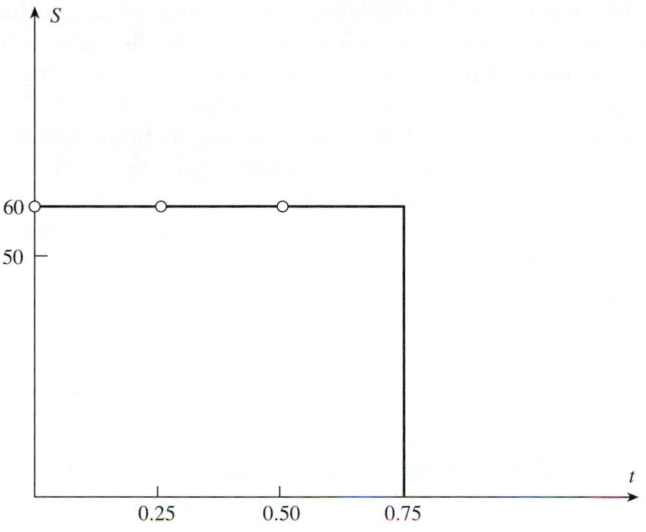

option with a strike price of 60. (We will refer to this as option B.) Black–Scholes formulas show that this is worth 4.33 at the 6-month point when $S = 60$. They also show that the position in option A is worth 11.54 at this point. The position we require in option B is therefore $-11.54/4.33 = -2.66$.

We next move on to matching the second boundary condition at $t = 0.25$. The option used should have the property that it has zero value on all boundaries that have been matched thus far. One possibility is a regular 6-month European call option with a strike price of 60. (We refer to this as option C.) This is worth 4.33 at the 3-month point when $S = 60$. Our position in options A and B is worth -4.21 at this point. The position we require in option C is therefore $4.21/4.33 = 0.97$.

Finally, we match the second boundary condition at $t = 0$. For this we use a regular 3-month European option with a strike price of 60. (We refer to this as option D.) Calculations similar to those above show that the required position in option D is 0.28.

The portfolio chosen is summarized in Table 22.1. (See also Sample Application F of the DerivaGem Application Builder.) It is worth 0.73 initially (i.e., at time zero when

Table 22.1 The portfolio of European call options used to replicate an up-and-out option.

Option	*Strike price*	*Maturity (years)*	*Position*	*Initial value*
A	50	0.75	1.00	+6.99
B	60	0.75	−2.66	−8.21
C	60	0.50	0.97	+1.78
D	60	0.25	0.28	+0.17

the stock price is 50). This compares with 0.31 given by the analytic formula for the up-and-out call earlier in this chapter. The replicating portfolio is not exactly the same as the up-and-out option because it matches the latter at only three points on the second boundary. If we use the same scheme, but match at 18 points on the second boundary (using options that mature every half month), the value of the replicating portfolio reduces to 0.38. If 100 points are matched, the value reduces further to 0.32.

To hedge a derivative, we short the portfolio that replicates its boundary conditions. This has the advantage over delta hedging that it does not require frequent rebalancing. The static replication approach can be used for a wide range of derivatives. The user has a great deal of flexibility in choosing the boundary that is to be matched and the options that are to be used. The portfolio must be unwound when any part of the boundary is reached.

SUMMARY

Exotic options are options with rules governing the payoff that are more complicated than standard options. We have discussed 12 different types of exotic options: packages, nonstandard American options, forward start options, compound options, chooser options, barrier options, binary options, lookback options, shout options, Asian options, options to exchange one asset for another, and options involving several assets. We have discussed how these can be valued using the same assumptions as those used to derive the Black–Scholes model in Chapter 13. Some can be valued analytically, but using much more complicated formulas than those for regular European calls and puts, some can be handled using analytic approximations, and some can be valued using extensions of the numerical procedures in Chapter 17. We will present more numerical procedures for valuing exotic options in Chapter 24.

Some exotic options are easier to hedge than the corresponding regular options; others are more difficult. In general, Asian options are easier to hedge because the payoff becomes progressively more certain as we approach maturity. Barrier options can be more difficult to hedge because delta is discontinuous at the barrier. One approach to hedging an exotic option, known as static options replication, is to find a portfolio of regular options whose value matches the value of the exotic option on some boundary. The exotic option is hedged by shorting this portfolio.

FURTHER READING

Clewlow, L., and C. Strickland, *Exotic Options: The State of the Art*. London: Thomson Business Press, 1997.

Derman, E., D. Ergener, and I. Kani, "Static Options Replication," *Journal of Derivatives*, 2, 4 (Summer 1995): 78–95.

Derman, E., I. Kani, and N. Chriss, "Static Options Replication," *Journal of Derivatives*, 1, 4 (Summer 1994): 6–14.

Geske, R., "The Valuation of Compound Options," *Journal of Financial Economics*, 7 (1979): 63–81.

Goldman, B., H. Sosin, and M. A. Gatto, "Path Dependent Options: Buy at the Low, Sell at the High," *Journal of Finance*, 34 (December 1979); 1111–27.

Margrabe, W., "The Value of an Option to Exchange One Asset for Another," *Journal of Finance*, 33 (March 1978): 177–86.

Milevsky, M. A., and S. E. Posner, "Asian Options: The Sum of Lognormals and the Reciprocal Gamma Distribution," *Journal of Financial and Quantitative Analysis*, 33, 3 (September 1998), 409–22.

Ritchken, P. "On Pricing Barrier Options," *Journal of Derivatives*, 3, 2 (Winter 1995): 19–28.

Ritchken P., L. Sankarasubramanian, and A. M. Vijh, "The Valuation of Path Dependent Contracts on the Average," *Management Science*, 39 (1993): 1202–13.

Rubinstein, M., and E. Reiner, "Breaking Down the Barriers," *Risk*, September (1991): 28–35.

Rubinstein, M., "Double Trouble," *Risk*, December/January (1991/1992): 53–56.

Rubinstein, M., "One for Another," *Risk*, July/August (1991): 30–32.

Rubinstein, M., "Options for the Undecided," *Risk*, April (1991): 70–73.

Rubinstein, M., "Pay Now, Choose Later," *Risk*, February (1991): 44–47.

Rubinstein, M., "Somewhere Over the Rainbow," *Risk*, November (1991): 63–66.

Rubinstein, M., "Two in One," *Risk* May (1991): 49.

Rubinstein, M., and E. Reiner, "Unscrambling the Binary Code," *Risk*, October 1991: 75–83.

Stulz, R. M., "Options on the Minimum or Maximum of Two Assets," *Journal of Financial Economics*, 10 (1982): 161–85.

Turnbull, S. M., and L. M. Wakeman, "A Quick Algorithm for Pricing European Average Options," *Journal of Financial and Quantitative Analysis*, 26 (September 1991): 377–89.

Zhang, P. G., *Exotic Options: A Guide to Second Generation Options*, 2nd edn. Singapore: World Scientific, 1998.

Questions and Problems (Answers in Solutions Manual)

22.1. Explain the difference between a forward start option and a chooser option.

22.2. Describe the payoff from a portfolio consisting of a lookback call and a lookback put with the same maturity.

22.3. Consider a chooser option where the holder has the right to choose between a European call and a European put at any time during a 2-year period. The maturity dates and strike prices for the calls and puts are the same regardless of when the choice is made. Is it ever optimal to make the choice before the end of the 2-year period? Explain your answer.

22.4. Suppose that c_1 and p_1 are the prices of a European average price call and a European average price put with strike price K and maturity T, c_2 and p_2 are the prices of a European average strike call and European average strike put with maturity T, and c_3 and p_3 are the prices of a regular European call and a regular European put with strike price K and maturity T. Show that

$$c_1 + c_2 - c_3 = p_1 + p_2 - p_3$$

22.5. The text derives a decomposition of a particular type of chooser option into a call maturing at time T_2 and a put maturing at time T_1. Derive an alternative decomposition into a call maturing at time T_1 and a put maturing at time T_2.

22.6. Section 22.6 gives two formulas for a down-and-out call. The first applies to the situation where the barrier, H, is less than or equal to the strike price, K. The second applies to the situation where $H \geqslant K$. Show that the two formulas are the same when $H = K$.

22.7. Explain why a down-and-out put is worth zero when the barrier is greater than the strike price.

22.8. Suppose that the strike price of an American call option on a non-dividend-paying stock grows at rate g. Show that if g is less than the risk-free rate, r, it is never optimal to exercise the call early.

22.9. How can the value of a forward start put option on a non-dividend-paying stock be calculated if it is agreed that the strike price will be 10% greater than the stock price at the time the option starts?

22.10. If a stock price follows geometric Brownian motion, what process does $A(t)$ follow where $A(t)$ is the arithmetic average stock price between time zero and time t?

22.11. Explain why delta hedging is easier for Asian options than for regular options.

22.12. Calculate the price of a 1-year European option to give up 100 ounces of silver in exchange for 1 ounce of gold. The current prices of gold and silver are \$380 and \$4, respectively; the risk-free interest rate is 10% per annum; the volatility of each commodity price is 20%; and the correlation between the two prices is 0.7. Ignore storage costs.

22.13. Is a European down-and-out option on an asset worth the same as a European down-and-out option on the asset's futures price for a futures contract maturing at the same time as the option?

22.14. Answer the following questions about compound options:
(a) What put–call parity relationship exists between the price of a European call on a call and a European put on a call? Show that the formulas given in the text satisfy the relationship.
(b) What put–call parity relationship exists between the price of a European call on a put and a European put on a put? Show that the formulas given in the text satisfy the relationship.

22.15. Does a lookback call become more valuable or less valuable as we increase the frequency with which we observe the asset price in calculating the minimum?

22.16. Does a down-and-out call become more valuable or less valuable as we increase the frequency with which we observe the asset price in determining whether the barrier has been crossed? What is the answer to the same question for a down-and-in call?

22.17. Explain why a regular European call option is the sum of a down-and-out European call and a down-and-in European call. Is the same true for American call options?

22.18. What is the value of a derivative that pays off \$100 in 6 months if the S&P 500 index is greater than 1,000 and zero otherwise? Assume that the current level of the index is 960, the risk-free rate is 8% per annum, the dividend yield on the index is 3% per annum, and the volatility of the index is 20%.

22.19. In a 3-month down-and-out call option on silver futures the strike price is \$20 per ounce and the barrier is \$18. The current futures price is \$19, the risk-free interest rate is 5%, and the volatility of silver futures is 40% per annum. Explain how the option works and calculate its value. What is the value of a regular call option on silver futures with the same terms? What is the value of a down-and-in call option on silver futures with the same terms?

22.20. A new European-style lookback call option on a stock index has a maturity of 9 months. The current level of the index is 400, the risk-free rate is 6% per annum, the dividend yield on the index is 4% per annum, and the volatility of the index is 20%. Use DerivaGem to value the option.

22.21. Estimate the value of a new 6-month European-style average price call option on a non-dividend-paying stock. The initial stock price is \$30, the strike price is \$30, the risk-free interest rate is 5%, and the stock price volatility is 30%.

22.22. Use DerivaGem to calculate the value of:

(a) A regular European call option on a non-dividend-paying stock where the stock price is \$50, the strike price is \$50, the risk-free rate is 5% per annum, the volatility is 30%, and the time to maturity is one year

(b) A down-and-out European call which is as in (a) with the barrier at \$45

(c) A down-and-in European call which is as in (a) with the barrier at \$45.

Show that the option in (a) is worth the sum of the values of the options in (b) and (c).

22.23. Explain adjustments that has to be made when $r = q$ for (a) the valuation formulas for lookback call options in Section 22.8 and (b) the formulas for M_1 and M_2 in Section 22.10.

Assignment Questions

22.24. What is the value in dollars of a derivative that pays off £10,000 in 1 year provided that the dollar/sterling exchange rate is greater than 1.5000 at that time? The current exchange rate is 1.4800. The dollar and sterling interest rates are 4% and 8% per annum, respectively. The volatility of the exchange rate is 12% per annum.

22.25. Consider an up-and-out barrier call option on a non-dividend-paying stock when the stock price is 50, the strike price is 50, the volatility is 30%, the risk-free rate is 5%, the time to maturity is 1 year, and the barrier at \$80. Use the software to value the option and graph the relationship between (a) the option price and the stock price, (b) the delta and the option price, (c) the option price and the time to maturity, and (d) the option price and the volatility. Provide an intuitive explanation for the results you get. Show that the delta, gamma, theta, and vega for an up-and-out barrier call option can be either positive or negative.

22.26. Sample Application F in the DerivaGem Application Builder Software considers the static options replication example in Section 22.13. It shows the way a hedge can be constructed using four options (as in Section 22.13) and two ways a hedge can be constructed using 16 options.

(a) Explain the difference between the two ways a hedge can be constructed using 16 options. Explain intuitively why the second method works better.

(b) Improve on the four-option hedge by changing Tmat for the third and fourth options.

(c) Check how well the 16-option portfolios match the delta, gamma, and vega of the barrier option.

22.27. Consider a down-and-out call option on a foreign currency. The initial exchange rate is 0.90, the time to maturity is 2 years, the strike price is 1.00, the barrier is 0.80, the domestic risk-free interest rate is 5%, the foreign risk-free interest rate is 6%, and the volatility is 25% per annum. Use DerivaGem to develop a static option replication strategy involving five options.

22.28. Suppose that a stock index is currently 900. The dividend yield is 2%, the risk-free rate is 5%, and the volatility is 40%. Use the results in the appendix to calculate the value of a 1-year average price call where the strike price is 900 and the index level is observed at the end of each quarter for the purposes of the averaging. Compare this with the price calculated by DerivaGem for a 1-year average price option where the price is observed continuously. Provide an intuitive explanation for any differences between the prices.

22.29. Use the DerivaGem Application Builder software to compare the effectiveness of daily delta hedging for (a) the option considered in Tables 15.2 and 15.3 and (b) an average price call with the same parameters. Use Sample Application C. For the average price option you will find it necessary to change the calculation of the option price in cell C16, the payoffs in cells H15 and H16, and the deltas (cells G46 to G186 and N46 to N186). Carry out 20 Monte Carlo simulation runs for each option by repeatedly pressing F9. On each run record the cost of writing and hedging the option, the volume of trading over the whole 20 weeks and the volume of trading between weeks 11 and 20. Comment on the results.

22.30. In the DerivaGem Application Builder Software modify Sample Application D to test the effectiveness of delta and gamma hedging for a call on call compound option on a 100,000 units of a foreign currency where the exchange rate is 0.67, the domestic risk-free rate is 5%, the foreign risk-free rate is 6%, the volatility is 12%. The time to maturity of the first option is 20 weeks, and the strike price of the first option is 0.015. The second option matures 40 weeks from today and has a strike price of 0.68. Explain how you modified the cells. Comment on hedge effectiveness.

APPENDIX

CALCULATION OF MOMENTS FOR VALUATION OF BASKET OPTIONS AND ASIAN OPTIONS

Consider first the problem of calculating the first two moments of the value of a basket of assets at a future time, T, in a risk-neutral world. The price of each asset in the basket is assumed to be lognormal. Define:

n: The number of assets

S_i: The value of the ith asset at time T[13]

F_i: The forward price of the ith asset for a contract maturing at time T

σ_i: The volatility of the ith asset between time zero and time T

ρ_{ij}: Correlation between returns from the ith and jth asset

P: Value of basket at time T

M_1: First moment of P in a risk-neutral world

M_2: Second moment of P in a risk-neutral world

Because $P = \sum_{i=1}^{n} S_i$, $\hat{E}(S_i) = F_i$, $M_1 = \hat{E}(P)$ and $M_2 = \hat{E}(P^2)$, where $\hat{E}$ denotes expected value in a risk-neutral world, it follows that

$$M_1 = \sum_{i=1}^{n} F_i$$

Also,

$$P^2 = \sum_{i=1}^{n}\sum_{j=1}^{n} S_i S_j$$

From the properties of lognormal distributions,

$$\hat{E}(S_i S_j) = F_i F_j e^{\rho_{ij}\sigma_i\sigma_j T}$$

Hence

$$M_2 = \sum_{i=1}^{n}\sum_{j=1}^{n} F_i F_j e^{\rho_{ij}\sigma_i\sigma_j T}$$

Asian Options

We now move on to the related problem of calculating the first two moments of the arithmetic average price of an asset in a risk-neutral world when the average is calculated from discrete observations. Suppose that the asset price is observed at times T_i $(1 \leqslant i \leqslant m)$. We redefine variables as follows:

S_i: The value of the asset at time T_i

F_i: The forward price of the asset for a contract maturing at time T_i

σ_i: The implied volatility for an option on the asset with maturity T_i

[13] If the ith asset is a certain stock and there are, say, 200 shares of the stock in the basket, then (for the purposes of the first part of the appendix) the ith "asset" is defined as 200 shares of the stock and S_i is the value of 200 shares of the stock.

ρ_{ij}: Correlation between return on asset up to time T_i and the return on the asset up to time T_j

P: Value of the arithmetic average

M_1: First moment of P in a risk-neutral world

M_2: Second moment of P in a risk-neutral world

In this case,

$$M_1 = \frac{1}{m}\sum_{i=1}^{m} F_i$$

Also,

$$P^2 = \frac{1}{m^2}\sum_{i=1}^{m}\sum_{j=1}^{m} S_i S_j$$

In this case,

$$\hat{E}(S_i S_j) = F_i F_j e^{\rho_{ij}\sigma_i\sigma_j\sqrt{T_i T_j}}$$

It can be shown that, when $i < j$,

$$\rho_{ij} = \frac{\sigma_i\sqrt{T_i}}{\sigma_j\sqrt{T_j}}$$

so that

$$\hat{E}(S_i S_j) = F_i F_j e^{\sigma_i^2 T_i}$$

and

$$M_2 = \frac{1}{m^2}\left[\sum_{i=1}^{m} F_i^2 e^{\sigma_i^2 T_i} + 2\sum_{j=1}^{m}\sum_{i=1}^{j-1} F_i F_j e^{\sigma_i^2 T_i}\right]$$

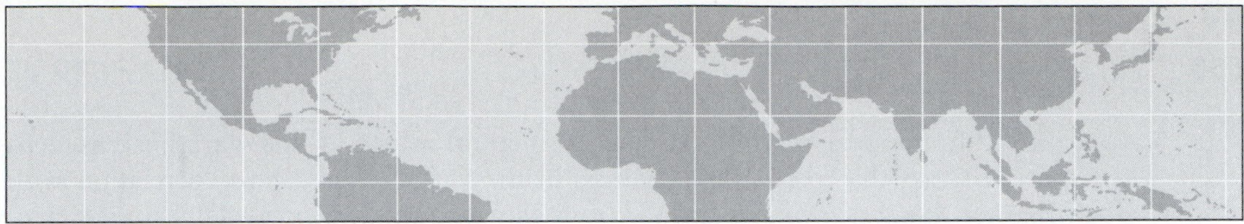

CHAPTER 23 Weather, Energy, and Insurance Derivatives

The most common underlying variables in derivatives contracts are stock prices, exchange rates, interest rates, and commodity prices. The futures, forward, option, and swap contracts on these variables have been outstandingly successful. As we discussed in Chapter 21, credit derivatives have also become very popular in recent years. Chapter 22 shows that one way dealers have expanded the derivatives market is by developing nonstandard (or exotic) structures for defining payoffs. This chapter discusses another way they have expanded the market. This is by trading derivatives on what might be termed "non-mainstream" underlying variables.

The chapter examines the products that have been developed to manage weather risk, energy price risk, and insurance risks. The markets that we will talk about are in some cases in the early stages of their development. As they evolve we may well see significant changes in both the products that are offered and the ways they are used.

23.1 REVIEW OF PRICING ISSUES

In Chapters 11 and 13, we explained the risk-neutral valuation result. This involves pricing the derivative on the assumption that investors are risk neutral. The expected payoff is calculated in a risk-neutral world and then discounted at the risk-free interest rate. The approach gives the correct price—not just in a risk-neutral world, but in all other worlds as well.

An alternative pricing approach sometimes adopted is to use historical data to calculate the expected payoff and then discount this expected payoff at the risk free rate to obtain the price. We will refer to this as the historical data approach. Historical data give an estimate of the expected payoff in the real world. It follows that the historical data approach is correct only when the expected payoff from the derivative is the same in both the real world and the risk-neutral world.

We showed in Section 11.7 that when we move from the real world to the risk-neutral world, the volatilities of variables remain the same, but their expected growth rates are liable to change. For example, the expected growth rate of a stock market index decreases by perhaps 4% or 5% when we move from the real world to the risk-neutral world. The expected growth rate of a variable can reasonably be assumed to be the same in both the real world and the risk-neutral world if the variable has zero systematic risk so that percentage changes in the variable have zero correlation with stock market returns.[1] We can deduce from this that the historical data approach to valuing a derivative gives the right answer if all underlying variables have zero systematic risk. A common feature of most of the derivatives we will consider in this chapter is that the historical data approach can be used. The underlying variables can reasonably be assumed to have zero systematic risk.

23.2 WEATHER DERIVATIVES

Many companies are in the position where their performance is liable to be adversely affected by the weather.[2] It makes sense for these companies to consider hedging their weather risk in much the same way as they hedge foreign exchange or interest rate risks.

The first over-the-counter weather derivatives were introduced in 1997. To understand how they work, we explain two variables:

HDD: Heating degree days

CDD: Cooling degree days

A day's HDD is defined as

$$\text{HDD} = \max(0,\ 65 - A)$$

and a day's CDD is defined as

$$\text{CDD} = \max(0,\ A - 65)$$

where A is the average of the highest and lowest temperature during the day at a specified weather station, measured in degrees Fahrenheit. For example, if the maximum temperature during a day (midnight to midnight) is 68° Fahrenheit and the minimum temperature is 44° Fahrenheit, then $A = 56$. The daily HDD is then 9 and the daily CDD is 0.

A typical over-the-counter product is a forward or option contract providing a payoff dependent on the cumulative HDD or CDD during a month (i.e., the total of the HDDs or CDDs for every day in the month). For example, a dealer could in January 2004 sell a client a call option on the cumulative HDD during February 2005 at the Chicago O'Hare Airport weather station with a strike price of 700 and a payment rate of $10,000 per degree day. If the actual cumulative HDD is 820, the payoff is $1.2 million. Contracts often include a payment cap. If the payment cap in our example is $1.5 million, the contract is the equivalent of a bull spread. The client has a long call option on cumulative HDD with a strike price of 700 and a short call option with a strike price of 850.

A day's HDD is a measure of the volume of energy required for heating during the day. A day's CDD is a measure of the volume of energy required for cooling during the day. Most weather derivative contracts are entered into by energy producers and energy consumers. But retailers, supermarket chains, food and drink manufacturers, health service companies, agricultural companies, and companies in the leisure industry are also potential users of weather derivatives. The Weather Risk Management Association

[1] We will discuss this further in Chapter 31.

[2] The US Department of Energy has estimated that one-seventh of the US economy is subject to weather risk.

(www.wrma.org) has been formed to serve the interests of the weather risk management industry.

In September 1999 the Chicago Mercantile Exchange began trading weather futures and European options on weather futures. The contracts are on the cumulative HDD and CDD for a month observed at a weather station.[3] The contracts are settled in cash just after the end of the month once the HDD and CDD are known. One futures contract is on \$100 times the cumulative HDD or CDD. The HDD and CDD are calculated by a company, Earth Satellite Corporation, using automated data-collection equipment.

The temperature at a certain location can reasonably be assumed to have zero systematic risk. It follows from Section 23.1 that weather derivatives can be priced using the historical data approach. Consider, for example, the call option on the February 2005 HDD at Chicago O'Hare airport mentioned earlier. We could collect 50 years of data and estimate a probability distribution for the HDD in February. This in turn could be used to provide a probability distribution for the option payoff. Our estimate of the value of the option would be the mean of this distribution discounted at the risk-free rate. We might want to adjust the probability distribution for temperature trends. For example, a linear regression might show that (perhaps because of global warming) the HDD in February is decreasing at a rate of 10 per year on average. If so the output from the regression could be used to estimate a trend-adjusted probability distribution for the HDD in February 2005.

23.3 ENERGY DERIVATIVES

Energy companies are among the most active and sophisticated users of derivatives. Many energy products trade in both the over-the-counter market and on exchanges. In this section we will examine the trading in crude oil, natural gas, and electricity derivatives.

Crude Oil

Crude oil is one of the most important commodities in the world, with global demand amounting to about 80 million barrels daily. Ten-year fixed-price supply contracts have been commonplace in the over-the-counter market for many years. These are swaps where oil at a fixed price is exchanged for oil at a floating price.

In the 1970s the price of oil was highly volatile. The 1973 war in the Middle East led to a tripling of oil prices. The fall of the Shah of Iran in the late 1970s again increased prices. These events led oil producers and users to a realization that they needed more sophisticated tools for managing oil-price risk. In the 1980s both the over-the-counter market and the exchange-traded market developed products to meet this need.

In the over-the-counter market, virtually any derivative that is available on common stocks or stock indices is now available with oil as the underlying asset. Swaps, forward contracts, and options are popular. Contracts sometimes require settlement in cash and sometimes require settlement by physical delivery (i.e., by delivery of the oil).

---

[3] The CME has introduced contracts for 10 different weather stations (Atlanta, Chicago, Cincinnati, Dallas, Des Moines, Las Vegas, New York, Philadelphia, Portland, and Tucson).

Exchange-traded contracts are also popular. The New York Mercantile Exchange (NYMEX) and the International Petroleum Exchange (IPE) trade a number of oil futures and futures options contracts. Some of the futures contracts are settled in cash; others are settled by physical delivery. For example the Brent crude oil futures traded on the IPE has cash settlement based on the Brent index price; the light sweet crude oil futures traded on NYMEX requires physical delivery. In both cases the amount of oil underlying one contract is 1,000 barrels. NYMEX also trades popular contracts on two refined products: heating oil and gasoline. In both cases one contract is for the delivery of 42,000 gallons.

Natural Gas

The natural gas industry throughout the world has been going through a period of deregulation and the elimination of government monopolies. The supplier of natural gas is now not necessarily the same company as the producer of the gas. Suppliers are faced with the problem of meeting daily demand.

A typical over-the-counter contract is for the delivery of a specified amount of natural gas at a roughly uniform rate over a one-month period. Forward contracts, options, and swaps are available in the over-the-counter market. The seller of gas is usually responsible for moving the gas through pipelines to the specified location.

NYMEX trades a contract for the delivery of 10,000 million British thermal units of natural gas. The contract, if not closed out, requires physical delivery to be made during the delivery month at a roughly uniform rate to a particular hub in Louisiana. The IPE trades a similar contract in London.

Electricity

Electricity is an unusual commodity because it cannot easily be stored.[4] The maximum supply of electricity in a region at any moment is determined by the maximum capacity of all the electricity-producing plants in the region. In the United States there are 140 regions known as *control areas*. Demand and supply are first matched within a control area, and any excess power is sold to other control areas. It is this excess power that constitutes the wholesale market for electricity. The ability of one control area to sell power to another control area depends on the transmission capacity of the lines between the two areas. Transmission from one area to another involves a transmission cost, charged by the owner of the line, and there are generally some transmission or energy losses.

A major use of electricity is for air-conditioning systems. As a result the demand for electricity, and therefore its price, is much greater in the summer months than in the winter months. The nonstorability of electricity causes occasional very large movements in the spot price. Heat waves have been known to increase the spot price by as much as 1000% for short periods of time.

Like natural gas, electricity has been going through a period of deregulation and the elimination of government monopolies. This has been accompanied by the development of an electricity derivatives market. NYMEX now trades a futures contract on the price

[4] Electricity producers with spare capacity sometimes use it to pump water to the top of their hydroelectric plants so that it can be used to produce electricity at a later time. This is the closest they can get to storing this commodity.

of electricity, and there is an active over-the-counter market in forward contracts, options, and swaps. A typical contract (exchange traded or over the counter) allows one side to receive a specified number of megawatt-hours for a specified price at a specified location during a particular month. In a 5×8 contract, power is received for 5 days a week (Monday to Friday) during the off-peak period (11 p.m. to 7 a.m.) for the specified month. In a 5×16 contract, power is received 5 days a week during the on-peak period (7 a.m. to 11 p.m.) for the specified month. In a 7×24 contract, it is received around the clock every day during the month. Option contracts have either daily exercise or monthly exercise. In the case of daily exercise, the option holder can choose on each day of the month (by giving one day's notice) to receive the specified amount of power at the specified strike price. When there is monthly exercise a single decision on whether to receive power for the whole month at the specified strike price is made at the beginning of the month.

An interesting contract in electricity and natural gas markets is what is known as a *swing option* or *take-and-pay option*. In this contract a minimum and maximum for the amount of power that must be purchased at a certain price by the option holder is specified for each day during a month and for the month in total. The option holder can change (or swing) the rate at which the power is purchased during the month, but usually there is a limit on the total number of changes that can be made.

Modeling Energy Prices

A realistic model for a energy and other commodity prices should incorporate both mean reversion and volatility. One possible model is:

$$d \ln S = [\theta(t) - a \ln S]\, dt + \sigma\, dz \qquad \textbf{(23.1)}$$

where S is the energy price, and a and σ are constant parameters. The $\theta(t)$ term captures seasonality and trends. In Chapter 31 we will show how to construct a trinomial tree for the model in equation (23.1) with $\theta(t)$ being estimated from futures prices. The parameters a and σ can be estimated from historical data.

The parameters a and σ are different for different sources of energy. For crude oil, the reversion rate parameter a in equation (23.1) is about 0.5 and the volatility parameter σ is about 20%; for natural gas, a is about 1.0 and σ is about 40%; for electricity, a is typically between 10 and 20, while σ is 100 to 200%. The seasonality of electricity prices is also greater.[5]

How an Energy Producer Can Hedge Risks

There are two components to the risks facing an energy producer. One is the price risk; the other is the volume risk. Although prices do adjust to reflect volumes, there is a less-than-perfect relationship between the two, and energy producers have to take both into account when developing a hedging strategy. The price risk can be hedged using the energy derivative contracts discussed in this section. The volume risks can be hedged using the weather derivatives discussed in the previous section.

[5] For a fuller discussion of the spot price behavior of energy products, see D. Pilipovic, *Energy Risk*. New York: McGraw-Hill, 1997.

Define:

Y: Profit for a month

P: Average energy prices for the month

T: Relevant temperature variable (HDD or CDD) for the month

An energy producer can use historical data to obtain a best-fit linear regression relationship of the form

$$Y = a + bP + cT + \epsilon$$

where ϵ is the error term. The energy producer can then hedge risks for the month by taking a position of $-b$ in energy forwards or futures and a position of $-c$ in weather forwards or futures. The relationship can also be used to analyze the effectiveness of alternative option strategies.

23.4 INSURANCE DERIVATIVES

When derivative contracts are used for hedging purposes, they have many of the same characteristics as insurance contracts. Both types of contracts are designed to provide protection against adverse events. It is not surprising that many insurance companies have subsidiaries that trade derivatives and that many of the activities of insurance companies are becoming very similar to those of investment banks.

Traditionally the insurance industry has hedged its exposure to catastrophic (CAT) risks such as hurricanes and earthquakes using a practice known as reinsurance. Reinsurance contracts can take a number of forms. Suppose that an insurance company has an exposure of \$100 million to earthquakes in California and wants to limit this to \$30 million. One alternative is to enter into annual reinsurance contracts that cover on a pro rata basis 70% of its exposure. If California earthquake claims in a particular year total \$50 million, the costs to the company would then be only $0.3 \times \$50$, or \$15 million. Another more popular alternative, involving lower reinsurance premiums, is to buy a series of reinsurance contracts covering what are known as *excess cost layers*. The first layer might provide indemnification for losses between \$30 million and \$40 million; the next layer might cover losses between \$40 million and \$50 million; and so on. Each reinsurance contract is known as an *excess-of-loss* reinsurance contract. The reinsurer has written a bull spread on the total losses. It is long a call option with a strike price equal to the lower end of the layer and short a call option with a strike price equal to the upper end of the layer.[6]

The principal providers of CAT reinsurance have traditionally been reinsurance companies and Lloyds syndicates (which are unlimited liability syndicates of wealthy individuals). In recent years the industry has come to the conclusion that its reinsurance needs have outstripped what can be provided from these traditional sources. It has searched for new ways in which capital markets can provide reinsurance. One of the events that caused the industry to rethink its practices was Hurricane Andrew in 1992, which caused about \$15 billion of insurance costs in Florida. This exceeded the total of relevant insurance premiums received in Florida during the previous seven years. If

---

[6] Reinsurance is also sometimes offered in the form of a lump sum if a certain loss level is reached. The reinsurer is then writing a cash-or-nothing binary call option on the losses.

Hurricane Andrew had hit Miami, it is estimated that insured losses would have exceeded $40 billion. Hurricane Andrew and other catastrophes have led to increases in insurance/reinsurance premiums.

Exchange-traded insurance futures contracts have been developed by the CBOT, but have not been highly successful. The over-the-counter market has come up with a number of products that are alternatives to traditional reinsurance. The most popular is a CAT bond. This is a bond issued by a subsidiary of an insurance company that pays a higher-than-normal interest rate. In exchange for the extra interest the holder of the bond agrees to provide an excess-of-cost reinsurance contract. Depending on the terms of the CAT bond, the interest or principal (or both) can be used to meet claims. In the example considered above where an insurance company wants protection for California earthquake losses between $30 million and $40 million, the insurance company could issue CAT bonds with a total principal of $10 million. In the event that the insurance company's California earthquake losses exceeded $30 million, bond holders would lose some or all of their principal. As an alternative the insurance company could cover this excess cost layer by making a much bigger bond issue where only the bondholders' interest is at risk.

CAT bonds typically give a high probability of an above-normal rate of interest and a low-probability of a high loss. Why would investors be interested in such instruments? The answer is that there are no statistically significant correlations between CAT risks and market returns.[7] CAT bonds are therefore an attractive addition to an investor's portfolio. They have no systematic risk, so that their total risk can be completely diversified away in a large portfolio. If a CAT bond's expected return is greater than the risk-free interest rate (and typically it is), it has the potential to improve risk–return trade-offs.

SUMMARY

This chapter has shown that when there are risks to be managed, derivative markets have been very innovative in developing products to meet the needs of market participants.

In the weather derivatives market, two measures, HDD and CDD, have been developed to describe the temperature during a month. These are used to define the payoffs on both exchange-traded and over-the-counter derivatives. No doubt, as the weather derivatives market develops, we will see contracts on rainfall, snow, and similar variables become more commonplace.

In energy markets, oil derivatives have been important for some time and play a key role in helping oil producers and oil consumers manage their price risk. Natural gas and electricity derivatives are relatively new. They became important for risk management when these markets were deregulated and government monopolies discontinued.

Insurance derivatives are now beginning to be an alternative traditional reinsurance as a way for insurance companies to manage the risks of a catastrophic event such as a hurricane or an earthquake. No doubt we will see other sorts of insurance (e.g., life insurance and automobile insurance) being securitized in a similar way as this market develops.

---

[7] See R. H. Litzenberger, D. R. Beaglehole, and C. E. Reynolds, "Assessing Catastrophe Reinsurance-Linked Securities as a New Asset Class," *Journal of Portfolio Management*, Winter (1996): 76–86.

Weather, energy, and insurance derivatives have the property that percentage changes in the underlying variables have negligible correlations with market returns. This means that we can value derivatives by calculating expected payoffs using historical data and then discounting the expected payoffs at the risk-free rate.

FURTHER READING

On Weather Derivatives

Arditti, F., L. Cai, M. Cao, and R. McDonald, "Whether to Hedge," *Risk*, Supplement on Weather Risk (1999): 9–12.

Cao, M., and J. Wei, "Weather Derivatives Valuation and the Market Price of Weather Derivatives," *Journal of Futures Markets*, 24, 11 (November 2004): 1065–89.

Hunter, R., "Managing Mother Nature," *Derivatives Strategy*, February (1999).

On Energy Derivatives

Clewlow, L., and C. Strickland, *Energy Derivatives: Pricing and Risk Management*, Lacima Group, 2000.

Eydeland, A., and H. Geman, "Pricing Power Derivatives," *Risk*, October (1998): 71–73.

Joskow, P., "Electricity Sectors in Transition," *The Energy Journal*, 19 (1998): 25–52.

Kendall, R., "Crude Oil: Price Shocking," *Risk* Supplement on Commodity Risk, May (1999).

On Insurance Derivatives

Canter, M. S., J. B. Cole, and R. L. Sandor, "Insurance Derivatives: A New Asset Class for the Capital Markets and a New Hedging Tool for the Insurance Industry," *Journal of Applied Corporate Finance*, Autumn (1997): 69–83.

Froot, K. A., "The Market for Catastrophe Risk: A Clinical Examination," *Journal of Financial Economics*, 60 (2001): 529–71.

Froot, K. A., *The Financing of Catastrophe Risk*. University of Chicago Press, 1999.

Geman, H., "CAT Calls," *Risk*, September (1994): 86–89.

Hanley, M., "A Catastrophe Too Far," *Risk* Supplement on Insurance, July (1998).

Litzenberger, R. H., D. R. Beaglehole, and C. E. Reynolds, "Assessing Catastrophe Reinsurance-Linked Securities as a New Asset Class," *Journal of Portfolio Management*, Winter (1996): 76–86.

Questions and Problems (Answers in Solutions Manual)

23.1. What is meant by HDD and CDD?

23.2. How is a typical natural gas forward contract structured?

23.3. Distinguish between the historical data and the risk-neutral approach to valuing a derivative. Under what circumstance do they give the same answer.

23.4. Suppose that each day during July the minimum temperature is 68° Fahrenheit and the maximum temperature is 82° Fahrenheit. What is the payoff from a call option on the cumulative CDD during July with a strike of 250 and a payment rate of $5,000 per degree-day?

23.5. Why is the price of electricity more volatile than that of other energy sources?

23.6. Why is the historical data approach appropriate for pricing a weather derivatives contract and a CAT bond?

23.7. "HDD and CDD can be regarded as payoffs from options on temperature." Explain this statement.

23.8. Suppose that you have 50 years of temperature data at your disposal. Explain carefully the analyses you would carry out to value a forward contract on the cumulative CDD for a particular month.

23.9. Would you expect the volatility of the 1-year forward price of oil to be greater than or less than the volatility of the spot price? Explain your answer.

23.10. What are the characteristics of an energy source where the price has a very high volatility and a very high rate of mean reversion? Give an example of such an energy source.

23.11. How can an energy producer use derivatives markets to hedge risks?

23.12. Explain how a 5×8 option contract for May 2006 on electricity with daily exercise works. Explain how a 5×8 option contract for May 2006 on electricity with monthly exercise works. Which is worth more?

23.13. Explain how CAT bonds work.

23.14. Consider two bonds that have the same coupon, time to maturity, and price. One is a B-rated corporate bond. The other is a CAT bond. An analysis based on historical data shows that the expected losses on the two bonds in each year of their life is the same. Which bond would you advise a portfolio manager to buy and why?

Assignment Question

23.15. An insurance company's losses of a particular type are to a reasonable approximation normally distributed with a mean of $150 million and a standard deviation of $50 million. (Assume no difference between losses in a risk-neutral world and losses in the real world.) The 1-year risk-free rate is 5%. Estimate the cost of the following:

(a) A contract that will pay in 1 year's time 60% of the insurance company's costs on a pro rata basis

(b) A contract that pays $100 million in 1 year's time if losses exceed $200 million

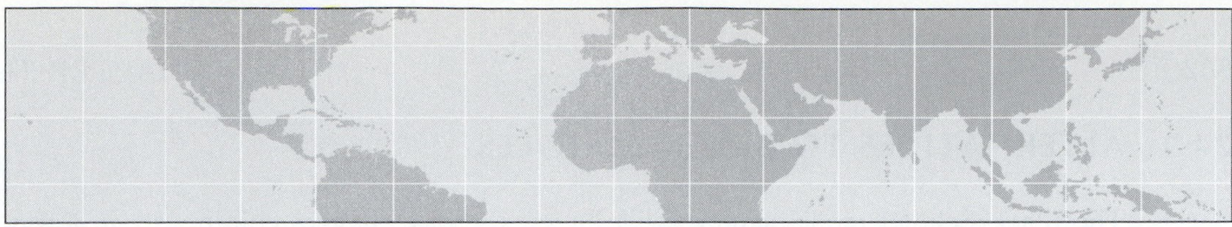

CHAPTER 24

More on Models and Numerical Procedures

Up to now the models we have used to value options have been based on the geometric Brownian motion model of asset price behavior that underlies the Black–Scholes formulas and the numerical procedures we have used have been relatively straightforward. In this chapter we introduce a number of new models and explain how the numerical procedures can be adapted to cope with particular situations.

In Chapter 16 we explained how traders overcome the weaknesses in the geometric Brownian motion model by using volatility surfaces. A volatility surface determines an appropriate volatility to substitute into Black–Scholes when pricing plain vanilla options. Unfortunately it says little about the volatility that should be used for exotic options when the pricing formulas of Chapter 22 are used. Suppose the volatility surface shows that the correct volatility to use when pricing a 1-year plain vanilla option with a strike price of \$40 is 27%. This is liable to be totally inappropriate for pricing a barrier option (or some other exotic option) that has a strike price of \$40 and a life of 1 year.

The first part of this chapter discusses a number of alternatives to geometric Brownian motion that are designed to deal with the problem of pricing exotic options consistently with plain vanilla options. These alternative asset price processes fit the market prices of plain vanilla options better than geometric Brownian motion. As a result, we can have more confidence in using them to value exotic options.

The second part of the chapter extends our discussion of numerical procedures. We explain how some types of path-dependent derivatives can be valued using trees. We discuss the special problems associated with valuing barrier options numerically and how these problems can be handled. Finally, we outline alternative ways of constructing trees for two correlated variables and show how Monte Carlo simulation can be used to value derivatives when there are early exercise opportunities.

As in earlier chapters our results are presented for derivatives dependent on an asset providing a yield at rate q. For an option on a stock index, q should be set equal to the dividend yield on the index; for an option on a currency, q should be set equal to the foreign risk-free rate; for an option on a futures contract, q should be set equal to the domestic risk-free rate.

24.1 ALTERNATIVES TO BLACK–SCHOLES

The Black–Scholes model assumes that an asset's price changes continously in a way that produces a lognormal distribution for the price at any future time. There are many alternative processes that can be assumed. One possibility is to retain the property that the asset price changes continuously, but assume a process other than geometric Brownian motion. Another alternative is to overlay continuous asset price changes with jumps. Yet another alternative is to assume a process where all the asset price changes that take place are jumps. We will consider examples of all three types of processes in this section. A model where stock prices change continuously is known as a *diffusion model*. A model where continuous changes are overlaid with jumps is known as a *mixed jump–diffusion model*. A model where all stock price changes are jumps is known as a *pure jump model*. These types of processes are known collectively as *Levy processes*.[1]

The Constant Elasticity of Variance Model

One alternative to Black–Scholes is the *constant elasticity of variance* (CEV) model. This is a diffusion model where the risk-neutral process for a stock price S is

$$dS = (r - q)S\,dt + \sigma S^{\alpha}\,dz$$

where r is the risk-free rate, q is the dividend yield, dz is a Wiener process, σ is a volatility parameter, and α is a positive constant.[2]

When $\alpha = 1$, the CEV model is the geometric Brownian motion model we have been using up to now. When $\alpha < 1$, the volatility increases as the stock price decreases. This creates a probability distribution similar to that observed for equities with a heavy left tail and less heavy right tail (see Figure 15.4).[3] When $\alpha > 1$, the volatility increases as the stock price increases. This creates a probability distribution with a heavy right tail and a less heavy left tail. This corresponds to a volatility smile where the implied volatility is an increasing function of the strike price. This type of volatility smile is sometimes observed for options on futures (see Assignment 14.46).

The valuation formulas for European call and put options under the CEV model are

$$c = S_0 e^{-qT}[1 - \chi^2(a, b+2, c)] - Ke^{-rT}\chi^2(c, b, a)$$
$$p = Ke^{-rT}[1 - \chi^2(c, b, a)] - S_0 e^{-qT}\chi^2(a, b+2, c)$$

when $0 < \alpha < 1$, and

$$c = S_0 e^{-qT}[1 - \chi^2(c, -b, a)] - Ke^{-rT}\chi^2(a, 2-b, c)$$
$$p = Ke^{-rT}[1 - \chi^2(a, 2-b, c)] - S_0 e^{-qT}\chi^2(c, -b, a)$$

[1] Roughly speaking, a Levy process is a continuous-time stochastic process with stationary independent increments.

[2] See J. C. Cox and S. A. Ross, "The Valuation of Options for Alternative Stochastic Processes," *Journal of Financial Economics*, 3 (March 1976): 145–66.

[3] The reason is as follows. As the stock price decreases, the volatility increases making even lower stock price more likely; when the stock price increases, the volatility decreases making higher stock prices less likely.

when $\alpha > 1$, with

$$a = \frac{[Ke^{-(r-q)T}]^{2(1-\alpha)}}{(1-\alpha)^2 v}, \qquad b = \frac{1}{1-\alpha}, \qquad c = \frac{S^{2(1-\alpha)}}{(1-\alpha)^2 v}$$

where

$$v = \frac{\sigma^2}{2(r-q)(\alpha-1)}[e^{2(r-q)(\alpha-1)T} - 1]$$

and $\chi^2(z, k, v)$ is the cumulative probability that a variable with a noncentral χ^2 distribution with noncentrality parameter v and k degrees of freedom is less than z. A procedure for computing $\chi^2(z, k, v)$ is provided in Technical Note 12 on the author's website.

The CEV model is particularly useful for valuing exotic equity options. The parameters of the model can be chosen to fit the prices of plain vanilla options as closely as possible by minimizing the sum of the squared differences between model prices and market prices.

Merton's Mixed Jump–Diffusion Model

Merton has suggested a model where jumps are combined with continuous changes.[4] Define:

λ: Average number of jumps per year

k: Average jump size measured as a percentage of the asset price

The percentage jump size is assumed to be drawn from a probability distribution in the model.

The probability of a jump in time Δt is $\lambda\,\Delta t$. The average growth rate in the asset price from the jumps is therefore λk. The risk-neutral process for the asset price is

$$\frac{dS}{S} = (r - q - \lambda k)\,dt + \sigma\,dz + dp$$

where dz is a Wiener process, dp is the Poisson process generating the jumps, and σ is the volatility of the geometric Brownian motion. The processes dz and dp are assumed to be independent.

An important particular case of Merton's model is where the logarithm of the size of the percentage jump is normal. Assume that the standard deviation of the normal distribution is s. Merton shows that a European option price can then be written

$$\sum_{n=0}^{\infty} \frac{e^{-\lambda' T}(\lambda' T)^n}{n!} f_n$$

where $\lambda' = \lambda(1 + k)$. The variable f_n is the Black–Scholes option price when the dividend yield is q, the variance rate is

$$\sigma^2 + \frac{ns^2}{T}$$

[4] See R.C. Merton, "Option Pricing When Underlying Stock Returns Are Discontinuous," *Journal of Financial Economics*, 3 (March 1976): 125–44.

and the risk-free rate is

$$r - \lambda k + \frac{n\gamma}{T}$$

where $\gamma = \ln(1 + k)$.

This model gives rise to heavier left and heavier right tails than Black–Scholes. It can be used for pricing currency options. As in the case of the CEV model we choose the model parameters by minimizing the sum of the squared differences between model prices and market prices.

Another particular case of Merton's model is the model we used in Section 21.9 for valuing convertible bonds. In this case the jump is always down and equal to the current stock price (see Problem 24.5).

The Variance-Gamma Model

An example of a pure jump model that is proving quite popular is the *variance-gamma model*.[5] For this model, we first define a variable g as the change over time T in a variable that follows a gamma process with mean rate of 1 and variance rate of v. A gamma process is a pure jump process where small jumps occur very frequently and large jumps occur only occasionally. The probability density for g is

$$\phi(g) = \frac{g^{T/v-1}e^{-g/v}}{v^{T/v}\Gamma(T/v)}$$

where $\Gamma(\cdot)$ denotes the gamma function. This can be computed in Excel using the GAMMADIST($\cdot, \cdot, \cdot, \cdot$) function. The first argument of the function is g, the second is T/v, the third is v, and the fourth is TRUE or FALSE, where TRUE returns the cumulative probability distribution function and FALSE returns the probability density function we have just given.

As usual, we define S_T as the asset price at time T, S_0 as the asset price today, r as the risk-free interest rate, and q as the dividend yield. In a risk-neutral world $\ln S_T$, under the variance-gamma model, has a probability distribution that, conditional on g, is normal. The conditional mean is

$$\ln S_0 + (r - q)T + \omega + \theta g$$

and the conditional standard deviation is

$$\sigma\sqrt{g}$$

where

$$\omega = \frac{T}{v}\ln(1 - \theta v - \sigma^2 v/2)$$

The variance-gamma model has three parameters: v, σ, and θ.[6] The parameter v is the variance rate of the gamma process, σ is the volatility, and θ is a parameter defining skewness. When $\theta = 0$, $\ln S_T$ is symmetric; when $\theta < 0$, it is negatively skewed (as for equities); and when $\theta > 0$, it is positively skewed.

---

[5] See D. B. Madan, P. P. Carr, and E. C. Chang, "The Variance-Gamma Process and Option Pricing," *European Finance Review*, 2 (1998): 7–105.

[6] Note that all these parameters are liable to change when we move from the real world to the risk-neutral world. This is in contract to pure diffusion models where the volatility remains the same.

Suppose that we are interested in using Excel to obtain 10,000 random samples of the change in an asset price between time 0 and time T using the variance-gamma model. As a preliminary, we set cells E1, E2, E3, E4, E5, E6, and E7 equal to T, v, θ, σ, r, q, and S_0, respectively. We also set E8 equal to ω by defining it as

$$= \$E\$1 * \mathrm{LN}(1 - \$E\$3 * \$E\$2 - \$E\$4 * \$E\$4 * \$E\$2/2)/\$E\$2$$

We then proceed as follows:

1. We sample values for g using the GAMMAINV function. We set the contents of cells A1, A2, ..., A10000 as

$$= \mathrm{GAMMAINV(RAND(),\ \$E\$1/\$E\$2,\ \$E\$2)}$$

2. For each value of g we sample a value for a variable that is normally distributed with mean θg and standard deviation $\sigma\sqrt{g}$. We do this by defining cell B1 as

$$= \mathrm{A1} * \$E\$3 + \mathrm{SQRT(A1)} * \$E\$4 * \mathrm{NORMSINV(RAND())}$$

   and cells B2, B3, ..., B10000 similarly.

3. The stock price S_T is given by

$$S_T = S_0 \exp[(r - q)T + \omega + \theta g]$$

   If we define C1 as

$$= \$E\$7 * \mathrm{EXP}((\$E\$5 - \$E\$6) * \$E\$1 + \mathrm{B1} + \$E\$8)$$

   and define C2, C3, ..., C10000 similarly, we have created random samples from the distribution of S_T in C1, C2, ..., C10000.

Figure 24.1 shows the probability distribution that is obtained using the variance-gamma model for S_T when $S_0 = 100$, $T = 0.5$, $v = 0.5$, $\theta = 0.1$, $\sigma = 0.2$, and $r = q = 0$. For comparison it also shows the distribution given by geometric Brownian motion when the volatility, σ is 0.2 (or 20%). Although not clear in Figure 24.1, the variance-gamma distribution has heavier tails than the lognormal distribution given by geometric Brownian motion.

One way of characterizing the variance-gamma distribution is that g defines the rate at which information arrives during time T. If g is large, a great deal of information arrives and the sample we take from a normal distribution in step 2 above has a relatively large mean and variance. If g is small, relatively little information arrives and the sample we take has a relatively small mean and variance. The parameter T is the usual time measure, and g is sometimes referred to as measuring economic time or time adjusted for the flow of information.

Semi-analytic European option valuation formulas are provided by Madan *et al.* (1998). The variance-gamma model tends to produce a U-shaped volatility smile. The smile is not necessarily symmetrical. It is very pronounced for short maturities and "dies away" for long maturities. The model can be fitted to either equity or foreign currency plain vanilla option prices.

Figure 24.1 Distributions obtained with variance-gamma process and geometric Brownian motion.

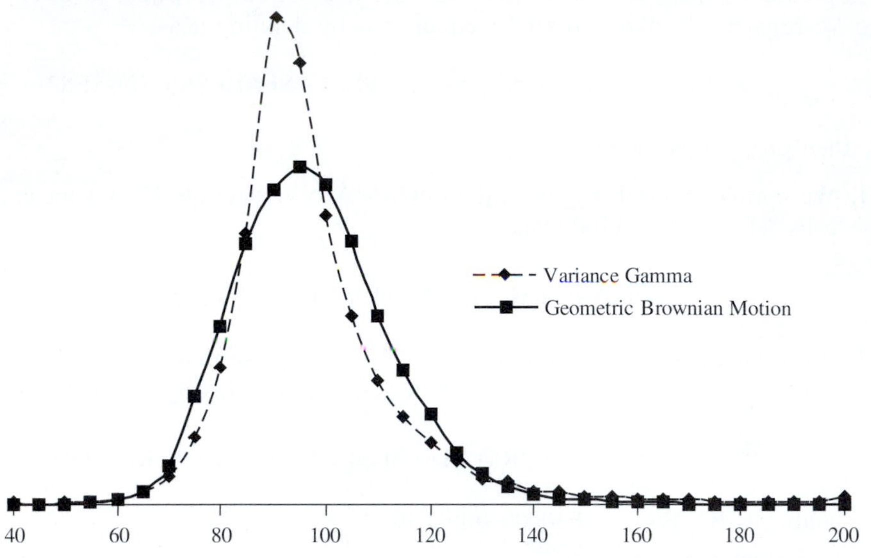

24.2 STOCHASTIC VOLATILITY MODELS

The Black–Scholes model assumes that volatility is constant. In practice as we saw in Chapter 19 volatility varies through time. The variance-gamma model reflects this with its g parameter. Low values of g correspond to a low arrival rate for information and a low volatility; high values of g correspond to a high arrival rate for information and a high volatility.

An alternative to the variance-gamma model is a model where the process followed by the volatility variable is specified explicitly. Suppose first that we make the volatility parameter in the geometric Brownian motion a known function of time. The risk-neutral process followed by the asset price is then

$$dS = (r - q)S\,dt + \sigma(t)S\,dz \tag{24.1}$$

The Black–Scholes formulas are then correct provided that the variance rate is set equal to the average variance rate during the life of the option (see Problem 24.6). The variance rate is the square of the volatility. Suppose that during a 1-year period the volatility of a stock will be 20% during the first 6 months and 30% during the second 6 months. The average variance rate is

$$0.5 \times 0.20^2 + 0.5 \times 0.30^2 = 0.065$$

It is correct to use Black–Scholes with a variance rate of 0.065. This corresponds to a volatility of $\sqrt{0.065} = 0.255$, or 25.5%.

Equation (24.1) assumes that the instantaneous volatility of an asset is perfectly predictable. In practice volatility varies stochastically. This has led to the development more complex models with two stochastic variables: the stock price and its volatility.

One model that has been used by researchers is

$$\frac{dS}{S} = (r - q)\,dt + \sqrt{V}\,dz_S \tag{24.2}$$

$$dV = a(V_L - V)\,dt + \xi V^{\alpha}\,dz_V \tag{24.3}$$

where a, V_L, ξ, and α are constants, and dz_S and dz_V are Wiener processes. The variable V in this model is the asset's variance rate. The variance rate has a drift that pulls it back to a level V_L at rate a.

Hull and White show that, when volatility is stochastic but uncorrelated with the asset price, the price of a European option is the Black–Scholes price integrated over the probability distribution of the average variance rate during the life of the option.[7] Thus a European call price is

$$\int_0^{\infty} c(\bar{V})g(\bar{V})\,d\bar{V}$$

where $\bar{V}$ is the average value of the variance rate, c is the Black–Scholes price expressed as a function of $\bar{V}$, and g is the probability density function of $\bar{V}$ in a risk-neutral world. This result can be used to show that Black–Scholes overprices options that are at the money or close to the money, and underprices options that are deep in or deep out of the money. The model is consistent with the pattern of implied volatilities observed for currency options (see Section 16.2).

The case where the asset price and volatility are correlated is more complicated. Option prices can be obtained using Monte Carlo simulation. In the particular case where $\alpha = 0.5$, Hull and White provide a series expansion and Heston provides an analytic result.[8] The pattern of implied volatilities obtained when the volatility is negatively correlated with the asset price is similar to that observed for equities (see Section 16.3).[9]

Chapter 19 discusses exponentially weighted moving average (EWMA) and GARCH(1, 1) models. These are alternative approaches to characterizing a stochastic volatility model. Duan shows that it is possible to use GARCH(1, 1) as the basis for an internally consistent option pricing model.[10] (See Problem 19.14 for the equivalence of GARCH(1, 1) and stochastic volatility models.)

Stochastic volatility models can be fitted to the prices of plain vanilla options and then used to price exotic options.[11] For options that last less than a year, the impact of a stochastic volatility on pricing is fairly small in absolute terms (although in percentage

---

[7] See J. C. Hull and A. White, "The Pricing of Options on Assets with Stochastic Volatilities," *Journal of Finance*, 42 (June 1987): 281–300. This result is independent of the process followed by the variance rate.

[8] See J. C. Hull and A. White, "An Analysis of the Bias in Option Pricing Caused by a Stochastic Volatility," *Advances in Futures and Options Research*, 3 (1988): 27–61; S. L. Heston, "A Closed Form Solution for Options with Stochastic Volatility with Applications to Bonds and Currency Options," *Review of Financial Studies*, 6, 2 (1993): 327–43.

[9] The reason is given in footnote 3.

[10] See J.-C. Duan, "The GARCH Option Pricing Model," *Mathematical Finance*, vol. 5 (1995), 13–32; and J.-C. Duan, "Cracking the Smile" *RISK*, vol. 9 (December 1996), 55-59.

[11] For an example of this, see J. C. Hull and W. Suo, "A Methodology for the Assessment of Model Risk and its Application to the Implied Volatility Function Model," *Journal of Financial and Quantitative Analysis*, 37, 2 (June 2002): 297–318.

terms it can be quite large for deep-out-of-the-money options). It becomes progressively larger as the life of the option increases. The impact of a stochastic volatility on the performance of delta hedging is generally quite large. Traders recognize this and, as described in Chapter 15, monitor their exposure to volatility changes by calculating vega.

24.3 THE IVF MODEL

The parameters of the models we have discussed so far can be chosen so that they provide an approximate fit to the prices of plain vanilla options on any given day. Financial institutions sometimes want to go one stage further and use a model that provides an exact fit to the prices of these options.[12] In 1994 Derman and Kani, Dupire, and Rubinstein developed a model that is designed to do this. It has become known as the *implied volatility function* (IVF) model or the *implied tree* model.[13] It provides an exact fit to the European option prices observed on any given day, regardless of the shape of the volatility surface.

The risk-neutral process for the asset price in the model has the form

$$dS = [r(t) - q(t)]S\,dt + \sigma(S, t)S\,dz$$

where $r(t)$ is the instantaneous forward interest rate for a contract maturing at time t and $q(t)$ is the dividend yield as a function of time. The volatility $\sigma(S, t)$ is a function of both S and t and is chosen so that the model prices all European options consistently with the market. It is shown both by Dupire and by Andersen and Brotherton-Ratcliffe that $\sigma(S, t)$ can be calculated analytically:[14]

$$[\sigma(K, T)]^2 = 2\frac{\partial c_{\text{mkt}}/\partial T + q(T)c_{\text{mkt}} + K[r(T) - q(T)]\partial c_{\text{mkt}}/\partial K}{K^2(\partial^2 c_{\text{mkt}}/\partial K^2)} \tag{24.4}$$

where $c_{\text{mkt}}(K, T)$ is the market price of a European call option with strike price K and maturity T. If a sufficiently large number of European call prices are available in the market, this equation can be used to estimate the $\sigma(S, t)$ function.[15]

Andersen and Brotherton-Ratcliffe implement the model by using equation (24.4) together with the implicit finite difference method. An alternative approach, the *implied tree* methodology suggested by Derman and Kani and Rubinstein, involves constructing a tree for the asset price that is consistent with option prices in the market.

When it is used in practice the IVF model is recalibrated daily to the prices of plain vanilla options. It is a tool to price exotic options consistently with plain vanilla options. As discussed in Chapter 16 plain vanilla options define the risk-neutral

---

[12] There is a practical reason for this. If the bank does not use a model with this property, there is a danger that traders working for the bank will spend their time arbitraging the bank's internal models.

[13] See B. Dupire, "Pricing with a Smile," *Risk*, February (1994): 18–20; E. Derman and I. Kani, "Riding on a Smile," *Risk*, February (1994): 32–39; M. Rubinstein, "Implied Binomial Trees" *Journal of Finance*, 49, 3 (July 1994), 771–818.

[14] See B. Dupire, "Pricing with a Smile," *Risk*, February (1994), 18–20; L. B. G. Andersen and R. Brotherton-Ratcliffe "The Equity Option Volatility Smile: An Implicit Finite Difference Approach," *Journal of Computation Finance* 1, No. 2 (Winter 1997/98): 5–37. Dupire considers the case where r and q are zero; Andersen and Brotherton-Ratcliffe consider the more general situation.

[15] Some smoothing of the observed volatility surface is typically necessary.

probability distribution of the asset price at all future times. It follows that the IVF model gets the risk-neutral probability distribution of the asset price at all future times correct. This means that options providing payoffs at just one time (e.g., all-or-nothing and asset-or-nothing options) are priced correctly by the IVF model. However, the model does not necessarily get the joint distribution of the asset price at two or more times correct. This means that exotic options such as compound options and barrier options may be priced incorrectly.[16]

24.4 PATH-DEPENDENT DERIVATIVES

We now move on to discuss how the numerical procedures we presented in Chapter 17 can be modified to handle particular valuation problems. We start by considering how trees can be used for path-dependent derivatives.

A path-dependent derivative (or history-dependent derivative) is a derivative where the payoff depends on the path followed by the price of the underlying asset, not just its final value. Asian options and lookback options are examples of path-dependent derivatives. As explained in Chapter 22, the payoff from an Asian option depends on the average price of the underlying asset; the payoff from a lookback option depends on its maximum or minimum price. One approach to valuing path-dependent options when analytic results are not available is Monte Carlo simulation, as discussed in Chapter 17. A sample value of the derivative can be calculated by sampling a random path for the underlying asset in a risk-neutral world, calculating the payoff, and discounting the payoff at the risk-free interest rate. An estimate of the value of the derivative is found by obtaining many sample values of the derivative in this way and calculating their mean.

The main problem with using Monte Carlo simulation is that the computation time necessary to achieve the required level of accuracy can be unacceptably high. Also, American-style path-dependent derivatives (i.e., path-dependent derivatives where one side has exercise opportunities or other decisions to make) cannot easily be handled. In this section, we show how the binomial tree methods presented in Chapter 17 can be extended to cope with some path-dependent derivatives.[17] The procedure can handle American-style path-dependent derivatives and is computationally more efficient than Monte Carlo simulation for European-style path-dependent derivatives.

For the procedure to work, two conditions must be satisfied:

1. The payoff from the derivative must depend on a single function, F, of the path followed by the underlying asset.
2. It must be possible to calculate the value of F at time $\tau + \Delta t$ from the value of F at time τ and the value of the underlying asset at time $\tau + \Delta t$.

[16] Hull and Suo test the IVF model by assuming that all derivative prices are determined by a stochastic volatility model. They found that the model works reasonably well for compound options, but sometimes gives serious errors for barrier options. See J. C. Hull and W. Suo, "A Methodology for the Assessment of Model Risk and its Application to the Implied Volatility Function Model," *Journal of Financial and Quantitative Analysis*, 37, 2 (June 2002): 297–318

[17] This approach was suggested in J. Hull and A. White, "Efficient Procedures for Valuing European and American Path-Dependent Options," *Journal of Derivatives*, 1, 1 (Fall 1993): 21 31.

Illustration Using Lookback Options

As a first illustration of the procedure, we consider an American lookback put option on a non-dividend-paying stock.[18] If exercised at time τ, this pays off the amount by which the maximum stock price between time 0 and time τ exceeds the current stock price. We suppose that the initial stock price is \$50, the stock price volatility is 40% per annum, the risk-free interest rate is 10% per annum, the total life of the option is three months, and that stock price movements are represented by a three-step binomial tree. With our usual notation this means that $S_0 = 50$, $\sigma = 0.4$, $r = 0.10$, $\Delta t = 0.08333$, $u = 1.1224$, $d = 0.8909$, $a = 1.0084$, and $p = 0.5073$.

The tree is shown in Figure 24.2. The top number at each node is the stock price. The next level of numbers at each node shows the possible maximum stock prices achievable on paths leading to the node. The final level of numbers shows the values of the derivative corresponding to each of the possible maximum stock prices.

The values of the derivative at the final nodes of the tree are calculated as the maximum stock price minus the actual stock price. To illustrate the rollback procedure, suppose that we are at node A, where the stock price is \$50. The maximum stock price achieved thus far is either 56.12 or 50. Consider first the situation where it is equal to 50. If there is an up movement, the maximum stock price becomes 56.12 and the value

Figure 24.2 Tree for valuing an American lookback option.

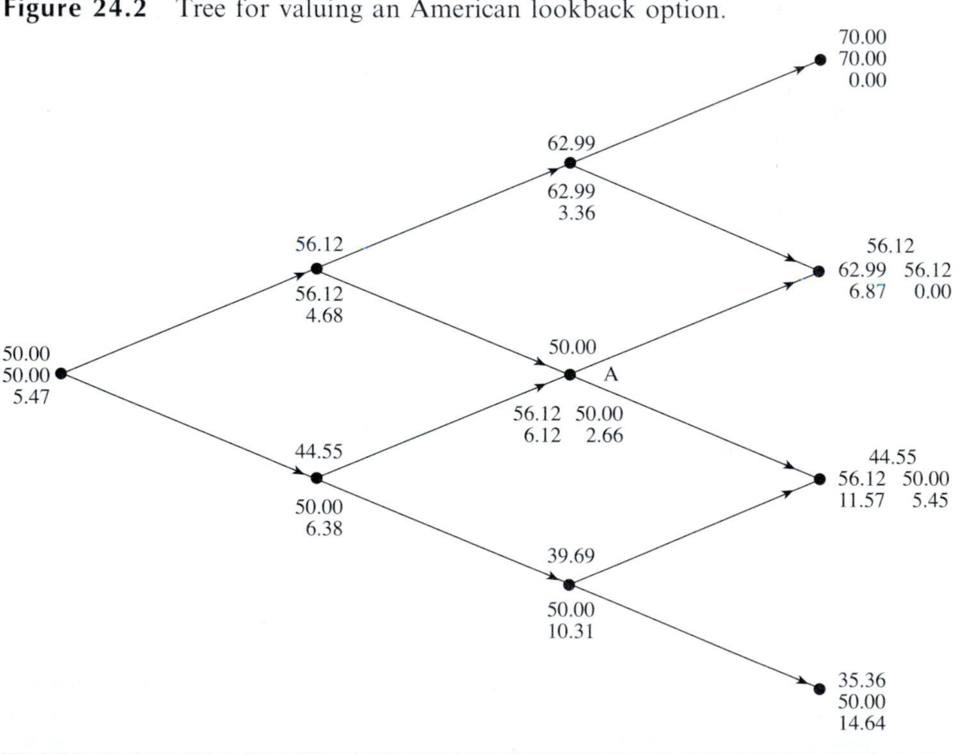

[18] This example is used as a first illustration of the general procedure for handling path dependence. For a more efficient approach to valuing American-style lookback options, see Technical Note 13 on the author's website.

of the derivative is zero. If there is a down movement, the maximum stock price stays at 50 and the value of the derivative is 5.45. Assuming no early exercise, the value of the derivative at A when the maximum achieved so far is 50 is, therefore,

$$(0 \times 0.5073 + 5.45 \times 0.4927)e^{-0.1\times0.08333} = 2.66$$

Clearly, it is not worth exercising at node A in these circumstances because the payoff from doing so is zero. A similar calculation for the situation where the maximum value at node A is 56.12 gives the value of the derivative at node A, without early exercise, to be

$$(0 \times 0.5073 + 11.57 \times 0.4927)e^{-0.1\times0.08333} = 5.65$$

In this case, early exercise gives a value of 6.12 and is the optimal strategy. Rolling back through the tree in the way we have indicated gives the value of the American lookback as \$5.47.

Generalization

The approach just described is computationally feasible when the number of alternative values of the path function, F, at each node does not grow too fast as the number of time steps is increased. The example we used, a lookback option, presents no problems because the number of alternative values for the maximum asset price at a node in a binomial tree with n time steps is never greater than n.

Luckily, the approach can be extended to cope with situations where there are a very large number of different possible values of the path function at each node. The basic idea is as follows. At a node, we carry out calculations for a small number of representative values of F. When the value of the derivative is required for other values of the path function, we calculate it from the known values using interpolation.

The first stage is to work forward through the tree establishing the maximum and minimum values of the path function at each node. Assuming the value of the path function at time $\tau + \Delta t$ depends only on the value of the path function at time τ and the value of the underlying variable at time $\tau + \Delta t$, the maximum and minimum values of the path function for the nodes at time $\tau + \Delta t$ can be calculated in a straightforward way from those for the nodes at time τ. The second stage is to choose representative values of the path function at each node. There are a number of approaches. A simple rule is to choose the representative values as the maximum value, the minimum value, and a number of other values that are equally spaced between the maximum and the minimum. As we roll back through the tree, we value the derivative for each of representative values of the path function.

We illustrate the nature of the calculation by considering the problem of valuing the average price call option in Example 22.2. We examine the case where the payoff depends on the arithmetic average stock price. The initial stock price is 50, the strike price is 50, the risk-free interest rate is 10%, the stock price volatility is 40%, and the time to maturity is 1 year. We use a tree with 20 time steps. The binomial tree parameters are $\Delta t = 0.05$, $u = 1.0936$, $d = 0.9144$, $p = 0.5056$, and $1 - p = 0.4944$. The path function is the arithmetic average of the stock price.

Figure 24.3 shows the calculations that are carried out in one small part of the tree. Node X is the central node at time 0.2 year (at the end of the fourth time step). Nodes Y and Z are the two nodes at time 0.25 year that are reachable from node X. The stock

Figure 24.3 Part of tree for valuing option on the arithmetic average.

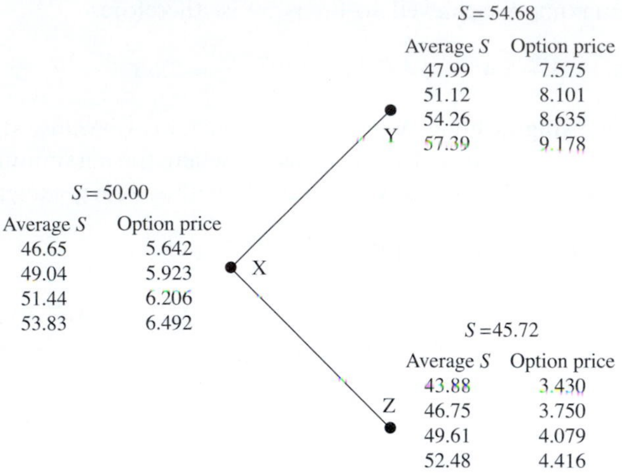

price at node X is 50. Forward induction shows that the maximum average stock price that is achievable in reaching node X is 53.83. The minimum is 46.65. (We include both the initial and final stock prices when calculating the average.) From node X we branch to one of the two nodes, Y and Z. At node Y, the stock price is 54.68 and the bounds for the average are 47.99 and 57.39. At node Z, the stock price is 45.72 and the bounds for the average stock price are 43.88 and 52.48.

Suppose that we have chosen the representative values of the average to be four equally spaced values at each node. This means that, at node X, we consider the averages 46.65, 49.04, 51.44, and 53.83. At node Y, we consider the averages 47.99, 51.12, 54.26, and 57.39. At node Z, we consider the averages 43.88, 46.75, 49.61, and 52.48. We assume that backward induction has already been used to calculate the value of the option for each of the alternative values of the average at nodes Y and Z. Values are shown in Figure 24.3 (e.g., at node Y when the average is 51.12, the value of the option is 8.101).

Consider the calculations at node X for the case where the average is 51.44. If the stock price moves up to node Y, the new average will be

$$\frac{5 \times 51.44 + 54.68}{6} = 51.98$$

The value of the derivative at node Y for this average can be found by interpolating between the values when the average is 51.12 and when it is 54.26. It is

$$\frac{(51.98 - 51.12) \times 8.635 + (54.26 - 51.98) \times 8.101}{54.26 - 51.12} = 8.247$$

Similarly, if the stock price moves down to node Z, the new average will be

$$\frac{5 \times 51.44 + 45.72}{6} = 50.49$$

and by interpolation the value of the derivative is 4.182.

The value of the derivative at node X when the average is 51.44 is, therefore,

$$(0.5056 \times 8.247 + 0.4944 \times 4.182)e^{-0.1\times 0.05} = 6.206$$

The other values at node X are calculated similarly. Once the values at all nodes at time 0.2 year have been calculated, we can move on to the nodes at time 0.15 year.

The value given by the full tree for the option at time zero is 7.17. As the number of time steps and the number of averages considered at each node is increased, the value of the option converges to the correct answer. With 60 time steps and 100 averages at each node, the value of the option is 5.58. The analytic approximation for the value of the option calculated in Example 22.2 is 5.62.

A key advantage of the method described here is that it can handle American options. The calculations are as we have described them except that we test for early exercise at each node for each of the alternative values of the path function at the node. (In practice, the early exercise decision is liable to depend on both the value of the path function and the value of the underlying asset.) Consider the American version of the average price call considered here. The value calculated using the 20-step tree and four averages at each node is 7.77; with 60 time steps and 100 averages, the value is 6.17.

The approach just described can be used in a wide range of different situations. The two conditions that must be satisfied were listed at the beginning of this section. Efficiency is improved somewhat if quadratic rather than linear interpolation is used at each node.

24.5 BARRIER OPTIONS

In Chapter 22 we presented analytic results for standard barrier options. Here we consider the numerical procedures that can be used for barrier options when there are no analytic results.

In principle, a barrier option can be valued using the binomial and trinomial trees discussed in Chapter 17. Consider an up-and-out option. We can value this in the same way as a regular option except that, when we encounter a node above the barrier, we set the value of the option equal to zero.

Trinomial trees work better than binomial trees but even for them convergence is very slow when this approach is used. A large number of time steps are required to obtain a reasonably accurate result. The reason for this is that the barrier being assumed by the tree is different from the true barrier.[19] Define the *inner barrier* as the barrier formed by nodes just on the inside of the true barrier (i.e., closer to the center of the tree) and *the outer barrier* as the barrier formed by nodes just outside the true barrier (i.e., farther away from the center of the tree). Figure 24.4 shows the inner and outer barrier for a trinomial tree on the assumption that the true barrier is horizontal. The usual tree calculations implicitly assume that the outer barrier is the true barrier because the barrier conditions are first used at nodes on this barrier. When the time step is Δt, the vertical spacing between the nodes is of order $\sqrt{\Delta t}$. This means that errors created by the difference between the true barrier and the outer barrier also tend to be of order $\sqrt{\Delta t}$.

---

[19] For a discussion of this, see P. P. Boyle and S. H. Lau, "Bumping Up Against the Barrier with the Binomial Method," *Journal of Derivatives*, 1, 4 (Summer 1994): 6–14.

Figure 24.4 Barriers assumed by trinomial trees.

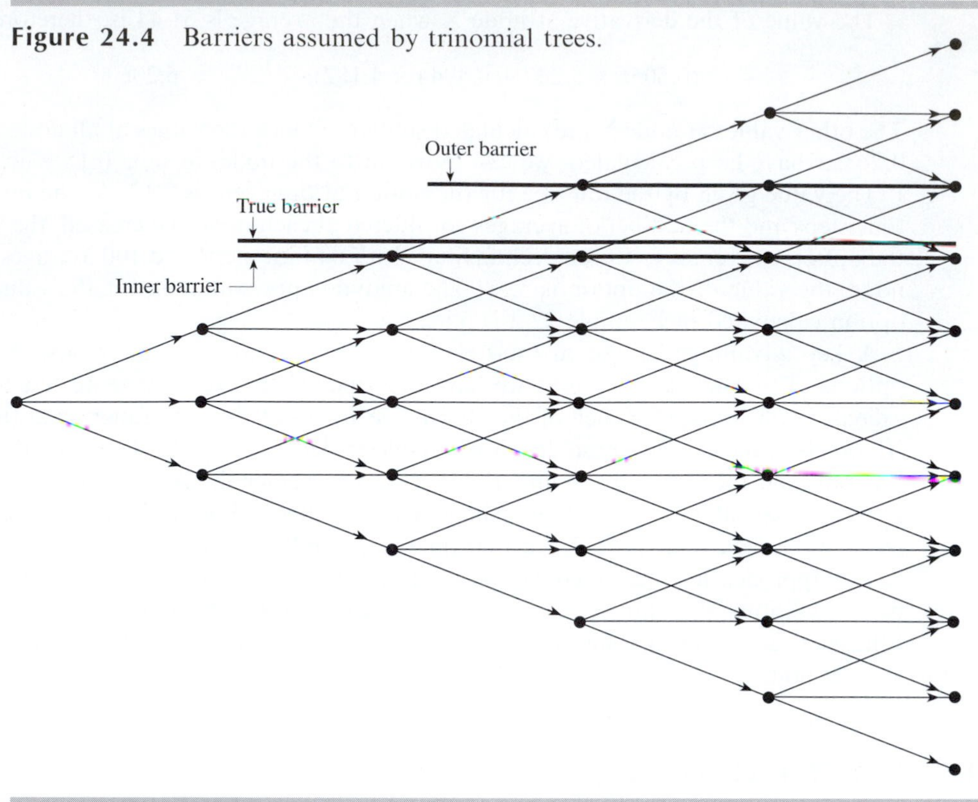

One approach to overcoming this problem is to

1. Calculate the price of the derivative on the assumption that the inner barrier is the true barrier.
2. Calculate the value of the derivative on the assumption that the outer barrier is the true barrier.
3. Interpolate between the two prices.

Another approach is to ensure that nodes lie on the barrier. Suppose that the initial stock price is S_0 and that the barrier is at H. In a trinomial tree, there are three possible movements in the asset's price at each node: up by a proportional amount u; stay the same; and down by a proportional amount d, where $d = 1/u$. We can always choose u so that nodes lie on the barrier. The condition that must be satisfied by u is

$$H = S_0 u^N$$

or

$$\ln H = \ln S_0 + N \ln u$$

for some positive or negative N.

When discussing trinomial trees in Section 17.4, the value suggested for u was $e^{\sigma\sqrt{3\Delta t}}$, so that $\ln u = \sigma\sqrt{3\Delta t}$. In the situation considered here, a good rule is to choose $\ln u$ as close as possible to this value, consistent with the condition given above. This means

Figure 24.5 Tree with nodes lying on barrier.

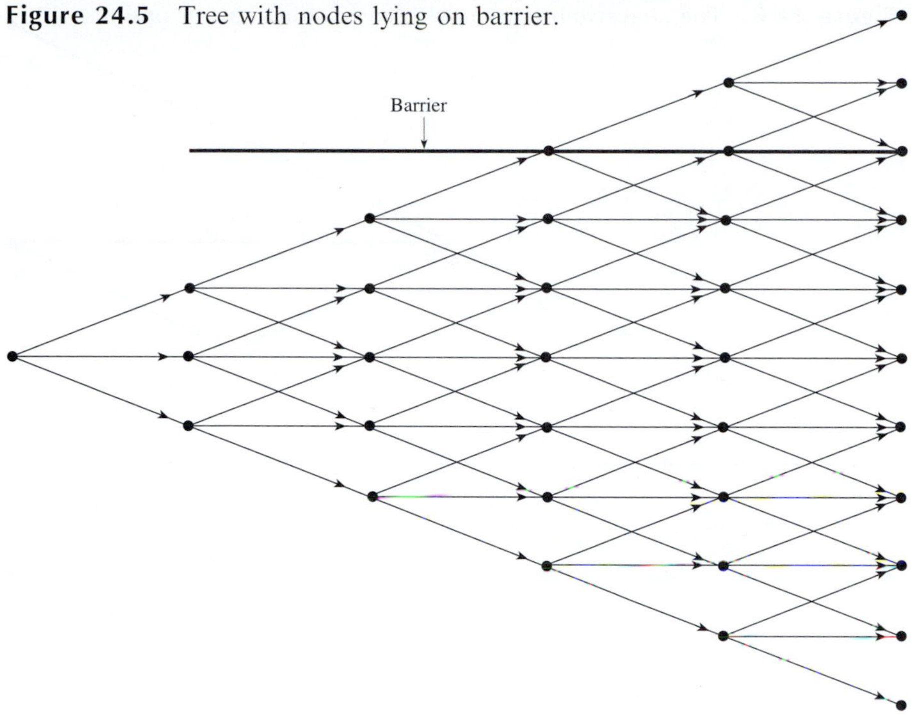

Barrier

that we set

$$\ln u = \frac{\ln H - \ln S_0}{N}$$

where

$$N = \text{int}\left[\frac{\ln H - \ln S_0}{\sigma\sqrt{3\Delta t}} + 0.5\right]$$

and $\text{int}(x)$ is the integral part of x.

This leads to a tree of the form shown in Figure 24.5. The probabilities p_u, p_m, and p_d on the upper, middle, and lower branches of the tree are chosen to match the first two moments of the return, so that

$$p_d = -\frac{(r - q - \sigma^2/2)\,\Delta t}{2\ln u} + \frac{\sigma^2 \Delta t}{2(\ln u)^2}, \quad p_m = 1 - \frac{\sigma^2 \Delta t}{(\ln u)^2}, \quad p_u = \frac{(r - q - \sigma^2/2)\,\Delta t}{2\ln u} + \frac{\sigma^2 \Delta t}{2(\ln u)^2}$$

where p_u, p_m, and p_d are the probabilities on the upper, middle, and lower branches.

The Adaptive Mesh Model

The methods we have presented so far work reasonably well when the initial asset price is not close to the barrier. When the initial asset price is close to a barrier, the adaptive mesh model, which we introduced in Section 17.4, can be used.[20] The idea behind the

[20] See S. Figlewski and B. Gao, "The Adaptive Mesh Model: A New Approach to Efficient Option Pricing," *Journal of Financial Economics*, 53 (1999): 313–51.

Figure 24.6 The adaptive mesh model used to value barrier options.

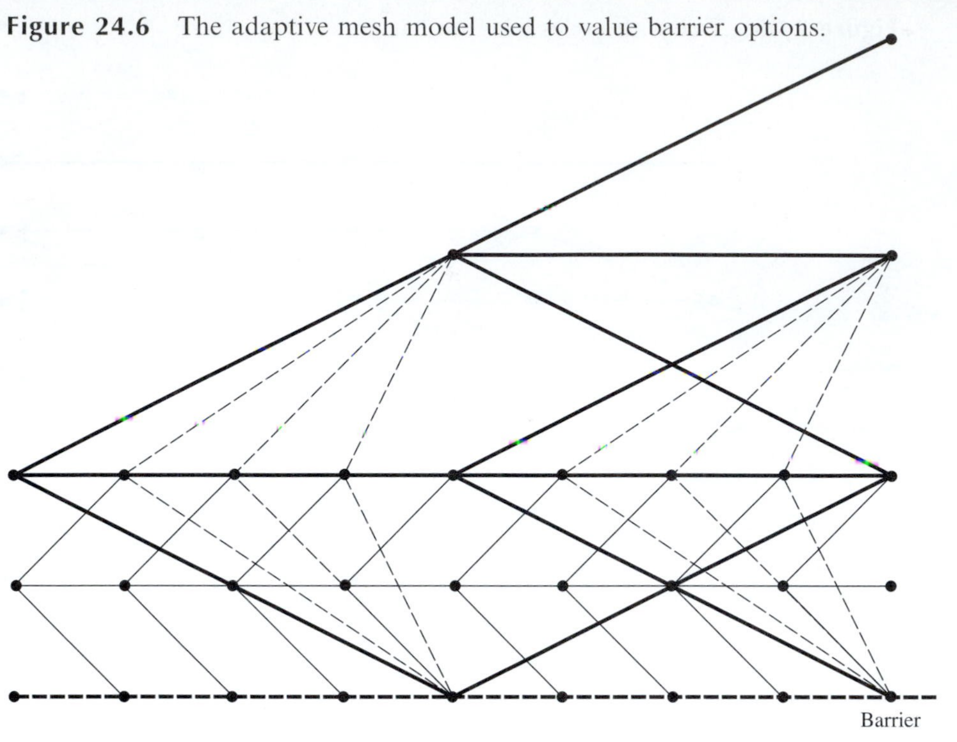

model is that computational efficiency can be improved by grafting a fine tree onto a coarse tree to achieve a more detailed modeling of the asset price in the regions of the tree where it is needed most.

To value a barrier option, it is useful to have a fine tree close to barriers. Figure 24.6 illustrates the design of the tree. The geometry of the tree is arranged so that nodes lie on the barriers. The probabilities on branches are chosen, as usual, to match the first two moments of the process followed by the underlying asset. The heavy lines in Figure 24.6 are the branches of the coarse tree. The light solid line are the fine tree. We first roll back through the coarse tree in the usual way. We then calculate the value at additional nodes using the branches indicated by the dotted lines. Finally we roll back through the fine tree.

24.6 OPTIONS ON TWO CORRELATED ASSETS

Another tricky numerical problem is that of valuing American options dependent on two assets whose prices are correlated. A number of alternative approaches have been suggested. We will explain three of these.

Transforming Variables

It is relatively easy to construct a tree in three dimensions to represent the movements of two *uncorrelated* variables. The procedure is as follows. First, we construct a two-dimensional tree for each variable. We then combine these trees into a single three-dimensional tree. The probabilities on the branches of the three-dimensional tree are the product of the corresponding probabilities on the two-dimensional trees. Suppose, for example, that the variables are stock prices, S_1 and S_2. Each can be represented in two dimensions by a Cox, Ross, and Rubinstein binomial tree. Assume that S_1 has a probability p_1 of moving up by a proportional amount u_1 and a probability $1 - p_1$ of moving down by a proportional amount d_1. Suppose further that S_2 has a probability p_2 of moving up by a proportional amount u_2 and a probability $1 - p_2$ of moving down by a proportional amount d_2. In the three-dimensional tree there are four branches emanating from each node. The probabilities are:

$$\begin{aligned} p_1 p_2 &: \; S_1 \text{ increases; } S_2 \text{ increases.} \\ p_1(1-p_2) &: \; S_1 \text{ increases; } S_2 \text{ decreases.} \\ (1-p_1)p_2 &: \; S_1 \text{ decreases; } S_2 \text{ increases.} \\ (1-p_1)(1-p_2) &: \; S_1 \text{ decreases; } S_2 \text{ decreases.} \end{aligned}$$

Consider next the situation where S_1 and S_2 are correlated. We suppose that the risk-neutral processes are:

$$dS_1 = (r - q_1)S_1\,dt + \sigma_1 S_1\,dz_1$$

$$dS_2 = (r - q_2)S_2\,dt + \sigma_2 S_2\,dz_2$$

and the instantaneous correlation between the Wiener processes, dz_1 and dz_2, is ρ. This means that

$$d\ln S_1 = (r - q_1 - \sigma_1^2/2)\,dt + \sigma_1\,dz_1$$

$$d\ln S_2 = (r - q_2 - \sigma_2^2/2)\,dt + \sigma_2\,dz_2$$

We define two new uncorrelated variables:[21]

$$x_1 = \sigma_2 \ln S_1 + \sigma_1 \ln S_2$$

$$x_2 = \sigma_2 \ln S_1 - \sigma_1 \ln S_2$$

These variables follow the processes

$$dx_1 = [\sigma_2(r - q_1 - \sigma_1^2/2) + \sigma_1(r - q_2 - \sigma_2^2/2)]\,dt + \sigma_1\sigma_2\sqrt{2(1+\rho)}\,dz_A$$

$$dx_2 = [\sigma_2(r - q_1 - \sigma_1^2/2) - \sigma_1(r - q_2 - \sigma_2^2/2)]\,dt + \sigma_1\sigma_2\sqrt{2(1-\rho)}\,dz_B$$

where dz_A and dz_B are uncorrelated Wiener processes.

The variables x_1 and x_2 can be modeled using two separate binomial trees. In time Δt, x_i has a probability p_i of increasing by h_i and a probability $1 - p_i$ of decreasing by h_i. The variables h_i and p_i are chosen so that the tree gives correct values for the first two moments of the distribution of x_1 and x_2. Because they are uncorrelated, the two trees can be combined into a single three-dimensional tree, as already described. At each node of the tree, S_1 and S_2 can be calculated from x_1 and x_2 using the inverse

[21] This idea was suggested in J. Hull and A. White, "Valuing Derivative Securities Using the Explicit Finite Difference Method," *Journal of Financial and Quantitative Analysis*, 25 (1990): 87–100.

relationships

$$S_1 = \exp\left[\frac{x_1 + x_2}{2\sigma_2}\right] \quad \text{and} \quad S_2 = \exp\left[\frac{x_1 - x_2}{2\sigma_1}\right]$$

The procedure for rolling back through a three-dimensional tree to value a derivative is analogous to that for a two-dimensional tree.

Using a Nonrectangular Tree

Rubinstein has suggested a way of building a three-dimensional tree for two correlated stock prices by using a nonrectangular arrangement of the nodes.[22] From a node (S_1, S_2), where the first stock price is S_1 and the second stock price is S_2, we have a 0.25 chance of moving to each of the following:

$$(S_1u_1, S_2A), \quad (S_1u_1, S_2B), \quad (S_1d_1, S_2C), \quad (S_2d_1, S_2D)$$

where

$$u_1 = \exp[(r - q_1 - \sigma_1^2/2)\,\Delta t + \sigma_1\sqrt{\Delta t}\,]$$
$$d_1 = \exp[(r - q_1 - \sigma_1^2/2)\,\Delta t - \sigma_1\sqrt{\Delta t}\,]$$

and

$$A = \exp[(r - q_2 - \sigma_2^2/2)\,\Delta t + \sigma_2\sqrt{\Delta t}\,(\rho + \sqrt{1 - \rho^2})]$$
$$B = \exp[(r - q_2 - \sigma_2^2/2)\,\Delta t + \sigma_2\sqrt{\Delta t}\,(\rho - \sqrt{1 - \rho^2})]$$
$$C = \exp[(r - q_2 - \sigma_2^2/2)\,\Delta t - \sigma_2\sqrt{\Delta t}\,(\rho - \sqrt{1 - \rho^2})]$$
$$D = \exp[(r - q_2 - \sigma_2^2/2)\,\Delta t - \sigma_2\sqrt{\Delta t}\,(\rho + \sqrt{1 - \rho^2})]$$

When the correlation is zero, this method is equivalent to constructing separate trees for S_1 and S_2 using the alternative binomial tree construction method in Section 17.4.

Adjusting the Probabilities

A third approach to building a three-dimensional tree for S_1 and S_2 involves first assuming no correlation and then adjusting the probabilities at each node to reflect the correlation.[23] We use the alternative binomial tree construction method for each of S_1 and S_2 in Section 17.4. This method has the property that all probabilities are 0.5.

Table 24.1 Combination of binomials assuming no correlation.

S_2-move	*S_1-move*	
	Down	*Up*
Up	0.25	0.25
Down	0.25	0.25

[22] See M. Rubinstein, "Return to Oz," *Risk*, November (1994): 67–70.

[23] This approach was suggested in the context of interest rate trees in J. Hull and A. White, "Numerical Procedures for Implementing Term Structure Models II: Two-Factor Models," *Journal of Derivatives*, Winter (1994): 37–48.

Table 24.2 Combination of binomials assuming correlation of ρ.

S_2-move	*S_1-move*	
	Down	*Up*
Up	$0.25(1-\rho)$	$0.25(1+\rho)$
Down	$0.25(1+\rho)$	$0.25(1-\rho)$

When the two binomial trees are combined on the assumption that there is no correlation, the probabilities are as shown in Table 24.1. When we adjust these probabilities to reflect the correlation they become as shown in Table 24.2.

24.7 MONTE CARLO SIMULATION AND AMERICAN OPTIONS

Monte Carlo simulation is well suited to valuing path-dependent options and options where there are many stochastic variables. Trees and finite difference methods are well suited to valuing American-style options. What happens if an option is both path dependent and American? What happens if an American option depends on several stochastic variables? In Section 24.4 we explained a way in which the binomial tree approach can be modified to value path-dependent options in some situations. A number of researchers have adopted a different approach by searching for a way in which Monte Carlo simulation can be used to value American-style options.[24] Here we explain two alternative ways of proceeding.

The Least-Squares Approach

In order to value an American-style option it is necessary to choose between exercising and continuing at each early exercise point. The value of exercising is normally easy to determine. A number of researchers including Longstaff and Schwartz provide a way of determining the value of continuing when Monte Carlo simulation is used.[25] Their approach involves using a least-squares analysis to determine the best-fit relationship between the value of continuing and the values of relevant variables at each time an early exercise decision has to be made. The approach is best illustrated with a numerical example. We use the one in the Longstaff–Schwartz paper.

Consider a 3-year American put option on a non-dividend-paying stock that can be exercised at the end of year 1, the end of year 2, and the end of year 3. The risk-free rate is 6% per annum (continuously compounded). The current stock price is 1.00 and the strike price is 1.10. Assume that we sample the eight paths for the stock price shown in Table 24.3. (This example is for illustration only; in practice many more paths would be sampled.) If the option can be exercised only at the 3-year point, it provides a cash flow equal to its intrinsic value at that point. This is shown in the last column of Table 24.4.

[24] Tilley was the first researcher to publish a solution to the problem. See J. A. Tilley, "Valuing American Options in a Path Simulation Model," *Transactions of the Society of Actuaries*, 45 (1993): 83–104.

[25] See F. A. Longstaff and E. S. Schwartz, "Valuing American Options by Simulation: A Simple Least-Squares Approach," *Review of Financial Studies*, 14, 1 (Spring 2001): 113–47.

Table 24.3 Sample paths for put option example.

Path	$t = 0$	$t = 1$	$t = 2$	$t = 3$
1	1.00	1.09	1.08	1.34
2	1.00	1.16	1.26	1.54
3	1.00	1.22	1.07	1.03
4	1.00	0.93	0.97	0.92
5	1.00	1.11	1.56	1.52
6	1.00	0.76	0.77	0.90
7	1.00	0.92	0.84	1.01
8	1.00	0.88	1.22	1.34

If the put option is in the money at the 2-year point the option holder must decide whether to exercise. From Table 24.3, we see that the option is in the money at the 2-year point for paths 1, 3, 4, 6, and 7. For these paths, we assume an approximate relationship:

$$V = a + bS + cS^2$$

where S is the stock price at the 2-year point and V is the value of continuing, discounted back to the 2-year point. Our five observations on S are: 1.08, 1.07, 0.97, 0.77, and 0.84. From Table 24.4 the corresponding values for V are: 0.00, $0.07e^{-0.06\times 1}$, $0.18e^{-0.06\times 1}$, $0.20e^{-0.06\times 1}$, and $0.09e^{-0.06\times 1}$. We use this data to calculate the values of a, b, and c that minimize

$$\sum_{i=1}^{5}(V_i - a - bS_i - cS_i^2)^2$$

where S_i and V_i are the ith observation on S and V, respectively. It turns out that $a = -1.070$, $b = 2.983$ and $c = -1.813$, so that the best-fit relationship is

$$V = -1.070 + 2.983S - 1.813S^2$$

This gives the value at the 2-year point of continuing for paths 1, 3, 4, 6, and 7 of 0.0369, 0.0461, 0.1176, 0.1520, and 0.1565, respectively. From Table 24.3 the value of exercising is 0.02, 0.03, 0.13, 0.33, and 0.26. This means that we should exercise at

Table 24.4 Cash flows if exercise only at the 3-year point.

Path	$t = 1$	$t = 2$	$t = 3$
1	0.00	0.00	0.00
2	0.00	0.00	0.00
3	0.00	0.00	0.07
4	0.00	0.00	0.18
5	0.00	0.00	0.00
6	0.00	0.00	0.20
7	0.00	0.00	0.09
8	0.00	0.00	0.00

Table 24.5 Cash flows if exercise only possible at 2- and 3-year point.

Path	$t = 1$	$t = 2$	$t = 3$
1	0.00	0.00	0.00
2	0.00	0.00	0.00
3	0.00	0.00	0.07
4	0.00	0.13	0.00
5	0.00	0.00	0.00
6	0.00	0.33	0.00
7	0.00	0.26	0.00
8	0.00	0.00	0.00

the 2-year point for paths 4, 6, and 7. Table 24.5 summarizes the cash flow assuming exercise at either the 2-year point or the 3-year point for the eight paths.

We next consider the paths that are in the money at the 1-year point. These are paths 1, 4, 6, 7, and 8. From Table 24.3 the values of S for the paths are 1.09, 0.93, 0.76, 0.92, and 0.88, respectively. From Table 24.5, the corresponding continuation values discounted back to $t = 1$ are 0.00, $0.13e^{-0.06\times 1}$, $0.33e^{-0.06\times 1}$, $0.26e^{-0.06\times 1}$, and 0.00, respectively. The least-squares relationship is

$$V = 2.038 - 3.335S + 1.356S^2$$

This gives the value of continuing at the 1-year point for paths 1, 4, 6, 7, 8 as 0.0139, 0.1092, 0.2866, 0.1175, and 0.1533, respectively. From Table 24.3 the value of exercising is 0.01, 0.17, 0.34, 0.18, and 0.22, respectively. This means that we should exercise at the 1-year point for paths 4, 6, 7, and 8. Table 24.6 summarizes the cash flows assuming that early exercise is possible at all three times. The value of the option is determined by discounting each cash flow back to time zero at the risk-free rate and calculating the mean of the results. It is

$$\tfrac{1}{8}(0.07e^{-0.06\times 3} + 0.17e^{-0.06\times 1} + 0.34e^{-0.06\times 1} + 0.18e^{-0.06\times 1} + 0.22e^{-0.06\times 1}) = 0.1144$$

Because this is greater than 0.10, it is not optimal to exercise the option immediately.

Table 24.6 Cash flows from option.

Path	$t = 1$	$t = 2$	$t = 3$
1	0.00	0.00	0.00
2	0.00	0.00	0.00
3	0.00	0.00	0.07
4	0.17	0.00	0.00
5	0.00	0.00	0.00
6	0.34	0.00	0.00
7	0.18	0.00	0.00
8	0.22	0.00	0.00

This method can be extended in a number of ways. If the option can be exercised at any time we can approximate its value by considering a large number of exercise points (just as a binomial tree does). The relationship between V and S can be assumed to be more complicated. For example we could assume that V is a cubic rather than a quadratic function of S. When the early exercise decision depends on several state variables, we proceed as we did in the example just considered. A functional form for the relationship between V and the variables is assumed and the parameters are estimated using the least-squares approach.

The Exercise Boundary Parameterization Approach

A number of researchers, such as Andersen, have proposed an alternative approach where the early exercise boundary is parameterized and the optimal values of the parameters are determined iteratively by starting at the end of the life of the option and working backward.[26] To illustrate the approach, we continue with the put option example and assume that the eight paths shown in Table 24.3 have been sampled. In this case, the early exercise boundary at time t can be parameterized by a critical value of S, $S^*(t)$. If the asset price at time t is below $S^*(t)$ we exercise at time t; if it is above $S^*(t)$ we do not exercise at time t. The value of $S^*(3)$ is 1.10. If the stock price is above 1.10 when $t = 3$ (the end of the option's life) we do not exercise; if it is below 1.10 we exercise. We now consider the determination of $S^*(2)$.

Suppose that we choose a value of $S^*(2)$ less than 0.77. The option is not exercised at the 2-year point for any of the paths. The value of the option at the 2-year point for the eight paths is then 0.00, 0.00, $0.07e^{-0.06\times 1}$, $0.18e^{-0.06\times 1}$, 0.00, $0.20e^{-0.06\times 1}$, $0.09e^{-0.06\times 1}$, and 0.00, respectively. The average of these is 0.0636. Suppose next that $S^*(2) = 0.77$. The value of the option at the 2-year point for the eight paths is then 0.00, 0.00, $0.07e^{-0.06\times 1}$, $0.18e^{-0.06\times 1}$, 0.00, 0.33, $0.09e^{-0.06\times 1}$, and 0.00, respectively. The average of these is 0.0813. Similarly when $S^*(2)$ equals 0.84, 0.97, 1.07, and 1.08, the average value of the option at the 2-year point is 0.1032, 0.0982, 0.0938, and 0.0963, respectively. This analysis shows that the optimal value of $S^*(2)$ (i.e., the one that maximizes the average value of the option) is 0.84. (More precisely, it is optimal to choose $0.84 \leqslant S^*(2) < 0.97$.) When we choose this optimal value for $S^*(2)$, the value of the option at the 2-year point for the eight paths is 0.00, 0.00, 0.0659, 0.1695, 0.00, 0.33, 0.26, and 0.00, respectively. The average value is 0.1032.

We now move on to calculate $S^*(1)$. If $S^*(1) < 0.76$ the option is not exercised at the 1-year point for any of the paths and the value at the option at the 1-year point is $0.1032e^{-0.06\times 1} = 0.0972$. If $S^*(1) = 0.76$, the value of the option for each of the eight paths at the 1-year point is 0.00, 0.00, $0.0659e^{-0.06\times 1}$, $0.1695e^{-0.06\times 1}$, 0.0, 0.34, $0.26e^{-0.06\times 1}$, and 0.00, respectively. The average value of the option is 0.1008. Similarly when $S^*(1)$ equals 0.88, 0.92, 0.93, and 1.09 the average value of the option is 0.1283, 0.1202, 0.1215, and 0.1228, respectively. The analysis therefore shows that the optimal value of $S^*(1)$ is 0.88. (More precisely, it is optimal to choose $0.88 \leqslant S^*(1) < 0.92$.) The value of the option at time zero with no early exercise is $0.1283e^{-0.06\times 1} = 0.1208$. This is greater than the value of 0.10 obtained by exercising at time zero.

In practice tens of thousands of simulations are carried out to determine the early

[26] See L. Andersen, "A Simple Approach to the Pricing of Bermudan Swaptions in the Multifactor LIBOR Market Model," *Journal of Computational Finance*, 3, 2 (Winter 2000): 1–32.

exercise boundary in the way we have described. Once we have obtained the early exercise boundary, we discard the paths for the variables and carry out a new Monte Carlo simulation using the early exercise boundary to value the option. Our American put option example is simple in that we know the early exercise boundary at a time can be defined entirely in terms of the value of the stock price at that time. In more complicated situations it is necessary to make assumptions about how the early exercise boundary should be parameterized.

Upper Bounds

The two approaches we have outlined tend to underprice American-style options because they assume a suboptimal early exercise boundary. This has led Andersen and Broadie to propose a procedure that provides an upper bound to the price.[27] This procedure can be used in conjunction with any algorithm that generates a lower bound and pinpoints the true value of an American-style option more precisely than the algorithm does by itself.

SUMMARY

A number of models have been developed to fit the volatility smiles that are observed in practice. The constant elasticity of variance model leads to a volatility smile similar to that observed for equity options. The jump–diffusion model leads to a volatility smile similar to that observed for currency options. Variance-gamma and stochastic volatility models are more flexible in that they can lead to either the type of volatility smile observed for equity options or the type of volatility smile observed for currency options. The implied volatility function model provides even more flexibility than this. It is designed to provide an exact fit to any pattern of European option prices observed in the market.

The natural technique to use for valuing path-dependent options is Monte Carlo simulation. This has the disadvantage that it is fairly slow and unable to handle American-style derivatives easily. Luckily, trees can be used to value many types of path-dependent derivatives. The approach is to choose representative values for the underlying path function at each node of the tree and calculate the value of the derivative for each alternative value of the path function as we roll back through the tree.

Trees can be used to value many types of barrier options, but the convergence of the option value to the correct value as the number of time steps is increased tends to be slow. One approach for improving convergence is to arrange the geometry of the tree so that nodes always lie on the barriers. Another is to use an interpolation scheme to adjust for the fact that the barrier being assumed by the tree is different from the true barrier. A third is to design the tree so that it provides a finer representation of movements in the underlying asset price near the barrier.

One way of valuing options dependent on the prices of two correlated assets is to apply a transformation to the asset price to create two new uncorrelated variables. These two variables are each modeled with trees and the trees are then combined to

[27] See L. Andersen and M. Broadie, "A Primal-Dual Simulation Algorithm for Pricing Multi-Dimensional American Options," *Management Science*, 50, 9 (2004), 1222–34.

form a single three-dimensional tree. At each node of the tree, the inverse of the transformation gives the asset prices. A second approach is to arrange the positions of nodes on the three-dimensional tree to reflect the correlation. A third approach is to start with a tree that assumes no correlation between the variables and then adjust the probabilities on the tree to reflect the correlation.

Monte Carlo simulation is not naturally suited to valuing American-style options, but there are two ways it can be adapted to handle them. The first involves using a least-squares analysis to relate the value of continuing (i.e, not exercising) to the values of relevant variables. The second involves parameterizing the early exercise boundary and determining it iteratively by working back from the end of the life of the option to the beginning.

FURTHER READING

Andersen, L., "A Simple Approach to the Pricing of Bermudan Swaptions in the Multifactor LIBOR Market Model," *Journal of Computational Finance*, 3, 2 (Winter 2000): 1–32.

Andersen, L. B. G., and R. Brotherton-Ratcliffe, "The Equity Option Volatility Smile: An Implicit Finite Difference Approach," *Journal of Computational Finance*, 1, 2 (Winter 1997/98): 3–37.

Boyle, P. P., and S. H. Lau, "Bumping Up Against the Barrier with the Binomial Method," *Journal of Derivatives*, 1, 4 (Summer 1994): 6–14.

Conze, A., and R. Viswanathan, "Path Dependent Options: The Case of Lookback Options," *Journal of Finance*, 46 (1991): 1893–1907.

Cox, J. C. and S. A. Ross, "The Valuation of Options for Alternative Stochastic Processes," *Journal of Financial Economics*, 3 (March 1976), 145–66.

Derman, E., and I. Kani, "Riding on a Smile," *Risk*, February (1994): 32–39.

Duan, J.-C., "The GARCH Option Pricing Model," *Mathematical Finance*, 5 (1995): 13–32.

Duan, J.-C., "Cracking the Smile," *Risk*, December (1996): 55–59.

Dupire, B., "Pricing with a Smile," *Risk*, February (1994): 18–20.

Figlewski, S., and B. Gao, "The Adaptive Mesh Model: A New Approach to Efficient Option Pricing," *Journal of Financial Economics*, 53 (1999): 313–51.

Heston, S. L., "A Closed Form Solution for Options with Stochastic Volatility with Applications to Bonds and Currency Options," *Review of Financial Studies*, 6, 2 (1993): 327–43.

Hull, J., and A. White, "Efficient Procedures for Valuing European and American Path-Dependent Options," *Journal of Derivatives*, 1, 1 (Fall 1993): 21–31.

Hull J. C., and A. White, "The Pricing of Options on Assets with Stochastic Volatilities," *Journal of Finance*, 42 (June 1987): 281–300.

Hull, J. C. and A. White, "An Analysis of the Bias in Option Pricing Caused by a Stochastic Volatility," *Advances in Futures and Options Research*, 3 (1988): 27–61.

Hull, J. C. and W. Suo, "A Methodology for the Assessment of Model Risk and its Application to the Implied Volatility Function Model," *Journal of Financial and Quantitative Analysis*, 37, 2 (2002): 297–318.

Longstaff, F. A. and E. S. Schwartz, "Valuing American Options by Simulation: A Simple Least-Squares Approach," *Review of Financial Studies*, 14, 1 (Spring 2001): 113–47.

Madan D. B., P. P. Carr, and E. C. Chang, "The Variance-Gamma Process and Option Pricing" *European Finance Review*, 2 (1998): 7–105.

Merton, R. C., "Option Pricing When Underlying Stock Returns Are Discontinuous," *Journal of Financial Economics*, 3 (March 1976): 125–44.

Rebonato, R., '*Volatility and Correlation: The Perfect Hedger and the Fox*, 2nd edn.Chichester: Wiley, 2004.

Ritchken, P, and R. Trevor, "Pricing Options Under Generalized GARCH and Stochastic Volatility Processes," *Journal of Finance* 54, 1 (February 1999): 377–402

Rubinstein, M., "Implied Binomial Trees," *Journal of Finance*, 49, 3 (July 1994): 771–818.

Rubinstein, M., "Return to Oz," *Risk*, November (1994): 67–70.

Stutzer, M., "A Simple Nonparametric Approach to Derivative Security Valuation," *Journal of Finance*, 51 (December 1996): 1633–52.

Tilley, J. A., "Valuing American Options in a Path Simulation Model," *Transactions of the Society of Actuaries*, 45 (1993): 83–104.

Questions and Problems (Answers in Solutions Manual)

24.1. Confirm that the CEV model formulas satisfy put–call parity.

24.2. Explain how you would use Monte Carlo simulation to sample paths for the asset price when Merton's jump–diffusion model is used.

24.3. Confirm that Merton's jump–diffusion model satisfies put–call parity when the jump size is lognormal.

24.4. Suppose that the volatility of an asset will be 20% from month 0 to month 6, 22% from month 6 to month 12, and 24% from month 12 to month 24. What volatility should be used in Black–Scholes to value a 2-year option?

24.5. Consider the case of Merton's jump–diffusion model where jumps always reduce the asset price to zero. Assume that the average number of jumps per year is λ. Show that the price of a European call option is the same as in a world with no jumps except that the risk-free rate is $r + \lambda$ rather than r. Does the possibility of jumps increase or reduce the value of the call option in this case? (*Hint*: Value the option assuming no jumps and assuming one or more jumps. The probability of no jumps in time T is $e^{-\lambda T}$).

24.6. At time zero the price of a non-dividend-paying stock is S_0. Suppose that the time interval between 0 and T is divided into two subintervals of length t_1 and t_2. During the first subinterval, the risk-free interest rate and volatility are r_1 and σ_1, respectively. During the second subinterval, they are r_2 and σ_2, respectively. Assume that the world is risk neutral.

(a) Use the results in Chapter 13 to determine the stock price distribution at time T in terms of r_1, r_2, σ_1, σ_2, t_1, t_2, and S_0.

(b) Suppose that $\bar{r}$ is the average interest rate between time zero and T and that $\bar{V}$ is the average variance rate between times zero and T. What is the stock price distribution as a function of T in terms of $\bar{r}$, $\bar{V}$, T, and S_0?

(c) What are the results corresponding to (a) and (b) when there are three subintervals with different interest rates and volatilities?

(d) Show that if the risk-free rate, r, and the volatility, σ, are known functions of time, the stock price distribution at time T in a risk-neutral world is

$$\ln S_T \sim \phi\left[\ln S_0 + \left(\bar{r} - \frac{\bar{V}}{2}\right)T,\ \sqrt{\bar{V}T}\right]$$

where $\bar{r}$ is the average value of r, $\bar{V}$ is equal to the average value of σ^2, and S_0 is the stock price today.

24.7. Write down the equations for simulating the path followed by the asset price in the stochastic volatility model in equations (24.2) and (24.3).

24.8. "The IVF model does not necessarily get the evolution of the volatility surface correct." Explain this statement.

24.9. "When interest rates are constant the IVF model correctly values any derivative whose payoff depends on the value of the underlying asset at only one time." Explain this statement.

24.10. Use a three-time-step tree to value an American lookback call option on a currency when the initial exchange rate is 1.6, the domestic risk-free rate is 5% per annum, the foreign risk-free interest rate is 8% per annum, the exchange rate volatility is 15%, and the time to maturity is 18 months. Use the approach in Section 24.4.

24.11. What happens to the variance-gamma model as the parameter v tends to zero?

24.12. Use a three-time-step tree to value an American put option on the geometric average of the price of a non-dividend-paying stock when the stock price is \$40, the strike price is \$40, the risk-free interest rate is 10% per annum, the volatility is 35% per annum, and the time to maturity is three months. The geometric average is measured from today until the option matures.

24.13. Can the approach for valuing path-dependent options in Section 24.4 be used for a 2-year American-style option that provides a payoff equal to $\max(S_{ave} - K, 0)$, where S_{ave} is the average asset price over the three months preceding exercise? Explain your answer.

24.14. Verify that the 6.492 number in Figure 24.3 is correct.

24.15. Examine the early exercise policy for the eight paths considered in the example in Section 24.7. What is the difference between the early exercise policy given by the least squares approach and the exercise boundary parameterization approach? Which gives a higher option price for the paths sampled?

24.16. Consider a European put option on a non-dividend paying stock when the stock price is \$100, the strike price is \$110, the risk-free rate is 5% per annum, and the time to maturity is one year. Suppose that the average variance rate during the life of an option has a 0.20 probability of being 0.06, a 0.5 probability of being 0.09, and a 0.3 probability of being 0.12. The volatility is uncorrelated with the stock price. Estimate the value of the option. Use DerivaGem.

24.17. When there are two barriers how can a tree be designed so that nodes lie on both barriers?

Assignment Questions

24.18. A new European-style lookback call option on a stock index has a maturity of 9 months. The current level of the index is 400, the risk-free rate is 6% per annum, the dividend yield on the index is 4% per annum, and the volatility of the index is 20%. Use the approach in Section 24.4 to value the option and compare your answer to the result given by DerivaGem using the analytic valuation formula.

24.19. Suppose that the volatilities used to price a 6-month currency option are as in Table 16.2. Assume that the domestic and foreign risk-free rates are 5% per annum and the current exchange rate is 1.00. Consider a bull spread that consists of a long position in a 6-month call option with strike price 1.05 and a short position in a 6-month call option with a strike price 1.10.

(a) What is the value of the spread?

(b) What single volatility if used for both options gives the correct value of the bull spread? (Use the DerivaGem Application Builder in conjunction with Goal Seek or Solver.)

(c) Does your answer support the assertion at the beginning of the chapter that the correct volatility to use when pricing exotic options can be counterintuitive?

(d) Does the IVF model give the correct price for the bull spread?

24.20. Repeat the analysis in Section 24.7 for the put option example on the assumption that the strike price is 1.13. Use both the least squares approach and the exercise boundary parameterization approach.

24.21. Consider the situation in Merton's jump–diffusion model where the underlying asset is a non-dividend-paying stock. The average frequency of jumps is one per year. The average percentage jump size is 2% and the standard deviation of the logarithm of the percentage jump size is 20%. The stock price is 100, the risk-free rate is 5%, the volatility, σ provided by the diffusion part of the process is 15%, and the time to maturity is six months. Use the DerivaGem Application Builder to calculate an implied volatility when the strike price is 80, 90, 100, 110, and 120. What does the volatility smile or skew that you obtain imply about the probability distribution of the stock price.

CHAPTER 25 Martingales and Measures

Up to now we have assumed that interest rates are constant when valuing options. In this chapter we relax this assumption in preparation for valuing interest rate derivatives in Chapters 26 to 30.

The risk-neutral valuation principle we have used up to now states that a derivative can be valued by (a) calculating the expected payoff on the assumption that the expected return from the underlying asset equals the risk-free interest rate and (b) discounting the expected payoff at the risk-free interest rate. When interest rates are constant, risk-neutral valuation provides a well-defined and unambiguous valuation tool. When interest rates are stochastic, it is less clear-cut. What does it mean to assume that the expected return on the underlying asset equals to the risk-free rate? Does it mean (a) that each day the expected return is the one-day risk-free rate, or (b) that each year the expected return is the 1-year risk-free rate, or (c) that over a 5-year period the expected return is the 5-year rate at the beginning of the period? What does it mean to discount expected payoffs at the risk-free rate? Can we, for example, discount an expected payoff realized in year 5 at today's 5-year risk-free rate?

In this chapter we explain the theoretical underpinnings of risk-neutral valuation when interest rates are stochastic and show that there are many different risk-neutral worlds that can be assumed in any given situation. We first define a parameter known as the *market price of risk* and show that the excess return over the risk-free interest rate earned by any derivative in a short period of time is linearly related to the market prices of risk of the underlying stochastic variables. What we will refer to as the *traditional risk-neutral world* assumes that all market prices of risk are zero, but we will find that other assumptions about the market price of risk are useful in some situations.

Martingales and *measures* are critical to a full understanding of risk neutral valuation. A martingale is a zero-drift stochastic process. A measure is the unit in which we value security prices. A key result in this chapter will be the *equivalent martingale measure result*. This states that if we use the price of a traded security as the unit of measurement then there is some market price of risk for which all security prices follow martingales.

In this chapter we illustrate the power of the equivalent martingale measure result by using it to value stock options when interest rates are stochastic and to value options to exchange one asset for another. In Chapter 26 we use the result to understand the standard market models for valuing interest rate derivatives, in Chapter 27 we use it to value some nonstandard derivatives, and in Chapter 29 it will assist us in developing the LIBOR market model.

25.1 THE MARKET PRICE OF RISK

We start by considering the properties of derivatives dependent on the value of a single variable θ. We will assume that the process followed by θ is

$$\frac{d\theta}{\theta} = m\,dt + s\,dz \tag{25.1}$$

where dz is a Wiener process. The parameters m and s are the expected growth rate in θ and the volatility of θ, respectively. We assume that they depend only on θ and time t. The variable θ need not be the price of an investment asset. It could be something as far removed from financial markets as the temperature in the center of New Orleans.

Suppose that f_1 and f_2 are the prices of two derivatives dependent only on θ and t. These can be options or other instruments that provide a payoff equal to some function of θ at some future time. We assume that during the time period under consideration f_1 and f_2 provide no income.[1]

Suppose that the processes followed by f_1 and f_2 are

$$\frac{df_1}{f_1} = \mu_1\,dt + \sigma_1\,dz$$

and

$$\frac{df_2}{f_2} = \mu_2\,dt + \sigma_2\,dz$$

where μ_1, μ_2, σ_1, and σ_2 are functions of θ and t. The "dz" in these processes must be the same dz as in equation (25.1) because it is the only source of the uncertainty in the prices of f_1 and f_2.

We now relate the prices f_1 and f_2 using an analysis similar to the Black–Scholes analysis described in Section 13.6. The discrete versions of the processes for f_1 and f_2 are

$$\Delta f_1 = \mu_1 f_1\,\Delta t + \sigma_1 f_1\,\Delta z \tag{25.2}$$

$$\Delta f_2 = \mu_2 f_2\,\Delta t + \sigma_2 f_2\,\Delta z \tag{25.3}$$

We can eliminate the Δz by forming an instantaneously riskless portfolio consisting of $\sigma_2 f_2$ of the first derivative and $-\sigma_1 f_1$ of the second derivative. If Π is the value of the portfolio, then

$$\Pi = (\sigma_2 f_2) f_1 - (\sigma_1 f_1) f_2 \tag{25.4}$$

and

$$\Delta\Pi = \sigma_2 f_2\,\Delta f_1 - \sigma_1 f_1\,\Delta f_2$$

Substituting from equations (25.2) and (25.3), this becomes

$$\Delta\Pi = (\mu_1\sigma_2 f_1 f_2 - \mu_2\sigma_1 f_1 f_2)\,\Delta t \tag{25.5}$$

[1] The analysis can be extended to derivatives that provide income (see Problem 25.7).

Because the portfolio is instantaneously riskless, it must earn the risk-free rate. Hence,

$$\Delta\Pi = r\Pi\,\Delta t$$

Substituting into this equation from equations (25.4) and (25.5) gives

$$\mu_1\sigma_2 - \mu_2\sigma_1 = r\sigma_2 - r\sigma_1$$

or

$$\frac{\mu_1 - r}{\sigma_1} = \frac{\mu_2 - r}{\sigma_2} \tag{25.6}$$

Note that the left-hand side of equation (25.6) depends only on the parameters of the process followed by f_1 and the right-hand side depends only on the parameters of the process followed by f_2. Define λ as the value of each side in equation (25.6), so that

$$\frac{\mu_1 - r}{\sigma_1} = \frac{\mu_2 - r}{\sigma_2} = \lambda$$

Dropping subscripts, we have shown that if f is the price of a derivative dependent only on θ and t with

$$\frac{df}{f} = \mu\,dt + \sigma\,dz \tag{25.7}$$

then

$$\frac{\mu - r}{\sigma} = \lambda \tag{25.8}$$

The parameter λ is known as the *market price of risk* of θ. It can be dependent on both θ and t, but it is not dependent on the nature of the derivative f. Our analysis shows that, for no arbitrage, $(\mu - r)/\sigma$ must at any given time be the same for all derivatives that are dependent only on θ and t.

It is worth noting that σ, which we are referring to as the volatility of f, is defined as the coefficient of dz in equation (25.7). It can be either positive or negative. If the volatility, s, of θ is positive and f is positively related to θ (so that $\partial f/\partial\theta$ is positive), σ is positive. But if f is negatively related to θ, then σ is negative. The volatility of f, as it is traditionally defined, is $|\sigma|$.

The market price of risk of θ measures the trade-offs between risk and return that are made for securities dependent on θ. Equation (25.8) can be written

$$\mu - r = \lambda\sigma \tag{25.9}$$

For an intuitive understanding of this equation, we note that the variable σ can be loosely interpreted as the quantity of θ-risk present in f. On the right-hand side of the equation we are, therefore, multiplying the quantity of θ-risk by the price of θ-risk. The left-hand side is the expected return in excess of the risk-free interest rate that is required to compensate for this risk. Equation (25.9) is analogous to the capital asset pricing model, which relates the expected excess return on a stock to its risk.

We will not be concerned with the measurement of the market price of risk in this chapter. But this will be discussed in Chapter 31 in the context of the evaluation of real options.

In Chapter 5, we distinguished between investment assets and consumption assets. An investment asset is an asset that is bought or sold purely for investment purposes by a significant number of investors. Consumption assets are held primarily for consumption.

Equation (25.8) is true for all investment assets that provide no income and depend only on θ. If the variable θ itself happens to be such an asset, then

$$\frac{m-r}{s}=\lambda$$

But, in other circumstances, this relationship is not usually true.

Example 25.1

Consider a derivative whose price is positively related to the price of oil and depends on no other stochastic variables. Suppose that it provides an expected return of 12% per annum and has a volatility of 20% per annum. Assume that the risk-free interest rate is 8% per annum. It follows that the market price of risk of oil is

$$\frac{0.12-0.08}{0.2}=0.2$$

Note that oil is a consumption asset rather than an investment asset, so its market price of risk cannot be calculated from equation (25.8) by setting μ equal to the expected return from an investment in oil and σ equal to the volatility of oil prices.

Example 25.2

Consider two securities, both of which are positively dependent on the 90-day interest rate. Suppose that the first one has an expected return of 3% per annum and a volatility of 20% per annum, and the second one has a volatility of 30% per annum. Assume that the instantaneous risk-free rate of interest is 6% per annum. The market price of interest rate risk is, using the expected return and volatility for the first security,

$$\frac{0.03-0.06}{0.2}=-0.15$$

From a rearrangement of equation (25.9), the expected return from the second security is, therefore,

$$0.06-0.15\times 0.3=0.015$$

or 1.5% per annum.

Alternative Worlds

The process followed by derivative price f is

$$df=\mu f\,dt+\sigma f\,dz$$

The value of μ depends on the risk preferences of investors. In a world where the market price of risk is zero, λ equals zero. From equation (25.9) $\mu=r$, so that the process followed by f is

$$df=rf\,dt+\sigma f\,dz$$

We will refer to this as the *traditional risk-neutral world.*

By making other assumptions about the market price of risk, λ, we define other worlds that are internally consistent. In general, we see from equation (25.9) that

$$\mu=r+\lambda\sigma$$

so that

$$df = (r + \lambda\sigma) f\, dt + \sigma f\, dz \tag{25.10}$$

The market price of risk of a variable determines the growth rates of all securities dependent on the variable. As we move from one market price of risk to another, the expected growth rates of security prices change, but their volatilities remain the same. This is a general property of variables following diffusion processes and was illustrated in Section 11.7. Choosing a particular market price of risk is also referred to as defining the *probability measure*. For some value of the market price of risk, we obtain the "real world" and the growth rates of security prices that are observed in practice.

25.2 SEVERAL STATE VARIABLES

Suppose that n variables, $\theta_1, \theta_2, \dots, \theta_n$, follow stochastic processes of the form

$$\frac{d\theta_i}{\theta_i} = m_i\, dt + s_i\, dz_i \tag{25.11}$$

for $i = 1, 2, \dots, n$, where the dz_i are Wiener processes. The parameters m_i and s_i are expected growth rates and volatilities and may be functions of the θ_i and time. The appendix at the end of this chapter provides a version of Itô's lemma that covers functions of several variables. It shows that the process for the price, f, of a security that is dependent on the θ_i has the form

$$\frac{df}{f} = \mu\, dt + \sum_{i=1}^{n} \sigma_i\, dz_i \tag{25.12}$$

In this equation, μ is the expected return from the security and $\sigma_i\, dz_i$ is the component of the risk of this return attributable to θ_i.

The appendix at the end of this chapter shows that

$$\mu - r = \sum_{i=1}^{n} \lambda_i \sigma_i \tag{25.13}$$

where λ_i is the market price of risk for θ_i. This equation relates the expected excess return that investors require on the security to the λ_i and σ_i. Equation (25.9) is the particular case of this equation when $n = 1$. The term $\lambda_i\sigma_i$ on the right-hand side measures the extent that the excess return required by investors on a security is affected by the dependence of the security on θ_i. If $\lambda_i\sigma_i = 0$, there is no effect; if $\lambda_i\sigma_i > 0$, investors require a higher return to compensate them for the risk arising from θ_i; if $\lambda_i\sigma_i < 0$, the dependence of the security on θ_i causes investors to require a lower return than would otherwise be the case. The $\lambda_i\sigma_i < 0$ situation occurs when the variable has the effect of reducing rather than increasing the risks in the portfolio of a typical investor.

Example 25.3

A stock price depends on three underlying variables: the price of oil, the price of gold, and the performance of a stock index. Suppose that the market prices of risk for these variables are 0.2, −0.1, and 0.4, respectively. Suppose also that the σ_i

factors in equation (25.12) corresponding to the three variables have been estimated as 0.05, 0.1, and 0.15, respectively. The excess return on the stock over the risk-free rate is

$$0.2 \times 0.05 - 0.1 \times 0.1 + 0.4 \times 0.15 = 0.06$$

or 6.0% per annum. If variables other than those considered affect the stock price, this result is still true provided that the market price of risk for each of these other variables is zero.

Equation (25.13) is closely related to arbitrage pricing theory, developed by Stephen Ross in 1976.[2] The continuous-time version of the capital asset pricing model (CAPM) can be regarded as a particular case of the equation. CAPM argues that an investor requires excess returns to compensate for any risk that is correlated to the risk in the return from the stock market, but requires no excess return for other risks. Risks that are correlated with the return from the stock market are referred to as *systematic*; other risks are referred to as *nonsystematic*. If CAPM is true, then λ_i is proportional to the correlation between changes in θ_i and the return from the market. When θ_i is uncorrelated with the return from the market, λ_i is zero.

25.3 MARTINGALES

A martingale is a zero-drift stochastic process. A variable θ follows a martingale if its process has the form

$$d\theta = \sigma\, dz$$

where dz is a Wiener process. The variable σ may itself be stochastic. It can depend on θ and other stochastic variables. A martingale has the convenient property that its expected value at any future time is equal to its value today. This means that

$$E(\theta_T) = \theta_0$$

where θ_0 and θ_T denote the values of θ at times zero and T, respectively. To understand this result, we note that over a very small time interval the change in θ is normally distributed with zero mean. The expected change in θ over any very small time interval is therefore zero. The change in θ between time 0 and time T is the sum of its changes over many small time intervals. It follows that the expected change in θ between time 0 and time T must also be zero.

The Equivalent Martingale Measure Result

Suppose that f and g are the prices of traded securities dependent on a single source of uncertainty. We assume that the securities provide no income during the time period under consideration.[3] We define

$$\phi = \frac{f}{g}$$

[2] See S.A. Ross, "The Arbitrage Theory of Capital Asset Pricing," *Journal of Economic Theory*, 13 (December 1976): 343–62.

[3] Problem 25.8 extends the analysis to situations where the securities provide income.

The variable ϕ is the relative price of f with respect to g. It can be thought of as measuring the price of f in units of g rather than dollars. The security price g is referred to as the *numeraire*.

The *equivalent martingale measure* result shows that, when there are no arbitrage opportunities, ϕ is a martingale for some choice of the market price of risk. What is more, for a given numeraire security g, the same choice of the market price of risk makes ϕ a martingale for all securities f. This choice of the market price of risk is the volatility of g. In other words, when the market price of risk is set equal to the volatility of g, the ratio f/g is a martingale for all security prices f.

To prove this result, we suppose that the volatilities of f and g are σ_f and σ_g. From equation (25.10), in a world where the market price of risk is σ_g, we have

$$df = (r + \sigma_g \sigma_f) f\, dt + \sigma_f f\, dz$$

$$dg = (r + \sigma_g^2) g\, dt + \sigma_g g\, dz$$

Using Itô's lemma, we have

$$d\ln f = (r + \sigma_g \sigma_f - \sigma_f^2/2)\, dt + \sigma_f\, dz$$

$$d\ln g = (r + \sigma_g^2/2)\, dt + \sigma_g\, dz$$

so that

$$d(\ln f - \ln g) = (\sigma_g \sigma_f - \sigma_f^2/2 - \sigma_g^2/2)\, dt + (\sigma_f - \sigma_g)\, dz$$

or

$$d\left(\ln \frac{f}{g}\right) = -\frac{(\sigma_f - \sigma_g)^2}{2}\, dt + (\sigma_f - \sigma_g)\, dz$$

Using Itô's lemma to determine the process for f/g from the process for $\ln(f/g)$, we obtain

$$d\left(\frac{f}{g}\right) = (\sigma_f - \sigma_g)\frac{f}{g}\, dz \tag{25.14}$$

showing that f/g is a martingale.

This provides the required result. We refer to a world where the market price of risk is the volatility of g, σ_g, as a world that is *forward risk neutral* with respect to g.

Because f/g is a martingale in a world that is forward risk neutral with respect to g, it follows from the result at the beginning of this section that

$$\frac{f_0}{g_0} = E_g\left(\frac{f_T}{g_T}\right)$$

or

$$f_0 = g_0 E_g\left(\frac{f_T}{g_T}\right) \tag{25.15}$$

where E_g denotes the expected value in a world that is forward risk neutral with respect to g.

25.4 ALTERNATIVE CHOICES FOR THE NUMERAIRE

We now present a number of examples of the equivalent martingale measure result. Our first example shows that it is consistent with the traditional risk-neutral valuation result we have used up to now. The other examples prepare the way for the valuation of bond options, interest rate caps, and swap options in Chapter 26.

Money Market Account as the Numeraire

The dollar money market account is a security that is worth \$1 at time zero and earns the instantaneous risk-free rate r at any given time.[4] The variable r may be stochastic. If we set g equal to the money market account, it grows at rate r so that

$$dg = rg\,dt \tag{25.16}$$

The drift of g is stochastic, but the volatility of g is zero. The world that is forward risk neutral with respect to g is therefore a world where the market price of risk is zero. This is the world we defined earlier as the traditional risk-neutral world. It follows from equation (25.15), that

$$f_0 = g_0 \hat{E}\left(\frac{f_T}{g_T}\right) \tag{25.17}$$

where $\hat{E}$ denotes expectations in the traditional risk-neutral world.

In this case, $g_0 = 1$ and

$$g_T = e^{\int_0^T r\,dt}$$

so that equation (25.17) reduces to

$$f_0 = \hat{E}\big(e^{-\int_0^T r\,dt} f_T\big) \tag{25.18}$$

or

$$f_0 = \hat{E}\big(e^{-\bar{r}T} f_T\big) \tag{25.19}$$

where $\bar{r}$ is the average value of r between time 0 and time T. This equation shows that one way of valuing an interest rate derivative is to simulate the short-term interest rate r in the traditional risk-neutral world. On each trial we calculate the expected payoff and discount at the average value of the short rate on the sampled path.

When the short-term interest rate r is assumed to be constant, equation (25.19) reduces to

$$f_0 = e^{-rT}\hat{E}(f_T)$$

or the risk-neutral valuation relationship we used in earlier chapters.

Zero-Coupon Bond Price as the Numeraire

Define $P(t, T)$ as the price at time t of a zero-coupon bond that pays off \$1 at time T. We now explore the implications of setting g equal to $P(t, T)$. We use E_T to denote

---

[4] The money account is the limit as Δt approaches zero of the following security. For the first short period of time of length Δt, it is invested at the initial Δt period rate; at time Δt, it is reinvested for a further period of time Δt at the new Δt period rate; at time $2\Delta t$, it is again reinvested for a further period of time Δt at the new Δt period rate; and so on. The money market accounts in other currencies are defined analogously to the dollar money market account.

expectations in a world that is forward risk neutral with respect to $P(t, T)$. Because $g_T = P(T, T) = 1$ and $g_0 = P(0, T)$, equation (25.15) gives

$$f_0 = P(0, T)E_T(f_T) \tag{25.20}$$

Notice the difference between equations (25.20) and (25.19). In equation (25.19), the discounting is inside the expectations operator. In equation (25.20) the discounting, as represented by the $P(0, T)$ term, is outside the expectations operator. By using a world that is forward risk neutral with respect to $P(t, T)$, we considerably simplify things for a security that provides a payoff solely at time T.

Consider any variable θ that is not an interest rate.[5] A forward contract on θ with maturity T is defined as a contract that pays off $\theta_T - K$ at time T, where θ_T is the value θ at time T. Define f as the value of this forward contract. From equation (25.20), we have

$$f_0 = P(0, T)[E_T(\theta_T) - K]$$

The forward price, F, of θ is the value of K for which f_0 equals zero. It therefore follows that

$$P(0, T)[E_T(\theta_T) - F] = 0$$

or

$$F = E_T(\theta_T) \tag{25.21}$$

Equation (25.21) shows that the forward price of any variable (except an interest rate) is its expected future spot price in a world that is forward risk neutral with respect to $P(t, T)$. Note the difference here between forward prices and futures prices. The argument in Section 14.7 shows that the futures price of a variable is the expected future spot price in the traditional risk-neutral world.

Equation (25.20) shows that we can value any security that provides a payoff at time T by calculating its expected payoff in a world that is forward risk neutral with respect to a bond maturing at time T and discounting at the risk-free rate for maturity T. Equation (25.21) shows that it is correct to assume that the expected value of the underlying variables equal their forward values when computing the expected payoff. These results will be critical to our understanding of the standard market model for bond options in the next chapter.

Interest Rates when a Bond Price is the Numeraire

For our next result, we define $R(t, T, T^*)$ as the forward interest rate as seen at time t for the period between T and T^* expressed with a compounding period of $T^* - T$. (For example, if $T^* - T = 0.5$, the interest rate is expressed with semiannual compounding; if $T^* - T = 0.25$, it is expressed with quarterly compounding; and so on.) The forward price, as seen at time t, of a zero-coupon bond lasting between times T and T^* is

$$\frac{P(t, T^*)}{P(t, T)}$$

We define a forward interest rate differently from the forward value of most variables.

[5] As we shall see later on, forward contracts for interest rates are defined differently from forward contracts for other variables.

A forward interest rate is the interest rate implied by the corresponding forward bond price. It follows that

$$\frac{1}{[1+(T^*-T)R(t,T,T^*)]} = \frac{P(t,T^*)}{P(t,T)}$$

so that

$$R(t,T,T^*) = \frac{1}{T^*-T}\left[\frac{P(t,T)}{P(t,T^*)} - 1\right]$$

or

$$R(t,T,T^*) = \frac{1}{T^*-T}\left[\frac{P(t,T)-P(t,T^*)}{P(t,T^*)}\right]$$

Setting

$$f = \frac{1}{T^*-T}[P(t,T) - P(t,T^*)]$$

and $g = P(t,T^*)$, the equivalent martingale measure result shows that $R(t,T,T^*)$ is a martingale in a world that is forward risk neutral with respect to $P(t,T^*)$. This means that

$$R(0,T,T^*) = E_{T^*}[R(T,T,T^*)] \tag{25.22}$$

where E_{T^*} denotes expectations in a world that is forward risk neutral with respect to $P(t,T^*)$.

We have shown that the forward interest rate equals the expected future interest rate in a world that is forward risk neutral with respect to a zero-coupon bond maturing at time T^*. This result, when combined with that in equation (25.20), will be critical to our understanding of the standard market model for interest rate caps in the next chapter.

Annuity Factor as the Numeraire

For our next application of equivalent martingale measure arguments we consider a swap starting at a future time T with payment dates at times $T_1, T_2, \ldots, T_N$. Define $T_0 = T$. Assume that the principal underlying the swap is \$1. Suppose that the forward swap rate (i.e., the interest rate on the fixed side that makes the swap have a value of zero) is $s(t)$ at time t ($t \leqslant T$). The value of the fixed side of the swap is

$$s(t)A(t)$$

where

$$A(t) = \sum_{i=0}^{N-1}(T_{i+1} - T_i)P(t, T_{i+1})$$

We showed in Chapter 7 that, when the principal is added to the payment on the last payment date swap, the value of the floating side of the swap on the initiation date equals the underlying principal. It follows that if we add \$1 at time T_N, the floating side is worth \$1 at time T. The value of \$1 received at time T_N is $P(t, T_N)$. The value of \$1 at time T_0 is $P(t, T_0)$. The value of the floating side at time t is, therefore,

$$P(t, T_0) - P(t, T_N)$$

Equating the values of the fixed and floating sides, we obtain

$$s(t)A(t) = P(t, T_0) - P(t, T_N)$$

or

$$s(t) = \frac{P(t, T_0) - P(t, T_N)}{A(t)} \tag{25.23}$$

We can apply the equivalent martingale measure result by setting f equal to $P(t, T_0) - P(t, T_N)$ and g equal to $A(t)$. This leads to

$$s(t) = E_A[s(T)] \tag{25.24}$$

where E_A denotes expectations in a world that is forward risk neutral with respect to $A(t)$. Therefore, in a world that is forward risk neutral with respect to $A(t)$, the expected future swap rate is the current swap rate.

For any security, f, the result in equation (25.15) shows that

$$f_0 = A(0)E_A\left[\frac{f_T}{A(T)}\right] \tag{25.25}$$

This result, when combined with the result in equation (25.24), will be critical to our understanding of the standard market model for European swap options in the next chapter.

25.5 EXTENSION TO SEVERAL FACTORS

The results presented in Sections 25.3 and 25.4 can be extended to cover the situation when there are many independent factors.[6] Assume that there are n independent factors and that the processes for f and g in the traditional risk-neutral world are

$$df = rf\,dt + \sum_{i=1}^{n} \sigma_{f,i} f\,dz_i$$

and

$$dg = rg\,dt + \sum_{i=1}^{n} \sigma_{g,i} g\,dz_i$$

It follows from Section 25.2 that we can define other worlds that are internally consistent by setting

$$df = \left[r + \sum_{i=1}^{n} \lambda_i \sigma_{f,i}\right] f\,dt + \sum_{i=1}^{n} \sigma_{f,i} f\,dz_i$$

and

$$dg = \left[r + \sum_{i=1}^{n} \lambda_i \sigma_{g,i}\right] g\,dt + \sum_{i=1}^{n} \sigma_{g,i} g\,dz_i$$

where the λ_i $(1 \leqslant i \leqslant n)$ are the n market prices of risk. One of these other worlds is the real world.

We define a world that is forward risk neutral with respect to g as a world, where $\lambda_i = \sigma_{g,i}$. It can be shown from Itô's lemma, using the fact that the dz_i are uncorrelated,

[6] The independence condition is not critical. If factors are not independent they can be orthogonalized.

that the process followed by f/g in this world has zero drift (see Problem 25.12). The rest of the results in the last two sections (from equation 25.15 onward) are therefore still true.

25.6 APPLICATIONS

In this section we provide two applications of the forward risk-neutral valuation argument. Several others are given in Chapters 26, 27, 29, and 30.

The Black–Scholes Result

We can use forward risk-neutral arguments to extend the Black–Scholes result to situations where interest rates are stochastic. Consider a European call option maturing at time T on a non-dividend-paying stock. From equation (25.20), the call option's price is given by

$$c = P(0, T)E_T[\max(S_T - K, 0)] \tag{25.26}$$

where S_T is the stock price at time T, K is the strike price, and E_T denotes expectations in a world that is forward risk neutral with respect to a zero-coupon bond maturing at time T. Define R as the zero rate for maturity T, so that

$$P(0, T) = e^{-RT}$$

and equation (25.26) becomes

$$c = e^{-RT} E_T[\max(S_T - K, 0)] \tag{25.27}$$

If we assume that S_T is lognormal in the forward risk-neutral world, we are considering with the standard deviation of $\ln(S_T)$ equal to w, the appendix at the end of Chapter 13 shows that

$$E_T[\max(S_T - K, 0)] = E_T(S_T)N(d_1) - KN(d_2) \tag{25.28}$$

where

$$d_1 = \frac{\ln[E_T(S_T)/K] + w^2/2}{w}$$

$$d_2 = \frac{\ln[E_T(S_T)/K] - w^2/2}{w}$$

From equation (25.21), $E_T(S_T)$ is the forward stock price for a contract maturing at time T. From the no-arbitrage arguments in Chapter 5, we have

$$E_T(S_T) = S_0 e^{RT} \tag{25.29}$$

Equations (25.27), (25.28), and (25.29) give

$$c = S_0 N(d_1) - Ke^{-RT} N(d_2)$$

where

$$d_1 = \frac{\ln[S_0/K] + RT + w^2/2}{w}$$

$$d_2 = \frac{\ln[S_0/K] + RT - w^2/2}{w}$$

If the stock price volatility σ is defined so that $\sigma\sqrt{T} = w$, the expressions for d_1 and d_2 become

$$d_1 = \frac{\ln[S_0/K] + (R + \sigma^2/2)T}{\sigma\sqrt{T}}$$

$$d_2 = \frac{\ln[S_0/K] + (R - \sigma^2/2)T}{\sigma\sqrt{T}}$$

showing that the call price is given by the Black–Scholes formula with r replaced by R. A similar result can be produced for European put options.

Option to Exchange One Asset for Another

Consider next an option to exchange an investment asset worth U for an investment asset worth V. This has already been discussed in Section 22.11. We suppose that the volatilities of U and V are σ_U and σ_V and the coefficient of correlation between them is ρ.

Suppose first that the assets provide no income. We choose the numeraire security g to be U. Setting $f = V$ in equation (25.15), we obtain

$$V_0 = U_0 E_U\left(\frac{V_T}{U_T}\right) \tag{25.30}$$

where E_U denotes expectations in a world that is forward risk neutral with respect to U.

Next we set f in equation (25.15) as the value the option under consideration, so that $f_T = \max(V_T - U_T, 0)$. It follows that

$$f_0 = U_0\, E_U\left[\frac{\max(V_T - U_T,\ 0)}{U_T}\right]$$

or

$$f_0 = U_0\, E_U\left[\max\left(\frac{V_T}{U_T} - 1,\ 0\right)\right] \tag{25.31}$$

The volatility of V/U is (see Problem 25.14) $\hat{\sigma}$, where

$$\hat{\sigma}^2 = \sigma_U^2 + \sigma_V^2 - 2\rho\sigma_U\sigma_V$$

From the appendix at the end of Chapter 13, equation (25.31) becomes

$$f_0 = U_0\left[E_U\left(\frac{V_T}{U_T}\right)N(d_1) - N(d_2)\right]$$

where

$$d_1 = \frac{\ln(V_0/U_0) + \hat{\sigma}^2 T/2}{\hat{\sigma}\sqrt{T}} \quad \text{and} \quad d_2 = d_1 - \hat{\sigma}\sqrt{T}$$

Substituting from equation (25.30), we get

$$f_0 = V_0 N(d_1) - U_0 N(d_2) \tag{25.32}$$

Problem 25.8 shows that, when f and g provide income at rate q_f and q_g, equation (25.15) becomes

$$f_0 = g_0 e^{(q_f - q_g)T} E_g\left(\frac{f_T}{g_T}\right)$$

This means that equations (25.30) and (25.31) become

$$E_U\left(\frac{V_T}{U_T}\right) = e^{(q_U - q_V)T} \frac{V_0}{U_0}$$

and

$$f_0 = e^{-q_U T} U_0 E_U\left[\max\left(\frac{V_T}{U_T} - 1,\ 0\right)\right]$$

and equation (25.32) becomes

$$f_0 = e^{-q_V T} V_0 N(d_1) - e^{-q_U T} U_0 N(d_2)$$

with d_1 and d_2 being redefined as

$$d_1 = \frac{\ln(V_0/U_0) + (q_U - q_V + \hat{\sigma}^2/2)T}{\hat{\sigma}\sqrt{T}} \quad \text{and} \quad d_2 = d_1 - \hat{\sigma}\sqrt{T}$$

This is the result given in equation (22.3).

25.7 CHANGE OF NUMERAIRE

In this section we consider the impact of a change in numeraire on the process followed by a market variable. In a world that is forward risk neutral with respect to g, the process followed by a traded security f is

$$df = \left[r + \sum_{i=1}^{n} \sigma_{g,i}\sigma_{f,i}\right] f\, dt + \sum_{i=1}^{n} \sigma_{f,i} f\, dz_i$$

Similarly, in a world that is forward risk neutral with respect to another security h, the process followed by f is

$$df = \left[r + \sum_{i=1}^{n} \sigma_{h,i}\sigma_{f,i}\right] f\, dt + \sum_{i=1}^{n} \sigma_{f,i} f\, dz_i$$

where $\sigma_{h,i}$ is the ith component of the volatility of h.

The effect of moving from a world that is forward risk neutral with respect to g to one that is forward risk neutral with respect to h (i.e., of changing the numeraire from g to h) is therefore to increase the expected growth rate of the price of any traded security f by

$$\sum_{i=1}^{n} (\sigma_{h,i} - \sigma_{g,i})\sigma_{f,i}$$

Consider next a variable v that is a function of the prices of traded securities (where v is not necessarily the price of a traded security itself). Define $\sigma_{v,i}$ as the ith component of the volatility of v. From Itô's lemma in the appendix at the end of this chapter, we can calculate what happens to the process followed by v when there is a change in numeraire causing the expected growth rate of the underlying traded securities to change. It turns out that the expected growth rate of v responds to a change in numeraire in the same way as the expected growth rate of the prices of traded securities (see Problem 12.6 for the situation where there is only one stochastic variable and Problem 25.13 for the general case). It increases by

$$\alpha_v = \sum_{i=1}^{n}(\sigma_{h,i} - \sigma_{g,i})\sigma_{v,i} \tag{25.33}$$

Define $w = h/g$ and $\sigma_{w,i}$ as the ith component of the volatility of w. From Itô's lemma (see Problem 25.14), we have

$$\sigma_{w,i} = \sigma_{h,i} - \sigma_{g,i}$$

so that equation (25.33) becomes

$$\alpha_v = \sum_{i=1}^{n} \sigma_{w,i}\,\sigma_{v,i} \tag{25.34}$$

We will refer to w as the *numeraire ratio*. Equation (25.34) is equivalent to

$$\alpha_v = \rho\sigma_v\sigma_w \tag{25.35}$$

where σ_v is the total volatility of v, σ_w is the total volatility of w, and ρ is the instantaneous correlation between v and w.[7]

This is a surprisingly simple result. The adjustment to the expected growth rate of a variable v when we change from one numeraire to another is the instantaneous covariance between the percentage change in v and the percentage change in the numeraire ratio. We will use this result when considering timing and quanto adjustments in Chapter 27.

SUMMARY

The market price of risk of a variable defines the trade-offs between risk and return for traded securities dependent on the variable. When there is one underlying variable, a derivative's excess return over the risk-free rate equals the market price of risk multiplied by the variable's volatility. When there are many underlying variables, the excess return is the sum of the market price of risk multiplied by the volatility for each variable.

A powerful tool in the valuation of derivatives is risk-neutral valuation. This was introduced in Chapters 11 and 13. The principle of risk-neutral valuation shows that, if we assume that the world is risk neutral when valuing derivatives, we get the right

[7] To see this, note that the changes Δv and Δw in v and w in a short period of time Δt are given by

$$\Delta v = \cdots + \sum \sigma_{v,i}\, v\epsilon_i\sqrt{\Delta t}$$
$$\Delta w = \cdots + \sum \sigma_{w,i}\, w\epsilon_i\sqrt{\Delta t}$$

Since the dz_i are uncorrelated, it follows that $E(\epsilon_i\epsilon_j) = 0$ when $i \neq j$. Also, from the definition of ρ, we have

$$\rho v\sigma_v w\sigma_w = E(\Delta v\,\Delta w) - E(\Delta v)\,E(\Delta w)$$

When terms of higher order than Δt are ignored this leads to

$$\rho\sigma_v\sigma_w = \sum \sigma_{w,i}\,\sigma_{v,i}$$

answer—not just in a risk-neutral world, but in all other worlds as well. In the traditional risk-neutral world, the market price of risk of all variables is zero. Furthermore, the expected price of any asset in this world is its futures price.

In this chapter we have extended the principle of risk-neutral valuation. We have shown that, when interest rates are stochastic, there are many interesting and useful alternatives to the traditional risk-neutral world. When there is only one stochastic variable, a world is defined as forward risk neutral with respect to a security price if the market price of risk for the variable is set equal to the volatility of the security price. A similar definition applies when there are many stochastic variables.

A martingale is a zero drift stochastic process. Any variable following a martingale has the simplifying property that its expected value at any future time equals its value today. We have shown that in a world that is forward risk neutral with respect to a security price g, the ratio f/g is a martingale for all security prices f. It turns out that, by appropriately choosing the numeraire security g, we can simplify the valuation of many interest rate dependent derivatives.

In this chapter we have shown how our extensions of risk-neutral valuation enable European options to exchange one asset for another to be valued when interest rates are stochastic. In Chapters 26, 27, 29, and 30, the extensions will be useful in valuing interest rate derivatives.

FURTHER READING

Baxter, M., and A. Rennie, *Financial Calculus*. Cambridge University Press, 1996.

Cox, J.C., J.E. Ingersoll, and S.A. Ross, "An Intertemporal General Equilibrium Model of Asset Prices," *Econometrica*, 53 (1985): 363–84.

Duffie, D., *Dynamic Asset Pricing Theory*. Princeton University Press, 1992

Garman, M., "A General Theory of Asset Valuation Under Diffusion State Processes," Working Paper 50, University of California, Berkeley, 1976.

Harrison, J.M., and D.M. Kreps, "Martingales and Arbitrage in Multiperiod Securities Markets," *Journal of Economic Theory*, 20 (1979): 381–408.

Harrison, J.M., and S.R. Pliska, "Martingales and Stochastic Integrals in the Theory of Continuous Trading," *Stochastic Processes and Their Applications*, 11 (1981): 215–60.

Questions and Problems (Answers in the Solutions Manual)

25.1. How is the market price of risk defined for a variable that is not the price of an investment asset?

25.2. Suppose that the market price of risk for gold is zero. If the storage costs are 1% per annum and the risk-free rate of interest is 6% per annum, what is the expected growth rate in the price of gold? Assume that gold provides no income.

25.3. Consider two securities both of which are dependent on the same market variable. The expected returns from the securities are 8% and 12%. The volatility of the first security is 15%. The instantaneous risk-free rate is 4%. What is the volatility of the second security?

25.4. An oil company is set up solely for the purpose of exploring for oil in a certain small area of Texas. Its value depends primarily on two stochastic variables: the price of oil and the quantity of proven oil reserves. Discuss whether the market price of risk for the second of these two variables is likely to be positive, negative, or zero.

25.5. Deduce the differential equation for a derivative dependent on the prices of two non-dividend-paying traded securities by forming a riskless portfolio consisting of the derivative and the two traded securities.

25.6. Suppose that an interest rate x follows the process

$$dx = a(x_0 - x)\,dt + c\,\sqrt{x}\,dz$$

where a, x_0, and c are positive constants. Suppose further that the market price of risk for x is λ. What is the process for x in the traditional risk-neutral world?

25.7. Prove that, when the security f provides income at rate q, equation (25.9) becomes $\mu + q - r = \lambda\sigma$. (*Hint*: Form a new security f^* that provides no income by assuming that all the income from f is reinvested in f.)

25.8. Show that when f and g provide income at rates q_f and q_g, respectively, equation (25.15) becomes

$$f_0 = g_0 e^{(q_f - q_g)T} E_g\left(\frac{f_T}{g_T}\right)$$

(*Hint*: Form new securities f^* and g^* that provide no income by assuming that all the income from f is reinvested in f and all the income in g is reinvested in g.)

25.9. "The expected future value of an interest rate in a risk-neutral world is greater than it is in the real world." What does this statement imply about the market price of risk for (a) an interest rate and (b) a bond price. Do you think the statement is likely to be true? Give reasons.

25.10. The variable S is an investment asset providing income at rate q measured in currency A. It follows the process

$$dS = \mu_S S\,dt + \sigma_S S\,dz$$

in the real world. Defining new variables as necessary, give the process followed by S, and the corresponding market price of risk, in:

(a) A world that is the traditional risk-neutral world for currency A
(b) A world that is the traditional risk-neutral world for currency B
(c) A world that is forward risk neutral with respect to a zero-coupon currency A bond maturing at time T
(d) A world that is forward risk neutral with respect to a zero coupon currency B bond maturing at time T.

25.11. Explain the difference between the way a forward interest rate is defined and the way the forward values of other variables such as stock prices, commodity prices, and exchange rates are defined.

25.12. Prove the result in Section 25.5 that when

$$df = \left[r + \sum_{i=1}^{n} \lambda_i \sigma_{f,i}\right] f\,dt + \sum_{i=1}^{n} \sigma_{f,i} f\,dz_i$$

and

$$dg = \left[r + \sum_{i=1}^{n} \lambda_i \sigma_{g,i}\right] g\,dt + \sum_{i=1}^{n} \sigma_{g,i} g\,dz_i$$

with the dz_i uncorrelated, f/g is a martingale for $\lambda_i = \sigma_{g,i}$.

25.13. Prove equation (25.33) in Section 25.7.

25.14. Show that when $w = h/g$ and h and g are each dependent on n Wiener processes, the ith component of the volatility of w is the ith component of the volatility of h minus the ith component of the volatility of g. Use this to prove the result that if σ_U is the volatility of U and σ_V is the volatility of V then the volatility of U/V is $\sqrt{\sigma_U^2 + \sigma_V^2 - 2\rho\sigma_U\sigma_V}$. (*Hint*: Use the result in Footnote 7.)

Assignment Questions

25.15. A security's price is positively dependent on two variables: the price of copper and the yen/dollar exchange rate. Suppose that the market price of risk for these variables is 0.5 and 0.1, respectively. If the price of copper were held fixed, the volatility of the security would be 8% per annum; if the yen/dollar exchange rate were held fixed, the volatility of the security would be 12% per annum. The risk-free interest rate is 7% per annum. What is the expected rate of return from the security? If the two variables are uncorrelated with each other, what is the volatility of the security?

25.16. Suppose that the price of a zero-coupon bond maturing at time T follows the process

$$dP(t, T) = \mu_P P(t, T)\,dt + \sigma_P P(t, T)\,dz$$

and the price of a derivative dependent on the bond follows the process

$$df = \mu_f f\,dt + \sigma_f f\,dz$$

Assume only one source of uncertainty and that f provides no income.

(a) What is the forward price F of f for a contract maturing at time T?
(b) What is the process followed by F in a world that is forward risk neutral with respect to $P(t, T)$?
(c) What is the process followed by F in the traditional risk-neutral world?
(d) What is the process followed by f in a world that is forward risk neutral with respect to a bond maturing at time T^*, where $T^* \neq T$? Assume that σ_P^* is the volatility of this bond.

25.17. Consider a variable that is not an interest rate:

(a) In what world is the futures price of the variable a martingale?
(b) In what world is the forward price of the variable a martingale?
(c) Defining variables as necessary, derive an expression for the difference between the drift of the futures price and the drift of the forward price in the traditional risk-neutral world.
(d) Show that your result is consistent with the points made in Section 5.8 about the circumstances when the futures price is above the forward price.

APPENDIX

HANDLING MULTIPLE SOURCES OF UNCERTAINTY

In this appendix we extend Itô's lemma to cover situations where there are multiple sources of uncertainty and prove the result in equation (25.13) relating the excess return to market prices of risk when there are multiple sources of uncertainty.

Itô's Lemma for a Function of Several Variables

Itô's lemma, as presented in the appendix to Chapter 12, provides the process followed by a function of a single stochastic variable. Here we present a generalized version of Itô's lemma for the process followed by a function of several stochastic variables.

Suppose that a function f depends on the n variables $x_1, x_2, \dots, x_n$ and time t. Suppose further that x_i follows an Itô process with instantaneous drift a_i and instantaneous variance b_i^2 $(1 \leqslant i \leqslant n)$, that is,

$$dx_i = a_i\,dt + b_i\,dz_i \qquad \textbf{(25A.1)}$$

where dz_i $(1 \leqslant i \leqslant n)$ is a Wiener process. Each a_i and b_i may be any function of all the x_i and t. A Taylor series expansion of Δf gives

$$\Delta f = \sum_{i=1}^{n} \frac{\partial f}{\partial x_i}\Delta x_i + \frac{\partial f}{\partial t}\Delta t + \tfrac{1}{2}\sum_{i=1}^{n}\sum_{j=1}^{n}\frac{\partial^2 f}{\partial x_i\,\partial x_j}\Delta x_i\,\Delta x_j + \tfrac{1}{2}\sum_{i=1}^{n}\frac{\partial^2 f}{\partial x_i\,\partial t}\Delta x_i\,\Delta t + \cdots \qquad \textbf{(25A.2)}$$

Equation (25A.1) can be discretized as

$$\Delta x_i = a_i\,\Delta t + b_i\epsilon_i\sqrt{\Delta t}$$

where ϵ_i is a random sample from a standardized normal distribution. The correlation ρ_{ij} between dz_i and dz_j is defined as the correlation between ϵ_i and ϵ_j. In the appendix to Chapter 12 it was argued that

$$\lim_{\Delta t\to 0} \Delta x_i^2 = b_i^2\,dt$$

Similarly,

$$\lim_{\Delta t\to 0} \Delta x_i\,\Delta x_j = b_i b_j \rho_{ij}\,dt$$

As $\Delta t \to 0$, the first three terms in the expansion of Δf in equation (25A.2) are of order Δt. All other terms are of higher order. Hence,

$$df = \sum_{i=1}^{n}\frac{\partial f}{\partial x_i}dx_i + \frac{\partial f}{\partial t}dt + \tfrac{1}{2}\sum_{i=1}^{n}\sum_{j=1}^{n}\frac{\partial^2 f}{\partial x_i\,\partial x_j}b_i b_j \rho_{ij}\,dt$$

This is the generalized version of Itô's lemma. Substituting for dx_i from equation (25A.1) gives

$$df = \left(\sum_{i=1}^{n}\frac{\partial f}{\partial x_i}a_i + \frac{\partial f}{\partial t} + \tfrac{1}{2}\sum_{i=1}^{n}\sum_{j=1}^{n}\frac{\partial^2 f}{\partial x_i\,\partial x_j}b_i b_j\rho_{ij}\right)dt + \sum_{i=1}^{n}\frac{\partial f}{\partial x_i}b_i\,dz_i \qquad \textbf{(25A.3)}$$

For an alternative generalization of Itô's lemma, suppose that f depends on a single variable x and that the process for x involves more than one Wiener process:

$$dx = a\,dt + \sum_{i=1}^{m} b_i\,dz_i$$

In this case,

$$\Delta f = \frac{\partial f}{\partial x}\Delta x + \frac{\partial f}{\partial t}\Delta t + \tfrac{1}{2}\frac{\partial^2 f}{\partial x^2}\Delta x^2 + \tfrac{1}{2}\frac{\partial^2 f}{\partial x\,\partial t}\Delta x\,\Delta t + \cdots$$

$$\Delta x = a\,\Delta t + \sum_{i=1}^{m} b_i \epsilon_i \sqrt{\Delta t}$$

and

$$\lim_{\Delta t \to 0} \Delta x_i^2 = \sum_{i=1}^{m}\sum_{j=1}^{m} b_i b_j \rho_{ij}\,dt$$

where, as before, ρ_{ij} is the correlation between dz_i and dz_j This leads to

$$df = \left(\frac{\partial f}{\partial x}a + \frac{\partial f}{\partial t} + \tfrac{1}{2}\frac{\partial^2 f}{\partial x^2}\sum_{i=1}^{m}\sum_{j=1}^{m} b_i b_j \rho_{ij}\right)dt + \frac{\partial f}{\partial x}\sum_{i=1}^{m} b_i\,dz_i \tag{25A.4}$$

Finally, consider the more general case where f depends on variables x_i $(1 \leqslant i \leqslant n)$ and

$$dx_i = a_i\,dt + \sum_{k=1}^{m} b_{ik}\,dz_k$$

A similar analysis shows that

$$df = \left(\sum_{i=1}^{n}\frac{\partial f}{\partial x_i}a_i + \frac{\partial f}{\partial t} + \tfrac{1}{2}\sum_{i=1}^{n}\sum_{j=1}^{n}\frac{\partial^2 f}{\partial x_i \partial dx_j}\sum_{k=1}^{m}\sum_{l=1}^{m} b_{ik}b_{jl}\rho_{kl}\right)dt + \sum_{i=1}^{n}\frac{\partial f}{\partial x_i}\sum_{k=1}^{m} b_{ik}\,dz_k \tag{25A.5}$$

The Return for a Security Dependent on Multiple Sources of Uncertainty

In Section 25.1 we prove a result relating return to risk when there is one source of uncertainty. We now prove the result in equation (25.13) for the situation where there are multiple sources of uncertainty.

Suppose that there are n stochastic variables following Wiener processes. Consider $n+1$ traded securities whose prices depend on some or all of the n stochastic variables. Define f_j as the price of the jth security $(1 \leqslant j \leqslant n+1)$. We assume that no dividends or other income is paid by the $n+1$ traded securities.[8] It follows from the previous

[8] This is not restrictive. A non-dividend-paying security can always be obtained from a dividend-paying security by reinvesting the dividends in the security.

section that the securities follow processes of the form

$$df_j = \mu_j f_j \, dt + \sum_{i=1}^{n} \sigma_{ij} f_j \, dz_i \tag{25A.6}$$

Since there are $n+1$ traded securities and n Wiener processes, it is possible to form an instantaneously riskless portfolio Π using the securities. Define k_j as the amount of the jth security in the portfolio, so that

$$\Pi = \sum_{j=1}^{n+1} k_j f_j \tag{25A.7}$$

The k_j must be chosen so that the stochastic components of the returns from the securities are eliminated. From equation (25A.6), this means that

$$\sum_{j=1}^{n+1} k_j \sigma_{ij} f_j = 0 \tag{25A.8}$$

for $1 \leqslant i \leqslant n$. The return from the portfolio is then given by

$$d\Pi = \sum_{j=1}^{n+1} k_j \mu_j f_j \, dt$$

The cost of setting up the portfolio is

$$\sum_{j=1}^{n+1} k_j f_j$$

If there are no arbitrage opportunities, the portfolio must earn the risk-free interest rate, so that

$$\sum_{j=1}^{n+1} k_j \mu_j f_j = r \sum_{j=1}^{n+1} k_j f_j \tag{25A.9}$$

or

$$\sum_{j=1}^{n+1} k_j f_j (\mu_j - r) = 0 \tag{25A.10}$$

Equations (25A.8) and (25A.10) can be regarded as $n+1$ homogeneous linear equations in the k_j. The k_j are not all zero. From a well-known theorem in linear algebra, equations (25A.8) and (25A.10) can be consistent only if, for all j,

$$f_j(\mu_j - r) = \sum_{i=1}^{n} \lambda_i \sigma_{ij} f_j \tag{25A.11}$$

or

$$\mu_j - r = \sum_{i=1}^{n} \lambda_i \sigma_{ij} \tag{25A.12}$$

for some λ_i $(1 \leqslant i \leqslant n)$ that are dependent only on the state variables and time. Dropping the j subscript, this shows that, for any security f dependent on the n

stochastic variables,

$$df = \mu f\, dt + \sum_{i=1}^{n} \sigma_i f\, dz_i$$

where

$$\mu - r = \sum_{i=1}^{n} \lambda_i \sigma_i$$

This proves the result in equation (25.13).

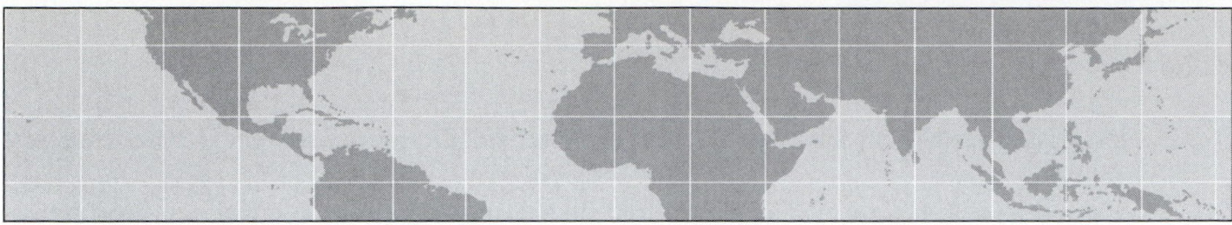

CHAPTER 26

Interest Rate Derivatives: The Standard Market Models

Interest rate derivatives are instruments whose payoffs are dependent in some way on the level of interest rates. In the 1980s and 1990s, the volume of trading in interest rate derivatives in both the over-the-counter and exchange-traded markets increased very quickly. Many new products were developed to meet particular needs of end users. A key challenge for derivatives traders is to find good, robust procedures for pricing and hedging these products.

Interest rate derivatives are more difficult to value than equity and foreign exchange derivatives. There are a number of reasons for this:

1. The behavior of an individual interest rate is more complicated than that of a stock price or an exchange rate.
2. For the valuation of many products it is necessary to develop a model describing the behavior of the entire zero-coupon yield curve.
3. The volatilities of different points on the yield curve are different.
4. Interest rates are used for discounting as well as for defining the payoff from the derivative.

In this chapter we look at the three most popular over-the-counter interest rate option products: bond options, interest rate caps/floors, and swap options. We explain the standard market models for valuing these products and use the analysis from Chapter 25 to show that the models are internally consistent.

26.1 BLACK'S MODEL

Since the Black–Scholes model was first published in 1973, it has become a very popular tool. As explained in Chapter 14, the model has been extended so that it can be used to value options on foreign exchange, options on indices, and options on futures contracts. Traders have become very comfortable with both the lognormal assumption that underlies the model and the volatility measure that describes uncertainty. It is not surprising that there have been attempts to extend the model so that it covers interest rate derivatives.

In this chapter we will discuss three of the most popular interest rate derivatives (bond options, interest rate caps/floors, and swap options) and describe how the lognormal assumption underlying the Black–Scholes model can be used to value these instruments. The model we will use is usually referred to as Black's model because it is structurally similar to the model suggested by Fischer Black for valuing options on commodity futures (see Section 14.8). If, in this model, the futures contract and the option have the same maturity date, then the futures price equals the spot price at the end of the option's life. This means that the model then gives the value of an option on spot as well as an option on futures.

Using Black's Model to Price European Options

Consider a European call option on a variable whose value is V. (The variable V does not have to be the price of a traded security.) Define:

T: Time to maturity of the option

F: Forward price of V for a contract with maturity T

F_0: Value of F at time zero

K: Strike price of the option

$P(t, T)$: Price at time t of a zero-coupon bond paying \$1 at time T

V_T: Value of V at time T

σ: Volatility of F

We value the option by:

1. Assuming $\ln V_T$ is normal with mean F_0 and standard deviation $\sigma\sqrt{T}$
2. Discounting the expected payoff at the T-year rate. (This is equivalent to multiplying the expected payoff by $P(0, T)$.)

The payoff from the option at time T is $\max(V_T - K, 0)$. As shown in the appendix to Chapter 13, the lognormal assumption for V_T implies that the expected payoff is

$$E(V_T)N(d_1) - KN(d_2)$$

where $E(V_T)$ is the expected value of V_T and

$$d_1 = \frac{\ln[E(V_T)/K] + \sigma^2 T/2}{\sigma\sqrt{T}}$$

$$d_2 = \frac{\ln[E(V_T)/K] - \sigma^2 T/2}{\sigma\sqrt{T}} = d_1 - \sigma\sqrt{T}$$

Because we are assuming that $E(V_T) = F_0$, the value of the option is

$$c = P(0, T)[F_0 N(d_1) - KN(d_2)] \qquad \textbf{(26.1)}$$

where

$$d_1 = \frac{\ln(F_0/K) + \sigma^2 T/2}{\sigma\sqrt{T}}$$

$$d_2 = \frac{\ln(F_0/K) - \sigma^2 T/2}{\sigma\sqrt{T}} = d_1 - \sigma\sqrt{T}$$

Similarly the value p of the corresponding put option is given by

$$p = P(0, T)[KN(-d_2) - F_0N(-d_1)] \quad \textbf{(26.2)}$$

This is the model we will refer to as Black's model from now on. An important feature of Black's model is that we do not have to assume geometric Brownian motion for the evolution of either V or F. All that we require is that V_T be lognormal at time T. The parameter σ is usually referred to as the volatility of F or the forward volatility of V. However, its only role is to define the standard deviation of $\ln V_T$ by means of the relationship

$$\text{Standard deviation of } \ln V_T = \sigma\sqrt{T}$$

The volatility parameter does not necessarily say anything about the standard deviation of $\ln V$ at times other than T.

Delayed Payoff

We can extend Black's model to allow for the situation where the payoff is calculated from the value of the variable V at time T, but the payoff is actually made at some later time T^*. The expected payoff is discounted from time T^* instead of time T so that equation (26.1) and (26.2) become

$$c = P(0, T^*)[F_0N(d_1) - KN(d_2)] \quad \textbf{(26.3)}$$

$$p = P(0, T^*)[KN(-d_2) - F_0N(-d_1)] \quad \textbf{(26.4)}$$

where

$$d_1 = \frac{\ln(F_0/K) + \sigma^2 T/2}{\sigma\sqrt{T}}$$

$$d_2 = \frac{\ln(F_0/K) - \sigma^2 T/2}{\sigma\sqrt{T}} = d_1 - \sigma\sqrt{T}$$

Validity of Black's Model

It is easy to see that Black's model is appropriate when interest rates are assumed to be either constant or deterministic. In this case, as explained in Chapter 5, the forward price of V equals its futures price and from Section 14.7 the $E(S_T) = F_0$ in a risk-neutral world.

When interest rates are stochastic, there are two aspects of the derivation of equations (26.1) to (26.4) that are open to question.

1. Why do we set $E(V_T)$ equal to the forward price F_0 of V? This is not the same as the futures price.
2. Why do we ignore the fact that interest rates are stochastic when discounting?

It turns out that these two assumptions offset each other. As we apply Black's model to bond options, caps/floors, and swap options, we will use the results in Section 25.4 to show that there are no approximations in equations (26.1) to (26.4) when interest rates are stochastic. Black's model therefore has a sounder theoretical basis and wider applicability than sometimes supposed.

26.2 BOND OPTIONS

A bond option is an option to buy or sell a particular bond by a particular date for a particular price. In addition to trading in the over-the-counter market, bond options are frequently embedded in bonds when they are issued to make them more attractive to either the issuer or potential purchasers.

Embedded Bond Options

One example of a bond with an embedded bond option is a *callable bond.* This is a bond that contains provisions allowing the issuing firm to buy back the bond at a predetermined price at certain times in the future. The holder of such a bond has sold a call option to the issuer. The strike price or call price in the option is the predetermined price that must be paid by the issuer to the holder. Callable bonds cannot usually be called for the first few years of their life. (This is known as the lock-out period.) After that the call price is usually a decreasing function of time. For example, in a 10-year callable bond, there might be no call privileges for the first 2 years. After that, the issuer might have the right to buy the bond back at a price of 110 in years 3 and 4 of its life, at a price of 107.5 in years 5 and 6, at a price of 106 in years 7 and 8, and at a price of 103 in years 9 and 10. The value of the call option is reflected in the quoted yields on bonds. Bonds with call features generally offer higher yields than bonds with no call features.

Another type of bond with an embedded option is a *puttable bond.* This contains provisions that allow the holder to demand early redemption at a predetermined price at certain times in the future. The holder of such a bond has purchased a put option on the bond as well as the bond itself. Because the put option increases the value of the bond to the holder, bonds with put features provide lower yields than bonds with no put features. A simple example of a puttable bond is a 10-year bond where the holder has the right to be repaid at the end of 5 years. (This is sometimes referred to as a *retractable bond.*)

Loan and deposit instruments also often contain embedded bond options. For example, a 5-year fixed-rate deposit with a financial institution that can be redeemed without penalty at any time contains an American put option on a bond. (The deposit instrument is a bond that the investor has the right to put back to the financial institution at its face value at any time.) Prepayment privileges on loans and mortgages are similarly call options on bonds.

Finally, we note that a loan commitment made by a bank or other financial institution is a put option on a bond. Consider, for example, the situation where a bank quotes a 5-year interest rate of 5% per annum to a potential borrower and states that the rate is good for the next 2 months. The client has, in effect, obtained the right to sell a 5-year bond with a 5% coupon to the financial institution for its face value any time within the next 2 months.

European Bond Options

Many over-the-counter bond options and some embedded bond options are European. We now consider the standard market models used to value European options.

The assumption usually made is that the bond price at the maturity of the option is lognormal. Equations (26.1) and (26.2) can be used to price the option with F_0 equal to the forward bond price F_B. The variable σ is set equal to the forward bond price volatility, σ_B. As explained in Section 26.1 σ_B is defined so that $\sigma_B\sqrt{T}$ is the standard deviation of the logarithm of the bond price at the maturity of the option. The equations for pricing a European bond option are therefore

$$c = P(0, T)[F_B N(d_1) - KN(d_2)] \tag{26.5}$$

$$p = P(0, T)[KN(-d_2) - F_B N(-d_1)] \tag{26.6}$$

where

$$d_1 = \frac{\ln(F_B/K) + \sigma_B^2 T/2}{\sigma_B\sqrt{T}} \quad \text{and} \quad d_2 = d_1 - \sigma_B\sqrt{T}$$

From Section 5.5, F_B can be calculated using the formula

$$F_B = \frac{B_0 - I}{P(0, T)} \tag{26.7}$$

where B_0 is the bond price at time zero and I is the present value of the coupons that will be paid during the life of the option. In this formula, both the spot bond price and the forward bond price are cash prices rather than quoted prices. The relationship between cash and quoted bond prices is explained in Section 6.2.

The strike price K in equations (26.5) and (26.6) should be the cash strike price. In choosing the correct value for K, the precise terms of the option are therefore important. If the strike price is defined as the cash amount that is exchanged for the bond when the option is exercised, K should be put equal to this strike price. If, as is more common, the strike price is the quoted price applicable when the option is exercised, K should be set equal to the strike price plus accrued interest at the expiration date of the option. Traders refer to the quoted price of a bond as the *clean price* and the cash price as the *dirty price*.

Example 26.1

Consider a 10-month European call option on a 9.75-year bond with a face value of \$1,000. (When the option matures, the bond will have 8 years and 11 months remaining.) Suppose that the current cash bond price is \$960, the strike price is \$1,000, the 10-month risk-free interest rate is 10% per annum, and the volatility of the forward bond price in 10 months is 9% per annum. The bond pays a semiannual coupon of 10% and coupon payments of \$50 are expected in 3 months and 9 months. (This means that the accrued interest is \$25 and the quoted bond price is \$935.) We suppose that the 3-month and 9-month risk-free interest rates are 9.0% and 9.5% per annum, respectively. The present value of the coupon payments is, therefore,

$$50e^{-0.25\times 0.09} + 50e^{-0.75\times 0.095} = 95.45$$

or \$95.45. The bond forward price is from equation (26.7) given by

$$F_B = (960 - 95.45)e^{0.1\times 0.8333} = 939.68$$

(a) If the strike price is the cash price that would be paid for the bond on exercise, the parameters for equation (26.5) are $F_B = 939.68$, $K = 1000$, $P(0, T) = e^{-0.1\times(10/12)} = 0.9200$, $\sigma_B = 0.09$, and $T = 10/12$. The price of the call option is \$9.49.

(b) If the strike price is the quoted price that would be paid for the bond on exercise, 1 month's accrued interest must be added to K because the maturity of the option is 1 month after a coupon date. This produces a value for K of

$$1{,}000 + 50 \times 0.16667 = 1{,}008.33$$

The values for the other parameters in equation (26.5) are unchanged (i.e., $F_B = 939.68$, $P(0, T) = 0.9200$, $\sigma_B = 0.09$, and $T = 0.8333$). The price of the option is \$7.97.

Figure 26.1 shows how the standard deviation of the logarithm of a bond's price changes as we look further ahead. The standard deviation is zero today because there is no uncertainty about the bond's price today. It is also zero at the bond's maturity because we know that the bond's price will equal its face value at maturity. Between today and the maturity of the bond, the standard deviation first increases and then decreases.

The volatility σ_B that should be used when a European option on the bond is valued is

$$\frac{\text{Standard deviation of logarithm of bond price at maturity of option}}{\sqrt{\text{Time to maturity of option}}}$$

What happens when we keep the underlying bond fixed and increase the life of the

Figure 26.1 Standard deviation of logarithm of bond price at future times.

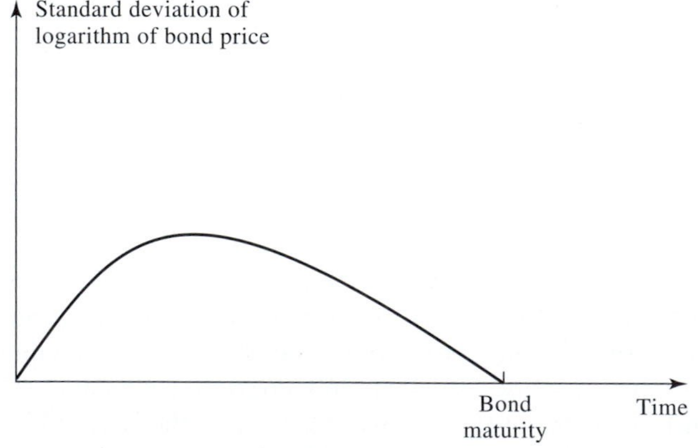

Figure 26.2 Variation of forward bond price volatility σ_B with life of option when bond is kept fixed.

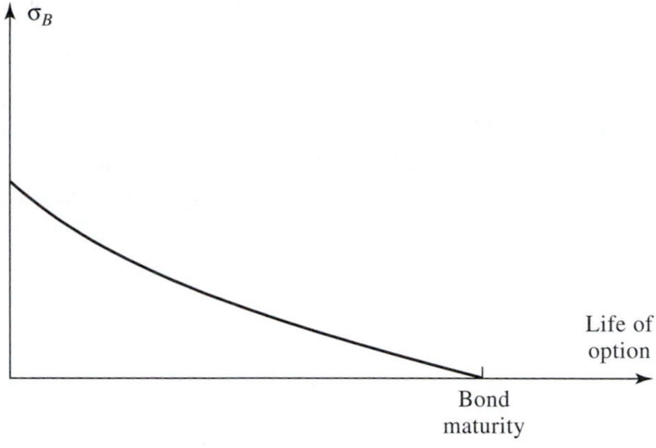

option? Figure 26.2 shows a typical pattern for σ_B as a function of the life of the option. In general, σ_B declines as the life of the option increases.

Yield Volatilities

The volatilities that are quoted for bond options are often yield volatilities rather than price volatilities. The duration concept, introduced in Chapter 4, is used by the market to convert a quoted yield volatility into a price volatility. Suppose that D is the modified duration of the bond underlying the option at the option maturity, as defined in Chapter 4. The relationship between the change ΔF_B in the forward bond price F_B and the change Δy_F in the forward yield y_F is

$$\frac{\Delta F_B}{F_B} \approx -D\Delta y_F$$

or

$$\frac{\Delta F_B}{F_B} \approx -Dy_F \frac{\Delta y_F}{y_F}$$

Volatility is a measure of the standard deviation of percentage changes in the value of a variable. This equation therefore suggests that the volatility of the forward bond price σ_B used in Black's model can be approximately related to the volatility of the forward bond yield σ_y by

$$\sigma_B = Dy_0\sigma_y \tag{26.8}$$

where y_0 is the initial value of y_F. When a yield volatility is quoted for a bond option, the implicit assumption is usually that it will be converted to a price volatility using equation (26.8), and that this volatility will then be used in conjunction with equation (26.5) or (26.6) to obtain a price. Suppose that the bond underlying a call option will have a modified duration of 5 years at option maturity, the forward yield is 8%, and the forward yield volatility quoted by a broker is 20%. This means that the market price of the option corresponding to the broker quote is the price given by equation (26.5) when the volatility variable σ_B is

$$5 \times 0.08 \times 0.2 = 0.08$$

or 8% per annum. Figure 26.2 shows that forward bond volatilities depend on the option considered. Forward yield volatilities as we have just defined them are more constant. This is why traders prefer them.

The Bond_Options worksheet of the software DerivaGem accompanying this book can be used to price European bond options using Black's model by selecting Black-European as the Pricing Model. The user inputs a yield volatility, which is handled in the way just described. The strike price can be the cash or quoted strike price.

Example 26.2

Consider a European put option on a 10-year bond with a principal of 100. The coupon is 8% per year payable semiannually. The life of the option is 2.25 years and the strike price of the option is 115. The forward yield volatility is 20%. The zero curve is flat at 5% with continuous compounding. DerivaGem shows that the quoted price of the bond is 122.84. The price of the option when the strike price is a quoted price is 2.37. When the strike price is a cash price, the price of the option is $1.74. (Note that DerivaGem's prices may not exactly agree with manually calculated prices because DerivaGem assumes 365 days per year and rounds times to the nearest whole number of days. See Problem 26.16 for the manual calculation.)

Theoretical Justification for the Model

In Section 25.4, we explored alternatives to the usual risk-neutral valuation assumption for valuing derivatives. One alternative was a world that is forward risk neutral with respect to a zero-coupon bond maturing at time T. We showed that:

1. The current value of any security is its expected value at time T in this world multiplied by the price of a zero-coupon bond maturing at time T (see equation 25.20).
2. The expected value of any variable (except an interest rate) at time T in this world equals its forward value (see equation 25.21).

The first of these results shows that the price of a call option with maturity T years on a bond is

$$c = P(0, T)E_T[\max(B_T - K, 0)] \tag{26.9}$$

where B_T is the bond price at time T and E_T denotes expected value in a world that is forward risk neutral with respect to a zero-coupon bond maturing at time T. The second result implies that

$$E_T(B_T) = F_B \tag{26.10}$$

Assuming the bond price is lognormal with the standard deviation of the logarithm of the bond price equal to $\sigma_B\sqrt{T}$, the appendix to Chapter 13 shows that equation (26.9) becomes

$$c = P(0, T)[E_T(B_T)N(d_1) - KN(d_2)]$$

where

$$d_1 = \frac{\ln[E_T(B_T)/K] + \sigma_B^2 T/2}{\sigma_B \sqrt{T}}$$

$$d_2 = \frac{\ln[E_T(B_T)/K] - \sigma_B^2 T/2}{\sigma_B \sqrt{T}} = d_1 - \sigma_B \sqrt{T}$$

Using equation (26.10), this reduces to the Black's model formula in equation (26.5). We have shown that we can use today's T-year maturity interest rate for discounting provided that we also set the expected bond price equal to the forward bond price.

26.3 INTEREST RATE CAPS AND FLOORS

A popular interest rate option offered by financial institutions in the over-the-counter market is an *interest rate cap*. Interest rate caps can best be understood by first considering a floating-rate note where the interest rate is reset periodically equal to LIBOR. The time between resets is known as the *tenor*. Suppose the tenor is 3 months. The interest rate on the note for the first 3 months is the initial 3-month LIBOR rate; the interest rate for the next 3 months is set equal to the 3-month LIBOR rate prevailing in the market at the 3-month point; and so on.

An interest rate cap is designed to provide insurance against the rate of interest on the floating-rate note rising above a certain level. This level is known as the *cap rate*. Suppose that the principal amount is \$10 million, the tenor is 3 months, the life of the cap is 3 years, and the cap rate is 4%. (Because the payments are made quarterly, this cap rate is expressed with quarterly compounding.) The cap provides insurance against the interest on the floating rate note rising above 4%.

For the moment we ignore day count issues and assume that there is exactly 0.25 year between each payment date. We will cover day count issues at the end of this section. Suppose that on a particular reset date the 3-month LIBOR interest rate is 5%. The floating rate note would require

$$0.25 \times 0.05 \times \$10{,}000{,}000 = \$125{,}000$$

of interest to be paid 3 months later. With a 3-month LIBOR rate of 4% the interest payment would be

$$0.25 \times 0.04 \times \$10{,}000{,}000 = \$100{,}000$$

The cap therefore provides a payoff of \$25,000. Note that the payoff does not occur on the reset date when the 5% is observed. It occurs 3 months later. This reflects the usual time lag between an interest rate being observed and the corresponding payment being required.

At each reset date during the life of the cap we observe LIBOR. If LIBOR is less than 4%, there is no payoff from the cap three months later. If LIBOR is greater than 4%, the payoff is one quarter of the excess applied to the principal of \$10 million. Note that caps are usually defined so that the initial LIBOR rate, even if it is greater than the cap rate, does not lead to a payoff on the first reset date. In our example, the cap lasts for 5 years. There are, therefore, a total of 19 reset dates (at times 0.25, 0.50, 0.75, ..., 4.75 years) and 19 potential payoffs from the caps (at times 0.50, 0.75, 1.00, ..., 5.00 years).

The Cap as a Portfolio of Interest Rate Options

We now consider a cap with a total life of T, a principal of L, and a cap rate of R_K. Suppose that the reset dates are $t_1, t_2, \dots, t_n$ and define $t_{n+1} = T$. Define R_k as the interest rate for the period between time t_k and t_{k+1} observed at time t_k ($1 \leqslant k \leqslant n$). The cap leads to a payoff at time t_{k+1} ($k = 1, 2, \dots, n$) of

$$L\delta_k \max(R_k - R_K, 0) \qquad \textbf{(26.11)}$$

where $\delta_k = t_{k+1} - t_k$.[1] Both R_k and R_K are expressed with a compounding frequency equal to the frequency of resets.

Equation (26.11) is a call option on the LIBOR rate observed at time t_k with the payoff occurring at time t_{k+1}. The cap is a portfolio of n such options. LIBOR rates are observed at times $t_1, t_2, t_3, \dots, t_n$ and the corresponding payoffs occur at times $t_2, t_3, t_4, \dots, t_{n+1}$. The n call options underlying the cap are known as *caplets*.

A Cap as a Portfolio of Bond Options

An interest rate cap can also be characterized as a portfolio of put options on zero-coupon bonds with payoffs on the puts occurring at the time they are calculated. The payoff in equation (26.11) at time t_{k+1} is equivalent to

$$\frac{L\delta_k}{1 + R_k\delta_k}\max(R_k - R_K, 0)$$

at time t_k. A few lines of algebra show that this reduces to

$$\max\left[L - \frac{L(1 + R_K\delta_k)}{1 + R_k\delta_k}, 0\right] \qquad \textbf{(26.12)}$$

The expression

$$\frac{L(1 + R_K\delta_k)}{1 + R_k\delta_k}$$

is the value at time t_k of a zero-coupon bond that pays off $L(1 + R_K\delta_k)$ at time t_{k+1}. The expression in equation (26.12) is therefore the payoff from a put option with maturity t_k on a zero-coupon bond with maturity t_{k+1} when the face value of the bond is $L(1 + R_K\delta_k)$ and the strike price is L. It follows that an interest rate cap can be regarded as a portfolio of European put options on zero-coupon bonds.

Floors and Collars

Interest rate floors and interest rate collars (sometimes called floor–ceiling agreements) are defined analogously to caps. A *floor* provides a payoff when the interest rate on the underlying floating-rate note falls below a certain rate. With the notation already introduced, a floor provides a payoff at time t_{k+1} ($k = 1, 2, \dots, n$) of

$$L\delta_k \max(R_K - R_k, 0)$$

Analogously to an interest rate cap, an interest rate floor is a portfolio of put options on interest rates or a portfolio of call options on zero-coupon bonds. Each of the

[1] Day count issues are discussed at the end of this section.

> **Business Snapshot 26.1** Put–Call Parity for Caps and Floors
>
> There is a put–call parity relationship between the prices of caps and floors. This is
>
> $$\text{Value of cap} = \text{Value of floor} + \text{Value of swap}$$
>
> In this relationship, the cap and floor have the same strike price, R_K. The swap is an agreement to receive LIBOR and pay a fixed rate of R_K with no exchange of payments on the first reset date. All three instruments have the same life and the same frequency of payments.
>
> To see that the result is true, consider a long position in the cap combined with a short position in the floor. The cap provides a cash flow of LIBOR $- R_K$ for periods when LIBOR is greater than R_K. The short floor provides a cash flow of $-(R_K - \text{LIBOR}) = \text{LIBOR} - R_K$ for periods when LIBOR is less than R_K. There is therefore a cash flow of LIBOR $- R_K$ in all circumstances. This is the cash flow on the swap. It follows that the value of the cap minus the value of the floor must equal the value of the swap.
>
> Note that swaps are usually structured so that LIBOR at time zero determines a payment on the first reset date. Caps and floors are usually structured so that there is no payoff on the first reset date. This is why the swap has to be defined as one with no payment on the first reset date.

individual options comprising a floor is known as a *floorlet*. A *collar* is an instrument designed to guarantee that the interest rate on the underlying floating-rate note always lies between two levels. A collar is a combination of a long position in a cap and a short position in a floor. It is usually constructed so that the price of the cap is initially equal to the price of the floor. The cost of entering into the collar is then zero.

As explained in Business Snapshot 26.1 there is a put–call parity relationship between caps and floors.

Valuation of Caps and Floors

As shown in equation (26.11), the caplet corresponding to the rate observed at time t_k provides a payoff at time t_{k+1} of

$$L\delta_k \max(R_k - R_K, 0)$$

If the rate R_k is assumed to be lognormal with volatility σ_k, equation (26.3) gives the value of this caplet as

$$L\delta_k P(0, t_{k+1})[F_k N(d_1) - R_K N(d_2)] \tag{26.13}$$

where

$$d_1 = \frac{\ln(F_k/R_K) + \sigma_k^2 t_k/2}{\sigma_k\sqrt{t_k}}$$

$$d_2 = \frac{\ln(F_k/R_K) - \sigma_k^2 t_k/2}{\sigma_k\sqrt{t_k}} = d_1 - \sigma_k\sqrt{t_k}$$

and F_k is the forward rate for the period between time t_k and t_{k+1}. The value of the corresponding floorlet is, from equation (26.4),

$$L\delta_k P(0, t_{k+1})[R_K N(-d_2) - F_k N(-d_1)] \tag{26.14}$$

Example 26.3

Consider a contract that caps the LIBOR interest rate on \$10,000 at 8% per annum (with quarterly compounding) for 3 months starting in 1 year. This is a caplet and could be one element of a cap. Suppose that the LIBOR/swap zero curve is flat at 7% per annum with quarterly compounding and the volatility of the 3-month forward rate underlying the caplet is 20% per annum. The continuously compounded zero rate for all maturities is 6.9394%. In equation (26.13), $F_k = 0.07$, $\delta_k = 0.25$, $L = 10,000$, $R_K = 0.08$, $t_k = 1.0$, $t_{k+1} = 1.25$, $P(0, t_{k+1}) = e^{-0.069394\times 1.25} = 0.9169$, and $\sigma_k = 0.20$. Also,

$$d_1 = \frac{\ln(0.07/0.08) + 0.2^2 \times 1/2}{0.20 \times 1} = -0.5677$$

$$d_2 = d_1 - 0.20 = -0.7677$$

so that the caplet price is

$$0.25 \times 10,000 \times 0.9169[0.07N(-0.5677) - 0.08N(-0.7677)] = \$5.162$$

(Note that DerivaGem gives \$5.146 for the price of this caplet. This is because it assumes 365 days per year and rounds times to the nearest whole number of days.)

Each caplet of a cap must be valued separately using equation (26.13). One approach is to use a different volatility for each caplet. The volatilities are then referred to as *spot volatilities*. An alternative approach is to use the same volatility for all the caplets comprising any particular cap but to vary this volatility according to the life of the cap. The volatilities used are then referred to as *flat volatilities*.[2] The volatilities quoted in the market are usually flat volatilities. However, many traders like to work with spot volatilities because this allows them to identify underpriced and overpriced caplets. Options on Eurodollar futures are very similar to caplets and the spot volatilities used for caplets on 3-month LIBOR are frequently compared with those calculated from the prices of Eurodollar futures options.

Spot Volatilities vs. Flat Volatilities

Figure 26.3 shows a typical pattern for spot volatilities and flat volatilities as a function of maturity. (In the case of a spot volatility, the maturity is the maturity of a caplet; in the case of a flat volatility, it is the maturity of a cap.) The flat volatilities are akin to cumulative averages of the spot volatilities and therefore exhibit less variability. As indicated by Figure 26.3, we usually observe a "hump" in the volatilities. The peak of the hump is at about the 2- to 3-year point. This hump is observed both when the volatilities are implied from option prices and when they are calculated from historical data. There is no general agreement on the reason for the existence of the hump. One possible explanation is as follows. Rates at the short end of the zero curve are controlled by central banks. By contrast, 2- and 3-year interest rates are determined to a large extent by the activities of traders. These traders may be

[2] Flat volatilities can be calculated from spot volatilities and vice versa (see Problem 26.20).

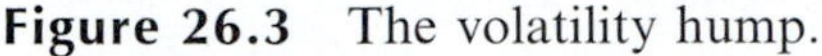

Figure 26.3 The volatility hump.

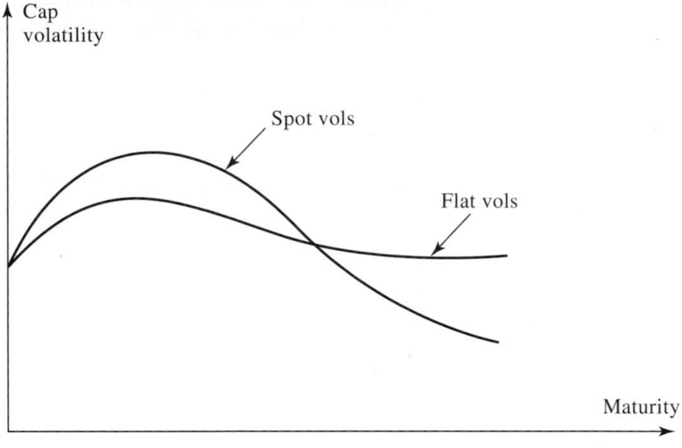

overreacting to the changes they observe in the short rate and causing the volatility of these rates to be higher than the volatility of short rates. For maturities beyond 2 to 3 years, the mean reversion of interest rates, which will be discussed in Chapter 28, causes volatilities to decline.

Brokers provide tables of flat implied volatilities for caps and floors. The instruments underlying the quotes are usually at the money. This means that the cap/floor rate equals the swap rate for a swap that has the same payment dates as the cap. Table 26.1 shows typical broker quotes for the US dollar market. The tenor of the cap is 3 months and the cap life varies from 1 to 10 years. The data exhibits the type of "hump" shown in Figure 26.3.

Theoretical Justification for the Model

We can show that Black's model for a caplet is internally consistent by considering a world that is forward risk neutral with respect to a zero-coupon bond maturing at

Table 26.1 Typical broker flat volatility quotes for US dollar caps and floors (% per annum).

Life	*Cap bid*	*Cap offer*	*Floor bid*	*Floor offer*
1 year	18.00	20.00	18.00	20.00
2 years	23.25	24.25	23.75	24.75
3 years	24.00	25.00	24.50	25.50
4 years	23.75	24.75	24.25	25.25
5 years	23.50	24.50	24.00	25.00
7 years	21.75	22.75	22.00	23.00
10 years	20.00	21.00	20.25	21.25

time t_{k+1}. The analysis in Section 25.4 shows that:

1. The current value of any security is its expected value at time t_{k+1} in this world multiplied by the price of a zero-coupon bond maturing at time t_{k+1} (see equation 25.20).
2. The expected value of an interest rate lasting between times t_k and t_{k+1} equals the forward interest rate in this world (see equation 25.22).

The first of these results shows that, with the notation introduced earlier, the price of a caplet that provides a payoff at time t_{k+1} is

$$L\delta_k P(0, t_{k+1}) E_{k+1}[\max(R_k - R_K, 0)]$$

where E_{k+1} denotes expected value in a world that is forward risk neutral with respect to a zero-coupon bond maturing at time t_{k+1}. From the appendix at the end of Chapter 13, when R_k is assumed to be lognormal, this becomes

$$L\delta_k P(0, t_{k+1})[E_{k+1}(R_k)N(d_1) - R_K N(d_2)]$$

where

$$d_1 = \frac{\ln[E_{k+1}(R_k)/R_K] + \sigma_k^2 t_k/2}{\sigma_k\sqrt{t_k}}$$

$$d_2 = \frac{\ln[E_{k+1}(R_k)/R_K] - \sigma_k^2 t_k/2}{\sigma_k\sqrt{t_k}} = d_1 - \sigma\sqrt{t_k}$$

The second result implies that

$$E_{k+1}(R_k) = F_k$$

Together the results lead to the cap pricing model in equation (26.13). They show that we can discount at the t_{k+1}-maturity interest rate observed in the market today providing we set the expected interest rate equal to the forward interest rate.

Use of DerivaGem

The software DerivaGem accompanying this book can be used to price interest rate caps and floors using Black's model. In the Cap_and_Swap_Option worksheet select Cap/Floor as the Underlying Type and Black-European as the Pricing Model. The zero curve is input using continuously compounded rates. The inputs include the start and end date of the period covered by the cap, the flat volatility, and the cap settlement frequency (i.e., the tenor). The software calculates the payment dates by working back from the end of period covered by the cap to the beginning. The initial caplet/floorlet is assumed to cover a period of length between 0.5 and 1.5 times a regular period. Suppose, for example, that the period covered by the cap is 1.22 years to 2.80 years and the settlement frequency is quarterly. There are six caplets covering the periods 2.55 to 2.80 years, 2.30 to 2.55 years, 2.05 to 2.30 years, 1.80 to 2.05 years, 1.55 to 1.80 years, and 1.22 to 1.55 years.

The Impact of Day Count Conventions

The formulas we have presented so far in this section do not reflect day count conventions (see Section 6.1 for an explanation of day count conventions). Suppose that the cap rate R_K is expressed with an actual/360 day count (as would be normal in the United States). This means that the time interval δ_k in our formulas should be replaced by a_k, the *accrual fraction* for the time period between t_k and t_{k+1}. Suppose, for example, that t_k is May 1 and t_{k+1} is August 1. Under actual/360 there are 92 days between these payment dates so that $a_k = 92/360 = 0.2521$. We must also express the forward rate F_k with an actual/360 day count. This means that we must set it by solving

$$1 + a_k F_k = \frac{P(0, t_k)}{P(0, t_{k+1})}$$

The impact of all this is much the same as converting R_K from actual/360 to actual/actual and calculating F_k on an actual/actual basis. In other words it is much the same as multiplying the quoted cap rate by 365/360 or 366/360 to get R_K and calculating F_k by solving

$$1 + \delta_k F_k = \frac{P(0, t_k)}{P(0, t_{k+1})}$$

26.4 EUROPEAN SWAP OPTIONS

Swap options, or *swaptions*, are options on interest rate swaps and are another popular type of interest rate option. They give the holder the right to enter into a certain interest rate swap at a certain time in the future. (The holder does not, of course, have to exercise this right.) Many large financial institutions that offer interest rate swap contracts to their corporate clients are also prepared to sell them swaptions or buy swaptions from them. As shown in Business Snapshot 26.2, a swaption can be viewed as a type of bond option. To give an example of how a swaption might be used, consider a company that knows that in 6 months it will enter into a 5-year floating-rate loan agreement and knows that it will wish to swap the floating interest payments for fixed interest payments to convert the loan into a fixed-rate loan (see Chapter 7 for a discussion of how swaps can be used in this way). At a cost, the company could enter into a swaption giving it the right to receive 6-month LIBOR and pay a certain fixed rate of interest, say 8% per annum, for a 5-year period starting in 6 months. If the fixed rate exchanged for floating on a regular 5-year swap in 6 months turns out to be less than 8% per annum, the company will choose not to exercise the swaption and will enter into a swap agreement in the usual way. However, if it turns out to be greater than 8% per annum, the company will choose to exercise the swaption and will obtain a swap at more favorable terms than those available in the market.

Swaptions, when used in the way just described, provide companies with a guarantee that the fixed rate of interest they will pay on a loan at some future time will not exceed some level. They are an alternative to forward swaps (sometimes called *deferred swaps*). Forward swaps involve no up-front cost but have the disadvantage of obligating the company to enter into a swap agreement. With a swaption, the company is able to benefit from favorable interest rate movements while acquiring protection from unfavorable interest rate movements. The difference between a swaption and a forward swap is analogous to the difference between an option on a foreign currency and a forward contract on the currency.

Business Snapshot 26.2 Swaptions and Bond Options

As explained in Chapter 7, an interest rate swap can be regarded as an agreement to exchange a fixed-rate bond for a floating-rate bond. At the start of a swap, the value of the floating-rate bond always equals the principal amount of the swap. A swaption can therefore be regarded as an option to exchange a fixed-rate bond for the principal amount of the swap—that is, a type of bond option.

If a swaption gives the holder the right to pay fixed and receive floating, it is a put option on the fixed-rate bond with strike price equal to the principal. If a swaption gives the holder the right to pay floating and receive fixed, it is a call option on the fixed-rate bond with a strike price equal to the principal.

Valuation of European Swap Options

As explained in Chapter 7 the swap rate for a particular maturity at a particular time is the (mid-market) fixed rate that would be exchanged for LIBOR in a newly issued swap with that maturity. The model usually used to value a European option on a swap assumes that the underlying swap rate at the maturity of the option is lognormal. Consider a swaption where we have the right to pay a rate s_K and receive LIBOR on a swap that will last n years starting in T years. We suppose that there are m payments per year under the swap and that the notional principal is L.

We saw in Chapter 7 that day count conventions may lead to the fixed payments under a swap being slightly different on each payment date. For now we will ignore the effect of day count conventions and assume that each fixed payment on the swap is the fixed rate times L/m. We consider the impact of day count conventions at the end of this section.

Suppose that the swap rate for an n-year swap starting at time T proves to be s_T. By comparing the cash flows on a swap where the fixed rate is s_T to the cash flows on a swap where the fixed rate is s_K, we see that the payoff from the swaption consists of a series of cash flows equal to

$$\frac{L}{m}\max(s_T - s_K,\ 0)$$

The cash flows are received m times per year for the n years of the life of the swap. Suppose that the swap payment dates are $T_1, T_2, \ldots, T_{mn}$, measured in years from today. (It is approximately true that $T_k = T + k/m$.) Each cash flow is the payoff from a call option on s_T with strike price s_K.

Using equation (26.3), the value of the cash flow received at time T_i is

$$\frac{L}{m}P(0, T_i)[s_0 N(d_1) - s_K N(d_2)]$$

where

$$d_1 = \frac{\ln(s_0/s_K) + \sigma^2 T/2}{\sigma\sqrt{T}}$$

$$d_2 = \frac{\ln(s_0/s_K) - \sigma^2 T/2}{\sigma\sqrt{T}} = d_1 - \sigma\sqrt{T}$$

s_0 is the forward swap rate at time zero calculated as indicated in equation (25.23), and σ is the volatility of the forward swap rate (so that $\sigma\sqrt{T}$ is the standard deviation of $\ln s_T$).

The total value of the swaption is

$$\sum_{i=1}^{mn} \frac{L}{m} P(0, T_i)[s_0 N(d_1) - s_K N(d_2)]$$

Defining A as the value of a contract that pays $1/m$ at times T_i $(1 \leqslant i \leqslant mn)$, the value of the swaption becomes

$$LA[s_0 N(d_1) - s_K N(d_2)] \tag{26.15}$$

where

$$A = \frac{1}{m} \sum_{i=1}^{mn} P(0, T_i)$$

If the swaption gives the holder the right to receive a fixed rate of s_K instead of paying it, the payoff from the swaption is

$$\frac{L}{m} \max(s_K - s_T, 0)$$

This is a put option on s_T. As before, the payoffs are received at times T_i $(1 \leqslant i \leqslant mn)$. Equation (26.4) gives the value of the swaption as

$$LA[s_K N(-d_2) - s_0 N(-d_1)] \tag{26.16}$$

Example 26.4

Suppose that the LIBOR yield curve is flat at 6% per annum with continuous compounding. Consider a swaption that gives the holder the right to pay 6.2% in a 3-year swap starting in 5 years. The volatility of the forward swap rate is 20%. Payments are made semiannually and the principal is \$100. In this case,

$$A = \tfrac{1}{2}[e^{-0.06\times5.5} + e^{-0.06\times6} + e^{-0.06\times6.5} + e^{-0.06\times7} + e^{-0.06\times7.5} + e^{-0.06\times8}] = 2.0035$$

A rate of 6% per annum with continuous compounding translates into 6.09% with semiannual compounding. It follows that, in this example, $s_0 = 0.0609$, $s_K = 0.062$, $T = 5$, and $\sigma = 0.2$, so that

$$d_1 = \frac{\ln(0.0609/0.062) + 0.2^2 \times 5/2}{0.2\sqrt{5}} = 0.1836 \quad \text{and} \quad d_2 = d_1 - 0.2\sqrt{5} = -0.2636$$

From equation (26.15), the value of the swaption is

$$100 \times 2.0035[0.0609 \times N(0.1836) - 0.062 \times N(-0.2636)] = 2.07$$

or \$2.07. (This is in agreement with the price given by DerivaGem.)

Broker Quotes

Brokers provide tables of implied volatilities for European swap options. The instruments underlying the quotes are usually at the money. This means that the strike swap rate equals the forward swap rate. Table 26.2 shows typical broker quotes provided for the US dollar market. The life of the option is shown on the vertical scale. This varies from 1 month to 5 years. The life of the underlying swap at the maturity of the option is shown on the horizontal scale. This varies from 1 to 10 years. The volatilities in the 1-year column of the table exhibit a hump similar to that discussed for caps earlier. As

Table 26.2 Typical broker quotes for US European swap options (mid-market volatilities percent per annum).

Expiration	*Swap length (years)*						
	1	*2*	*3*	*4*	*5*	*7*	*10*
1 month	17.75	17.75	17.75	17.50	17.00	17.00	16.00
3 months	19.50	19.00	19.00	18.00	17.50	17.00	16.00
6 months	20.00	20.00	19.25	18.50	18.75	17.75	16.75
1 year	22.50	21.75	20.50	20.00	19.50	18.25	16.75
2 years	22.00	22.00	20.75	19.50	19.75	18.25	16.75
3 years	21.50	21.00	20.00	19.25	19.00	17.75	16.50
4 years	20.75	20.25	19.25	18.50	18.25	17.50	16.00
5 years	20.00	19.50	18.50	17.75	17.50	17.00	15.50

we move to the columns corresponding to options on longer-lived swaps, the hump persists but it becomes less pronounced.

Theoretical Justification for the Swap Option Model

We can show that Black's model for swap options is internally consistent by considering a world that is forward risk neutral with respect to the annuity A. The analysis in Section 25.4 shows that:

1. The current value of any security is the current value of the annuity multiplied by the expected value of
$$\frac{\text{Security price at time } T}{\text{Value of the annuity at time } T}$$
in this world (see equation (25.25)).
2. The expected value of the swap rate at time T in this world equals the forward swap rate (see equation (25.24)).

The first result shows that the value of the swaption is

$$LAE_A[\max(s_T - s_K,\ 0)]$$

From the appendix at the end of Chapter 13, this is

$$LA[E_A(s_T)N(d_1) - s_K N(d_2)]$$

where

$$d_1 = \frac{\ln[E_A(s_T)/s_K] + \sigma^2 T/2}{\sigma\sqrt{T}}$$

$$d_2 = \frac{\ln[E_A(s_T)/s_K] - \sigma^2 T/2}{\sigma\sqrt{T}} = d_1 - \sigma\sqrt{T}$$

The second result shows that $E_A(s_T)$ equals s_0. Taken together, the results lead to the swap option pricing formula in equation (26.15). They show that we are entitled to treat interest rates as constant for the purposes of discounting provided that we also set the expected swap rate equal to the forward swap rate.

The Impact of Day Count Conventions

We now make the above formulas more precise by considering day count conventions. The fixed rate for the swap underlying the swap option is expressed with a day count convention such as actual/365 or 30/360. Suppose that $T_0 = T$ and that, for the applicable day count convention, the accrual fraction corresponding to the time period between T_{i-1} and T_i is a_i. (For example, if T_{i-1} corresponds to March 1 and T_i corresponds to September 1 and the day count is actual/365, $a_i = 184/365 = 0.5041$.) The formulas we have presented are then correct with the annuity factor A being defined as

$$A = \sum_{i=1}^{mn} a_i P(0, T_i)$$

As indicated by equation (25.23) the forward swap rate s_0 is given by solving

$$s_0 A = P(0, T) - P(0, T_{mn})$$

26.5 GENERALIZATIONS

We have presented three different versions of Black's model: one for bond options, one for caps, and one for swap options. Each of the models is internally consistent, but they are not consistent with each other. For example, when future bond prices are lognormal, future zero rates and swap rates are not lognormal; when future zero rates are lognormal, future bond prices and swap rates are not lognormal.

The results we have produced can be generalized:

1. Consider any instrument that provides a payoff at time T dependent on the value of a variable observed at time T. Its current value is $P(0, T)$ times the expected payoff provided that expectations are calculated in a world where the expected value of the underlying variable equals its forward price.
2. Consider any instrument that provides a payoff at time T^* dependent on the interest rate observed at time T for the period between T and T^*. Its current value is $P(0, T^*)$ times the expected payoff provided that expectations are calculated in a world where the expected value of the underlying interest rate equals the forward interest rate.
3. Consider any instrument that provides a payoff in the form of an annuity. We suppose that the size of the annuity is determined at time T as a function of the n-year swap rate at time T. We also suppose that annuity lasts for n years and payment dates for the annuity are the same as those for the swap. The value of the instrument is A times the expected payoff per year where (a) A is current value of the annuity when payments are at the rate \$1 per year and (b) expectations are taken in a world where the expected future swap rate equals the forward swap rate.

The first of these results is a generalization of the European bond option model; the second is a generalization of the cap/floor model; the third is a generalization of the swap option model.

26.6 HEDGING INTEREST RATE DERIVATIVES

This section discusses how the material on Greek letters in Chapter 15 can be extended to cover interest rate derivatives. In the context of interest rate derivatives, delta risk is the risk associated with a shift in the zero curve. Because there are many ways in which the zero curve can shift, many deltas can be calculated. Some alternatives are:

1. Calculate the impact of a 1-basis-point parallel shift in the zero curve. This is sometimes termed a DV01.
2. Calculate the impact of small changes in the quotes for each of the instruments used to construct the zero curve.
3. Divide the zero curve (or the forward curve) into a number of sections (or buckets). Calculate the impact of shifting the rates in one bucket by 1 basis point, keeping the rest of the initial term structure unchanged. (This is described in Business Snapshot 6.3.)
4. Carry out a principal components analysis as outlined in Section 18.9. Calculate a delta with respect to the changes in each of the first few factors. The first delta then measures the impact of a small, approximately parallel, shift in the zero curve; the second delta measures the impact of a small twist in the zero curve; and so on.

In practice, traders tend to prefer the second approach. They argue that the only way the zero curve can change is if the quote for one of the instruments used to compute the zero curve changes. They therefore feel that it makes sense to focus on the exposures arising from changes in the prices of these instruments.

When several delta measures are calculated, there are many possible gamma measures. Suppose that 10 instruments are used to compute the zero curve and that we measure deltas with respect to changes in the quotes for each of these. Gamma is a second partial derivative of the form $\partial^2\Pi/\partial x_i\,\partial x_j$, where Π is the portfolio value. We have 10 choices for x_i and 10 choices for x_j and a total of 55 different gamma measures. This may be "information overload". One approach is ignore cross-gammas and focus on the 10 partial derivatives where $i = j$. Another is to calculate a single gamma measure as the second partial derivative of the value of the portfolio with respect to a parallel shift in the zero curve. A further possibility is to calculate gammas with respect to the first two factors in a principal components analysis.

The vega of a portfolio of interest rate derivatives measures its exposure to volatility changes. One approach is to calculate the impact on the portfolio of the making the same small change to the Black volatilities of all caps and European swap options. However, this assumes that one factor drives all volatilities and may be too simplistic. A better idea is to carry out a principal components analysis on the volatilities of caps and swap options and calculate vega measures corresponding to the first 2 or 3 factors.

SUMMARY

Black's model provides a popular approach for valuing European-style interest rate options. The essence of Black's model is that the value of the variable underlying the option is assumed to be lognormal at the maturity of the option. In the case of a European bond option, Black's model assumes that the underlying bond price is lognormal at the option's maturity. For a cap, the model assumes that the interest rate underlying each of the constituent caplets is lognormally distributed. In the case of a swap option, the model assumes that the underlying swap rate is lognormally distributed. Each of these models is internally consistent, but they are not consistent with each other.

Black's model involves calculating the expected payoff based on the assumption that the expected value of a variable equals its forward value and then discounting the expected payoff at the zero rate observed in the market today. This is the correct procedure for the "plain vanilla" instruments we have considered in this chapter. However, as we will see in the next chapter it is not correct in all situations.

FURTHER READING

Black, F., "The Pricing of Commodity Contracts," *Journal of Financial Economics*, 3 (March 1976): 167–79.

Questions and Problems (Answers in Solutions Manual)

26.1. A company caps 3-month LIBOR at 10% per annum. The principal amount is \$20 million. On a reset date, 3-month LIBOR is 12% per annum. What payment would this lead to under the cap? When would the payment be made?

26.2. Explain why a swap option can be regarded as a type of bond option.

26.3. Use the Black's model to value a 1-year European put option on a 10-year bond. Assume that the current value of the bond is \$125, the strike price is \$110, the 1-year interest rate is 10% per annum, the bond's forward price volatility is 8% per annum, and the present value of the coupons to be paid during the life of the option is \$10.

26.4. Explain carefully how you would use (a) spot volatilities and (b) flat volatilities to value a 5-year cap.

26.5. Calculate the price of an option that caps the 3-month rate, starting in 15 months' time, at 13% (quoted with quarterly compounding) on a principal amount of \$1,000. The forward interest rate for the period in question is 12% per annum (quoted with quarterly compounding), the 18-month risk-free interest rate (continuously compounded) is 11.5% per annum, and the volatility of the forward rate is 12% per annum.

26.6. A bank uses Black's model to price European bond options. Suppose that an implied price volatility for a 5-year option on a bond maturing in 10 years is used to price a 9-year option on the bond. Would you expect the resultant price to be too high or too low? Explain.

26.7. Calculate the value of a 4-year European call option on bond that will mature 5 years from today using Black's model. The 5-year cash bond price is \$105, the cash price of a 4-year bond with the same coupon is \$102, the strike price is \$100, the 4-year risk-free interest rate is 10% per annum with continuous compounding, and the volatility for the bond price in 4 years is 2% per annum.

26.8. If the yield volatility for a 5-year put option on a bond maturing in 10 years time is specified as 22%, how should the option be valued? Assume that, based on today's interest rates the modified duration of the bond at the maturity of the option will be 4.2 years and the forward yield on the bond is 7%.

26.9. What other instrument is the same as a 5-year zero-cost collar where the strike price of the cap equals the strike price of the floor? What does the common strike price equal?

26.10. Derive a put–call parity relationship for European bond options.

26.11. Derive a put–call parity relationship for European swap options.

26.12. Explain why there is an arbitrage opportunity if the implied Black (flat) volatility of a cap is different from that of a floor. Do the broker quotes in Table 26.1 present an arbitrage opportunity?

26.13. When a bond's price is lognormal can the bond's yield be negative? Explain your answer.

26.14. What is the value of a European swap option that gives the holder the right to enter into a 3-year annual-pay swap in 4 years where a fixed rate of 5% is paid and LIBOR is received? The swap principal is \$10 million. Assume that the yield curve is flat at 5% per annum with annual compounding and the volatility of the swap rate is 20%. Compare your answer with that given by DerivaGem.

26.15. Suppose that the yield R on a zero-coupon bond follows the process

$$dR = \mu\, dt + \sigma dz$$

where μ and σ are functions of R and t, and dz is a Wiener process. Use Itô's lemma to show that the volatility of the zero-coupon bond price declines to zero as it approaches maturity.

26.16. Carry out a manual calculation to verify the option prices in Example 26.2.

26.17. Suppose that the 1-year, 2-year, 3-year, 4-year, and 5-year zero rates are 6%, 6.4%, 6.7%, 6.9%, and 7%. The price of a 5-year semiannual cap with a principal of \$100 at a cap rate of 8% is \$3. Use DerivaGem to determine:
(a) The 5-year flat volatility for caps and floors
(b) The floor rate in a zero-cost 5-year collar when the cap rate is 8%

26.18. Show that $V_1 + f = V_2$, where V_1 is the value of a swap option to pay a fixed rate of s_K and receive LIBOR between times T_1 and T_2, f is the value of a forward swap to receive a fixed rate of s_K and pay LIBOR between times T_1 and T_2, and V_2 is the value of a swap option to receive a fixed rate of s_K between times T_1 and T_2. Deduce that $V_1 = V_2$ when s_K equals the current forward swap rate.

26.19. Suppose that zero rates are as in Problem 26.17. Use DerivaGem to determine the value of an option to pay a fixed rate of 6% and receive LIBOR on a 5-year swap starting in 1 year. Assume that the principal is \$100 million, payments are exchanged semiannually, and the swap rate volatility is 21%.

26.20. Describe how you would (a) calculate cap flat volatilities from cap spot volatilities and (b) calculate cap spot volatilities from cap flat volatilities.

Assignment Questions

26.21. Consider an 8-month European put option on a Treasury bond that currently has 14.25 years to maturity. The current cash bond price is \$910, the exercise price is \$900, and the volatility for the bond price is 10% per annum. A coupon of \$35 will be paid by the bond in 3 months. The risk-free interest rate is 8% for all maturities up to 1 year. Use Black's model to determine the price of the option. Consider both the case where the strike price corresponds to the cash price of the bond and the case where it corresponds to the quoted price.

26.22. Calculate the price of a cap on the 90-day LIBOR rate in 9 months' time when the principal amount is \$1,000. Use Black's model and the following information:
(a) The quoted 9-month Eurodollar futures price = 92. (Ignore differences between futures and forward rates.)
(b) The interest rate volatility implied by a 9-month Eurodollar option = 15% per annum.
(c) The current 12-month interest rate with continuous compounding = 7.5% per annum.
(d) The cap rate = 8% per annum. (Assume an actual/360 day count.)

26.23. Suppose that the LIBOR yield curve is flat at 8% with annual compounding. A swaption gives the holder the right to receive 7.6% in a 5-year swap starting in 4 years. Payments are made annually. The volatility of the forward swap rate is 25% per annum and the principal is \$1 million. Use Black's model to price the swaption. Compare your answer with that given by DerivaGem.

26.24. Use the DerivaGem software to value a 5-year collar that guarantees that the maximum and minimum interest rates on a LIBOR-based loan (with quarterly resets) are 5% and 7%, respectively. The LIBOR zero curve (continuously compounded) is currently flat at 6%. Use a flat volatility of 20%. Assume that the principal is \$100.

26.25. Use the DerivaGem software to value a European swap option that gives you the right in 2 years to enter into a 5-year swap in which you pay a fixed rate of 6% and receive floating. Cash flows are exchanged semiannually on the swap. The 1-year, 2-year, 5-year, and 10-year zero-coupon interest rates (continuously compounded) are 5%, 6%, 6.5%, and 7%, respectively. Assume a principal of \$100 and a volatility of 15% per annum. Give an example of how the swap option might be used by a corporation. What bond option is equivalent to the swap option?

CHAPTER 27

Convexity, Timing, and Quanto Adjustments

A popular two-step procedure for valuing a European-style derivative is:

1. Calculate the expected payoff by assuming that the expected value of each underlying variable equals its forward value.
2. Discount the expected payoff at the risk-free rate applicable for the time period between the valuation date and the payoff date.

We first used this procedure in Chapter 4 when valuing FRAs. We found that an FRA can be valued by calculating the payoff on the assumption that the forward interest rate will be realized and then discounting the payoff at the risk-free rate. Similarly, in Chapter 7 we found that swaps can be valued by calculating cash flows on the assumptions that forward rates will be realized and discounting them at risk-free rates. In Chapter 26 we found that Black's model provides a general approach to valuing a wide range of European options—and Black's model, as we saw in Section 26.1, is an application of this two-step procedure. The models presented in Chapter 26 for bond options, caps/floors, and swap options are all examples of the two-step procedure.

This raises the issue of whether it always correct to value European-style interest rate derivatives by using the two-step procedure? The answer is no! For nonstandard interest rate derivatives it is sometimes necessary to modify the two-step procedure so that an adjustment is made to the forward value of the variable in the first step. In this chapter we consider three types of adjustments: convexity adjustments, timing adjustments, and quanto adjustments.

27.1 CONVEXITY ADJUSTMENTS

We start by discussing the valuation an instrument that provides a payoff dependent on a bond yield observed at the time of the payoff.

Usually the forward value of a variable S is calculated with reference to a forward contract that pays off $S_T - K$ at time T. It is the value of K that causes the contract to have zero value. As we discussed in Section 25.4, forward interest rates and forward yields are defined differently. A forward interest rate is the rate implied by a forward zero-coupon bond. More generally, a forward bond yield is the yield implied by the forward bond price.

Suppose that B_T is the price of a bond at time T, y_T is its yield, and the (bond pricing) relationship between B_T and y_T is

$$B_T = G(y_T)$$

Define F_0 as the forward bond price at time zero for a contract maturing at time T and y_0 as the forward bond yield at time zero. The definition of a forward bond yield means that

$$F_0 = G(y_0)$$

The function G is nonlinear. This means that, when the expected future bond price equals the forward bond price (so that we are a world that is forward risk neutral with respect to a zero-coupon bond maturing at time T), the expected future bond yield does not equal the forward bond yield.

This is illustrated in Figure 27.1, which shows the relationship between bond prices and bond yields at time T. For simplicity, we suppose that there are only three possible bond prices, B_1, B_2, and B_3 and that they are equally likely in a world that is forward risk neutral with respect to $P(t, T)$. We assume that the bond prices are equally spaced, so that $B_2 - B_1 = B_3 - B_2$. The forward bond price is the expected bond price B_2. The bond prices translate into three equally likely bond yields: y_1, y_2, and y_3. These are not equally spaced. The variable y_2 is the forward bond yield because it is the yield corresponding to the forward bond price. The expected bond yield is the average of y_1, y_2, and y_3 and is clearly greater than y_2.

Consider now a derivative that provides a payoff dependent on the bond yield at time T. We know from equation (25.20) that it can be valued by (a) calculating the expected payoff in a world that is forward risk neutral with respect to a zero-coupon bond maturing at time T and (b) discounting at the current risk-free rate for maturity T. We

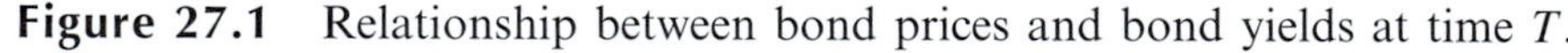

Figure 27.1 Relationship between bond prices and bond yields at time T.

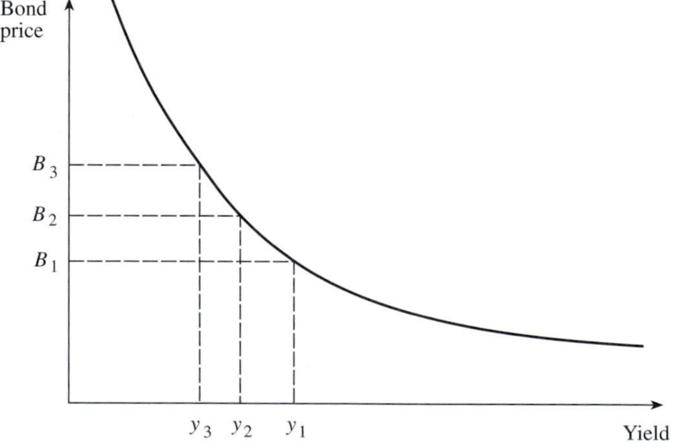

know that the expected bond price equals the forward price in the world being considered. We therefore need to know the value of the expected bond yield when the expected bond price equals the forward bond price. The analysis in the appendix at the end of this chapter shows that an approximate expression for the required expected bond yield is

$$E_T(y_T) = y_0 - \tfrac{1}{2}y_0^2\sigma_y^2 T\frac{G''(y_0)}{G'(y_0)} \tag{27.1}$$

where G' and G'' denote the first and second partial derivatives of G, E_T denotes expectations in a world that is forward risk neutral with respect to $P(t, T)$, and σ_y is the forward yield volatility. It follows that we can discount expected payoffs at the current risk-free rate for maturity T providing we assume that the expected bond yield is

$$y_0 - \tfrac{1}{2}y_0^2\sigma_y^2 T\frac{G''(y_0)}{G'(y_0)}$$

rather than y_0. The difference between the expected bond yield and the forward bond yield

$$-\tfrac{1}{2}y_0^2\sigma_y^2 T\frac{G''(y_0)}{G'(y_0)}$$

is the known as a *convexity adjustment*. It corresponds to the difference between y_2 and the expected yield in Figure 27.1. (The convexity adjustment is positive because $G'(y_0) < 0$ and $G''(y_0) > 0$.)

Application 1: Interest Rates

As our first application of equation (27.1) we consider an instrument that provides a cash flow at time T equal to the interest rate between times T and T^* applied to a principal of L. (This example will be useful when we consider LIBOR-in-arrears swaps in Chapter 30.) Note that the interest rate applicable to the time period between times T and T^* is normally paid at time T^*; here we are assuming that it is paid early, at time T.

The cash flow at time T in the instrument we are considering is $LR_T\tau$, where $\tau = T^* - T$ and R_T is the zero-coupon interest rate applicable to the period between T and T^* (expressed with a compounding period of τ).[1] The variable R_T can be viewed as the yield at time T on a zero-coupon bond maturing at time T^*. The relationship between the price of this bond and its yield is

$$G(y) = \frac{1}{1 + y\tau}$$

From equation (27.1),

$$E_T(R_T) = R_0 - \tfrac{1}{2}R_0^2\sigma_R^2 T\frac{G''(R_0)}{G'(R_0)}$$

or

$$E_T(R_T) = R_0 + \frac{R_0^2\sigma_R^2\tau T}{1 + R_0\tau} \tag{27.2}$$

[1] As usual, for ease of exposition we assume actual/actual day counts in our examples.

where R_0 is the forward rate applicable to the period between T and T^* and σ_R is the volatility of the forward rate.

The value of the instrument is therefore

$$P(0,T)L\tau\left[R_0+\frac{R_0^2\sigma_R^2\tau T}{1+R_0\tau}\right]$$

Example 27.1

Consider a derivative that provides a payoff in 3 years equal to the 1-year zero-coupon rate (annually compounded) at that time multiplied by \$1000. Suppose that the zero rate for all maturities is 10% per annum with annual compounding and the volatility of the forward rate applicable to the time period between year 3 and year 4 is 20%. In this case, $R_0 = 0.10$, $\sigma_R = 0.20$, $T = 3$, $\tau = 1$, and $P(0, 3) = 1/1.10^3 = 0.7513$. The value of the derivative is

$$0.7513\times 1000\times 1\times\left[0.10+\frac{0.10^2\times 0.20^2\times 1\times 3}{1+0.10\times 1}\right]$$

or \$75.95. (This compares with a price of \$75.13 when no convexity adjustment is made.)

Application 2: Swap Rates

Consider next a derivative providing a payoff at time T equal to a swap rate observed at that time. A swap rate is a par yield. For the purposes of calculating a convexity adjustment we can make an approximation and assume that the N-year swap rate at time T equals the yield at that time on an N-year bond with a coupon equal to today's forward swap rate. This enables equation (27.1) to be used.

Example 27.2

Consider an instrument that provides a payoff in 3 years equal to the 3-year swap rate at that time multiplied by \$100. Suppose that payments are made annually on the swap, the zero rate for all maturities is 12% per annum with annual compounding, the volatility for the 3-year forward swap rate in 3 years (implied from swap option prices) is 22%. We approximate the swap rate as the yield on a 12% bond, so that the relevant function $G(y)$ is

$$G(y)=\frac{0.12}{1+y}+\frac{0.12}{(1+y)^2}+\frac{1.12}{(1+y)^3}$$

$$G'(y)=-\frac{0.12}{(1+y)^2}-\frac{0.24}{(1+y)^3}-\frac{3.36}{(1+y)^4}$$

$$G''(y)=\frac{0.24}{(1+y)^3}+\frac{0.72}{(1+y)^4}+\frac{13.44}{(1+y)^5}$$

In this case the forward yield y_0 is 0.12, so that $G'(y_0) = -2.4018$ and $G''(y_0) = 8.2546$. From equation (27.1),

$$E_T(y_T)=0.12+\tfrac{1}{2}\times 0.12^2\times 0.22^2\times 3\times\frac{8.2546}{2.4018}=0.1236$$

We should therefore assume a forward swap rate of 0.1236 (=12.36%) rather than 0.12 when valuing the instrument. The instrument is worth

$$\frac{100 \times 0.1236}{1.12^3} = 8.80$$

or \$8.80. (This compares with a price of 8.54 obtained without any convexity adjustment.)

27.2 TIMING ADJUSTMENTS

In this section we consider the situation where we observe a market variable V at time T and use its value to calculate a payoff that occurs at a later time T^*. Define:

V_T: Value of V at time T

$E_T(V_T)$: Expected value of V_T in a world that is forward risk-neutral with respect to $P(t, T)$

$E_{T^*}(V_T)$: Expected value of V_T in a world that is forward risk-neutral with respect to $P(t, T^*)$

The numeraire ratio when we move from the $P(t, T)$ numeraire to the $P(t, T^*)$ numeraire (see Section 25.7) is

$$W = \frac{P(t, T^*)}{P(t, T)}$$

This is the forward price of a zero-coupon bond lasting between times T and T^*. Define:

σ_V: Volatility of V

σ_W: Volatility of W

ρ_{VW}: Correlation between V and W

From equation (25.35) the change of numeraire increases the growth rate of V by α_V, where

$$\alpha_V = \rho_{VW}\sigma_V\sigma_W \tag{27.3}$$

We can express this result in terms of the forward interest rate between times T and T^*. Define:

R: Forward interest rate for period between T and T^*, expressed with a compounding frequency of m

σ_R: Volatility of R

The relationship between W and R is

$$W = \frac{1}{(1 + R/m)^{m(T^*-T)}}$$

The relationship between the volatility of W and the volatility of R can be calculated from Itô's lemma as[2]

$$\sigma_W = \frac{\sigma_R R(T^* - T)}{1 + R/m}$$

Hence equation (27.3) becomes

$$\alpha_V = -\frac{\rho_{VR}\sigma_V\sigma_R R(T^* - T)}{1 + R/m}$$

where $\rho_{VR} = -\rho_{VW}$ is the instantaneous correlation between V and R. As an approximation we can assume that R remains constant at R_0 and that the volatilities and correlation in this expression are constant to get at time zero

$$E_{T^*}(V_T) = E_T(V_T)\exp\left[-\frac{\rho_{VR}\sigma_V\sigma_R R_0(T^* - T)}{1 + R_0/m}T\right] \tag{27.4}$$

Example 27.3

Consider a derivative that provides a payoff in 6 years equal to the value of a stock index observed in 5 years. Suppose that 1,200 is the forward value of the stock index for a contract maturing in 5 years. Suppose that the volatility of the index is 20%, the volatility of the forward interest rate between years 5 and 6 is 18%, and the correlation between the two is –0.4. Suppose further that the zero curve is flat at 8% with annual compounding. We apply the results we have just produced to the situation where V is equal the value of the index. In this case $T = 5$, $T^* = 6$, $m = 1$, $R_0 = 0.08$, $\rho_{VR} = -0.4$, $\sigma_V = 0.20$, and $\sigma_R = 0.18$, so that

$$E_{T^*}(V_T) = E_T(V_T)\exp\left[-\frac{-0.4 \times 0.20 \times 0.18 \times 0.08 \times 1}{1 + 0.08} \times 5\right]$$

or $E_{T^*}(V_T) = 1.00535 E_T(V_T)$. From the arguments in Chapter 25 we know that $E_T(V_T)$ is the forward price of the index, or 1,200. It follows that $E_{T^*}(V_T) = 1{,}200 \times 1.00535 = 1206.42$. Using again the arguments in Chapter 25, it follows from equation (25.20) that the value of the derivative is $1206.42 \times P(0, 6)$. In this case $P(0, 6) = 1/1.08^6 = 0.6302$, so that the value of the derivative is 760.25.

Application 1 Revisited

The analysis just given provides a different way of producing the result in Application 1 of Section 27.1. Using the notation from that application, we define R_T as the interest rate between T and T^* and R_0 as the forward rate for the period between time T and T^*. We know from equation (25.22) that

$$E_{T^*}(R_T) = R_0$$

We can apply equation (27.4) with V equal to R to get

$$E_{T^*}(R_T) = E_T(R_T)\exp\left[-\frac{\sigma_R^2 R_0 \tau}{1 + R_0\tau}T\right]$$

[2] Instead of Itô's lemma we can use the duration result in Section 26.2

where $\tau = T^* - T$ (note that $m = 1/\tau$). It follows that

$$R_0 = E_T(R_T)\exp\left[-\frac{\sigma_R^2 R_0 T\tau}{1 + R_0\tau}\right]$$

or

$$E_T(R_T) = R_0 \exp\left[\frac{\sigma_R^2 R_0 T\tau}{1 + R_0\tau}\right]$$

Approximating the exponential function, we see that

$$E_T(R_T) = R_0 + \frac{R_0^2\sigma_R^2\tau T}{1 + R_0\tau}$$

This is the same result as equation (27.2).

27.3 QUANTOS

A *quanto* or *cross-currency derivative* is an instrument where two currencies are involved. The payoff is defined in terms of a variable that is measured in one of the currencies and the payoff is made in the other currency. One example of a quanto is the CME futures contract on the Nikkei discussed in Business Snapshot 5.3. The market variable underlying this contract is the Nikkei 225 index (which is measured in yen), but contract is settled in US dollars.

Consider a quanto that provides a payoff in currency X at time T. We assume that the payoff depends on the value V of a variable that is observed in currency Y at time T. Define:

$P_X(t, T)$: Value at time t in currency X of a zero-coupon bond paying off 1 unit of currency X at time T

$P_Y(t, T)$: Value at time t in currency Y of a zero-coupon bond paying off 1 unit of currency Y at time T

V_T: Value of V at time T

$E_X(V_T)$: Expected value of V_T in a world that is forward risk neutral with respect to $P_X(t, T)$

$E_Y(V_T)$: Expected value of V_T in a world that is forward risk neutral with respect to $P_Y(t, T)$

The numeraire ratio when we move from the $P_Y(t, T)$ numeraire to the $P_X(t, T)$ numeraire is

$$W(t) = \frac{P_X(t, T)}{P_Y(t, T)} S(t)$$

where $S(t)$ is the spot exchange rate (units of Y per unit of X) at time t. It follows from this that the numeraire ratio $W(t)$ is the forward exchange rate (units of Y per unit of X) for a contract maturing at time T. Define:

σ_W Volatility of W

σ_V: Volatility of V

ρ_{VW}: Instantaneous correlation between V and W.

From equation (25.35) the change of numeraire increases the growth rate of V by α_V where

$$\alpha_V = \rho_{VW}\sigma_V\sigma_W \tag{27.5}$$

If as an approximation we assume that the volatilities and correlation are constant, this means that

$$E_X(V_T) = E_Y(V_T)e^{\rho\sigma_V\sigma_W T}$$

or as an approximation

$$E_X(V_T) = E_Y(V_T)(1 + \rho\sigma_V\sigma_W T) \tag{27.6}$$

We will apply this equation to the valuation of what are known as diff swaps in Chapter 30.

Example 27.4

Suppose that the current value of the Nikkei stock index for a 1-year contract is 15,000 yen, the 1-year dollar risk-free rate is 5%, the 1-year yen risk-free rate is 2%, and the Nikkei dividend yield is 1%. The forward price of the Nikkei for a contract denominated in yen can be calculated in the usual way from equation (5.8) as

$$15{,}000e^{(0.02-0.01)\times 1} = 15{,}150.75$$

Suppose that the volatility of the index is 20%, the volatility of the 1-year forward yen per dollar exchange rate is 12%, and the correlation between the two is 0.3. In this case $F(0) = 15{,}150.75$, $\sigma_F = 0.20$, $\sigma_W = 0.12$ and $\rho = 0.3$. From equation (27.6), the expected value of the Nikkei in a world that is forward risk neutral with respect to a dollar bond maturing in 1 year is

$$15{,}150.75e^{0.3\times 0.2\times 0.12\times 1} = 15{,}260.23$$

This is the forward price of the Nikkei for a contract that provides a payoff in dollars rather than yen. (As an approximation, it is also the futures price of such a contract.)

Using Traditional Risk-Neutral Measures

The forward risk-neutral measure we have been using works well when payoffs occur at only one time. In other situations it is sometimes more appropriate to use the traditional risk-neutral measure. Suppose we know the process followed by a variable V in the traditional currency-Y risk-neutral world and we wish to estimate its process in the traditional currency-X risk-neutral world. Define:

S: Spot exchange rate (units of Y per unit of X)

σ_S: Volatility of S

σ_V: Volatility of V

ρ: Instantaneous correlation between S and V

In this case, the change of numeraire is from the money market account in currency Y to the money market account in currency X (with both money market accounts being denominated in currency X). Define g_X as the value of the money market account in

Business Snapshot 27.1 Siegel's Paradox

Consider two currencies, X and Y. Suppose that the interest rates in the two currencies, r_X and r_Y, are constant. Define S as the number of units of currency Y per unit of currency X. As explained in Chapter 5, a currency is an asset that provides a yield at the foreign risk-free rate. The traditional risk-neutral process for S is therefore

$$dS = (r_Y - r_X)S\,dt + \sigma_S S\,dz$$

From Itô's lemma, this implies that the process for $1/S$ is

$$d(1/S) = (r_X - r_Y + \sigma_S^2)(1/S)\,dt - \sigma_S(1/S)\,dz$$

This leads to what is known as *Siegel's paradox*. Since the expected growth rate of S is $r_Y - r_X$ in a risk-neutral world, symmetry suggests that the expected growth rate of $1/S$ should be $r_X - r_Y$ rather than $r_X - r_Y + \sigma_S^2$.

To understand Siegel's paradox it is necessary to appreciate that the process we have given for S is the risk-neutral process for S in a world where the numeraire is the money market account in currency Y. The process for $1/S$, because it is deduced from the process for S, therefore also assumes that this is the numeraire. Because $1/S$ is the number of units of X per unit of Y, to be symmetrical we should measure the process for $1/S$ in a world where the numeraire is the money market account in currency X. Equation (27.7) shows that when we change the numeraire, from the money market account in currency Y to the money market account in currency X, the growth rate of a variable V increases by $\rho\sigma_V\sigma_S$, where ρ is the correlation between S and V. In this case, $V = 1/S$, so that $\rho = -1$ and $\sigma_V = \sigma_S$. It follows that the change of numeraire causes the growth rate of $1/S$ to increase by $-\sigma_S^2$. This neutralizes the $+\sigma_S^2$ in the process given above for $1/S$. The process for $1/S$ in a world where the numeraire is the money market account in currency X is therefore

$$d(1/S) = (r_X - r_Y)(1/S)\,dt - \sigma_S(1/S)\,dz$$

This is symmetrical with the process we started with for S. The paradox has been resolved!

currency X and g_Y as the value of the money market account in currency Y. The numeraire ratio is

$$\frac{g_X}{g_Y}S$$

The variables $g_X(t)$ and $g_Y(t)$ have a stochastic drift but zero volatility as explained in Section 25.4. From Itô's lemma it follows that the volatility of the numeraire ratio is σ_S. The change of numeraire therefore involves increasing the expected growth rate of V by

$$\rho\sigma_V\sigma_S \tag{27.7}$$

The market price of risk changes from zero to $\rho\sigma_S$. An application of this result is to Siegel's paradox (see Business Snapshot 27.1).

Example 27.5

A 2-year American option provides a payoff of $S - K$ pounds sterling where S is the level of the S&P 500 at the time of exercise and K is the strike price. The current level of the S&P 500 is 1,200. The risk-free interest rates in sterling and dollars are both constant at 5% and 3%, respectively, the correlation between the dollars/sterling exchange rate and the S&P 500 is 0.2, the volatility of the S&P 500 is 25%, and the volatility of the exchange rate is 12%. The dividend yield on the S&P 500 is 1.5%.

We can value this option by constructing a binomial tree for the S&P 500 using as the numeraire the money market account in the UK (i.e., using the traditional risk-neutral world as seen from the perspective of a UK investor). From equation (27.7), the change in numeraire from the US to UK money market account leads to an increase in the expected growth rate in the S&P 500 of

$$0.2 \times 0.25 \times 0.12 = 0.006$$

or 0.6%. The growth rate of the S&P 500 using a US dollar numeraire is $3\% - 1.5\% = 1.5\%$. The growth rate using the sterling numeraire is therefore 2.1%. The risk-free interest rate in sterling is 5%. The S&P 500 therefore behaves like an asset providing a dividend yield of $5\% - 2.1\% = 2.9\%$ under the sterling numeraire. Using the parameter values of $S = 1{,}200$, $K = 1{,}200$, $r = 0.05$, $q = 0.029$, $\sigma = 0.25$, and $T = 2$ with 100 time steps, DerivaGem estimates the value of the option as £179.83.

SUMMARY

When valuing a derivative providing a payoff at a particular future time it is natural to assume that the variables underlying the derivative equal their forward values and discount at the rate of interest applicable from the valuation date to the payoff date. This chapter has shown that this is not always the correct procedure.

When a payoff depends on a bond yield y observed at time T the expected yield should be assumed to be higher than the forward yield as indicated by equation (27.1). This result can be adapted for situations where a payoff depends on a swap rate. When a variable is observed at time T but the payoff occurs at a later time T^* the forward value of the variable should be adjusted as indicated by equation (27.4). When a variable is observed in one currency but leads to a payoff in another currency the forward value of the variable should also be adjusted. In this case the adjustment is shown in equation (27.6).

We will use these results when we look at nonstandard swaps in Chapter 30.

FURTHER READING

Brotherton-Ratcliffe, R., and B. Iben, "Yield Curve Applications of Swap Products," in *Advanced Strategies in Financial Risk Management* (R. Schwartz and C. Smith, eds.). New York Institute of Finance, 1993.

Jamshidian, F., "Corralling Quantos," *Risk*, March (1994): 71–75.

Reiner, E., "Quanto Mechanics," *Risk*, March (1992), 59–63.

Questions and Problems (Answers in Solutions Manual)

27.1. Explain how you would value a derivative that pays off $100R$ in 5 years, where R is the 1-year interest rate (annually compounded) observed in 4 years. What difference would it make if the payoff were in 4 years? What difference would it make if the payoff were in 5 years?

27.2. Explain whether any convexity or timing adjustments are necessary when:
(a) We wish to value a spread option that pays off every quarter the excess (if any) of the 5-year swap rate over the 3-month LIBOR rate applied to a principal of \$100. The payoff occurs 90 days after the rates are observed.
(b) We wish to value a derivative that pays off every quarter the 3-month LIBOR rate minus the 3-month Treasury bill rate. The payoff occurs 90 days after the rates are observed.

27.3. Suppose that in Example 26.3 of Section 26.3 the payoff occurs after 1 year (i.e., when the interest rate is observed) rather than in 15 months. What difference does this make to the inputs to Black's models?

27.4. The yield curve is flat at 10% per annum with annual compounding. Calculate the value of an instrument where, in 5 years' time, the 2-year swap rate (with annual compounding) is received and a fixed rate of 10% is paid. Both are applied to a notional principal of \$100. Assume that the volatility of the swap rate is 20% per annum. Explain why the value of the instrument is different from zero.

27.5. What difference does it make in Problem 27.4 if the swap rate is observed in 5 years, but the exchange of payments takes place in (a) 6 years, and (b) 7 years? Assume that the volatilities of all forward rates are 20%. Assume also that the forward swap rate for the period between years 5 and 7 has a correlation of 0.8 with the forward interest rate between years 5 and 6 and a correlation of 0.95 with the forward interest rate between years 5 and 7.

27.6. The price of a bond at time T, measured in terms of its yield, is $G(y_T)$. Assume geometric Brownian motion for the forward bond yield y in a world that is forward risk neutral with respect to a bond maturing at time T. Suppose that the growth rate of the forward bond yield is α and its volatility σ_y.
(a) Use Itô's lemma to calculate the process for the forward bond price in terms of α, σ_y, y, and $G(y)$.
(b) The forward bond price should follow a martingale in the world considered. Use this fact to calculate an expression for α.
(c) Show that the expression for α is, to a first approximation, consistent with equation (27.1).

27.7. The variable S is an investment asset providing income at rate q measured in currency A. It follows the process

$$dS = \mu_S S\,dt + \sigma_S S\,dz$$

in the real world. Defining new variables as necessary, give the process followed by S, and the corresponding market price of risk, in:
(a) A world that is the traditional risk-neutral world for currency A
(b) A world that is the traditional risk-neutral world for currency B

(c) A world that is forward risk neutral with respect to a zero-coupon currency A bond maturing at time T

(d) A world that is forward risk neutral with respect to a zero-coupon currency B bond maturing at time T

27.8. A call option provides a payoff at time T of $\max(S_T - K, 0)$ yen, where S_T is the dollar price of gold at time T and K is the strike price. Assuming that the storage costs of gold are zero and defining other variables as necessary, calculate the value of the contract.

27.9. Suppose that an index of Canadian stocks currently stands at 400. The Canadian dollar is currently worth 0.70 US dollars. The risk-free interest rates in Canada and the US are constant at 6% and 4%, respectively. The dividend yield on the index is 3%. Define Q as the number of Canadian dollars per U.S dollar and S as the value of the index. The volatility of S is 20%, the volatility of Q is 6%, and the correlation between S and Q is 0.4. Use DerivaGem to determine the value of a 2-year American-style call option on the index if:

(a) It pays off in Canadian dollars the amount by which the index exceeds 400.

(b) It pays off in US dollars the amount by which the index exceeds 400.

Assignment Questions

27.10. Consider an instrument that will pay off S dollars in 2 years, where S is the value of the Nikkei index. The index is currently 20,000. The yen/dollar exchange rate is 100 (yen per dollar). The correlation between the exchange rate and the index is 0.3 and the dividend yield on the index is 1% per annum. The volatility of the Nikkei index is 20% and the volatility of the yen/dollar exchange rate is 12%. The interest rates (assumed constant) in the US and Japan are 4% and 2%, respectively.

(a) What is the value of the instrument?

(b) Suppose that the exchange rate at some point during the life of the instrument is Q and the level of the index is S. Show that a US investor can create a portfolio that changes in value by approximately ΔS dollar when the index changes in value by ΔS yen by investing S dollars in the Nikkei and shorting SQ yen.

(c) Confirm that this is correct by supposing that the index changes from 20,000 to 20,050 and the exchange rate changes from 100 to 99.7.

(d) How would you delta hedge the instrument under consideration?

27.11. Suppose that the LIBOR yield curve is flat at 8% (with continuous compounding). The payoff from a derivative occurs in 4 years. It is equal to the 5-year rate minus the 2-year rate at this time, applied to a principal of \$100 with both rates being continuously compounded. (The payoff can be positive or negative.) Calculate the value of the derivative. Assume that the volatility for all rates is 25%. What difference does it make if the payoff occurs in 5 years instead of 4 years? Assume all rates are perfectly correlated.

27.12. Suppose that the payoff from a derivative will occur in 10 years and will equal the 3-year US dollar swap rate for a semiannual-pay swap observed at that time applied to a certain principal. Assume that the yield curve is flat at 8% (semiannually compounded) per annum in dollars and 3% (semiannually compounded) in yen. The forward swap rate volatility is 18%, the volatility of the 10-year "yen per dollar" forward exchange rate is 12%, and the correlation between this exchange rate and US dollar interest rates is 0.25.

(a) What is the value of the derivative if the swap rate is applied to a principal of \$100 million so that the payoff is in dollars?

(b) What is its value of the derivative if the swap rate is applied to a principal of 100 million yen so that the payoff is in yen?

27.13. The payoff from a derivative will occur in 8 years. It will equal the average of the 1-year interest rates observed at times 5, 6, 7, and 8 years applied to a principal of \$1,000. The yield curve is flat at 6% with annual compounding and the volatilities of all rates are 16%. Assume perfect correlation between all rates. What is the value of the derivative?

APPENDIX

PROOF OF THE CONVEXITY ADJUSTMENT FORMULA

This appendix calculates a convexity adjustment for forward bond yields. Suppose that the payoff from a derivative at time T depends on a bond yield observed at that time. Define:

y_0: Forward bond yield observed today for a forward contract with maturity T

y_T: Bond yield at time T

B_T: Price of the bond at time T

σ_y: Volatility of the forward bond yield

We suppose that

$$B_T = G(y_T)$$

Expanding $G(y_T)$ in a Taylor series about $y_T = y_0$ yields the following approximation:

$$B_T = G(y_0) + (y_T - y_0)G'(y_0) + 0.5(y_T - y_0)^2 G''(y_0)$$

where G' and G'' are the first and second partial derivatives of G. Taking expectations in a world that is forward risk neutral with respect to a zero-coupon bond maturing at time T, we get

$$E_T(B_T) = G(y_0) + E_T(y_T - y_0)G'(y_0) + \tfrac{1}{2}E_T[(y_T - y_0)^2]G''(y_0)$$

where E_T denotes expectations in this world. The expression $G(y_0)$ is by definition the forward bond price. Also, because of the particular world we are working in, $E_T(B_T)$ equals the forward bond price. Hence $E_T(B_T) = G(y_0)$, so that

$$E_T(y_T - y_0)G'(y_0) + \tfrac{1}{2}E_T[(y_T - y_0)^2]G''(y_0) = 0$$

The expression $E_T[(y_T - y_0)^2]$ is approximately $\sigma_y^2 y_0^2 T$. Hence it is approximately true that

$$E_T(y_T) = y_0 - \tfrac{1}{2}y_0^2\sigma_y^2 T\frac{G''(y_0)}{G'(y_0)}$$

This shows that, to obtain the expected bond yield in a world that is forward risk neutral with respect to a zero-coupon bond maturing at time T, we should add

$$-\tfrac{1}{2}y_0^2\sigma_y^2 T\frac{G''(y_0)}{G'(y_0)}$$

to the forward bond yield. This is the result in equation (27.1). For an alternative proof, see Problem 27.6.

CHAPTER 28

Interest Rate Derivatives: Models of the Short Rate

The models for pricing interest rate options that we have presented so far make the assumption that the probability distribution of an interest rate, a bond price, or some other variable at a future point in time is lognormal. They are widely used for valuing instruments such as caps, European bond options, and European swap options. However, they have limitations. They do not provide a description of how interest rates evolve through time. Consequently, they cannot be used for valuing interest rate derivatives such as American-style swap options, callable bonds, and structured notes.

This chapter and the next discuss alternative approaches for overcoming these limitations. These involve building what is known as a *term structure model*. This is a model describing the evolution of all zero-coupon interest rates.[1] This chapter focuses on term structure models constructed by specifying the behavior of the short-term interest rate, r.

28.1 BACKGROUND

The short rate, r, at time t is the rate that applies to an infinitesimally short period of time at time t. It is sometimes referred to as the *instantaneous short rate*. Bond prices, option prices, and other derivative prices depend only on the process followed by r in a risk-neutral world. The process for r in the real world is irrelevant. The risk-neutral world we consider here will be the traditional risk-neutral world where, in a very short time period between t and $t + \Delta t$, investors earn on average $r(t)\,\Delta t$. All processes for r that we present will be processes in this risk-neutral world.

From equation (25.19), the value at time t of an interest rate derivative that provides a payoff of f_T at time T is

$$\hat{E}[e^{-\bar{r}(T-t)} f_T] \tag{28.1}$$

where $\bar{r}$ is the average value of r in the time interval between t and T, and $\hat{E}$ denotes expected value in the traditional risk-neutral world.

[1] Note that when a term structure model is used we do not need to make the convexity, timing, and quanto adjustments discussed in the previous chapter.

As usual we define $P(t, T)$ as the price at time t of a zero-coupon bond that pays off \$1 at time T. From equation (28.1),

$$P(t, T) = \hat{E}[e^{-\bar{r}(T-t)}] \tag{28.2}$$

If $R(t, T)$ is the continuously compounded interest rate at time t for a term of $T - t$, then

$$P(t, T) = e^{-R(t,T)(T-t)} \tag{28.3}$$

so that

$$R(t, T) = -\frac{1}{T-t} \ln P(t, T) \tag{28.4}$$

and, from equation (28.2),

$$R(t, T) = -\frac{1}{T-t} \ln \hat{E}[e^{-\bar{r}(T-t)}] \tag{28.5}$$

This equation enables the term structure of interest rates at any given time to be obtained from the value of r at that time and the risk-neutral process for r. It shows that once we have fully defined the process for r, we have fully defined everything about the initial zero curve and its evolution through time.

28.2 EQUILIBRIUM MODELS

Equilibrium models usually start with assumptions about economic variables and derive a process for the short rate, r. They then explore what the process for r implies about bond prices and option prices.

In a one-factor equilibrium model, the process for r involves only one source of uncertainty. Usually the risk-neutral process for the short rate is described by an Itô process of the form

$$dr = m(r)\,dt + s(r)\,dz$$

The instantaneous drift, m, and instantaneous standard deviation, s, are assumed to be functions of r, but are independent of time. The assumption of a single factor is not as restrictive as it might appear. A one-factor model implies that all rates move in the same direction over any short time interval, but not that they all move by the same amount. The shape of the zero curve can therefore change with the passage of time.

We now consider three one-factor equilibrium models:

$m(r) = \mu r$; $s(r) = \sigma r$ (Rendleman and Bartter model)

$m(r) = a(b - r)$; $s(r) = \sigma$ (Vasicek model)

$m(r) = a(b - r)$; $s(r) = \sigma\sqrt{r}$ (Cox, Ingersoll, and Ross model)

The Rendleman and Bartter Model

In Rendleman and Bartter's model, the risk-neutral process for r is[2]

$$dr = \mu r\,dt + \sigma r\,dz$$

[2] See R. Rendleman and B. Bartter, "The Pricing of Options on Debt Securities," *Journal of Financial and Quantitative Analysis*, 15 (March 1980): 11–24.

Figure 28.1 Mean reversion.

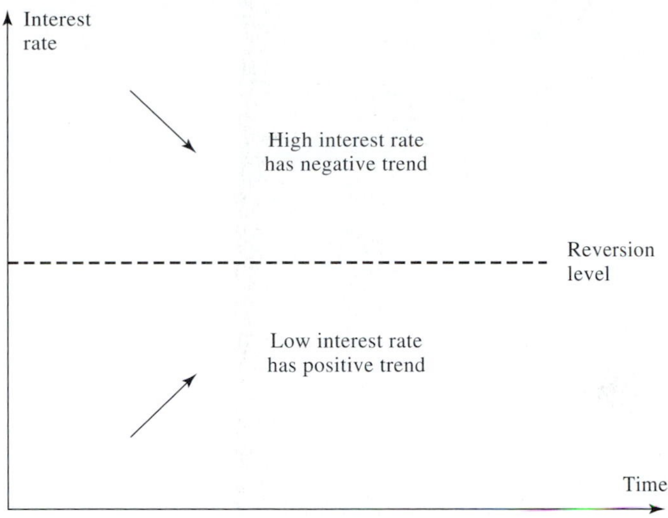

where μ and σ are constants. This means that r follows geometric Brownian motion. The process for r is of the same type as that assumed for a stock price in Chapter 13. It can be represented using a binomial tree similar to the one used for stocks in Chapter 11.[3]

The assumption that the short-term interest rate behaves like a stock price is a natural starting point but is less than ideal. One important difference between interest rates and stock prices is that interest rates appear to be pulled back to some long-run average level over time. This phenomenon is known as *mean reversion*. When r is high, mean reversion tends to cause it to have a negative drift; when r is low, mean reversion tends to cause it to have a positive drift. Mean reversion is illustrated in Figure 28.1. The Rendleman and Bartter model does not incorporate mean reversion.

There are compelling economic arguments in favor of mean reversion. When rates are high, the economy tends to slow down and there is low demand for funds from borrowers. As a result, rates decline. When rates are low, there tends to be a high demand for funds on the part of borrowers and rates tend to rise.

The Vasicek Model

In Vasicek's model, the risk-neutral process for r is

$$dr = a(b - r)\,dt + \sigma\,dz$$

where a, b, and σ are constants.[4] This model incorporates mean reversion. The short rate is pulled to a level b at rate a. Superimposed upon this "pull" is a normally distributed stochastic term $\sigma\,dz$.

[3] The way that the interest rate tree is used is explained later in the chapter.

[4] See O.A. Vasicek, "An Equilibrium Characterization of the Term Structure," *Journal of Financial Economics*, 5 (1977): 177–88.

Vasicek shows that equation (28.2) can be used to obtain the following expression for the price at time t of a zero-coupon bond that pays \$1 at time T:

$$P(t, T) = A(t, T)e^{-B(t,T)r(t)} \tag{28.6}$$

In this equation $r(t)$ is the value of r at time t,

$$B(t, T) = \frac{1 - e^{-a(T-t)}}{a} \tag{28.7}$$

and

$$A(t, T) = \exp\left[\frac{(B(t, T) - T + t)(a^2 b - \sigma^2/2)}{a^2} - \frac{\sigma^2 B(t, T)^2}{4a}\right] \tag{28.8}$$

When $a = 0$, $B(t, T) = T - t$ and $A(t, T) = \exp[\sigma^2 (T - t)^3/6]$.

Using equation (28.4), we get

$$R(t, T) = -\frac{1}{T - t} \ln A(t, T) + \frac{1}{T - t} B(t, T)r(t) \tag{28.9}$$

showing that the entire term structure can be determined as a function of $r(t)$ once a, b, and σ are chosen. The shape can be upward-sloping, downward-sloping, or slightly "humped" (see Figure 28.2).

Figure 28.2 Possible shapes of term structure when Vasicek's model is used.

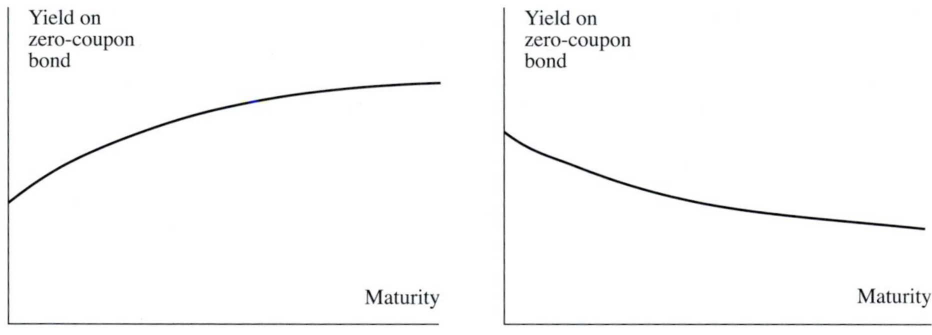

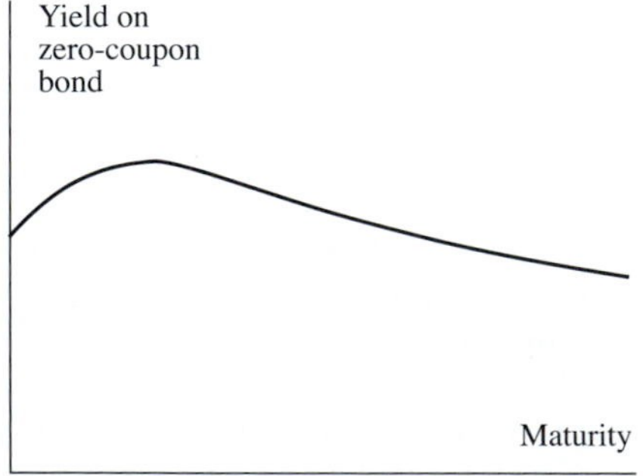

The Cox, Ingersoll, and Ross Model

In Vasicek's model the short-term interest rate, r, can become negative. Cox, Ingersoll, and Ross have proposed an alternative model where rates are always non-negative.[5] The risk-neutral process for r in their model is

$$dr = a(b - r)\,dt + \sigma\sqrt{r}\,dz$$

This has the same mean-reverting drift as Vasicek, but the standard deviation of the change in the short rate in a short period of time is proportional to $\sqrt{r}$. This means that, as the short-term interest rate increases, its standard deviation increases.

Cox, Ingersoll, and Ross show that, in their model, bond prices have the same general form as those in Vasicek's model,

$$P(t, T) = A(t, T)e^{-B(t,T)r}$$

but the functions $B(t, T)$ and $A(t, T)$ are different,

$$B(t, T) = \frac{2(e^{\gamma(T-t)} - 1)}{(\gamma + a)(e^{\gamma(T-t)} - 1) + 2\gamma}$$

and

$$A(t, T) = \left[\frac{2\gamma e^{(a+\gamma)(T-t)/2}}{(\gamma + a)(e^{\gamma(T-t)} - 1) + 2\gamma}\right]^{2ab/\sigma^2}$$

with $\gamma = \sqrt{a^2 + 2\sigma^2}$. Upward-sloping, downward-sloping, and slightly humped yield curves are possible. As in the case of Vasicek's model, the long rate, $R(t, T)$, is linearly dependent on $r(t)$. This means that the value of $r(t)$ determines the level of the term structure at time t. The general shape of the term structure at time t is independent of $r(t)$, but does depend on t.

Two-Factor Equilibrium Models

A number of researchers have investigated the properties of two-factor equilibrium models. For example, Brennan and Schwartz have developed a model where the process for the short rate reverts to a long rate, which in turn follows a stochastic process.[6] The long rate is chosen as the yield on a perpetual bond that pays \$1 per year. Because the yield on this bond is the reciprocal of its price, Itô's lemma can be used to calculate the process followed by the yield from the process followed by the price of the bond. The bond is a traded security. This simplifies the analysis because the expected return on the bond in a risk-neutral world must be the risk-free interest rate.

---

[5] See J. C. Cox, J. E. Ingersoll, and S. A. Ross, "A Theory of the Term Structure of Interest Rates," *Econometrica*, 53 (1985): 385–407.

[6] See M. J. Brennan and E. S. Schwartz, "A Continuous Time Approach to Pricing Bonds," *Journal of Banking and Finance*, 3 (July 1979): 133–55; M. J. Brennan and E. S. Schwartz, "An Equilibrium Model of Bond Pricing and a Test of Market Efficiency," *Journal of Financial and Quantitative Analysis*, 21, 3 (September 1982): 301–29.

Another two-factor model, proposed by Longstaff and Schwartz, starts with a general equilibrium model of the economy and derives a term structure model where there is stochastic volatility.[7] The model proves to be analytically quite tractable.

28.3 NO-ARBITRAGE MODELS

The disadvantage of the equilibrium models we have presented is that they do not automatically fit today's term structure of interest rates. By choosing the parameters judiciously, they can be made to provide an approximate fit to many of the term structures that are encountered in practice. But the fit is not usually an exact one and, in some cases, no reasonable fit can be found. Most traders find this unsatisfactory. Not unreasonably, they argue that they can have very little confidence in the price of a bond option when the model does not price the underlying bond correctly. A 1% error in the price of the underlying bond may lead to a 25% error in an option price.

A *no-arbitrage model* is a model designed to be exactly consistent with today's term structure of interest rates. The essential difference between an equilibrium and a no-arbitrage model is therefore as follows. In an equilibrium model, today's term structure of interest rates is an output. In a no-arbitrage model, today's term structure of interest rates is an input.

In an equilibrium model, the drift of the short rate (i.e., the coefficient of dt) is not usually a function of time. In a no-arbitrage model, the drift is, in general, dependent on time. This is because the shape of the initial zero curve governs the average path taken by the short rate in the future in a no-arbitrage model. If the zero curve is steeply upward-sloping for maturities between t_1 and t_2, then r has a positive drift between these times; if it is steeply downward-sloping for these maturities, then r has a negative drift between these times.

It turns out that some equilibrium models can be converted to no-arbitrage models by including a function of time in the drift of the short rate. We now consider the Ho–Lee, Hull–White (one- and two-factor), and Black–Karasinski models.

The Ho–Lee Model

Ho and Lee proposed the first no-arbitrage model of the term structure in a paper in 1986.[8] They presented the model in the form of a binomial tree of bond prices with two parameters: the short-rate standard deviation and the market price of risk of the short rate. It has since been shown that the continuous-time limit of the model is

$$dr = \theta(t)\,dt + \sigma\,dz \tag{28.10}$$

where σ, the instantaneous standard deviation of the short rate, is constant and $\theta(t)$ is a function of time chosen to ensure that the model fits the initial term structure. The variable $\theta(t)$ defines the average direction that r moves at time t. This is independent of the level of r. Interestingly, Ho and Lee's parameter that concerns the market price of

[7] See F. A. Longstaff and E. S. Schwartz, "Interest Rate Volatility and the Term Structure: A Two Factor General Equilibrium Model," *Journal of Finance*, 47, 4 (September 1992): 1259–82.

[8] See T. S. Y. Ho and S.-B. Lee, "Term Structure Movements and Pricing Interest Rate Contingent Claims," *Journal of Finance*, 41 (December 1986): 1011–29.

Figure 28.3 The Ho–Lee model.

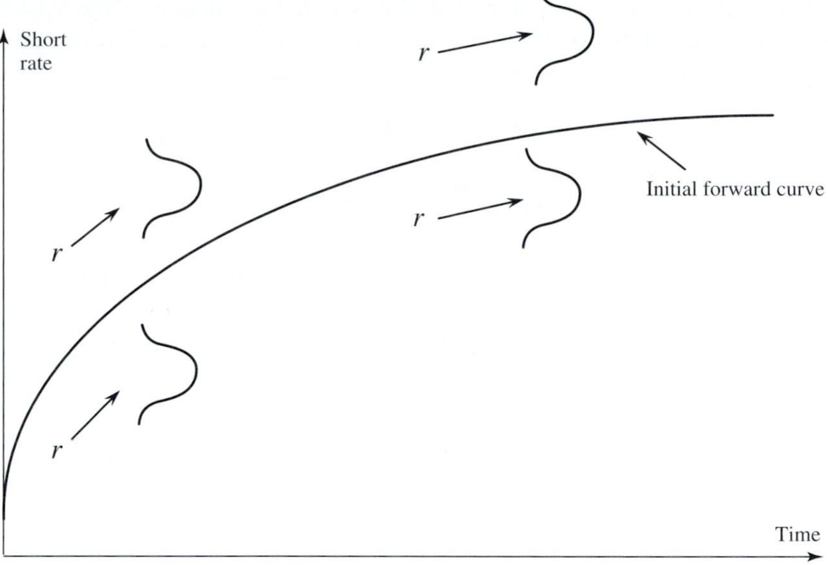

risk proves to be irrelevant when the model is used to price interest rate derivatives. This is analogous to risk preferences being irrelevant in the pricing of stock options.

The variable $\theta(t)$ can be calculated analytically (see Problem 28.13). It is

$$\theta(t) = F_t(0, t) + \sigma^2 t \tag{28.11}$$

where the $F(0, t)$ is the instantaneous forward rate for a maturity t as seen at time zero and the subscript t denotes a partial derivative with respect to t. As an approximation, $\theta(t)$ equals $F_t(0, t)$. This means that the average direction that the short rate will be moving in the future is approximately equal to the slope of the instantaneous forward curve. The Ho–Lee model is illustrated in Figure 28.3. The slope of the forward curve defines the average direction that the short rate is moving at any given time. Superimposed on this slope is the normally distributed random outcome.

In the Ho–Lee model, zero-coupon bonds and European options on zero-coupon bonds can be valued analytically. The expression for the price of a zero-coupon bond at time t in terms of the short rate is

$$P(t, T) = A(t, T)e^{-r(t)(T-t)} \tag{28.12}$$

where

$$\ln A(t, T) = \ln \frac{P(0, T)}{P(0, t)} + (T - t)F(0, t) - \tfrac{1}{2}\sigma^2 t(T - t)^2$$

In these equations, time zero is today. Times t and T are general times in the future with $T \geqslant t$. The equations, therefore, define the price of a zero-coupon bond at a future time t in terms of the short rate at time t and the prices of bonds today. The latter can be calculated from today's term structure.

The Hull–White (One-Factor) Model

In a paper published in 1990, Hull and White explored extensions of the Vasicek model that provide an exact fit to the initial term structure.[9] One version of the extended Vasicek model that they consider is

$$dr = [\theta(t) - ar]\, dt + \sigma\, dz \tag{28.13}$$

or

$$dr = a\left[\frac{\theta(t)}{a} - r\right] dt + \sigma\, dz$$

where a and σ are constants. This is known as the Hull–White model. It can be characterized as the Ho–Lee model with mean reversion at rate a. Alternatively, it can be characterized as the Vasicek model with a time-dependent reversion level. At time t, the short rate reverts to $\theta(t)/a$ at rate a. The Ho–Lee model is a particular case of the Hull–White model with $a = 0$.

The model has the same amount of analytic tractability as Ho–Lee. The $\theta(t)$ function can be calculated from the initial term structure (see Problem 28.14):

$$\theta(t) = F_t(0, t) + aF(0, t) + \frac{\sigma^2}{2a}(1 - e^{-2at}) \tag{28.14}$$

The last term in this equation is usually fairly small. If we ignore it, the equation implies that the drift of the process for r at time t is $F_t(0, t) + a[F(0, t) - r]$. This shows that, on

Figure 28.4 The Hull–White model.

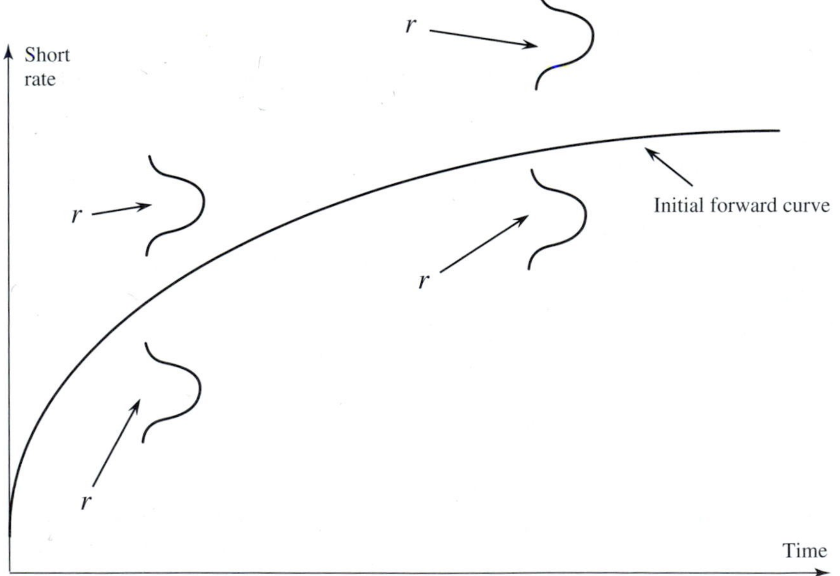

[9] See J. Hull and A. White, "Pricing Interest Rate Derivative Securities," *Review of Financial Studies*, 3, 4 (1990): 573–92.

average, r follows the slope of the initial instantaneous forward rate curve. When it deviates from that curve, it reverts back to it at rate a. The model is illustrated in Figure 28.4.

Bond prices at time t in the Hull–White model are given by

$$P(t, T) = A(t, T)e^{-B(t,T)r(t)} \quad \textbf{(28.15)}$$

where

$$B(t, T) = \frac{1 - e^{-a(T-t)}}{a} \quad \textbf{(28.16)}$$

and

$$\ln A(t, T) = \ln \frac{P(0, T)}{P(0, t)} + B(t, T)F(0, t) - \frac{1}{4a^3}\sigma^2(e^{-aT} - e^{-at})^2(e^{2at} - 1) \quad \textbf{(28.17)}$$

Equations (28.15), (28.16), and (28.17) define the price of a zero-coupon bond at a future time t in terms of the short rate at time t and the prices of bonds today. The latter can be calculated from today's term structure.

The Black–Karasinski Model

The Ho–Lee and Hull–White models have the disadvantage that the short-term interest rate, r, can become negative. A model that allows only positive interest rates is a model propose by Black and Karasinski:[10]

$$d \ln r = [\theta(t) - a(t)\ln(r)]\, dt + \sigma(t)\, dz \quad \textbf{(28.18)}$$

The variable $\ln r$ follows the same process as r in the Hull–White model. Whereas the value of r at a future time is normal in the Ho–Lee and Hull–White models, it is lognormal in the Black–Karasinski model.

The Black–Karasinski model does not have as much analytic tractability as Ho–Lee or Hull–White. For example, it is not possible to produce formulas for valuing bonds in terms of r using the model.

The Hull–White Two-Factor Model

A no-arbitrage model that involves a similar idea to the two-factor equilibrium model suggested by Brennan and Schwartz is[11]

$$df(r) = [\theta(t) + u - af(r)]\, dt + \sigma_1\, dz_1 \quad \textbf{(28.19)}$$

where u has an initial value of zero and follows the process

$$du = -bu\, dt + \sigma_2\, dz_2$$

As in the one-factor models just considered, the parameter $\theta(t)$ is chosen to make the model consistent with the initial term structure. The stochastic variable u is a component of the reversion level of r and itself reverts to a level of zero at rate b. The

[10] See F. Black and P. Karasinski, "Bond and Option Pricing When Short Rates Are Lognormal," *Financial Analysts Journal*, July/August (1991), 52–59.

[11] See J. Hull and A. White, "Numerical Procedures for Implementing Term Structure Models II: Two-Factor Models," *Journal of Derivatives*, 2, 2 (Winter 1994): 37–48.

parameters a, b, σ_1, and σ_2 are constants and dz_1 and dz_2 are Wiener processes with instantaneous correlation ρ.

This model provides a richer pattern of term structure movements and a richer pattern of volatilities than one-factor models of r. For more information on the model, see Technical Note 14 on the author's website.

28.4 OPTIONS ON BONDS

Some of the models we have presented allow options on zero-coupon bonds to be valued analytically. For the Vasicek, Ho–Lee, and Hull–White models, the price at time zero of a call option that matures at time T on a zero-coupon bond maturing at time s is

$$LP(0, s)N(h) - KP(0, T)N(h - \sigma_P) \tag{28.20}$$

where L is the principal of the bond, K is its strike price, and

$$h = \frac{1}{\sigma_P}\ln\frac{LP(0, s)}{P(0, T)K} + \frac{\sigma_P}{2}$$

The price of a put option on the bond is

$$KP(0, T)N(-h + \sigma_P) - LP(0, s)N(-h)$$

In the case of the Vasicek and Hull–White models,

$$\sigma_P = \frac{\sigma}{a}[1 - e^{-a(s-T)}]\sqrt{\frac{1 - e^{-2aT}}{2a}}$$

In the case of the Ho–Lee model,

$$\sigma_P = \sigma(s - T)\sqrt{T}$$

Equation (28.20) is essentially the same as Black's model for pricing bond options in Section 26.2. The bond price volatility is $\sigma_P/\sqrt{T}$ and the standard deviation of the logarithm of the bond price at time T is σ_P. As explained in Section 26.3, an interest rate cap or floor can be expressed as a portfolio of options on zero-coupon bonds. It can, therefore, be valued analytically using the equations just presented.

There are also formulas for valuing options on zero-coupon bonds in the Cox, Ingersoll, and Ross model, which we presented in Section 28.2. These involve integrals of the noncentral chi-square distribution.

Options on Coupon-Bearing Bonds

In a one-factor model of r, all zero-coupon bonds move up in price when r decreases and all zero-coupon bonds move down in price when r increases. As a result, a one-factor model allows us to express a European option on a coupon-bearing bond as the sum of European options on zero-coupon bonds. The procedure is as follows:

1. Calculate r^*, the critical value of r for which the price of the coupon-bearing bond equals the strike price of the option on the bond at option maturity.

2. Calculate the prices of options on the zero-coupon bonds that comprise the coupon-bearing bond. Set the strike price of each option equal to the value the corresponding zero-coupon bond will have at time T when $r = r^*$.
3. Set the price of the option on the coupon-bearing bond equal to the sum of the prices on the options on zero-coupon bonds calculated in step 2.

This allows options on coupon-bearing bonds to be valued for the Vasicek, Cox, Ingersoll, and Ross, Ho–Lee, and Hull–White models As explained in Business Snapshot 26.2, a European swap option can be viewed as an option on a coupon-bearing bond. It can, therefore, be valued using this procedure. For more details on the procedure, see Technical Note 15 on the author's website.

28.5 VOLATILITY STRUCTURES

The models we have looked at give rise to different volatility environments. In Figure 28.5 we show the volatility of the 3-month forward rate as a function of maturity for Ho–Lee, Hull–White one-factor and Hull–White two-factor models. The term structure of interest rates is assumed to be flat.

For Ho–Lee the volatility of the 3-month forward rate is the same for all maturities. In the one-factor Hull–White model the effect of mean reversion is to cause the volatility of the 3-month forward rate to be a declining function of maturity. In the Hull–White two-factor model when parameters are chosen appropriately, the volatility

Figure 28.5 Volatility of 3-month forward rate as a function of maturity for (a) the Ho–Lee model, (b) the Hull–White one-factor model, and (c) the Hull–White two-factor model (when parameters are chosen appropriately).

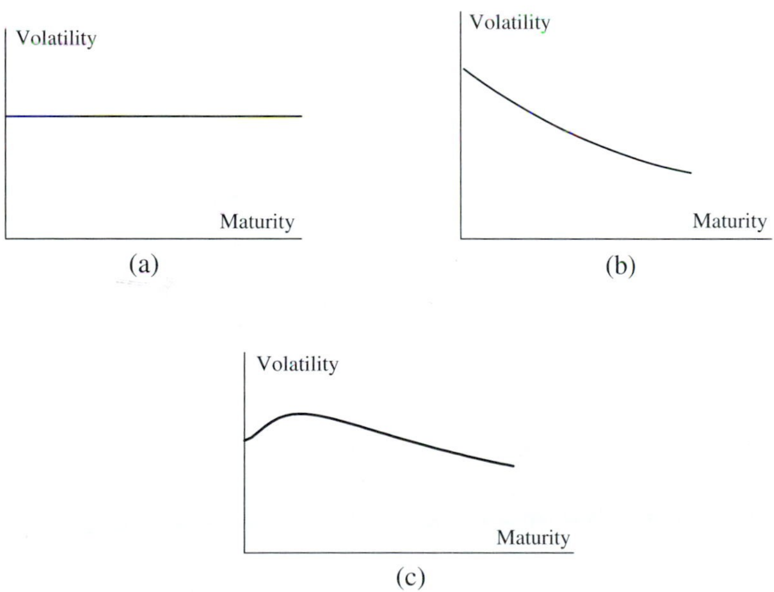

of the 3-month forward rate has a "humped" look. The latter is consistent with empirical evidence and implied cap volatilities discussed in Section 26.3.

28.6 INTEREST RATE TREES

An interest rate tree is a discrete-time representation of the stochastic process for the short rate in much the same way as a stock price tree is a discrete-time representation of the process followed by a stock price. If the time step on the tree is Δt, the rates on the tree are the continuously compounded Δt-period rates. The usual assumption when a tree is constructed is that the Δt-period rate, R, follows the same stochastic process as the instantaneous rate, r, in the corresponding continuous-time model. The main difference between interest rate trees and stock price trees is in the way that discounting is done. In a stock price tree, the discount rate is usually assumed to be the same at each node (or a function of time). In an interest rate tree, the discount rate varies from node to node.

It often proves to be convenient to use a trinomial rather than a binomial tree for interest rates. The main advantage of a trinomial tree is that it provides an extra degree of freedom, making it easier for the tree to represent features of the interest rate process such as mean reversion. As mentioned in Section 17.8, using a trinomial tree is equivalent to using the explicit finite difference method.

Illustration of Use of Trinomial Trees

To illustrate how trinomial interest rate trees are used to value derivatives, we consider the simple example shown in Figure 28.6. This is a two-step tree with each time step equal to 1 year in length so that $\Delta t = 1$ year. We assume that the up, middle, and down

Figure 28.6 Example of the use of trinomial interest rate trees. Upper number at each node is rate; lower number is value of instrument.

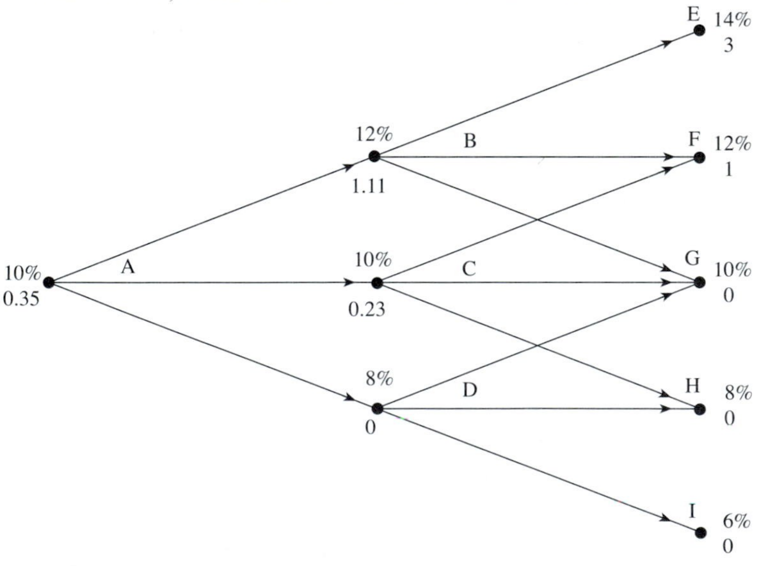

probabilities are 0.25, 0.50, and 0.25, respectively, at each node. The assumed Δt-period rate is shown as the upper number at each node.[12]

The tree is used to value a derivative that provides a payoff at the end of the second time step of

$$\max[100(R - 0.11), 0]$$

where R is the Δt-period rate. The calculated value of this derivative is the lower number at each node. At the final nodes, the value of the derivative equals the payoff. For example, at node E, the value is $100 \times (0.14 - 0.11) = 3$. At earlier nodes, the value of the derivative is calculated using the rollback procedure explained in Chapters 11 and 17. At node B, the 1-year interest rate is 12%. This is used for discounting to obtain the value of the derivative at node B from its values at nodes E, F, and G as

$$[0.25 \times 3 + 0.5 \times 1 + 0.25 \times 0]e^{-0.12\times 1} = 1.11$$

At node C, the 1-year interest rate is 10%. This is used for discounting to obtain the value of the derivative at node C as

$$(0.25 \times 1 + 0.5 \times 0 + 0.25 \times 0)e^{-0.1\times 1} = 0.23$$

At the initial node, A, the interest rate is also 10% and the value of the derivative is

$$(0.25 \times 1.11 + 0.5 \times 0.23 + 0.25 \times 0)e^{-0.1\times 1} = 0.35$$

Nonstandard Branching

It sometimes proves convenient to modify the standard branching pattern, which is used at all nodes in Figure 28.6. Three alternative branching possibilities are shown in Figure 28.7. The usual branching is shown in Figure 28.7(a). It is "up one/straight along/down one". One alternative to this is "up two/up one/straight along", as shown in Figure 28.7(b). This proves useful for incorporating mean reversion when interest rates are very low. A third branching pattern shown in Figure 28.7(c) is "straight along/down one/down two". This is useful for incorporating mean reversion when interest rates are very high. We illustrate the use of different branching patterns in the following section.

Figure 28.7 Alternative branching methods in a trinomial tree.

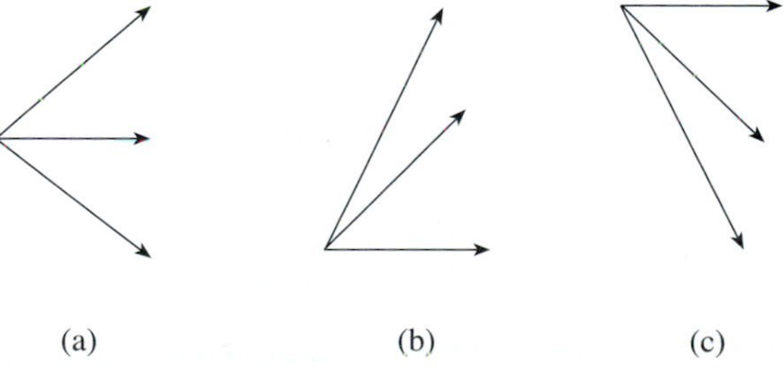

[12] We explain later how the probabilities and rates on an interest rate tree are determined.

28.7 A GENERAL TREE-BUILDING PROCEDURE

Hull and White have proposed a robust two-stage procedure for constructing trinomial trees to represent a wide range of one-factor models.[13] This section first explains how the procedure can be used for the Hull–White model in equation (28.13) and then shows how it can be extended to represent other models.

First Stage

The Hull–White model for the instantaneous short rate r is

$$dr = [\theta(t) - ar]\,dt + \sigma\,dz$$

We suppose that the time step on the tree is constant and equal to Δt.[14]

We assume that the Δt rate, R, follows the same process as r.

$$dR = [\theta(t) - aR]\,dt + \sigma\,dz$$

Clearly, this is reasonable in the limit as Δt tends to zero. The first stage in building a tree for this model is to construct a tree for a variable R^* that is initially zero and follows the process

$$dR^* = -aR^*\,dt + \sigma\,dz$$

This process is symmetrical about $R^* = 0$. The variable $R^*(t + \Delta t) - R^*(t)$ is normally distributed. If terms of higher order than Δt are ignored, the expected value of $R^*(t + \Delta t) - R^*(t)$ is $-aR^*(t)\Delta t$ and the variance of $R^*(t + \Delta t) - R^*(t)$ is $\sigma^2 \Delta t$.

We define ΔR as the spacing between interest rates on the tree and set

$$\Delta R = \sigma\sqrt{3\Delta t}$$

This proves to be a good choice of ΔR from the viewpoint of error minimization.

Our objective during the first stage of this procedure is to build a tree similar to that shown in Figure 28.8 for R^*. To do this, we must resolve which of the three branching methods shown in Figure 28.7 will apply at each node. This will determine the overall geometry of the tree. Once this is done, the branching probabilities must also be calculated.

Define (i, j) as the node where $t = i\,\Delta t$ and $R^* = j\,\Delta R$. (The variable i is a positive integer and j is a positive or negative integer.) The branching method used at a node must lead to the probabilities on all three branches being positive. Most of the time, the branching shown in Figure 28.7(a) is appropriate. When $a > 0$, it is necessary to switch from the branching in Figure 28.7(a) to the branching in Figure 28.7(c) for a sufficiently large j. Similarly, it is necessary to switch from the branching in Figure 28.7(a) to the branching in Figure 28.7(b) when j is sufficiently negative. Define $j_{\max}$ as the value of j where we switch from the Figure 28.7(a) branching to the Figure 28.7(c) branching and $j_{\min}$ as the value of j where we switch from the Figure 28.7(a) branching to the Figure 28.7(b) branching. Hull and White show that probabilities are always positive if

[13] See J. Hull and A. White, "Numerical Procedures for Implementing Term Structure Models I: Single-Factor Models," *Journal of Derivatives*, 2, 1 (1994): 7–16; and J. Hull and A. White, "Using Hull–White Interest Rate Trees," *Journal of Derivatives*, (Spring 1996): 26–36.

[14] See Technical Note 16 on the author's website for a discussion of how nonconstant time steps can be used.

Figure 28.8 Tree for R^* in Hull–White model (first stage).

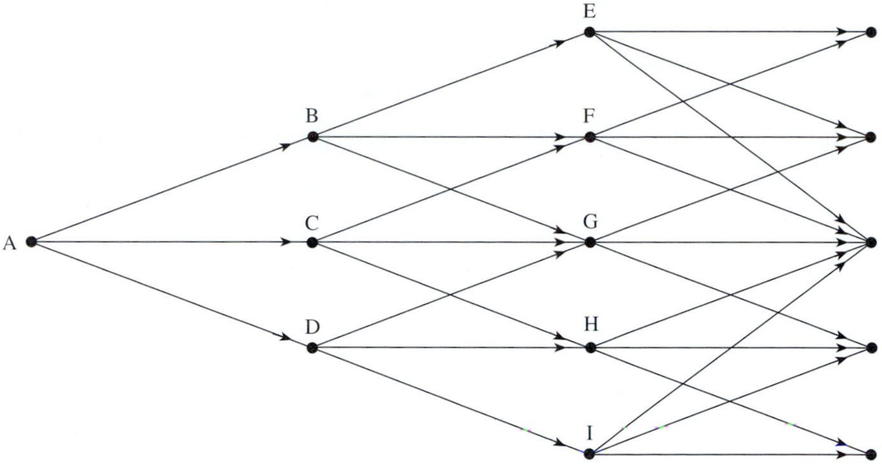

Node:	A	B	C	D	E	F	G	H	I
R(%)	0.000	1.732	0.000	−1.732	3.464	1.732	0.000	−1.732	−3.464
p_u	0.1667	0.1217	0.1667	0.2217	0.8867	0.1217	0.1667	0.2217	0.0867
p_m	0.6666	0.6566	0.6666	0.6566	0.0266	0.6566	0.6666	0.6566	0.0266
p_d	0.1667	0.2217	0.1667	0.1217	0.0867	0.2217	0.1667	0.1217	0.8867

we set j_{max} equal to the smallest integer greater than $0.184/(a\,\Delta t)$ and j_{min} equal to $-j_{max}$.[15] Define p_u, p_m, and p_d as the probabilities of the highest, middle, and lowest branches emanating from the node. The probabilities are chosen to match the expected change and variance of the change in R^* over the next time interval Δt. The probabilities must also sum to unity. This leads to three equations in the three probabilities.

As already mentioned, the mean change in R^* in time Δt is $-aR^*\Delta t$ and the variance of the change is $\sigma^2\Delta t$. At node (i, j), $R^* = j\,\Delta r$. If the branching has the form shown in Figure 28.7(a), the p_u, p_m, and p_d at node (i, j) must satisfy the following three equations:

$$p_u\Delta R - p_d\Delta R = -aj\,\Delta R\,\Delta t$$
$$p_u\Delta R^2 + p_d\Delta R^2 = \sigma^2\Delta t + a^2j^2\Delta R^2\Delta t^2$$
$$p_u + p_m + p_d = 1$$

Using $\Delta R = \sigma\sqrt{3\Delta t}$, the solution to these equations is

$$p_u = \tfrac{1}{6} + \tfrac{1}{2}(a^2j^2\Delta t^2 - aj\,\Delta t)$$
$$p_m = \tfrac{2}{3} - a^2j^2\Delta t^2$$
$$p_d = \tfrac{1}{6} + \tfrac{1}{2}(a^2j^2\Delta t^2 + aj\,\Delta t)$$

[15] The probabilities are positive for any value of j_{max} between $0.184/(a\,\Delta t)$ and $0.816/(a\,\Delta t)$ and for any value of j_{min} between $-0.184/(a\,\Delta t)$ and $-0.816/(a\,\Delta t)$. Changing the branching at the first possible node proves to be computationally most efficient.

Similarly, if the branching has the form shown in Figure 28.7(b), the probabilities are

$$p_u = \tfrac{1}{6} + \tfrac{1}{2}(a^2 j^2 \Delta t^2 + aj\,\Delta t)$$
$$p_m = -\tfrac{1}{3} - a^2 j^2 \Delta t^2 - 2aj\,\Delta t$$
$$p_d = \tfrac{7}{6} + \tfrac{1}{2}(a^2 j^2 \Delta t^2 + 3aj\,\Delta t)$$

Finally, if the branching has the form shown in Figure 28.7(c), the probabilities are

$$p_u = \tfrac{7}{6} + \tfrac{1}{2}(a^2 j^2 \Delta t^2 - 3aj\,\Delta t)$$
$$p_m = -\tfrac{1}{3} - a^2 j^2 \Delta t^2 + 2aj\,\Delta t$$
$$p_d = \tfrac{1}{6} + \tfrac{1}{2}(a^2 j^2 \Delta t^2 - aj\,\Delta t)$$

To illustrate the first stage of the tree construction, suppose that $\sigma = 0.01$, $a = 0.1$, and $\Delta t = 1$ year. In this case, $\Delta R = 0.01\sqrt{3} = 0.0173$, $j_{\max}$ is set equal to the smallest integer greater than 0.184/0.1, and $j_{\min} = -j_{\max}$. This means that $j_{\max} = 2$ and $j_{\min} = -2$ and the tree is as shown in Figure 28.8. The probabilities on the branches emanating from each node are shown below the tree and are calculated using the equations above for p_u, p_m, and p_d.

Note that the probabilities at each node in Figure 28.8 depend only on j. For example, the probabilities at node B are the same as the probabilities at node F. Furthermore, the tree is symmetrical. The probabilities at node D are the mirror image of the probabilities at node B.

Second Stage

The second stage in the tree construction is to convert the tree for R^* into a tree for R. This is accomplished by displacing the nodes on the R^*-tree so that the initial term structure of interest rates is exactly matched. Define

$$\alpha(t) = R(t) - R^*(t)$$

We calculate the α's iteratively so that the initial term structure is matched exactly.[16] Define α_i as $\alpha(i\,\Delta t)$, the value of R at time $i\,\Delta t$ on the R-tree minus the corresponding value of R^* at time $i\,\Delta t$ on the r^*-tree. Define $Q_{i,j}$ as the present value of a security that pays off \$1 if node (i, j) is reached and zero otherwise. The α_i and $Q_{i,j}$ can be calculated using forward induction in such a way that the initial term structure is matched exactly.

Illustration of Second Stage

Suppose that the continuously compounded zero rates in the example in Figure 28.8 are as shown in Table 28.1. The value of $Q_{0,0}$ is 1.0. The value of α_0 is chosen to give the

[16] It is possible to estimate $\alpha(t)$ analytically. Since

$$dR = [\theta(t) - aR]\,dt + \sigma\,dz \quad \text{and} \quad dR^* = -aR^*\,dt + \sigma\,dz$$

it follows that

$$d\alpha = [\theta(t) - a\alpha(t)]\,dt$$

If we ignore the distinction between r and R, the solution to this is

$$\alpha(t) = F(0, t) + \frac{\sigma^2}{2a^2}(1 - e^{-at})^2$$

However, these are instantaneous α's and do not lead to the tree calculations exactly matching the term structure of interest rates.

Table 28.1 Zero rates for example in Figures 28.8 and 28.9.

Maturity	*Rate (%)*
0.5	3.430
1.0	3.824
1.5	4.183
2.0	4.512
2.5	4.812
3.0	5.086

right price for a zero-coupon bond maturing at time Δt. That is, α_0 is set equal to the initial Δt-period interest rate. Because $\Delta t = 1$ in this example, $\alpha_0 = 0.03824$. This defines the position of the initial node on the R-tree in Figure 28.9. The next step is to calculate the values of $Q_{1,1}$, $Q_{1,0}$, and $Q_{1,-1}$. There is a probability of 0.1667 that the (1, 1) node is reached and the discount rate for the first time step is 3.82%. The value of $Q_{1,1}$ is therefore $0.1667e^{-0.0382} = 0.1604$. Similarly, $Q_{1,0} = 0.6417$ and $Q_{1,-1} = 0.1604$.

Once $Q_{1,1}$, $Q_{1,0}$, and $Q_{1,-1}$ have been calculated, we are in a position to determine α_1. This is chosen to give the right price for a zero-coupon bond maturing at time $2\Delta t$. Because $\Delta R = 0.01732$ and $\Delta t = 1$, the price of this bond as seen at node B is $e^{-(\alpha_1+0.01732)}$. Similarly, the price as seen at node C is $e^{-\alpha_1}$ and the price as seen at

Figure 28.9 Tree for R in Hull–White model (the second stage).

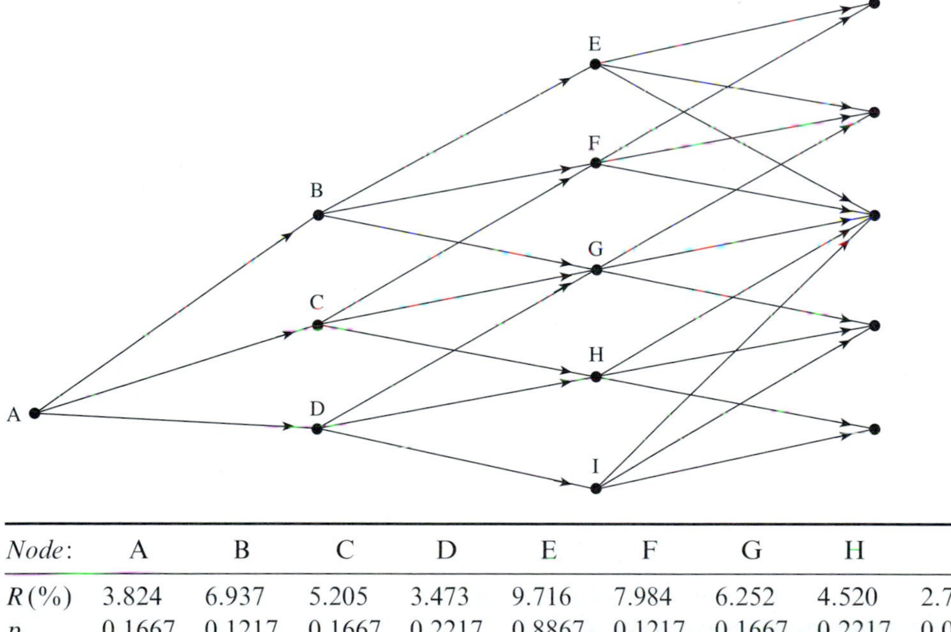

Node:	A	B	C	D	E	F	G	H	I
R(%)	3.824	6.937	5.205	3.473	9.716	7.984	6.252	4.520	2.788
p_u	0.1667	0.1217	0.1667	0.2217	0.8867	0.1217	0.1667	0.2217	0.0867
p_m	0.6666	0.6566	0.6666	0.6566	0.0266	0.6566	0.6666	0.6566	0.0266
p_d	0.1667	0.2217	0.1667	0.1217	0.0867	0.2217	0.1667	0.1217	0.8867

node D is $e^{-(\alpha_1-0.01732)}$. The price as seen at the initial node A is therefore

$$Q_{1,1}e^{-(\alpha_1+0.01732)} + Q_{1,0}e^{-\alpha_1} + Q_{1,-1}e^{-(\alpha_1-0.01732)} \tag{28.21}$$

From the initial term structure, this bond price should be $e^{-0.04512\times 2} = 0.9137$. Substituting for the Q's in equation (28.21), we obtain

$$0.1604e^{-(\alpha_1+0.01732)} + 0.6417e^{-\alpha_1} + 0.1604e^{-(\alpha_1-0.01732)} = 0.9137$$

or

$$e^{\alpha_1}(0.1604e^{-0.01732} + 0.6417 + 0.1604e^{0.01732}) = 0.9137$$

or

$$\alpha_1 = \ln\left[\frac{0.1604e^{-0.01732} + 0.6417 + 0.1604e^{0.01732}}{0.9137}\right] = 0.05205$$

This means that the central node at time Δt in the tree for R corresponds to an interest rate of 5.205% (see Figure 28.9).

The next step is to calculate $Q_{2,2}$, $Q_{2,1}$, $Q_{2,0}$, $Q_{2,-1}$, and $Q_{2,-2}$. The calculations can be shortened by using previously determined Q values. Consider $Q_{2,1}$ as an example. This is the value of a security that pays off \$1 if node F is reached and zero otherwise. Node F can be reached only from nodes B and C. The interest rates at these nodes are 6.937% and 5.205%, respectively. The probabilities associated with the B–F and C–F branches are 0.6566 and 0.1667. The value at node B of a security that pays \$1 at node F is therefore $0.6566e^{-0.06937}$. The value at node C is $0.1667e^{-0.05205}$. The variable $Q_{2,1}$ is $0.6566e^{-0.06937}$ times the present value of \$1 received at node B plus $0.1667e^{-0.05205}$ times the present value of \$1 received at node C; that is,

$$Q_{2,1} = 0.6566e^{-0.0693} \times 0.1604 + 0.1667e^{-0.05205} \times 0.6417 = 0.1998$$

Similarly, $Q_{2,2} = 0.0182$, $Q_{2,0} = 0.4736$, $Q_{2,-1} = 0.2033$, and $Q_{2,-2} = 0.0189$.

The next step in producing the R-tree in Figure 28.9 is to calculate α_2. After that, the $Q_{3,j}$'s can then be computed. We can then calculate α_3; and so on.

Formulas for α's and Q's

To express the approach more formally, we suppose that the $Q_{i,j}$ have been determined for $i \leqslant m$ ($m \geqslant 0$). The next step is to determine α_m so that the tree correctly prices a zero-coupon bond maturing at $(m+1)\,\Delta t$. The interest rate at node (m, j) is $\alpha_m + j\,\Delta R$, so that the price of a zero-coupon bond maturing at time $(m+1)\Delta t$ is given by

$$P_{m+1} = \sum_{j=-n_m}^{n_m} Q_{m,j}\exp[-(\alpha_m + j\,\Delta R)\Delta t] \tag{28.22}$$

where n_m is the number of nodes on each side of the central node at time $m\,\Delta t$. The solution to this equation is

$$\alpha_m = \frac{\ln \sum_{j=-n_m}^{n_m} Q_{m,j}e^{-j\Delta R\Delta t} - \ln P_{m+1}}{\Delta t}$$

Once α_m has been determined, the $Q_{i,j}$ for $i = m+1$ can be calculated using

$$Q_{m+1,j} = \sum_k Q_{m,k} q(k, j) \exp[-(\alpha_m + k\,\Delta R)\,\Delta t]$$

where $q(k, j)$ is the probability of moving from node (m, k) to node $(m+1, j)$ and the summation is taken over all values of k for which this is nonzero.

Extension to Other Models

The procedure that has just been outlined can be extended to more general models of the form

$$df(r) = [\theta(t) - af(r)]\,dt + \sigma\,dz \tag{28.23}$$

This family of models has the property that they can fit any term structure.[17]

As before, we assume that the Δt period rate, R, follows the same process as r:

$$df(R) = [\theta(t) - af(R)]\,dt + \sigma\,dz$$

We start by setting $x = f(R)$, so that

$$dx = [\theta(t) - ax]\,dt + \sigma\,dz$$

The first stage is to build a tree for a variable x^* that follows the same process as x except that $\theta(t) = 0$ and the initial value is zero. The procedure here is identical to the procedure already outlined for building a tree such as that in Figure 28.8.

As in Figure 28.9, we then displace the nodes at time $i\,\Delta t$ by an amount α_i to provide an exact fit to the initial term structure. The equations for determining α_i and $Q_{i,j}$ inductively are slightly different from those for the $f(R) = R$ case. The value of Q at the first node, $Q_{0,0}$, is set equal to 1. Suppose that the $Q_{i,j}$ have been determined for $i \leqslant m$ ($m \geqslant 0$). The next step is to determine α_m so that the tree correctly prices an $(m+1)\Delta t$ zero-coupon bond. Define g as the inverse function of f so that the Δt-period interest rate at the jth node at time $m\,\Delta t$ is

$$g(\alpha_m + j\,\Delta x)$$

The price of a zero-coupon bond maturing at time $(m+1)\Delta t$ is given by

$$P_{m+1} = \sum_{j=-n_m}^{n_m} Q_{m,j} \exp[-g(\alpha_m + j\,\Delta x)\Delta t] \tag{28.24}$$

This equation can be solved using a numerical procedure such as Newton–Raphson. The value α_0 of α when $m = 0$, is $f\big(R(0)\big)$.

Once α_m has been determined, the $Q_{i,j}$ for $i = m+1$ can be calculated using

$$Q_{m+1,j} = \sum_k Q_{m,k} q(k, j) \exp[-g(\alpha_m + k\,\Delta x)\Delta t]$$

---

[17] Not all no-arbitrage models have this property. For example, the extended-CIR model, considered by Cox, Ingersoll, and Ross (1985) and Hull and White (1990), which has the form

$$dr = [\theta(t) - ar]\,dt + \sigma\sqrt{r}\,dz$$

cannot fit yield curves where the forward rate declines sharply. This is because the process is not well defined when $\theta(t)$ is negative.

Figure 28.10 Tree for lognormal model.

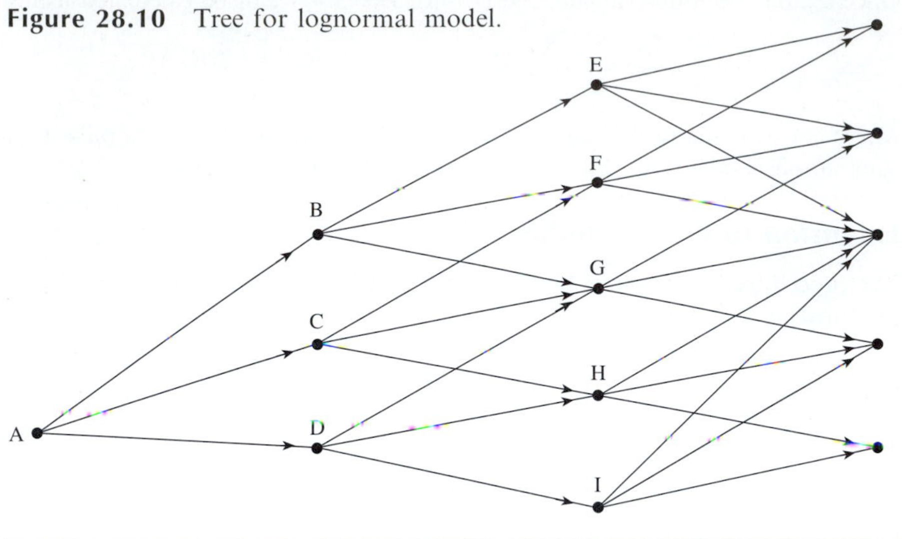

Node:	A	B	C	D	E	F	G	H	I
x	−3.373	−2.875	−3.181	−3.487	−2.430	−2.736	−3.042	−3.349	−3.655
R (%)	3.430	5.642	4.154	3.058	8.803	6.481	4.772	3.513	2.587
p_u	0.1667	0.1177	0.1667	0.2277	0.8609	0.1177	0.1667	0.2277	0.0809
p_m	0.6666	0.6546	0.6666	0.6546	0.0582	0.6546	0.6666	0.6546	0.0582
p_d	0.1667	0.2277	0.1667	0.1177	0.0809	0.2277	0.1667	0.1177	0.8609

where $q(k, j)$ is the probability of moving from node (m, k) to node $(m + 1, j)$ and the summation is taken over all values of k where this is nonzero.

Figure 28.10 shows the results of applying the procedure to the model

$$d\ln(r) = [\theta(t) - a\ln(r)]\,dt + \sigma\,dz$$

when $a = 0.22$, $\sigma = 0.25$, $\Delta t = 0.5$, and the zero rates are as in Table 28.1.

Choosing $f(r)$

When $f(r) = r$ we obtain the Hull–White model in equation (28.13); when $f(r) = \ln(r)$ we obtain the Black–Karasinksi model in equation (28.18). In most circumstances these two models appear to perform about equally well in fitting market data on actively traded instruments such as caps and European swap options. The main advantage of the $f(r) = r$ model is its analytic tractability. Its main disadvantage is that negative interest rates are possible. In most circumstances, the probability of negative interest rates occurring under the model is very small, but some analysts are reluctant to use a model where there is any chance at all of negative interest rates. The $f(r) = \ln r$ model has no analytic tractability, but has the advantage that interest rates are always positive. Another advantage is that traders naturally think in terms of σ's arising from a lognormal model rather than σ's arising from a normal model.

There is a problem in choosing a satisfactory model for countries with low interest rates. The normal model is unsatisfactory because, when the initial short rate is low, the probability of negative interest rates in the future is no longer negligible. The lognormal model is unsatisfactory because the volatility of rates (i.e., the σ parameter in the lognormal model) is usually much greater when rates are low than when they are high. (For example, a volatility of 100% might be appropriate when the short rate is less than 1%, while 20% might be appropriate when it is 4% or more.) A model that appears to work well is one where $f(r)$ is chosen so that rates are lognormal for r less than 1% and normal for r greater than 1%.[18]

Using Analytic Results in Conjunction with Trees

When a tree is constructed for the $f(r) = r$ version of the Hull–White model, the analytic results in Section 28.3 can be used to provide the complete term structure and European option prices at each node. It is important to recognize that the interest rate on the tree is the Δt-period rate R. It is not the instantaneous short rate r.

From equations (28.15), (28.16), and (28.17) it can be shown (see Problem 28.21) that

$$P(t, T) = \hat{A}(t, T)e^{-\hat{B}(t,T)R} \tag{28.25}$$

where

$$\ln \hat{A}(t, T) = \ln\frac{P(0, T)}{P(0, t)} - \frac{B(t, T)}{B(t, t + \Delta t)}\ln\frac{P(0, t + \Delta t)}{P(0, t)} - \frac{\sigma^2}{4a}(1 - e^{-2at})B(t, T)[B(t, T) - B(t, t + \Delta t)] \tag{28.26}$$

and

$$\hat{B}(t, T) = \frac{B(t, T)}{B(t, t + \Delta t)}\Delta t \tag{28.27}$$

(In the case of the Ho–Lee model, we set $\hat{B}(t, T) = T - t$ in these equations.)

We should, therefore, calculate bond prices using equation (28.25), not equation (28.15).

Example 28.1

As an example, we use the zero rates in Table 28.2. The rates for maturities between those indicated are generated using linear interpolation.

We price a 3-year ($= 3 \times 365$ days) European put option on a zero-coupon bond that will expire in 9 years ($= 9 \times 365$ days). Interest rates are assumed to follow the Hull–White ($f(r) = r$) model. The strike price is 63, $a = 0.1$, and $\sigma = 0.01$. We construct a 3-year tree and calculate zero-coupon bond prices at the final nodes analytically as just described. As shown in Table 28.3, the results from the tree are consistent with the analytic price of the option.

This example provides a good test of the implementation of the model because the gradient of the zero curve changes sharply immediately after the expiration of the option. Small errors in the construction and use of the tree are liable to have a big effect on the option values obtained. (The example is used in Sample Application G of the DerivaGem Application Builder software.)

[18] See J. Hull and A. White "Taking Rates to the Limit," *Risk*, December (1997): 168–69.

Table 28.2 Zero curve with all rates continuously compounded.

Maturity	*Days*	*Rate* (%)
3 days	3	5.01772
1 month	31	4.98284
2 months	62	4.97234
3 months	94	4.96157
6 months	185	4.99058
1 year	367	5.09389
2 years	731	5.79733
3 years	1,096	6.30595
4 years	1,461	6.73464
5 years	1,826	6.94816
6 years	2,194	7.08807
7 years	2,558	7.27527
8 years	2,922	7.30852
9 years	3,287	7.39790
10 years	3,653	7.49015

Tree for American Bond Options

The DerivaGem software accompanying this book implements the normal and the lognormal model, as well as Black's model, for valuing European bond options, caps/floors, and European swap options. In addition, American-style bond options can be handled. Figure 28.11 shows the tree produced by the software when it is used to value a 1.5-year American call option on a 10-year bond using four time steps and the lognormal model. The parameters used in the lognormal model are $a = 5\%$ and $\sigma = 20\%$. The underlying bond lasts 10 years, has a principal of 100, and pays a coupon of 5% per annum semiannually. The yield curve is flat at 5% per annum. The strike price is 105. As explained in Section 26.2 the strike price can be a cash strike price or a quoted strike price. In this case it is a quoted strike price. The bond price shown on the tree is the cash bond price. The accrued interest at each node is shown below the tree. The cash strike price is calculated as the quoted strike price plus accrued interest.

Table 28.3 Value of a three-year put option on a nine-year zero-coupon bond with a strike price of 63: $a = 0.1$ and $\sigma = 0.01$; zero curve as in Table 28.2.

Steps	*Tree*	*Analytic*
10	1.8658	1.8093
30	1.8234	1.8093
50	1.8093	1.8093
100	1.8144	1.8093
200	1.8097	1.8093
500	1.8093	1.8093

Figure 28.11 Tree, produced by DerivaGem, for valuing an American bond option.

At each node:
Upper value = Cash Bond Price
Middle value = Option Price
Lower value = dt-period Rate
Shaded values are as a result of early exercise

Strike price = 105
Time step, dt = 0.3753 years, 137.00 days

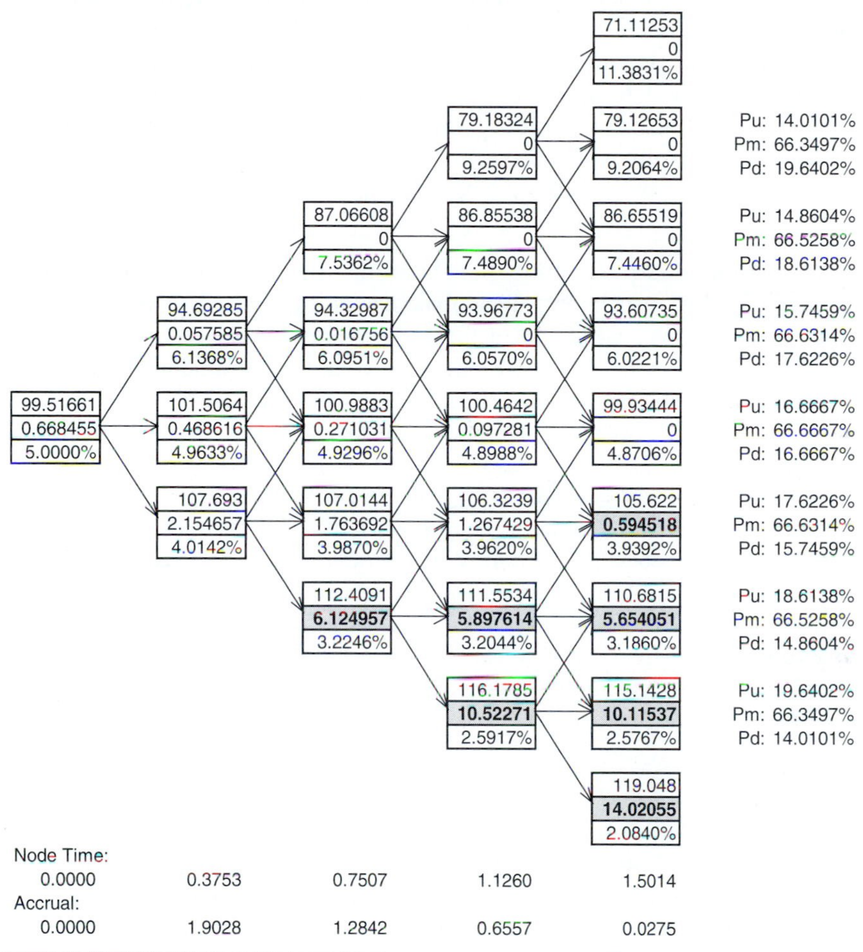

The quoted bond price is the cash bond price minus accrued interest. The payoff from the option is the cash bond price minus the cash strike price. Equivalently it is the quoted bond price minus the quoted strike price.

The tree gives the price of the option as 0.668. A much larger tree with 100 time steps gives the price of the option as 0.699. Two points should be noted about Figure 28.11:

1. The software measures the time to option maturity as a whole number of days. For example, when an option maturity of 1.5 years is input, the life of the option is assumed to be 1.5014 years (or 1 year and 183 days).

2. The price of the 10-year bond cannot be computed analytically when the lognormal model is assumed. It is computed numerically by rolling back through a much larger tree than that shown.

28.8 CALIBRATION

Up to now, we have assumed that the volatility parameters a and σ are known. We now discuss how they are determined. This is known as calibrating the model.

The volatility parameters are determined from market data on actively traded options (e.g., broker quotes on caps and swap options such as those in Tables 26.1 and 26.2). These will be referred to as the *calibrating instruments*. The first stage is to choose a "goodness-of-fit" measure. Suppose there are n calibrating instruments. A popular goodness-of-fit measure is

$$\sum_{i=1}^{n}(U_i - V_i)^2$$

where U_i is the market price of the ith calibrating instrument and V_i is the price given by the model for this instrument. The objective of calibration is to choose the model parameters so that this goodness-of-fit measure is minimized.

If a and σ are constant, there are only two volatility parameters. The models can be extended so that a or σ, or both, are functions of time. Step functions can be used. Suppose, for example, we elect to make a constant and σ a function of time. We might choose times $t_1, t_2, \dots, t_n$ and assume $\sigma(t) = \sigma_0$ for $t \leqslant t_1$, $\sigma(t) = \sigma_i$ for $t_i < t \leqslant t_{i+1}$ $(1 \leqslant i \leqslant n-1)$, and $\sigma(t) = \sigma_n$ for $t > t_n$. There would then be a total of $n+2$ volatility parameters: a, σ_0, $\sigma_1, \dots,$ and σ_n. The number of volatility parameters should not be greater than the number of calibrating instruments.

The minimization of the goodness-of-fit measure can be accomplished using the Levenberg–Marquardt procedure.[19] When a or σ, or both, are functions of time, a penalty function is often added to the goodness-of-fit measure to that the functions are "well behaved". In the example just mentioned, where σ is a step function, we would choose the objective function as

$$\sum_{i=1}^{n}(U_i - V_i)^2 + \sum_{i=1}^{n} w_{1,i}(\sigma_i - \sigma_{i-1})^2 + \sum_{i=1}^{n-1} w_{2,i}(\sigma_{i-1} + \sigma_{i+1} - 2\sigma_i)^2$$

The second term provides a penalty for large changes in σ between one step and the next. The third term provides a penalty for high curvature in σ. Appropriate values for $w_{1,i}$ and $w_{2,i}$ are based on experimentation and are chosen to provide an appropriate level of smoothness in the σ function.

The calibrating instruments chosen should be as similar as possible to the instrument being valued. Suppose, for example, that we wish to value a Bermudan-style swap option that lasts 10 years and can be exercised on any payment date between year 5 and year 9 into a swap maturing 10 years from today. The most relevant calibrating instruments are 5×5, 6×4, 7×3, 8×2, and 9×1 European swap options. (An $n \times m$ European swap option is an n-year option to enter into a swap lasting for m years beyond the maturity of the option.)

[19] For a good description of this procedure, see W. H. Press, B. P. Flannery, S. A. Teukolsky, and W. T. Vetterling, *Numerical Recipes in C: The Art of Scientific Computing*. Cambridge University Press, 1988.

The advantage of making a or σ, or both, functions of time is that the models can be fitted more precisely to the prices of instruments that trade actively in the market. The disadvantage is that the volatility structure becomes nonstationary. The volatility term structure given by the model in the future is liable to be quite different from that existing in the market today.[20]

A somewhat different approach to calibration is to use all available calibrating instruments to calculate "global-best-fit" a and σ parameters. The parameter a is held fixed at its best-fit value. The model can then be used in the same way as Black–Scholes. There is a one-to-one relationship between options prices and the σ parameter. The model can be used to convert tables such as Table 26.1 and 26.2 into tables of implied σ's.[21] These tables can be used to assess the σ most appropriate for pricing the instrument under consideration.

28.9 HEDGING USING A ONE-FACTOR MODEL

We outlined some general approaches to hedging a portfolio of interest rate derivatives in Section 26.6. They can be used with the term structure models discussed in this chapter. The calculation of deltas, gammas, and vegas involves making small changes to either the zero curve or the volatility environment and recomputing the value of the portfolio.

Note that, although we often assume there is one factor when pricing interest rate derivatives, we do not assume only one factor when hedging. For example, the deltas we calculate allow for many different movements in the yield curve, not just those that are possible under the model chosen. The practice of taking account of changes that cannot happen under the model considered, as well as those that can, is known as *outside model hedging* and is standard practice for traders.[22] The reality is that relatively simple one-factor models if used carefully usually give reasonable prices for instruments, but good hedging schemes must explicitly or implicitly assume many factors.

SUMMARY

The traditional models of the term structure used in finance are known as equilibrium models. These are useful for understanding potential relationships between variables in the economy, but have the disadvantage that the initial term structure is an output from the model rather than an input to it. When valuing derivatives, it is important that the model used be consistent with the initial term structure observed in the market. No-arbitrage models are designed to have this property. They take the initial term structure as given and define how it can evolve.

---

[20] For a discussion of the implementation of a model where a and σ are functions of time, see Technical Note 16 on the author's website.

[21] Note that in a term structure model the implied σ's are not the same as the implied volatilities calculated from Black's model in Tables 26.1 and 26.2. The procedure for computing implied σ's is as follows. The Black volatilities are converted to prices using Black's model. An iterative procedure is then used to imply the σ parameter in the term structure model from the price.

[22] A simple example of outside model hedging is in the way that the Black–Scholes model is used. The Black–Scholes model assumes that volatility is constant—but traders regularly calculate vega and hedge against volatility changes.

This chapter has provided a description of a number of one-factor no-arbitrage models of the short rate. These are very robust and can be used in conjunction with any set of initial zero rates. The simplest model is the Ho–Lee model. This has the advantage that it is analytically tractable. Its chief disadvantage is that it implies that all rates are equally variable at all times. The Hull–White model is a version of the Ho–Lee model that includes mean reversion. It allows a richer description of the volatility environment while preserving its analytic tractability. Lognormal one-factor models have the advantage that they avoid the possibility of negative interest rates but, unfortunately, they have no analytic tractability.

FURTHER READING

Equilibrium Models

Cox, J. C., J. E. Ingersoll, and S. A. Ross, "A Theory of the Term Structure of Interest Rates," *Econometrica*, 53 (1985): 385–407.

Longstaff, F. A. and E. S. Schwartz, "Interest Rate Volatility and the Term Structure: A Two Factor General Equilibrium Model," *Journal of Finance*, 47, 4 (September 1992): 1259–82.

Vasicek, O. A.,"An Equilibrium Characterization of the Term Structure," *Journal of Financial Economics*, 5 (1977): 177–88.

No-Arbitrage Models

Black, F., and P. Karasinski, "Bond and Option Pricing When Short Rates Are Lognormal," *Financial Analysts Journal*, July/August (1991): 52–59.

Ho, T. S. Y., and S.-B. Lee, "Term Structure Movements and Pricing Interest Rate Contingent Claims," *Journal of Finance*, 41 (December 1986): 1011–29.

Hull, J., and A. White, "Bond Option Pricing Based on a Model for the Evolution of Bond Prices," *Advances in Futures and Options Research*, 6 (1993): 1–13.

Hull, J., and A. White, "Pricing Interest Rate Derivative Securities," *The Review of Financial Studies*, 3, 4 (1990): 573–92.

Hull, J., and A. White, "Using Hull–White Interest Rate Trees," *Journal of Derivatives*, Spring (1996): 26–36.

Kijima, M., and I. Nagayama, "Efficient Numerical Procedures for the Hull–White Extended Vasicek Model," *Journal of Financial Engineering*, 3 (September/December 1994): 275–92.

Kijima, M., and I. Nagayama, "A Numerical Procedure for the General One-Factor Interest rate Model" *Journal of Financial Engineering*, 5 (December 1996): 317–37.

Li, A., P. Ritchken, and L. Sankarasubramanian, "Lattice Models for Pricing American Interest Rate Claims," *Journal of Finance*, 50, 2 (June 1995): 719–37.

Rebonato, R., *Interest Rate Option Models*. Chichester: Wiley, 1998.

Questions and Problems (Answers in Solutions Manual)

28.1. What is the difference between an equilibrium model and a no-arbitrage model?

28.2. Suppose that the short rate is currently 4% and its standard deviation is 1% per annum. What happens to the standard deviation when the short rate increases to 8% in (a) Vasicek's model; (b) Rendleman and Bartter's model; and (c) the Cox, Ingersoll, and Ross model?

28.3. If a stock price were mean reverting or followed a path-dependent process there would be market inefficiency. Why is there not a market inefficiency when the short-term interest rate does so?

28.4. Explain the difference between a one-factor and a two-factor interest rate model.

28.5. Can the approach described in Section 28.4 for decomposing an option on a coupon-bearing bond into a portfolio of options on zero-coupon bonds be used in conjunction with a two-factor model? Explain your answer.

28.6. Suppose that $a = 0.1$ and $b = 0.1$ in both the Vasicek and the Cox, Ingersoll, Ross model. In both models, the initial short rate is 10% and the initial standard deviation of the short-rate change in a short time Δt is $0.02\sqrt{\Delta t}$. Compare the prices given by the models for a zero-coupon bond that matures in year 10.

28.7. Suppose that $a = 0.1$, $b = 0.08$, and $\sigma = 0.015$ in Vasicek's model, with the initial value of the short rate being 5%. Calculate the price of a 1-year European call option on a zero-coupon bond with a principal of \$100 that matures in 3 years when the strike price is \$87.

28.8. Repeat Problem 28.7 valuing a European put option with a strike of \$87. What is the put–call parity relationship between the prices of European call and put options? Show that the put and call option prices satisfy put–call parity in this case.

28.9. Suppose that $a = 0.05$, $b = 0.08$, and $\sigma = 0.015$ in Vasicek's model with the initial short-term interest rate being 6%. Calculate the price of a 2.1-year European call option on a bond that will mature in 3 years. Suppose that the bond pays a coupon of 5% semiannually. The principal of the bond is 100 and the strike price of the option is 99. The strike price is the cash price (not the quoted price) that will be paid for the bond.

28.10. Use the answer to Problem 28.9 and put–call parity arguments to calculate the price of a put option that has the same terms as the call option in Problem 23.9.

28.11. In the Hull–White model, $a = 0.08$ and $\sigma = 0.01$. Calculate the price of a 1-year European call option on a zero-coupon bond that will mature in 5 years when the term structure is flat at 10%, the principal of the bond is \$100, and the strike price is \$68.

28.12. Suppose that $a = 0.05$ and $\sigma = 0.015$ in the Hull–White model with the initial term structure being flat at 6% with semiannual compounding. Calculate the price of a 2.1-year European call option on a bond that will mature in 3 years. Suppose that the bond pays a coupon of 5% per annum semiannually. The principal of the bond is 100 and the strike price of the option is 99. The strike price is the cash price (not the quoted price) that will be paid for the bond.

28.13. Use a change of numeraire argument to show that the relationship between the futures rate and forward rate for the Ho–Lee model is as shown in Section 6.4. Use the relationship to verify the expression for $\theta(t)$ given for the Ho–Lee model in equation (28.11). (*Hint*: The futures price is a martingale when the market price of risk is zero. The forward price is a martingale when the market price of risk is a zero-coupon bond maturing at the same time as the forward contract.)

28.14. Use a similar approach to that in Problem 28.13 to derive the relationship between the futures rate and the forward rate for the Hull–White model. Use the relationship to verify the expression for $\theta(t)$ given for the Hull–White model in equation (28.14).

28.15. Suppose $a = 0.05$, $\sigma = 0.015$, and the term structure is flat at 10%. Construct a trinomial tree for the Hull–White model where there are two time steps, each 1 year in length.

28.16. Calculate the price of a 2-year zero-coupon bond from the tree in Figure 28.6.

28.17. Calculate the price of a 2-year zero-coupon bond from the tree in Figure 28.9 and verify that it agrees with the initial term structure.

28.18. Calculate the price of an 18-month zero-coupon bond from the tree in Figure 28.10 and verify that it agrees with the initial term structure.

28.19. What does the calibration of a one-factor term structure model involve?

28.20. Use the DerivaGem software to value 1×4, 2×3, 3×2, and 4×1 European swap options to receive fixed and pay floating. Assume that the 1-, 2-, 3-, 4-, and 5-year interest rates are 6%, 5.5%, 6%, 6.5%, and 7%, respectively. The payment frequency on the swap is semiannual and the fixed rate is 6% per annum with semiannual compounding. Use the Hull–White model with $a = 3\%$ and $\sigma = 1\%$. Calculate the volatility implied by Black's model for each option.

28.21. Prove equations (28.25), (28.26), and (28.27).

Assignment Questions

28.22. Construct a trinomial tree for the Ho–Lee model where $\sigma = 0.02$. Suppose that the the initial zero-coupon interest rate for a maturities of 0.5, 1.0, and 1.5 years are 7.5%, 8%, and 8.5%. Use two time steps, each 6 months long. Calculate the value of a zero-coupon bond with a face value of $100 and a remaining life of 6 months at the ends of the final nodes of the tree. Use the tree to value a 1-year European put option with a strike price of 95 on the bond. Compare the price given by your tree with the analytic price given by DerivaGem.

28.23. A trader wishes to compute the price of a 1-year American call option on a 5-year bond with a face value of 100. The bond pays a coupon of 6% semiannually and the (quoted) strike price of the option is $100. The continuously compounded zero rates for maturities of 6 months, 1 year, 2 years, 3 years, 4 years, and 5 years are 4.5%, 5%, 5.5%, 5.8%, 6.1%, and 6.3%. The best-fit reversion rate for either the normal or the lognormal model has been estimated as 5%.

A 1-year European call option with a (quoted) strike price of 100 on the bond is actively traded. Its market price is $0.50. The trader decides to use this option for calibration. Use the DerivaGem software with 10 time steps to answer the following questions:

(a) Assuming a normal model, imply the σ parameter from the price of the European option.
(b) Use the σ parameter to calculate the price of the option when it is American.
(c) Repeat (a) and (b) for the lognormal model. Show that the model used does not significantly affect the price obtained providing it is calibrated to the known European price.
(d) Display the tree for the normal model and calculate the probability of a negative interest rate occurring.
(e) Display the tree for the lognormal model and verify that the option price is correctly calculated at the node where, with the notation of Section 28.7, $i = 9$ and $j = -1$.

28.24. Use the DerivaGem software to value 1×4, 2×3, 3×2, and 4×1 European swap options to receive floating and pay fixed. Assume that the 1-, 2-, 3-, 3-, and 5-year interest rates are 3%, 3.5%, 3.8%, 4.0%, and 4.1%, respectively. The payment frequency on the swap is semiannual and the fixed rate is 4% per annum with semiannual compounding. Use the lognormal model with $a = 5\%$, $\sigma = 15\%$, and 50 time steps. Calculate the volatility implied by Black's model for each option.

28.25. Verify that the DerivaGem software gives Figure 28.11 for the example considered. Use the software to calculate the price of the American bond option for the lognormal and normal models when the strike price is 95, 100, and 105. In the case of the normal model, assume that $a = 5\%$ and $\sigma = 1\%$. Discuss the results in the context of the heaviness of the tails arguments of Chapter 16.

28.26. Modify Sample Application G in the DerivaGem Application Builder software to test the convergence of the price of the trinomial tree when it is used to price a 2-year call option on a 5-year bond with a face value of 100. Suppose that the strike price (quoted) is 100, the coupon rate is 7% with coupons being paid twice a year. Assume that the zero curve is as in Table 28.2. Compare results for the following cases:
(a) Option is European; normal model with $\sigma = 0.01$ and $a = 0.05$
(b) Option is European; lognormal model with $\sigma = 0.15$ and $a = 0.05$
(c) Option is American; normal model with $\sigma = 0.01$ and $a = 0.05$
(d) Option is American; lognormal model with $\sigma = 0.15$ and $a = 0.05$

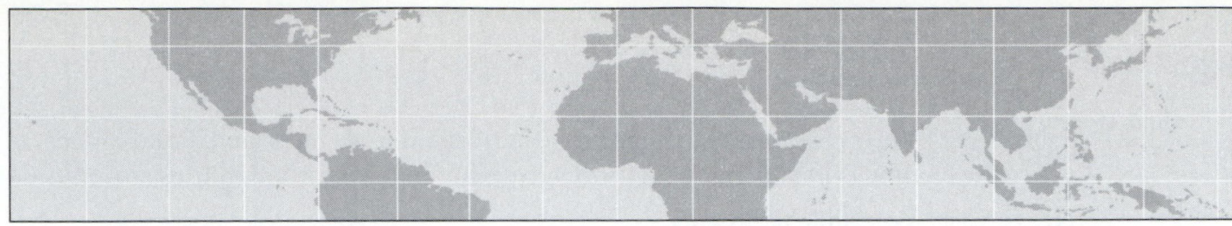

CHAPTER 29

Interest Rate Derivatives: HJM and LMM

The interest rate models discussed in Chapter 28 are widely used for pricing instruments when the simpler models in Chapter 26 are inappropriate. They are easy to implement and, if used carefully, can ensure that most nonstandard interest rate derivatives are priced consistently with actively traded instruments such as interest rate caps, European swap options, and European bond options. Two limitations of the models are:

1. Most involve only one factor (i.e., one source of uncertainty).
2. They do not give the user complete freedom in choosing the volatility structure.

By making the parameters a and σ functions of time, an analyst can use the models so that they fit the volatilities observed in the market today, but as mentioned in Section 28.8 the volatility term structure is then nonstationary. The volatility structure in the future is liable to be quite different from that observed in the market today.

This chapter discusses some general approaches to building term structure models that give the user more flexibility in specifying the volatility environment and allow several factors to be used. The models require much more computation time than the models in Chapter 28. As a result, they are often used for research and development rather than routine pricing.

This chapter also covers the mortgage-backed security market in the United States and describes how some of the ideas presented in the chapter can be used to price instruments in that market.

29.1 THE HEATH, JARROW, AND MORTON MODEL

In 1990 David Heath, Bob Jarrow, and Andy Morton (HJM) published an important paper describing the no-arbitrage conditions that must be satisfied by a model of the yield curve.[1] To describe their model, we will use the following notation:

$P(t, T)$: Price at time t of a zero-coupon bond with principal \$1 maturing at time T

[1] See D. Heath, R. A. Jarrow, and A. Morton, "Bond Pricing and the Term Structure of Interest Rates: A New Methodology," *Econometrica*, 60, 1 (1992): 77–105.

Ω_t: Vector of past and present values of interest rates and bond prices at time t that are relevant for determining bond price volatilities at that time

$v(t, T, \Omega_t)$: Volatility of $P(t, T)$

$f(t, T_1, T_2)$: Forward rate as seen at time t for the period between time T_1 and time T_2

$F(t, T)$: Instantaneous forward rate as seen at time t for a contract maturing at time T

$r(t)$: Short-term risk-free interest rate at time t

$dz(t)$: Wiener process driving term structure movements

Processes for Zero-Coupon Bond Prices and Forward Rates

We start by assuming there is just one factor and will use the traditional risk-neutral world. A zero-coupon bond is a traded security providing no income. Its return in the traditional risk-neutral world must therefore be r. This means that its stochastic process has the form

$$dP(t, T) = r(t)P(t, T)\,dt + v(t, T, \Omega_t)P(t, T)\,dz(t) \tag{29.1}$$

As the argument Ω_t indicates, the zero-coupon bond's volatility v can be, in the most general form of the model, any well-behaved function of past and present interest rates and bond prices. Because a bond's price volatility declines to zero at maturity, we must have[2]

$$v(t, t, \Omega_t) = 0$$

From equation (4.5), the forward rate $f(t, T_1, T_2)$ can be related to zero-coupon bond prices as follows:

$$f(t, T_1, T_2) = \frac{\ln[P(t, T_1)] - \ln[P(t, T_2)]}{T_2 - T_1} \tag{29.2}$$

From equation (29.1) and Itô's lemma,

$$d\ln[P(t, T_1)] = \left[r(t) - \frac{v(t, T_1, \Omega_t)^2}{2}\right]dt + v(t, T_1, \Omega_t)\,dz(t)$$

and

$$d\ln[P(t, T_2)] = \left[r(t) - \frac{v(t, T_2, \Omega_t)^2}{2}\right]dt + v(t, T_2, \Omega_t)\,dz(t)$$

so that

$$df(t, T_1, T_2) = \frac{v(t, T_2, \Omega_t)^2 - v(t, T_1, \Omega_t)^2}{2(T_2 - T_1)}\,dt + \frac{v(t, T_1, \Omega_t) - v(t, T_2, \Omega_t)}{T_2 - T_1}\,dz(t) \tag{29.3}$$

Equation (29.3) shows that the risk-neutral process for f depends solely on the v's. It depends on r and the P's only to the extent that the v's themselves depend on these variables.

[2] The $v(t, t, \Omega_t) = 0$ condition is equivalent to the assumption that all discount bonds have finite drifts at all times. If the volatility of the bond does not decline to zero at maturity, an infinite drift may be necessary to ensure that the bond's price equals its face value at maturity.

When we put $T_1 = T$ and $T_2 = T + \Delta T$ in equation (29.3) and then take limits as ΔT tends to zero, $f(t, T_1, T_2)$ becomes $F(t, T)$, the coefficient of $dz(t)$ becomes $v_T(t, T, \Omega_t)$, and the coefficient of dt becomes

$$\frac{1}{2}\frac{\partial[v(t, T, \Omega_t)^2]}{\partial T} = v(t, T, \Omega_t)\, v_T(t, T, \Omega_t)$$

where the subscript to v denotes a partial derivative. It follows that

$$dF(t, T) = v(t, T, \Omega_t)\, v_T(t, T, \Omega_t)\, dt - v_T(t, T, \Omega_t)\, dz(t) \tag{29.4}$$

Once the function $v(t, T, \Omega_t)$ has been specified, the risk-neutral processes for the $F(t, T)$'s are known.

Equation (29.4) shows that there is a link between the drift and standard deviation of an instantaneous forward rate. This is the key HJM result. Integrating $v_\tau(t, \tau, \Omega_t)$ between $\tau = t$ and $\tau = T$, we obtain

$$v(t, T, \Omega_t) - v(t, t, \Omega_t) = \int_t^T v_\tau(t, \tau, \Omega_t)\, d\tau$$

Because $v(t, t, \Omega_t) = 0$, this becomes

$$v(t, T, \Omega_t) = \int_t^T v_\tau(t, \tau, \Omega_t)\, d\tau$$

If $m(t, T, \Omega_t)$ and $s(t, T, \Omega_t)$ are the instantaneous drift and standard deviation of $F(t, T)$, so that

$$dF(t, T) = m(t, T, \Omega_t)\, dt + s(t, T, \Omega_t)\, dz$$

then it follows from equation (29.4) that

$$m(t, T, \Omega_t) = s(t, T, \Omega_t) \int_t^T s(t, \tau, \Omega_t)\, d\tau \tag{29.5}$$

This is the HJM result.

The process for the short rate r in the general HJM model is non-Markov. To understand what this means, suppose that we are at time zero and calculate the process followed by r at a future time T. We would find that the process is liable to depend on the particular path followed by the Wiener process $z(t)$ in equation (29.1) between time 0 and time t.[3]

This highlights the key problem in implementing a general HJM model. We have to use Monte Carlo simulation. Trees create difficulties. When we construct a tree representing term structure movements, it is usually nonrecombining. Assuming the model has one factor and the tree is binomial as in Figure 29.1, there are 2^n nodes after n time steps. If the model has two factors, the tree must be constructed in three dimensions and there are then 4^n nodes after n time steps. Therefore, for $n = 30$, the number of terminal nodes in a one-factor model is about 10^9; in a two-factor model, it is about 10^{18}.

[3] For more details, see Technical Note 17 on the author's website.

Figure 29.1 A nonrecombining tree such as that arising from the general HJM model.

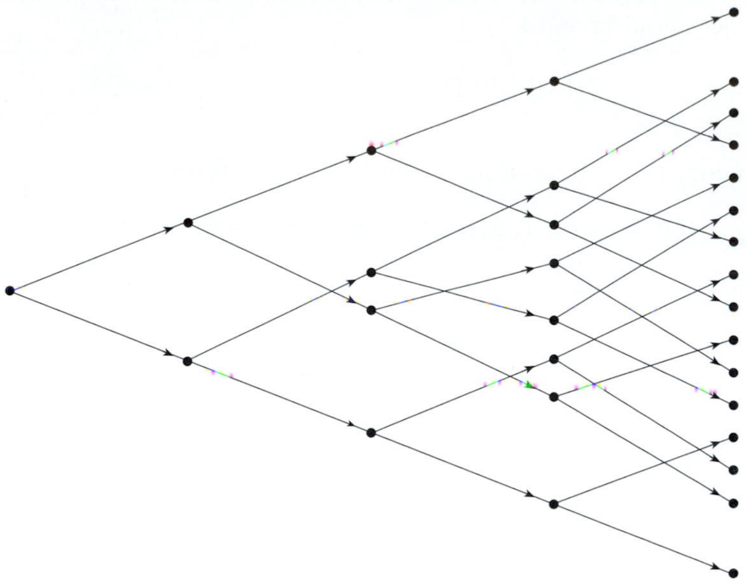

Extension to Several Factors

The HJM result can be extended to the situation where there are several independent factors. Suppose

$$dF(t, T) = m(t, T, \Omega_t)\,dt + \sum_k s_k(t, T, \Omega_t)\,dz_k$$

A similar analysis to that just given (see Problem 29.2) shows that

$$m(t, T, \Omega_t) = \sum_k s_k(t, T, \Omega_t) \int_t^T s_k(t, \tau, \Omega_t)\,d\tau \tag{29.6}$$

29.2 THE LIBOR MARKET MODEL

One drawback of the HJM model is that it is expressed in terms of instantaneous forward rates and these are not directly observable in the market. Another drawback is that it is difficult to calibrate the model to prices of actively traded instruments. This has led Brace, Gatarek, and Musiela (BGM), Jamshidian, and Miltersen, Sandmann, and Sondermann to propose an alternative.[4] It is known as the *LIBOR market model* (LMM) or the *BGM model* and it is expressed in terms of the forward rates that traders are used to working with.

[4] See A. Brace, D. Gatarek, and M. Musiela "The Market Model of Interest Rate Dynamics," *Mathematical Finance* 7, 2 (1997): 127–55; F. Jamshidian, "LIBOR and Swap Market Models and Measures," *Finance and Stochastics*, 1 (1997): 293–330; and K. Miltersen, K. Sandmann, and D. Sondermann, "Closed Form Solutions for Term Structure Derivatives with LogNormal Interest Rate," *Journal of Finance*, 52, 1 (March 1997): 409–30.

The Model

Define $t_0 = 0$ and let $t_1, t_2, \ldots$ be the reset times for caps that trade in the market today. In the United States, the most popular caps have quarterly resets, so that it is approximately true that $t_1 = 0.25$, $t_2 = 0.5$, $t_3 = 0.75$, and so on. Define $\delta_k = t_{k+1} - t_k$, and

- $F_k(t)$: Forward rate between times t_k and t_{k+1} as seen at time t, expressed with a compounding period of δ_k and an actual/actual day count
- $m(t)$: Index for the next reset date at time t; this means that $m(t)$ is the smallest integer such that $t \leqslant t_{m(t)}$
- $\zeta_k(t)$: Volatility of $F_k(t)$ at time t
- $v_k(t)$: Volatility of the zero-coupon bond price $P(t, t_k)$ at time t

Initially, we will assume that there is only one factor. As shown in Section 25.4, in a world that is forward risk neutral with respect to $P(t, t_{k+1})$, $F_k(t)$ is a martingale and follows the process

$$dF_k(t) = \zeta_k(t)F_k(t)\,dz \tag{29.7}$$

where dz is a Wiener process.

In practice, it is often most convenient to value interest rate derivatives by working in a world that is always forward risk neutral with respect to a bond maturing at the next reset date. We refer to this as a *rolling forward risk-neutral world.*[5] In this world we can discount from time t_{k+1} to time t_k using the zero rate observed at time t_k for a maturity t_{k+1}. We do not have to worry about what happens to interest rates between times t_k and t_{k+1}.

At time t the rolling forward risk-neutral world is a world that is forward risk neutral with respect to the bond price, $P[t, t_{m(t)}]$. Equation (29.7) gives the process followed by $F_k(t)$ in a world that is forward risk neutral with respect to $P(t, t_{k+1})$. From Section 25.7, it follows that the process followed by $F_k(t)$ in the rolling forward risk-neutral world is

$$dF_k(t) = \zeta_k(t)[v_{m(t)}(t) - v_{k+1}(t)]F_k(t)\,dt + \zeta_k(t)F_k(t)\,dz \tag{29.8}$$

The relationship between forward rates and bond prices is

$$\frac{P(t, t_i)}{P(t, t_{i+1})} = 1 + \delta_i F_i(t)$$

or

$$\ln P(t, t_i) - \ln P(t, t_{i+1}) = \ln[1 + \delta_i F_i(t)]$$

Using Itô's lemma we can calculate the process followed the left-hand side and the right-hand side of this equation. Equating the coefficients of dz, we obtain

$$v_i(t) - v_{i+1}(t) = \frac{\delta_i F_i(t)\zeta_i(t)}{1 + \delta_i F_i(t)} \tag{29.9}$$

---

[5] In the terminology of Section 25.4, this world corresponds to using a "rolling CD" as the numeraire. A rolling CD (certificate of deposit) is one where we start with \$1, buy a bond maturing at time t_1, reinvest the proceeds at time t_1 in a bond maturing at time t_2, reinvest the proceeds at time t_2 in a bond maturing at time t_3, and so on. Strictly speaking, the interest rate trees we constructed in Chapter 28 are in a rolling forward risk-neutral world rather than the traditional risk-neutral world. The numeraire is a CD rolled over at the end of each time step.

so that from equation (29.8) the process followed by $F_k(t)$ in the rolling forward risk-neutral world is

$$\frac{dF_k(t)}{F_k(t)} = \sum_{i=m(t)}^{k} \frac{\delta_i F_i(t)\zeta_i(t)\zeta_k(t)}{1+\delta_i F_i(t)}\, dt + \zeta_k(t)\, dz \tag{29.10}$$

The HJM result in equation (29.4) is the limiting case of this as the δ_i tend to zero (see Problem 29.7).

Forward Rate Volatilities

We now simplify the model by assuming that $\zeta_k(t)$ is a function only of the number of whole accrual periods between the next reset date and time t_k. Define Λ_i as the value of $\zeta_k(t)$ when there are i such accrual periods. This means that $\zeta_k(t) = \Lambda_{k-m(t)}$ is a step function.

The Λ_i can (at least in theory) be estimated from the volatilities used to value caplets in Black's model (i.e., from the spot volatilities in Figure 26.3).[6] Suppose that σ_k is the Black volatility for the caplet that corresponds to the period between times t_k and t_{k+1}. Equating variances, we must have

$$\sigma_k^2 t_k = \sum_{i=1}^{k} \Lambda_{k-i}^2\, \delta_{i-1} \tag{29.11}$$

This equation can be used to obtain the Λ's iteratively.

Example 29.1

Assume that the δ_i are all equal and the Black caplet spot volatilities for the first three caplets are 24%, 22%, and 20%. This means that $\Lambda_0 = 24\%$. Since

$$\Lambda_0^2 + \Lambda_1^2 = 2 \times 0.22^2$$

Λ_1 is 19.80%. Also, since

$$\Lambda_0^2 + \Lambda_1^2 + \Lambda_2^2 = 3 \times 0.20^2$$

Λ_2 is 15.23%.

Example 29.2

Consider the data in Table 29.1 on caplet volatilities σ_k. These exhibit the hump discussed in Section 26.3. The Λ's are shown in the second row. Notice that the hump in the Λ's is more pronounced than the hump in the σ's.

Table 29.1 Volatility data; accrual period = 1 year.

Year, k:	*1*	*2*	*3*	*4*	*5*	*6*	*7*	*8*	*9*	*10*
σ_k (%):	15.50	18.25	17.91	17.74	17.27	16.79	16.30	16.01	15.76	15.54
Λ_{k-1} (%):	15.50	20.64	17.21	17.22	15.25	14.15	12.98	13.81	13.60	13.40

[6] In practice the Λ's are determined using a least-squares calibration that we will discuss later.

Implementation of the Model

The LIBOR market model can be implemented using Monte Carlo simulation. Expressed in terms of the Λ_i's, equation (29.10) is

$$\frac{dF_k(t)}{F_k(t)} = \sum_{i=m(t)}^{k} \frac{\delta_i F_i(t)\Lambda_{i-m(t)}\Lambda_{k-m(t)}}{1+\delta_i F_i(t)}\,dt + \Lambda_{k-m(t)}\,dz \tag{29.12}$$

or

$$d\ln F_k(t) = \left[\sum_{i=m(t)}^{k} \frac{\delta_i F_i(t)\Lambda_{i-m(t)}\Lambda_{k-m(t)}}{1+\delta_i F_i(t)} - \frac{(\Lambda_{k-m(t)})^2}{2}\right]dt + \Lambda_{k-m(t)}\,dz \tag{29.13}$$

If, as an approximation, we assume in the calculation of the drift of $\ln F_k(t)$ that $F_i(t) = F_i(t_j)$ for $t_j < t < t_{j+1}$, then

$$F_k(t_{j+1}) = F_k(t_j)\exp\left[\left(\sum_{i=j+1}^{k} \frac{\delta_i F_i(t_j)\Lambda_{i-j-1}\Lambda_{k-j-1}}{1+\delta_i F_i(t_j)} - \frac{\Lambda_{k-j-1}^2}{2}\right)\delta_j + \Lambda_{k-j-1}\epsilon\sqrt{\delta_j}\right] \tag{29.14}$$

where ϵ is a random sample from a normal distribution with mean equal to zero and standard deviation equal to one.

Extension to Several Factors

The LIBOR market model can be extended to incorporate several independent factors. Suppose that there are p factors and $\zeta_{k,q}$ is the component of the volatility of $F_k(t)$ attributable to the qth factor. Equation (29.10) becomes (see Problem 29.11)

$$\frac{dF_k(t)}{F_k(t)} = \sum_{i=m(t)}^{k} \frac{\delta_i F_i(t)\sum_{q=1}^{p}\zeta_{i,q}(t)\zeta_{k,q}(t)}{1+\delta_i F_i(t)}\,dt + \sum_{q=1}^{p}\zeta_{k,q}(t)\,dz_q \tag{29.15}$$

Define $\lambda_{i,q}$ as the qth component of the volatility when there are i accrual periods between the next reset date and the maturity of the forward contract. Equation (29.14) then becomes

$$F_k(t_{j+1}) = F_k(t_j)\exp\left[\left(\sum_{i=j+1}^{k} \frac{\delta_i F_i(t_j)\sum_{q=1}^{p}\lambda_{i-j-1,q}\lambda_{k-j-1,q}}{1+\delta_i F_i(t_j)} - \frac{\sum_{q=1}^{p}\lambda_{k-j-1,q}^2}{2}\right)\delta_j + \sum_{q=1}^{p}\lambda_{k-j-1,q}\,\epsilon_q\sqrt{\delta_j}\right] \tag{29.16}$$

where the ϵ_q are random samples from a normal distribution with mean equal to zero and standard deviation equal to one.

The approximation that the drift of a forward rate remains constant within each accrual period allows us to jump from one reset date to the next in the simulation. This is convenient because as already mentioned the rolling forward risk-neutral world allows us to discount from one reset date to the next. Suppose that we wish to simulate a zero curve for N accrual periods. On each trial we start with the forward rates at time zero. These are $F_0(0), F_1(0), \dots, F_{N-1}(0)$ and are calculated from the initial zero curve. We use equation (29.16) to calculate $F_1(t_1), F_2(t_1), \dots, F_{N-1}(t_1)$. We then use equation (29.16) again to calculate $F_2(t_2), F_3(t_2), \dots, F_{N-1}(t_2)$; and so on until $F_{N-1}(t_{N-1})$ is obtained. Note that as we move through time the zero curve gets shorter and shorter. For example, suppose each accrual period is 3 months and $N = 40$. We start with a 10-year zero curve. At the 6-year point (at time t_{24}), the simulation gives us information on a 4-year zero curve.

We can test the drift approximation by valuing caplets using equation (29.16) and comparing the prices to those given by Black's model. The value of $F_k(t_k)$ is the realized rate for the time period between t_k and t_{k+1} and enables the caplet payoff at time t_{k+1} to be calculated. This payoff is discounted back to time zero, one accrual period at a time. The caplet value is the average of the discounted payoffs. The results of this type of analysis show that the cap values from Monte Carlo simulation are not significantly different from those given by Black's model. This is true even when the accrual periods are 1 year in length and a very large number of trials is used.[7] This suggests that the drift assumption is innocuous in most situations.

Ratchet Caps, Sticky Caps, and Flexi Caps

The LIBOR market model can be used to value some types of nonstandard caps. Consider ratchet caps and sticky caps. These incorporate rules for determining how the cap rate for each caplet is set. In a *ratchet cap* it equals the LIBOR rate at the previous reset date plus a spread. In a *sticky cap* it equals the previous capped rate plus a spread. Suppose that the cap rate at time t_j is K_j, the LIBOR rate at time t_j is R_j, and the spread is s. In a ratchet cap, $K_{j+1} = R_j + s$. In a sticky cap, $K_{j+1} = \min(R_j, K_j) + s$.

Tables 29.2 and 29.3 provides valuations of a ratchet cap and sticky cap using the LIBOR market model with one, two, and three factors. The principal is \$100. The term

Table 29.2 Valuation of ratchet caplets.

Caplet start time (years)	*One factor*	*Two factors*	*Three factors*
1	0.196	0.194	0.195
2	0.207	0.207	0.209
3	0.201	0.205	0.210
4	0.194	0.198	0.205
5	0.187	0.193	0.201
6	0.180	0.189	0.193
7	0.172	0.180	0.188
8	0.167	0.174	0.182
9	0.160	0.168	0.175
10	0.153	0.162	0.169

[7] See J. C. Hull and A. White, "Forward Rate Volatilities, Swap Rate Volatilities, and the Implementation of the LIBOR Market Model," *Journal of Fixed Income*, 10, 2 (September 2000): 46–62. The only exception is when the cap volatilities are very high.

Table 29.3 Valuation of sticky caplets.

Caplet start time (years)	*One factor*	*Two factors*	*Three factors*
1	0.196	0.194	0.195
2	0.336	0.334	0.336
3	0.412	0.413	0.418
4	0.458	0.462	0.472
5	0.484	0.492	0.506
6	0.498	0.512	0.524
7	0.502	0.520	0.533
8	0.501	0.523	0.537
9	0.497	0.523	0.537
10	0.488	0.519	0.534

structure is assumed to be flat at 5% per annum and the caplet volatilities are as in Table 29.1. The interest rate is reset annually. The spread is 25 basis points. Tables 29.4 and 29.5 show how the volatility was split into components when two- and three-factor models were used. The results are based on 100,000 Monte Carlo simulations incorporating the antithetic variable technique described in Section 17.7. The standard error of each price is about 0.001.

A third type of nonstandard cap is a *flexi cap*. This is like a regular cap except that there is a limit on the total number of caplets that can be exercised. Consider an annual-pay flexi cap when the principal is \$100, the term structure is flat at 5%, and the cap volatilities are as in Tables 29.1, 29.4, and 29.5. Suppose that all in-the-money caplets are exercised up to a maximum of five. With one, two, and three factors, the LIBOR market model gives the price of the instrument as 3.43, 3.58, and 3.61, respectively (see Problem 29.15 for other types of flexi caps).

The pricing of a plain vanilla cap depends only on the total volatility and is independent of the number of factors. This is because the price of a plain vanilla caplet depends the behavior of only one forward rate. The prices of caplets in the nonstandard instruments we have looked at are different in that they depend on the joint probability distribution of several different forward rates. As a result they do depend on the number of factors.

Table 29.4 Volatility components in two-factor model.

Year, k:	*1*	*2*	*3*	*4*	*5*	*6*	*7*	*8*	*9*	*10*
$\lambda_{k-1,1}$ (%):	14.10	19.52	16.78	17.11	15.25	14.06	12.65	13.06	12.36	11.63
$\lambda_{k-1,2}$ (%):	−6.45	−6.70	−3.84	−1.96	0.00	1.61	2.89	4.48	5.65	6.65
Total volatility (%):	15.50	20.64	17.21	17.22	15.25	14.15	12.98	13.81	13.60	13.40

Table 29.5 Volatility components in a three-factor model.

Year, k:	*1*	*2*	*3*	*4*	*5*	*6*	*7*	*8*	*9*	*10*
$\lambda_{k-1,1}$ (%):	13.65	19.28	16.72	16.98	14.85	13.95	12.61	12.90	11.97	10.97
$\lambda_{k-1,2}$ (%):	−6.62	−7.02	−4.06	−2.06	0.00	1.69	3.06	4.70	5.81	6.66
$\lambda_{k-1,3}$ (%):	3.19	2.25	0.00	−1.98	−3.47	−1.63	0.00	1.51	2.80	3.84
Total volatility (%):	15.50	20.64	17.21	17.22	15.25	14.15	12.98	13.81	13.60	13.40

Valuing European Swap Options

As shown by Hull and White, there is an analytic approximation for valuing European swap options in the LIBOR market model.[8] Let T_0 be the maturity of the swap option and assume that the payment dates for the swap are $T_1, T_2, \ldots, T_N$. Define $\tau_i = T_{i+1} - T_i$. From equation (25.23), the swap rate at time t is given by

$$s(t) = \frac{P(t, T_0) - P(t, T_N)}{\sum_{i=0}^{N-1} \tau_i P(t, T_{i+1})}$$

It is also true that

$$\frac{P(t, T_i)}{P(t, T_0)} = \prod_{j=0}^{i-1} \frac{1}{1 + \tau_j G_j(t)}$$

for $1 \leqslant i \leqslant N$, where $G_j(t)$ is the forward rate at time t for the period between T_j and T_{j+1}. These two equations together define a relationship between $s(t)$ and the $G_j(t)$. Applying Itô's lemma (see Problem 29.12), the variance $V(t)$ of the swap rate $s(t)$ is given by

$$V(t) = \sum_{q=1}^{p} \left[\sum_{k=0}^{N-1} \frac{\tau_k \beta_{k,q}(t) G_k(t) \gamma_k(t)}{1 + \tau_k G_k(t)} \right]^2 \tag{29.17}$$

where

$$\gamma_k(t) = \frac{\prod_{j=0}^{N-1} [1 + \tau_j G_j(t)]}{\prod_{j=0}^{N-1} [1 + \tau_j G_j(t)] - 1} - \frac{\sum_{i=0}^{k-1} \tau_i \prod_{j=i+1}^{N-1} [1 + \tau_j G_j(t)]}{\sum_{i=0}^{N-1} \tau_i \prod_{j=i+1}^{N} [1 + \tau_j G_j(t)]}$$

and $\beta_{j,q}(t)$ is the qth component of the volatility of $G_j(t)$. We approximate $V(t)$ by setting $G_j(t) = G_j(0)$ for all j and t. The swap volatility that is substituted into the

[8] See J. C. Hull and A. White, "Forward Rate Volatilities, Swap Rate Volatilities, and the Implementation of the LIBOR Market Model," *Journal of Fixed Income*, 10, 2 (September 2000): 46–62. Other analytic approximations have been suggested by A. Brace, D. Gatarek, and M. Musiela "The Market Model of Interest Rate Dynamics," *Mathematical Finance*, 7, 2 (1997): 127–55 and L. Andersen and J. Andreasen, "Volatility Skews and Extensions of the LIBOR Market Model," *Applied Mathematical Finance*, 7, 1 (March 2000), 1–32.

standard market model for valuing a swaption is then

$$\sqrt{\frac{1}{T_0}\int_{t=0}^{T_0} V(t)\, dt}$$

or

$$\sqrt{\frac{1}{T_0}\int_{t=0}^{T_0} \sum_{q=1}^{p}\left[\sum_{k=0}^{N-1} \frac{\tau_k \beta_{k,q}(t) G_k(0)\gamma_k(0)}{1+\tau_k G_k(0)}\right]^2 dt} \tag{29.18}$$

In the situation where the length of the accrual period for swap underlying the swaption is the same as the length of the accrual period for a cap, $\beta_{k,q}(t)$ is the qth component of volatility of a cap forward rate when the time to maturity is $T_k - t$. This can be looked up in a table such as Table 29.5

The accrual periods for the swaps underlying broker quotes for European swap options do not always match the accrual periods for the caps and floors underlying broker quotes. For example, in the United States, the benchmark caps and floors have quarterly resets, while the swaps underlying the benchmark European swap options have semiannual resets on the fixed side. Fortunately, the valuation result for European swap options can be extended to the situation where each swap accrual period includes M subperiods that could be accrual periods in a typical cap. Define $\tau_{j,m}$ as the length of the mth subperiod in the jth accrual period so that

$$\tau_j = \sum_{m=1}^{M} \tau_{j,m}$$

Define $G_{j,m}(t)$ as the forward rate observed at time t for the $\tau_{j,m}$ accrual period. Because

$$1 + \tau_j G_j(t) = \prod_{m=1}^{M} [1 + \tau_{j,m} G_{j,m}(t)]$$

we can modify the analysis leading to equation (29.18) so that the volatility of $s(t)$ is obtained in terms of the volatilities of the $G_{j,m}(t)$ rather than the volatilities of the $G_j(t)$. The swap volatility to be substituted into the standard market model for valuing a swap option proves to be (see Problem 29.13)

$$\sqrt{\frac{1}{T_0}\int_{t=0}^{T_0} \sum_{q=1}^{p}\left[\sum_{k=n}^{N-1}\sum_{m=1}^{M} \frac{\tau_{k,m} \beta_{k,m,q}(t) G_{k,m}(0)\gamma_k(0)}{1+\tau_{k,m} G_{k,m}(0)}\right]^2 dt} \tag{29.19}$$

Here $\beta_{j,m,q}(t)$ is the qth component of the volatility of $G_{j,m}(t)$. It is the qth component of the volatility of a cap forward rate when the time to maturity is from t to the beginning of the mth subperiod in the (T_j, T_{j+1}) swap accrual period.

The expressions in equations (29.18) and (29.19) for the swap volatility do involve the approximations that $G_j(t) = G_j(0)$ and $G_{j,m}(t) = G_{j,m}(0)$. Hull and White compared the prices of European swap options calculated using equations (29.18) and (29.19) with the prices calculated from a Monte Carlo simulation and found the two to be very close. Once the LIBOR market model has been calibrated, equations (29.18) and (29.19) therefore provide a quick way of valuing European swap options. Analysts can determine whether European swap options are overpriced or underpriced relative to caps. As we will see shortly, they can also use the results to calibrate the model to the market prices of swap options.

Calibrating the Model

To calibrate the LIBOR market model, we must determine the Λ_j and how they are split into $\lambda_{j,q}$. The first step is usually to use a principal components analysis such as that in Section 18.9 to determine the way the Λ's are split into λ's. The principal components model is

$$\Delta F_j = \sum_{q=1}^{M} \alpha_{j,q} x_q$$

where M is the total number of factors, ΔF_j is the change in the forward rate for a forward contract maturing in j accrual periods, $\alpha_{j,q}$ is the factor loading for the jth forward rate and the qth factor, x_q is the factor score for the qth factor, and

$$\sum_{j=1}^{M} \alpha_{j,q_1} \alpha_{j,q_2}$$

equals 1 when $q_1 = q_2$ and 0 when $q_1 \neq q_2$. Define s_q as the standard deviation of the qth factor score. If the number of factors used in the LIBOR market model, p, is equal to the total number of factors, M, it is correct to set

$$\lambda_{j,q} = \alpha_{j,q}\, s_q$$

for $1 \leqslant j,q \leqslant M$. When $p < M$, the $\lambda_{j,q}$ must be scaled so that

$$\Lambda_j = \sqrt{\sum\nolimits_{q=1}^{p} \lambda_{j,q}^2}$$

This involves setting

$$\lambda_{j,q} = \frac{\Lambda_j\, s_q\, \alpha_{j,q}}{\sqrt{\sum\nolimits_{q=1}^{p} s_q^2\, \alpha_{i,q}^2}} \qquad \textbf{(29.20)}$$

Equation (29.11) provides one way to determine the Λ's so that they are consistent with caplet prices. In practice it is not usually used because it often leads to wild swings in the Λ's.[9] Also, although the LIBOR market model is designed to be consistent with the prices of caplets, analysts sometimes like to calibrate it to European swaptions.

The most commonly used calibration procedure for the LIBOR market model is similar to that described for one-factor models in Section 28.8. Suppose that U_i is the market price of the ith calibrating instrument and V_i is the model price. We choose the Λ's to minimize

$$\sum_i (U_i - V_i)^2 + P$$

[9] Sometimes there is no set of Λ's consistent with a set of cap quotes.

where P is a penalty function chosen to ensure that the Λ's are "well behaved". Similarly to Section 28.8, P has the form

$$P = \sum_i w_{1,i}(\Lambda_{i+1} - \Lambda_i)^2 + \sum_i w_{2,i}(\Lambda_{i+1} + \Lambda_{i-1} - 2\Lambda_i)^2$$

When some calibrating instruments are European swaptions the formulas in equations (29.18) and (29.19) make the minimization feasible using the Levenberg–Marquardt procedure. Equation (29.20) is used to determine the λ's from the Λ's.

Volatility Skews

Brokers provide quotes on caps that are not at the money as well as on caps that are at the money. In some markets a volatility skew is observed, that is, the quoted (Black) volatility for a cap or a floor is a declining function of the strike price. This can be handled using the CEV model. (See Section 24.1 for the application of the CEV model to equities.) The model is

$$dF_i(t) = \cdots + \sum_{q=1}^{p} \zeta_{i,q}(t) F_i(t)^{\alpha}\, dz_q \tag{29.21}$$

where α is a constant ($0 < \alpha < 1$). It turns out that this model can be handled very similarly to the lognormal model. Caps and floors can be valued analytically using the cumulative noncentral χ^2 distribution. There are similar analytic approximations to those given above for the prices of European swap options.[10]

Bermudan Swap Options

A popular interest rate derivative is a Bermudan swap option. This is a swap option that can be exercised on some or all of the payment dates of the underlying swap. Bermudan swap options are difficult to value using the LIBOR market model because the LIBOR market model relies on Monte Carlo simulation and it is difficult to evaluate early exercise decisions when Monte Carlo simulation is used. Fortunately, the procedures described in Section 24.7 can be used. Longstaff and Schwartz apply the least-squares approach when there are a large number of factors. The value of not exercising on a particular payment date is assumed to be a polynomial function of the values of the factors.[11] Andersen shows that the optimal early exercise boundary approach can be used. He experiments with a number of ways of parameterizing the early exercise boundary and finds that good results are obtained when the early exercise decision is assumed to depend only on the intrinsic value of the option.[12]. Most traders value Bermudan options using one of the one-factor no-arbitrage models discussed in

[10] For details, see L. Andersen and J. Andreasen, "Volatility Skews and Extensions of the LIBOR Market Model," *Applied Mathematical Finance*, 7, 1 (2000): 1–32; J.C. Hull and A. White, "Forward Rate Volatilities, Swap Rate Volatilities, and the Implementation of the LIBOR Market Model," *Journal of Fixed Income*, 10, 2 (September 2000): 46–62.

[11] See F.A. Longstaff and E.S. Schwartz, "Valuing American Options by Simulation: A Simple Least Squares Approach," *Review of Financial Studies*, 14, 1 (2001): 113–47.

[12] L. Andersen, "A simple Approach to the Pricing of Bermudan Swaptions in the Multifactor LIBOR Market Model," *Journal of Computational Finance*, 3, 2 (Winter 2000): 5–32.

Chapter 28. However, the accuracy of one-factor models for pricing Bermudan swap options has become a controversial issue.[13]

29.3 MORTGAGE-BACKED SECURITIES

One application of the models presented in this chapter is to the mortgage-backed security (MBS) market in the United States. A mortgage-backed security is created when a financial institution decides to sell part of its residential mortgage portfolio to investors. The mortgages sold are put into a pool and investors acquire a stake in the pool by buying units. The units are known as mortgage-backed securities. A secondary market is usually created for the units so that investors can sell them to other investors as desired. An investor who owns units representing $X\%$ of a certain pool is entitled to $X\%$ of the principal and interest cash flows received from the mortgages in the pool.

The mortgages in a pool are generally guaranteed by a government-related agency such as the Government National Mortgage Association (GNMA) or the Federal National Mortgage Association (FNMA) so that investors are protected against defaults. This makes an MBS sound like a regular fixed-income security issued by the government. In fact, there is a critical difference between an MBS and a regular fixed-income investment. This difference is that the mortgages in an MBS pool have prepayment privileges. These prepayment privileges can be quite valuable to the householder. In the United States, mortgages typically last for 25 years and can be prepaid at any time. This means that the householder has a 25-year American-style option to put the mortgage back to the lender at its face value.

In practice, prepayments on mortgages occur for a variety of reasons. Sometimes interest rates fall and the owner of the house decides to refinance at a lower rate. On other occasions, a mortgage is prepaid simply because the house is being sold. A critical element in valuing an MBS is the determination of what is known as the *prepayment function*. This is a function describing expected prepayments on the underlying pool of mortgages at a time t in terms of the yield curve at time t and other relevant variables.

A prepayment function is very unreliable as a predictor of actual prepayment experience for an individual mortgage. When many similar mortgage loans are combined in the same pool, there is a "law of large numbers" effect at work and prepayments can be predicted more accurately from an analysis of historical data. As mentioned, prepayments are not always motivated by pure interest rate considerations. Nevertheless, there is a tendency for prepayments to be more likely when interest rates are low than when they are high. This means that investors require a higher rate of interest on an MBS than on other fixed-income securities to compensate for the prepayment options they have written.

Collateralized Mortgage Obligations

The MBSs we have described so far are sometimes referred to as *pass-throughs*. All investors receive the same return and bear the same prepayment risk. Not all mortgage-

[13] For opposing viewpoints, see "Factor Dependence of Bermudan Swaptions: Fact or Fiction," by L. Andersen and J. Andreasen, and "Throwing Away a Billion Dollars: The Cost of Suboptimal Exercise Strategies in the Swaption Market," by F. A. Longstaff, P. Santa-Clara, and E. S. Schwartz. Both articles are in *Journal of Financial Economics*, 62, 1 (October 2001).

Business Snapshot 29.1 IOs and POs

In what is known as a *stripped MBS*, principal payments are separated from interest payments. All principal payments are channeled to one class of security, known as a *principal only* (PO). All interest payments are channeled to another class of security known as an *interest only* (IO). Both IOs and POs are risky investments. As prepayment rates increase, a PO becomes more valuable and an IO becomes less valuable. As prepayment rates decrease, the reverse happens. In a PO, a fixed amount of principal is returned to the investor, but the timing is uncertain. A high rate of prepayments on the underlying pool leads to the principal being received early (which is, of course, good news for the holder of the PO). A low rate of prepayments on the underlying pool delays the return of the principal and reduces the yield provided by the PO. In the case of an IO, the total of the cash flows received by the investor is uncertain. The higher the rate of prepayments, the lower the total cash flows received by the investor, and vice versa.

backed securities work in this way. In a *collateralized mortgage obligation* (CMO) the investors are divided into a number of classes and rules are developed for determining how principal repayments are channeled to different classes.

As an example of a CMO, consider an MBS where investors are divided into three classes: class A, class B, and class C. All the principal repayments (both those that are scheduled and those that are prepayments) are channeled to class A investors until investors in this class have been completely paid off. Principal repayments are then channeled to class B investors until these investors have been completely paid off. Finally, principal repayments are channeled to class C investors. In this situation, class A investors bear the most prepayment risk. The class A securities can be expected to last for a shorter time than the class B securities, and these, in turn, can be expected to last less long than the class C securities.

The objective of this type of structure is to create classes of securities that are more attractive to institutional investors than those created by the simpler pass-through MBS. The prepayment risks assumed by the different classes depend on the par value in each class. For example, class C bears very little prepayment risk if the par values in classes A, B, and C are 400, 300, and 100, respectively. Class C bears rather more prepayment risk in the situation where the par values in the classes are 100, 200, and 500.

The creators of mortgage-backed securities have created many more exotic structures than the one we have just described. Business Snapshot 29.1 gives an example.

Valuing Mortgage-Backed Securities

Mortgage-backed securities are usually valued using Monte Carlo simulation. Either the HJM or LIBOR market models can be used to simulate the behavior of interest rates month by month throughout the life of an MBS. Consider what happens on one simulation trial. Each month, expected prepayments are calculated from the current yield curve and the history of yield curve movements. These prepayments determine the expected cash flows to the holder of the MBS and the cash flows are discounted to time zero to obtain a sample value for the MBS. An estimate of the value of the MBS is the average of the sample values over many simulation trials.

Option-Adjusted Spread

In addition to calculating theoretical prices for mortgage-backed securities and other bonds with embedded options, traders also like to compute what is known as the *option-adjusted spread* (OAS). This is a measure of the spread over the yields on government Treasury bonds provided by the instrument when all options have been taken into account.

An input to any term structure model is the initial zero-coupon yield curve. Usually this is the LIBOR zero curve. However, to calculate an OAS for an instrument, we first price it using the zero-coupon government Treasury curve. The price of the instrument given by the model is compared to the price in the market. A series of iterations is then used to determine the parallel shift to the input Treasury curve that causes the model price to be equal to the market price. This parallel shift is the OAS.

To illustrate the nature of the calculations, suppose that the market price is \$102.00 and that the price calculated using the Treasury curve is \$103.27. As a first trial we might choose to try a 60-basis-point parallel shift to the Treasury zero curve. Suppose that this gives a price of \$101.20 for the instrument. This is less than the market price of \$102.00 and means that a parallel shift somewhere between 0 and 60 basis points will lead to the model price being equal to the market price. We could use linear interpolation to calculate

$$60 \times \frac{103.27 - 102.00}{103.27 - 101.20} = 36.81$$

or 36.81 basis points as the next trial shift. Suppose that this gives a price of \$101.95. This indicates that the OAS is slightly less than 36.81 basis points. Linear interpolation suggests that the next trial shift be

$$36.81 \times \frac{103.27 - 102.00}{103.27 - 101.95} = 35.41$$

or 35.41 basis points; and so on.

SUMMARY

The HJM and LMM models provide approaches to valuing interest rate derivatives that give the user complete freedom in choosing the volatility term structure. The LMM model has two key advantages over the HJM model. First, it is developed in terms of the forward rates that determine the pricing of caps, rather than in terms of instantaneous forward rates. Second, it is relatively easy to calibrate to the price of caps or European swap options. The HJM and LMM models both have the disadvantage that they cannot be represented as recombining trees. In practice, this means that they must be implemented using Monte Carlo simulation.

The mortgage-backed security market in the United States has given birth to many exotic interest rate derivatives: CMOs, IOs, POs, and so on. These instruments provide cash flows to the holder that depend on the prepayments on a pool of mortgages. These prepayments depend on, among other things, the level of interest rates. Because they are heavily path dependent, mortgage-backed securities usually have to be valued using

Monte Carlo simulation. These are, therefore, ideal candidates for applications of the HJM and LMM models.

FURTHER READING

Amin, K., and A. Morton, "Implied Volatility Functions in Arbitrage-Free Term Structure Models," *Journal of Financial Economics*, 35 (1994): 141–80.

Andersen, L., "A Simple Approach to the Pricing of Bermudan Swaption in the Multi-Factor LIBOR Market Model," *The Journal of Computational Finance*, 3, 2 (2000): 5–32.

Andersen, L., and J. Andreasen, "Volatility Skews and Extensions of the LIBOR Market Model," *Applied Mathematical Finance*, 7, 1 (March 2000): 1–32.

Brace A., D. Gatarek, and M. Musiela "The Market Model of Interest Rate Dynamics," *Mathematical Finance*, 7, 2 (1997): 127–55.

Buhler, W., M. Ulrig-Homberg, U. Walter, and T. Weber, "An Empirical Comparison of Forward and Spot-Rate Models for Valuing Interest Rate Options," *Journal of Finance*, 54, 1 (February 1999): 269–305.

Carverhill, A., "When is the Short Rate Markovian," *Mathematical Finance*, 4 (1994): 305–12.

Cheyette, O., "Term Structure Dynamics and Mortgage Valuation," *Journal of Fixed Income*, (March 1992): 28–41.

Duffie, D. and R. Kan, "A Yield-Factor Model of Interest Rates," *Mathematical Finance* 6, 4 (1996), 379–406.

Heath, D., R. Jarrow, and A. Morton, "Bond Pricing and the Term Structure of Interest Rates: A Discrete Time Approximation," *Journal of Financial and Quantitative Analysis*, 25, 4 (December 1990): 419–40.

Heath, D., R. Jarrow, and A. Morton, "Bond Pricing and the Term Structure of the Interest Rates: A New Methodology," *Econometrica*, 60, 1 (1992): 77–105.

Hull, J., and A. White, "Forward Rate Volatilities, Swap Rate Volatilities, and the Implementation of the LIBOR Market Model," *Journal of Fixed Income*, 10, 2 (September 2000): 46–62.

Inui, K., and M. Kijima, "A Markovian Framework in Multifactor Heath, Jarrow, and Morton Models," *Journal of Financial and Quantitative Analysis*, 33, 3 (September 1998): 423–40.

Jamshidian, F., "LIBOR and Swap Market Models and Measures," *Finance and Stochastics*, 1 (1977): 293–330.

Jarrow, R. A., *Modeling Fixed Income Securities and Interest Rate Options*. New York: McGraw-Hill, 1995.

Jarrow, R. A., and S. M. Turnbull, "Delta, Gamma, and Bucket Hedging of Interest Rate Derivatives," *Applied Mathematical Finance*, 1 (1994): 21–48.

Jeffrey, A., "Single Factor Heath-Jarrow-Morton Term Structure Models Based on Markov Spot Interest Rate Dynamics," *Journal of Financial and Quantitative Analysis*, 30 (1995): 619–42.

Miltersen, K., K. Sandmann, and D. Sondermann, "Closed Form Solutions for Term Structure Derivatives with Lognormal Interest Rates," *Journal of Finance*, 52, 1 (March 1997): 409–30.

Rebonato, R., *Interest Rate Option Models* 2nd edn. Chichester, UK: Wiley, 1998.

Ritchken, P., and L. Sankarasubramanian, "Volatility Structures of Forward Rates and the Dynamics of the Term Structure," *Mathematical Finance*, 5 (1995): 55–72.

Questions and Problems (Answers in Solutions Manual)

29.1. Explain the difference between a Markov and a non-Markov model of the short rate.

29.2. Prove the relationship between the drift and volatility of the forward rate for the multifactor version of HJM in equation (29.6).

29.3. "When the forward rate volatility $s(t, T)$ in HJM is constant, the Ho–Lee model results." Verify that this is true by showing that HJM gives a process for bond prices that is consistent with the Ho–Lee model in Chapter 28.

29.4. "When the forward rate volatility, $s(t, T)$, in HJM is $\sigma e^{-a(T-t)}$, the Hull–White model results." Verify that this is true by showing that HJM gives a process for bond prices that is consistent with the Hull–White model in Chapter 28.

29.5. What is the advantage of LMM over HJM?

29.6. Provide an intuitive explanation of why a ratchet cap increases in value as the number of factors increase.

29.7. Show that equation (29.10) reduces to (29.4) as the δ_i tend to zero.

29.8. Explain why a sticky cap is more expensive than a similar ratchet cap.

29.9. Explain why IOs and POs have opposite sensitivities to the rate of prepayments.

29.10. "An option adjusted spread is analogous to the yield on a bond." Explain this statement.

29.11. Prove equation (29.15).

29.12. Prove the formula for the variance $V(T)$ of the swap rate in equation (29.17).

29.13. Prove equation (29.19).

Assignment Questions

29.14. In an annual-pay cap, the Black volatilities for caplets with maturities 1, 2, 3, and 5 years are 18%, 20%, 22%, and 20%, respectively. Estimate the volatility of a 1-year forward rate in the LIBOR Market Model when the time to maturity is (a) 0 to 1 year, (b) 1 to 2 years, (c) 2 to 3 years, and (d) 3 to 5 years. Assume that the zero curve is flat at 5% per annum (annually compounded). Use DerivaGem to estimate flat volatilities for 2-, 3-, 4-, 5-, and 6-year caps.

29.15. In the flexi cap considered in Section 29.2 the holder is obligated to exercise the first N in-the-money caplets. After that no further caplets can be exercised. (In the example, $N = 5$.) Two other ways that flexi caps are sometimes defined are:

(a) The holder can choose whether any caplet is exercised, but there is a limit of N on the total number of caplets that can be exercised.

(b) Once the holder chooses to exercise a caplet all subsequent in-the-money caplets must be exercised up to a maximum of N.

Discuss the problems in valuing these types of flexi caps. Of the three types of flexi caps, which would you expect to be most expensive? Which would you expect to be least expensive?

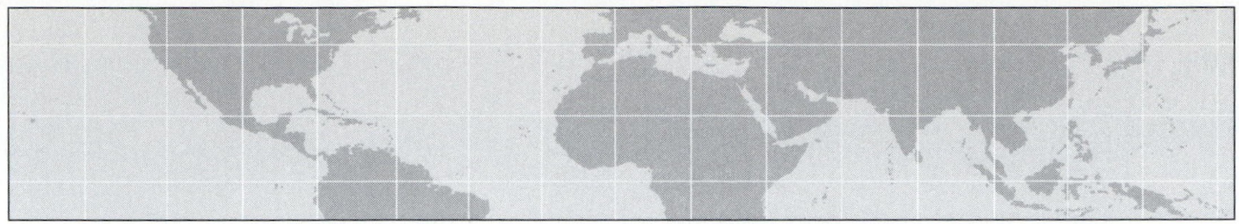

CHAPTER 30 Swaps Revisited

Swaps have been central to the success of over-the-counter derivatives markets in the 1980s and 1990s. They have proved to be very flexible instruments for managing risk. Based on the range of different contracts that now trade and the total volume of business transacted each year, swaps are arguably one the most successful innovations in financial markets ever.

In Chapter 7 we discussed how plain vanilla interest rate swaps can be valued. The standard approach can be summarized as: "Assume forward rates will be realized." The steps are as follows:

1. Calculate the swap's net cash flows on the assumption that LIBOR rates in the future equal the forward rates calculated from today's LIBOR/swap zero curve.
2. Set the value of the swap equal to the present value of the net cash flows using the LIBOR/swap zero curve for discounting.

In this chapter we describe a number of nonstandard swaps. Some can be valued using the "assume forward rates will be realized" approach; some require the application of the convexity, timing, and quanto adjustments we encountered in Chapters 27; some contain embedded options that must be valued using the techniques described in Chapters 26, 28, and 29.

30.1 VARIATIONS ON THE VANILLA DEAL

Many interest rate swaps involve relatively minor variations to the plain vanilla structure we discussed in Chapter 7. In some swaps the notional principal changes with time in a predetermined way. Swaps where the notional principal is an increasing function of time are known as *step-up swaps*. Swaps where the notional principal is a decreasing function of time are known as *amortizing swaps*. Step-up swaps could be useful for a construction company that intends to borrow increasing amounts of money at floating rates to finance a particular project and wants to swap it to fixed-rate funding. An amortizing swap could be used by a company that has fixed-rate borrowings with a certain prepayment schedule and wants to swap them to borrowings at a floating rate.

Business Snapshot 30.1 Hypothetical Confirmation for Nonstandard Swap

Trade date:	5-January-2004
Effective date:	11-January-2004
Business day convention (all dates):	Following business day
Holiday calendar:	US
Termination date:	11-January-2009
Fixed amounts	
Fixed-rate payer:	Microsoft
Fixed-rate notional principal:	USD 100 million
Fixed rate:	6% per annum
Fixed-rate day count convention:	Actual/365
Fixed-rate payment dates	Each 11-July and 11-January commencing 11-July, 2004, up to and including 11-January, 2009
Floating amounts	
Floating-rate payer	Goldman Sachs
Floating-rate notional principal	USD 120 million
Floating rate	USD 1-month LIBOR
Floating-rate day count convention	Actual/360
Floating-rate payment dates	11-July, 2004, and the 11th of each month thereafter up to and including 11-January, 2009

The principal can be different on the two sides of a swap. Also the frequency of payments can be different. Business Snapshot 30.1 illustrates this by showing a hypothetical swap between Microsoft and Goldman Sachs where the notional principal is \$120 million on the floating side and \$100 million on fixed side. Payments are made every month on the floating side and every 6 months on the fixed side. These type of variations to the basic plain vanilla structure do not affect the valuation methodology. We can still use the "assume forward rates are realized" approach.

The floating reference rate for a swap is not always LIBOR. In some swaps for instance, it is the commercial paper (CP) rate. A *basis swap* involves exchanging cash flows calculated using one floating reference rate for cash flows calculated using another floating reference rate. An example would be a swap where the 3-month CP rate plus 10 basis points is exchanged for 3-month LIBOR with both being applied to a principal of \$100 million. A basis swap could be used for risk management by a financial institution whose assets and liabilities are dependent on different floating reference rates.

Swaps where the floating reference rate is not LIBOR can be valued using the "assume forward rates are realized" approach. A zero curve other than LIBOR is necessary to calculate future cash flows on the assumption that forward rates are realized. The cash flows are discounted at LIBOR.

Business Snapshot 30.2 Hypothetical Confirmation for Compounding Swap

Trade date:	5-January-2004
Effective date:	11-January-2004
Holiday calendar:	US
Business day convention (all dates):	Following business day
Termination date:	11-January-2009
Fixed amounts	
Fixed-rate payer:	Microsoft
Fixed-rate notional principal:	USD 100 million
Fixed rate:	6% per annum
Fixed-rate day count convention:	Actual/365
Fixed-rate payment date:	11-January, 2009
Fixed-rate compounding:	Applicable at 6.3%
Fixed-rate compounding dates	Each 11-July and 11-January commencing 11-July, 2004, up to and including 11-July, 2008
Floating amounts	
Floating-rate payer:	Goldman Sachs
Floating-rate notional principal:	USD 100 million
Floating rate:	USD 6-month LIBOR plus 20 basis points
Floating-rate day count convention:	Actual/360
Floating-rate payment date:	11-January, 2009
Floating-rate compounding:	Applicable at LIBOR plus 10 basis points
Floating-rate compounding dates:	Each 11-July and 11-January commencing 11-July, 2004, up to and including 11-July, 2008

30.2 COMPOUNDING SWAPS

Another variation on the plain vanilla swap is a *compounding swap*. A hypothetical confirmation for a compounding swap is in Business Snapshot 30.2. In this example there is only one payment date for both the floating-rate payments and the fixed-rate payments. This is at the end of the life of the swap. The floating rate of interest is LIBOR plus 20 basis points. Instead of being paid, the interest is compounded forward until the end of the life of the swap at a rate of LIBOR plus 10 basis points. The fixed rate of interest is 6%. Instead of being paid this interest is compounded forward at a fixed rate of interest of 6.3% until the end of the swap.

We can use the "assume forward rates are realized" approach for valuing a compounding swap such as that in Business Snapshot 30.2. It is straightforward to deal with the fixed side of the swap because the payment that we will make at maturity is known with certainty. The "assume forward rates are realized" approach for the floating part is justifiable because we can devise a series of forward rate agreements (FRAs) where the floating-rate cash flows are exchanged for the values they would have if each floating rate equaled the corresponding forward rate.[1]

Example 30.1

A compounding swap with annual resets has a life of 3 years. A fixed rate is paid and a floating rate is received. The fixed interest rate is 4% and the floating interest rate is 12-month LIBOR. The fixed side compounds at 3.9% and the floating side compounds at 12-month LIBOR minus 20 basis points. The LIBOR zero curve is flat at 5% with annual compounding and the notional principal is $100 million.

On the fixed side, interest of $4 million is earned at the end of the first year. This compounds to $4 \times 1.039 = \$4.156$ million at the end of the second year. A second interest amount of $4 million is added at the end of the second year bringing the total compounded forward amount to $8.156 million. This compounds to $8.156 \times 1.039 = \$8.474$ million by the end of the third year when there is the third interest amount of $4 million. The cash flow at the end of the third year on the fixed side of the swap is therefore $12.474 million.

On the floating side we assume all future interest rates equal the corresponding forward LIBOR rates. Given the LIBOR zero curve, this means that we assume all future interest rates are 5% with annual compounding. The interest calculated at the end of the first year is $5 million. Compounding this forward at 4.8% (forward LIBOR minus 20 basis points) gives $5 \times 1.048 = \$5.24$ million at the end of the second year. Adding in the interest, the compounded forward amount is $10.24 million. Compounding forward to the end of the third year, we get $10.24 \times 1.048 = \$10.731$ million. Adding in the final interest gives $15.731 million.

We can value the swap by assuming that it leads to an inflow of $15.731 million and an outflow of $12.474 million at the end of year 3. The value of the swap is therefore

$$\frac{15.731 - 12.474}{1.05^3} = 2.814$$

or $2.814 million. (This analysis ignores day count issues.)

30.3 CURRENCY SWAPS

We introduced currency swaps in Chapter 7. These enable an interest rate exposure in one currency to be swapped for an interest rate exposure in another currency. Usually two principals are specified, one in each currency. The principals are exchanged at both the beginning and the end of the life of the swap as described in Section 7.8.

Suppose that the currencies involved in a currency swap are US dollars (USD) and British pounds (GBP). In a fixed-for-fixed currency swap, a fixed rate of interest is specified in each currency. The payments on one side are determined by applying the fixed rate of interest in USD to the USD principal; the payments on the other side are determined by applying the fixed rate of interest in GBP to the GBP principal. We discussed the valuation of this type of swap in Section 7.9.

Another popular type of currency swap is floating-for-floating. In this, the payments

[1] See Technical Note 18 on the author's website for the details.

on one side are determined by applying USD LIBOR (possibly with a spread added) to the USD principal; similarly the payments on the other side are determined by applying GBP LIBOR (possibly with a spread added) to the GBP principal. A third type of swap is a cross-currency interest rate swap where a floating rate in one currency is exchanged for a fixed rate in another currency.

Floating-for-floating and cross-currency interest rate swaps can be valued using the "assume forward rates are realized" rule. Future LIBOR rates in each currency are assumed to equal today's forward rates. This enables the cash flows in the currencies to be determined. The USD cash flows are discounted at the USD LIBOR zero rate. The GBP cash flows are discounted at the GBP LIBOR zero rate. The current exchange rate is then used to translate the two present values to a common currency.

An adjustment to this procedure is sometimes made to reflect the realities of the market. In theory, a new floating-for-floating swap should involve exchanging LIBOR in one currency for LIBOR in another currency (with no spreads added). In practice, macroeconomic effects give rise to spreads. Financial institutions often adjust the discount rates they use to allow for this. As an example, suppose that market conditions are such that USD LIBOR is exchanged for Japanese yen (JPY) LIBOR minus 20 basis points in new floating-for-floating swaps of all maturities. In its valuations a US financial institution would discount USD cash flows at USD LIBOR and it would discount JPY cash flows at JPY LIBOR minus 20 basis points.[2] It would do this in all swaps that involved both JPY and USD cash flows.

30.4 MORE COMPLEX SWAPS

We now move on to consider some examples of swaps where the simple rule "assume forward rates will be realized" does not work. In each case we must make adjustments to forward rates.

LIBOR-in-Arrears Swap

A plain vanilla interest rate swap is designed so that the floating rate of interest observed on one payment date is paid on the next payment date. An alternative instrument that is sometimes traded is a *LIBOR-in-arrears swap*. In this, the floating rate paid on a payment date equals the rate observed on the payment date itself.

Suppose that the reset dates in the swap are t_i for $i = 0, 1, \dots, n$, with $\tau_i = t_{i+1} - t_i$. Define R_i as the LIBOR rate for the period between t_i and t_{i+1}, F_i as the forward value of R_i, and σ_i as the volatility of this forward rate. (The value of σ_i is typically implied from caplet prices.) In a LIBOR-in-arrears swap the payment on the floating side at time t_i is based on R_i rather than R_{i-1}. As explained in Section 27.1, it is necessary to make a convexity adjustment to the forward rate when the payment is valued. The valuation should be based on the assumption that the forward rate is

$$F_i + \frac{F_i^2 \sigma_i^2 \tau_i t_i}{1 + F_i \tau_i} \tag{30.1}$$

rather than F_i.

[2] This adjustment is *ad hoc*, but, if it is not made, traders make an immediate profit or loss every time they trade a new JPY/USD floating-for-floating swap.

Example 30.2

In a LIBOR-in-arrears swap, the principal is \$100 million. A fixed rate of 5% is received annually and LIBOR is paid. Payments are exchanged at the ends of years 1, 2, 3, 4, and 5. The yield curve is flat at 5% per annum (measured with annual compounding). All caplet volatilities are 22% per annum.

The forward rate for each floating payment is 5%. If this were a regular swap rather than an in-arrears swap, its value would (ignoring day count conventions, etc.) be exactly zero. Because it is an in-arrears swap, we must make convexity adjustments. In equation (30.1), $F_i = 0.05$, $\sigma_i = 0.22$, and $\tau_i = 1$ for all i. The convexity adjustment changes the rate assumed at time t_i from 0.05 to

$$0.05 + \frac{0.05^2 \times 0.22^2 \times 1 \times t_i}{1 + 0.05 \times 1} = 0.05 + 0.000115t_i$$

The floating rates for the payments at the ends of years 1, 2, 3, 4, and 5 should therefore be assumed to be 5.0115%, 5.0230%, 5.0345%, 5.0460%, and 5.0575%, respectively. The net exchange on the first payment date is equivalent to a cash outflow of 0.0115% of \$100 million or \$11,500. Equivalent net cash flows for other exchanges are calculated similarly. The value of the swap is

$$-\frac{11{,}500}{1.05} - \frac{23{,}000}{1.05^2} - \frac{34{,}500}{1.05^3} - \frac{46{,}000}{1.05^4} - \frac{57{,}500}{1.05^5}$$

or −\$144,514.

CMS and CMT Swaps

A constant maturity swap (CMS) is an interest rate swap where the floating rate equals the swap rate for a swap with a certain life. For example, the floating payments on a CMS swap might be made every 6 months at a rate equal to the 5-year swap rate. Usually there is a lag so that the payment on a particular payment date is equal to the swap rate observed on the previous payment date. Suppose that rates are set at times $t_0, t_1, t_2, \dots,$ payments are made at times $t_1, t_2, t_3, \dots,$ and L is the notional principal. The floating payment at time t_{i+1} is

$$\tau_i L S_i$$

where $\tau_i = t_{i+1} - t_i$ and S_i is the swap rate at time t_i.

Suppose that y_i is the forward value of the swap rate S_i. To value the payment at time t_{i+1}, it turns out to be correct to make a convexity adjustment to the forward swap rate, so that the swap rate is assumed to be

$$y_i - \tfrac{1}{2} y_i^2 \sigma_{y,i}^2 t_i \frac{G_i''(y_i)}{G_i'(y_i)} - \frac{y_i \tau_i F_i \rho_i \sigma_{y,i} \sigma_{F,i} t_i}{1 + F_i \tau_i} \tag{30.2}$$

rather that y_i. In this equation, $\sigma_{y,i}$ is the volatility of the forward swap rate, F_i is the current forward interest rate between times t_i and t_{i+1}, $\sigma_{F,i}$ is the volatility of this forward rate, and ρ_i is the correlation between the forward swap rate and the forward interest rate. $G_i(x)$ is the price at time t_i of a bond as a function of its yield x. The bond pays coupons at rate y_i and has the same life and payment frequency as the swap from which the CMS rate is calculated. $G_i'(x)$ and $G_i''(x)$ are the first and second partial derivatives of G_i with respect to x. The volatilities $\sigma_{y,i}$ can be implied from swap options; the volatilities $\sigma_{F,i}$ can be implied from caplet prices; the correlation ρ_i can be estimated from historical data.

Equation (30.2) involves a convexity and a timing adjustment. The term

$$-\tfrac{1}{2}y_i^2\sigma_{y,i}^2 t_i \frac{G_i''(y_i)}{G_i'(y_i)}$$

is an adjustment similar the one we calculated in Example 27.2 of Section 27.1. It is based on the assumption that the swap rate S_i leads to only one payment at time t_i. The term

$$-\frac{y_i\tau_i F_i\rho_i\sigma_{y,i}\sigma_{F,i}\,t_i}{1+F_i\tau_i}$$

is similar to the one we calculated in Section 27.2 and allows for the fact that the payment calculated from S_i is made at time t_{i+1} rather than t_i.

Example 30.3

In a 6-year CMS swap, the 5-year swap rate is received and a fixed rate of 5% is paid on a notional principal of \$100 million. The exchange of payments is semiannual (both on the underlying 5-year swap and on the CMS swap itself). The exchange on a payment date is determined from the swap rate on the previous payment date. The term structure is flat at 5% per annum with semiannual compounding. All options on five-year swaps have a 15% implied volatility and all caplets with a 6-month tenor have a 20% implied volatility. The correlation between each cap rate and each swap rate is 0.7.

In this case, $y_i = 0.05$, $\sigma_{y,i} = 0.15$, $\tau_i = 0.5$, $F_i = 0.05$, $\sigma_{F,i} = 0.20$, and $\rho_i = 0.7$ for all i. Also,

$$G_i(x) = \sum_{i=1}^{10}\frac{2.5}{(1+x/2)^i} + \frac{100}{(1+x/2)^{10}}$$

so that $G_i'(y_i) = -437.603$ and $G_i''(y_i) = 2261.23$. Equation (30.2) gives the total convexity/timing adjustment as $0.0001197t_i$, or 1.197 basis points per year until the swap rate is observed. For example, for the purposes of valuing the CMS swap, the 5-year swap rate in 4 years' time should be assumed to be 5.0479% rather than 5% and the net cash flow received at the 4.5-year point should be assumed to be $0.5 \times 0.000479 \times 100{,}000{,}000 = \$23{,}940$. Other net cash flows are calculated similarly. Taking their present value, we find the value of the swap to be \$159,811.

A constant maturity Treasury swap (CMT swap) works similarly to a CMS swap except that the floating rate is the yield on a Treasury bond with a specified life. The analysis of a CMT swap is essentially the same as that for a CMS swap with S_i defined as the par yield on a Treasury bond with the specified life.

Differential Swaps

A *differential swap*, sometimes referred to as a *diff swap*, is an interest rate swap where the floating interest rate is observed in one currency and applied to a principal in another currency. Suppose that we observe the LIBOR rate for the period between t_i

and t_{i+1} in currency Y and apply it to a principal in currency X with the payment taking place at time t_{i+1}. Define V_i as the forward interest rate between t_i and t_{i+1} in currency Y and W_i as the forward exchange rate for a contract with maturity t_{i+1} (expressed as the number of units of currency Y that equal one unit of currency X). If the LIBOR rate in currency Y were applied to a principal in currency Y we would value the cash flow on the assumption that the LIBOR rate equaled F_i. From the analysis in Section 27.3, a quanto adjustment is necessary when it is applied to a principal in currency X. It is correct to value the cash flow on the assumption that the LIBOR rate equals

$$V_i + V_i \rho_i \sigma_{W,i} \sigma_{V,i} t_i \tag{30.3}$$

where $\sigma_{V,i}$ is the volatility of V_i, $\sigma_{W,i}$ is the volatility of W_i, and ρ_i is the correlation between V_i and W_i.

Example 30.4

Zero rates in both the US and Britain are flat at 5% per annum with annual compounding. In a 3-year diff swap agreement with annual payments, USD 12-month LIBOR is received and sterling 12-month LIBOR is paid with both being applied to a principal of 10 million pounds sterling. The volatility of all 1-year forward rates in the US is estimated to be 20%, the volatility of the forward USD/sterling exchange rate (dollars per pound) is 12% for all maturities, and the correlation between the two is 0.4.

In this case, $V_i = 0.05$, $\rho_i = 0.4$, $\sigma_{W,i} = 0.12$, $\sigma_{V,i} = 0.2$. The floating-rate cash flows dependent on the 1-year USD rate observed at time t_i should therefore be calculated on the assumption that the rate will be

$$0.05 + 0.05 \times 0.4 \times 0.12 \times 0.2 \times t_i = 0.05 + 0.00048t_i$$

This means that the net cash flows from the swap at times 1, 2, and 3 years should be assumed to be 0, 4,800, and 9,600 pounds sterling for the purposes of valuation. The value of the swap is therefore

$$\frac{0}{1.05} + \frac{4,800}{1.05^2} + \frac{9,600}{1.05^3} = 12,647$$

or 12,647 pounds sterling.

30.5 EQUITY SWAPS

In an equity swap, one party promises to pay the return on an equity index on a notional principal, while the other promises to pay a fixed or floating return on a notional principal. Equity swaps enable a fund managers to increase or reduce their exposure to an index without buying and selling stock. An equity swap is a convenient way of packaging a series of forward contracts on an index to meet the needs of the market.

The equity index is usually a total return index where dividends are reinvested in the stocks comprising the index. An example of an equity swap is in Business Snapshot 30.3. In this, the 6-month return on the S&P 500 is exchanged for LIBOR. The principal on either side of the swap is $100 million and payments are made every 6 months.

For an equity-for-floating swap such as that in Business Snapshot 30.3 the value at the start of its life is zero. This is because a financial institution can arrange to costlessly

Business Snapshot 30.3 Hypothetical Confirmation for an Equity Swap

Trade date:	5-January-2004
Effective date:	11-January-2004
Business day convention (all dates):	Following business day
Holiday calendar:	US
Termination date:	11-January-2009
Equity amounts	
Equity payer:	Microsoft
Equity principal	USD 100 million
Equity index:	Total Return S&P 500 index
Equity payment:	$100(I_1 - I_0)/I_0$, where I_1 is the index level on the payment date and I_0 is the index level on the immediately preceding payment date. In the case of the first payment date, I_0 is the index level on 11-January, 2004
Equity payment dates:	Each 11-July and 11-January commencing 11-July, 2004, up to and including 11-January, 2009
Floating amounts	
Floating-rate payer:	Goldman Sachs
Floating-rate notional principal:	USD 100 million
Floating rate:	USD 6-month LIBOR
Floating-rate day count convention:	Actual/360
Floating-rate payment dates:	Each 11-July and 11-January commencing 11-July, 2004, up to and including 11-January, 2009

replicate the cash flows to one side by borrowing the principal on each payment date at LIBOR and investing it in the index until the next payment date with any dividends being reinvested. A similar argument shows that the swap is always worth zero immediately after a payment date.

Between payment dates we must value the equity cash flow and the LIBOR cash flow at the next payment date. The LIBOR cash flow was fixed at the last reset date and so can be valued easily. The value of the equity cash flow is LE/E_0, where L is the principal, E is the current value of the equity index, and E_0 is its value at the last reset date.[3]

30.6 SWAPS WITH EMBEDDED OPTIONS

Some swaps contain embedded options. In this section we consider some commonly encountered examples.

[3] See Technical Note 19 on the author's website for a more detailed discussion of this.

Accrual Swaps

Accrual swaps are swaps where the interest on one side accrues only when the floating reference rate is within a certain range. Sometimes the range remains fixed during the entire life of the swap; sometimes it is reset periodically.

As a simple example of an accrual swap, consider a deal where a fixed rate Q is exchanged for 3-month LIBOR every quarter. We suppose that the fixed rate accrues only on days when 3-month LIBOR is below 8% per annum. Suppose that the principal is L. In a normal swap the fixed-rate payer would pay QLn_1/n_2 on each payment date where n_1 is the number of days in the preceding quarter and n_2 is the number of days in the year. (This assumes that the day count is actual/actual.) In an accrual swap, this is changed to QLn_3/n_2, where n_3 is the number of days in the preceding quarter that the 3-month LIBOR was below 8%. The fixed-rate payer saves QL/n_2 on each day when 3-month LIBOR is above 8%.[4] The fixed-rate payer's position can therefore be considered equivalent to a regular swap plus a series of binary options, one for each day of the life of the swap. The binary options pay off QL/n_2 when the 3-month LIBOR is above 8%.

To generalize, we suppose that the LIBOR cutoff rate (8% in the case just considered) is R_K and that payments are exchanged every τ years. Consider day i during the life of the swap and suppose that t_i is the time until day i. Suppose that the τ-year LIBOR rate on day i is R_i so that interest accrues when $R_i < R_K$. Define F_i as the forward value of R_i and σ_i as the volatility of F_i. (The latter is estimated from spot caplet volatilities.) Using the usual lognormal assumption, the probability that LIBOR is greater than R_K in a world that is forward risk neutral with respect to a zero-coupon bond maturing at time $t_i + \tau$ is $N(d_2)$, where

$$d_2 = \frac{\ln(F_i/R_K) - \sigma_i^2 t_i/2}{\sigma_i \sqrt{t_i}}$$

The payoff from the binary option is realized at the swap payment date following day i. We suppose that this is at time s_i. The probability that LIBOR is greater than R_K in a world that is forward risk neutral with respect to a zero-coupon bond maturing at time s_i is given by $N(d_2^*)$, where d_2^* is calculated using the same formula as d_2, but with a small timing adjustment to F_i reflecting the difference between time $t_i + \tau$ and time s_i.

The value of the binary option corresponding to day i is

$$\frac{QL}{n_2} P(0, s_i) N(d_2^*)$$

The total value of the binary options is obtained by summing this expression for every day in the life of the swap. The timing adjustment (causing d_2 to be replaced by d_2^*) is so small that, in practice, it is frequently ignored.

Cancelable Swap

A cancelable swap is a plain vanilla interest rate swap where one side has the option to terminate on one or more payment dates. Terminating a swap is the same as entering

[4] The usual convention is that, if a day is a holiday, the applicable rate is assumed to be the rate on the immediately preceding business day.

into the offsetting (opposite) swap. Consider a swap between Microsoft and Goldman Sachs. If Microsoft has the option to cancel, it can regard the swap as a regular swap plus a long position in an option to enter into the offsetting swap. If Goldman Sachs has the cancelation option, Microsoft has a regular swap plus a short position in an option to enter into the swap.

If there is only one termination date, a cancelable swap is the same as a regular swap plus a position in a European swap option. Consider, for example, a 10-year swap where Microsoft will receive 6% and pay LIBOR. Suppose that Microsoft has the option to terminate at the end of 6 years. The swap is a regular 10-year swap to receive 6% and pay LIBOR plus long position in a 6-year European option to enter into a 4-year swap where 6% is paid and LIBOR is received. (The latter is referred to as a 6×4 European option.) The standard market model for valuing European swap options is described in Chapter 26.

When the swap can be terminated on a number of different payment dates, it is a regular swap option plus a Bermudan-style swap option. Consider, for example, the situation where Microsoft has entered into a 5-year swap with semiannual payments where 6% is received and LIBOR is paid. Suppose that the counterparty has the option to terminate on the swap on payment dates between year 2 and year 5. The swap is a regular swap plus a short position in a Bermudan-style swap option where the Bermudan style swap option is an option to enter into a swap that matures in 5 years and involves a fixed payment at 6% being received and a floating payment at LIBOR being paid. The swap option can be exercised on any payment date between year 2 and year 5. We discussed methods for valuing Bermudan swap options in Chapters 28 and 29.

Cancelable Compounding Swaps

Sometimes compounding swaps can be terminated on specified payment dates. On termination the floating-rate payer pays the compounded value of the floating amounts up to the time of termination and the fixed-rate payer pays the compounded value of the fixed payments up to the time of termination.

Some tricks can be used to value cancelable compounding swaps. Suppose first that the floating rate is LIBOR and it is compounded at LIBOR. We assume that the principal amount of the swap is paid on both the fixed and floating sides of the swap at the end of its life. This is similar to moving from Table 7.1 to Table 7.2 for a vanilla swap. It does not change the value of the swap and has the effect of ensuring that the value of the floating side is always equals the notional principal on a payment date. To make the cancelation decision, we need only look at the fixed side. We construct an interest rate tree as outlined in Chapter 28. We roll back through the tree in the usual way valuing the fixed side. At each node where the swap can be canceled, we test whether it is optimal to keep the swap or cancel it. Canceling the swap in effect sets the fixed side equal to par. If we are paying fixed and receiving floating, our objective is to minimize the value of the fixed side; if we are receiving fixed and paying floating, our objective is to maximize the value of the fixed side.

When the floating side is LIBOR plus a spread compounded at LIBOR, we can subtract cash flows corresponding to the spread rate of interest from the fixed side instead of adding them to the floating side. The option can then be valued as in the case where there is no spread.

When the compounding is at LIBOR plus a spread, an approximate approach is as follows:[5]

1. Calculate the value of the floating side of the swap at each cancelation date assuming forward rates are realized.
2. Calculate the value of the floating side of the swap at each cancelation date assuming that the floating rate is LIBOR and it is compounded at LIBOR.
3. Define the excess of step 1 over step 2 as the "value of spreads" on a cancelation date.
4. Treat the option in the way described above. In deciding whether to exercise the cancelation option, subtract the value of the spreads from the values calculated for the fixed side.

30.7 OTHER SWAPS

This chapter has discussed just a few of the different types of swaps that trade. In practice, the number of instruments that trade is limited only by the imagination of financial engineers and the appetite of corporate treasurers for innovative risk management tools.

A swap that was very popular in the United States in the mid-1990s is an *index amortizing rate swap* (sometimes also called an *indexed principal swap*). In this, the principal reduces in a way dependent on the level of interest rates. The lower the interest rate, the greater the reduction in the principal. The fixed side of an indexed amortizing swap was originally designed to mirror, at least approximately, the return obtained by an investor on a mortgage-backed security after prepayment options are taken into account. The swap therefore exchanged the return on a mortgage-backed security for a floating-rate return.

Commodity swaps are now becoming increasingly popular. A company that consumes 100,000 barrels of oil per year could agree to pay $4 million each year for the next 10 years and to receive in return $100{,}000S$, where S is the market price of oil per barrel. The agreement would in effect lock in the company's oil cost at $40 per barrel. An oil producer might agree to the opposite exchange, thereby locking in the price it realized for its oil at $40 per barrel. We discussed energy derivatives in Chapter 23.

A recent innovation in swap markets is a *volatility swap*. In this, the payments depend on the volatility of a stock (or other asset). Suppose that the principal is L. On each payment date, one side pays $L\sigma$, where σ is the historical volatility calculated in the usual way by taking daily observations on the stock during the immediately preceding accrual period and the other side pays $L\sigma_K$, where σ_K is a constant prespecified volatility level. Variance swaps, correlation swaps, and covariance swaps are defined similarly.

A number of other types of swaps are discussed elsewhere in this book. For example, asset swaps are discussed in Chapter 20, and total return swaps and various types of credit default swaps are covered in Chapter 21.

[5] This approach is not perfectly accurate in that it assumes that the decision to exercise the cancelation option is not influenced by future payments being compounded at a rate different from LIBOR.

Business Snapshot 30.4 Procter and Gamble's Bizarre Deal

A particularly bizarre swap is the so-called "5/30" swap entered into between Bankers Trust (BT) and Procter and Gamble (P&G) on November 2, 1993. This was a 5-year swap with semiannual payments. The notional principal was \$200 million. BT paid P&G 5.30% per annum. P&G paid BT the average 30-day CP (commercial paper) rate minus 75 basis points plus a spread. The average commercial paper rate was calculated by taking observations on the 30-day commercial paper rate each day during the preceding accrual period and averaging them.

The spread was zero for the first payment date (May 2, 1994). For the remaining nine payment dates, it was

$$\max\left[0,\ \frac{98.5\left(\dfrac{\text{5-year CMT\%}}{5.78\%}\right)-(\text{30-year TSY price})}{100}\right]$$

In this, 5-year CMT is the constant maturity Treasury yield (i.e., the yield on a 5-year Treasury note, as reported by the Federal Reserve). The 30-year TSY price is the midpoint of the bid and offer cash bond prices for the 6.25% Treasury bond maturing on August 2023. Note that the spread calculated from the formula is a decimal interest rate. It is not measured in basis points. If the formula gives 0.1 and the CP rate is 6%, the rate paid by P&G is 15.25%.

P&G were hoping that the spread would be zero and the deal would enable them to exchange fixed-rate funding at 5.30% for funding at 75 basis points less than the commercial paper rate. In fact, interest rates rose sharply in early 1994, bond prices fell, and the swap proved very, very expensive (see Problem 30.10).

Bizarre Deals

Some swaps have payoffs that are calculated in quite bizarre ways. An example is a deal entered into between Procter and Gamble and Bankers Trust in 1993 (see Business Snapshot 30.4). The details of this transaction are in the public domain because it later became the subject of litigation.[6]

SUMMARY

Swaps have proved to be very versatile financial instruments. Many swaps can be valued by (a) assuming that LIBOR (or some other floating reference rate) will equal its forward value and (b) discounting the resulting cash flows at the LIBOR/swap rate. These include plain vanilla interest swaps, most types of currency swaps, swaps where the principal changes in a predetermined way, swaps where the payment dates are different on each side, and compounding swaps.

---

[6] See D. J. Smith, "Aggressive Corporate Finance: A Close Look at the Procter and Gamble–Bankers Trust Leveraged Swap," *Journal of Derivatives* 4, 4 (Summer 1997): 67–79.

Some swaps require adjustments to the forward rates when they are valued. These adjustments are termed convexity, timing, or quanto adjustments. Among the swaps that require adjustments are LIBOR-in-arrears swaps, CMS/CMT swaps, and differential swaps.

Equity swaps involve the return on an equity index being exchanged for a fixed or floating rate of interest. They are usually designed so that they are worth zero immediately after a payment date, but they may have nonzero values between payment dates.

Some swaps involve embedded options. An accrual swap turns out to be a regular swap plus a large portfolio of binary options (one for each day of the life of the swap). A cancelable swap turns out to be a regular swap plus a Bermudan swap option.

FURTHER READING

Chance, D., and Rich, D., "The Pricing of Equity Swap and Swaptions," *Journal of Derivatives* 5, 4 (Summer 1998): 19–31.

Demeterfi, K., Derman, E., Kamal, M., and Zou, J., "A Guide to Volatility and Variance Swaps," *Journal of Derivatives* 6, 4 (Summer 1999): 9–32.

Smith D. J., "Aggressive Corporate Finance: A Close Look at the Procter and Gamble–Bankers Trust Leveraged Swap," *Journal of Derivatives*, 4, 4 (Summer 1997): 67–79.

Questions and Problems (Answers in Solutions Manual)

30.1. Calculate all the fixed cash flows and their exact timing for the swap in Business Snapshot 30.1. Assume that the day count conventions are applied using target payment dates rather than actual payment dates.

30.2. Suppose that a swap specifies that a fixed rate is exchanged for twice the LIBOR rate. Can the swap be valued using the "assume forward rates are realized" rule?

30.3. What is the value of a 2-year fixed-for-floating compound swap where the principal is $100 million and payments are made semiannually. Fixed interest is received and floating is paid? The fixed rate is 8% and it is compounded at 8.3% (both semiannually compounded). The floating rate is LIBOR plus 10 basis points and it is compounded at LIBOR plus 20 basis points. The LIBOR zero curve is flat at 8% with semiannual compounding.

30.4. What is the value of a 5-year swap where LIBOR is paid in the usual way and in return LIBOR compounded at LIBOR is received on the other side? The principal on both sides is $100 million. Payment dates on the pay side and compounding dates on the receive side are every 6 months and the yield curve is flat at 5% with semiannual compounding.

30.5. Explain carefully why a bank might choose to discount cash flows on a currency swap at a rate slightly different from LIBOR.

30.6. Calculate the total convexity/timing adjustment in Example 30.3 of Section 30.4 if all cap volatilities are 18% instead of 20% and volatilities for all options on 5-year swaps are 13% instead of 15%. What should the 5-year swap rate in 3 years' time be assumed for the purpose of valuing the swap? What is the value of the swap?

30.7. Explain why a plain vanilla interest rate swap and the compounding swap in Section 30.2 can be valued using the "assume forward rates are realized" rule, but a LIBOR-in-arrears swap in Section 30.4 cannot.

30.8. In the accrual swap discussed in the text, the fixed side accrues only when the floating reference rate lies below a certain level. Discuss how the analysis can be extended to cope with a situation where the fixed side accrues only when the floating reference rate is above one level and below another.

Assignment Questions

30.9. LIBOR zero rates are flat at 5% in the United States and flat at 10% in Australia (both annually compounded). In a 4-year swap Australian LIBOR is received and 9% is paid with both being applied to a USD principal of $10 million. Payments are exchanged annually. The volatility of all 1-year forward rates in Australia is estimated to be 25%, the volatility of the forward USD/AUD exchange rate (AUD per USD) is 15% for all maturities, and the correlation between the two is 0.3. What is the value of the swap?

30.10. Estimate the interest rate paid by P&G on the 5/30 swap in Section 30.7 if (a) the CP rate is 6.5% and the Treasury yield curve is flat at 6% and (b) the CP rate is 7.5% and the Treasury yield curve is flat at 7% with semiannual compounding.

30.11. Suppose that you are trading a LIBOR-in-arrears swap with an unsophisticated counterparty who does not make convexity adjustments. To take advantage of the situation, should you be paying fixed or receiving fixed? How should you try to structure the swap as far as its life and payment frequencies?

Consider the situation where the yield curve is flat at 10% per annum with annual compounding. All cap volatilities are 18%. Estimate the difference between the way a sophisticated trader and an unsophisticated trader would value a LIBOR-in-arrears swap where payments are made annually and the life of the swap is (a) 5 years, (b) 10 years, and (c) 20 years. Assume a notional principal of $1 million.

30.12. Suppose that the LIBOR zero rate is flat at 5% with annual compounding. In a 5-year swap, company X pays a fixed rate of 6% and receives LIBOR. The volatility of the 2-year swap rate in 3 years is 20%.

(a) What is the value of the swap?
(b) Use DerivaGem to calculate the value of the swap if company X has the option to cancel after 3 years.
(c) Use DerivaGem to calculate the value of the swap if the counterparty has the option to cancel after 3 years.
(d) What is the value of the swap if either side can cancel at the end of 3 years?

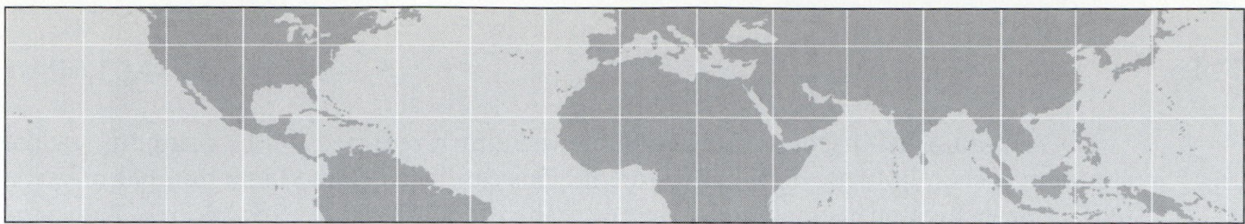

CHAPTER 31 Real Options

Up to now we have been almost entirely concerned with the valuation of financial assets. In this chapter we explore how the ideas we have developed can be extended to assess capital investment opportunities in real assets such as land, buildings, plant, and equipment. Often there are options embedded in these investment opportunities (the option to expand the investment, the option to abandon the investment, the option to defer the investment, and so on.) These options are very difficult to value using traditional capital investment appraisal techniques. The approach known as *real options* attempts to deal with this problem using option-pricing theory.

The chapter starts by explaining the traditional approach to evaluating investments in real assets and shows how difficult it is to correctly value embedded options when this approach is used. It explains how the risk-neutral valuation approach can be extended to handle the valuation of real assets and presents a number of examples illustrating the application of the approach in a range of different situations.

31.1 CAPITAL INVESTMENT APPRAISAL

The traditional approach to valuing a potential capital investment project is known as the "net present value" (NPV) approach. The NPV of a project is the present value of its expected future incremental cash flows. The discount rate used to calculate the present value is a "risk-adjusted" discount rate, chosen to reflect the risk of the project. As the riskiness of the project increases, the discount rate also increases.

As an example, consider an investment that costs \$100 million and will last 5 years. The expected cash inflow in each year is estimated to be \$25 million. If the risk-adjusted discount rate is 12% (with continuous compounding), the net present value of the investment is (in millions of dollars)

$$-100 + 25e^{-0.12\times 1} + 25e^{-0.12\times 2} + 25e^{-0.12\times 3} + 25e^{-0.12\times 4} + 25e^{-0.12\times 5} = -11.53$$

A negative NPV, such as the one we have just calculated, indicates that the project will reduce the value of the company to its shareholders and should not be undertaken. A positive NPV indicates that the project should be undertaken because it will increase shareholder wealth.

The risk-adjusted discount rate should be the return required by the company, or the company's shareholders, on the investment. This can be calculated in a number of ways. One approach often recommended involves the capital asset pricing model. The steps are as follows:

1. Take a sample of companies whose main line of business is the same as that of the project being contemplated.
2. Calculate the betas of the companies and average them to obtain a proxy beta for the project.
3. Set the required rate of return equal to the risk-free rate plus the proxy beta times the excess return of the market portfolio over the risk-free rate.

One problem with the traditional NPV approach is that many projects contain embedded options. Consider, for example, a company that is considering building a plant to manufacture a new product. Often the company has the option to abandon the project if things do not work out well. It may also have the option to expand the plant if demand for the output exceeds expectations. These options usually have quite different risk characteristics from the base project and require different discount rates.

To understand the problem here, return to the example at the beginning of Chapter 11. This involved a stock whose current price is \$20. In three months the price will be either \$22 or \$18. Risk-neutral valuation shows that the value of a three-month call option on the stock with a strike price of 21 is 0.633. Footnote 1 of Chapter 11 shows that if the expected return required by investors on the stock in the real world is 16% then the expected return required on the call option is 42.6%. A similar analysis shows that if the option is a put rather than a call the expected return required on the option is −52.5%. These analyses mean that if the traditional NPV approach were used to value the call option the correct discount rate would be 42.6%, and if it were used to value a put option the correct discount rate would be −52.5%. There is no easy way of estimating these discount rates. (We know them only because we are able to value the options another way.) Similarly, there is no easy way of estimating the risk-adjusted discount rates appropriate for cash flows when they arise from abandonment, expansion, and other options. This is the motivation for exploring whether the risk-neutral valuation principle can be applied to options on real assets as well as to options on financial assets.

Another problem with the traditional NPV approach lies in the estimation of the appropriate risk-adjusted discount rate for the base project (i.e., the project without embedded options). The companies that are used to estimate a proxy beta for the project in the three-step procedure above have expansion options and abandonment options of their own. Their betas reflect these options and may not therefore be appropriate for estimating a beta for the base project.

31.2 EXTENSION OF THE RISK-NEUTRAL VALUATION FRAMEWORK

In Section 25.1 we defined the market price of risk for a variable θ as

$$\lambda = \frac{\mu - r}{\sigma} \tag{31.1}$$

where r is the risk-free rate, μ is the return on a traded security dependent only on θ, and σ is its volatility. As we showed in Section 25.1, we get the same market price of risk, λ, regardless of the traded security chosen.

Suppose that a real asset depends on several variables θ_i ($i = 1, 2, \dots$). Let m_i and s_i be the expected growth rate and volatility of θ_i so that

$$\frac{d\theta_i}{\theta_i} = m_i\, dt + s_i\, dz_i$$

where z_i is a Wiener process. Define λ_i as the market price of risk of θ_i. We can extend risk-neutral valuation to show that any asset dependent on the θ_i can be valued by[1]

1. Reducing the expected growth rate of each θ_i from m to $m - \lambda s$
2. Discounting cash flows at the risk-free rate.

Example 31.1

The cost of renting commercial real estate in a certain city is quoted as the amount that would be paid per square foot per year in a new 5-year rental agreement. The current cost is \$30 per square foot. The expected growth rate of the cost is 12% per annum, its volatility is 20% per annum, and its market price of risk is 0.3. A company has the opportunity to pay \$1 million now for the option to rent 100,000 square feet at \$35 per square foot for a 5-year period starting in 2 years. The risk-free rate is 5% per annum (assumed constant). Define V as the quoted cost per square foot of office space in 2 years. We make the simplifying assumption that rent is paid annually in advance. The payoff from the option is

$$100{,}000A\max(V - 35,\ 0)$$

where A is an annuity factor given by

$$A = 1 + 1 \times e^{-0.05\times 1} + 1 \times e^{-0.05\times 2} + 1 \times e^{-0.05\times 3} + 1 \times e^{-0.05\times 4} = 4.5355$$

The expected payoff in a risk-neutral world is therefore

$$100{,}000 \times 4.5355 \times \hat{E}[\max(V - 35,\ 0)] = 453{,}550 \times \hat{E}[\max(V - 35,\ 0)]$$

where $\hat{E}$ denotes expectations in a risk-neutral world. Using the result in equation (13A.1), this is

$$453{,}550[\hat{E}(V)N(d_1) - 35N(d_2)]$$

where

$$d_1 = \frac{\ln[\hat{E}(V)/35] + .2^2 \times 2/2}{0.2\sqrt{2}}$$

$$d_2 = \frac{\ln[\hat{E}(V)/35] - .2^2 \times 2/2}{0.2\sqrt{2}}$$

The expected growth rate in the cost of commercial real estate in a risk-neutral

[1] To see that this is consistent with regular risk-neutral valuation, suppose that θ_i is the price of a non-dividend-paying stock. Since this is the price of a traded security, equation (31.1) implies that $(m_i - r)/s_i = \lambda_i$, or $m_i - \lambda_i s_i = r$. The expected growth-rate adjustment is therefore the same as setting the return on the stock equal to the risk-free rate. For a proof of the more general result, see Technical Note 20 on the author's website.

world is $m - \lambda s$, where m is the real-world growth rate, s is the volatility, and λ is the market price of risk. In this case, $m = 0.12$, $s = 0.2$, and $\lambda = 0.3$, so that the expected risk-neutral growth rate is 0.06, or 6%, per year. It follows that $\hat{E}(V) = 30e^{0.06\times 2} = 33.82$. Substituting this in the expression above gives the expected payoff in a risk-neutral world as \$1.5015 million. Discounting at the risk-free rate the value of the option is $1.5015e^{-0.05\times 2} = \$1.3586$ million. This shows that it is worth paying \$1 million for the option.

31.3 ESTIMATING THE MARKET PRICE OF RISK

The real-options approach to evaluating an investment avoids the need to estimate risk-adjusted discount rates in the way described in Section 31.1, but it does require market price of risk parameters for all stochastic variables. When historical data are available for a particular variable, its market price of risk can be estimated using the capital asset pricing model. To show how this is done, we consider an investment asset dependent solely on the variable and define:

μ: Expected return of the investment asset

σ: Volatility of the return of the investment asset

λ: Market price of risk of the variable

ρ: Instantaneous correlation between the percentage changes in the variable and returns on a broad index of stock market prices

μ_m: Expected return on broad index of stock market prices

σ_m: Volatility of return on the broad index of stock market prices

r: Short-term risk-free rate

Because the investment asset is dependent solely on the market variable, the instantaneous correlation between its return and the broad index of stock market prices is also ρ. From the continuous-time version of the capital asset pricing model, we have

$$\mu - r = \frac{\rho\sigma}{\sigma_m}(\mu_m - r)$$

From equation (31.1), another expression for $\mu - r$ is

$$\mu - r = \lambda\sigma$$

It follows that

$$\lambda = \frac{\rho}{\sigma_m}(\mu_m - r) \tag{31.2}$$

This equation can be used to estimate λ.

Example 31.2

A historical analysis of company's sales, quarter by quarter, show that percentage changes in sales have a correlation of 0.3 with returns on the S&P 500 index. The volatility of the S&P 500 is 20% per annum and based on historical data the expected excess return of the S&P 500 over the risk-free rate is 5%. Equation (31.2) estimates the market price of risk for the company's sales as

$$\frac{0.3}{0.2} \times 0.05 = 0.075$$

When no historical data are available for the particular variable under consideration, other similar variables can sometimes be used as proxies. For example, if a plant is being constructed to manufacture a new product, data can be collected on the sales of other similar products. The correlation of the new product with the market index can then be assumed to be the same as that of these other products. In some cases, the estimate of ρ in equation (31.2) must be based on subjective judgment. If an analyst is convinced that a particular variable is unrelated to the performance of a market index, its market price of risk should be set to zero.

For some variables, it is not necessary to estimate the market price of risk because the process followed by a variable in a risk-neutral world can be estimated directly. For example, if the variable is the price of an investment asset, its total return in a risk-neutral world is the risk-free rate. If the variable is the short-term interest rate r, Chapter 28 shows how a risk-neutral process can be estimated from the initial term structure of interest rates. Later in this chapter we will show how the risk-neutral process for a commodity can be estimated from futures prices.

31.4 APPLICATION TO THE VALUATION OF A BUSINESS

Traditional methods of business valuation, such as applying a price/earnings multiplier to current earnings, do not work well for new businesses. Typically a company's earnings are negative during its early years as it attempts to gain market share and establish relationships with customers. The company must be valued by estimating future earnings and cash flows under different scenarios.

The company's future cash flows typically depend on a number of variables such as sales, variable costs as a percent of sales, fixed costs, and so on. Single estimates should be sufficient for some of the variables. For key variables, a risk-neutral stochastic process should be estimated as outlined in the previous two sections. A Monte Carlo simulation can then be carried out to generate alternative scenarios for the net cash flows per year in a risk-neutral world. It is likely that under some of these scenarios the company does very well and under others it becomes bankrupt and ceases operations. (The simulation must have a built in rule for determining when bankruptcy happens.) The value of the company is the present value of the expected cash flow in each year using the risk-free rate for discounting. Business Snapshot 31.1 gives an example of the application of the approach to Amazon.com.

31.5 COMMODITY PRICES

Many investments involve uncertainties related to future commodity prices. Often futures prices can be used to estimate the risk-neutral stochastic process for a commodity price directly. This avoids the need to explicitly estimate a market price of risk for the commodity.

Business Snapshot 31.1 Valuing Amazon.com

One of the earliest published attempts to value a company using the real options approach was Schwartz and Moon (2000), who considered Amazon.com at the end of 1999. They assumed the following stochastic processes for the company's sales revenue R and its revenue growth rate μ:

$$\frac{dR}{R} = \mu\, dt + \sigma(t)\, dz_1$$

$$d\mu = \kappa(\bar{\mu} - \mu)\, dt + \eta(t)\, dz_2$$

They assumed that the two Wiener processes dz_1 and dz_2 were uncorrelated and made reasonable assumptions about $\sigma(t)$, $\eta(t)$, κ, and $\bar{\mu}$ based on available data.

They assumed the cost of goods sold would be 75% of sales, other variable expenses would be 19% of sales, and fixed expenses would be \$75 million per quarter. The initial sales level was \$356 million, the initial tax loss carry forward was \$559 million and the tax rate was assumed to be 35%. The market price of risk for R was estimated from historical data using the approach described in the previous section. The market price of risk for μ was assumed to be zero.

The time horizon for the analysis was 25 years and the terminal value of the company was assumed to be ten times pretax operating profit. The initial cash position was \$906 million and the company was assumed to go bankrupt if the cash balance became negative.

Different future scenarios were generated in a risk-neutral world using Monte Carlo simulation. The evaluation of the scenarios involved taking account of the possible exercise of convertible bonds and the possible exercise of employee stock options. The value of the company to the share holders was calculated as the present value of the net cash flows discounted at the risk-free rate.

Using these assumptions, Schwartz and Moon provided an estimate of the value of Amazon.com's shares at the end of 1999 equal to \$12.42. The market price at the time was \$76.125 (although it declined sharply in 2000). One of the key advantages of the real-options approach is that identifies the key assumptions. Schwartz and Moon found that the estimated share value was very sensitive to $\eta(t)$, the volatility of the growth rate. This was an important source of optionality. A small increase in $\eta(t)$ leads to more optionality and a big increase in the value of Amazon.com shares.

From Section 14.7 the expected future price of a commodity in the traditional risk-neutral world is its futures price. If we assume that the expected growth rate in the commodity price is dependent solely on time and that the volatility of the commodity price is constant, then the risk-neutral process for the commodity price S has the form

$$\frac{dS}{S} = \mu(t)\, dt + \sigma\, dz \tag{31.3}$$

and we have

$$F(t) = \hat{E}[S(t)] = S(0)e^{\int_0^t \mu(\tau)d\tau}$$

where $F(t)$ is the futures price for a contract with maturity t and $\hat{E}$ denotes expected value in a risk-neutral world. It follows that

$$\ln F(t) = \ln S(0) + \int_0^t \mu(\tau)d\tau$$

Differentiating both sides with respect to time gives

$$\mu(t) = \frac{\partial}{\partial t}[\ln F(t)]$$

Example 31.3

Suppose that the futures prices of live cattle at the end of July 2005 are (in cents per pound) as follows:

August 2005	62.20
October 2005	60.60
December 2005	62.70
February 2006	63.37
April 2006	64.42
June 2006	64.40

These can be used to estimate the expected growth rate in live cattle prices in a risk-neutral world. For example, when the model in equation (31.3) is used, the expected growth rate in live cattle prices between October and December 2005, in a risk-neutral world is

$$\ln\left(\frac{62.70}{60.60}\right) = 0.034$$

or 3.4% with continuous compounding. On an annualized basis, this is 20.4% per annum.

Example 31.4

Suppose that the futures prices of live cattle are as in Example 31.3. A certain breeding decision would involve an investment of \$100,000 now and expenditures of \$20,000 in 3 months, 6 months, and 9 months. The result is expected to be that an extra cattle will be available for sale at the end of the year. There are two major uncertainties: the number of pounds of extra cattle that will be available for sale and the price per pound. The expected number of pounds is 300,000. The expected price of cattle in 1 year in a risk-neutral world is, from Example 31.3, 64.40 cents per pound. Assuming that the risk-free rate of interest is 10% per annum, the value of the investment (in thousands of dollars) is

$$-100 - 20e^{-0.1\times 0.25} - 20e^{-0.1\times 0.50} - 20e^{-0.1\times 0.75} + 300 \times 0.644e^{-0.1\times 1} = 17.729$$

This assumes that any uncertainty about the extra amount of cattle that will be available for sale has zero systematic risk and that there is no correlation between the amount of cattle that will be available for sale and the price.

A Mean-Reverting Process

It can be argued that the process in equation (31.3) for commodity prices is too simplistic. In practice, most commodity prices follow mean-reverting processes. They tend to get pulled back to a central value. A more realistic process than equation (31.3) for the risk-neutral process followed by the commodity price S is

$$d \ln S = [\theta(t) - a \ln S]\, dt + \sigma\, dz \qquad \textbf{(31.4)}$$

This incorporates mean reversion and is analogous to the lognormal process assumed for the short-term interest rate in Chapter 28. The trinomial tree methodology in Section 28.7 can be adapted to construct a tree for S and determine the value of $\theta(t)$ such that $F(t) = \hat{E}[S(t)]$

We will illustrate this process by building a three-step tree for oil. Suppose that the spot price of oil is \$20 per barrel and the 1-year, 2-year, and 3-year futures prices are \$22, \$23, and \$24, respectively. Suppose that $a = 0.1$ and $\sigma = 0.2$ in equation (31.4). We first define a variable X that is initially zero and follows the process

$$dX = -a\, dt + \sigma\, dz \qquad \textbf{(31.5)}$$

Using the procedure in Section 28.7, a trinomial tree can be constructed for X. This is shown in Figure 31.1.

The variable $\ln S$ follows the same process as X except for a time-dependent drift. Analogously to Section 28.7, we can convert the tree for X to a tree for $\ln S$ by displacing the positions of nodes. This tree is shown in Figure 31.2. The initial node corresponds to an oil price of 20, so the displacement for that node is $\ln 20$. Suppose

Figure 31.1 Tree for X. Constructing this tree is the first stage in constructing a tree for the spot price of oil, S. Here p_u, p_m, and p_d are the probabilities of "up", "middle", and "down" movements from a node.

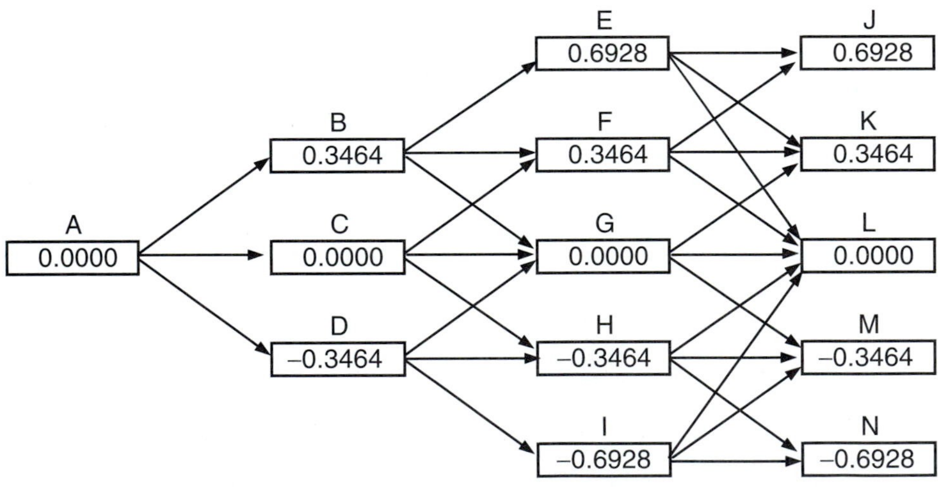

Node:	A	B	C	D	E	F	G	H	I
p_u:	0.1667	0.1217	0.1667	0.2217	0.8867	0.1217	0.1667	0.2217	0.0867
p_m:	0.6666	0.6566	0.6666	0.6566	0.0266	0.6566	0.6666	0.6566	0.0266
p_d:	0.1667	0.2217	0.1667	0.1217	0.0867	0.2217	0.1667	0.1217	0.8867

Figure 31.2 Tree for spot price of oil: p_u, p_m, and p_d are the probabilities of "up", "middle", and "down" movements from a node.

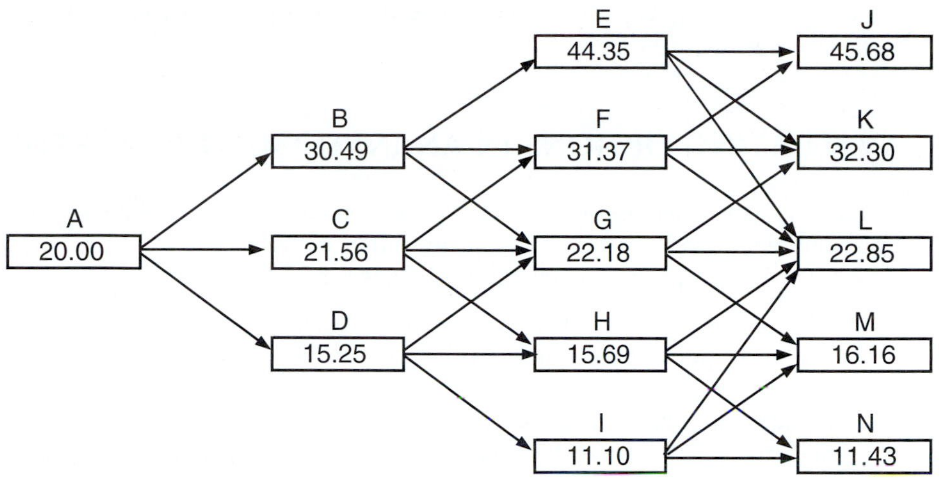

Node:	A	B	C	D	E	F	G	H	I
p_u:	0.1667	0.1217	0.1667	0.2217	0.8867	0.1217	0.1667	0.2217	0.0867
p_m:	0.6666	0.6566	0.6666	0.6566	0.0266	0.6566	0.6666	0.6566	0.0266
p_d:	0.1667	0.2217	0.1667	0.1217	0.0867	0.2217	0.1667	0.1217	0.8867

that the displacements of the nodes at 1 year is α_1. The values of the X at the three nodes at the 1-year point are +0.3464, 0, and −0.3464. The corresponding values of ln S are $0.3464+\alpha_1$, α_1, and $-0.3464+\alpha_1$. The values of S are therefore $e^{0.3464+\alpha_1}$, e^{α_1}, and $e^{-0.3464+\alpha_1}$, respectively. We require the expected value of S to equal the futures price. This means that

$$0.1667e^{0.3464+\alpha_1}+0.6666e^{\alpha_1}+0.1667e^{-0.3464+\alpha_1}=22$$

The solution to this is $\alpha_1=3.071$. The values of S at the 1-year point are therefore 30.49, 21.56, and 15.25.

At the 2-year point, we first calculate the probabilities of nodes E, F, G, H, and I being reached from the probabilities of nodes B, C, and D being reached. The probability of reaching node F is the probability of reaching node B times the probability of moving from B to F plus the probability of reaching node C times the probability of moving from C to F. This is

$$0.1667\times 0.6566+0.6666\times 0.1667=0.2206$$

Similarly the probabilities of reaching nodes E, G, H, and I are 0.0203, 0.5183, 0.2206, and 0.0203, respectively. The amount α_2 by which the nodes at time 2 years are displaced must satisfy

$$0.0203e^{0.6928+\alpha_2}+0.2206e^{0.3464+\alpha_2}+0.5183e^{\alpha_2}+0.2206e^{-0.3464+\alpha_2}+0.0203e^{-0.6928+\alpha_2}=23$$

The solution to this is $\alpha_2 = 3.099$. This means that the values of S at the 2-year point are 44.35, 31.37, 22.18, 15.69, and 11.10, respectively.

A similar calculation can be carried out at time 3 years. Figure 31.2 shows the resulting tree for S. We will illustrate how the tree can be used in the valuation of a real option in the next section.

31.6 EVALUATING OPTIONS IN AN INVESTMENT OPPORTUNITY

As already mentioned, most investment projects involve options. These options can add considerable value to the project and are often either ignored or valued incorrectly. Examples of the options embedded in projects are:

1. *Abandonment options*. This is an option to sell or close down a project. It is an American put option on the project's value. The strike price of the option is the liquidation (or resale) value of the project less any closing-down costs. When the liquidation value is low, the strike price can be negative. Abandonment options mitigate the impact of very poor investment outcomes and increase the initial valuation of a project.
2. *Expansion options*. This is the option to make further investments and increase the output if conditions are favorable. It is an American call option on the value of additional capacity. The strike price of the call option is the cost of creating this additional capacity discounted to the time of option exercise. The strike price often depends on the initial investment. If management initially choose to build capacity in excess of the expected level of output, the strike price can be relatively small.
3. *Contraction options*. This is the option to reduce the scale of a project's operation. It is an American put option on the value of the lost capacity. The strike price is the present value of the future expenditures saved as seen at the time of exercise of the option.
4. *Options to defer*. One of the most important options open to a manager is the option to defer a project. This is an American call option on the value of the project.
5. *Options to extend*. Sometimes it is possible to extend the life of an asset by paying a fixed amount. This is a European call option on the asset's future value.

As a simple example of the evaluation of an investment with an embedded option, consider a company that has to decide whether to invest \$15 million to obtain 6 million barrels of oil from a certain source at the rate of 2 million barrels per year for 3 years. The fixed costs of operating the equipment are \$6 million per year and the variable costs are \$17 per barrel. We assume that the risk-free interest rate is 10% per annum for all maturities, that the spot price of oil is \$20 per barrel, and that the 1-, 2-, and 3-year futures prices are \$22, \$23, and \$24 per barrel, respectively. We assume that the stochastic process for oil prices has been estimated as equation (31.4) with $a = 0.1$ and $\sigma = 0.2$. This means that the tree in Figure 31.2 describes the behavior of oil prices in a risk-neutral world.

First assume that the project has no embedded options. The expected prices of oil in 1, 2, and 3 years' time in a risk-neutral world are \$22, \$23, and \$24, respectively. The expected payoff from the project (in millions of dollars) in a risk-neutral world can be calculated from the cost data as 4.0, 6.0, and 8.0 in years 1, 2, and 3, respectively. The value of the project is therefore

$$-15.0 + 4.0e^{-0.1\times 1} + 6.0e^{-0.1\times 2} + 8.0e^{0.1\times 3} = -0.54$$

This analysis indicates that the project should not be undertaken because it would reduce shareholder wealth by 0.54 million.

Figure 31.3 shows the value of the project at each node of Figure 31.2. This is calculated from Figure 31.2. Consider, for example, node H. There is a 0.2217 probability that the price of oil at the end of the third year is 22.85, so that the third-year profit is $2 \times 22.85 - 2 \times 17 - 6 = 5.70$. Similarly, there is a 0.6566 probability that the price of oil at the end of the third year is 16.16, so that the profit is −7.68 and there is a 0.1217 probability that the price of oil at the end of the third year is 11.43, so that the profit is −17.14. The value of the project at node H in Figure 31.3 is therefore

$$[0.2217 \times 5.70 + 0.6566 \times (-7.68) + 0.1217 \times (-17.14)]e^{-0.1\times 1} = -5.31$$

As another example, consider node C. There is a 0.1667 chance of moving to node F where the oil price is 31.37. The second year cash flow is then $2 \times 31.37 - 2 \times 17 - 6 = 22.74$. The value of subsequent cash flows at node F is 21.42. The total value of the project if we move to node F is therefore $21.42 + 22.74 = 44.16$. Similarly the total value of the project if we move to nodes G and H are 10.35 and −13.93, respectively. The value

Figure 31.3 Valuation of base project with no embedded options: p_u, p_m, and p_d are the probabilities of "up", "middle", and "down" movements from a node.

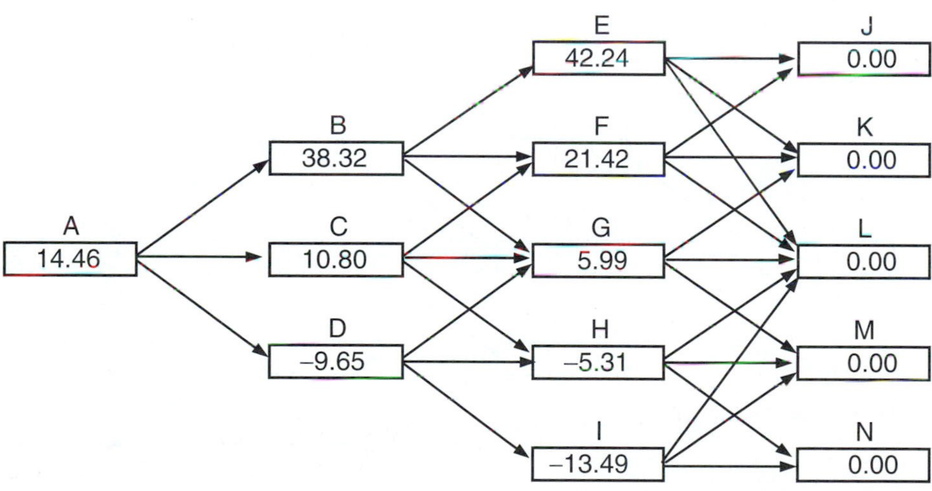

Node:	A	B	C	D	E	F	G	H	I
p_u:	0.1667	0.1217	0.1667	0.2217	0.8867	0.1217	0.1667	0.2217	0.0867
p_m:	0.6666	0.6566	0.6666	0.6566	0.0266	0.6566	0.6666	0.6566	0.0266
p_d:	0.1667	0.2217	0.1667	0.1217	0.0867	0.2217	0.1667	0.1217	0.8867

of the project at node C is therefore

$$[0.1667 \times 44.16 + 0.6666 \times 10.35 + 0.1667 \times (-13.93)]e^{-0.1\times 1} = 10.80$$

Figure 31.3 shows that the value of the project at the initial node A is 14.46. When the initial investment is taken into account the value of the project is therefore −0.54. This is in agreement with our earlier calculations.

Suppose now that the company has the option to abandon the project at any time. We suppose that there is no salvage value and no further payments are required once the project has been abandoned. Abandonment is an American put option with a strike price of zero and is valued in Figure 31.4. The put option should not be exercised at nodes E, F, and G because the value of the project is positive at these nodes. It should be exercised at nodes H and I. The value of the put option is 5.31 and 13.49 at nodes H and I, respectively. Rolling back through the tree, the value of the abandonment put option at node D if it is not exercised is

$$(0.1217 \times 13.49 + 0.6566 \times 5.31 + 0.2217 \times 0)e^{-0.1\times 1} = 4.64$$

The value of exercising the put option at node D is 9.65. This is greater than 4.64, and so the put should be exercised at node D. The value of the put option at node C is

$$[0.1667 \times 0 + 0.6666 \times 0 + 0.1667 \times (5.31)]e^{-0.1\times 1} = 0.80$$

Figure 31.4 Valuation of option to abandon the project: p_u, p_m, and p_d are the probabilities of "up", "middle", and "down" movements from a node.

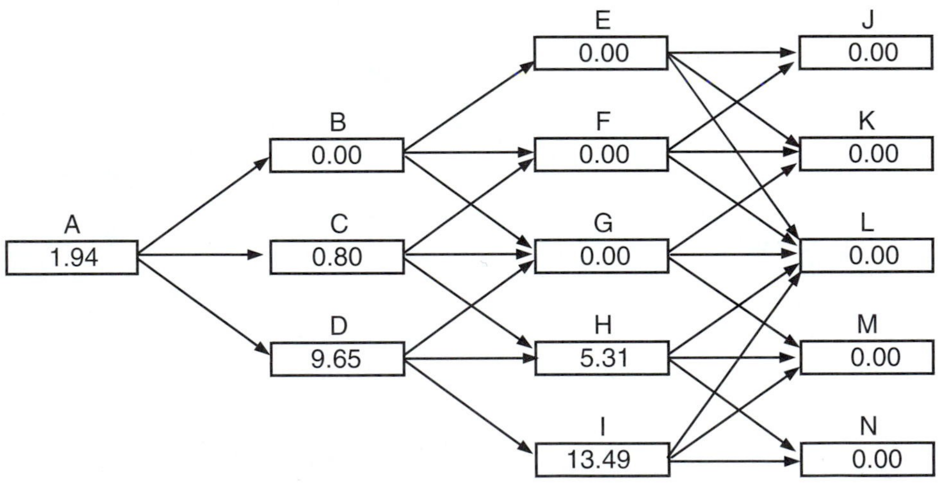

Node:	A	B	C	D	E	F	G	H	I
p_u:	0.1667	0.1217	0.1667	0.2217	0.8867	0.1217	0.1667	0.2217	0.0867
p_m:	0.6666	0.6566	0.6666	0.6566	0.0266	0.6566	0.6666	0.6566	0.0266
p_d:	0.1667	0.2217	0.1667	0.1217	0.0867	0.2217	0.1667	0.1217	0.8867

Figure 31.5 Valuation of option to expand the project: p_u, p_m, and p_d are the probabilities of "up", "middle", and "down" movements from a node.

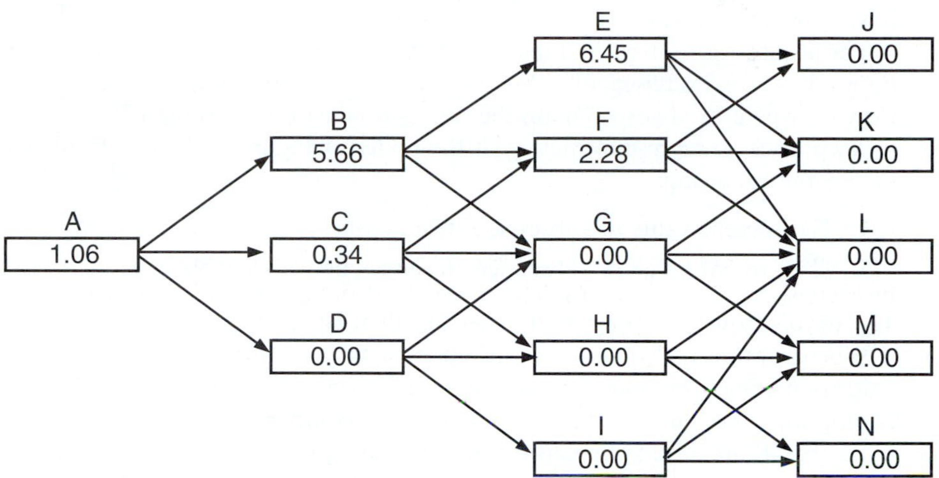

Node:	A	B	C	D	E	F	G	H	I
p_u:	0.1667	0.1217	0.1667	0.2217	0.8867	0.1217	0.1667	0.2217	0.0867
p_m:	0.6666	0.6566	0.6666	0.6566	0.0266	0.6566	0.6666	0.6566	0.0266
p_d:	0.1667	0.2217	0.1667	0.1217	0.0867	0.2217	0.1667	0.1217	0.8867

and the value at node A is

$$(0.1667 \times 0 + 0.6666 \times 0.80 + 0.1667 \times 9.65)e^{-0.1\times 1} = 1.94$$

The abandonment option is therefore worth \$1.94 million. It increases the value of the project from −\$0.54 million to +\$1.40 million. A project that was previously unattractive now has a positive value to shareholders.

Suppose next that the company has no abandonment option. Instead it has the option at any time to increase the scale of the project by 20%. The cost of doing this is \$2 million. Oil production increases from 2.0 to 2.4 million barrels. Variable costs remain \$17 per barrel and fixed costs increase by 20% from \$6.0 million to \$7.2 million. This is an American call option to buy 20% of the base project in Figure 31.3 for \$2 million. The option is valued in Figure 31.5. At node E, the option should be exercised. The payoff is $0.2 \times 42.24 - 2 = 6.45$. At node F, it should also be exercised for a payoff of $0.2 \times 21.42 - 2 = 2.28$. At nodes G, H, and I, the option should not be exercised. At node B, exercising is worth more than waiting and the option is worth $0.2 \times 38.32 - 2 = 5.66$. At node C, if the option is not exercised, it is worth

$$(0.1667 \times 2.28 + 0.6666 \times 0.00 + 0.1667 \times 0.00)e^{-0.1\times 1} = 0.34$$

If the option is exercised, it is worth $0.2 \times 10.80 - 2 = 0.16$. The option should therefore not be exercised at node C. At node A, if not exercised, the option is worth

$$(0.1667 \times 5.66 + 0.6666 \times 0.34 + 0.1667 \times 0.00)e^{-0.1\times 1} = 1.06$$

If the option is exercised it is worth $0.2 \times 14.46 - 2 = 0.89$. Early exercise is therefore not optimal at node A. In this case, the option increases the value of the project from -0.54 to $+0.52$. Again we find that a project that previously had a negative value now has a positive value.

The expansion option in Figure 31.5 is relatively easy to value because, once the option has been exercised, all subsequent cash inflows and outflows increase by 20%. In the case where fixed costs remain the same or increase by less than 20%, it is necessary to keep track of more information at the nodes of Figure 31.3. Specifically we need to record the following:

1. The present value of subsequent fixed costs
2. The present value of subsequent revenues net of variable costs

The payoff from exercising the option can then be calculated.

When a project has two or more options, they are typically not independent. The value of having both option A and option B is typically not the sum of the values of the two options. To illustrate this, suppose that the company we have been considering has both abandonment and expansion options. The project cannot be expanded if it has already been abandoned. Moreover, the value of the put option to abandon depends on whether the project has been expanded.[2]

These interactions between the options in our example can be handled by defining four states at each node:

1. Not already abandoned; not already expanded
2. Not already abandoned; already expanded
3. Already abandoned; not already expanded
4. Already abandoned; already expanded

When we roll back through the tree we calculate the combined value of the options at each node for all four alternatives. This approach to valuing path-dependent options is discussed in more detail in Section 24.4.

When there are several stochastic variables, the value of the base project is usually determined by Monte Carlo simulation. The valuation of the project's embedded options is then more difficult because a Monte Carlo simulation works from the beginning to the end of a project. When we reach a certain point, we do not have information on the present value of the project's future cash flows. However, the techniques mentioned in Section 24.7 for valuing American options using Monte Carlo simulation can sometimes be used.

As an illustration of this point, Schwartz and Moon (2000) explain how their Amazon.com analysis outlined in Busness Snapshot 31.1 could be extended to take account of the option to abandon (i.e. the option to declare bankruptcy) when the value of future cash flows is negative.[3] At each time step, a polynomial relationship between the value of not abandoning and variables such as the current revenue, revenue growth rate, volatilities, cash balances, and loss carry forwards is assumed. Each simulation trial

[2] As it happens, the two options do not interact in Figures 31.4 and 31.5. However, the interactions between the options would become an issue if a larger tree with smaller time steps were built.

[3] The analysis in Section 31.4 assumed that bankruptcy occurs when the cash balance falls below zero, but this is not necessarily optimal for Amazon.com.

provides an observation for obtaining a least-squares estimate of the relationship at each time. This is the Longstaff and Schwartz approach of Section 24.7.[4]

SUMMARY

In this chapter, we have investigated how the ideas developed earlier in the book can be applied to the valuation of real assets and options on real assets. We have shown how the risk-neutral valuation principle can be used to value an asset dependent on any set of variables. The expected growth rate of each variable is adjusted to reflect its market price of risk. The value of the asset is then the present value of its expected cash flows discounted at the risk-free rate.

Risk-neutral valuation provides an internally consistent approach to capital investment appraisal. It also makes it possible to value the options that are embedded in many of the projects that are encountered in practice. We have illustrated the approach by applying it to the valuation of Amazon.com at the end of 1999 and the valuation of an oil project.

FURTHER READING

Amran, M., and N. Kulatilaka, *Real Options*, Boston, MA: Harvard Business School Press, 1999.

Copeland, T., T. Koller, and J. Murrin, *Valuation: Measuring and Managing the Value of Companies*, 3rd edn. New York: Wiley, 2000.

Copeland, T., and V. Antikarov, *Real Options: A Practitioners Guide*, New York: Texere, 2001.

Schwartz, E. S., and M. Moon, "Rational Pricing of Internet Companies," *Financial Analysts Journal*, May/June (2000): 62–75.

Trigeorgis, L., *Real Options: Managerial Flexibility and Strategy in Resource Allocation*, Cambridge, MA: MIT Press, 1996.

Questions and Problems (Answers in Solutions Manual)

31.1. Explain the difference between the net present value approach and the risk-neutral valuation approach for valuing a new capital investment opportunity. What are the advantages of the risk-neutral valuation approach for valuing real options?

31.2. The market price of risk for copper is 0.5, the volatility of copper prices is 20% per annum, the spot price is 80 cents per pound, and the 6-month futures price is 75 cents per pound. What is the expected percentage growth rate in copper prices over the next 6 months?

31.3. Consider a commodity with constant volatility σ and an expected growth rate that is a function solely of time. Show that, in the traditional risk-neutral world,

$$\ln S_T \sim \phi[(\ln F(T) - \tfrac{1}{2}\sigma^2 T, \sigma\sqrt{T}]$$

[4] F. A. Longstaff and E. S. Schwartz, "Valuing American Options by Simulation: A Simple Least-Squares Approach," *Review of Financial Studies*, 14, 1 (Spring 2001): 113–47.

where S_T is the value of the commodity at time T and $F(t)$ is the futures price at time 0 for a contract maturing at time t.

31.4. Derive a relationship between the convenience yield of a commodity and its market price of risk.

31.5. The correlation between a company's gross revenue and the market index is 0.2. The excess return of the market over the risk-free rate is 6% and the volatility of the market index is 18%. What is the market price of risk for the company's revenue?

31.6. A company can buy an option for the delivery of 1 million barrels of oil in 3 years at \$25 per barrel. The 3-year futures price of oil is \$24 per barrel. The risk-free interest rate is 5% per annum with continuous compounding and the volatility of the futures price is 20% per annum. How much is the option worth?

31.7. A driver entering into a car lease agreement can obtain the right to buy the car in 4 years for \$10,000. The current value of the car is \$30,000. The value of the car, S, is expected to follow the process

$$dS = \mu S\,dt + \sigma S\,dz$$

where $\mu = -0.25$, $\sigma = 0.15$, and dz is a Wiener process. The market price of risk for the car price is estimated to be -0.1. What is the value of the option? Assume that the risk-free rate for all maturities is 6%.

Assignment Questions

31.8. Suppose that the spot price, 6-month futures price, and 12-month futures price for wheat are 250, 260, and 270 cents per bushel, respectively. Suppose that the price of wheat follows the process in equation (31.4) with $a = 0.05$ and $\sigma = 0.15$. Construct a two-time-step tree for the price of wheat in a risk-neutral world.

A farmer has a project that involves an expenditure of \$10,000 and a further expenditure of \$90,000 in 6 months. It will increase wheat that is harvested and sold by 40,000 bushels in 1 year. What is the value of the project? Suppose that the farmer can abandon the project in 6 months and avoid paying the \$90,000 cost at that time. What is the value of the abandonment option? Assume a risk-free rate of 5% with continuous compounding.

31.9. In the oil example considered in Section 31.6:

(a) What is the value of the abandonment option if it costs \$3 million rather than zero?

(b) What is the value of the expansion option if it costs \$5 million rather than \$2 million?

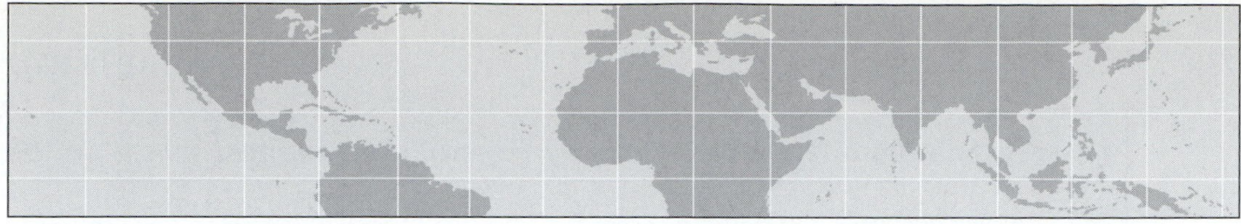

CHAPTER 32

Derivatives Mishaps and What We Can Learn from Them

Since the mid-1980s there have been some spectacular losses in derivatives markets. Some of the losses made by financial institutions are listed in Business Snapshot 32.1, and some of those made by nonfinancial organizations in Business Snapshot 32.2. What is remarkable about these lists is the number of situations where huge losses arose from the activities of a single employee. In 1995, Nick Leeson's trading brought a 200-year-old British bank, Barings, to its knees; in 1994, Robert Citron's trading led to Orange County, a municipality in California, losing about $2 billion. Joseph Jett's trading for Kidder Peabody lost $350 million. John Rusnak's losses of $700 million for Allied Irish Bank came to light in 2002. The huge losses at Daiwa, Shell, and Sumitomo were also each the result of the activities of a single individual.

The losses should not be viewed as an indictment of the whole derivatives industry. The derivatives market is a vast multitrillion dollar market that by most measures has been outstandingly successful and has served the needs of its users well. The events listed represent a tiny proportion of the total trades (both in number and value). Nevertheless, it is worth considering carefully the lessons we can learn from them. This is what we will do in this final chapter.

32.1 LESSONS FOR ALL USERS OF DERIVATIVES

First, we consider the lessons appropriate to all users of derivatives, whether they are financial or nonfinancial companies.

Define Risk Limits

It is essential that all companies define in a clear and unambiguous way limits to the financial risks that can be taken. They should then set up procedures for ensuring that the limits are obeyed. Ideally, overall risk limits should be set at board level. These should then be converted to limits applicable to the individuals responsible for managing particular risks. Daily reports should indicate the gain or loss that will be

Business Snapshot 32.1 Big Losses by Financial Institutions

Allied Irish bank

This bank lost about $700 million from speculative activities of one of its foreign exchange traders, John Rusnak, that lasted a number of years. Rusnak covered up his losses by creating fictitious option trades.

Barings (see page 15)

This 200-year-old British bank was wiped out in 1995 by the activities of one trader, Nick Leeson, in Singapore. The trader's mandate was to arbitrage between Nikkei 225 futures quotes in Singapore and Osaka. Instead, he made big bets on the future direction of the Nikkei 225 using futures and options. The total loss was close to $1 billion.

Daiwa Bank

A trader working in New York for this Japanese bank lost more than $1 billion in the 1990s.

Kidder Peabody (see page 103)

The activities of a single trader, Joseph Jett, led to this New York investment dealer losing $350 million trading U.S. government securities and their strips. (Strips are created when each of the cash flows underlying a bond is sold as a separate security.) The loss arose because of a mistake in the way the company's computer system calculated profits.

Long-Term Capital Management (see page 30)

This hedge fund lost about $4 billion in 1998. The strategy followed by the fund was convergence arbitrage. This involved attempting to identify two nearly identical securities whose prices were temporarily out of line with each other. The company would buy the less expensive security and short the more expensive one, hedging any residual risks. In mid-1998 the company was badly hurt by widening credit spreads resulting from defaults on Russian bonds. The hedge fund was considered too large to fail. The New York Federal Reserve organized a $3.5 billion bailout by encouraging 14 banks to invest in the fund.

Midland Bank

This British bank lost $500 million in the early 1990s largely because of a wrong bet on the direction of interest rates. It was later taken over by the Hong Kong and Shanghai bank.

National Westminster Bank

This British bank lost about $130 million from using an inappropriate model to value swap options in 1997.

experienced for particular movements in market variables. These should be checked against the actual gains and losses that are experienced to ensure that the valuation procedures underlying the reports are accurate.

It is particularly important that companies monitor risks carefully when derivatives are used. This is because, as we saw in Chapter 1, derivatives can be used for hedging, speculation, and arbitrage. Without close monitoring, it is impossible to know whether

Business Snapshot 32.2 Big Losses by Nonfinancial Organizations

Allied Lyons
The treasury department of this drinks and food company lost $150 million in 1991 selling call options on the US dollar–sterling exchange rate.

Gibson Greetings
The treasury department of this greeting card manufacturer in Cincinnati lost about $20 million in 1994 trading highly exotic interest rate derivatives contracts with Bankers Trust. They later sued Bankers Trust and settled out of court.

Hammersmith and Fulham *(see page 173)*
This British Local Authority lost about $600 million on sterling interest rate swaps and options in 1988. All its contracts were later declared null and void by the British courts, much to the annoyance of the banks on the other side of the transactions.

Metallgesellschaft *(see page 68)*
This German company entered into long-term contracts to supply oil and gasoline and hedged them by rolling over short-term futures contracts. It lost $1.8 billion when it was forced to discontinue this activity.

Orange County *(see page 86)*
The activities of the treasurer, Robert Citron, led to this California municipality losing about $2 billion in 1994. The treasurer was using derivatives to speculate that interest rates would not rise.

Procter & Gamble *(see page 709)*
The treasury department of this large U.S. company lost about $90 million in 1994 trading highly exotic interest rate derivatives contracts with Bankers Trust. They later sued Bankers Trust and settled out of court.

Shell
A single employee working in the Japanese subsidiary of this company lost $1 billion dollars in unauthorized trading of currency futures.

Sumitomo
A single trader working for this Japanese company lost about $2 billion in the copper spot, futures, and options market in the 1990s.

a derivatives trader has switched from being a hedger to a speculator or switched from being an arbitrageur to being a speculator. Barings is a classic example of what can go wrong. Nick Leeson's mandate was to carry out low-risk arbitrage between the Singapore and Osaka markets on Nikkei 225 futures. Unknown to his superiors in London, Leeson switched from being an arbitrageur to taking huge bets on the future direction of the Nikkei 225. Systems within Barings were so inadequate that nobody knew what he was doing.

The argument here is not that no risks should be taken. A treasurer working for a corporation, or a trader in a financial institution, or a fund manager should be allowed to take positions on the future direction of relevant market variables. What we are arguing is that the sizes of the positions that can be taken should be limited and the systems in place should accurately report the risks being taken.

Take the Risk Limits Seriously

What happens if an individual exceeds risk limits and makes a profit? This is a tricky issue for senior management. It is tempting to ignore violations of risk limits when profits result. However, this is shortsighted. It leads to a culture where risk limits are not taken seriously, and it paves the way for a disaster. In many of the situations listed in Business Snapshots 32.1 and 32.2, the companies had become complacent about the risks they were taking because they had taken similar risks in previous years and made profits.

The classic example here is Orange County. Robert Citron's activities in 1991–93 had been very profitable for Orange County, and the municipality had come to rely on his trading for additional funding. People chose to ignore the risks he was taking because he had produced profits. Unfortunately, the losses made in 1994 far exceeded the profits from previous years.

The penalties for exceeding risk limits should be just as great when profits result as when losses result. Otherwise, traders who make losses are liable to keep increasing their bets in the hope that eventually a profit will result and all will be forgiven.

Do Not Assume You Can Outguess the Market

Some traders are quite possibly better than others. But no trader gets it right all the time. A trader who correctly predicts the direction in which market variables will move 60% of the time is doing well. If a trader has an outstanding track record (as Robert Citron did in the early 1990s), it is likely to be a result of luck rather than superior trading skill.

Suppose that a financial institution employs 16 traders and one of those traders makes profits in every quarter of a year. Should the trader receive a good bonus? Should the trader's risk limits be increased? The answer to the first question is that inevitably the trader will receive a good bonus. The answer to the second question should be no. The chance of making a profit in four consecutive quarters from random trading is 0.5^4 or 1 in 16. This means that just by chance one of the 16 traders will "get it right" every single quarter of the year. We should not assume that the trader's luck will continue and we should not increase the trader's risk limits.

Do Not Underestimate the Benefits of Diversification

When a trader appears good at predicting a particular market variable, there is a tendency to increase the trader's limits. We have just argued that this is a bad idea because it is quite likely that the trader has been lucky rather than clever. However, let us suppose that we are really convinced that the trader has special talents. How undiversified should we allow ourselves to become in order to take advantage of the trader's special skills? The answer is that the benefits from diversification are huge, and it is unlikely that any trader is so good that it is worth foregoing these benefits to speculate heavily on just one market variable.

An example will illustrate the point here. Suppose that there are 20 stocks, each of which have an expected return of 10% per annum and a standard deviation of returns of 30%. The correlation between the returns from any two of the stocks is 0.2. By dividing an investment equally among the 20 stocks, an investor has an expected return of 10% per annum and standard deviation of returns of 14.7%. Diversification enables the investor to reduce risks by over half. Another way of expressing this is that diversification enables an investor to double the expected return per unit of risk taken. The investor would have to be extremely good at stock picking to get a better risk–return tradeoff by investing in just one stock.

Carry out Scenario Analyses and Stress Tests

The calculation of risk measures such as VaR should always be accompanied by scenario analyses and stress testing to obtain an understanding of what can go wrong. These techniques were mentioned in Chapter 18. They are very important. Human beings have an unfortunate tendency to anchor on one or two scenarios when evaluating decisions. In 1993 and 1994, for example, Procter & Gamble and Gibson Greetings were so convinced that interest rates would remain low that they ignored the possibility of a 100-basis-point increase in their decision making.

It is important to be creative in the way scenarios are generated. One approach is to look at 10 or 20 years of data and choose the most extreme events as scenarios. Sometimes there is a shortage of data on a key variable. It is then sensible to choose a similar variable for which much more data is available and use historical daily percentage changes in that variable as a proxy for possible daily percentage changes in the key variable. For example, if there is little data on the prices of bonds issued by a particular country, we can look at historical data on prices of bonds issued by other similar countries to develop possible scenarios.

32.2 LESSONS FOR FINANCIAL INSTITUTIONS

We now move on to consider lessons that are primarily relevant to financial institutions.

Monitor Traders Carefully

In trading rooms there is a tendency to regard high-performing traders as "untouchable" and to not subject their activities to the same scrutiny as other traders. Apparently Joseph Jett, Kidder Peabody's star trader of Treasury instruments, was often "too busy" to answer questions and discuss his positions with the company's risk managers.

It is important that all traders—particularly those making high profits—be fully accountable. It is important for the financial institution to know whether the high profits are being made by taking unreasonably high risks. It is also important to check that the financial institution's computer systems and pricing models are correct and are not being manipulated in some way.

Separate the Front, Middle, and Back Office

The *front office* in a financial institution consists of the traders who are executing trades, taking positions, and so forth. The *middle office* consists of risk managers who are monitoring the risks being taken. The *back office* is where the record keeping and accounting takes place. Some of the worst derivatives disasters have occurred because these functions were not kept separate. Nick Leeson controlled both the front and back office for Barings in Singapore and was, as a result, able to conceal the disastrous nature of his trades from his superiors in London for some time. Although full details are not available, it appears that a lack of separation of the front and back office was at least partially responsible for the huge losses experienced by Sumitomo in copper trading.

Do Not Blindly Trust Models

Some of the large losses in by financial institutions arose because of the models and computer systems being used. We discussed how Kidder Peabody was misled by its own systems on page 103. Another example of an incorrect model leading to losses is provided by National Westminster Bank. This bank had an incorrect model for valuing swap options that led to significant losses.

If large profits are reported when relatively simple trading strategies are followed, there is a good chance that the models underlying the calculation of the profits are wrong. Similarly, if a financial institution appears to be particularly competitive on its quotes for a particular type of deal, there is a good chance that it is using a different model from other market participants, and it should analyze what is going on carefully. To the head of a trading room, getting too much business of a certain type can be just as worrisome as getting too little business of that type.

Be Conservative in Recognizing Inception Profits

When a financial institution sells a highly exotic instrument to a nonfinancial corporation, the valuation can be highly dependent on the underlying model. For example, instruments with long-dated embedded interest rate options can be highly dependent on the interest rate model used. In these circumstances, a phrase used to describe the daily marking to market of the deal is *marking to model*. This is because there are no market prices for similar deals that can be used as a benchmark.

Suppose that a financial institution manages to sell an instrument to a client for \$10 million more than it is worth—or at least \$10 million more than its model says it is worth. The \$10 million is known as an *inception profit*. When should it be recognized? There appears to be quite a variation in what different investment banks do. Some recognize the \$10 million immediately, whereas others are much more conservative and recognize it slowly over the life of the deal.

Recognizing inception profits immediately is very dangerous. It encourages traders to use aggressive models, take their bonuses, and leave before the model and the value of the deal come under close scrutiny. It is much better to recognize inception profits slowly, so that traders have the motivation to investigate the impact of several different models and several different sets of assumptions before committing themselves to a deal.

Do Not Sell Clients Inappropriate Products

It is tempting to sell corporate clients inappropriate products, particularly when they appear to have an appetite for the underlying risks. But this is shortsighted. The most dramatic example of this is the activities of Bankers Trust (BT) in the period leading up to the spring of 1994. Many of BT's clients were persuaded to buy high-risk and totally inappropriate products. A typical product (e.g., the 5/30 swap discussed on page 709) would give the client a good chance of saving a few basis points on its borrowings and a small chance of costing a large amount of money. The products worked well for BT's clients in 1992 and 1993, but blew up in 1994 when interest rates rose sharply. The bad publicity that followed hurt BT greatly. The years it had spent building up trust among corporate clients and developing an enviable reputation for innovation in derivatives were largely lost as a result of the activities of a few overly aggressive salesmen. BT was forced to pay large amounts of money to its clients to settle lawsuits out of court. It was taken over by Deutsche Bank in 1999.

Do Not Ignore Liquidity Risk

Financial engineers usually base the pricing of exotic instruments and other instruments that trade relatively infrequently on the prices of actively traded instruments. For example:

1. A financial engineer often calculates a zero curve from actively traded government bonds (known as on-the-run bonds) and uses it to price bonds that trade less frequently (off-the-run bonds).
2. A financial engineer often implies the volatility of an asset from actively traded options and uses it to price less actively traded options.
3. A financial engineer often implies information about the behavior of interest rates from actively traded interest rate caps and swap options and uses it to price products that are highly structured.

These practices are not unreasonable. However, it is dangerous to assume that less actively traded instruments can always be traded at close to their theoretical price. When financial markets experience a shock of one sort or another there is often a "flight to quality." Liquidity becomes very important to investors, and illiquid instruments often sell at a big discount to their theoretical values. Trading strategies that assume large volumes of relatively illiquid instruments can be sold at short notice at close to their theoretical values are dangerous.

An example of liquidity risk is provided by Long-Term Capital Management (LTCM), which we discussed in Business Snapshot 2.2. This hedge fund followed a strategy known as *convergence arbitrage*. It attempted to identify two securities (or portfolios of securities) that should in theory sell for the same price. If the market price of one security was less that of the other, it would buy that security and sell the other. The strategy is based on the idea that if two securities have the same theoretical price their market prices should eventually be the same.

In the summer of 1998 LTCM made a huge loss. This was largely because a default by Russia on its debt caused a flight to quality. LTCM tended to be long illiquid instruments and short the corresponding liquid instruments (for example, it was long off-the-run bonds and short on-the-run bonds). The spreads between the prices of illiquid instruments and the corresponding liquid instruments widened sharply after the Russian default. LTCM was highly leveraged. It experienced huge losses and there were margin calls on its positions that it was unable to meet.

The LTCM story reinforces the importance of carrying out scenario analyses and stress testing to look at what can happen in the worst of all worlds. LTCM could have tried to examine other times in history when there have been extreme flights to quality to quantify the liquidity risks it was facing.

Beware When Everyone Is Following the Same Trading Strategy

It sometimes happens that many market participants are following essentially the same trading strategy. This creates a dangerous environment where there are liable to be big market moves, unstable markets, and large losses for the market participants.

We gave one example of this in Chapter 15 when discussing portfolio insurance and the market crash of October 1987. In the months leading up to the crash, increasing numbers of portfolio managers were attempting to insure their portfolios by creating synthetic put options. They bought stocks or stock index futures after a rise in the market and sold them after a fall. This created an unstable market. A relatively small decline in stock prices could lead to a wave of selling by portfolio insurers. The latter would lead to a further decline in the market, which could give rise to another wave of selling, and so on. There is little doubt that without portfolio insurance the crash of October 1987 would have been much less severe.

Another example is provided by LTCM in 1998. Its position was made more difficult by the fact that many other hedge funds were following similar convergence arbitrage strategies. After the Russian default and the flight to quality, LTCM tried to liquidate part of its portfolio to meet margin calls. Unfortunately, other hedge funds were facing similar problems to LTCM and trying to do similar trades. This exacerbated the situation, causing liquidity spreads to be even higher than they would otherwise have been and reinforcing the flight to quality. Consider, for example, LTCM's position in U.S. Treasury bonds. It was long the illiquid off-the-run bonds and short the liquid on-the-run bonds. When a flight to quality caused spreads between yields on the two types of bonds to widen, LTCM had to liquidate its positions by selling off-the-run bonds and buying on-the-run bonds. Other large hedge funds were doing the same. As a result, the price of on-the-run bonds rose relative to off-the-run bonds and the spread between the two yields widened even more than it had done already.

A further example is provided by the activities of British insurance companies in the late 1990s. These insurance companies had entered into many contracts promising that the rate of interest applicable to an annuity received by an individual on retirement would be the greater of the market rate and a guaranteed rate. At about the same time, all insurance companies decided to hedge part of their risks on these contracts by buying long-dated swap options from financial institutions. The financial institutions they dealt with hedged their risks by buying huge numbers of long-dated sterling bonds. As a result, bond prices rose and long sterling rates declined. More bonds had to be bought to maintain the dynamic hedge, long sterling rates declined further, and so on. Financial institutions lost money and, because long rates declined, insurance companies found themselves in a worse position on the risks that they had chosen not to hedge.

The chief lesson to be learned from these stories is that it is important to see the big picture of what is going on in financial markets and to understand the risks inherent in situations where many market participants are following the same trading strategy.

32.3 LESSONS FOR NONFINANCIAL CORPORATIONS

We now consider lessons primarily applicable to nonfinancial corporations.

Make Sure You Fully Understand the Trades You Are Doing

Corporations should never undertake a trade or a trading strategy that they do not fully understand. This is a somewhat obvious point, but it is surprising how often a trader working for a nonfinancial corporation will, after a big loss, admit to not knowing what was really going on and claim to have been misled by investment bankers. Robert Citron, the treasurer of Orange County did this. So did the traders working for Hammersmith and Fulham, who in spite of their huge positions were surprisingly uninformed about how the swaps and other interest rate derivatives they traded really worked.

If a senior manager in a corporation does not understand a trade proposed by a subordinate, the trade should not be approved. A simple rule of thumb is that if a trade and the rationale for entering into it are so complicated that they cannot be understood by the manager, it is almost certainly inappropriate for the corporation. The trades undertaken by Procter & Gamble and Gibson Greetings would have been vetoed using this criterion.

One way of ensuring that you fully understand a financial instrument is to value it. If a corporation does not have the in-house capability to value an instrument, it should not trade it. In practice, corporations often rely on their investment bankers for valuation advice. This is dangerous, as Procter & Gamble and Gibson Greetings found out. When they wanted to unwind their deals, they found they were facing prices produced by Bankers Trust's proprietary models, which they had no way of checking.

Make Sure a Hedger Does Not Become a Speculator

One of the unfortunate facts of life is that hedging is relatively dull, whereas speculation is exciting. When a company hires a trader to manage foreign exchange, commodity price, or interest rate risk, there is a danger that the following might happen. At first, the trader does the job diligently and earns the confidence of top management. He or she assesses the company's exposures and hedges them. As time goes by, the trader becomes convinced that he or she can outguess the market. Slowly the trader becomes a speculator. At first things go well, but then a loss is made. To recover the loss, the trader doubles up the bets. Further losses are made—and so on. The result is likely to be a disaster.

As mentioned earlier, clear limits to the risks that can be taken should be set by senior management. Controls should be put in place to ensure that the limits are obeyed. The trading strategy for a corporation should start with an analysis of the risks facing the corporation in foreign exchange, interest rate, commodity markets, and so on. A decision should then be taken on how the risks are to be reduced to acceptable levels. It is a clear sign that something is wrong within a corporation if the trading strategy is not derived in a very direct way from the company's exposures.

Be Cautious about Making the Treasury Department a Profit Center

In the last 20 years there has been a tendency to make the treasury department within a corporation a profit center. This appears to have much to recommend it. The treasurer is motivated to reduce financing costs and manage risks as profitably as possible. The problem is that the potential for the treasurer to make profits is limited. When raising funds and investing surplus cash, the treasurer is facing an efficient market. The treasurer can usually improve the bottom line only by taking additional risks. The company's hedging program gives the treasurer some scope for making shrewd decisions that increase profits. But it should be remembered that the goal of a hedging program is to reduce risks, not to increase expected profits. As pointed out in Chapter 3, the decision to hedge will lead to a worse outcome than the decision not to hedge roughly 50% of the time. The danger of making the treasury department a profit center is that the treasurer is motivated to become a speculator. This is liable to lead to the type of outcome experienced by Orange County, Procter & Gamble, or Gibson Greetings.

SUMMARY

The huge losses experienced from the use of derivatives have made many treasurers very wary. Since the spate of mishaps in 1994 and 1995, some nonfinancial corporations have announced plans to reduce or even eliminate their use of derivatives. This is unfortunate because derivatives provide treasurers with very efficient ways to manage risks.

The stories behind the losses emphasize the point, made as early as Chapter 1, that derivatives can be used for either hedging or speculation; that is, they can be used either to reduce risks or to take risks. Most losses occurred because derivatives were used inappropriately. Employees who had an implicit or explicit mandate to hedge their company's risks decided instead to speculate.

The key lesson to be learned from the losses is the importance of *internal controls*. Senior management within a company should issue a clear and unambiguous policy statement about how derivatives are to be used and the extent to which it is permissible for employees to take positions on movements in market variables. Management should then institute controls to ensure that the policy is carried out. It is a recipe for disaster to give individuals authority to trade derivatives without a close monitoring of the risks being taken.

FURTHER READING

Dunbar, N. *Inventing Money: The Story of Long-Term Capital Management and the Legends Behind It*. Chichester, UK: Wiley, 2000.

Jorion, P. *Big Bets Gone Bad: Derivatives and Bankruptcy in Orange County*. New York: Academic Press, 1995.

Jorion, P. "How Long-Term Lost Its Capital," *Risk* (September 1999).

Ju, X., and N. Pearson. "Using Value at Risk to Control Risk Taking: How Wrong Can You Be?" *Journal of Risk*, 1 (1999): 5–36.

Persaud, A. D. (ed.) *Liquidity Black Holes: Understanding, Quantifying and Managing Financial Liquidity Risk*. London, Risk Books, 2003.

Thomson, R. *Apocalypse Roulette: The Lethal World of Derivatives*. London: Macmillan, 1998.

Zhang, P. G. *Barings Bankruptcy and Financial Derivatives*. Singapore: World Scientific Publishing, 1995.

Glossary of Terms

Accrual Swap An interest rate swap where interest on one side accrues only when a certain condition is met.

Accrued Interest The interest earned on a bond since the last coupon payment date.

Adaptive Mesh Model A model developed by Figlewski and Gao that grafts a high-resolution tree on to a low-resolution tree so that there is more detailed modeling of the asset price in critical regions.

American Option An option that can be exercised at any time during its life.

Amortizing Swap A swap where the notional principal decreases in a predetermined way as time passes.

Analytic Result Result where answer is in the form of an equation.

Arbitrage A trading strategy that takes advantage of two or more securities being mispriced relative to each other.

Arbitrageur An individual engaging in arbitrage.

Asian Option An option with a payoff dependent on the average price of the underlying asset during a specified period.

Ask Price The price that a dealer is offering to sell an asset.

Asked Price *See* Ask Price.

Asset-or-Nothing Call Option An option that provides a payoff equal to the asset price if the asset price is above the strike price and zero otherwise.

Asset-or-Nothing Put Option An option that provides a payoff equal to the asset price if the asset price is below the strike price and zero otherwise.

Asset Swap Exchanges the coupon on a bond for LIBOR plus a spread.

As-You-Like-It Option *See* Chooser Option.

At-the-Money Option An option in which the strike price equals the price of the underlying asset.

Average Price Call Option An option giving a payoff equal to the greater of zero and the amount by which the average price of the asset exceeds the strike price.

Average Price Put Option An option giving a payoff equal to the greater of zero and the amount by which the strike price exceeds the average price of the asset.

Average Strike Option An option that provides a payoff dependent on the difference between the final asset price and the average asset price.

Back Testing Testing a value-at-risk or other model using historical data.

Backwards Induction A procedure for working from the end of a tree to its beginning in order to value an option.

Barrier Option An option whose payoff depends on whether the path of the underlying asset has reached a barrier (i.e., a certain predetermined level).

Basel II New international regulations for calculating bank capital expected to come into effect in about 2007.

Basis The difference between the spot price and the futures price of a commodity.

Basis Point When used to describe an interest rate, a basis point is one hundredth of one percent (= 0.01%)

Basis Risk The risk to a hedger arising from uncertainty about the basis at a future time.

Basis Swap A swap where cash flows determined by one floating reference rate are exchanged for cash flows determined by another floating reference rate.

Basket Credit Default Swap Credit default swap where there are several reference entities.

Basket Option An option that provides a payoff dependent on the value of a portfolio of assets.

Bear Spread A short position in a put option with strike price K_1 combined with a long position in a put option with strike price K_2 where $K_2 > K_1$. (A bear spread can also be created with call options.)

Bermudan Option An option that can be exercised on specified dates during its life.

Beta A measure of the systematic risk of an asset.

Bid–Ask Spread The amount by which the ask price exceeds the bid price.

Bid–Offer Spread *See* Bid–Ask Spread.

Bid Price The price that a dealer is prepared to pay for an asset.

Binary Credit Default Swap Instrument where there is a fixed dollar payoff in the event of a default by a particular company.

Binary Option Option with a discontinuous payoff, e.g., a cash-or-nothing option or an asset-or-nothing option.

Binomial Model A model where the price of an asset is monitored over successive short periods of time. In each short period it is assumed that only two price movements are possible.

Binomial Tree A tree that represents how an asset price can evolve under the binomial model.

Bivariate Normal Distribution A distribution for two correlated variables, each of which is normal.

Black's Approximation An approximate procedure developed by Fischer Black for valuing a call option on a dividend-paying stock.

Black's Model An extension of the Black–Scholes model for valuing European options on futures contracts. As described in Chapter 26, it is used extensively in practice to value European options when the distribution of the asset price at maturity is assumed to be lognormal.

Black–Scholes Model A model for pricing European options on stocks, developed by Fischer Black, Myron Scholes, and Robert Merton.

Board Broker The individual who handles limit orders in some exchanges. The board broker makes information on outstanding limit orders available to other traders.

Bond Option An option where a bond is the underlying asset.

Bond Yield Discount rate which, when applied to all the cash flows of a bond, causes the present value of the cash flows to equal the bond's market price.

Bootstrap Method A procedure for calculating the zero-coupon yield curve from market data.

Boston Option *See* Deferred Payment Option.

Box Spread A combination of a bull spread created from calls and a bear spread created from puts.

Break Forward *See* Deferred Payment Option.

Brownian Motion *See* Wiener Process.

Bull Spread A long position in a call with strike price K_1 combined with a short position in a call with strike price K_2, where $K_2 > K_1$. (A bull spread can also be created with put options.)

Butterfly Spread A position that is created by taking a long position in a call with strike price K_1, a long position in a call with strike price K_3, and a short position in two calls with strike price K_2, where $K_3 > K_2 > K_1$ and $K_2 = 0.5(K_1 + K_3)$. (A butterfly spread can also be created with put options.)

Calendar Spread A position that is created by taking a long position in a call option that matures at one time and a short position in a similar call option that matures at a different time. (A calendar spread can also be created using put options.)

Calibration Method for implying a model's parameters from the prices of actively traded options.

Callable Bond A bond containing provisions that allow the issuer to buy it back at a predetermined price at certain times during its life.

Call Option An option to buy an asset at a certain price by a certain date.

Cancelable Swap Swap that can be canceled by one side on prespecified dates.

Cap *See* Interest Rate Cap.

Cap Rate The rate determining payoffs in an interest rate cap.

Capital Asset Pricing Model A model relating the expected return on an asset to its beta.

Caplet One component of an interest rate cap.

Cash Flow Mapping A procedure for representing an instrument as a portfolio of zero-coupon bonds for the purpose of calculating value at risk.

Cash-or-Nothing Call Option An option that provides a fixed predetermined payoff if the final asset price is above the strike price and zero otherwise.

Cash-or-Nothing Put Option An option that provides a fixed predetermined payoff if the final asset price is below the strike price and zero otherwise.

Cash Settlement Procedure for settling a futures contract in cash rather than by delivering the underlying asset.

CAT Bond Bond where the interest and, possibly, the principal paid are reduced if a particular category of "catastrophic" insurance claims exceed a certain amount.

CDD Cooling degree days. The maximum of zero and the amount by which the daily average temperature is greater than 65° Fahrenheit. The average temperature is the average of the highest and lowest temperatures (midnight to midnight).

CDO *See* Collateralized Debt Obligation.

CDO Squared An instrument in which the default risks in a portfolio of CDO tranches are allocated to new securities.

Cheapest-to-Deliver Bond The bond that is cheapest to deliver in the Chicago Board of Trade bond futures contract.

Cholesky Decomposition A method of sampling from a multivariate normal distribution.

Chooser Option An option where the holder has the right to choose whether it is a call or a put at some point during its life.

Class of Options *See* Option Class.

Clean Price of Bond The quoted price of a bond. The cash price paid for the bond (or dirty price) is calculated by adding the accrued interest to the clean price.

Clearinghouse A firm that guarantees the performance of the parties in an exchange-traded derivatives transaction (also referred to as a clearing corporation).

Clearing Margin A margin posted by a member of a clearinghouse.

CMO Collateralized Mortgage Obligation.

Collar *See* Interest Rate Collar.

Collateralization A system for posting collateral by one or both parties in a derivatives transaction.

Collateralized Debt Obligation A way of packaging credit risk. Several classes of securities (known as tranches) are created from a portfolio of bonds and there are rules for determining how the cost of defaults are allocated to classes.

Collateralized Mortgage Obligation (CMO) A mortgage-backed security where investors are divided into classes and there are rules for determining how principal repayments are channeled to the classes.

Combination A position involving both calls and puts on the same underlying asset.

Commission Brokers Individuals who execute trades for other people and charge a commission for doing so.

Commodity Futures Trading Commission A body that regulates trading in futures contracts in the United States.

Commodity Swap A swap where cash flows depend on the price of a commodity.

Compound Option An option on an option.

Compounding Frequency This defines how an interest rate is measured.

Compounding Swap Swap where interest compounds instead of being paid.

Conditional Value at Risk (C-VaR) Expected loss during N days conditional on being in the $(100 - X)\%$ tail of the distribution of profits/losses. The variable N is the time horizon and $X\%$ is the confidence level.

Confirmation Contract confirming verbal agreement between two parties to a trade in the over-the-counter market.

Constant Elasticity of Variance (CEV) Model Model where the variance of the change in a variable in a short period of time is proportional to the value of the variable.

Constant Maturity Swap A swap where a swap rate is exchanged for either a fixed rate or a floating rate on each payment date.

Constant Maturity Treasury Swap A swap where the yield on a Treasury bond is exchanged for either a fixed rate or a floating rate on each payment date.

Consumption Asset An asset held for consumption rather than investment.

Contango A situation where the futures price is above the expected future spot price.

Continuous Compounding A way of quoting interest rates. It is the limit as the assumed compounding interval is made smaller and smaller.

Control Variate Technique A technique that can sometimes be used for improving the accuracy of a numerical procedure.

Convenience Yield A measure of the benefits from ownership of an asset that are not obtained by the holder of a long futures contract on the asset.

Conversion Factor A factor used to determine the number of bonds that must be delivered in the Chicago Board of Trade bond futures contract.

Convertible Bond A corporate bond that can be converted into a predetermined amount of the company's equity at certain times during its life.

Convexity A measure of the curvature in the relationship between bond prices and bond yields.

Convexity Adjustment An overworked term. For example, it can refer to the adjustment necessary to convert a futures interest rate to a forward interest rate. It can also refer to the adjustment to a forward rate that is sometimes necessary when Black's model is used.

Copula A way of defining the correlation between variables with known distributions.

Cornish–Fisher Expansion An approximate relationship between the fractiles of a probability distribution and its moments.

Cost of Carry The storage costs plus the cost of financing an asset minus the income earned on the asset.

Counterparty The opposite side in a financial transaction.

Coupon Interest payment made on a bond.

Covariance Measure of the linear relationship between two variables (equals the correlation between the variables times the product of their standard deviations).

Covered Call A short position in a call option on an asset combined with a long position in the asset.

Credit Default Swap An instrument that gives the holder the right to sell a bond for its face value in the event of a default by the issuer.

Credit Derivative A derivative whose payoff depends on the creditworthiness of one or more companies or countries.

Credit Rating A measure of the creditworthiness of a bond issue.

Credit Ratings Transition Matrix A table showing the probability that a company will move from one credit rating to another during a certain period of time.

Credit Risk The risk that a loss will be experienced because of a default by the counterparty in a derivatives transaction.

Credit Spread Option Option whose payoff depends on the spread between the yields earned on two assets.

Credit Value at Risk The credit loss that will not be exceeded at some specified confidence level.

CreditMetrics A procedure for calculating credit value at risk.

Cross Hedging Hedging an exposure to the price of one asset with a contract on another asset.

Cumulative Distribution Function The probability that a variable will be less than x as a function of x.

Currency Swap A swap where interest and principal in one currency are exchanged for interest and principal in another currency.

Day Count A convention for quoting interest rates.

Day Trade A trade that is entered into and closed out on the same day.

Default Correlation Measures the tendency of two companies to default at about the same time.

Default Intensity *See* Hazard Rate.

Default Probability Density Measures the unconditional probability of default in a future short period of time.

Deferred Payment Option An option where the price paid is deferred until the end of the option's life.

Deferred Swap An agreement to enter into a swap at some time in the future (also called a forward swap).

Delivery Price Price agreed to (possibly some time in the past) in a forward contract.

Delta The rate of change of the price of a derivative with the price of the underlying asset.

Delta Hedging A hedging scheme that is designed to make the price of a portfolio of derivatives insensitive to small changes in the price of the underlying asset.

Delta-Neutral Portfolio A portfolio with a delta of zero so that there is no sensitivity to small changes in the price of the underlying asset.

DerivaGem The software accompanying this book.

Derivative An instrument whose price depends on, or is derived from, the price of another asset.

Deterministic Variable A variable whose future value is known.

Diagonal Spread A position in two calls where both the strike prices and times to maturity are different. (A diagonal spread can also be created with put options.)

Differential Swap A swap where a floating rate in one currency is exchanged for a floating rate in another currency and both rates are applied to the same principal.

Diffusion Process Model where value of asset changes continuously (no jumps).

Dirty Price of Bond Cash price of bond.

Discount Bond *See* Zero-Coupon Bond.

Discount Instrument An instrument, such as a Treasury bill, that provides no coupons.

Discount Rate The annualized dollar return on a Treasury bill or similar instrument expressed as a percentage of the final face value.

Dividend A cash payment made to the owner of a stock.

Dividend Yield The dividend as a percentage of the stock price.

Down-and-In Option An option that comes into existence when the price of the underlying asset declines to a prespecified level.

Down-and-Out Option An option that ceases to exist when the price of the underlying asset declines to a prespecified level.

Downgrade Trigger A clause in a contract that states that the contract will be terminated with a cash settlement if the credit rating of one side falls below a certain level.

Drift Rate The average increase per unit of time in a stochastic variable.

Duration A measure of the average life a bond. It is also an approximation to the ratio of the proportional change in the bond price to the absolute change in its yield.

Duration Matching A procedure for matching the durations of assets and liabilities in a financial institution.

Dynamic Hedging A procedure for hedging an option position by periodically changing the position held in the underlying asset. The objective is usually to maintain a delta-neutral position.

Early Exercise Exercise prior to the maturity date.

Efficient Market Hypothesis A hypothesis that asset prices reflect relevant information.

Electronic Trading System of trading where a computer is used to match buyers and sellers.

Embedded Option An option that is an inseparable part of another instrument.

Empirical Research Research based on historical market data.

Equilibrium Model A model for the behavior of interest rates derived from a model of the economy.

Equity Swap A swap where the return on an equity portfolio is exchanged for either a fixed or a floating rate of interest.

Eurocurrency A currency that is outside the formal control of the issuing country's monetary authorities.

Eurodollar A dollar held in a bank outside the United States.

Eurodollar Futures Contract A futures contract written on a Eurodollar deposit.

Eurodollar Interest Rate The interest rate on a Eurodollar deposit.

European Option An option that can be exercised only at the end of its life.

EWMA Exponentially weighted moving average.

Exchange Option An option to exchange one asset for another.

Ex-dividend Date When a dividend is declared, an ex-dividend date is specified. Investors who own shares of the stock just before the ex-dividend date receive the dividend.

Executive Stock Option A stock option issued by company on its own stock and given to its executives as part of their remuneration.

Exercise Limit Maximum number of option contracts that can be exercised within a five-day period.

Exercise Price The price at which the underlying asset may be bought or sold in an option contract (also called the strike price).

Exotic Option A nonstandard option.

Expectations Theory The theory that forward interest rates equal expected future spot interest rates.

Expected Shortfall *See* Conditional Value at Risk.

Expected Value of a Variable The average value of the variable obtained by weighting the alternative values by their probabilities.

Expiration Date The end of life of a contract.

Explicit Finite Difference Method A method for valuing a derivative by solving the underlying differential equation. The value of the derivative at time t is related to three values at time $t + \Delta t$. It is essentially the same as the trinomial tree method.

Exponentially Weighted Moving Average Model A model where exponential weighting is used to provide forecasts for a variable from historical data. It is sometimes applied to variances and covariances in value at risk calculations.

Exponential Weighting A weighting scheme where the weight given to an observation depends on how recent it is. The weight given to an observation i time periods ago is λ times the weight given to an observation $i - 1$ time periods ago where $\lambda < 1$.

Exposure The maximum loss from default by a counterparty.

Extendable Bond A bond whose life can be extended at the option of the holder.

Extendable Swap A swap whose life can be extended at the option of one side to the contract.

Factor Source of uncertainty.

Factor analysis An analysis aimed at finding a small number of factors that describe most of the variation in a large number of correlated variables (similar to a principal components analysis).

FASB Financial Accounting Standards Board.

Financial Intermediary A bank or other financial institution that facilitates the flow of funds between different entities in the economy.

Finite Difference Method A method for solving a differential equation.

Flat Volatility The name given to volatility used to price a cap when the same volatility is used for each caplet.

Flex Option An option traded on an exchange with terms that are different from the standard options traded by the exchange.

Flexi Cap Interest rate cap where there is a limit on the total number of caplets that can be exercised.

Floor *See* Interest Rate Floor.

Floor–Ceiling Agreement *See* Collar.

Floorlet One component of a floor.

Floor Rate The rate in an interest rate floor agreement.

Foreign Currency Option An option on a foreign exchange rate.

Forward Contract A contract that obligates the holder to buy or sell an asset for a predetermined delivery price at a predetermined future time.

Forward Exchange Rate The forward price of one unit of a foreign currency.

Forward Interest Rate The interest rate for a future period of time implied by the rates prevailing in the market today.

Forward Price The delivery price in a forward contract that causes the contract to be worth zero.

Forward Rate Rate of interest for a period of time in the future implied by today's zero rates.

Forward Rate Agreement (FRA) Agreement that a certain interest rate will apply to a certain principal amount for a certain time period in the future.

Forward Risk-Neutral World A world is forward risk-neutral with respect to a certain asset when the market price of risk equals the volatility of that asset.

Forward Start Option An option designed so that it will be at-the-money at some time in the future.

Forward Swap *See* Deferred Swap.

Futures Contract A contract that obligates the holder to buy or sell an asset at a predetermined delivery price during a specified future time period. The contract is settled daily.

Futures Option An option on a futures contract.

Futures Price The delivery price currently applicable to a futures contract.

Gamma The rate of change of delta with respect to the asset price.

Gamma-Neutral Portfolio A portfolio with a gamma of zero.

GARCH Model A model for forecasting volatility where the variance rate follows a mean-reverting process.

Generalized Wiener Process A stochastic process where the change in a variable in time t has a normal distribution with mean and variance both proportional to t.

Geometric Average The nth root of the product of n numbers.

Geometric Brownian Motion A stochastic process often assumed for asset prices where the logarithm of the underlying variable follows a generalized Wiener process.

Greeks Hedge parameters such as delta, gamma, vega, theta, and rho.

Haircut Discount applied to the value of an asset for collateral purposes.

Hazard Rate Measures probability of default in a short period of time conditional on no earlier default.

HDD Heating degree days. The maximum of zero and the amount by which the daily average temperature is less than 65° Fahrenheit. The average temperature is the average of the highest and lowest temperatures (midnight to midnight).

Hedge A trade designed to reduce risk.

Hedger An individual who enters into hedging trades.

Hedge Ratio The ratio of the size of a position in a hedging instrument to the size of the position being hedged.

Historical Simulation A simulation based on historical data.

Historic Volatility A volatility estimated from historical data.

Holiday Calendar Calendar defining which days are holidays for the purposes of determining payment dates in a swap.

Implicit Finite Difference Method A method for valuing a derivative by solving the underlying differential equation. The value of the derivative at time $t + \Delta t$ is related to three values at time t.

Implied Distribution A distribution for a future asset price implied from option prices.

Implied Tree A tree describing the movements of an asset price that is constructed to be consistent with observed option prices.

Implied Volatility Volatility implied from an option price using the Black–Scholes or a similar model.

Implied Volatility Function (IVF) Model Model designed so that it matches the market prices of all European options.

Inception Profit Profit created by selling a derivative for more than its theoretical value.

Index Amortizing Swap See indexed principal swap.

Index Arbitrage An arbitrage involving a position in the stocks comprising a stock index and a position in a futures contract on the stock index.

Index Futures A futures contract on a stock index or other index.

Index Option An option contract on a stock index or other index.

Indexed Principal Swap A swap where the principal declines over time. The reduction in the principal on a payment date depends on the level of interest rates.

Initial Margin The cash required from a futures trader at the time of the trade.

Instantaneous Forward Rate Forward rate for a very short period of time in the future.

Interest Rate Cap An option that provides a payoff when a specified interest rate is above a certain level. The interest rate is a floating rate that is reset periodically.

Interest Rate Collar A combination of an interest-rate cap and an interest rate floor.

Interest Rate Derivative A derivative whose payoffs are dependent on future interest rates.

Interest Rate Floor An option that provides a payoff when an interest rate is below a certain level. The interest rate is a floating rate that is reset periodically.

Interest Rate Option An option where the payoff is dependent on the level of interest rates.

Interest Rate Swap An exchange of a fixed rate of interest on a certain notional principal for a floating rate of interest on the same notional principal.

In-the-Money Option Either (a) a call option where the asset price is greater than the strike price or (b) a put option where the asset price is less than the strike price.

Intrinsic Value For a call option, this is the greater of the excess of the asset price over the strike price and zero. For a put option, it is the greater of the excess of the strike price over the asset price and zero.

Inverted Market A market where futures prices decrease with maturity.

Investment Asset An asset held by at least some individuals for investment purposes.

IO Interest Only. A mortgage-backed security where the holder receives only interest cash flows on the underlying mortgage pool.

Itô Process A stochastic process where the change in a variable during each short period of time of length Δt has a normal distribution. The mean and variance of the distribution are proportional to Δt and are not necessarily constant.

Itô's Lemma A result that enables the stochastic process for a function of a variable to be calculated from the stochastic process for the variable itself.

Kurtosis A measure of the fatness of the tails of a distribution.

Jump–Diffusion Model Model where asset price has jumps superimposed on to a diffusion process such as geometric Brownian motion.

LEAPS Long-term equity anticipation securities. These are relatively long-term options on individual stocks or stock indices.

LIBID London interbank bid rate. The rate bid by banks on Eurocurrency deposits (i.e., the rate at which a bank is willing to borrow from other banks).

LIBOR London interbank offer rate. The rate offered by banks on Eurocurrency deposits (i.e., the rate at which a bank is willing to lend to other banks).

LIBOR Curve LIBOR zero-coupon interest rates as a function of maturity.

LIBOR-in-Arrears Swap Swap where the interest paid on a date is determined by the interest rate observed on that date (not by the interest rate observed on the previous payment date).

Limit Move The maximum price move permitted by the exchange in a single trading session.

Limit Order An order that can be executed only at a specified price or one more favorable to the investor.

Liquidity Preference Theory A theory leading to the conclusion that forward interest rates are above expected future spot interest rates.

Liquidity Premium The amount that forward interest rates exceed expected future spot interest rates.

Liquidity Risk Risk that it will not be possible to sell a holding of a particular instrument at its theoretical price.

Locals Individuals on the floor of an exchange who trade for their own account rather than for someone else.

Lognormal Distribution A variable has a lognormal distribution when the logarithm of the variable has a normal distribution.

Long Hedge A hedge involving a long futures position.

Long Position A position involving the purchase of an asset.

Lookback Option An option whose payoff is dependent on the maximum or minimum of the asset price achieved during a certain period.

Low Discrepancy Sequence *See* Quasi-random Sequence.

Maintenance Margin When the balance in a trader's margin account falls below the maintenance margin level, the trader receives a margin call requiring the account to be topped up to the initial margin level.

Margin The cash balance (or security deposit) required from a futures or options trader.

Margin Call A request for extra margin when the balance in the margin account falls below the maintenance margin level.

Market Maker A trader who is willing to quote both bid and offer prices for an asset.

Market Model A model most commonly used by traders.

Market Price of Risk A measure of the trade-offs investors make between risk and return.

Market Segmentation Theory A theory that short interest rates are determined independently of long interest rates by the market.

Marking to Market The practice of revaluing an instrument to reflect the current values of the relevant market variables.

Markov Process A stochastic process where the behavior of the variable over a short period of time depends solely on the value of the variable at the beginning of the period, not on its past history.

Martingale A zero drift stochastic process.

Maturity Date The end of the life of a contract.

Maximum Likelihood Method A method for choosing the values of parameters by maximizing the probability of a set of observations occurring.

Mean Reversion The tendency of a market variable (such as an interest rate) to revert back to some long-run average level.

Measure Sometimes also called a probability measure, it defines the market price of risk.

Modified Duration A modification to the standard duration measure so that it more accurately describes the relationship between proportional changes in a bond price and actual changes in its yield. The modification takes account of the compounding frequency with which the yield is quoted.

Money Market Account An investment that is initially equal to $1 and, at time t, increases at the very short-term risk-free interest rate prevailing at that time.

Monte Carlo Simulation A procedure for randomly sampling changes in market variables in order to value a derivative.

Mortgage-Backed Security A security that entitles the owner to a share in the cash flows realized from a pool of mortgages.

Naked Position A short position in a call option that is not combined with a long position in the underlying asset.

Netting The ability to offset contracts with positive and negative values in the event of a default by a counterparty.

Newton–Raphson Method An iterative procedure for solving nonlinear equations.

No-Arbitrage Assumption The assumption that there are no arbitrage opportunities in market prices.

No-Arbitrage Interest Rate Model A model for the behavior of interest rates that is exactly consistent with the initial term structure of interest rates.

Nonstationary Model A model where the volatility parameters are a function of time.

Nonsystematic Risk Risk that can be diversified away.

Normal Backwardation A situation where the futures price is below the expected future spot price.

Normal Distribution The standard bell-shaped distribution of statistics.

Normal Market A market where futures prices increase with maturity.

Notional Principal The principal used to calculate payments in an interest rate swap. The principal is "notional" because it is neither paid nor received.

Numeraire Defines the units in which security prices are measured. For example, if the price of IBM is the numeraire, all security prices are measured relative to IBM. If IBM is $80 and a particular security price is $50, the security price is 0.625 when IBM is the numeraire.

Numerical Procedure A method of valuing an option when no formula is available.

OCC Options Clearing Corporation. *See* Clearinghouse.

Offer Price *See* Ask Price.

Open Interest The total number of long positions outstanding in a futures contract (equals the total number of short positions).

Open Outcry System of trading where traders meet on the floor of the exchange

Option The right to buy or sell an asset.

Option-Adjusted Spread The spread over the Treasury curve that makes the theoretical price of an interest rate derivative equal to the market price.

Option Class All options of the same type (call or put) on a particular stock.

Option Series All options of a certain class with the same strike price and expiration date.

Order Book Official *See* Board Broker.

Out-of-the-Money Option Either (a) a call option where the asset price is less than the strike price or (b) a put option where the asset price is greater than the strike price.

Over-the-Counter Market A market where traders deal by phone. The traders are usually financial institutions, corporations, and fund managers.

Package A derivative that is a portfolio of standard calls and puts, possibly combined with a position in forward contracts and the asset itself.

Par Value The principal amount of a bond.

Par Yield The coupon on a bond that makes its price equal the principal.

Parallel Shift A movement in the yield curve where each point on the curve changes by the same amount.

Path-Dependent Option An option whose payoff depends on the whole path followed by the underlying variable—not just its final value.

Payoff The cash realized by the holder of an option or other derivative at the end of its life.

Plain Vanilla A term used to describe a standard deal.

P-Measure Real-world measure.

PO Principal Only. A mortgage-backed security where the holder receives only principal cash flows on the underlying mortgage pool.

Poisson Process A process describing a situation where events happen at random. The probability of an event in time Δt is $\lambda\,\Delta t$, where λ is the intensity of the process.

Portfolio Immunization Making a portfolio relatively insensitive to interest rates.

Portfolio Insurance Entering into trades to ensure that the value of a portfolio will not fall below a certain level.

Position Limit The maximum position a trader (or group of traders acting together) is allowed to hold.

Premium The price of an option.

Prepayment function A function estimating the prepayment of principal on a portfolio of mortgages in terms of other variables.

Principal The par or face value of a debt instrument.

Principal Components Analysis An analysis aimed at finding a small number of factors that describe most of the variation in a large number of correlated variables (similar to a factor analysis).

Program Trading A procedure where trades are automatically generated by a computer and transmitted to the trading floor of an exchange.

Protective Put A put option combined with a long position in the underlying asset.

Pull-to-Par The reversion of a bond's price to its par value at maturity.

Put–Call Parity The relationship between the price of a European call option and the price of a European put option when they have the same strike price and maturity date.

Put Option An option to sell an asset for a certain price by a certain date.

Puttable Bond A bond where the holder has the right to sell it back to the issuer at certain predetermined times for a predetermined price.

Puttable Swap A swap where one side has the right to terminate early.

Q-Measure Risk-neutral measure.

Quanto A derivative where the payoff is defined by variables associated with one currency but is paid in another currency.

Quasi-random Sequences A sequences of numbers used in a Monte Carlo simulation that are representative of alternative outcomes rather than random.

Rainbow Option An option whose payoff is dependent on two or more underlying variables.

Range Forward Contract The combination of a long call and short put or the combination of a short call and long put.

Ratchet Cap Interest rate cap where the cap rate applicable to an accrual period equals the rate for the previous accrual period plus a spread.

Real Option Option involving real (as opposed to financial) assets. Real assets include land, plant, and machinery.

Rebalancing The process of adjusting a trading position periodically. Usually the purpose is to maintain delta neutrality.

Recovery Rate Amount recovered in the event of a default as a percent of the face value.

Repo Repurchase agreement. A procedure for borrowing money by selling securities to a counterparty and agreeing to buy them back later at a slightly higher price.

Repo Rate The rate of interest in a repo transaction.

Reset Date The date in a swap or cap or floor when the floating rate for the next period is set.

Reversion Level The level that the value of a market variable (e.g., an interest rate) tends to revert.

Rho Rate of change of the price of a derivative with the interest rate.

Rights Issue An issue to existing shareholders of a security giving them the right to buy new shares at a certain price.

Risk-Free Rate The rate of interest that can be earned without assuming any risks.

Risk-Neutral Valuation The valuation of an option or other derivative assuming the world is risk neutral. Risk-neutral valuation gives the correct price for a derivative in all worlds, not just in a risk-neutral world.

Risk-Neutral World A world where investors are assumed to require no extra return on average for bearing risks.

Roll Back *See* Backwards Induction.

Scalper A trader who holds positions for a very short period of time.

Scenario Analysis An analysis of the effects of possible alternative future movements in market variables on the value of a portfolio.

SEC Securities and Exchange Commission.

Settlement Price The average of the prices that a contract trades for immediately before the bell signaling the close of trading for a day. It is used in mark-to-market calculations.

Short Hedge A hedge where a short futures position is taken.

Short Position A position assumed when traders sell shares they do not own.

Short Rate The interest rate applying for a very short period of time.

Short Selling Selling in the market shares that have been borrowed from another investor.

Short-Term Risk-Free Rate *See* Short Rate.

Shout Option An option where the holder has the right to lock in a minimum value for the payoff at one time during its life.

Simulation *See* Monte Carlo Simulation.

Specialist An individual responsible for managing limit orders on some exchanges. The specialist does not make the information on outstanding limit orders available to other traders.

Speculator An individual who is taking a position in the market. Usually the individual is betting that the price of an asset will go up or that the price of an asset will go down.

Spot Interest Rate *See* Zero-Coupon Interest Rate.

Spot Price The price for immediate delivery.

Spot Volatilities The volatilities used to price a cap when a different volatility is used for each caplet.

Spread Option An option where the payoff is dependent on the difference between two market variables.

Spread Transaction A position in two or more options of the same type.

Static Hedge A hedge that does not have to be changed once it is initiated.

Static Options Replication A procedure for hedging a portfolio that involves finding another portfolio of approximately equal value on some boundary.

Step-up Swap A swap where the principal increases over time in a predetermined way.

Sticky Cap Interest rate cap where the cap rate applicable to an accrual period equals the capped rate for the previous accrual period plus a spread.

Stochastic Process An equation describing the probabilistic behavior of a stochastic variable.

Stochastic Variable A variable whose future value is uncertain.

Stock Dividend A dividend paid in the form of additional shares.

Stock Index An index monitoring the value of a portfolio of stocks.

Stock Index Futures Futures on a stock index.

Stock Index Option An option on a stock index.

Stock Option Option on a stock.

Stock Split The conversion of each existing share into more than one new share.

Storage Costs The costs of storing a commodity.

Straddle A long position in a call and a put with the same strike price.

Strangle A long position in a call and a put with different strike prices.

Strap A long position in two call options and one put option with the same strike price.

Stress Testing Testing of the impact of extreme market moves on the value of a portfolio.

Strike Price The price at which the asset may be bought or sold in an option contract (also called the exercise price).

Strip A long position in one call option and two put options with the same strike price.

Swap An agreement to exchange cash flows in the future according to a prearranged formula.

Swap Rate The fixed rate in an interest rate swap that causes the swap to have a value of zero.

Swaption An option to enter into an interest rate swap where a specified fixed rate is exchanged for floating.

Swing Option Energy option in which the rate of consumption must be between a minimum and maximum level. There is usually a limit on the number of times the option holder can change the rate at which the energy is consumed.

Synthetic CDO A CDO created by selling credit default swaps.

Synthetic Option An option created by trading the underlying asset.

Systematic Risk Risk that cannot be diversified away.

Tail Loss *See* Conditional Value at Risk.

Take-and-Pay Option *See* Swing Option.

Term Structure of Interest Rates The relationship between interest rates and their maturities.

Terminal Value The value at maturity.

Theta The rate of change of the price of an option or other derivative with the passage of time.

Time Decay *See* Theta.

Time Value The value of an option arising from the time left to maturity (equals an option's price minus its intrinsic value).

Timing Adjustment Adjustment made to the forward value of a variable to allow for the timing of a payoff from a derivative.

Total Return Swap A swap where the return on an asset such as a bond is exchanged for LIBOR plus a spread. The return on the asset includes income such as coupons and the change in value of the asset.

Tranche One of several securities that have different risk attributes. Examples are the tranches of a CDO or CMO.

Transaction Costs The cost of carrying out a trade (commissions plus the difference between the price obtained and the midpoint of the bid–offer spread).

Treasury Bill A short-term non-coupon-bearing instrument issued by the government to finance its debt.

Treasury Bond A long-term coupon-bearing instrument issued by the government to finance it debt.

Treasury Bond Futures A futures contract on Treasury bonds.

Treasury Note *See* Treasury Bond. (Treasury notes have maturities of less than 10 years.)

Treasury Note Futures A futures contract on Treasury notes.

Tree Representation of the evolution of the value of a market variable for the purposes of valuing an option or other derivative.

Trinomial Tree A tree where there are three branches emanating from each node. It is used in the same way as a binomial tree for valuing derivatives.

Triple Witching Hour A term given to the time when stock index futures, stock index options, and options on stock index futures all expire together.

Underlying Variable A variable on which the price of an option or other derivative depends.

Unsystematic Risk *See* Nonsystematic Risk.

Up-and-In Option An option that comes into existence when the price of the underlying asset increases to a prespecified level.

Up-and-Out Option An option that ceases to exist when the price of the underlying asset increases to a prespecified level.

Uptick An increase in price.

Value at Risk A loss that will not be exceeded at some specified confidence level.

Variance–Covariance Matrix A matrix showing variances of, and covariances between, a number of different market variables.

Variance-Gamma Model A pure jump model where small jumps occur often and large jumps occur infrequently.

Variance Rate The square of volatility.

Variance Reduction Procedures Procedures for reducing the error in a Monte Carlo simulation.

Variation Margin An extra margin required to bring the balance in a margin account up to the initial margin when there is a margin call.

Vega The rate of change in the price of an option or other derivative with volatility.

Vega-Neutral Portfolio A portfolio with a vega of zero.

Volatility A measure of the uncertainty of the return realized on an asset.

Volatility Skew A term used to describe the volatility smile when it is nonsymmetrical.

Volatility Smile The variation of implied volatility with strike price.

Volatility Surface A table showing the variation of implied volatilities with strike price and time to maturity.

Volatility Swap Swap where the realized volatility during an accrual period is exchanged for a fixed volatility. Both percentage volatilities are applied to a notional principal.

Volatility Term Structure The variation of implied volatility with time to maturity.

Warrant An option issued by a company or a financial institution. Call warrants are frequently issued by companies on their own stock.

Weather Derivative Derivative where the payoff depends on the weather.

Wiener Process A stochastic process where the change in a variable during each short period of time of length Δt has a normal distribution with a mean equal to zero and a variance equal to Δt.

Wild Card Play The right to deliver on a futures contract at the closing price for a period of time after the close of trading.

Writing an Option Selling an option.

Yield A return provided by an instrument.

Yield Curve *See* Term Structure.

Zero-Coupon Bond A bond that provides no coupons.

Zero-Coupon Interest Rate The interest rate that would be earned on a bond that provides no coupons.

Zero-Coupon Yield Curve A plot of the zero-coupon interest rate against time to maturity.

Zero Curve *See* Zero-Coupon Yield Curve.

Zero Rate *See* Zero-Coupon Interest Rate.

DerivaGem Software

The software accompanying this book is DerivaGem for Excel, Version 1.51. It requires Excel Version 7.0 or later. The software consists of three files: dg151.dll, DG151.xls, and DG151functions.xls To install the software, you should create a directory with the name DerivaGem (or some other name of your own choosing) and load DG151.xls and DG151functions.xls into the directory. You should load dg151.dll into the Windows\System directory (Windows 95 and 98 users) or the WINNT\System32 directory (Windows 2000 and Windows NT users).[1]

Excel 2000 users should ensure that Security for Macros is set at *Medium* or *Low*. Check *Tools* followed by *Macros* in Excel to change this. While using the software, you may be asked whether you want to enable macros. You should click *Enable Macros*.

Updates to the software can be downloaded from the author's website:

http://www.rotman.utoronto.ca/~hull

There are two parts to the software: the Options Calculator (DG151.xls) and the Applications Builder (DG151functions.xls). Both parts require dg151.dll to be loaded into the Windows\System or WINNT\System32 directory.

New users are advised to start with The Options Calculator.

THE OPTIONS CALCULATOR

DG151.xls is a user-friendly options calculator. It consists of three worksheets. The first worksheet is used to carry out computations for stock options, currency options, index options, and futures options; the second is used for European and American bond options; the third is used for caps, floors, and European swap options.

The software produces prices, Greek letters, and implied volatilities for a wide range of different instruments. It displays charts showing the way that option prices and the

[1] Note that it is not uncommon for Windows Explorer to be set up so that *.dll files are not displayed. To change the setting so that the *.dll file can be seen, proceed as follows. In Windows 95, click *View*, followed by *Options*, followed by *Show All Files*. In Windows 98 click *View*, followed by *Folder Options*, followed by *View*, followed by *Show All Files*. In Windows 2000, click *Tools*, followed by *Folder Options*, followed by *View*, followed by *Show Hidden Files and Folders*.

Greek letters depend on inputs. It also displays binomial and trinomial trees, showing how the computations are carried out.

General Operation

To use the options calculator, you should choose a worksheet and click on the appropriate buttons to select Option Type, Underlying Type, and so on. You should then enter the parameters for the option you are considering, hit *Enter* on your keyboard, and click on *Calculate*. DerivaGem will then display the price or implied volatility for the option you are considering, together with Greek letters. If the price has been calculated from a tree, and you are using the first or second worksheet, you can then click on *Display Tree* to see the tree. Sample displays of the tree are shown in Chapters 11 and 17. Many different charts can be displayed in all three worksheets. To display a chart, you must first choose the variable you require on the vertical axis, the variable you require on the horizontal axis, and the range of values to be considered on the horizontal axis. Following that you should hit *Enter* on your keyboard and click on *Draw Graph*. Note that, whenever the values in one or more cells are changed, it is necessary to hit *Enter* on your keyboard before clicking on one of the buttons.

If your version of Excel is later than 7.0, you will be asked whether you want to update to the new version when you first save the software. You should choose the *Yes* button.

Options on Stocks, Currencies, Indices, and Futures

The first worksheet (Equity_FX_Index_Futures) is used for options on stocks, currencies, indices, and futures. To use it you should first select the Underlying Type (Equity, Currency, Index, or Futures). You should then select the Option Type (Analytic European, Binomial European, Binomial American, Asian, Barrier Up and In, Barrier Up and Out, Barrier Down and In, Barrier Down and Out, Binary Cash or Nothing, Binary Asset or Nothing, Chooser, Compound Option on Call, Compound Option on Put, or Lookback). You should then enter the data on the underlying asset and data on the option. Note that all interest rates are expressed with continuous compounding.

In the case of European and American equity options, a table pops up allowing you to enter dividends. Enter the time of each ex-dividend date (measured in years from today) in the first column and the amount of the dividend in the second column. Dividends must be entered in chronological order.

You must click on buttons to choose whether the option is a call or a put and whether you wish to calculate an implied volatility. If you do wish to calculate an implied volatility, the option price should be entered in the cell labeled Price.

Once all the data has been entered you should hit *Enter* on your keyboard and click on *Calculate*. If Implied Volatility was selected, DerivaGem displays the implied volatility in the Volatility (% per year) cell. If Implied Volatility was not selected, it uses the volatility you entered in this cell and displays the option price in the Price cell.

Once the calculations have been completed, the tree (if used) can be inspected and charts can be displayed.

When Analytic European is selected, DerivaGem uses the Black–Scholes equations in Chapters 13 and 14 to calculate prices, and the equations in Chapter 15 to calculate Greek letters. When Binomial European or Binomial American is selected, a binomial tree is constructed as described in Chapter 17. Up to 500 time steps can be used.

The input data are largely self-explanatory. In the case of an Asian option, the Current Average is the average price since inception. If the Asian option is new (Time since Inception equals zero), then the Current Average cell is irrelevant and can be left blank. In the case of a Lookback Option, the Minimum to Date is used when a Call is valued and the Maximum to Date is used when a Put is valued. For a new deal, these should be set equal to the current price of the underlying asset.

Bond Options

The second worksheet (Bond_Options) is used for European and American options on bonds. You should first select a pricing model (Black-European, Normal-Analytic European, Normal-Tree European, Normal-American, Lognormal-European, or Lognormal-American). You should then enter the Bond Data and the Option Data. The coupon is the rate paid per year and the frequency of payments can be selected as Quarterly, Semi-Annual, or Annual. The zero-coupon yield curve is entered in the table labeled Term Structure. Enter maturities (measured in years) in the first column and the corresponding continuously compounded rates in the second column. The maturities should be entered in chronological order. DerivaGem assumes a piecewise linear zero curve similar to that in Figure 4.1. Note that, when valuing interest rate derivatives, DerivaGem rounds all times to the nearest whole number of days.

When all data have been entered, hit *Enter* on your keyboard. The quoted bond price per $100 of Principal, calculated from the zero curve, is displayed when the calculations are complete. You should indicate whether the option is a call or a put and whether the strike price is a quoted (clean) strike price or a cash (dirty) strike price. (See the discussion and example in Section 26.2 to understand the difference between the two.) Note that the strike price is entered as the price per $100 of principal. You should indicate whether you are considering a call or a put option and whether you wish to calculate an implied volatility. If you select implied volatility and the normal model or lognormal model is used, DerivaGem implies the short-rate volatility, keeping the reversion rate fixed.

Once all the inputs are complete, you should hit *Enter* on your keyboard and click *Calculate*. After that the tree (if used) can be inspected and charts can be displayed. Note that the tree displayed lasts until the end of the life of the option. DerivaGem uses a much larger tree in its computations to value the underlying bond.

Note that, when Black's model is selected, DerivaGem uses the equations in Section 26.2. Also, the procedure in Section 26.2 is used for converting the input yield volatility into a price volatility.

Caps and Swap Options

The third worksheet (Caps_and_Swap_Options) is used for caps and swap options. You should first select the Option Type (Swap Option or Cap/Floor) and Pricing Model (Black-European, Normal-European, or Lognormal-European). You should then enter data on the option you are considering. The Settlement Frequency indicates the frequency of payments and can be Annual, Semi-Annual, Quarterly, or Monthly. The software calculates payment dates by working backward from the end of the life of the cap or swap option. The initial accrual period may be a nonstandard length between 0.5 and 1.5 times a normal accrual period. The software can be used to imply either a volatility or a cap rate/swap rate from the price. When a normal model or a lognormal model is used, DerivaGem implies the short rate volatility keeping the reversion rate fixed. The zero-coupon yield curve is entered in the table labeled Term Structure. Enter maturities (measured in years) in the first column and the corresponding continuously compounded rates in the second column. The maturities should be entered in chronological order. DerivaGem assumes a piecewise linear zero curve similar to that in Figure 4.1.

Once all the inputs are complete, you should click *Calculate*. After that, charts can be displayed. Note that, when Black's model is used, DerivaGem uses the equations in Sections 26.3 and 26.4.

Greek Letters

In the Equity_FX_Index_Futures worksheet, the Greek letters are calculated as follows.

Delta: Change in option price per dollar increase in underlying asset.

Gamma: Change in delta per dollar increase in underlying asset.

Vega: Change in option price per 1% increase in volatility (e.g., volatility increases from 20% to 21%).

Rho: Change in option price per 1% increase in interest rate (e.g., interest increases from 5% to 6%).

Theta: Change in option price per calendar day passing.

In the Bond_Options and Caps_and_Swap_Options worksheets, the Greek letters are calculated as follows:

DV01: Change in option price per one basis point upward parallel shift in the zero curve.

Gamma01: Change in DV01 per one basis point upward parallel shift in the zero curve, multiplied by 100.

Vega: Change in option price when volatility parameter increases by 1% (e.g., volatility increases from 20% to 21%)

THE APPLICATIONS BUILDER

The Applications Builder is DG151functions.xls. It is a set of 21 functions and seven sample applications from which users can build their own applications.

The Functions

The following is a list of the 21 functions included in the Applications Builder. Full details are on the first worksheet (FunctionSpecs).

1. Black_Scholes. This carries out Black–Scholes calculations for a European option on a stock, stock index, currency, or futures contract.
2. TreeEquityOpt. This carries out binomial tree calculations for a European or American option on a stock, stock index, currency, or futures contract.

3. BinaryOption. This carries out calculations for a binary option on a stock, stock index, currency, or futures contract.
4. BarrierOption. This carries out calculations for a barrier option on a non-dividend-paying stock, stock index, currency, or futures contract.
5. AverageOption. This carries out calculations for an Asian option on a non-dividend-paying stock, stock index, currency, or futures contract.
6. ChooserOption. This carries out calculations for a chooser option on a non-dividend-paying stock, stock index, currency, or futures contract.
7. CompoundOption. This carries out calculations for compound options on non-dividend-paying stocks, stock indices, currencies, and futures.
8. LookbackOption. This carries out calculations for a lookback option on a non-dividend-paying stock, stock index, currency, or futures contract.
9. EPortfolio. This carries out calculations for a portfolio of options on a stock, stock index, currency, or futures contract.
10. BlackCap. This carries out calculations for a cap or floor using Black's model.
11. HullWhiteCap. This carries out calculations for a cap or floor using the Hull–White model.
12. TreeCap. This carries out calculations for a cap or floor using a trinomial tree.
13. BlackSwapOption. This carries out calculations for a swap option using Black's model.
14. HullWhiteSwap. This carries out calculations for a swap option using the Hull–White model.
15. TreeSwapOption. This carries out calculations for a swap option using a trinomial tree.
16. BlackBondOption. This carries out calculations for a bond option using Black's model.
17. HullWhiteBondOption. This carries out calculations for a bond option using the Hull–White model.
18. TreeBondOption. This carries out calculations for a bond option using a trinomial tree.
19. BondPrice. This values a bond.
20. SwapPrice. This values a plain vanilla interest rate swap. Note that it ignores cash flows arising from reset dates prior to start time.
21. IPortfolio. This carries out calculations for a portfolio of interest rate derivatives.

Sample Applications

DG151functions.xls includes seven worksheets with sample applications:

A. Binomial Convergence. This investigates the convergence of the binomial model in Chapters 11 and 17.

B. GreekLetters. This provides charts showing the Greek letters in Chapter 15.

C. Delta Hedge. This investigates the performance of delta hedging as in Tables 15.2 and 15.3.

D. Delta and Gamma Hedge. This investigates the performance of delta plus gamma hedging for a position in a binary option.

E. Value and Risk. This calculates Value at Risk for a portfolio consisting of three options on a single stock using three different approaches.

F. Barrier Replication. This carries out calculations for the static options replication example in Section 22.13.

G. Trinomial Convergence. This investigates the convergence of the trinomial tree model in Chapter 28.

Major Exchanges Trading Futures and Options

American Stock Exchange	AMEX	www.amex.com
Australian Stock Exchange	ASX	www.asx.com.au
Bolsa de Mercadorias y Futuros, Brazil	BM&F	www.bmf.com.br
Chicago Board of Trade	CBOT	www.cbot.com
Chicago Board Options Exchange	CBOE	www.cboe.com
Chicago Mercantile Exchange	CME	www.cme.com
Coffee, Sugar & Cocoa Exchange, New York	CSCE	www.csce.com
Commodity Exchange, New York	COMEX	www.nymex.com
Copenhagen Stock Exchange	FUTOP	www.xcse.dk
Deutsche Termin Börse, Germany	DTB	www.exchange.de
Eurex	EUREX	www.eurexchange.com
Euronext	EURONEXT	www.euronext.com
Hong Kong Futures Exchange	HKFE	www.hkfe.com
International Petroleum Exchange, London	IPE	www.ipe.uk.com
International Securities Exchange	ISE	www.iseoptions.com
Kansas City Board of Trade	KCBT	www.kcbt.com
London International Financial Futures & Options Exchange	LIFFE	www.liffe.com
London Metal Exchange	LME	www.lme.co.uk
Malaysian Derivatives Exchange	MDEX	www.mdex.com.my
Marché à Terme International de France	MATIF	www.matif.fr
Marché des Options Négociables de Paris	MONEP	www.monep.fr
MEFF Renta Fija and Variable, Spain	MEFF	www.meff.es
Mexican Derivatives Exchange	MEXDER	www.mexder.com
Minneapolis Grain Exchange	MGE	www.mgex.com
Montreal Exchange	ME	www.me.org
New York Board of Trade	NYBOT	www.nybot.com
New York Cotton Exchange	NYCE	www.nyce.com
New York Futures Exchange	NYFE	www.nyce.com
New York Mercantile Exchange	NYMEX	www.nymex.com
New York Stock Exchange	NYSE	www.nyse.com
OMHEX	MHEX	www.omhex.com
Osaka Securities Exchange	OSA	www.ose.or.jp
Pacific Exchange	PXS	www.pacificex.com
Philadelphia Stock Exchange	PHLX	www.phlx.com
Singapore International Monetary Exchange	SIMEX	www.simex.com.sg
Sydney Futures Exchange	SFE	www.sfe.com.au
Swiss Exchange	SWX	www.swx.com
Tokyo Grain Exchange	TGE	www.tge.or.jp
Tokyo International Financial Futures Exchange	TIFFE	www.tiffe.or.jp
Winnipeg Commodity Exchange	WCE	www.wce.ca

A number of exchanges have merged or formed alliances. For example, Eurex is jointly operated by DTB and SWX, and Euronext owns LIFFE, MATIF, and MONEP.

Table for $N(x)$ When $x \leqslant 0$

This table shows values of $N(x)$ for $x \leqslant 0$. The table should be used with interpolation. For example,

$$\begin{aligned} N(-0.1234) &= N(-0.12) - 0.34[N(-0.12) - N(-0.13)] \\ &= 0.4522 - 0.34 \times (0.4522 - 0.4483) \\ &= 0.4509 \end{aligned}$$

x	.00	.01	.02	.03	.04	.05	.06	.07	.08	.09
−0.0	0.5000	0.4960	0.4920	0.4880	0.4840	0.4801	0.4761	0.4721	0.4681	0.4641
−0.1	0.4602	0.4562	0.4522	0.4483	0.4443	0.4404	0.4364	0.4325	0.4286	0.4247
−0.2	0.4207	0.4168	0.4129	0.4090	0.4052	0.4013	0.3974	0.3936	0.3897	0.3859
−0.3	0.3821	0.3783	0.3745	0.3707	0.3669	0.3632	0.3594	0.3557	0.3520	0.3483
−0.4	0.3446	0.3409	0.3372	0.3336	0.3300	0.3264	0.3228	0.3192	0.3156	0.3121
−0.5	0.3085	0.3050	0.3015	0.2981	0.2946	0.2912	0.2877	0.2843	0.2810	0.2776
−0.6	0.2743	0.2709	0.2676	0.2643	0.2611	0.2578	0.2546	0.2514	0.2483	0.2451
−0.7	0.2420	0.2389	0.2358	0.2327	0.2296	0.2266	0.2236	0.2206	0.2177	0.2148
−0.8	0.2119	0.2090	0.2061	0.2033	0.2005	0.1977	0.1949	0.1922	0.1894	0.1867
−0.9	0.1841	0.1814	0.1788	0.1762	0.1736	0.1711	0.1685	0.1660	0.1635	0.1611
−1.0	0.1587	0.1562	0.1539	0.1515	0.1492	0.1469	0.1446	0.1423	0.1401	0.1379
−1.1	0.1357	0.1335	0.1314	0.1292	0.1271	0.1251	0.1230	0.1210	0.1190	0.1170
−1.2	0.1151	0.1131	0.1112	0.1093	0.1075	0.1056	0.1038	0.1020	0.1003	0.0985
−1.3	0.0968	0.0951	0.0934	0.0918	0.0901	0.0885	0.0869	0.0853	0.0838	0.0823
−1.4	0.0808	0.0793	0.0778	0.0764	0.0749	0.0735	0.0721	0.0708	0.0694	0.0681
−1.5	0.0668	0.0655	0.0643	0.0630	0.0618	0.0606	0.0594	0.0582	0.0571	0.0559
−1.6	0.0548	0.0537	0.0526	0.0516	0.0505	0.0495	0.0485	0.0475	0.0465	0.0455
−1.7	0.0446	0.0436	0.0427	0.0418	0.0409	0.0401	0.0392	0.0384	0.0375	0.0367
−1.8	0.0359	0.0351	0.0344	0.0336	0.0329	0.0322	0.0314	0.0307	0.0301	0.0294
−1.9	0.0287	0.0281	0.0274	0.0268	0.0262	0.0256	0.0250	0.0244	0.0239	0.0233
−2.0	0.0228	0.0222	0.0217	0.0212	0.0207	0.0202	0.0197	0.0192	0.0188	0.0183
−2.1	0.0179	0.0174	0.0170	0.0166	0.0162	0.0158	0.0154	0.0150	0.0146	0.0143
−2.2	0.0139	0.0136	0.0132	0.0129	0.0125	0.0122	0.0119	0.0116	0.0113	0.0110
−2.3	0.0107	0.0104	0.0102	0.0099	0.0096	0.0094	0.0091	0.0089	0.0087	0.0084
−2.4	0.0082	0.0080	0.0078	0.0075	0.0073	0.0071	0.0069	0.0068	0.0066	0.0064
−2.5	0.0062	0.0060	0.0059	0.0057	0.0055	0.0054	0.0052	0.0051	0.0049	0.0048
−2.6	0.0047	0.0045	0.0044	0.0043	0.0041	0.0040	0.0039	0.0038	0.0037	0.0036
−2.7	0.0035	0.0034	0.0033	0.0032	0.0031	0.0030	0.0029	0.0028	0.0027	0.0026
−2.8	0.0026	0.0025	0.0024	0.0023	0.0023	0.0022	0.0021	0.0021	0.0020	0.0019
−2.9	0.0019	0.0018	0.0018	0.0017	0.0016	0.0016	0.0015	0.0015	0.0014	0.0014
−3.0	0.0014	0.0013	0.0013	0.0012	0.0012	0.0011	0.0011	0.0011	0.0010	0.0010
−3.1	0.0010	0.0009	0.0009	0.0009	0.0008	0.0008	0.0008	0.0008	0.0007	0.0007
−3.2	0.0007	0.0007	0.0006	0.0006	0.0006	0.0006	0.0006	0.0005	0.0005	0.0005
−3.3	0.0005	0.0005	0.0005	0.0004	0.0004	0.0004	0.0004	0.0004	0.0004	0.0003
−3.4	0.0003	0.0003	0.0003	0.0003	0.0003	0.0003	0.0003	0.0003	0.0003	0.0002
−3.5	0.0002	0.0002	0.0002	0.0002	0.0002	0.0002	0.0002	0.0002	0.0002	0.0002
−3.6	0.0002	0.0002	0.0001	0.0001	0.0001	0.0001	0.0001	0.0001	0.0001	0.0001
−3.7	0.0001	0.0001	0.0001	0.0001	0.0001	0.0001	0.0001	0.0001	0.0001	0.0001
−3.8	0.0001	0.0001	0.0001	0.0001	0.0001	0.0001	0.0001	0.0001	0.0001	0.0001
−3.9	0.0000	0.0000	0.0000	0.0000	0.0000	0.0000	0.0000	0.0000	0.0000	0.0000
−4.0	0.0000	0.0000	0.0000	0.0000	0.0000	0.0000	0.0000	0.0000	0.0000	0.0000

Table for $N(x)$ When $x \geqslant 0$

This table shows values of $N(x)$ for $x \geqslant 0$. The table should be used with interpolation. For example,

$$\begin{aligned} N(0.6278) &= N(0.62) + 0.78[N(0.63) - N(0.62)] \\ &= 0.7324 + 0.78 \times (0.7357 - 0.7324) \\ &= 0.7350 \end{aligned}$$

x	.00	.01	.02	.03	.04	.05	.06	.07	.08	.09
0.0	0.5000	0.5040	0.5080	0.5120	0.5160	0.5199	0.5239	0.5279	0.5319	0.5359
0.1	0.5398	0.5438	0.5478	0.5517	0.5557	0.5596	0.5636	0.5675	0.5714	0.5753
0.2	0.5793	0.5832	0.5871	0.5910	0.5948	0.5987	0.6026	0.6064	0.6103	0.6141
0.3	0.6179	0.6217	0.6255	0.6293	0.6331	0.6368	0.6406	0.6443	0.6480	0.6517
0.4	0.6554	0.6591	0.6628	0.6664	0.6700	0.6736	0.6772	0.6808	0.6844	0.6879
0.5	0.6915	0.6950	0.6985	0.7019	0.7054	0.7088	0.7123	0.7157	0.7190	0.7224
0.6	0.7257	0.7291	0.7324	0.7357	0.7389	0.7422	0.7454	0.7486	0.7517	0.7549
0.7	0.7580	0.7611	0.7642	0.7673	0.7704	0.7734	0.7764	0.7794	0.7823	0.7852
0.8	0.7881	0.7910	0.7939	0.7967	0.7995	0.8023	0.8051	0.8078	0.8106	0.8133
0.9	0.8159	0.8186	0.8212	0.8238	0.8264	0.8289	0.8315	0.8340	0.8365	0.8389
1.0	0.8413	0.8438	0.8461	0.8485	0.8508	0.8531	0.8554	0.8577	0.8599	0.8621
1.1	0.8643	0.8665	0.8686	0.8708	0.8729	0.8749	0.8770	0.8790	0.8810	0.8830
1.2	0.8849	0.8869	0.8888	0.8907	0.8925	0.8944	0.8962	0.8980	0.8997	0.9015
1.3	0.9032	0.9049	0.9066	0.9082	0.9099	0.9115	0.9131	0.9147	0.9162	0.9177
1.4	0.9192	0.9207	0.9222	0.9236	0.9251	0.9265	0.9279	0.9292	0.9306	0.9319
1.5	0.9332	0.9345	0.9357	0.9370	0.9382	0.9394	0.9406	0.9418	0.9429	0.9441
1.6	0.9452	0.9463	0.9474	0.9484	0.9495	0.9505	0.9515	0.9525	0.9535	0.9545
1.7	0.9554	0.9564	0.9573	0.9582	0.9591	0.9599	0.9608	0.9616	0.9625	0.9633
1.8	0.9641	0.9649	0.9656	0.9664	0.9671	0.9678	0.9686	0.9693	0.9699	0.9706
1.9	0.9713	0.9719	0.9726	0.9732	0.9738	0.9744	0.9750	0.9756	0.9761	0.9767
2.0	0.9772	0.9778	0.9783	0.9788	0.9793	0.9798	0.9803	0.9808	0.9812	0.9817
2.1	0.9821	0.9826	0.9830	0.9834	0.9838	0.9842	0.9846	0.9850	0.9854	0.9857
2.2	0.9861	0.9864	0.9868	0.9871	0.9875	0.9878	0.9881	0.9884	0.9887	0.9890
2.3	0.9893	0.9896	0.9898	0.9901	0.9904	0.9906	0.9909	0.9911	0.9913	0.9916
2.4	0.9918	0.9920	0.9922	0.9925	0.9927	0.9929	0.9931	0.9932	0.9934	0.9936
2.5	0.9938	0.9940	0.9941	0.9943	0.9945	0.9946	0.9948	0.9949	0.9951	0.9952
2.6	0.9953	0.9955	0.9956	0.9957	0.9959	0.9960	0.9961	0.9962	0.9963	0.9964
2.7	0.9965	0.9966	0.9967	0.9968	0.9969	0.9970	0.9971	0.9972	0.9973	0.9974
2.8	0.9974	0.9975	0.9976	0.9977	0.9977	0.9978	0.9979	0.9979	0.9980	0.9981
2.9	0.9981	0.9982	0.9982	0.9983	0.9984	0.9984	0.9985	0.9985	0.9986	0.9986
3.0	0.9986	0.9987	0.9987	0.9988	0.9988	0.9989	0.9989	0.9989	0.9990	0.9990
3.1	0.9990	0.9991	0.9991	0.9991	0.9992	0.9992	0.9992	0.9992	0.9993	0.9993
3.2	0.9993	0.9993	0.9994	0.9994	0.9994	0.9994	0.9994	0.9995	0.9995	0.9995
3.3	0.9995	0.9995	0.9995	0.9996	0.9996	0.9996	0.9996	0.9996	0.9996	0.9997
3.4	0.9997	0.9997	0.9997	0.9997	0.9997	0.9997	0.9997	0.9997	0.9997	0.9998
3.5	0.9998	0.9998	0.9998	0.9998	0.9998	0.9998	0.9998	0.9998	0.9998	0.9998
3.6	0.9998	0.9998	0.9999	0.9999	0.9999	0.9999	0.9999	0.9999	0.9999	0.9999
3.7	0.9999	0.9999	0.9999	0.9999	0.9999	0.9999	0.9999	0.9999	0.9999	0.9999
3.8	0.9999	0.9999	0.9999	0.9999	0.9999	0.9999	0.9999	0.9999	0.9999	0.9999
3.9	1.0000	1.0000	1.0000	1.0000	1.0000	1.0000	1.0000	1.0000	1.0000	1.0000
4.0	1.0000	1.0000	1.0000	1.0000	1.0000	1.0000	1.0000	1.0000	1.0000	1.0000

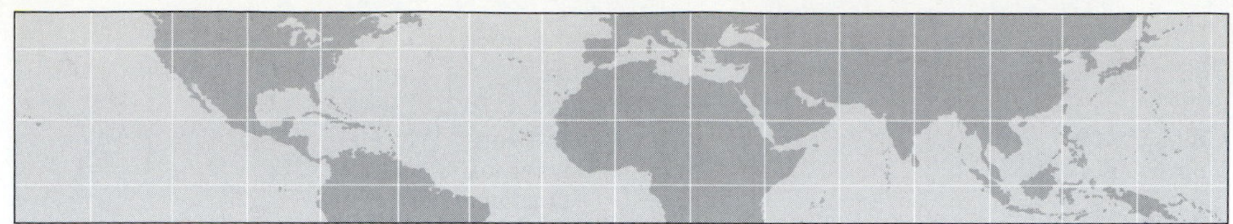

Author Index

Subject Index

References to items in the Glossary of Terms are **bolded**

DATA DISK LICENSE AGREEMENT AND LIMITED WARRANTY

READ THIS LICENSE CAREFULLY BEFORE USING THIS PACKAGE. BY USING THIS PACKAGE, YOU ARE AGREEING TO THE TERMS AND CONDITIONS OF THIS LICENSE. IF YOU DO NOT AGREE, DO NOT USE THE PACKAGE. PROMPTLY RETURN THE UNUSED PACKAGE AND ALL ACCOMPANYING ITEMS TO THE PLACE YOU OBTAINED THEM. ***THESE TERMS APPLY TO ALL LICENSED SOFTWARE ON THE DISK EXCEPT THAT THE TERMS FOR USE OF ANY SHAREWARE OR FREEWARE ON THE DISKETTES ARE AS SET FORTH IN THE ELECTRONIC LICENSE LOCATED ON THE DISK:***

1. GRANT OF LICENSE and OWNERSHIP: The enclosed data disk ("Software") is licensed, not sold, to you by Pearson Education, Inc., publishing as Prentice Hall ("We" or the "Company") for academic purposes and in consideration of your purchase or adoption of the accompanying Company textbooks and/or other materials, and your agreement to these terms. This license allows instructors and students enrolled in the course using the Company textbook that accompanies this Software (the "Course") to use, display and manipulate the data for academic use only, so long as you comply with the terms of this Agreement. We reserve any rights not granted to you. You own only the disk(s) but we and our licensors own the Software itself.

2. RESTRICTIONS ON USE AND TRANSFER: You may not transfer, distribute or make available the Software or the Documentation, except to instructors and students in your school in connection with the Course. You may not reverse engineer, disassemble, decompile, modify, adapt, translate or create derivative works based on the Software or the Documentation. You may be held legally responsible for any copying or copyright infringement that is caused by your failure to abide by the terms of these restrictions.

3. TERMINATION: This license is effective until terminated. This license will terminate automatically without notice from the Company if you fail to comply with any provisions or limitations of this license. Upon termination, you shall destroy the Documentation and all copies of the Software. All provisions of this Agreement as to limitation and disclaimer of warranties, limitation of liability, remedies or damages, and our ownership rights shall survive termination.

4. DISCLAIMER OF WARRANTY: THE COMPANY AND ITS LICENSORS MAKE NO WARRANTIES ABOUT THE SOFTWARE, WHICH IS PROVIDED "AS-IS." IF THE DISK IS DEFECTIVE IN MATERIALS OR WORKMANSHIP, YOUR ONLY REMEDY IS TO RETURN IT TO THE COMPANY WITHIN 30 DAYS FOR REPLACEMENT UNLESS THE COMPANY DETERMINES IN GOOD FAITH THAT THE DISK HAS BEEN MISUSED OR IMPROPERLY INSTALLED, REPAIRED, ALTERED OR DAMAGED. THE COMPANY DISCLAIMS ALL WARRANTIES, EXPRESS OR IMPLIED, INCLUDING WITHOUT LIMITATION, THE IMPLIED WARRANTIES OF MERCHANTABILITY AND FITNESS FOR A PARTICULAR PURPOSE. THE COMPANY DOES NOT WARRANT, GUARANTEE OR MAKE ANY REPRESENTATION REGARDING THE ACCURACY, RELIABILITY, CURRENTNESS, USE, OR RESULTS OF USE, OF THE SOFTWARE.

5. LIMITATION OF REMEDIES AND DAMAGES: IN NO EVENT, SHALL THE COMPANY OR ITS EMPLOYEES, AGENTS, LICENSORS OR CONTRACTORS BE LIABLE FOR ANY INCIDENTAL, INDIRECT, SPECIAL OR CONSEQUENTIAL DAMAGES ARISING OUT OF OR IN CONNECTION WITH THIS LICENSE OR THE SOFTWARE, INCLUDING, WITHOUT LIMITATION, LOSS OF USE, LOSS OF DATA, LOSS OF INCOME OR PROFIT, OR OTHER LOSSES SUSTAINED AS A RESULT OF INJURY TO ANY PERSON, OR LOSS OF OR DAMAGE TO PROPERTY, OR CLAIMS OF THIRD PARTIES, EVEN IF THE COMPANY OR AN AUTHORIZED REPRESENTATIVE OF THE COMPANY HAS BEEN ADVISED OF THE POSSIBILITY OF SUCH DAMAGES. SOME JURISDICTIONS DO NOT ALLOW THE LIMITATION OF DAMAGES IN CERTAIN CIRCUMSTANCES, SO THE ABOVE LIMITATIONS MAY NOT ALWAYS APPLY.

6. GENERAL: THIS AGREEMENT SHALL BE CONSTRUED IN ACCORDANCE WITH THE LAWS OF THE UNITED STATES OF AMERICA AND THE STATE OF NEW YORK, APPLICABLE TO CONTRACTS MADE IN NEW YORK, AND SHALL BENEFIT THE COMPANY, ITS AFFILIATES AND ASSIGNEES. This Agreement is the complete and exclusive statement of the agreement between you and the Company and supersedes all proposals, prior agreements, oral or written, and any other communications between you and the company or any of its representatives relating to the subject matter. If you are a U.S. Government user, this Software is licensed with "restricted rights" as set forth in subparagraphs (a)–(d) of the Commercial Computer-Restricted Rights clause at FAR 52.227-19 or in subparagraphs (c)(1)(ii) of the Rights in Technical Data and Computer Software clause at DFARS 252.227-7013, and similar clauses, as applicable.

Should you have any questions concerning this agreement or if you wish to contact the Company for any reason, please contact in writing:

Director, Media Production
Prentice Hall
1 Lake Street
Upper Saddle River, NJ 07458